THE OXFORD ENCYCLOPEDIA OF
LATINOS AND LATINAS IN THE UNITED STATES

THE OXFORD ENCYCLOPEDIA

OF

LATINOS AND LATINAS
IN THE
UNITED STATES

Suzanne Oboler and Deena J. González

Editors in Chief

VOLUME 1

Acequias

—

Dual Nationality

OXFORD
UNIVERSITY PRESS
2005

OXFORD
UNIVERSITY PRESS

Oxford University Press, Inc., publishes works that further
Oxford University's objective of excellence
in research, scholarship, and education.

Oxford   New York

Auckland   Cape Town   Dar es Salaam   Hong Kong   Karachi
Kuala Lumpur   Madrid   Melbourne   Mexico City   Nairobi
New Delhi   Shanghai   Taipei   Toronto

With offices in

Argentina   Austria   Brazil   Chile   Czech Republic   France   Greece
Guatemala   Hungary   Italy   Japan   Poland   Portugal   Singapore
South Korea   Switzerland   Thailand   Turkey   Ukraine   Vietnam

Published by Oxford University Press, Inc.
198 Madison Avenue, New York, New York, 10016
www.oup.com/us

Library of Congress Cataloging-in-Publication Data

The Oxford encyclopedia of Latinos and Latinas in the United States/Suzanne Oboler
and Deena J. González, editors in chief.
p. cm.
Includes bibliographical references and index.
ISBN-13: 978-0-19-515600-3 (set: acid-free paper)
ISBN-10: 0-19-515600-5 (set: acid-free paper)
1. Hispanic Americans—Encyclopedias. I. Oboler, Suzanne.
II. González, Deena J., 1952- III. Title: Encyclopedia of
Latinos and Latinas in the United States.
E184.S75O97 2005
973'.0468'003—dc22

2005007764

Printing number: 9 8 7 6 5 4 3
Printed 2006 in the United States of America
on acid-free paper

EDITORIAL AND PRODUCTION STAFF

ACQUIRING EDITOR
Ralph Carlson

DEVELOPMENT EDITORS
Erin K. Carter   Sarah Feehan   Meera Vaidyanathan

MANAGING EDITOR
Georgia Shepherd Maas

EDITORIAL ASSISTANT
Cassandra Snyder

COPYEDITORS AND PROOFREADERS
Jonathan G. Aretakis   Robert A. Arlt Sr.   Johanna M. Baboukis   Sylvia J. Cannizzaro
Jean Fortune Kaplan   Susan McCloskey   Jason Philip Miller   Matthew Edmund Miller
Marina Padakis   Robin L. Perlow   Brennen Wysong

INDEXER
Katharyn Dunham, Paragraphs Indexing and Editorial Services

COMPOSITOR
Macmillan India Ltd.

MANUFACTURING CONTROLLER
Chris Critelli

DESIGNER
Joan Greenfield

ILLUSTRATION RESEARCHER
Nina Whitney, Picture Vision

EXECUTIVE EDITOR
Stephen Wagley

DIRECTOR OF EDITORIAL DEVELOPMENT AND PRODUCTION
Timothy J. DeWerff

PUBLISHER, REFERENCE DIVISION
Casper Grathwohl

Contents

Topical Outline of Articles

Directory of Contributors

Index

Introduction

Organize, organize, organize!

—Dolores Huerta

Nothing is built on stone; all is built on sand, but we must build as if the sand were stone.
—Jorge Luis Borges

A book is more than a verbal structure or series of verbal structures; . . . it is not an isolated being: it is a relationship, an axis of innumerable relationships.
—Jorge Luis Borges

The unprecedented growth of the Latino and Latina population in the United States has been well documented in many different sources. These include the U.S. census, which in March 2003 announced that Latinos and Latinas had become the largest minority population in the nation. There is no doubt that the roughly forty million people known as Latinos and Latinas in the United States are having a significant impact on this society's political, economic, social, and cultural institutions.

Developing a comprehensive understanding of the distinct historical, political, economic, cultural, and sociological experiences of what are in fact very diverse communities grounded in distinct national experiences has been an ongoing challenge for both U.S. society and the various Latino and Latina groups themselves. Similarly, it has been difficult to elaborate an in-depth and critical appreciation of the implications for U.S. society of this growing population. Substantive, reliable, and useful information concerning U.S. Latinos and Latinas is still hard to find, and what exists is found primarily in scholarly publications and professional journals that are not always easily accessible.

In this context, we were first led to conceive this project as a result of the obvious and glaring need to give expression to as many of the most important intellectual, social, cultural, and political developments of our times and in our field of Latino and Latina Studies. At the same time, we were also prompted to embark on this Encyclopedia project by the multiple possibilities and openings of human knowledge that the exploration and classification of learning about Latinos and Latinas in the United States could create for all of us today—Latinos and non-Latinos alike.

As the history of the word itself indicates, putting together an encyclopedia is an ambitious endeavor. First used in 1531, "encyclopedia" includes the Greek *enkyklios* (meaning "circular") and *paideia* (meaning "education" or "child-rearing"). The word therefore refers to the attempt to encompass knowledge on a particular topic that every child should be taught as part of a society's child-rearing. Given the invisibility that characterizes the history and experience of Latinos and Latinas in U.S. society since the early colonial period of this country, this project has indeed been driven by the idea of making available information that is essential to all—knowledge that every child, whether Latino or non-Latino, should possess about the historical experience of Latinos and Latinas in the United States.

What gave us the necessary self-assurance to undertake such a task is not so much excessive conceit or lightmindedness as a shared belief and concern for the virtues of citizenship inherent in education and the acquisition of knowledge—articulated as far back as the Enlightenment, when what is considered the first alphabetically arranged encyclopedia, the *Encylopédie; ou, Dictionnaire raisonné des sciences, des artes, et des métiers* was published between 1751 and 1765.

This is and has been a daunting project. In accepting the challenge it has posed to us, our aim was to provide a useful reference beyond the academic sphere and to do our best to contribute to the arduous task of dispelling the many and persistent prejudices and bigotries regarding Latinas and Latinos in this country. We see this Encyclopedia today as a *máquina de guerra*, a tool in the continuous struggle to unshackle the human spirit and to propagate as far and as wide as possible the enlightened ideas of our own time. And "memory, imagination and reason"—the guiding muses of the Encyclopedists at the brink of modernity—still inform, inspire, and support all attempts at harmonizing political reality and intellectual striving, particularly among Latinos and Latinas.

Using the Encyclopedia

Clearly, the acquisition and dissemination of knowledge is an ongoing process that is never complete. Our aim, therefore, could never be to produce a finished product. Rather, by providing these four volumes of exemplary and thoroughly researched essays, we strive, instead, to point to the necessity for the publication of additional works such as this.

Our collaborative effort to assemble and make available knowledge about Latinos and Latinas has produced over nine hundred articles, each of which has been written by a scholar-specialist. In addition to the articles, this project includes over four hundred illustrations, charts, and maps. The contributors have sought to write in clear language with a minimum of technical vocabulary. The articles give important terms and titles in their original languages, with English translations when needed. A selective bibliography at the end of each article directs readers who wish to pursue a topic in more detail to primary sources and important scholarly works on the subject.

At the end of most of the articles, we have added end references to guide readers to related discussions elsewhere in the Encyclopedia. In addition, there are cross-references within the body of a few articles. Blind entries direct the user from an alternate form of an entry term to the entry itself. For example, the blind entry for "Yerberia" tells the reader to look under "Botánicas." Readers interested in finding all the articles on a particular subject (e.g., Religion, Folklore, and Festivals) may consult the systematic outline at the end of Volume 4. A comprehensive index at the end of Volume 4 lists all the topics covered in the Encyclopedia, including those that are not headwords themselves.

In thinking about the kinds of articles documenting the complex and vast historical and contemporary experience of U.S. Latinos and Latinas that we wanted to include, we focused on two major goals: first, to provide for nonspecialists a general source of information—one that could be as comprehensive, accurate, and useful as we could possibly make it—on the diverse historical and contemporary experiences of Latinos and Latinas in the United States; and second, to offer more specialized readers (educators, policy makers, professionals, practitioners, students, and others) substantive and rigorous discussions, grounded in the most up-to-date research available, on the history, status, and circumstances of Latinos and Latinas in the United States. With these two goals in mind, in these four volumes we have made every effort to bring together and give coherence to the shared political, cultural, and socioeconomic experiences of Latinos and Latinas, while simultaneously acknowledging their diverse and distinct histories, trajectories, and traditions.

To attempt to compile and organize a systematic and comprehensive presentation of relevant information on the U.S. Latino and Latina population is undoubtedly an enterprise worthy of a madman or a believer. From its inception, throughout its execution, and to its completion, we have experienced this process as both—and hence have lived the joys of a labor of love. The ultimate aim of all knowledge is to produce a "living encyclopedia"—that is, a human being who is a conscious, responsive, and appreciative heir to the rich experiences of the past, and who is thus capable of facing with courage the challenges inherent in the adventures of the unquenchable human spirit.

The Scope of This Project

In designing this project, in considering how best to introduce the Latino and Latina population to a mainstream audience, we found ourselves continuously addressing the following questions: Do we approach this population as a statistical fact of the demography of the nation? Or is this "ethnic group" best understood as a living and increasingly self-conscious community of citizens and denizens, rather than as a set of numbers? What should we make of these numbers in which living human beings are continually categorized, empowered, and/or entrapped? How, for example, should we address the fact that the exact numbers of Latinos and Latinas would vary according to the particular scholar discussing this population? Indeed, who are "Latinos and Latinas"? Are recently arrived Latin Americans also Latinos and Latinas? Are Latin Americans in their home countries Latinos and Latinas? When does a Latin American become a Latino or Latina?

These are some of the key questions currently debated and discussed within the field of Latino and Latina Studies, and they were essential for us to address as we developed the contents of this Encyclopedia. In determining the scope of the project, it was important to take into account the fact that in its current usage the term "Latino" emerged during the 1980s as an alternative—and to some a corrective—to the term "Hispanic." The latter term was officially adopted in 1977 through Directive 15 of the U.S. Office of Budget and Management for purposes of data collection. Like the official term, "Latino and Latina" refers specifically to a U.S.–based population and is used to group people formerly classified as Mexican, Puerto Rican, Cuban, Dominican, Central American, South American, Latin American, Spanish-surnamed, Spanish-speaking, and Spanish American. Both terms, "Hispanic" and "Latino and Latina," highlight the extent to which populations of diverse cultural, regional, and national origins have come together in the U.S. context and emphasize the growing interaction between and among disparate groups. For detailed definitions of these and other terms used to name and define the Hispanic and Latino population, see the essays titled "Latino" and "Latino Identities and Ethnicities." In this Encyclopedia and in this introductory essay, we have chosen to use the term "Latino and Latina."

Contrary to popular thought, Latinos and Latinas are not a homogeneous population with a common history and evolution. In fact, Latinos and Latinas became American citizens or residents in a variety of ways and over a period of centuries. Difference marks the Latino and Latina experience—whether this be difference of class, ethnicity, color, social location, national origin, or generation. Undoubtedly, the differing circumstances of individual and group incorporation into U.S. society and their distinct historical experiences have consequences for how these different individuals and groups interact with its institutions, participate in its civic life, adopt its modes and manners, and take on its values and beliefs.

Some Latino and Latina populations, for example, are historical minorities and have been in this country for centuries; others only began to arrive in large numbers in the post–World War II period and, more specifically, during the 1980s and 1990s. The former include the descendants of persons living in what is now the U.S. Southwest who were granted U.S. residency in the aftermath of the United States–Mexican War (1846–1848). Similarly, inhabitants of the island of Puerto Rico were made U.S. citizens in 1917, following their colonization as a result of the Spanish American War of 1898. To this day, the initial colonization of the island continues to make the complex implications of U.S. nationality and citizenship of Puerto Ricans an anomaly in this nation's history as well as among Latinos and Latinas themselves.

Moreover, the term "Latino and Latina" combines the histories, cultures, and experiences of these two U.S. historical minorities with those of millions of recent immigrants from Mexico, Cuba, the Dominican Republic, and the various Central American and South American countries, as well as their U.S.–born children. While representatives of all of these nationalities were present on U.S. territory as early as the first decades of the 1800s—and in the case of Mexicans as far back as the Spanish conquest of New Mexico in 1598—the majority are economic immigrants who came to the United States during the course of the twentieth century in search of jobs or a better standard of living. The term "Latino and Latina," however, also encompasses more recent political refugees, such as large numbers of Guatemalans, Nicaraguans, and Salvadorans, who augment the older political exile community, which since the early 1960s consisted principally of Cubans who emigrated to the United States following the Cuban Revolution of 1959. In addition, the U.S. government also officially includes nationals from Spain under the rubric of Hispanic or Latino. From conqueror/migrant, to immigrant and refugee or exile, the sum of the historical experiences, along with the linguistic mixtures of Spanish and indigenous dialects, of religious and spiritual traditions, together make up this culturally and ethnically enriched population.

Further complicating the question of terminology is the fact that the use of the term "Latino and Latina" overlooks the cultural, linguistic, ethnic, and racial diversity of this population, whether as historical minorities or immigrants: the various indigenous peoples; the descendants of African slaves; the immigrants from every country in Europe, Asia, and the Middle East. Whatever their cultural, ethnic, or racial background, in the United States they too are categorized as Latinos and Latinas.

In view of both the complex historical, geopolitical, and sociocultural diversity of Latinos and Latinas and their growing numbers in the United States, it is imperative that, as citizens of a global society in a new millennium, we all come together to learn about the disparate populations known as Latinos and Latinas in the United States. In presenting this Encyclopedia as a substantial four-volume source of information on the U.S. Latino and Latina experience, our aim is not—indeed necessarily cannot be—to cover all the events in which Latinos and Latinas have been present, nor is it to include every "famous person" or define every cultural practice and tradition of this complex and irreducible population group. Instead, we aim more generally to facilitate greater national awareness and knowledge of a relatively long historical experience of Chicanos and Chicanas, or Mexican Americans, and Puerto Ricans, as well as of forced and/or voluntary immigrants from all the Spanish American countries, and more generally of the contemporary Latino and Latina experience in the U.S. context. In so doing we are affirming the significance of the task of the growing field of Latino and Latina Studies today—an endeavor first pioneered by scholar-activists in the 1970s who fought for the creation of Chicano and Chicana Studies and Puerto Rican Studies in the universities, so that knowledge about this long-excluded sector of the U.S. citizenry could be researched and taught and thus become part of the required historical knowledge of this country.

Conceptual Framework

Given that our primary goal was, above all, to *marcar presencia*—that is, to document and record the long and unacknowledged presence of Latinos and Latinas in all spheres of U.S. history and society—we decided that this project would emphasize a substantive discussion of the historical, economic, sociocultural, and geopolitical structural issues that have shaped the Latino and Latina experience in the United States particularly, although not only, during the twentieth and early twenty-first centuries. While it was essential to us that we carefully document the long history and presence of Chicanos and Chicanas, or Mexican Americans, and Puerto Ricans in the United States, we were also interested in providing some understanding of the political, economic, and sociocultural consequences of the flow and counterflow of the Latino and Latin American populations in the hemisphere.

Indeed, globalization has made all of us aware of the ongoing impact of Latin American national cultures and values in shaping the daily lives of Latinos and Latinas, their cultural and sociopolitical interactions, and their influence on U.S. society and its institutions. Hence, in addition to ensuring a marked presence of U.S.–born and raised Chicanos and Chicanas and Puerto Ricans, a significant aspect of the process of conceptualizing this project entailed achieving a balance in the information we provided about each of the various national origin groups.

Thus, the uniqueness of *The Oxford Encyclopedia of Latinos and Latinas in the United States* resides precisely in our efforts to incorporate, at all levels, the significance of the wider and fundamentally interdisciplinary and transnational geographical scope from which research on Latinos and Latinas is being produced. Key to the integrity of this project is the incorporation of historical antecedents and their impact and influence on the present and future of the Latino and Latina experience and, more broadly, of U.S. society as a whole. Moreover, we ensured that the articles incorporate issues pertaining to the specific ways that gender, sexuality, social status, generation, and national origin serve to shape and further distinguish the commonalities and differences among Latinos and Latinas in the United States.

Editorial Structure and Organization of the Project

In view of the historical and contemporary complexity of the Latino and Latina experience in the United States, the composition and structure of the editorial board became an essential component of the success of a project of this scope and ambition. Our editorial board consisted of seven senior scholars in the field of Latino and Latina Studies, who served as our senior editors. They were invited to participate in this project on the basis of three criteria: their particular area of expertise, their standing in the field, and their national origin. Each senior editor was ultimately responsible for articles covering a specific area of expertise, in categories outlined below.

In our effort to produce a comprehensive, reliable, useful, and accessible *Oxford Encyclopedia of Latinos and Latinas in the United States*, our editorial team worked very closely to conceptualize, name, and define the over nine hundred entries that together constitute the roughly twenty-one hundred pages in these four volumes. The exceptions were the essays on the fifty states of the United States—a task for which we thank Barbara Tenenbaum and Tracy North, who made sure that a general overview of the presence of Latinos and Latinas in each state was documented in this project.

Conceptualizing this massive project was a challenging task. We began by identifying seven general areas that served to guide us in developing the Encyclopedia's table of contents. The seven individual areas, with the respective senior editor in charge, are:

(1) Culture, Language, Hollywood, and the Media: Frances R. Aparicio
(2) International Relations and Political Economy: Pedro Cabán
(3) Museums, Architecture and Urban Landscapes, Religion and Folklore, and Education: Norma E. Cantú
(4) Race, Laws and Customs, and Court Cases: Tanya Katerí Hernández
(5) The Environment, Science, Technology, and Health and Nutrition: Devon Peña
(6) Contemporary Political Participation, Access, and Citizenship: Maria de los Angeles Torres
(7) Literature, Poetry, the Arts, and Sports: Silvio Torres-Saillant

Together, our editorial team agreed on the table of contents and identified more than five hundred eminent Latino and Latina Studies academics, writers, intellectuals, and artists in the country. We then invited each of them to contribute their expertise in essays, both long and short, aimed at producing a cutting-edge, groundbreaking compilation of the latest knowledge about Latinos and Latinas in the United States.

Indeed, we cannot underscore enough the extent to which this Encyclopedia has been a collective and collaborative project. While the editors in chief coordinated the entire project, the work of coordinating and defining the above areas was roughly divided according to each senior editor's individual area of expertise. Our team met several times in the course of the three years that it took to take this work to completion, and all of us worked together to ensure the integrity of the project, the general organization of the Encyclopedia, and the identification of various issues pertaining to each of the areas. The meetings we held also allowed us to continually strengthen the conceptual and editorial direction of the Encyclopedia and to ensure appropriate representation, in all the categories, of the myriad national and other perspectives, both past and present, among Latinos and Latinas in U.S. society. Thus, each senior editor was able to draw on the disciplinary and national-origin expertise of all the scholars on the editorial board, as well as of both editors in chief. Finally, together with the editors in chief, each senior editor read the essays in his or her area of specialization, and collaborated with the authors to ensure the editorial integrity of the project.

From the beginning, we envisioned various kinds of essays, some longer, some shorter, all of which would be based on high-quality and rigorous scholarship that draws on the expertise and work of renowned scholars, intellectuals, artists, and researchers in Latino and Latina Studies. Because there are so few works that bring together the accumulated knowledge of the Latino and Latina scholarly community in one project, we wanted to ensure that the key historical events, the main issues, and the principal concerns of Latinos and Latinas were substantively covered.

Historical essays. While the focus of the Encyclopedia is undoubtedly the United States, we also sought to incorporate, particularly through longer general-overview essays devoted specifically to each respective national-origin group, the necessary historical and sociocultural background information on the countries and societies from which they came. In addition, we included a substantive essay on the border region between Mexico and the United States. As the author of that essay so clearly explains, the history and culture of that region of the United States is created by and has in turn produced a very specific socioeconomic, political, and cultural context within which Latino and Latinas in that region have historically lived their lives.

Within each category, we also identified the key themes that have shaped and that continue to have a substantial impact on the lives and experiences of Latinos and Latinas in the United States. Having defined the major themes we wanted to ensure were covered as substantive overview essays, we then identified issues, events, and individuals that stemmed from or were related to each theme. These allowed us to provide additional information on each major theme in smaller and more focused articles.

In other words, in addition to the long overview essays documenting the historical experiences of each of the principal national-origin groups, including the growing population of the border region, we further divided and organized the Encyclopedia.

Thematic essays. These are survey essays, broadly conceived and interdisciplinary in character, that provide the reader with general background information on each group, identify significant individuals, events, and issues that have shaped the history and experience of the group in question, and document the group's contribution to the development of the nation.

Issue essays. These essays focus on various aspects of the broader thematic articles described above. Interdisciplinary articles of varying lengths were broadly or narrowly conceived according to both existing and available research and the significance of the topic. Wherever possible, we tried to ensure that these essays, like all of the articles, incorporate discussions that resonate (or not) in the histories and/or cultures of all the various national-origin groups. Whether longer or shorter, they allowed us to include, albeit not extensively, particular developments or individuals.

Biographies. Finally, we included a relatively small number of short biographies that aim to document the lives of particular Latinos and Latinas. While the members of the editorial board all agreed that the structural conditions that shape the historical experiences and lives of Latinos and Latinas are undoubtedly the focus of this Encyclopedia, we also wanted to profile certain pioneering individuals whose resourcefulness and creativity have helped to pave the way for Latinos and Latinas.

It is important to note that we are fully aware of the many Latinos and Latinas whom we could not include but who have also contributed in myriad ways to making life in this society better for both other Latinos and Latinas and non-Latinos and non-Latinas alike. In deciding to include some biographies, our aim was certainly not to be inclusive. Because there are other works that do focus on and provide biographical information on a number of Latinos and Latinas, we decided to include primarily—and in most areas solely—the pioneers, that is, those who were the first in their respective fields or those who, by their lives, actions, and/or writings, have left their indelible marks in U.S. history and in the history of Latinos and Latinas in the United States. Hence, given the limitations of space, and while biography was by no means the focus of this project, we tried to include substantial case-study material and discussions of the significant historical and contemporary contributions to U.S. society of (exemplary) individual members of each Latino and Latina national origin group.

Caveats

A project of this size cannot but have its shortcomings, some of which (for example those caused, as we suggest above, by the limitations of space) are beyond our control. While from the beginning we envisioned this Encyclopedia as merely a modest contribution toward shaping what we referred to earlier in this essay as a "living encyclopedia," we were eventually forced to acknowledge that we would be unable to fulfill the expectations—our own, and those of others—that even in these more modest terms this massive undertaking entailed. Hence, there will be those who will undoubtedly point to gaps, as well as some who may disagree with the perspective, the decisions, the direction, that we chose to adopt.

Indeed, a project of this size is a daunting undertaking for anyone. Above all, it entailed on the one hand an awareness—which brought us together as a collective—of the significance of our task (the production of these four volumes documenting the experience of U.S. Latinos and Latinas), and on the other hand its corollary, the need to arrive at a consensus even when we did not necessarily agree with one another. Given the varied experiences that have structured our own lives and knowledge, achieving these two prerequisites required questioning and engaging in an ongoing dialogue about our own political stances, historical knowledge, and disciplinary understandings. These discussions often involved acknowledging the integrity of our personal histories and politics as much as they did negotiating our regional positioning and disciplinary understandings. In addition, our awareness of the implications of producing a project that we all agreed had to be accessible to the mainstream was complicated by the knowledge that even the placement—let alone the naming of a group—was in itself a pedagogical act, given the appalling lack of knowledge about Latinos and Latinas.

Given the multiple labels—whether defined by Latinos and Latinas themselves or by others—and their importance in the definition of both groups and individuals, we opted to write an essay, which we called "Latino Identities and Ethnicities," discussing all the terms as a way of highlighting the complexity of the very issue of naming a population whose exclusion from belonging to this society as full citizens has been partially ensured through invisibility. Labels, like names, do have a life of their own, sometimes quite removed from those who create them, even as they provide us with an ongoing signal of the meaning of our social, political, cultural, and historical experiences. In bringing together in one essay all the labels by which various groups within the Latino and Latina population are known—instead of scattering them alphabetically throughout the four volumes—we affirm the diversity of the historical, national, social, and cultural experiences that each term inherently contains.

We want to emphasize that we do not see this Encyclopedia as a finished product. Rather, for us, it is only a beginning—a perhaps audacious but clearly necessary beginning of the compilation of knowledge about Latinos and Latinas in the United States. At the same time, putting this project together and seeing it through completion—all the time knowing that no matter how hard we tried our very humanity along with the humanity and complexity of the population we are presenting here ensures that we could not produce the perfect project we all wanted—has also been a new experience for all of us. Still, as an editorial team, we learned with and from each other as well as from all our contributors, and we taught ourselves and others about this population's complex experience. It is a beginning that we decided to undertake not only for the sake of Latinos and Latinas but also for the sake of all those who, like us, believe that only through inclusion of all populations in this country's historical knowledge and contemporary events will we truly achieve a community of equals—or its modern synonym, a citizenry—in this country.

From this point of view, for all of us on this project's editorial team, knowledge, systematically classified and organized, is by no means a passive meditative activity. Rather, as this project has shown us, it is and has been an invaluable constructive experience of collaboration and discovery, both for us as the organizers as well as for the practitioners in our particular intellectual fields. At the same time, we hope that it is, or at least that it can also be, something more.

Acknowledgments

Finally, as coeditors, we want to express our very deep appreciation to everyone who helped us and contributed to this project. First and foremost, of course, *mil gracias* to the seven senior editors without whom this Encyclopedia would never have seen the light of day. As we have tried to document above, their commitment, participation, and involvement in this project—to say nothing of their wonderful sense of humor and solidarity, kept us focused and ensured its successful completion. Thanks also go to our contributors, for their enthusiastic collaboration and participation. We owe immense gratitude to the editorial staff and professional editors at Oxford University Press, who followed our dream and insisted on a timely completion, including Karen Day, Timothy DeWerff, Stephen Wagley, Georgia Maas, Ralph Carlson, Meera Vaidyanathan, Sarah Feehan, and Erin Carter, as well as all the other assistants who were on board at various times during the three years this project took to come to fruition; to all those family members and friends who supported us for three years in spite of our arrogant audacity in agreeing to take this project on and to completion; and last, but not least, to each other.

SUZANNE OBOLER AND DEENA J. GONZÁLEZ

THE OXFORD ENCYCLOPEDIA OF

LATINOS AND LATINAS IN THE UNITED STATES

A

ACEQUIAS. In its current context, the term *acequia* has three distinct but interrelated meanings. First, it refers to the irrigation ditches established by the Spanish Mexican settlers in the northernmost frontier of New Spain, a region that became part of Mexico after the country gained independence in 1821, which the United States then acquired in 1848, comprising most of the American Southwest. Second, it refers to the subsistence-based farming cultures and communities that have coevolved with, and depend upon, acequia irrigation systems. Third, it refers to acequia associations, common property resource institutions that oversee irrigation-ditch maintenance, operations, and water distribution, and often serve as the only formal local political organization in acequia communities.

Acequias—irrigation systems, farming communities, and local common property resource institutions—remain vital to the economic and cultural survival of traditional Indo-Hispano communities in the American Southwest, particularly in a stretch of the Rio Grande Basin from its headwaters in southern Colorado through New Mexico. While it is estimated that roughly a thousand acequias and their corresponding acequia associations still exist in New Mexico and southern Colorado, they are the subject of much political discussion and debate as their rights and vitality are threatened by unprecedented growth, changing economies, and increasing demands and new priorities for water use throughout the region.

Community Irrigation Systems

In the late 1590s, Spanish Mexican settlers crossed the Rio Grande, which forms part of the current United States–Mexico border, to expand the northern frontier of New Spain beyond present-day Mexico. At the time, the northern frontier was populated by indigenous Tiwa, Tewa, and Keresan Pueblo Indians who had developed irrigated agriculture systems based on natural flood cycles and the domestication of small-scale waterways. Archaeological evidence demonstrates that these systems were likely adapted from more primitive ones developed by the Anasazi Indians, who predated the Pueblos. Prior to the arrival of Spanish Mexican colonists, Pueblo Indian tribes had established their agricultural settlements in flood-prone areas and along easily diverted watercourses.

The arid rugged mountains and grasslands of the northern frontier of New Spain resembled the settlers' own native landscapes in many ways and were appropriate for transplanting their own irrigation methods, accompanying settlement patterns, and agricultural practices. As they colonized the region and began establishing agricultural settlements, the newcomers integrated elements of the flood irrigation methods and environmental knowledge used by the indigenous Pueblo farmers with their own agricultural system brought from Spain and Mexico, which had its roots in Roman and Arabic irrigation technologies.

Acequia technology enabled large quantities of water to be diverted from major waterways, including the Rio Grande, Rio Chama, Rio Taos, and Rio Pecos, facilitating the proliferation of Spanish settlements in previously undeveloped areas that lacked immediate water sources or that did not flood regularly. The first colonial settlement in New Spain, located close to the junction of the Rio Grande and the Rio Chama, at what is now the town of Española, New Mexico, was established in 1598 by Capitán General Juan de Oñate. The San Juan Acequia de Común, laid out by Oñate for the colony and still in operation, is reputed to be the oldest continuously operating irrigation canal in the United States.

The resulting acequia irrigation systems are typically composed of networks of gravity-driven, earthen ditches, which are fed by the snowmelt from high alpine streams and individual flood-irrigated farm plots, the latter known as long lots or *varas*, extending from the ditches. Typically, a diversion dam redirects water from a river or stream. *Compuertas* (head gates) constructed out of locally available materials release water into an *acequia madre* (mother ditch), or main canal, which forms the main water diversion channel. Smaller ditches branch off downstream and distribute water to individual varas. Drainage channels, or *desagues*, redirect water from the fields back to the original waterway. Each acequia was constructed by hand without the convenience of modern tools.

Acequia irrigation methods, technologies, and governing practices are derived from those that were common in

ACEQUIA. Acequia near Penasco, New Mexico, 1940. (Prints and Photographs Division, Library of Congress)

regions of southern Spain, especially Andalusia and Valencia, which were founded upon Roman irrigation strategies that included aqueducts for water transport, floodgates, and customs of Arabic influence introduced by the Moorish occupation of Spain. Like many other Spanish terms related to water, the word acequia is derived from an Arabic term, *as-Saquia*, meaning "the water bearer." Acequias, with technological influences dating back hundreds of years in northern Africa, the Iberian Peninsula, and the Middle East, have proven to be effective strategies for harnessing and evenly distributing water resources in arid and semiarid climates.

Acequia irrigation systems defined the settlement patterns and boundaries for towns and villages in the Spanish colonial Southwest. In fact, because of their centrality in the development of agricultural communities, Spanish colonial law, las Leyes de las Indias (Law of the Indies), required that irrigation systems be constructed, along with churches and military forts, prior to populating frontier settlements. Varas along acequias were granted to individual families, and common lands for grazing, firewood gathering, timber and medicinal plant harvesting, and hunting were made available to all of the members of the community who presented themselves for inspection and approval. *Parciantes,* those who had farm plots along acequias, participated in the construction and maintenance of early acequia ditches, as they continue to do today. In early cases, separate acequias were established for indigenous Pueblo farmers adjacent to Hispano settlements. Although not always successfully secured, cooperation from native Pueblo populations was considered critical in

protecting settlements against attacks from hostile Indian bands, which forced the abandonment of many early settlements.

Although many acequias, especially in the Middle Rio Grande Basin, have been lined with concrete or covered to prevent water from leaching into the ground or evaporating, traditional earthen acequia construction has been shown to be ecologically regenerative, supporting a variety of ecological processes. Water leached from the ditches replenishes the water table, and it creates wetland oases and riparian corridors that house migratory birds and other wildlife. Additionally, flood irrigation methods have been shown to distribute minerals and nutrients that continuously improve soil quality.

Farming Cultures

Multigenerational environmental knowledge has made acequia farming practices highly sustainable and adaptive to local circumstances. For example, acequia farmers grow heirloom varieties of corn, beans, squash, and other crops that have been refined to suit the particular microclimatic, soil, and hydrological conditions of family farm locations, thus minimizing the need for external inputs. Medicinal and edible native plants are often integrated into planting schemes to complement introduced domestic crops. Irrigation schedules and water distribution decisions are made according to keen understandings of precipitation regimes and climatic fluctuations. For these reasons, acequia agricultural traditions have been highly adaptive and resilient in the face of drought and other environmental changes. Their persistence has enabled them to provide the economic, cultural, and social foundations of rural Hispano communities in the Southwest for hundreds of years.

Political Institutions

Acequia governing practices in the Southwest have roots in the diverse water traditions of southern Spain, which were influenced by Islamic customs during the period of Moorish occupation. The "Customary Law of the Acequias" established democratic institutions with a membership of all parciantes along an irrigation ditch. Each parciante gets one vote in the annual election of three commissioners and a mayordomo, or "ditch boss," who make decisions regarding water distribution and usage, as well as a plethora of other important community matters. In many unincorporated towns in the Southwest, acequia associations have been the only formally organized local political body, handling all sorts of community and social issues. Acequias de común are, by definition, community resources and cannot be privately held, and thus acequia associations are common property resource governing institutions, managing acequias for the benefit of the entire community, and sharing in the cost and labor of ditch maintenance.

The customary government of acequia associations in the Southwest, which remain virtually unchanged since colonial times, was codified in Spanish colonial law. The Leyes de las Indias included instructions for settling disputes, distributing water, determining labor contributions for constructing and maintaining ditches, and appointing officials through democratic election. The annual spring cleaning of the acequias is a community event, in which representatives from every parciante must participate. The cost and labor for other ditch maintenance activities, such as repairing compuertas and dams, and building additional diversions or bridges, are also shared by parciantes.

The Spanish colonial period ended in 1821, when the northern frontier region became part of independent Mexico. Almost thirty years later, it was annexed by the United States following the United States–Mexican War. Acequia laws and customs remained virtually unchallenged by the Mexican and early U.S. territorial governments in New Mexico. The first water laws adopted by the Territorial Assembly of New Mexico in 1851 assured that acequia customs would be continued in territorial New Mexico. Acequia associations continued to operate as autonomous bodies and to freely determine surface water uses until the turn of the twentieth century.

However, U.S. occupation introduced an Anglo-American property rights system that recognizes only private and public forms of property, which would eventually erode the Spanish-derived system. The Anglo-American legal designations contributed to the dismantling of the Spanish and Mexican communal land grants in New Mexico during the late nineteenth century. During this period, most land grants, which had contained forms of private property (varas) and communal property to be shared among community members (grazing land, forest resources, water), were divided and either privatized or handed over to the state. U.S. law did not accommodate communal property, even though access to these resources had been guaranteed to land grant heirs by the Treaty of Guadalupe Hidalgo, the agreement that ended the war between the United States and Mexico in February 1848. The U.S. government failed to honor the customary laws that had been applied to the regulation of communal resources for centuries.

Legal distinctions similar to those applied to land in the division of Spanish Mexican land grants were ultimately applied to water by the territorial government. The 1907 Water Code adopted by the New Mexico Territorial Assembly turned surface water resources over to the public domain and established the territorial government as the sole administrator and decision maker in matters of water distribution. The 1907 Water Code was carried over when the territory of New Mexico became a state in 1912. The Office of the State Engineer (OSE) was later established to oversee water distribution and management in the state of New Mexico. The shift in water management eroded the sovereignty that had previously been afforded to acequia associations. This was especially true in the Middle Rio Grande Basin, where water development projects spearhead by federal and state bureaucratic agencies forced the seventy-two acequias in the region to operate under the oversight of the Middle Rio Grande Conservancy District. However, farther north in the Upper Rio Grande Basin (colloquially known as Río Arriba), acequias continued to operate primarily as self-governing bodies despite the formal change in governance over water.

As in other parts of the western United States, water in the Southwest was primarily distributed according to a doctrine of prior appropriation, which holds that the first users to appropriate water resources are granted senior water rights to their full shares of water, and excess available water is granted to junior water rights holders if it is available. Junior water rights are fulfilled depending on the availability of water resources in a given year, which means that in drought years, junior water rights holders may not get their full shares.

Such a system is at odds with acequia customary law, which puts the welfare of the community over that of the individual and considers water to be a communal, not an individual or "public," resource. Water is customarily distributed amongst parciantes according to a system of *repartamiento de agua*, or water sharing. Thus, senior water rights holders share in scarcity in years when each parciante's water rights cannot be met. Many acequias continued to practice communal repartamiento, even though it was inconsistent with Anglo-American legal designations.

In New Mexico, acequia associations regained some of their previously recognized decision-making authority when the state legislature acknowledged them as political subdivisions of the state in 1978, after a long lobbying effort by organized acequia advocates (Section 7-2-28 NMSA 1978). An estimated eight hundred acequias are still in operation in the state. As descendants of the earliest settlers to inhabit the area, members of acequia communities hold the second most senior rights in the state, following only the Pueblo tribes' rights. Consistent with Anglo-American property law, individual parciantes hold individual rights to water and can sell their rights in water markets or forfeit their rights for failure of use. The 1978 legislation, however, granted acequia associations the authority to distribute water within acequias according to their customary laws. The New Mexico legislature also established an acequia commission to advise the legislature on acequia-related issues.

The state of Colorado, on the other hand, with nearly two hundred acequias, operates exclusively on the basis of prior appropriation laws and does not officially grant acequias the authority to distribute water according to their customary laws. Many Colorado acequias have continued to exercise self-governance and distribute water according to acequia customs, but they are not protected in doing so by law as they are in New Mexico. Therefore, Colorado acequias are even more vulnerable to disruption by new water uses and claims to water rights than are the acequias across the state line in New Mexico.

Contemporary Struggles

Unprecedented population and industrial growth, and amplified environmental and endangered species–protection regulations, have increased the demand for water in New Mexico and Colorado. Since the 1960s, re-adjudication processes in both states, intended to allocate water according to "priority uses," have required acequias to engage in costly legal procedures in order to maintain their historic water rights. Some struggles have endured for decades, such as the heated struggle over Rio Taos resources in the 1980s and 1990s, which brought out tensions between acequia communities and a burgeoning tourist economy in the Taos Valley. Acequias in New Mexico have been somewhat successful in legally protecting their rights by invoking a 1985 state statute that prevents the Office of the State Engineer, which oversees water allocation and makes recommendations to the courts in

adjudications, from approving water transfers that would be deleterious to the public welfare of the state or to conservation efforts. These legal battles have been widely publicized and have attracted the attention of the general public and the media, as well as regional, national, and international activists for environmental justice and civil rights. John Nichols's 1974 novel *The Milagro Beanfield War*, and a 1988 film version directed by Robert Redford, helped introduce to a mainstream audience acequia struggles over traditional and new priorities for water use in acequia watersheds.

Acequias have adapted to changing social and environmental circumstances for four centuries. The legal, political, and cultural successes of acequias have been achieved through the collective action of acequia communities, as well as through the support of grassroots networks and individual advocates working to promote traditional resource rights and the preservation of traditional communities. As is the case for many rural agricultural communities in the western United States, acequia communities are finding it increasingly difficult to maintain their lands and their livelihoods.

Unfortunately, acequia cohesion is threatened not only by the strain of outside forces but also by pressures exerted from within acequia communities. Many acequia farmers have found the contemporary economic and social hardship of maintaining their lands and their livelihoods too difficult and have migrated away from their ancestral communities. Others have invoked the rights guaranteed to parciantes under prior appropriation in order to sell their shares of water on the market, leaving less communal water available to others along the acequias. Every drop of water removed from acequias takes water away from the rest of the community, and every farmer who leaves diminishes the community's capacity for collective action. The viability of acequia farming and irrigation systems, acequia community vitality, and acequia associations' political sovereignty over their common property resources all depend on the cohesion of the community and mutual participation in traditional acequia practices, laws, and norms.

See also Border, The; Colorado Acequia Association; Environmental Justice; Land Grants; *and* New Mexico Acequia Association.

VANESSA MAZAL

ACOSTA, IVÁN (b. 1943), playwright and screenplay writer. Iván Acosta was born in Oriente Province, Cuba. He left Cuba in 1961, emigrating to the New York area, where he started in theater as an actor and discovered his interest in playwriting. He studied film at New York University and gained instant attention with *El súper*. This play was presented in 1977 at the Centro Cultural Cubano—a vital and instrumental agent in promoting and preserving Cuban theater in New York in the 1970s. *El súper* became an instant hit of the Hispanic theater, receiving good reviews and winning awards. Among the many awards that Acosta has received over the course of his career are the Cintas Fellowships for Cuban writers and artists, the ACE Award for Best Writer, the Thalia Best Writer Award, and the Ariel Best Writer Award.

El súper was later adapted into a film directed by León Ichaso and Orlando Jiménez Leal. The popularity of *El súper* marked a milestone in the Latino and Latina art scene in the United States. Both works drew attention to the experiences of Cubans and other immigrants while broadening the scope of Cuban cultural productions in the United States.

El súper is the quintessential Cuban film. A dramatic comedy, it focuses on the domestic experiences of a Cuban family that left Cuba after the outbreak of the revolution. It tells the story of Roberto Amador González, his wife, Aurelia, and their daughter, Aurelita, in New York City. Roberto, a middle-aged man of humble origins and underprivileged background, works as a building superintendent in Manhattan. The film concentrates on his family's experiences as marginal people in a country with a language and traditions different from their own. The fact that they live in the basement of the building where Roberto works underscores the sense of imprisonment and marginalization that the characters suffer. Cold weather and snow enhance the sense of desolation in the film.

Like many of Acosta's works, the film is concerned with alienation in the Cuban family. The tone of the film is bitter and satiric. The three characters, Roberto, Aurelia, and Aurelita, express different forms and degrees of frustration. Roberto is a reflexive and melancholic character who is dissatisfied with his life in New York City. Many of the scenes that present Roberto fulfilling his duties as a building superintendent show that he is incapable of connecting with others. Aurelia is at home and concerned with family and health care issues. Aurelita does not understand why her parents talk so much about Cuba. She represents a new generation—one that is assimilated and that chooses to speak English instead of Spanish.

The play and the film are unique in the scope of their representations of Cuban exiles. In an interview published in *OLLANTAY Theater Magazine*, Acosta stated that he wrote the screenplay because he felt that his message was important and because people needed to see works with this particular point of view.

Many of Acosta's plays are concerned with Cuban sociopolitical themes and the exploration of the impact of the revolution on the lives of Cubans living abroad and those still on the island. His plays *Abdalá-José Martí, Un cubiche en la luna*, and *Recojan las serpentinas que se acabó el carnaval* present political commentaries. *Abdalá-José Martí* was the first play in Spanish to be part of the Lincoln Center Theater Festival. While *Abdalá-José Martí*—inspired by a text by José Martí—deals with issues of freedom, *Un cubiche en la luna* explores in a humorous way issues of language, identity, freedom, and alienation in revolutionary Cuba. The play, which opens with one of the characters asking, "What will the future bring?" uses humor and irony to attack revolutionary ideology and dogmatism. Among the issues presented are the influence of the Russian language in spoken Cuban Spanish, housing problems, scarcity of food, and political repression and propaganda.

Like other Cuban artists and writers during the 1980s, Acosta turned his attention to the wave of Cuban immigration associated with the Mariel boatlift. His film *Amigos* (1986) centers on the experiences of Cubans who came to the United States as part of the Mariel crisis. His documentary *Como se forma una rumba*, an entertaining and educational film chronicling the roots of Cuban dance rhythms, premiered at the Latin Jazz Festival and was shown with great success in New York, New Jersey, and Miami, as well as in several film festivals.

Acosta has served as the producer of the Latin Jazz USA concerts at Carnegie Hall, Lincoln Center, and at the Jackie Gleason Theater in Miami Beach.

See also **Cuban Americans; Film; Marielitos; Performing Arts and Theater;** *and* **Playwrights.**

BIBLIOGRAPHY

Acosta, Iván. *El súper*. Miami, Fla.: Ediciones Universal, 1982.
Acosta, Iván. *Tres obras teatrales*. Houston, Tex.: Arte Público Press, 1989.
Febles, Jorge. "*El súper*: Epic Resonance within a Nondialectic Construct." *Michigan Academician* 18, no. 2 (Spring 1986): 295–302.
"The Playwrights Speak: Iván Acosta. ¿Qué cómo comenzó todo? Como son las cosas cuando son del alma." *OLLANTAY Theater Magazine* 2, no. 1 (1994): 59–62.

ELENA M. MARTÍNEZ

ACOSTA, OSCAR "ZETA" (1935–1974), writer and lawyer. Oscar Acosta was born in El Paso, Texas, on April 8, 1935 (though biographical records differ slightly on this date). Soon after his birth, in search of work, his Mexican émigré parents moved to a small town at the outskirts of Modesto, California. Acosta grew up in this largely agricultural belt of the San Joaquin Valley, where he learned early on of his differences both racially as a Mexican American and in physical size. On the school grounds, he was regularly the target of racist epithets, especially from his white, working-class "Okie" classmates but also from

bigoted teachers. In his autobiography, he powerfully recalls his childhood: "I grew up a fat, dark Mexican—a Brown Buffalo—and my enemies called me a nigger" (Acosta 1972, p. 86). As a teenager, Acosta continued to rub up against a racist America, and he survived by learning to laugh at and make fun of his xenophobic world. This spirit later transformed into a playfully satiric writing style.

After barely making the grades to graduate from high school (a fact he later extolled as part of his comedic tendency to play up his mediocrity), Acosta first worked as a missionary in Panama and then attended creative writing and French classes at a junior college in Modesto. He spent some time in Los Angeles, where he sat for and passed the sheriff's exams (he campaigned unsuccessfully to become the LA County sheriff). Later, he settled in San Francisco. After years of taking night-school law courses, he eventually passed the California bar exam on June 28, 1966. During the civil rights movement, Acosta worked as a lawyer representing the urban poor in Oakland, California. Relocating to Los Angeles, he worked as a defense attorney for activist Chicanos and Chicanas wrongfully incarcerated during the height of the Brown Power movement in the late 1960s. He became well known among Chicanos and Chicanas and was a media headliner because of his sharp wit yet playful and sardonic defense style.

From an early age, Acosta was fascinated by stories, including his father's experiences as a horse trader and as a U.S. sailor during World War II and his mother's experiences as a naturalized Mexican growing up in El Paso. Although he did not excel at school, Acosta as a young man was greatly influenced by writers such as Federico García Lorca, Ernest Hemingway, Jack Kerouac, Henry Miller, and Bob Dylan. He sensed that one day he would be a writer, and he saved all his notes, journals, stories written on scraps of paper, and poems. In 1970, he published his first short story, "Perla Is a Pig," in the Chicano and Chicana literary magazine *Con Safos*. The story was later included in Ilan Stavan's collection *Oscar "Zeta" Acosta: The Uncollected Works* (1996). His playful tone and mixing of fact and fiction became a trademark in books such as *The Autobiography of a Brown Buffalo* (1972) and *The Revolt of the Cockroach People* (1973). Acosta's blurring of fact and fiction and quick-paced, drug-induced writing style informed Hunter S. Thompson's "gonzo style" of reportage. Thompson's alleged failure to acknowledge Acosta's creative contribution to his work tore their friendship apart, according to Acosta's published account of their rupture in the October 15, 1973, issue of *Playboy* magazine. This account was later included in Stavan's *Oscar "Zeta" Acosta: The Uncollected Works*.

When Acosta published *The Autobiography of a Brown Buffalo*, many Chicanos and Chicanas celebrated its satiric irreverence not just toward mainstream society but also toward its critique of categories of racial self-identification that stifle one's experiences in the world. In this picaresque odyssey, he continually blurs the line between fact and fiction, reordering biographical chronology to announce his age as the same "as Jesus when he died," for example (Acosta 1972, p. 18). He playfully identifies himself variously as Samoan and American Indian to disrupt prejudice and finally comes into his sense of self, declaring: "I am neither a Mexican nor an American. I am neither a Catholic nor a Protestant. I am a Chicano by ancestry and a Brown Buffalo by choice" (Acosta 1972, p. 199). Acosta wrote *The Revolt of the Cockroach People* in the same playful and parodic style, creatively refashioning the time he worked in Los Angeles defending activists incarcerated during the explosive civil rights battles over racist education systems and public policy making that discriminated against Chicanos and Chicanas. Acosta brings to life both the pains and the pleasures of the landmark case *Castro v. The Superior Court of Los Angeles*, in which he defended with his trademark wit and bravado those indicted during the East Los Angeles high school walk outs.

Sometime in June 1974, Acosta disappeared off the coast of Mazatlán on a friend's sailing boat. It is believed that he died at sea, but his body was never found. Many have speculated that Acosta relocated to somewhere in Mexico, having staged his death to slide off the "wanted" list of the Central Intelligence Agency's (CIA). Acosta's creative spirit was a step ahead of his time and certainly far ahead of many so-called "first-wave" writers who often portrayed Chicanos and Chicanas as cut off from the mainstream and in an essentialist light. A Chicano writer, activist, and social critic, he dared to experiment with storytelling form and to self-reflexively contour Chicano and Chicana experience as intricately woven into U.S. mainstream culture.

See also Literature.

BIBLIOGRAPHY
Acosta, Oscar Zeta. *The Autobiography of a Brown Buffalo*. San Francisco: Straight Arrow Books, 1972.
Acosta, Oscar Zeta. *The Revolt of the Cockroach People*. San Francisco: Straight Arrow Books, 1973.
Aldama, Frederick Luis. *Postethnic Narrative Criticism: Magicorealism in Oscar "Zeta" Acosta, Ana Castillo, Julie Dash, Hanif Kureishi, and Salman Rushdie*. Austin: University of Texas Press, 2003.
Rivera, Tomás. "Into the Labyrinth: The Chicano in Literature." *Southwestern American Literature* 2, no. 2 (1972): 90–97.
Rodríguez, Joe D. "The Chicano Novel and the North American Narrative of Survival." *Denver Quarterly* 16 (Fall 1981): 229–235.
Rodríguez, Joe D. "God's Silence and the Shrill of Ethnicity in the Chicano Novel." *Explorations in Ethnic Studies* 4 (July 1981): 14–21.
Rodríguez, Joe D. "The Sense of Mestizaje in Two Latino Novels." *Revista Chicano-Riqueña* 12 (Spring 1984): 57–63.
Smith, Norman D. "Buffalos and Cockroaches: Acosta's Siege at Aztlán." *Latin American Literary Review* 5 (Spring–Summer 1977): 85–97.
Stavans, Ilan. *Bandido: Oscar "Zeta" Acosta and the Chicano Experience*. New York: IconEditions, 1995.
Stavans, Ilan. *Oscar "Zeta" Acosta: The Uncollected Works*. Houston, Tex.: Arte Público Press, 1996.

FREDERICK LUIS ALDAMA

ACTORS AND ACTRESSES. Latinos and Latinas have been a part of the Hollywood film industry since Cecil B. DeMille brought his Lasky Players to the Golden State in 1913. Los Angeles had a large Mexican American population, and many secured employment in the new start-up industry as extra players, stunt people, and actors.

Western film dramas were a staple of the new industry, and stock characters in these films presented opportunities for Latino and Latina players. Such characters were usually the most negative stereotypes of Latinos and Latinas: mustachioed, sombrero-wearing, dark and swarthy banditos; light-skinned Spanish grandees; virginal senoritas; sexually available, hip-swinging, heel-clicking cantina girls; and vamps. These stereotypes had their origins in the popular literature of the time.

Because of strict racial codes, the Latino and Latina actors working in leading roles were generally light skinned and Caucasian; and though some were Mexican born, they were generally of Spanish heritage. Darker-skinned actors usually played villains, banditos, poor peons, or Native Americans. Actors with strong indigenous features were never seen on screen in lead roles.

Silent Films

In the early days of silent filmmaking, most movie audiences in the United States were undedicated immigrant masses. Movies were considered a curiosity and a low form of entertainment. Theater, literature, and music were the legitimate and accepted forms of entertainment. Silent cinema was an international phenomenon, yet it was not dependent on language. An actor's voice and ability to speak, while essential in the theater, were unimportant in silent cinema. Language barriers were nonexistent. Some actors had stage training, and others had a natural affinity for the camera with no previous stage experience. Both could be equally effective with audiences. Indeed, the influence of these actors was immediately apparent; their films played all over the world, and everyone knew the stars. The power of film images to create characters and tell stories that would leave an impression on people was enormous.

Latinos. Antonio Moreno was born and grew up in Spain. He moved to New York at an early age to pursue a career on the stage. Moreno traveled to California and worked in bit parts in films until he was discovered by the famed film pioneer D. W. Griffith, who launched him on a screen career in 1914. Moreno was a romantic leading man and was actually the screen's first "Latin Lover," before the term took on new meaning with the arrival of the Italian-born silent screen superstar Rudolph Valentino. Dark good looks and smoldering intensity on screen made Valentino a film icon of enormous stature that eclipsed Moreno's career. Thus, the Latin Lover of this time was a Mediterranean type character, not necessarily Hispanic, South American, or Mexican. That assignation came later with the ascendancy of actors who followed in Valentino's footsteps, including Mexican-born Ramon Novarro and Gilbert Roland and the actress Dolores Del Rio, who was first promoted as a "Female Valentino."

Moreno starred with many of the leading ladies of the silent period, including Gloria Swanson, Clara Bow, and Greta Garbo in her second Hollywood film. When sound films arrived, Moreno made the transition from silent pictures to talkies as a character actor. He also spent some

RAMON NAVARRO. (© Topham Picture Point/The Image Works)

time in Mexico directing and starring in a number of Spanish-language films that helped to establish the Mexican film industry. As he matured, Moreno worked increasingly as a supporting actor in many important Hollywood productions in a variety of roles. His white hair, handsome features, and diction lent themselves to contemporary, western, and period dramas such as *Rose of the Rio Grande* (1938), *Captain from Castille* (1947), and *The Searchers* (1956).

Ramon Novarro was born in Durango, Mexico, but in 1913 his family fled to the United States to escape the Mexican Revolution. Dark and handsome, Novarro was discovered, in a theater production, by the famed Hollywood director Rex Ingram, who cast him in the 1922 film version of *The Prisoner of Zenda*. Novarro was an immediate hit with the public. In 1925, he starred in the worldwide hit *Ben-Hur*, the picture that saved Metro Pictures from bankruptcy.

Novarro was followed into stardom shortly thereafter by another young man, Luis Antonio Damaso de Alonso, better known as Gilbert Roland. Roland's career spanned over sixty years, from matinee idol to consummate supporting actor. Born in 1905 in Juarez, Mexico, he moved with his family to El Paso, Texas, during the Mexican Revolution, when Pancho Villa threatened the lives of Mexicans of Spanish ancestry. Roland became enamored of all the people he saw on the silent screen and drifted to Los Angeles, where he obtained work as an extra player and even became a stunt double for Ramon Novarro on a film. The son of a former bullfighter, Roland also taught Valentino how to bullfight in preparation for *Blood and Sand*. Discovered by an agent in 1925, he soon starred opposite Clara Bow in *The Plastic Age*. A year later, he attained stardom opposite Norma Talmadge in *Camille* (1926).

Leo Carrillo was born in an adobe structure in Los Angeles, of true Californio, Spanish-Mexican parentage. He attended grammar school and college, and after stints as a railroad engineer, cartoonist, and vaudevillian began his legitimate stage career in 1914 on Broadway. He appeared in numerous plays and shows until he made his film debut in 1929 in *Mr. Antonio*. Carrillo became a gifted supporting player and character actor in films, playing every kind of ethnicity and character.

Latinas. The first Latina actor of any prominence was Beatriz Michelina, an actress of the Spanish theater who performed in San Francisco. She starred in sixteen silent films that were made in California and distributed nationwide. Myrtle Gonzalez, a Mexican American actress, costarred in more than thirty outdoor action feature films for the Vitagraph Company from 1914 until her untimely death from influenza in 1918.

Dolores Del Rio was discovered at a party in Mexico by an American director, Edwin Carewe. Although she was

DOLORES DEL RIO. (Getty Images/General Photographic Agency)

A number of actresses played assorted Polynesian, Indian, and Mexican types during the 1930s. Mexican-born Raquel Torres starred in the Academy Award–winning film *White Shadows in the South Seas* (1928), and Lupita Tovar starred in the Spanish-Language version of *Drácula* (1931), filmed at Universal Studios at night on the sets of the Bela Lugosi version that was filmed during the day. The Mexican actress and dancer Margo had an important role in Frank Capra's *Lost Horizon* (1937) as the beautiful girl who withered and died upon leaving the enchanted valley. Maria Casteneda achieved brief popularity when, known as Movita, she played a native girl in Metro-Goldwyn-Mayer's 1935 production of *Mutiny on the Bounty*.

Sound

The development of sound in cinema allowed for the rise of films spoken in the language of the nations producing them. From 1927 until 1938, Hollywood, wishing to retain its dominance in the worldwide marketplace, produced foreign-language versions of English-language films and also original works. This gave writers, actors, and directors from Spain, Mexico, and other Latin American countries the opportunity to come to Hollywood and work in their own language. Despite having accents and with limited or no English-language capability, the majority of the actors made the transition from silent to sound films. Bilingual actors such as Gilbert Roland and Antonio Moreno were able to work in several versions of the same film. However, once dubbing techniques were perfected, multiple-language versions of films were discontinued.

Latino and Latina actors continued to work in a variety of roles in films throughout the 1930s. Most of these were supporting or character roles, but there was plenty of employment in the booming Hollywood movie industry. This period led to the rise of the actor of Hispanic/Latino origins who was born and/or raised in the United States and spoke English without an accent.

Latinas. Rita Hayworth was born Rita Cansino in Brooklyn, New York, to a Spanish father, Eduardo Cansino, and an Irish mother, Volga Haworth. Eduardo was a dancer and taught his whole family to perform. They appeared in theaters all across America and migrated to Hollywood, where they found work in nightclubs and in the movies. As Rita Cansino, Hayworth appeared with her father in countless westerns and period dramas as a Spanish or Mexican dancer.

She was later renamed Rita Hayworth, a variation on her mother's name, by a Columbia Pictures executive. Cosmetically altered and groomed for stardom, in a relatively short time she became the All-American girl starring in such pictures as *The Strawberry Blonde* (1941), returned to her Spanish and dance roots as Dona Sol in

not an actress, Del Rio's captivating dark beauty and dancing ability caught the attention of Carewe, who convinced the young Dolores to come to Hollywood in 1925. He immediately cast her in several motion pictures. Del Rio finally received attention when the director Raoul Walsh cast her as the feisty French farm girl in the hit film *What Price Glory?* (1926). Del Rio was considered one of the most beautiful women of the screen. She made the transition to sound films and later returned to Mexico, where she became a leading actress during the "Golden Age" of Mexican cinema in the 1940s and 1950s.

Lupe Velez began her career as Douglas Fairbanks's leading lady in *The Gaucho* (1927) and worked for all the leading directors of her time. She was typecast and later starred in a series of "Mexican Spitfire" B-films during the 1930s, modeled somewhat on her outrageous real-life personality.

Blood and Sand (1941) opposite Tyrone Power, and became Fred Astaire's and Gene Kelly's dance partner in several musicals. She reached the height of her screen fame with her role as Gilda (1946) in the film of the same name opposite Glenn Ford. She became one of the first stars to start her own production company through Columbia Pictures. One of her first productions was a film version of Prosper Merimee's novella *Carmen*. Though she changed her look and her name, Rita never denied her Spanish heritage, and on the production of *The Loves of Carmen* (1948) she hired her father to choreograph all the Spanish dance sequences.

Carmen Miranda was already an established film, stage, and recording star in Brazil before she came to the United States in 1939 and captivated audiences with her energy and Brazilian music on the Broadway stage in *The Streets of Paris*. She was offered a film contract by Twentieth Century Fox Studios in Hollywood, but was at first unable to leave the musical because of contractual commitments. So she performed on the stage at night and filmed her musical numbers during the day at a New York studio, and the footage was inserted into the film *Down Argentine Way* (1940). Her gyrating hips, mangling of the English language, and fruit-topped headdresses and platform shoes made her one of the highest-paid performers in Hollywood during the 1940s. A series of film appearances also transformed her into a caricature of the Latin woman. She made such a strong impression that by the end of the decade the public had grown tired of her image, which had never quite evolved or changed.

Maria Montez was born to a Spanish diplomat in the Caribbean nation of the Dominican Republic. Montez played sultry and beautiful Arabian princesses and native women in a series of Technicolor fantasy adventure dramas at Universal Pictures. Although she had a strong accent and a limited acting range, Montez found audience favor, especially when teamed with Jon Hall, her leading man in several films. She became one of the top money-making stars during the 1940s. Her beauty was so well suited to the Technicolor film photography of the period that she was proclaimed "Universal Pictures Queen of Technicolor."

Mapy Cortés, a Puerto Rican comedienne, appeared in two films at RKO Radio Pictures, but her film career fizzled in Hollywood, although she did continue performing in her native Puerto Rico and in Latin America. Olga San Juan, a Puerto Rican singer, actress, and dancer, was put under contract to Paramount Pictures during the mid-1940s, and she danced the torrid "Heat Wave" number with Fred Astaire in *Blue Skies* (1946) and costarred in *Variety Girl* (1947) and in *One Touch of Venus* (1948). San Juan appeared on Broadway in the original production of *Paint Your Wagon* (1951).

MARIA MONTEZ. (Walter Sanders/Time Life Pictures/Getty Images)

The American-born Lina Romay was a beautiful lead singer for the bandleader Xavier Cugat, a Spaniard who popularized Latin American band music in the United States. She landed a contract at MGM and appeared in several musical segments with Cugat and appeared opposite Clark Gable in *Adventure* (1945). Elena Verdugo, a California-born direct descendant of the Spanish settlers of early California, also started as a dancer and singer in Cugat's band. A contract at Twentieth Century Fox Studios, where she appeared as featured dancer in *Down Argentine Way* at the age of thirteen, led to a major role as a Tahitian beauty in *The Moon and the Sixpence* (1943). At

Universal, Verdugo starred in *House of Frankenstein* (1944) and *Little Giant* (1946).

As a result of the extension of President Roosevelt's "Good Neighbor Policy," Mexican actresses began to appear in American films. Esther Fernandez played the virginal senorita opposite Alan Ladd in *Two Years before the Mast* (1946); Maria Elena Marquez played a Native American opposite Clark Gable in *Across the Wide Missouri* (1951); and Sarita Montiel played a lovely cantina girl opposite Gary Cooper in *Vera Cruz* (1953).

In 1952, the Mexican actress Katy Jurado was considered for the part of Helen Ramirez, a wealthy woman with a dark past in the western *High Noon* (1952). The producer Stanley Kramer and the director Fred Zinnemann thought she was too young for the part and were concerned about her acting experience. They invited her to Hollywood for a screen test. Jurado, a veteran leading actress of seven years in Mexican films would not audition but instead asked Kramer to go to any Mexican movie house in downtown Los Angeles and watch any one of her films. He did, and she got the part, even though she did not speak one word of English. Her friend Antonio Moreno, the former silent-screen matinee idol, coached her, and she learned the lines phonetically. Her nuanced portrayal combined with her sultry and unique screen presence won over critics and audiences alike. A year later, she was nominated for an Academy Award for Best Supporting Actress as Spencer Tracy's Indian wife in *Broken Lance* (1954).

Susan Kohner, daughter of the Mexican actress Lupita Tovar and the Hollywood agent Paul Kohner, was nominated for an Oscar for Best Supporting Actress for her role in the film *Imitation of Life* in 1959. The Argentine-born actress Linda Cristal achieved popularity in the United States after working for six years in Mexican films. Her most important film role was as an available Mexican widow in John Wayne's *The Alamo* (1960).

Puerto Rican–born and New York–raised, Rita Moreno made her Broadway stage debut at seventeen in the play *Skydrift* (1945) opposite Eli Wallach. Spotted by an MGM talent scout, who put her under contract, she was soon on her way to Hollywood. Moreno thought she would be a star and appeared in bit parts in *Singin' in the Rain* (1952) and *Pagan Love Song* (1950) She was loaned out to other studios, but there was no place for a Latina except in the traditional mostly stereotypical roles. In order to make a living, she worked in what she called several variations of the one-dimensional "Rosita, Pepita" type roles in a number of motion pictures. Her big break came when she was cast as the oriental ingénue in the Oscar-winning musical film *The King and I* (1956). This led to her being cast in the role of the fiery Puerto Rican Anita, opposite the virginal non-Latina Natalie Wood as Maria in *West Side Story* (1961). Moreno won the Academy Award as Best Supporting Actress for her role. An Oscar usually promises the actor a better and wider variety of roles, but Moreno did not work for seven years after winning hers, because the roles offered were more of the same stereotypes. The actress returned to the stage, where she played in many productions in a variety of roles without restrictions, both on Broadway and in London. Moreno did eventually find suitable film roles; she worked with Marlon Brando in *Night of the Following Day* (1968) and with Jack Nicholson in *Carnal Knowledge* (1971). Moreno won Broadway's coveted Tony Award in 1975 for her performance as the wacky aspiring actress Googie Gomez in *The Ritz*. She later re-created the role in the film version. Moreno is one of a few woman performers to have earned the four major awards an actor can receive: an Oscar, an Emmy, a Tony, and a Grammy.

Raquel Welch, born Raquel Tejada in Chicago, Illinois, of a Bolivian father and an American mother, was one of the last of the studio-promoted film sex goddesses. She went from a struggling single mother with two small children to international screen fame during the decades of the late sixties and early seventies. Welch attended school near San Diego, California. She won numerous local beauty contests and secured modeling jobs. After several small roles in films, she landed a contract at Twentieth Century Fox. The actress retained her married name, Welch, and she found stardom as a fur-clad bikini cave woman in the film *One Million Years B.C.* (1966) This led to her being cast opposite the leading men of the period, including James Stewart, Dean Martin, and Frank Sinatra. Welch played a scientist in *Fantastic Voyage* (1966), a sexy female spy in *Fathom* (1967), and a Mexican heiress in *Bandolero!* (1968). She was also seen in a comedic role in Richard Lester's *The Three Musketeers* (1973).

The Cuban actress Elizabeth Peña found fame playing a sultry maid in *Down and out in Beverly Hills* (1986). Cuban-born and Venezuelan-raised, Maria Conchita Alonso was an established actress and singer when she was picked to play Robin Williams's Italian American girlfriend in *Moscow on the Hudson* (1984). The Mexican actress Elpidia Carillo, who has a dark, ethereal, indigenous beauty, played the quintessential native Latina girl in *The Border* (1982) with Jack Nicholson, *Predator* (1987), and *Salvador* (1986). The Mexican American filmmaker Gregory Nava used her in the same way in *My Family–Mi Familia* (1995), but with a difference. Her character is a human being with a point of view on the pain and joy of the immigrant experience.

The Nicaraguan-born fashion-model-turned-actress Barbara Carrera played a virginal senorita in *The Master Gunfighter* (1975), and a vamp, Fatima Bush, opposite Sean Connery in the James Bond adventure *Never Say*

OSCAR WINNERS AND NOMINEES

Latinos and Latinas who have won an Oscar		Latinos and Latinas who have been nominated for Oscars	
Jose Ferrer	Best Actor, *Cyrano de Bergerac* (1949)	Katy Jurado	Best Supporting Actress, *High Noon* (1952)
Anthony Quinn	Best Supporting Actor, *Viva Zapata!* (1952)	Anthony Quinn	Best Actor, *Wild Is the Wind* (1957)
	Best Supporting Actor, *Lust for Life* (1956)		Best Actor, *Zorba the Greek* (1964)
		Edward James Olmos	Best Actor, *Stand and Deliver* (1988)
Rita Moreno	Best Supporting Actress, *West Side Story* (1961)	Andy Garcia	Best Supporting Actor, *The Godfather, Part III* (1990)
Mercedes Ruehl	Best Supporting Actress, *The Fisher King* (1991)	Rosie Perez	Best Supporting Actress, *Fearless* (1993)
		Salma Hayek	Best Actress, *Frida* (2002)
Benicio Del Toro	Best Supporting Actor, *Traffic* (2000)	Benicio Del Toro	Best Supporting Actor, *26 Grams* (2003)
		Catalina Sandino Moreno	Best Supporting Actress, *Maria Full of Grace* (2005)

MARY BELTRÁN

Never Again (1983). New York–born Rachel Ticotin played a nurse who dies of a drug overdose in *Fort Apache the Bronx* (1981). Luis Valdez's *La Bamba* (1987) presents a strong-willed determined single mother in Connie, the rock and roll singer Ritchie Valens's mother, played by Rosana De Soto.

The Brazilian actress Sonia Braga gained international attention in a number of sexy Brazilian films and achieved the attention of Hollywood in Hector Babenco's worldwide hit film *Kiss of the Spider Woman* (1985). Braga has appeared in a number of American films, but her dark looks and accent have limited her opportunities in Hollywood.

Latinos. Cesar Romero was born in Manhattan to Cuban parents. He started as a ballroom dancer and made the transition into legitimate theater. Tall, dark, and handsome, Romero played gigolos, gangsters, and romantic leads on stage and was brought out to Hollywood under contract to Metro-Goldwyn-Mayer Studios, which placed him in several films then quickly dropped his contract. Romero found employment at Twentieth Century Fox Studios, which cast him in roles similar to those he had played on stage as well as in some nontraditional roles. He had a flair for musical comedy and so appeared in musicals, as well. Romero spoke with no accent and became quite adept at dialects in an ever-expanding character repertoire.

Anthony Quinn, perhaps the most important and versatile Hispanic American actor of his generation, was born in 1915 inside a railroad boxcar in Chihuahua, Mexico, during the Mexican Revolution. Quinn immigrated with his family to the United States and settled in East Los Angeles. The elder Quinn died when Anthony was a young boy, and Anthony worked at odd jobs to help support his family. Quinn was tall, and his Irish Mexican heritage gave him strong facial features that lent themselves to a wide variety of ethnic characters as defined by the Hollywood film standards of the time.

After appearing in several plays, the young actor broke into movies in 1936 in a bit part as a prison convict in *Parole*. He followed this with a role as a Cheyenne Indian in Cecil B. DeMille's *The Plainsman* (1937). Quinn applied for the job on the strength of being able to say he could ride a horse and that he was a member of the Cheyenne tribe, neither of which was true. Quinn appeared in numerous films, usually in supporting roles encompassing a variety of ethnic characters, between 1936 and 1947.

Anthony Quinn won two Oscars for Best Supporting Actor—in 1952 for his role as Eufemio, the troubled brother of the Mexican revolutionary Emiliano Zapata in *Viva Zapata*, and in 1956 for his role as the French painter Paul Gauguin in *Lust for Life*. He left Hollywood for a time to seek more challenging film roles in Europe and became an international film star after appearing in the Italian film director Federico Fellini's *La Strada* (The Way) as the brutish circus strongman, Zamapanò. He was nominated twice in the category of Best Actor, as an Italian rancher in *Wild Is the Wind* in 1957, and for his signature role as Zorba, the earthy Greek peasant in *Zorba the Greek*, in 1964.

Pedro Armendariz was a Mexican-born leading man who was educated in the United States. He was a huge star of the Mexican cinema of the 1940s and 1950s and was considered the Mexican John Wayne because of the way he came to symbolize a national identity through his on-screen roles. Armendariz had strong mestizo features and a commanding screen presence and was frequently cast in Mexican films with Dolores Del Rio. He was never cast as a leading man in American films; he always played a second lead or supporting player in such films as *Three Godfathers* (1948), *Fort Apache* (1948), and *Tulsa* (1949).

Metro-Goldwyn-Mayer, the biggest and most powerful studio, signed two Latino actors to a term contract: the Mexican-born Ricardo Montalbán in 1946 and the Argentine Fernando Lamas in 1950. Fernando Lamas had been a swimmer and a film star in his native Argentina when MGM signed him to a contract. Handsome and charming with an obvious accent, Lamas was typecast as a Latin Lover in film after film.

Montalbán was born and raised in Mexico but came to the United States as a teenager to live with his older brother in Los Angeles. He attended Fairfax High School, where he studied English and theater. He appeared in a number of school productions. He went to New York and appeared in a play with the Broadway actress Tallulah Bankhead. He was offered and given an MGM screen test for a role in the film *Tortilla Flat* but was told he was too Mexican, and the actor John Garfield got the role. He returned to Mexico in 1941, found work in Mexican films, and quickly became a popular young leading man, making thirteen Spanish-language films in four years. He was rediscovered by the MGM producer Jack Cummings, who went to Mexico to find a leading man to star opposite Esther Williams in *Fiesta* (1947).

For the next eight years, Montalbán performed under contract in film roles that ran the gamut from romantic leads in musicals to serious dramatic roles in films such as *Border Incident* (1949), *Battleground* (1949), and *Across the Wide Missouri* (1951). He excelled at everything he did, but was typecast as a Latin Lover. Montalbán danced so well with Cyd Charrise, that everyone thought him a trained dancer. When his MGM contract expired, he moved on to the new medium of television and guest starred in countless series episodes and performed in occasional film roles, most notably starring opposite Marlon Brando in *Sayonara* (1957) as a Japanese Kabuki dancer. In the 1980s, he starred in the hit feature films *Star Trek II: The Wrath of Khan* (1982) and *The Naked Gun* (1988).

The New York–born Puerto Rican actor Perry Lopez went to California and in 1953 won a contract at Warner Bros. Pictures, where he appeared in Raoul Walsh's *Battle Cry* (1955), John Ford's *Mister Roberts* (1955), and other motion pictures. He is best known for his role as Lt. Escobar in Roman Polanski's classic *Chinatown* (1974) opposite Jack Nicholson.

In 1950, the Puerto Rican–born Jose Ferrer became the first Hispanic American to win an Academy Award as Best Actor, for his title role in the film *Cyrano de Bergerac*. In his tripartite career as an actor, director, and writer, Ferrer also won three New York Drama Critics awards, five Tony Awards, and two Oscar nominations for Best Actor and one for Best Supporting Actor. At the first Tony Awards in 1947, he shared the Best Actor honors with Frederic March, receiving the award for his leading role in *Cyrano de Bergerac*. When he won the Academy Award for the same role in the film version, he became the first actor to win an Oscar for re-creating a theatrical role on film. In 1952, he won his second Tony for Best Actor for *The Shrike*. In that same year, he also won a Tony as the

season's Best Director for three separate plays: *Stalag 17*, *The Fourposter*, and *The Shrike*. He re-created his role in *The Shrike* in his directorial debut in the 1955 film version. In 1948, he had received his first Oscar nomination, for Best Supporting Actor for his role as the Dauphin opposite Ingrid Bergman in *Joan of Arc*, which marked his first on-screen appearance. Ferrer was later nominated for an Oscar for his role as the diminutive French painter Toulouse-Lautrec in John Huston's *Moulin Rouge* (1952). Ferrer went on to appear in more than seventy films. He directed thirteen Broadway productions and seven feature films. His classic diction, unconventional looks, and classical demeanor defied all the stereotypes.

Resisting Stereotypes

Throughout most of the 1970s, 1980s, and 1990s, Hispanic actors were cast in traditional roles that evolved and changed over time but not necessarily for the better. The banditos of the West became urban drug dealers or gang members, the cantina girls became streetwalkers, and the jovial mamacitas became household maids or the street gang members' suffering mothers. Latin Lovers became Mambo Kings, and border crossings were full of illegal immigrants.

In 1970, Ricardo Montalbán, along with other actors, started the organization NOSOTROS (Spanish for "we the people") in Hollywood to improve the image of Latinos and Latinas in film and television and to provide a training ground for talented artists. There was much discrimination and ignorance in Hollywood that limited opportunities for Latino and Latina actors. Most lead Latino and Latina roles went to non-Latino and non-Latina actors. Latino and Latina actors were told by producers that a box-office name was needed to ensure financial success, but by 1976 films such as *Rocky*, starring a then-unknown Sylvester Stallone, proved the argument invalid. Thus, in effect, this policy would keep Latino and Latina actors from gaining access to lead and starring roles in motion pictures, and they would never be considered for non-Latino or non-Latina leading parts. Still, there was hope for change. The civil rights movements of the 1960s and cable television's MTV music videos of the 1980s, which showcased the diversity of musical artists in a youth-oriented, multicultural, and multiethnic society, were groundbreaking in audience acceptance of people of color on the screen in nontraditional roles.

The New Generation

Puerto Rican–born Raul Julia was one of the finest American actors of his generation. He knew he wanted to be an actor since he was in the first grade. He went on to study at the University of Puerto Rico and in 1964 headed for Manhattan. There he met the theatrical impresario Joseph Papp, whose New York Shakespeare Festival company had a unique vision of reinterpreting Shakespeare's works with contemporary tones and multiethnic casting. Papp cast Julia in *Two Gentlemen of Verona*, which became a turning point in the young actor's career. In 1972, he was nominated for a Tony Award as Best Actor for his performance in the play. Raul became a Broadway star and was nominated for an additional three Tony Awards over his career, for roles in *Where's Charley* (1974), *Three Penny Opera* (1977), and *Nine* (1981).

Although he began appearing in movies in 1971, Julia did not become well known as a film actor until he costarred as a political prisoner opposite William Hurt and Sonia Braga in the Oscar-winning film *Kiss of the Spider Woman* in 1985. Julia became a star in the dark, zany comedy *The Addams Family* (1991), which was one of the first films to generate over $100 million in domestic box-office receipts, as did its sequel, *Addams Family Values* (1993). The character of the dashing, love-struck Gomez utilized all the best characteristics of Julia's theatrical background and is the film role he will be remembered for. Julia died unexpectedly at the age of fifty-four from heart failure in 1994. He won an Emmy Award posthumously for his role as the Brazilian activist Chico Mendes in the Home Box Office cable film *The Burning Season* (1994).

The Argentine actress Norma Aleandro earned an Oscar nomination as Best Supporting Actress for her role as an indigenous Mexican servant in *Gaby: A True Story* (1987), and the Brazilian Fernanda Montenegro became the first Latina to win an Oscar nomination in the Best Actress category for her role in the Brazilian film *Central Station* (1998).

The handsome, Cuban-born charismatic leading actor Andy Garcia was nominated for an Academy Award as Best Supporting Actor for his role as the hot-headed, illegitimate son Vincent Mancini in *Godfather III* (1990) and had impressed audiences as the Italian-American treasury agent George Stone in *The Untouchables* (1987).

The Panamanian Salsa-musician-turned-actor Rubén Blades (*The Milagro Beanfield War*, 1988) and the New York–born Puerto Rican actors Hector Elizondo (*Pretty Woman*, 1990) and Jimmy Smits (*Old Gringo*, 1989) have demonstrated versatility in a number of films and television shows.

Edward James Olmos, a Mexican American actor, was born and raised in the barrios of East Los Angeles. He achieved prominence with his role as the omnipotent 1940s street warrior El Pachuco in Luis Valdez's hit musical drama *Zoot Suit*. Originating in Los Angeles, the show went on to Broadway, where Olmos was nominated for a Tony Award as Best Actor, in the first play written by a Mexican American ever to be performed on "The Great White Way" with an all–Latino and Latina cast. Olmos received national recognition when he landed the role of the sullen, no-nonsense Lt. Castillo on the trend-setting TV series *Miami Vice*

(1984). For this role, he won an Emmy Award as Best Supporting Actor in a regular series.

In 1988, Olmos executive produced and starred in the feature film *Stand and Deliver*. His performance as the quirky and inspirational real life high school calculus teacher Jaime Escalante earned Olmos an Academy Award nomination as Best Actor. He cowrote, directed, and starred in the stark prison drama *American Me* (1992). Some of his more notable feature film credits include *The Ballad of Gregorio Cortez* (1982), *Bladerunner* (1982), *My Family–Mi Familia* (1995), and *Selena* (1997).

Benicio Del Toro, a Puerto Rican–born actor won an Academy Award in 2000 as Best Supporting Actor for his role as a conflicted Mexican policeman in the Oscar-winning film *Traffic*. A New York–born actress of Puerto Rican heritage, Rosie Perez was nominated for Best Supporting Actress for her role as a woman coping with grief in the film *Fearless* (1994).

The superstar Jennifer Lopez was born in the Bronx, New York, of Puerto Rican parents. She emerged from small roles on television to her film debut as the young mother in Gregory Nava's *My Family–Mi Familia* (1995). Lopez was catapulted to stardom with her starring role as the young slain Tejana singer Selena in the film *Selena* (1997), also directed by Nava. The actress became the first Latina to be paid a million dollars for a starring film role. Lopez's dark features and shapely body matched the deceased singer's, and she consequently became a symbol of young contemporary Latin femininity. Lopez has starred in a number of successful films, but so far her acting ability has been overshadowed by her beauty and glamorous image.

Salma Hayek left a successful acting career in Mexico to pursue a career in Hollywood. She learned English and studied acting while she appeared in several films. The Texas-born wunderkind filmmaker Robert Rodriquez, despite studio objections, cast her opposite Antonio Banderas in *Desperado* (1995). Her unique beauty and acting ability found tremendous audience favor, and she followed with a role as a sexy Aztec snake dancer in Rodriquez's *From Dusk til Dawn* (1996) and a starring role in the romantic comedy *Fools Rush In* (1997).

After a ten-year struggle to get the film made, Hayek starred in and produced *Frida* (2002), the story of Mexican artist Frida Kahlo. The film won two Academy Awards, and Hayek received an Oscar nomination as Best Actress. This moved her away from a sex symbol and established her as a legitimate actress. Expanding on her artistic ambitions, the actress directed her first film, *The Maldonado Miracle* (2003), for the Showtime cable network.

The Spanish-born, classically handsome actor Antonio Banderas found worldwide recognition with his work for the Spanish director Pedro Almodóvar. He was soon typecast by Hollywood as a modern sensitive Latin Lover in his first Hollywood film role in *The Mambo Kings* (1992). He had parts in various films, but success eluded him until he played the role of Che in Alan Parker's film version of the musical *Evita* (1996) opposite Madonna. He soon solidified his star status when he took up the role of Zorro, the swashbuckling fictional hero of early California, in *The Mask of Zorro* (1998).

The beautiful young actress Cameron Diaz was born in Long Beach, California, to a Cuban father and an American mother. She made her film debut in *The Mask* in 1994 at the age of twenty-one, and has since followed with roles in many motion pictures including *Charlie's Angels* (2003) and Martin Scorsese's *Gangs Of New York* (2002).

Penélope Cruz, from Spain, has played every kind of role in Spain, but in Hollywood she is cast as a traditional virginal Mexican senorita in *The Hi-Lo Country* (1998), as a prostitute in *All the Pretty Horses* (2000), and as a sexy drug-induced wife of a drug lord in *Blow* (2001).

Patricia Cardoso directed *Real Woman Have Curves* (2002), a cross-generational story about a young Latina on the verge of womanhood and her old world mother. The screenplay is by Josefina Lopez and is based on her play. It features standout performances by the veteran character actress Lupe Ontiveros and the newcomer America Ferrera. Other Latina actresses working in a variety of diverse roles in feature films are Wanda De Jesus, Julie Carmen, Rosario Dawson, Michelle Rodriguez, and Laura Herring. Linda Mendoza directed the Latina bonding comedy feature *Chasing Papi* (2003).

Assessment

Latino and Latina actors have made their mark on Hollywood and will continue to build on the foundations of the past. The growing U.S. Latino and Latina market and the international film market will certainly affect the future of Latino and Latina artists. Their achievements have been recognized by the film industry in the work presented and in the awards that have been earned. The rise of such bankable box office stars as Antonio Banderas, Jennifer Lopez, Salma Hayek, Penélope Cruz, and Cameron Diaz, coupled with the emergence of important directors including Robert Rodriquez, Gregory Nava, and Alfonso Cuarón, has allowed for more range in artistic expression. Universities, colleges, and film schools are preparing and graduating young people around the United States and across the globe for careers in the arts. Regional and community theaters and Latino/Latina community centers are acting as focal points for the arts. Previous economic and cultural barriers are fast disappearing, and the successes of Latinos and Latinas in the performing arts have encouraged and inspired a new generation of talent. Both in front of and behind the cameras, Latinos and Latinas will continue to be a present and

SELMA HAYEK. Selma Hayek walks the red carpet in Hollywood. (Latin Focus)

growing artistic force in Hollywood, defying stereotypes and common misrepresentations.

See also Film; Film Producers; Hollywood, Latinas in; Stereotypes; *and biographies of figures mentioned in this article*.

BIBLIOGRAPHY

Bell, Geoffrey. *The Golden Gate and the Silver Screen*. New York: Cornwall Books, 1984.

Berumen, Frank Javier Garcia. *The Chicano/Hispanic Image in American Film*. New York: Vantage, 1995.

Buscombe, Edward, ed. *The BFI Companion to the Western*. New York: Atheneum, 1988.

Cardoso Júnior, Abel. *Carmen Miranda, a cantora do Brasil*. São Paulo, Brazil: Cardoso Júnior, 1978.

Eames, John Douglas. *The MGM Story*. New York: Crown, 1976.

Fregoso, Rosa Linda. *The Bronze Screen: Chicana and Chicano Film Culture*. Minneapolis: University of Minnesota Press, 1993.

Gunning, Tom. *D. W. Griffith and the Origins of American Narrative Film*. Urbana: University of Illinois Press, 1994.

Hadley-Garcia, George. *Hispanic Hollywood: The Latins in Motion Pictures*. New York: Carol, 1990.

Haskell, Molly. *From Reverence to Rape*. New York: Holt, Rinehart & Winston, 1974.

Hirschhorn, Clive. *The Columbia Story*. New York: Crown, 1989.

Hirschhorn, Clive. *The Warner Bros. Story*. New York: Crown, 1979.

Keller, Gary, ed. *Chicano Cinema: Research, Reviews, and Resources*. Binghamton, N.Y.: Bilingual Review, 1985.

List, Christine. *Chicano Images: Refiguring Ethnicity in Mainstream Film*. New York: Garland, 1996.

Marín, Cheech, et al. *Chicano Visions: American Painters on the Verge*. Boston: Bulfinch Press, 2002.

Mason, Wiley, and Damien Bona. *Inside Oscar: The Unofficial History of the Academy Awards*. New York: Ballantine, 1988.

Montalbán, Ricardo, with Bob Thomas. *Reflections: A Life in Two Worlds*. New York: Doubleday, 1980.

Morella, Joe, and Edward Z. Epstein. *Rita: The Life of Rita Hayworth*. New York: Delacorte, 1983.

Noriega, Chon, ed. *Chicanos and Film*. New York: Garland, 1992.

Pettit, Arthur. *Images of the Mexican American in Fiction and Film*. Edited with an afterword by Dennis E. Showalter. College Station, Tex.: A&M University Press, 1980.

Quinn, Anthony. *One Man Tango*. New York: HarperCollins, 1995.

Quinn, Anthony. *Original Sin*. New York: Little Brown, 1972.

Reyes, Luis, and Peter Rubie. *Hispanics in Hollywood: An Encyclopedia of Film and Television*. New York: Garland 1994.

Richard, Alfred Charles. *The Hispanic Image on the Silver Screen: An Interpretive Filmography from Silents into Sound, 1898–1935*. Westport, Conn.: Greenwood, 1992.

Roberts-Frenzel, Caren. *Rita Hayworth: A Photographic Retrospective*. New York: Abrams, 2001.

Thomas, Victoria. *Hollywood's Latin Lovers: Latino, French, and Italian Men Who Make the Screen Smolder*. Santa Monica, Calif.: Angel City Press, 1998.

Walsh, Raoul. *Each Man in His Own Time*. New York: Farrar, Strauss & Giroux, 1974.

LUIS REYES

ACUÑA, RODOLFO F. (b. 1932), writer, political activist, and professor. Known by many as the father of Chicano/a Studies, the historian Rodolfo Acuña is a prolific writer, political activist, and professor. Beginning his career before the Chicano/a movement of the late 1960s and 1970s, Acuña has worked tirelessly for Chicana and Chicano civil rights and representation in multiple social and political arenas.

Education and Early Career

Born in Los Angeles into a traditional Mexican family originally from northern Mexico, Acuña attended the University of Southern California, completing a PhD in history in the 1950s, an era when few Chicanas and Chicanos were represented in the discipline. Acuña sought in his dissertation and subsequent work to fuse an entirely new field that served both the scholarly or academic community as well as the workers and laborers whose interests he supported and studied.

The quintessential scholar-activist, Acuña worked with others in the Chicano/a civil rights movement to produce *El Plan de Santa Barbara* (1969), a plan of action for establishing curriculum and structures that would help Chicanos and Chicanas gain access to higher education. The plan resulted in the founding of several Chicano/a studies programs and departments across the country. One prominent Chicano/a Studies Department, the oldest and largest at the beginning of the twenty-first century, was at California State University, Northridge, where Acuña was the founding chair.

During his tenure as chair and while teaching thousands of students in the many courses a public and large university requires, Acuña published the widely read *Occupied America: A History of Chicanos* (1972), a survey of Chicano history since the Spanish conquest. This text serves as one of the core books in introductory Chicano/a studies courses and is continually revised and reprinted. *Occupied America* is only one of the many scholarly books Acuña has written in the field of Chicano/a studies. Throughout his career, he has written monographs dealing with such issues as racism, affirmative action, labor rights, resistance movements, and ethnic/cultural identity.

Political Activism

In addition to his scholarly contributions to the Chicano and Latino community, Acuña is known and highly regarded for his activism in the political arena. Acuña is involved with the Southwest Voter Registration and Education Project, an organization committed to educating the Latino community about the electoral process as well as helping them register to vote. His continued participation in political and social activism is illustrated in his work as an expert on racism and desegregation with the American Civil Liberties Union (ACLU), including its 1998 challenge to California Proposition 209, which argued against bilingual education. Acuña also writes several editorial columns and contributes to many newspapers and magazines as well as to talk shows and public radio.

Acuña's continued involvement in social and political activism has involved him in heated debates and situations in which he is required to defend his political beliefs. Acuña made no secret of his participation in the Movimiento Estudiantil Chicano de Aztlán (MEChA), the Chicano Student Movement of Aztlán; in addition to being a former member, he is also an advisor to the organization. During the 2003 California gubernatorial election, the college membership in MEChA of the lieutenant governor and candidate for governor Cruz Bustamante was questioned and attacked by opponents identifying the organization as racist and separatist. Acuña came to the defense of MEChA and questioned the media's bias and purpose.

In 1989, the National Association for Chicana and Chicano Studies (NACCS) recognized Acuña's great commitment to the Chicano community and awarded him the NACCS Scholar Award. This association awards the title to scholars recognized as having contributed to the development of Chicano/a Studies as a discipline and whose work significantly influences the study of the Chicano community. Although Acuña received this award in 1989, his activism and contributions to scholarship continued thorough the 1990s and into the twenty-first century.

In 1992, Professor Acuña, with some lawyers and other supporters, including the ACLU, launched a lawsuit challenging the decision of the University of California, Santa Barbara, to deny him an appointment in the Department of Chicana and Chicano Studies. Although it was evident that the judge was directly linked to the university, Acuña's young attorneys—whose work and careers were placed on hold while they took on a lawsuit they viewed as a question of social justice—prevailed in one of the few successful challenges to institutionalized racism as it exists in academe. Acuña won the lawsuit, but not on the basis of ethnic or racial prejudice. Rather, because a faculty committee had mentioned his age and the possibility of "undue" influence based on his age, the university was forced to compensate him with $325,000 for the loss of the appointment. Agism carried the day in the Acuña case, despite any number of other critical discoveries that lawyers found, ranging from outright racial discrimination to hostile racist invective. That a few Chicanas and Chicanos also supported the university in its case against his hiring sheds light on the matter of how much Chicano/a studies has become a part of the mainstream in some academic environments, at least to the extent that it is marked by many of the same divisions that plague all other fields and disciplines. In the final analysis, however, Acuña instructed a sympathetic jury in the reasons university officials and some university professors dislike Chicano/a studies as an area of study; jurors later told the Acuña team that they were keenly aware

of the methods being used to discredit his scholarship and his professorial training. The mostly working-class jury saw through the lies and ruses presented by the university to discredit Acuña's scholarship, and jurors were undeterred in seeking proper compensation for discriminatory treatment. More than anything else in his career, this court case occurred because Professor Acuña refused to let the University of California use improper grounds or methods in its hiring practices. The challenge would have enormous implications for the future of Chicano and Chicana higher education.

Along with this legal challenge, his numerous books and articles, editorials, interviews, and commitments to social justice, Acuña's decades-long commitment to scholarly activism ensures him a place in Chicano and Chicana history. In the early 2000s, Acuña lived with his wife, Lupita Compeán, and daughter, Angela, in the San Fernando Valley. He remained engaged as professor emeritus at his campus (CSUN), and supported young scholars and others seeking assistance with legal challenges through the foundation he created with the gains from his lawsuit.

See also **California; Chicano/a Movement; Chicanos and Chicanas; Mexican-Origin People in the United States; Movimiento Estudiantil Chicano de Aztlán;** *and* **Plan de Santa Barbara.**

BIBLIOGRAPHY

Acuña, Rodolfo. *A Community under Siege: A Chronicle of Chicanos East of the Los Angeles River, 1945–1975.* Los Angeles: UCLA Chicano Studies Research Center, 1984.

Acuña, Rodolfo. *Anything but Mexican: Chicanos in Contemporary Los Angeles.* New York: Verso, 1996.

Acuña, Rodolfo. *Occupied America: A History of Chicanos.* 5th ed. New York: Pearson Longman, 2004.

Acuña, Rodolfo. *Sometimes There Is No Other Side: Chicanos and the Myth of Equality.* Notre Dame, Ind.: University of Notre Dame Press, 1998.

DEENA J. GONZÁLEZ AND YVETTE SAAVEDRA

ADÁL (b. 1948), artist. Adál was born Adál Maldonado in Utuado, Puerto Rico, in 1948 and relocated to New York City at the age of seventeen. Known by his first name, he is one of the most innovative and celebrated Puerto Rican–Nuyorican artists working in the early twenty-first century. Trained as a photographer and master printer at the San Francisco Art Institute in the early 1970s, Adál was the cofounder and codirector (with Alex Coleman) of Foto Gallery in Soho, New York City, an experimental gallery solely devoted to photography and photo-derived works as a fine arts medium.

As have many other photographers of his generation (most notably Cindy Sherman, Robert Mapplethorpe, and Lucas Samaras) and as a result of his complex view of identity, Adál has systematically explored identity issues to their ultimate consequences. From suggestive, "surreal" photographic collages in the early 1970s to the ironic concreteness of his auto-portraits series and finally to the creation of an ethereal, ubiquitous country where he and his out-of-focus Nuyorican colleagues live, Adál has collapsed self-portraiture's allegedly self-referential quality. Indeed, a great deal of his work's satiric trademark arises from the constant mockery of the possibility of ever achieving an ultimate, definitive picture of one's self.

By exposing the absurdity behind the search for ultimate reference to selfhood in art, Adál challenges the notion of literalness by stretching it to its limits. His relentless punning on literal meanings has become the most privileged artistic principle in his work and has enabled him to address perhaps the most slippery characteristic of his own biography: his double cultural allegiance as a Nuyorican. Through this mechanism, he has been able to successfully incorporate the potentially satiric quality of the Spanglish language sandwich and bilingual code-switching into his self-portraiture without making it strenuously conceptual and to tackle the scandals of the day with theatrical irony.

Most importantly, though, such exploration of the literal has allowed Adál to go against the grain in terms of self-portraiture by moving from self to type. If in his early series of photographs, like *The Evidence of Things Not Seen . . .*, the masterful use of the photo collage creates a disorienting effect that supposedly resembles his most intimate and individual mental landscapes, his *Out of Focus Nuyoricans* series is an exercise in collective portraiture that literally takes these Nuyoricans' "out-of-focus" cultural and political conditions and turns them into a guiding aesthetic principle. Adál has once more taken this principle to its limits by creating an imaginary world, *El Spirit Republic of Puerto Rico*, where he and his colleagues can live in an out-of-focus world.

Outside this imaginary territory, Adál works in the passport agency, quietly issuing passports to anyone who wants to be an honorary citizen of El Spirit Republic. Neither demiurge, king, nor president of his own imaginary territory, Adál merely works for his own creation like any other bureaucrat—his latest self-refashioning.

His first series of photographs, *The Evidence of Things Not Seen . . .* was published by Da Capo Press in 1975 and has become a collector's item. Four more books followed: *Falling Eyelids: A Foto Novela* (1981), *Portraits of the Puerto Rican Experience* (1984), *Galería Luigi Marrozzino presenta Mango mambo* (1987), and *Out of Focus Nuyoricans* (2004).

Adál is also known for his collaborations with many different artists. In the mid-1970s Adál met the late Pedro Pietri, with whom he started a long and fruitful collaboration that lasted until Pietri's death in 1994. Together they developed *El Puerto Rican Embassy Project* (1994) and *Mondo Mambo: A Mambo Rap Sodi* (a collaboration with the musician Tito Puente and the choreographer Eddie Torres), presented at the Public Theater in New York City in 1990. Adál has also collaborated with Ntozake Shange in creating the photographic environmental design of the play *Love Space Demands* (1992) and in the early 1970s with Robert Mapplethorpe developing his distinct photographic printing style.

Adál's work has been exhibited in and is in the permanent collections of the Museum of Modern Art in New York City, the San Francisco Museum of Modern Art, the Houston Museum of Fine Arts, the Metropolitan Museum of Art in New York City, the Museo del Barrio in New York City, the Musée Modern de la Ville de Paris in France, Musée de la Photographie a Charleroi, Belgium, and the Lehigh University Art Galleries. A retrospective of his work was exhibited in 2004–2005 at the David Rockefeller Center for Latin American Studies at Harvard University in Cambridge, Massachusetts.

See also **Art, Puerto Rican; Photographers;** *and* **Puerto Ricans.**

BIBLIOGRAPHY

Coleman, A. D. *The Grotesque in Photography*. New York: Summit Books, 1977.

Maldonado, Adál. *The Evidence of Things Not Seen … .* New York: Da Capo, 1975.

Maldonado, Adál. *Falling Eyelids: A Foto Novela*. New York: Foto-Graphic Editions, 1981.

Maldonado, Adál. *Galería Luigi Marrozzino presenta Mango mambo*. San Juan, P.R.: Ilustres Studios, 1987.

Maldonado, Adál. *Portraits of the Puerto Rican Experience*. Bronx, N.Y.: IPRUS, 1984.

Merlo, Lorenzo, and Claude Nori, eds. *Fantastic Photographers*. New York: Pantheon, 1977.

JOSÉ LUIS FALCONI

ADOBE. The Spanish word *adobe* means the soil used to make earthen bricks shaped in molds. However, it can also mean adobe bricks themselves, an architectural design, a house built of adobe bricks, and the mud plaster used as raw material to make earthen bricks.

"Adobe" comes from the Arabic *attubab*, which means "the brick." During the colonial period the word was brought by the Spaniards to the Americas, where it was adapted from its original meaning. The word "adobe" is well-known in the United States and in Spanish-speaking countries. However, all around the world people use other names to describe this material, such as unbaked earth, *pisé de terre*, *tierra*, puddling, and rammed earth.

Adobe is important for several reasons. First, it composes almost three-quarters of the earth's crust, which

means it is a cheap and easily available construction material. Also it does not need any industrial processing, nor does it need transportation because of its availability. Adobe has been used as a construction material for dwellings for thousands of years on every continent. In fact ten thousand years ago the first farming villages in the world, in the Middle East and Egypt, were built principally of unbaked earth. Throughout the globe archaeological adobe sites have withstood the passage of time in places such as Acoma in New Mexico, Las Casas Grandes in northern Mexico, and Chan-Chan in Peru. Therefore it is not surprising that more than half of the world's population lives in houses made from unbaked earth.

The use of adobe is understandable because people generally use materials readily at hand for shelter, keeping to a basic principle: make it as simple as possible and make it yourself. Adobe does not require specialized labor. It is cheap, and it requires only water and hands to sculpt it.

Around the world there are different ways to use earth construction. However, one can classify two basic types, adobe bricks and rammed earth. Adobe bricks are made from dirt and water shaped in rectangular molds that are allowed to dry and harden in the sun for several weeks. Most of the time the dirt is mixed with another ingredient, such as chopped straw, to form a cohesive material. The bricks are then used to build such structures as walls, domes, vaults, arches, and fireplaces.

Rammed earth is a technique by which mud is rammed to build a compacted wall. Walls are at least half a meter (about 1.75 feet) thick, and wooden frames are used to support the dirt while it dries. After the wall is completely dried, the frames are removed. A special technique for building roofs and walls using rammed earth is called wattle. In this case dirt is daubed over a framework made from brush, wood, or both. The mud dries and sticks to the framework, providing a hardened structure.

Adobe, however, has some vulnerability. It is susceptible to water damage. To overcome this flaw, various solutions have been developed, such as including a waterproof material like cement or asphalt in the adobe and architectural designs like building walls and roofs that repel or drain off water. In some cases regular maintenance is needed, such as annual mud replastering to avoid erosion.

Besides cheapness and availability, the manufacturing of adobe requires far less energy than the manufacturing of modern industrialized building materials. Cement, steel, and conventional raw materials for construction require a relatively high level of energy to manufacture them. For instance, the equivalent of four gallons of gasoline is expended in the production of a single bag of cement. Adobe bricks or rammed earth, on the other hand, require a minimum amount of energy to convert them into usable building materials. Adobe bricks require little energy conversion beyond the labor of the brick maker (*adobero* in Spanish). The raw materials for adobe building are simple: soil, water, hand labor, and solar energy. Adobe represents an environmentally friendly option for shelter because its sources are virtually unlimited, it can be recycled, it does not pollute, and it does not deplete natural resources.

Although adobe is an adaptable material, it gained a bad reputation during the second half of the twentieth century, when it became associated with poverty and was considered a primitive and fragile material. This reputation resulted from Western economic policies that privileged the use of new, highly processed materials, such as aluminum, steel, cement, and oil derivatives. These building materials were produced by transnational and industrial corporations, who influenced these economic policies.

Adobe can be a luxurious and artistic building material, and the trend is toward rediscovering its importance. In the southwestern United States, unbaked earth has been revived and has regained its reputation and symbolic status. Santa Fe, New Mexico, is the most famous city where adobe is found widely in both old and new construction. Adobe constructions in Santa Fe have been given a new appearance, which suggests that "traditional" and "modern" architectures are compatible.

Adobe in some parts of New Mexico became a fashionable trend that established a new pattern of construction called pueblo style or Santa Fe style, deriving from the New Mexican indigenous architecture. This name stems from the word "pueblo," which means "village" in Spanish. The pueblo style is characterized by rammed walls using roof beams (*vigas*) and wood structure. The modern style is complex and requires skilled labor. Santa Fe style homes are often luxurious, artistic structures made from adobe that have added expensive materials, such as ceramic tile and plaster. Although adobe has limited use in contemporary building in the United States, it will continue to be an essential raw material for shelter around the world because it is cheap, easy to use, and readily available, whether people build expensive homes or basic rooms for protection against the environment.

See also Architecture *and* Santa Fe Style.

BIBLIOGRAPHY

Bunting, Bainbridge. *Of Earth and Timbers Made*. Albuquerque: University of New Mexico Press, 1974.

Dethier, Jean. *Down to Earth: Adobe Architecture, an Old Idea, a New Future*. Translated by Ruth Eaton. New York: Facts on File, 1983.

Facey, William. *Back to Earth: Adobe Building in Saudi Arabia*. London: Al-Turath in association with the London Centre of Arab Studies, 1997.

McHenry, Paul G., Jr. *The Adobe Story: A Global Treasure*. Albuquerque: Center for Aging, University of New Mexico, 1996.

GABRIEL FERREYRA-OROZCO

ADOLESCENCE. Adolescence is a socially constructed category. For this reason, it should not be seen strictly as a developmental stage that is an inherent category separate from the social environment that assigns attributes, expectations, and limitations to this period of life. Lawrence Friedman and Elizabeth Goodman describe adolescence in the U.S. context as "a time of profound physiologic and psychosocial change during which the process of family separation begins, independent thought and action develop, and sexual identity emerges" (Friedman and Goodman, p. 171).

While this has become an increasingly important stage of life in the United States, research involving Latina and Latino adolescents and youth is fraught with gaps and limitations. Very little research has been done on the social and personality development of Latina and Latino youth. Rather, most research emphasizes "problem" behaviors such as school dropout, pregnancy, and substance abuse. In addition, adolescents' experiences involving Latina and Latino minority status such as discrimination, self-concept, and personal aspirations have not been researched sufficiently.

Research on Latina and Latino adolescents sometimes refers to Latinas and Latinos without discussing the cultural or socioeconomic differences among ethnic subgroups or stating whether the sample is representative of the Latina and Latino population nationally, regionally, or locally. At other times, the research is available for only one ethnic subgroup, such as Mexicans, but nothing may be written on the subject about other subgroups, such as Puerto Ricans. Therefore, information on different topics may often originate from either nonrepresentative samples of various subgroups, or from a sample of a particular Latina and Latino group.

Because of the limited research involving Latina and Latino youth, the information available on a particular subject may be based on only one or two studies rather than on a body of scholarship in the area. While more research is needed on a variety of topics, it is most important that research take a contextual approach considering multiple individual, familial, and societal factors in describing the developmental course of Latina and Latino youth. Among the macrosocietal factors affecting Latinas and Latinos, acculturation, poverty, and various forms of social oppression should be granted special attention.

In the following sections, a summary of findings in key areas will be provided. It is important to remember that there is diversity within and among the Latina and Latino ethnic groups and that while these findings are useful, they do not always address, for a variety of reasons, intra- and intergroup differences.

Latina and Latino Adolescents

Latinas and Latinos are not only the fastest growing minority in the United States, but also one of the youngest groups in the country. According to the 2000 census, while the median age for Latinas and Latinos was 25.9 years, the median age of the rest of the U.S. population was 35.3 years. At that time, Latinas and Latinos under the age of twenty-one were the fastest-growing age group in the United States. The U.S. population under age eighteen reached 25.7 percent in 2000. About 17 percent of these youth and children were of Latina and Latino origin. The Mexican and Puerto Rican populations had the greatest numbers of youth under twenty-one, while the Cuban population had the lowest number. According to this growth trend, Latina and Latino youth will continue to comprise a significant proportion of the U.S. population, and therefore issues affecting this group should be granted special attention. Moreover, the growth of this population may necessitate policies and funding related to family planning, child care, education, and youth services that may be in conflict with the needs or wants of an older general population, particularly during budget crises.

Living Conditions

Like other American youth, Latina and Latino adolescents grow up in different kinds of household arrangements. In 1994, 68 percent of Latina and Latino adolescents lived in two-parent homes as compared to 79 percent of non-Latina and non-Latino white youth. Moreover, 25 percent of Latinas and Latinos lived in single-female-headed households as compared to 17 percent of non-Latina and non-Latino white youth. More Latina and Latino youth live with relatives other than their parents than do non-Latina and non-Latino white adolescents. Latina and Latino adolescents are also much more likely than non-Latina and non-Latino white adolescents to have parents under thirty years old. Their parents are more likely to be poor, less educated, and unemployed or underemployed than parents of white youth.

Latinas and Latinos are three times more likely to be living in poverty than are whites. The percentage of Latinas and Latinos under age eighteen living below the poverty level is 34.4, versus 10.6 percent of non-Latina and non-Latino whites under age eighteen. The percentage of Latina and Latino youth living in poor two-parent families is 19.5. Among poor youth living in a mother-headed household, Latinas and Latinos are the third largest group (47.2 percent) after American Indians (50 percent) and blacks (47.4 percent). Among the three largest Latina and Latino populations, Puerto Rican youth have the highest rates of poverty and Cuban youth have the lowest.

Latina and Latino adolescents are more likely to reside in urban or inner-city areas as compared to white adolescents. Limited resources affecting schools, housing, and other institutions have plagued these areas. Latino and Latina youth usually have employment rates as high as, if not higher than, those of white male adolescents. They are also more likely to be in full-time employment. Latina youth have lower labor participation than either Latino youth or white adolescent females. The overall labor participation does not differ significantly for the different subgroups, except in the case of Puerto Rican youth, who have the lowest employment rates. Mexicans, Cubans, and Central and South Americans have rates similar to white youth. Since Latino youth are more likely to work full time as compared to white male adolescents, it is not surprising that while teenagers their earnings are higher. However, after age nineteen Latino youths' earnings decrease to less than those of white males.

Physical Development and Pubertal Changes

Two important milestones in adolescence are the growth spurt and pubertal development. Research on pubertal timing, or development relative to one's peers, indicates that timing influences the adolescent's feelings about puberty, body satisfaction, and overall psychological adjustment. Early sexual maturation has a more negative impact on girls, whereas late sexual maturation is most distressing for boys.

Latina and Latino youth ages twelve to seventeen are more likely to be at low height for age as compared to their white counterparts. Among Latina and Latino subgroups the percentages of low-height youth are higher among females than males and also higher for Mexican Americans of both sexes. In terms of development of secondary sexual characteristics, Puerto Ricans reach stages of sexual maturation at rates similar to those of other U.S. adolescents, while Mexican American youth experience such changes later than youth in other Latina and Latino subgroups and in the general U.S. adolescent population. Among Latina and Latino adolescents, females are more likely to develop a positive body image if they perceive their pubertal changes to be on time rather than if they mature early or late. For males, maturing early or on time is perceived as more positive than developing late.

Education

In 1998, only 63 percent of Latinas and Latinos were high school graduates. Latina and Latino adolescents are significantly more likely than white adolescents to drop out of school. A large percentage of them drop out before entering high school. This makes them less likely ever to obtain a high school degree, since the closer one is to graduating when dropping out of high school the more likely one will be to complete high school at some later point. Latino adolescents are more likely to drop out than their female counterparts. Other factors associated with Latina and Latino youth school-dropout rates include marriage, living independently or with relatives, and living in poverty.

Latina and Latino youth are also more likely to be one or two school grades behind throughout their adolescence. Grade delay is higher among Mexicans and Puerto Ricans than among Cubans and Central and South Americans. Those born outside the United States are also more likely to have grade delay than those born in the United States. Those Latina and Latino youth with the lowest English language abilities have the highest rate of grade delay. The use of Spanish to communicate at home seems to be unrelated to their grade delay.

Even if Latina and Latino youth stay in the school system, they tend to score lower on standardized tests for reading, math, and science than do white adolescents. Latina and Latino students are more likely to be placed in remedial and vocational classes, and less likely to be placed in gifted or advanced programs. Not only have Latina and Latino students been found to be placed in vocational classes earlier than the non-Latina and non-Latino white counterparts, but also the vocational programs where Latinas and Latinos are placed are different from those of non-Latina and non-Latino white students. The former are more likely to be assigned to low-status occupational training (for example, building maintenance), versus the latter's placement in management-oriented training programs.

Latinas and Latinos also have the lowest college attainment rates as compared to African American, Asian, and white adolescents. There are subgroup variations in college graduation rates, with Cubans having the largest rates, followed by Puerto Ricans, Central and South Americans, and Mexican Americans, who are the least likely to graduate from college. Latinas have higher rates of high school completion than Latinos, but both sexes graduate from college at similar rates.

The educational issues of Latina and Latino youth need to be understood within the context of multiple factors, such as immigration status, English language proficiency, acculturation, geographic location, and economic status. A report by the National Alliance for Hispanic Health (NAHH) concludes that: "contrary to popular stereotypes, greater acculturation among Hispanic girls is tied to poorer . . . educational outcomes" (National Alliance for Hispanic Health, p. 59).

Family Relations, Gender, and Sexuality

In spite of the dramatic changes in gender roles that have occurred in U.S. society over the last decades of the twentieth century, a parental and social gender-based double standard continues to shape gender socialization in the twenty-first century. Latina and Latino culture has been described as being more traditional regarding gender roles than the mainstream American culture. Latino adolescents are granted more privileges, such as freedom to go places or later curfews, than are females. Latinas are expected to help more with household chores and are encouraged to act in "feminine" ways. Also, females experience stricter rules about dating and sexuality than do their male counterparts. Studies on parents of Latina and Latino youth reveal that the same-sex parent tends to engage in more socialization of traditional gender-appropriate behavior than the cross-sex parent.

In various studies, Latinas and Latinos have consistently been found to place great value in being part of a family and in having a family as compared to non-Latina and non-Latino whites. Latina and Latino adolescents have a higher rate of marriage than either African American or white adolescents. It has been found that there are significant racial and ethnic differences in girls' sexual, marital, birth, school, and job expectations. Mexican American girls as compared to black, white, and Southeast Asian girls were found to want to pass through these transitions earlier and more rapidly. Unlike girls from other racial and ethnic categories, Mexican American girls were socialized for marriage and childbearing to the exclusion of work and educational roles.

Reproductive and Sexual Health

Latina adolescents' birth rates are between those of African American, who have the highest, and white adolescents, who have the lowest. Mexican adolescent females have the highest birth rates among all Latina and Latino groups. Rates of marriage for teenagers who give birth are the highest for Mexicans and Cubans and the lowest for Puerto Ricans. As compared to other ethnic groups, Latina adolescents are the least likely to be sexually active but the most likely to give birth. Also, they have been found to use contraception less than either white or African American adolescents. Latinas are less likely to terminate their pregnancy than white and African American youth and are more likely to report their pregnancy as intentional. Early childbearing has been found to be associated with lower socioeconomic status.

Initiation of sexual intercourse for Latina and Latino adolescents is between that of African American adolescents (the earliest) and white adolescents (the latest). There are gender differences, with males having first intercourse younger than females. Latina adolescents have less knowledge of sexuality, birth control, or condom use than either Latino adolescents or white females. Anne Driscoll and others observe that there seems to be a pattern for sexual activity among Latina adolescents that is different from those found for African American and white youth. Latinas are more likely to belong to three categories in terms of sexual activity: (1) those that initiate sexual activity before eighteen years of age; (2) those who wait to have intercourse until eighteen or nineteen years of age; and (3) those who by age twenty are still "virgins" (38 percent of Latinas belong to this group). In contrast, African American and white female adolescents are gradually more likely to have sexual intercourse as they age. Latino adolescents have on average more sexual partners than Latinas. Those Latinas who are sexually active are as likely as Latino males to continue their sexual activity. Latina adolescents who were born outside the United States are more conservative in terms of initiation of sexual activity and numbers of sex partners when compared to those born in the United States. They are also more likely to have planned their pregnancies, to be married, or to be living with their partner when they become mothers. It has been found that, contrary to beliefs about the relation between dropping out of school and pregnancy, Mexican American girls tend to drop out prior to getting pregnant and to be married at the time of conception.

Latina and Latino adolescents report using contraception less than white and African American youth. DuRant and others found that Mexican American and Central and South American females were more likely to use effective birth control than were Puerto Ricans, Cubans, and adolescents of other Latina and Latino backgrounds. These differences in contraceptive use among the different segments of the Latina and Latino adolescent community demonstrate that Latina and Latino "culture" is not the only source of influence on the gender roles and sexuality of Latina and Latino youth.

Latina and Latino adolescents are overrepresented in the number of AIDS cases in the United States. Adolescent Latinos are significantly less likely to use condoms than white or African American males. In 1998, the chlamydia, gonorrhea, and syphilis rates among Latino adolescents were between those of African American teens (the highest) and white teens (the lowest). Latina adolescents have higher rates of these sexually transmitted infections (STIs) than do Latino males, since females have higher risks than males in acquiring STIs from sexual intercourse.

Mental Health

Several social factors pose serious risks to the optimal development and mental health of Latina and Latino youth. Research has documented the deterioration of mental-health status that occurs intergenerationally among Latinas and Latinos after their migration to the United States. Thus, U.S.–born Latina and Latino youth are in general at greater risk of developing mental health problems than are immigrant Latina and Latino youth.

In addition to migration status, opportunities for healthy development among Latina and Latino youth depend greatly on the interplay of family, community, and individual factors. Poverty is associated with a host of conditions (for example, bad schools, impoverished neighborhood quality) that are detrimental to quality of life across the lifespan. Research findings about mental health issues among Latinas and Latinos should be interpreted with caution, because of possible biases in the design and instruments used. Also, the majority of studies are based on Mexican Americans, Cubans, and Puerto Ricans, and therefore the findings may not be representative of other Latina and Latino groups.

Depression and suicide. Studies indicate that Latina and Latino adolescents have higher rates of suicide attempts than those observed in other ethnic groups. Also, Latina and Latino immigrant youth show lower self-esteem and are considered to be at greater risk of manifesting suicidal ideation than U.S.–born youth. However, the discrepancy in suicide rates between these two groups has diminished over time. Although suicide ideation and attempts are high among Latinas and Latinos, their suicide completion rates are lower when compared to other ethnic groups. There is some limited evidence that links acculturative stress and drug use with greater vulnerability to suicidal behavior.

Although research is not conclusive, studies suggest that prevalence of depressive symptoms among Latina and Latino adolescents is the highest of any ethnic group. Particularly, among Latinas and Latinos, Mexican Americans consistently report significantly higher symptoms of depression than other subgroups. As is the case in the general adolescent population, Latina adolescents are twice as likely to report depressive symptoms as are Latino adolescents. However, for both male and female immigrant Latina and Latino youth the risk of developing depressive symptoms increases, as they face contradictory expectations regarding gender roles from their culture of origin and the new culture.

Eating disorders. Body dissatisfaction among female adolescents has traditionally been associated with being white and middle or upper class. However, studies have shown that Latina adolescents may be at greater risk for adopting disordered eating behaviors than previously recognized. Low-income Latina adolescents are as likely as white adolescent females to resort to maladaptive strategies, such as diet pills and purging, to lose weight. Adolescents who are overweight and are exposed to these behaviors in their families are at an increased risk for engaging in these maladaptive weight control behaviors. While normal weight or overweight Latina girls are as likely as females from other ethnic groups to report body dissatisfaction, lean Latina girls report greater body dissatisfaction than lean white adolescent females.

Conduct problems and substance abuse. U.S.–born Latina and Latino adolescents are more likely to exhibit conduct problems such as school misbehavior, delinquency, early sexual intercourse, drug use, and truancy than Latina and Latino immigrant youth. Latina and Latino youth report rates of heavy drinking and illicit drug use that are comparable to those reported by white American youth. Among Latina and Latino subgroups, Mexican Americans (30 percent) and Puerto Ricans (28 percent) report more frequent use of illicit drug use than Cubans (16 percent). However, no significant differences in alcohol consumption are found among these groups (average rates are between 12 and 16 percent).

Latina and Latino adolescents ages twelve to eighteen are more likely to drink alcohol more often and in larger quantities if they are male, older, live in father-absent homes, come from higher income families, and are not enrolled in school. In addition, research reveals that increased alcohol consumption among both Latino and Latina adolescents is associated with: most friends drinking, siblings drinking, smoking cigarettes, marijuana use, and finding it easy to obtain alcohol. Based on these findings, adolescent alcohol prevention programs need to directly affect social factors related to drinking and involve family members.

Use of mental-health services. Studies conducted among the general population of youth indicate that Latina and Latino children and adolescents have lower rates of mental-health service utilization. Mental-health service use is especially low among Puerto Rican youth living on the island, although use rates are low among youth of various ethnic backgrounds living on the U.S. mainland as well. More research is needed in order to assess and improve the adequacy of health services provided to Latina and Latino youth. Also, issues such as insurance availability, information about mental health services, and having Spanish-speaking support and treatment staff should be included in the mental health agenda for Latinas and Latinos.

See also **Drug Abuse; Education; Female-headed Households; Poverty;** *and* **Teenage Pregnancy.**

BIBLIOGRAPHY

Asencio, Marysol. *Sex and Sexuality among New York's Puerto Rican Youth.* Boulder, Colo.: Rienner, 2002.

Breitkopf, Carmen R., and Abbey B. Berenson. "Correlates of Weight Loss Behaviors among Low-Income African-American, Caucasian, and Latina Women." *Obstetrics and Gynecology* 103 (2004): 231–239.

Carrasquillo, Angela L. "Profile of Hispanic Students in United States Public Schools." In *Education of Hispanics in the United States: Politics, Policies, and Outcomes*, edited by Abbas Tashakkori and Salvador Hector Ochoa. New York: AMS, 1999.

Choi, Heeseung. "Understanding Adolescent Depression in Ethnocultural Context." *Advances in Nursing Science* 25 (2002): 71–85.

Driscoll, Anne K., M. Antonia Briggs, Claire D. Brindins, et al. "Adolescent Latino Reproductive Health: A Review of the Literature." *Hispanic Journal of Behavioral Sciences* 23 (2001): 255–326.

DuRant, R., et al. "Contraceptive Behaviors among Sexually Active Hispanic Adolescents." *Journal of Adolescent Health* 11 (1990): 440–496.

East, Patricia. "Racial and Ethnic Differences in Girls' Sexual, Marital, and Birth Expectations." *Journal of Marriage and the Family* 60 (1998): 150–162.

Epstein, Jennifer A., et al. "Impact of Social Influences and Problem Behavior on Alcohol Use among Inner-City Hispanic and Black Adolescents." *Journal of Studies on Alcohol* 60 (1999): 595–604.

Flores, Glenn, and Ruth Enid Zambrana. "The Early Years: The Health of Children and Youth." In *Health Issues in the Latino Community*, edited by Marilyn Aguirre-Molina, Carlos W. Molina, and Ruth Enid Zambrana. San Francisco: Jossey-Bass, 2001.

Flores-Ortiz, Yvette. "The Role of Cultural and Gender Values in Alcohol Use Patterns among Chicana/Latina High School and University Students: Implications for AIDS Prevention." *International Journal of the Addictions* 29 (1994): 1149–1171.

Friedman, Lawrence S., and Elizabeth Goodman. "Adolescents at Risk for HIV Infection." *Primary Care* 19 (1992): 171–190.

National Alliance for Hispanic Health (NAHH). *The State of Hispanic Girls.* Washington, D.C.: Estrella, 2000.

Raffaelli, Marcela, and Lenna L. Ontai. "Gender Socialization in Latina and Latino Families: Results from Two Retrospective Studies" *Sex Roles* 50 (2004): 287–299.

Robinson, Thomas, et al. "Ethnicity and Body Dissatisfaction: Are Hispanic and Asian Girls at Increased Risk for Eating Disorders?" *Journal of Adolescent Health* 19 (1996): 384–393.

Solis, Julie. "The Status of Latino Children and Youth: Challenges and Prospects." In *Understanding Latino Families: Scholarship, Policy, and Practice*, edited by Ruth E. Zambrana. Thousand Oaks, Calif.: Sage, 1995.

Sorenson, Susan B., and Haikang Shen. "Youth Suicide Trends in California: An Examination of Immigrant and Ethnic Group Risk." *Suicide and Life Threatening Behavior* 26 (1996): 143–154.

U.S. Bureau of the Census. *The Hispanic Population in the United States: Population Characteristics.* Washington, D.C.: U.S. Department of Commerce, 1999.

U.S. Census Bureau. *Marital Status: Census 2000 Brief.* Washington, D.C.: U.S. Department of Commerce, 2003.

U.S. Bureau of the Census. *Poverty in the United States: Current Population Reports.* Washington, D.C.: U.S. Department of Commerce, 2002.

Vega, William, and Margarita, Alegria. "Latino Mental Health and Treatment in the United States." In *Health Issues in the Latino Community.* edited by Marilyn Aguirre-Molina, Carlos W. Molina, and Ruth Enid Zambrana. San Francisco: Jossey-Bass, 2001.

Vigil, James D. *A Rainbow of Gangs: Street Cultures in the Mega-city.* Austin: University of Texas Press, 2002.

Villarruel, Antonia. "Health of Hispanic Adolescents." In *Hispanic Voices: Hispanic Health Educators Speak Out*, edited by Sara Torres. New York: National League for Nursing, 1996.

MARYSOL ASENCIO AND KAREN RIPOLL-NÚÑEZ

ADOPTION. At the turn of the twenty-first century, Latino children constitute 17 percent of the child population in the United States and 13 percent of the child population waiting to be adopted. In California, where Latino children constitute 40 percent of the child population, they account for 31 percent of the children in foster care (U.S. Department of Health and Human Services).

Significant historical, economic, and cultural factors influence Latino patterns of adoption and may contribute to the high number of Latino children in nonfamilial foster care who are waiting to be adopted.

Historical and Cultural Factors

Among Latinos a tradition of informal adoption exists; it includes children being raised by aunts, uncles, and grandparents. In Latin America, families that have more financial resources incorporate children from poorer relatives into their households. Likewise, through the practice of *compadrazgo* (co-parentship based on the ritual of baptism), a child's godparents (particularly if childless) might raise their godchild as their own. Likewise, many young Latino parents allow their firstborn child to be raised by a grandmother, particularly if the couple needs time to solidify the marriage or travels to a different region to seek employment. In such cases, the child generally knows who his or her parents are and is not stigmatized for not living with them. The practice of informal adoption has been facilitated by the fact that Latino families tend to be larger than non-Latino families (3.65 members versus 2.56, respectively) (Zambrana). In addition, Latino families tend to be extended, rather than nuclear in nature. Regardless of household size, Latinos tend to consider grandparents, aunts, uncles, cousins, and godparents as immediate family.

With increased migration of Latinos to the United States, the practice of informal adoption in nations with high emigration rates has increased significantly, as adults generally migrate alone and later send for their children. Moreover, studies indicate that families can be adversely affected by migration in terms of health status and family functioning, thereby potentially increasing the number of families that are unable to care for their children once their family reunites in the United States. One or two generations after migration to the United States, Latino families become smaller in size, reducing the familial resources for informal adoption; thus the process of migration may loosen familial ties and disrupt the practice of informal adoption.

Economic Factors

U.S. Latinos are a highly diverse population with considerable differences in family and social structure, depending on the country of origin. Furthermore, Latino families are generally more economically disadvantaged than European Americans. There is scant information indicating why Latinos of various national origins place their children for adoption or lose their children to foster care. However, several factors may contribute to the high number of Latino children in this situation. First, Latinas have a high rate of teen pregnancy. In the past, if the young woman did not marry, the teen's family raised her children. In recent years, however, adoption has become a more acceptable option. Second, the rate of marriage has decreased, and the divorce rate has increased among Latinos, creating a burden on Latina single parents who are generally undereducated and underemployed. In the absence of extended family with the economic means to take care of children temporarily, a single parent unable to care for them may lose

ADOPTION. Parents at home with their adopted Colombian American daughters, ages 11 and 14, in Schenectady, New York. (Ellen Senisi/The Image Works)

custody of her children. Third, the majority of children involved in the child welfare system have been removed from the home due to parental abuse or neglect. Maternal alcohol and drug abuse is a key predictor of loss of custody. The epidemic of addiction to opiates and cocaine in the 1980s and 1990s affected large numbers of poor women in Mexican American and Puerto Rican communities, resulting in their children being placed in foster care if the mother lacked extended family members to raise them.

Barriers to Latino Adoption

Despite a history of informal adoption, data indicate that Latinos are underrepresented among foster and adoptive families. Of states able to provide statistics for 1998, only 127 of a total of 31,128 licensed or approved adoptive families were identified as Latino (CWLA 1999). In addition, a number of barriers may exist for the placement of Latino children with families from the same ethnic or national origin group.

First, Latinos may be unaware of the extent of the need. The general perception within and outside the culture that Latinos are highly familistic and well adapted may obscure the reality that many Latinos are unable to care for and raise their own children temporarily or permanently. Second, a large percentage of the children in the welfare system are sibling groups, which are harder to place together in foster care and harder to place in common adoptive homes. The socioeconomic condition of most Latinos may preclude adoption or foster care of more than one child. Third, childless Latinos may feel that their inability to have children is a punishment from God and that they do not deserve to have a child, even an adopted one. In addition, there are misconceptions about children with special needs, especially among Latinos who are less educated and who are less acculturated to the United States. Fourth, about one quarter of the Latino population in the United States speaks little or no English, and one third does not speak English well (Zambrana). Children from such households need Spanish-speaking foster placements and adoptive or foster parents who understand their cultural background. Yet linguistic requirements for adoptive placements preclude many Spanish-speaking families who otherwise meet criteria for serving as foster or adoptive parents.

Other barriers to adoption include lack of information, unavailability of financial resources, and absence of bilingual caseworkers. In addition, Quintanilla found that bureaucracy deters people who might apply because of a lack of Spanish-speaking staff and forms written in Spanish. Agencies sometimes view individuals who do not speak "perfect" English as inappropriate for adoption and hold the view that Latino children should be removed from their communities and placed with non-Latinos to afford them better opportunities.

Thus, to promote adoption by individuals from similar ethnic and national backgrounds, specific recruitment and information strategies must be developed. For children in foster care, the ultimate goal is family reunification. When that is not an option, an adoptive family who will support the child's cultural and emotional needs is needed. Once Latinos become aware of the need by Latino children, they will come forth to adopt, since taking care of children is highly valued in Latino cultures.

See also Familia *and* Teenage Pregnancy.

BIBLIOGRAPHY

Child Welfare League of America. *State Child Welfare Agency Survey.* Washington, D.C.: Child Welfare League of America (CWLA), 1999.

Flores-Ortiz, Y. "Injustice in Latino Families: Considerations for Family Therapists." In *Family Therapy with Hispanics*, edited by M. T. Flores and G. Carey, 251–264. Boston: Allyn and Bacon, 2000.

Quintanilla, M. "Adoption and the Latino Community." In *Race, Culture, and National Origin: The Issues. . .the Values.* Conference Proceedings, Ethics and Adoption: Challenges for Today and the Future, Anaheim, Calif. November 4 1999.

U.S. Department of Health and Human Services. *Child Welfare Outcomes 1998, Annual Report.* Washington, D.C.: U.S. Department of Health and Human Services, 2000. Available at www.acf.dhhs.gov/programs/cb

Zambrana, R. E. "Economic and Social Vulnerability of Latino Children and Families by Subgroup: Implications for Child Welfare." *Child Welfare* 77, no. 1 (1998): 5–27.

YVETTE G. FLORES

ADVERTISING AND MARKETING. The millennium brought an explosion of Latina and Latino names and faces in film, music, television, and, most recently, advertising. As with other media industries, the social and historical forces responsible for the unprecedented increase of revenues flowing into Latino marketing and advertising campaigns are varied and complex. Spearheading efforts to tap into the more lucrative advertising budgets of multinational advertisers are agencies owned and operated by Latinas and Latinos. These agencies are redefining industry perceptions and expectations of Latinas and Latinos as a viable commodity audience—in other words, as a profitable audience worthy of marketing attention. Their long-term efforts are finally paying off with record-breaking but modest (by general industry standards) gains. The result is a barrage of advertising campaigns, from Gap jeans to L'Oreal products, using Latinas and Latinos and *Latinidad* to sell products and services to Latinas and Latinos and non-Latinas and non-Latinos alike.

Although some multinational corporations are eager to exploit Latino ethnicity to sell products, for a variety of reasons many remain resistant to allocating significant portions of their advertising budgets to the largest and one of the fastest-growing ethnic/racial groups in the United States. Research by the Association of Hispanic Advertising Agencies suggests that some companies still believe that marketing to Latinas and Latinos is not profitable or that they can more effectively target Latina and Latino audiences through general English-media campaigns (Santiago and Valdés). The reasons for this reluctance have their roots in the historical development of Latinas and Latinos as a commodity market, the complex issues surrounding contemporary marketing and advertising campaigns targeting Latinas and Latinos, and the commodification of pan-ethnic Latinidad to sell products to Latina and Latino and non-Latina and non-Latino audiences.

Developing the Latino Market

Although "Latina" and "Latino" is the more ethnically inclusive and contemporary terminology, "Hispanic" is the preferred term of U.S. advertising and marketing companies that are owned and operated by Latinos and Latinas. Many in the industry believe that "Hispanic," the official term used by the U.S. Census Bureau, is more recognizable and meaningful since it is the label familiar to most people. This article uses both the terms "Latina" and "Latino," when discussing general developments and issues, and the term "Hispanic advertising and marketing," when specifically referring to the industry or companies owned by Latinas and Latinos.

The historical roots of Latina and Latino advertising and marketing lie in two primary developments. In the nineteenth and early twentieth centuries, the Southwest border region was one of the earliest sites for Latino marketing and advertising (Rodriguez, pp. 13–34). Driven by both the politics of community building and the search for untapped audiences, Spanish-language newspapers and radio stations sprouted from Texas to Southern California. These media were primarily dependent on local and regional advertisers and specifically aimed at local, regional, and transnational Mexican and Mexican American communities. Given the divisive racial politics of that era, few non-Latino companies advertised in these channels, and most Spanish-language radio stations and newspapers were supported by wealthy individuals or community organizers. Despite continuing difficulties in attracting non-Latino advertisers, many of the media outlets that arouse during this period, such as *La opinion*, are still in existence today.

The second major wave of Latino advertising and marketing developed during the 1960s in Miami and New York with the migration of exiled Cuban media professionals to the United States. Unlike the regional media in the Southwest, these professionals sought to work with

Para tu papá parrillero.

Sᴇᴀʀs Aᴅᴠᴇʀᴛɪsᴇᴍᴇɴᴛ. (Courtesy of the Sears Corporation)

national media outlets throughout the United States and Latin America. Rather than specializing in a particular region or local ethnic group, such as Mexican Americans in Los Angeles, these agencies specialized in selling a diversity of specific ethnic Latina and Latino audiences to national advertisers. In other words, they would take a national brand, such as Dole, and develop simultaneous marketing campaigns targeted at Puerto Ricans in the Northeast, Cubans in the South, or Mexicans in the Southwest. Each campaign would be tailored to the specific Latina or Latino group, using their own Spanish dialect and cultural practices. These Hispanic advertising and marketing agencies were the first to market to Latinas and Latinos actively as a commodity audience for U.S. products. Much of the advertising during the 1960s and 1970s centered on connecting U.S. companies with Latina and Latino consumers through national Spanish-language broadcast outlets such as Univision and Telemundo.

The Cuban exiles brought with them to the United States the commercial relationships with international advertisers, like Colgate and Del Monte, that they had already established in pre-communist Cuba. The most important national Hispanic advertising agencies created during this period were founded by Cuban exiles. They include the Spanish Advertising and Marketing Services (SAMS), founded in 1962 by Luis Díaz Albertini; Conill Advertising, founded in 1968 by Rafael and Alicia Conill; and Siboney U.S.A., founded by José Luis Cubas.

The release of the 1980 U.S. census report revealed the dramatic growth of the Latina and Latino community and predicted radical demographic shifts in the composition of the U.S. population. This information signaled a watershed moment in the construction of the Latina and Latino market. Since that time, Hispanic advertising and marketing agencies have sought to extend their reach in both English- and Spanish-language media by moving away from ethnic-specific Latina and Latino marketing to pan-ethnic Latina and Latino marketing. Unlike the pre-1980s marketing strategies that emphasized differences among Cubans, Puerto Ricans, and Mexicans, Hispanic advertising and marketing campaigns of the 1980s and 1990s constructed a pan-ethnic and unified image of Latina and Latino consumers, emphasizing the similarities, rather than the differences, among the more than fifty Latina and Latino groups that live in the United States.

Contemporary Latino Marketing and Advertising

The contemporary marketing and advertising landscape has built on this image of a unified Latina and Latino market. Using Census Bureau data, consumer data reports, and market research studies, Hispanic marketing and advertising agencies have continued to shift the focus away from nationality-specific marketing targeted at particular groups or regions and toward the notion of Latinas and Latinos as one unified market that shares common cultural values and norms. At the center of this strategy in the early 2000s is the demographic group to which Hispanic industry insiders refer as Generation Ñ, the 18- to 38-year-olds who make up the largest segment of the U.S. Latina and Latino population. The goal of the strategy is to highlight Generation Ñ's lucrative spending potential to national advertisers. The Generation Ñ strategy highlights the facts that:

- U.S. Latinas and Latinos are younger than the general population and wealthier than non–U.S. Latinas and Latinos based on annual per capital income.
- U.S. Latinas and Latinos had a combined spending power of $630 billion in 2000.
- U.S. Latinas and Latinos consume at a higher rate than the population at large (Valdés, pp. 60–70).

In emphasizing the relative wealth and numbers of U.S. Latinas and Latinos, the goal is to shift advertisers' focus away from the less lucrative Spanish-language outlets to the more profitable English-language general media. Because it is more expensive to advertise in English-language outlets, Hispanic advertising and marketing agencies stand to profit by developing a pan-ethnic strategy with a broad enough appeal to succeed in multiple markets. This marketing strategy is at the core of the mission of the Association of Hispanic Advertising Agencies (AHAA), an umbrella organization established in 1996 to raise awareness about the Latina and Latino market and to provide a forum for professionalizing the Hispanic advertising industry.

The Generation Ñ marketing strategy is slowly paying off for Hispanic advertising agencies. In less than six years, AHAA increased its membership from forty to fifty-seven Latina- and Latino-oriented advertising companies throughout the United States. Furthermore, at a time when general market advertising agencies saw a decline in their profits because of the terrorist attacks of September 11, 2001, the premier Hispanic advertising agencies experienced record-breaking earnings. Expenditures on Latina and Latino advertising increased from $1.4 billion in 1997 to $2.7 billion in 2002. This is a remarkable but underwhelming increase, considering that companies spend more than $233.7 billion per year advertising in the general media (Kramer, pp. 3 and 21). Among the Hispanic advertising companies benefiting most from the economic upturn are Bravo Group (New York); Casanova Pendrill (Irvine, California); Lopez Negrete Communications (Houston); Lumina America (New York); Vidal Parternship (New York); and Zubi Advertising (Coral Gables, Florida). These companies represent national and international clients such as Cingular Wireless, Citibank, Coca Cola Co., Jim Beam Brands Co., Heineken, McDonald's, Sears Roebuck & Co., and Wendy's International Inc.

Despite the contemporary success of Hispanic advertising agencies, the future development of the Latina and Latino market faces challenges as many corporations remain resistant to allocating advertising money for Latina- and Latino-centered campaigns. According to one industry report, advertisers consistently ignore the data regarding Latina and Latino consumer spending and potential buying power (Santiago and Valdés, p. 4). The report found that two-thirds of major U.S. companies are not targeting the Latina and Latino market. Of those who are, more than 64 percent spend less than 3.2 percent of their overall advertising budget on Latina- and Latino-oriented campaigns. The majority of those advertisers allocate most of the budget to the less lucrative Spanish-language market. Of the total U.S. advertising in the Hispanic market, 70 percent, or $1.7 billion, is spent at Univision and the Sony-owned Telemundo. Approximately $570 million is spent on Latino print media, which means that the highest-circulation magazines, *Latina* and *People en Español*, still face problems attracting advertisers (Villano, pp. 24–28).

Barriers to Latino Advertising and Marketing

The expansion of Latino advertising and marketing into general English-language media faces three main barriers: complex demographics, Spanish-language media, and Latina and Latino stereotypes. First, Latina and Latino demographics are complex. People defined as Latinas and Latinos come from a variety of national backgrounds and racial identities and posses a diversity of language competencies, education levels, income levels, and levels of acculturation. These differences make it difficult to conceptualize Latinas and Latinos as a unified market. Before the emergence of pan-ethnic national and transnational marketing strategies, potential advertisers had to make decisions about language, Spanish dialect, and cultural practices, for example.

Second, advertising in Spanish-language media remains less expensive. Because many advertisers stereotype Latinas and Latinos as Spanish-dominant, they are reluctant to spend money targeting Latina and Latino consumers through English-language media or campaigns. The underlying assumption in the marketing industry is that English-dominant or bilingual Latinas and Latinos are familiar enough with the culture, norms, and values of the United States to respond to general advertising campaigns. Therefore, most advertisers who target the Latina and Latino market at all focus their campaigns on first-generation Spanish-dominant Latinas and Latinos with low levels of acculturation. As a result, the top five Latina and Latino media markets, California, Florida, Illinois, New York, and Texas, are also geographical areas with high numbers of first-generation Latina and Latino immigrants.

Recent data demonstrating a growth in the audience shares for Spanish-format media have made it even more difficult to persuade advertisers to enter the English market. For example, the top-rated radio station in New York (WSKG-FM) and the top-rated television stations in the San Francisco area (KDTV) and Los Angeles (KMEX-TV) broadcast in Spanish. In Miami the circulation for the Spanish-language newspapers, *El nuevo herald* and *Diarios las Americas*, almost equals that of the English-language *Miami Herald* (Villano, p. 26).

The academic research on the effectiveness of English- versus Spanish-language advertising is mixed. A 1996 study found that Spanish-language advertisements are more persuasive and cost-effective than English-language advertisements regardless of the audience's English fluency (Roslow and Nicholls, p. 45). However, a 1997 study argued that mainstream media outlets are just as effective as the ethnic media in reaching minority audiences by suggesting that an advertisement's effectiveness is primarily determined by the level of acculturation (Ueltschy and Krampf, p. 89). For instance, first-generation Mexican Americans with low levels of acculturation prefer Spanish-language advertisements with Anglo models, while third-generation Mexican Americans with high levels of acculturation prefer English-language advertisements with Latina and Latino models. As of the early 2000s, there is no definitive academic study on the effectiveness of Spanish versus English advertising.

Last, but most important, U.S. advertisers continue to hold a myriad of stereotypes about Latinas and Latinos as consumers. The primary ones are that Latinas and Latinos are Spanish-speaking, lower-income, and uneducated. Surveys actually demonstrate that a majority of Latinas and Latinos are bilingual or English-dominant and consume both Spanish- and English-language media (Suro, p. 4). In lectures and public appearances, Christy Hauberger, founder of *Latina*, one of the more successful Hispanic niche magazines, argues that her magazine still faces resistance by major advertisers who stereotype Latinas as submissive stay-at-home mothers or uneducated welfare recipients. In contrast to these stereotypes, the market data demonstrate that Latinas spend more on make-up, hair products, and baby products than other demographic groups. Hauberger says that industry officials are often surprised by and skeptical of the numbers. Advertisers also tend to believe that Latinas and Latinos are not a stable long-term revenue market and that, despite their sizable spending potential, Latinas and Latinos are not likely to spend money on luxury or nonutilitarian goods.

Consequently, much of the work of Latina and Latino media producers and Hispanic advertising and marketing agencies centers on breaking down stereotyped assumptions about Latinas and Latinos as a market and on informing potential advertisers about Latina and Latino population statistics and consumer data. It is only recently that many industries, such as pharmaceuticals, financial services, apparel, health and beauty aids, and traditional and online retail, have begun to enter the Latina and Latino market.

The Politics and Content of Latino Advertising

The racialized stereotype of the Frito Bandito and the sexualized stereotype of Chiquita Banana have been displaced by a different yet equally problematic set of representations. Advertising, as a kind of linguistic and visual code, conveys both implicit and explicit messages about social norms and values and the social status of ethnic, racial, and gender groups. In this code, the representations of Latinas and Latinos in advertisements face three main difficulties: (1) Latinas and Latinos remain relatively invisible in advertising representation; (2) Latinas and Latinos in advertisements remain racially and sexually stereotyped; (3) pan-ethnic Latina and Latino representations contribute to homogenization of a diverse group.

First, despite recent increases, Latina and Latino actors and models, like Asians and Asian Americans, remain underrepresented in mainstream advertising. For instance, in a content analysis of magazine advertisements, Latina and Latino models appeared in 4.7 percent of advertisements, Asian in 4 percent, and African American in 11.4 percent. Second, when Latinas and Latinos are depicted in advertisements, they are more likely to be represented as less educated and working-class rather than professional, and are most often associated with family and ethnic signifiers like food and music. Many of the Latina and Latino representations in Spanish- and English-language advertisements remain couched in what Arlene Dávila labels the "Hispanic archetype," or the representation of Latinas and Latinos as "family-oriented, Catholic, traditional, conservative, and immigrant Spanish-speaking individuals" who live primarily in urban areas with large extended families (p. 60). Ironically, the Hispanic advertising and marketing agencies established during the 1960s are largely responsible for the continuing dominance of this representation.

Third, in order to reach English-language media advertisers, Hispanic advertising and marketing agencies are distancing themselves from the "Hispanic archetype" by circulating an alternative pan-ethnic image of Latinas and Latinos and Latinidad that erases racial and national differences and favors whiteness. In other words, rather than encouraging advertisers to develop Spanish-language advertisements specifically tailored for Mexican American, Latin American, or Spanish Caribbean audiences, Hispanic advertising and marketing agencies are promoting a broader, more unifying notion of Latinas and Latinos with a shared culture, foods, music, and language. This approach allows them to be targeted as one homogeneous group. At the center of this strategy is the use of English and non-accented Spanish, Anglo-appearing models with stereotypical black hair and dark eyes, and generic appeals to Latino values, traditions, family, and other community structures. The result is a problematic trend toward economic, racial, and ethnic homogenization, where Latinas and Latinos are increasingly represented as white, and Latinidad is expressed only through stereotypical notions of food, music, and hypersexuality.

Latina and Latino bodies, music, and other cultural elements of Latinidad are used to sell a myriad of products and services. Among the most visible Latina spokespeople are Penelope Cruz (Ralph Lauren), Salma Hayek (Lincoln Continental), Jennifer Lopez (Pepsi), and Christina Aguillera (Versace). In addition, Jessica Alba, Salma Hayek, and Jennifer Lopez have all been awarded coveted contracts as L'Oreal spokeswomen. Recent television campaigns for Cuervo and Budweiser prominently feature Latina and Latino models dressed seductively in stereotypically bright colors with salsa background music. Other television campaigns for the Institute of Information and Technology feature a Latina actress speaking accented English. Among companies recently targeting Latinas and Latinos are Levi's, Adidas, Target, Wal-Mart and Blockbuster. On one hand, the increasing number of advertisements targeting Latinas and Latinos and using elements of Latina and Latino culture to sell products denotes a shift for Latinas and Latinos from the social periphery to the social center. On the other hand, it raises questions about the use of stereotyped representations and homogenizing images and the ethics of proliferating alcohol and tobacco advertisements in Latina and Latino communities.

In fact, alcohol and tobacco companies in particular have led the charge in Latina and Latino marketing. Latinas and Latinos, and more specifically urban and low-income Latinas and Latinos, are both a primary target and a representational vehicle for alcohol and tobacco campaigns. Five of the top twenty corporations in terms of revenue spent on advertising and marketing to Latinas and Latinos are Anheuser-Busch, Coors Brewing, Miller Brewing, Phillip Morris, and United Distillers and Vendors (Santiago and Valdés, p. 4). Most alcohol and tobacco advertising campaigns are conducted through Spanish-language media such as billboard and magazine advertisements targeted at urban Latina and Latino audiences. Telemundo and Univision are restricted by FCC regulations from airing such advertisements.

Most research indicates that advertising for alcohol and cigarettes exerts an indirect and negligible influence compared to that of family and peers. Nonetheless, the aggressive targeting of young urban Latina and Latino men and women through high-density billboard campaigns poses an ethical dilemma for Hispanic advertising and marketing agencies. A 2002 study confirmed that African American and Latina and Latino neighborhoods had more alcohol and tobacco billboards per capita than any other neighborhood (Mastro and Atkin, p. 131). Most of these billboards were located near schools. While researchers have found minimal but measurable connections between exposure to alcohol advertisements and adolescent behavior, many remain concerned about the long-term indirect effects of these campaigns targeted at Latina and Latino communities. Regardless of the effects, however, it is possible to question whether Hispanic advertising and marketing agencies should be profiting by promoting activities that pose a documented health risk and threat to Latina and Latino families and communities, many of whom are already economically and educationally at risk.

See also Alcoholism; Census; Film; Lopez, Jennifer; Media; Media and Latino Identity; Television, Spanish Language; *and* Univision.

BIBLIOGRAPHY

Bowen, Lawrence, and Jill Schmid. "Minority Presence and Portrayal in Mainstream Magazine Advertising: An Update." *Journalism and Mass Communication Quarterly* 74 (1997): 134–146.

Bucholz, Kathleen K., and Lee N. Robins. "Sociological Research on Alcohol Use, Problems, and Policy." *Annual Review of Sociology* 15 (1989): 163–186.

Dávila, Arlene M. *Latinos, Inc.: The Marketing and Making of a People.* Berkeley: University of California Press, 2001.

Domenech Rodríguez, Melanie, Michael Slater, and Frederick Beauvais. "Beer Advertising to Latino Youth: The Effects of Spanish- vs. English-Language Targeting." In *Facing Differences: Race, Gender, and Mass Media*, edited by Shirley Biagi and Marilyn Kern-Foxworth. Thousand Oaks, Calif.: Pine Forge Press, 1997.

Goodson, Sabrina, and Mary Alice Shaver. "Hispanic Marketing: National Advertisers, Spending Patterns, and Media Choices." *Journalism Quarterly* 71 (1994): 191–198.

Kanellos, Nicolás, and Claudio Esteva-Fabregat, eds. *Handbook of Hispanic Cultures in the United States.* Vol. 3: *Sociology*, edited by Félix M. Padilla. Houston, Tex.: Arte Público Press, 1994.

Kramer, Louise. "Ethnic Ad-vances: Hispanic Agencies Are Industry's Hot Spots." *Crain's New York Business* 18, no. 1 (January 7–13, 2002): 3, 21.

LaChausse, Robert G. "Attitudes toward Tobacco Advertising among Hispanic Migrant Farm Workers." *Journal of Immigrant Health* 3 (2001): 107–110.

Mastro, Dana E., and Charles Atkin. "Exposure to Alcohol Billboards and Beliefs and Attitudes toward Drinking among Mexican American High School Students." *Howard Journal of Communications* 13 (2002): 129–151.

Rodriguez, América. *Making Latino News: Race, Language, Class.* Thousand Oaks, Calif.: Sage, 1999.

Roslow, Peter, and J. A. F. Nicholls. "Targeting the Hispanic Market: Comparative Persuasion of TV Commercials in Spanish and English." *Journal of Advertising Research* 36 (1996): 67–77.

Santiago, Carlos, and Isabel Valdés. *Missed Opportunities: Vast Corporate Underinvestment in the U.S. Hispanic Market.* McLean, Va.: Association of Hispanic Advertising Agencies, April 2002. Available at www.ahaa.org/research/Missedopportunities.pdf

Schooler, Caroline, Michael Basil, and David G. Altman. "Alcohol and Cigarette Advertising on Billboards: Targeting with Social Cues." *Health Communication* 8 (1996): 109–129.

Stevenson, Thomas H., and Patricia E. McIntyre. "A Comparison of the Portrayal and Frequency of Hispanics and Whites in English Language Television Advertising." *Journal of Current Issues and Research in Advertising* 17 (1995): 65–74.

Suro, Roberto. *Changing Channels and Crisscrossing Cultures: A Survey of Latinos on the News Media.* Pew Hispanic Center: University of Southern California. 2004.

Ueltschy, Linda, and Robert Krampf. "The Influence of Acculturation on Advertising Effectiveness to the Hispanic Market." *Applied Business Research* 13, no. 2 (1997): 87–101.

Valdés, M. Isabel. *Marketing to American Latinos: A Guide to the In-Culture Approach.* 2 vols. Ithaca, N.Y.: Paramount Market Publishing, 2000.

Villano, Matt. "Hispanic Media Flourishes." *Editor & Publisher* 132, no. 11 (1999): 24–28.

Isabel Molina Guzmán

AFDC. *See* Aid to Families with Dependent Children.

AFFIRMATIVE ACTION. Affirmative action is legally defined as a system designed to remedy past discrimination and eliminate current and future discrimination. Historically, affirmative action involved voluntary and mandatory efforts by federal, state, and local governments; private employers; and schools to combat discrimination and foster fair hiring and promotion of qualified individuals. The initial origin was a recognition that practices in the past did not guarantee such fairness and that there was evidence for discriminatory practices.

Until the mid-1960s, legal barriers prevented Latinos and Latinas, blacks, and other racial minorities in the United States from entering many jobs and educational institutions. The Civil Rights Act of 1964, which prohibited discrimination in public accommodations and employment, was the first modern legislation to address these barriers.

Historical Background

The term "affirmative action" was first used by President John F. Kennedy in a 1961 executive order that created the Committee on Equal Employment Opportunity and was designed to encourage contractors on projects financed with federal funds to racially integrate their workforces. Kennedy's executive order declared that federal contractors should "take affirmative action to ensure that applicants are employed, and employees are treated during their employment, without regard to race, creed, color or national origin" (Executive Order No. 10,925, 26 Federal Register 1977 [1961]). (Employment discrimination on the basis of a person's sex was first prohibited by Title VII of the Civil Rights Act of 1964.) The original goal of the civil rights movement had been "color-blind" laws. However, many people believed that simply ending a long-standing policy of discrimination did not go far enough. They believed that affirmative, or proactive, measures to increase equality were necessary. As President Lyndon B. Johnson stated in a 1965 speech at Howard University, "You do not take a person who, for years, has been hobbled by chains and liberate him, bring him up to the starting line of a race and say, 'you are free to compete with all the others,' and still justly believe that you have been completely fair."

President Richard Nixon was the first to implement federal policies designed to guarantee minority hiring.

Responding to continuing racial inequalities in the workforce, the Nixon administration in 1969 developed the Philadelphia Plan requiring that contractors on federally assisted projects set specific goals for hiring minorities. Federal courts upheld this plan in 1970 and 1971.

Affirmative action plans do not mandate "preferences" or "quotas" (the U.S. Supreme Court has ruled that quotas are illegal). However, opponents of affirmative action routinely use such terms interchangeably with the term "affirmative action." From its beginnings in the United States in the 1960s, affirmative action has been highly controversial, yet the research of many psychologists demonstrates that how the concept is defined often shapes public opinion. When appropriately defined as a remedy for both past and continuing discrimination based on race, ethnicity, and gender, public support for affirmative action increases as demonstrated in public opinion surveys.

Affirmative action plans are usually based on an analysis of how well women and minorities are represented in targeted areas, such as employment settings, and the percentage of qualified individuals from these backgrounds who are part of the larger pool of potential employees, students, and so forth. At their core, however, affirmative action plans are designed to create opportunity and eliminate both conscious and inadvertent discrimination. The scope and limitations of affirmative action policy have been defined through a series of legislative initiatives and decisions by the Supreme Court of the United States.

Affirmative Action Challenged and Defended

Starting in the mid-1990s, politicians and grassroots groups began to attack affirmative action at the state level with some success. The regents of the University of California system voted in 1995 to end all affirmative action in hiring and admissions, and minority enrollment in the system's entering undergraduate class plummeted in 1998, when the changes took effect. In 1996, California voters approved Proposition 209, an initiative that ended affirmative action throughout the state in public hiring, purchasing, and other government business. In 1998, Washington State voters passed Initiative 200, a measure that banned affirmative action in state and local government hiring, contracting, and education.

Around the same time, federal courts began considering lawsuits from white students denied admission to state universities with affirmative action programs. In some cases, the courts have invalidated such programs on the grounds that they promote reverse racial discrimination. For example, in *Hopwood v. Texas* (1996) a federal appeals court barred the University of Texas Law School from "any consideration of race or ethnicity" in its admissions decisions. As in California, the termination of the school's affirmative action program led to a sharp drop in minority enrollment. One of the immediate effects of the *Hopwood* decision was to decrease the number of Latinos and Latinas who applied and were admitted to many of the most selective publicly funded higher education programs in the state. The amount of financial aid available to Latino and Latina students was also drastically decreased because of *Hopwood*.

Yet in 2003 the Supreme Court, in the case of *Grutter v. Bollinger*, reaffirmed the premise that affirmative action was constitutionally permissible because the state has a compelling interest in assuring racial diversity. In *Grutter v. Bollinger*, the affirmative action policy for law school admissions at the University of Michigan had been challenged. In the 5 to 4 majority decision Justice Sandra Day O'Connor wrote, "In order to cultivate a set of leaders with legitimacy in the eyes of the citizenry, it is necessary that the path to leadership be visibly open to talented and qualified individuals of every race and ethnicity." Amicus (friend of the court) briefs from the heads of major corporations and from retired military officers argued that affirmative action was essential to produce qualified corporate managers and military leaders and to encourage industrial innovation. These amicus briefs and Justice O'Connor's references to them in her opinion suggest that affirmative action has become a key tool not only to achieve greater equality in the nation but also to help manage sustained economic growth and secure the national defense.

Affirmative action programs have increased the racial, ethnic, and gender diversity of many educational and workplace settings in the United States. During the period from 1976 to 1993 the numbers of Latinos and Latinas attending college rose 160.1 percent, and the proportional representation of Latinos and Latinas in college doubled from 3.6 percent to 7.4 percent. This diversity helps to enrich the lives of U.S. residents in many ways. For instance, empirical studies document that racial, ethnic, and gender diversity in collegiate settings helps to stimulate students' personal growth and intellectual development. Many Latino and Latina politicians, academicians, and community leaders owe their educational or career opportunities to legislation that used ethnicity as one determining factor.

However, on the same day the Supreme Court's *Grutter* decision validated the use of affirmative action in the University of Michigan's law school admissions policy, the Court also issued a separate decision rejecting the affirmative action program used in the University of Michigan's undergraduate program, which was challenged in *Gratz v. Bollinger*. The undergraduate program used a point system in deciding how to weigh applicants, with minority applicants receiving a large number of points. The Court ruled that this method was too "mechanistic" and amounted to a quota system. The law school program, the Court said, was permissible because it evaluated each applicant individually and used race as one of many factors in deciding whom to admit.

Simultaneously, civil rights organizations hailed the *Grutter* decision because it clearly reaffirmed the value of affirmative action programs even though it did not overturn state laws that prohibit affirmative action, such as those in California and Washington. Opponents of affirmative action vowed to continue fighting and noted the Court's opinion that "enshrining a permanent justification of racial preferences would offend [the] equal protection principle" of the Constitution. "We expect that 25 years from now, the use of racial preferences will no longer be necessary to further the interest approved today," O'Connor wrote.

However, even after thirty years of federally mandated affirmative action policies bringing about undeniable progress, inequalities persist. Latinos and Latinas still lag behind in overall college enrollment numbers, college graduation rates, and completion of master's and doctoral degree programs. There is much evidence of continuing discrimination against Latinos and Latinas and other racial minorities and women of all colors. In fact, the evidence is overwhelming that the problems affirmative action seeks to address—widespread discrimination and exclusion and their ripple effects—continue to exist.

See also Civil Rights Act (1964); Employment Discrimination; Race and Racialization; *and* Racial Profiling.

BIBLIOGRAPHY
Anderson, Terry H. *The Pursuit of Fairness: A History of Affirmative Action*. New York: Oxford University Press, 2004.
Curry, George E., ed. *The Affirmative Action Debate*. Reading, Mass.: Addison-Wesley, 1996.
Edley, Christopher, Jr. *Not All Black and White: Affirmative Action, Race, and American Values*. New York: Hill and Wang, 1996.
Executive Order No. 10,925, 26 Federal Register 1977 (1961). Establishing the President's Committee on Equal Employment Opportunity. Available at www.lib.umich.edu/govdocs/jfkeo/eo/10925.htm
Johnson, Lyndon B. "To Fulfill These Rights." Commencement Address at Howard University, Washington, D.C., June 4, 1965. In *Public Papers of the Presidents of the United States: Lyndon B. Johnson, 1965*. vol. 2, entry 301, 635–640. Washington, D.C.: Government Printing Office, 1966.

TANYA KATERÍ HERNANDEZ

AFRICA AND LATINOS AND LATINAS.

The historical and cultural significance of Africa in the lives of Latinas and Latinos in the United States is fully comprehensible only when considered within the context of the specific cultures and histories of their countries of origin, not least the connection to continental Africa. The transatlantic slave trade and the institution of slavery in the Americas, spanning the sixteenth to the nineteenth centuries, frame the relationship between Africa and Latin America. The arrival of Africans in the Americas occasioned the development of communities that bore the unmistakable stamp of the African continent, no more so than in Latin America, where a number of factors account for the relative prominence of African cultural and religious traditions. These factors include the nature and duration of contact with Africa, a Catholicism that accommodated African and African-derived institutions, and African demographics. (African-descent populations range from 45 percent of 170 million in Brazil, to 62 percent of 11 million in Cuba, to 84 percent of 9 million in the Dominican Republic, to 26 percent of 40 million in Colombia.) But varying histories have meant that Africa in, for example, Argentina and Chile assumes a quite distinct profile from Africa in the Dominican Republic, Cuba, Colombia, and Ecuador. Complex historical and cultural developments resist categorization under an unwieldy, catchall Latin American or Latina or Latino. Since the pioneering work of Frank Tannenbaum, Fernando Ortiz, and Roger Bastide, various scholars have examined the African connection to the Americas and its consequences. Recent additions to the list are Anani Dzidzienyo, Michael Conniff, Thomas Davis, and Peter Wade.

One feature of Africana is common to all Latin American societies. In the hierarchy of desirable religious, cultural, and even demographic qualities, those associated with Africa and Africans were early on considered a blight on civilized, Christianized lifestyles and so were to be extirpated where possible or stringently contained and improved upon. The ultimate object was to de-Africanize society, religion, and culture. Throughout colonial Latin America official decrees uniformly sought to regulate African lifestyles and institutions by banning public worship, drumming, and dancing. No such obvious attempts to quash a controversial heritage exist in the early twenty-first century. In fact one sees in many places concerted efforts to incorporate Africana into the larger culture. This nationalized blackness, as Robin Moore characterizes the Cuban example, celebrates the African contribution to the religious pantheon, to dance, and to music. What it does not do, however, is remove the ages-old negativity associated with Africa, nor does it permit an acknowledgment of African contributions beyond the restricted spheres of religion, dance, music, and sports. One cannot overemphasize the centrality of the historical context in any assessment of Africana among present-day Latin Americans and their Latina and Latino progeny. The work of Magnus Mörner, for example, helps unravel the deep roots of race mixture and its consequences within Latin America.

Societies that have uniformly associated Africana with vice, ugliness, crudeness, and the need to improve the

MADONA AFRO-LATINA. Painting by Alfredo Arreguin, 1994. (Courtesy University of Washington Press)

race through selective de-Africanization of physical features, hair texture, skin tone, and the like confront a persisting conundrum: how to celebrate what in other contexts it denigrates. For individuals and groups who are recognizably of African descent, the consequences are etiquettes beyond dispute. Leslie Rout Jr.'s work helped focus attention on the continuing relevance of Africa in Latin America.

What then is to be made of the oft-repeated claim that mass participation in Africa-derived religious traditions suggests that Africana has no effect on patterns of social and political mobility? Witness, one is told, the blackest of priests and priestesses who are revered by a multiracial group of adherents and the whitest of practitioners who partake of culinary tidbits that taste of Africa and who pour libations to deities of Africa. Does this not argue powerfully for the essential benignity of the treatment of things African among Latin Americans and Latinas and Latinos?

Unfortunately, an overview based on the available history reveals a general "unfriendliness" to Africa. An unin-

tended consequence of this negativity has been the enormous burden shouldered by those who take on the task of promoting positive images of Africana, advocating candid discussions in public discourses, rescuing Africana from the restricted cultural and folkloric spaces to which it has been consigned, and daring to link the much-touted money-as-whitener trope to a racial hierarchy that has historically demonized Africanity.

In the United States, Afro-Latinas and Afro-Latinos assume rather more than a label, for with it comes possible criticism from their fellow Latinas and Latinos that their identity undermines the solidarity and unity of Latinas and Latinos. Indeed Afro-Latinism threatens to blur the lines separating the multiracial rainbow of the Latin universe from its vilified antipode, the binary race-relations structure of the United States. And it is here that the African factor reemerges for those Latinas and Latinos who may be mistaken for blacks. What are these individuals to do within a socioracial context that offers limited symbolic and physical space for denying or ignoring blackness?

Piri Thomas's and Evélio Grilló's autobiographies illustrate this problem. Recognizing that blackness is burdened with extreme negativity in U.S. society, Latin Americans may opt for whiteness or for classifications that are not associated with blackness. Prevailing norms may of course all but negate those self-designations. As Peter Winn has observed, in the Dominican Republic colonels are never black, no matter how dark their complexion. But what becomes the predicament of those with visibly dark complexions who are now stuck between a more restrictive U.S. conceptualization of blackness and a Latin American and Latina and Latino variant? How are Afro-Latinas and Afro-Latinos to negotiate this narrow passage? It would be presumptuous to offer a single response precisely because all choices carry particular consequences, especially for Afro-Latinas and Afro-Latinos. What is incontrovertible is that, throughout the Americas, Africa and Africana have traditionally symbolized the antithesis of both advancement and prestige in the world. Ironically perhaps, the increasing demographic presence of Latinas and Latinos in the United States has opened possibilities for tackling the conundrum of Africa in the Americas.

Increasingly, the encounter between Africans and Latinas and Latinos will encompass historical, cultural, and religious Africa and a living, contemporary Africa, some of whose peoples actually live in the United States and will inevitably cross paths with Latinas and Latinos. Such face-to-face contact or its symbolic variants will have to be factored into the long and complex histories of Latin American and Latina and Latino relations with Africa at home and abroad, especially within the United States. The vigorous debates on the Afrolatino Connection Web site are a clear indication of the seriousness attached to the Africa connection by some Latinas and Latinos.

See also Afro-Latinos; Black-Latino Relations; Blanqueamiento; Internalized Racism; Leyes de Castas; Mestizaje; Negrophobia; Pigmentocracy; *and* Race and Racialization.

BIBLIOGRAPHY
Bastide, Roger. *African Civilisations in the New World.* Translated by Peter Green. New York: Harper and Row, 1971.
Conniff, Michael L., and Thomas J. Davis, eds. *Africans in the Americas: A History of the Black Diaspora.* New York: St. Martin's Press, 1994.
Dzidzienyo, Anani, and Suzanne Oboler, eds. *Neither Enemies nor Friends: Latinos, Blacks, Afro-Latinos.* New York: Palgrave Macmillan, 2005.
Grilló, Evélio. *Black Cuban, Black American: A Memoir.* Houston, Tex.: Arte Público, 2000.
Inter-American Dialogue. Race Report. Washington, D.C., 2003. www.iadialog.org/publications/race/afro-descendants.pdf
Moore, Robin. *Nationalizing Blackness: Afrocubanismo and Artistic Revolution in Havana, 1920–1940.* Pittsburgh, Pa.: University of Pittsburgh Press, 1997.
Mörner, Magnus. *Race Mixture in the History of Latin America.* Boston: Little, Brown, 1967.
Ortiz, Fernando. *Cuban Counterpoint: Tobacco and Sugar.* Durham, N.C.: Duke University Press, 1995.
Rout, Leslie B., Jr. *The African Experience in Spanish America: 1502 to the Present Day.* Cambridge, U.K.: Cambridge University Press, 1976.
Wade, Peter. *Race and Ethnicity in Latin America.* Chicago: Pluto Press, 1997.
Winn, Peter. *The Changing Face of Latin America and the Caribbean.* Berkeley: University of California Press, 1999.

ANANI DZIDZIENYO

AFRO-LATINOS. The terms "Afro-Latino" and "Afro-Latina" refer to those Latinos and Latinas in the United States who are of African ancestry and choose to identify with blackness as a racial identity in addition to identifying along ethnic lines with their Latino national origins. (It should also be noted that activists of African descent in Latin America and the Caribbean have begun to use the same term to refer to their own persons of African descent.) As the Latino population has grown in the United States, so has the number of Latinos and Latinas of African descent. According to the 2000 U.S. census, the 35.3 million Latinos and Latinas in the United States (the nation's largest pan-ethnic group) account for 12.5 percent of the country's population. About 2 percent of those Latinos and Latinas also identified themselves as "black" on the 2000 census. That compares with close to half who said they were also "white" and the 42.5 percent who described themselves as "some other race." (The census permits Latinos and Latinas to select a "Hispanic/Latino" ethnic origin category in addition to selecting any number of the racial categories of black, white, Asian, or "some other race.")

Most Afro-Latinos in the United States can trace their origins to the Dominican Republic and Puerto Rico, though nearly a quarter of a million people of Mexican heritage also defined themselves as black in the 2000 census. As compared to other Latinos, Afro-Latinos are much less likely to be immigrants and are more likely to speak English in their homes. In fact many Afro-Latino families have had a historical presence in the United States for many generations. Some scholars trace the first Afro-Latino in the United States to Estebanico, an explorer from Spain. Estebanico was one of four survivors of the infamous voyage of the Spanish explorer Pánfilo de Narvaez, which shipwrecked along the Florida coast in 1528 and was later immortalized in the memoirs of Cabeza de Vaca.

Other Afro-Latino personages are the writers Junot Díaz, Loida Maritza Pérez, Pedro Pietri, and Piri Thomas; the musicians Mario Bauzá, Frank Grillo "Machito," Chano Pozo, and Mongo Santamaría; the journalists Jesús Colón, Pablo Guzmán, and Felipe Luciano; the athlete Roberto Clemente; and the esteemed bibliophile Arturo Schomburg (one of the foremost collectors and bibliophiles of the African diasporic experience). In addition a number of celebrities recognized as African Americans were also of Afro-Latino heritage; for instance, Sammy Davis Jr.'s mother, the Harlem vaudeville dancer Elvera "Baby" Sanchez, was Puerto Rican.

The beginnings of a sizable Afro-Latino community in the United States began in the mid-nineteenth century with the migration of Afro-Cubans to southern Florida. The burgeoning cigar industry brought thousands of Afro-Cubans to the cities of Tampa, Key West, and Ybor City as cigar workers. With the decline of the cigar industry, the main locus of Afro-Latino density slowly shifted from Florida to New York City, and its members shifted from Afro-Cuban to Afro–Puerto Rican. With Operation Bootstrap in the 1940s and 1950s bringing hundreds of thousands of Puerto Rican migrants to New York, many Puerto Ricans of African descent migrated as well. After 1966 massive immigration from the Dominican Republic accounted for the increase in the U.S. Afro-Latino population. (After 1966 U.S.–influenced changes in the economic development policies of the Dominican Republic encouraged massive emigration from the country.)

Although Latinos and Latinas who explicitly identify themselves as black by using the terms "Afro-Latino" and "Afro-Latina" make up a small percentage of the U.S. Latino and Latina population, they often trace their origins to Latin American and Caribbean countries with significant numbers of people of African descent. Indeed 90 percent of the estimated 10 million African slaves brought to the Americas were transported to Mexico, Central and South America, and the Caribbean, whereas only 4.65 percent were transported to the United States. The number of people of African origin in Latin American and the Caribbean varies widely from country to country (See Table 1). Most Afro-Latinos and Afro-Latinas in the United States come from the Dominican Republic and Puerto Rico, though nearly a quarter of a million people of Mexican heritage also defined themselves as black in the 2000 census.

TABLE 1. *Afro-Descendants in Latin America and the Caribbean*

COUNTRY	TOTAL POPULATION	PERCENTAGE OF AFRO-DESCENDANTS
Dominican Republic	9 million	84%
Cuba	11 million	62%
Brazil	170 million	45%
Colombia	40 million	26%
Panama	3 million	14%
Venezuela	23 million	10%
Ecuador	12 million	10%
Nicaragua	5 million	9%
Peru	27 million	5%

SOURCE: Inter-Agency Consultation on Race in Latin America (IAC), "Inter-American Dialogue Race Report," January 2003.

But despite the varying numbers of people of African descent in Latin America and the Caribbean, the historical legacy of slavery is pervasive throughout the region, and thus people of African descent are actively discouraged from identifying as Afro-Latinos. In Latin America and the Caribbean, like in the United States, having lighter skin and European features increases the chances of socioeconomic opportunity, whereas having darker skin and African features severely limits such opportunity and mobility. In general the poorest socioeconomic class is populated primarily by people of African (and indigenous) descent, and the most privileged class is populated by whites. An elastic intermediary class with socioeconomic standing exists for some light-skinned (mixed-race) mulattos and mestizos. Negative stereotypes about blackness abound in a region that simultaneously denies the existence of racism. Instead, residents are encouraged to disassociate from their blackness in favor of national identities mythologized as a harmonious blend of all races in the discourse of *mestizaje*.

As a consequence many people of African descent from Latin America and the Caribbean harbor internalized racist norms and initially may choose not to self-identify as Afro-Latino regardless of how pronounced their African ancestry may be in their features and skin colors. The internalized racism manifests itself in a widespread concern with the degree of darkness in pigmentation, width of nose, thickness of lips, and quality of hair, with straight, European-textured hair denominated literally as "good"

hair. This concern with European features and white skin also influences the choice of marriage partners. Marrying someone lighter is called *adelantando la raza* (improving the race) under the theory of *blanqueamiento* (whitening), which prizes the mixture of races precisely to help diminish the existence of Afro-Latinos and Afro-Latinas.

Thus migrants from Latin America and the Caribbean (Afro-Latinos and Afro-Latinas included) often arrive in the United States with their culture of antiblack racism well intact along with other manifestations of their cultures to transmit to younger generations of Afro-Latinos and Afro-Latinas in the country. Negative racial stereotypes are then reinforced by the racial hierarchy of Spanish-language programming broadcast throughout the United States. The two dominant Spanish-language television networks, Univision and Telemundo, reserve the newscaster slots for whites and permit Afro-Latinos and Afro-Latinas to portray only the demeaning roles of maids, gardeners, chauffeurs, or witchcraft practitioners on the soap operas that are the focus of the television programming.

It is thus not so surprising that Afro-Latinos in the United States consistently report receiving racist treatment at the hands of other Latinos in addition to being perceived as outsiders to the construction of Latino entity. For example, Afro-Latinos and Afro-Latinas are frequently mistaken for African Americans in their own communities and upon identifying themselves as Afro-Latinos and Afro-Latinas are told, "But you don't look Latino." Indeed the 2002 National Survey of Latinos sponsored by the Pew Hispanic Center and the Kaiser Family Foundation indicated that Latinos and Latinas with more pronounced African ancestry, such as many Dominicans, more readily identify color discrimination as an explanation for the bias they experience from other Latinos and Latinas. In turn such experiences of bias within the U.S. culture of racial consciousness motivate Latinos and Latinas of African descent to begin self-identifying as Afro-Latino and Afro-Latina.

In addition studies suggest that the socioeconomic status of Afro-Latinos in the United States is more akin to that of African Americans than to other Latinos or white Americans. According to "How Race Counts for Hispanic Americans," a study by the State University of New York at Albany released in July 2004, Latinos who define themselves as "black" have lower incomes, higher unemployment rates, higher rates of poverty, less education, and fewer opportunities and are more likely to reside in segregated neighborhoods than those who identify themselves as "white" or "other." Based on such data, the study concluded that there are stark differences between the standard of living for Afro-Latinos and that of all other Latinos in the United States. The disparities in living standards among Latinos and Latinas of different races may thus also account for the increased willingness to identify as Afro-Latino and Afro-Latina in the United States. Furthermore the segregated residential patterns of Afro-Latinos in areas of African American settlement provide Afro-Latino youth with an exposure to African American culture and racial consciousness that also influences their choice to identify as Afro-Latinos and Afro-Latinas. Indeed, one study of Afro-Dominicans found that the longer Afro-Dominicans resided in the United States, the more likely they were to identify with African Americans.

Other forces of increased racial consciousness include the organization of Afro-Latino identity-based social justice organizations and networks in the United States and abroad. For instance, Washington, D.C., is home to the community-based Afro-Latino Institute and the Institute for Afro–Latin American Studies. The premier predominantly black university, Howard University, uses "Cimarrones," the Spanish term for fugitive black slaves, for its black student union, whose members include Afro-Latinos and Afro-Latinas. In New York City the Franklin H. Williams Caribbean Cultural Center is a cultural arts organization that represents all of the diverse artistic expressions and traditions of the African diaspora, including those of Afro-Latinos and Afro-Latinas in the United States.

In addition a number of Latin American and Spanish-speaking Caribbean countries have begun to experience an increase in Afro-Latino activism. This activism garnered public attention when numerous Afro-Latino organizations from abroad organized an agenda of racial issues for the 2001 United Nations World Conference against Racism held in Durban, South Africa. The activism of those Afro-Latino/Afro-Latina organizations continues to get attention in the United States through the cooperative effort in Washington, D.C., called the Inter-Agency Consultation on Race in Latin America, a consortium that includes the World Bank, the United Nations Development Program, and the Ford Foundation, formed to address the special problems of Afro-Latino populations in Latin America and the Caribbean. Other sources of racial pride empowerment emanate from Internet Web sites. In short, Afro-Latinos and Afro-Latinas compose a growing community in the United States with an evolving racial consciousness connected to the racial issues in the United States and throughout the African diaspora. The issues of Afro-Latinos and Afro-Latinas will attract greater attention as they continue to develop their social justice networks and the public continues to seek them out as potential links between Latino and African American communities.

See also Bauzá, Mario; Black-Latino Relations; Blanqueamiento; Census; Clemente, Roberto; Colón, Jesús; Díaz, Junot; Dominicans; Guzmán, Pablo; Internalized Racism; Latino Identities and Ethnicities; Luciano, Felipe; Machito; Mestizaje; Mongo Santamaría; Native Americans/Mexicanos; Operation Bootstrap/Section 936; Pérez, Loida Maritza; Pietri, Pedro; Schomburg, Arturo; Thomas, Piri; *and* Whiteness.

BIBLIOGRAPHY

Afrolatino Web site. www.afrolatino.com

Colón, Jesús. *A Puerto Rican in New York and Other Sketches*. New York: International Publishers, 1982.

Colón, Jesús. *The Way It Was and Other Writings*. Houston, Tex.: Arte Público Press, 1993.

Dzidzienyo, Anani, and Suzanne Oboler, eds. *Neither Enemies nor Friends: Latinos, Blacks, Afro Latinos*. New York: Palgrave Macmillian, 2004.

Franklin H. Williams Caribbean Cultural Center Web site. caribbean culturalcenter.citysearch.com/

Glasser, Ruth. *My Music Is My Flag: Puerto Rican Musicians and Their New York Communities, 1917–1940*. Latinos in American Society and Culture, Berkeley: University of California Press, 1995.

Grillo, Evelio. *Black Cuban, Black American: A Memoir*. Houston, Tex.: Arte Público Press, 2000.

Inter-Agency Consultation on Race in Latin America (IAC). "Inter-American Dialogue Race Report." Inter-American Dialogue, 2003. Available at www.iac-race.org.

Las Culturas Web site. www.lasculturas.com.

Logan, John R. "How Race Counts for Hispanic Americans." Lewis Mumford Center, University at Albany, July 14, 2003. Available at mumford1.dyndns.org/cen2000/BlackLatinoReport/BlackLatinoReport.pdf

Morris, Margaret Lindsay. *An Introduction to Selected Afro-Latino Writers*. Studies in Comparative Literature, 53. Lewiston, N.Y.: Mellen Press, 2003.

MundoAfroLatino Web site. www.mundoafrolatino.com

Sinnette, Elinor Des Verney. *Arthur Alfonso Schomburg, Black Bibliophile and Collector*. Detroit, Mich.: Wayne State University Press, 1989.

Thomas, Piri. *Down These Mean Streets*. New York: Vintage Press, 1974.

2002 National Survey of Latinos. Pew Hispanic Center. Available at www.pewhispanic.org

TANYA KATERÍ HERNÁNDEZ

AGOSÍN, MARJORIE (b. 1955), writer. Marjorie Agosín is an artist who has committed most of her life to the defense of human rights through her writings. Agosín, who considers herself as being from both the United States and Chile, was born in the United States while her father was doing research in Maryland. When only a few months old, Agosín was taken to Chile, where she grew up. Chile remains the country that she re-creates and reinvents in most of her literary work.

Agosín attended the Hebrew School in Santiago, Chile. After the coup d'état of September 11, 1973, she left with her family to live in the United States. She studied in Georgia and later attended Indiana University in Bloomington, where she obtained her PhD in Latin American Literature. After receiving her degree, her first job was as an assistant

MARJORIE AGOSÍN. (Courtesy of Wellesley College)

professor at Wellesley College, the same Massachusetts women's college at which, at the age of thirty-seven, she became one of the youngest women ever to obtain the rank of full professor in the history of the institution, and at which, after more than twenty years, she continues to teach.

Agosín is a political activist, an educator, but, above all things, a poet. She began to write poetry in Spanish when she was ten years old, and although she speaks both English and Yiddish, she has written her extensive work in Spanish. Her poetry has been translated and published in bilingual editions in the United States and abroad. She has indicated on many occasions that she will continue to write her work only in Spanish. Since the publication of her first collection, *Conchali* (1981), which includes a prologue by the distinguished Chilean writer Maria Luisa Bombal, Agosín has published twenty-seven books of poetry. Her poetry covers a broad range of themes from

Anne Frank, to the Mothers of Plaza de Mayo, in Argentina, to the political struggles of people in South America, Europe, Africa, and North America. Although her first poetry was mostly about the world she left behind when she immigrated to the United States, her later books have increasingly tackled the Jewish experience, not only in Latin America, but also as it relates to her own life in the United States.

She has published several books of fiction, among them two collections of short stories: *La Felicidad* (1991) and *Las Alfareras* (1994). Agosín also has written memoirs, and this aspect of her work has drawn considerable attention from reviewers. Her series of memoirs began with a trilogy about her family's history. The first book was about her mother's life in the south of Chile, *A Cross and a Star: Memoirs of a Jewish Girl in Chile* (1995). The later two volumes related the story of her father's life, *Always from Somewhere Else* (1998), and Agosín's own story, *The Alphabet in My Hands* (2000). In each of these books, the prevailing theme is that of the Jewish immigrant who is trying to find a place in Latin American society.

Agosín writes poetry, fiction, and nonfiction, but she has also done extensive work editing and translating the literary efforts of Latin American women writers so that they can be read and studied outside of their own countries. In the process of giving a new life to neglected or forgotten art, Agosín has published several collections of essays on women artists from Latin America. In addition, she began to put together anthologies of the work of Latin American Jewish writers, works that have been previously unknown in most of the world.

Agosín is an example of a writer who lives the life she writes about. From the moment she left Chile, she has continuously returned to her adopted country to work, write, and speak in defense of the victims of the dictatorship. She became a spokesperson for the "mothers of the disappeared" and her voice traveled around the world denouncing the abuses committed in Chile by the military junta. Her work with the women of Chile was the inspiration for the first documentary that focused on the lives and work of the women who made tapestries, called *arpilleras*, to protest the disappearance of their loved ones from 1973 to 1989.

Agosín has often been recognized for her writing and her work in defense of human rights. In Chile, she was granted the Gabriela Mistral Medal, one of the most esteemed awards given to writers. In the United States, she has received the Letras de Oro, the Latino Literary Prize, and the Peabody Award, together with the United Nations Leadership Award in Human Rights.

See also Literature; Poetry; *and* South Americans.

EMMA SEPULVEDA

AGRICULTURE AND AGRIBUSINESS.

Over the second half of the twentieth century, agriculture in the United States underwent an extraordinary series of revolutionary changes affecting its technological, sociocultural, and ecological character. The transformation of American agriculture that began at mid-century is often described in neoclassical economic commentaries as a "productivity revolution" and is said to have been the result of the unleashing of "progress" through the application of modern science and technology to the problems and limitations of traditional agriculture. Often left unsaid in the neoclassical tale of a glorious "green revolution" of highly productive "miracle crops" is the fact that the industrialization of agriculture also involved a corresponding concentration in the ownership of land, water, and other resources with grave social, economic, and environmental consequences.

Starting around mid-century, capitalist corporations took effective control of the agricultural means of production in the United States and this led to the end of America's "agrarian ideal" and the mass displacement of small-scale family farms, which virtually collapsed in a wave of bankruptcy between 1960 and 1990.

It is important not to hold a "romantic" view of the family farm as if it represents a perfect social institution that promotes balance with nature and equality among people across the locations of class, gender, and race. Guthman notes that

> there are significant problems with the small-scale family farm ideal . . . [and] the agrarian imaginary is equally bound up with a sort of cultural conservatism and even with Christian fundamentalism. . . . [A]grarian populism [has] roots in conservative notions of an organic society. . . . Moreover, by failing to question the race and gender relations that enabled the family farm . . . [the agrarian ideal] inherently glorifies them . . . [it] also ultimately uphold[s] white privilege by ignoring the racial history of U.S. land policy
>
> (p. 174)

The point in highlighting the decline of the family farm is merely to identify a particularly significant structural change that occurred during the post-1950 transformation of U.S. agriculture.

The size in acreage of the new "factories in the fields" grew to as much as ten times larger than the traditional family farm. This shift in the ownership and scale of agriculture involved an alliance among industrial capitalist interests, the producers and purveyors of scientific knowledge in the universities, and the state sector (for example, U.S. Department of Agriculture, USDA, and the Bureau of Reclamation). After 1950, the federal government provided massive crop subsidies, research support, and infrastructure development, like the construction of dams, reservoirs, and transportation systems, to support the expansion of agribusiness. (The era of big dam construction in the western United States dates to shortly after 1902, when the Bureau of Reclamation was established.) The triad of agribusiness-university-government bureaucracy jointly developed and sought to manage the process of scientific, technological, and political economic development of agriculture for the benefit of American corporations.

It is often overlooked that the industrialization or "modernization" of agriculture was also accompanied by a process of sociocultural transformation involving the "Latinoization" of rural America. The flip side of the decline of the family farm was the growth in the number of nonfamily workers in agriculture, which increased from 1.5 million in 1950 to 3.3 million in 1997. This increase corresponds with the process over the past five decades through which farm work was essentially transformed from a system characterized by cooperative labor in mostly white farming families to a system based on the hiring of seasonal and temporary migratory workers by agribusiness farm operations. About 80 percent of nonfamily farm laborers today are of Mexican origin. They constitute the heart of a new transnational rural proletariat, created by the rise of an increasingly globalized corporate agribusiness, and employed across rural America from the Pacific Northwest to the Deep South.

The mainstream neoclassical narrative of the triumph and progress of American agriculture hides another story, one that chronicles persistent patterns of class, race, and gender inequality and exploitation, social and racial conflict, displacement from the land and forced migration, and ultimately the devastation of rural communities. The neoclassical tale of modernity's progress obscures decades of environmental abuse and socioeconomic upheaval that accompanied the two modern scientific revolutions in American agriculture: the so-called "green" and "biotechnology" revolutions.

The scientific reorganization of agriculture by industrial capitalist corporations is a central force underlying the decline of family farms and rural communities, disruption of local food security, destruction of traditional forms of agriculture and environmental knowledge, threats to wildlife and its habitat, and a growing epidemic of hunger, malnutrition, and obesity in the "midst of plenty." Finally, this radical transformation of agriculture has been confronted by the rise of social movements including struggles by Latina and Latino farm workers, farmers, urban workers and consumers, the elderly and low-income communities, and environmentalists in search of sustainable agriculture and environmental justice.

Some Indicators of Agricultural Transformation

The history of agriculture in the United States during the twentieth-century involved a transition from a nation of independent farmers and craft workers to a nation of landless workers and urban consumers dependent on increasingly transnational corporate agribusiness producers, processors, and distributors of food. According to the U.S. Bureau of Census, in 1900, over one out of every three Americans was part of the farm-based population (29.8 million out of a total population of 76.2 million). By 1940, there were still 30.5 million individuals in the farm-based population out of a total population of 132.1 million or 23.1 percent. Rapid change followed after mid-century, and by 1970 only 9.7 million persons remained categorized as farm-based or roughly 5 percent of the total population of 203.3 million. The downward trend has continued, and in 1990 only 4.5 million persons were categorized as farm-based, or less than 2 percent of a total population of 248.7 million.

This transformation is further illustrated by data on the changing number and size (acreage) of farms and ranches. Again, according to the U.S. Bureau of Census, the decline in the number of farms between 1910 and 1940 was gradual with a loss of 100,000 farms (from 6.4 to 6.3 million). After 1950, however, the rate of decline accelerated so that only 2.9 million farms remained in 1970 and only 2.146 million in 1990. This decline seems to have stabilized recently, and in 2002 there was a slight increase to 2.158 million farms. Some of this increase is undoubtedly due to the dramatic growth in the number of Latina and Latino owned farms, ranches, and orchards, an effect of the Latinoization of rural America. These data are indicative of the structural transformation of agriculture involving a shift from small and medium-sized family-based farms to industrial agribusinesses, which are corporate-owned factory farms in which only one type of crop is mass produced (monoculture) under the rules of "economies of scale."

The rise of mass production agriculture involved the concentration of capital in the form of fewer but larger agricultural operations: In 1935, there were only 89,000 farms in the U.S. larger than 1,000 acres or about 1.3 percent of all farms; still, these managed about 29 percent of all the farm land. By 1993, the number of farms larger than 1,000 acres had increased to make up 9 percent of all farms but these controlled nearly 65 percent of all productive farmland (Sofranko, Frerichs, Samy, et al. 2001).

Concentration of Capital and the Globalization of Food Production

The period since 1950 has witnessed the emergence and widening influence of industrial monocultures controlled by transnational corporations such as Monsanto, ConAgra, Archer Daniels Midland (ADM), Iowa Beef Processors (IBP), Cargill, and others. The concentration of capital, industrial economies of scale, and uniform monoculture models of farming were the most significant developments in twentieth-century agriculture. This concentration is so advanced that by 1997 all major food products were controlled by groups composed of no more than four corporations. In livestock slaughtering and processing:

- more than 55 percent of the production of broilers (meat chickens) was controlled by Tyson Foods, Gold Kist, Perdue Farms, and ConAgra;
- 87 percent of beef production was controlled by IBP, ConAgra, Cargill, and Farmland Industries;
- 60 percent of pork production was controlled by Smithfield, IBP, ConAgra, and Cargill; and
- 73 percent of sheep production was controlled by ConAgra, Superior Packing, High Country, and Denver Lamb (Heffernan 2000, p. 65, table 1).

Similar extreme levels of industrial concentration were already evident in the milling and processing of all major commodity crop categories:

- 62 percent of flour milling was controlled by ADM, ConAgra, Cargill, and Cereal Food Processors;
- 76 percent of soybean processing was controlled by ADM, Cargill, Bunge, and Ag Processors;
- 57 percent of dry corn milling was controlled by Bunge, Illinois Cereal Mills, ADM, and ConAgra; and
- 74 percent of wet corn milling was controlled by ADM, Cargill, Tate and Lyle, and CPC.

The concentration of capital in agriculture has been extended through the process of globalization. This domination of agriculture by a handful of corporations has meant that local communities everywhere have increasingly lost the ability to control access, affordability, and safety of their food supplies. The globalization of food production was evident in data from the late 1980s when agribusiness giants like Cargill, ADM, and Monsanto already operated in dozens of countries. Cargill—perhaps the most global of these firms in 1990—operated in forty-nine countries including Mexico, where it had six different operations.

Ecological Consequences of the Global-Industrial Agribusiness Model

There are well-documented ecological consequences resulting from the historical patterns of capital concentration, monocultures, and growing disconnection between local communities and their food sources. Between the 1950s and 1970s, a first wave of environmental problems developed out of excessive reliance on mechanized monocultures and their associated inputs of chemical fertilizers, pesticides, and herbicides. Since the publication of Rachel Carson's classic *Silent Spring* (1962), the use of pesticides and other agro-industrial chemicals has increased dramatically. For example, in California the use of pesticides increased between 1950 and 1999 by a factor of five

AGRICULTURAL WORKERS. Women packing organic broccoli for PurePak, Inc., in Oxnard, Calif., 1999. (AP)

accounting for $1 billion in agribusiness-related expenditures or about 12 percent of the U.S. total that year.

What was this green revolution? It was an effort by the United States to launch a modern industrial revolution in agriculture based on scientific research conducted for the development of high-yield varieties of food crops including maize, wheat, and rice. The high yields of the new select miracle crops were only possible under a new regime of chemically-intensive agriculture. For this reason, critics note that the so-called miracle crops were not so much high-yield as high-input varieties. Of course, low-income and subsistence farmers could ill-afford to make the substantial investments required to pursue this type of agriculture. Many of the first pesticides developed in the U.S. were derived from chemical weapons the military developed during World War II. The technologies and practices of the so-called green revolution led to accelerated soil erosion and compaction, depletion of soil fertility, salinization and alkalinization of soils, pollution of surface and ground waters, loss of traditional farm land to infrastructure development, displacement of small subsistence-oriented farmers, destruction of wild life habitat, and loss of agricultural biodiversity.

In the 1950s, the United States exported its so-called green revolution to the rest of the world when Mexico became a major site for research on "improved" high-input varieties of hybrid wheat, corn, and other crops.

The establishment in 1945 in Mexico of what became the CIMMYT, the Centro Internacional para el Mejoramiento de Maíz y Trigo (International Center for the Improvement of Corn and Wheat), is an important chapter in the history of agricultural modernization and globalization. Less well understood is the role this model of industrial monocultures played in endangering the diversity of agricultural biodiversity and traditional farming communities in the U.S., Mexico, India, Brazil, the Philippines, and other countries that were the centers of green revolution research.

A second wave of scientific and technological change began in the late 1970s and early 1980s with the advent of research in plant genetics, which eventually resulted in the rise of a very large and globalized commercial agricultural biotechnology industry. The number of patented transgenic (genetically engineered) plants on the market has grown at an astonishing pace since 1990, and transgenic crops are now more than 50 to 60 percent of the critical commodity crops of soy, rapeseed, cotton, and maize grown in the United States. The same corporations that were behind the miracle crops of the green revolution are now leading the biotechnology revolution and many of these are agrochemical interests that have recently absorbed smaller agricultural biotechnology companies. Instead of reducing the use of agro-industrial chemicals, transgenic crops have increased the use of herbicides and pesticides in almost all cases with increased hazards for farmers, farm workers, and wildlife. The rise of commercial agricultural biotechnology also represents a serious threat to the preservation of the diversity of agricultural crops by creating conditions for crop uniformity in rural landscapes. The simplification of cropping systems results in the loss of domesticated plant genetic resources because older varieties, most of them developed and preserved by small family farmers, become extinct.

Latinas and Latinos and Industrial Agribusiness

Since the mid-twentieth century, the historical experiences of Latinas and Latinos in the development of American agribusiness have been largely shaped by their status as temporary and seasonal migratory laborers. Government-sanctioned recruitment of Mexican workers for agriculture has a long history, dating back to the guest worker programs of the early to mid-twentieth century. During World War I and II, the U.S. and Mexican governments agreed to a bilateral policy for the importation of massive numbers of Mexican workers, presumably to meet wartime labor shortages. The World War II policy was called the bracero program and resulted in the importation of several million workers between 1942 and 1964. The majority of braceros were destined for the agricultural sector although many worked on the railroads, mining, and even manufacturing.

Many Latinas and Latinos have experienced persistent poverty, hunger, and malnutrition in the midst of an agricultural revolution that increased the productivity of farming and the volume of food available for consumption. The availability of food for consumption (supply) has not translated into equitable access. The American agribusiness revolution did not lead to less hunger or to the elimination of malnutrition and related health problems. On the contrary, the advent of agribusiness has resulted in wider disparities in access to nutritious foods and at the same time has undermined the viability of traditional foods and foodways.

As we have seen, the advent of industrialized agribusiness is a major storyline in American agricultural history. But the contributions of Latinas and Latinos to that history are more than a matter of a presumed and limited role as "unskilled" and "cheap labor" for growers. For Latina and Latino workers a job in American corporate agriculture has meant earning less than a living wage, exposure to toxics and nominal environmental protection, lack of access to clean drinking water or toilets, lack of humane housing and medical care, and the underlying problem of the suppression of workers's right to organize and engage in collective bargaining.

The USDA also has a deep-rooted pattern of discrimination against farmers of color (African American, Latina and Latino, and Native American). Discriminatory treatment of farmers of color is part of the history of the land grant college-agricultural extension service complex and its research programs and development priorities, which have favored large-scale monoculture farming. Latina and Latino farmers have experienced inequitable access to private and public credit markets resulting in land loss due to predatory lending practices, real estate speculation, and rural gentrification.

This issue is of utmost importance, particularly because Latinas and Latinos represent one of the few ethnic/national-origin groups to have experienced an increase in the number of owner-operated farms, ranches, and orchards. According to official agricultural census data, between 1987 and 1997 the number of Latina and Latino owned or operated farms in the United States increased by nearly 40 percent. The increase was most salient in the Southwest and Northwest. For example, in the state of Washington, the number of Latina and Latino owned or operated farms (including commercial orchards) increased by 343 percent during that period. Significant growth of the Latina and Latino farm sector was also observed in Arizona, California, Colorado, Florida, New Mexico, Oregon, and Texas. Michigan, Wisconsin, Minnesota, and other Midwestern states also experienced growth. There are Latina and Latino farm owners and operators in every state in the nation. There were 16,183 farms operated by Latinas and

Latinos in 1982; 17,476 in 1987; 20,956 in 1992; and an estimated 23,000 in 1997. At this rate, there will be at least 50,000 Latina and Latino operated farms by 2022.

Latinas and Latinos and the Prospects for Sustainable and Equitable Agriculture

A critical history of Latinas and Latinos in agriculture must acknowledge the loss of local food security caused by the globalization and concentration of agriculture. It must address the failure by the organic agriculture movement to integrate environmental justice principles into its visions of sustainable production. It must include discussion of the failure by the academic establishment to recognize and value the legitimacy of the local agroecological knowledge of farmers of color. Despite these scholarly shortcomings, Latina and Latino rural and urban communities are playing a significant role in social movement struggles seeking to make agriculture more sustainable and socially just.

The Latina and Latino environmental justice movement is developing a progressive vision of sustainable agriculture to affect changes in the direction of public policy discourses. Environmental justice scholars and activists are contributing to the analysis of food production and consumption as social justice problems in local, regional, national, and global contexts. They are demonstrating the role of racial and class discrimination in the experiences of people of color with land loss, farm labor exploitation, hunger, malnutrition, and health problems. Environmental justice frames the goals of sustainable agriculture according to the values and objectives of social justice, equity, and autonomy. The environmental justice framework for sustainable agriculture is pursuing the following types of objectives:

- Farmworker rights to organize to attain workplace health and safety and economic justice;
- Elimination of racial and class discrimination in federal and state agricultural policies and especially in farm loan, subsidy, and conservation programs;
- Survival and flourishing of family farms owned and operated by people of color; restoration of the lost lands of African, Native, Latina and Latino, and Asian American farmers and recovery of traditional customary systems of local management of natural resources and watersheds;
- Local food security to promote self-sufficiency, autonomy, and health of communities of color;
- Development of organic, community-supported, and alternative methods of farming to serve low-income families and the elderly in urban and rural communities of color;
- Protection of traditions of seed saving of heirloom crop varieties by farmers of color and resistance against the "patenting of life";

- Adoption of the "Precautionary Principle" and solidarity with farmers, seed savers, and food consumers of color opposed to the commercialization and environmental release of GEOs (genetically-engineered organisms) and the marketing of transgenic foods;
- Recognition of the contributions of farmers of color in the development of place-based agroecological knowledge;
- Recognition of the ecological, economic base, and social services and benefits provided by farmers of color as managers of millions of acres of farmland, open space, wildlife habitat, and diverse and healthy cultural landscapes.

These objectives represent a clear challenge to the dominant industrial agribusiness model of food production and are redefining the struggle for sustainable agriculture as a movement that integrates environmental sustainability with human rights and social justice.

See also Environmental Justice; Environmental Racism; Genetic Sciences; Land Grants; Scientific Racism; Sustainable Development; *and* Transgenic Maize.

BIBLIOGRAPHY

Allensworth, Elain M., and Refugio I. Rochin. "Ethnic Transformation in Rural California: Looking Beyond the Immigrant Farmworker." *Rural Sociology* 63 (1998): 26–50.

Altieri, Miguel. *Genetic Engineering in Agriculture: The Myths, Environmental Risks, and Alternatives.* 2nd ed. San Francisco: Food First Books, 2004.

Altieri, Miguel. "Ecological Impacts of Industrial Agriculture and the Possibilities for Truly Sustainable Farming." In *Hungry for Profit: The Agribusiness Threat to Farmers, Food, and the Environment*, edited by Fred Magdoff, John Bellamy Foster, and Frederick H. Buttel. New York: Monthly Review Press, 2000.

Benbrook, C. M. "Troubled Times amid Commercial Success for Roundup Ready Soybeans: Glyphosate Efficacy is Slipping and Unstable Transgene Expression Erodes Plant Defenses and Yields." *AgBioTech InfoNet Technical Paper* 4 (May 3, 2001).

Bonnano, Alessandro, et al., eds. *From Columbus to ConAgra: The Globalization of Agriculture and Food.* Lawrence: University Press of Kansas, 1994.

Busch, L. "The State of Agricultural Science and the Agricultural Science State." In *From Columbus to ConAgra: The Globalization of Agriculture and Food*, edited by Alessandra Bonnano et al. Lawrence: University Press of Kansas, 1994.

Craig, Richard B. *The Bracero Program: Interest Groups and Foreign Policy.* Austin: University of Texas Press, 1971.

Fowler, Cary, and Pat R. Mooney. *Shattering: Food, Politics, and the Loss of Genetic Diversity.* Tucson: University of Arizona Press, 1990.

Guthman, Julie. *Agrarian Dreams: The Paradox of Organic Farming in California.* Berkeley: University of California Press, 2004.

Heffernan, W. D. "Concentration of Ownership and Control in Agriculture." In *Hungry for Profit: The Agribusiness Threat to Farmers, Food, and the Environment*, edited by F. Magdoff, J. Bellamy Foster, and F. H. Buttel. New York: Monthly Review Press, 2000.

Heffernan, W. D., and D. H. Constance. "Transnational Corporations and the Globalization of the Food System." In *From Columbus to ConAgra: The Globalization of Agriculture and Food*, edited by Alessandro Bonnano, et al. Lawrence: University Press of Kansas, 1994.

Lappé, Francis Moore, Jospeh Collins, P. Rosset, et al. *World Hunger: Twelve Myths.* New York: Grove Press, 1998. www.foodfirst. org/pubs/backgrdrs/1998/s98v5n3.html

Lyson, Thomas A. *Civic Agriculture: Reconnecting Farm, Food, and Community.* Medford, Mass.: Tufts University Press, 2004.

Martin, Philip. "Mexico-U.S. Migration." Institute for International Economics. www.iie.com/publications/papers/nafta-migration.pdf.

Mullen, J. D., et al. *Returns to University of California Pest Management R&D: Overview and Case Studies Emphasizing IPM.* Davis: University of California, Division of Agriculture and Natural Resources, Agricultural Issues Center, 2000.

Peña, Devon G. *Mexican Americans and the Environment: Tierra y Vida.* Tucson: University of Arizona Press, 2005.

Peña, Devon G. "Sustainable Agriculture and Environmental Justice: Linking Ecological and Social Sides of Sustainability." *Resource Paper* (2002), no. 7. Second National People of Color Environmental Leadership Summit, Washington, D.C. www.ejrc.cau.edu/ summit2/SustainableAg.pdf

Rochin, Refugio I. "Hispanic Americans in the Rural Economy: Conditions, Issues, and Probable Future Adjustments." In *National Rural Studies Committee: A Proceedings*, edited by E.N. Castle and B. Baldwin. Corvalis: Western Rural Development Center, Oregon State University, 1992.

Rochin, Refugio I. "Rural Latinos: Evolving Conditions and Issues." In *The Changing American Countryside: Rural People and Places*, edited by Emery N. Castle. Lawrence: University Press of Kansas, 1995.

Shiva, Vandana. *The Violence of the Green Revolution: Third World Agriculture, Ecology, and Politics.* London: Zed Books, 1991.

Sofranko, A., R. Frerichs, M. Samy, et al. *Will Farmers Organize? Structural Change and Loss of Control Over Production.* 2001. Unpublished survey research report. www.aces.uiuc.edu/value/research/organize.html

Taylor, J. Edward, Philip L. Martin, and Michael Fix. *Poverty Amid Prosperity: Immigration and the Changing Face of Rural California.* Washington, D.C.: The Urban Institute Press, 1997.

Wright, A. "Innocents Abroad: American Agricultural Research in Mexico." In *Meeting the Expectations of the Land: Essays in Sustainable Agriculture and Stewardship*, edited by W. Jackson, W. Berry, and B. Colman. San Francisco: North Point Press, 1984.

United States Bureau of the Census. 2003. *Statistical Abstract of the United States.* Washington, D.C.: U.S. Government Printing Office, 2003.

United States Department of Agriculture. *Census of Agriculture: State and County Summaries.* www.usda.gov

DEVON G. PEÑA

AGROECOLOGY. Agroecology is the scientific study of traditional, alternative, and sustainable agricultural systems. It involves an interdisciplinary approach to research that relies heavily on the integration of the methods and materials of ecosystem ecology, ethnobotany, conservation biology, environmental history, environmental anthropology, political ecology, and other fields that focus on the study of anthropogenesis (human-effected change in the environment). A fundamental premise of agroecology is that a farm does not end at the edge of the field and is not a self-enclosed system. Farms are ecological units but they exist within the broader context of their ecosystems, watersheds, and social framework.

Agroecology emerged in the 1970s as part of the widening critique of the science and technology promulgated by the so-called Green Revolution. The Green Revolution was a global effort led by the United States and initiated in the mid-1940s to modernize and westernize agriculture by introducing high-yield/high-input varieties of hybrid crops in a presumed effort to solve the persistent and growing problems of world hunger and malnutrition. Observers rightly noted that the modernization of agriculture had numerous harmful effects on the land, water, wildlife, farmworkers, and farmers and their communities.

The Green Revolution exported the American model of chemically intensive, mechanized, and mass production agriculture. It imposed that model's high inputs of agrochemicals (pesticides, herbicides, and fertilizers), the use of large-scale machinery, a preference for uniform cultivation of single crops (monoculture), and reliance on heavily subsidized investments in the construction of large-scale irrigation systems, dams, and reservoirs, port facilities, roads, bridges, power plants, and other infrastructure. The policies of high capital investment and the use of mass production technologies have favored industrial monocultures over smaller and more sustainable traditional polycultures (farms that grow a diversity of native landrace crops). Local farmers everywhere have been displaced by the expropriation of land, water, and other resources by state and market forces for the benefit of industrial agriculture. Displacement has also resulted from the construction of dams, reservoirs, highways, and other infrastructure that supports industrial monocultures. Local, indigenous, and independent smallholder farmers have been driven out of the market by the dumping of cheap grains from the United States and other Western countries that have long benefited from subsidies and other programs to support mass production surpluses and agricultural exports.

The scientists, technicians, and technocrats behind the Green Revolution ignored and marginalized the traditional environmental knowledge (TEK) of third-world farmers. The architects of agricultural modernization misunderstood traditional farming systems. They mistakenly reduced complex agroecosystems to simple and vulgar stereotypes. Traditional farming practices were depicted as primitive, inefficient, and environmentally destructive. So-called backward peasants were depicted as mindlessly devastating the rainforests to grow meager food crops.

This view was challenged in 1954 when the anthropologist Harold Conklin published his study of Hanunuo agroecosystems in the Philippines. Since then, environmental anthropologists and agroecologists have worked to "dismantle the dominant view of shifting cultivation as a haphazard, destructive, and primitive way of making a living" (Nazarea, p. 3). Over the past five decades, an increasing number of these anthropologists have documented the logic, complexity, and sophistication of local knowledge while exploring its scientific qualities.

Agroecology revalues local knowledge and seeks to understand and promote the traditional practices of indigenous and other local farmers who may embrace alternative and sustainable methods of farming. Contrary to the dominant stereotype of primitive, inefficient, and destructive farming practices, indigenous agroecosystems are characterized by high crop diversity, optimal use of space and available resources, recycling of nutrients and other inputs, effective communal water and soil conservation and management, natural control of weeds and pests, and sustainable income and subsistence for the farmer and local community.

The comparative study of agroecosystems reveals that, over the long term, traditional polyculture farms are more stable, diverse, and productive than are modern monocultures because they are usually better adapted to the uncertainties of climate, moisture, and insect predation. In contrast to monoculture agribusinesses, traditional polyculture farming systems provide vital services to communities including the provisioning of local food security, preservation of the genetic diversity of domesticated crops and their wild relatives, and a wide range of other ecological and economic base services that contribute to local community stability and vitality.

During the first three decades (1970–2000), the focus of agroecological research was largely on so-called third world farmers. Few research scholars have paid much attention to the agroecological knowledge and practices of farmers in the United States, especially Latinas and Latinos. One exception is the work of the Rio Grande Bioregions Project, an informal network of more than forty research scholars, farmers, and sustainable agriculture advocates who have dedicated fifteen years to the collaborative interdisciplinary study of Hispana and Hispano agroecosystems in the Rio Grande corridor in Colorado, New Mexico, and Texas. The Rio Grande Bioregions Project has documented the sustainable agroecological practices of Hispana and Hispano *acequia* farms, offering evidence of the ecological and economic base services provided by these human-made landscape mosaics.

See also **Acequias; Environmental Justice;** *and* **Genetic Sciences.**

BIBLIOGRAPHY

Altieri, Miguel A. *Agroecology: The Science of Sustainable Agriculture.* Boulder, Colo.: Westview Press, 1995.

Conklin, Harold. "The Relation of Hanunuo Culture to the Plant World." PhD diss., Yale University, 1954.

Conklin, Harold. "The Study of Shifting Cultivation." *Current Anthropology* 2 (1961): 27–61.

Nazarea, Virginia D. *Ethnoecology: Situated Knowledge/Located Lives.* Tucson: University of Arizona Press, 1999.

Peña, Devon G., ed. *Chicano Culture, Ecology, Politics: Subversive Kin*. Tucson: University of Arizona Press, 1998.

Peña, Devon G. "Cultural Landscapes and Biodiversity: The Ethnoecology of an Upper Rio Grande Watershed Commons." In *Ethnoecology: Situated Knowledge/Located Lives*, edited by Virginia D. Nazarea. Tucson: University of Arizona Press, 1999.

Peña, Devon G. *Mexican Americans and the Environment: Tierra y Vida*. Tucson: University of Arizona Press, 2005.

Peña, Devon G. "The Watershed Commonwealth of the Upper Rio Grande." In *Natural Assets: Democratizing Environmental Ownership*, edited by James K. Boyce and Barry G. Shelley. Washington, D.C.: Island Press, 2003.

Peña, Devon G., and Rubén O. Martínez. *Upper Rio Grande Hispano Farms Study: A Cultural and Environmental History of Land Ethics in Transition, 1598–1998*. Final report to the National Endowment for the Humanities, Collaborative, and Interdisciplinary Research Grant R0-22707-94 (April 1994).

Peña, Devon G., Rubén O. Martínez, and Joseph C. Gallegos, eds. *Voces de agua y tierra: Four Hundred Years of Acequia Farms in the Rio Arriba, 1598-1998*. Tucson: University of Arizona Press. Forthcoming.

Shiva, Vandana. *The Violence of the Green Revolution: Third World Agriculture, Ecology, and Politics*. London: Zed Books, 1993.

Wright, Angus. "Innocents Abroad: American Agricultural Research in Mexico." In *Meeting the Expectations of the Land: Essays in Sustainable Agriculture and Stewardship*, edited by Wes Jackson, Wendell Berry, and Bruce Colman. San Francisco: North Point, 1984.

DEVON G. PEÑA

AGUILAR, LAURA (b. 1959), photographer and videographer. Laura Aguilar, a Chicana lesbian artist who works in photography and video, was born in San Gabriel, California, in 1959. Her refined sense of formal composition and her unconventional subject matter have earned her an international reputation: her work has been exhibited in the United States, Latin America, and Europe. Most of her work involves black-and-white portraits of people whose bodies and social identities have been denigrated, dismissed, or ignored in mainstream art and culture. Most often, she produces these images in large formats, increasing the visual impact with the sheer size of the print (16 × 20 or larger).

Aguilar is largely a self-taught artist. She began taking photographs at age fourteen. Her photography served as a means of self-expression when the public school system failed to teach her to read or write—Aguilar is severely dyslexic and was not properly diagnosed in school or provided appropriate instruction. Nonetheless, she graduated from high school and attended East Los Angeles College (ELAC) for two years. Aguilar credits Suda House, an instructor at ELAC, with introducing her to Chicano/a art and encouraging her to pursue photography.

Aguilar subsequently attended a number of photography workshops that influenced her work. She participated in the Friends of Photography workshop on portraiture and the nude in 1989 and the Santa Fe Photographic Workshops in 1991. Aguilar cites photographers Judy

Dater, Joyce Tenneson, and Arnold Newman as formative influences on her photographic sensibility. Aguilar's *oeuvre* includes dramatic black-and-white portraits, a substantial number of which are self-portraits. Her work has been exhibited extensively. She has participated in both solo and group exhibits at the Armand Hammer Museum, Los Angeles Photography Center, Los Angeles Contemporary Exhibitions (LACE), Self Help Graphics, New Museum of Contemporary Art in New York, Archivo General de la Nación in Mexico City, the Venice Biennial in Italy, and the Fundacio la Caixa in Barcelona, Spain.

Aguilar's early works feature the "Latina Lesbian" series (1986–1994) and the "Plush Pony" series (1992). The first consists of photographs of the members and friends of a Los Angeles grassroots organization called Lesbianas Unidas (Lesbians United). The women in this series—who are diverse in terms of education, age, career, and national origin—affirm their strong Latina lesbian identity in brief handwritten autobiographical statements appearing below their respective images. In "Plush Pony," Aguilar sets out to document another Latina lesbian community, this one centered around a working-class bar of that name situated east of Los Angeles. Aguilar set up a makeshift studio in the back of Plush Pony and offered to photograph women alone, in couples, or in groups. The resulting series of photographs is an amazing document of working-class Chicana lesbian culture, a group whose existence is relegated to the margins of both Chicana and lesbian social formations. The "Plush Pony" series records the highly stylized bodies of the women—in particular, their Chicana configuration of butch/femme tattoos and hairstyles and their poses. Both "Latina Lesbian" and "Plush Pony" provide important historical records of Latina lesbian identity and community of the late 1980s and 1990s.

Aguilar's "Clothed/Unclothed" series (1990–1994) marks a transitional moment in which Aguilar became increasingly interested in the nude subject. However, even by this time she had already produced several nude self-portraits, such as "In Sandy's Room" (1990), which shows a side view of Aguilar reclining in a chair, a fan blowing across her nude body. Another photograph from that same year, "Three Eagles Flying" (1990), is a stunning commentary on the embodiment and alienation of Chicana identity. "Three Eagles" is a triptych: the center panel is a self-portrait of Aguilar's nude body bound by the Mexican and U.S. flags, while the left and right panels show the U.S. and Mexican flags.

In "Clothed/Unclothed," Aguilar presents her subjects in elegant diptychs. The first panel shows them clothed while the second panel shows them nude. Aguilar worked closely with the subjects, listening to how they wanted to pose. She used Polaroid technology to immediately obtain her sitters' feedback on their images. Such a collaborative method allowed Aguilar to represent each sitter's vulnerability and openness to the camera. In this series, Aguilar photographed friends from the multiple communities of which she is a part, including fellow artists, lesbians, queer men, and people of color. While the individual images are not titled and her subjects go unnamed, many spectators will recognize some important figures in Latina and Latino Los Angeles, including Luis Alfaro, Monica Palacios, and the late Gil Cuadros (1962–1996).

In the late 1990s, following the deaths of her close friend Gil Cuadros, her father, and her beloved aunt, Aguilar began several series that picture her own nude body in desolate natural surroundings. The photographs evoke feelings of mourning and sadness. In the "Stillness" (1990) series, Aguilar photographs her nude body in a stark, barren landscape. Her body functions as the visual equivalent of a boulder, or the trunk of a tree, or a reflecting pond. In her subsequent work "Motion" (2000), Aguilar appears as if, regaining her mobility, she emerged from the earth. The images in these series have been well received. In a glowing review in *Art Week*, Victoria Martin writes, "Aguilar's vision is daring, one where women are able to be open and neutral about their bodies. . . . [She creates] a world where humans and earth coalesce, a monumental work where formal elegance supersedes personality; where strength is more valuable than seductiveness" (p. 24).

In addition, Aguilar's work has been recognized by art scholars, eliciting a number of major articles (Yarbro-Bejarano 1998; Jones 1998) and earning consideration in several important books (Bright 1998; Hammond 2000). Yvonne Yarbro-Bejarano argues that "Aguilar's work invites us to rethink/re-vision [the notion of] "Chicano" and its bodies" (p. 277). Amelia Jones, in keeping with poststructuralist critiques of the unitary subject, contends further that "Aguilar's work . . . exuberantly plays out the dissolution of the notion of the 'individual' " (p. 208).

See also **Art, Chicano; Lesbians;** *and* **Photographers.**

BIBLIOGRAPHY

Bright, Deborah, ed. *The Passionate Camera: Photography and Bodies of Desire*. New York: Routledge, 1998.

Hammond, Harmony. *Lesbian Art in America: A Contemporary History*. New York: Rizzoli, 2000.

Hulick, Diana E. "Laura Aguilar." *Latin American Art* 5, no. 3 (1993): 52–54.

Jones, Amelia. "Bodies and Subjects in the Technologized Self-Portrait: The Work of Laura Aguilar." *Aztlán* 23, no. 2 (Fall 1998): 203–219.

Martin, Victoria. "Laura Aguilar at Susanne Vielmetter Los Angeles Projects." *Art Week* 31, no. 5 (May 2000): 24.

Yarbro-Bejarano, Yvonne. "Laying It Bare: The Queer/Colored Body in Photography by Laura Aguilar." In *Living Chicana Theory*, edited by Carla Trujillo. Berkeley, Calif.: Third Woman Press, 1998.

LUZ CALVO

AID TO FAMILIES WITH DEPENDENT CHILDREN. The Aid to Families with Dependent Children (AFDC) program was established by Congress during the height of the Great Depression as part of the 1935 Social Security Act (Title IV). The original program provided financial assistance to needy children. In order to be eligible, the child had to live with a parent or other close relative. Since the 1960s Congress has expanded the criteria for those eligible for assistance under the program. Eligibility was added for the child of an unemployed parent (and that parent); a second parent in a family with an incapacitated or unemployed parent; any other individual deemed "essential" to the child; and unborn children in the third trimester of the mother's pregnancy. In 1974 all AFDC families were qualified to receive food stamps unless they lived in a larger household. In 1967 Congress required states to establish programs to determine paternity and locate absent parents in order to secure support from them and in 1975 required families to assign to the state their rights to support as a condition of AFDC eligibility. The Medicaid program added medical assistance to the AFDC household. Over the years, work requirements were added to the program. In 1996 Congress severely limited the AFDC program with the passage of the Personal Responsibility and Work Opportunity Reconciliation Act. The details of those changes are set forth below.

At the inception of AFDC, most AFDC families were headed by a mother without a father in the home. AFDC was an income support program which states administered under federal regulations and supervision. The states provided cash grants to needy families as long as they included a "dependent" child, as defined by federal law and regulations, and were financially eligible as defined by state standards. While federal law did not require states to participate in the program, all states did so.

AFDC was an "entitlement" program for two reasons. First, states were entitled to federal matching funds since the federal government guaranteed the necessary funds to match state expenditures. Second, eligible families were entitled to AFDC benefits because states were required to provide benefits to all eligible persons who applied and to continue benefits as long as they remained eligible. The federal government reimbursed 50 percent of the state's administrative costs and at least 50 percent of the AFDC payment, with a higher federal "matching" rate available for states with per capita income below the national average. States were required to establish a standard of need (a minimum amount necessary for subsistence) and a payment standard. In reality, families received whatever funds the state legislature appropriated.

Some Latinos and Latinas faced obstacles in receiving AFDC benefits because of their immigration status. AFDC benefits were limited to citizens, legal permanent residents,

AFDC RALLY. Members of the Kensington Welfare Rights Union of Philadelphia at a rally in New York City to protest federal and state welfare reform laws, 1997. (Kathy Willens/AP)

and "aliens" permanently residing in the United States under color of law, which meant persons permanently residing in the United States with the knowledge of the Immigration and Naturalization Service (INS) (see 42 U.S.C. §602 (a)(33)). Receipt of AFDC benefits also had immigration law implications. The U.S. Citizenship and Immigration Services (formerly the INS) can refuse to allow someone to enter or reenter the United States or become a legal permanent resident if it believes that the person is unable to support himself or herself and will rely on public benefits in the future. Receipt of cash benefits, such as AFDC, is one of the considerations, among others, under the "public charge" doctrine. The misapplication of the doctrine, however, has a chilling effect on the willingness of immigrant families to request assistance.

Puerto Rico was also treated differently from the states by being given less assistance than the states. As a result, the benefits of the people living in the U.S. commonwealth of Puerto Rico were lower (see 42 U.S.C. §§ 1308(a)(1) and 1396d(b)). This differential level of benefits was allowed to stand by the Supreme Court in *Harris v. Rosario* (1980).

The Personal Responsibility and Work Opportunity Reconciliation Act of 1996 replaced AFDC with Temporary Assistance to Needy Families (TANF). Under the act, there is no entitlement to TANF though some states provide for one. States are given control over the program and broad discretion to determine who is eligible for assistance. Despite this flexibility, they must establish objective criteria.

States receive a block grant from the federal government, which is a flat amount that can be used for a wide range of activities. The most significant aspect of TANF is its five-year lifetime limit on receipt of assistance. The program also has work participation requirements.

The 1996 act further limited immigrants' access to cash assistance. The act created two categories of immigrants for purposes of benefits eligibility—"qualified" and "not qualified." "Qualified" immigrants include legal permanent residents; refugees; asylum seekers; and a few other groups, including certain abused immigrants and their children and parents. The Department of Health and Human Services has designated "unqualified" immigrants as ineligible for TANF benefits with the exception of those who are victims of trafficking. The act also barred immigrants entering the United States after the passage of the law on August 22, 1996, from receiving TANF for five years. The law also gave states the option of barring current immigrants from TANF and new immigrants from TANF following the five-year bar.

Latinos and Latinas do not seem to act as one group for the purpose of receipt of welfare benefits—there are differences within the subgroups. Latinas face greater risks of long-term welfare dependency than white women. Latino families are overrepresented on welfare, composing 25 percent of TANF caseloads. They are also overrepresented among long-term recipients—51 percent of Latinas as opposed to 27 percent of whites will receive welfare for more than five years. Latinas are less likely than whites to leave welfare even when they work. A number of complex factors account for this particularized experience with the welfare system. To begin with, Latinas on and off welfare earn less than whites in comparable circumstances, and they are more likely to be unemployed than white women. In addition, white women on welfare are more likely to be cohabiting than Latinas, and they receive more financial support from friends, family, and child support. Latinos and Latinas tend to have very low levels of education and large families. As a result, they may bear the heaviest burden of welfare reform due to TANF's time limits and its shift away from education and skills building.

See also Education; Employment Discrimination; Familia; Female-headed Households; Harris v. Rosario; *and* Race and Racialization.

BIBLIOGRAPHY

Assistant Secretary for Planning and Evaluation. AFDC Baseline Report, 1998, Human Services Policy. U.S. Department of Health and Human Services. aspe.hhs.gov/hsp/AFDC/afdcbase98.htm

Blong, Adele M., and Timothy J. Casey, "AFDC Program Rules for Advocates: An Overview." *Clearinghouse Review*, February 1994, 1164–1183.

Broder, Tanya, and Dinah Wiley. "Immigrants' Eligibility for Federal Benefits." Poverty Law Manual for New Lawyers. National

Center on Poverty Law. www.povertylaw.org./legalresearch/manual/index.cfm

Fix, Michael, and Wendy, Zimmerman. "The Legacies of Welfare Reform's Immigrant Restrictions." *Interpreter Releases* 75, no. 24 (November 16, 1998): 1577–1587.

Harknett, Kristen. "Working and Leaving Welfare: Does Race or Ethnicity Matter?" *Social Science Review* 65 (September 2001): 359–385.

Pollack, Wendy. "An Introduction to the Temporary Assistance for Needy Families Program." Poverty Law Manual for New Lawyers. National Center on Poverty Law. www.povertylaw.org./legalresearch/manual/index.cfm

Vélez, William. "Welfare Dependency among Chicanos and Puerto Ricans: The Milwaukee Case." *Hispanic Journal of Behavioral Sciences* 14 (February 1992): 91–106.

ALICIA ALVAREZ

ALABADOS AND ALABANZAS. *Alabados*, also called *alabanzas*, are religious hymns found in Mexico and the U.S. Southwest. Juan B. Rael describes alabados as ballads that turn into prayers.

In New Mexico the hymns are closely associated with the Hermandad de Nuestro Padre Jesús Nazareno (Brotherhood of Our Father Jesus Nazarene), a Hispano/a Catholic organization native to this area of the Sangre de Cristo Mountains. The first collection of alabados outside the brotherhood was published in 1877 by Father Raillere. The *hermanos* (brothers) are commonly known as the *penitentes*, although many object to the term as vulgar and derogatory. Most discussions of the hermanos define them exclusively as a flagellant order (practicing mortification of the flesh), but Alberto López Pulido has argued that such a definition grossly distorts the religious practice of *caridad* (charity and commitment to community) that defines the hermanos.

Alabado of the Passion

Ven Pecador y Verás
Ven pecador y verás
Al señor sacramentado
Padeciendo por el hombre
Tan cruelmente azotado
Come, sinner, and see
The Lord sacrificed
Suffering for Man,
Flogged so cruelly

The name *alabado* comes from the opening phrase of many of the hymns, *alabado sea* (blessed be, or praise be). Alabados can be defined narrowly as sorrowful hymns, which differentiates them from other religious hymns of the region: *salves* addressed to María and other saints; *albas*, morning songs of thanksgiving; and *cánticos* addressed to el Santo Niño. In his 1998 history of the *hermandad* and collection of alabados, Ray John de Aragón adds that *cuadernos* (handwritten notebooks) of the hermanos contain mainly sorrowful hymns, whereas those of

women's religious organizations (las Carmelitas) contain mainly salves.

Alabado in praise of the Virgin

Dios te salve, Dolorosa
Madre de Dolores
madre de tormentos,
ay, triste madre,
qué sentimiento!
Mother of Sorrows
Mother of torments,
Oh, sad mother,
what emotion!

Rael, in his 1967 collection of eighty-nine alabados, includes cánticos, salves, and albas under a broader definition of alabados. Rael identifies eight categories of alabados: (1) the Passion, (2) in praise of the Lord, (3) in praise of the Virgin, (4) farewell to the Virgin, (5) in praise of the Virgin and begging her intercession, (6) entreating the protection of the Virgin, (7) sung during communion, and (8) miscellaneous. The two largest categories are the Passion and miscellaneous, and many of the other categories could be classified as songs to the Virgin. Enrique Lamadrid indicates that praise hymns to the Virgin and to other saints are sometimes known as alabanzas.

Alabado in praise of a saint

Salve Santa Rita
Salve Santa Rita
Salve vea aurora
De los imposibles
Eres vencedora
Hail, Saint Rita
Hail, the beautiful dawn
In [the face of] impossible odds,
You are victorious

The historical origin of alabados is a subject of debate. Competing theories trace them to thirteenth-century Spanish hymns (de Aragón) and to Moorish and Sephardic peoples of Spain (Loeffler). Whatever its origin, the alabado has evolved in the unique environment of Spanish and Native American *mestizaje* in the mountains of New Mexico and Colorado and elsewhere in the Southwest. Rael suggests that a small number of alabados predate the nineteenth century and that in the mid-twentieth century new alabados were written and have not yet become anonymous. He does not include twentieth-century alabados in his collection because they are not in the public domain.

Alabados are sung at devotional ceremonies at the hermandad's private chapels (*moradas*) and at public ceremonies for Lent, for the saint's day of the village, for *velorios* (religious funeral vigils), and for private devotions in the home. They are sung without musical accompaniment, although in some cases a *pito* (indigenous flute) may be played between stanzas.

In the case of the hermandad, each hermano copies the alabados into his own cuaderno. These handwritten notebooks are subject to regular use, and few survive longer than thirty years, although some have been passed down from father to son. The oldest extant cuaderno outside of the brotherhood dates from the 1880s. A 1992–2004 Smithsonian Institution exhibition, American Encounters, featured cuadernos from the early twentieth century. De Aragón and López Pulido both argue that the alabados and cuadernos together describe the brothers' service to their communities.

As the devotions of the hermanos focus on Christ's Passion, his five wounds, and the Virgin in her aspect of Nuestra Señora de Dolores (Our Lady of Sorrows), these are common themes of alabados. Many alabados have dozens of stanzas, which may be why they are written down rather than memorized. Songs are often led by the *rezador* (*rezadores*)—one or two brothers singing stanzas while the rest of the community joins in on the refrain (repetition of first stanza). Some alabados specify a particular form of worship, as when they call to the public to join a procession, recite the stations of the cross, or describe an encounter between the Virgin and Jesus during the Passion (acted out when a procession of hermanos meets a procession of Carmelitas). Most alabados are named for the first verse of the first stanza, as in the sample songs above.

In 1940 Rael recorded over eighty alabados as sung by Hermanos Ricardo Archuleta, Narciso Arrellano, José Ignacio Cantú, Luis Montoya, and Alfredo Romero. His recordings are in the historical collections of the National Digital Library at the Library of Congress, and many of the original recordings are digitized on the library's Web site with transcriptions of all songs and some English translations. Rael's study suggests that whereas there are many commonalities among the songs, there are no definite rules all must follow. For example, more than half of the alabados studied were written with eight-syllable lines, but of these some used assonance and others used rhyme. The remaining songs were largely of six-syllable lines, though others used five-, seven-, or ten-syllable lines. Alabado collections are also in the New Mexico State Archives. Many alabados or alabanzas survive in the oral tradition, which is the case of the *alabanzas a la Virgin* sung in San Ygnacio, Texas.

See also Catholicism; New Mexico; Penitentes; *and* Religion and Spirituality.

BIBLIOGRAPHY
Cervantes, Leo. *Los alabados*. Tucson, Ariz.: Orbis Press, 2000.
De Aragón, Ray John. *Hermanos de la Luz/Brothers of the Light*. Santa Fe, N.Mex.: Heartsfire Books, 1998.
Lamadrid, Enrique R. "Juan Bautista Rael, 1900–1993: Pioneer Hispano Folklorist." Available at memory.loc.gov/ammem/rghtml/rgrael.html
Lamadrid, Enrique R. "La Musica Nuevo Mexicana: Religious and Secular Music from the Juan B. Rael Collection." *The Juan B. Rael Collection, 1940–1999*, Library of Congress. 1999.
Lamadrid, Enrique R. "Nuevo Mexicanos of the Upper Rio Grande: Culture, History, and Society." Available at memory.loc.gov/ammem/rghtml/rgculture.html
Loeffler, Jack, with Katherine Loeffler, and Enrique R. Lamadrid. *La música de los Viejitos*. Albuquerque: University of New Mexico Press, 1999.
López Pulido, Alberto. *The Sacred World of the Penitentes*. Washington, D.C., and London: Smithsonian Institution Press, 2000.
Rael, Juan Bautista. *The New Mexican Alabado* (1951). Musical transcription by Elizabeth Hague, translation of some songs by Elsie T. Stebbins. Language and Literature series, vol. 9, no. 3. New York: AMS Press, 1967.
Weigle, Marta. *Brothers of Light, Brothers of Blood*. Albuquerque: University of New Mexico Press, 1976.

CATRIONA RUEDA ESQUIBEL

ALABAMA. Alabama became a new immigrant destination at the end of the twentieth century. Latino immigrants and migrants, primarily from Mexico and Central America, have brought dramatic demographic, economic, and cultural change to this part of the Deep South. U.S. census statistics reveal the dimensions of this powerful migration stream. Latinos and Latinas in Alabama numbered 24,629 in 1990, 75,830 in 2000, and an estimated 87,617 in 2003. Since Latinos and Latinas tend to be undercounted in the census, the Latino and Latina population of the state is probably considerably higher, with some unofficial estimates reaching 150,000. Mexicans made up almost 59 percent of Alabama Latinos and Latinas in 2000, and Central and South Americans 30 percent. Alabama has few Puerto Ricans or Cubans, 8 and 3 percent respectively.

The new Latino and Latina migration to Alabama began in the late 1980s. Scholars attribute it to the impact of the 1986 Immigration Reform and Control Act, which legalized 3 million undocumented workers in the United States, mostly from Mexico and Central America. New job opportunities and the moderate climate of the southern states attracted both amnestied and undocumented Latinos and Latinas from California and the Southwest. During the 1990s, chain migration brought family and friends from sending communities in Mexico and Guatemala directly to Alabama towns and cities.

Shifting economic currents in the 1990s created a demand for cheap, reliable, nonunion labor throughout the United States. Latinos and Latinas found themselves in demand for many farming, factory, construction, and service jobs. In small north Alabama towns, such as Russellville, Collinsville, and Albertville, Latinos and Latinas work in agriculture, in poultry plants, and in hosiery, garment, textile, carpet, and furniture factories. In south Alabama, they provide migrant agricultural labor, replant timberland, process poultry and seafood, and work on farms and in sawmills. In metropolitan areas such as Birmingham, Latinos and Latinas work in restaurants, landscaping, construction, and warehouse jobs. Latinos fill most of the city's janitorial jobs, and Latinas work as hotel housekeepers.

At first, Latino newcomers were primarily young, single men who shared cramped housing, worked in teams or crews, and sent earnings to families in home countries. Eventually, entire families resettled in Alabama from California, Texas, Mexico, and Guatemala, establishing new ethnic communities in new residential spaces, purchasing homes, establishing businesses (primarily groceries and restaurants) and sending their children to local schools. Alabama's Latinos and Latinas have found strength in communal activities focused on homeland foods, musical traditions, holiday festivals, and weekend soccer leagues. Traditional religious practice, such as universal veneration of the Virgin of Guadalupe, along with several Spanish-language newspapers and radio stations, have also helped them to preserve their culture. The new communities are transnational in that they stay in close contact with relatives and travel back and forth regularly to their homeland. Thus, while adapting to life in Alabama, Latinos and Latinas have found ways of maintaining their cultural identity and connection to home.

Alabamians have exhibited mixed reactions to the Latino and Latina influx and its concentration in small towns and urban neighborhoods. It has complicated Alabama's historic racial divide between black and white. In the late 1990s, anti-immigrant sentiment surfaced in some north Alabama towns. Some have complained about job competition from Latino and Latina workers. Spanish language use has become controversial. An unknown number of Latinos and Latinas in the state are undocumented immigrants, which is a matter of concern to many Alabamians. For the most part, however, churches, schools, and public agencies have responded in positive ways to Latino and Latina newcomers. Several organizations have emerged to serve and advocate for Latinos and Latinas. Project Aprende, for example, works with migrant farm workers in several north Alabama counties, providing information on schooling, health care, and environmental safety. In Hoover, a Birmingham suburb, the Multicultural Resource Center sponsored by Catholic Family Services works with government and community agencies in providing assistance to immigrants. The Hispanic Interest Coalition of Alabama, founded in Birmingham in 1999, coordinates service and advocacy work for Latinos and Latinas. The Latinization process in Alabama, although only in its formative stage, has brought social and cultural change to parts of this Deep-South state.

See also Central Americans; Census; Chicanos and Chicanas; Demographics; Education; Immigration Reform and Control Act of 1986; *and* Mexican-Origin People in the United States.

BIBLIOGRAPHY
Connolly, Daniel. "Sueño de Alabama." *Birmingham Post-Herald*, July 26–30, 2004.
Mohl, Raymond A. "Latinization in the Heart of Dixie: Hispanics in Late-Twentieth-Century Alabama." *The Alabama Review* 55 (2002): 243–274.
Short, Dale. "Mexico in the Heart of Dixie." *UAB Magazine* 21 (2001): 2–9.

RAYMOND A. MOHL

ALAMO. Shortly after the battle of the Alamo (March 6, 1836), Texans turned the story of that military engagement into a founding epic for their new society and a symbol of the triumphal westward expansion of the United States. Through the years the Alamo story has been repeated in popular and scholarly books and in films, and it is told again and again to schoolchildren in Texas.

This first battle of the Texas Revolution had the elements for an epic. Facing an overwhelming force of approximately 2,500 Mexican soldiers, all the Alamo defenders—possibly as many as 250—perished in a twilight engagement. Word of their sacrifice traveled quickly and emboldened other Texans to continue the fight against Mexico.

The Alamo story also confirmed the depiction of Texas's revolt against Mexico as a cosmic struggle between good and evil that cast all Mexicans as villains. Such a portrayal justified the appropriation of Tejanos' (Mexican Texans') lands in the nineteenth century, the exploitation of Mexican labor in the twentieth century, and the segregation that subsequently excluded Mexican Americans from full participation in the state's society.

The Alamo, originally named San Antonio de Valero, had been established in 1718 as a missionary-led Indian community. Because it was a walled complex, the town was occupied by military troops in the Mexican period, long after the mission had been secularized (unincorporated). The contingent stationed there carried the name of its old home in northern Mexico, la Compañía Volante de Parras del Alamo (the Flying Company from Parras del Alamo), hence the fortress's new name.

There were other mission communities in the San Antonio River valley and across the Province of Texas, and there were also several soldier-settler garrison towns (*presidios*) and some civilian communities (*villas*). These settlements were all part of the northward movement from the central Mexican Highlands. In the semiarid north, including Texas, settlers relied on farming for self-subsistence and on grazing livestock for money to purchase

clothing, tools, and other goods. However, as permanent and impressive as the Texas communities in this far northeastern frontier were, they never attracted large numbers of settlers, and by the time of the Texas Revolution, the population did not exceed six thousand.

By contrast, the westward movement from the United States was aggressive, fueled by a growing population in search of land to grow cash crops to sell in a world trade network. Overexpansion in land speculation sparked periodic "panics" or recessions that left many on the frontier in debt, forcing them to move westward to begin anew. For them, Texas, particularly the fertile lands in the eastern half of the state, was attractive. Additionally the Mexican government's offer of free land in order to populate Texas and make it more productive proved irresistible, and by 1835 approximately thirty thousand Americans had taken Mexican citizenship and settled in Texas.

The arrival of these newcomers created conflicts. They arose from the different legal and political traditions and the requirements that settlers accept the Catholic faith and use Spanish for official transactions. In partisan politics, Texans understandably sided with the Federalists, who favored states' rights, against the Centralists, but in all likelihood the political controversy, like the cultural issues, could have been resolved.

What could not be negotiated was the economic conflict that resulted when President Antonio López de Santa Anna stationed troops on the Mexico–United States border, an action taken to prevent Texas from drifting to the United States. The troops on the border blocked Texans' trade with the United States and the world and shut off the flow of immigrants, ending Texans' prospects for selling their cash crops and excess farmland.

Clashes between Texans and the Mexican troops on the border led to armed confrontations elsewhere and eventually to all-out rebellion. To quash this, Santa Anna led an army across northern Mexico and arrived at Béxar (the San Antonio settlement) on February 23, 1836. At this point Santa Anna paused to await the arrival of the trained troops garrisoned in northern Mexico. Santa Anna's delay in the assault on the Alamo is described as a "siege" in the Alamo story. Actually some of the defenders left and reentered the Alamo, and one, possibly two, contingents arrived to assist in the expected engagement.

The battle of March 6 was bloody but short. Santa Anna had positioned most of his troops on the north wall, which was the most vulnerable. The attack began even before the first light appeared, and scaling the wall took some thirty minutes. Then the fighting continued in the courtyard for another quarter of an hour. The last of the defenders took refuge in one of the buildings, but they were overwhelmed, taken out, and executed. Santa Anna lost some six hundred soldiers in the battle.

After taking the Alamo, Santa Anna marched eastward to Goliad, where on March 19 he captured and executed some 350 men fighting under General James Fannin. Santa Anna then hurried farther east to engage the forces of General Sam Houston at the bayou of San Jacinto. In a surprise attack on April 21, Houston overtook the Mexican army, and Texans decimated the retreating Mexican forces. Santa Anna was captured and forced to commit to independence for Texas. The Mexican government, however, refused to concede, and a period of attack and counterattack ensued for the decade in which Texas proclaimed itself a republic. Texas became a part of the United States in 1846, which Mexico only recognized in the Treaty of Guadalupe Hidalgo (1848) ending the United States–Mexican War.

The Texan victory at San Jacinto and the eventual annexation of Texas into the United States were not enough, however, to avenge the defeat at the Alamo, and violence and fraud against Mexicans and Mexican Americans, justified as settling the score for the Mexican "slaughter" of the Alamo defenders, continued for decades. Ironically Tejanos were among the Alamo defenders, and they fought against Santa Anna for Texas independence. Their participation was not included in the Alamo epic or in the Texas Revolution narrative until the late twentieth century, when the growing numbers of Latinas and Latinos in the state necessitated their inclusion in the founding stories.

See also Missions and Other Colonial Churches; Treaty of Guadalupe Hidalgo; *and* United States–Mexican War.

BIBLIOGRAPHY

Flores, Richard R. *Remembering the Alamo: Memory, Modernity, and the Master Symbol.* Austin: University of Texas Press, 2002.

Harding, Stephen L. *Texian Iliad: A Military History of the Texas Revolution, 1835–1936.* Austin: University of Texas Press, 1994.

Montejano, David. *Anglos and Mexicans in the Making of Texas, 1836–1986.* Austin: University of Texas Press, 1987.

GILBERTO M. HINOJOSA

ALARCÓN, NORMA (b. 1943), feminist literary scholar. Norma Alarcón has dedicated most of her work to the representation of Latina women in all aspects of life. She is perhaps one of the most widely recognized Chicana feminist activist scholars. She was born in Villa Frontera, Coahuila, Mexico, a small town near the United States–Mexico border, on November 30, 1943. Life in Frontera proved difficult for the Alarcón family during the 1950s, and in the summer of 1955 they began their move northward to find work in the United States. They first moved to San Antonio, Texas, and by the end of the year settled in Chicago, Illinois, where Alarcón's father became a steelworker and her mother worked as a candy packer for Marshall Fields.

At a young age, Alarcón dedicated her life to her education. She was a gifted student and showed promise as a scholar. She graduated from Saint Thomas the Apostle, an all-girl Catholic school, in 1961 as a member of the National Honor Society. She received a scholarship to college in Wisconsin, but her father would not allow her to move out of state alone to continue her education. Instead, she started college at De Paul University, where she met her first husband, Jon McKesson. They married in 1962 and moved to Newark, Ohio. Alarcón had to forgo college to take care of her husband. She gave birth to her only child, Joe McKesson, in 1964.

Her desire for learning grew in those early years of married life. She briefly attended night school at Marion College in Indianapolis, Indiana. In 1968, she transferred to Indiana University in Bloomington, where she graduated Phi Beta Kappa in 1973, having completed a degree in Spanish literature with an emphasis in Latin American literature and a minor in comparative literature. She subsequently entered the PhD program in Spanish literature at Indiana University and completed a year of study in Madrid, Spain, in 1971. The countercultural and feminist movements influenced her intellectual development, and it was in these movements that Alarcón found the focus of her studies.

In the spring of 1974, Alarcón completed her doctoral examinations and was determined to finish the PhD program. The rigors of academic life greatly affected her personal life, and in 1976 she divorced her husband Jon. On her own, Alarcón balanced raising her son Joe and working to complete her dissertation during the next five years. She found work with the Social Center for Bilingual-Bicultural Education, where she conducted workshops for migrants in the Bloomington area. She met her second husband, Jim Opiat, in her last year of graduate school.

Alarcón's passion for literature and expression grew in many ways. She took an interest in feminism among women of color while attending the Midwestern Women's Conference in Chicago in the late 1970s. The idea for a journal about Latina women forming alliances with other women of color was born at the Latina Caucus meeting, where she met writers Ana Castillo and Sandra Cisneros. *Third Woman* grew out of a desire to create a journal dedicated to the writings of women living on the margins of society. Third Woman Press was officially founded in 1979 by Alarcón. Since then, it has offered a forum for the written and visual expressions of women of color, supporting intellectual activism by publishing the works of young writers.

In 1983, Alarcón completed her dissertation, "Ninfomanía: El Discurso feminista en la obre de Rosario Castellanos," a theoretical study of Mexican feminist literary criticism. She began her academic career in the Foreign Language department at Purdue University in Lafayette, Indiana in the fall of 1983. In 1986, she received the Chancellors Postdoctoral Fellowship at the University of California, Berkeley, and the following year she was hired by the Ethnic Studies department. She received tenure in the summer of 1993, and eventually taught in Women's Studies and Spanish as well.

A specialist in feminist critical theory, cultural criticism, and studies of Chicana literature, Alarcón published several major articles on Latinas throughout her years at Berkeley. Her study of Anglo-American feminism and women of color had a significant influence on other Chicano and Chicana students and colleagues. She examined the institutional role of gender and social politics in her studies "The Theoretical Subjects of 'This Bridge Called My Back' " and "Traddutora, Traditora: A Paradigmatic Figure of Chicana Feminism." Her other publications include "Chicana Feminism: In the Tracks of the Native Woman," "Anzaldúa's Frontera: Inscribing Gynetics," and "Conjugating Subjects: The Heteroglossia of Essence and Resistance."

An ardent supporter of student activism, Alarcón joined the student hunger strike in May of 1999 to protest Berkeley's policies on affirmative action that had taken effect under Proposition 209. As editor of Third Woman Press, she was able to promote the careers of such aspiring Latina writers as Sandra Cisneros, Judith Ortiz Cofer, Cherríe Moraga, Gloria Anzaldua, Lucha Corpi, and Carla Trujillo, to name but a few.

The demands of university life greatly affected her personal well-being, and after eighteen years of marriage to Jim, Alarcón divorced him in the summer of 1999. She continues her social activism and remains dedicated to the intellectual life that she has always loved.

See also Literary Criticism and Theory; Literature; *and* Publishing.

ELLIE HERNÁNDEZ

ALASKA. Place names like Valdez and Cordova reveal that there has been a Hispanic presence in Alaska since 1791, when Spanish sailors on the famous Malaspina Expedition visited the area. In the early twenty-first century, out of a total state population of 626,932, Latinos and Latinas number 25,765. Of this number, 14,738 reside in Anchorage, Alaska's most populous urban area, which contains 42 percent of the state's entire population.

According to the 2000 U.S. census, Latinos and Latinas formed the third-largest minority group in the state. This population is projected to double in size by 2010. The Alaska Native population (Northwest Coast Indians, Inupiaqs, Yup'iks, Aleuts, and Athabascans) makes up 15 percent of the state's population and is the largest minority group. The second largest consists of those who self-identified as persons of "one or more races" during the 2000 U.S. census.

Latinos and Latinas are concentrated in Alaska's three major urban areas (Anchorage, Fairbanks, and Juneau), although they can also be found in other areas like the Aleutian Chain, Kodiak Island, Sitka, Valdez, Petersburg, and even Barrow (the northernmost city located within the Arctic Circle). One can run into Latinos and Latinas in Bethel, located in southwest Alaska, and in Nome, along Norton Sound, and even in some of the state's smallest villages, like Angoon. Latinos and Latinas hold a variety of white- and blue-collar jobs, ranging from small business owners, professors, and army officers to hotel clerks and cooks. Some are new immigrants; others are fourth-generation U.S. citizens who have migrated from other parts of the country to Alaska.

Latinos and Latinas come to Alaska for the same reasons others do. Although the state economy had begun to decline by the end of the 1990s, there were still plenty of job opportunities for wageworkers in the canneries in the southeast and for professionals in private practice, in various institutions such as schools and universities, or in business. A significant number return to live in Alaska after serving in the military. As in other parts of the country, Latinos and Latinas are valued for their work ethic and are rewarded for it. Their ability to interact and communicate effectively with members of the state's largest minority group, the Alaska Natives, is also a significant factor in their success in the workplace.

There are other reasons Latinos and Latinas come to Alaska. The pace of life is slower than in other parts of the country, and the sheer size of the state and the isolation it offers make state residents dependent on each other when necessary. Yet the independence that is part of the Alaska character is also attractive to many Latinos and Latinas.

In places where large numbers of Latinos and Latinas reside (Anchorage, Fairbanks, Juneau, and Sitka), they celebrate their culture in various ways. The urban areas have one or more Latino and Latina organizations that plan various social events throughout the year. The focus of these events is usually Latino and Latina music and food and sometimes education. Military bases also sponsor cultural or educational activities with a focus on the Latino and Latina culture because of their large number in the military. At the University of Alaska Fairbanks, the first Latino and Latina club in the state was founded by the school's first tenured Latina professor in the fall of 1999.

See also Census; Demographics; Education; Immigrant Incorporation into U.S. Society; *and* Immigration.

BIBLIOGRAPHY

Olson, Wallace M. *Through Spanish Eyes: Spanish Voyages to Alaska, 1774–1792.* Auke Bay, Alaska: Heritage Research, 2002.
United States Census. 2000 Census Summary File. Alaska Department of Labor. 146.63.75.45/census2000/Census_lv2.asp

MARIA ELENA REYES

ALBIZU CAMPOS, PEDRO (1891–1965). The Puerto Rican nationalist leader Pedro Albizu Campos has attained a degree of historical preeminence approximating that of Luis Muñoz Marín as the foremost Puerto Rican public figure of the twentieth century. Unlike Muñoz Marín's, though, his prestige and acceptance continue to grow. The resistance against U.S. colonialism that he embodies has become a significant component of cultural identity for both island and mainland Puerto Ricans.

Albizu Campos was born in Ponce, on September 21, 1891. In 1912 he won a scholarship to the University of Vermont. He went on from there to Harvard where he obtained an undergraduate degree in 1916 and a law degree in 1921.

Much has been made of the supposed mistreatment of Albizu Campos, a multiracial Puerto Rican, in the United States as a catalyst for his nationalism. Yet the historical record fails to establish overt acts of discrimination. He was actively involved in student organizations at Harvard, succeeding John Reed as president of the prestigious Cosmopolitan Club. He was exposed to experiences that contributed to his ideological formation, acting as commentator for Rabindranath Tagore and Eamon de Valera. There is no record of mistreatment during his military service.

However racialized he may have been as a Puerto Rican in the United States, assuming a direct relationship between this and his subsequent political development misrepresents Albizu Campos's capacity to theorize Puerto Rico's colonial situation and to strategize against it. His engagement with political justice and nationalism was based on a solid ideological foundation and historical knowledge rather than on psychologized injury.

Returning to Ponce to practice law in 1921, Albizu Campos joined the centrist Union Party to work within the system. In 1924, when the Unionists removed independence from their platform, he joined the Nationalist Party. After traveling throughout Latin America to publicize Puerto Rico's plight, he became party president in 1930 and launched one of the most sustained struggles against colonialism that Puerto Ricans have ever experienced.

The 1936 execution of police chief Elisha Riggs by two Nationalist youths led the U.S. government to bring charges of seditious conspiracy against Albizu Campos. Along with other Nationalist leaders, he was convicted and sentenced to ten years in the federal penitentiary in Atlanta, Georgia.

Returning in 1947, Albizu Campos continued his struggle. His efforts culminated in the Nationalist Insurrection of 1950, spurred by the impending establishment of commonwealth status for Puerto Rico. The insurrection remains a significant event for Puerto Rican nationalism. Albizu Campos was prosecuted and sentenced to eighty years in the local penitentiary. Muñoz Marín pardoned

PEDRO ALBIZU CAMPOS. Albizu Campos under arrest, San Juan, Puerto Rico, November 2, 1950. (©Bettmann/CORBIS)

him in 1953 but revoked the pardon in 1954 when a group of Nationalists attacked the U.S. Congress.

Albizu Campos died in San Juan on April 21, 1965, a year after ill health led to another executive pardon. His legacy has been reevaluated and recontextualized, recognizing his stature as a significant national and international icon of political resistance. The impact of his struggle is evident in the public use and circulation of his name and image, both on the island and in the United States, as embodiments of Puerto Rican sovereignty and dignity.

See also **Muñoz Marín, Luis** *and* **Peuerto Ricans.**

BIBLIOGRAPHY
López, Adalberto, and James Petras, eds. *Puerto Rico and Puerto Ricans: Studies in History and Society.* Cambridge, Mass: Schenkman, 1974.

Torres, Andrés, and José E. Velázquez, eds. *The Puerto Rican Movement: Voices from the Diaspora.* Philadelphia: Temple University Press, 1998.

Young Lords Party and Michael Abramson. *Palante: Young Lords Party.* New York: McGraw-Hill, 1971.

VILMA SANTIAGO-IRIZARRY

ALCOHOLISM. Alcohol abuse and alcoholism are significant problems for Latinos and Latinas, affecting individuals and families as a result of ill health, premature death due to cirrhosis and other liver diseases and accidents, and social and family violence. It has been estimated that nearly 50 percent of Latino men between eighteen and thirty-five years of age exhibit problematic drinking (Caetano). Moreover, comparative studies find differences in the patterns of drinking exhibited by Anglo and Latino and Latina men and women that have been explained in terms of cultural and structural factors.

Etiology

In the late twentieth and early twenty-first centuries, Latino and Latina drinking patterns and alcoholism have been studied by anthropologists and health scholars. In his early writings William Madsen associated alcohol abuse with anomie, the result of the social and economic marginality endured by Mexican-origin individuals in the United States. Madsen argued that pervasive racism toward Mexicans impeded the social and economic advancement of the group, leading to collective and individual despair. Moreover, among Mexicans who attempted to assimilate, alcohol abuse was seen as an effort to drown the cultural alienation experienced by those whose efforts to abandon their cultural roots and embrace those of the Anglo were met with rejection and continued marginalization. While Madsen's conclusions have been challenged by later writers, his recognition of the influence of racism on substance abuse remains important.

Since the 1970s, studies of Latino and Latina drinking patterns have examined both the social and the structural forces that promote problematic drinking as well as cultural patterns and familial problems that may be related to alcohol abuse and dependence. Raul Caetano conducted a number of studies comparing drinking patterns in Mexico and the United States and found that men in Mexico tend to drink large quantities of alcohol at one time but generally only during the weekend. Furthermore, alcoholism is viewed more as moral weakness and less as an "illness" influenced by both environmental and genetic factors. However, when Mexican men migrate to the United States, their pattern of drinking shifts to frequent (often daily) and heavy drinking (six or more drinks at one time). Binge drinking is associated with increased economic and social problems (arrests for driving while intoxicated, accidents, homicides, and domestic violence).

While Mexican women are mostly abstainers, women who migrate to the United States often begin to drink. Moreover, Latino men tend to begin drinking at an earlier age (fourteen to sixteen years of age); their drinking peaks at about age thirty-five and generally decreases by age fifty, often as a result of illness (diabetes and liver disease). U.S.–born Latinas, in particular those who are educated and more acculturated, are social drinkers, although binge drinking is not uncommon among Latina college students. However, it is generally the less-educated and less- privileged Latinas who demonstrate problematic drinking (arrests for driving under the influence, accusations of child abuse or neglect, or criminal activity). Moreover, Latinos and Latinas of different national origins vary with regard to the prevalence of alcohol-related problems. Among men, those of Mexican and Puerto Rican origin show more frequent and problematic drinking than those of Cuban origin of similar socioeconomic backgrounds. Among women, Puerto Ricans and Chicanas show more problematic drinking than Cuban and Mexican-born women.

Cultural Factors

Prior to the conquest of the American continent, indigenous men used alcohol primarily for ceremonial purposes. However, during the colonial period alcohol was used as payment to the indigenous indentured servants. Thus alcohol abuse became associated with the disempowerment and despair suffered by indigenous men during and following the conquest. Over time, alcohol became an integral part of family life, as celebrations of births and deaths and other important family rituals included alcohol. Traditionally drinking alcohol was considered a rite of passage for men, and a man's worth was equated with his ability to "hold his liquor" and not lose control. Women were not supposed to drink, and those who did were looked upon unfavorably. Men who were controlled by alcohol were considered weak, particularly if their drinking adversely affected their role as provider for the family.

It is in fact these cultural patterns that have been transformed into stereotypical depictions of Mexican men as drinkers and womanizers. In both Mexican and U.S. cinema, Latino working-class men are frequently depicted as out-of-control drunkards. These men, not coincidentally, are usually darker and more indigenous-looking than their middle-class counterparts. *El borracho* (the drunk) is a cultural archetype of the dispossessed and downtrodden Mexican man. These stereotypical and classist depictions obscure the fact that alcohol abuse crosses class, gender, and national borders.

Migration and Acculturation

Epidemiological findings indicate that the longer Latinos and Latinas live in the United States, the worse their overall health status becomes. Scholars posit that immigrant Latinos and Latinas bring with them a number of protective factors (better nutrition, cohesive family relations, and less smoking). However, within a few years after migration Latinos and Latinas begin to emulate the dietary and exercise patterns of urban Americans, with disastrous health results (increased incidence of hypertension, diabetes, and smoking- and alcohol-related illnesses). Research findings suggest that the stress inherent in negotiating new environmental demands, limited economic and social resources, and experiences of marginality affect the physical and psychological well-being of immigrants. Caetano's studies highlight the role of cultural dislocation and the stress of acculturation in Latino and Latina drinking patterns.

Family Disintegration

Latino cultures are highly familistic, valuing family over individual well-being. The idealized Latino family is characterized by respect, mutuality, interdependence, and solidarity. However, migration may result in family separation, changed gender roles, intergenerational conflicts, and ultimately family disintegration. For those facing the stress of family problems in a new social and cultural context, alcohol may serve as a coping mechanism. In a study of migration and intimate partner violence, several themes emerged as key predictors of alcohol misuse and domestic violence: missing the family left behind, economic pressures, lack of work opportunities in the United States, and among men *la falta de comprensión de las mujeres de su necesidad de tomar* (women's lack of understanding of the men's need to drink).

Summary

Latinos and Latinas evidence significant problems with alcohol misuse and alcoholism. To better understand and treat the problem, however, it is essential to consider the historical role of alcohol in the lives of Latinos and Latinas, particularly the poor and marginalized; the stresses of migration and acculturation; and the roles of nationality, gender, and social class in the incidence and prevalence of alcoholism.

See also Health *and* Latinas and Intimate Partner Violence.

BIBLIOGRAPHY

Alvarez, Louis. "Substance Abuse in the Hispanic Population." In *The Latino Psychiatric Patient: Assessment and Treatment*, edited by Alberto G. López and Ernestina Carrillo, 93–217. Washington, D.C.: American Psychiatric Publishing, 2001.

Caetano, Raul. "Drinking Patterns and Alcohol-Related Problems among Hispanics in the United States: A Review." *Drug and Alcohol Dependence* 12 (1983): 37–59.

Flores-Ortiz, Yvette. "The Role of Cultural and Gender Values in Alcohol Use Patterns among Chicana/Latina High School and University Students: Implications for AIDS Prevention." *International Journal of Addictions* 29, no. 9 (1994): 1149–1171.

Flores-Ortiz, Yvette. "Theorizing Justice in Chicano Families." Occasional paper no. 43. East Lansing, Mich.: Julian Zamora Research Institute, 2000.

Flores-Ortiz, Yvette, and Enriqueta Valdez Curiel. "Intimate Partner Violence and Couple Interaction among Women from Mexico City and Jalisco, Mexico." *Journal of Border Health* 1 (2002): 33–42.

Gilbert, Jean. M. "Alcohol-Related Practices, Problems, and Norms among Mexican-Americans: An Overview." In *Alcohol Use among U.S. Ethnic Minorities*, edited by Danielle Spiegler et al., 115–134. Rockville, Md.: U.S. Department of Health and Human Services, National Institute on Alcohol Abuse and Alcoholism, 1989.

Madsen, William. "The Alcoholic Agringado." *American Anthropologist* 66 (1964): 355–361.

Mora, Juana, and Jean M. Gilbert. "Issues for Latinas: Mexican American Women." In *Alcohol and Drugs Are Women's Issues*, edited by Paula Roth, vol. 1, 43–47. Metuchen, N.J.: Women's Action Alliance and Scarecrow Press, 1991.

YVETTE G. FLORES

ALEXANDER V. SANDOVAL. Until 1991, Alabama, like forty-eight other states, offered the written part of its general driver's license examination in at least fourteen languages besides English. One of those languages was Spanish. The practice was a response to demographic trends on the rise throughout the United States. In Alabama alone, the number of Spanish-speaking residents doubled to more than 20,000 from 1990 to 2000. But after the 1990 passage of a constitutional amendment declaring English to be the state's official language, Alabama's director of public safety implemented a new rule forbidding applicants from taking the written driver's license exam in any other language. Translators, dictionaries, and other interpretative aids were banned.

Martha Sandoval, a Spanish-speaking Mexican national, had settled in Mobile, Alabama, where she worked as a housekeeper. A permanent U.S. resident, Sandoval could understand posted traffic signs but not questions on the written part of the driver's license exam. In 1996, on behalf of herself and thousands of non-English speakers, Sandoval filed a class action lawsuit. Her target was the director of public safety, whom she sued under regulations promulgated by two federal agencies exercising powers granted by Title VI of the Civil Rights Act of 1964. Sandoval demanded that the English-only rule be thrown out and that written examinations in Spanish be restored.

Title VI is a statute prohibiting any program or activity that receives federal funds from excluding anyone from participation "on the ground of race, color, or national origin." One of the regulations invoked by Sandoval forbids any such program to "utilize criteria or methods of administration which have the effect of subjecting individuals to discrimination." The regulation applies to all state government agencies and private contractors that receive shares of the billions of dollars in federal funds appropriated by Congress each year to pay for local services. Alabama's department of public safety received some of this largess to fund its system for licensing drivers of motor vehicles. Sandoval argued that the department's English-only rule amounted to discrimination based on national origin, because it had the effect of excluding non-English–speaking people from other countries from obtaining driver's licenses in violation of federal regulations.

In 1998, a federal trial judge ruled in Sandoval's favor. According to the judge, people like Sandoval were no more likely than English-speaking drivers to become involved in accidents or threaten the public safety. The following year, a federal appeals court agreed with the ruling. But in 2001, a divided U.S. Supreme Court reversed. By a five to four vote, the Court held that Congress did not intend to permit private individuals like Sandoval to sue to enforce the regulations. Writing for the majority, Justice Antonin Scalia reasoned that Title VI lacked plain language authorizing such lawsuits. "Having sworn off the habit of venturing beyond Congress' intent," he wrote, "we will not accept [the] invitation to have one last drink."

In dissent, Justice John Paul Stevens argued that the question before the Court already had been answered in *Lau v. Nichols* (1974), a nearly identical case decided twenty-seven years earlier. He wrote that the majority's attempt to distinguish this case, and others that came after it, was "muddled." Title VI authorized agencies to issue "broad" and "prophylactic" rules necessary to realize the goals of the statute, Stevens wrote. Therefore, "It makes no sense" to differentiate between private actions to enforce Title VI and private actions to enforce the regulations promulgated under Title VI.

The Supreme Court's decision in *Alexander v. Sandoval* (2001) has had a sweeping effect on the enforcement of civil rights laws applying to federally funded programs. The decision makes it more difficult to challenge a wide range of practices whose burdens fall disproportionately on minorities, such as assigning hospital beds based on whether the patient has insurance or limiting the number of Medicare patients allowed in a nursing home. Moreover, the ruling applies not only to regulations outlawing racial and ethnic discrimination under Title VI but also to regulations forbidding gender bias in education under Title IX and disability discrimination in public accommodations under the Americans with Disabilities Act.

Since the ruling, people like Sandoval cannot sue for violations of anti-discrimination regulations; they must rely exclusively on federal agencies to do so. But few of these agencies have the will or resources to enforce their own regulations. In fact, two years before *Alexander v. Sandoval* was decided, the U.S. Commission on Civil Rights had already concluded that "timid and ineffective enforcement efforts . . . have fostered, rather than combated . . . the segregation, disparate treatment, and racism experienced by African Americans, Hispanic Americans, Native Americans, Asian Americans, and Pacific Islanders."

Private individuals may still recover damages and obtain injunctive relief by suing fund recipients directly under Title VI, but only to challenge forms of mistreatment that the Supreme Court classifies as "intentional discrimination." Title VI alone does not outlaw "disparate impact" practices, in which a seemingly neutral rule has an unintentionally discriminatory effect based on race, national origin, or other protected status. To permit private individuals to sue directly under these regulations,

Congress would have to pass an amendment—a reform in which it has yet to express serious interest.

To advocates of judicial restraint, *Alexander v. Sandoval* is a logical application of the settled principle that it is the job of legislatures, not courts, to create new rights to bring lawsuits. After all, members of Congress must answer to voters at the polls; federal judges are largely immune from politics because they are appointed for life. To advocates of civil rights, however, the case presents a paradox: one the one hand, agencies have the power to issue sweeping regulations to implement federal laws; on the other hand, the people most affected by those regulations are forbidden to help enforce them.

See also Bilingualism and Biculturalism; Civil Rights Act (1964); Race and Racialization; *and* Title VI.

BIBLIOGRAPHY

Alexander v. Sandoval. United States Reports. Volume 532 (2001): 275–317.

Commission on Civil Rights, a Report of the United States. "The Health Care Challenge: Acknowledging Disparity, Confronting Discrimination, and Ensuring Equality: The Role of Federal Civil Rights Enforcement Efforts." Vol. II (1999): 1-438. Sections available at academic.udayton.edu/health/08civilrights/

Department of Justice. *Code of Federal Regulations* 28 (2001): § 42.104(b)(2).

Department of Transportation. *Code of Federal Regulations* 49 (2001): § 21.5(b)(2). ecfr.gpoaccess.gov/cgi/t/text/text-idx?&c=ecfr&tpl=/ecfr browse/Title49/49tab_02.tpl

Mann, Jonathan M., Sofia Gruskin, Michael A. Grodin, and George J. Annas. *Health and Human Rights: A Reader.* Routledge, 1999.

Rosenbaum, Sara, and Joel Teitelbaum. "Civil Rights Enforcement in the Modern Healthcare System: Reinvigorating the Role of the Federal Government in the Aftermath of *Alexander v. Sandoval.*" *Yale Journal of Health Policy, Law, and Ethics* 3, no. 2 (Summer 2003): 215–252.

CHRISTOPHER DAVID RUIZ CAMERON

ALFARO, LUIS (b. 1961), playwright. Luis Alfaro is a Los Angeles–based playwright, performance artist, and director whose artistic work was recognized in 1997 with a MacArthur Foundation "Genius" Fellowship. Alfaro was born and raised in the Pico-Union district of Los Angeles, a poor working-class and mainly immigrant neighborhood in the city's downtown area. He grew up in a deeply religious Mexican American household amidst an extended family structure. Alfaro's relatives and neighbors became the subject of his early writing and formed the basis of *Downtown* (1990), his signature performance piece. *Downtown* is a multicharacter monologue that scrutinizes Los Angeles by laying bare the glorification of the city and the glamorization of its people fabricated by Hollywood and the entertainment industry. In *Downtown*, as in much of his work, Alfaro brings to life an alternative city, one readily visible but rarely examined and

one that shaped Alfaro's sense of self as a gay Chicano. *Downtown* is also one of the first explicit ruminations on homosexuality and Chicano identity. Alfaro's unequivocal refusal to prioritize one facet of his identity over the other was novel for its time. *Downtown*'s matter-of-fact presentation of his sexuality and his ethnicity as noncompetitive identities signaled a break from earlier models where these aspects were viewed as oppositional.

Downtown is a poetic meditation on growing up gay and Chicano told through performance, narrative, and movement. The piece was performed throughout the United States and was recorded as a spoken word CD in 1993. In the introduction to *Downtown* published in *O Solo Homo: The New Queer Performance*, Alfaro writes,

> I call myself a gay Chicano. I create work that asks questions about identity and social power and addresses the intersection of nationality and sexuality. More than all of that, I am trying to tell the story of my people, of what it means to live in a city like Los Angeles, to give voice to the stories that have not been heard
>
> (p. 316)

Alfaro's commitment to art and politics is reflected in the various projects—creative, cultural, political—that he has helped inaugurate over the years. He was a cofounder of VIVA!, one of the first Latina and Latino lesbian and gay arts organizations in the United States. VIVA advocated for queer Latina and Latino artists and provided a space where they could meet. In the early 1990s, VIVA's "Teatro VIVA!" provided fundamental AIDS information to the diverse Latina and Latino communities throughout Southern California. Presented in the agit-prop style of

Teatro Campesino, Teatro VIVA's short comic sketches were among the most innovative HIV-prevention efforts directed to Latinas and Latinos. In 1995, Alfaro was named co-director of the Latino Theatre Initiative (LTI) at the Mark Taper Forum, the premiere regional theater in Los Angeles. The Latino Theatre Initiative was designed to develop new work by Latina and Latino playwrights and to provide opportunities for Latina and Latino actors, directors, and designers. In this capacity, Alfaro, along with Diane Rodriguez, LTI's co-director, worked with a wide range of Latina and Latino playwrights and performers. The roster of artists supported by LTI is a who's who of Latino and Latina theater and includes such names as Culture Clash, Nilo Cruz, José Rivera, Carmelita Tropicana, and Oliver Mayer.

Alfaro's script for the short film *Chicanismo* (1997) was produced by PBS and nominated for an Emmy Award. *Chicanismo* is composed of four character sketches of two men and two women who provide diverse representations of Chicana and Chicano life in late-twentieth-century Los Angeles. Alfaro wrote the script and performed each of the characters. He has also collaborated with a number of other Latina and Latino artists, including Alberto "Beto" Araiza and Monica Palacios, his VIVA! cofounders, on *Deep in the Crotch of My Latino Psyche* (1993), the first performance collaboration between queer Chicanos and Chicanas. Other collaborations include one with the photographer Laura Aguilar, another with the performance artist Marisela Norte, and various projects with the performer and director Diane Rodriguez.

Alfaro also has a distinguished career as a playwright. His plays *Bitter Homes and Gardens*; *Breakfast, Lunch, & Dinner*; and *Straight as a Line* have been produced in Los Angeles and at premiere regional theaters throughout the United States. His most recent plays include *Electricidad*, a retelling of the classical story of Elektra told within the context of Chicana and Chicano culture, which held its world premiere at Tucson's Borderlands Theatre in 2003, and *Body of Faith*, a play about the role of religion and spirituality in the lives of lesbian, gay, bisexual, and trans-gendered people of all backgrounds, which was presented in collaboration with Los Angeles's highly regarded Cornerstone Theatre in 2003. The range of Alfaro's interests, both as a dramatist and as a performer, challenges efforts to reduce his work to a set of shared themes. Alfaro's work cuts across genres, and he is as adept at writing autobiographical performance pieces as he is at writing satiric comedies, adaptations of classical tragedy, or community-based activist works. Alfaro's writings are currently under contract to the University of Michigan Press, which plans to publish *Downtown and Elsewhere: A Luis Alfaro Reader*.

See also HIV and AIDS; Gays; Performing Arts and Theater; *and* Playwrights.

BIBLIOGRAPHY

Alfaro, Luis. "Downtown." In *O Solo Homo: The New Queer Performance*, edited by Holly Hughes and David Román. New York: Grove, 1998.

Alfaro, Luis. *Downtown and Elsewhere: A Luis Alfaro Reader*, edited by David Román. Ann Arbor: University of Michigan Press. Forthcoming.

Allatson, Paul. "Siempre Feliz en Mi Falda: Luis Alfaro's Simulative Challenge." *GLQ: A Journal of Lesbian and Gay Studies* 5, no. 2 (1999): 199–230.

Román, David. *Acts of Intervention: Performance, Gay Culture, and AIDS*. Bloomington: Indiana University Press, 1998.

Román, David. "Latino Performance and Identity." *Aztlán: A Journal of Chicano Studies* 22, no. 2 (Fall 1997): 151–168.

DAVID ROMÁN

ALFONZO, CARLOS J. (1950–1991), artist. Carlos José Alfonzo studied art at Havana's San Alejandro Academy of Fine Arts and earned recognition and support as a young and promising intellectual in the strict cultural circles of the Revolución. To the surprise of many of his *compatriotas*, he seized the first opportunity to leave the country, traveling across the treacherous Florida Straits on a crowded fishing boat as part of the Mariel exodus in 1980. Throughout the rest of his life, he would remain wounded by politics even as he became a fearless artist willing to push all the limits.

At the beginning, Alfonzo had to take whatever jobs were offered to start his new life. Soon he began to have free time and, confident in his artistic style and solid technical education, he first painted small works, slowly moving to larger formats. As he became more established, he experienced a boundless release of emotions and ideas, which bolstered his constant artistic expression, his relentless *descarga*, his "unloading."

The art of Alfonzo reveals the dizzying world of a driven visionary who expressed his evolving artistic selves and recorded an immigrant's longings and tears. Because he had grown up in a Marxist, nationalist culture, his imagery was initially driven by social concerns and by the pictorial tradition of Cuban modernism. In the United States, intensifying his vivid interest in the human body as a subject, he began to paint "the drama and poetry of the everyday."

After living in Los Angeles briefly in 1983, he set up his home in Miami. He traveled to New York and Texas for his exhibitions and visited museums and galleries to see work by contemporary artists he admired. In 1986, walking through Italian churches and museums, he felt "fulfilled, inspired and energized" by the Old Masters. By the mid-1980s, Alfonzo was working in a large studio, solely dedicated to his art, producing dynamic, charged compositions of great presence, scale, and power.

His mature paintings are full of tension and movement, often composed like a stage where some drama is unfolding. For *Aurora Borealis*, he found inspiration in a scene from Lezama Lima's *Paradiso*. *Anunciación* is suffused with the baroque images and golden light Alfonzo encountered in Italy. In *Gulfstream*, he recalled his own perilous maritime flight from Cuba. *La Noche Oscura*, *In Peace*, *Three Drops*, and *Bullfight* feature his striking large compositions and demonstrate his vast range as a painter.

Alfonzo was thoroughly familiar with art history and art theory. He also had a special interest in arcane symbols and the iconography of Santería. In 1987, he produced an important suite of paintings intended for a temple that was never built. Each panel included the image of a specific *orisha*, or diety. Extending their pictorial syncretism, he painted symbols familiar to initiates (Changó's double ax, Babalú Ayé's *muletas*, or crutches) in several works. As a Santería practitioner and believer, Alfonzo's involvement with sacred images was motivated by faith and informed by peers, *padrinos* (Santero elders), and Lydia Cabrera's books. Eventually, he became involved with the philosophy and practice of the Rosicrucians, strengthening and deepening his religious convictions.

Producing sculptural versions of his complex pictorial visions, Alfonzo worked in ceramics and welded steel. In a group of large sculptures, Ballerina Suite, he transformed his painted prima donnas into life-size metal divas. Using delicate lines, he painted the Santería pantheon in a group of small ceramic plates. With clay, he made models for benches and park furniture. In the tradition of playful modernists, Alfonzo enjoyed painting and incising dishes as well as forming them by hand. A group of large plates criticized "Cuba's false cultural freedom and the use of ballet and folklore as smoke screens." He would occasionally paint a campy teapot or a wild ashtray, "so I won't be taken so seriously." By 1986, life and art had merged seamlessly, and Alfonzo was becoming a celebrity.

Curators who organized surveys and touring exhibitions immediately recognized Alfonzo's genius. Invitations to important exhibitions followed and continued through the years. Critics reviewing these exhibitions received his works favorably, and broad audiences came to experience his paintings in museums and galleries across the United States. One of his paintings is featured on the cover of the catalog of *Hispanic Artists in the United States* (1987), an ambitious survey of Latina and Latino artists. He worked with various dealers, and his exhibitions usually sold out. Collectors also courted Alfonzo, acquiring paintings for their homes and to donate to museums.

Alfonzo's growing prestige as an artist was bolstered by important public-art commissions. In *Ceremony of the Tropics*, a ceramic mural for a Miami public transport station, he references the neighborhood's markets, where Santeros buy the offerings for their gods. The mural depicts "the ritual of taking fruits and vegetables and turning them into objects of devotion and worship." In the lower part of the composition, a representation of Eleggua alludes to the deity's power of closing and opening doors as the guardian of transfers between physical and spiritual realms. In *Brainstorm*, at the Engineering and Computer Science Building on the campus of Florida International University, Alfonzo celebrates an inner world of "exploding ideas and thinking."

In 1989, Alfonzo began to produce his "black" paintings. Witnessing his body becoming frail and weak as he endured living with the AIDS virus, he recorded the transcendence of his own person from flesh into spirit. The exhibition at the Bass Museum revealed the artist's immense drive and gravity. This time, he acknowledged his looming mortality and the peaceful passage he was seeking. The late Giulio V. Blanc, a friend and avid critic, wrote:

> The "black paintings" are attempts to fathom, and thus conquer, existence at the end of the millennium. One has to return to the heroic paintings filled with myth and universality, that were the Abstract Expressionists' answers to the war, the Holocaust and the birth of the atomic age, to find comparable intentions and results in the art of the past fifty years.
>
> (Blanc)

Alfonzo's death at the age of forty of a cerebral hemorrhage meant that, despite his prodigious career, his potential as an artist was only partially fulfilled. In acknowledgement of his singular contribution, some of his paintings were included in the 1991 Biennial of American Art at New York's Whitney Museum, and the Miami Art Museum organized a major retrospective in 1997.

See also **Art, Cuban American; Painters;** *and* **Sculptors.**

BIBLIOGRAPHY

Alfonzo, Carlos. Conversations with César Trasobares on various dates.

Blanc, Giulio V. "Carlos Alfonzo's Black Paintings." In *Carlos Alfonzo: New Work*, catalog of the exhibition. Miami Beach, Fla.: Bass Museum of Art, 1990.

Carlos Alfonzo: Triumph of the Spirit: A Survey, 1975–1991. Catalog of the exhibition. Olga M. Viso, guest curator. Miami, Fla.: Miami Art Museum, 1997.

CÉSAR TRASOBARES

ALIANZA DOMINICANA. Alianza Dominicana, a comprehensive nonprofit organization founded in 1987 in New York City, offers a broad range of services. The Arts and Culture component teaches traditional arts from the Dominican Republic; Youth Development and Education offers job training to adolescents, drug counseling, after-school programming, and other initiatives; Child Welfare and Family Services offers child care and foster care; Economic Developments is home to the Triangle Project, a real estate project that developed Centro Cultural Afro-Quisqueya, an artistic and cultural institution in the heart of Washington Heights, the well-established Dominican enclave in Manhattan; Health Services includes programs for HIV-positive individuals and offers community-oriented health programs; and the Community Technology Projects hopes to show the connection between a community's economic growth and technology. This is just a sampling. Alianza not only addresses the issues of the residents of Washington Heights but the agency also deals with national and international crises. Community efforts included helping flood victims in Haiti and the Dominican Republic and aiding in relief efforts after September 11, 2001.

At the beginning of the twenty-first century, Dominicans were the fourth largest Latino and Latina group in the United States and the second-largest Latino and Latina group in New York State. Dominicans seeking political asylum from the regime of Rafael Trujillo, dictator of the Dominican Republic from 1930 to 1961, migrated to the United States in significant numbers. Dominican migration to the United States increased dramatically after the U.S. invasion of the Dominican Republic in 1965, and the number continued to grow throughout the 1970s and 1980s. In 2004, it was estimated that half a million Dominicans lived in New York City, and half of those were said to live in Washington Heights. Like many other Latino and Latina groups, Dominicans found their immigrant community plagued with social problems.

Alianza offers services to children, adolescents, and families in an effort to alleviate the burdens of poverty and break the cycle. Services are offered in eleven different sites in Manhattan and the Bronx. Alianza is one of the largest nonprofit organizations in the state, serving over seventeen thousand people a year.

Alianza is considered the definitive community development organization for Dominicans and Dominican Americans. It has also won many awards, including an Annie E. Casey Foundation Families Count National Honors Program Award of $500,000 in 2002, one of eight U.S. agencies to receive this award. The organization also won the Hispanic Federation of New York City Latino Agency of the Year Award; the Imagen Latino Award for aiding New York's Dominican community; and the Reliance Award for Excellence in Education for striving to improve New York City's public schools. Alianza was cited by former Vice President Al Gore for its role as an important community-based organization. Queen Noor of Jordan singled out Alianza for its START program that focused on preventing teen drug use. Moisés Pérez, the executive director of Alianza, has also won awards for his work with the agency, including the First Annual New York State Governor's Award for Hispanic-Americans of Distinction, the Columbia University Mailman School of Public Health Dean's Award for Distinguished Service, and the Points of Light Foundation President's Award.

Milagros Ricourt, in *Dominicans in New York City*, suggests that organizations such as Alianza Dominicana help the Dominican community to create a Dominican American identity. Alianza encourages Dominicans to invest in their lives by tackling their immediate problems rather than considering the United States their temporary home and remaining polarized from the politics and activities of New York City.

Alianza Dominicana was established to alleviate those immediate problems. Rafael Lantigua, Moisés Pérez, and a host of other young Dominican professionals were instrumental in its founding. Lantigua, who at the time was a doctor at Columbia-Presbyterian Medical Center in Washington Heights, and Pérez were troubled by the massive budget cuts in New York during the 1980s that adversely affected hospital employees and patients. Seeing how poorly these people were treated, they decided to start a nonprofit agency to tackle many of the issues facing residents of Washington Heights. At the time, few service agencies addressed the needs of the burgeoning Dominican community.

Initially, Lantigua and Pérez had difficulty obtaining the funds relegated to such community-oriented agencies by New York State and New York City. In 1989, they engaged in political activity and supported the successful mayoral candidate David Dinkins. Consequently, they secured lucrative city grants for Alianza. Funding for their programs was substantially cut in 1993 with the ascendancy of the Republican mayor Rudolph Guiliani. Undeterred, Alianza developed relationships with the new administration that allowed the nonprofit's continued growth.

Rafael Lantigua was a professor of clinical medicine at Columbia University and served as the director for the Columbia Center for the Active Life of Minority Elders, dedicated to studying minority aging. He was a board member of several Latino- and Latina-oriented nonprofit organizations, including the Latino Commission on AIDS, the Puerto Rican Legal Defense Fund, and the Puerto Rican/Hispanic Institute for the Elderly.

Moisés Pérez has been recognized for his service to Dominicans in New York City. He began his career as a community activist and educator when he earned his BA at Brooklyn College. He was a founding member of the Agenda for Children Tomorrow; Northern Manhattan Collaborates, a wide-ranging planning group that worked with the Harlem and Washington Heights communities; and the Hispanic Federation of New York City.

See also **Dominicans; Mutualista Organizations;** *and* **Washington Heights.**

BIBLIOGRAPHY

Alianza Dominicana, Inc. Web site www.alianzadom.org/aboutus.html

Rau, Jordan. "The Dominican Factor: Group Struggles with Political Growing Pains." Newsday.com, August 26, 2002. Available at mumford1.dyndns.org/cen2000/newspdf/Newsday082602.pdf

Ricourt, Milagros. *Dominicans in New York City: Power from the Margins.* New York: Routledge, 2002.

IVELISSE RODRIGUEZ

ALLENDE, ISABEL (b. 1942), writer. Born in Lima, Peru, to Chilean parents, Francisca Llona Barros and Tomas Allende, Isabel Allende is the most widely read Latin American woman writer. She has written over a dozen books, including novels, short fiction, a memoir, and stories for young adults, that have been translated into more than twenty-seven languages. Some have become best sellers in Europe, the United States, Latin America, and Australia, and two, *The House of the Spirits* and *Of Love and Shadows*, have been made into Hollywood films. The remarkable success of her literary career has earned Allende numerous awards and honors, including eight honorary degrees from American universities and induction in 2004 as a member of the prestigious American Academy of Arts and Letters. On July 7, 1988, Allende married the American attorney William Gordon, and the couple settled in San Rafael, California.

Novels and Nonfiction

Since the publication of her novel *The Infinite Plan* (1993) originally published in Madrid as *El plan infinito* (1991), which, like all her fiction, she wrote in Spanish, Allende has increasingly chosen the United States as the setting of her stories. The book tells of the harrowing journey of Gregory Reeves, a San Francisco lawyer, who is beset by the ghosts of an unsavory past that can only be appeased by the young man's ultimate search for love and acceptance among family and his native roots.

Allende had two children in her first marriage in 1962 to the Chilean engineer Miguel Frias. Paula was born in 1963, and Nicolas was born in 1966. Life dealt Allende a harsh emotional blow in December 1991, when her daughter became gravely ill and fell into a coma in Madrid while Allende launched the original Spanish edition of *The Infinite Plan*. Paula died on December 6, 1992, and her prolonged comatose condition is the core of Allende's memoir *Paula*, which was published in 1994 in Spanish, English, Dutch, and German editions. The book opens with these prefatory words: "These pages were written during the interminable hours spent in the corridors of a Madrid hospital and in the hotel room where I lived for several months, as well as beside her bed in our home in California during the summer and fall of 1992" (Allende). The book works as a tapestry into which are woven episodes of the writer's life with family members and the world of her literary imagination, and as it comes to a close with an account of her daughter's death, the California landscape provides the soothing setting for the foreseeable healing: "I watched the sky grow dark beyond the large windows. At that hour, the view from the hill where we live is extraordinary; the water of the Bay is like phosphorescent steel as the landscape turns to a fresco of shadows and lights" (Allende).

In 1997, Allende published a playful book entitled *Aphrodite*, in which she treads the territory of literary texts that engage the erotics of food, a project she undertook as a celebration of life after the years of sadness that followed Paula's untimely death. Her 1999 novel *Daughter of Fortune* became a *New York Times* best seller and a selection of Oprah's Book Club, ensuring its popularity with large audiences in the United States. The story is centered around the life and times of Eliza Sommers, a young woman raised by English traders in Valparaiso, Chile, who follows her lover to San Francisco during the gold rush of 1849. Joaquin Andieta, a young man of humble origins and a noble heart, has made the trek to California to secure the means necessary to lift his mother out of abject poverty. When Eliza realizes she was pregnant by Joaquin, she immediately resolves to travel to the unknown to find her beloved. Eliza is able to complete her personal odyssey with the help of her loyal companion Tao Chi'en. The reader comes into contact with the nineteenth-century colonial network that explains the presence in Chile of a Chinese man uprooted from his homeland by the English domination of China. The novel further shows Tao Chi'en's subsequent incorporation into a trade route created by the economic dynamism unleashed by the discovery of gold in California soon after the land was surrendered by Mexico to the United States. The novel draws on the history that linked Chileans to San Francisco, re-creating the lives, the hopes, and the struggles of Latin Americans, whose arrival at the site of the gold find preceded that of Anglos coming from the Northeast and the Midwest.

Portrait in Sepia (2000), a novel published a year after *Daughter of Fortune*, revisits the characters from the previous story, bringing the life of each to its peculiar conclusion against the backdrop of the political geography that in the nineteenth century linked Chile to England and the United States. Together, the novels invite the reader to consider the importance of South Americans as part of the Hispanic population living in the United States over 150 years ago. They show the writer invested in the task of utilizing to advantage the insights stemming from her acquaintance with the American experience, a familiarity she has developed during her years of residence in California. Her nonfiction book on Chile, *My Invented Country* (2003), written in the aftermath of the September 11, 2001, terrorist attacks against the World Trade Center in New York and the Pentagon in Washington, D.C., to a large extent narrates her life against the backdrop of Chilean history in a manner that seems to make it logical for her to have ended up in the United States, where she, with the love of her understanding husband Willie, has attained her fullest realization.

Allende's Place in Latino and Latina Literature

Because of the enormous appeal of her books among all sectors of the American reading public and also because of her dedication to creating stories set in the United States, Allende's name has begun to appear in several compilations and anthologies of Latino and Latina literature. In 1997, when only one of her U.S.–based texts (*The Infinite Plan*) had appeared, her work was covered in Frances Ann Day's reference book *Latina and Latino Voices in Literature for Children and Teenagers*, a text for middle schools and high schools in which Allende shares space comfortably with the likes of Julia Alvarez, Rudolfo Anaya, Gloria Anzaldúa, Judith Ortiz Cofer, and Pat Mora. Not everyone will agree with Day's decision to include Allende among "Latino/Latina" writers. As a classification, the more meticulous scholars tend to reserve the term for U.S. authors of Hispanic descent born in this country or those who immigrated while young enough to have been shaped by the experience of living as an ethnic minority in American society. This is clearly not the case with Allende, who was already a Latin American author of note when she fell in love with Willie and chose to settle in California. She had achieved an international reputation with her first novel *The House of the Spirits* (1982), followed by *Of Love and Shadows* (1984) and *Eva Luna* (1985), compelling fiction works that gave her a firm footing in contemporary Latin American literature.

Even the details of Allende's biography may be said to place her quite apart from the community of writers typically called Latinos and Latinas. Her father, first cousin of Salvador Allende, the man who in 1970 became president of Chile, was a Chilean diplomat serving in Peru when Isabel Allende was born in Lima. She lived there until the age of three, when her mother relocated with her children to Santiago, Chile. In 1953, her mother married another diplomat, Ramon Huidobro, and his posts to foreign shores caused the family to live in Bolivia, where young Isabel attended an American private school, and in Lebanon, where she studied in a British private school. Returning to Santiago, Chile, in 1958, Allende continued her secondary education. After she graduated she obtained employment as a secretary at the Santiago branch of the United Nation's Food and Agriculture Organization. Her marriage in 1962 was followed by extended periods of residence in Europe until 1966. She began collaborating with Chilean publications in 1967, especially as a humor columnist, and by 1970 she had joined the television industry, specializing in humor and interviews.

President Allende was overthrown by a military coup on September 11, 1973, and Isabel Allende's family stayed in Santiago until they no longer felt safe. In 1975, they moved to Caracas, Venezuela, where they lived for the next thirteen years. Isabel wrote for the Venezuelan national press until the great explosion of her literary career with the publication in 1982 of *The House of the Spirits* by a major press in Spain. But as the inclusion of Allende's name among Latino and Latina writers in anthologies and compilations continues, scholars will have to consider revisiting the classification of "Latinos and Latinas" to make space for atypical authors whose membership in the U.S. Hispanic population may result primarily from their own decision to belong and the ensuing consent of their readers.

See also **Literature** *and* **South Americans.**

BIBLIOGRAPHY
Allende, Isabel. *Paula*. New York: HarperCollins, 1995.
Boland, Roy C., ed. *Rebelling in the Garden: Isabel Allende, Cristina Peri Rossi, and Luisa Valenzuela*. Auckland: VOX, 1996.
Correas Zapata, Celia, ed. *Isabel Allende: Vida y espíritus*. Barcelona: Plaza and Janés, 1998.
Day, Frances Ann. *Latina and Latino Voices in Literature for Children and Teenagers*. Portsmouth, N.H.: Heinemann, 1997.
Isabel Allende. www.isabelallende.com

SILVIO TORRES-SAILLANT

ALMANZA, SUSANA (b. 1952), community activist. Susana Almanza is a founding member and executive director of People Organized in Defense of Earth and Her Resources (PODER), a grassroots environmental, economic, and social justice organization based in Austin, Texas. Almanza was born in East Austin, Texas. Raised in poverty, Almanza and her nine siblings experienced prejudice and school segregation. Neither of her parents was formally educated, and both spoke only Spanish. By age five, Almanza became the translator for her parents, assisting them at the grocery store and the ballot box. She observed how they were treated as "second-class citizens" and often did not translate the cruel words spoken to them.

Acutely aware of racism, educational inequities, and economic inequality, Almanza was driven to become a powerful grassroots organizer who challenges local government and transnational corporations on issues of environmental racism. Her fervor is matched only by her knowledge of the technical aspects of issues that she pursues. Her commitment is to the pursuit of justice, bringing passion and perseverance to her organizing efforts. Almanza, who describes herself as "an indigenous woman of the continent of America," is the mother of four and grandmother of four. Her son, Librado, follows in her footsteps as an organizer with PODER.

Almanza inherited her parents' love of Mother Earth and still carries on their practices of nourishing the soil to produce food as well as plants and flowers for healing. She maintains a personal altar and honors her spiritual connections to the universe. This commitment to Mother Earth also motivates her grassroots activity against the injustices that she sees against humanity and nature. During the 1960s and 1970s, Almanza participated in the Chicano and Chicana movement as a Brown Beret, tackling issues of police brutality, quality and equitable education, and health care as a right.

As executive director of PODER, Almanza is responsible for office administration, personnel management, resource development, program work, and fiscal activities including financial management, writing grants, and reporting to foundations. Almanza served on the City of Austin Environmental Board and is a former planning commissioner for the City of Austin. She currently sits on the Saltillo District Redevelopment Master Plan Community Advisory Group. On the national level, Almanza has served on numerous committees, including the Environmental Protection Agency's Title VI Implementation Advisory Committee.

Almanza has been cochair of the Southwest Network for Environmental and Economic Justice, a regional network of environmental- and economic-justice organizations. She was integral to the Network's high-tech campaign and land use–rights campaign. She is a founding member of the Texas Network for Environmental and

Economic Justice and the former coordinator of the Electronic Industry Good Neighbor Campaign, which is a campaign to bring together community, labor, and environmental organizations and to demand a genuinely democratic approach to high-tech development that begins with community and worker empowerment.

Almanza and her good friend Sylvia Herrera, who also grew up in East Austin, decided in May of 1991 that they would form an organization to battle the poisoning of their community. They wanted to address the social, cultural, economic, and environmental impacts of the toxic industries that plagued East Austin. In 1928, a City of Austin master plan zoned areas of Austin as "white residential" but directed "Mexicans" and "Negroes" into the area where "undesirable industry" was being zoned. From that time on, the Mexican American and African American communities of East Austin battled the health impacts and economic and social inequalities of heavy industry. Their successful efforts to close the fifty-two-acre petrochemical Tank Farm in East Austin began an intensive period of activism for Almanza and for Sylvia Herrera. Herrera, born March 4, 1951, was raised in circumstances similar to Almanza's. She was the first Mexicana from her neighborhood to receive a PhD, from the nearby University of Texas, Austin. She attributes her ability to finish her doctorate in heath education to her connection to PODER, which enabled her to focus on how her education was going to benefit her community. Despite Herrera's vivid memory of having her mouth taped shut when she was seven years old for speaking Spanish, her voice is strong and clear on issues of environmental justice.

In 2000, Almanza and Herrera received a $130,000 "Leadership for a Changing World" Ford Foundation award. The funds have been used to address pressing issues in the community. Through various contributions and fund-raisers, PODER purchased a small house on Garden Street in East Austin. The house bears a wrought iron screen door, designed and welded by Herrera's father. The house and other small houses like it are in contrast to the industrial infrastructure such as voltage power lines and metal towers that are laced throughout the area. The two women proudly operate their grassroots organization from this house, where they have successfully organized women in their community to confront the toxic contamination in their neighborhoods from fuel storage tanks, landfills, power plants, metal casting factories, and chemical storage facilities. They have also changed land-use designations and regulations for East Austin.

The Tank Farm victory earned PODER a 1993 Special Service Award from the Sierra Club. The organizing effort against the six oil companies—Exxon, Texaco, Mobile, Chevron, Coastal States Crude Gather Company, and Citgo Petroleum Corporation—drew national attention, with CNN and CBS news responding to the media campaign.

Consistent with the environmental-justice principle "we speak for ourselves," Almanza believed that the place to begin their organizing effort was with the voices of local residents who were affected by the toxic contamination.

A key to PODER's success is the strategy of going door to door to ascertain and document residents' health conditions, thus discovering patterns of health impacts. For example, the family who thought it was just their child who experienced frequent nose bleeds found out that other children in the area were experiencing the same thing. By providing training and structures for participation, Susana Almanza and the organizers of PODER mobilized the people of East Austin to confront local government and big corporations on their practices and policies that concentrated toxic industrial activity in Chicana and Chicano and African American neighborhoods.

Susana Almanza is a warrior woman who battles effectively for human rights and environmental, economic, and social justice.

See also Environmental Justice; Environmental Justice and Latinas; Environmental Justice Networks; People Organized in Defense of Earth and Her Resources, Austin; *and* Southwest Network for Environmental and Economic Justice.

TERESA CÓRDOVA

ALMARAZ, CARLOS (1941–1989), painter. In 1981, Carlos Almaraz, a major figure of the Chicano art movement and a founding member of the Los Angeles Chicano collective, Los Four, received a commission for a poster celebrating the Los Angeles bicentennial. This was the first recognition at such a level for the work of an artist who had, as a Chicano, overtly protested the marginalization of a sociocultural segment of the community through a visual language originating in large measure from a non-Western cultural heritage. Three years later, he received a commission for a poster celebrating the 1984 Los Angeles Olympic Games and was the subject of a retrospective exhibition at the Los Angeles Municipal Gallery. This was followed by an invitation in 1987 to be interviewed for the Archives of American Art Oral History Project for the Smithsonian Institution. Almaraz thus became the first Latino painter to be selected for the Smithsonian Oral History Project. In 1987 and 1989, he was included in two exhibitions: Hispanic Art in the United States (1987) and the European exhibition Le Démon des Anges (1989). These commissions and exhibitions, as well as the interview, demonstrate that Chicano and Chicana artists were moving into the mainstream of contemporary American art by the late 1980s.

Carlos Almaraz was born October 5, 1941, in Mexico City. When he was six months old, his parents moved to Chicago, Illinois. The family traveled frequently to Mexico.

GROWING CITY. Screenprint by Carlos Almaraz, 1988. (Courtesy of Elsa Flores Almaraz)

As a consequence, Almaraz was both bilingual and bicultural. In 1949 the family moved to Los Angeles and initially lived on the west side before establishing themselves in East Los Angeles.

After graduating from Garfield High School, Almaraz attended Otis Art Institute on scholarship. There he developed a monochromatic, nonrepresentational form of abstract expressionism. In the sixties he went with Frank Romero to New York, where in response to the tumultuous changes in styles and concepts in the art world, combined with the difficulty of trying to make art and earn a living, he fell into depression. In 1969, after a brief visit to Europe, Almaraz returned to Los Angeles, still under medication and drinking heavily. By 1971 he began to develop a signature grid-like structure in his work, a style which in this early period experimented with graffiti as well as sacred and profane images, including crosses, bleeding hearts, and phallic references.

In 1971 Almaraz suffered a near-fatal attack of pancreatitis, and his younger brother died of a drug overdose.

He underwent a kind of epiphany. Pondering his brother's death and his own survival, he began volunteering for the community arts program at Plaza de la Raza. A new activism was emerging as a result of the grape boycotts, the 1968 Chicano Moratorium, and the struggle for civil rights. The Chicano mural renaissance was just beginning, especially in the housing projects of East Los Angeles. Gilbert "Magú" Luján, a prominent activist-artist whom Almaraz met in 1972, engaged him in the movement, and Almaraz began painting murals as early as 1973. That year he also met Luis Valdez and, through him, César Chávez; both becoming his friends. He painted a mural for the United Farm Workers (UFW) headquarters in Keene, California, and a banner for the UFW marches.

Activism resolved Almaraz's depression, which he realized lay rooted in a search for his identity. Though he had long called himself "Charles," he now called himself "Carlos," his birth name. His commitment to social and public art spanned the years from 1973 to 1979. He cofounded the Public Art Center in Highland Park. He also worked on the Citywide Mural Projects and with *Chismearte* magazine and the Concilio de Arte Popular. He turned away from easel painting and the studio. His ideological shift led to trips to China and Cuba in the mid-1970s.

In February 1974, Los Four, an artists collective that consisted of Almaraz, Frank Romero, Beto de la Rocha, and Luján, became the first Chicano artists to have an exhibition in the Los Angeles County Museum of Art. All four of these artists were academically trained and based in Los Angeles. The exhibition reveled in graffiti, lowriders, and bleeding hearts. Initiated by Luján, it also marked the naming of the collective itself. The aesthetics of the collective and of the Chicano/a movement itself are interrelated. The sociopolitical focus of the movement informed and motivated their art making. They aspired to use art to effect ideological and practical changes in the Chicano and Chicana community.

In 1979 Almaraz showed a breakthrough series of pastels of car crashes and landscapes of Echo Park, near downtown Los Angeles. Through this dichotomy of images—violence and serenity—his work reached new levels of expression, and he returned to easel painting. A key work from this period is the four-panel oil on linen *Echo Park* (1979), a simultaneous homage to the French impressionist painter Claude Monet and to urban Los Angeles. He began showing in galleries and was represented, until his death, by the Jan Turner Gallery in West Hollywood.

Almaraz's urban landscapes combine images of eroticism, violence, and death beneath a shimmering palette of rich greens, blues, and reds, already evident in his early pastels. His grids became ever more dynamic with soaring skyscrapers and a constant twilight sky of shimmering blues, stars, and careening projectiles. Couples run fleeing from or after each other among empty chairs. Chaos overcomes order. In his last exhibition, in March 1989, the paintings are outlined in black. He was already aware that he was HIV-positive. Carlos Almaraz died of AIDS on December 11, 1989. *California Dreamscape* (1990), a mural produced in collaboration with his wife, Elsa Flores, was unveiled posthumously at the Ronald Reagan State Office building, Los Angeles.

See also Art, Chicano; CARA Exhibition; Chávez, César; Chicanos and Chicanas; Luján, Gilbert Sánchez; Mexican-Origin People in the United States; Painters; *and* United Farm Workers.

BIBLIOGRAPHY

Almaraz, Carlos. *Carlos Almaraz: A Survey of Works on Paper.* Los Angeles: Jan Turner Gallery, 1990.

Beardsley, John, and Jane Livingston. *Hispanic Art in the United States: Thirty Contemporary Painters and Sculptors.* New York: Abbeville, 1987.

Griswold del Castillo, Richard, Teresa McKenna, and Yvonne Yarbro-Bejerano, eds. *Chicano Art: Resistance and Affirmation, 1965–1985.* Los Angeles: Wight Art Gallery, University of California, Los Angeles, 1991.

Marin, Cheech. *Chicano Visions: American Painters on the Verge.* Boston: Bullfinch, 2002.

MARGARITA NIETO

ALTARES. The tradition of Mexican American *altares* (home altars) began in pre-Columbian Mesoamerica, when a wide array of religious beliefs and practices existed. During this time, places of holy and ceremonial significance were marked by small stone structures, which often took the form of altars and shrines. With the coming of Catholicism in the sixteenth century, many of these indigenous sites of worship were either eradicated or driven into the home. The *altarcito de casa* (personal home altar) developed as a direct response to these events, and because of the lack of Catholic priests the altars became a necessary focal point for formal and informal prayer.

Traditional Altars

Blending European and indigenous American systems of belief, home altars continue to fulfill personal, familial, and spiritual needs. Often arranged in living rooms, bedrooms, or on dressers, especially in the American Southwest, they are traditionally maintained by women and form continuities with maternal legacies that are passed on through the family line. Sacred statues and pictures that have been handed down, bric-a-brac, memorabilia, and other personal and decorative elements are all incorporated into the altar's eclectic design. While seemingly random in their selection, the particular emplacement of these objects is nonetheless deliberate and symbolic. When ornately framed photographs of relatives are placed around a central devotional icon, their location not only establishes family histories but also creates a spiritual interconnectedness between deceased family members and the holy or divine. The constant addition of other items often multiplies or embellishes this significance, suggesting further historic connections between personal and spiritual lives.

Surrounding the images or statues of the central deity, the other objects that make up the altar are laid out in an artistic and fairly symmetrical way. The assembled *santos* (saints) are often engulfed with flowers, especially roses, and are then surrounded by a number of objects associated with ritual and religious rites. These include candles, incense burners, rosaries, crucifixes, and *milagros* (miracle cure amulets). Other frequently used elements in the altar-making tradition include formal constructions such as *nichos* (niches) and *retablos* (boxlike containers), which are used to highlight the significance of special icons and saints.

An Ofrenda for Dolores del Rio. Mixed media altar installation, including plywood, mirrors, fabric, framed items, and decorative element in honor of the actress Dolores del Rio by Amalia Mesa-Bains, 1984/1990. (American Art Museum, Smithsonian Institution)

Seasonal shrines such as the *nacimiento* as well as those made in order to honor the dead are other significant forms of traditional altar making. *Nacimientos* are usually constructed to celebrate Christmas and often have a replica manger or nativity scene consisting of the holy couple and the infant Jesus situated centrally in the middle ground. Subsidiary scenes consist of miniaturized landscapes with animals and carved wooden or clay figures of the shepherds and magi. The colors used in the nacimiento are generally of sonorous tones.

Perhaps the most popularly known of all Mexican American altars, the *día de los muertos* (day of the dead)

altar, appears on November 1 and 2. This is the time when families celebrate and remember the lives of deceased relatives and friends. Along with personal belongings of the dead, the altar is decorated with objects that are specific to this time. Particular flowers are used, especially the *cempasúchil* (marigold), which is also known as the *flor de muerto* (flower of the dead). Specific kinds of food also serve to distinguish día de los muertos altars from other shrines. Fruits and other consumable items such as *pan de muerto* (bread of the dead) and *calaveras* (sugar skeletons and skulls) collectively form an *ofrenda* (offering) that is meant to tempt the deceased into visiting their surviving relatives and friends. Traditionally, día de los muertos celebrations were private, but they have recently become more public, consisting of community processions to the *camposanto* (cemetery), which are then followed by personal vigils at the graveside. Día de los muertos has a long history of ceremony and ritual that evokes many familial relationships and cultural and spiritual meanings dating back to pre-Columbian times.

Aesthetic and Political Altars

The political and aesthetic significance of the altar-making tradition is often made more explicit in shrine installations that are located outside the home. These kinds of shrines frequently mark apparition sites, or the places where religious visions have occurred. They commonly appear in the country and on roadsides. Most often, however, shrines are constructed in front or back yards, in grottoes, and on porches. Their decoration is distinguished by its *rasquache* aesthetic, which is an exaggerated mode of artistic practice that reflects the owner's particular economic and sociocultural class. In the front-yard shrine or *capilla* (little chapel), replicas of traditional icons are often juxtaposed with brightly colored objects from mass culture such as Christmas lights, plastic figurines, coffee cans, and reconstituted statuary. The combination of these objects often evokes an ironic and witty interplay between the provocative contrasts made in high and low, secular and religious cultures, and between textures and tone.

A politicized aesthetic is also a significant factor in the growing tradition of altar making within Chicana artistic practice. Structurally these altars usually consist of a table and other flat surfaces such as overturned boxes or crates, which are placed in graduated tiers against a wall or a corner of a room. The wall is used to display holy images and *alabanzas* (prayer sheets), or flowers made from *papel picado* (colorful tissue paper), and can be covered in various fabrics ranging from plastic and paper to linen and silk. Often richly embroidered by hand, the cloths sometimes form decorative connections to crocheted doilies arranged around the altar, or are used to draw attention to special objects or favored images located within the shrine. With *An Ofrenda for Dolores del Río* (1984/1990) the nationally renowned Chicana artist Amalia Mesa Bains uses canopies made from various luxury fabrics, including lace and satin, to dynamically frame a central photographic image of the glamorous and successful Mexican film star of the altar's title. Other Chicana artists, such as María Almeida Natividad and Patssi Valdez, use fabrics for similar effects, though usually to honor the most central deity of Mexican Catholicism and the patron saint of all indigenous peoples in the Americas, La Virgen de Guadalupe (the Virgin of Guadalupe).

See also Día de los Muertos; Festivals; Piñatas and Paper Arts; Saints and Border Saints; *and* Virgen de Guadalupe.

BIBLIOGRAPHY

Gaspar de Alba, Alicia. *Chicano Art: Inside/Outside The Master's House: Cultural Politics and The CARA Exhibition.* Austin: University of Texas Press, 1998.

Griswold del Castillo, Richard, Teresa McKenna, and Yvonne Yarbro-Bejarano, eds. *Chicano Art: Resistance and Affirmation, 1965–1985.* Los Angeles: Wight Art Gallery, University of California, 1991.

Gutiérrez, Ramón A., ed. *Home Altars of Mexico.* Albuquerque: University of New Mexico Press, 1997.

Turner, Kay. *Beautiful Necessity: The Art and Meaning of Women's Altars.* New York: Thames and Hudson, 1999.

ELIZABETH JACOBS

ALURISTA (b. 1947), Chicano author. Alberto Baltazar Urista, who combines his first and last names to form the nom de plume Alurista, has contributed greatly to Chicano literature, as well as to the Chicano movement in general. He stood out as a pivotal poet, cultural leader, thinker, teacher, and social activist in his community's efforts at recovery and self-affirmation during the mid-1960s. In 1968, spurred by a spirit of linguistic innovation and political activism, Alurista embraced poetry in the code-switching mode as a legitimate form of expression. Although not the first to write poetry that mixed Spanish and English, he was the first to promote its acceptance in American literary circles. He encouraged bilingual and bicultural Chicanos to see their dual backgrounds as a source of great cultural synthesis. Alurista not only advocated inclusion, but also explored practical ways of incorporating a Chicano worldview into the political contexts of civil rights, ethnic pride, and social mobilization. He sought to formulate a Chicano nationhood connected to Aztlán, the mythic homeland of the Aztecs. This link provided a springboard to explain the Chicano past within a cultural nationalist framework, thus creating a foundation for an extensive Native American ideology based on a pre-Columbian system of values that could somehow merge with urban concerns. Of all the Chicano movement's leaders in the 1960s, Alurista demonstrated the greatest breadth and versatility by developing a social agenda, an artistic plan, a cultural design, and, most important, a new language.

Early Life and Influences

Born in Mexico City on August 8, 1947, Alurista studied for a short time in an all-boys Jesuit seminary where he stood out among his peers, displaying an early command of words, and earning small fees by writing poems and drafting love letters for his classmates. He migrated to San Diego, California, when he was thirteen, and around 1966 he began to attempt what he called "serious poetry"

ALURISTA. (© Nic Paget-Clarke)

with the intention of publishing. He briefly attended Chapman College near Los Angeles before transferring to San Diego State University, where he received his psychology degree in 1970. Here he blossomed with a new awareness of his cultural self and a desire to make educational institutions responsive to Chicanos. Around 1967 he came across an article in a popular magazine—either *Life* or *Look*—that introduced him to Aztec culture. Thus he discovered Aztlán as a viable concept for cultural nationalism, became inspired by Aztec civilization, and gained an appreciation for the expressive potential of mixing Spanish and English.

His social and artistic purpose crystallized into a vision that construed Chicanos as direct heirs of ancient Mexico. By 1968 Alurista was already a spokesman for Chicano civil rights in San Diego, and his reputation skyrocketed in 1969 when he wrote the manifesto "El Plan Espiritual de Aztlán" (The Spiritual Plan of Aztlán) for the First National Chicano Youth Liberation Conference in Denver, Colorado. This document defined "La Causa" (The Cause), including the ideological framework and political program of the Chicano movement, which emphasized nationalism, pride, liberation, and self-determination. Alurista revolutionized Chicano writing when he submitted unconventional and daring poetry to the vanguard Berkeley journal *El Grito*. Blending Spanish and English naturally with an artistic flair, he invoked a pre-Columbian background that many Chicanos had repressed. He became an overnight sensation for young Chicanos by validating their language and heritage. He incited a neo-indigenist movement that freely weaved barrio argot with standard English, popular Spanish with black English, and various slangs with highbrow poetic utterance. Alurista became a guru in Chicano poetics, leaving an indelible imprint on much Chicano writing of the late 1960s and early 1970s.

Overview of Works

Alurista has written numerous books in various genres, including poetry, drama, criticism, and children's literature, often breaking new ground with themes about Chicanos' and Chicanas' place in American society. Generally regarded as the poet laureate of Chicano letters, he led a literary renaissance by serving as an exemplary practitioner and theorist of a renewed sociocultural mission in ethnic politics. He can be viewed as the lightning rod of the literary movement at a time when a messianic spirit prevailed among Chicanos. Deeply motivated to accomplish concrete community-building, he dared to test new techniques as well as push for a reconceptualized notion of minorities.

Alurista's poetic works include *Floricanto en Aztlán* (1971), *Nationchild Plumaroja* (1972), *Cantares arrullos* (1975), *Timespace Huracán* (1976), *A'nque* (1979), *Spik in Glyph?* (1981), *Return: Poems Collected and New* (1982), *Et tú ... Raza?* (1995), and *Z Eros* (1995). He has also published a play, *Dawn* (1974), a novel, *As Our Barrio Turns... Who the Yoke B On?* (2000), the coedited poetry collections *El ombligo de Aztlán: An Anthology of Chicano Student Poetry* (1972) and *Festival de Flor y Canto: An Anthology of Chicano Literature* (1976), and a short-story anthology, *Southwest Tales: A Contemporary Collection* (1986). He has also edited a nine-volume series of children's books collectively titled *Colección Tula y Tonán: Textos generativos* (1973). In addition to his creative and editorial work, he also helped found a variety of community and intellectual enterprises, including an artist's group called Toltecas en Aztlán in San Diego, the Chicano Studies Program as well as a Chicano Studies Center at San Diego State University, the Flor y Canto literary festivals, and a literary journal called *Maize* (1980).

Alurista's first landmark work, *Floricanto en Aztlán* (1971), consisting of his first one hundred poems, made an immediate impact by establishing a bilingual poetics while inscribing the symbol of "Aztlán" in a Chicano text for the first time. The work contains many frequently anthologized poems that inspired a whole new generation of aspiring poets. Fundamentally, the book is a result of a revelation from Alurista's cultural past, which he so aptly suggests in the poem "me habló en el sueño" (it spoke to me in a dream). By referring to the bird *tenoch*, he brings to mind the Aztec capital Tenochtitlán and with it a neo-indigenist perspective.

Alurista subsequently took various directions in his writings, experimenting with various forms and genres, creating neologisms along the way. He continued his neo-indigenous slant in *Nationchild Plumaroja* (1972) by professing a higher level of cultural nationalism. More contemplative than his first collection, the second work delivers a cosmic message, going beyond institutionalized religions and Western philosophies. As Francisco A. Lomelí and Donaldo Urioste have observed: "That explains the metaphor-filled expression because Alurista thinks in images and symbolism powered by a drum-like rhythm" (p. 18). Clearly, the poet is appealing to Chicanos to concentrate on their rich pre-Columbian background while he also pays close attention to the needs of the barrios: "let the barrio/ be a barrio, barrio, barrio, / barrio and not blood sweating colonia" (poem #11). *Cantares arrullos* (1975) is a chapbook of high lyrical poems about more personal sentiments, whereas *Timespace Huracán* (1976) marks a return to myth-building and Mexican values while continuing in the lyrical vein. Here, however, Alurista underscores an indigenous sensibility in preparation for a new age, using internal rhyme and alliteration to give his writing movement and dynamism. Most of his subsequent works reflect a fundamental shift toward lyricism by focusing more on form and linguistic economy than on a specific social agenda. Ideology still figures centrally, but a more global approach becomes prominent. *A'nque, Spik in Glyph?, Et tú . . . Raza?*, and *Z Eros* are short collections fueled by cleverness, virtuosity, and pyrotechnics. Alurista often breaks language down to its essence, a single letter or syllable for example, to maximize its meaning. The titles of these works show a writer enveloped in double or triple puns, double entendres, and a conflation of modalities, thereby suggesting a multiplicity of meanings and messages. For example, *Spik in Glyph?* offers a variety of connotations: "spik" alludes either to "spic," a derogatory term for Latinas and Latinos, or to "speak." When the double entendre is combined with "in," the statement extends to either "spik-ing" or "speaking." Combining either possibility with "glyph," denoting a symbolic figure or character carved in relief, creates a poetic statement about the nature of language and communication as forms that automatically imply multiple dimensions, nuances, and signification. By putting a question mark at the end of title, he further problematizes what he is proposing, consequently expanding the possibilities that much more.

These last works contain Alurista's poetic meditations, through which he experiments with melodies, accents, echoes, and alliteration. In *A'nque*, a popular pronunciation of *"aunque"* (although), he includes songs, chants, and short narratives, with prose and verse mixing freely, oftentimes enhanced by onomatopoeia and musicality: "swoosh, swoosh, swoosh, clinkclinkclink . . ." (p. 54) and "too way out, two güey [an 'ox,' rhyming with 'way'] out en la com pañía [com pany] del *mayor* [oldest] to b sellin his color tv too caro [expensive], to carol?" (p. 57). He also includes such modified sayings as "cada loco con su dogma" (everyone with their dogma, which plays on the Spanish saying "every one is entitled to their own view"). In *Z Eros*, Alurista continues his wordplay with shifting signifiers and clever abbreviations: "u b u as i b i and we b we/ u b history u, i, we make/ b herstory u, i, we bake" (p. 9).

Although falling into distinct genres, his play *Dawn* (1974) and his only novel, *As Our Barrio Turns … Who the Yoke B On?*, both express many of Alurista's central concerns: The former personifies modern "gods" in Pepsicóatl and Cocacóatl, a spoof on how corporations appropriate real gods such as the Aztec Quetzalcóatl who represented the arts and regeneration. In the latter work, really an antinovel, the author presents a veiled autobiography about his budding activism in San Diego (called San Dedo or "Saint Finger") in the late 1960s and early 1970s, providing an insider's view of various factors and personalities crucial to the movement. Here Alurista takes much poetic license, employing verse or prose depending on which style fits the mood, or vice versa. Besides presenting an extended version of his worldview, he also produces a modern codex, a manuscript that requires deciphering much like a Maya text.

Legacy

Alurista has had a long and creative career as a poet, community organizer, professor, social activist, and artist. He inspired generations with his effective code-switching and bilingual compositions, but his pro-indigenous philosophy has been central in influencing a new way of looking at the world. His rediscovery of Aztlán helped create a symbolic nation, which in turn helped Chicanos establish a cultural identity and carve out a place in American society during the tumultuous 1960s. And most important, he achieved a new acceptance and credibility for Chicano poets.

See also Chicanos and Chicanas; Literature; Mexican-Origin People in the United States; *and* Plan de Aztlán.

BIBLIOGRAPHY

PRIMARY WORKS

As Our Barrio Turns . . . Who the Yoke B On? San Diego, Calif.: Calaca Press, 2000.

A'unque. San Diego, Calif.: Maize, 1979.

Cantares arrullos. Binghamton, N.Y.: Bilingual Press, 1975.

Colección Tula y Tonán: Textos generativos. San Diego, Calif. : Toltecas de Aztlan Publications, 1973.

Dawn. El Grito 7 (June–August 1974): 55–84.

Et tú . . . Raza? Tempe, Ariz.: Bilingual Press/Editorial Bilingüe, 1994.

Floricanto en Aztlán. Los Angeles: University of California, Center for Chicano Studies, 1971.

Nationchild Plumaroja. San Diego, Calif.: Toltecas de Aztlán Publications, 1972.

Return: Poems Collected and New. Ipsilanti, Mich.: Bilingual Press/ Editorial Bilingüe, 1982.

Spik in Glyph? Houston, Tex.: Arte Público, 1981.

Timespace Huracán. Albuquerque, N.Mex.: Pajarito Publications, 1976.

Zeros. Tempe, Ariz.: Bilingual Press/Editorial Bilingüe, 1995.

SECONDARY WORKS

Bruce-Novoa, Juan. *Chicano Authors: Inquiry by Interview.* Austin: University of Texas Press, 1980.

Candelaria, Cordelia. *Chicano Poetry: A Critical Introduction.* Westport, Conn.: Greenwood Press, 1986.

Corti, Erminio. *Da Aztlán all'Amerindia: Multiculturalismo e difesa dell'identità chicana nella poesia di Alurista.* Viareggio, Italy: Baroni Editore, 1999.

Ginsberg, Judith. "Alurista (Alberto Baltazar Urista)." In *Dictionary of Literary Biography; Chicano Writers; First Series,* edited by Francisco A. Lomelí and Carl S. Shirley, 16–23. Detroit: Gale Research, 1989.

Grandjeat, Yves-Charles. *Aztlán: Terre volée, terre promise: Les pérégrinations du peuple chicano.* Paris: Presses de l'Ecole Normale Supérieure, 1989.

Keller, Gary D. "Alurista, Poeta-Antropólogo, and the Recuperation of the Chicano Identity." In *Return: Poems Collected and New,* by Alurista, xi–xlix. Ypsilanti, Mich.: Bilingual Press/Editorial Bilingüe, 1982.

Lomelí, Francisco A., and Donaldo W. Urioste. *Chicano Perspectives in Literature: A Critical and Annotated Bibliography.* Albuquerque, N. Mex.: Pajarito Publications, 1976.

Rojas, Guillermo. "Alurista." In *Chicano Literature: A Reference Guide,* edited by Julio A. Martínez and Francisco A. Lomelí, 19–34. Westport, Conn.: Greenwood Press, 1985.

FRANCISCO A. LOMELÍ

ALVAREZ, JULIA (b. 1950), Dominican American author. Born in New York on March 27, 1950, Julia Alvarez spent her early childhood in the Dominican Republic. She moved to the United States with her parents and three sisters ten years later when her father had to seek refuge from the ruthless persecutions of the Trujillo regime, which accused him of conspiracy. Alvarez received most of her primary education in boarding schools. She began her higher education at Connecticut College in 1967 and transferred two years later to Middlebury College, where she received her bachelor's degree in English in 1971. In 1975, Alvarez received her MFA. in creative writing from Syracuse University.

Alvarez has since held teaching positions at numerous colleges and universities throughout the country, including the Phillips Andover Academy in Massachusetts (1979–1981), the University of Vermont (1981–1983), and the University of Illinois (1985–1988). In 1984, she was the Jenny McKean Moore Visiting Writer at George Washington University. In 1988, she took a full-time position as professor of English at her alma mater, Middlebury College, a position she held until 1995 when she resigned to devote herself exclusively to writing. Alvarez still teaches occasional courses and workshops at Middlebury, where she is now a writer-in-residence.

Julia Alvarez is the author of four novels, three collections of poetry, one collection of essays, one children's book, two young adult novels, and one cookbook, in addition to articles and essays published in journals, newspapers, and other publications. She is also the recipient of numerous awards, fellowships, and other forms of recognition for her literary work. Her debut novel, *How the García Girls Lost Their Accents* (Algonquin, 1991), won the 1991 PEN Oakland/Josephine Miles Award and in 1992 was named a "Notable Book" by the American Library Association. The novel tells the story of a Dominican family (parents and four daughters) fleeing the Trujillo dictatorship in 1960. Belonging to a well-to-do Dominican family, the García girls have a difficult time adjusting to a country where they are considered outsiders and no longer the wealthy *García de la Torre.* Throughout the novel, the notion of home is riddled with ambivalent feelings of loss and nostalgia for the familiar sanctuary of a home country that is at the same time perceived as a place of punishment and oppression. A bestseller, *How the García Girls Lost Their Accents* sheds light on issues integral to the process of immigration: cultural adjustment, separation from family, changing perceptions of the home culture, and the negotiation of traditional values concerning the role of women, as well as the definition of an identity that can balance both cultures.

Alvarez's second novel, *In the Time of the Butterflies* (Algonquin, 1994), was also named a "Notable Book" by the American Library Association. It was nominated as a finalist for the 1995 National Book Critics Circle Award in fiction, selected as a Book of the Month Club choice, and chosen as one of the Best Books for Young Adults by the Young Adult Library Services Association and the American

JULIA ALVAREZ. (©Bill Eichner, reprinted by permission of Susan Bergholz Literary Services, New York. All rights reserved.)

Library Association. *In the Time of the Butterflies* is the fictionalized account of the lives of the Mirabal sisters, Dominican heroines who fought against the Trujillo regime. Their assassination on November 25, 1960, a mere three months after Alvarez's own family escaped, was a watershed moment in Dominican history. The dominant themes of this novel are the cruel and oppressive nature of Trujillo's rule, its impact on the behavior of the population as people became fearful and subservient, and finally the revolutionary ideas in vogue during those days, notably after the success of the Cuban Revolution. The novel also explores the role of the Catholic Church in supporting the dictatorship, and it portrays the characters' search for answers to political and social injustice while taking an unflinching look at the machismo of male characters who echo the oppressive values of the dictatorial regime.

The novel *¡Yo!* (Algonquin, 1997), a sequel to *How the García Girls Lost Their Accents*, further examines the life and cultural adaptation of its main character, Yolanda García. This time the novel is told from the perspective of the relatives, friends, and acquaintances who were only secondary players in the previous novel. The theme of identity is central to the structure of this novel, as illustrated by the title. The Spanish word for "I," "Yo" is also the short form of Yolanda—Alvarez's alter ego. *¡Yo!*'s structure is built upon the wide range of perspectives of its characters, who take Yolanda and her impact on their lives as *their* subject and use the opportunity to tell *their* version of events. Experimental in form, the novel maintains its cohesiveness and progression through multiple narratives centered on Yolanda García. The themes of the novel, which invoke Alvarez's earlier works, include poverty and class difference, cultural adaptation and displacement, and finally machismo and the role of Catholicism in supporting patriarchy.

Alvarez's novel *In the Name of Salomé* (Algonquin, 2000) is a fictionalized account of the lives of two exceptional Dominican women: poet laureate Salomé Ureña de Henríquez and her daughter Camila Henríquez Ureña. A historical novel, *In the Name of Salomé* is also a deep examination of identity, exploring the intimate struggles of the two women to affirm themselves in different ways. Camila, a professor at Vassar College, decides upon her retirement to join the ranks of Fidel Castro in the literacy campaign of the Cuban Revolution, and she devotes herself to the life of an educator. In doing so, she follows the path of her mother, a National Poet in the Dominican Republic who also established herself as the first female educator to devote herself actively to the education of other women, putting into practice the ideas of positivist thinker and educator Eugenio María de Hostos. *In the Name of Salomé* not only provides a richly textured overview of the historical contexts that surrounded these women, it also inspires those seeking modern-day female role models.

In this novel as in *¡Yo!*, Alvarez continues her experimentation with form, intertwining characters with the vagaries of time. The stories of Salomé and Camila are recounted in alternating chapters, with Salomé's story progressing chronologically from childhood to death and Camila's story moving backwards from her retirement as a professor to her mother's death, which occurred during Camila's early childhood.

As with *How the García Girls Lost Their Accents* and *¡Yo!*, Alvarez's poetry collections—*Homecoming* (Grove Press, 1984), *The Other Side/El otro lado* (Dutton, 1995), and *Homecoming: New and Collected Poems* (Plume, 1996)—deal with the loss of the home culture and adaptation to the new unfamiliar world. As in the novels, themes of gender, class, and race recur in Alvarez's poetry. *The Other Side/El otro lado*, especially the title series, examines the narrator's return to the Dominican Republic.

It portrays the tribulations of a Dominican American poet filled with homesickness, confusion, emptiness, and need for meaning as she struggles to overcome writer's block. Widely praised in literary circles, Alvarez's poetry has been included in the exhibition "The Hand of the Poet," which displayed "original manuscripts by 100 masters" at the New York Public Library.

Other books by Julia Alvarez include *Something to Declare* (Algonquin, 1998), a collection of essays on writing and the immigrant experience; *A Cafecito Story* (Chelsea Green, 2001), a tale about coffee growing and its implications for learning how to live in the natural world; *The Secret Footprints* (Knopf, 2002), a children's book based on the Taino mythical figure the Ciguapa, a beautiful creature that has backwards-facing feet and that enchants humans; *How Tía Lola Came to Stay* (Random House, 2002), a young adult novel that tells how second-generation immigrants can bond with relatives from the homeland; and *Before We Were Free* (Knopf, 2002), a young adult novel about a Dominican girl growing up under Trujillo's dictatorship in the 1960s. With some of her books regularly assigned to students in high schools and colleges throughout the country, Alvarez enjoys one of the most prestigious literary careers among Latina and Latino authors writing today.

See also **Dominican Writers in the United States** *and* **Literature.**

BIBLIOGRAPHY

Jacques, Ben. "Julia Alvarez: Real Flights of Imagination." *Américas* 53, no. 1 (January–February 2001): 23–29.

Luis, William. *Dance between Two Cultures: Latino-Caribbean Literature Written in the United States.* Nashville, Tenn.: Vanderbilt University Press, 1997.

Sirias, Silvio. *Julia Alvarez: A Critical Companion.* Westport, Conn.: Greenwood Press, 2001.

Torres-Saillant, Silvio, and Ramona Hernández. *The Dominican Americans.* Westport, Conn.: Greenwood Press, 1998.

SOPHIE MARÍÑEZ

AMERICAN G.I. FORUM. The American G.I. Forum was founded by Dr. Hector P. García in Corpus Christi, Texas, in March 1948, to serve Mexican American veterans returning from World War II. Before the war, these veterans and their families throughout the southwestern and midwestern United States had experienced severe social, political, and economic repression in regional law and custom. Such constraints prohibited Mexican Americans, much like former slaves of African American descent in the American South, from participating in fundamental civic processes, including voting and serving on juries. They also severely precluded Mexican Americans in many locations from accessing basic educational programs, dining establishments, and public health and recreational facilities.

Origins

Upon returning from overseas campaigns against foreign systems of racist totalitarianism, Mexican American soldiers, many of them Congressional Medal of Honor recipients and otherwise decorated combatants, were unwilling to further accept discriminatory conditions in America. The American G.I. Forum was accordingly established to advance postwar Mexican American rights and opportunities. Originally, the Forum was envisioned as a regional organization that would address the particular needs of Mexican American veterans in South Texas. Shortly after the Forum's creation, however, the family of a Mexican American killed in the Philippines at the war's conclusion was refused burial services by a white-owned South Texas funeral home. Hector García and other Forum leaders organized multistate protest efforts that resulted in an intervention by newly elected U.S. Senator Lyndon B. Johnson to have the felled soldier buried with honors at Arlington National Cemetery in Washington, D.C. The episode attracted national media attention with major reports appearing in the *New York Times* and in Walter Winchell's nationally syndicated column.

The Forum's local victory led to other major gains for Mexican American ex-servicemen and their families, related to veterans' benefits and health care access throughout South Texas. These gains, in turn, inspired interest among Mexican American veterans throughout the United States to organize American G.I. Forum chapters in their own communities and states. By 1958, the Forum had become a national membership organization, expanding to thirteen states and over 100,000 members; by 1977, it was active in over thirty states and boasted a national membership exceeding 150,000 individuals.

The Forum's activities were especially significant and far-reaching during the late 1940s through the mid-1960s. These were especially difficult times for civil rights groups in America because of the fervent anticommunist and racist sentiments of the era, and the efforts of political figures such as then U.S. senator Joseph P. McCarthy to quell more progressive voices and causes. The Forum, however, was uniquely positioned to successfully challenge accusations that its members were "communists" or otherwise "un-American," owing to the impressive record of Hispanic soldiers in recent overseas combat on America's behalf. This record of distinguished service gave the Forum the latitude to advocate that other social justice organizations lacked at the time.

During these years, therefore, often in partnership with the League of United Latin American Citizens (LULAC),

AMERICAN G.I. FORUM OF TEXAS. (Courtesy Dr. Hector P. Garcia Papers, Special Collections, Bell Library, Texas A&M University, Corpus Christi)

Forum leaders aggressively pursued groundbreaking efforts to advance Latino and Latina civil and political rights in America. They successfully challenged school and jury segregation in Texas and other states through various federal court cases, several of which were reviewed by the U.S. Supreme Court. They mobilized unprecedented voter registration drives that resulted for the first time in substantial Mexican American voter participation in U.S. political elections. In the process, following a decade-long struggle, Forum principals were able to influence repeal of the poll tax in Texas (which by requiring voter fees substantially prohibited the participation of poor Mexican Americans in state and local elections).

National Influence

American G.I. Forum principals were the first Mexican American leaders to do serious business with national elected and appointed officials throughout the United States. As a result, during the 1960s, Forum leaders were able to negotiate multimillion-dollar federal Department of Labor grants to develop job training programs for needy Latino and Latina workers and veterans. These were the first major federal grants ever awarded to an Hispanic organization. Forum principals were also able to secure initial federal support for bilingual education programs, through the then U.S. Department of Health, Education, and Welfare. Finally, during these years, Forum leaders themselves were among the first Latinos and Latinas ever to be appointed to presidential administration posts: Hector García served as a special ambassador under President Kennedy, and García and Forum New Mexico leader Vicente Ximenes were appointed to important posts in the Johnson administration. García was appointed to serve as the first Hispanic member of the U.S. Commission on Civil Rights. Ximenes was the first Hispanic ever appointed to the U.S. Equal Employment Opportunity Commission.

In 1972, the Forum established the National Veterans Outreach Program (NVOP), the United States' leading veterans support organization targeting services to Latino and Latina Americans. Today, the NVOP administers a multimillion-dollar budget and oversees training and employment programs, a light manufacturing facility, and a housing weatherization program. Since its founding, the NVOP has served more than 350,000 veterans, most of them Latinos.

During the 1980s, the Forum, under the leadership of then national chairman Jose R. Cano, was one of the few civil rights organizations to effectively engage President Ronald Reagan. From 1980 to 1984, Forum lobbying efforts persuaded Reagan to reverse his long-standing opposition to federally supported bilingual education programs. At Cano's invitation, Reagan also became the first U.S. president to address a national Latino and Latina civil rights group when he spoke at the Forum's annual convention in El Paso in 1983. In 1984, Reagan named Forum founder Hector García a Presidential Medal of Freedom recipient; the Medal of Freedom is the highest honor a president can bestow upon a civilian citizen of the United States.

Leading historians agree that the organizing vitality of contemporary Latino and Latina communities in the United States has been heavily informed by the efforts of returning Latino World War II veterans. The leading organization advancing this work during the initial decades following the war was the American G.I. Forum. Its veterans-driven advocacy established a secure foundation for subsequent Latino and Latina community efforts designed to press American leaders and institutions to meaningfully address long-standing social, political, and economic challenges facing Latinos and Latinas.

See also **García, Hector Pérez** *and* **League of United Latin American Citizens.**

BIBLIOGRAPHY

Allsup, Carl. *The American G.I. Forum: Origins and Evolution.* Austin: University of Texas Center for Mexican American Studies, 1982.

Caro, Robert A. *The Years of Lyndon Johnson: Master of the Senate.* New York: Knopf, 2002.

García, Ignacio M. *Hector P. García: In Relentless Pursuit of Justice.* Houston, Tex.: Arte Público, 2002.
Leininger Pycior, Julie. *LBJ and Mexican Americans: The Paradox of Power.* Austin: University of Texas Press, 1997.
Ramos, Henry A. J. *The American G.I. Forum: In Pursuit of the Dream, 1948–1983.* Houston, Tex.: Arte Público, 1998.

HENRY A. J. RAMOS

AMERICANIZATION. By the end of World War I, the United States had indisputably become a global power. The country's growth was driven by a history of territorial conquest and massive immigration. After defeating Mexico militarily in the United States–Mexican War, the United States forced the Mexican government to relinquish almost half of its land in the 1848 Treaty of Guadalupe Hidalgo. Those Mexicans who remained in U.S. territory were quickly relegated to a second-class citizenship. A half-century later, the United States defeated Spain and forced it to cede Puerto Rico and the Philippines and to relinquish its control of Cuba. In the 1898 Treaty of Paris, the United States acquired the authority to determine the political future and citizenship status of millions of people in the former Spanish colonies.

After the Mexican Revolution of 1910, the Mexican presence in the United States increased dramatically. Between 1910 and 1930, over one million Mexicans migrated north. Most left to escape a war that had devastated their country. They came to the United States in the hope of finding security and employment. Like the millions of Europeans who immigrated during the 1880s and 1890s, Puerto Ricans and Mexicans were popularly depicted as indolent foreigners who undermined the country's fabled Anglo-Saxon racial composition. However, Mexicans and Puerto Ricans were also racialized, and, like African Americans and Native Americans, were portrayed as biologically inferior to the white Europeans. This racism was justified by a warlike Anglo-Saxon ideology that defined nationhood as a male-centric and racially exclusive notion that blended patriotism, whiteness, and xenophobia.

Although Mexicans and Puerto Ricans were portrayed as incapable of completely assimilating because of their presumed racial inferiority, their conversion into loyal English-speaking citizens and obedient workers was an important part of the nation-building process in the early twentieth century. According to the authors of a 1928 Americanization study, assimilating Spanish-speaking peoples from Mexico was one of the great problems confronting the Southwest. Through aggressive Americanization, the distinctive cultural identity of the immigrants and their patriotic ties to their countries of origin would be eradicated. The purpose of Americanization was to unify a culturally diverse people by obliterating ethnic identities and forcing the immigrants to rapidly divest themselves of values that were portrayed as antiquated and antidemocratic. The acquisition of the English language, familiarity with U.S. political beliefs and institutions, and manual training for a rapidly expanding industrial economy were seen as the core of Americanization.

The United States employed various approaches in its attempts to Americanize Puerto Ricans and Mexicans. Puerto Rico was seen as a social laboratory in which to test radical Americanization approaches. The goal was not to prepare Puerto Ricans for citizenship, but to effect the complete transformation of their institutions and culture and to displace their language. The legal and political institutions established by the Spanish during four centuries of rule were replaced by a new colonial government that undertook Puerto Rico's transformation. Educational reform, with English-language immersion training, was the centerpiece of the Americanization effort. The school system was used to instill civic values and patriotism toward the United States, to train Puerto Ricans for civil service jobs, and to socialize and train young girls in hygiene, nutrition, cooking, sewing, and gardening. Boys were taught manual and industrial trades, and girls took classes in needlework and domestic service. The educational system was a vast enterprise that absorbed most of the colonial government's budget. But in the end the hoped-for goals were only partially achieved, and English never became the dominant language. Puerto Rican cultural institutions remain vibrant into the early twenty-first century, and the island's culture, art, music, and literature are consumed in the United States.

As was the case in Puerto Rico, the customs and traditions of Mexican immigrants were seen as impediments to thorough integration into the U.S. social and political order. The governments of states with large Mexican populations, primarily California, Texas, and Arizona, used the schools to conduct Americanization campaigns. Between 1915 and 1929, the California state government targeted Mexican women for Americanization in the belief that they were more amenable to cultural transformation and more likely, given their roles as homemakers and mothers, to transmit new values to their children. Moreover, job training was important since Mexican women were targeted for eventual employment in the Southwest as domestic and service workers, as well as seamstresses and laundresses. Programs to instruct Mexican women on hygiene and diet and to control fertility were remarkably similar to those in Puerto Rico. The Americanization campaigns had limited success and were uniformly abandoned during the Great Depression of the 1930s. Latinas and Latinos have negotiated their own terms of integration into U.S. culture and society.

AMERICANIZATION. Migrant school children saying the Pledge of Allegiance in school in Moreno Valley, Calif. (©Jimmy Dorantes/Latin Focus.com)

See also Education; Mexican Revolution; *and* Puerto Ricans.

BIBLIOGRAPHY

Cabán, Pedro. *Constructing a Colonial People: Puerto Rico and the United States, 1898–1932*. Boulder, Colo.: Westview Press, 2000.

Cabán, Pedro. "Subjects and Immigrants during the Progressive Era," *Discourse* 23, no. 3 (Fall 2001): 24–51.

Foner, Eric. *The Story of American Freedom*. New York: Norton, 1998.

Hill, Merton E. "The Development of an Americanization Program." In *Aspects of the Mexican American Experience*, edited by Carlos E. Cortés. New York: Arno Press, 1976.

Reyes, Ignacio. *A Survey of the Problems Involved in the Americanization of the Mexican-American*. San Francisco: R and E Research Associates, 1972.

Sánchez, George. " 'Go after the Women': Americanization and the Mexican Immigrant Woman, 1915–1929." In *Unequal Sisters: A Multicultural Reader in U.S. Women's History*, 2nd ed., edited by Vicki L. Ruiz and Ellen Carol DuBois. New York: Routledge, 1994.

PEDRO CABÁN

AMNESTY MOVEMENT. The early-twenty-first-century movement to regularize the status of undocumented immigrants brought together various immigrant groups across the United States not only to bring the undocumented "out of the shadows of the law," but also to publicly identify the major contribution that immigrants make to the economy and to society. In many ways movement leaders, in their calls for blanket (or total) amnesty, were following the lead of a previous generation that saw some of their aims and goals partially realized in the 1986 Immigration Reform and Control Act (IRCA).

Initial Projects for Immigrants' Rights (1951–1986)

The notion that undocumented workers should qualify for legal status runs counter to many popular notions and carefully crafted representations of "illegal aliens" by anti-immigrant special interest groups and lobbies. According to Chicano activist Bert Corona (1918–2001) this belief system is what informed much of the debate on immigration restrictions. He saw part of his life's work as countering "anti-immigrant legislation, which portrays undocumented immigrants as economic and social threats to American society" (Garcia, p. 300). In *Memories of Chicano History*, his personal narrative or *testimonio*, Corona credits La Hermandad Mexicana Nacional, a San Diego–based *mutualista* or mutual aid society, for the initial attempts at undocumented immigrant advocacy work.

As early as 1951, Mexican labor organizers Phil and Albert Usquiano in San Diego were challenging Immigration and Naturalization Service (INS) deportations of Mexican workers who had been given visas (and permanent residency status) to work in the United States during World War II but who, because of housing shortages, lived in Tijuana. When the INS attempted to revoke the visas and deport the workers, La Hermandad provided representation and successfully filed suit in many cases. Bert Corona's often-recognized Centers for Autonomous Social Action (Centros de Acción Social Autónomo; CASA) in Los Angeles grew out of the structure of La Hermandad and were instrumental in providing housing and economic, legal, and medical assistance for undocumented workers from Mexico and Central America. The CASAs disintegrated as a result of internal strife and a failed attempt at radical political organizing, but the Hermandad weathered the storm, grew to nearly thirty thousand members, and served as a lobbyist to both state and federal governments on behalf of undocumented workers. It also provided citizenship classes and legal assistance for those who qualified under the legalization provision of IRCA.

Another related push for legalization came from the situation faced by many Central American immigrants (predominately from El Salvador and Guatemala but also Nicaragua and Honduras) during the Reagan administration. President Ronald Reagan's foreign policy was based on the "domino" theory, which posits that Communist movements in particular nations would lead to Communist movements in neighboring nations, which would reject capitalism as the mode of development. The Reagan administration went to great pains, covert and overt, to fund and arm political regimes in Central America that supported U.S. corporate interests and capitalist ideologies by squashing radical insurgent movements. As people fled the civil wars and violence, only those who supported capitalism and U.S. aims but were living in socialist nations such as Nicaragua were given refugee status (at a rate of around 80 percent). Those attempting to escape state-sponsored death squads and violence in El Salvador and Guatemala were deemed economic migrants because of their governments' favorable status with the Reagan administration, and the refugee status approval rate from those countries was closer to 2–3 percent.

Sanctuary movement. The result was a sizable group of U.S. citizens who challenged the foreign policy and selective application of immigration and refugee laws by providing sanctuary for those fleeing the violence of U.S.–sponsored military regimes. The sanctuary movement was an organization of approximately two hundred churches, often supported by Latina and Latino–serving organizations similar to the CASAs previously mentioned, some universities and university towns, and eventually the state of New Mexico, when then-Governor Toney Anaya declared the state a sanctuary. The idea was based on biblical scripture calling for the church to provide safe passage for those persecuted under unjust and oppressive laws. The leaders of the sanctuary movement contended that the Reagan administration was not only defying the 1951 United Nations Convention and Protocol on Refugees but also the 1980 U.S. Refugee Act, which committed the United States to provide refugee status for those who had a "well-founded fear of persecution" or whose "life and liberty would be threatened" in their homeland. The selective application of this refugee status determination was based almost wholly on nation of origin and on whether the administration of that nation was on good terms with the U.S. administration or not. In addition, refugee status did not translate into permanent residency status. Much of the impetus for legalization from the Central American immigrant population arose out of these particular circumstances.

IRCA Legalization Provisions (1986–1993)

Congress passed the Simpson–Rodino sponsored–Immigration Reform and Control Act (IRCA) in 1986. It was the first major overhaul of immigration law since the passage of the Refugee Act in 1980. Predominately a restrictive law aimed at reducing the number of undocumented immigrants, IRCA contained several provisions that extended temporary worker visa programs and introduced employer sanctions for those who knowingly hired laborers unauthorized to work in the United States. Pressure by Latina and Latino and immigrant advocacy groups led to the provisions within IRCA that specifically barred discrimination in the hiring process and offered limited amnesty for undocumented immigrants who could prove they had lived continuously in the United States since 1982. This excluded the large influx of individuals without documentation who entered the country after 1982 and those transnational migrants who went back and forth in a circular migration pattern.

Another provision, the Seasonal Agricultural Workers program (SAW), allowed agricultural laborers who could prove ninety days of continuous employment in the previous year to legalize their status. The Replenishment Agricultural Worker program (RAW) provided additional admittances to the agricultural industry if there was deemed to be a labor shortage. It was designed to meet grower concerns that legalized workers would leave agriculture. When the list of interested RAW workers expired in 1993, it contained 100,000 applicants. Susan González Baker notes that the SAW program was expected to net 50,000 applicants but that the amount was closer to 1.3 million. Overall, legalization included approximately 3 million undocumented immigrants. The RAW program was never put into place because a labor shortage was never identified. Studies found that legalization did not lead to a departure from agricultural employment, and, if anything, SAW workers were working more days per year in agriculture after legalization than before they were documented.

Early calls for amnesty. The first calls for total or blanket amnesty (a legalization of status for all undocumented immigrants, regardless of their date of entry) were voiced during the debate leading up to the passage of IRCA. Groups like the United Farm Workers (UFW) union were for the first time identifying with the struggle for securing immigrant rights and calling for total amnesty. This represented a marked shift from earlier UFW positions that characterized undocumented and temporary immigrant laborers as detrimental to labor organizing. Other groups like La Hermandad and CASA stated their previously held views that legalization would be viable only if it were a plan for total amnesty coupled with the unequivocal right to U.S. citizenship. In her analysis of the "Hispanic lobby" that influenced the long debate over immigration reform, Christine Sierra claims that five major Latina and Latino constituencies (single-issue groups, professional-provider groups, membership organizations, national advocacy groups, and elected political representatives) were responsible for shaping the political debate and eventual passage of IRCA with its limited protections for immigrants. Without the lobby, even with the major internal dissension, it is likely that IRCA would have passed ten years earlier as simply a piece of legislation aimed exclusively at restriction and punishment.

The Question of Immigrant Rights (1993–2004)

But the legalization provisions with IRCA legislation were only partial and were particularly cumbersome for the applicants seeking amnesty. The provisions were never aimed at reaching the entire undocumented population, and the overall aim of IRCA was to restrict unauthorized entry into the United States. On this account, IRCA failed to reduce the in-migration of undocumented immigrants significantly. Renewed calls for full or blanket amnesty came in the late 1990s and early 2000s—an era of reduced immigrant rights and increased dangers associated with migration. With an increase in the enforcement of the United States–Mexico border, special operations designed to arrest and deport undocumented immigrants, and nativist (anti-immigrant) sentiments as evidenced by the California propositions aimed at reducing the number and rights of the Latina and Latino and immigrant population, the amnesty movement was required to deal with numerous challenges and setbacks.

Militarized border. In the late 1990s and early 2000s the United States–Mexico border became increasingly militarized. Timothy Dunn argues that the INS applied the military doctrine of low-intensity conflict (LIC) to "defend" the border. The equipment used to patrol the border (helicopters, night-vision equipment, electronic intrusion-detection ground sensors), operational tactics and strategies of border enforcement (combining police, military, and paramilitary forces), and overall aim of social control of a targeted civilian population all embody the LIC doctrine that has been put into action by the U.S. military in Vietnam, Somalia, Libya, Kuwait, Panama, Grenada, Afghanistan, and Iraq.

The most visible physical manifestation of this militarization of the border region is the construction of walls and fences to separate the urban sister cities. A series of INS campaigns from 1993 to the early 2000s (such as Operation Blockade and Operation Hold-the-Line in El Paso, Texas, Operation Gatekeeper in San Diego, California, and Operation Guardian—the "Light Up the Border" campaign—in Douglas and Nogales, Arizona) physically defined the line in the sand or rivers that had previously only symbolically marked the border between Mexico and the United States. As the sociologist Néstor Rodríguez notes,

> nation-state boundaries are social constructions. They do not exist independent of our volition. . . . Nation-state borders exist primarily because state governments agree, voluntarily or through coercion, that they delimit political divisions. Solemn treaties formalize international boundaries, but it is the daily reproduction of ideas and myths that socially construct borders.

(p. 223)

Mary Romero investigated the joint operation between the Border Patrol and Chandler Police Department to target

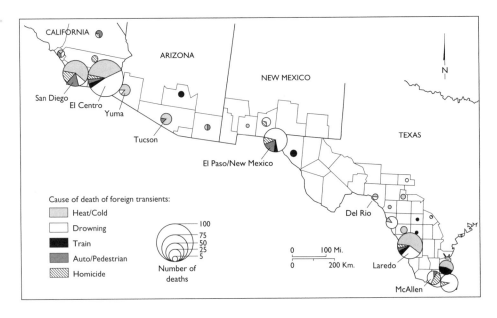

FIGURE 1. Immigrant deaths along the United States–Mexico Border, 1998. (Source: Eschbach, Hagan, and Rodriguez)

CALIFORNIA

ARIZONA

NEW MEXICO

N

San Diego
El Centro
Yuma

Tucson

TEXAS

El Paso/New Mexico

Del Rio

Cause of death of foreign transients:

Heat/Cold

Drowning

Train

Auto/Pedestrian

Homicide

100
75
50
25
5

Number of deaths

0   100 Mi.
0   200 Km.

Laredo

McAllen

AMNESTY MOVEMENT.
Amnesty International
consultants advising illegal
immigrants about
immigration laws. (Bruce
Berman/Time Life
Pictures/Getty Images)

AMNESTY MOVEMENT.
Amnesty International
consultants advising illegal
immigrants about
immigration laws. (Bruce
Berman/Time Life
Pictures/Getty Images)

working-class, Chicano neighborhoods in the Phoenix, Arizona, metropolitan area. In what has come to be known as the Chandler Round-Up, the detainment and inspection of papers of those who looked like "illegals" or were of Mexican ancestry relates to the issue of racial profiling. Romero contends that a practice of class profiling was conducted as well, given the neighborhood targeted (which not coincidentally was slated for redevelopment) and the reliance on stopping pedestrians in public shopping areas, residential streets, unannounced house-to-house visits, and bus stops.

The overall effect of the criminalization of the undocumented is that entry into the United States became much more dangerous. With the increased enforcement of the border, immigrants were forced to cross in the least defended stretches of the two-thousand-mile border, which are the most treacherous and dangerous crossing points. Researchers at the University of Houston worked to identify the total number of deaths associated with the increased militarization of the border (see Figure 1). In San Diego, the American Friends Service Committee (a Quaker organization) took on immigrant rights as a major focus for the California-Mexico border region. In addition to numerous direct action activities, they maintained a banner updated daily with a running tally of immigrants who lost their lives attempting to cross the border. The banner was visible on Interstate 5 to those driving by the Coronado Bridge and Chicano Park (the world's largest display of public murals, which chronicles the Chicano experience in San Diego) on their commute to downtown jobs. The public critique of border militarization created a link between Chicano activists who took over Chicano Park thirty-four years ago to keep the city from placing a highway patrol station in the heart of Barrio Logan and those immigrants who deal daily with the increased threats associated with undocumented border crossing. Karl Eschbach, Jacqueline Hagan, and Néstor Rodríguez estimate that nearly five thousand immigrants died on the U.S. side of the border from 1985 to 2002.

Immigrant bashing. Also in California, political elites overseeing one of California's worst recessions in the 1990s found an easy target and scapegoat in the form of the "illegal alien." The resulting series of voter-approved propositions designed to punish undocumented workers created a political environment in which immigrant bashing was the norm, and Latinas and Latinos and other immigrants were blamed for the state's economic woes. Proposition 187, the so-called Save Our State initiative, was designed to deny public services to undocumented immigrants. Then-Governor Pete Wilson was a staunch supporter of the proposition, although it was disclosed during the campaign that his family employed undocumented laborers as maids. The hypocrisy was lost on the Californians who in 1994 voted overwhelmingly to pass the proposition mandating state employees to turn in suspected undocumented immigrants and to refuse education, medical, and social services to those who could not provide sufficient documentation. Proposition 187 was preceded in 1986 by California Proposition 63, which was designed to make English the "official language of the state," and was followed in 1998 by Proposition 227, the so-called Save Our Children initiative, which stipulated that Limited English Proficiency students be placed in English-only classrooms (so-called immersion programs) after one year of English as a Second Language instruction. In 1996, affirmative action was in the crosshairs of the conservative groups that had backed each of the previous propositions; when Proposition 209 was passed by voters, it effectively ended affirmative action in state hiring and school admittance decisions. This hostile climate prompted cultural critic George Lipsitz to call "California in the 1990s the human rights equivalent of Mississippi in the 1960s" (p. xviii).

The Amnesty Movement in the Early 2000s

Yet within this context, and the even more repressive post–September 11 era of reduced civil liberties and restricted immigrants' rights, tireless activists continued the movement for amnesty begun in the previous era and broadened it across the entire United States. In many ways, a shared opposition to the Patriot Act united Latina and Latino advocacy organizations, refugee and immigrant service providers, labor unions, socially conscious church groups, and members of all racialized communities (black, Latina and Latino, Arab, Middle Eastern, Asian, and Native American).

Efforts by life-long Latina activist Emma Lozano in Chicago exemplify the trends in these calls for amnesty. Lozano worked tirelessly to develop three organizations advocating on behalf of amnesty and immigrant rights. She founded and served as president of the community-based membership organization Pueblo Sin Fronteras and two related nonprofits, Centro Sin Fronteras and Sin Fronteras. She was recognized by the Cook County Board of Commissioners for her work on educational reform, legal advocacy for undocumented immigrants, and union representation regardless of citizenship status, and for being one of the national leaders in the amnesty movement. She shared the stage with Middle Eastern and African American leaders not only to push the Chicago city council to urge the federal administration to repeal the Patriot Act, but also to identify and challenge the increased use of racial profiling as a result of the far-reaching powers of the act.

In Providence, Rhode Island, Guatemalan-born activist Juan Garcia waged a similarly broad-based campaign around the issue of amnesty. Employed as a community organizer with Saint Teresa's Catholic Church, he founded "Immigrants in Action/Comité de Inmigrantes en Acción" to secure amnesty for the undocumented population. The efforts of the Comité were slowed because of the overall nativist reaction to the attacks on the World Trade Center and the Pentagon. Using models of self-education reminiscent of Brazilian author Paulo Friere, the pre–September 11 work of Garcia involved helping undocumented workers educate themselves about their rights and mobilize for amnesty. After September 11, he coordinated his efforts with local Middle Eastern activists in challenging racial profiling. He worked with immigrant workers/labor

organizers who lost their fish-processing jobs after organizing and detailing abuses and careless workplace practices that had led to the death of one undocumented worker. The need for amnesty becomes all the clearer within this context.

Garcia's Comité was part of a nationwide network of amnesty advocates that organized the Immigrant Worker Freedom Ride of 2003. The National Coalition for Dignity and Amnesty was composed of labor unions, church organizations, civil rights organizations, immigrant rights organizations, community-based organizations, and elected officials. Together, they coordinated the Freedom Ride connecting the struggles of undocumented immigrants with the struggle against racial segregation of blacks in the southern United States during the civil rights era. The most prominent labor unions working to organize the undocumented (SEIU, HERE, UFW, UFCW, and UNITE!), along with original Freedom Ride organizers and national immigrant advocacy organizations, sponsored nine buses in a cross-country journey to Queens, New York, for a rally in support of a blanket amnesty program. The Freedom Riders were successful in publicizing the plight in local newspapers, but the event did not receive national television coverage.

President George W. Bush initially attempted to make immigration a visible aspect of his political platform. When the administration leaked its interest in pursuing a legalization program for undocumented immigrants residing in the United States, the negative reaction it received put an immediate end to administrative support for amnesty. Most likely this was at the behest of the Mexican president, Vicente Fox, who wished to address Mexico's immigration dilemma by regularizing the migrant flow through legalization and/or temporary guest-worker arrangements. But in the 2004 State of the Union address, Bush stated unequivocally that he opposed amnesty and called for a large-scale temporary worker program based on the model of the Bracero Program (1942–1964) as his solution to the immigration dilemma.

Political discourse in the 2000s shifted the blame for undocumented laborers onto immigrants, not employers, with little to no discussion of enforcing employer sanctions or dealing with the impetus for undocumented migration in the first place. Yet one member of Congress, Rep. Luis Gutierrez (D-Ill.), with the assistance of amnesty movement leaders, created legislation that would overhaul immigration policies that criminalize the undocumented and provide pathways for full amnesty. The Unity, Security, Accountability, and Family Act (USA Family Act, H.R. 440) would have allowed any undocumented immigrant residing in the United States for five years on January 29, 2003, who had not been convicted of certain criminal or civil violations, to apply for and automatically receive permanent resident-alien status. Those residing in the United States for less than five years would be granted "conditional" permanent resident-alien status, including work authorization. An updated version of this bill, referred to as the Safe, Orderly, Legal Visas & Enforcement Act (S.O.L.V.E.), also came under consideration but, given the political climate, it was not expected to make it out of committee. Nevertheless, amnesty advocates and the elected officials who supported their efforts continued the daily struggle to ensure the rights of the undocumented.

See also Ballot Propositions 187, 209, and 227; Border, The; Bracero Program; CASA HGT; Central Americans; Corona, Bert; Immigration Policy, Twentieth Century; Immigration Reform and Control Act of 1986; Mutualista Organizations; Sanctuary Movement; *and* United States Interventions in Latin America.

BIBLIOGRAPHY

Acuña, Rodolfo. *Occupied America: A History of Chicanos.* 4th ed. New York: Longman, 2000.

Chavez, Leo. *Shadowed Lives: Undocumented Immigrants in American Society.* 2nd ed. Fort Worth, Tex.: Harcourt Brace Jovanovich College Publishers, 1992.

Dunn, Timothy. *The Militarization of the U.S.–Mexico Border.* Austin: CMAS Books, University of Texas Press, 1996.

Eschbach, Karl, Jacqueline Hagan, and Néstor Rodríguez. "Deaths during Undocumented Migration: Trends and Policy Implications in the New Era of Homeland Security." Presented at the 26th Annual National Legal Conference on Immigration and Refugee Policy. Washington, D.C., 2003.

Garcia, Mario T. *Memories of Chicano History: The Life and Narrative of Bert Corona.* Berkeley: University of California Press, 1994.

González Baker, Susan. *The Cautious Welcome: The Legalization Programs of the Immigration Reform and Control Act.* Santa Monica, Calif.: Rand Corporation; Washington, D.C.: Urban Institute Press, 1990.

Lipsitz, George. *The Possessive Investment in Whiteness: How White People Profit from Identity Politics.* Philadelphia: Temple University Press, 1998.

MacEoin, Gary, ed. *Sanctuary: A Resource Guide for Understanding and Participating in the Central American Refugees' Struggle.* San Francisco: Harper and Row, 1985.

Rodríguez, Néstor. "The Social Construction of the U.S.–Mexico Border." In *Immigrants Out! The New Nativism and the Anti-Immigrant Impulse in the United States,* edited by Juan Perea, 223–243. New York: New York University Press, 1997.

Romero, Mary. "Racial Profiling and Immigration Law Enforcement." *Critical Sociology.* Forthcoming.

Romero, Mary. "Violation of Latino Civil Rights Resulting from INS and Local Police's Use of Race, Culture, and Class Profiling: The Case of the Chandler Roundup in Arizona." With Marwah Serag. *Cleveland State University Law Review* 51 (2004).

Sierra, Christine. "In Search of National Power: Chicanos Working the System of Immigration Reform, 1976–1986." In *Chicano Politics and Society in the Late Twentieth Century,* edited by David Montejano, 131–153. Austin: University of Texas Press, 1999.

RONALD L. MIZE

ANAYA, RUDOLFO A. (b. 1937), Mexican American author. Rudolfo Anaya reached the apex of his career in April 2002 when he received the National Medal of Arts from President George W. Bush. Sharing the stage with other American cultural icons, Anaya stood as a singular representative of Chicana and Chicano letters and culture. He was honored for his untiring efforts to support and promote Latina and Latino writers, and for enriching the American literary landscape. It was an auspicious and historic moment in that no other Chicano writer has achieved that level of official recognition.

Early Life

Anaya was born October 30, 1937, in Pastura, a small village in the northeast region of New Mexico. The seemingly endless grasslands of this region, called *el llano estacado* (staked plains), were the farming and hunting grounds of early Hispanic settlers. Local myths and legends, and the haunting, wind-swept landscape, indelibly marked Anaya's literary imagination. His family spoke Spanish at home, but in school he began to learn English, the language that would shape his experience in poetry and myth. In *Rudolfo Anaya, Autobiography as Written in 1985,* he recounts his family history. His mother, Rafaelita Mares, grew up in the Puerto de Luna Valley, near the Pecos River. She married Solomon Bonney and gave birth to a son and a daughter. But the harsh life on the plains often brought early death, and soon Rafaelita was a widow. She then married Martín Anaya, who already had a daughter of his own, and together they produced seven more children, including Rudolfo.

In 1939, the Anaya family moved to Santa Rosa, near the Pecos River. There, as Anaya has recounted in interviews and autobiographical writings, he first heard the terrorizing wailings of *La Llorona* (the wailing woman). La Llorona is the restless spirit of the woman who drowned her children and searches for them near rivers, lakes, and other bodies of water. La Llorona would become a dominant myth in Anaya's work.

Anaya graduated from Albuquerque High School in 1956, then attended the Browning Business School for two years before enrolling at the University of New Mexico, where he earned bachelor's and master's degrees in English in 1963 and 1968, respectively. After earning a second master's degree in guidance and counseling in 1972, he served as director of counseling at the University of Albuquerque until 1974.

Writing Career

It was while teaching in La Joya and then in Albuquerque that the memories, images, and myths of his childhood began to reemerge and give shape to his narrative voice. Anaya recalls how late one night, an old woman dressed

Rudolfo Anaya. (Loretta Jaramillo Reynolds)

in black appeared to him. She became the *curandera* (medicine woman) of *Bless Me, Ultima* (1972).

Anaya received the national Premio Quinto Sol literary award in 1971 for his first novel, which was published the following year. Consequently, the English Department at the University of New Mexico invited him to join the faculty in 1974. Anaya, well respected as a teacher by both his students and his colleagues, became a full professor in 1988. In 1993, he retired as professor emeritus to devote more time to writing.

Anaya imbues his work—be it novels, plays, poems, essays, or lectures—with the wonderment of *el inocente* (the innocent), a character suffused with awe of the miraculous, the magic of words, and an enduring belief in a divine power in the material and spiritual worlds. In an autobiographical essay published in 2003, Anaya pays homage to the river voices that beckoned him, the night spirits that glided above the rushing waters, and the

unearthly cries of La Llorona. The stones, hills, and animals that inhabited the landscape of his boyhood were not simply a fantasy but a marvelous reality lived by el inocente and later captured by the writer Anaya became.

Although nurtured on American and world literature, Anaya has stayed true to his New Mexican roots. The use of mythology, a spiritual wellspring for him and the subject of his lifelong study, allowed him to introduce into the literary scene a new kind of novel, quite unlike the work of the leading Chicano writers of the time. Anaya's artistic and philosophical vision holds that Chicanos have created their traditions, ceremonies, and history within a unique, deeply rooted culture that gives them the foundations of their identity. His work references mythology, legends, and traditions based in an Indo-Hispano culture infused with themes of love, strength, and endurance, and at the same time distinguished by a unique landscape that is a source of inspiration and spiritual sensibilities. His work has received much critical attention, in particular because of his thematic interests in imagination, power, and originality. Critics have recognized and applauded the mythical world Anaya has created.

Luis Leal writes that the Chicano must create mythical images to bring about a new discursive amalgamation of history, traditions, culture, and daily life. And Antonio Márquez notes that in this sense, Anaya's novelistic vision is informed by mythopoesis. Anaya's work, particularly *Bless Me, Ultima*, has inspired an impressive body of critical studies analyzing themes central to his creative impulse, such as landscape and the sense of identity of the Chicano people.

In *Bless Me, Ultima*, Anaya explores the passage from innocence to maturity of nine-year-old Antonio Marez and his relationship with Ultima, a *curandera* or spiritual healer. *Heart of Aztlán* (1976) portrays Clemente Chávez and his family struggling to cope with the pressures of a hostile urban life in Albuquerque. This novel explores religion, mythology, and contemporary themes such as technology and capitalism. *Tortuga* (1979) centers on alienation, loss of faith, mythology, and spirituality as experienced by a disabled young man nicknamed Tortuga (Turtle), who is confined to a hospital along with other disabled and powerless children.

Anaya's numerous multifaceted works also include *Who Killed Don José?* (1987), a mystery play, and four mystery novels—*Albuquerque* (1992), *Zia Summer* (1995), *Rio Grande Fall* (1996), and *Shaman Winter* (1999)—which form a major part of the small but growing boom in the Latina and Latino mystery genre. Sonny Baca, Anaya's detective, investigates political corruption, international spying, land and environmental issues, and New Mexican history.

Anaya's literary project also extends to writing children's books intended to instill pride in a rich cultural heritage and to preserve the tradition of storytelling. His books *The Farolitos of Christmas* (1995) and *My Land Sings: Stories from the Rio Grande* (1999) received the Tomás Rivera Mexican American Children's Book Award in 1995 and 1999 respectively. *Maya's Children: The Story of La Llorona* (1997), *Farolitos for Abuelo* (1998), and the *Roadrunner's Dance* (2000) have significantly enhanced the growing body of literature for young Latino readers. Always willing to explore new genres, Anaya wrote *La Llorona*, a opera libretto (unpublished) based on his short novel *The Legend of La Llorona* (1984).

Collections of critical thought, such as *The Magic of Words: Rudolfo A. Anaya and His Writings* (1982), *Rudolfo A. Anaya: Focus on Criticism* (1990), and *Rudolfo A. Anaya: A Critical Companion* (1999), offer positive assessments of Anaya's place in Chicano letters, as well as significant analyses of Anaya's trilogy: *Bless Me, Ultima, Heart of Aztlán*, and *Tortuga*. Dissertations, theses, articles, reviews, and countless interviews explore Anaya's focus on traditions, customs, and beliefs, attesting to his national and international critical reputation. Translation of his work into Japanese, Russian, Spanish, French, German, and Italian confirms his international importance and role in world literature.

Awards and Honors

Anaya has received awards and honors throughout his career. In 1978 he received the New Mexico Governor's Public Service Award and the National Chicano Council on Higher Education Fellowship. His novel *Tortuga* won the Before Columbus Foundation's American Book Award. From 1983 to 1986, he participated in the highly regarded W. K. Kellogg Foundation Fellowship program. In 1984 he received the distinguished Award for Achievement in Chicano Literature from the Hispanic Caucus of the National Council of Teachers of English. The list of accolades goes on, culminating in the National Medal of Arts in 2002. His critically acclaimed work has also been the object of controversy and censorship, however. For its alleged violence and profanity, *Bless Me, Ultima* was banned and burned in Bloomfield, New Mexico, in 1981; removed from the Laton, California, Unified School District in 1999; and censored by John Jay High School in Wappingers Falls, New York.

Rudolfo Anaya continues to write actively. His other interests range from painting, photography, farming, collecting Chicana and Chicano art, and owning horses to philanthropy. He endowed the Premio Aztlán, a literary award for emerging Chicana and Chicano writers, and the Critica Nueva, an award for critics of Chicana and Chicano literature. Whether appreciated or misunderstood, praised or disparaged, Anaya has made and continues to make a singular contribution to Chicano literature and

culture. He has created a body of work of lasting influence likely to inspire generations of readers and writers.

See also Chicanos and Chicanas; Curanderismo; Literature; *and* Mexican-Origin People in the United States.

BIBLIOGRAPHY

Bruce-Novoa, Juan D. *Chicano Authors: Inquiry by Interview*. Austin: University of Texas Press, 1980.

Fernández Olmos, Margarite. *Rudolfo A. Anaya: A Critical Companion*. Westport, Conn.: Greenwood Press, 1999.

González-T., César A., ed. *Rudolfo A. Anaya: Focus on Criticism*. La Jolla, Calif.: Lalo Press, 1990.

González-T., César A., and Phyllis S. Morgan. *A Sense of Place: Rudolfo A. Anaya: An Annotated Bio-Bibliography*. Berkeley: University of California Ethnic Studies Library Publications, 2000.

Hurt, Jeanette. "Trying to Unite Racine With One Book." www.jsonline.com/news/racine/sep01/readr23092201a.asp

Lomelí, Francisco A., and Carl R. Shirley, eds. *Dictionary of Literary Biography: Chicano Writers First Series*. Detroit, Mich.: Gale, 1989.

"Rudolfo Anaya Receives National Medal of Arts." University of New Mexico. www.unm.edu/news/Releases/April23anaya.htm

Vassallo, Paul, ed. *The Magic of Words: Rudolfo A. Anaya and his Writings*. Albuquerque: University of New Mexico Press, 1982.

Teresa Marquez

ANTHONY, MARC (b. 1969), musician and actor. Born on September 16, 1968, in Spanish Harlem, New York City, to Puerto Rican parents, Marc Anthony (Marco Antonio Muñiz) is a well-known performer of Latin pop, salsa, and freestyle music as well as a successful film and stage actor. By the early 1990s, Anthony had sold more salsa records than any other performer on the planet, solidifying his position among the most important new salsa artists to emerge in the 1990s. Unlike the more socially conscious New York salsa musicians of the 1960s and 1970s, or the highly produced "romantic" salsa artists of the 1980s, Anthony gained fame performing a salsa style that borrowed more heavily from the African American and urban genres that he listened to growing up, such as rhythm and blues and house. Working for famed salsa producer Ralph Mercado's RMM record label and then completing his first mainstream English pop album for Sony, Anthony has become known in the international media as one of the most successful "crossover" stars of the so-called Latin music boom of the late 1990s, a label he has repeatedly rejected.

Originally named for famed Mexican singer Marco Antonio Muñiz, Anthony changed his name at the beginning of his career in order to avoid confusion between the two artists. His musical education began at home, where he learned to sing in both Spanish and English under the guidance of his father, Felipe, himself a professional guitarist. As a child, Anthony listened to a variety of musical genres and performers, including rock, rhythm and blues, pop

MARC ANTHONY. (© Brooks Kraft/CORBIS)

stars José Feliciano (Puerto Rico), Air Supply (United States), as well as salsa legends Héctor Lavoe (Puerto Rico), Willie Colón (Puerto Rico), and Rubén Blades (Panama), among others. According to Anthony, renowned Puerto Rican percussionist and bandleader Tito Puente in particular wielded a profound personal and professional influence throughout his life.

Marc Anthony gained much of his early professional experience singing in New York dance clubs, where he performed English-language house and freestyle music. In the early 1990s, he recorded "When the Night Is Over" (1991) with Nuyorican producer and DJ "Little" Louie Vega. Tito Puente and India (Linda Caballero), another Nuyorican salsa singer who also began her artistic career in the city's freestyle scene, appeared on the recording as well. One year later, Puente invited Anthony and Vega to participate in a concert in Madison Square Garden celebrating the release of his 100th record. Anthony later revealed that it was

Puente who inspired him to pursue a career as a *salsero* (salsa singer). In 1993, Anthony released his first salsa record, *Otra nota* (Another Note), which was well received by both international and domestic audiences. His subsequent recordings, *Todo a su tiempo* (All in Good Time, 1996) and *Contra la corriente* (Against the Current, 1997), were also highly successful, the former becoming the first salsa album to be certified gold by the Recording Industry Association of America, and the latter winning a 1998 Grammy for best Latin/tropical performance. Throughout the 1990s, Anthony collaborated on numerous other popular recordings, among them his duets with India ("Vivir lo nuestro," Living Our Life Together, 1993), Nuyorican actress/singer Jennifer Lopez ("No me ames," Don't Love Me, 1999), and the artists on the soundtrack for *Romance del Cumbanchero* (The Cumbanchero's Romance, 1998). He also earned the distinctions of being the first salsa soloist ever invited to perform in historic Madison Square Garden and the only performer to sell out the entire venue at each of his concerts to date. As an actor, Anthony has earned critical notice for his roles in films such as *Bringing Out the Dead* by director Martin Scorsese (1999) and the short-lived Broadway musical *The Capeman*, written by musician Paul Simon and Nobel Laureate Derek Walcott, which opened in January 1998 and closed because of lagging ticket sales a few months later. Based on a real-life crime involving 1960s Nuyorican gang member Salvador Agrón, *The Capeman* engendered some controversy for its portrayal of U.S. Latino life and its commercialization of a violent historical episode in particular.

Notably, *Contra la corriente* marked Anthony's final album of new material with New York–based RMM Records. The subsequent release of *Marc Anthony* in 1999 under the Sony label thus signaled a departure from Anthony's previous salsa hits, as he shifted to performing ballads and Latin-influenced pop music. While the record contained a few Spanish-language tracks, it clearly marked a return to his earlier performances in English. Following a publicity campaign in which, curiously, he was marketed as a new musical "discovery," *Marc Anthony* captured the attention of non-Latino audiences, gaining triple platinum status, while its first single, "Dímelo" (Tell Me), won the Latin Grammy for best song of 2000. Despite the media's constant efforts to label Anthony a "crossover" star in the vein of his Latin American peers who have released successful English-language albums, Anthony has consistently rejected the crossover label on the grounds that as a U.S. Latino he is as much American as he is Puerto Rican and that therefore the very notion of a need to "cross over" to English-speaking culture does not apply to him.

Anthony's eponymous record was immediately followed by *Desde un principio/From the Beginning* (1999), a collection of his previous Spanish-language hits under the RMM label that ultimately reached number one on the Billboard Latin charts. His 2001 salsa recording, *Libre* (Free), was released to fair reviews, while his 2002 English-language pop album, *Mended*, struggled to achieve the visibility of his previous recordings.

See also **Latin Grammys; Mercado, Ralph; Puente, Tito;** *and* **Salsa.**

BIBLIOGRAPHY

Cepeda, María Elena. "'Columbus Effects': Chronology and Crossover in the Latin(o) Music 'Boom'." *Discourse* 23, no. 1 (2001): 63–81.
McLane, Daisann. "Salsa for the High-Tops Generation." *The New York Times*, August 11, 1996.

MARÍA ELENA CEPEDA

ANZALDÚA, GLORIA (1942–2004), writer. Born on September 26, 1942, in South Texas, Gloria E. Anzaldúa, self-described Chicana Tejana lesbian feminist poet and writer, is most well known for her book *Borderlands/La frontera: The New Mestiza* (1987). She revolutionized both Chicano and Chicana studies and critical race theories with her critiques of heterosexism and machismo, traditionally accepted academic ways of theorizing, and dualisms. Informed by her experiences growing up in South Texas, Anzaldúa infused her work with both personal and poetic writings that spoke not only to her experience but also to the larger experiences of Chicanas in the United States. Anzaldúa's other influential works include the edited collections *Making Face, Making Soul/Haciendo caras: Creative and Critical Perspectives by Feminists of Color* (1990); *This Bridge Called My Back: Writings by Radical Women of Color* (1981), with Cherríe Moraga; and *This Bridge We Call Home: Radical Visions for Transformation* (2002), with AnaLouise Keating. Anzaldúa also published several children's books, including *Friends from the Other Side/Amigos del otro lado* (1993) and *Prietita and the Ghost Women/Prietita y la llorona* (1995). The theories advanced in her books contributed to Anzaldúa's status as an internationally recognized scholar.

Within the realm of Chicana/Chicano and Latina/ Latino literary studies, Anzaldúa's work has been far-reaching. She extended previous work by not simply rehabilitating Chicana and Chicano identity through the reappropriation of precolonial imagery but by reclaiming mixed-race identity or a full accounting of all the heritages within Chicana and Chicano identities. Thus, Anzaldúa built on and moved beyond her predecessors in the Chicana and Chicano movement. She subverted the essentialism that hurt the movement, the privileging of a male, heterosexual, precolonial image. Using the metaphor of borderlands both symbolically and literally, Anzaldúa claimed the middle space as a one of empowerment for mestiza and mestizo or mixed-race Chicana and Chicano peoples.

GLORIA ANZALDÚA.

Due to a legacy of internalized colonialism or psychic trauma as the result of Spanish colonialism in Mexico, mixed-race identity in Chicana and Chicano and Mexican cultures symbolically traced back to the Spanish conqueror Hernán Cortés and his interpreter, a native woman named Malintzin Tenépal, and the birth of their son Martin Cortés, has been stigmatized. As described by the prominent Mexican philosopher Octavio Paz in *The Labyrinth of Solitude: Life and Thought in Mexico* (1962), Mexican and Chicana and Chicano identity as a result of the aforementioned union exists as a space of nothingness, an abstraction without a history. However, by reclaiming ambiguity or mixed-race identity from its previously negative connotations, Anzaldúa uses the borderlands as a metaphor for the space in between cultures or biculturalism. This theory of the borderlands disrupts subject-object binaries that have traditionally denounced the middle space or rendered Chicanas and Chicanos passive. Instead, she reconceptualizes Chicanas and Chicanos as the ultimate border crossers or translators of culture whose ambiguity is the very source of their potential. Thus, theorizing Chicana and Chicano identity through the trope of borderlands creates a sense of agency or activity for Chicanas and Chicanos by placing them at the center of their own self-constructions. Anzaldúa's positioning of Chicanas as translators is further pronounced through her constant switching among Spanish, English, and caló (Chicano/Chicana English) in *Borderlands/La frontera: The New Mestiza*. This moving between languages has the effect of forcing the reader to occupy the position of the new mestiza, who is constantly code switching in her everyday lived experience. Therefore, in the book Anzaldúa poetically performs that which she describes.

In addition to the centering of racial and cultural differences, Anzaldúa, like other Chicana feminists before her, privileges queerness as a space of difference that allows the usurping of potentially dangerous binaries to remind readers that queer is not an exclusively white property, and Chicano is not simply a male-centered identity. The Chicana feminists Cherríe Moraga, Adelaida del Castillo, and Carla Trujillo offered powerful critiques of sexism and homophobia in Chicana and Chicano communities. Anzaldúa furthered these critiques by positioning her lesbian identity alongside her mestiza identity as another space that enabled multiple border crossings or translations. This move in turn challenged dominant negative associations of lesbianism within Chicana and Chicano and Mexican cultures by placing it in the center of a powerful space. It also challenged traditional ways of theorizing identity as separate subjectivities and instead accounted for intersecting sites of race, class, sexuality, and gender. The rhetorical critic Lisa A. Flores observed that, as a result of the multiple sites of psychic trauma (heterosexism, sexism, and racism), Chicana feminists craft rhetorical spaces through their writings that account for these multiple sites of difference and contribute to the creation of a new symbolic home.

In constructing such a new symbolic home or identity, Anzaldúa continued the work of Chicana feminists. She traced the long lineages of mother goddess worship in precolonial and Chicana and Chicano cultures to supplant virgin-whore dichotomies strengthened in Mexican and Chicana and Chicano cultures through the strategic uses of the patron saint of Mexico, the Virgin of Guadalupe, and Malintzin Tenépal. By reclaiming these religious, historical, and mythic figures, Anzaldúa contributed to the Chicana feminist project of creating more complex images and understandings of Chicana and Mexican sexuality.

Anzaldúa's use of the borderlands extends beyond the symbolic realm into the literal through her reclamation of Aztlán, the Chicana and Chicano homeland, the Mexican land lost to the southwestern United States in the Treaty of Guadalupe Hidalgo. Anzaldúa rewrote the dominant histories of the land and granted Chicanas and Chicanos and Mexicans precedence. She thereby challenged narratives that continually render Chicanas and Chicanos and Mexicans as foreigners to the land. She further connected each of these cultures to the land organically, which in turn displaced human-constructed borders.

Anzaldúa's reach extends beyond Chicana and Chicano and Latina and Latino literary studies into U.S. critical theories alongside the prominent scholars bell hooks and Patricia Hill Collins. Much like that of other feminists of color, Anzaldúa's work challenged dominant or mainstream theories of feminism that either erased or ignored entirely the situation of women of color, who experience oppression through the intersecting tropes of race, class, and gender. Rather than privileging female identity over a racial identification, Anzaldúa argued, as have other feminists of color, for the recognition of the unique challenges faced by women of color because of the intersecting nature of their oppression. Her book *This Bridge Called My Back: Writings by Radical Women of Color*, coedited with Moraga, brought the concerns and issues relating to women of color to the forefront and offered an important intervention in women's studies and ethnic studies. Similarly, in 2002 Anzaldúa and Keating edited a third-wave feminist text, *This Bridge We Call Home: Radical Visions for Transformation*, which extended the work of *This Bridge Called My Back*. As Flores noted, Anzaldúa's use of the bridge metaphor is highly relevant in that once Chicana feminists have created their own space or home discursively, they then employ bridges to make connections or alliances with others, particularly other feminist communities.

Anzaldúa was also central in challenging prevailing academic notions of intellectualizing or theorizing. Responding to Eurocentric biases that privilege the mind as the sole site of knowledge and locate the body as a site of excess or pleasure while upholding the written over the oral, Anzaldúa and Moraga called for an understanding of theories of the flesh or indigenous ways of theorizing. In defining theories of the flesh, Anzaldúa turned to the idea of body knowledge or knowledge through experience. She called attention to the problematic history of theorizing in the academy that fails to recognize that marginalized communities such as women of color have historically not had access or the means to authorize or produce written texts. She thus reconceptualized theorizing through the everyday lived experience. For example, women of color have not necessarily theorized about resistance and survival through traditional academic writings but through their everyday experiences that they orally pass on through generations. However, because of the bias toward textuality in academia, the voices and theories of women of color are often ignored or deemed valueless. Anzaldúa's theories of the flesh challenged these assumptions and attempted to write the experiences and theories of women of color into the academy while also questioning what constituted theory and the process of theorizing.

Anzaldúa's disruption of dualities, reclamation of mixed-race identity, and privileging of indigenous ways of theorizing made her well known not only in Chicana and Chicano and Latina and Latino literary circles but also as a preeminent critical theorist. Her key significance lies in the introduction of a new academic discourse, theories of borderlands and borderland identities, which has changed the landscape of academia since they were introduced in 1987. Anzaldúa was awarded the Before Columbus Foundation American Book Award, the Lambda Lesbian Small Press Book Award, a National Endowment for the Arts Fiction Award, and the Sappho Award of Distinction for her revolutionary work. When she passed away on May 16, 2004, the Latina and Latino intellectual and artistic community lost one of its most influential voices.

See also **Border Art; Chicanos and Chicanas; Critical Race Theory and Lat Crit Theory; Lesbians; Literature; Mexican-Origin People in the United States; Moraga, Cherríe;** *and* **Sexuality.**

BIBLIOGRAPHY
Anzaldúa, Gloria. *Borderlands/La frontera: The New Mestiza.* 2nd ed. San Francisco: Aunt Lute Books, 1999. The original was published in 1987.

Anzaldúa, Gloria. *Friends from the Other Side/Amigos de otro lado.* San Francisco: Children's Book Press, 1993.

Anzaldúa, Gloria. *Prietita and the Ghost Woman/Prietita y la llorona.* San Francisco: Children's Book Press, 1995.

Anzaldúa, Gloria, ed. *Making Face, Making Soul/Haciendo caras: Creative and Critical Perspectives by Feminists of Color.* San Francisco: Aunt Lute Books, 1990.

Anzaldúa, Gloria E., and AnaLouise Keating, eds. *This Bridge We Call Home: Radical Visions for Transformation.* New York and London: Routledge, 2002.

Del Castillo, Adelaida R. "Malintzin Tenepal: A Preliminary Look into a New Perspective." In *Chicana Feminist Thought: The Basic Historical Writings,* edited by Alma M. García. New York: Routledge, 1997.

Flores, Lisa A. "Creating Discursive Space through a Rhetoric of Difference: Chicana Feminists Craft a Homeland." *Quarterly Journal of Speech* 82 (1996): 142–156.

Keating, AnaLouise, ed. *Interviews/Entrevistas: Gloria E. Anzaldúa.* New York and London: Routledge, 2000.

Moraga, Cherríe. *Loving in the War Years: Lo que nunca pasó por sus labios.* Boston: South End Press, 1983.

Moraga, Cherríe, and Gloria Anzaldúa, eds. *This Bridge Called My Back: Writings by Radical Women of Color.* Watertown, Mass.: Persephone Press, 1981.

Paz, Octavio. *The Labyrinth of Solitude: Life and Thought in Mexico.* Translated by Lysander Kemp. New York: Grove, 1962.

Trujillo, Carla. "Chicana Lesbians: Fear and Loathing in the Community." In *Chicana Feminist Thought: The Basic Historical Writings,* edited by Alma M. García. New York: Routledge, 1997.

BERNADETTE MARIE CALAFELL

ARCHITECTURE. This essay explores the historical features and evolution of a group of unique architectural elements, including forms, colors, structures, materials, textures, spatial enclosures, geometries, and symbols that characterize the "Latino and Latina culture" of the United States. Latino and Latina culture is by nature a multiethnic subgroup of American society comprised of a mixture of Iberian, pre-Columbian, and African peoples, referred to as "mestizo," "mulatto," or a combination of all three.

The Expansion of Latino and Latina Culture

Latino and Latina civilization in the United States is both the oldest and the newest cultural force reshaping the urban form and architecture of many American cities. The pattern of distribution was dramatically altered during the twentieth century, especially after World War II. By the end of the century, large concentrations of Latinos and Latinas had settled in the Northeast, Midwest, Southeast, and Northwest of the United States. The Latino and Latina population and its culture are expanding not only demographically but also geographically, impacting numerous urban settlements that historically had no Latino and Latina influence. This reality is having both positive and negative consequences. In the Midwest the Latino and Latina influx has saved many towns and communities from extinction, but in other areas the Latino and Latina expansion is causing fiscal havoc, racial conflict, and other sociopolitical problems.

The Latino and Latina population in the United States in the early twenty-first century is estimated at about 30 million, making it the nation's largest ethnic minority. In Los Angeles; San Antonio, Texas; Miami, Florida; and many other United States cities, Latinos and Latinas make up the majority of the population.

Paralleling the impact of the Latino and Latina population expansion are changes in the character of the cities' traditional forms. An apparent Latino and Latina image is beginning to appear within the American urban landscape, at times dramatic and in other instances subtle.

Historical Influences

Historically the features of U.S. Latino and Latina architecture are the same as those that characterize architecture throughout Latin America. Although most of these characteristics can be traced directly to the Iberian Peninsula—Spain and Portugal—others are unique to the Americas and stem from its pre-Columbian and mestizo culture. This is especially true of Mexican and Andean architecture. Mexico has by far had the most direct impact on Latino and Latina architecture in the United States, both in the past and in the present. Most early colonial towns were founded directly through the Spanish and later Mexican capital of New Spain, Mexico City.

Modern influences can be traced to the geographic proximity of Mexico and the fact that many prominent Mexican architects, such as Ricardo Ligorreta and Teodoro González de León, are doing significant projects in the United States. In addition, most Latino and Latina architects, including José Jimenez, continue to look at the work of modern Mexican architects as a fountain of inspiration.

Other sources of influence come from the published works of Iberian and Latin American architects via the increasing availability of books, magazines, the Internet, and other communication media in the United States. The United States publishes little work by U.S. Latino and Latina architects, but a few, like Carlos Jimenez of Houston and the firm Aquitectonica of Miami, have achieved national attention and are becoming a major source of influence on other U.S. Latino and Latina architects.

Common Characteristics of Latino and Latina Architecture

The specific characteristics of U.S. Latino and Latina architecture are too numerous, varied, and complex to permit detailed analysis here. Furthermore, the manifestations of these features in Miami, Los Angeles, New York, San Antonio, and other major Latino and Latina cities are not necessarily the same. Yet some features are amazingly alike, certainly produced by similar historical

SAN ANTONIO PUBLIC LIBRARY. (Photograph by José Jimenez)

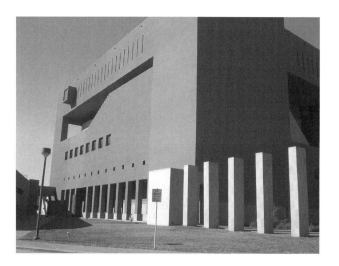

influences. These archetypical traits can be categorized into the following groups:

- primary geometric forms
- polychrome
- texture, materials, and pattern
- geometry
- ornament
- spatial enclosure

Primary geometric forms. Primary geometric forms have historically dominated Latino and Latina architecture. Among these forms are squares; cubes; circles; cylindrical shapes in the form of domes; vaults and triangles, mainly in pyramidal shapes; and various combinations. Pre-Columbian architects made great use of these forms, and their use continued throughout the Spanish and Portuguese colonial period. A modern example of primary geometric forms in contemporary Latino and Latina architecture is the San Antonio Public Library by Ricardo Ligorreta.

Polychrome. The extensive use of color on both the exterior and the interior of buildings is an outstanding feature of Latino and Latina architecture. Contrasting sharply with the prevailing pastels and subdued colors of the dominant Anglo architecture, its use at times has irritated and ruffled the feathers of the establishment. Such was the case with the house of the internationally acclaimed writer Sandra Cisneros in San Antonio. The irony is that with time Cisneros's "purple house" has become one of the city's major tourist attractions.

Polychrome has become the most dramatic indicator of Latino and Latina influence on American architecture. Popular colors are pink, blue, yellow, green, turquoise, and red. Historically the extensive use of color has deep roots stretching back to Iberia, Africa, and pre-Columbian civilizations. Although much of the original meaning and symbolism has been lost, its use in the Latino and Latina culture has survived through modern times irrespective of changing socioeconomic standings, religious beliefs, and educational levels.

Texture, materials, and pattern. Elaborate textures and patterns have traditionally been an inherent element in Latino and Latina architecture. While the modern movement in architecture separated painting, sculpture, and the crafts from architecture elsewhere, this did not happen in Latin America. Most modern Latino and Latina buildings contain highly textured surfaces, murals, graphic elements, sculpture, and other decorative features integrated with the architecture.

Latin American architecture has always used the great variety and beauty of the natural materials available, such as marble, onyx, cantera, brick, and granite. The traditional art of *yeseria* or plasterwork imported from Iberia,

SOUTHWESTERN BELL TELEPHONE BUILDING, SAN ANTONIO. (Photograph by José Jimenez)

especially in areas with Arabic influence, was highly developed among the indigenous cultures of the Americas and has also survived into modern times. In areas of Latin America and the United States where these rich materials were not available or were too costly, plaster or painted ornament was used. Examples have survived in the mission architecture of the Southwest. In the early twenty-first century modern means of transportation and trade have made these traditional materials more available. Practically every new house and building in places such as San Antonio contains either stone or tile from sources in Mexico or Spain. Ornament and the placement of doors, windows, and other elements in public and domestic architecture also have used geometric patterns and guidelines. The most common traditional materials used in American Latino and Latina architecture are cantera stone, ceramic tile, and Spanish roof tile.

Geometry. Geometry, both as a proportional element and as a method for laying out ornament, is a natural part of Latino and Latina architecture. Its roots can be traced to the Islamic architecture of Iberia and to extensive use in pre-Columbian architecture. The shapes of almost all structures and public spaces have been based on the laws of geometry. Early in the colonial period new Spanish towns in the Americas were laid out according to strict principles spelled out in the Laws of the Indies. The Laws of the Indies were the first city planning codes in the areas that became the United States. All Spanish settlements were designed according to the regulations of these laws, which specified the proportions, dimensions, and orientations of plazas, public buildings, streets, and other civic spaces. José Jimenez used many of the original planning principles to restore Milam Plaza (Plaza del Zacate), one of the original public spaces in San Antonio, which had been completely destroyed during the twentieth century. Its geometry is based on the square and the golden section rectangle, which was used extensively in Spanish colonial architecture throughout the Americas.

Ornament. Ornament in Latino and Latina architecture is used to enrich the aesthetic quality of a surface or space, but in many instances it has a symbolic, political, religious, or social function. Latino and Latina ornament is made of a great variety of materials, including tile, wood, iron, stuccowork, or paint. It is placed on both exterior and interior surfaces, on walls, ceilings, floors, or trim. Symbolic ornament usually reflects a sacred belief (a saint, the Virgin) or a family tradition, and at times it is placed simply for nostalgic reasons to remind one of the motherland or place of origin. Ornament can take the form of a shrine or altar placed in the interior or exterior of a structure or house. Almost all American Latino and Latina cultures have their virgin or patron saint. In San Antonio several images of the Virgin are venerated, such as the Virgen de Guadalupe, the Virgen San Juan de los Lagos, or

MILAM PLAZA (PLAZA DEL ZACATE), SAN ANTONIO. (Photograph by José Jimenez)

CANDELARIA OF LA VIRGEN DE GUADALUPE. Work by Jesse Trevino, Guadalupe Cultural Center, San Antonio. (Photograph by José Jimenez)

new Latino and Latina owners of the house shown have introduced a walled enclosure that separates the house from the public domain of the street and sidewalk. They have also marked off a secondary enclosure in the form of an arcade for small group gatherings in the evenings. The surrounding houses do not have porches. The front yard is mostly paved, reflecting the traditional plaza. One can see a fountain and shrine in the front yard. Plants are in containers. There is a definite sense of ordered space articulated by walls, arcades, and other spatial dividers. Examples of modern American Latino and Latina public space show similar characteristics.

Assessment

The study of American Latino and Latina architecture is as complex as the Latino and Latina society itself. Historical Latino and Latina architecture is easier to grasp because its form is clearly connected to specific roots from Iberia. Its manifestation in the modern context is not as easily discernable due to many factors. Foremost is the fact that in many cities, especially those with no traditional Latino and

SAN ANTONIO PUBLIC LIBRARY. (Photograph by José Jimenez)

the Virgen of Candelaria. In other instances it may be the Virgen de la Regla or the Virgen del Cobre, reflecting the religious devotional practices of the community.

Spatial enclosure. Latinos and Latinas relate to space differently from Anglos. Historically Latino and Latina cities and dwellings were organized according to a system of enclosed spaces that led one from the public domain to the private. Cities were organized around plazas, dwellings around a private courtyard. The source of this traditional pattern can be traced to both the pre-Columbian and the Iberian cultures.

The spatial pattern of the modern American Latino and Latina city and dwelling is emerging as a hybrid version with elements reflecting both the characteristics of the traditional past and the American influences. The San Antonio house in the illustration is an example of this pattern. The setting is a typical American subdivision composed of bungalow houses set back from the street with open front yards that are mostly landscaped. The

HOME IN SAN ANTONIO. (Photograph by José Jimenez)

experiencing a renaissance in the United States distinct from that of Mexico and other Latino and Latina sources. Its expressive qualities, however, have definite linkages to their pre-Columbian, Iberian, and African heritages.

See also Altares; Resolana; *and* Santa Fe Style.

BIBLIOGRAPHY

Arreola, Daniel. "Mexican American Housescapes." *Geographical Review* 78 (July 1988): 299–315.

Bolton, Herbert Eugene. *Bolton and the Spanish Borderlands*. Edited by John Francis Bannon. Norman: University of Oklahoma Press, 1964.

Castedo, Leopoldo. *A History of Latin American Art and Architecture from Pre-Columbian Times to the Present*. Translated and edited by Phyllis Freeman. New York: Praeger, 1969.

Chipman, Donald E. *Spanish Texas: 1519–1821*. Austin: University of Texas Press, 1992.

Cruz, Gilbert R. *Let There Be Towns: Spanish Municipal Origins in the American Southwest, 1610–1810*. College Station: Texas A&M University Press, 1988.

Kanellos, Nicolás. *Thirty Million Strong: Reclaiming the Hispanic Image in American Culture*. Golden, Colo.: Fulcrum Publishing, 1998.

Kingston, Mike. *A Concise History of Texas*. Houston, Tex.: Gulf Publishing, 1991.

Oles, James. *South of the Border: Mexico in the American Imagination, 1917–1947*. Washington, D.C.: Smithsonian Institution Press, 1993.

Reps, John W. *Town Planning in Frontier America*. Princeton, N.J.: Princeton University Press, 1969.

Sanford, Trent Elwood. *The Architecture of the Southwest*. Tucson: University of Arizona Press, 1997. Originally published in 1950.

Stierlin, Henri. *Living Architecture: Mayan*. New York: Grosset and Dunlap, 1964.

Williams, Norma. *The Mexican American Family: Tradition and Change*. Dix Hills, N.Y.: General Hall, 1990.

Yorba, Jonathan. *Arte Latino: Treasures from the Smithsonian American Art Museum*. New York: Watson-Guptill Publications, 2001.

JOSÉ JIMENEZ

Latina heritage, the Latino and Latina architectural style is just emerging. In cities with a historically strong Latino and Latina culture, like San Antonio and Los Angeles, it may seem easier to comprehend on the surface. However, the architecture takes many forms. After the 1850s much of the original Latino and Latina architecture of these cities was destroyed. Though the culture survived, its architecture became Anglo-American. Latinos and Latinas simply adapted and modified Anglo-American forms to suit their needs and lived in barrios that were pretty much isolated from the dominant Anglo city. San Antonio, for example, is in reality two cities, one Latino and Latina and the other Anglo.

A truly new American Latino and Latina architecture began to emerge after the 1960s, primarily because of the rising economic and social-political power of the Latino and Latina community. The late twentieth century saw the rise of an American Latino and Latina middle class as well as a cadre of American Latino and Latina architects producing their own architecture but practicing mostly in the offices of Anglo-dominated firms. Their architectural vocabulary and production reflected the values of the dominant culture. In the early twenty-first century this has begun to change. The Latino and Latina population, at least its middle class, though more fully integrated into the mainstream culture, is not totally adopting the architectural values of the Anglo culture but in many cases is trying to find its own expression.

Whereas early American Latino and Latina architecture simply copied American models, it appears that Latinos and Latinas are beginning to seek an architecture that more closely expresses their values. Like Latino and Latina art, music, and literature, Latino and Latina architecture is

AREÍTO. *Areíto* is a socioreligious music and dance ritual of the Taíno Arawak peoples. In the late sixties, it was the name given to a group of young, radical Cuban Americans that organized for political and social change in the United States. Identifying politically as progressive, socialist, and Communist, Areíto aligned itself with and came out of the social movements of the sixties and seventies. Primarily exiled Cubans living in the northeastern and southeastern United States, most members of Areíto came from white middle- and upper-middle-class Cuban families that emigrated to the United States in the early sixties.

Basis for Areíto

Before they formed Areíto, many of its participants were activists working in the civil rights movement, the American Indian Movement (AIM), the anti–Vietnam War protests, and the Chicano and Chicana and farmworker struggles. They formed part of the sixties hippy counterculture and the antiestablishment and Puerto Rican independence struggles. As college students, they began a process of political interrogation that led them not only to question the politics of the Cuban American exile community, but also to reassess their position toward the Cuban Revolution. Areíto members established a journal called *Areíto* in 1971 and published a book, *Contra viento y marea* (Against All Odds), in 1978. *Areíto* published academic articles, editorials, arts, and poetry that explored issues of identity and politics in Cuba and the Latino and Latina and Cuban community in the United States. The book captured the voices of Areíto members and chronicled their political awakenings, experiences, and visions for the future.

Areíto came out of the collective experiences of young Cuban American college students at the University of Florida in Gainesville struggling with issues of identity and social awareness. Experiences of downward mobility, loss of social status, and racial discrimination had created general disenchantment with the United States. Often perceived as "spics," these young Cuban women and men confronted language and cultural discrimination in educational institutions and in the wider society and culture. They became conscious that their "exile" status did not preclude the denigration they faced. They also saw themselves as members of a marginal group at the receiving end of racist attitudes and practices similar to those confronted by members of other racial and ethnic minority groups in the United States. As they sought to make sense out of their experiences of racism, discrimination, and social alienation, they realized how other marginal groups fighting for their rights shared these experiences as well. Understanding themselves as minorities instead of exiles set in motion a process of examining their social location and actively engaging with social justice struggles. These Cuban women and men aligned themselves with blacks, Chicanos and Chicanas, Puerto Ricans, and American Indians and worked with them to achieve social change and justice.

Engaging in Politics

Besides activism in the civil rights movements of the sixties, Cuban Americans joined the debates and articulated identities in solidarity with anti-imperialist, internationalist struggles that were oppositional to the dominant Cuban American community and its anti-Cuba politics. The radical, anticapitalist politics, including Marxism, studied and discussed on college campuses during the sixties and seventies helped Areíto members form their ideology. The U.S. invasion of the Dominican Republic, the death of Che Guevara, and the overthrow, backed by the Central Intelligence Agency (CIA), of the democratically elected president Salvador Allende in Chile also shaped their political principles. These positions put

them in direct confrontation with the politics of the larger Cuban American community.

Members of Areíto faced conflict and hostility within their families and the right-wing Cuban American community. Many came to feel a "double exile," in which they suffered alienation from both the Cuban exile community and U.S. society. In *Contra viento y marea* a member of Areíto expresses this paradox:

> Me friquié porque no encajaba en eso. No encajaba en las fiestas de los cubanos, así que dejé de ir. No encajaba con los norteamericanos tampoco, así que pasé la mayor parte de los años de secundaria sola. Me sentía como "en el medio" y no podia aceptarme yo misma. Eso es lo que mata. Yo tenia que ser una cosa o la otra, y no podia.
> [I freaked out because I didn't fit into that. I didn't fit into the Cuban parties, so I stopped going. I didn't fit in with North Americans either, so I spent the majority of high school years alone. I felt like "in the middle" and I could not accept myself. That is what kills. I had to be one thing or another, and I couldn't]
>
> (Grupo Areíto, p. 37)

In claiming independence from and opposition to the conservative right-wing Cuban American community, Areíto members were able to reexamine their position toward the Cuban Revolution. The revaluation led to their support for and commitment to the Cuban revolutionary project. Unfortunately, this put them at the receiving end of terrorist assaults and retaliations from conservative Cuban American groups. Right-wing terrorist threats, bombs, firebombings, and killings targeted members of Areíto and anyone else in the Cuban community who did not advocate antagonism toward the Cuban government. One of the founders of Areíto, Carlos Muniz Varela, was killed on April 28, 1979, in Puerto Rico by right-wing Cubans. His killers were never brought to justice.

Areíto's development came out of the experiences of Cuban American participants in political movements and radical politics and out of previous, short-lived Cuban American groups. For example, in 1967 young Cuban Americans from cities in the Northeast came together in Union City, New Jersey, to discuss issues related to Cuba and the Cuban Revolution. They called themselves La Cosa, or The Thing, for lack of a better name. La Cosa's posture toward Cuba was initially one of aggression, but a subgroup of radicals broke off to explore dialogue with Cuba and a better understanding of socialism. Areíto's direct genesis, however, came from a group called Juventud Cubana Socialista (Cuban Socialist Youth) that started in Miami in December 1970. The aims of Juventud Cubana Socialista were to return to Cuba and in the meantime to be engaged in the Puerto Rican independence movement. By 1971 they had expanded into New York City and Puerto Rico. The Estudios Cubanos, or Cuban Studies, meetings that took place in Washington, D.C., also provided a space for discussion and open exploration of issues related to Cuba and Cuban American politics. Members of Areíto participated in these organizations and in the Brigada Antonio Maceo, founded in 1977.

Areíto surged at a time of radical leftist politics in the United States but from within a right-wing intolerant community. Members faced many challenges, including alienation and ostracism from their families and their communities, terrorist attacks, and general intimidation. But they created a space for dialogue within the Cuban community where none had previously existed. They called for reconciliation and reassessment of the Cuban Revolution within a context of threats, intimidation, and violence. They faced these challenges from their families and communities and re-created their identities and political visions.

See also Brigada Antonio Maceo *and* Cuban Americans.

BIBLIOGRAPHY

Grupo Areíto. *Contra viento y marea*. Havana, Cuba: Casa de las Américas, 1978.

García, Cristina. *The Aguero Sisters*. New York: Knopf, 1997.

García, Cristina. *Dreaming in Cuban*. New York: Knopf, 1992.

Torres, Maria de los Angeles. *In the Land of Mirrors: Cuban Exile Politics in the United States*. Ann Arbor: University of Michigan Press, 1999. Notes the political changes in the Cuban exile community over the forty years since the Cuban revolution.

AMALIA CABEZAS

ARENAS, REINALDO (1943–1990), Cuban American author. Reinaldo Arenas is one of the most innovative and provocative Latin American authors of the twentieth century. His most important works include the novels *El mundo alucinante, una novela de aventuras* (1969), *La loma del angel* (1987), and *El portero* (1989); the play *Persecución* (1986); the collection of essays *Necesidad de libertad* (1986); and four collections of poems and short stories. Nevertheless, Arenas's masterpiece is the sequence of novels "La Pentagonía," one of the most ambitious works of narrative fiction produced in Latin America.

Arenas was born in 1943 in the small town of Holguín, Cuba. At the age of fifteen, he left home and joined Fidel Castro's revolution. When Castro came to power, Arenas benefited from the new regime's mass education programs and moved to Havana, where he began to study literature at the university and was introduced to Havana's homosexual subculture. In 1963 Arenas quit school and a job at the National Library and began his career as a writer. In 1965 he won the First Mention Award at the Cirilo Villaverde National Competition for his first novel, *Celestino antes del alba*, which was published in 1967 by the Unión Nacional de Escritores y Artistas Cubanos

(UNEAC). Although it received critical recognition, the novel's lack of realism clashed with the cultural orthodoxy of a socialist regime that was more interested in producing realistic fiction. Consequently, *El mundo alucinante*, his second novel, was disapproved and had to be smuggled to France to be published. This rebellious act resulted in a campaign of police harassment that culminated in 1973, when Arenas was arrested, falsely accused of sexual molestation. He was charged and convicted of "ideological deviation" and of publishing abroad without official permission. Arenas escaped, but he was recaptured and sent to the prison of El Morro, where he continued writing and smuggling his work out of prison and out of Cuba. He was discovered and, threatened with death, was forced to renounce his work and abide by the Revolutionary doctrine.

Soon after his release, Arenas took advantage of the situation created by the mass exodus from the Mariel harbor in 1980 and left Cuba undetected. He settled in New York, where he continued writing, but his new freedom was soon embittered when he was diagnosed with AIDS. Arenas struggled to finish writing the last two novels of "La Pentagonía" and his autobiography, *Antes que anochezca* (1990). Dying and depressed, Arenas committed suicide in 1990.

For its intradependent structure and thematic unity, "La Pentagonía" reflects better than any other single text Arenas's literary concerns: the struggle for self-expression and the need for literary experimentation in societies seized by ignorance and intolerance. It reflects Arenas's attempts to cope with social practices determined to suppress his gay identity and the writer's will to create an alternative reality in which the individual liberates himself. This artistic endeavor, which has been taken as an attack against Castroism, made him the quintessential voice for literary and individual resistance inside and outside Cuba, where he still had no official recognition by the early twenty-first century. For its political stance against Castro's regime, the Cuban community in exile warmly welcomed Arenas and appropriated his work. However, Arenas soon expressed his disappointment with the community for embodying the same repressive practices as those of Castro's regime, from the opposite end of the political spectrum.

The title of "La Pentagonía" is a neologism highlighting the agony that the characters of the novels suffer for their repression and persecution by authoritative discourses of power. It opens with *Celestino* and is followed by *El palacio de las blanquísimas mofetas* (1975), *Otra vez el mar* (1982), *El color del verano* (1990), and *El asalto* (1991). The protagonist of each novel experiences the same urge for self-expression as a means to survive an oppressive reality, which Arenas subverts through an aesthetic of disjunction

REINALDO ARENAS. (CORBIS)

and discomfort. With no structured plot, chronology, or delineation of characters, the novels underscore the psychological and social dimensions of the Cuban subject: uncertainty, contradiction, and inconsistency.

Celestino, the protagonist of the first novel, is the alter ego the narrator creates as a means to gain freedom through literary expression. Celestino has a poetic sensibility that drives him to write poetry on the trunks and leaves of trees. Being creations of the narrator's imagination, Celestino and his poetic drive are indestructible. They even endure when the narrator's grandfather cuts his head or all the trees with his hatchet, a tool of censorship that is translated into the novel when the word "hatchet" graphically cuts the narrative for several pages.

The narrator finally dies, but reappears as Fortunato in *El palacio*. Fortunato expresses the same compulsion for self-expression, which aids him in trying to survive the alienation he suffers within his repressive family. He steals paper from his grandfather and writes in secret, inventing, like Celestino, a magical world completely different from that in which he lives, an act that is perceived by the reader not only as an expression of individual freedom, but also as a search for aesthetic beauty.

Fortunato dies at the end of *El palacio* only to reappear as Héctor in *Otra vez el mar*, Arenas's finest work. The novel, which Arenas had to rewrite three times because his manuscripts were confiscated, takes place during Castro's Revolution. Like the narrator of *Celestino*, Héctor, a political dissident and a homosexual, invents an alter ego to fulfill his desire for expression and survive his desperation, which goes beyond the political and the sexual. Héctor struggles against the irrelevance of man's existence in a society that denies him the satisfaction of his desires and the possibility of plenitude as a human being.

The last two novels of "La Pentagonía" were written in and affected by exile. *El color del verano* (The Color of the Summer) and *El asalto* (The Assault) more deeply explore the future of the subject in a tyrannized society. While *The Color of the Summer* is a pastiche of several plots composed of many independent but interrelated chapters narrated by multiple voices, *The Assault* mimics the realistic fiction authoritative regimes praise, since the protagonist is now an accomplice of the tyrannical political regime. But the monstrous absurdity of the story undermines the ability of realistic fiction to mirror reality. The unnamed protagonist roams the country searching for his mother to kill her and end her domination, while committing all kind of atrocities to his fellow citizens. At the end, he learns that his mother is in fact the "Reprimero," the head of the state, whom he rapes and kills, liberating society from despotism.

"La Pentagonía" illustrates the significance of writing as an act of individual liberation. Therefore, the function of language cannot be to mirror reality, but to subordinate reality to fiction. The novels in this sequence never sacrifice the aesthetic experience for the transparency of the discourse, demanding an active reader who internalizes and interprets the disjointed elements of the texts. Even though Arenas inscribes his particular experiences into his works, the subversion of narrative conventions reminds us that such conventions are nothing else but fiction, and we cannot presume a uneqivocal political use of them.

See also Cuban American Writers; HIV and AIDS; Literature; Marielitos; *and* Sexuality.

BIBLIOGRAPHY

Béjar, Eduardo C. *La textualidad de Reinaldo Arenas: Juegos de la escritura posmoderna*. Madrid, Spain: Editorial Playor, 1987.

Lugo Nazario, Félix. *La alucinación y los recursos literarios en las novelas de Reinaldo Arenas*. Miami, Fla: Ediciones Universal, 1995.

Rozencvaig, Perla. *Reinaldo Arenas: Narrativa de un transgresión*. Mexico City, Mexico: Editorial Oasis, 1986.

Soto, Francisco. *Conversación con Reinaldo Arenas*. Madrid, Spain: Betania, 1990.

Soto, Francisco. *Reinaldo Arenas*. New York: Twayne, 1998.

CÉSAR F. SIERRA

ARIZONA. The establishment of economic and political control by the United States in the Southwest during the nineteenth century shaped the history of Latinos and Latinas in Arizona. After the United States defeated Mexico in the United States–Mexican War (1846–1848), the peace accord known as the Treaty of Guadalupe Hidalgo was signed (1848). For $15 million, the United States acquired the vast territories of New Mexico, Arizona, California, and parts of Nevada, Utah, and Colorado. Southwest Mexicans who remained in United States territory were granted the constitutional rights of citizens, and the treaty theoretically protected their property, culture, and religion. The territory acquired by the treaty did not include southern Arizona and southwestern New Mexico. General Antonio López de Santa Anna sold this region to the United States in 1853 in a transaction known as the Gadsden Purchase, creating the modern-day boundary that separates Arizona from the Mexican state of Sonora. This treaty provided Mexicans in the territory the same rights supposedly guaranteed by the Treaty of Guadalupe Hidalgo. The population of Mexicans in what is now Arizona did not exceed one thousand, all of whom lived in the Gadsden Purchase region.

Early Cooperation

Many Mexicans emigrated from northern Mexico after the Purchase. They held onto political and economic power, although their influence declined during the course of the century. In 1863, when Arizona separated from New Mexico, Tucson became the territorial capital. Initially, Anglos and Mexicans cooperated in the importation of European and American goods into Arizona across the Isthmus of Nicaragua. By the 1880s, the railroads replaced this system. A new influx of Anglos who did not need to cooperate with Mexicans displaced the older non-Mexican population. Prescott in northern Arizona became the new territorial seat, away from the Mexican population. As Phoenix grew in importance, that city became the seat, and it remained the capital when Arizona became a state in 1912.

Arizona prospered in the early twentieth century as a source of raw materials for eastern industrial markets. In 1903, the Newlands Reclamation Act allowed Anglo American farmers to plant cotton and lettuce on irrigated acreage in the desert surrounding Phoenix and Yuma. Industrial metals such as copper were abundant in the eastern part of the state. Both industries relied on Mexico as their main labor source. Railroad transportation not only allowed the marketing of these new raw materials, but it greatly stimulated Mexican immigration as well. By 1910, Mexicans made up 13 percent of Arizona's population of 200,000.

Regaining Rights

As Mexicans lost political power, the need to combat civil rights violations and to protect themselves in the workplace became apparent. This spurred the formation of organizations such as La Alianza Hispano Americana (Hispanic American Alliance), started in Tucson in 1894, and La Liga Protectora Latina (Latin Protective League), formed in 1914 in Phoenix. The Mexican government also sponsored self-help organizations through its consular service. The activism of Arizona Mexicans led to the first successful school desegregation case in the United States, in Tempe in 1925. Mexicans were the first to be involved in intensive unionization efforts in Arizona, beginning with a number of mining strikes in 1903. During World War I, the Western Federation of Miners and the Industrial Workers of the World (IWW) instigated numerous strikes with sizable Mexican participation. In spite of the widespread use of Mexican labor in agriculture, few efforts were made to unionize farm workers at this time.

By the 1930s the ethnic Mexican population had reached over 60,000, out of a total state population of 400,000. About half of these had been born in the United States. The young Mexicans who were born and raised in Arizona were strongly influenced by Anglo society and culture. These young Hispanics practiced "Mexican Americanism," an ideology that committed them to Americanizing, breaking down segregation in the schools, and fighting discrimination in general. Essentially, they asked that America's professed democratic values be honored in practice. The Latin American Club was formed to encourage greater political participation. Students at the Arizona Normal School in Tempe started Los Conquistadores (The Conquistadors) to advocate for greater educational opportunities. Both groups adamantly opposed discrimination and segregation.

When the United States entered World War II in 1941, Mexican Americans in Arizona enthusiastically enlisted in the armed forces. Civilians organized "Home Front" efforts such as bond drives. Women took jobs as wartime workers. But after the war, discrimination continued, prompting even more intensive efforts to eliminate barriers to social and economic mobility. Returning veterans, for example, broke down restrictive housing policies in Phoenix. In 1952, Mexican Americans united to abolish the last vestiges of segregation in Tolleson and Peoria, agricultural communities near Phoenix.

Arizona's economy changed drastically after the war, as electronic manufacturing overshadowed mining and agriculture. Thousands of non-Mexican migrants from the Midwest and the East settled in the state. By 1965, Arizona's population passed the one million mark. Some Mexicans were able to take advantage of the new prosperity. By the 1960s and early 1970s, more Mexican Americans were enrolled in Arizona colleges than at any time in the past. These students, especially at the University of Arizona in Tucson and at Arizona State University in the Phoenix area, became involved in the Chicano/a movement. The activists rejected the assimilation strategy of the older generation and took on the task of ending the subordination and poverty that persisted for Mexican Americans in spite of a general economic improvement in the state. The fervor of the movement eventually subsided, but it spawned a generation of political activists such as Ed Pastor and Raul Grijalva, both of whom became Democratic congressmen.

Immigration to Arizona from Mexico and Latin America continues unabated, and the state continues to grow faster than most other parts of the country in terms of economy and population. The Hispanic population increased from 720,561 to 1,295,617—25 percent of the state's population—during the 1990s. This massive influx of Hispanic immigrants since the 1960s has reinforced Hispanic culture in the United States. The culture and identity of Mexican Americans in Arizona will continue to change, reflecting both the inevitable acculturation to Anglo society and the continuing influence of immigrants, not only from Mexico but also from throughout Latin America.

See also **Border, The; Cananea Miners' Strike; Census; Chicanos and Chicanas; Demographics; Education; Immigration; Industrial Workers of the World; Mexican-Origin People in the United States; Treaty of Guadalupe Hidalgo;** *and* **United States–Mexican War.**

BIBLIOGRAPHY
Luckingham, Bradford. *Minorities in Phoenix: A Profile of Mexican American, Chinese American, and African American Communities, 1860–1992.* Tucson: University of Arizona Press, 1994.
Luey, Beth, and Noel J. Stowe. *Arizona at Seventy-Five: The Next Twenty-Five Years.* Tucson: Arizona State University Public History Program and the Arizona Historical Society, 1987.
Mellinger, Philip J. *Race and Labor in Western Copper: The Fight for Equality, 1896–1918.* Tucson: University of Arizona Press, 1995.
Officer, James. *Hispanic Arizona: 1536–1856.* Tucson: University of Arizona Press, 1987.
Sheridan, Thomas E. *Los Tucsonenses: The Mexican Community in Tucson, 1854–1941.* Tucson: University of Arizona Press, 1986.

F. ARTURO ROSALES

ARKANSAS. In the mid-sixteenth century, Spaniard Hernando de Soto became one of the first European explorers to visit the territory of what is now Arkansas. After being named governor of Cuba by Holy Roman Emperor Charles V (who was also the king of Spain as Charles I), he led an expedition that left Spain in 1538 in search of gold and silver. De Soto journeyed up the Arkansas River into Oklahoma but died along the river banks. Arkansas was originally part of the Spanish Louisiana Territory, but it was Henri de Tonti of France who founded the first permanent white settlement, the

Arkansas Post, near the Arkansas River in 1686. Part of the Territory of Missouri from 1812, the area became an official territory in 1819 when a large wave of settlers arrived. The Arkansas Territory included what is today Arkansas and Oklahoma (excluding the panhandle), with Arkansas Post as its capital. A few years later the capital moved to Little Rock.

In 1836, Arkansas became the twenty-fifth state with an approximate population of 50,000. Subsequent decades were marked by the development of the cotton industry and the spread of the southern plantation system west into Arkansas. Arkansas joined the Confederacy in 1861, but from 1863 the northern part of the state was occupied by Union troops. Around 1870, railroads came to the state, and Mexican labor came to work them. During World War I, the war department agreed to transport workers to labor camps in the United States, where they would be housed and fed while working on government construction contracts at defense plants and military bases. In many of these camps, workers were subjected to harsh conditions and even forced labor. Rafael Marchán was one of the first to provide an account of such incidents to the commissioner of Puerto Rico in 1918. Workers like Marchán appealed to the U.S. government to improve sanitary conditions, provide adequate food, and stop widespread beatings. In 1918 and 1919, almost one hundred Puerto Rican immigrants died in Arkansas labor camps.

Documentation of Mexicans in the state of Arkansas can be found in early labor history. In fact, the earliest Census documentation of Latinas and Latinos in the state was in the 1920s when Mexicans were recruited to the state to work the aluminum mines in Saline County. Mexicans were also actively recruited to work cotton farms around 1949. The labor history of Latinas and Latinos in Arkansas was rife with racial tensions, which grew from lower wages being offered to farmworkers due to the influx of Mexican laborers. At the 1952 Congressional hearings that focused on farmworker complaints about foreign labor, the first piece of testimony came from a Gould, Arkansas, cotton plantation worker. Such complaints resulted in racist legislation, exemplified by the federal government's "Operation Wetback," which resulted in the expulsion of nearly 4 million Mexican nationals and U.S. citizens of Mexican origin back to Mexico between 1950 and 1955.

The state census did not record Latinas and Latinos during the twentieth century, and in fact it was not until 1960 that the state of Arkansas census recorded Native Americans in their own category. Thus, religious institutions and cultural activities provide much of the documentation of Mexicans and other Latina and Latino groups in the state. Some community leaders in the state assert that the unification of a visible Latina and Latino population can be traced through the Catholic Church, particularly since the early 1970s when the Mexican American Spanish Center was formed in Little Rock under the auspices of the Little Rock Catholic Diocese. This center has since been renamed the Hispanic Council in order to be more representative of other Latina and Latino populations. Between 1990 and 2000, the Latina and Latino population increased 336 percent, making Arkansas the U.S. state with the second-fastest-growing Latina and Latino population, behind North Carolina. In 1990, the Hispanic population was 19,876. According to the 2000 U. S. Census, there are 86,866 Hispanics and/or Latinas and Latinos living in Arkansas, composing 3.2 percent of the state's total population. Of this percentage, 61,204 are Mexican, 2,473 Puerto Rican, 950 Cuban, and 22,239 "other Hispanic."

Emerging organizations and cultural visibility reflect this population spurt. Some examples include the Hispanic Women's Organization of Arkansas, founded in 1999 by a group of Latina women concerned with their families' well-being. *¡Hola! Arkansas*, the first statewide bilingual Spanish-English language newspaper was published in 2000. Formed by a group of Latinas and Latinos in Northwest Arkansas who were concerned about the absence of an effective voice for Latinas and Latinos in the area, the Arkansas branch of the League of United Latin American Citizens (LULAC), one of the nation's oldest Latina and Latino political organizations, received its charter as Council 754 on February 23, 2001. Elected government officials in Arkansas have also made adjustments to better serve their Spanish-speaking constituents. In 2001 Arkansas governor Mike Huckabee became the first Arkansas state governor to translate (via interpreter) his weekly radio addresses into Spanish. Most recently, negotiations have begun to establish a Mexican consulate in Little Rock to serve the state's 150,000 Mexican residents.

See also Census; Demographics; Education; Immigration; *and* League of United Latin American Citizens.

DEBORAH R. VARGAS

ARNAZ, DESI (1917–1986), actor, musician, and television producer. The "I" in the title of the 1950s television comedy *I Love Lucy*, Desi Arnaz was subordinate to the comedic genius of his wife Lucille Ball. But Arnaz's pioneer status owes as much to his talents as a showman and businessman who critically shaped early television production practices as to his prominence as costar in one of the most successful comedy shows.

Desiderio Alberto Arnaz y de Acha III was born March 2, 1917, to an elite family in Santiago, Cuba. His father was Santiago's mayor, and his paternal grandfather was

the doctor for Teddy Roosevelt's Rough Riders. His maternal grandfather was one of the cofounders of the Bacardí Rum Company. In 1933, a few months after Arnaz's father was elected to the Cuban Congress, Gerardo Machado's government was overthrown, and Arnaz's father was jailed for six months. After his release he moved to Miami, where Desi Arnaz soon joined him.

In his unsentimental and often salty autobiography *A Book* (1976), Arnaz renders his early years in the United States as a picaresque series of episodes in which he bluffs his way to success. Less than a year after he was hired by the renowned bandleader Xavier Cugat, Arnaz quit, forming his own band. With twenty dollars in his pocket and a ton of nerve, he parlayed his brief New York stint into a twelve-week contract for five times what he made with Cugat. Gustavo Pérez-Firmat, in *Life on the Hyphen* (1994), calls *A Book* the life story of a *vivo*, someone who lives and thrives by his wits.

Arnaz is considered at best a minor talent by many music historians. His conga playing, the drum showily slung over his shoulder and his arms waving wildly, served more to rouse the crowd than to carry the beat. But he made up for less-than-stellar musical abilities with shrewd showmanship. He is most closely identified with the song "Babalú," first recorded by the Cuban crooner Miguelito Valdés. Arnaz also took credit for starting the conga craze in the United States, which the gossip columnist Walter Winchell dubbed "the Desi chain" (Pérez-Firmat, p. 100). However, as John Storm Roberts noted in *The Latin Tinge* (1979), the carnival dance was performed in New York in 1936, a year before Arnaz's arrival. Nonetheless, Arnaz was spotted by the Broadway lyricists Richard Rodgers and Lorenz Hart, who asked him to audition for the part of Manuelito Lynch in the musical *Too Many Girls*. Arnaz played the girl-crazed football phenom from Argentina on Broadway and in the film version. During the filming he met Lucille Ball, whom he married in 1940.

The couple spent the first years of their marriage largely apart. Ball was "Queen of the Bs" in Hollywood, and Arnaz was in New York, on the road with his band, or making movies for RKO. Arnaz was drafted in 1943, but because he injured his knee, he served the rest of his tour entertaining injured troops at a southern California hospital.

In 1950 CBS signed Ball to make a television version of her hit radio show *My Favorite Husband*. She asked that Arnaz be cast as her husband, but CBS executives and the show's sponsors balked. To prove that audiences could accept them as a couple, they embarked on a vaudeville tour. The act was successful and later was incorporated into the pilot for the show. Renamed *I Love Lucy*, it was about Ricky Ricardo, a Cuban bandleader, whose wife Lucy continually tries to get into his nightclub act.

Sponsors wanted to produce the show in New York because shows shot live on the West Coast were shown in the East in kinescope, an inferior technology. To maintain high quality without moving his family, which now included their daughter Lucie, Arnaz devised a production system never before used in television. The show was shot on film in a movie studio in front of an audience and edited in a specially built three-headed Moviola.

To make up for increased production costs, Arnaz negotiated an unprecedented deal that cut their salaries but gave Desilu, the company he and Ball formed, complete ownership, single-handedly creating syndication, which allowed producers to deal directly with local stations and bypass the networks. This deal earned Arnaz and Ball much more as producers of the show than as its stars. Arnaz's producing talents and Desilu's unique capabilities attracted other shows. By 1956, the sixth season for *I Love Lucy*, Desilu was a $12 million operation with eight hundred employees. During the 1955–1956 and 1956–1957 seasons, Desilu produced 691 half-hour shows, making it the top television production company at the time.

I Love Lucy remains one of the most successful comedies in American television. During the second season the episode dramatizing the birth of Little Ricky Ricardo (broadcast January 19, 1953, the same day their son Desi Arnaz IV was born) was seen by a record 44 million viewers. By the end of that season *I Love Lucy* had been the top-rated show for eleven consecutive months.

While Ricky Ricardo's ethnicity was fodder for jokes—Lucy often made fun of his accent, and his rapid-fire tirades in Spanish were played for laughs—it was not an object of ridicule. Ricky Ricardo was restorer of the order upset by his wacky wife. Variations on this sitcom husband can be found in just about every family television comedy. The image of Ricky Ricardo, and Desi Arnaz, as a stylish, hardworking Latino integrated into an American family remains a potent symbol for many Hispanics. For example, Arnaz is featured in a pivotal plot point in Oscar Hijuelos's Pulitzer Prize–winning novel *The Mambo Kings Sing Songs of Love* (1989) when its two protagonists appear on *I Love Lucy*.

After he and Ball divorced in 1960, Arnaz sold his share of Desilu to Ball in 1962 for $3 million. He retired to breed horses, and he married again, to Edie Mack Hirsch in 1962. He attempted to return to television production but never regained the success he had had with Desilu. He died of lung cancer on December 2, 1986, at his home in Del Mar, California.

The only time Arnaz spoke openly about politics was to defend Ball when she was accused of being a communist in 1953. Nevertheless he was honored posthumously in 2004 by Veterans of the Bay of Pigs invasion for his anonymous $50,000 donation to help free those captured in Cuba.

FILMS AND TELEVISION SHOWS

Bataan. Directed by Tay Garnett, written by Robert D. Andrews. Metro-Goldwyn-Mayer, 1943.

Cuban Pete. Directed by Jean Yarbrough, story by Bernard Feins, written by Robert Presnell Sr., 1946.

The Escape Artist. Directed by Caleb Deschanel, written by Melissa Mathiso. Zoetrope Studios, 1982.

Father Takes a Wife. Directed by Jack Hively, written by Dorothy and Herbert Fields, 1941.

Forever, Darling. Directed by Alexander Hall, written by Helen Deutsch. Zanra Productions, 1955.

Four Jacks and a Jill. Directed by Jack Hively, written by Monte Brice and John Twist, 1942.

Holiday in Havana. Directed by Jean Yarbrough, written by Karen De-Wolf, 1949.

I Love Lucy. CBS, 1951–1957.

The Long, Long Trailer. Directed by Vicente Minelli, written by Albert Hackett. Metro-Goldwyn-Mayer, 1954.

The Lucy-Desi Comedy Hour. CBS, 1957–1960.

The Navy Comes Through. Directed by A. Edward Sutherland, story by Borden Chase. RKO, 1942.

Too Many Girls. Directed by George Abbott, written by George Marion Jr. and John Twist. RKO, 1940.

See also Cuban Americans; Media; *and* Stereotypes.

BIBLIOGRAPHY
Arnaz, Desi. *A Book*. New York: Morrow, 1976.
Ball, Lucille, with Betty Hannah Hoffman. *Love, Lucy*. New York: Putnam, 1996.
De Valle, Elaine. "The Late Desi Arnaz Honored for Bay of Pigs Contributions." *Miami Herald*, May 8, 2004, B3.
Pérez-Firmat, Gustavo. *Life on the Hyphen: The Cuba-American Way*. Austin: University of Texas Press, 1994.
Roberts, John Storm. *The Latin Tinge: The Impact of Latin American Music on the United States*. New York: Oxford University Press, 1979.
Sanders, Coyne Steven, and Tom Gilbert. *Desilu: The Story of Lucille Ball and Desi Arnaz*. New York: Morrow, 1993.

CAROLINA GONZÁLEZ

ARQUITECTONICA. *See* Architecture.

ART, CHICANO. Chicano and Chicana art arose at the end of the 1960s as part of the Chicano/a movement, a national political and social mobilization initiated and led by farm workers, student activists, third-party electorates, dispossessed land-grant owners, and critics of police brutality and of the war in Vietnam. Following the successes of the civil rights movement and the Native American movement and developing in tandem with the feminist movement and gay and lesbian movements, El Movimiento developed throughout the United States, not just the Southwest, between 1965 and 1985. Fluctuations in the Chicano/a movement were largely due to regional differences, but the characteristics of resistance, cultural affirmation, anti-assimilation, and self-determination were evident in all locations, although some communities did not embrace the term "Chicano/a" itself. For instance, artists in New Mexico continued traditional arts, such as that of the *santero*, a person who makes images of saints, and sometimes added contemporary visual vocabulary from the Chicano/a movement. Artists in Chicago identified with the philosophy and politics of El Movimiento, but they preferred the term "Mexicana/o."

Born out of the civil rights movement and the other liberation movements it inspired, the work of Chicano/a artists echoed the social and political struggle for self-determination, liberation, and equality. Chicano/a art is fundamentally a politicized art form. It is politicized in content and aesthetic style, and both are used to challenge the status quo. Furthermore, in the early decades of its formation, Chicano/a artists found inspiration abroad as well as at home, especially in the Cuban Revolution, and developed a visual language and strategy to explore the patterns of disempowerment that they faced in education, labor, health care, housing, and the media. The crafting of cultural icons, images, histories, and futures is a goal for Chicano/a artists—all of which are political acts in the context of oppression, expectations of assimilation, and denial of historical presence.

For some art historians and cultural critics, however, political art is primarily found in the early period or during the height of the Chicano/a movement, in which artists directly challenged art for art's sake. They assert that circulation through commercial galleries and participation in multicultural agendas signified a fundamental shift in the nature of Chicano/a art. This assessment of Chicano/a art is the underlying criterion for the periodization used by art historians who divide it into three periods (1965–1975, 1975–1985, and 1985 onward). In general, the periodization for art mirrors scholars' claims about the Chicano/a movement, which they suggest ended or stalled out in the mid-1980s. This evaluation is based on changes in the political realm, when strategies of organizing were replaced with less confrontational tactics. Certainly, the national and mass engagement brought on by the grape and lettuce boycotts, student activism, and anti–Vietnam War protests was transformed into regional mobilizations, whereas the Midwest and the South witnessed a groundswell of activism well into the 1980s and 1990s. In addition, artist activism around AIDS/SIDA also emerged in the mid-1980s. Scholars suggest that Chicano/a art was neutralized

SUN MAD. Screenprint by Ester Hernández, 1981. (Ester Hernández)

or commercialized during the Reagan and Bush administrations, riding the wave of multiculturalism in the 1980s and early 1990s. Recent assessments, however, look more closely at regional variations, immigration histories, the gender and sexuality of the artist, as well as the use of conceptual art as early as 1972. It is increasingly difficult to evaluate the periods in terms of a noncommercial orientation or iconography limited to patriarchal or urban symbols. For example, in the early 2000s, mass mobilizations were again seen around issues of global capitalism, education, anti-immigration, affirmative action, U.S. imperialism, and workers' rights, and artists were participating in social-change activities.

While patterns might be observable for the artists who have had gallery successes, it is difficult to assess a national trend for two reasons. First, critics tend to argue that personal imagery or self-referential art is evidence that an artist has diverted from the cultural and political expression of El Movimiento, yet Chicana artists working at the height of the movement used private and family histories as visual sources. Second, the criticism against the commercialization of Chicano/a art, loudest during the 1980s and 1990s, cannot reconcile this notion with the fact that Chicano/a art is still produced, exhibited, collected, and interpreted predominantly within Chicano/a communities and is still seen to be outside the mainstream art world. Public museums have yet to acquire significant works, although a few university libraries have developed important archival collections of artists' papers, print media, and exhibition catalogues. Private collections of artists and Chicano/a professionals continue to be the major sources for national exhibitions. In addition, many artists continue to produce and experiment with figurative, abstract, political, conceptual, and referential art and draw on the live experience of Chicanas/os. Certainly, the conditions that made the Chicano/a movement are still present, and therefore this essay concerns itself with visual art production, exhibition, interpretation, content, style, and aesthetics from 1965 to the early years of the twenty-first century.

Artistic Forms and Functions: Chicano/a Murals and Posters

In the late 1960s and throughout the 1970s and 1980s, over one hundred cultural centers and artist collectives, such as Galería de la Raza in San Francisco; Royal Chicano Air Force (RCAF and originally the Rebel Chicano Art Front) in Sacramento; Mechicano Art Center (no longer in existence) in Los Angeles; La Extensión Cultural Art Collective in Seattle; the Mexican Fine Arts Center Museum in Chicago; La Raza Art and Media Collective of Ann Arbor, Michigan; Con Safo, Esperanza Peace and Justice Center, and the Guadalupe Cultural Arts Center in San Antonio; MARCH, initially in Indiana and later in Chicago; El Grito de Aztlán Gallery, "the first Chicano gallery in Colorado" (quoted in "Chicano Art in Colorado"); and Ariztlán in Phoenix emerged from and participated in the sociopolitical mobilizations within Mexican American communities and in the ideological undercurrent of the Chicano/a movement. For arts centers, organizations, and collectives, the political and cultural project of the Chicano/a movement became the source for community expression and forms of artistic display.

Though artists experimented with a range of forms during the height of El Movimiento, many chose media such as the mural, poster, flyer, and leaflet that allowed them to publicly proclaim a Chicano/a position on local political issues while rejecting notions of "high" or "fine" art. Even after the period of intense social upheaval, artists continued to use art forms that were inexpensive, immediate, and flexible, including cartoons, photocopies, computer-generated images, and other ordinary and synthetic forms that emerged from their ability to borrow from the cultures around them while drawing on collective and personal histories. Of these forms, the mural and the poster remain the most important expressions of cultural and political opposition.

Murals. "Metafísica," a geometrically abstract mural of Mesoamerican motifs, painted in 1968 by Mario Castillo and local youths at the Urban Progress Center in Chicago, is the first recorded Chicano/a mural. The Mesoamerican design lays claim to an indigenous heritage, providing a historical and cultural genealogy that defies assimilation and predates a European experience. Castillo drew from an established artistic genre, as Chicago was home to an important African American mural movement that began in the 1950s. West Coast Chicano/a muralism did not flourish until the early 1970s, and many artists looked to David Alfaro Siquieros for political and aesthetic inspiration. By 1974, the mural became one of the most popular visual forms throughout the United States as artists painted their messages of self-determination and liberation on churches, hospitals, schools, public buildings, private establishments, storefronts, meeting halls, freeway pillars, bridge piers, and river canals. Artists took advantage of nearly every type of public surface, and thus murals reached a large and diverse audience. Even in the damp climate of the Pacific Northwest, where artists painted most of their murals indoors—and thus complicated the public aspect of this art form—the murals continued to reach a Chicano/a audience. They were painted where people gathered—inside community-based organizations and educational institutions, such as Northwest Rural Opportunities in Grander, Washington, and Colegio César Chávez in Mount Angel, Oregon—and they were monumental. Nevertheless, the public nature of murals has often led to their demise as they challenge the most intimate desires and stories of nationhood.

The mural exemplifies two important qualities of the Chicano/a movement and its legacy of activism and empowerment; moreover, it can serve as an allegory of that message. First, a mural is declarative. Because it is created in and for public view, a mural is a visual proclamation of position. This practice resonates with a Chicano/a nationalist stance because the latter requires its supporters to announce their position publicly by adopting the cultural and political referent "Chicano/a." Likewise, a mural emphatically declares the artist's or artists' image of the world, visually stating "we are here" and discarding the conventions of the art world, the museum, and the social hierarchy in the United States. By making themselves present in the landscape, Chicanas/os defy the status quo. Second, a mural is collective. Because of its scale, a mural requires the coordination and communal action of a group of people. Even murals designed and painted by a single artist confound the myth of individualism in the art world and mainstream America because the mural's survival depends upon a community to safeguard it against urban calligraphy or whitewashing. Thus, more than any other visual form of expression, the mural can operate to publicly affirm a collective identity, culture, or politics without the prerequisite (dis)approval of the museum, gallery, or art patron's living room (and checkbook). In fact, the mural does not require the approval of these places but mocks the culture of the museum and the art market because it is created as part of the architecture of a building or structure—not as a canvas—and thus escapes commoditization or individual possession. It cannot be sold on the art market, hidden in a museum's basement, or ignored.

However, the qualities of a mural—declarative and collective—are precisely what leads to its highly contested existence. (Internal criticism about Chicano/a murals points to overly romantic views of indigenous culture and a bias toward the heterosexual nuclear family.) Murals are challenged on the basis of content, location, and design. Some arguments against Chicano/a murals use legal channels, such as the defense's claim in *Botello v. Shell Oil Co.* (1991) that a mural is not "fine art," or the point of view that a mural is a sign and thus subject to strict municipal codes. Others use vigilantism under the cloak of darkness to white out a mural. In addition, Chicano/a murals have not been safe from attack, even when artists follow municipal regulations. In cities such as Los Angeles, graffiti-abatement programs obliterate murals that incorporate graffiti and graffiti techniques as well as murals that have been tagged by graffiti writers. Even the federal Visual Artists Rights Act is no guarantee of protection. Though it gives ownership rights to artists, it leaves the definition of art open to interpretation. It gives the right of legal redress to artists but creates no enforcement protocol.

Posters. The poster shares many similarities with the mural. First, both flourished during the height of the Chicano/a movement because of a dialectic relationship between the art form and community activism. Second, both support democratic ownership of art. Third, both illustrate how Chicano/a artists are focused on opening up the art world and speaking directly to populations that have not had access to it; no intermediary is required for Chicano/a communities to read the message or see the images. Fourth, both represent a democratizing art form that, by its very nature, is political in concept and execution. However, though a mural communicates its message to anyone who sees it, it is a fixed and immovable medium.

In contrast, the poster is created for mass distribution, rapid production, and cost-effectiveness (in the 1980s and 1990s this was also said of digital art and photography). Because of these qualities, the poster functioned more than did the mural as a part of the movement itself because of its portability and technical simplicity (in comparison to mural productions, which required several people, municipal regulators, scaffolding, dozens of gallons of paint—among the most difficult factors). This made for wide distribution of the message, imagery, and style. More important, the poster's graphic nature means that it uses images and narrative text, thereby speaking directly to communities in the languages Chicanas/os prefer—Spanish, English, *caló*, or any combination of these. Furthermore, the medium does not depend upon literacy in any language, as the visual design conveys concepts and narrates stories.

Created to communicate information about events or to support a specific cause, the poster is a unique mix of fine art and mass media. Produced and distributed by cultural centers and collectives, such as the Centro de Artistas Chicanos and Galería Posada in Sacramento; La Raza Silkscreen Center and Mission Cultural Center in San Francisco; La Broche del Valle in Fresno; Mechicano Art Center and Self-Help Graphics and Art in Los Angeles; Coronado Studio in Austin, Texas; and Centro Cultural de la Raza in San Diego, the poster quickly transformed itself into a collector's item for many Chicanas/os, who kept them on the walls of their homes, businesses, and gathering places long after the events had ended. In line with their purpose, they were printed in large numbers and thus were not initially a rare item. Most art historians and curators focus on California poster production in part because of the presence of several important archives in the state that allow for systematic analysis. However, future scholars will turn up significant poster productions in Illinois, North Carolina, and Georgia—major centers of Mexican migration since 1980. Historians also view the poster as a permanent record of the mass mobilizations against war (starting with anti-Vietnam protests and continuing in the twenty-first century with criticism against the U.S. invasion of Iraq), worker exploitation, human-rights violations, educational inequity, AIDS/SIDA, and military or police brutality. The poster records community coalitions that support or announce Chicana empowerment; boycotts; immigration reform; cultural activities; and affordable, safe, and decent housing. The poster documents the complexity of the Chicano/a movement and its legacy because it demonstrates the range of political beliefs: nationalism and internationalism, prolabor and cultural essentialism, a feminist critique of patriarchy and reinforcement of gender and sex norms, consumerism and anticapitalism, and reformism and separatism.

Just as posters give scholars the means to expand their knowledge of the Chicano/a movement, they also give artists the means to expand the medium's form. Arts collectives and community centers provide artists with the resources and opportunities to advance the aesthetic and technique of the poster. Silkscreen print workshops are experimental and have led to new artistic possibilities. In 1983, Self-Help Graphics and Art established the Experimental Silkscreen Atelier; the Chicano/a poster became a refined form, a limited-edition fine-art print, which made important aesthetic and technical advances that paralleled those in Puerto Rican and Cuban *talleres*. Inspired by the work of Self-Help Graphics and Art, in 1994 Coronado Studio in Austin, Texas initiated Serie Print Project. No longer concerned with announcing an event or a specific political agenda, artists enjoyed greater experimentation through these and other workshops. In some ways the expansion of the aesthetic range and content of the poster validated the iconographic strategies and messages that Chicanas/os had been using since the 1970s. With access to and the creation of Chicano/a art collectors, especially through Galería Sin Fronteras of Austin, Texas, the print workshops proved successful strategies for economic autonomy, an important tactic in the 1980s as federal and local state funds for mural production and the arts were diverted to the prison system, militarization of the border, and other components of a police state.

Sources of Originality

Central to the artistic project of Chicano/a art is the taking of a stance in opposition to the dominant views on art and Mexican Americans. Chicano/a artists consciously invoke and evoke the daily life of the Chicano/a community in their art. Rituals and traditions are one foundation for artistic expression, providing imagery and subtext. Chicano/a artists also draw on cultural heritages that cross time and space, particularly their indigenous, African, Spanish, and North American roots. Chicano/a artists also mined Chicano/a youth, and later hip-hop, culture, animation, and the magical realism of Latin America. This source material is not merely duplication or mimicry but rather a reinterpretation and revision according to the ideological project of the artist.

Artistic consciousness emerged from everyday, collective, and complex experiences, including charged relationships with Mexico as homeland or heritage. Even though artists are trained in formalism, they transform the boundaries of visual expression by rejecting imposed images, aesthetic styles, and standards. For example, Chicano/a artists draw on neoindigenous visual vocabularies; they reveal the condition of urban and rural life, the popular culture of Mexico and the United States, and Catholic and indigenous rituals and beliefs. In short, the sources of their originality come from their historical location as a people who are both native and foreign to this land and as a people of mixed race and culture that learn to inhabit a range of social spaces.

The vernacular or quotidian component of Chicano/a art is not conservative. Chicana artists do not unthinkingly reproduce images of La Virgen de Guadalupe; they transform her into a feminist, an activist, a lesbian, or a goddess, equal to masculine representations of God and the Holy Spirit, and yet she is unambiguously Chicana. Aztec mythology, typically available to Chicano/a communities through calendars that were reproduced and distributed by businesses, is reformulated to make women into active agents in history rather than passive maidens. In other areas, youth culture, such as graffiti and tattoos, punk fashion, prison art, and lowrider cars, is elevated and parodied. Experiments with the *altar*, a religious home shrine typically created and moderated by elder women, are an important example of the fusion of traditional sources and modern contexts.

The hybrid character of Chicano/a art is considered emblematic of what Yvonne Yarbro-Bejarano (*The Female Subject*) and Tomás Ybarra-Frausto (*Rasquachismo*) have identified as *rasquache* style. It encapsulates the fluid, the exploratory, and the nonlinear qualities of Chicano/a art. Resourcefulness and adaptability are other important aspects of rasquache style, reflecting as well a willingness to recycle and reuse in order to survive. Rasquache sensibility rejects polish, order, and simplicity; although the slick artistic styles, which include technology, commercial and graphic design, and formalism, may appear to mock rasquachismo, the response from Chicano/a audiences, particularly collectors, suggests that artists parody particular styles of art in an effort to critique trends in the art world and expectations about Chicano/a art.

The parody of slickness, therefore, is another strategy of rasquachismo. The rasquache strategy subverts hierarchies and legitimates the perspective of those on the margins by anchoring the ordinary, the everyday, and the routine. Sometimes the dialogue is internal—an inside joke—which suggests that rasquachismo functions best when it does not address "the center" or the dominant society.

The home altar, and its recreation in the art world, is one of the best examples of a rasquache point of reference. Set up on dressers, televisions, stereos, and tables, *altares* as well as *nichos* (shelves) include pictures of the deceased, figures of saints and other holy persons, trinkets, and candles to serve as daily homage and connections to family members. As a domestic representation of intimate knowledge, the sacred afterlife, and the deceased, altars map emotions and family ties. These connections are articulated through the arrangement of objects; each item has a particular place on the altar, and this spot depends on the other objects with which it is placed. For example, the *recuerdo* (memento) of someone's wedding sits next to photographs of the bride and groom; family members who quarreled in life are placed at opposite ends of the altar; *santos* (saints) are placed in the background as if to observe the celestial and earthly family; and candles illuminate the space but are offered in remembrance of the most recently deceased, whose photograph or treasured object is centrally placed. To the uninitiated, the altar looks chaotic, but the relationships are spatially maintained while simultaneously producing vertical or horizontal symmetry on the altar.

Installations of altars in museums and galleries make use of all of these codes, although some conventions are parodied or refracted. For instance, the layers, symmetry, balance, use of space, and baroque sensibility are elements of installation art that originate from home altars, particularly those created for Día de los Muertos (Day of the Dead), a largely indigenous celebration that honors the deceased but that overlaps with the Catholic feast days for All Saints and All Souls. Once relocated inside a museum's walls or in community galleries, *ofrendas* (offerings) for the dead shift in meaning, combining secular interpretations of the altar's content and style with a public display of intimate memories, emotions, and faith. As a result of the new location, ofrendas invite both an aesthetic response based on public standards and a religious experience based on private understanding.

Ofrenda installations made on the occasion of Día de los Muertos frequently recast private matters (pain, sorrow, loss, and injury) as a communal tragedy and thus contribute to the declarative aspect of the Chicano/a movement. Increasingly, Day of the Dead exhibitions include at least one ofrenda/installation that addresses the pain of youth homicide and asks for an end to violence in *nuestra comunidad* (our community). These public appeals to communal peace elevate personal pain to public discourse and insist upon collective action to eradicate gang violence instead of the individualist's strategy of "Just Say No." By joining collective memory with social commentary, ofrenda/installations operate as political art.

Although artists fuse multiple styles, the rasquache position of the ofrenda/installation is not a pastiche of free-floating images disconnected from or indifferent to its source. The practice—from ephemeral displays to two-dimensional paintings—consistently foregrounds the indigenous and Catholic blending found in El Día de los Muertos. The installations are clearly for the dead. The foregrounding of a particular cultural history challenges nations' perceptions of themselves as geographically separate entities with decisive boundaries in time and space. The aesthetic sensibility of the altar or installation indicates its vitality as an original art form.

Significance in the Art World

To understand the significance of Chicano/a art in the art world, one must have a perspective on the assumptions and boundaries of art history. Despite accomplishments in creating a visual vocabulary, changing historical awareness, and validating new forms and goals, art historians have yet to document, analyze, and integrate Chicano/a artists into their scholarship. The findings of curator and videographer Rita González (*Undocumented History*) reveal a significant lack of literature on successful Chicano/a artists. Exhibition catalogs and reference encyclopedias are the major source of information on Chicano/a art, though Alicia Gaspar de Alba's book is the first scholarly monograph on Chicano/a art from an interdisciplinary perspective that includes ethnic, feminist, cultural, and American studies with an emphasis on the political and social contexts of exhibition. This blackout in art history is the result of a formalist bias, the attention to form over meaning and content. Art history is also built up around European notions of art and an evolutionary or developmental view that pronounces modernism as the zenith. Contemporary art favors conceptualism, and thus Chicano/a artists, whose major style is representational, enter at a time when their aesthetic styles are not valued. Art criticism often attacks Chicano/a art as "simplistic," "anecdotal," "propagandistic," or "ethnic." Furthermore, the use of imagery outside of European or European American experiences is considered "narrow" or "different." The universal standard has yet to be questioned in this discipline, even after the postmodern deconstructionist trend transformed most disciplines in the 1980s and 1990s. However, a small group of art historians who received their doctorates in the 1990s with a specialty in Chicano/a art have begun a systematic challenge to the discipline.

The irony is that Chicano/a artists are products of the mainstream art culture of the United States. What separates them and defines them as Chicano/a artists, rather than artists of Mexican origin, is that while they have been trained within the realm of the mainstream art world, they do not participate in its continuance. Rather, they use trends in mainstream art to inform their own production. For instance, performance art, installation, and pop art are used as vehicles to communicate the ideology of the Chicano/a movement. The aesthetics of modernism help Chicano/a artists refine the presentation of altares. Chicano/a posters integrate various styles with Chicano/a imagery and messages to create powerful statements for social action and solidarity. At the same time, Chicano/a artists' adaptation and development of mainstream art trends feed back into the larger art world. Co-optation of altars, without the socially relevant message, by mainstream artists is one example of the unacknowledged influence of Chicano/a art.

Significance in the Community

While the mainstream art world does not systematically value Chicano/a art, Chicano/a communities do. Moreover, they engage in a dialectical relationship with Chicano/a art—finding it to be of value but also endowing it with meaning. Two artists from the San Francisco Bay area, Malaquías Montoya and Lezlie Salkowitz-Montoya, articulated one of the most significant meanings assigned to Chicano/a art. In *A Critical Perspective* (p. 4) they state that Chicano/a art is "art of liberation," "art of protest," and "political art" that functions as "a social tool to combat" social inequities. According to the Montoyas, Chicano/a art cannot function as a tool of liberation within a capitalist institution (such as major metropolitan museums) that promotes the economic exploitation and racist oppression of Chicanas/os and other third world peoples. Blending an anti-imperialist position with Chicano/a cultural affirmation, they imply that art has significance for Chicanas/os only if it is created and exhibited in community spaces. From this position, Chicano/a artists should reject the art market, styles, and venues inaccessible to local Chicano/a communities, and mainstream methods of recognition and success. In part they echo the pop art movement in New York City, which aimed for popular control of the arts. Furthermore, they question artists who display their work in public museums or who receive federal or corporate sponsorship.

Art historian Shifra M. Goldman, one of the most prolific proponents of Chicano/a art, offers another interpretation. Her response to the Montoyas does not question the notion of political art, but her project differs from that of the Montoyas in that she challenges the assumption that co-optation is signaled by entry into the museum or private gallery. Rather, Goldman focuses on a matrix of beliefs and behaviors found within capitalism and individualism. Co-optation, she suggests, involves a competitive focus, accumulation of capital and goods, and the simultaneous investment in the rhetoric of individualism, artistic freedom, and meritocracy. She argues that a flexible artistic style is valued within Chicano/a communities, particularly the hybrid incorporation of commercial and mass media, vernacular materials, digital technology, and fine art styles.

The position that the Montoyas make public is based on a widely held belief that community-based cultural centers and museums are sanctuaries geographically and ideologically separate from the dominant society. Historians, cultural critics, and other scholars have documented the community formation and collective identity that result from arts organizations. Scholar of ethnic and American studies George Lipsitz refers to this process as art-based community making and community-based art making. For example, the Mission Cultural Center serves San Francisco's Latina/o neighborhood; Self-Help Graphics and Art operates in the predominantly Chicano/a community of East Los Angeles; the Mexican Fine Arts Center Museum is centrally located between Pilsen and Little Village in Chicago (the second-largest concentration of Mexican-origin people in the United States); and the Guadalupe Cultural Arts Center caters to San Antonio's Chicano/a community. The physical location of arts institutions has become a symbol of their ideological distance from the public museum and mainstream society. Designed as ideologically different spaces of self-definition, the cultural centers and museums offer via arts and cultural programming an alternative vision of the nation and the citizen. Not only do they validate the creative products of artists, but the subject and content of the art also give authority to the daily experiences and memories of Chicanas/os. These institutions aim to rectify the absence of Mexicans in the public museum as well as in the nation's imagination.

Chicano/a arts organizations, however, are more than places of cultural exhibition and production because their artistic goals are often inseparable from social, educational, and political goals. The effort to preserve the daily culture of Chicanas/os and their communities necessarily overlaps with the drive for political empowerment. For example, at the height of the Chicano/a movement, artists affiliated with the galleries and print shops created posters to announce political rallies, demonstrations, and cultural events. In Chicago, Casa Aztlán and the Mexican Fine Arts Center Museum opened their doors to other community-based organizations for meetings and receptions. In San Antonio, the physical presence of the Guadalupe Cultural Arts Center helped re-establish Mexican and Chicano/a economic and cultural authority in the neighborhood by inspiring other Mexican- and Chicano/a-focused organizations and businesses. As gathering places for the community, cultural centers and museums were central to grassroots organizing and dialogue. Thus, by promoting cultural identity as well as political self-determination, arts institutions function as advocates for their communities, at times becoming directly involved in community development, political action, and protest.

Challenges in the Twenty-first Century

Through arts organizations, Chicano/a art fills a void. Ironically, as local institutions gain exposure in the media and break boundaries in scholarship, they develop a regional and national audience. Thus, while community-based institutions were designed for local constituents, since the 1990s they have often been asked to address Chicano/a populations outside of their immediate neighborhood or municipality. National and international traveling Chicano/a art exhibitions and funding options are the most typical reasons that arts organizations extend themselves to a larger audience. While the connections of arts and activism have been expanded and refocused to suit the needs of a national geographic constituency, the emphasis on a Chicano/a audience remains.

Chicano, IL. Mixed media on paper by Hector Duarte, 1993. (Hector Duarte)

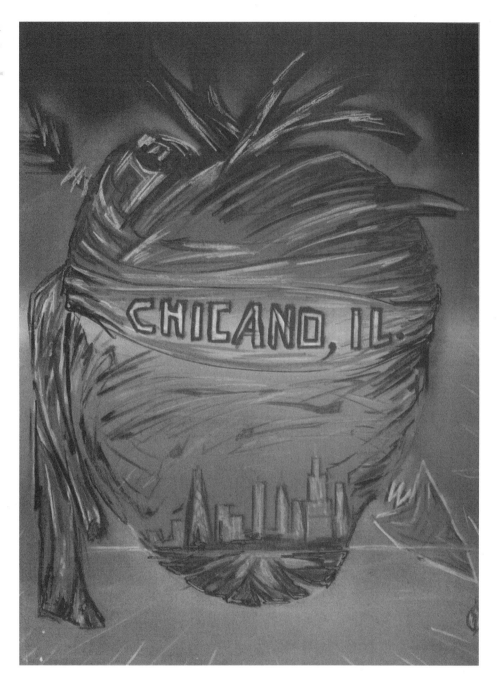

The challenge for the twenty-first-century Chicano/a artist and audience is to develop and support arts organizations without undermining the strengths of the Chicano/a art movement. Increased professionalization of Chicano/a artists and community arts institutions is only valuable if it maintains a healthy critique of meritocracy, liberalism, assimilation, and consumerism. Expansion of artistic goals should not duplicate the national homogenization of Latinas/os, a strategy that supports assimilation rhetoric by lumping twenty-two national groups, hundreds of indigenous cultures, and a range of racial heritages into one culture. Simultaneously, Chicano/a art and arts institutions should continue to challenge separatist strategies that rigidly determine who belongs or does not belong to the community or to an arts organization or in the category of Chicano/a art. Relevance in the new millennium will come from the social condition of the majority of Chicanos and Chicanas, just as it has since the 1960s. Chicano/a art will continue to find its sources, meanings, and styles in the lived experience of Mexicans and Mexican Americans living in the United States.

See also: Altares; Chicanos and Chicanas; Mexican-Origin People in the United States; Murals; Painters; Photographers; Political Organizations; Sculptors; *and* Self-Help Graphics.

BIBLIOGRAPHY

Carrasco, Davíd. "Aztec Moments and Chicano Cosmovision: Aztlán Recalled to Life." In *Moctezuma's Mexico: Vision of the Aztec World*, edited by Davíd Carrasco and Eduardo Matos Moctezuma. Boulder: University Press of Colorado, 2003.

Cockcroft, Eva Sperling, and Holly Barnet-Sánchez, eds. *Signs from the Heart: California Chicano Murals*. Venice, Calif.: SPARC; Albuquerque: University of New Mexico Press, 1993.

Colburn, Bolton T. *Across the Street: Self-Help Graphics and Chicano Art in Los Angeles*. Laguna Beach, Calif.: Laguna Art Museum, 1995.

Davalos, Karen Mary. *Exhibiting Mestizaje: Mexican (American) Museums in the Diaspora*. Albuquerque: University of New Mexico Press, 2001.

Fields, Virginia M., and Victor Zamudio-Taylor, eds. *The Road to Aztlan: Art from a Mythic Homeland*. Los Angeles: Los Angeles County Museum of Art, 2001.

Gaspar de Alba, Alicia. *Chicano Art Inside/Outside the Master's House: Cultural Politics and the CARA Exhibition*. Austin: University of Texas Press, 1998.

Goldman, Shifra M. *Dimensions of the Americas: Art and Social Change in Latin America and the United States*. Chicago: University of Chicago Press, 1994.

Goldman, Shifra M., and Tomás Ybarra-Frausto. *Arte Chicano: A Comprehensive Annotated Bibliography of Chicano Art, 1965–1981*. Berkeley: Chicano Studies Library Publications Unit, University of California, 1985.

Gómez-Peña, Guillermo. "The Multicultural Paradigm: An Open Letter to the National Arts Community." *High Performance* (Sept. 1989): 18–27. Reprinted in *Negotiating Performance: Gender, Sexuality, and Theatricality in Latina/o America*, edited by D. Taylor and J. Villegas. Durham, N.C.: Duke University Press, 1994.

González, Rita. "An Undocumented History: A Survey of Index Citations for Latino and Latina Artists." *CSRC Research Report* no. 2. Los Angeles: UCLA Chicano Studies Research Center, 2003.

Griswold del Castillo, Richard, Teresa McKenna, and Yvonne Yarbro-Bejarano, eds. *Chicano Art: Resistance and Affirmation, 1965–1985*. Los Angeles: Wight Art Gallery, University of California, 1991.

Keller, Gary D., Mary Erickson, Kaytie Johnson, and Joaquín Alvarado. *Contemporary Chicana and Chicano Art: Artists, Works, Cultures, and Education*. Edited by Gary Keller. Vols. I and II. Tempe, Ariz.: Bilingual Press/Editorial Bilingüe, 2002.

Lipsitz, George. "Not Just Another Social Movement: Poster Art and the Movimiento Chicano." In *Just Another Poster? Chicano Graphic Arts in California*, edited by Chon A. Noriega. Santa Barbara: University of California Art Museum, 2001.

Mesa-Bains, Amalia. "Art of the Other México: Sources and Meanings." In *Art of the Other México: Sources and Meanings*. Chicago: Mexican Fine Arts Center Museum, 1993.

Mesa-Bains, Amalia. "Domesticana: The Sensibility of Chicana Rasquache." *Aztlán* 24 (1999): 157–170.

Montoya, Malaquías, and Lezlie Salkowitz-Montoya. "A Critical Perspective on the State of Chicano Art." *Metamórfosis* 3 (1980): 3–7.

Noriega, Chon A., ed. *Just Another Poster? Chicano Graphic Arts in California*. Santa Barbara: University of California Art Museum, 2001.

Ochoa, María. *Creative Collectives: Chicana Painters Working in Community*. Albuquerque: University of New Mexico Press, 2003.

Pérez, Laura E. "Spirit Glyphs: Reimaging Art and Artist in the Work of Chicana Tlamatinime." *Modern Fiction Studies* 44 (1998): 36–76.

Rivera, George. "Chicano Art in Colorado." University of Colorado, Boulder. www.colorado.edu/finearts/rivera/chicano_art/flash/ interface_low.html.

Sánchez-Tranquilino, Marcos. "Space, Power, and Youth Culture: Mexican American Graffiti and Chicano Murals in East Los Angeles, 1972–1978." In *Looking High and Low: Art and Cultural Identity*, edited by Brenda Jo Bright and Liza Bakewell. Tucson: University of Arizona Press, 1995.

Sorell, Victor. "Barrio Murals in Chicago: Painting the Hispanic-American Experience on 'Our Community' Walls." *Revista Chicano-Riqueña* 4 (1976): 51–72.

Yarbro-Bejarano, Yvonne. "The Female Subject in Chicano Theatre: Sexuality, 'Race,' and Class." *Theatre Journal* 38 (1986): 389–407.

Ybarra-Frausto, Tomás. "The Chicano Movement/The Movement of Chicano Art." In *Exhibiting Cultures: The Poetics and Politics of Museum Display*, edited by Ivan Karp and Steven D. Lavine. Washington, D.C. and London: Smithsonian Institution Press, 1991.

Ybarra-Frausto, Tomás. "Rasquachismo: A Chicano Sensibility." (1989) Reprint in *Chicano Art: Resistance and Affirmation, 1965–1985*, edited by Richard Griswold del Castillo, Teresa McKenna, and Yvonne Yarbro-Bejarano, 155–162. Los Angeles: Wight Art Gallery, University of California, 1991.

KAREN MARY DAVALOS

ART, CUBAN AMERICAN.

Throughout the twentieth century, crossing political and cultural boundaries, artists from various countries migrated to the United States seeking freedom, adventure, and fortune. Other artists became exiles escaping war, tyrannical repression, and persecution. By 1959, in opposition to the revolution, thousands of Cubans began to flee Cuba with their families. Some of these people were already painters and sculptors; others were young men and women who would later study and practice art in the United States. Arriving as individuals and in subsequent waves, generations of Cuban American artists have made significant contributions to the culture of the United States.

The exhibition catalog *Outside Cuba: Contemporary Cuban Visual Artists* presented an overview of the field in 1988. The timeline begins with the pioneer Cuban masters followed by two generations studying and working in Cuba until 1959. The fourth generation matured in exile in the 1960s, and includes some of the young artists trained in U.S. universities who would be working by the early 1980s. Other artists escaped through the Mariel boatlift or left via Mexico and Spain on the way to America, while some settled in Paris. In time, the demographics expanded with younger Cuban Americans who were beginning their careers. These generations of artists were joined by another group of mid-career artists trained in the advanced art schools in Havana who opted in the early 1990s for life in the United States. In the early twenty-first century, Cuban American artists worked in every possible medium, ideological territory, and conceptual approach. Many made their work independent of

THE JUNGLE. Gouache on paper mounted on canvas by Wilfredo Lam, 1943. (Museum of Modern Art, New York/Art Resource)

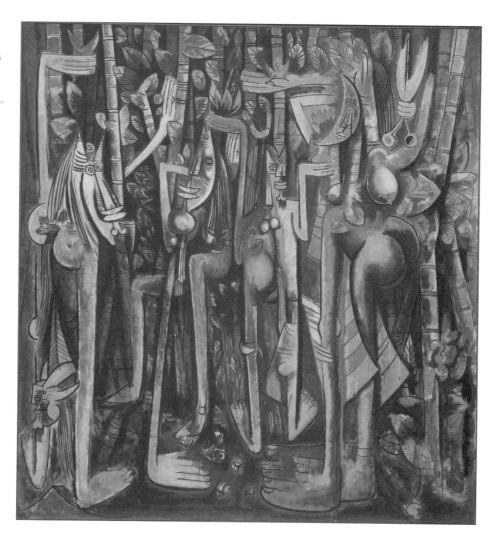

vested theories about Cuban art, hoping to shed ethnic associations and connect to the expanding international art world.

Cuban art in the United States developed beyond and apart from the art produced at home on the island. Miami museums could not show the work of artists staying on the island. Inside Cuba the work and histories of all artists who had defected were banned from publications and exhibitions. After four tough decades of cultural impasse, the "iron curtain" began to open by the late 1990s, as a larger collective cultural identity became possible. Through exhibitions and publications, some of the art produced in Cuba became both part and shadow of the larger terrain of Cuban American art in the United States.

Who can be considered a Cuban American artist today? Only Cuban-born Americans and their descendants can apply to the prestigious Cintas Foundation for the fellowships that have bolstered the careers of hundreds of Cuban artists, architects, composers, and creative writers.

Exhibitions

The history of Cuban American art in the United States is documented in the catalogs of important and ambitious exhibitions that presented the expanding population of expatriate artists. After the economic and identity struggles of early exile, by the mid-1970s, as Miami's Cuban community became prosperous and active, four generations of artists started to show together. An evolving new Cuban art began to gain visibility with the support of the Miami Art Center, the Miami-Dade Public Library, and the Bacardi Gallery, as well as highlighted media coverage, the formation of different artists' groups, and the opening of galleries.

In 1976, the Museo Cubano de Arte y Cultura was established, and began a series of inspiring exhibitions. An early Retrospectiva de Pintura Cubana provided a historical overview of Cuban painters still grouped by the pattern of colonial and republican epochs. For a few years, the Re-Encuentro Cubano, hosted by different institutions, included other art forms in exhibitions that presented only the works

CASABLANCA. Photograph by Mario Algaze, 1985. (Jane Voorhees Zimmerli Art Museum, Rutgers, The State University of New Jersey, Gift of J. D. Montgomery/Photo by Jack Abraham [1986.0992])

of artists living outside Cuba. Other institutions sponsored solo and group exhibitions of artists living in the area.

In 1978, the exhibition Contemporary Latin American Artists of the Southeastern United States, organized by Jose Gomez Sicre, offered the first comprehensive grouping of exiled Cuban artists of all the generations. This show was paired with an exhibition of the Esso Latin American Art Collection of the Lowe Art Museum of the University of Miami. While the selection featured most of the active professionals, some serious artists working in Miami were not invited. Through other exhibitions, a broader territory emerged.

Organized by the Museo Cubano de Arte y Cultura in 1983, The Miami Generation chronicled nine emerging U.S.–trained artists: Mario Bencomo, Maria Brito-Avellana, Humberto Calzada, Pablo Cano, Emilio Falero, Fernando Garcia, Juan Gonzalez, Carlos Macia, and César Trasobares. The curator, Giulio Blanc, wrote in his essay, "There remains the generation of the '*casi niños*,' those who were children or almost children when they left the island. For them, Cuba is revolution, exile, coming of age in a foreign land, myth" (*The Miami Generation*).

In 1988, *Outside Cuba* accomplished its comprehensive effort to document significant expatriate Cuban artists. The catalog includes the seminal essay, "Cuban Visual Thinking in Exile since 1959," and other texts that present the roots of Cuban art in revolutionary politics, the "inevitable" position of exile of artists, and an acknowledgement of women artists.

CUBA USA: The First Generation was organized by the Fondo del Sol Visual Arts Center in Washington, D.C., and traveled to various venues. The exhibition featured installations, photography, and video, with performances by younger Cuban diaspora artists, uniting sensibilities with media, acknowledging the amplitude of the field, and transcending clichéd ideas of "nostalgic exile art." In addition to popular and sacred music, the project celebrated the Santería altars of Caridad Salome.

Taking a more traditional approach, Breaking Barriers: Selections from the Museum's Permanent Contemporary Collection presented an amazing selection of ninety artists in 1997, casting a broad net and discovering a few new talents.

In the early twenty-first century, important exhibitions and publications consolidated the comprehensive field of the art of Cubans. The stellar presentation of artists living in Cuba with a few living elsewhere, CUBA SIGLO XX: Modernidad y Sincretismo, produced a weighty catalog with significant critical essays providing background and perspective.

MEMORIA: Cuban Art of the Twentieth Century is a mammoth effort that treats Cuban modern art as an evolving field with shifting boundaries. It includes articles, a chronology of exhibitions, and resumes of artists living in Cuba and in other countries. Produced by a team of curators, writers, historians, and archivists, *MEMORIA* charts the landscape of contemporary Cuban art and provides information on 474 artists.

Across the United States, other exhibitions were constructing larger definitions of Latino and Latina and Hispanic art, often including Cuban American artists. Beyond the commonality of language, Latino and Latina and Hispanic artists have radically different historical sources, diverse political tracks, and individual aesthetic interests. As a distinct field, Cuban American art in the United States is a historical phenomenon moving toward global culture.

Foundation: Cuban Vanguardia

Cuban modern art emerged in Havana in the early decades of the twentieth century. Various aspiring men and women traveled to Europe to see and study art and returned home to create their versions of the "isms" and go on to invent their own forms and fusions of contemporary art. These artists found support and fame by staying and working in the motherland, decreasing the need to seek renown and recognition elsewhere. By the late 1940s, many of the Havana-based stars—Amelia Pelaez, Eduardo Abela, Carlos Enriquez, Victor Manuel, Fidelio Ponce, and others, including the reigning Cuban expatriate artist in Europe, Wifredo Lam—were celebrated and valued internationally.

The renown of these Vanguardia artists was bolstered by the acquisition of a group of their paintings by the Museum of Modern Art (MoMA). The project was made possible by the influential Alfred Barr, who agreed to access the works into The Latin American Collection of the Museum of Modern Art. In *Pintura Cubana de Hoy*, published in 1944, the group was presented by Jose Gomez-Sicre, who became a powerful advocate for Cuban and Latin American artists as Director of the Organization of American States Museum from its founding in 1976 until his retirement. MoMA eventually acquired Lam's *La Jungla*, showing it in a place of honor in the building's lobby. The collective contribution of these artists influenced evolving perceptions about Cuban modern art.

Vanguardia art was colorful, lively, and joyful, celebrating the noble *campesino* and the beautiful *guajira*; it extolled the beauty of the island, its vegetation, flowers, and fruits; it recorded its light, color, landscapes, architecture, and baroque interiors. For some, it also extended remnants of provincialism and the lingering aesthetics of colonial days. By all accounts, the celebration of the insular beauty would be the primary model of "Cuban art" sold to tourists, exported and constructed beyond the mainland. Despite the modernist focus of the Vanguardia, with the ongoing formal training of artists at Academia San Alejandro, a separate official academic style kept alive older stylistic traditions.

Early emigrant artists like Enrique Riveron and Antonio Gattorno moved to New York in the 1930s. They traveled and studied in Europe, strongly rebelling against the academic aesthetic and nationalist iconography and embracing abstraction and the evolving art of the machine age. Mario Carreño lived in the United States for short periods and eventually moved to Chile. In New York, these artists were part of larger gatherings with fellow Latin American and Mexican artists, musicians, dancers, and poets working in the city. Like others, Emilio Sanchez went to New York in 1944 to study at the Art Students League and stayed there for the rest of his life. Until the early years of exile, these artists traveled to Cuba freely and participated in exhibitions with the resident artists.

In Cuba, those who followed the Vanguardia generation began with the benefit of the aesthetic climate that the pioneers had established, making it possible for young artists to work within a more personal vocabulary and a broader interest of subjects. René Portocarrero and Mariano Rodriguez were influential mentors, even as other artists like Osvaldo Gutierrez Aleman were cultivating their own styles. The groups Los Menores de 30 and Grupo de Los Once were formed circa 1953, consolidating a new stage in Cuban modern art, separating the emerging interest in abstraction: Guido Llinas, Tomas Oliva, Hugo Consuegra, Jose Mijares, Roberto Diago, and Jose Ignacio Bermudez, among others. Sculptors were making works for public spaces: Alfredo Lozano, Roberto Estopiñán, Tomas Oliva, and Rita Longa, with the enduring presence of Sandú Darié. Others like Antonia Eiriz and Gina Pellón were creating their own expressive pictorial realms. Many of these artists would eventually escape from the island.

Moving to the United States in the 1960s

The first wave of mature Cuban artists arrived in the United States with developed styles but devastated by an uncertain future and shocked by unavoidable circumstances. As politically defeated and economically disowned Cubans, labeled *gusanos* (worms) by their compatriots back home, some had to work in other trades but continued to paint in their free time during the difficult first decade of exile.

Cuban art in the United States was nurtured in Miami, as individuals and institutions coalesced to present and encourage the art being produced. The Miami-Dade Public Library encouraged and showed artists from all areas of the artistic continuum. The Lowe Art Museum at the University of Miami developed its own collection and hosted significant exhibitions. The Art Museum at Florida International University also staged group and solo exhibitions over the years.

The painter Baruj Salinas was an enthusiastic catalyst in the early days of exile in Miami, forging artistic associations with Rafael Soriano and Enrique Riveron. In 1969, they formed GALA (Group of Latin American Artists) with Jose Mijares, Osvaldo Gutierrez Aleman, and Roxana McCallister-Kelly from Argentina. They began to invite other artists to show, like Cundo Bermudez and Alfredo Lozano, and the group became a visible presence in Miami's fledgling art community.

As more exhibitions became possible, the public saw other artists who had continued to paint: Miguel Jorge, Dionisio Perkins, and Lourdes Gomez Franca. Younger artists, sometimes with the mentoring of the old guard, continued their work in Miami: Gabriel Sorzano, Ricardo Pedreguera, Maria Tuma, Rafael Consuegra, Vicente Dopico, Siro del Castillo, Fernando Luis, Efraim Oliver, Rafael Mirabal, Thorvald Sanchez, Anibal Marrero, and Susana Sori.

Other Cuban artists had settled in New York like Daniel Serra Badué, Hugo Consuegra, Carmen Herrera, Julio Girona, Oscar Magnin, Roberto Estopiñan, Julio Larraz, and Hugo Consuegra. Some moved to Puerto Rico: Cundo Bermudez, Alfredo Lozano, Agustin Fernandez, Gay Garcia, Victor Piedra, and Zilia Sanchez. The work of these artists would be presented in traveling group exhibitions, collectively forming and giving identity to the larger community of artists living outside their island homeland.

Although deciding to study art did not seem like a viable option in the first decade of exile, a few first-generation emigrants enrolled in Miami-Dade Community College and continued their studies at the University of Miami and other Florida universities. Youngsters who had formed part of the Pedro Pan group, the rescue campaign led by the Catholic Church to bring Cuban children without their parents to the United States, enrolled in U.S. universities to study art and art history. Most of these artists were trained in the MFA tradition, with an emphasis on making and craft. The first were graduating in the 1970s, and began working beyond their immediate ethnic enclave in cities nationwide. Their art was initially visible in survey exhibitions and later in major solo exhibitions.

Traditional artists had also settled in Miami, including Domingo Ramos, a leading landscape painter, and the Scull Sisters, unparalleled in their populist satire, as well as society portraitists like Pedro Menocal and Felix Cossio. Numerous other painters specialized in flowers, buildings, and birds. Maria Capdevila was an octogenarian outsider artist, and Maria Luisa Rios explored the destruction of the environment. Teok Carrasco, a leading muralist, painted the interior of the Ermita de la Caridad, the community's main religious venue. This branch of Cuban aesthetics is perpetuated by the Academy of Painting and Sculpture of San Alejandro in Exile, among other organizations, and is enabled by the nostalgia art market. In parts of Miami, especially the Calle Ocho gallery district, dozens of self-proclaimed artists continue to work within the pictorial traditions of prerevolutionary Cuba. This phenomenon, known as *los congelados* (the frozen ones), is also evident in other aspects of exile culture. Ironically, the imagery of the Cuban modern masters acquired the patina of nostalgia, tainted with the sentimentality and sense of loss of uprooted individuals.

Eventually, some of the younger artists questioned political alignments while diminishing the centrality of the exile experience. With new perspectives and options, they stressed their situation as bicultural artists, impacted by mass media and consumerism. In 1990, the exhibition Post-Miami Generation presented yet another wave of young graduates sharing an "identity crisis" with others in Miami's art scene of the early 1990s.

Mariel Generation and Balseros

Through the years, there were smaller waves of departure from Cuba. Images emerged in Cuban art as exodus archetypes. The *balsa*, a floating raft made of various materials, became a potent icon.

The Mariel boatlift of 1980 brought a number of artists who had trained at San Alejandro Academy and the emerging art schools, infusing the ongoing culture of the gusanos with renewed connections to Cuba's artistic threads. Carlos Alfonzo, the star of the Mariel generation, produced a profound body of work in a decade. Like Alfonzo, Juan Boza worked with the iconography of Santería. Others, like Juan Abreu, Gilberto Ruiz, and Humberto Dionisio, focused on their existential condition of displacement. Victor Gomez, Agustin Gainza, Laura Luna, and others worked with printmaking, ceramics, and traditional materials. Moving to San Francisco, Eduardo Michaelsen is a singular visionary outsider artist. Having a committed identity, the group had its own publication, *Mariel Magazine*, dedicated to a broader sense of art, including contributions by Reinaldo Arenas.

Compañeros Artists

In the late 1980s, another wave of artists fled Cuba. Unlike the initial gusanos or those in the Mariel group, these younger artists had trained in the most advanced art schools in Havana, embracing conceptual approaches to art. Because many of the artists were in transition, Mexico City became a convenient and energizing point of convergence. There was also the support of cultural leader Nina Menocal, who organized a historic exhibition, 15 Artistas Cubanos, that brought together for the first time in thirty years some of the young artists who had studied in Cuba with others who had formed in the United States. One of the texts in the catalog acknowledges that the exhibition "has gained the irony, imperfect and incomplete, of upsetting both sides, knowing how to escape the control of each" (*15 Artistas Cubanos*). With work by Luis Cruz-Azaceta, Felix Gonzalez Torres, and Trasobares, the exhibiting artists were willing to take "small risks" together.

This opening was the conduit for most of these artists into the United States. The stellar contribution of Jose Bedia transcends any definition of native versus imported or insular versus universal. Glexis Novoa and Ruben Torres-Llorca set up studios in Miami to continue active careers. Alejandro Aguilera, Nestor Arenas, Adriano Buergo, and Ana Albertina Delgado also moved to Florida, while Carlos Cardenas and Arturo Cuenca continued their work in New York. Consuelo Castañeda and

Quisqueya Henriquez collaborated for a few years and went on to pursue individual careers. Also of this generation, Juan Si, Carlos Perez Vidal, Tomas Esson, Florencio Gelabert, and others eventually settled in the United States. This group could be considered *gusañeros*, half gusanos and half compañeros.

Twenty-first Century

After decades of separation and distance, the climate of the relationships among the split peoples of Cuba shifted, infused by the initial efforts to establish a constructive dialogue among academics and artists to reconnect, like *el dialogo*, and the visits from *mariposas* (butterflies, the returning gusanos) carrying dollars and hope. Maintaining a strict distance between Castro and the population in exile was crucial in the early decades of the separation. Artists, thinkers, writers, and curators in the twenty-first century welcomed the integration of Cuban culture to include those on the island and *la comunidad*. Art served as a major bridge among Cubans, connecting and healing individuals as they faced the issues of reintegration and the option to return to the homeland.

Focusing on artists living in Cuba, important publications document the art being produced on the island. Some of the credit for the high profile of Cuban art is due to dedicated curators and collectors who support different sectors of the stylistic spectrum. Numerous museums include Cuban American artists in their collections. Important galleries present their work.

Reflecting on the impact of AIDS, the immense loss of talent was chronicled by the exhibition Touched by AIDS in 1997. The catalog included an essay, "Lost and Found: Saving the Legacy of Miami Artists," presenting promising artists whose careers ended prematurely.

Other exhibitions acknowledged Cuban American artists with immense talent, many dying young, their potential curtailed by fate: Felix Gonzalez-Torres at the Guggenheim, Ana Mendieta: Earth Body organized by the Hirshhorn Museum and debuting at the Whitney Museum of American Art, and the retrospective of Carlos Alfonzo initiated by the Miami Art Museum. Across the United States, Cuban American artists continue to create and show the wondrous products of their talent everywhere.

See also Balseros; Cuban Americans; Exilio; Marielitos; Painters; *and* Sculptors.

BIBLIOGRAPHY
15 Artistas Cubanos. Curated by Nina Menocal with essays by Osvaldo Sánchez and Iván de la Nuez. Ninart. Mexico: Centro de Cultura, 1991.

Block, Holly. *Art Cuba: The New Generation*. New York: Abrams, 2001.

Borràs, Maria Lluïsa, and Antonio Zaya, eds. *CUBA SIGLO XX: Modernidad y Sincretismo*. Las Palmas de Gran Canaria: Centro Atlántico de Arte Moderno; Barcelona: Fundació "La Caixa": Centre d'Art Santa Mònica, 1995.

Camnitzer, Luis. *New Art of Cuba*. Austin: University of Texas Press, 2003.

Castro, Martha de. *El Arte en Cuba*. Miami: Ediciones Universal, 1970.

CUBA USA: The First Generation: Exhibition Tour, 1991–1992. Essays by Zuver, Wayne S. Smith, Leslie Judd Ahlander, Giulio Blanc, Carlos Alfonzo, Ileana Fuentes-Perez, Robert Farris Thompson, Ricardo Viera, and Jane Addams Allen. Washington, D.C.: Fondo del Sol Visual Arts Center, 1991.

Fuentes-Perez, Ileana, et al., eds. *Outside Cuba: Contemporary Cuban Visual Artists*. New Brunswick, N.J.: Office of Hispanic Arts, and Miami: Research Institute for Cuban Studies, 1989.

Latin American Art in Miami Collections. Catalog with essay by Giulio Blanc. Miami: The Lowe Art Museum, 1995.

Martinez, Juan. *Cuban Art and National Identity: The Vanguard Painters 1927–1950*. Gainesville: University Press of Florida, 1994.

McCabe, Cynthia Jaffee, guest curator. *The American Experience: Contemporary Immigrant Artists*. Exhibition catalog. Miami: Bass Museum of Art, 1985.

McCabe, Cynthia Jaffee. *The Golden Door: Artist-Immigrants of America, 1876–1976*. Washington: D.C.: Smithsonian Institution, 1985.

The Miami Generation: Nine Cuban-American Artists. Exhibition catalog. Miami: Cuban Museum of Arts and Culture, 1983.

Santis, Jorge H., ed. *Breaking Barriers: Selections from the Museum of Art's Permanent Contemporary Collection*. Fort Lauderdale, Fla.: Museum of Art, 1997.

Spector, Nancy. *Felix Gonzalez-Torres*. New York: Guggenheim Museum, 1995.

Trasobares, César, curator. *RIVERON, 1925–1950: Paris, La Habana, New York*. Exhibition catalog. Coral Gables, Fla.: Lowe Art Museum, 1980.

Veigas, José, et al. *MEMORIA: Cuban Art of the Twentieth Century*. Los Angeles: California/International Art Foundation, 2001.

Viso, Olga M. *Ana Mendieta, Earth Body: Sculpture and Performance, 1972–1985*. Washington, D.C.: Hirshhorn Museum, 2004.

Viso, Olga M., guest curator. *Triumph of the Spirit: Carlos Alfonzo, A Survey*. Exhibition catalog. Miami: Miami Art Museum, 1997.

CÉSAR TRASOBARES

ART, DOMINICAN. The presence of Dominicans in painting, sculpture, graphic design, and mixed media in the United States defies coherent descriptions. Since Dominican artists have traveled to North America for different reasons, at different times, and under different circumstances, an overview of their work here can follow no easy pattern.

Dominican Artists Visiting the United States

Historically, the contact of Dominicans with the art world in the United States dates back at least to 1922, when Celeste Woss y Gil, "the grand dame of Dominican modernist painting," began the first of two sojourns in New York. By the end of her second stay in the city in 1931, Woss y Gil had spent a total of five years in New York, studying at the prestigious Art Student League and absorbing the aesthetic currents then transforming the plastic arts in the cultural capitals of the West. The daughter of former President Alejandro Woss y Gil, who had ruled the Dominican Republic from 1885 to 1887, she lived in France, Cuba, and the United States during her father's exile. She was born into a privileged social rank that permitted her to pursue the highest artistic education in each of the countries she lived in.

New York's Art Student League has continued to be a desirable school for aspiring artists from the Dominican Republic to pursue their training. A late-twentieth-century painter, Alberto Bass, born in Santo Domingo in 1949, came to study in that school in 1967. From the biographical information in *Historia y bachata: Colonización y neo-colonización*, a catalogue/lecture he published in Santo Domingo in 1993, during his years in New York, Bass established contact with the working-class Dominican community that had already emerged in Washington Heights. He lectured at the community organization Club Orlando Martínez in northern Manhattan, and, back in Santo Domingo, in 1981, he launched an exhibit titled La vida del dominicano en Nueva York (The Life of Dominicans in New York). Bass is separated from Woss y Gil by a vast difference of class, generation, and circumstances, which probably explains his rapport with the community; but, like her, he returned to practice his art in the native land.

Artists Living in the United States

Among those who stayed in the United States, the most senior are Tito Enrique Cánepa, born in San Pedro de Macorís in 1916, and Dario Suro, who was born in La Vega in 1917 and died in 1997. Cánepa left his native land fleeing the Trujillo dictatorship in 1935. "After two years in Puerto Rico, he moved to New York where he worked in the Sisqueiros Workshop and studied art and composition in WPA art schools" (Pellegrini 1996b, p. 114). The WPA art projects in the 1930s stimulated Cánepa, and the cultural dynamism of the city fueled his work with rich possibilities for expression. He has exhibited work in New York at least since 1938. This brings on a question about the outright omission of his name from the survey *The Latin American Spirit: Art and Artists in the United States, 1920–1970*, a retrospective overview published in 1988 based on an exhibition sponsored by The Bronx Museum of the Arts that failed to include even a single Dominican among the 165 artists considered. Though reflecting a wide range of aesthetic lessons drawn from diverse international currents and retaining a thematic interest in episodes of Dominican history, Cánepa's artistic production emanates from his nearly seven decades living in the United States.

Suro, on the other hand, spent time in Mexico, where he studied under Diego Rivera and other master muralists. He came to the United States only after he had attained recognition in the Dominican Republic as a first-rate painter. He

traveled widely and received distinctions at home and abroad. In 1962, he had a solo exhibition at Poindexter Gallery in New York. For many years he lived in Washington, D.C., where he continued to paint vigorously and to write art criticism while serving in the Dominican Embassy as cultural attaché until his death. Although Suro was far from his country, his work continued to reflect a concern with highlighting the uniqueness of Dominican culture, as art historian Elena Pellegrini has noted (Pellegrini 1996a, p. 28).

Next among the recognized Dominican masters is Clara Ledesma, who was born in Santiago in 1924. She began exhibiting as a solo artist in 1952, has achieved much international recognition, and today her work forms part of the permanent exhibit of the major museums in her country. Art historian Jeannette Miller says that Ledesma "resided a long time in New York, where she held exhibits and maintained her own art gallery, following which she moved to Santo Domingo" (Miller, p. 122). In the late 1980s, Ledesma has resettled in New York, where she lives and works largely unbeknownst to the Dominican community that has become the second largest immigrant component of the city's population.

The late Eligio Pichardo (1929–1984), who lived for seventeen years in New York, where he had solo shows in several private galleries, has had his work included in the collection of the Metropolitan Museum of Art. Without a doubt, however, the 1980s marked a turning point for Dominican artists, who began to take major strides towards visibility in this country. Early in that decade several expatriate Dominican painters and sculptors formed a loose association known as the Dominican Visual Artists of New York (DVANY) "with the goal of presenting the works of its members to an American public that knew almost nothing about these artists or their Dominican heritage" (Kaplan, pp. 14–15). The group included Bismarck Victoria, Freddy Rodríguez, Eligio Reynoso, Magno Laracuente, and Tito Cánepa. They, for the most part, felt dissatisfied with the lack of venues for their work. The gallery establishment did not seem interested enough in displaying their work. In 1984, the members of DVANY launched a collective exhibit with considerable success at the gallery of the Department of Cultural Affairs of the City of New York on Columbus Circle in midtown Manhattan. The divergent styles and diversity of expressions and forms surprised many who had not expected such richness. The following year, in November 1995, Gulf and Western "turned over the lobby of its 59th Street headquarters" to an exhibition, the first ever in that space, by the New York-based Dominican sculptor Victoria, one of the members of DVANY (Kaplan, p. 15).

Stephen D. Kaplan, himself a founding member of DVANY and the Rector of the Altos de Chavón/The School of Design in La Romana, Dominican Republic, the alma mater of many of the young Dominican artists currently in the United States, believes that the group drew extensively on "the vast new art stream flooding the international media" as well as from the dynamism of life in New York (Kaplan, p. 15). But, most importantly, the "burgeoning Dominican community in Manhattan" offered these artists a cultural framework and an emotional context that often proved profitable. One remarkable case of the cross-fertilization of the artist with the community is that of Carlos Reynoso, a 1996 recipient of the prestigious "Artist's Projects" grant awarded by the National Endowment for the Arts, the Rockefeller Foundation, and the Andy Warhol Foundation for the Visual Arts. Reynoso has shunned the "gallery circuit," preferring "instead the creation of pieces that are anonymous and ephemeral—often done in conjunction with Dominican students in Washington Heights, whom he voluntarily teaches," according to Alanna Lockward in her words of presentation of the artist for a brochure describing his exhibit in the Santo Domingo Museum Casa de Bastidas on August 5, 1996.

Important Exhibitions in the 1990s and Later

On the whole, the Dominican art scene in the United States is probably best summarized via several important exhibits that have been presented in New York since 1992. The first, entitled Dominicaras Dominicosas, an exhibition of photography, painting, and "utilitarian sculpture" seeking to document and celebrate Dominican migration, was shown at the Hostos Art Gallery, from April 14 to May 29, 1992, under the curatorship of Josefina Báez. The exhibit featured the artists Onorio Pérez, Richard Powel, Radhames Morales, Scherezade García Vázquez, and Pilar Gonzales. The second, entitled 500 Yolas, displayed paintings, sculptures, and drawings by New York–based Dominican artists on topics inspired by the quincentenary of the conquest of the Americas. Held from November 4, 1992 through January 15, 1993 at the Hostos Art Gallery in the Bronx, the exhibit featured works by Scherezade García, Danilo González, Hochi Asiático, Moses Rios, and Germán Pérez, all successful young artists. The third, entitled Modern and Contemporary Art of the Dominican Republic, opened, first in New York at the contiguous galleries of the main sponsoring institutions, the Americas Society and The Spanish Institute, June 14 through August 4, 1996, and then at the Bass Museum of Art in Miami, Florida, from October 3 through December 1, 1996. While this exhibit was primarily a survey of the artistic production of the Dominican Republic, it did include four U.S.–based names in the selection of thirty-two artists that made up the show: Cánepa, Rodríguez, Suro, and Victoria. The fourth exhibit, held at INTAR Latin American Gallery in Manhattan, was called Art in Transit: A Dominican Experience. Part One,

featuring the work of Hochi Asiático, Raquel Paiewonsky, Julia Santos Solomon, and Dario Suro, opened from September 26 to October 26, 1996. Part Two, presenting work by Crucelyn Ferreira, Freddy Rodríguez, Etienne H. Stanley, and Julio Valdez, opened from November 4 to November 30, 1996. Unlike previous efforts, this art show, conceived originally by Pellegrini when she directed the Gallery at INTAR, specifically concentrated on "Dominican artists currently living in the United States," so as to give an idea of how contemporary Dominican artists have developed outside of their native country (Casares, p. 9).

Since residence in the United States at the time of the exhibit was the only commonality linking the artists included in INTAR's program (apart from the curators' aesthetic considerations about the quality of the pieces displayed), the show allowed for much disparity as to the nature of the artists' relationship with American society. The duration of their stay in this country, for instance, ranged from five years, in the cases of Stanley and Valdez, to nearly three decades in the case of Solomon. Nor could the exhibit, or any other of the art shows mentioned in this overview, exhaust the wide range of artistic talent and activity produced by Dominican immigrants in the United States. For instance, thirty-five-year-old Magno Laracuente, who has lived in New York since 1979 and formed part of the original DVANY group in 1984, did not appear in any of the three exhibits listed above despite his relative success both in the Dominican Republic and in the United States. Also absent was the painter Gerardo Phillips, a Dominican residing in New York, who has been influenced by Wildredo Lam and Marc Chagall, as he acknowledges in the book Caribbean Visions, an overview of Contemporary Caribbean painters and sculptors that includes work of his (Phillips, p. 124). There are also lesser known Dominican artists of the diaspora like Diógenes Abreu, who has participated in exhibitions in New York and Tokyo galleries. Abreu, unlike many of the artists herein surveyed, began to paint in New York, where he, by virtue of his own working-class origin, has shared the immigrant experience of his people on a day-to-day basis in marginal social settings such as the Dominican neighborhood of Washington Heights.

Involvement with Memorial Art

Ironically, the visual artists who are most closely and painfully connected with the plight of the Dominican community are the practitioners of memorial art, an "offspring" of the graffiti movement that emerged in the 1980s (Camacho, pp. 126–127). Jhovanny Camacho, former curator of the Museum of Contemporary Hispanic Art in New York City, speaks of memorial art as "an underground" expression whereby "a community or elements within it" seek "to perpetuate the remembrance of members gone before their time." While the street murals normally depict the plight of the deviant, primarily young men who have "fallen in territorial drug wars," they also include some who have died of other causes (Camacho, p. 127). The majority of the Dominican youngsters honored with memorials are unknown to a large sector of the community where the work is exhibited. As Camacho puts it, "anonymity is one of the most interesting facts in Dominican memorial art. Both the artist and the honored subject remain anonymous" (Camacho, pp. 133–34). Their anonymity, plus their thematic engagement with death and "shattered dreams," painfully reflects the harshness of the immigrant experience for many Dominicans in the United States.

Growing Institutional Support

The CUNY-Dominican Studies Institute, as the only university-based Dominican institution, has contributed to the promotion of Dominican arts in the United States. It has cosponsored activities in which Dominican artists showcase their works and share their experience with the audience. In 1998, CUNY-DSI organized a two-day symposium on visual arts, spiritual traditions, popular and folk music, and history of the Dominican people in the homeland and the United States. The first panel, "Dominican Visual Artists: Between Here and There," brought together the curator Leonora Vega, the New York-based Dominican artist Scherezade García, the Miami-based Charo Oquet, the Dominican sculptor David Medina, and the art critic Sara Hermann.

Over six years later, the CUNY-Dominican Studies Institute, with financial support from the New York City Council for the Humanities, launched an exhibition entitled Crossroads: An Exhibition of Contemporary Dominican-American Art. Held from February 5 through April 5, 2004, at the Aaron Davis Hall Grand Lobby, City College, the exhibit featured works by eight young New York–area based Dominican artists: Hochi Asiático, Delsa Camacho, Niccolo Cataldi, Luis Leonor, Luanda Lozano, Doris Rodríguez, Julia Santos Solomón, and Miguel Tió. The aim of the exhibition was to create a network among professional Dominican artists, Dominican art students, and the community to explore various themes of Dominican life in the diaspora.

Looking to the Future

As the Dominican population in the United States continues to grow, there is greater demand for a more visible representation. Dominican artists are venturing off on their own by establishing galleries and businesses throughout the nation to open the doors to their fellow Dominicans and Latino and Latina artists. In 2003, Charo Oquet cofounded Edge Zones, a nonprofit art organization that sponsors a series of collective exhibitions at the World Arts Building in Wynwood, Miami. The Dominican-born curator Camilo Alvarez is the director and cofounder of Samson Projects, a Boston-based gallery that "has chosen not to represent a defined group of artists, but rather introduce emerging and under-recognized artists as well as established artists" (samsonprojects.com). In 2005, Camilo Alvarez curated ¡Dominicanazo!, an exhibition that displays the works of nine Dominican artists living in the Dominican Republic and the United States featuring Elia Alba, Tony Capellán, José García Cordero, Nicolás Dumít Estévez, Mónica Ferreras, Iliana Emilia García, Scherezade García, Pascal Meccariello, and Belkis Ramírez.

See also Dominicans; Painters; Photographers; *and* Sculptors.

BIBLIOGRAPHY

Camacho, Jhovanny. "Dominican Memorial Art: Testimonials of Pain in a Diaspora." *Punto 7 Review: A Journal of Marginal Discourse* 3 (1996): 126–134.

Casares, Eduardo. "Preface." In *Art in Transit: A Dominican Experience*, by Stephen D. Kaplan et al., 9. New York: INTAR Latin American Gallery, 1996.

Kaplan, Stephen D. "The Shaping of Contemporary Dominican Art." In *Art in Transit: A Dominican Experience*, by Stephen D. Kaplan et al., 13–16. New York: INTAR Latin American Gallery, 1996.

Miller, Jeannette. *Historia de la pintura dominicana*. 3rd ed. Santo Domingo: Amigo del Hogar, 1984.

Pellegrini, Elena. "Locating Sites of Memory in Art of the Dominican Diaspora." In *Art in Transit: A Dominican Experience*, by Stephen D. Kaplan et al., 23–29. New York: INTAR Latin American Gallery, 1996a.

Pellegrini, Elena. "Artist Biographies." In *Modern and Contemporary Art of the Dominican Republic*, edited by Suzanne Stratton, 113–122. New York: Americas Society and the Spanish Institute, 1996b.

Phillips, Genaro. "Remarks." In *Caribbean Visions: Contemporary Painting and Sculpture*, Samella Lewis, guest curator, 124–125. Alexandria, Virginia: Art Services International, 1995.

Samson Projects. samsonprojects.com

SARAH APONTE AND SILVIO TORRES-SAILLANT

ART, PUERTO RICAN. During the Spanish-American War of 1898, Spain ceded Puerto Rico to the United States. In 1917, Puerto Ricans became U.S. citizens, and by 1952 the island became a commonwealth (a political unit having local autonomy but voluntarily united with the United States). In the early twenty-first century, Puerto Rico remains a U.S. possession. Residents of the island carry U.S. passports. They are subject to military service and most federal laws, but they do not pay federal income tax, lack official voting representation in Congress, and do not participate in presidential elections. In the late twentieth and early twenty-first centuries, popular and political opinion has been dominated by the maintenance of the existing commonwealth association

ALL COLOURED CAST (PART II). Acrylic and pencil and collage on wood support by Jean-Michel Basquiat, 1982. (Banque d'Images, ADAGP/Art Resource, NY)

and/or the impetus to transform the island into the fifty-first state. Artists and political activists have remained a vocal contingent promoting independence.

In the late 1940s and 1950s, Operation Bootstrap was created by the island's first freely elected governor, Luis Muñoz Marín, in collaboration with U.S. president Harry S. Truman. The program encouraged a massive migration of unemployed Puerto Ricans to large cities on the "mainland" to serve the postwar boom. The majority of these low-wage workers based themselves in El Barrio, an area on the Upper East Side of Manhattan located between 96th Street, 125th Street, Central Park, and the East River. Also known as Spanish Harlem, the neighborhood became the most important center for Puerto Ricans in the United States By 2005, the island's population was estimated at 3.9 million; the U.S. census revealed 3.4 million Puerto Ricans living in the United States in 2000—primarily in New York, but also in Hartford, Philadelphia, Chicago, Houston, New Orleans, and Hawaii.

Puerto Rico is politically and culturally linked to the United States while remaining geographically and so-

cially kindred to the Caribbean and Latin America. The relationship between Puerto Rico and New York is strong. Puerto Ricans' fluid commute on "La Guagua Aéra" (The Airbus) is symbolic of the translocal Puerto Rican nation. Similarly, the reference to the seas between the island and the United States as "El Charco" (The Puddle) poetically sustains an ideological contraction of the spatial divide. For artists, a bifurcated sense of belonging is common, and many have developed careers with a dual presence on both the island and New York City. While in the past, the two locations were more clearly separate, and being Puerto Rican was very different than being Nuyorican (Puerto Rican born in New York). In the digital age old-fashioned physical coordinates are no longer so absolute, as communications and information continuously exchange. Second- and third-generation Puerto Ricans in the United States have moved across the nation, and El Barrio now welcomes many Mexican and Central American immigrants. The artistic contributions of Puerto Ricans in the United States over the past one hundred years often refers to this history.

Early Twentieth Century and the Fifties Generation

An independent Puerto Rican art within the United States did not truly emerge until after World War II, spurred on by developments on the island. For example, to foster graphics and filmmaking in the service of the community, Muñoz Marín in 1949 created the División de la Educación de la Communidad (Division of Community Education, DIVEDCO). The Centro de Arte Puertorriqueño (Puerto Rican Art Center, CAP) existed from 1950 to 1952. CAP followed the ideals of Mexico's printmaking workshop, Taller de Gráfica Popular (the People's Print Workshop, TGP): to create an ideal space for the development of the national arts. This era is known as the Puerto Rican Renaissance. The generation of artists at this time, La Generación del Cincuenta (the Fifties Generation), initiated the Puerto Rican print tradition. The leading Puerto Rican artists looked to Mexican modernism of the 1920s and 1930s; Lorenzo Homar, Rafael Tufiño, and Antonio Maldonado trained with Mexican artists and translated their effective approaches, such as muralism and printmaking.

Homar and Tufiño are central figures in modern Puerto Rican art, both on the island and in New York. Distinguished poster makers, draftsmen, and calligraphers, their striking combinations of image and text became hallmarks of Puerto Rican graphics during the 1950s and 1960s. Lorenzo Homar (1913–2004; b. San Juan, Puerto Rico) created precisely lettered prints and posters. He moved to New York in 1928. In 1931, he attended the Art Students League. By 1937, he began a design apprenticeship at Cartier jewelers and attended Pratt Institute. He interacted with the American social realist Ben Shahn and the German expressionist Max Beckmann. Homar served in the Philippines during World War II, and in 1946 returned to Cartier. He enrolled in the Brooklyn Museum School of Art where the Mexican painter, Rufino Tamayo, had just been appointed. Homar returned to Puerto Rico in 1950, but traveled frequently to the United States, remaining in close contact with the artists and his relatives here.

From age five, Rafael Tufiño (b. 1922; Brooklyn, New York) moved between the island and New York. He apprenticed with artists in Puerto Rico, where he began his career. After serving with the U.S. Army in Panama from 1943 to 1946, he opened a sign-painting shop in El Barrio. On the G.I. Bill, Tufiño moved to Mexico and studied art at Academia de San Carlos from 1947 to 1949. He returned to Puerto Rico but lived in New York from 1970 to 1974, when he was active in the nascent organizations, El Museo del Barrio, a museum devoted to Puerto Rican and Latina/Latino art, and the community workshop, Taller Boricua. Tufiño's work encompasses linoleum block prints, book illustrations, posters, and paintings of dance and music.

Carlos Osorio (1927–1984; b. Caguas, Puerto Rico) grappled with abstraction, creating thickly layered, expressionistic surfaces covered in graffiti-like symbols. Osorio served with the U.S. military in Korea and Japan in 1951. In 1953, he moved to New York and studied at the School of Visual Arts. He absorbed the lessons of the abstract expressionists before returning to Puerto Rico in 1954. Osorio moved again to the Lower East Side of New York in 1964, which remained his base until 1977. In 1967, he secured a studio at the Friends of Puerto Rico building. This group, founded in 1953, is often considered the first collective of Puerto Rican artists in New York City. Like Tufiño, Osorio was a early participant in both El Museo del Barrio and Taller Boricua. From 1973 to 1975, he lived in Massachusetts. In 1976, he helped found the artist's organization Grupo Morivivi. In 1977, he left for Austin, Texas, where he worked with Chicano/a community organizations to paint murals before returning to Puerto Rico in 1979.

In contrast to Homar, Tufiño, and Osorio, Wilfredo "Eloy" Blanco (1933–1984; b. Aguadilla, Puerto Rico) developed completely apart from Puerto Rican artists. In 1938, his family moved to New York. At fourteen, he received a scholarship to the Brooklyn Museum School of Art, where he remained for five years, until 1953. He became acquainted with the German expressionist Max Beckmann and studied with the American abstract expressionist painter William Baziotes. Blanco was prolific and is best remembered for his early abstract canvases, expressive portraits, and his later stick-figure surfaces, which Blanco himself compared to cave paintings. In 1976, when he had a solo exhibition, he first came into contact with Puerto Rican artists.

Other artists working in the United States during the 1950s and 1960s are known for their realistic styles. Juan DePrey (1904–1962; b. San Juan, Puerto Rico), a self-taught, part-Haitian artist who lived in New York for a long period, was recognized for his portraits and depictions of children. Félix Cordero (b. 1931; Ponce, Puerto Rico) worked and studied in the United States from 1954 to 1986. He is best known for his architectural images of Ponce, Puerto Rico, although he has also developed an abstract series. Pedro Villarini (b. 1933; Hato Rey, Puerto Rico) came to the United States in 1947 and studied until 1956, when he began exhibiting his carefully crafted landscapes and figurative paintings.

Abstraction

The abstract painting movement had several strong Puerto Rican exponents during the 1950s and 1960s. Julio Rosado del Valle (b. 1922; Cataño, Puerto Rico) attended the New School for Social Research in New York in 1946. After his return to the island, he moved into abstraction by 1950. He was an initiator of the development of non-figurative formal languages. Other early and prominent artists who developed abstract works—including Luis Hernández Cruz, Diego Garcia, Francisco Rodón, and Myrna Báez—studied in the United States, but few embraced the U.S. community like Olga Albizu (b. 1924; Ponce, Puerto Rico). After training in Puerto Rico with Miguel Pou and the Spanish painter Esteban Vicente, she came to New York where she remained. From 1948 to 1949, she studied with the prominent German abstract expressionist Hans Hoffman. Between 1949 and 1951, she attended the Art Students League where her teachers included Vaclav Vytlacil, a Czech abstractionist and student of Hoffman's. After working in Europe, Albizu returned to New York in 1956 and had a solo exhibition at Gallery Panoras that was positively reviewed in the *New York Times*. Albizu's impressionistic or organic abstraction was utilized on several RCA album covers for musicians, including Stan Getz.

Several abstract artists following Albizu were integral to the New York arts scene. Tony Bechara (b. 1942; San Juan, Puerto Rico), a painter, printmaker, and mosaic artist, studied at Georgetown University in Washington, D.C. After completing his degree, he traveled in Europe and returned to New York in the early 1960s, where he remains. During the 1968 to 1970 period, he attended the School of Visual Arts, studying with American minimalist sculptor Richard Serra and African American printmaker Robert Blackburn, among others. By 1971 Bechara began to work in geometric, hard-edge paintings and prints that address color and optics. Bechara was also an early participant with both Taller Boricua and El Museo del Barrio, where he continues to serve in the early 2000s.

Evelyn López de Guzman (b. 1947, New York City) also paints in a hard-edge style, at times on shaped supports. She studied at Hunter College with Mark Rothko, the Russian-born New York School painter, and the color field painter Helen Frankenthaler. While completing her master's degree, she began to exhibit annually. Similar to Blanco, the first time de Guzman came into contact with other Puerto Rican artists was during a 1979 exhibition.

Avant-Garde Tendencies

Several artists who worked abstractly also contributed to avant-garde tendencies, including performative or body works and installation, during the late 1960s and 1970s. Lope Max Díaz, Antonio Navia, and Joaquín Mercado all enrolled in graduate studies in New York.

Rafael Ferrer (b. 1933; Santurce, Puerto Rico) went to military school in Virginia. Returning to Puerto Rico in 1952, he was influenced by his university teacher, the Spanish surrealist Eugenio Fernández Granell. He joined Granell in Paris in 1954, and met a surrealist circle that included Afro-Cuban painter Wifredo Lam. Ferrer worked as a Latin jazz musician in New York and traveled between the island and the United States prior to settling in Philadelphia. In both New York and Philadelphia between 1969 and 1971, he developed ephemeral, interventionist projects with leaves, hay, grease, ice, water, and his body. He associated with the major minimalists and conceptual artists of the time, including Robert Morris, and participated in several key exhibits of American avant-garde work. Since that time, he has drawn freely from art historical sources, including Parisian surrealism and German expressionism. His large figurative paintings, elaborately drawn maps and prints, sculptural assemblages, kayaks, and tents, and his paper-bag faces have all utilized words, color, and witty draftsmanship.

Rafael Montañez Ortiz (b. 1934; Brooklyn, New York) was a central figure in the New York avant-garde and fluxus movements, and was a key participant in the legendary "Destruction in Art Symposium" (DIAS) held in London in 1966. There he presented his *Destruction Realizations* involving chairs, mattresses, pianos, paper bags, and his own body in the context of international artists working with this concept. He achieved public notoriety for his *Piano Destruction Concerts* (performed on *The Tonight Show with Johnny Carson*, 1968 and 1970) and for performances in which he sacrificed live chickens, held at the Judson Church in 1968. Montañez Ortiz was the founding director of El Museo del Barrio in Spanish Harlem in 1969. Mandated only to create an educational program, he instead envisioned an advanced museum that would celebrate not only Taíno culture and the popular arts, but also support the development of avant-garde practices and multimedia explorations by Puerto Rican and Latina/Latino artists. The museum straddles New York's Museum Mile and El Barrio, presenting quality exhibitions on Latina/Latino art and preserving a richly diverse collection of over 6,500 works. His doctoral thesis, "Physio-Psycho-Alchemy" (Columbia University, 1982) informed his performative work through the early 1980s. In the early 2000s, he creates large-scale digital productions and serves as a tenured professor at Rutgers University, in New Brunswick, New Jersey. Always an innovator in digital media, Montañez Ortiz produced a number of recycled films between 1956 and 1958 that had a great impact on experimental filmmaking.

Carlos Irizarry (b. 1938; Santa Isabel, Puerto Rico) spent his formative years in New York and graduated from Manhattan's School of Art and Design in 1958. His work developed at an intersection between the simple geometric color forms of the minimalists, and the pop artists, who appropriated images from mass media and popular culture. Irizarry opened Galería 63, an experimental space, in San Juan in 1963. He began to play an active role on the island while maintaining a studio in New York, but by 1972 he had made San Juan his primary residence.

Irizarry created two notorious conceptual works. He announced he would blow up U.S. president Gerald Ford at a meeting of the superpowers in Puerto Rico; later he created a flyer announcing he would bomb an airplane flying between New York and San Juan, to protest Puerto Rico's colonial status. Indicted for this act, he was sent to a U.S. federal prison in 1979 and released in 1983. During that time, Irizarry continued to develop his work. His work in the early twenty-first century includes complex digital prints and large-scale, mixed-media portraits.

The Taíno Revival

From the late 1960s through the 1970s, during the civil rights struggles, Puerto Rican artists in New York initiated a resurgence in the use of Taíno visual symbols. This development was concurrent to similar movements by other groups, including African Americans, Native Americans, and Chicanos and Chicanas, who also sought to distinguish and affirm their cultural legacies. Like the Chicanos/as who utilized Aztec imagery in their campaigns, Nuyorican artists reclaimed the petroglyphs and patterns of the island's indigenous peoples to express their affinity and continuity. At the same time, they explored their African lineage. The Taíno revival took root as a backlash against the dominant colonial and Catholic presence of the Spanish, and by extension the United States.

José Caraballo (1930–1992; b. Santurce, Puerto, Rico) moved to New York at the age of fourteen. In 1947, he studied graphics and sculpture in Greenwich Village. Caraballo was among the earliest artists in the United States to use indigenous iconography in his paintings, drawings, graphics, and tapestries. Another important artist working early on in this tradition is Rafael Colón Morales (b. 1941; Trujillo Alto, Puerto Rico). An artist, art historian, and curator who served at El Museo del Barrio, Colón Morales lived between Puerto Rico and New York for many years. His free-flowing narrative paintings combine African and primitive art, cubo-surrealist forms, and Taíno mythology. He developed a painting method by pouring layers of acrylic paint. He then peeled these thick skins—which he called *pellejos*—and suspended, stretched, or twisted them.

Taller Boricua is closely associated with the Taíno revival. El Taller Alma Boricua was established in 1969 in El Barrio by Marcos Dimas, Adrian García, Manuel (Neco) Otero, Armando Soto, and Martín Rubio. The founding artists were active in the Art Worker's Coalition, an arts advocacy group that championed the decentralization of art institutions, the development of programs within museums that would relate to local communities, and the inclusion of African Americans, Asians, Latinos, and women in mainstream museum exhibitions. Montañez Ortiz organized a group called Puerto Rican Art

Workers. As artist-activists, Taller Boricua members aspired to "take art to the people." In addition to creating posters for everything from protest rallies to poetry readings, members made murals and participated in "traveling exhibitions" that took place on the streets. Taller Boricua membership quickly expanded in the early 1970s to include Sandra María Esteves, Gilberto Hernández, Martín "Tito" Pérez, Fernando Salicrup, Jorge Soto, Sammy Tanco, and Nitza Tufiño, with Rafael Tufiño and Carlos Osorio as the group's senior mentors.

In the early twenty-first century, Marcos Dimas and Fernando Salicrup codirect Taller Boricua. Marcos Dimas (b. 1943; Cabo Rojo, Puerto Rico) migrated to the United States before his tenth birthday. He grew up in the South Bronx and earned his graduate degree from the School of Visual Arts in 1970. Dimas is a painter, sculptor, graphic artist, and filmmaker who uses mythical and metaphorical spiritual images in his work. Fernando Salicrup (b. 1946, New York City) is a painter and printmaker, recognized for his work in experimental digital methods. Salicrup served in the U.S. military in Vietnam, and studied at the Philadelphia Academy of Art as well as at the School of Visual Arts, where he worked with the American portrait painter Chuck Close, the printmaker Robert Blackburn, and Carlos Osorio.

The paintings, linoleum prints, and public ceramic murals of Nitza Tufiño (b. 1949; Mexico City, Mexico) are also inspired by the art of the Taíno, particularly her mural in the 103rd Street Lexington Avenue subway station in New York. The Taíno called the island of Puerto Rico "Boriken," meaning "land of the brave lord." By titling a group of her works Neo-Boriken, Tufiño indicates that the series represents contemporary interpretations of Taíno designs. Tufiño was born and trained in Mexico City and grew up in Puerto Rico, guided by her father, artist Rafael Tufiño. In 1970, she moved to New York, joined Taller Boricua, and began working with El Museo del Barrio. The tropical Taíno figures of Tufiño's mural are the first thing that subway riders see as they enter El Barrio.

Jorge Soto Sánchez (1947–1985; b. Bronx, New York) was another influential figure among Latina/Latino painters and poets active in New York during the 1970s and early 1980s. Trained as a commercial artist, Soto Sánchez joined Taller Boricua in 1971 and helped direct its operations from 1972 to 1982. During his decade-long association, he developed an artistic vocabulary drawn from Pre-Columbian, Oceanic, and African art. A prolific draftsman, Soto Sánchez's utilizes surreal, curvilinear forms. He died before his prime; he is remembered as a profound teacher and an under-recognized master. Diogénes Ballester (b. 1956; Playa Ponce, Puerto Rico) moved to New York in 1981. As he became aware of the multiple threads within Puerto Rican spiritual traditions, he began to create expressionistic paintings, artist's books, prints, installations, and altars. Ballester was also an early member of Taller Boricua and El Museo del Barrio.

Other fertile artists of this period include Manny Vega (b. 1956; New York City) and Carlos Sueños (b 1952; San Juan, Puerto Rico). Vega's works include prints, drawings, elaborate ceremonial beadwork objects, and celebratory festivals. His public murals range from painted walls to a ceramic mosaic related to Afro-Brazilian religious experience at the 110th Street Lexington Avenue subway station in El Barrio. Sueños worked closely both with the Taíno holdings at El Museo del Barrio, as well as with the print collection of Robert Blackburn's Printmaking Workshop in New York, where he created graphics in the 1970s and 1980s.

Several strong feminist artists emerged in New York from this socially conscious, historically aware tradition. Miriam Hernández (b. 1947; Santurce, Puerto Rico) is known for her feminist and Buddhist imagery. Her delicately figurative drawings and paintings address the spiritual and mental battles of the contemporary world. Marina Gutierrez (b. 1954; New York City) creates mobile and public sculpture, as well as two- and three-dimensional works in which the female figure and its attributes are important metaphorical symbols of both women's rights and Puerto Rican self-determination.

The works of Gloria Rodríguez (Arecibo, Puerto Rico) also address the contemporary construction of identity. Her acrylic painting collages—acrollages—use photographs, torn papers, metallics, and lushly colored paint to form figurative images that address sexism, racism, and the urban condition. The painter María Domínguez has created a number of community murals and public art, in which numerous figures engaged in everyday business, celebration, and motion create complex narratives. Anaida Hernández (b. 1954; Mayaguez, Puerto Rico) has been a major innovator in graphic arts. She is recognized for her politically conscious prints, paintings and installations that address immigration, domestic violence, human rights, and cultural dislocation, often in the form of a multipart game or puzzle.

José Morales (b. 1947; Bronx, New York) is known for his sharply drawn caricatures, beautifully drafted images, and exquisitely painted, elegiac urban scenes. His installations incorporate cast-off furniture, mattress springs, shower curtains, chairs, machetes, and fish heads. In other work, his fantastical, fragile bridges, which are composed of large numbers of simple wooden crutches, lead to elegantly drawn doorways. Néstor Otero (b. 1948; Caguas, Puerto Rico) has spent considerable time in New York. A painter, printmaker, digital artist, and graphic designer in the late 1970s and 1980s, he began creating assemblage-objects and environments that incorporate

objects. He combined ladders, knives, targets, and chairs with elegant striped or patterned minimalist paintings. While Morales and Otero are both closely affiliated with El Barrio, Taller Boricua, and El Museo del Barrio, and the artists of the neo-Taíno movements, their mature artworks lead to postmodern installation.

Multiculturalism and Postmodernism

The generation that flourished during and after the Vietnam War combined practices of visual art, performance, writing, and mixed-media interventions with an activist or political intent. Their works celebrated difference. This explosion of forms in the 1970s led to the multicultural era of the 1980s, where expression found outlets in underdeveloped areas of major cities. The coexistence of so many formal strategies and visual languages fed the development of postmodernism.

Adál (b. 1947; Utuado, Puerto Rico) utilizes mixed-media installation, performance, language, and photography to humorously explore the political and psychological condition of Puerto Ricans' hybrid culture. Adál is an accomplished photographer who cofounded the Foto Gallery in New York in 1975. His work stakes out a whimsical yet complex conceptual territory.

Papo Colo (b. 1946; Santurce, Puerto Rico) is a painter, performer, photographer, poet, mixed-media artist, curator, and provocateur. In addition to his own diverse artistic production, he has successfully staked a claim as an important New York culture broker; in 1982, Colo cofounded the alternative contemporary art space Exit Art with his partner, Jeanette Ingberman. Colo champions the concept of "zero identity": freeing oneself of the burden of specificity, ethnicity, or culture, and accepting the contemporary reality of the "hybrid state." In 1977, Colo's action, *Superman*, involved running on the West Side Highway with fifty-one pieces of lumber tied and trailing from his body, until he collapsed in exhaustion. This project has been understood as a commentary on the conflicted status of Puerto Rico.

During the late 1970s and 1980s, the graffiti movement was related to the rap and hip-hop scene. Jean-Michel Basquiat (1960–1988; Brooklyn, New York) was born to a Haitian immigrant father and a Brooklyn-born, Puerto Rican mother. His work drew inspiration in part from music and the downtown New York club scene in which he was active, as well as his peers including the writer Rammellzee and DJ Fab 5 Freddy. His early contributions include graffitied aphorisms, in collaboration with Al Diaz, tagged "Samo©." Basquiat's mature paintings and drawings incorporated petroglyphic figures, diagrammatic lines, and shallow pictorial space. Basquiat's neo-expressionism juxtaposed images with language and symbols, in a form kindred to musical sampling or mixing.

Other graffiti writers, including Lee Quiñones, have transformed their street practice into Twenty-first-century paintings and three-dimensional works. The styles of the 1980s also inspired later generations, who created their own contemporary versions. For example, Dzine (b. 1970; Chicago, Illinois), who from a young age followed the graffiti writers, today straddles a boundary between art and music in abstract, lyrical murals, Envirotex paintings, and glass-beaded abstractions. In El Barrio, James de la Vega (b. 1972, New York City) paints both full-fledged wall murals of musicians, local heroes, or classic works of art, and he chalks temporary drawings and quips on sidewalks and construction-site plywoods. The Graffiti Hall of Fame, located in a school courtyard in East Harlem at 106th Street and Park Avenue, is a showcase of writers, periodically reinvigorated under the leadership of artist Joe Whippler. The work of Rigoberto Torres (b. 1960; Aguadilla, Puerto Rico) is ideologically linked to graffiti. Growing up in the South Bronx, by 1978 Torres apprenticed with John Ahearn, casting their neighbor's faces and bodies, and mounting the painted plaster reliefs on buildings or staging them as public sculpture. Although the two still collaborate, Torres moved to Florida where he continues his individual practice.

Juan Sánchez (b. 1954; Brooklyn, New York) grew up and trained in the greater New York metropolitan area. His mixed-media canvases and prints entice viewers to visually excavate them, much like the strata of a postered, graffitied wall within an urban environment. Active color fields jostle snapshots and newspaper clippings. Texts scrawled in English and Spanish cover laminas and drawings of petroglyphs. His works combine all elements into lush, visually dense surfaces, which are both personal and political reflections on the emotions and experiences of the contemporary Puerto Rican community. Pepón Osorio (b. 1955; Santurce, Puerto Rico) moved to New York in 1975 and relocated to Philadelphia in 2000. His complex mixed-media installations also remix objects from popular culture, but with a flamboyancy whose essence is transformative. Osorio's belief that "more is more" feeds his impulse to embellish. His works are not solely celebratory adornments; trained in social work and art education, Osorio explores complicated topics relating to Latina/Latino realities, including violence, machismo, crime and punishment, race, and class.

Other artists who came of age in the mid- and late 1980s addressed gay rights and AIDS. For example, the minimal, conceptual artist Felix Gonzalez-Torres (1957–1996; b. Guaimaro, Cuba) created deceptively simple works about memory, loss, love, and sexuality. Gonzalez-Torres lived in Puerto Rico for eight years (1971–1979) and attended the university there before moving to the United States. During a time of raging debates over identity and sexuality, and of

fury over the lack of action to fight the devastating AIDS pandemic, Gonzalez-Torres's piles of candy or hanging light bulb curtains galvanized a broad community. His compatriot, Ernesto Pujol (b. 1957; Havana, Cuba), also moved to Puerto Rico in 1961, and then to the United States in 1979. Pujol creates psychologically charged, elegant installations and paintings. Utilizing religious habits, shoes, and other elements, Pujol's work deals with gender construction, and ideas of nationality and ethnicity, Roman Catholicism, loss, and memory. The mixed-media surfaces of Rafael Collazo (1943–1990; b. San Juan, Puerto Rico) relate to both abstract expressionism and tapestries. Collazo came to New York City with his family at age four. Raised on the Lower East Side, his lyrical abstract and figurative paintings summon the parks, streets, and cityscapes of his adopted home.

Other New York–based artists continue to work with related themes. Hiram Alfredo Rodríguez-Mora (b. 1948; San Juan, Puerto Rico) creates delicate, hand-sewn works with found elements that are diaristic explorations of life's fragility. José Luis Cortes (b. 1962; Philadelphia, Pennsylvania), in expressionistic paintings on attached sheets of newspaper, evokes the days of Times Square peep shows and majestic movie theatres. Luis Carle (b. 1962; San Juan, Puerto Rico) utilizes photography in his personal works that allude to the transcendence of everyday life. Carle founded OP Art (Organization of Puerto Rican Artists), which documents and promotes the work of contemporary Puerto Rican artists.

Early Twenty-first Century

The greater New York area still remains the major hub for Puerto Rican artists, although it is no longer as a result of immigration patterns, but rather, like all artists, they wish to be at the center of the global art scene. Cutting-edge, younger painters, photographers, and conceptual and installation artists born in the 1960s and 1970s include Manuel Acevedo, Desirée Alvarez, Javier Cambre, Nayda Collazo-Llórens, Fernando Colón González, Yasmin Hernández, Ivelisse Jiménez, CIG Lang, Miguel Luciano, Malika, Soraya Marcano, Rosanna Martínez, Arnaldo Morales, Wanda Ortiz, Enoc Pérez, Aixa Requena, Rita Rivera, Leticia Stella-Serra, and Miguel Trelles; other artists, such as Allora and Calzadilla, and Cari González Casanova, maintain bases in the United States, Europe, and Puerto Rico. Chicago is an important locus for contemporary Puerto Rican artists as well; the conceptual painter Bibiana Suárez has been based there since 1980; in 1982, the influential painter Arnaldo Roche Rabell went to the Art Institute of Chicago to train, and painter Cándida Álvarez teaches at the School of the Art Institute of Chicago. Younger artists, born in the 1960s and 1970s, with a strong Chicago connection include the conceptual artists Ryan Rivera, Luis Romero, Edra Soto, and Pedro Velez.

Younger Puerto Rican artists can be found working in nearly every major city. The multimedia installation artist Charles Juhász-Alvardo spent eight years (1984–1992) in New Haven, Connecticut, while completing his bachelor's and master's degrees at Yale University. The digital artist and sculptor Ana Rosa Rivera Marrero also spent time at Yale and in Norwalk, Connecticut. Pablo Delano, a photographer who also attended Yale, lives and works in the Hartford area and teaches at Trinity College. Sylvia Benítez, a significant sculptor, is based in Maryland. The performative photographer and installation artist, Carlos Betancourt, lives and works in Miami. The painter Angel Rodríguez Díaz lives and works in San Antonio, Texas.

While it might not yet be known what Puerto Rican artists in the twenty-first century will contribute, the development of the Puerto Rican arts in the twentieth century in the United States is, in many ways, best encapsulated by the life and work of Antonio Martorell (b. 1939; Santurce, Puerto Rico). Martorell divides his time between the island, where he is the artist in residence at the University of Puerto Rico, Cayey, and New York. Renowned as a contemporary and experimental graphic artist, Martorell is recognized for his baroque, multi-textural and multi-textual installations that compile narrative images, calligraphic literary texts, textiles, carved wooden surfaces, photos, and decorated domestic objects. While his prints, posters, installations and artist's books frequently employ literary allusions, biographical elements, and poetic or punning wordplay, he also often deploys biting political and social criticism. Martorell embodies the contemporary fluid interchange between the island and mainland; as a student of Lorenzo Homar and the Fifties Generation, he bridges that fundamental production to contemporary practice, bringing it full circle to the twenty-first century.

See also Museo del Barrio; Painters; Puerto Ricans; Sculptors; *and* Spanish Harlem.

BIBLIOGRAPHY

Báez, Myrna, and José A. Torres Martinó, eds. *Puerto Rico: Arte e identidad*. San Juan: Editorial de la Universidad de Puerto Rico, 1998.

Benítez, Marimar. "Neurotic Imperatives: Contemporary Art from Puerto Rico." *Art Journal* 57, no. 4 (Winter 1998): 74–85.

Bercht, Fatima, and Deborah Cullen, eds. *Voces y Visiones: Highlights from El Museo del Barrio's Permanent Collection*. 5 vols. New York: El Museo del Barrio, 2003.

Cancel, Luis R., et al. *The Latin American Spirit: Art and Artists in the United States, 1920–1970*. New York: Bronx Museum of the Arts in association with Harry N. Abrams, 1988.

Cullen, Deborah, ed. *None of the Above: Contemporary Work by Puerto Rican Artists*. Hartford, Conn.: Real Art Ways, and San Juan: Museo de Arte de Puerto Rico, 2005.

El Museo del Barrio and the Metropolitan Museum of Art. *The Art Heritage of Puerto Rico: Pre-Columbian to the Present*. New York: El Museo del Barrio and the Metropolitan Museum of Art, 1974.

Pérez-Lizano Manuel. *Arte contemporáneo de Puerto Rico, 1950–1983: cerámica, escultura, pintura*. Puerto Rico: Universidad Central de Bayamon, Ediciones Cruz-Ansata, 1983.

Poupeye, Veerle. *Caribbean Art*. New York and London: Thames and Hudson, 1998.

Ramírez, Mari Carmen. *Puerto Rican Painting: Between Past and Present*. Princeton, N.J.: Squibb Corporation, 1987.

Roulet, Laura. *Contemporary Puerto Rican Installation Art: The Guagua Aérea, The Trojan Horse, and The Termite*. San Juan, P.R.: Editorial de la Universidad de Puerto Rico, 2000.

Sullivan, Edward J., ed. *Latin American Artists of the Twentieth Century*. London: Phaidon Press, 1996.

Wilson Cryer, Patricia L. "Puerto Rican Art in New York: The Aesthetic Analysis of Eleven Artists and Their Work." PhD diss., New York University, 1984.

DEBORAH CULLEN

ASIAN LATINOS. The multiple and diverse voices of Asian Latinas and Latinos in the United States have been muted, inaudible, ignored, discounted, or simply silenced for the simple reason that the category of Asian Latinas and Latinos is not a widely recognized and acknowledged cultural or social category in the United States. It is a byproduct of a peculiar kind of *mestizaje* unique to America, a multiracial, multicultural project all its own, as well as a reflection of the massive post-1965 emigration from Mexico, the Spanish Caribbean, and Central and South America. Yet Asian Latinas and Latinos are practically absent from the discourses of Asian American Studies and Latina and Latino Studies and are nowhere to be found in treatises on multiracialism and mixed-race peoples of the United States. For example, in the two volumes titled *The Multiracial Experience* and *Racial Mixed People in America*, edited by the Filipina American psychologist Maria Root, and in the popular reader *Voices of Mixed-Race Young People*, edited by Pearl Fuyo Gaskins, all major combinations are well represented: black-white, white-Asian, black-Asian, Hispanic/Latina- and Hispanic/Latino-white, Hispanic/Latina- and Hispanic/Latino-black, and different combinations with native peoples. But these volumes offer no case study at all of Asian Latina and Latino mixtures nor do they even hint at such a possibility. As well, Martha Menchaca's well-timed exploration of the racial history of Mexican Americans includes "the Indian, Black, and White roots" but leaves out the Asian.

Voices of Asian Latinas and Latinos

Yet the voices of Asian Latinas and Latinos are fairly easy to find. They are diverse in ethnicity, gender, age, and regional location in the United States. Asian Latinas and Latinos clearly have announced their social presence in the United States, despite their apparent absence, if not outright erasure, in the academic scholarship of race and ethnic studies. Following are some of their voices.

Latino and Latina Studies professor Alicia Rodríguez describes her search for an elusive ancestor:

Around the beginning of the 1900s, my maternal great-grandfather came from China and went to Jamaica, where he met my great-grandmother. Story has it that he was a sailor on a merchant ship. After my grandmother was born (who is still alive and living in Cuba), her mother migrated to Santiago de Cuba while my great-grandfather returned to China (my great-grandmother was very independent and didn't want to go with him to China). Anyway, supposedly he died on the way to China. Although they never married, my great-grandmother made up a surname for herself and my grandmother to make it sound like his (which we think was "Chung Fak") and to adapt to Jamaican surnames. She came up with "Thompson." This remains my grandmother's surname. My great-grandfather has been such a mysterious, curious figure in our family history ("China" was a nickname of one of my sisters because of her eyes, and I have several cousins in Cuba who were given pseudo-Chinese names because of their looks).

(Alicia Rodríguez, associate director of the Latina/Latino Studies Program at the University of Illinois at Urbana-Champaign, 2003).

A Japanese Peruvian who was interned in the United States during World War II and later became an American citizen wrote:

In our family, too, the language spoken in our home gradually shifted from Japanese to English as our children grew up. At some imperceptible point, English became the common language in our home. Of course, when my wife and I led the conversation we mainly used a brand of broken Japanese that embraced an odd mixture of English and Spanish. But even that gradually lost its ability to communicate our thoughts and feelings accurately. After a certain point, if we wanted to communicate with our children at all, we were forced to rely on the English language.

(Higashide, p. 219)

Isabel Singh García of Imperial Valley, California, told an interviewer,

I also wanted to let you know that the first generation of Hindus that came here married Mexican women and there are a large amount of half-breed children born from those marriages. The East Indians of today would like to forget we exist, because they are ashamed that their people came to this country and found the Mexican women very compatible with them. . . . Our fathers and mothers lived a very rich life. They raised us to be very proud, and gave us the best and the finest quality of life that one could ask for.

(quoted in Leonard, p. 195)

Frances Bu, born in Havana in 1956, emigrated to New York City and told a researcher

I hate to say that, but race is an American hang-up. . . . And one of the things I hated the most when I came to this country, and my brother, too, was to have to fill out an application where it asks your "race." My brother used to put "human" all the time—I mean, all the time. It would bug the heck out of him to have somebody ask him, "What race are you?" Yet they've got to know what your race is. And in Cuba, everybody was Cuban. . . . I never felt any different. I actually didn't even realize that I wasn't Cuban. I always thought of myself as Cuban.

(quoted in Cynthia Ai-fen Lee, p. 46)

Lamgen Antonio Léon, born in Azua in the Dominican Republic in 1959 and now living in New York City, described the difficulties of moving between cultures.

While studying in Hong Kong, we always missed our rice and beans. At the beginning, we didn't know how to speak Chinese, so we always said, "We want *arroz y habichuelas*. We want our rice and beans, rice and beans." We cried for our rice and beans. Because there were no beans in Hong Kong, so we missed our rice and beans, our beef stew, our Dominican food. But then we get used to it, and it's OK. And we learned. . . . We learned Chinese.

(quoted in Cynthia Ai-fen Lee, p. 56)

Fabiana Chiu-Rinaldi, born in Lima, Peru, in 1964, became a resident of New York City in the 1980s and encountered problems with the bureaucracy.

When I applied for a new SOCIAL Security card in Brooklyn, the form instructed me to check only one racial/ethnic category. I decided to be accurate and checked both Hispanic and Asian. Minutes after I turned in my form, the clerk and later her supervisor called me to their desks to try to persuade me to choose between the categories. After my tiresome recitation about who my parents were, what language we spoke, and what our last names were, they—fully confused—shrugged their shoulders and left the form unchanged. Unwilling to give in, I wanted every part of my identity, China/Peruana/Asian/Latina/American, to be counted and accounted for.

(Chiu-Rinaldi, p. 183)

Cristina Hwang, who was born in São Paolo, Brazil, in 1968 and now lives in Fort Lee, New Jersey, recalls her childhood.

My father had his store. And until I was ten, he used to work in a market in the south part of São Paolo. The market—it was a small one, I should say a very small one. And whenever the trucks came, you had to unload them, and sometimes it was 3 A.M. or 3 P.M. And these trucks would come from all over Brazil. And there was no business hours. . . . it was whenever you need it. So this is why I think my parents understood they could not force me to speak Chinese, because they couldn't spend enough time with me for me to learn Chinese.

(quoted in Cynthia Ai-fen Lee, p. 54)

Marian Lim, who was born in Guaymas, Sonora, Mexico, in 1903 and later lived in Tucson, remembers life in a town on the United States–Mexico border.

We used to have problems in Nogales when we were going to school. The Mexican kids used to tease us because we were

Chinese. There were some Mexican boys in our neighborhood who would always take my brother and beat him up. My brother Frank, who was smaller and younger, would cry. One day I told them that if they didn't stop bothering him, I was going to go after them. So they didn't believe me. One day they teased my brother so much I went after them and I beat one up something terrible. Oh, I just beat him to a fare-thee-well.

(quoted in Fong, p. 19)

Rudy Guevarra of Santa Barbara wrote a poem titled "Clueless" to capture his feelings:

I'm not the brown unknown
But a Filipino dragon flying high up in the clouds
  I'm the ancient serpent of pre-Columbian
  cultures,
  Among the warriors of the inner cities and
  yuppies of the suburbs
I am your illusion, your reality, your future
Mestizo you call me,
  But what the hell is that?
    Does that include all of me?
    My Asian, Indian, African, and Spanish roots?

(Guevarra, "Clueless," pp. 14–17).

Historical Perspective

Ironically, one very prominent place in which the Asian Latina and Latino presence has been noted is the 2000 U.S. census. According to the U.S. government, "Hispanic," unlike "white," "black," and "Asian," is not a racial category. Rather, it is a cultural category that allows the members to self-identify racially any way they want. Thus, after the category "Hispanic," the census form asks for a racial check-off. Among the 35,305,818 Hispanics counted in the 2000 census, about half (16,907,852) chose to identify as white, another 710,353 as black, and, notably, 119,829 as Asian, considerably more than chose to identify as American Indian—45,326. Thus, from the Hispanic perspective, an Asian heritage was prominently noted.

The question of Asian Latinas and Latinos can also be explored from the Asian perspective expressed on the census. When, in 2000, they were given the option for the first time of checking more than one racial category, fully 15 percent of Asians chose to express their multiracialism, much higher than the 6 percent of Hispanics who did so (with blacks at 5 percent and whites at only 2.5 percent). Furthermore, while 52 percent of multiracial Asians identified "white" as their other heritage, and only 6 percent identified with blacks and 8 percent with Native Hawaiians and other Pacific Islanders, an impressive 15 percent identified with Latinas and Latinos and "other races," totaling almost 249,000, compared to the 119,829 Hispanics who identified with an Asian heritage. In the absence of any other available count of this elusive category, it is reasonable to accept the two figures from the

census as the range of the size of the Asian Latina and Latino population in the United States.

It is impossible to ascertain what made Hispanics identify themselves also as Asian, and vice versa. From stories gathered from both the historical record and contemporary sources, it appears that Asian Latinas and Latinos are of two major types. They are either a unique kind of mestizaje that brings together Asian with Latina and Latino or a special group of immigrants or border crossers from Latin American countries who were originally Asian immigrants to those countries or descendants of those immigrants. The two are actually closely related, for many of the Asian immigrants from Latin America and the Caribbean were already racially mixed, the result in turn of the heavily male-Asian migration to those multiracial regions with, moreover, racial customs that were more relaxed than the rigid legal system of segregation that prevailed in the United States through the 1960s, when immigration reform once again permitted immigration from the nonwhite "Third World." We will explore some of the most poignant and striking stories that illustrate both kinds of Asian Latinas and Latinos, reaching deep into the historical record of the Americas as well as surveying the contemporary scene in different parts of the United States.

The history of Asia and America began, of course, with Columbus, who set out to explore "Las Indias" and got lost in what we now know as the Caribbean. He insisted, however, that Cuba, which he partially explored, was really "Cipango," or Japan. Shortly after the Spanish empire established itself in Mexico as New Spain, it inaugurated the highly lucrative trans-Pacific commercial enterprise known as the Manila Galleon Trade, exchanging Mexican silver for mostly luxury items from Japan and especially China, using the Spanish colony of Manila in the Philippines as entrepôt. The sailors manning these ships were known as *chinos de manila*; some of them jumped ship and settled in Mexico City, setting up small businesses such as barbershops. The story of who might be termed the first Asian Latina or Latino was probably apocryphal, but it came out of this context and is worth reviewing, because if it were true, history would have to be rewritten. The popular historian Stan Steiner asserted in his book *The Chinese Who Built America* that Chinese from Mexico City helped found the city of Los Angeles in 1781. However, he may have misunderstood a colonial racial label when he described one Antonio Rodriguez as a "Mexican of Chinese blood" because he was labeled a "chino." According to the preeminent scholar of race in colonial New Spain, Magnus Mörner, "chino" was actually a designation for a dark-skinned mestizo of black and Indian heritage.

Within one hundred years, however, many Chinese had immigrated to Mexico and settled all over the country, especially along the northern border with the United States, an area vibrant with economic development around U.S. investment in mines and railroads. Because of Chinese exclusion from the United States beginning in l882, Chinese laborers and merchants went to Mexico instead, congregating along the border, where their compatriots had already established businesses in California, Arizona, and Texas, just on the other side of the international line. Historians locate the first appearance of Asian Latinas and Latinos in this long and wide border region because the Chinese from Mexico routinely crossed the border to work and to do business with both Chinese and American merchants in the United States. Because Chinese were forbidden to enter the United States, Chinese in Mexico took out Mexican citizenship papers and crossed the border as Mexicans, with surprising facility in many instances. These Chinese often had families in the Imperial Valley of California and in towns throughout Arizona, such as Nogales, Tucson, and Phoenix. During the mining boom, some Chinese in Arizona moved to Mexico to capitalize on available opportunities; there they established families with Mexican-born wives, both Chinese and Mexican, later moving the families back to Arizona. Along the Texas-Mexico border in cities such as El Paso, Chinese merchants operated on both sides of the border; some eventually formed families with Mexican wives in Mexico, then moved the family back to the United States. In 1932, the prosperous Chinese community of Sonora was actually expelled from Mexico, their businesses and properties confiscated and Mexicanized. Many were deported back to China, but others managed to reestablish themselves in the United States.

These are the stories represented by Marian Lim (quoted above), born in Guaymas, Sonora, and brought back to Nogales as a child with her parents and siblings. She spoke Spanish, grew up along the border, and always considered herself culturally Mexican, although she felt the sting of being taunted by Mexican children as being different. From the beginning, these early Asian Latinas and Latinos were binational, bicultural border crossers with transnational families, businesses, and social relationships; in this regard, they were no different from Mexicans and other immigrant groups who lived in the same multiracial, multicultural, and politically contested space. But more than Mexicans and Mexican Americans, they occupied a deeper layer of in-between space that tended to marginalize them and often rendered them invisible.

Forced Removal and Displacement

Other case studies in the history of Asian Latinas and Latinos can be described as "accidents of history"; they are poignant stories of forced removal and displacement. Two episodes stand out. In 1917, when President Woodrow Wilson sent General John Pershing into Chihuahua, Mexico, to hunt down the popular revolutionary leader Pancho Villa, he enlisted some five hundred Chinese men in Mexico to provide food and services for his 6,000-strong army. When he retreated one year later—sans Villa—he petitioned the U.S. government to allow these Chinese men to enter the United States with his army, knowing they would suffer retribution if they stayed. Most of these Chinese were sent to Fort Sam Houston in San Antonio, where they quadrupled the small Chinese community already established there. In 1921, the U.S. Congress granted the right of residency to the 365 remaining Chinese, and today their descendants are still known around San Antonio.

The most egregious act of history that contributed to the formation of the Asian Latina and Latino population in the United States began with the internment of 2,118 Japanese Latin Americans during World War II. Rounded up by the U.S. military from twelve different countries in Central and South America, with the vast majority (84 percent) from Peru, they were interned in Texas and New Mexico in two camps maintained just for them by the U.S. Immigration and Naturalization Services. In 1946, rubbing salt on an open wound, the U.S. government accused them of being "illegal aliens." Almost all returned to Japan because countries like Peru refused to take most of them back. Three hundred and sixty-four of the internees remained in the United States and built new lives in the face of enormous challenges and hardships. Seiichi Higashide, cited above, was one of them. His children are Americanized, but like others of their generation, they fought for their parents to be included in the redress movement, which would win them an apology from the U.S. government for wrongful imprisonment and a token $10,000 to compensate for their pain and suffering. It is interesting to note that the Japanese Peruvian parents, while unable to maintain the Spanish language in the family, nevertheless gave all their children Spanish names: Elsa, Carlos, and Irma (born in Peru) and Arturo and Marta (born in the U.S. camps).

Interesting and Unusual Situations

Perhaps the most intriguing and certainly least-known of the Asian Latina and Latino mestizos in the United States are the Punjabi Mexicans, also known at one time as Hindu Mexicans. Their place in history is temporally and spatially restricted to the first half of the twentieth century, along the cotton belt of the United States–Mexico border, from Texas to the southern part of the Imperial Valley of California. Between 1899 and 1914, 6,800 Punjabi men—Hindus, Muslims, and especially Sikhs, noted for wearing their uncut hair in an elaborate turban—arrived to work the land. They were immediately racially marked and had difficulty accumulating enough savings to finance their families' emigration from India. They soon began to form families with women newly arrived from Mexico, brothers and good friends often marrying Mexican sisters. Most of their offspring bore names reflecting their dual heritage (the ubiquitous "Singh" that all Sikh men use combined with Spanish first names); Isabel Singh García, cited above, has a typical Punjabi Mexican name. Raised mainly by their Mexican mothers and their families, they were for the most part Catholic and Spanish speaking but proud to claim their East Indian heritage. However, given their small numbers and their estrangement from the East Indian communities that formed after their Punjabi fathers' generation, they have not invented a Punjabi Mexican tradition that can be passed on.

Mexican Filipino Rudy Guevarra has named his own mestizo identity "Mexipina" or "Mexipino." Having Spanish surnames and brown complexions has complicated the identity issue for Mexipinas and Mexipinos, for usually they are perceived as Chicana and Chicano or Latina and Latino. Unlike the Punjabis who preceded them, the Filipina and Filipino community in California today is largely made up of women. Hence Filipina and Filipino Americans and mixed-race Filipinas and Filipinos have strong cultural traditions that compete for attention and space with the equally assertive Chicana and Chicano identity in the Mexipina and Mexpino imagination and subjectivity. "As a rule," Guevarra notes, "we all grew up in both cultures, knowing that we were Mexican and Filipino, Chicano and Pinoy." (This second pair of terms signifies the more political identity adopted by young Mexican Americans and Filipina and Filipino Americans in their respective civil rights struggles.) In practice, some feel they have "the best of both worlds" while others struggle with an "ambiguous identity." Yet, like few others in American society, they can enjoy or deploy the option of "multiple passing," being also perceived as Middle Easterners (Persian, Greeks) and Polynesians.

Immigration in the Late Twentieth Century

The majority of Asian Latinas and Latinos are recent immigrants from Latin America and the Caribbean. The voices of Fabiana Chiu-Rinaldi (Peruvian Chinese), Lamgen Antonio Léon (Dominican Chinese), Frances Bu (Cuban Chinese), and Cristina Hwang (Brazilian Chinese) represent these new voices; they are also the most self-consciously Asian Latina and Latino. As Fabiana Chiu-Rinaldi notes, "Asian Latinos represent a unique link between two of the largest immigrant groups in the United States"—Asian and Latin American.

Among these immigrants, the largest group is the Cuban Chinese, who have introduced a new experience and a new term into the U.S. multicultural lexicon, the *restaurantes chino-cubanos*. When a large wave of Chinese Cubans joined other Cubans in fleeing Cuba for the United States after Fidel Castro took power in 1959 and nationalized their small businesses, many reestablished small restaurants in Miami, New York, and New Jersey, and, more recently, in Los Angeles, catering to a largely Cuban clientele. Few Chinese other than those from Cuba patronize these restaurants because they serve mainly Cuban food made in the Chinese way, or Chinese food inflected with Cuban flavors adapted to the Cuban palate. Other Americans, however, especially sophisticated New York City and Los Angeles connoisseurs, have long gravitated to the Chinese Cuban restaurants. Mike Yip, owner of La Caridad in New York City, had to expand his restaurant to accommodate the large crowds. Yip was born in Cuba of Chinese parents; he is fluent in Spanish, Cantonese, and English, "sometimes cramming all three languages into one short sentence." Yip also notes wistfully, however, that few in his generation of Cuban Americans want to continue the restaurants that their exiled parents started.

For Cuban Americans such as the celebrated writer Cristina García, whose novel *Monkey Hunting* describes the Chinese immigrant experience from their arrival as coolies in the mid-nineteenth century through several generations to the early part of the twenty-first century, these Chinese Cuban cultural relics help maintain Cuban American culture in the United States. For the Chinese Cuban Americans themselves, such as Iris and Mike Louk of Miami, who at the beginning of the twenty-first century owned and operated a restaurant with their grown children Sandra and Wayne, this was one way to maintain their unique identity as Cuban Americans of Chinese descent. As American-born Sandra described it, she was born in an environment that was *"chinocubano y americano."* When it came to her identity, *"Nunca me he podido sentir parte de un grupo, ni con los chinos, ni con los americanos, ni con los cubanos. Pero me identifico más con los cubanoamericanos, aunque ellos me ven como chinacubana."* ("I have never been able to feel part of a group, not with the Chinese, nor with the Americans, nor with the Cubans. But I identify most with the Cuban Americans, although they see me as a Chinese Cuban.") (Villaverde). With these poignant words, Sandra has captured all the possibilities and all the challenges of being Asian Latina or Latino.

Assessment

The Asian Latina or Latino is an old phenomenon historically speaking but an emerging new identity that is still in the process of formation, fueled in large part by new immigrants of the post–civil rights era, in which Americans of all races and heritages jostle to claim their space on the crowded multicultural stage. In finding their voices to celebrate cultural traditions and protest against discrimination and injustices, they may yet build a self-conscious community of Asian Latinas and Latinos that does not currently exist (except in small pockets in places like Flushing, Queens, New York City). On the other hand, Asian Latinas and Latinos may continue to form and re-form, dissolve, and regroup, as they have done over the course of the histories of the Americas. As with every other identity and community, it is a process of invention and imagination, based on cold, hard reality and lived experiences.

See also **Chicanos and Chicanas; Cuban Americans; García, Cristina; Immigration; Mestizaje;** *and* **Mexican-Origin People in the United States.**

BIBLIOGRAPHY

"Census 2000 and Asian and Pacific Islander American Basic Facts." Leadership Institute for Asian Pacifics, January 2002.

Chiu-Rinaldi, Fabiana. "China Latina." In *Re/Collecting Early Asian America: Essays in Cultural History*, edited by Josephine Lee, Imogene L. Lim, and Yuko Matsukawa. Philadelphia: Temple University Press, 2002.

Delgado, Grace Peña. "At Exclusion's Southern Gate: Changing Categories of Race and Class among Chinese *Fronterizos*, 1882–1904." In *Continental Crossroads: Remapping U.S.–Mexican Borderlands History*, edited by Samuel L. Truett and Elliott Young. Durham, N.C.: Duke University Press, 2004.

Dubs, H. H. "The Chinese in Mexico City in 1635." *Far Eastern Quarterly* 1 (1942): 387–389.

Farrar, Nancy. "The Chinese in El Paso." *Southwestern Studies* Monograph no. 33 (1972): 13–14.

Fong, Lawrence Michael. "Sojourners and Settlers: The Chinese Experience in Arizona." *Journal of Arizona History*, 21 (Autumn 1980): 1–30.

García, Cristina. *Monkey Hunting*. New York: Knopf, 2003.

Gardiner, C. Howard. *Pawns in a Triangle of Hate: The Peruvian Japanese and the United States*. Seattle: University of Washington Press, 1981.

Gaskins, Pearl Fuyo. *What Are You? Voices of Mixed-Race Young People*. New York: Henry Holt, 1999.

Guevarra, Rudy P., Jr. "Burritos and Bagoong: Mexipinos and Multiethnic Identity in San Diego, California." In *Crossing Lines: Race and Mixed Race across the Geohistorical Divide*, edited by Marc Coronado, Rudy P. Guevarra, Jr. Jeffrey Moniz, and Laura Furlan Szanto. Santa Barbara: University of California Multiethnic Student Outreach, 2003.

Guevarra, Rudy P., Jr. Excerpted from "Clueless." In *Crossing Lines: Race and Mixed Race Across the Geohistorical Divide*, edited by Marc Coronado, Rudy P. Guevarra, Jr., Jeffrey Moniz, and Laura Furlan Szanto. Santa Barbara: University of California Multiethnic Student Outreach, 2003.

Higashide, Seiichi. *Adios to Tears: The Memoirs of a Japanese-Peruvian Internee in U.S. Concentration Camps*. Honolulu: E & E Kudo, 1993.

Hu-DeHart, Evelyn. "Huagong and Huashang: The Chinese as Laborers and Merchants in Latin America and the Caribbean." *Amerasia Journal* 28, no. 2 (2002): 64–90.

Hu-DeHart, Evelyn. "Immigrants to a Developing Society: The Chinese in Northern Mexico, 1875–1932." *Journal of Arizona History* 21 (Autumn 1980): 275–312.

Lee, Cynthia Ai-fen. "Our Histories in Conversation." In *Tomie Arai: Double Happiness* (exhibit catalogue with essays and photos). New York: Bronx Museum of the Arts, 1998.

Lee, Erika. "Enforcing the Borders: Chinese Exclusion along the U.S. Borders with Canada and Mexico, 1882–1924." *Journal of American History* 89, no. 1 (June 2002): 54–86.

Leonard, Karen Isaksen. *Making Ethnic Choices. California's Punjabi Mexican Americans*. Philadelphia: Temple University Press, 1992.

Lii, Jane. "Neighborhood Report: Upper West Side; Olé Fat Chou! A Restaurant Returns." *New York Times* (Sunday), February 16, 1997, section 13, page 8.

Menchaca, Martha. *Recovering History, Constructing Race: The Indian, Black, and White Roots of Mexican Americans*. Austin: University of Texas Press, 2001.

Mörner, Magnus. *Race Mixture in the History of Latin America*. Boston: Little, Brown, 1967. According to Mörner, a "mulatto and Indian woman begets chino," p. 59.

"The Nature of Inheritance: A Conversation with Cristina García." *Atlantic Unbound*, April 22, 2003. www.theatlantic.com

Rhoads, Edward J. M. "The Chinese in Texas." *Southwestern Historical Quarterly* 81 no. 1 (July 1977): 1–36.

Rodriguez, Alicia. Email to Evelyn Hu-Dehart. February 11, 2003.

Root, Maria P. P., ed. *The Multiracial Experience: Racial Borders as the New Frontier*. Thousand Oaks, Calif.: Sage, 1996.

Root, Maria P. P., ed. *Racially Mixed People in America*. Newbury Park, Calif.: Sage, 1992.

Steiner, Stan. *Fusang: The Chinese Who Built America*. New York: Harper & Row, 1979.

Villaverde, Minuca. "Feliz Año del Jabalí." *El Nuevo Heraldo*, January 29, 1995, 1E and 5E.

EVELYN HU-DEHART

ASPIRA. ASPIRA, the organization considered by its founder, Antonia Pantoja, to be "the most important work of my life" (*Memoir of a Visionary*, p. 93), was established in New York City in 1961 to help in the education and leadership development of Puerto Rican and other Latino and Latina youth. The name "ASPIRA" derives from the Spanish verb *aspirar*, "to aspire." Thus the members of the club are called "Aspirantes."

A group of Puerto Rican New Yorkers led by Pantoja received the funding that served as the cornerstone for the creation of ASPIRA. In 1961 Latinas and Latinos in New York suffered from very high school–dropout rates, high unemployment, and terrible living conditions in the slums of the city. The school system seemed indifferent to the concerns of Latino parents and students, and there were very few leaders willing to advocate for this community. There was an urgency in the community to "design ways to attack the root causes" of these problems and to "begin to develop in the community other people who could join the battle at different points in the problem" (Pantoja, p. 98). This small group of concerned Puerto Rican educators and professionals decided to address the dismal state of education for this community: two out of three Puerto Rican eighth graders were three years behind in reading; in 1963, 331 Puerto Rican students—out of 179,000—received their high school diplomas, and only 28 went on to higher education studies. The urgency of the situation mandated the creation

ASPIRA MEMBERS. (Courtesy of ASPIRA)

of an organization to work with youth, the success of which would, in a very short time, have a major impact upon thousands of Puerto Rican and other Latino students.

Since its founding, ASPIRA has grown from a community-based New York City agency to a national organization with its headquarters, the ASPIRA Association, in Washington, D.C., and associate affiliate offices in Connecticut, Florida, Illinois, New Jersey, New York, Pennsylvania, and Puerto Rico.

ASPIRA emerged from months of brainstorming discussions among New York leaders of the Puerto Rican Forum, an organization whose purpose was to launch other community agencies. With the financial backing of major foundations, ASPIRA opened its first facility in the City of New York. With Pantoja as its first executive director, ASPIRA established objectives designed to help empower, educate, and develop future leaders in the Puerto Rican community.

The organization planned to set up a series of ASPIRA clubs in schools to help students stay in high school and pursue higher educational opportunities and eventually to contribute to solving the problems of the community in New York. Part of the youth training included the study of Puerto Rican history and immigration. Schools and other community groups were encouraged to establish ASPIRA clubs.

In her autobiography, *Memoir of a Visionary*, Pantoja explains why launching ASPIRA was significant to her dream of lifting the Puerto Rican community from poverty. She reported that between the years 1963 and 1999, close to thirty-six thousand young Puerto Rican and Latino and Latina youths participated in ASPIRA clubs. A fundamental principle of these clubs is the belief that people grow and develop their skills best in their own communities. Another principle that guided Pantoja's vision for ASPIRA is the idea that "leadership emerges in a continuum" (p. 106) in the contact and nurturing offered through mentoring by leaders of one's own culture. She also aimed to establish an institution where, through high expectations, youths could be educated to develop their full potential. She served as executive director until 1966.

ASPIRA's mission included three major objectives. The first was to organize and develop in youth in the Puerto Rican community leadership and problem-solving skills that would help them begin to identify and solve the problems of the community. The second goal was to engage the youth in the study of the history and culture of Puerto Rico as well as the history of immigration in order to help them develop a commitment to and positive identification with the community that would result in advocacy and activism. Lastly, high school retention and graduation and higher education were the most important goals. Tied to this goal was the expectation that the youths would use the knowledge and skills acquired to work as leaders in the Puerto Rican community.

There were some roadblocks to the development of the ASPIRA clubs in the public school system. In her autobiography, Pantoja describes receiving hate mail and threats of violence opposing ASPIRA. Some protested under the guise that ASPIRA was segregating Puerto Rican youth, and others were angered by yet another agency that was tapping and diminishing the low level of existing funding for minority groups. However, it was the school system that proved the most difficult. The New York City Board of Education was opposed to the establishment of ASPIRA Leadership Development Clubs because the counselors were not formally licensed. At best the board allowed the organization of ASPIRA clubs only if a teacher were present at all times. Ultimately ASPIRA prevailed when it demonstrated that teachers attended the meetings during nonschool hours and were not compensated by the board for their time.

The clubs were successful in the number of members they recruited around the city and in the programs they developed, which included summer leadership study programs in Puerto Rico, annual conferences, the Areyto Leadership Initiation Ceremony, the annual graduation dance, and annual college and university fairs. The ASPIRA clubs also provided college and career counseling and financial aid and scholarship information. Remarkably, the ASPIRA programs were developed and organized by the youth members themselves.

ASPIRA was dedicated to the advancement of Puerto Rican youth through education. As a presence in the school system, ASPIRA witnessed and documented the underachievement of Puerto Rican and Latino and Latina children. In addition, ASPIRA was represented on many committees and task forces that addressed issues affecting this community. By the 1970s, based on ASPIRA's experiences and collected data, it was evident that substantive change was needed in the New York City educational system's approach to Spanish-speaking children. Bilingual education, although recognized as a valid approach, was used in teaching only a small number of children. The drop-out rate of Latino and Latina students was extremely high, and there was no indication that the board of education was willing to address the problem. The leadership of ASPIRA made the decision to seek remedy through the courts, and on September 20, 1972, it filed suit against the Board of Education of the City of New York. Three years later a landmark agreement resulting from the suit, the ASPIRA Consent Decree, was signed by both parties and approved by the court. It provided mandatory bilingual instruction for limited-English-ability students.

In the early twenty-first century ASPIRA runs its programs nationally, with offices in six states and Puerto Rico. It has grown from an initial staff of seven to over one hundred serving over twenty-five thousand youths and their families yearly. It is believed that since its founding, ASPIRA has provided over a quarter of a million Puerto Rican and Latino and Latina youths with the support needed for them to stay in school. Over the years the organization has formalized the involvement of the students' families through the Parents for Education Excellence (APEX) and the Teachers, Organizations, and Parents for Students (TOPS) programs. Both bring together teachers, parents, and members of the business community to support and promote academic achievement. ASPIRA's Public Policy Leadership Program offers students internships through which they experience policy making and implementation. ASPIRA's National Health Careers Program provides experiences and academic support to high school students interested in this field. Similarly the ASPIRA Math and Science Academy and its Web page CASA MAS (Community Allies for Smart Access to Math and Science) provide high school students and their families with a range of resources for improving their math and science skills. Through the Youth Ventures and Entrepreneurship Program, ASPIRA hopes to prepare young people for business ownership and careers in financial institutions, industries, and service businesses. In 1985 the ASPIRA Institute for Policy Research was created to address the needs of the Latino and Latina community through research and advocacy activities nationwide. Their data indicate that 98 percent of Aspirantes stay in school, and close to 90 percent of those go on to institutions of higher education.

After almost four decades of existence, through its national network and thousands of Aspirantes alumni, ASPIRA enjoys great visibility and respect throughout the country. In the early twenty-first century ASPIRA no longer limits itself to serving the Latino and Latina community. Nationally the organization serves over twenty-five thousand students in over four hundred schools. Numerous former Aspirantes who graduated and attended universities have become well-known figures, including Fernando Ferrer, the former Bronx borough president and former New York City candidate for mayor; Aida Alvarez, former television news anchor and director of the Small Business Administration during the presidency of Bill Clinton; Nelson Díaz, the first Latino judge in Pennsylvania; and Jimmy Smits, the actor.

See also ASPIRA Consent Decree; Bilingual Education; Education; New York; Pantoja, Antonia; *and* Puerto Ricans.

BIBLIOGRAPHY

Aspira.org: An Investment in Latino Youth Web site. www.aspira.org

Gonzalez, Juan. "Puerto Ricans Mourn an Inspiration." *New York Daily News*, May 30, 2002: p 40.

Pantoja, Antonia. *Memoir of a Visionary: Antonia Pantoja*. Houston, Tex.: Arte Público Press, 2002.

Santiago, Isaura. *ASPIRA v. Board of Education of the City of New York: A History*. New York: Aspira of New York, 1977.

GAIL A. CUETO

ASPIRA CONSENT DECREE.

In the 1970s, with bilingual education classes reaching only a small number of the large Puerto Rican school population in New York City, parents and citizens represented by the nonprofit organization ASPIRA were concerned that these children were not being provided the opportunity to participate meaningfully in the learning process. Particularly poignant was the fact that New York City boasted the largest school system in the country. The lawsuit *ASPIRA of New York, Inc. v. Board of Education of the City of New York* was filed on September 20, 1972.

Three years later the landmark agreement ASPIRA Consent Decree was approved by the court and signed by the parties. The result of this suit, which is still in effect in the early twenty-first century, mandates transitional bilingual education programs for students with limited English proficiency in the New York City public school system.

Founded in 1961 by Antonia Pantoja and other New York City educators and community leaders, ASPIRA, among other objectives, aimed to improve the quality of education for Latino and Latina and Puerto Rican students. In trying to make the educational system more responsive to its students, ASPIRA engaged in numerous research surveys that indicated Hispanic children were languishing in schools that did not accommodate their home language. The data submitted by ASPIRA indicated that, in addition to high drop-out rates, the Puerto Rican community had the highest rates of unemployment in New York City, the poorest housing and medical care, and the lowest wages. These terrible conditions, ASPIRA stated, were directly related to the city school system's failure to provide equal educational opportunity. The organization produced research evidence documenting both the ineffectiveness of monolingual education in New York City schools and the connection between inadequate quality of education and poor socioeconomic conditions.

In the meetings that preceded the filing of the case, Pantoja suggested involving the judicial system. She saw the possibilities for this case in light of recent federal legislation, the Civil Rights Act of 1964 and the Bilingual Education Act of 1968, as well as civil rights litigation from the 1950s and 1960s that set precedents for this case. Professional and community organizations, including the Puerto Rican Educators Association, the Puerto Rican Educators Task Force, educators from New York City Community School District No. 1, and the American Jewish Committee, were also involved in the case.

ASPIRA began its research and preparation for the suit in 1971 by soliciting legal assistance from the Community Agency for Legal Services (CALS), which served until 1972. Then the newly established Puerto Rican Legal Defense and Education Fund (PRLDEF), under the leadership of its first executive director, the attorney César Perales, took over the case and filed its first suit, *ASPIRA v. Board of Education*, on behalf of fifteen schoolchildren and their parents. The original suit was broadened to become a class action suit and included ASPIRA of New York and ASPIRA of America. The case now incorporated over 170,000 Spanish-speaking public school children who had limited proficiency in English and were not receiving any educational services that took into consideration their linguistic needs. A second class of twelve thousand other primarily Spanish-speaking public school students was also included. These twelve thousand children were given some educational services in their native language, but those services were deemed by the plaintiffs to be inadequate and were also included.

The ASPIRA case requested that the Board of Education of the City of New York be required to provide "bilingual education services and courses of study which take into account the linguistic needs and cultural differences of the plaintiffs and assure . . . an equal education opportunity" (Santiago 1977, p. 55). The plan also asked for special programs to compensate for defendants' past failures and called for the establishment of adequate evaluation and classification of the students' language ability and achievement.

In January 1974 a unanimous U.S. Supreme Court mandated in *Lau v. Nochols* that the San Francisco Board of Education had to rectify educational inequity by addressing the language needs of students who could not communicate with their teachers, such as the eighteen hundred Chinese children in San Francisco's public schools who brought the case. The Supreme Court ruled that an identical education was not the same as equal education under the 1964 Civil Rights Act, and that to be denied access to an equal education was a civil rights violation.

As a result of the *Lau* decision, the attorneys for ASPIRA, Herbert Teitelbaum and Richard Hiller, petitioned the court for a summary judgment that would apply the legal precedent established in the *Lau* decision to the ASPIRA case. The New York City Board of Education was opposed, but in April 1974 Judge Frankel ordered both parties to develop, by the following month, an adequate bilingual education plan for the students. During June and July both parties met and reviewed the submitted documents, and they presented their plan to the judge, who then approved the issuance of a court-ordered consent decree.

This agreement included a number of provisions. The first directed the New York City Board of Education to implement bilingual programs in the schools for children in grades one through twelve. Second, it mandated that the board develop a classification system that would identify, on the basis of his or her language ability, an individual child's eligibility for the program. The basic elements the bilingual program would provide were clearly delineated, and a number of schools, identified as pilot schools, would serve as models for the bilingual education program and for the training of personnel. The teachers implementing the program were required to be professionally trained and fluent in both Spanish and English. All of these conditions were required to be in place by September 1974. This agreement established the order that survives in the early twenty-first century and mandates quality bilingual education services for limited-English students in New York City's public schools.

Two major studies analyzing the implementation of the decree have been published. In 1979 Lois Steinberg reported that although the consent decree created jobs for Latinos and Latinas in the school system, it weakened the Latino and Latina community's control over policy implementation because the courts had turned over this responsibility to board of education administrators, the very people who had fought against the issue. Inasmuch as the courts were limited in their ability to monitor the implementation of the bilingual programs, it was difficult for the community to enforce compliance. Steinberg also concluded that the lack of political representation and power in proportion to the size of its population restricted the Latino and Latina community's ability to promote its educational interests through the school system.

Ten years after the decree, in an overview of its implementation, a report authored by Isaura Santiago Santiago found that the board of education had been unsuccessful in providing bilingual education to the majority of eligible students and had also failed in monitoring and evaluating the educational outcomes of the program. She conceded that access to a quality education provided gains for Latino and Latina children, but that changes in the educational system came as a result of continued legal pressure by ASPIRA of New York and the Puerto Rican Legal Defense and Education Fund.

In 2001 the board of education, under the leadership of then-mayor Rudolph Giuliani, pushed for the dismantling of bilingual education programs. Even though some major revisions were made to the program, the effort to permanently abolish the program failed because of the legal standing of the 1974 ASPIRA Consent Decree.

See also **ASPIRA; Bilingual Education; Bilingual Education Act; Civil Rights Act (1964); New York; Pantoja, Antonia;** *and* **Puerto Rican Legal Defense and Education Fund.**

BIBLIOGRAPHY

Aspira of New York, Incorporated v. Board of Education of the City of New York, et al. 72 Civ. 4002 S.D.N.Y. (MEF) Consent Decree, August 29, 1974. (a).

Gonzalez, Juan. "Face Facts on Bilingual Education." *New York Daily News*, October 31, 2000, p. 28.

Gonzalez, Juan. "Language Lesson in '70s Ruling." *New York Daily News*, October 24, 2000, p. 35.

Holloway, Lynette. "Board of Education Votes, 7–0, to Revamp Bilingual Programs." *New York Times*, February 28, 2001, p. A1.

Steinberg, Lois. "Can Federal Laws Protect the Educational Interests of Language Minorities? Implementation of the Bilingual Act and the ASPIRA Consent Decree in New York City." Paper presented at the American Educational Research Association Meeting, San Francisco, California, April 8–12, 1979.

Santiago, Isaura. ASPIRA v. Board of Education of the City of New York: *A History*. New York: ASPIRA of New York, 1977.

Santiago, Isaura. "*ASPIRA v. Board of Education* Revisited." *American Journal of Education* 95 (November 1986): 149–199.

GAIL CUETO

ASSIMILATION AND ACCULTURATION. In the United States at the beginning of the twentieth century, the study of immigrants was closely wedded with the beginnings of social science. Immigrants and their plight were the focus of vivid studies from the early days of the Chicago school, whose work on immigration, racial and ethnic studies, and urban studies laid the very foundations of American sociology. Despite varying emphases, they shared the expectation that the outcome to the process of integrating those who arrived at its shores would be a process of assimilation. Yet from the outset there was an ambiguity in the idea that Robert E. Park underscored in *Race and Culture* (1913). That ambiguity remained until Milton Gordon distinguished between types of assimilation: cultural versus structural. But the fundamental characteristic of assimilation theory was already evident. Assimilation was expected to be a one-way process that would also be natural and evolutionary, a process that as time passed would yield an inevitable outcome.

Assimilation Theory

As Gordon defined it, cultural assimilation entailed a process of acculturation on the part of the immigrants, of becoming "like" in cultural patterns, such as language, behavior, customs, dress, beliefs, and values. Structural assimilation resulted only when the immigrants had been "taken up and incorporated" and entailed the full integration of the immigrants and their descendants into the major institutions of the society (educational, occupational, political) and into the social cliques, clubs, and institutions of the core society that lead to intimate primary relationships, including intermarriage. This distinction aimed to provide a more exact conceptual tool to gauge the reality of the assimilation of immigrants and racial minorities in the United States.

The Chicago school in the early part of the century also emphasized the "natural history" of ethnic relations, as best expressed in Park's race relations cycle. Park evolved his theory of the race relations cycle as stages of interaction through which immigrant or racial groups progressed irreversibly: contact, competition, and accommodation, culminating in eventual assimilation. Because at the root of his thinking was the ecological emphasis on race relations as spatial relations that defined the Chicago school of urban sociology, Park expected that the notion of assimilation and the stages of the race relations cycle could be extended to immigrants and racial minorities alike. From his point of view, both European immigrants and American blacks came from rural, peasant backgrounds and, upon migration to the urban ghetto, confronted a similar clash of cultures. Thus, immigration and race and ethnic relations could both be viewed within the same frame of reference.

This perspective was clearly apparent in another of the classics of the Chicago school, William I. Thomas and Florian Znaniecki's *The Polish Peasant in Europe and America* (1927). Drawing from the work of Thomas, Park also was responsible for disseminating the theory of the "marginal man." In "Human Migration and the Marginal Man," (1928), Park stressed that marginal human beings—those who, as a result of migration, ended up by living simultaneously in two separate worlds—were not only marginal, never fully belonging to the one or the other, but also enormously creative and intelligent, as experiencing more than one social world had sharpened their vision and sensibilities. Again Park extended the concept of the marginal man from its origins in the notion of the human being caught between two cultures—the immigrant, the mixed-blood person (Eurasians, mestizos, mulattoes), the outcast and stranger (the Jew)—to encompass the experience of American blacks, who shared the same national culture but lived at the margins of society in social, rather than cultural or ethnic, marginality. Thus, it was left to E. Franklin Frazier, student of the Chicago school and black sociologist, to demarcate the difference between race relations and ethnic relations. He underscored that American blacks had experienced successive forms of economic subordination (slavery, the plantation society, "Jim Crow") with the outcome of extensive cultural assimilation and, rather than final structural assimilation, complete social and institutional segregation. Sociologists in the early part of the twentieth century were concerned with what the experience of immigration had done to the immigrants' lives and with the outcomes to the process of integrating those who arrived at the country's shores, outcomes that were usually conceptualized as acculturation and assimilation—becoming like the dominant population, which at the beginning of the century clearly meant conformity to Anglo-Saxon ways.

Research on immigrants and the eventual outcomes of the processes of immigration therefore was at the very foundations of American sociology. But that emphasis began to wane until, in the 1960s, it all but disappeared. Several different trends promoted its disappearance. First, the Immigration and Nationality Act of 1924 cut the massive waves of European immigration to the United States. Second, under the pressures of Anglo conformity, the children of those European immigrants went on to assimilate in American society at a time when the price of success was often one's ethnicity and identity. And third, as Alejandro Portes stressed in "Immigrant Aspirations" (1978), the research focus on immigrants and immigration was also lost as a result of the arrival of the racial demands and militancy of the civil rights movement so that the analytical focus shifted to that of racial and ethnic relations. And in the process what is really distinctive about immigrants was lost. What is distinctive about immigrants? At the micro level, they have experienced another whole life in another country and culture, which they bring with them and which decisively continues to influence them; and, at the macro level, that the state in two societies permits the immigrants to exit and enter. As gatekeeper, the state regulates and directs migration through a body of law.

From the theoretical vantage point, immigrants are also distinct in that they bring with them a whole host of social resources (their social classes, educations, occupations, cultures, and values) from other societies, and their outcomes in American society, their assimilation and acculturation, will be partly a function of those initial resources, partly a function of the nature of their migration (whether they are political or economic immigrants, victims of genocide, settlers, or sojourners), and partly a function of the social context that greeted them, of the amount of opportunity available to them in their new society (in the particular cities and industries where they become concentrated, and in the nature of the discrimination or exclusion they afterward face).

Indeed, the major questions in immigration research can be summarized briefly as follows: What led people to make the decision to move—what "push" and "pull" factors impelled them to displace and uproot themselves? What is the nature of the crossing—not only literally but also, more abstractly, the policies of two governments that can, in societies that have developed long histories of emigration and immigration, result in their developing systems of economic and political migration? And what can they attain afterward? A recurrent question in studies of immigration is: How does one best describe that process—as assimilation and acculturation, adaptation, integration, incorporation, or transnationalism and diasporic citizenship?

In the United States, the most commonplace statement is also the truest. With the exception of the Native American, everyone else is an immigrant to American soil. American history can be broadly understood as consisting of four major waves of migration. The first wave consisted of northwest Europeans who immigrated up to the mid-nineteenth century; the second consisted of southern and eastern Europeans at the end of the nineteenth century and the beginning of the twentieth; the third can be said to be the movement from the South to the North of black Americans, Mexicans, and Puerto Ricans precipitated by two world wars; and the fourth wave from 1965 into the early twenty-first century consists of immigrants mostly from Latin America and Asia. Not only has each of the major waves been characterized by a different racial or ethnic composition, but also over the course of this time span profound changes were taking place in the very nature of American society. The immigrants of the first wave came to an essentially colonial, agrarian society; the immigrants of the second and third waves arrived to an urban society where they provided the cheap labor essential to the process of industrialization and expansion in the United States; and the immigrants of the fourth wave are arriving into an increasingly postindustrial service-oriented society embedded in a new era of globalization.

Internal Colonialism and Incorporation

In sociology, the major challenge to assimilation theory came from the proponents of the internal colonialism model, the theoretical effort to delineate in what ways the experiences of the racial minorities (blacks, Puerto Ricans, Mexicans, Native Americans—some of its oldest immigrants and most indigenous native sons and daughters) differed significantly from the experiences and eventual assimilation of the white European immigrants at the beginning of the century. The internal colonialism model underscored that the experience of these groups was different in that they had suffered a process of internal colonization due to their place and role in the system of production, the place and role they came to occupy because of their color, their race. An important corrective to the assimilation model, the internal colonialism model suffered from stretching the colonial analogy overly far, not recognizing the essential differences between the domestic situation of race relations in the United States and what happened in Africa and Asia. Thereafter several theorists (among them, Joe R. Feagin, Portes, and Silvia Pedraza-Bailey) sought to transcend the shortcomings of both the assimilation and internal colonialism models by focusing on the varying ways different ethnic groups were incorporated, became a part of the society, by paying attention to the initial and continuing placement and access of various groups within the economic, political, and educational institutions of the society. Still, as a central concept that guided research, incorporation, like its predecessors assimilation and acculturation, assumed a one-way process, failing to take into account that immigrants not only become incorporated into a new society, they also transform it. Immigrants did not just become incorporated into American society, they made and remade America and continue to fashion her still.

As a result of the fourth wave of American immigration, sociology refocused research on immigrants as a social category distinct from racial and ethnic minorities and on immigration as an international process that reshuffles persons and cultures across nations, producing a veritable explosion of immigration research. New concepts, such as those of transnationalism and diasporic citizenship, also emerged with which to describe the new realities and to challenge the older notions of assimilation and acculturation.

Transnationalism and Diasporic Citizenship

Transnationalism—the process by which immigrants "forge and sustain multi-stranded social relations that link together their societies of origin and settlement"—is not really new, however (Basch et al., p. 7). As Nancy Foner showed in "What's New about Transnationalism?" (1997), many transnational patterns—keeping communication alive with loved ones back home, sending remittances, supporting particular political causes, return migration—actually have a long history. Nonetheless, at the beginning of the twenty-first century much is distinctive about transnationalism. In the global economy, changes in the technologies of trans-

portation and communication (jet air travel, faxes, cable television, electronic mail, the Internet, videos) have enabled immigrants to maintain more frequent and closer contact with their home countries and to participate both actually and vicariously in the lives they once left behind. Rather than being substantially cut off from the past, twenty-first-century immigrants live—existentially speaking—in both the past and the present at once. A strong emotional thread now ties the two realities as never before. As David Hollinger underscored, the new immigration, like the old, "displays a variety of degrees of engagement with the United States and with prior homelands, and it yields some strong assimilationist impulses along vivid expressions of diasporic consciousness" (Hollinger, p. 153).

However, transnationalism may have consequences for the extent to which immigrants can assimilate—both culturally and structurally—in the United States. For example, participation in transnational practices and the exercise of a diasporic citizenship has consequences for the extent to which immigrants can engage in domestic politics, particularly ethnic politics in American life.

Despite the challenges the concept of assimilation and acculturation received from other concepts, such as internal colonialism, incorporation, transnationalism, and diasporic citizenship, Richard Alba and Victor Nee argued in *Remaking the American Mainstream* (2003) that it is still a necessary concept. In their view assimilation is a grand narrative that served to describe well the experience of the southern and eastern European immigrants as well as the Asian immigrants who arrived at the beginning of the twentieth century and, over the course of several generations, went on to join the mainstream of American life in terms of their levels of educational attainment, patterns of suburbanization, and intermarriage. As Alba and Nee emphasized, the process by which they achieved parity in terms of their life chances was partly historically contingent—dependent on two world wars, the G.I. Bill, and the like. It was also racialized—that is, exclusive to those who had become "white" in the process. Banks, other credit lenders, and real estate developers kept blacks, Mexicans, Puerto Ricans, and Native Americans from joining the mainstream of life in suburbia due to their races. Still, even for those formerly excluded groups there has been progress. Reynolds Farley and Richard Alba, in "The New Second Generation in the U.S.," (2002) examined the patterns of occupational distribution for older immigrants and for the new second generation in the United States in the 1998–2000 period. They showed that even for those groups dominated by low-wage labor immigrants in the first generation (such as Mexicans, Central Americans, and Afro-Caribbeans), there has been considerable improvement in the average occupational position in the second generation, though not to the point of parity with native-born whites, as is the case for Asians and South Americans, immigrants who arrived with high levels of human capital. Hence, it would seem that for all the challenges to the concepts of assimilation and acculturation over time, the concepts are still useful in exactly the way Gordon intended them to be: as a conceptual yardstick with which to measure the extent to which various groups have joined the American mainstream over the course of time.

See also Immigrant Incorporation into U.S. Society; Immigration; *and* Race and Racialization.

BIBLIOGRAPHY

Alba, Richard, and Victor Nee. *Remaking the American Mainstream: Assimilation and Contemporary Immigration.* Cambridge, Mass.: Harvard University Press, 2003.

Barrera, Mario. *Race and Class in the Southwest.* Notre Dame, Ind.: University of Notre Dame Press, 1979.

Basch, Linda, Nina Glick Schiller, and Cristina Szanton Blanc. *Nations Unbound: Transnational Projects, Postcolonial Predicaments, and Deterritorialized Nation States.* Langhorne, Pa.: Gordon and Breach, 1994.

Blauner, Robert. "Internal Colonialism and Ghetto Revolt." *Social Problems* 16 (1969): 393–408.

Burawoy, Michael. "The Functions and Reproduction of Migrant Labor: Comparative Material from Southern Africa and the United States." *American Journal of Sociology* 81 (1976): 1050–1087.

Cowan, Paul. *An Orphan in History: Retrieving a Jewish Legacy.* Garden City, N.Y.: Doubleday, 1982.

Farley, Reynolds, and Richard Alba. "The New Second Generation in the U.S." *International Migration Review* 36 (Fall 2002): 669–701.

Feagin, Joe R. *Racial and Ethnic Relations.* Englewood Cliffs, N.J.: Prentice-Hall, 1978.

Foner, Nancy. "What's New about Transnationalism? New York Immigrants Today and at the Turn of the Century." *Diaspora* 6 (1997): 355–376.

Frazier, E. Franklin. *The Negro in the United States.* New York: Macmillan, 1957.

Frazier, E. Franklin. *Race and Culture Contacts in the Modern World.* New York: Knopf, 1957.

Gordon, Milton M. *Assimilation in American Life.* New York: Oxford University Press, 1964.

Hollinger, David A. *Postethnic America.* New York: BasicBooks, 1995.

Lora, Eduardo Antonio. "Changing Patterns in the Supply of Labor." *Economic and Social Progress in Latin America–2004 Report.* Washington, D.C.: Inter-American Development Bank, 2004.

Lee, Everett S. "A Theory of Migration." *Demography* 3 (1966): 47–57.

Muller, Thomas, and Thomas J. Espenshade. *The Fourth Wave: California's Newest Immigrants.* Washington, D.C.: Urban Institute, 1985.

Park, Robert E. "Human Migration and the Marginal Man." *American Journal of Sociology* 33 (1928): 881–893.

Park, Robert E. *Race and Culture.* Reprint Glencoe, Ill.: Free Press, 1950.

Park, Robert E., and Ernest W. Burgess. *Introduction to the Science of Sociology.* Chicago: University of Chicago Press, 1921.

Pedraza, Silvia, and Rubén G. Rumbaut. *Origins and Destinies: Immigration, Race, and Ethnicity in America.* Belmont, Calif.: Wadsworth Press, 1996.

Pedraza-Bailey, Silvia. *Political and Economic Migrants in America: Cubans and Mexicans.* Austin: University of Texas Press, 1985.

Portes, Alejandro. "Immigrant Aspirations." *Sociology of Education* 51 (1978): 241–260.

Portes, Alejandro. "Modes of Structural Incorporation and Present Theories of Labor Immigration." In *Global Trends in Migration: Theory and Research on International Population Movements*, edited by Mary M. Kritz, Charles B. Keely, and Silvano M. Tomasi, 279–297. New York: Center for Migration Studies, 1981.

Thomas, William I., and Florian Znaniecki. *The Polish Peasant in Europe and America.* 2 vols. New York: Knopf, 1927.

SILVIA PEDRAZA

ASTHMA. Asthma is a serious public health problem in the United States. It is estimated that some 14 million people in the nation have asthma, 11 million people experience an asthma attack each year, and 5,000 people die annually of asthma and related conditions. Asthma takes a significant financial toll on the families of individuals with the disease, the health care system, and society at large. The disease accounts for 1.8 million hospital emergency department visits and 500,000 inpatient hospitalizations each year. Asthma is a leading cause of school absence and hospitalization in children, and a major reason for time lost at work among adults. In 1998, it was estimated that $12.7 billion was spent nationally on the direct and indirect costs of asthma.

Differences among Latino and Latina Groups

There are dramatic differences in asthma prevalence, morbidity, and mortality rates among Latino and Latina ethnic groups living in the United States. Puerto Ricans have the highest prevalence of asthma, the earliest onset of the disease, and the greatest morbidity and mortality rates. In sharp contrast, Mexican Americans have the lowest prevalence, morbidity, and mortality rates. Other Latino and Latina groups such as Cubans and Central and South Americans have asthma rates that fall somewhere between these two groups. The reasons for these differences are unknown.

Low-income inner city blacks and Puerto Ricans in particular suffer from asthma. Black residents in New York's central Harlem area and Puerto Ricans in Chicago's Humboldt Park and West Town communities have some of the highest rates of asthma in the nation. In these communities, one of every four children has asthma.

Asthma is a chronic disease in which the airflow in and out of the lungs is partially blocked by swelling, muscle squeezing, and mucus in the lower airways. The most common symptoms of asthma include shortness of breath, coughing, wheezing, and tightness or discomfort in the chest. People with asthma have "sensitized" airways. Many things can cause or trigger asthma "flares" or "attacks," and such attacks may vary in intensity from mild to severe and life threatening. The etiology of asthma is complex and not well understood, but the occurrence of the disease appears to be related to such factors as genetics, the environment, socioeconomic status, and the lifestyles of individuals and families.

Asthma is known to cluster in families. Genetic factors appear to play an important role in determining individual susceptibility of developing the disease. It has been found, for example, that children whose mothers have asthma are themselves at a higher risk of developing the disease. Researchers in the United States are currently attempting to identify which gene, or combination of genes, is associated with asthma. As of this writing, the disease seems likely to be caused by multiple genes interacting with each other within the body as it develops and also various agents in the environment.

Many agents in the environment are known to trigger asthma. Exposure to allergens such as plant pollens, mold spores, animal dander from cats and dogs, house dust mites, cockroaches, and certain foods and medicines can trigger asthma attacks. The disease can also be triggered or made worse by irritating substances in the air, such as fresh paint, cleaning products, perfumes, workplace chemicals, and air pollution. Other possible triggers include cold air, sudden changes in air temperature, exercise, and infections of the airways, such as a cold or the flu.

Low socioeconomic status is associated with many factors that contribute to the increased prevalence, morbidity, and mortality rates of asthma. Latinos and Latinas with low-paying jobs, for example, frequently live in older substandard housing that may have many allergens such as molds and cockroaches. They live in overcrowded households, which cause a greater likelihood of respiratory infections. Many live in inner city areas near factories and expressways with high concentrations of air pollution. Low-income Latinos and Latinas also frequently work at jobs that do not provide any health insurance coverage, which leads to a lack of access to needed medical care. As a result, they may have poorly controlled asthma, because they do not have a regular source of care. When experiencing asthma problems, many Latinos are forced to use hospital emergency departments. And many hospitals do not have culturally and linguistically appropriate asthma education programs for Latinos.

Lifestyle factors also appear to play a role in the occurrence of asthma. One of the most important lifestyle factors is smoking. Secondhand smoke from cigarettes, cigars, or pipes is a risk factor for developing childhood asthma. It may also trigger asthma attacks and make the disease's symptoms more severe.

Diagnosing the Illness

Physicians diagnose asthma by taking a detailed medical history of the patient, conducting a thorough medical examination, and taking several laboratory tests. Laboratory tests for asthma include skin allergy and lung-function tests. A skin allergy test is used to identify which specific things a person is allergic to. Lung-function tests measure the amount of air going in and out of the lungs, using a device called a spirometer, and how fast a person can breathe air out of the lungs, using a peak flow meter.

With careful management, it is possible for the majority of people to control their asthma. Besides avoiding and reducing exposure to asthma triggers, the disease can be effectively treated with various medicines. Asthma medicines can be taken for long-term control of the disease, and for short-term relief when a person is having an asthma attack. Long-term control medicines are taken every day and include such drugs as inhaled or oral corticosteroids, which prevent and reduce swelling in the airways. Short-term relief medicines, such as inhaled short-acting bronchodilators, are taken when needed to quickly relax and open airways. People with well-controlled asthma have few, if any, symptoms. They can take part in everyday activities, including sports and exercise.

To better understand the underlying causes of asthma and to develop more effective means of preventing and treating it, as well as other acute and chronic diseases among Latinos and Latinas, the nation's health care policies, health delivery system, and medical and public health researchers need to study pertinent Latino and Latina ethnic groups. As their dramatically different asthma rates illustrate, Latinos and Latinas should not be considered to be a single, uniform group. Latinos and Latina ethnic groups greatly differ in terms of their susceptibility to disease, exposure to environmental agents, health beliefs and practices, and health outcomes.

See also **Health; Health, Children's;** *and* **Health Care Access.**

BIBLIOGRAPHY

Berg, Jill, Dennis R. Wahlgren, Richard Hofstetter, et al. "Latino Children with Asthma: Rates and Risks for Medical Care Utilization." *Journal of Asthma* 41, no. 2 (April 2004): 147–157.

Blumenthal, Jacob Bryan, and Malcolm N. Blumenthal. "Genetics of Asthma." *Medical Clinics of North America* 86, no. 5 (September 2002): 937–950.

Burchard, Esteban Gonzalez, Pedro C. Avila, Sylvette Nazario, et al. "Lower Bronchodilator Responsiveness in Puerto Rican than in Mexican Subjects with Asthma." *American Journal of Respiratory and Critical Care Medicine* 169, no. 3 (February 2004): 386–392.

Carter-Pokras, Olivia Denise, and Peter Joseph Gergen. "Reported Asthma among Puerto Rican, Mexican-American, and Cuban Children, 1982 through 1984." *American Journal of Public Health* 83, no. 4 (1993): 580–582.

Flores, Glenn, Elena Fuentes-Afflick, Oxiris Barbot, et al. "The Health of Latino Children: Urgent Priorities, Unanswered Questions, and a Research Agenda." *Journal of the American Medical Association* 288, no. 1 (July 2002): 82–90.

Homa, David M., David M. Mannino, and Marielena Lara. "Asthma Mortality in U.S. Hispanics of Mexican, Puerto Rican, and Cuban Heritage, 1990–1995." *American Journal of Respiratory and Critical Care Medicine* 161, no. 2 (February 2000): 504–509.

Kinnert, Mary D., Marcella R. Price, Andrew H. Liu, et al. "Unraveling the Ecology of Risks for Early Childhood Asthma among Ethnically Diverse Families in the Southwest." *American Journal of Public Health* 95, no. 5 (May 2002): 792–798.

Ledogar, Robert J., Analia Penchaszadeh, C. Cecilia Garden, et al. "Asthma and Latino Cultures: Different Prevalence Reported among Groups Sharing the Same Environment." *American Journal of Public Health* 90, no. 6 (2000): 929–935.

McDermott, Michael, Julio Silva, Robert Rydman, et al. "Practice Variations in Treating Urban Minority Asthmatics in Chicago." *Journal of Medical Systems* 20, no. 5 (October 1996): 255–266.

Pachter, Lee M., Susan C. Weller, Roberta D. Baer, et al. "Variation in Asthma Beliefs and Practices among Mainland Puerto Ricans, Mexican-Americans, Mexicans, and Guatemalans." *Journal of Asthma* 39, no. 2 (April 2002): 119–134.

Weiss, Kevin B., A. Sonia Buist, and Sean D. Sullivan, eds. *Asthma's Impact on Society: The Social and Economic Burden.* Lung Biology in Health Disease, vol. 138. New York: Marcel Dekker, 1999.

Whitman, Steven, Cynthia Williams, and Ami M. Shah. *Sinai Health System's Community Health Survey: Report 1.* Chicago: Sinai Health System, 2004.

ROSS MULLNER AND AIDA L. GIACHELLO

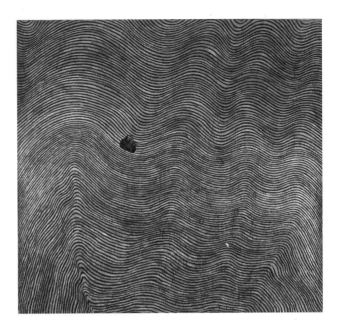

CROSSING. Acrylic on canvas by Luis Cruz Azaceta, 1999. (Galeria Ramis Barquet)

AZACETA, LUIS CRUZ (b. 1942), Cuban American artist. Luis Cruz Azaceta was born in Cuba in 1942 and came to the United States in 1960. He received a bachelor of arts degree from the School of Visual Arts in New York City, where he studied under Leon Golub, a politically concerned painter. Cruz Azaceta's work has been shown in galleries and museums in the United States, including the Cayman Gallery in New York, Miami Dade Community College, University of California at Davis, Louisiana State University, the Chicago Art Institute, and the Lowe Art Museum of the University of Miami, among others. He has received many important awards, including fellowships and grants from the Guggenheim Foundation, the National Endowment for the Arts, the New York Foundation for the Arts, and the Cintas Fellowships for Cuban artists and writers.

According to the categories established by Ricardo Pau-Llosa in his essay "Identity and Variation: Cuban Visual Thinking in Exile since 1959," Cruz Azaceta belongs to the fourth generation of twentieth-century Cuban painters. The other painters of this generation, Ramón Alejandro, Juan Boza, Humberto Chávez, Humberto Calzada, Julio Larraz, and Juan González, left Cuba in the 1960s and through their works have created intense variations on their respective milieus. Like other painters of his generation, Cruz Azaceta creates works that denote great social awareness and make strong statements about human reality and circumstances.

Cruz Azaceta's paintings are characterized by transgressive ways of looking at reality. In the 1970s, he investigated the possibilities of the self and subject representation while exploring Pop Art aesthetics. One of his major contributions as a painter is related to the transgressive nature of his representations, the renovation of the language of the urban space, and the connection he makes between the experience of his own exile and the concerns of the urban subject. While underscoring the tension and chaos that characterize urban life, he breaks away from traditional representations of the city.

Parodic self-representation and a powerful sense of distortion and agony are central to many of Cruz Azaceta's paintings. As he has stated, Goya and Picasso have been two important influences on the development of his style and pictorial language. Like Goya's *Desastres de la guerra*, Cruz Azaceta's paintings explore themes of violence, agony, and extreme human experiences. While his works from the 1960s and the 1970s are manifestations of the Pop Art movement, the works from the 1980s onward are concerned with darker human experiences.

In the 1980s, themes of violence and pain became central to his aesthetics. In *The City Painter of Hearts* (1981), a large acrylic on canvas, he presents a turbulent view of New York City with skyscrapers and fire, in which human destruction is typified by the representation of broken parts of the human body. In *Traveler III* (1985), the experiences of isolation and disconnection are underscored by the representation of a human figure at the center of the painting, surrounded and seized by what seem to be numerous eyes. In both paintings, the use of red creates an effect of intensity that suggests blood, decomposition, and human fragmentation.

The theme of pain appears in various manifestations in Cruz Azaceta's painting series on the AIDS epidemic (1987–1989), which was part of the Best of Annual Exhibition in 1989 at the Queens Museum of Art. This series locates itself within the trends of socially conscious visual and literary works, exploring the impact of the AIDS epidemic on both the individual and the collective.

The pictorial representations of death, human pain, and disease are diverse and singular in paintings such as *AIDS: Suicidal Leap, Hope, The Virus, Young Man Looking in a Mirror, The Plague: AIDS Epidemic, Babies with AIDS, Ghost II, S.O.S,* and *Isolation* (1990). Using original motifs, Cruz Azaceta explores the devastating effect of the epidemic from several perspectives. In paintings such as *Babies with AIDS,* Cruz Azaceta presents one of the most common symbolic representations of the United States, an American flag, but he transforms the stars into skulls from which ropes or umbilical cords are connected to babies. Thus, he makes a strong statement about the AIDS crisis in the United States and the future of a country threatened by the epidemic. *Memorial,* a painting notable for its sobriety and economy of language, is divided horizontally into two sections: the top part in blue, the lower section in black. In the black area of the canvas, a line of white numbers from one to thirty-two appears, thus attesting to the increasingly large numbers of AIDS victims. By presenting clocks, numbers, and skulls, which are common motifs in this series, he links the concerns of time, the painful statistics of people who die from the disease, and the inevitable threat of death.

Another manifestation of Cruz Azaceta's sociopolitically conscious work is his series on the Mariel boat lift. As it has been for many other Cuban visual artists and writers, the Mariel boatlift has been an important theme for Cruz Azaceta. Like other painters of his generation, Cruz Azaceta has reflected on the experiences of isolation, displacement, and marginalization of the 1980s wave of Cuban immigrants. *Caught* (1993), one of the most powerful and representative paintings on the Mariel theme, portrays the torso of a terrified male figure on a raft at the center of the canvas, surrounded by knives, guns, and a cage coming down on his head. It suggests both physical and psychological danger. In addition to the threat of guns and knives, the figure is surrounded by small dark circles with white dots, which serve as metaphors for staring eyes. The economy of elements in the representation of the oppressive experience and the terror of an isolated individual on a raft is singular.

Cruz Azaceta's works about the Mariel theme—like his previous works on the urban space, his series on the AIDS epidemic, and his more contemporary paintings and drawings—expand the range of themes and motifs of visual representation. By elaborating metaphors on issues of displacement and alienation, his work also helps to raise consciousness about his community's exile. Moreover, his aesthetic concerns go well beyond reflection on the individual and one particular community; they underscore a universal preoccupation with human existence. Cruz Azaceta's works contribute to a renovation of abstract and figurative painting and broaden the scope of Cuban and Latino and Latina artistic discourses.

See also Art, Cuban American; Cuban Americans; HIV and AIDS; *and* Marielitos.

BIBLIOGRAPHY

Anreus, Alejandro. "Luis Cruz Azaceta." In *Encyclopedia of Cuba: People, History, Culture,* edited by Luis Martínez-Fernández, 471. Westport, Conn.: Greenwood Press, 2003.

Pau-Llosa, Ricardo. "Identity and Variations: Cuban Visual Thinking in Exile since 1959." In *Outside Cuba/Fuera de Cuba: Contemporary Cuban Visual Artists,* edited by Ileana Fuentes-Pérez, Graciella Cruz-Taura, and Ricardo Pau-Llosa. New Brunswick, N.J.: Rutgers University Press, 1989.

Torruella Leval, Susana, Philip Yenawine, and Ileen Sheppard. *Luis Cruz Azaceta: The AIDS Epidemic Series.* Exhibition catalog. New York: Queens Museum of Art, 1990.

ELENA M. MARTÍNEZ

AZTLÁN. Since the 1960s Aztlán, the original homeland of the Aztecs, has been a powerful symbol of cultural pride and social and political empowerment for many activists and other persons of Mexican descent in the United States. The story of Aztlán is shrouded in myth. The Aztecs described Aztlán as an earthly paradise located northwest of their city of Tenochtitlán (present-day Mexico City). According to the Aztecs, their ancestors lived a life of leisure in Aztlán because of its plentiful trees, water supply, and other natural resources. An abundance of white-plumed waterfowl in the area led them to call it Aztlán, meaning either "land of the herons" or "land of whiteness" in the Aztec language Nahuatl. Legend has it that the Aztecs abandoned Aztlán after their gods told them to build a city wherever they beheld an eagle with a snake in its beak perched atop a cactus. They marched southward and witnessed such a spectacle in the Valley of Mexico, where they then founded Tenochtitlán in about 1325 C.E.

No one has been able to determine the exact location of the real Aztlán. Most likely it was situated in the present-day Mexican state of Nayarit. There Spanish explorers under the command of Nuño de Guzmán encountered a place called Aztatlán in 1530. Aztatlán fit the description of Aztlán to some extent, but the Spaniards still considered the area too unlike the wondrous homeland of Aztec lore. Hoping to find lost Aztec treasures and other riches, they decided to keep searching for Aztlán farther north. In 1538 Juan de la Asuncíon and Pedro Nadal, two Franciscan friars, looked for Aztlán as far north as the Colorado

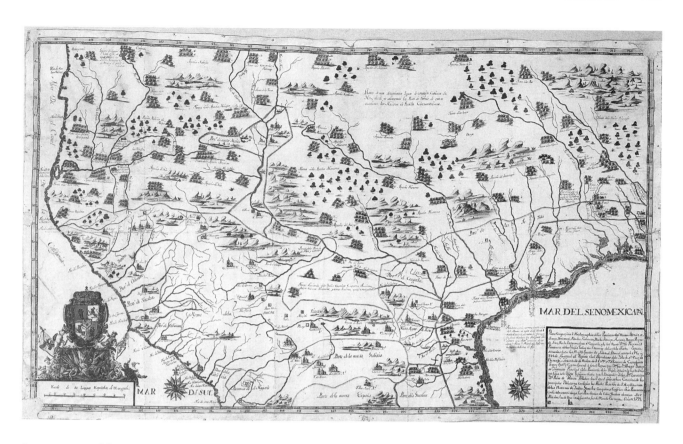

AZTLANAHUAC-MESOAMERICA IN NORTH AMERICA. Map by Francisco Alvarez Barreiro Plano, 1729. (Courtesy of The Hispanic Society of America, New York)

River, near the present-day boundary between California and Arizona. Their journey led to the centuries-old belief that Aztlán was located in what is now the American Southwest.

Beginning in the 1960s the story of Aztlán resurfaced amid a new political climate. To many Mexican Americans, their chronic poverty, inadequate schools, and disproportionately high casualty rates in the Vietnam War demonstrated the U.S. government's neglect of people of Mexican descent. Consequently a new generation of Mexican American activists grew to distrust the established values and institutions of American society. It rejected the notion that Mexican Americans should assimilate into the larger population. Instead, the goal for many activists involved making Mexican Americans self-reliant and proud of their unique heritage. Mexican American youths in particular dropped the terms "Spanish" and "Latin American," called themselves "Chicanos" and "Chicanas," and glorified their Aztec ancestry. In this atmosphere the story of Aztlán, with its notion of the Aztecs as native to the Southwest, attained popularity among the many Chicanos and Chicanas of the region.

Aztlán acquired new meanings as a result of the developments of the era. Chicanos and Chicanas pointed to the story of the Aztec homeland as proof that Mexicans held a better claim to the Southwest than Anglo-Americans. Refuting the stereotype of Mexicans as culturally backward, they regarded the U.S. conquest of this territory after the United States–Mexican War (1846–1848), along with prejudice and racial discrimination, as the main reason for the poverty and low social status of the Mexican-origin population. They also believed that all persons of Mexican descent in the United States should unite on the basis of their shared history as a conquered people to regain political, social, and economic control of the Southwest.

Many Chicano and Chicana leaders and organizers employed the symbol of Aztlán. Its use gained widespread popularity after Rodolfo "Corky" Gonzáles and other activists issued El Plan Espiritual de Aztlán (The Spiritual Plan of Aztlán) at the first Chicano Youth Liberation Conference in 1969. Written by the poet Alurista, the document reaffirmed the indigenous heritage of Chicanos and Chicanas, declared their spiritual independence from U.S. culture, and proclaimed the Southwest as the Chicano and

Chicana homeland. In the early 1970s, activists in Texas organized El Partido de La Raza Unida (The United People's Party), a Chicano and Chicana third party geared toward reclaiming political control of the Southwest. Party leaders relied on the symbol of Aztlán and advertisements with indigenous motifs to gain followers from all over the Southwest. Meanwhile thousands of Chicano and Chicana students on college campuses joined El Movimiento Estudiantil Chicano de Aztlán (MEChA, The Chicano Student Movement of Aztlán) and demanded, among other things, the implementation of Chicano and Chicana studies in the curricula and more inclusive admissions policies.

The Chicano and Chicana visual and performing arts also referred to the Aztecs and their ancient homeland. For example, the performances of El Teatro Campesino (The Farmworkers' Theater), the premier Mexican American theatrical troupe to emerge out of the 1960s and 1970s, drew on Aztec sacred rituals and addressed themes related to the indigenous roots of persons of Mexican descent. In 1971 theatrical companies such as El Teatro de la Gente (The Theater of the People), El Teatro Mestizo (The Mestizo Theater), and El Teatro de la Causa de los Pobres (The Theater of the Poor People's Cause) joined El Teatro Campesino to form an association called El Teatro Nacional de Aztlán (TENAZ, The National Theater of Aztlán). This group sought to raise the political awareness of Chicanos and Chicanas and instill pride in their cultural background. Similar goals inspired Chicano and Chicana artists to paint murals on public and private buildings across the Southwest. Many of the murals depicted Aztec calendars, Mesoamerican pyramids, and such Mexican historical figures as Benito Juárez and Emiliano Zapata. Muralists and other artists formed collectives like the Casa Aztlán (Aztlán House) and El Grito Aztlán (The Aztlán Roar) for mutual support and to help gain exposure for their works.

Intellectuals and novelists likewise attempted to empower the Chicano and Chicana community. The titles of many of their publications linked the Southwest to Aztlán. These books included the novels *Peregrinos de Aztlán* (1974) by Miguel Méndez M. and *Heart of Aztlán* (1976) by Rudolfo A. Anaya and the compilation *Aztlán: An Anthology of Mexican American Literature* (1972), edited by Luis Valdez and Stan Steiner. In 1970 Aztlán Publications at the University of California, Los Angeles, released the first issue of the scholarly journal *Aztlán: Chicano Journal of the Social Sciences and the Arts*.

Many activists, artists, and intellectuals still employ the theme of Aztlán. The ancient homeland of the Aztecs remains a powerful symbol for Chicanos and Chicanas across the country.

See also **Art, Chicano; Chicanos and Chicanas; Gonzáles, Rodolfo Corky; Movimiento Estudiantil Chicano de Aztlán; Mexican-Origin People in the United States;** *and* **Murals.**

BIBLIOGRAPHY

Anaya, Rudolfo A., and Francisco A. Lomelí. *Aztlán: Essays on the Chicano Homeland*. Albuquerque, N.Mex.: Academia/El Norte Publications, 1989.

Chávez, John R. *The Lost Land: The Chicano Image of the Southwest*. Albuquerque: University of New Mexico Press, 1984.

JOSÉ A. RAMÍREZ

B

BACA, JUDY (b. 1946), artist and activist. Judith Baca was born September 20, 1946, into a woman-centered, Spanish-speaking family in Huntington Park, California. When her family moved to Pacoima, Judy was not yet fluent in English, so to keep her occupied during class, her teacher gave her art materials to work with. Her interest in art developed, and she went on to study art at California State University in Northridge. After her grandmother questioned the usefulness of her art, Judy had an epiphany: her art had to "be connected with something that had meaning or purpose beyond my self gratification and could speak to the people I cared most about, my family and community" (http://gac.edu/~cgamble/).

Murals and SPARC

Baca went on to teach art at her alma mater, Bishop Alemany High School, but was fired in 1970 along with other activists who opposed the Vietnam War. She then found employment with Los Angeles's Cultural Affairs Division, where she organized a group of gang members and community youth from Hollenbeck Park to design and paint a mural. Baca recalls,

> I needed to engage young people to work together. The idea occurred to me that if you made something too big for one person to do . . . it would force cooperation. I was really interested in all the underlying social architecture, where you really try to build something between people.
>
> (Isenberg, p. 155)

The success of this radical project led her to found the Los Angeles Citywide Mural Project in 1974, which over a ten-year period created more than four hundred murals using the talent of over two thousand multicultural participants.

Baca's perspectives on public art and community are reflected in the spirit and mission of the Social and Public Art Resource Center (SPARC), founded by Baca, the printmaker Christina Schlesinger, and the filmmaker Donna Deitch in 1976 in Venice, California. SPARC described its mission as a

> multi-ethnic arts center that produces, distributes, preserves and documents community based public art works. SPARC espouses public art as an organizing tool for addressing social

issues, fostering cross-cultural understanding and promoting civic dialogue. Over the last twenty-five years SPARC has created murals in almost every ethnic community in Los Angeles.

In the early 2000s, SPARC housed a collection of sixty thousand slides of public art from around the world.

Baca notes that mural art is "denigrated," and not considered "fine art," because it is not individualistic and is associated with marginalized communities, be they Mexican or even the Works Progress Administration's (WPA) murals produced during the Depression. In interviews with Amalia Mesa-Bains (1986) and Diane Neumaier (1990), Baca discusses her aesthetic and conceptual approach to public art. Scale is important, as is putting "back into public consciousness information that has been lost (1990, p. 267). In the 1970s, Baca added an important dimension to her approach when she discovered the work of the Mexican muralists Diego Rivera, David Alfaro Siqueiros, and José Clemente Orozco, and traveled to Mexico to study materials and techniques at Siqueiros's studio. There she was influenced by "Siqueiros's concept of the musical ratio, [the] harmonious musical ratio of composition and his division of space" (Baca 1986). For Baca, these concepts underlie the structure of a mural, where "any directional line that falls through a form will hit a point that is in mathematical ratio one to another." These points have a relationship to each other, a ratio, which is akin to musical time and which creates "a rhythm within the piece" (Baca 1986).

Works

What Baca learned at Siqueiros's studio she applied to what became one of her best-known projects, *The Great Wall of Los Angeles*. This collective endeavor (1974–1983) is a half-mile-long narrative mural painted on the walls of the Tujunga Wash Canal, in the San Fernando Valley northwest of Los Angeles. Baca supervised teams of young artists who researched, envisioned, and painted images of the multicultural history of the Los Angeles area from prehistoric times to the 1950s. Baca notes that, "Each panel depicts a different era of California's history from the perspective of women and minorities" (Hammond, p. 68). The Tujunga Wash is located on the site where the Los Angeles River used to run. The river has

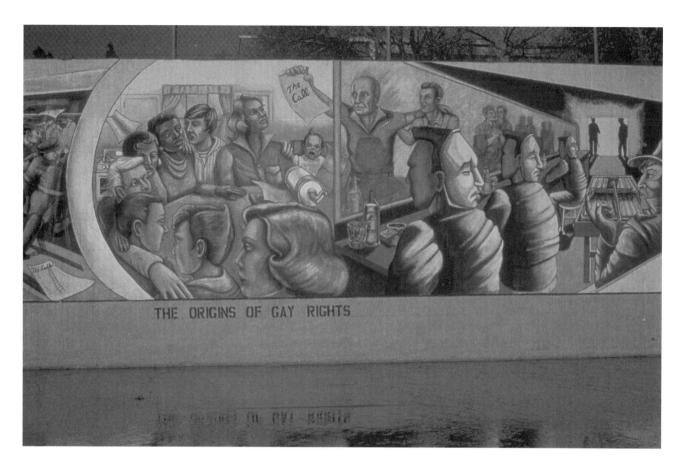

THE GREAT WALL OF LOS ANGELES: THE ORIGINS OF GAY RIGHTS. Mural by Judy Baca, 1983.
(SPARC www.sparcmurals.org)

been paved over with concrete. Baca thinks of the *Great Wall* mural as a "tattoo on the [concrete] scar where the river once ran" (Isenberg, p. 158).

In 1984, as part of the Los Angeles Olympic festivities, Baca was one of ten local artists chosen to create murals along the Los Angeles freeways. Her mural *Hitting the Wall* celebrated the sports accomplishments of women of color. In 1987, Baca began work on *World Wall: A Vision of the Future without Fear*, a project that depicts global awareness, peace, cooperation, and the futility of war. According to Baca, "The World Wall is an international piece and the global geography involved makes it inherently different [from other mural projects]. It has to rely on media information, ecological information, media systems and technology" (Roth 11/21, p. 10) for portions of its collaborative process. Baca recalls that in planning the project, collaborators were at a loss to imagine what the absence of war and the presence of peace would look like: "It was not imagining destruction that was so hard for us, but rather imagining peace" (Baca 1986). The portable mural is made up of seven ten-by-thirty-foot panels painted by Baca and arranged in a semicircle. The plan

called for additional panels to be painted by artists in other countries and arranged in an outer circle.

For another project, SPARC works in partnership with the César Chávez Center and the World Arts and Cultures Department at the University of California, Los Angeles. At the Digital Mural Lab participants make use of "state-of-the-art digital technology stretching widely held notions about the definition of murals." Digital imaging is flexible and allows a new generation of muralists to apply images onto aluminum panels, a medium that deteriorates more slowly than do conventional surfaces and that is less expensive. The Lab also addresses the digital divide by encouraging community education and participation. One Lab project concerns the mural *America Tropical*, painted in La Plazita Olvera in Los Angeles by Siqueiros in 1932. The work, an allegory depicting U.S. imperialism in Latin America, was considered politically unacceptable by Anglo city leaders and was whitewashed. Efforts are underway to restore the Siqueiros mural, and students at the Digital Lab have created another mural near the original. According to the SPARC Web site, "The murals depict historical comparisons between Siqueiros' vision of

Los Angeles of the 1930s and young people's vision of Los Angeles at the end of the 20th century."

In addition to working on mural projects, Baca has been SPARC's artistic director since 1976 and, since 1996, has also been a full professor of art at the University of California at Los Angeles. Her awards include an Arts Award from Hispanic Women, City of San Francisco (1986); a Rockefeller Fellowship (1991); and a Creative Vision Award, Liberty Hill Foundation (2001). Her work appears in *Dialectics of Isolation: An Exhibition of Third World Women Artists of the United States* (1980) and *Saber es Poder/Interventions* (1994). Her experiences as a developing artist and public art activist are described in several interviews.

While Baca identifies as lesbian, she does not focus her work on this part of her life. Like a number of lesbian, gay, bisexual, and transgender activists and artists of color who work in culture-specific environments, rather than underscore this aspect of herself, Baca has chosen to integrate it into her work, noting that, "in terms of a lesbian identity, it is only one of multiple identities for me" (Hammond, p. 68). According to the art critic Harmony Hammond, "Baca does not see sexuality as a separate issue but stresses that a female voice underlies her work and that women play an important role in representing histories of many peoples. Within Chicano cultural projects, that in itself is a radical act" (p. 68).

See also Murals *and* Social and Public Art Resource Center.

BIBLIOGRAPHY
Baca, Judith. Interview with Ann Malaspina. August, 1992.
Baca, Judith. "Our People Are the Internal Exiles." From an interview with Diane Neumaier. In *Making Face, Making Soul/Haciendo Caras: Creative and Critical Perspectives by Feminists of Color*, edited by Gloria Anzaldúa, 256–270. San Francisco: Aunt Lute Foundation, 1990.
Baca, Judith. Interview with Amalia Mesa-Bains. Archives of American Art, Smithsonian Institution, 1986. artarchives.si.edu/oralhist/baca86.htm
Hammond, Harmony. *Lesbian Art in America: A Contemporary History*. New York: Rizzoli, 2000.
Isenberg, Barbara. *State of the Arts: California Artists Talk about Their Work*. New York: Morrow, 2000.
Roth, Moira. "Towards a World in Balance, Part 1." *Artweek* November 14, 1991: 10–11.
Roth, Moira. "Towards a World in Balance, Part 2." *Artweek* November 21, 1991: 10–11.

YOLANDA RETTER VARGAS

BACHATA. *Bachata* is a popular music form that originated in the Dominican Republic in the 1960s. It was initially characterized by a guitar-centered ensemble; an unpolished singing style; a predilection for sexual double entendres and/or melodramatic expressions of romantic love, despair, and heartbreak; highly colloquial language; and, most notably, its low social status. Although its roots were in guitar-based musical traditions preferred by *campesinos*, bachata emerged as a distinct genre in the squalid urban shantytowns where rural migrants seeking work usually ended up; thus its aesthetics and lyrical concerns reflected the disrupted and often desperate lives of its musicians and fans. Until the late 1980s, bachata was contained within lower-class spaces by the media's refusal to give it access to the normal means of production and dissemination. Moreover, it was recorded in technologically antiquated studios that were cheaper to rent but that produced sounds markedly inferior in quality to those of bachata's more socially acceptable counterpart, merengue. Bachatas was thus perceived as the artless, if not vulgar, expression of its constituents' unsophisticated and provincial culture.

In the 1990s bachata's image improved noticeably, and it is now accepted as a legitimate form of Dominican music whose popularity has been growing dramatically within the Dominican Republic as well as internationally. The origins of the improvement in bachata's social status have often been ascribed to the impact of Juan Luis Guerra's 1990 Grammy-winning recording *Bachata Rosa*, whose sophisticated bachatas, composed and sung by a highly respected musician, opened doors for Guerra's grassroots counterparts. Once legitimized by Guerra and subsequent middle-class-oriented imitators, bachata's popularity began crossing class lines, securing its access to critically important national and international media. But bachata's post-1990 success must also be attributed to the social and economic influences of Dominican immigrants in the United States. With 10 percent of the Dominican population living in the United States and eager to hear sounds reminding them of home, the bachateros' fan base expanded rapidly, but more important, it came to include consumers with considerably more disposable income to spend on recordings and live performances than their counterparts in the Dominican Republic.

Some aesthetic changes have occurred as bachata has moved into the Latin music mainstream, but generally, the changes have not altered bachata's signature guitar-based sound and lyrical focus on gender relationships. However, although lyrics were originally more likely to reflect conflict between men and women, later bachatas tend to be highly romantic, and as a result are appealing more to women than in the past.

U.S.–based Dominicans particularly appreciate bachata's ability to invoke traditional Dominican lifestyles. Indeed, bachata's qualities of artlessness and simplicity, once responsible for the music's rejection, have been embraced by nostalgic immigrants because those qualities are perceived to effectively capture the cultural essence of their homeland. While a handful of new U.S.–based bachata groups, such as Aventura, have successfully experimented with incorporating English and Spanglish lyrics, none has reached a level of success comparable to that of musicians whose musical aesthetics and language more directly index the Dominican Republic. This is not to suggest that bachata's fans are musical Luddites pining for an imaginary past. Many of bachata's fans are young and U.S.–born, and they are fully familiar and engaged with contemporary urban genres from salsa to hip hop to rock. Rather, for fans of Dominican descent, bachata effectively articulates their unique identity as Dominicans in a sea of undifferentiated "Latinos," and it expresses their desires to belong and be connected to a specific locality. At the same time, Latinas and Latinos of other national backgrounds have turned to bachata because of its ability to effectively articulate emotions of love and longing. Puerto Ricans are bachata's second largest group of consumers, and growing numbers of Central American and Mexican immigrants in the United States have become fans as well.

Although most of the revenue from bachata comes from the United States, most bachata is still recorded in the Dominican Republic. It is cheaper to record there than in the United States, and it is easier to obtain the services of studio musicians competent in the style. More significantly, bachata is initially released there as well. A bachata has to "break" in the Dominican Republic before it is exported, as an established hit, to the United States. After bachata musicians become well known in the United States, they begin lucrative tours in a circuit of Dominican-oriented clubs, beginning in New York City, then fanning out to smaller northeastern cities with substantial Dominican populations, such as Lawrence, Massachusetts, and Providence, Rhode Island. Many of them also travel to Puerto Rico, and as bachata's popularity continues to grow, to European and Latin American capitals as well. The profits from bachata sales and performances in the United States and beyond are then reinvested in the Dominican Republic for producing and promoting new material. A handful of the biggest bachata stars—pioneer Luis Segura as well as younger musicians such as Anthony Santos and Raulin Rodriguez—have become wealthy thanks to these tours, but even the less successful bachateros can expect some income from their music—royalties for airplay and composing, for example—which they never received in the era before the 1990s, when the bachata business was still highly informal and musicians were often exploited by producers and promoters.

The Dominican Republic itself, beset by extensive and chronic poverty, now accounts for a relatively small portion of the earnings derived from record sales and live performances. The main offices of the record companies that promote and distribute bachata are now based where the consumers—and hence the money—are, in the United States. This does not mean that the Dominican Republic is irrelevant to bachata, but that the Dominican popular music industry, following its fans, is now dispersed, functioning in several distinct but interconnected national and cultural settings—the Dominican Republic, the northeastern United States, and Puerto Rico. More recently, a fourth node, unconnected to a Dominican community, has emerged: Miami, where bachata producers have established offices. The logic of this new development reflects Miami's role as the center of the international Latin music industry. Bachata producers are clearly preparing for bachata's presence to increase within the Latin music market. In short, while bachata's aesthetics and symbolic associations have remained firmly rooted in the Dominican Republic, the music's economy has become thoroughly transnational.

See also Dominicans *and* Music, Popular.

BIBLIOGRAPHY

Pacini Hernandez, Deborah. *Bachata: A Social History of a Dominican Popular Music*. Philadelphia: Temple University Press, 1995.

DEBORAH PACINI HERNANDEZ

BAEZ, JOAN (b. 1941), musician and activist. Joan Chandos Baez was born in Staten Island, New York, to immigrant parents. Her father, Albert Baez, left Mexico as a child with his family when his father became a Methodist minister in New York City. Her mother, Joan Bridge Baez, left Scotland with her father, an Episcopal minister, and sister to live in New York City. Baez's parents met at a college dance at Drew University in Madison, New Jersey. They married and had three children while Baez's father continued his education. Each of the Baez children was born in a different state, reflecting the nomadic live that accompanied their father's academic career. By the time Joan Baez completed high school, she had lived in the university communities of Stanford University, Cornell University, Redlands University, and the University of Baghdad.

In her autobiography, *And a Voice to Sing With*, Baez states that her passion for social justice was probably born in Baghdad because there she saw the effects of extreme poverty, especially on children. In 1951, after moving from Baghdad to Southern California, she began to confront her bicultural identity. She felt isolated from most of her peers and found it hard to fit in. Her school was largely Mexican, but because she did not speak Spanish, she could not form connections with many Mexican students. Anglo and Mexican students during that time period often formed separate groups and expressed animosity toward one another within the school grounds.

JOAN BAEZ, 1967. (Associated Press)

After attending Boston University's School of Drama for a month, Baez dropped out to dedicate herself to playing her guitar and singing popular songs in the coffeehouses on Harvard Square in Cambridge, Massachusetts. Students followed her performances, and she was soon invited to perform at the Gate of Horn nightclub in Chicago. There she met the singer Bob Gibson and the "Queen of Folk," Odetta. Gibson invited Baez to perform with him at the first Newport Folk Festival in the summer of 1959. Only twenty years old, Baez was a sensation with the audience and the media. Both Columbia Records and Vanguard Records offered her a recording contract in New York City. During this same period, Baez met Bob Dylan, and they were romantically involved for a brief time. Introducing Dylan to audiences in 1963, Baez performed with him at this stage in her career.

During the 1960s, Baez became a celebrity as well as an activist for pacifism and equal rights. She joined civil rights demonstrations and worked for racial integration in the South. While touring southern college campuses, she noticed that no blacks attended her concerts. After this realization, Baez insisted that her contracts stipulate that she would not perform unless blacks were allowed into the concert halls. Her 1962 college tour included four black colleges in the heart of the South. Her repertoire included the classic protest songs "Oh, Freedom" and "We Shall Overcome." Her third album, which came out in 1963, featured "Amazing Grace," "Swing Low," "What Have They Done to the Rain," and "Joe Hill," songs expressing her civil rights and peace sentiments. In 1963 she sang at the March on Washington, where King gave his famous "I have a dream" speech. She also demonstrated with the University of California, Berkeley, Student Free Speech movement and at early anti–Vietnam War rallies. In 1966 Baez and King led a group of black children to school in Grenada, Mississippi. Even though they were not allowed into the school, the event was televised as a peaceful demonstration for integration.

In 1964 Baez opened the Institute for the Study of Nonviolence in Carmel, California, to teach the concepts, history, and theory of nonviolence. Supporting the United Farm Workers strike against grape growers in Delano, California, organized by César Chávez, she held teach-ins about the strike at her institute and visited the strikers in the field and in jail. Based on Baez's institute, the Resource Center for Nonviolence was founded in Santa Cruz, California, in 1978. This center continues to work toward the achievement of peace and social justice in the early twenty-first century. In the late sixties Baez spent time in jail for practicing civil disobedience by blocking the Armed Forces Induction Center in Oakland, California, in October 1967. At this protest she met David Harris, an antiwar activist who refused to be drafted into the

Because she had a Mexican last name, brown skin, and brown eyes, Baez did not feel accepted by the white students either. She came to experience her ethnicity as a condition of double rejection. To fight her isolation and as a way to express herself, Baez learned to play stringed instruments and to sing. During her ninth- and tenth-grade years, Baez entertained her classmates, family, and family friends by playing a ukulele and singing blues, country, rock, and rhythm and blues songs.

In 1956, while living in Palo Alto, California, Baez attended a three-day conference with the American Friends Service Committee, a Quaker organization, at Asilomar in Monterey, California, where she met Martin Luther King Jr. King became a major influence on Baez and instilled in her a doctrine of nonviolent activism and a commitment to peace and equality. Baez further developed her pacifism while attending the Quaker First Day School, where as a teenager she read texts by Leo Tolstoy, Lao-tze, Aldous Huxley, and the Bhagavad Gita. These experiences provided the foundation for Baez's nonviolent organizing and demonstrating. Throughout her life she used her music to express her concerns for social justice and equality.

military and who also served a jail sentence for his civil disobedience. Baez and Harris married and had one child, Gabriel, born in 1969.

In 1972 Baez joined Amnesty International and took a year off from her music to organize the Amnesty International West Coast with Ginetta Sagan. In the summer of 1972 she also helped organize Ring around Congress, a demonstration of American mothers and their children holding hands, symbolizing solidarity with the women of Vietnam. In December 1972, while Baez was visiting Hanoi, Vietnam, the city was bombarded by American B-52s. She survived the attack by taking refuge in a shelter with the North Vietnamese group called the Committee for Solidarity with the American People. After she saw the devastation of the war and experienced the fear of being bombarded, Baez's pacifism grow stronger.

Throughout the 1970s Baez continued to tour nationally and internationally, although she never regained the success she had enjoyed in the 1960s. However, her commitment to peace and social justice continue in the twenty-first century. Because of her mixed heritage, she is sometimes not perceived as a Latina. But her commitment to justice for all aligns her with the struggles of Latinas and Latinos in the United States.

See also Bilingualism and Biculturalism; Folklore; Mestizaje; *and* Social Movements.

BIBLIOGRAPHY

Baez, Joan. *And a Voice to Sing With: A Memoir.* New York: Summit Books, 1987.

Baez, Joan. *Daybreak.* New York: Dial Press, 1968.

Bessman, Jim. "Baez Turns to New Generation for Latest Songs." *Billboard,* September 13, 2003, 48.

Fuss, Charles J. *Joan Baez: A Bio-Bibliography.* Westport, Conn.: Greenwood Press, 1996.

Hajdu, David. *Positively 4th Street: The Lives and Times of Joan Baez, Bob Dylan, Mimi Baez Fariña, and Richard Fariña.* New York: Farrar, Straus, and Giroux, 2001.

EMMA GARCÍA

BALLOT PROPOSITIONS 187, 209, AND 227.

During the late 1990s, California's minority communities, particularly its Latina and Latino community, faced a series of challenges to their civil rights. These rights were challenged not by the legislature but by ballot propositions placed on the ballot by petition drives and evaluated by California's voters. These ballot initiatives were Proposition 187 (1994), which prohibited the delivery of state-provided health care and education to undocumented immigrants and required that state and local government employees report on the immigration status of their clients; Proposition 209 (1996), which prevented the state of California from implementing affirmative action programs in public education, public employment, and pub-

lic contracting; and Proposition 227 (1998), which limited the ability of school districts in California to use bilingual education programs lasting more than one year. Each of these policy initiatives was considered in several other states during the 1990s, but California was the only state to consider all three over successive election cycles.

Despite strong opposition from California Latinas and Latinos, each of these initiatives received support from a majority of California voters. Two factors explain these defeats for California's Latinas and Latinos. First, California has among the most expansive palette of direct democracy tools of any state. Second, California's electorate includes a lower share of minorities than does the population of the state as a whole (in large part because of high rates of non–United States citizenship in Latino and Asian American communities and the relative youth of California minorities). As a result Latinas and Latinos do not have a political voice commensurate with their numbers.

California's tools of direct democracy include three elements: referendum, initiative, and recall. Referenda block the implementation of a law passed by the legislature and signed by the governor (or passed over a governor's veto). Referenda ensure that ultimate authority over legislation (with some narrow exceptions, particularly for taxation and appropriations) rests with the people. Initiatives, what are referred to as ballot propositions, allow citizens to propose laws and constitutional amendments without requiring that the legislature agree. These place the power of law making in the electorate's hands. Finally, recalls allow the citizenry to remove officeholders from office through special elections. In 2003 Governor Gray Davis was recalled from office and, in a replacement election held at the same time as the recall, Arnold Schwarzenegger defeated Cruz Bustamante to win the remainder of Davis's term.

California's Ongoing Experiment with Direct Democracy

The roots of California's use of the initiative and referendum appeared early in the twentieth century. Political reformers of that era sought to limit the power of political parties, political machines, and organized interests. Under the leadership of Progressive governor Hiram Johnson, California voters considered and approved constitutional amendments in 1911 that provided for the use of initiative and referendum (as well as recall). California is one of twenty-one states that employ both referendum and initiative in statewide elections.

Not all referenda or initiatives will be considered by the electorate, nor will all officeholders be subjected to recall. Instead, the state constitution sets minimum requirements for placement on statewide ballots. Referenda require petitions to be submitted with signatures numbering at least 5 percent of the vote cast in the most recent gubernatorial election. These signatures must be collected within ninety days of the enactment of the bill. Initiatives require signatures totaling 8 percent of the vote in the most recent gubernatorial election for state constitutional amendments and 5 percent of the vote for statutory initiatives. The signatures must be collected within a 150-day period. Recall petitions require the signatures of 12 percent of the vote cast in the last election for the office being recalled. The signatures must be collected over a period of no more than 160 days.

These requirements for the number of signatures are generally more lax than in other states with referendum, initiative, or recall, ensuring that more referenda, recalls, and particularly initiatives reach the California ballots. In the 2003 gubernatorial recall, for example, recall proponents needed only 897,158 valid signatures (in part because of the relatively low statewide turnout in the 2002 gubernatorial election). Although this number may seem high, advocates of specific initiatives, referenda, or recall drives can hire professional signature gatherers to collect signatures. Conventional wisdom among California politicos suggests that most initiatives, referenda, and recall drives can make a statewide ballot as long as their proponents have sufficient funding. Professional signature-gathering firms charge between $1.00 and $1.25 per signature. Many of the people who sign the petitions are unclear about what exactly they are calling for a vote on and, in many cases, are misled by the paid signature gatherers, who have an interest only in collecting as many signatures as possible.

Each of these tools of direct democracy has seen increased use since the 1980s. In part this reflects a growing distrust among California's electorate in the ability of the state legislature to represent their interests. It also reflects an increasing partisan divide in legislative districts and a reduced need to compromise in the legislature. Finally, it reflects an era of limited budgets in California, in large part because in 1978 California voters passed Proposition 13, which limited the ability of the state to raise new revenues through the increasing value of property in the state. While the increased use of referenda, initiatives, and recalls can be explained with each of these political factors, it is also important to note that the period since the 1980s has seen a dramatic increase in Latina and Latino political power and the emergence of Latina and Latino officeholders who can influence policy.

Propositions 187, 209, and 227

Proposition 187 because a turning point in California politics, but as late as one month before the election few Californians, and few California Latinas and Latinos, were

CELEBRATION. David Cervantes, an organizer of the campaign to nullify Proposition 187, celebrates success in July 1999 in Los Angeles. (AP/Neil Jacobs)

paying attention. A poll in this period showed support for 187 among all California electorates, including Latinas and Latinos. In that poll approximately two-thirds of Latinas and Latinos supported Proposition 187.

The debate around 187 changed considerably in October 1994. Governor Pete Wilson, facing a difficult reelection campaign, began to echo the anti-immigrant message of 187 and to blend it into his own campaign advertising. As the campaign neared, the airwaves filled with pro-187 and pro-Wilson ads with a common message: "They Keep Coming." The campaign quickly escalated from a discussion of a set of policies to limit state spending to a more profound challenge to the presence of Latinas and Latinos in California.

Opponents of 187 also galvanized in the month before the election. These opponents included Latina and Latino elites, who conducted public information, voter registration, and get-out-the-vote campaigns, and community activists, who organized street protests. These protests, which included Latinas and Latinos carrying the flags of their countries of origin or ancestry, generated much debate in the media and may well have solidified pro-187 votes.

These anti-187 efforts succeeded in converting Latina and Latino support for 187 to opposition. More important for longer-term Latina and Latino empowerment, they highlighted the connection between the pro-187 campaign, the Wilson campaign, and the state Republican Party. This had the effect of solidifying Latina and Latino support for the Democrats, which laid the foundation for a shift from Republican to Democratic dominance in statewide politics in the years after 1994.

Proposition 187 received support from 59 percent of California voters. Support for the proposition was highest in California's rural counties. Its supporters did not include the majority of California's minority communities. According to exit polls, just 23 percent of Latinas and Latinos and 47 percent of African Americans and Asian Americans supported the proposition (see Table 1). Considering the preelection poll showing that two-thirds of Latinas and Latinos supported 187, this low level of Latina and Latino support on election day should be seen as a considerable victory for Latina and Latino and immigrant leaders who opposed the proposition.

TABLE 1. *Support for Propositions 187, 209, and 227 by Race or Ethnic Group*

	PROPOSITION 187 %	PROPOSITION 209 %	PROPOSITION 227 %
White	63	63	67
Black	47	26	48
Latino and Latina	23	24	37
Asian American	47	39	57

SOURCES: *Los Angeles Times* Poll 1994; 1996; 1998.

Ultimately the proposition had little impact on public policy in California. The federal courts held most of it unconstitutional (the exception had to do with a minor provision to make it a state offense to use fraudulent documents to falsely assert legal residence or citizenship). Its impact on national policy was greater. Members of Congress quickly introduced legislation to make 187's provisions into national legislation. Although the proposals did not result in legislation, they spurred fear in immigrant communities and encouraged many legal residents to pursue U.S. citizenship.

The success at the ballot box of Proposition 187 encouraged other leaders seeking to roll back civil rights protections in California. The first of these to be challenged was affirmative action, led by the University of California regent Ward Connerly. Connerly had already led a successful effort to eliminate affirmative action in admissions to the University of California. With financial support from many of the same interests who had supported 187 as well as Governor Pete Wilson, Connerly was able to quickly gather a sufficient number of signatures to qualify Proposition 209 for the 1996 general election.

Perhaps learning a lesson from the 187 campaign, 209's opponents organized much earlier than 187's had in 1994. More important, they built a broader coalition that included blacks, Latinas and Latinos, Asian Americans, white women, and civil rights leaders. The opposition to 209 in the Latina and Latino electorate consequently coalesced much earlier in the campaign. The anti-209 coalition was much more elite driven than had been the anti-187 organization; there were no comparable protests in the streets or nationalistic protests in 1996. Anti-209 organizers were also able to tap national civil rights organizations for support.

Proposition 209 passed with 55 percent of the vote. Of the three 1990s ballot propositions with significant impacts on the Latina and Latino community, Proposition 209 engendered the most pan-minority unity. Latinas and Latinos were the most opposed to 209, with just 24 percent supporting the proposition. Support from African Americans was equally tepid (26 percent), and support was only slightly greater among Asian Americans (39 percent). Just 39 percent of women statewide supported the proposition. As with 187, the anti–affirmative action agenda of 209 quickly spread outside California. Just as quickly, though, these efforts disappeared from the national agenda, speaking perhaps to the ease of ballot access in California. As federal issues were not at stake in 209, there was no federal judicial intervention. In the early twenty-first century California continued not to use affirmative action in public education, public employment, and government contracting.

The final ballot issue with significant impact on California Latina and Latino communities to come before state voters in the 1990s was the 1998 Proposition 227 to severely restrict the ability of school districts to use bilingual education in classrooms. One-year transitional programs would be permitted and, in districts that could offer alternatives, parents could petition to place their children into multiyear bilingual programs. According to its proponents, the impetus for 227 was organized efforts by some parent organizations in Los Angeles and other immigrant-concentration school districts to move their children out of bilingual classes. Although these parent

TABLE 2. *Adult Population and Electorate, Statewide and Latinos and Latinas, 1990–2002*

	ADULTS			VOTED		
	Statewide	Latina/ Latino	Latina/ Latino (%)	Statewide	Latina/ Latino	Latina/ Latino (%)
1990	21,289,000	4,739,000	22.3	9,027,000	844,000	9.3
1992	22,340,000	5,443,000	24.4	11,789,000	1,135,000	9.6
1994	22,639,000	5,736,000	25.3	10,184,000	1,134,000	11.1
1996	22,871,000	5,723,000	25.0	11,079,000	1,291,000	11.7
1998	23,696,000	6,264,000	26.4	9,593,000	1,388,000	13.9
2000	24,749,000	6,514,000	26.3	11,489,000	1,597,000	13.9
2002	24,405,000	6,964,000	28.5	8,355,000	1,206,000	14.4

SOURCE: Author's compilation from U.S. Bureau of the Census, 1992–2004.
Note: Adult population includes non–United States citizens and others ineligible to vote.

organizations were few, they received a great deal of press attention and support from a software entrepreneur, Ron Unz, who led and financed the pro-227 effort. Unz had opposed 187 and tried to distance the 227 campaign from the nativist organizations that had led the 187 campaign. In the mass electorate, however, the core of 227 support came from the same voters who had supported 187.

Both pro- and anti-227 leaders had learned from 187 and 209. Unz was careful not to follow the lead of 187 and to expand the scope of his efforts beyond the question on the ballot. The anti-227 campaign was not as active as had been the opposition to the two earlier ballot initiatives. Part of the explanation for this was the fact that 227 appeared on the primary ballot, whereas the other two had been on the general election ballot (limiting the spillover effect it could have on other races). Perhaps more important were the lessons of 187 and 209. Bilingual advocates recognized that defeating 227 would require changing the anti-bilingual education biases of the white electorate, and they had neither the resources nor a strategy to accomplish this goal.

On election day Proposition 227 passed with 61 percent of the vote statewide. It received its highest levels of support from rural counties and its lowest levels in the Bay Area. Although the majority of Latinas and Latinos opposed 227, a higher share supported it than did 187 or 209. Exit polls indicate that 37 percent of Latinas and Latinos supported the elimination of bilingual education. Proposition 227 also failed to galvanize California's minority communities: 57 percent of Asian Americans and 48 percent of African Americans supported the proposition.

Although each of these initiatives addressed a separate issue, taken together they came to be understood as a direct challenge to Latina and Latino power in the state. In the short term the presence of each on the ballot worked to the advantage of California Republicans. In 1994, for

example, having Proposition 187 on the ballot reinvigorated Pete Wilson's lagging campaign for reelection. Once 187 achieved ballot status, Wilson linked the rhetoric and advertising of his campaign to the anti-immigrant message of 187. This anti-immigrant message mobilized many potential voters who also voted for Wilson (and would not have necessarily turned out had it not been for Proposition 187). Wilson went from 15 percent behind in the polls to a 10-point victory.

The short-term reward for state Republicans of Propositions 209 and 227 were less than for Proposition 187. In both cases leading state and national Republicans opposed the initiatives (after being largely silent on 187). The nature of the initiative certification process, however, limits the ability of party leaders to control factions who have a policy or ideological agenda. Ward Connerly led efforts to eliminate affirmative action in California in 1996, and Ron Unz led the antibilingual measure in 1998. In each of these cases the presence of these initiatives on the ballot mobilized some Republican voters, but neither can be said to have changed the outcomes of other elections.

The increasing hesitation on the part of California Republican leaders if not on the part of issue advocates resulted from a realization that Proposition 187 had mobilized Latina and Latino voters and not just for the 1994 elections (see Table 2). The 1994 election saw a dramatic increase in Latina and Latino turnout, particularly notable because 1994 was an off-year federal election in which congressional races were on the ballot but not a presidential race. The number of Latina and Latino voters increased by almost 300,000 over 1990. This surge in Latina and Latino voting (which was matched by a surge in Latina and Latino applications for U.S. citizenship) remained throughout the 1990s. Consequently Latinas and Latinos increased their share of the statewide vote from 9 percent in 1990 to over 14 percent in 2002. These votes have produced dramatic increases in Latina and Latino officeholders at all levels of California government.

Conclusions: Direct Democracy and California Latina and Latino Interests

As should be evident, Latinas and Latinos in California have not been served by the state's tools of direct democracy. As the Latina and Latino population grows, initiative and to a lesser degree referendum and recall will increasingly be used as tools to limit gains made by the election of Latinas and Latinos to state offices and the passage of legislation that addresses the Latina and Latino policy agenda.

The statewide electorate for referenda, initiatives, and recalls will remain less Latina and Latino than the state's population as a whole for the foreseeable future. In 2000, for example, Latinas and Latinos made up more than 26 percent of the state's adult population but just 14 percent of the electorate.

With the steady growth of the Latina and Latino population (and its concentration), Latinas and Latinos have seen considerable gains in the numbers of Latinas and Latinos in state legislative offices. For example, the number of Latina and Latino legislators in California increased from seven in 1992 to twenty-six in 2002. Twice during the 1990s a Latino served as speaker of the assembly, a position of considerable power. By 2004 Latinas and Latinos made up 22.5 percent of the members of each body. Latina and Latino officeholders also included several statewide officeholders (including the lieutenant governor, Cruz Bustamante). With this new concentration of Latina and Latino officeholders and their importance to the Democratic Party in the legislature, Latina and Latino influence over legislation and state government has grown.

The potential influence of this newly emergent Latina and Latino leadership is limited, however, by the institutions of direct democracy. Statewide electorates can overrule the acts of legislatures or put issues on the ballot that the legislature would prefer to neglect. As Latina and Latino power in the state continues to increase, angry statewide electorates will increasingly use these resources to slow Latina and Latino influence. To the extent that these efforts directly challenge the status of Latinas and Latinos in the state, as did Proposition 187 in particular, these challenges may serve as short-term barriers to and long-term forces for Latina and Latino mobilization. With more cautiously run initiative campaigns, such as the Proposition 227 campaign, however, Latinas and Latinos can see the loss of legislative gains without a commensurate gain in community activism or mobilization. Just as Latinas and Latinos learned from the anti–Latina and Latino ballot initiatives of the 1990s, so did the forces that use fear of Latina and Latino gains to mobilize Anglo voters.

See also California *and* Immigration.

BIBLIOGRAPHY

Baldassare, Mark. *California in the New Millennium: The Changing Social and Political Landscape*. Berkeley: University of California Press, 2000.

Bowler, Shaun, and Bruce Cain, eds. *The Historic California Recall Election*. Englewood Cliffs, N.J.: Prentice Hall. Forthcoming.

Chávez, Lydia. *The Color Bind: California's Battle to End Affirmative Action*. Berkeley: University of California Press, 1998.

DeSipio, Louis. "After Proposition 187, the Deluge: Reforming Naturalization Administration while Making Good Citizens." *Harvard Journal of Hispanic Policy* 9 (1996): 7–24.

DeSipio, Louis. *Counting on the Latino Vote: Latinos as a New Electorate*. Charlottesville: University Press of Virginia, 1996.

Los Angeles Times Poll. *Demographic Profile of the Electorate: California General Election, November 8, 1994*. Los Angeles: Los Angeles Times, 1994.

Los Angeles Times Poll. *Study #389/Exit Poll: The General Election*. Los Angeles: Los Angeles Times, 1996.

Los Angles Times Poll. *Study #413/Exit Poll: June 2, 1998*. Los Angeles: Los Angeles Times, 1998.

MacDonald, Karin, and Bruce E. Cain. "Nativism, Partisanship, and Immigration: An Analysis of Prop. 187." In *Racial and Ethnic Politics in California*, edited by Bryan O. Jackson and Michael B. Preston. Vol. 2, edited by Michael B. Preston, Bruce E. Cain, and Sandra Bass, 277–304. Berkeley: Institute of Governmental Studies Press, University of California at Berkeley, 1991–1998.

Ono, Kent A., and John M. Sloop. *Shifting Borders: Rhetoric, Immigration, and California's Proposition 187*. Philadelphia, Pa.: Temple University Press, 2002.

Schrag, Peter. *Paradise Lost: California's Experience, America's Future*. New York: New Press, 1998.

U.S. Bureau of the Census. *Voting and Registration in the Election of November*, 1990–2002. Washington, D.C.: U.S. Bureau of the Census, 1992–2004.

LOUIS DESIPIO

BALMASEDA, LIZ (b. 1959), journalist. The Pulitzer Prize–winning columnist Liz Balmaseda is an author and screenwriter based in Miami. Her writings reflect the concerns and aspirations of a generation of Cuban Americans born in exile.

Since the 1980s, the Cuban-born writer has chronicled Miami's political, social, and cultural evolution. Her columns in the *Miami Herald* cast a revealing light on the city's silenced, politically diverse communities. From its start in late 1991, her column sparked debate in a Cuban American population where hardliners controlled public opinion. In 1992, she was named as one of three finalists for the Pulitzer Prize in commentary. In 1993, she won the Pulitzer for columns on Cuban American and Haitian issues. She was the first Latina or Latino to receive a Pulitzer Prize.

In 2001, Balmaseda shared a second Pulitzer Prize, joining the *Herald*'s staff in winning the award for breaking news, for the coverage of the federal raid to seize the refugee boy Elián González. That year she was also

LIZ BALMASEDA. Balmaseda at the 2001 Hispanic Heritage Awards Ceremony. (Associated Press/Pablo Martinez)

honored with the Hispanic Heritage Award for writing excellence.

Balmaseda's journalistic career has brought her a range of assignments as a news reporter, feature and magazine writer, and network television producer. In the mid-1980s, she was based in El Salvador as the Central America bureau chief for *Newsweek* magazine. Later, before returning to the *Miami Herald*, she worked as a Central America–based field producer for NBC News.

Balmaseda's writing career also includes published essays and the book *Waking Up in America* (1999), which she coauthored. The book is a memoir of Dr. Pedro José Greer Jr., an advocate for the homeless. Knopf published her essays in two anthologies of Latina and Latino writings, titled *Las Christmas* and *Las Mamis*. She was featured in the book *Mothers and Daughters* along with her mother, Ada, and her sister, Elaine. She also appears in *By*

Heart, a collection of writings by Cuban women, and she is a contributor to national magazines.

Balmaseda's radio essays have been aired on NPR's *All Things Considered*, *Latino USA*, and the BBC's Radio Four, for which she wrote and hosted a critically acclaimed documentary on Miami's ethnic relations. The BBC has called her "an expressive writer who is known for being unafraid of controversy."

Balmaseda began her film work in 2000 as an associate producer and writer for the HBO film *For Love of Country*, which focuses on the jazz trumpeter Arturo Sandoval. Another film project for HBO is based on Balmaseda and Greer's book *Waking Up in America*.

Balmaseda has appeared in various documentaries about the Cuban exile experience, including Mari Rodríguez Ichaso's *Marcadas por el Paraiso* and the nationally aired *Café con Leche*. Her independent film projects have included the documentary *American Purgatory*, shot by hidden camera inside the Guantánamo refugee camps in 1995. In 2002, she narrated the PBS documentary *José Martí, Legacy of Freedom*. Other film work includes a documentary about a landmark bombing case in Miami.

Balmaseda's writing, honored by Amnesty International, has proved influential beyond any one issue or any one community, and it has prompted political and social action. In 1994, she brought to light the plight of refugee children in detention at the U.S. naval base at Guantánamo Bay, Cuba, sparking the court case that won the children's release.

For her commentaries on Haiti, she has also been honored by the National Association of Black Journalists. In 1984, she won second place in the Scripps-Howard Foundation's Ernie Pyle Award for Writing Excellence. She was awarded first prize in commentary by the Florida Society of Newspaper Editors in 1993 and 1994. In July 1994, she was awarded the Ruben Salazar award by the National Council of La Raza.

See also Cuban American Writers; Cuban Americans; González, Elián; National Council of La Raza; *and* Sandoval, Arturo.

MARÍA DE LOS ANGELES TORRES

BALSEROS. During the summer of 1994, thirty-six thousand Cubans, dubbed *balseros* (rafters), risked and survived the dangerous voyage from Cuba to South Florida in homemade rafts, inner tubes, and flimsy vessels. The exodus was triggered by many factors, but chief among them were the deterioration of the Cuban economy after the disintegration of the Soviet Union, the country's main trading partner; the Cuban government's response to a series of hijackings and embassy invasions in Havana by political asylum seekers; and the lack of safe and normal migratory channels between Cuba and the United States. As could be expected, the uncontrolled exodus was chaotic and tragic. An estimated one of every five people who attempted the crossing died trying.

Irregular and uncontrolled migration was not new to Cuban culture. Since the triumph of the Cuban Revolution in 1959, more than sixty-three thousand had made and survived the illegal and risky ninety-mile voyage north, and in 1980, as a result of a diplomatic dispute involving Cuba, Peru, and the United States, an additional 125,000 Cubans came to the United States as part of the Mariel boatlift, unilaterally authorized by the Cuban government. The balseros crisis of 1994, as it came to be known, can only be understood within the framework of United States–Cuba relations during the preceding forty years. The important political role that migration played in both countries must also be considered. The Cuban government followed a strategy that welcomed the departure of its political enemies and anyone disaffected with the revolutionary process. The exportation of the opposition facilitated and accelerated the consolidation of revolutionary power. Likewise, the U.S. government implemented a cold war immigration strategy designed to welcome all Cuban migrants as political refugees fleeing Communist repression. The results of these migration strategies were two uncontrolled boatlifts and one major airlift prior to the balseros crisis of 1994.

The balseros crisis, like most waves of Cuban migration to the United States since 1959, was a direct consequence of an unwritten U.S. open-door policy that was formalized with the passing of the Cuban Adjustment Act in 1966. Still in effect in the early 2000s, the law grants permanent resident status to all Cuban immigrants one year and one day after their arrival in the United States. However, despite their historic categorization as "political refugees," by 1994 most Cuban rafters and migrants seemed to be motivated mainly by the increased economic hardships Cubans experienced as a consequence of the Soviet Union's disintegration in 1991, which had resulted in Cuba losing 75 percent of its international trade.

In September 1994, after more than thirty-five thousand balseros had been rescued by the U.S. Coast Guard and placed in detention camps at the U.S. naval base in Guantánamo Bay, Cuba, the U.S. and Cuban governments entered into secret negotiations that led to two important migration agreements. Ironically, what began as a serious crisis provided the basis for the most extensive direct talks between the two countries in forty years. The crisis forced them to respond to the urgent need to create appropriate channels for legal migration from Cuba to the United States. The agreements established: (1) Cuba would increase border patrols to stop illegal emigration, but not punish those caught trying; (2) those who were rescued by the U.S. Coast Guard before reaching U.S. soil would be returned to Cuba, where they would be encouraged to apply for legal exit permits to emigrate to the United States; (3) the United States would issue a minimum of twenty thousand visas per year for Cubans wishing to emigrate to the United States; and (4) the United States would create a special visa lottery for Cubans who wished to emigrate but did not have relatives in the United States to claim them.

The 1994 and 1995 immigration accords effectively stopped the 1994 balseros crisis, but they were far from perfect, as they failed to produce a safe and regular migratory process that would end illegal migration. A major loophole in the accords was the "wet feet/dry feet" policy: Cubans rescued at sea by the U.S. Coast Guard would be, in accordance with the migratory agreements, automatically returned to Cuba, while those who made it to U.S. soil would be allowed to stay, in accordance with the Cuban Adjustment Act of 1966. The exploitation of this loophole by unscrupulous speedboat operators, who charge up to $10,000 per passenger, has led to hundreds of deaths and thousands of illegal entries. It is estimated that an average of three thousand Cubans per year arrive on U.S. shores illegally.

No one can predict if another uncontrolled and massive exodus from Cuba will take place in the future. What is certain is that there are hundreds of thousands of Cubans hoping to emigrate legally and safely to the United States. During the first three visa lottery drawings held in Havana, the number of applicants increased dramatically every time: 189,000 in 1994, 433,000 in 1996, and 541,000 in 1998. The numbers could possibly decrease if the political relations between Cuba and the United States improve, but the future does not look very promising. The passing of the Cuban Liberty and Democratic Solidarity Act (also known as the Helms-Burton Act) by the U.S. Congress in 1996 strengthened and internationalized the U.S. economic blockade against Cuba and, as intended, increased economic hardship for the Cuban people. In 2004, the Bush administration's adoption of the recommendations of the Commission for Assistance to a Free Cuba raised tensions between the two countries to dangerously high levels. In addition to outlining a plan to "hasten the end of the Cuban dictatorship," the commission recommended regulations that imposed harsh travel restrictions and severe penalties for American citizens who travel to Cuba; eliminated most academic exchanges between Cuba and the United States; and restricted the travel of Cuban Americans back to their homeland to once every three years, and only to visit close relatives. President George W. Bush approved these regulations. Most experts agree that as long as these conditions persist, Cubans are likely to continue taking to the sea heading north.

See also Bay of Pigs; Castro, Fidel; Cuban Americans; Detainees, Cuban; Guantánamo Bay; Helms-Burton Act; Immigration; Marielitos; United States Foreign Policy; *and* United States Interventions in Latin America.

BIBLIOGRAPHY

Ackerman, Holly. "The Cuban Rafter Phenomenon: A Unique Sea Exodus." The University of Miami Digital Library Program. http://www.balseros.miami.edu

Fernández, Alfredo A. *Adrift: The Cuban Raft People*. Translated by Susan Giersbach Rascón. Houston, Tex.: Arte Público Press, 2000.

García, Maria Cristina. *Havana USA: Cuban Exiles and Cuban Americans in South Florida, 1959–1994*. Berkeley: University of California Press, 1996.

Grenier, Guillermo J., and Lisandro Pérez. *The Legacy of Exile: Cubans in the United States*. Boston: Allyn and Bacon, 2003.

Masud-Piloto, Félix. *From Welcomed Exiles to Illegal Immigrants: Cuban Migration to the U.S., 1959–1995*. Lanham, Md.: Rowman and Littlefield, 1996.

Morley, Morris, and Chris McGillion. *Unfinished Business: America and Cuba after the Cold War, 1989–2001*. Cambridge, UK: Cambridge University Press, 2002.

Rodríguez Chávez, Ernesto. *Cuban Migration Today*. Havana, Cuba: Editorial José Martí, 1999.

Torres, María de los Angeles. *In the Land of Mirrors*. Ann Arbor: University of Michigan Press, 1999.

FÉLIX MASUD-PILOTO

BANDA. *Banda* (band) is a generic term for a variety of ensembles consisting of brass, woodwind, and percussion instruments found throughout Spain's former colonies. Banda is a pure male tradition; there are no female performers (except for a couple of *ranchera* singers who also sing with banda accompaniment); there are no female musicians or groups. In the mid-1800s civilian bands were introduced into every European colony, where they took root and flourished in their new environment. The so-called *bandas populares* (popular bands or village bands) or *bandas de viento* (wind bands) were ubiquitous features of Mexico's musical life in the late nineteenth century and thrived in both rural and urban areas. The instrumentation of early village bands, however, was variable. Around the beginning of the twentieth century, specific combinations of brass, woodwind, and percussion instruments evolved in different regions of Mexico. The revolutionary movement of the first two decades of the twentieth century was crucial in the development of the bands' regional characteristics inasmuch as it was a major impetus to both patriotism and regionalism. After the Mexican Revolution, the lineup in regional bands became more and more standardized.

Regional Bands

Among the many regional bands, *banda sinaloense* (Sinaloan band) stands out, as this type gained a reputa-tion in the international popular music market at the close of the twentieth century. The ensemble dates back to the military bands of European colonists and to the brass music of German immigrants to Mexico's northern Pacific coast in the mid-nineteenth century. After its consolidation in the early twentieth century, band membership in Sinaloa averaged from nine to twelve musicians playing clarinets, cornets or trumpets, trombones with valves, saxhorns (commonly called *armonía* or *charcheta*), tuba, snare drum (*tarola*), and *tambora*, a double-headed bass drum with attached cymbals. Though the brass and reed instruments were imported from Europe, the drums were manufactured locally.

Bandas performed at various outdoor celebrations—bullfights, cockfights, horse races, parades, saints' days, weddings, funerals, and fandangos (popular dances). Like the military bands of that time, bandas populares played an eclectic repertory of marches, operatic selections, and popular pieces. Since their beginnings in the late nineteenth century, bandas populares have been shunned by the upper classes, labeled as "vulgar" and "backward." Although brass band music had long served as one of the educated classes' favorite pastimes, bandas eventually became associated with lower-class music, rejected by the elite as a crude imitation of their venerable military bands by ignorant peasants who could do no better. Banda musicians' low social status was related to the alleged low quality of their music and to the rather disreputable locales where some of them found work. Urbanization, capitalism, and eventually the culture industry altered Sinaloa's society, lifestyles, habits, and popular musical tastes, but bandas remained popular among the rural population and the lower-class urbanites throughout the twentieth century.

In the 1920s *orquestas* (orchestras with predominantly stringed instruments) throughout Mexico began to adjust to music from the United States by replacing the traditional double bass with the tuba, integrating a percussion set, and adding such instruments as saxophone and banjo. This new formation became known as the jazz band. Inspired by these new trends in popular music, Sinaloan bandas too began to play the new upper-class ballroom dances of the time, the fox-trot, the Charleston, and the tango.

The main appeal of the banda was and continues to be its danceable music, which includes a variety of rhythms, ranging from the local *son*, *guaracha*, polka, waltz, and schottische to fox-trot, Cuban *danzón*, bolero, cha-cha, mambo, and *cumbia*. Unaffected by the developing radio, film, and recording industries of the early 1930s that revolutionized Mexico's musical world, Banda musicians continued to play in their traditional surroundings; they also found ample work in the cantinas (bars and brothels) of the lower-class urban neighborhoods.

In the 1950s and 1960s some of those who had moved to the cities of Mazatlán and Culiacán eventually became involved with the newer technological media—radio and recordings. To broaden their appeal, a few leaders with entrepreneurial spirit began to modify the makeup of the traditional banda by incorporating such new elements as Cuban percussion instruments (bongo drums, maracas, and *cencerros* [shakers and cowbells]), slide trombones, and saxophones. These commercially oriented bandas, known as banda-orquestas, performed a more cosmopolitan repertory of mainstream dance music and popular international pieces, such as big band mambo. A more polished and precise playing style was aspired to, and note-reading skills became more important for professional musicians. Although the big band jazz and mambo era left its imprint, banda kept a distinct character usually referred to as *sabor sinaloense* (Sinaloan flavor). This character results from the contrast of clarinet and brass timbres, the juxtaposition of tutti-soli (that is, an alternation between the whole banda and the individual instrument groups of the front line: trumpets, trombones, and clarinets), and the improvisation of countermelodies on one of the frontline instruments, a technique often used while accompanying vocalists. There is a strong emphasis on volume and pulse. Dynamics is mainly generated by alternating tutti and soli sections, the latter executed on the frontline instruments.

Addition of Technology

In the mid-1980s a *grupo* version of the acoustic *banda sinaloense* emerged in Guadalajara (the grupo ensemble, including synthesized instruments and a lead vocalist, plays easy-listening Mexican and international pop ballads and is one of Mexico's commercially most successful forms of popular music). This fusion became known as *tecnobanda* (technobanda) or simply banda. Although technobanda retained the trumpets, trombones, and percussion instruments and saxophones may have been added, the characteristic *tambora* (double-headed bass drum with attached cymbals) and the clarinets were eliminated, and the traditional tuba and *charchetas* (horns) were replaced with electric bass and keyboard synthesizer. Because of these changes in the instrumentation, a typical technobanda consists of seven to eleven musicians only (compared to fourteen to seventeen musicians of a traditional, acoustic Sinaloan banda). With profound roots in regional Mexican music, technobanda was highly innovative on its own. The integration of a vocalist allowed technobanda to develop a new and independent repertory. Technobanda and its associated *quebradita* dance style spread in the late 1980s from Guadalajara, Jalisco, to Los Angeles, California, where it gained great popularity among immigrants as well as U.S.–born

youths of Mexican heritage. Crucial for technobanda's success was the emergence of new Spanish-language FM radio stations that aired a variety of Mexican music with rural roots.

The demand for both recorded and live music grew rapidly. Record labels soon competed with each other to sign promising new groups, chief among them Banda Machos, Banda Maguey, and Banda Arkángel R-15. The vibrant and youthful new style was electrifying, and the quebradita dancing fever spread rapidly throughout Latin dance halls in Mexican Los Angeles and the Southwest. The name "quebradita" came from the dance's most characteristic gesture, "the little break," in which the male dancer dips his partner with a sudden but controlled movement into a backward bend. Like other dance crazes, the quebradita came along with a characteristic style of dress, the *vaquero* (cowboy) attire. But jeans, boots, hat, and the various accessories that explicitly demonstrated regional and national identities were more than a fashion statement. The quebradita dress style helped forge unity among the participants and at the same time expressed difference and social boundaries. The newfound confidence and pride in one's ethnic roots expressed in dancing, music, and dress style was encouraged by California's prevailing anti-immigrant climate of the early 1990s. Propositions such as "Save Our State" and "English Only" made not only recent immigrants feel unwelcome in California. Longtime Latino and Latina residents and Mexican Americans of several generations were also faced with growing resentments, open hostility, and hardly disguised racism. As young people of Mexican descent became more sensitive to racial discrimination and exploitation, they began to take an increased interest in their own, their parents', and their grandparents' heritage and traditions. Banda music was something new for a generation of Mexicans who had grown up listening to mainstream rock and rap music. The musical replenishment from south of the border encouraged them to reaffirm and to bolster their ethnic particularities and to express their cultural loyalty.

By the mid-1990s a large number of young Latinos and Latinas engaged in technobanda and quebradita as cultural affirmation. For many individuals who sensed their ambiguous social position as Chicanos and Chicanas in the United States, the participation in banda events was an alternative musical activity that also affirmed their political standing. In sum, accelerating processes of globalization, including mass mediaization and transmigration, helped the growing acceptance and popularity of technobanda and banda in the United States. *Billboard*, the U.S. magazine for popular music, declared 1993 as "the banda year" (without making a distinction between technobanda and acoustic Sinaloan banda). After its success in the United States, technobanda flowed back to Mexico and was eventually embraced by Mexico City and its culture industries. The early-twenty-first century's transnational, commercially oriented Sinaloan bandas, such as Banda El Recodo and Banda La Costeña, have included many of technobanda's innovations, in particular a lead vocalist. With an emphasis on the visual and the verbal and a shift in their musical repertory toward the more universally appealing and danceable cumbia and the romantic *balada*, high-profile Sinaloan bandas entered the circuit of commercial popular mass music.

Influence of Drugs

Banda's growing popularity north of the border was not only triggered by the technobanda craze, it was also a result of its appropriation of the *narcocorrido* (a ballad that narrates the adventurous life of drug traffickers), which originally belonged to the repertory of the *conjunto norteño* (an accordion-based ensemble type from northern Mexico). The flourishing business with narcocorridos in Los Angeles nightclubs and recording studios began around 1990. The Sinaloan singer and songwriter Chalino Sánchez, who immortalized and embodied the narco-subculture that encompasses both the United States and Mexico, was largely responsible for this development. In order to be competitive in an international music market, renowned Sinaloan bandas began to focus more and more on the reinterpretation of this repertory. By the late 1990s *narcomúsica* (music related to drug trafficking or traffickers) had become popular among a predominantly young Spanish-speaking audience—not just in the regions where cultivation of marijuana is prevalent but also in the cities north of the border where traffickers make a fortune by selling the illegal goods. The commercially most successful bands that play the narco-repertory—the accordion-based *norteño* groups Los Tigres del Norte, Los Tucanes de Tijuana, and Banda El Recodo—all originate from Sinaloa, a state with a long history of cultivating and trading drugs.

Narco-music is a fast-growing business, notably in the United States, where big music corporations sign promising narco-bands and where Grammy Awards officially recognize and validate this type of popular music. In the early twenty-first century commercial narco-music brings in the sounds, images, values, and language from a rural, premodern culture and mixes them with the technology and aesthetics of an urban, postmodern culture. This syncretic fusion of traditional elements and contemporary features is an expression of its creators' and listeners' own senses of identity. A decade after Sánchez's death, a handful of young, mostly U.S.–born singers from Greater Los Angeles transcended his legacy and created a raw but urban sound that appeals to a young audience that derives its social conventions, fashions, and aspirations

from both the narco-world and the American youth culture. Chief among them is Lupillo Rivera, whose CD *Despreciado* (2001) was listed by *Billboard* magazine as the fifth best-selling Latin music album in 2001.

The driving force of Sinaloan banda music and its strength to cope with changing fashions and cultural trends can be ascribed to its versatility and adaptability. Although banda music became less community centered and more universally appealing when bandas began to record for a mass market and perform stage shows for a transnational mass audience in the late 1990s, it has not lost its regional flavor. Similarly technobanda remained rooted in local identity, categorized by the record industry as "regional Mexican," despite its eclectic mixing, stylistic borrowing, and efforts to expand to a more global market.

See also Music, Popular *and* Norteño.

BIBLIOGRAPHY

Flores Gastélum, Manuel. *Historia de la música popular en Sinaloa.* Culiacán, Sinaloa, Mexico: Dirección de Investigación y Fomento de Cultura Regional, 1980.

Quiñones, Sam. "The Ballad of Chalino Sánchez." In *True Tales from Another Mexico: The Lynch Mob, the Popsicle Kings, Chalino, and the Bronx,* edited by Sam Quinones. Albuquerque: University of New Mexico Press, 2001.

Simonett, Helena. *Banda: Mexican Musical Life across Borders.* Middletown, Conn.: Wesleyan University Press, 2001.

Simonett, Helena. *En Sinaloa nací: Historia de la música de banda.* Mazatlán, Sinaloa, Mexico: Asociación de Gestores del Patrimonio Histórico y Cultural de Mazatlán, 2004.

Wald, Elijah. *Narcocorrido: A Journey into the Music of Drugs, Guns, and Guerrillas.* New York: Rayo, 2001.

HELENA SIMONETT

BAPTISM. *See* Bautizo.

BARBIE. *See* Puerto Rican Barbie.

BARRAZA, SANTA, artist. Santa Barraza's career mirrors her commitment to recording her personal history as a descendant of people of the Texas borderlands and to interpreting that history as an archetype of cultural experience. As a feminist artist, muralist, academic, and activist, she has explored the history and mythologies that connect the past and present realities of the border experience.

Born in Kingsville, Texas, to a family with deep roots in the Texas borderlands and specifically the King Ranch area, Barraza grew up with a deep awareness of the relationships between land and peoples and the conflicting worlds of the border. Those conflicts—economic, political, national, and geographic—have been the source of her art, and the landscape itself, which for her is timeless, is her *Popol Vuh*, her creation myth.

Barraza entered Texas Arts and Industry University in 1969 with the intention of majoring in mathematics. An art history course on pre-Columbian and Mexican art and a printmaking course changed her academic plans. Moreover she became involved with the nascent Chicano/a movement, the antiwar movement, and the feminist movement. Her fellow students included the artists Amado Peña and Carmen Lomas Garza and the activist José Angel Gutiérrez. Her art studies led her in 1971 to the University of Texas at Austin, where she studied with Jacinto Quirarte, the first art historian to offer a course in Mexican American art.

Barraza exhibited her work during her senior year through her fellow artist César Martínez, who organized exhibitions of Chicano and Chicana art in alternative spaces, given the lack of acceptance for this work in mainstream galleries and museums. After she earned her BFA, Barraza worked as a graphic designer, encouraged by Garza. By 1976 Barraza was invited to join an association of Chicano and Chicana visual artists, Los Quemados (The Burnt Out), an offshoot of the earlier Con Safos group, based in Austin and San Antonio, Texas. Los Quemados consisted of seven males and four females, including Peña, Martínez, and Garza. But upon the departure of the last, Barraza felt outnumbered by the males. With Nora González-Dodson, an artist she had met at the University of Texas at Austin, Barraza founded Mujeres Artistas del Suroeste (MAS), and the group had its first exhibition in 1976. In 1979 MAS and the League of United Chicano Artists (LUCHA), a cultural center at Juarez-Lincoln University in Austin, organized the Conferencia Plástica Chicana, the first encounter to include Chicano and Chicana and Mexican American visual artists, North American art historians, and Mexican visual artists and art historians.

The conference and the ensuing discussions led Barraza to enroll in the graduate program in studio art at the University of Texas at Austin. However, her first proposal, a three-dimensional fiberglass mural, was rejected because murals were not deemed art. Barraza persevered, and while pursuing her studies, she opened Diseño Studios, a gallery and studio. In 1981, in conjunction with José Treviño, a fellow artist who shared the studio, she began a series of exhibitions, the first of which was La Lupe, con Safos, c/s, in honor of the Virgin of Guadalupe. The concept began a new direction in Barraza's exploration of cultural imagery. She began a teaching career in Austin, and in 1990 she accepted a position at Pennsylvania State University. Continuing to integrate printmaking with drawing and painting, she fused lithographs with collage and stitching, concentrating on images of women, specifically the Virgin of Guadalupe, Coatlicue, and Soldaderas. In 1990 the university awarded Barraza a grant to do research on Mexican imagery, particularly the Guadalupana (imagery and iconography of the Virgin of Guadalupe). She traveled to Mexico City, where she began to incorporate *retablo* (altarpiece) painting into her aesthetic vision. In 1993 she won a Reader's Digest Lila Wallace Grant to study religious iconography in Oaxaca, Mexico. Also that year she became an associate professor at the Art Institute of Chicago. In 1994 Barraza organized a series of workshops for elementary and high school students in collaboration with the Mexican Fine Arts Center Museum as part of the Reader's Digest Lila Wallace Grant.

In 1995 Barraza worked on Entre Americas: El Taller Nepantla in Saratoga, California. Directed by the writer Gloria Anzaldúa, the project focused on exploring *nepantla*, a Nahuatl word Anzaldúa defined as "an in-between state . . . traveling from the present identity into a new identity." This project initiated the discourse on the mutilated Mechica moon goddess, Coyolhauhqui, as a focus for retelling and reinterpreting the narratives about controversial female figures like La Llorona and La Malinche. Barraza created a series of works exploring the narratives from this viewpoint, including *Cenote* (Sacred Well; 1995), which brought together images responding to personal memories, stories, and cultural mythologies.

In 1996 and 1997 Barraza was commissioned to create two murals for the Biosciences Building at the University of Texas at San Antonio in collaboration with Alice Adams, the New York–based artist. Incorporating concepts, forms, structures, and images from preconquest codices and petrographs, these murals combine three forms, the codex, the mural, and the retablo.

Barraza subsequently became chair of the Department of Art at Texas A&M University in Kingsville. She has continued to explore the painterly world she has created, using a vibrant palette and a flat surface reminiscent of the ex-voto and retablo, often incorporating photographs into her work. Barraza is a rare combination of artist-teacher who grows and develops even as she proffers herself to her students and her community. She married but divorced and has one daughter, Andrea.

See also **Anzaldúa, Gloria; Gutiérrez, José Angel; Lomas Garza, Carmen; Llorona, La;** *and* **Virgen de Guadalupe.**

BIBLIOGRAPHY
Barraza, Santa Contreras. "Manifestations of the Struggling Inner Force." MFA thesis, University of Texas at Austin, 1982.
Herrera-Sobek, Maria, ed. *Santa Barraza, Artist of the Borderlands.* College Station: Texas A&M University Press, 2001.
Santa Barraza: March 8–April 11, 1992. Exhibition catalog from Galería Posada, Sacramento. Sacramento, Calif.: La Raza/Galéria Posada, 1992.

MARGARITA NIETO

BARRERA, AÍDA, television producer and author. Aída Nydia Barrera has been a pioneer in the development of bilingual children's television programming. Born in Rio Grande City, Texas, Barrera grew up in various South Texas towns. She discovered at an early age through her family and her surroundings the cultural and social borderless connections between Mexico and the United States. However, while studying in a mostly white Catholic school in Edinburg, Texas, she became acutely aware of the ethnic, racial, cultural, and linguistic distinctions that divided Mexican Americans and white Americans. Barrera's experiences as a bilingual Mexican American child in the still racially segregated Texas of the 1940s and 1950s left an indelible mark that influenced her future career as a television producer and as an educator.

In 1962, after Barrera completed her bachelor's degree in journalism at the University of Texas at Austin, KLRN (the Austin–San Antonio Public Broadcasting Service [PBS] station) hired her to create a series of Spanish-English instructional programs for children. From 1962 to 1968 Barrera conceptualized, produced, wrote, and performed sixty to ninety programs a year for KLRN. In 1970, after two years of navigating through the federal bureaucracy, Barrera gained funds for *Carrascolendas*, a thirty-minute bilingual show targeting Latino and Latina children. Initially aired on Texas PBS stations (1970–1972), *Carrascolendas* became the first bilingual children's television program broadcast nationally (1972–1976). Barrera served as the creator, executive producer, writer, and actress for this innovative children's musical comedy program. *Carrascolendas* was also pathbreaking in that Barrera assembled a multiethnic staff that included Cuban Americans, Puerto Ricans, and Mexican Americans as part of both the technical crew and the on-camera talent.

AÍDA BARRERA.

CARRASCOLENDAS. Uncle Andy the Shoemaker and friends. (*Austin Chronicle*)

Although *Carrascolendas* has been considered Barrera's most important contribution in the area of children's television, her professional accomplishments have transcended the realm of children's programming. She created and served as the executive producer of the PBS and National Public Radio (NPR) series *Checking It Out* (1982), a newsmagazine television and radio show centered on Latino and Latina communities across the United States. Barrera also conceptualized, produced, and served as the commentator of NPR's *Sabor del pueblo* (1982–1983), which focused on Mexican American folklore. Additionally, Barrera created and produced the PBS documentary series *Somebody Else's Place* (1986), which addressed ethnic and race relations in the United States. As a television producer she has received numerous national and international awards.

Alongside her career as a media professional, Barrera pursued graduate studies at the Lyndon B. Johnson School of Public Affairs at the University of Texas at Austin and the Woodrow Wilson School of Public and International Affairs at Princeton University. In 1992 she earned a doctoral degree in American Studies from the University of Texas at Austin. Barrera has held academic positions at universities in the United States, Mexico,

Ecuador, Brazil, and the Dominican Republic. In 2001 Barrera published her first book, *Looking for* Carrascolendas: *From a Child's World to Award-Winning Television*, and she is working on a second book, *The Mysterious Death of Irene Garza: Forty Years of Community Voices*.

See also Bilingualism and Biculturalism; Carrascolendas; *and* Media and Latino Identity.

BIBLIOGRAPHY

Barrera, Aída. *Looking for* Carrascolendas: *From a Child's World to Award-Winning Television*. Louann Atkins Temple Women and Culture Series. Austin: University of Texas Press, 2001.

Berkman, Dave. "Minorities in Public Broadcasting." *Journal of Communication* (Summer 1980): 178–188.

Mayer, Vicki. *Producing Dreams, Consuming Youth: Mexican Americans and Mass Media*. New Brunswick, N.J.: Rutgers University Press, 2003.

Noriega, Chon A. *Shot in America: Television, the State, and the Rise of Chicano Cinema*. Minneapolis: University of Minnesota Press, 2000.

Williams, Frederick, and Geraldine Van Wart. Carrascolendas: *Bilingual Education through Television*. New York: Praeger, 1974.

YEIDY M. RIVERO

BARRETTO, RAY (b. 1929), salsa and jazz musician. Ray Barretto was born in April 1929, in Brooklyn, New York, to Puerto Rican parents. He was raised in Spanish Harlem ("El Barrio") and the Bronx, where he learned firsthand the pressures of "urban ghetto culture." In an effort to escape the low-income reality of the New York Puerto Rican community, he joined the army in 1946 at the tender age of seventeen. While in Munich, Germany, Barretto discovered a deep love for music after hearing "Manteca" by the jazz trumpeter Dizzy Gillespie with Latin *conguero* Chano Pozo. Years earlier, his mother had introduced him to Latin music, such as the bolero, *danza*, and *plena*, as well as to the big-band sounds of Tommy Dorsey and Glenn Miller, but his introduction to "CuBop" (a mixture of Cuban Afro-Caribbean rhythms and bebop) was what inspired him to transform himself into the world-renowned percussionist known as "Las Manos Duras" (Hard Hands).

After returning home in 1949 from his stint of military service abroad, Barretto dedicated himself to learning the diverse musical articulations of the conga drum, taking lessons and jamming with some of the greatest figures in both jazz and Latin music. He began his musical career playing in pickup bands and jamming with whoever would give him a gig. His first big break came in 1957, when he was asked to replace the percussionist Mongo Santamaría on Tito Puente's now-legendary album *Dance Mania*. Through his perseverance and good work, Barretto gradually built up a reputation as one of the top percussionists in both Latin and jazz music.

In 1961, Barretto was approached by Riverside Records to organize his own band, Charanga la Moderna, and record his first album, *Barretto para Bailar/Pachanga with Barretto*. In 1962, on the heels of his success on Riverside Records, Barretto switched to Tico Records and released the album *Charanga Moderna*, which contained the hit single "El Watusi." The Watusi became a short-lived craze of the mid-1960s, like other examples of "Latin soul" such as the jala jala, the boogaloo, and the shing-a-ling, all of which combined Spanish and English lyrics and mixed

RAY BARRETTO. The artist performs at the Nice Jazz Festival in 1996. (© Amet Jean Pierre/Corbis Sygma)

Latin rhythms and instruments with the instruments, melodies, and technologies of music popular in the United States. Barretto modernized charanga's flute- and violin-dominated sound by adding brass to the instrumentation while covering rock and pop tunes, as in his 1966 album *Señor 007*. Between 1963 and 1966, Barretto recorded eight albums in this mixed stylistic vein, but it wasn't until 1967, when he signed with the Fania Records label, that he began to enjoy wider recognition for his work.

Barretto's first album for Fania, *Acid* (1968), was heralded as "mind-expanding." Its hip mixture of Latin, jazz, and soul music allowed a diverse group of people access to the cultural revolution of the late 1960s. *Acid* was to mark the beginning of a string of hit albums for Fania Records from 1968 until 1975. Barretto was in the forefront of the Fania-led revolution in Latin music—salsa. His work with the Fania All-Stars is legendary, and his musical contributions at that time are some of the most memorable of the era. During this period, he worked with a plethora of talented musicians and vocalists. His first notable vocalist was Adalberto Santiago, who sang with Barretto from 1966 until 1972; Tito Allen replaced Santiago from 1972 until 1975.

Allen's stint with Barretto was especially notable because he was the lead vocalist on Barretto's 1973 hit *Indestructible*. The title song was important in the civil rights–initiated Puerto Rican Power Movement of the late 1960s and 1970s, which developed a sense of pride, respect, and love within the Puerto Rican diaspora living in the United States. The song's call to the blood of young people as an indestructible force in the face of an overwhelmingly powerful opposing force served as a rallying cry for Puerto Ricans throughout the struggle—especially young people, ranging from gang members and student radicals to Vietnam vets and many others from within the multitude of Puerto Rican barrios in the United States and Puerto Rico. And songs such as "El Hijo de Obatalá" (Obatala's Child), which also appeared on *Indestructible*, were a direct call to Puerto Ricans to recognize and be proud of their African heritage. In fact, throughout Barretto's "salsa repertoire" there are a number of songs that challenged the status quo. Songs such as "Quítate la máscara" (Take Off Your Mask) and "Hipocresía y falsedad" (Hypocrisy and Falsehood) question the nature of all relationships, from the smallest and most intimate to those at the larger, systemic level.

After Barretto dismantled his salsa band in 1975, he moved into his other musical love—jazz. In 1977, he released his debut album with Atlantic Records, *Barretto Live: Tomorrow*, a two-disc recording of his concert at the Beacon Theatre, New York, in May 1976. This "crossover" album meant that Barretto was one of Fania's few musi-

cians who were "big" enough to merit a special two-year agreement between Atlantic Records and Fania Records, which was famous for maintaining strict and exclusive business contracts with all of its artists.

Because of a hand injury, Barretto took a break from music from 1978 until 1979, when he reunited with Adalberto Santiago to record *Rican/Struction* for Fania in 1979. Beginning in 1968, he had recorded off and on for Fania Records, producing such hit albums as *Hard Hands* (1968), *Together* (1970), *From the Beginning* (1971), *Message* (1972), *Barretto Power* (1972), *Cocinando* (Cooking, 1972), and *The Other Road* (1973). His final recording for Fania came in 1989 with *Irresistible*. Since the 1990s, Barretto has focused his efforts on playing with his newest band, New World Spirit, and on demonstrating his ability to play jazz "straight ahead" or with a Latin flavor.

See also Fania All-Stars *and* Music, Popular.

ADAM A. PAGÁN

BARRIOS. With certain national variations, the Spanish word *barrio* refers to any distinguishable section (commercial, industrial, or residential) of a larger urban community. In the United States, the term typically identifies Latino residential and commercial districts, mostly working class and poorer, often located in the inner city, and relatively densely populated. They are also ethnic "minority" districts in comparison to the whole urban population, except for those cities, primarily in the southwestern border states, in which Latinas and Latinos are a majority. Barrios also have a subjective status in peoples' minds as distinct cultural zones. This subjective perception may be reinforced geographically, since they are often across rivers, railroad tracks, and urban infrastructure from the rest of the city. Additionally, historical practices of de jure and de facto residential segregation have isolated barrio residents socially from their cities at large. The best-known barrios are those of Greater East Los Angeles, with a population of mostly Mexican descent, and those of the South Bronx, with a population of Caribbean, primarily Puerto Rican, origin. Less widely known but historically significant are such barrios as the Westside in San Antonio, the Mission in San Francisco, El Barrio (Spanish Harlem) in New York City, Little Village and Pilsen in Chicago, the Calle Ocho district in Miami, El Segundo Barrio in El Paso, and the central-southside barrios of Tucson and Albuquerque.

From outside, barrios are generally considered foreign places in the city. If this difference is seen as exotic, outsiders may visit for ethnic shopping, dining, or cultural events. More negatively, barrios are demonized as dangerous slums. Similarly, barrio residents' own views reveal

GHOSTS OF THE BARRIO. Mural by Wayne Healy in the Ramona Gardens section of East Los Angeles. (Latin Focus Photo Agency)

contrasting attitudes. If they internalize the negative imagery, they may feel uncomfortable or unwelcome in other urban districts. Alternately, the feeling of difference can produce a strong cultural and territorial identification.

Although barrios are distinct areas, they are closely linked to the political economy of the cities that contain them. Their typical geographical centrality, population density, and class status combine to maintain a readily accessible, low-wage labor force. In spite of—or because of—their necessary labor, barrio communities are socially marginal in their urban contexts, as structural conditions hinder their general political and economic advancement. These conditions include racially restrictive and biased housing policies, electoral gerrymandering, separate and inferior educational resources, two-tiered wage scales, and stigmatization by the police and the judicial system. When monumental urban renewal and highway construction projects gained steam in the mid-twentieth century, many long-settled barrios were razed in the name of the greater public good. Additionally, continuing in-migration more than offsets the growing number of Latinas and Latinos who have moved out of the barrios. So, even as Latinas and Latinos have historically shown some social mobility, the barrios continue to exist and experience the effects of their historical subordination—poverty, crime, arrests, incarceration, youth pregnancy, drug use, and gang activity.

Yet these negative indicators do not tell the whole story. Barrio communities have positive qualities that help offset problems. The awareness of a common social condition within a larger, often hostile, urban milieu produces a certain solidarity. Its expressions range from the sharing of information and resources to the allocation of housing, to bartering for services in lieu of payment. These networks of assistance circulate the social capital essential to communities with limited economic capital. In the best case, these informal strategies inspire or reinforce bonds of communal identity. Early in barrio history, these practices led to the formation of community benevolent or protective societies, mutual aid groups, and cultural or religious associations. Such organizations drew on the same ethos of everyday cooperation. Formal community groups also generated institutional structures that provided public leadership training and organizational experience for residents. Such formal and informal self-help strategies are continuing elements in barrio culture.

The sharing of common space in the barrio also allows practices of public culture and community identity to emerge, by facilitating (or forcing) conversation, recreation, and a sense of familiarity or belonging in the neighborhood. Whether sitting on stoops or talking out windows in the apartment blocks of East Harlem or chatting across shared fences in the front yards of East Los Angeles, daily barrio life blurs the lines between the public and private domains of street and home. The well-being felt in such informal settings is expanded during formal occasions of public ceremony or festivity, often tied to Latin American civic or religious holidays. On these occasions, the display and consumption of culture through music, dance, oratory, food, games, and sports publicly promotes shared ethnic tastes, values, and social history.

Of course, even as barrio residents gather in leisure, drugs may be traded down the street, or a gunshot blast may signal a very different kind of contact. Obviously the public culture of the barrio cannot be romanticized. However, the debilitating behaviors and conditions that do exist are too often singled out to represent barrio culture in the larger public imagination through mainstream journalism, film, television, literature, and music. For most of the twentieth century, these media, and the barrio imagery they propagate, had no effective input from the barrios themselves. Thus, the barrios' image in the broader culture has largely been a chronicle of dysfunction and pathology.

The Early Period: Between World Wars

The earliest external representations of barrio residents came from reports and studies by Anglo-American reformers and investigators that evaluated the potential for assimilation among recent Mexican immigrants in California in the 1920s and 1930s. Their principal theme was the perceived maladjustment of Mexicans to the norms of the American culture, supported by a checklist of cultural or racial traits that would stereotype barrio residents for decades to come as dirty, lazy, clannish, prone to violence, intellectually inferior, non–goal oriented, and superstitious.

But while reformers and sociologists were considering the nature of the "Mexican problem," and later the Puerto Rican variety, the barrios were publicly representing their own experiences, feelings, and ideas through journalism and music. With a mostly immigrant audience, early Latino newspapers favored homeland news. But internal barrio concerns were also reported and interpreted. Editorials rebutted specific insults of the Anglo-American press and other institutions and promoted the virtues of the various Latino cultures. In Los Angeles and elsewhere, the early journalism of the barrio scene was published in cities with substantial Latina and Latino populations. In New York, Puerto Rican *cronista* (chronicle writer) Jesús Colón commented on local and global issues from the 1920s through the 1960s, first in the Spanish-language press, then in English.

Music was also a vital medium for early barrio residents. Homeland music was broadcast on Spanish-language radio programs, sold in stores, and played in restaurants, dance halls, and homes. Radio personalities were barrio celebrities, sometimes using their medium to engage with social issues, as Pedro J. Gonzalez did in 1920s and 1930s Los Angeles. Popular song forms like the Mexican *corrido* and the Caribbean *son* often described experiences of barrio residents confronting their new world. Through song, Latinas and Latinos gave public voice to their concerns and cultures.

The Middle Period: World War II to the 1960s

At this time, the supposed "problem" of the barrios assumed a more aggressive form, as newspapers and film discovered the selling power of inner-city criminality. "Juvenile delinquency" crossed ethnic lines, but black and brown gangs sent a special chill down the spine of Middle America, who imagined wild packs or incipient armies of colored man-children roaming urban streets. The depth of white America's antipathy was demonstrated, in full view of the national and international press, in the Zoot Suit Riots of 1943, the most spectacular of them in Los Angeles. For several nights, under the blind eye of police and inspired by misguided patriotism and inflammatory journalism about Mexican gang crime waves, white civilians and servicemen assaulted young Chicanos and Chicanas, not all of whom were gang members or wore zoot suits. In the dominant view, youth delinquency was just one indicator of the barrio's general slum degeneracy. It supported the ideas of urban planners who would soon clear many of the barrios for urban renewal and highway construction projects. As a Broadway hit and then a 1961 film, *West Side Story* offered another mass vision of Latino delinquency. In a telling coincidence, the actual New York street set for the film was in the ruins of a historic West Side barrio razed by urban renewal. Delinquency and blight were buzzwords for the barrios, and bulldozers were icons for this period of aggression against their communities.

While their barrios were under siege, Latinas and Latinos continued to represent their own perspectives. Now more locally focused, barrio journalists responded to the images and assaults of the media, police, and urban planners, as when Jesús Colón denounced *West Side Story* in an English-language *cronica*. It would take another generation for a full-fledged barrio-centric literature to emerge, but the seeds were there. In the late 1940s Mario Suarez published several vignettes in the *Arizona Quarterly*. He portrayed characters and events in the Tucson barrios from an affectionate and opinionated native perspective. His account of the *pachucos* (youthful urban "toughs" or hipsters, and sometimes gang members) and zoot suiters, for example, is critical but not pathological. Though not Latina herself, Beatrice Griffith offered in *American Me* (1948) a remarkably varied consideration of Los Angeles Chicana and Chicano youth, including pachucos and pachucas, during the zoot suit era. Critics have faulted the authors' narratives of victimization, but the protagonists are drawn with full personalities and clear voices, although within a restricted, almost naturalistic environment. In José Antonio Villarreal's 1959 novel *Pocho*, the identity-conflicted, non-barrio Chicano protagonist briefly explores the barrio, noting its earthy and informal pleasures. Along the way, he encounters young pachucos who attract him with their confident nonconformity while alienating him with their apparent fatalism.

Music continued to be central to the cultural identity of the barrio and its expression. "Pachuco boogie" emerged in postwar southwestern barrios. The notable recordings of Don Tosti, with the Pachuco Boogie Boys, and Lalo Guerrero wedded traditional Mexican, popular American, Latino Caribbean, and black jazz and rhythm and blues styles. Its meter, melody, and lyrics reflected the creative multicultural synthesis of language, fashion, and dance being crafted by barrio youth.

Nationally, the rising popularity of "tropical" musical styles allowed genres like rumba, *plena*, *guaguanco*, and *guaracha*, which emerged primarily in the barrios of the Caribbean islands and New York City, to both enhance barrio culture and entertain the world. So even as the "problem" of Puerto Ricans now emerged in full force, corresponding to their massive postwar migration, the American public eagerly consumed their popular rhythms and melodies. Lyrics often celebrated the vitality of the barrios. In "La gente del Bronx" (The Folks in the Bronx) and "Como se goza en el barrio" (It's a Blast in the barrio) (1953), Arsenio Rodriguez, the renowned Cuban *conjunto* (small band) leader, praised the predominantly Puerto Rican enclaves in East Harlem and the Bronx, noting that "los que viven en downtown vienen a gozar en el barrio" (those who live downtown come to the barrio to enjoy themselves). A genre of urban *jibaro* (mountain peasant) songs emerged in the late 1950s, often documenting the quirks of life in the new city environment, with titles like "Culpando el subway" (Blame It on the Subway) and "Un jibaro en New York."

The Contemporary Period: 1965 to the Present

Beginning in the mid-1960s, white suburbanites watched, with concern or terror, as barrios and ghettos erupted in a series of urban insurrections (riots, school walkouts, demonstrations) to protest their continuing neglect and degradation. By the early 1980s, the most searing images of urban decline emerged from the barrio and ghetto districts of New York's South Bronx. Devastated by postindustrial economic and political abandonment in the 1970s and 1980s, its rows of gutted and torched apartment houses became a global image of inner-city devastation and the primal setting for popular cultural narratives about a new urban frontier of civilization and savagery. *Fort Apache, The Bronx* (1981) in cinema and *Bonfire of the Vanities* in both its novel (1987) and film (1990) versions portrayed the South Bronx as an urban wasteland of junkies, pimps, prostitutes, muggers, rapists, and other criminals or outcasts. On the West Coast, similar imagery emerged from Los Angeles's extensive black and Latino gang culture, now with the added menace of

Salvadoran sets or *clicas* coming out of their own territory in the newer Central American barrios. The earlier moral panic of juvenile delinquency is echoed and updated in such West Coast gang-banger films as *Colors* (1988) or *American Me* (1992) and more indirectly in *Falling Down* (1993).

But in the tense climate of the 1960s and early 1970s, barrio residents more actively confronted the dominant culture that subordinated them. New, invigorating ethnic nationalist identities emerged in the barrios, under the loose banner of Brown Power. Barrio artists who directly or indirectly supported the political *causas* (causes) through the early 1980s fueled a renaissance of barrio-centric expressive culture. Murals, new to the barrios, became a powerful medium for expressing community cultural ideals and social history. Los Angeles emerged as the capital of Latina and Latino mural production. San Francisco's pan-Latino Mission District, the overlapping Chicano and Puerto Rican barrios of Chicago, and the Boricua (Puerto Rican) heart of New York's Loisaida (Lower East Side) have also produced especially rich street galleries of wall art.

Multiple artistic activities were also coordinated in new barrio cultural *centros* (centers) that disbursed essential grant funds among different projects and hosted community *talleres* (workshops) in the arts. The works of writers, graphic artists, musicians, dancers, and actors were presented in regular arts events at the centros. Editorial collectives published many new literary and cultural journals in and about the barrios. *Flor y canto* (flower and song) festivals were early "spoken word" happenings, while smaller literary readings and informal artists' "salons" abounded. Anthologies published the diversity of the new barrio literary culture, exposing it to a potentially wider audience.

Poetry was the most popular form of expression, but writers in all genres produced barrio-based literature for the American cultural landscape. San Francisco, East Los Angeles, and New York were major centers. Facilitated by writers' groups like the Pocho Che Collective in the Mission, the East Los Angeles Barrio Writer's Workshop, and the Nuyorican Poets Café, Latina and Latino writers narrated to a hungry barrio audience and laid the groundwork for some of them to cross over into the literary mainstream. The New York writers stood out for their consistent thematic focus on the dramatic complexities of Puerto Rican barrio life. Beginning with Piri Thomas's autobiography, *Down These Mean Streets* (1967), over the next decade this generation published important works in every genre (novel, short story, poetry, and drama). Nuyorican writers were keen to represent both the objective social circumstances and the subjectively felt experiences and consciousness of their narrators and protagonists, as

LA TIENDITA

Every Latina and Latino neighborhood has a *tiendita*, a general store roughly equivalent to the corner store. In Mexican American communities it is the *tendajo* or *tendajito*, and in Puerto Rican communities, the bodega. In these days of Circle K or 7-Eleven, such "little stores" may be disappearing, but in the heart of the barrio, one can still find these family-owned stores. They often sell products at a much higher price than the chain stores like Kroger or Safeway and certainly higher than Wal-Mart. But the tienditas, like the *fruterías* (fruit stands or fruit stores), survive because they supply the community with a number of goods and services. In the tiendita one can find the basic necessities and also keep a running tab that is due on payday. In Laredo, Texas, as in many other communities, these tienditas evolved into full-fledged grocery stores, and in some cases offered small loans that would also be collected on payday. In the early 2000s, they also sell phone cards.

For Latino and Latina baby boomers, childhood memories of la tiendita elicit feelings of nostalgia for certain products, as well as for a time when the neighborhoods were almost independent commercial units where small businesses served the needs of the barrio. Because Mexican Americans were often segregated into their own neighborhoods, small businesses helped make the community a self-contained entity that invariably included a shoe store (often attached to a shoe repair shop), a barbershop, a beauty shop, a fruit stand, a *yerberia*, and a *molino* that sold corn *masa* and corn tortillas. Of these, only the tiendita has survived, for it is where a large variety of products—canned goods, pasta, cold cuts, bread, flour, eggs, and some produce—can be bought. Traditionally, flour tortillas were made at home; only in the 1970s did they become a commodity that could be bought in a store. In many midwestern cities where the Mexican community had settled from the migrant stream, there were certain women who made flour tortillas to sell from their homes to the increasing number of dual-income households where the woman no longer had time to prepare the daily ration of tortillas for the family meals.

All over the Southwest, the tienditas served a dual purpose: they made products available to people who often did not have transportation to, or were not allowed into, the larger grocery stores, and they were a center for the social interactions of the community. Young men usually gathered outside, and often the local artists painted murals on its walls. The tiendita supported a strong social structure and served as a focus for economic and social activity in the neighborhoods.

These small businesses constituted the base for a growing middle class in the 1940s and 1950s, as many families managed to grow very small enterprises, like a *raspa* stand or a small taco stand, into a full-fledged grocery store or restaurant. These entrepreneurial projects provided economic advantages for the children of these families, and many of them

went on to higher education. Among prominent Chicanos and Chicanas whose parents had such a business is Henry Cisneros, former mayor of San Antonio and secretary of Housing and Urban Development under President Clinton; his family's tiendita was a mainstay in San Antonio's west side barrio community. Although in most cases the owners of these stores were Mexican Americans, in Tucson the earliest tienditas were owned and operated by Chinese. Popular tradition holds that these Chinese business owners came from Mexico when Mexico told them to leave or be killed. They relocated to Arizona and set up their family-run stores that the barrio residents called "El Chino," and many remember buying Chinese delicacies as well as Mexican foods there.

In the early twenty-first century, variants of these multipurpose stores have sprung up wherever Latinos and Latinas live, especially where the Latino and Latina immigrant population is significant. These stores are often named after the family who owns them (Peñita's, Mama Luz's, or Dovalina's) or the place where the family came from (Tienda Latina Nuevo Leon or Zacatecas). Everywhere in the United States, these stores supply the Latino/Latina population with goods that they would find in their places of origin, such as brand names from Mexico and Central America. They also provide Spanish-language video rentals and can arrange for money to be sent via Western Union to the countries of origin. Often they also carry clothing, hats, shoes, and leather goods. If there is a large enough population, there may be a restaurant and a bakery along with the stores. But these larger *tiendas* are fairly recent, and although they resemble the older tienditas, they function in a different way within the market economy of their community.

Tienditas still function as a basic resource in the barrio. They offer staple foods such as tortillas, bread, milk, eggs, and a variety of canned goods. They also often have a well-stocked medical shelf with aspirin, Mexican products like Iodex, and traditional medicinal herbs such as chamomile and *yerbanis*. They may sell plumbing and basic carpentry needs, such as nails and screwdrivers. These stores also carry reading material, such as *Vanidades* or *Selecciones* (*Reader's Digest* in Spanish), the local Spanish-language newspaper such as *Rumbo* or *La Prensa* in San Antonio, or a few of the thousands of Latino and Latina newspapers such as *Hola Berks* in Reading, Pennsylvania. Along the border, they also sell newspapers and magazines from Mexico. Although mostly a phenomenon of small towns and cities, tienditas exist in cities and even in rural areas, where the tiendita may be operated out of someone's home. These cultural business institutions may someday cease to exist as the chain stores replace them. However, in view of the growing Latino and Latina population in the United States, it is unlikely to happen any time soon.

NORMA E. CANTÚ

shaped by barrio life. In the fiction of Nicolasa Mohr and the poetry of Sandra María Esteves, the specific experiences of barrio women were emphasized. This marked a significant new ideological turn in barrio cultural representation, and it was echoed in other contexts. Many critics say it was a decisive shift in which women would then

enlarge the scope of the issues that could and should be treated in Latino arts, not to mention in everyday life.

Coincident with the crippling effects of deindustrialization and Reaganomics in many barrios, the ideological fervor of ethnic power waned in the 1980s, but its cultural legacy did not. Many artists of the Brown Power or political movement period would become part of a new cultural sector of the national Latina and Latino community, still active in the early 2000s. Among them, a new generation of barrio artists produced innovative, expressive forms that sought to rebut the pathological image of urban decay. Hip-hop culture was born and raised in the interwoven black and Puerto Rican neighborhoods of the South Bronx in the late 1970s and early 1980s. Long before they reached MTV, its related arts of dance, scratch, rap, fashion, and graffiti were being perfected by competitive and cooperative play among African Americans, West Indian blacks, and Puerto Ricans. Its artistic and festive qualities were not entirely different from the barrio-based youth culture of the previous generation. But its gritty tone and style were of a new sort, less clearly inclined toward social critique. Nonetheless, the Afro-Rican arts of hip-hop expressed a deep creativity and aspiration to pleasure amidst despair. And in rap and graffiti, it could articulate, by direct or indirect allusion, critical insights about the wounded social milieu shared by the ghetto and barrio artists and their audience.

In the early twenty-first century, the variety and complexity of barrio-centric cultural expressions defy easy description. But some general trends can be noted. The call for critical self-scrutiny within barrio cultural practice, arguably introduced by women writers and artists, has not abated and has led, for example, to representations of gay and lesbian experience in barrios. New or previously unavailable media have been drafted into the cause of representing barrio culture and counteracting lingering stereotypes. Film, television, comedy, photography, graphic novels, comic strips, and the Internet have all added significantly to the existing repertoire of barrio expressive culture.

Finally, civil strife and globalization in Latin America continue to push new immigrants into existing and emerging barrios of the United States. There are now major barrios of Central Americans in Los Angeles and of Dominicans in New York. And although there have always been multinational Latino districts, such as the early barrios of Manhattan and San Francisco's Mission District since the 1950s, more of these will emerge, like the exceptionally diverse Jackson Heights community of Queens in New York. Today's barrios, like those of the past, are complex sites of Latino community formation, survival, reproduction, recreation, and cultural identity. Although problems persist, their productive and creative capacity is unquestionable.

See also **East Los Angeles; Loisaida; Immigration; Literature; Music, Popular; Murals; New York; Nuyorican Poets Café; Socio-Economic Profile; Spanish Harlem; Zoot Suit;** *and biographies of figures mentioned in this article.*

BIBLIOGRAPHY

Davis, Mike. *Magical Urbanism: Latinos Reinvent the U.S. City.* New York: Verso, 2000.

Flores, Juan. *From Bomba to Hip-Hop: Puerto Rican Culture and Latino Identity.* New York: Columbia University Press, 2000.

Galarza, Ernesto. *Barrio Boy.* Notre Dame, Ind.: University of Notre Dame Press, 1971.

Haslip-Viera, Gabriel, and Sherrie L. Baver. *Latinos in New York: Communities in Transition.* Notre Dame, Ind.: University of Notre Dame Press, 1996.

Laó-Montes, Agustín, and Arlene Dávila. *Mambo Montage: The Latinization of New York.* New York: Columbia University Press, 2001.

Leclerc, Gustavo, Raúl Villa, and Michael J. Dear, eds. *Urban Latino Cultures: La vida Latina en L.A.* Thousand Oaks, Calif.: Sage, 1999.

Moore, Joan, and Raquel Pinderhughes, eds. *In the Barrios: Latinos and the Underclass Debate.* New York: Russell Sage Foundation, 1993.

Romo, Ricardo. "The Urbanization of Southwestern Chicanos in the Early Twentieth Century. In *New Directions in Chicano Scholarship,* edited by Ricardo Romo and Raymund Paredes, 183–207. La Jolla: Chicano Studies Program, University of California, San Diego, 1978.

Vega, Bernardo. *Memoirs of Bernardo Vega: A Contribution to the History of the Puerto Rican Community in New York.* Edited by César Andreu Iglesias. Translated by Juan Flores. New York: Monthly Review Press, 1984.

Villa, Raúl Homero. *Barrio-Logos: Space and Place in Urban Chicano Literature and Culture.* Austin: University of Texas Press, 2000.

RAÚL HOMERO VILLA

BASEBALL. The fascination of early-twenty-first-century baseball fans with Alex Rodríguez, Sammy Sosa, and Nomar Garciaparra and with Hispanic ballplayers as a whole belies a longer history of participation in the sport long heralded as the U.S. national pastime. Hispanic participation in baseball in the late 1990s and early 2000s illuminates the power and capriciousness of the segregationist system that, dictated by U.S. racial understandings, divided the U.S. professional game from 1889 until 1947. During baseball's era of racial segregation, Hispanics performed on either side of baseball's color line, some appearing in the major leagues and its affiliated minor leagues, which excluded African Americans, while most participated in the African American circuits, which did not discriminate against them on the basis of skin color or racial status. Just as importantly, Latin American–descended players made an impression with their fine play and passion for the game wherever they performed while also attaching their own meaning to their participation.

Hispanic participation in a major professional baseball league dates back to the late nineteenth century, before a formal color line was imposed, when Cuban-born Esteban "Steve" Bellan played in the National Association (1871–1873). Nine years later, the first U.S.–born Latino player, San Francisco–raised Vincent "Sandy" Nava, broke into the big leagues. Introduced to baseball enthusiasts as a "Spaniard," Nava was the son of a Mexican mother and the stepson of English-born William Irwin. Thus, the first Latino in the majors initially performed professionally under his stepfather's surname, Irwin. The years he spent in the majors, from 1882 to 1887, set a precedent for the different racial situation that Latinos would encounter on U.S. playing fields compared with African Americans, who endured total exclusion until the majors dismantled their color line in 1947.

Fifteen years passed between Nava's departure from the majors and the appearance of the next Latino big leaguer. In 1902, Colombian-born and U.S. college-educated Louis Castro signed with the Philadelphia Athletics. In the interim, Hispanics continued to play in California's professional circuits and with lower minor-league teams that were unaffiliated with the majors. The uninterrupted participation of Latinos in the segregated major leagues started in 1908, when the Boston Red Sox purchased the contract of Mexican American pitcher Frank Arellanes from a California league team. Arellanes's entry into the majors reiterated the peculiar criteria established for Latinos. Because of their restrictive racial policy, the major leagues focused on ensuring that players who participated in the circuit were not African American. Thus, Hispanics who were lighter skinned and could "prove" European ancestry—for example, Castilian, Spanish, or Basque—garnered consideration. This was the case with the Cuban natives Rafael Almeida and Armando Marsans, who were introduced to National League fans as "two of the purest bars of Castilian soap" when they made their 1911 debut with the Cincinnati Reds.

While opportunities to play in the major leagues were governed by exclusionary racial policy, the African American baseball circuits represented the highest level of professional baseball open to U.S. and foreign-born Hispanics. From 1899, when the Havana-based team All Cubans toured the United States, through the collapse of the Negro Leagues in 1950, approximately three hundred Hispanics played in the African American baseball circuits while only fifty-five played in the major leagues. The establishment of Negro Leagues based in the Midwest (Negro National League, 1920) and East (Eastern Colored League, 1923) formalized their participation in African American baseball, as each circuit featured a team of all-Hispanic performers, both, ironically, naming themselves the Cuban Stars. Significantly, Latino participation in these circuits included roles as team owners and league executives, most prominently the Afro-Cuban American Alejandro Pompez, and as umpires, such as Cuban-born Hector Magrinat.

Both in the segregated majors and in the Negro Leagues, cultural practices such as language were at the center of a racialization process where individuals from the Spanish-speaking Americas were distinguished from African Americans and white Americans. Latin Americans who secured entry into the majors during this era carried nicknames such as "the Goofy Castilian" or "Señor" and were occasionally subjected to ridicule, brushback pitches, spikings, and verbal abuse. This was surely the case for players such as Roberto Estalella and Roberto Ortiz, who played on the Washington Senators from the mid-1930s into the late 1940s. Their case demonstrates that although they secured entry into the segregated majors, they did not necessarily gain acceptance as fellow whites from teammates, team management, fans, or journalists. Similarly, in the Negro Leagues at times they were treated differently than their African American teammates when dealing with segregated facilities. Their Spanish accents and other factors prompted some Americans to differentiate between darker-skinned Hispanics and African Americans.

With the start of integration, major-league organizations began to capitalize on the available Hispanic talent. Subsequent decades witnessed the first generation to enter U.S. professional baseball without racial restriction. Cuban-born Orestes "Minnie" Miñoso and Dominican-born Osvaldo "Ozzie" Virgil were pioneers of integration, being the first black players on the Chicago White Sox and the Detroit Tigers, respectively. The 1950s through the 1970s witnessed the emergence of such Latin American perennial all-stars as Orlando Cepeda, Roberto Clemente, Juan Marichal, Miñoso, and Vic Power, among others. Wider recognition did not necessarily alleviate the challenge of cultural adjustment for foreign-born Hispanics, and regardless of their origins, the often ambivalent if not antagonistic relationship with the English-language press continued.

Economic conditions and policy shifts between the United States and Latin American countries increasingly affected the origins of Hispanic players entering the major leagues in the post-1947 integrated era. The ending of diplomatic relations with Cuba, political upheaval in the Dominican Republic, and economic restructuring in Mexico produced waves of immigrants that would yield players such as Jose Canseco, Alex Rodríguez, and Nomar Garciaparra, all of whom came from U.S. Latino communities. The advent of free agency in the late 1970s produced greater interest in foreign-born Latin American talent, mainly Dominicans and Venezuelans, as organizations sought to offset the high salaries paid to star performers. By the late 1990s, political and economic forces together contributed to Hispanics eclipsing African Americans as the largest minority group participating in the major leagues.

See also **Clemente, Roberto.**

BIBLIOGRAPHY

Burgos, Adrian. "Playing Ball in a Black and White Field of Dreams: Afro-Caribbean Ballplayers in the Negro Leagues, 1910–1950." *Journal of Negro History* 82, no. 1 (Winter 1997): 67–104.

Regalado, Samuel O. *Viva Baseball!: Latin Major Leaguers and Their Special Hunger*. Urbana: University of Illinois Press, 1998.

ADRIAN BURGOS

BAUTIZO. *Bautizo* or baptism, the rite of initiation into the Christian community, has some essential elements: the proclamation of faith, the witness of the community, and the *compadrazgo* or godparent. The proclamation of faith in the sacrament is a basic belief that the child, born in original sin, is free of sin and merits heaven after baptism. This belief is sometimes playfully articulated as *cortar la cola*, cutting off of the tail that links the child to evil, or *sacarle el diablo*, taking the devil out of the child.

The second essential element, community witness, sometimes happens in church, where the child is baptized. Other times that aspect happens at the fiesta, where family and friends gather in honor of the newly baptized. The compadrazgo serves two roles. First is the spiritual bond established between the child's parents and the *padrino* and *madrina*, the godparents. Second is the willingness of the godparents to assume responsibility for the care of the child if such becomes necessary.

Traditional symbols that accompany the rite include *el ropón*, *el bolo*, and *la fiesta*. El ropón is the Mexican and Cuban tradition of dressing the child in a long, white baptismal gown for the religious ceremony. The dress, worn by all infants, is ordinarily passed down from ancestors, so the grandfather's ropón may be worn by his children and grandchildren. *El bolo*, a Mexican custom that some Mexican Americans have continued, is associated with the practice of throwing rice at weddings or with the popular piñata. Upon emerging from the church, the godfather throws coins into the air for the children as a sign of abundance or good fortune. The fiesta includes food, drink, music, and sometimes dance.

Latinos and Latinas of different countries, generations, and statuses have modified the baptismal rituals in a variety of ways. Mexicans and new immigrants are familiar with the practices of el bolo and el ropón, whereas Cubans uphold the tradition of el ropón but not el bolo.

In other countries, such as Argentina, the lower economic levels disregard el ropón and dress the child in whatever white clothing they have, and a baptismal bib is provided by the godparents. Most Mexican Americans prefer the white dress for a girl and white pants for a boy with a simple bib provided by the parish. All the baptized wear the same bibs, but the baptismal gowns, purchased by the godparents, are indicators of economic means. Historically, Mexicans sought godparents who were better off than the child's parents; however, Mexicans and Mexican Americans in the twenty-first century tend to stay in similar economic levels and ask relatives to be godparents.

See also Catholicism; Chicanos and Chicanas; Cuban Americans; Mexican-Origin People in the United States; *and* Religion and Spirituality.

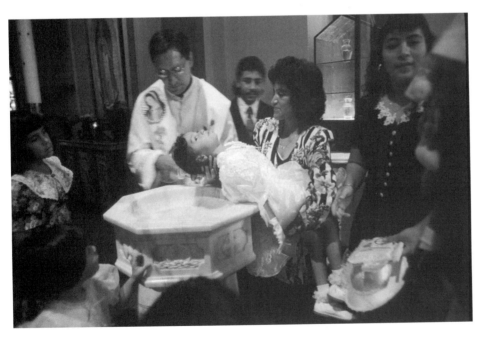

BAPTISM IN EAST LOS ANGELES. (© Paul Rodriguez/Latin Focus.com)

BIBLIOGRAPHY

Francis, Mark R., and Arturo Pérez-Rodríguez. *Primero Dios: Hispanic Liturgical Resource*. Chicago: Liturgy Training Publications, 1997.

Workshops on Hispanic Liturgy and Popular Piety. *Faith Expressions of Hispanics in the Southwest*. 2nd ed. San Antonio, Tex.: Mexican American Cultural Center, 1990.

ANITA DE LUNA

BAUZÁ, MARIO (1911–1993), Cuban jazz musician. Mario Bauzá was one of the founders of Latin Jazz, a term he disliked, preferring to describe his music as Afro-Cuban jazz. He was born on April 28, 1911, in Havana and raised by his godparents, Arturo Andrade, a *solfegio* teacher, and Sofía Domínguez. Bauzá began his musical education early, studying at a Havana conservatory, and at the age of sixteen he joined the Havana Symphony as a clarinetist. In the late 1920s, during a visit to New York with the Antonio María Romeu *charanga* for a *danzón* recording date, Bauzá fell in love with jazz.

In 1930 he left Cuba with the Don Azpiazu band and settled in New York City, where flutist Alberto Socarrás introduced him to several American jazz musicians. Bauzá played clarinet with Noble Sissle, became musical director of Chick Webb's band, and also played with Fletcher Henderson, Don Redman, and Cab Calloway. Simultaneously he continued to play Cuban music with New York bands and played trumpet in several recordings by Antonio Machín. With his brother-in-law "Machito" (Frank Grillo), Mario Bauzá launched Machito and His Afro-Cubans in 1940. This revolutionary orchestra consciously and deliberately sought to combine the rhythms of Afro-Cuban music with the harmonies, timbres and cadences characteristic of jazz. Under Bauzá's musical leadership, with arrangements first by John Bartee, sometimes by saxophonist José "Pin" Madera, and later by pianist and arranger René Hernández, Machito and the Afro-Cubans provided the cauldron for a new musical brew. For some critics, Machito and the Afro-Cubans sounded like the Duke Ellington Orchestra with a Latin beat.

The most successful early fruit of this labor was the tune "Tanga," played for the first time in 1943. Inspired by the opening bars of a popular Cuban tune, "Tanga" sounded like jazz, but of a kind never before heard. The horns employed typical jazz phrasing without clashing with the authentic Cuban rhythms laid out by the piano, percussion, and bass. "Tanga" is considered by many to be the first true example of Latin jazz, and it thrilled audiences to the point that Bauzá made it the band's signature song. Mario Bauzá's sister-in-law Graciela joined the band in 1943 and sang Cuban boleros with jazz arrangements by Chico O'Farrill, providing another element in

MARIO BAUZÁ. Mario Bauzá and Frank "Machito" Grillo, 1948. (Frank Driggs Collection/Getty Images)

the ongoing process of blending Caribbean music with jazz. Bauzá's work influenced Dizzy Gillespie, Stan Kenton, and an entire generation of jazz musicians that became enamored of the sound of Latin jazz, including George Shearing, Tito Puente, and Cal Tjader. Bauzá's role as conductor overtook his playing but he continued to play and record on his own in a strictly Cuban style. For example, in 1954 he played trumpet in a series of bolero recordings by famed Cuban crooner Panchito Riset, which became the rage throughout Latin America.

Bauzá left the Machito orchestra in the 1970s and continued to work in relative obscurity until the 1990s when a revival of interest in his mastery allowed him to release three CDs in his characteristic Afro-Cuban jazz style. Mario Bauzá will be long remembered as the musician who transformed the music of both his native Cuba and his adopted homeland, the United Sates. Bauzá passed away on July 11, 1993.

See also Latin Jazz.

BIBLIOGRAPHY
Fernández, Raúl. *Latin Jazz: The Perfect Combination.* San Francisco: Chronicle Books/Smithsonian Institution Traveling Exhibition Service, 2002.
Leymarie, Isabelle. *Cuban Fire: The Story of Salsa and Latin Jazz.* London and New York: Continuum, 2002.

RAÚL FERNÁNDEZ

BAY OF PIGS. Counting on the element of surprise and hoping to trigger a popular uprising that would topple the newly established Cuban Revolutionary Government, an invasion force of 1,500 Cuban exiles—organized, trained, and armed by the U.S. government—landed at the Bay of Pigs (Playa Girón) in southeastern Cuba on April 17, 1961. After only forty-eight hours of combat, the invasion force, Brigade 2506, was crushed by a fierce and well-coordinated Cuban defense that killed more than one hundred invaders, took 1,179 prisoners, and put them on trial, charged as "mercenaries at the service of Yankee imperialism." The prisoners spent twenty months in Cuban prisons before the U.S. government negotiated their release in exchange for $50 million worth of medicine, baby food, and farm equipment.

Planning for the invasion of Cuba and training of Cuban exiles began in 1960, during the administration of Dwight Eisenhower, who hoped to keep the U.S. role secret and deliver a quick knockout punch against Fidel Castro's government, as part of his crusade against Communism. Thus the invasion was modeled after the CIA's successful operation that led to the overthrow of Guatemala's reformist government in 1954. The plans were inherited by the Kennedy administration, which allowed the invasion to proceed, a decision the president would later regret, since in Cuba, nothing went as planned. The CIA failed to coordinate preinvasion operations with the Cuban internal opposition, and seriously underestimated the Cuban government's popular support and military strength.

The Cuban army's triumph over the invasion force was instrumental in the consolidation of revolutionary power in Cuba, and of Fidel Castro's leadership in Cuba and abroad. Throughout Latin America and the third world, the invasion's defeat was interpreted as a victory for oppressed and colonized peoples everywhere, and it served as inspiration for revolutionary and national liberation movements, now convinced that imperialism could be defeated. For President Kennedy, the invasion's defeat, only three months into his presidency, was a humiliating embarrassment. Embittered by the invasion's failure, Cuban exiles charged the Kennedy administration with treason to the cause of Cuban liberation.

Despite the fact that to this day the Cuban government celebrates April 19 as "Victoria de Girón" and proclaims the victory as the "first defeat of Yankee imperialism in the Americas," time has healed some wounds. To commemorate the invasion's fortieth anniversary, the Cuban government hosted a conference in Havana that brought together, for the first time, key policymakers from the Kennedy administration and the Soviet Union, veterans of Brigade 2506, and Fidel Castro. In 2004, the Cuban government reinstated Cuban citizenship for six brigade veterans who advocate a policy of dialogue and reconciliation among all Cubans. The Brigade Veterans Organization, however, officially rejects any dialogue or reconciliation with the Cuban government.

See also **Castro, Fidel; Cuban Americans; Exilio; United States Foreign Policy;** *and* **United States Interventions in Latin America.**

BIBLIOGRAPHY
Blight, James G., and Peter Kornbluh, eds. *The Politics of Illusion: The Bay of Pigs Invasion Reexamined.* Boulder, Colo.: Lynne Rienner Publishers, 1998.
Johnson, Haynes, with Manuel Artime, José Pérez San Román, et al. *The Bay of Pigs: The Leaders' Story of Brigade 2506.* New York: Norton, 1964.
Rodríguez Cruz, Juan Carlos. *The Bay of Pigs and the CIA.* Translated by Mary Todd. Melbourne, Australia: Ocean Press, 1999.
Torres, María de los Angeles. *In the Land of Mirrors.* Ann Arbor: University of Michigan Press, 1999.
Wyden, Peter. *Bay of Pigs: The Untold Story.* New York: Simon and Schuster, 1979.

FÉLIX MASUD-PILOTO

BEANS. Many valuable foods and ingredients that originated in North and South America continue to play a significant role in the food habits of people throughout the world. Maize, manioc, potatoes, sweet potatoes, yams, peanuts, squash, pineapples, avocados, tomatoes, chocolate, vanilla, chilies, and beans—all these foods and ingredients are used all over the world to make recipes more delicious, more attractive, or in some cases to help define a dish. Guacamole requires avocados; peanut butter needs peanuts; sweet potato pie needs sweet potatoes; chocolate cake needs chocolate, and refried beans need beans.

These foods can be referred to by different names, depending on the culture and region. In some areas or urban neighborhoods in the United States, for example, people have arguments over the meaning of the words "yams" and "sweet potatoes." Similarly in some ethnically diverse neighborhoods, people might use the words "yucca" and "manioc" interchangeably. The same linguistic diversity can be seen in relation to hot peppers; some refer to them as "chili," some as "aji." Overall a food item or ingredient can be three different things. It can be a food, a sign, or a symbol that has the potential to embody an enormous amount of history, language, and culture. This essay focuses on the cultural history of the beans that originated in Mesoamerica and discusses the importance of understanding their significance in Mexican food and culture.

History, Language, and Culture

In Mesoamerica, several key plant foods formed the culinary complex of the cultures encountered by the Spanish when they discovered the "New World." One of these foods is the bean, which developed into many species. Four species were domesticated in Mesoamerica: tepary beans (*Phaseolus acutifolius*), scarlet runner beans (*Phaseolus coccineus*), lima beans (*Phaseolus lunatus*), and pinto and black beans (*Phaseolus vulgaris*).

The tepary bean was domesticated around 3000 BCE in the most northern region of Mesoamerica—that is, the hot area that is now the southwestern United States and northern Mexico and especially those Mexican states bordering on the United States. The Papago Indians of the Southwest are associated with the tepary bean. The Opata Indians of Mexico assigned the bean the name "tepary," which means "desert-adapted," and the name "Papago" is a short form of Papavi Kuadam, or Tepary Eaters. It is believed that the Papagos were given this name because they were associated with the cultivation and consumption of tepary beans. Another explanation for the origin of the word is that the Spaniards changed the Papago word for bean *t'pawi* to "tepary."

The tepary bean is well suited for the arid desert environment. It has drought- and heat-tolerant genetic traits. Its deep roots enable it to access the reservoirs of lower levels of soil moisture, and it generates pollen and seeds at 105°F. The tepary bean seems to rank higher in the nutritional scale than many other beans in protein, niacin, and calcium content. This makes it a good choice for people who do not consume dairy products or who are breast-feeding. White and huge, tepary beans are a major food staple among Native Americans along the United States–Mexico border, who prepare them by boiling them with salt, a ham bone, or fatty bacon and eat them whole or in soups or with rice. In the early twenty-first century the tepary bean continues to play a significant role in the cuisine of many people not only in the United States but also around the world. They are also cultivated in Africa, for example.

A relative of the tepary bean, the scarlet runner bean was also a primary food item of Mesoamerica. Its wild beans were collected in Oaxaca around 8750–6750 BCE and in Tehuacan during 7050 BCE. The scarlet runner bean plant can be recognized by its beautiful red flowers, and unlike other domesticated bean plants, which were considered annuals, the scarlet runner plant is short-lived, less than a year. The Aztecs called these beans *ayacotli*, *ayecotli*, or *ayocotli*, referring to the large scarlet

runner beans, which were white, purple, or black. According to Spanish chroniclers, these large beans were eaten mostly by the Aztec working class, and the smaller beans were consumed by the Spanish aristocracy. Scarlet runner beans continue to be important in the diets of Mexicans and indigenous people. In Mexican outdoor markets, one can find a variety of scarlet runner beans in different colors.

There are an estimated two to four hundred varieties of *Phaseolus vulgaris*. These are smaller beans, including adzuki, white, roman, canary, cranberry, black, and pinto beans. The wild strain of *Phaseolus vulgaris* appears to have been growing on the eastern slopes of the Andes and also in Mexico and Central America. The early domestication of *Phaseolus vulgaris* took place around 5000 BCE. In Tehuacan, Mexico, it happened around 5680 BCE and in the highlands of Peru around 2550 BCE, mainly along the coast. In the northern part of Mexico, the most popular varieties of *Phaseolus vulgaris* beans are black and pinto beans.

There are many different kinds of recipes that include black and pinto beans in Mexican cuisine, and many of these recipes also embody the culture and history of a particular region. Making beans within Mexican culture is not a simple task; it requires skill and attention to the process of cooking them and transforming them into a particular dish, for instance, a main dish, an accompaniment to meat, eggs, or a condiment on an appetizer.

Frijoles de olla (beans in a pot), *frijoles a la charra* (charro beans), *frijoles borachos* (drunken beans), *frijoles maneados* (tied-up beans), *frijoles fronterizos* or *frijoles rancheros* (border beans or ranch-style beans), and *frijoles refritos* (refried beans) are the most traditional bean dishes in the northern region of Mexico. All these bean recipes can be made with either pinto or black beans, and there is not a clear consensus on the correct ingredients or cooking procedures. The process of cooking frijoles de olla (pot beans) is the most important, because from this stage on the beans become an accompaniment to grilled meats, in the form of refried beans, frijoles borachos, frijoles a la charra, frijoles fronterizos or frijoles rancheros, or frijoles maneados.

Food and Culture

Foods and ingredients can be impregnated with cultural, historical, and linguistic meaning and can connote a way of life that makes statements about class and gender. For example, lard is often associated with poor, working-class people but is also an important ingredient in Mexican folk foodways. In the particular world of the Texas-Mexico border working class, some ingredients signal class position. For example, many people substitute for lard by using canola or olive oil. Cooking beans with canola or

HOW TO COOK MEXICAN BEANS

For *frijoles de olla* (pot beans), the beans, either pinto or black, are cooked in a pot with water, usually three times more water than beans. Whether one cooks them in an earthenware pot or an iron pot can be a major decision. In these times of great social and economic change, many people of Mexican descent grew up eating frijoles de olla made in an earthenware pot but now make them in aluminum or cast-iron pots, pressure cookers, and Crock-Pots. Most would say there is a difference in taste; however, most would agree that some of the difference might lie in whether the beans are first soaked. Another difference comes from the kinds of flavorings and spices added to the beans. For example, some might add an onion, garlic, a sprig of epazote, avocado leaves, salt, or two tablespoons of lard. Once the frijoles de olla are made, one can serve them in a bowl along with the broth and eat them with a tortilla or scoop them with a spoon. Also one can garnish the beans with favorite kinds of cheese, such as a cream cheese or a hard cheese.

Frijoles a la charra is one of the signature dishes of northern Mexico and the Texas-Mexico border region. This bean dish requires some extra ingredients, such as cubed tomatoes, cilantro, sliced onions, garlic, chopped chilies serranos, cubed pork shoulder, and bacon. One adds the pork shoulder to the pot of beans and lets it cook. In the meantime one fries the bacon in a skillet and then removes the bacon. With the bacon drippings, one cooks the tomatoes, cilantro, onions, garlic, and chili serrano and makes a sauce. Afterward one adds this sauce to the pot of beans with the pork shoulder. If one decides to make them into *frijoles borrachos*, one adds a beer or tequila or, if one is in the southern region of Mexico, some pulque (fermented agave drink).

Frijoles fronterizos or *frijoles rancheros* require replacing the pork with lard, bacon drippings, and chorizo. They can be a main meal, or they can be an accompaniment to *cabrito al pastor*, *carne asadas*, *tacos al carbon*, or other barbecued meats. All these bean dishes require that the beans remain whole, not mashed, crushed, squashed, or pulverized. Once the cook mashes the beans, he or she enters another hotly contested area of cooking beans known as *frijoles refritos*, along with its many variations.

Frijoles refritos is the most popular dish among many Mexicans, regardless of region, whether it is the Yucatán Peninsula, central Mexico, northern Mexico, or South Texas. All these regions have their own specific regional variation on frijoles refritos. They might use different kinds of beans, different techniques to mash them, and different procedures to fry them, using pork lard, bacon drippings, or vegetable oil. There is no real secret in frying beans. Most cookbooks or home cooks will instruct one to fry the whole beans in a skillet and with lard or oil until they are dry and toasty and when the beans are shiny and slide off the pan. In Oaxaca women are known to sieve the beans to form a smooth puree, then fry them and use them in chalupas, *guarnachas*, and tacos. This method of cooking refried beans is called *chinitos*.

Another variation is *frijoles maneados*. This Sonoran bean dish requires frijoles refritos, but even within the state of Sonora there are many variations. For example, some versions require adding milk, baking the beans in the oven, and garnishing them with cheese and some roasted chilies. Other versions of frijoles maneados require no milk products and are not baked but are prepared in a skillet. These cooking techniques and cooking processes prompt intense discussion. At times these discussions can become rancorous, even among longtime friends and family members.

---

olive oil connotes aspirations of a non-working-class lifestyle. More importantly it runs the risk of insulting people who use lard instead of vegetable oil. Thus the use of particular ingredients can embody a way of life, reflect certain class aspirations, signal one's class position, or signal a cooking preparation associated with a lifestyle particular to a social class.

Conclusion

Mesoamerican foods continue to have an important role in the diets of people throughout the world. Beans of many varieties have influenced the diet and cuisines of many cultures, especially those of Mexico, Central America, and South America. Beans come in many varieties and are assigned different names, prepared in different ways, and used to convey messages related to history, culture, language, class, and gender. Many times these significant cultural messages are embedded in the cooking and consumption process and can reveal the region and class arrangement of the people who prepare them and eat them. For example, the cooking process itself can expose the structuring of gender and class relations related to the preparation of certain foods. Some social classes use particular food ingredients that might be viewed as status symbols or that signify the social aspirations of the cook. In some cultural situations, the mention of the word bean acts as a referent that encapsulates all the above-mentioned messages about culture, region, class, and gender.

The names for the different bean dishes and their accompaniments of spices and herbs signify different cultural regions in Mexico and at the same time convey a way of life particular to that region. In the early twenty-first century a simple excursion into a Mexican *tiendita*, or grocery store, in the United States can reveal the different regions of their customers by the different kinds of beans sold. A person can visit the Grand Central Market in Los Angeles or walk east on Whittier Boulevard and encounter all the gastronomic regions of Mexico.

See also Cuisine; Food and Literature; Quelites (Lambsquarters); *and* Barrios, *sidebar on* Tiendita.

BIBLIOGRAPHY

Bauer, Laurie. *Introducing Linguistic Morphology.* Edinburgh, U.K.: University of Edinburgh Press, 1992.

Bayless, Rick, with Deann Groen Bayless. *Authentic Mexican: Regional Cooking from the Heart of Mexico*. New York: Morrow, 1987.

Bayless, Rick, with Deann Groen Bayless and Jean Marie Brownson. *Mexican Kitchen: Capturing the Vibrant Flavors of a World-Class Cuisine*. New York: Scribner, 1996.

Bayless, Rick, with Deann Groen Bayless and Jean Marie Brownson. *Mexico One Plate at a Time*. New York: Scribner, 2000.

Castetter, Edward, and Ruth Underhill. "Ethnobiology of the Papago Indians." *University of New Mexico Bulletin* 4, no. 3 (1935): 32.

Coe, Sophie D. *America's First Cuisines*. Austin: University of Texas Press, 1994.

De'Angeli, Alicia, and Jorge De'Angeli. *Espazote y molcajete: Productos y técnicas de la cocina Mexicana*. Mexico City: Ediciones Larousse, 1993.

Freeman, G. F. *Southwestern Beans and Teparies*. Rev. ed. Tucson: University of Arizona Press, 1918.

Johnson, Jean B. *The Opata: An Inland Tribe of Sonora*. Albuquerque: University of New Mexico Press, 1950.

Kennedy, Diane. *Recipes from the Regional Cooks of Mexico*. New York: Harper and Row, 1978.

Nabhan, Gary. *Gathering the Desert*. Tucson: University of Arizona Press, 1985.

Niethammer, Carolyn J. *American Indian Food and Lore*. New York: Macmillan, 1974.

Niethammer, Carolyn J. *The Tumbleweed Gourmet: Cooking with Wild Southwestern Plants*. Tucson: University of Arizona Press, 1987.

Rodriguez Rivera, Virginia. *La comida en el México antiguo y moderno*. Mexico City: Editorial Pormaca, 1966.

Santamaria, Francisco J. *Diccionario de Mexicanismos*. Mexico City: Editorial Porrua, 1974.

Wiesmantel, Mary J. *Food, Gender, and Poverty in the Ecuadorian Andes*. Philadelphia: University of Pennsylvania Press, 1988.

MARIO MONTAÑO

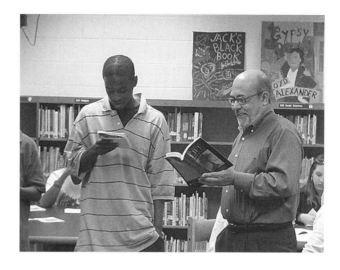

MARIO BENCASTRO. The writer reads from his book *Three of Life: Stories of Civil War* while visting a school in Jacksonville, Fla. (Arte Público Press)

BENCASTRO, MARIO

BENCASTRO, MARIO (b. 1949), Salvadoran American author. Born in Ahuachapán, El Salvador, on March 20, 1949, Mario Bencastro has become the leading novelist of Salvadoran immigration to the United States. His novels, plays, and stories document the political as well as the economic reasons for leaving Central America and resettling in the United States. In this, he is unique among the Central American writers who have migrated to our shores during the last three decades, because most of them see themselves and their literary characters either as political exiles—as do many writers of Cuban, Chilean, and Argentine nationality—or as economic refugees, who migrate from Mexico, the Caribbean, and Central America in search of work with which to sustain their families. The dual sensitivity in Bencastro's works stems from his continuous contact with and participation in expatriate communities in Washington, D.C., where he is a social worker for the Fannie Mae Corporation, as well as in other major cities that he tours as a popular writer.

Initially trained as a painter, Bencastro set out to become an artist after winning El Salvador's "National Drawing Competition" in 1961. He devoted himself full-time to his art beginning in 1975, and in 1978 he was given a show of his twenty-five *Monograms* at the National Exposition Hall. He went on to show his works internationally at more than forty-five individual and group exhibits. Despite his success as a painter of geometric abstracts, Bencastro gave up his brushes and canvas when he found them incapable of recording and expressing the tragedy of the civil wars in his country. He began to write stories about the wars and migrated to the United States in 1978. Since 1979, Bencastro has concentrated on writing that reflects the social and political life of his communities, both in El Salvador and in the United States.

In 1989, his first novel, *Disparo en la catedral*, was a finalist in the Novedades y Diana International Literary Prize competition, and it was published in the original Spanish in Mexico in 1990. The novel was subsequently translated into English by Susan Giersbach Rascón, as were all of his books, and it was published in the United States in 1996 as *A Shot in the Cathedral*. A separate edition of the Spanish original was also published in the United States that year. His short fiction collection, *Arbol de la vida: historias de la guerra civil*, was published in Spanish in El Salvador in 1993. Some of the stories were adapted as plays and staged, while others appeared in various anthologies in both the United States and El Salvador. The collection was translated and published in the United States in 1997 as *The Tree of Life: Stories of Civil War*. His best-known novel, *Odyssey to the North* (1999), was published first in translation in the United States, then in the original Spanish the following year. *Odyssey* is a classic novel of immigration, following economic and political refugees from their homes in Central America and Mexico into poor-paying and hazardous jobs in the Washington, D.C., area. Bencastro is also the author of unpublished plays and a short novel, *The Flight of the Lark*, which was a finalist for the Felipe Trigo Literary Prize in Badajoz, Spain. *The Flight of the Lark* is the only novel by Bencastro that reflects his background in visual arts: here, painting is used as a metaphor to reflect universal truths and portray portions of Salvadoran history.

A Shot in the Cathedral documents the establishment of martial law in El Salvador after a coup d'état; a religious leader takes the initiative of rallying the common people against the U.S.–backed military junta. More important than the actual historical events on which the novel is based are Bencastro's sensitivity and deep restraint in focusing on the tragedy caused by civil war. *Publishers Weekly* (July 22, 1996) characterized the novel as a "dramatic, powerful first novel . . . a vivid newsreel of a country disintegrating." *Kirkus Reviews* (August 1, 1996) called it a "skillful balance between journalistic reportage and a subjective focus."

The Tree of Life: Stories of Civil War continues Bencastro's preoccupation with the violence and turmoil in El Salvador that produced the large exodus of people seeking safety and economic stability. With a decidedly magic-realist tone, as opposed to the reportorial tone in his previous book, these civil war tales take up the perspective of the common man caught up in the maelstrom. Each of the twelve stories depicts a separate aspect of the brutality inflicted by the military junta on everyday people, their lives not only besieged but also determined by the actions of the military.

In *Odyssey to the North*, Bencastro tells the tale of a Salvadoran fleeing from persecution in his country toward safety and a job in the United States. Along the way, he meets other economic and political refugees from Central and South America heading to Washington, D.C. Through the protagonist Calixto's ears, the reader learns the stories of the other migrants and through his eyes observes the discrimination and poor living conditions they experience, as well as the underground culture they create in the United States. Bencastro includes a montage of newspaper articles, court transcripts, and other *realia* to lend authenticity to this otherwise fictional narrative, which sensitively portrays Calixto and his comrades. *Publishers Weekly* (October 26, 1998) found that "Bencastro's tone is welcomely understated—and his message all the more powerful for it." *Kirkus Reviews* (November 15, 1998) agreed that "Bencastro's directness and understated compassion make Calixto's disillusionment credible and quite moving."

Writing about Bencastro's art in general, Edward Hood has stated, "Bencastro is more interested in presenting the impact of the conflict upon ordinary people and their families than in expounding upon the ideological or poetical causes that motivated it."

See also **Central Americans; Literature;** *and* **South Americans.**

BIBLIOGRAPHY
Harris, John. "Artist's Books Create a Picture of El Salvador." *The Bellingham Herald*, June 10, 1999, C3.
Hood, Edward Waters. "Bencastro, Mario. *Odisea del Norte*." *World Literature Today* 74, no. 4 (Autumn 2000).
Lértora, Juan Carlos. "Bencastro, Mario. *The Tree of Life: Stories of Civil War*." *MultiCultural Review* (March 1998): 66.

NICOLÁS KANELLOS

BILINGUAL EDUCATION. Bilingual education generally involves using two languages for school instruction with the goal that students will develop proficiency in the two languages. During its long history in the United States, it has sometimes been surrounded by controversy when it reflected accommodations between ethnic groups. It is a form of schooling that Spanish-speaking *mexicanos*, Puerto Ricans on the mainland, Cubans, and other Latinos and Latinas in the United States have long sought and demanded for their children, so that they could understand the language of instruction in public schools and be understood by their teachers. For the last third of the twentieth century, bilingual education in U.S. public schools was practiced using two languages for instruction, one of which was English, with the goal of teaching sufficient English that the students could transition into all-English classrooms. It was intended for, and generally available only to, those students who spoke a non-English language and were not proficient in English—known as "non-English-proficient" or "limited-English-proficient" (LEP) students or "English language learners" (ELL). Most English language learners are Spanish-speaking. Support by the federal and state governments led to debates over the purposes and use of bilingual education. At the beginning of the twenty-first century, the federal government had withdrawn its support and put considerable pressure on state and local educational agencies to move away from bilingual education toward English-only instruction.

History of Spanish in the United States

The number of languages in use on the North American continent on the eve of contact with Europeans in 1492 has been estimated at over 500. Five hundred years later, less than half of those languages survive. At the same time, colonial languages—Spanish, English, and French—have become hegemonic throughout this region. Spanish was the first European language to take root in the Americas.

BILINGUAL EDUCATION. A math teacher writes instructions in English and Spanish. (© Bob Dammrich/Photo Edit)

Unlike colonial languages in other parts of the world, Spanish in the Americas became the native language of much of the indigenous, native-born majority over time. The overwhelming majority of Latinos and Latinas today are Spanish speakers with a small proportion of the various national populations speaking indigenous languages. This pattern holds for most of Latin America, except for Brazil, which substitutes Portuguese for Spanish. In the Caribbean, few of the indigenous languages survived the colonial period, and most of the populations speak the colonial languages of their given islands (for example, Spanish in Puerto Rico, Cuba, and the Dominican Republic, English in Jamaica and Bahamas).

English is the legacy of the British colonies in North America, settled starting in the early 1600s. The colonies along the northern Atlantic coast declared their independence from the English king in 1776, and the United States was founded in 1789 with the ratification of the Constitution by the thirteen former British colonies. English was the default national language. (A "national" language is one that is numerically dominant throughout a country. An "official" language is one that has an authoritative status within a nation.)

Between 1803 and 1848, the United States expanded 2,500 miles westward from the Atlantic coast to the Pacific coast of this continent, adding two million square miles to the nation, almost tripling its size. In this expansion, it gained, through purchase (for example, Louisiana, 1803) and military conquest (for example, the United States–Mexico War, 1846–1848), a substantial amount of new territory, already occupied by indigenous populations and other settlers.

As a result of this political history, nearly two-thirds of the current mainland jurisdiction of the United States was, at one time, under a Spanish-speaking sovereign—Spain or Mexico. In 1848, in fact, the United States gained more than 900,000 square miles of territory as spoils of the United States–Mexican War, adding about 100,000 Spanish-speaking Mexicans already settled on the lands ceded to the national population.

At the end of the nineteenth century, the United States intervened in the Cuban war of independence from Spain (the Spanish American War), and in the process gained the former Spanish colonies of Cuba, Puerto Rico, and the Philippines. Under the Teller Amendment (1898), the United States was forbidden to annex Cuba, but it acquired Puerto Rico. This intervention resulted in over 950,000 Spanish-speaking Puerto Ricans being added to the United States. The United States still includes Puerto Rico within its jurisdiction. In recognition of the prior sovereign, and of the predominantly Spanish-speaking populations of these areas, the federal government of the United States recognized an official status for Spanish for varying periods of time, and for various purposes. It currently still recognizes the official bilingual status, in English and Spanish, of Puerto Rico.

During the twentieth century, the Spanish-speaking population of the United States grew at a higher rate than the rest of the country and benefited from a continuous stream of immigration of Spanish speakers, primarily from Mexico. Puerto Ricans became citizens in 1917, and many have migrated to the mainland—to New York, the Northeast, and Chicago—since the 1920s. Since 1959, many Spanish-speaking Cubans have come to the United States to escape the Cuban Revolution and many of these have settled in southern Florida. Spanish-speaking Central Americans came to the United States during the 1980s and 1990s, mainly to escape the repressive regimes and civil wars in Guatemala, Nicaragua, and El Salvador. In 1900, the Spanish-speaking population was estimated at 2 percent of the national population, while in 2000, it was estimated at 11 percent of the national population.

The Nineteenth Century: Educational Services Withheld

Public schools as we know them today date to the middle of the nineteenth century. Between 1840 and 1860, the Common School Movement established public, secular, universal schooling, replacing in part the religious-based schooling that dominated previously. Both before and after the establishment of public schools for Euro-Americans during the nineteenth century, the language of instruction often reflected the languages of the surrounding communities. There were many schools that taught in German, for example, in communities with large German-origin populations. For Amerindians, Mexicans, and, after 1898, Puerto Ricans, however, there were few instances where bilingual instruction was practiced in their schools within the United States. More generally, the purpose of public schooling for these groups was to wipe away the "native" language and culture of the students, and often they were denied basic schooling services altogether.

It took a while to expand public schools in the new territories and states that had formerly been Mexican lands. As the population of the territories and states became more Euro-American, and political power shifted from Mexicans to Anglos, Spanish was tossed aside and English embraced. As California and Texas became states, measures were introduced to restrict teaching in the public schools to English. In 1856, Texas passed a law stating that only public schools where "the English language is principally taught therein" could receive state funds (MacDonald, p. 59). However, particularly in rural areas far from governmental oversight, Spanish-speaking and German-speaking communities continued to practice bilingual schooling in Texas throughout the nineteenth century.

In 1855, the California State Bureau of Public Instruction stipulated that all schools must teach exclusively in English. The Catholic Church initially led the fight opposing the imposition of English in California schools, even by partially encouraging bilingual schooling, but soon after 1855, under the direction of the Baltimore Diocese, the church became a primary proponent of assimilation. In 1870, the California state legislature enacted a statute providing that all the schools in the state (religious and public) be taught in the English language. This law superseded the State Bureau of Public Instruction's similar regulation of 1855.

In the territory of New Mexico, which included what is today the states of New Mexico and Arizona and parts of Colorado, the school laws of 1863 and 1869 continued with no specific language provisions. Since the Mexican population continued in the majority into the early twentieth century, there is little doubt that the schools were taught predominantly in Spanish. An 1876 article in *Harper's New Monthly Magazine* reported on the condition of the New Mexican schools: "Education is making slow headway. Until 1871 there were no public schools in the Territory, but there are now no less than 133 with 5,625 pupils. In twelve schools both English and Spanish are taught, in ten English only, and in 111 Spanish only."

1900–1960: Legal Segregation and English-Only

In Puerto Rico, the United States immediately introduced English into the public schools as part of its Americanization measures. Between 1899 and 1954, Spanish and English were utilized in Puerto Rico's public schools, with varying emphasis on one language or the other as the language of instruction or as a subject. The U.S. attempt at imposing English on the population greatly politicized the issue, reflecting the political tensions between the federal government and the island. Currently, Puerto Rican public schools are taught in Spanish, with English as a subject, while the federal government recognizes the official bilingual status, in English and Spanish, of the government of Puerto Rico.

On the mainland, by the beginning of the twentieth century, most states had subjugated non-English languages, especially Spanish, had made English the exclusive and official language of instruction in the schools, required English literacy for voting, and used English as the language for administration of government. Reflecting a growing nativism and Americanization movement, state legislation changed early in the century. In 1903, there were fourteen states with laws requiring that instruction in the elementary schools be conducted in English. In 1913, there were seventeen such states. By 1923, thirty-four states required English as the medium of instruction in the schools.

Reflecting the nationalist spirit of the war era, Texas passed a stringent English-only law in 1918. The act made it a criminal offense for teachers, principals, superintendents, and other school personnel to teach in a language other than English. For decades, Spanish-speaking children in the Southwest were punished for speaking Spanish in school, even at recess or lunch. Oral histories relate incidents such as pupils being hit for speaking Spanish or having their mouths washed out with soap.

Chicana and Chicano parents in the Southwest and Puerto Rican parents in New York City continued to resist these measures. They formed local advocacy organizations to battle discrimination, to promote and maintain the Spanish language and their cultures, and to assure that their children were prepared in English. As the Puerto Rican population in New York City grew during the 1930s and 1940s, organizations such as Madres y Padres Por Niños Hispanos (Mothers and Fathers in Support of Hispanic Children) questioned the indiscriminate use of intelligence testing, which channeled Puerto Rican children into classrooms for "backward" pupils rather than recognizing language biases in testing.

Until the 1960s, the official policy of the New York City public schools mandated "English-only instructional programs steeped in convention and inflexibility" for the Spanish-speaking American citizens (Sánchez-Korrol 1996, p. 86). *The Puerto Rican Study, 1953–1957* (1958), commissioned by the New York City Board of Education, recommended extensive bilingual education for Puerto Rican children, but implementation of this programming did not occur until the 1970s.

In the 1930s and 1940s, Chicana and Chicano parents filed lawsuits challenging segregation. School districts used Mexican students' lack of English-speaking ability as a subterfuge to segregate them. A successful lawsuit against Westminster School District in Orange County, California, challenging the segregation of Mexican children in the schools, foreshadowed the success of *Brown v. Board of Education* in 1954, which overturned legal segregation.

In response to the successful launch of Sputnik by the Union of Soviet Socialist Republics (USSR) in 1957, the United States Congress created foreign-language programs through the National Defense and Education Act (1958). The law and these new programs began to erode the resistance to the use of non-English languages in the elementary schools.

The Cold War and Bilingual Education: The Cuban Experience

The Cuban Revolution of 1959 caused major changes on the island, especially after Fidel Castro declared the new government socialist. Many Cuban political elites, professionals, and members of the upper class left the island. Many of these expatriates settled in southern Florida. The federal government provided financial and other support by expanding a little-known category in the immigration laws—the refugee. The policies developed in local Florida communities in response to the arrival of Cuban refugees in the early 1960s differed from the Americanization and "English-only" policies directed at Spanish-speaking children in the Southwest. Situated within the context of cold war politics, school policies toward the Cuban refugees were more flexible and open. The Cubans saw themselves and were seen as temporary visitors. A good number of these refugees were bilingual, and many were provided with English-language assistance and recertification of their Cuban professional credentials so that they could practice in the United States.

As early as 1961, Miami's public schools offered Cuban students a variety of separate "pull-out" English-as-a-Second-Language programs at elementary schools and junior and senior high schools. In 1963, with funding from the Ford Foundation and Dade County Schools, and the availability of recertified bilingual Cuban teachers, Coral Way Elementary School in Miami, Florida, became the first two-way bilingual, bi-ethnic public school in the post–World War II era. According to James and Judith Olson, "the field of bilingual education was born in those Dade County schools when it became clear that when Cuban American children were able to become literate in their mother tongue as well as learn English, their success rates in school were dramatic" (p. 99). Between 1960 and 1972, Dade County public schools spent more than

$130 million for bilingual education programs. In 1973, Dade County even adopted an ordinance declaring it officially bilingual in English and Spanish. This successful program, along with new research on bilingualism in Canada and developments in civil rights, resulted in a renewed support for and promotion of bilingual education to improve the education of Spanish-speaking groups in other parts of the country.

Federal Initiatives

The civil rights movement of the 1950s and 1960s caused the federal passage of the Civil Rights Act (1964), the Voting Rights Act (1965), the Elementary and Secondary Education Act (1965), and the Bilingual Education Act (1968). A new era was afoot. The Civil Rights Act and the Voting Rights Act were concerned with the protection of the rights of individuals and members of minority groups. The Elementary and Secondary Education Act provided formula-driven funding for programs for poor children, early childhood education, migrant education, adult education, and teacher preparation. The Bilingual Education Act, however, was only intended to demonstrate the effectiveness and utility of using two languages for instruction to improve the academic achievement of language minorities, and it was funded as a voluntary, discretionary, competitive program. It would take litigation and civil rights laws to get school districts to provide bilingual education more widely.

The passage of the federal Bilingual Education Act in 1968, however, caused three things to happen: (1) it encouraged states to amend or repeal the state laws that prohibited the use of non-English languages or that mandated using only English as the medium of instruction in public schools, most of which had been adopted between 1890 and 1920; (2) it signaled that it was acceptable to use non-English languages to teach language minority students, particularly Chicanas and Chicanos in the Southwest and Puerto Ricans in the Northeast; and (3) it made the condition and problems of Latinas and Latinos and other language minority students visible nationally. It took almost a decade for these programs to be widely implemented, and to develop a theoretical and research base. These developments were assisted by a broader, more inclusive set of language policies:

- The Office of Civil Rights in the Department of Health, Education, and Welfare, on May 5, 1970, issued a memorandum to school districts throughout the country indicating that in order to be in compliance with the 1964 Civil Rights Act regarding national-origin discrimination, they must take affirmative steps to address the language needs of students who are limited in English ability, stop high-stakes testing of these students in the

English language, and communicate with their parents in a language they can understand.

- The 1974 *Lau v. Nichols* U.S. Supreme Court decision affirmed the legality of the May 25th memorandum that required school districts to proactively provide language services for students who were not proficient in English in the public schools.
- The 1974 Equal Educational Opportunity Act prohibited language discrimination.
- In 1974, the advocacy group ASPIRA (founded in 1961 by educator Antonia Pantoja) and the Puerto Rican Legal Defense and Education Fund (founded in 1972) sued the New York City Board of Education, the largest school district in the nation, for its failure to provide an adequate education for Spanish-speaking Puerto Rican pupils. The lawsuit resulted in a legally binding agreement called a consent decree, which required the schools to provide students dominant in Spanish with transitional bilingual education programs.
- The 1975 amendments to the Voting Rights Act of 1965 provided for bilingual ballots and electoral services for Latinos and Latinas, American Indians, and Asian language groups.
- The 1978 Court Interpreters Act required that interpreters be provided in federal court for deaf and hard-of-hearing criminal defendants, as well as for language-minority criminal defendants who could not understand English well enough to participate in court proceedings, so as to meet *their* needs as well as the courts' needs. The act also provided funds for the training of translators and interpreters.

By 1980, there were several federal laws that reflected the national linguistic diversity in national language policies. In addition, many of the restrictive English-only language policies established at the beginning of the twentieth century by the states were eliminated in the name of an expanded understanding of civil rights.

Bilingual Education Grows and Matures, 1970–1990

The 1970s implementation of bilingual education programs was a rollercoaster, establishing new standards for teacher preparation, materials development, and language assessment, and deciding which language to use for how long to teach what to whom. Things stabilized in the second half of the decade as federal resources and state resources increased and combined to develop programs, and as civil rights law enforcement and litigation promoted standards. An infrastructure of bilingual education was put in place in local school districts, state education agencies, colleges, materials publishers, and professional associations.

Federally supported research in bilingual education began to flower in the 1980s, contributing to a broader understanding of language teaching and learning. A combined theoretical framework was developed for language acquisition and bilingualism, which is recognized in bilingual education, teaching of English as a Second Language (ESL), and the foreign language education fields. Numerous bilingual and ESL teacher certification programs were developed, providing critical numbers of trained teachers. Yet program implementation was still very uneven. Many school districts resisted the new programs until forced by litigation to implement them, and then undermined their implementation and continued discriminatory practices. Even with the tremendous growth in efforts to address the language needs of limited-English-proficient Latinos and Latinas (to learn English, have access to the curriculum, and make sociocultural adjustment to the schools), bilingual education has been available to only a fraction of those students who need it. Most LEP students receive some form of ESL instruction.

In a 1997 report, the National Research Council described the educational services received by LEP students as follows:

> Data on program types are difficult to collect and interpret because program philosophy and objectives do not always translate into program practice. However, it is safe to say that ESL-only (with some variants of content-based ESL and sheltered instruction) and transitional bilingual education are the two prevalent models. A recent study found over 1,600 schools that reported offering content ESL (content-based ESL and/or sheltered instruction) (Sheppard, 1995). Structured immersion programs are very few in number, as evidenced by the fact that a recent study examining the effects of structured immersion (Ramirez et al., 1991) had to select the universe of these programs. Maintenance programs are also relatively rare, while a recent survey of two-way bilingual programs, which are increasingly popular, identified just 182 schools nation-wide where this method is used (Christian and Whitcher, 1995).
>
> (August and Hakuta, p. 20)

California had 40 percent of the national LEP enrollment in 1998, making it a significant state in terms of bilingual educational services. In 1998, only about 30 percent of the state's LEP enrollment was receiving transitional bilingual education (academic instruction in English and the non-English language). The other 70 percent of the LEP enrollment received a form of ESL.

1980–2000: Challenges to Bilingual Education

In the last two decades of the twentieth century, a nativist English-only movement developed that made bilingual education the controversial centerpiece of its political agenda to eliminate the use of all non-English languages in the country. This movement has attempted to make English the official language of the states and the nation, and to return to the English-only policies of earlier periods. Seventeen states declared English their official language between 1981 and 1990, nine between 1986 and 1988. The English-only movement was also successful in reversing the bilingual education policies of California (1998), Arizona (2000), and Massachusetts (2002), and replacing them with a form of ESL called Structured English Immersion for all LEP students in those states. The consequence of these educational policy changes was that Latino and Latina LEP students had even fewer bilingual education services available to them in public schools, even though almost all of these programs had been transitional in nature.

Bilingual Education in the Twenty-First Century

The 2000 census for the United States estimated there were 45 million people in the country who spoke a language other than English at home, with almost 27 million (60 percent) of these people speaking Spanish. Most language groups in the United States, however, had a high degree of bilingualism, some as high as 90 percent. Almost 55 percent of Latinos and Latinas reported being bilingual in Spanish and English; 21 percent reported they only spoke English; and 24 percent reported speaking Spanish and very little or no English.

There were 4.6 million students from pre-kindergarten to the twelfth grade who were reported as having limited proficiency in English in the United States in the 2000–2001 school year. This was about 9.6 percent of the national total enrollment of 47.7 million students. While there is no racial, ethnic, or national-origin determination in these enrollments, an overwhelming majority of these Spanish-language background LEP students are Latinos and Latinas. They represented almost four-fifths (3.6 million) of the national LEP enrollment in 2000–2001.

While the LEP enrollment increases, recent federal policies have echoed the more restrictive educational language policies of the early twentieth century with the adoption into law of the No Child Left Behind Act of 2001 (2002), which expanded the use of English-only instruction for LEP students and constrained the delivery of these educational services to three years. The law also eliminated the use of the term "bilingual education" from government offices and programs. It has also required a greater participation of LEP students in standardized testing done in English, even for students not proficient in the language.

Latino and Latina participation in bilingual education continues to be dismal. In the 2000–2001 school year, according to a survey by Anneka Kindler, the states reported that only 22.7 percent of the LEP enrollment was receiving instruction that incorporated the "native" language.

Much of this "incorporation" of the native language is presumed to be for informal communication and not academic instruction. Only about 10 percent of the national LEP enrollment was reclassified from LEP to fluent English proficient the same year. Approximately 9 percent of secondary school LEP students were retained in grade across the nation.

Schools enrolling Latinas and Latinos are also becoming more segregated. A recent study by Jennifer Van Hook and Kelly Balistreri of the institutional contexts of California Spanish-speaking LEP students between 1985 and 2000 found that Spanish-speaking LEP children increasingly attended schools with low-income, minority, and LEP students—more than other non-LEP and LEP groups—as a result of district-level patterns of segregation by income, race or ethnicity, and language. The greater concentration of these characteristics suggests that in order for students to be successful, they need higher-quality and more relevant schooling.

Chicano and Chicana, Puerto Rican, and other Latino and Latina communities are still asking for high-quality educational services through which their children can learn, understand the language of instruction, and be understood in the classroom. Bilingual education was an option for the last third of the twentieth century, and has been much reduced as an option in the early twenty-first century.

Legacy

Language politics in the United States in the last two decades of the twentieth century challenged and shifted some of the principles around which educational policy was built. One principle of educational policy was that a student who was not proficient in English had a right to be taught in a language he or she could understand. While the implementation of this left much to be desired, it guided much of the educational policy, teacher education, and program standards for thirty years. This was challenged successfully by the English-only movement in several states. The principle still lives, albeit in diminished capacity, in the persistence of bilingual instruction demanded by parents and executed by bilingual teachers and administrators.

There was a definite cultural policy backlash against Chicanos and Chicanas, Puerto Ricans, Cubans, other Latinos and Latinas, and other immigrants and language minorities during the last decade of the last millennium. It is not clear that this backlash has run its course, or that the above-stated principle will not be reaffirmed. However, it may require a substantial increase in the political representation of the different Latino and Latina populations for these bilingual education interests to be reflected in future law and educational policies.

See also ASPIRA; Bilingual Education Act; Bilingual Teacher Training; Civil Rights Act (1964); Education; English as a Second Language; Schools, Parochial; Schools, Public; *and* United States–Mexican War.

BIBLIOGRAPHY

August, Diane, and Kenji Hakuta, eds. *Improving Schooling for Language-Minority Children: A Research Agenda.* Report of the National Research Council. Washington, D.C.: National Academy Press, 1997.

Kindler, Anneka. *Survey of the States' Limited English Proficient Students and Available Educational Programs and Services: 2000–2001 Summary Report.* Washington, D.C.: National Clearinghouse for English Language Acquisition and Language Instruction Educational Programs, 2002.

Leibowitz, Arnold. "English Literacy: Legal Sanction for Discrimination." *Notre Dame Lawyer* 45, no. 7 (Fall 1969): 7–67.

Leibowitz, Arnold. "The Imposition of English as the Language of Instruction in American Schools." *Revista de Derecho Puertorriqueño* no. 38, año 10 (octubre-diciembre 1970): 175–244.

MacDonald, Victoria-María, ed. *Latino Education in U.S. History, 1513–2000.* New York: Palgrave/Macmillan, 2004.

Macías, Reynaldo F. "The Flowering of America: Linguistic Diversity in the United States." In *New Immigrants in the United States: Readings for Second Language Educators*, edited by Sandra Lee McKay and Sau-ling Cynthia Wong. Cambridge, U.K.: Cambridge University Press, 2000.

Macías, Reynaldo F. "Language and Ethnic Classification of Language Minorities: Chicano and Latino Students in the 1990s." *Hispanic Journal of Behavioral Sciences* 15, no. 2 (1993): 230–257.

Macías, Reynaldo F. "Language Politics and the Sociolinguistic Historiography of Spanish in the United States." In *Language in Action: New Studies of Language in Society*, edited by Joy Kreeft Peyton, Peg Griffin, Walt Wolfram, and Ralph Fasold. Cresskill, N.J.: Hampton Press, 2001.

Mackey, William Francis, and Von Nieda Beebe. *Bilingual Schools for a Bicultural Community: Miami's Adaptation to the Cuban Refugees.* Rowley, Mass.: Newbury House Publishers, 1977.

Moran, Carrol E., and Kenji Hakuta. "Bilingual Education: Broadening Research Perspectives." In *Handbook of Research on Multicultural Education*, edited by James A. Banks and Cherry A. McGee Banks. New York: Macmillan, 1995.

Olson, James S., and Judith E. Olson. *Cuban Americans: From Trauma to Triumph.* New York: Twayne Publishers, 1995.

Perlmann, Joel. "Historical Legacies: 1840–1920." *The Annals of the American Academy of Political and Social Science* 508 (March 1990): 27–37.

Sánchez-Korrol, Virginia E. *From Colonia to Community: The History of Puerto Ricans in New York City.* Berkeley: University of California Press, 1994.

Sánchez-Korrol, Virginia. "Toward Bilingual Education: Puerto Rican Women Teachers in New York City Schools, 1947–1967." In *Puerto Rican Women and Work: Bridges in Transnational Labor*, edited by Altagarcía Ortiz. Philadelphia: Temple University Press, 1996.

San Miguel, Guadalupe, Jr. *Contested Policy: The Rise and Fall of Federal Bilingual Education in the United States, 1960–2001.* Denton: University of North Texas Press, 2004.

San Miguel, Guadalupe, Jr. *"Let All of Them Take Heed:" Mexican Americans and the Campaign for Educational Equality in Texas, 1910–1981.* Austin: University of Texas Press, 1987.

Shin, Hyon, and Rosalind Bruno. *Language Use and English Speaking Ability: 2000.* Census 2000 Brief, C2KBR-29, October. Washington, D.C.: U.S. Census Bureau, 2003.

U.S. Census Bureau. *Language Spoken at Home and Ability to Speak English for the United States, Regions, and States: 1990.* Special tabulation of the 1990 Census of Population. 1990 CPH-L-133. Washington, D.C.: U.S. Census Bureau, Education and Social Stratification Branch, 1993.

U.S. Census Bureau. *Statistical Abstract of the U.S.: 1999.* Washington, D.C.: U.S. Government Printing Office, 1999.

Valenzuela, Angela, ed. *Leaving Children Behind: Why "Texas-style" Accountability Fails Latino Youth.* Albany: State University of New York Press, 2004.

Van Hook, Jennifer, and Kelly Balistreri. "Diversity and Change in the Institutional Context of Immigrant Adaptation: California Schools, 1985–2000." *Demography* 39, no. 4 (November 2002): 639–654.

Weinberg, Meyer. *A Chance to Learn: The History of Race and Education in the United States.* 2nd ed. Long Beach: University Press, California State University–Long Beach, 1995.

REYNALDO F. MACÍAS, VICTORIA-MARÍA MACDONALD,
AND JUAN F. CARRILLO

BILINGUAL EDUCATION ACT. The Bilingual Education Act has been mired in controversy since it was enacted. The act reflects a desire both to improve the educational opportunities of English language learners and to incorporate burgeoning numbers of immigrant children into American society. There are deep divisions among educational experts, policy makers, and the general public about how to achieve these goals, and these disagreements have greatly complicated efforts to fund and implement the act.

First passed in 1968, the Bilingual Education Act began as a grant-in-aid program to promote research and experimentation on educational programs for students who speak a language other than English. Rather than create an enforceable right, the act simply provided school districts with modest sums of money to foster innovative instruction. Put on the national agenda by Senator Ralph Yarborough of Texas, the act was the first piece of federal legislation to focus exclusively on the needs of linguistic minority children. During congressional hearings, the bill's supporters argued that the act would begin to rectify the educational neglect and disadvantage that non–English-speaking children had suffered in America's public schools. However, there was not complete agreement about how best to remedy this legacy of educational failure. Parents and community leaders typically favored enrichment models based on multilingual, multicultural curricula, while educators largely endorsed programs of compensatory education that would assimilate children to traditional English-speaking classrooms. Enrichment models treated the non-English language as an asset to be preserved, while compensatory models treated it as a barrier to be overcome in learning English.

Throughout the act's history, controversy over the role of native-language instruction and English immersion has persisted. Some experts argue that students are best served by programs that incorporate the child's native language. Transitional bilingual education, which uses the native language as a bridge to acquiring English, is a temporary program, and when it is completed, children are placed in English-speaking classrooms. Bilingual-bicultural education programs (also referred to as maintenance programs) are designed to preserve fluency and literacy in both the native language and English. To avoid potentially long-term segregative effects, some school districts use dual-immersion programs in which English speakers and non-English speakers together acquire proficiency in multiple languages.

Other experts question the benefits of using native-language instruction to acquire English. In their view, programs should promote rapid acquisition of English, and children learn English best when immersed in the language to the greatest extent possible. Again there are different methods for promoting rapid English acquisition. English-as-a-Second-Language programs pull children out of English-speaking classrooms for a portion of the day to concentrate on acquiring English language skills. Other programs rely on structured immersion. That is, English language learners receive all of their lessons in English without special pull-out programs, but the instruction is specially structured to reflect their limited proficiency.

Initially the act did not endorse a particular pedagogical method. Although designed to sidestep controversy, this ambiguity left Congress uneasy about making a full financial commitment, and in the early years after the act's passage, appropriations fell well below the authorized funding levels. As the population of linguistic minority students grew dramatically due to immigration, appropriations under the act increased substantially. Faced with growing demand and limited resources, state and local educational agencies regularly converted research grants into desperately needed funds for service delivery. In the early twenty-first century the act does far more than promote experimentation. Grants can be used to build the capacity to deliver high-quality programs, to train teachers, and to provide technical assistance.

In 2002 the No Child Left Behind Act imposed extensive requirements for accountability testing in districts that serve linguistic minority students. As part of the 2002 reforms, the Bilingual Education Act was renamed the English Language Acquisition, Language Enhancement, and Academic Achievement Act. Although the act continues to allow state and local educators to choose from instructional methods "based on scientifically based research," the statement of purpose and accountability requirements make clear that the primary objective is English acquisition. As a result, programs "may make use of both English and a child's native language to enable the child to develop and attain English proficiency."

Currently the act makes clear that its provisions must be interpreted consistently with federal civil rights laws. Under Title VI of the Civil Rights Act of 1964, schools must take "affirmative steps" to rectify a language barrier that "excludes national origin–minority group children from effective participation in the educational program." The Equal Educational Opportunities Act (EEOA) requires school districts to take "appropriate action to overcome language barriers that impede equal participation by its students in the instructional process." As interpreted by the U.S. Supreme Court, Congress, and federal civil rights officials, these provisions rely on terms like "affirmative steps" and "appropriate action" that give school districts the discretion to use a range of instructional approaches. As a result, under both Title VI and the EEOA, courts and federal enforcement agencies must decide on a case-by-case basis whether programs are in fact overcoming linguistic barriers to full participation.

The current version of the act also states that its provisions do not "negate or supersede State law." In some states critics of native-language instruction have crafted state ballot initiatives that codify a preference for intensive English instruction. By the early twenty-first century these initiatives have succeeded in Arizona, California, and Massachusetts but not in Colorado, and where enacted, the initiatives have successfully withstood judicial challenge. Supporters of the measures argue that they have enhanced academic achievement among English language learners, while opponents contend that the initiatives have created a "one size fits all" approach that damages educational opportunity and innovation. The latest skirmishes over language policy make plain that decades of research and experimentation have not resolved the conflicts that surround bilingual education. In the early twenty-first century debates about language policy remain highly contentious, whether that policy is made in Congress or at the state ballot box.

See also **Bilingual Education; Bilingualism and Biculturalism; Civil Rights Act (1964);** *and* **Education.**

BIBLIOGRAPHY

Crawford, James. *Bilingual Education: History, Politics, Theory, and Practice.* 4th ed. Los Angeles: Bilingual Educational Services, 1999.

Cummins, Jim, and David Corson, eds. *Bilingual Education.* Boston: Kluwer Academic Publishers, 1997.

Moran, Rachel F. "Bilingual Education and the Culture of Disinvestment." *Journal of Gender, Race, and Justice* 2 (1999): 163–211.

Ovando, Carlos J., and Peter McLaren, eds. *The Politics of Multiculturalism and Bilingual Education: Students and Teachers Caught in the Cross Fire.* Boston: McGraw-Hill, 2000.

Wiese, Ann-Marie, and Eugene E. Garcia. "The Bilingual Education Act: Language Minority Students and U.S. Federal Educational Policy." *International Journal of Bilingual Education and Bilingualism* 4, no. 4 (2001): 29–48.

RACHEL F. MORAN

BILINGUALISM AND BICULTURALISM. Identity, language, and culture are intrinsically linked. We cannot talk about bilingualism without biculturalism. People who speak two languages usually also have knowledge and experience of the cultures identified with those languages. Culture is related to language and the development of basic communication and social skills. In a generic sense, to be bicultural is to have the ability to function effectively within two different cultural systems. However, Latinas and Latinos are not a monolith. They do not all have the same values, beliefs, or points of view. Some are newly arrived to the United States, and others were born and raised there. These two groups of Latinas and Latinos many times see things through different lenses. Latinas and Latinos in the United States come from a variety of Latin American countries, whose particular dialects of Spanish have a broad range of colloquial variations in diction, speech patterns, and vocabulary. The way each country enunciates and uses Spanish creates a sense of identity and pride distinct to each region. Latinas and Latinos are also a racially mixed group that includes European whites, and African and Caribbean blacks, as well as indigenous American Indians. Some individuals identify themselves ethnically as Latina or Latino and racially as black or white. The legacy of Spanish colonization and the resulting establishment of the Spanish language as the vernacular in their countries of origin are what provide a common group identity for Latinas and Latinos. In addition to that, there are important aspects that run through "Latina and Latino culture," such as the importance of family and community. A growing body of research indicates a tendency for Latinas and Latinos to acculturate rather than assimilate, largely preserving their cultural traits, while adopting a complementary mainstream cultural know-how.

Defining Bilingualism

Over the years, many scholars have tried to construct exact definitions of bilingualism that range from having native-like fluency in two languages to knowledge of two languages. Many scholars have agreed that a distinction should be made between types of bilingual language ability. On the one hand, there is academic language proficiency—the type of ability needed to function in an academic classroom setting—which requires higher-order thinking in the language, such as analysis and synthesis. On the other hand, there is conversational competence, which requires vocabulary and grammar sufficient to communicate meaning with the help of body language and gestures. The latter is the kind of communication where "situations provide . . . non verbal support to secure understanding," somewhat like the words and gestures used to communicate on the street or with a waiter

or a shopkeeper when engaged in foreign travel (Baker, p. 151). Linguist and researcher James Cummins described this distinction in bilingual language proficiency as cognitive academic language proficiency (CALP) and basic interpersonal communicative skills (BICS).

Bilingualism can also be an individual's choice—in cases in which a person decides to learn another language—or an external policy, in which the state decides the languages of instruction. Escobar defines bilingualism as the result of contact between or among ethnic groups "that coexist and compete" (Escobar, p. 33). More recently, Colin Baker has moved the definition further to include the use of language or what he terms "functional bilingualism," stressing that considering "when, where and with whom people use their two languages" brings the concept closer to reality and everyday life (Baker, p. 11).

The last two definitions are a good match for looking at bilingualism in the context of Latinas and Latinos in the United States. However, bilingualism is not only a Latina and Latino phenomenon. Throughout the history of the United States, English has not always been the only language spoken or used for instruction. Until the Dutch lost it to the British in 1664, Manhattan—then known as New Amsterdam—had a diverse population, speaking no fewer than eighteen languages. In the 1700s and 1800s, wherever European immigrants established their own schools, the vernacular was the language of instruction. These languages included German in places such as Cincinnati, Ohio, Cleveland, Ohio, and Indianapolis, Indiana; French in Louisiana; and Spanish in New Mexico and other parts of the Southwest. As early as 1839, the first bilingual education laws were enacted in Ohio. Louisiana followed in 1847. Nationally, by the late 1800s, 4 percent of the elementary school population was receiving its education in a language other than English.

Varied Sources of Spanish

The use of Spanish in America dates back to the fifteenth century and the Spanish colonization, which included such areas as Florida, Texas, Arizona, Colorado, and New Mexico—territories that became part of the United States during the nineteenth century. However, the Spanish spoken in the United States nowadays is also a consequence of large-scale immigration during the nineteenth and twentieth centuries, mainly from Mexico, Cuba, and Puerto Rico, and more recently from Central America. Spanish has even had an influence on American English. Words such as *salsa, coyote, armadillo, apache, canyon, ranch,* and *vigilante* are but a few examples of Spanish words that are now part of the American English lexicon.

With the 2000 census reporting that the Hispanic population has surpassed the 37 million mark, it is not uncommon to walk down the street of any major U.S. city and

hear Spanish being spoken. Bilingualism and biculturalism, once discouraged as divisive and not conducive to the Americanization process, are becoming the norm among Latinas and Latinos. A number of developments over the years have propelled Latina- and Latino-related issues into the national spotlight. Increases in the Latina and Latino population around the turn of the twenty-first century made Latinas and Latinos the largest minority in the country, surpassing African Americans. During the 1990s, debates about the primacy of English over Spanish and other immigrant languages reached a boiling point. The topic of bilingualism in the delivery of educational and other services to the Latina and Latino community became a primary focus of the political discourse. The rapidly expanding Latina and Latino population has been embraced and exploited by advertisers, politicians, and the media. Mass media, modern transportation, banking, and the Internet all provide translation of their services into Spanish in a way inconceivable to earlier immigrants. National media chains such as Telemundo and Univision are instrumental in maintaining the vernacular as a force in the community. Add to that the availability of Spanish videos and compact discs, supermarket chains, and easy access to travel to and from Latin America, all of which also help keep the old language and customs alive. Another phenomenon that reinforces bilingual and bicultural identity in Latinas and Latinos is the adherence to tradition and strong family and religious values. In her case studies, Sonia Nieto found that high school students were proud of their Latina and Latino heritage and wanted to maintain their culture and language. Her research also notes that there was more academic success among students who acculturated rather than assimilated.

Even Spanglish, a fusion of English and Spanish, for many years snubbed by academia, has become popular, entering the lexicon of many young urban U.S.–born Latinas and Latinos. Characterized by "code-switching" or substituting words from one language into another, Spanglish appears frequently in the works of well-established Latina and Latino writers such as Sandra Cisneros, Julia Alvarez, and Roberto Fernández. It is also common to hear Spanglish in the lyrics of contemporary Latina and Latino rappers and hip-hop singers. And so we arrange the *furnitura* (furniture); we buy *Bibaporú* (Vicks VapoRub) for our colds; and we complain about the lack of *el estín* (steam heat) that results in our colds. "Man, me dieron un ticket por parquear en una zona no-parking" (Man, I got a ticket for parking in a no parking zone). The actor and the governor of California, Arnold Schwarzenegger, coined one of the most popular Spanglish phrases of all time, "Hasta la vista, baby." A Latina executive explained her usage of this dialect as a manifestation of her bicultural identity and as part of the acculturation process, "You pick and choose and accommodate, and that's what Spanglish is" (Alvarez).

Bilingual Education and Other Issues

Bilingual education was established by congressional mandate in 1968. This approach, which espouses the philosophy of teaching academic subjects to immigrant children in their native languages while gradually instructing them in English so that after a few years they are able to join regular classes, is one of the initiatives at the core of intense public debate over bilingual education in the schools. Through initiatives such as the English-only movement, efforts have been made to eliminate these programs from the public school system. Nationally, the controversy over bilingual education intensified in 1998. In California, voters endorsed a proposition to end the instruction of immigrant children in their native languages. In Chicago and Denver, Colorado, school boards voted to limit bilingual classes to three years. The Arizona Legislature voted to limit bilingual education to four years.

As the number of Latinas and Latinos working in the corporate sector has grown over the past decade, companies have begun to tailor special programs to their needs—from offering free English classes to publishing bilingual company newsletters. In major cities with large Latina and Latino populations, Spanish-language media provide information about housing and tips to help Latinas and Latinos become more knowledgeable about their rights and obligations. Over the years the government has made these accommodations, including interpretive services and translation of documents, available to non–English speakers. This widespread use of Spanish has generated public debate over language. Some point to Canada, where the existence of English and French has been linked to a secessionist movement, as an example of where this debate could lead. But however strong the opinions of groups opposing the use of all languages but English in the United States, one must keep in mind that the authors of the U.S. Constitution discussed and discarded proposals to establish an official language. Historically, perhaps as a consequence of the fact that the U.S. population has been drawn from all parts of the world, language differences (with some exceptions such as censorship of German during World War I) have been accepted, accommodated, and respected in much the same way as religious differences. However, since 1981 there has been congressional interest in designating English as the official language of the United States, and over twenty-seven states have established English as their official language.

Reasons for Bilingualism and Biculturalism

Many wonder why bilingualism and biculturalism characterize the Latina and Latino community, young and old. Some point to the multiculturalism movement that has permeated the educational system for more than twenty years, which fosters the "coexistence of separate but equal cultures," in essence rejecting assimilation as well as the "melting pot" theory (Rodríguez). Others point to the existence of media and the continued immigration from Latin America. There isn't a definitive answer as to why Latinas and Latinos have maintained a strong attachment to their language and their identity. Wall Street, however, has taken great interest in bilingual and bicultural Latinas and Latinos: "acculturated Hispanics represent the prime market—sophisticated consumers . . . who differentiate themselves by maintaining their Hispanic heritage" (Ramírez Magaña p. 26).

Although most waves of immigration to the United States have had clear beginnings and endings, Latina and Latino immigration has been continuous for nearly a century. Latinas and Latinos are branching out and making significant contributions in many different fields while staying true to their roots. The "salad bowl" metaphor is a good way to describe the Latina and Latino acculturation process: each item in the salad remains a distinguishable element of the entity as a whole.

See also **Alexander v. Sandoval; Ballot Propositions 187, 209, and 227; Code-Switching; Mestizaje;** *and* **Spanglish.**

BIBLIOGRAPHY

Alvarez, Lizette. "It's the Talk of Nueva York: The Hybrid Called Spanglish." *New York Times*, March 25, 1997.

Andersson, Theodore, and Mildred Boyer. *Bilingual Schooling in the United States*. 2nd ed. Austin, Tex.: National Educational Laboratory Publishers, 1978.

Baker, Colin. *Foundations of Bilingual Education and Bilingualism*. 2nd ed. Clevedon, U.K.: Multilingual Matters, 1996.

Bloomfield, Leonard. *Language*. New York: Holt, 1933.

Cummins, Jim. "Wanted: A Theoretical Framework for Relating Language Proficiency to Academic Achievement among Bilingual Students." In *Language Proficiency and Academic Achievement*, edited by Charlene Rivera. Clevedon, U.K.: Multilingual Matters, 1984.

Escobar, Alberto. *Variaciones sociolingüísticas del castellano en el Perú*. Lima, Peru: Instituto de Estudios Peruanos, 1978.

Glazer, Nathan, and Daniel Patrick Moynihan. *Beyond the Melting Pot: The Negroes, Puerto Ricans, Jews, Italians, and Irish of New York City*. 2nd ed. Cambridge, Mass.: MIT Press, 1970.

Nieto, Sonia. *Affirming Diversity: The Sociopolitical Context of Multicultural Education*. 2nd ed. New York: Longman, 1996.

Oboler, Suzanne. *Ethnic Labels, Latino Lives: Identity and the Politics of (Re)presentation in the United States*. Minneapolis: University of Minnesota Press, 1995.

Ramírez Magaña, Abel. "A Bicultural Bias." *Hispanic Business* 25, no. 12 (December 2003): 24, 26.

Rodriguez, Gregory. "The Nation: Mexican-Americans; Forging a New Vision of America's Melting Pot." *New York Times*, February 11, 2001.

Von Maltitz, Frances Willard. *Living and Learning in Two Languages: Bilingual-Bicultural Education in the United States*. New York: McGraw-Hill, 1975.

GAIL CUETO

BILINGUAL TEACHER TRAINING.

In 1968 the federal government passed the Bilingual Education Act in an effort to provide equal educational opportunities for non–English-background students. An innovative yet controversial approach, it introduced a new area of study into the field of teacher education.

From a historical perspective, bilingual education has existed for many centuries. As early as the 1600s, Philadelphia's German-speaking Americans operated schools in their native language. In the eighteenth century the Continental Congress published many of its official documents, including the Articles of Confederation, in German and French as well as in English to accommodate politically significant groups of non-English speakers. In the 1700s and 1800s, wherever European immigrants established their own schools the vernacular was the language of instruction. The first bilingual education laws were enacted in Ohio in 1839, followed by Louisiana in 1847. Nationally, by the late 1800s, 4 percent of the elementary school population were receiving their education in a language other than English.

In *Bilingual Schooling in the United States* (1978) Theodore Andersson and Mildred Boyer divide bilingual education into two periods, 1840–1920 and post-1963. During that first period three languages other than English were used in schools: German in the Midwest, Spanish in the Southwest, and French in Louisiana. In *The Best of Two Worlds* (1983), Diego Castellanos describes the educational system of the time as a setting where immigrants' languages and cultures were acceptable in the classroom. Throughout much of the United States' educational history during this period, however, while there was tolerance for the inclusion of different languages and cultures in some educational settings, there was no curriculum or teacher training attached to it.

The events that initiated bilingual education as it is understood in the early twenty-first century and the subsequent development of bilingual teacher training began with the influx of Cuban refugees into Miami during the late 1950s and the 1960s. In 1963, striving to meet the educational needs of thousands of Cuban children entering the Miami school system, educators in Dade County, Florida, pioneered contemporary bilingual schooling in the Coral Way Elementary School. With support from the Ford Foundation, the school initiated a bilingual education program designed for both Spanish-speaking and English-speaking students. It was during this time that the first bilingual teacher training was conducted. Thirty Cuban teachers were retrained at the University of Miami and earned temporary certificates to work as paraprofessionals.

The number of non–English-speaking children increased dramatically during the early 1960s, and in 1967 Senator Ralph Yarborough of Texas proposed a bill to establish bilingual education programs in U. S. schools. In 1968 Title VII of the Elementary and Secondary Education Act (ESEA), known as the Bilingual Education Act, was authorized by Congress to provide funds to school districts for direct services to students and teacher training and support services. It supported bilingual education programs that buttressed students' cultural heritages and supported native-language instruction while they acquired English. Although this was the initial purpose of the law, over the years the federal and state bilingual education laws have changed the focus to a remedial effort designed to transition students as quickly as possible to monolingual English classrooms. This focus continues to shape the development of bilingual education in the nation and has been the cause of heated ideological battles between critics and supporters of bilingual education.

Initially not all teachers in the field had received formal training in the native language. There were no established standards to evaluate the degree of language competence needed to provide instruction in all areas of the curriculum. Even though the federal government began to make monies available to school districts to prepare professionals to participate in bilingual programs, not until 1974 were institutions of higher education allowed to apply for bilingual teacher training funds under Public Law 93-380. This legislation also created a bilingual education fellowship program at the graduate level to train future teacher trainers. However, up to this time there were few if any established bilingual teacher training programs. The literature regarding bilingual teacher education before 1974 is quite scarce, and some scholars have attributed this to the shortage of funding until the Bilingual Education Act was passed.

California was one of the first states to enact legislation on bilingual education, resulting in the Teacher Preparation and Licensing Standards for the certification of bilingual education teachers. The competencies Californians identified serve as the foundation for most bilingual teacher certifications nationwide. They include fluency in the primary language or dialect as well as English and familiarity with the cultural heritage of the students. In addition, teachers are required to have knowledge of the methodologies needed to effectively adapt and revise curricula for students with limited English proficiency (LEP).

By 1976 eleven states had developed teacher certification requirements and had begun to establish ways to assess bilingual teachers. Two years earlier in New York the landmark case *ASPIRA v. New York City Board of Education* mandated both bilingual education and qualified teachers to implement the program. In 1978 the United States Office of Bilingual Education published *Competencies for University Programs in Bilingual Education*, which includes language proficiency and courses in bilingual education materials and methodologies. In 1992 the National Association for Bilingual Education (NABE), as a policy statement, issued its standards for the preparation of bilingual and multicultural teachers in the United States. The standards were developed with the belief that bilingual and multicultural teachers should have "the same quality of academic preparation as all teachers" and that they "need to meet additional standards related to proficiency in non-English languages, cultural diversity and bilingual and second language pedagogy" (p. 3).

Still, in the early twenty-first century only twenty-four states and the District of Columbia offer bilingual teacher certification. Not surprisingly there is a severe shortage of bilingual teachers nationwide amid a large and rapidly growing population of language minority students.

The field of bilingual education has been highly politicized and at times swathed in controversy from the English Only movement to a number of legislative initiatives proposed in various states. However, the social, linguistic, and cultural characteristics of the language minority students continue to require the bilingual teacher education programs and the competencies these programs develop to address the reality of the student population.

See also **ASPIRA; ASPIRA Consent Decree; Bilingual Education; Bilingual Education Act;** *and* **Education.**

BIBLIOGRAPHY

Andersson, Theodore, and Mildred Boyer. *Bilingual Schooling in the United States*. Austin, Tex.: National Educational Laboratory Publishers, 1978.

Canales, JoAnn, and José Agustín Ruíz-Escalante. "A Pedagogical Framework for Bilingual Education Teacher Preparation Programs." *Proceedings of the Third National Research Symposium on Limited English Proficient Students' Issues: Focus on Middle and High Schools*, vol 1, 113–153. 1993.

Castellanos, Diego. *The Best of Two Worlds: Bilingual-Bicultural Education in the United States*. Trenton, N.J.: New Jersey State Department of Education, 1983.

Crawford, James. *Bilingual Education: History, Politics, Theory, and Practice*. Los Angeles: Bilingual Educational Services, 1991.

National Association for Bilingual Education. *Professional Standards for the Preparation of Bilingual/Multicultural Teachers*. Washington, D.C.: Author, 1992.

Riojas Clark, Ellen. "The State of the Art in Research on Teacher Training Model with Special Reference to Bilingual Education Teachers." *Proceedings of the First Research Symposium on Limited English Proficient Students' Issues*. Washington, D.C.: U.S. Department of Education, 1990. Available at www.ncela.gwu.edu/pubs/symposia/first/state-dis.htm

GAIL CUETO

BIRTH DEFECTS. From the early 1900s to the first decade of this century, U.S. infant and maternal mortality rates continually decreased as a direct result of better public-health and clinical practices, greater access to prenatal and postpartum care, and major drug advances that directly reduced morbidity and mortality from infection. More recently, the focus on reducing infant mortality has shifted to reducing the incidences of low-birth-weight (LBW) babies and of birth defects or congenital anomalies, since both these health outcomes are the leading causes of infant mortality in the United States today. Many LBW infants experience severe neurological problems at birth, impairing their physical, emotional, and intellectual development. As Table 1 illustrates, between 1995 and 1997 there was a lower rate of infant mortality but a higher rate of low-birth-weight babies born to women of all ethnic groups than there was between 1989 and 1991.

Latinas and Latinos only recently have surfaced as an important focus of study for this health problem. A limited but growing body of research on this topic has emerged and is based on a demographic shift—the high rate of fertility of Latinas, as well as slightly different observations of birth defect distributions, relative to non-Latina and non-Latino groups in the United States.

For Latinas and Latinos, the adverse health outcomes associated with LBW babies and birth defects is complicated by the fact that the distribution of both differs significantly by Latina and Latino subpopulation. For example, Puerto Rican women have a much higher incidence of

LBW babies compared to Cuban women. In addition, despite relatively good birth outcomes for immigrant Mexican women, there may be significant underreporting of birth outcomes since they are more than twice as likely as women in other racial or ethnic groups to give birth outside a hospital. Thus, despite the overall finding that Latinas and Latinos experience lower rates of infant mortality as compared to other high-risk groups, this "epidemiological paradox" should be viewed with caution as variations in Latina and Latino subpopulations, along with data limitations, reduce our ability to make generalizations from these findings. A final caveat is the comparability of birth-defect data across states with respect to Latina and Latino subpopulations. That is, data are limited because of variations in the way states collect data on birth defects. In California, for example, about one in thirty-three children are born with structural birth defects (e.g., missing limbs, malformed hearts). According to Becerra et al., birth-defect risk factors for foreign-born and non-foreign-born mothers were roughly the same for both groups, and as the mother's age increased, so did the risk factors for chromosome birth defects such as Down's Syndrome. Another California study highlighted that Latina and Latino children with birth defects stayed longer in the hospital and had higher mortality rates than other groups, even though they generally had lower rates of hospitalization than black children with respect to birth defects and genetic diseases.

A more detailed study by the Texas Department of Health (2003) indicated that the highest percentage of birth defects experienced by Latinas and Latinos included: spina bifida without anencephaly (absence of a part of brain and skull), hydrocephaly, cleft lip with or without cleft palate, and defects in the large intestine, heart, and upper limbs. In Texas, cardiovascular and respiratory birth defects are the most prevalent in the Latina and Latino population, as well as the other two comparison groups, as Figure 1 illustrates.

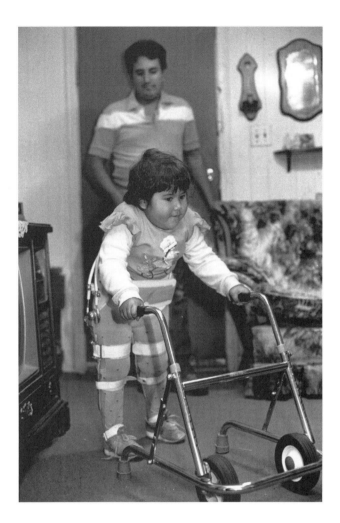

YOUNG GIRL WITH SPINA BIFIDA. The child uses braces and a walker. (© David H. Wells/CORBIS)

TABLE 1. *Rates of Adverse Pregnancy Outcomes by Ethnicity, United States, 1989–1991 to 1995–1997*

OUTCOME	NON-HISPANIC WHITE		MEXICAN		PUERTO RICAN		CUBAN		CENTRAL/SOUTH AMERICAN		OTHER HISPANIC	
	1989–1991	1995–1997	1989–1991	1995–1997	1989–1991	1995–1997	1989–1991	1995–1997	1989–1991	1995–1997	1989–1991	1995–1997
Preterm rate (per 100 live births)	8.47	9.52	10.55	10.58	13.36	13.16	9.35	10.21	10.70	10.81	11.04	11.77
Low-birth-weight rate (per 100 live births)	5.55	6.25	5.45	5.75	9.06	9.16	5.45	6.39	5.63	5.95	6.71	7.55
Infant mortality rate (per 100 live births)	6.25	4.98	6.17	4.73	8.39	6.35	5.03	4.28	5.47	4.02	6.63	5.71
N (in 1000s)	7683.7	7025	1088.6	1413.2	163.2	154.9	32	36.7	217.5	262.7	159.3	127.7

SOURCE: Frisbie, p. 237.

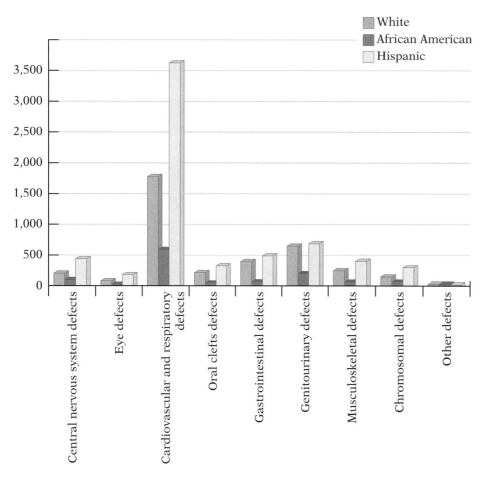

FIGURE 1. BIRTH DEFECTS IN TEXAS AMONG 1996–1997 DELIVERIES: PREVALENCE AT BIRTH BY MOTHER'S RACE/ETHNICITY (Source: Texas Birth Defects Monitoring Division: http://www.tdh.state. tx.us/tbdmd/Data/prevalence_at _birth_by_race_ethnic.htm)

There is growing evidence that environmental factors, including exposure to toxins and pollutants, may contribute to the development of birth defects. Between 1988 and 1992, twenty-five children were born with spina bifida and more than thirty were born with anencephaly in the border town of Brownsville, Texas. The cause was never identified. The Texas Department of Health later began a program to monitor and investigate the prevalence of birth defects, and reports from the department (1995 and 1997) identified, in various border regions, clusters of significantly elevated rates of gastroschisis (an abdominal wall defect causing the intestines to protrude), Down's Syndrome, neural tube defects (relating to the spinal cord and brain), and anophthalmia (the complete absence of an eye). In Piedras Negras, Mexico, during February and March of 1995, there were three babies born with anencephaly, which is 3.8 times the expected number of such neural tube defects. In another border town, Chilpancingo, a community of about 2,000 people located in a canyon below an industrial park near Tijuana, there were reported to be nine anencephaly births (newborns having a partial or total absence of a brain) in 1993 and fourteen in 1994.

A study conducted by the Pew Environmental Health Commission at the Johns Hopkins School of Public Health indicated that causes are known for only about 20 percent of birth defects. Research has established that the consumption of alcohol, caffeine, and tobacco by a pregnant woman can have detrimental effects on a baby's development. It is difficult to determine causal factors, trends, and clusters for lack of tracking systems or variations between those that do exist. It is particularly difficult to make links between environmental toxins and birth defects because of the need to determine levels of exposure. However, environmental factors that have been associated with low birth weight include exposure to lead, solvents, pesticides, carbon monoxide, radiation, altitude, noise, and stress. The California Birth Defects Monitoring Program has made various associations between environmental factors and birth defects. These include high-level exposure to solvents and higher risk of gastroschisis; exposure to colorants and higher risk of gastroschisis; proximity to a U.S. Environmental Protection Agency Superfund site (an area being cleaned of hazardous wastes) and higher risk of heart defects and neural tube defects; exposure to high levels of nitrates (in water) and increased risk of anencephaly;

exposure to carbon monoxide and increased incidence of heart defects; exposure to ozone and heart problems having to do with defects in the pulmonary artery and valve and aortic artery and valve.

See also Health; Health, Children's; Health Care Access; *and* Pesticides.

BIBLIOGRAPHY

Becerra, Jose E., Carol J. R. Hogue, Hani K. Atrash, et al. "Infant Mortality among Hispanics: A Portrait of Heterogeneity." *Journal of the American Medical Association* 265 (January 1991): 217–221.

California Birth Defects Monitoring Program. "All Birth Defects Combined." 2003. www.cbdmp.org/bd_intro.htm.

Centers for Disease Control and Prevention. "CDC on Infant and Maternal Mortality in the United States: 1900–1999." *Population and Development Review* 25 (1999): 821–826.

"Danger Still Great, but Activism along Border Paying off Slowly for Maquiladora Workers." *The Nation's Health* 26 (1996): 1.

Feldstein, Mark, and S. Singer. "The Border Babies." *Time* 149, no. 21 (May 26, 1997): 72.

Frisbie, W. Parker, and Seung-eun Song. "Hispanic Pregnancy Outcomes: Differentials over Time and Current Risk Factor Effects." *Policy Studies Journal* 31 (May 2003): 237–252.

March of Dimes. "Leading Cause of Infant Death, 1999." 2002. www.marchofdimes.com.

Texas Department of Health. "Report on Birth Defect Investigations Conducted by the Texas Birth Defects Monitoring Division and the Health Studies Program." 1994. www.tdh.state.tx.us/tbdmd/ClusterPage/clus94.pdf.

Texas Department of Health. "Birth Defect Investigations conducted in 1997." www.tdh.state.tx.us/tbdmd/ClusterPage/clus97.pdf.

Yoon, Paula W., Richard S. Olney, Muin J. Khoury, et al. "Contribution of Birth Defects and Genetic Diseases to Pediatric Hospitalizations: A Population-Based Study." *Pediatric Adolescent Medicine* 151 (November 1997): 1096–1103.

ADELA DE LA TORRE AND TERENCE VALENZUELA

BIRTH RATES. *See* Family Planning.

BISEXUALITY. The concept of bisexuality can encompass a range of topics from bisexual individuals to emotions, erotic attractions, and sexual behaviors. Cultural variations in the identification of sexual acts and identities complicate definitions, as do dichotomous conceptions of sexuality as either heterosexual or homosexual, since they often render bisexuality invisible.

National studies suggest that women are more likely to report attractions to both men and women than are men, but few people self-identify as bisexual, perhaps because bisexuality is generally stigmatized in both heterosexual and lesbian and gay contexts. Of the social science studies on bisexuality that exist, few discuss ethnic or racial variation. However, Paula Rodriguez Rust (1999) reported that rates of bisexual self-identification are higher among African Americans and Latinos and Latinas than among whites.

Rodriguez Rust (2000) also found that it is easier for mixed-race bisexual women of color to take on a bisexual identity since they were already more aware of "nonbipolar thinking." Bisexual Latinas (Leyva 1991) report that they experience extreme biphobia from both gay and heterosexual people and that although some Latinas might practice bisexuality, they are reluctant to discuss this openly.

While there is little documentation on Latina bisexuality, many studies suggest that, although Latinos do not tend to label themselves as bisexual, sexual contact between men is not all that unusual. There may be a number of reasons why Latinos do not identify as bisexual. One is that the idea of basing one's identity on sexual attraction or behavior is culturally specific. Unlike in the United States, in Latin America there is not a tendency to self-identify according to sexual behavior or attraction. Latin Americans prefer to self-identify according to roles assumed in familial relationships; this is also the case for Latinos who are recent immigrants to the United States.

Tomas Almaguer points out that Mexican and Latin American sexual systems also differ from Euro-American sexual systems in their emphasis on sexual acts rather than object choice. Whereas Euro-Americans tend to define sexuality according to the biological sex of the desired object, that is, same sex, homosexual, other sex, heterosexual, the Latin American system is based on the sexual act that a person carries out with another person. Sexual roles are understood as active or inserter and passive or receptor. Under this system those who enact a passive role are stigmatized as feminine and subordinate, whereas the active party retains macho status regardless of the sex of his partner. According to Almaguer, "This 'bisexual' option, an exemption from stigma for the 'masculine' homosexual, can be seen as part of the ensemble of gender privileges and sexual prerogatives accorded Mexican men" (p. 260). This idea works within an economy of sexual dominance where the macho is interpreted as so dominant that his sexuality is not threatened by having penetrative sex with another man. Men who engage in bisexual behavior are not stigmatized as long as they take on the inserter "masculine" role exclusively. The passive partner is considered the homosexual and stigmatized as effeminate. Interestingly, this system renders bisexual behavior totally compatible with both machismo and heterosexual identity.

On the other hand, it is important not to suggest absolute differences between nationalities that get reduced to cultural stereotypes, especially as interaction and exchange between cultures is abundant. In Mexico, men who adapt to the Euro-American sexual system and take on both active and passive roles are called *internacionales* or *modernos*, which clearly indicates that a range of systems may operate in one context. As Latinos are acculturated in the U.S. sexual system, more tend to take on gay and bisexual identities.

See also Gays; Lesbians; *and* Sexuality.

BIBLIOGRAPHY

Almaguer, Tomas. "Chicano Men: A Cartography of Homosexual Identity and Behavior." In *The Lesbian and Gay Studies Reader*, edited by Henry Abelove, Michèle Aina Barale, and David M. Halperin, 255–273. New York: Routledge, 1993.

Espin, Oliva. *Latina Realities: Essays on Healing, Migration, and Sexuality*. Boulder, Colo.: Westview Press, 1997.

Leyva, Obie. "Que es un bisexual?" In *Bi Any Other Name: Bisexual People Speak Out*, edited by Loraine Hutchins and Lani Kaahumanu, 201–202. Boston: Alyson, 1991.

Rodriguez Rust, Paula C. "Bisexuality: A Contemporary Paradox for Women." *Journal of Social Issues* 56, no. 2 (2000): 205–211.

Rodriguez Rust, Paula C., ed. *Bisexuality in the United States: A Social Science Reader*. New York: Columbia University Press, 1999.

LOURDES TORRES

BLACK-LATINO RELATIONS. The study of black-Latino relations is in its infancy. The dramatic growth of Latino immigrants after the 1964 immigration reform act has spurred interest in the topic since that time. Most important here were the conflicts and debates associated with a Latino expansion that coincided with civil rights reforms. Largely branded as black, this movement created opportunities that many people claimed belonged primarily to blacks. Hence, the dramatic growth of other minorities made the gains of the movement more limited as they all depended on the same source for their advancement. Such immigrants, many argued, would be enjoying benefits that they had not fought for and were therefore not entitled to—at least not until blacks were satisfied.

Mainstream Explanations

This rationalization continues the rationale constructed to explain relationships between European immigrants who had organized along nationality lines to preempt competition from other immigrants. Newcomers were supposed to wait in line for their turn: as the economy expanded, earlier immigrants would move up the ladder leaving their lower positions for the next in line. Eventually, everybody would be accommodated. It was a matter of time, hard work, and patience. The end result was a "melting pot." In the case of blacks, the rationale was that, when they finally reached the front of the line, others came to take their turn.

Mainstream America, the Chicago School, and the media have played a major role in promoting this rationalization and, in fact, taking sides with particular groups. A well-known article in the *Atlantic Monthly* (Miles, 1992) presented black-Latino relationships as innately conflictive, claiming that Latinos were taking the jobs of blacks—accepting or assuming along the way a legitimate hierarchy/ownership of jobs by race. Similarly, in the black-Korean conflict in New York, the *New York Times*

MURAL DE LA RAZA. Proponents to change the name of King Road to Martin Luther King Street stand in front of a mural in San Jose, Calif. The Latino and Latina residents of the neighborhood objected to the proposal. (Jeff Chiu/Associated Press)

sided with the former against the latter. In contrast, the *Los Angeles Times* sided with Koreans against blacks in Los Angeles. The issue is, however, more complex.

Alternative Explanations

Omi and Winant argue that race is socially constructed and suggest the need to understand the manner in which each minority group was incorporated into U.S. society, the racial condition it was assigned, and changes over time in the relationships between races. Such analysis questions the adequacy of the above reductionist and biased "one-size-fits-all" explanations. Reductionist explanations are inadequate because they ignore the unique process of incorporation of each group. Biased explanations are inadequate because they pretend that the process follows a rational and fair logic depicting incorporation as a progression from the country of origin to Americanization—regardless of the group at stake. In fact, the history of incorporation and race relations includes elements of manipulation, suppression, disenfranchisement, exploitation, and racism. It is driven by uneven structural dynamics of labor recruitment, geopolitical interests, colonial and postcolonial relations, and cultural hegemony. To fully understand this, the history of racialization of each group must be examined, along with the specific process and context of its incorporation into U.S. society, its relationship to European Americans, and the ways in which it fits into the process of construction of American society.

Blacks were originally forcibly incorporated into the U.S. economy as slaves specifically to work on plantations and in other slave occupations. Although African American slaves were fully emancipated in 1868 by the fourteenth amendment, only in 1964 did African Americans gain—at least formally—the same rights as European Americans. Meanwhile, different Latino nationals were incorporated through separate colonial and postcolonial processes and at different times and conjunctures. Colonization of their homelands turned Puerto Ricans and many Mexicans into U.S. residents. Although the Treaty of Guadalupe Hidalgo, which formalized the annexation of nearly half of Mexico to the United States, granted citizenship to residents of the territories conquered, in practice most of them were denied such rights and treated as foreign, often temporary, immigrant labor. The United States extended citizenship to Puerto Ricans in 1917; however, America always viewed and treated them as "second-class citizens." Cubans became part of the United States briefly through conquest; they became foreigners when they gained independence—although remaining under U.S. "protectionism"; finally, they became political or economic refugees after the Cuban Revolution. The rest of Latin America was Americanized before nationals from one country or another emigrated to join the Third World labor reserve in the United States.

These forms of incorporation ascribed blacks and Latinos a different status from the one granted to European immigrants—and from each other's status. The white majority in power excluded them from full partnership in the construction of the United States. European American views and incorporation of blacks became the basis for construction of Latinos as "other" blacks—and of all minorities as "colored" people. Although Latinos never bore the formal condition of slaves, they were denied full political participation, segregated socially and economically, and excluded from the "melting pot." Centuries of racism shaped the structural condition, image, and standing of both groups. Other immigrants from Latin America, the Caribbean and Africa—perhaps with the

exception of Cubans—inherited the status and structural limitations of their respective ancestors. At the end, a combination of accumulated structural factors, social stereotypes, and ascribed conditions turned them into separate groups situated at the bottom of society—only because of their race and origin.

Although the white majority in power constructed all minorities into the same racially inferior "other," it differentiated them legally, economically, and socially, ascribing different roles and representations to each. Original conditions carried—even after they acquired equal rights under the law—not only in the American mindset and institutions but also in a labor market highly fragmented by race.

Within these general matrices, there were local differences related to factors such as specific histories of incorporation, proportions of each group, nationalities of origin, timing of their immigration, and preexisting conditions. Similarly, America developed different stereotypes for different races. While the overall "white–non-white" divide distributed advantage and disadvantage universally, the specific conditions of each minority group produced separate communities with differential social processes and internal structures. Under these circumstances, blacks and Latinos inherited a shared common destiny of race-based exclusion but, at the same time, have separate histories, identities, and conditions that often pit them against each other. These conditions are further complicated by internal differences (e.g., class, gender, shades of color, internal racism, nationality of origin, beliefs, and politics).

Ignoring such factors, race relations were constructed into a bipolar, white-black paradigm characterized as "the black problem" and "the white man's burden"—ignoring factors that might have turned race relations into "a problem" while defining the solution as a "burden." Contrarily, recent research has defined them as relationships of domination, racism, and suppression while emphasizing the differences mentioned. Also, to construct their identities or address their specific issues, minorities have been trying to change these representations or have caved in to constraints pitting them against each other.

Meanwhile, questions inspiring research on non-black–white relations (e.g., black-Latino, white-Latino, Korean-black, Asian-Latino, and so forth) have come largely from institutionalized conflicts associated with recent urban changes often intensifying segregation and increasing the concentration of minorities in central cities and old suburbs or in separate municipalities. Although blacks and Latinos immigrated to cities a long time ago, they were contained for the most part in segregated "black belts" and barrios, respectively. As whites suburbanized and third world migration exploded with globalization, minorities came to occupy the spaces vacated by whites. Along with this, economic restructuring promoted a polarized labor market of high- and low-end industries and occupations, removing the traditional mobility ladder of manufacturing and further limiting the possibility of racial minorities to join the mainstream. This happened when Latinos and blacks were accessing mobility jobs in manufacturing, hence throwing them back into dead-end, low-end jobs. Mediated by race, this economic bifurcation consolidated a polarized job market with European Americans over-represented at the high end and Latinos, blacks, and other racial and pan-ethnic groups at the bottom. The result has been a new geography concentrating racialized minorities (both citizens and immigrants) in selected geographies (central cities in particular) and jobs and European Americans in others. This form of restructuring, not the growth of racialized minorities per se, has exacerbated tensions among minorities. It is, in fact, the result of accumulated white advantage and minority disadvantage in a context of globalization.

Black-Latino Relations

Black-Latino relations are as old as these groups' presence in the United States. They include the contextual issues mentioned earlier. They take place at all levels and spaces: federal, state, and local; economic, political, and social; geographical and cultural. Little, however, has been written about their interactions, collaborations, contentions, or anything else. Much of it has been featured by the media—often in sensationalist and stereotyped contexts. Most of what has been documented consists of instances of conflict. The study and documentation of relations at many levels has not even started. Some points have been made about extent of political representation, participation, and organizations and agendas, but little about interactions, commonalities, and differences, and much less about ways in which racism and discrimination shape or impact relations.

Relations vary by class, race, nationality, gender, and multiple other factors to the point that analyses of their interactions and ascriptions (as with all blacks and all Latinos) can be limited to vague generalities and can be misleading or irrelevant. Referring to the conflict between blacks and Koreans in Los Angeles and New York, Chang and Diaz-Veizades (1999) specify that it was between Korean "merchants" operating in low-income black neighborhoods and their "customers"—rather than between generic Koreans and generic blacks. Similarly, black-Latino relations assume as many forms and variations as divisions can be established within these communities. Hence, any analysis of their interactions should establish the proper contexts and qualifications.

Ultimately, the closest relations between blacks and Latinos take place locally. Here, we need to understand not only the specific histories of each group and the context of the relationship but also the specific subgroups involved. Similarly, interactions can be examined from a subjective or from an institutional or systemic perspective. The former includes studies of individual attitudes, opinions, and experiences. In a review of such studies, Flores Nieman (1999) concluded that race-based prejudices between blacks and Latinos may be a function of disparities between them. The author points to differences by generation, Latino nationality, and geography. To this, we can add differences of age; actual experiences of interaction; gender, class, political, religious, or other affiliation; and occupation. Subjective views can also reflect white or media views internalized by Latinos and blacks. Meanwhile, perceptions can change according to the moment, the environment, the locality, and the issue at stake.

Analyses focused on structural or institutional factors include other dynamics and findings. Comparing electoral politics and grassroots interactions between blacks and Latinos in New York, Bush and Sales (1997) conclude that the former tended to be more short lived and contentious than the latter. Similarly, examining the black-Latino coalition leading to the mayoral election of Harold Washington in Chicago, Betancur and Gills (2000) argue that, although agreeing on the major tenets of the coalition, Latino political, professional, and economic elites clashed over the distribution of divisible goods. Bonilla and Stafford (2000) point to a similar experience in New York.

Meanwhile, black-Latino relations vary between cities and regions—depending on local contexts, the groups involved the level of community formation, and the ways in which whites in power mediate or define relationships, among other factors. Cases from the main regions and cities of concentration of Latinos and blacks illustrate this.

In the Southwest, the U.S. occupation turned Mexicans into foreigners in their own land. Meanwhile, although they arrived after Mexicans, blacks moved ahead of them in the political and public sectors, especially as a result of the outcomes of the civil rights and black power movements. Mexicans responded with their own movement. Then, threatened by Latino demands and organizing, black leadership subscribed to civil rights entitlements claiming that Latinos were taking black jobs and trying to snatch black gains. Meanwhile, ongoing mass immigration of political and economic refugees from Central America and the accelerated immigration of Mexicans in a context of limited jobs, housing, and social services, generated new tensions, actors, and often contending agendas within the Latino community itself. Competition for a fixed "minority pie" (both within and between the

BLACK-LATINO RELATIONS.
Job seekers at the new
Sheraton Hotel in Chicago,
1992. (Ralf-Finn
Herstoft/CORBIS)

two communities) detracted from the deeper problem of distribution and opportunity for both races. Differences over bilingual education accelerated divisions within and without the communities, making race relations tense and, in fact, leading to the most unexpected coalitions around migration policy and bilingual education (e.g.,

subsectors of the Latino and black community coalescing against bilingual education or in favor of tougher immigration laws).

In Washington, D.C., a city traditionally shaped by the black-white divide, immigration of refugees from Central America introduced new dynamics. The desperate condition (both economic and legal) of Central Americans expressed itself in the 1991 Mount Prospect Riots demanding attention from local and national authorities. In turn, a decreasing black community feared the impact of the new claimants on their meager social services, housing, and job situations, straining relations between the two groups. Yet Afro-Latinos were welcomed into the Anglo-black community.

Black-white relations in the Miami area were deeply changed by Cuban migration just when the civil rights movement was opening doors to blacks. The latter resented the red carpet treatment of Cubans and their quick local ascension—with significant U.S. government help. Relations suffered a major blow as blacks saw Cubans move ahead of them while they remained confined to their traditional neighborhoods and positions. Efforts to compensate through improvements in the black community have produced only a bandage, and resentment between the two continues. Once again Afro-Cubans were segregated into Anglo-black areas by the racism of white Cubans, as discussed in the autobiography of Evilio Grillo, *Black Cuban, Black American*.

In New York, blacks benefited more than Latinos from the minority programs of the 1960s and 1970s. In spite of their racial closeness to and partnership with blacks, Puerto Ricans and Dominicans felt ignored by the civil rights movement, thus having to form their own movements apart from blacks. Yet there were instances of joint projects and cooperation such as described by Luis Aponte-Pares in his essay "Lessons from El Barrio: The East Harlem Real Great Society/Urban Planning Studio."

In Chicago, white-black relations dominated the racial scene until the 1970s. Their smaller size and isolation in clusters turned Latinos into an "invisible minority." However, a dramatic increase of Puerto Ricans in the 1950s and 1960s and of Mexicans since the 1950s, together with the fervor of the Puerto Rican and Chicano movements, produced strong joint struggles for political representation and opportunities. Although blacks feared Latino ascension, the two groups coalesced in the 1980s around a grassroots movement leading to the mayoral election of Harold Washington. Yet leaders disagreed over the distribution of public power and opportunity and the coalition fell apart when Washington, the glue that held them together, died in 1977.

Intra-community racism exists among both blacks (based on color shades and interracial mixing) and Latinos (comprising almost any race and racial mixing). For instance, intergroup relations between Latinos and blacks have tended to be more harmonious for Latinos and Latinas of African descent who have experienced anti-black racism from other Latinos and Latinas. This topic is the least documented. We should differentiate, however,

Illinois Black Panther Party. Deputy defense minister Bobby Rush speaks in 1969. Cha Cha Jimenez of the Chicago Young Lords is at left. (Jeff Chiu/Associated Press)

between the power of European Americans controlling white-black interactions and the ability of lighter blacks or white Latinos to inflict upon their own the disadvantages that white power has inflicted on blacks and Latinos as groups.

Challenges Ahead

Institutional analyses suggest uneasy relationships between blacks and Latinos in the United States. There are, however, others aspects and perspectives. For Barbaro (1977), manipulation of the civil rights movement after 1964 caused the modern black-Latino split. To gain black support, the Kennedy-Johnson administration steered War on Poverty and affirmative action programs to them. Moreover, as blacks moved into the black power movement, the struggle went from a general all-minority front to multiple ones by racial group. Hence, Mexicans and Puerto Ricans—and Latinos generally—engaged in separate processes and created their own movements. This split points to institutional factors beyond the communities' control, most specifically to decisions and interventions of the white establishment pitting blacks against Latinos.

Researchers point to intervening factors such as class and wars of position. Betancur and Gills (2000) document the divisive role of self-serving black and Latino elites in interactions between the two groups. Confronting the unwillingness of the white establishment to engage in the deep reforms required to make up for accumulated racial deficiencies, blacks and Latinos are consistently pushed into wars of position to get ahead of the other in the distribution of limited minority opportunities.

This, however, tells only part of the story. Blacks and Latinos interact daily around the issues, geographies, and institutions they share. They collaborate around common goods such as education and services or negotiate through "give and take" their daily interactions. They often learn from each other, help each other on a daily basis, and agree and disagree while carrying on their daily lives side to side. Unfortunately, successes and examples of collaboration don't get the attention of the media nor get properly documented as researchers are often influenced to look from the prism of institutionalized conflict. Perhaps the largest challenge for the two communities is to gain control of the ways in which they and their relations are portrayed and manipulated. Along with this, they need to insist on institutional and informal joint action and consciousness around their shared conditions and problems. For this, not only do they need to learn more about each other's conditions and develop a sense of shared histories and destiny but they also need to construct common agendas supported by strong efforts to overcome preconceived images of each other—often coined by a white-dominated media or minority elites exploiting their communities for their individual advancement. Antagonisms only benefit the status quo and the continuation of race-based distribution of opportunities and access. Moreover, much of their hope for the future may depend on their construction of collective struggles that recognize, accommodate and celebrate their differences while building together around their commonalities.

See also **Afro-Latinos; Americanization; Blanqueamiento; Civil Rights Act (1964); Internalized Racism; Mestizaje; Negrophobia; Pigmentocracy; Race and Racialization;** *and* **Treaty of Guadalupe Hidalgo.**

BIBLIOGRAPHY

Aponte-Pares, Luis. "Lessons from El Barrio: The East Harlem Real Great Society/Urban Planning Studio." In *Latino Social Movements*, edited by Rodolfo Torres and George Katsiaficas. New York: Routledge, 1999.

Barbaro, Fred. "Ethnic Resentment." In *Black/Brown/White Relations: Race Relations in the 1970s*, edited by Charles V. Willie, 77–94. New Brunswick, N.J.: Transaction Books, 1977.

Betancur, John J., and Douglas C. Gills. "The African American and Latino Coalition Experience in Chicago under Mayor Harold Washington." In *The Collaborative City: Opportunities and Struggles for Blacks and Latinos in U.S. Cities*, edited by John J. Betancur and Douglas C. Gills, 59–88. New York: Garland, 2000.

Bonilla, Frank, and Walter Stafford. "African Americans and Puerto Ricans in New York: Cycles and Circles of Discrimination." In *The Collaborative City: Opportunities and Struggles for Blacks and Latinos in U.S. Cities*, edited by John J. Betancur and Douglas C. Gills, 41–58. New York: Garland, 2000.

Bush, Roderick, and William Sales. "Black and Latino Coalitions: Propsects for New Social Movements in New York." In *Race and Politics: New Challenges and Responses for Black Activism*, edited by James Jennings, 135–148. London and New York: Verso, 1997.

Chang, Edward T., and Jeannette Diaz-Veizades. *Ethnic Peace in the American City: Building Community in Los Angeles and Beyond*. New York: New York University Press, 1999.

Dávila, Arlene. *Barrio Dreams: Puerto Ricans, Latinos, and the Neoliberal City*. Berkeley: University of California Press, 2004.

Dzidzienyo, Anani, and Suzanne Oboler, eds. *Neither Enemies nor Friends: Latinos, Blacks, Afro-Latinos*. New York: Palgrave Press, 2005.

Flores Nieman, Yolanda. "Social Ecological Contexts of Prejudice between Hispanics and Blacks." In *Race, Ethnicity, and Nationality in the United States: Toward the Twenty-First Century*, edited by Paul Wong, 170–190. Boulder, Colo.: Westview Press, 1999.

Grillo, Evilio. *Black Cuban, Black American: A Memoir*. Houston, Tex.: Arte Público Press, 2000.

Mann, Coramae Richey, and Marjorie S. Zats, eds. *Images of Color, Images of Crime: Readings*, 2nd Edition. Los Angeles: Roxbury, 2002.

Miles, Jack. "Blacks vs. Browns." *Atlantic Monthly* 270, no. 4 (1992): 41–68.

Moore, J. W. "Minorities and the American Class System." *Daedalus* 110, no. 2 (1981): 275–299.

Omi, Michael, and Howard Winant. *Racial Formation in the United States: From the 1960s to the 1990s*. New York: Routledge, 1994.

Pedraza, Silvia. "Cuba's Refugees: Manifold Experiences." In *Origins and Destinies: Immigration, Race, and Ethnicity in America*, edited by Silvia Pedraza and Rubén G. Rumbaut, 263–279. Belmont, Calif.: Wadsworth, 1996.

Yans-McLaughlin, Virginia, ed. *Immigration Reconsidered: History, Sociology, and Politics*. New York: Oxford University Press, 1990.

JOHN BETANCUR

BLADES, RUBÉN

BLADES, RUBÉN (b. 1948), singer, songwriter, actor, lawyer, and public servant. Born in Panama City in 1948, Rubén Blades is a transnational celebrity acclaimed for his artistic versatility and his enduring commitment to "making *salsa* with a thinker's edge" (Schnabel).

A prodigious musician of humble origins and keen intellect, Blades emerged out of the cultural and political turbulence of Panama in the sixties embracing the tenets of the evolving *nueva canción latinoamericana* movement: recovery and celebration of folk and national/regional music, styles, and instrumentation; substantive and expressive lyrics that reflect the cultural reality of Latin America, and a well-defined and relevant message. Blades pursued these tenets as he made his way to center stage of the U.S. Latino music scene in the mid-1980s. He is recognized for stretching the limits of salsa through innovative experimentation with rhythm and instrumentation and for broadening the thematic range of salsa with lyrics documenting the lives, beliefs, and shared struggles of people on both sides of the U.S. southern border.

RUBÉN BLADES. Performance at Concierto Para Los Heroes in Los Angeles. (Getty Images)

Blades was born the second of five children to Rubén Blades Bosques, a Panamanian-born policeman and bongo player, and Anoland Bellido de Luna, a Cuban-born singer, pianist, and radio actress. It was his Colombian-born paternal grandmother, Emma Bosques, however, with whom Blades spent much time growing up and who had the most profound influence on his intellectual development. Well educated by Panamanian standards, Emma Bosques was a woman before her time with a wide range of interests. She was a painter and writer, a vegetarian and yoga practitioner, a member of the Rosicrucians, and a feminist. She taught Rubèn how to read at the age of four with the aid of comic books and nurtured his enthusiasm for modern art and cinema. Most importantly, she instilled in him the idea that "justice is important and we can all serve and be part of the solution" (Marton, p. 26).

Early Career

Music was always a part of Blades's life in his youth. His family's cross-cultural background and the complex cultural milieu of Panama predisposed him to the precocious eclecticism that became his signature style. A self-taught musician, he grew up steeped in the rich Afro-Caribbean rhythms of Beny Moré, traditional boleros, and the folk music and ballads of Panama. A love for radio and the close proximity of the U.S. Canal Zone also exposed Blades to U.S. big band, swing, and jazz greats, as well as to the "mambomania" of Damaso Perez Prado, the postwar crossover phenomenon. But it was rock and roll that first engaged Blades's talent and creativity. At fourteen, following a Frankie Lymon and the Teenagers concert in Panama, Blades wrote to the singing idol requesting an audition and then gave the letter to his mother to mail. Anoland Blades did not mail the letter but instead bought Blades a plastic guitar with a decal commemorating Elvis Presley's hit, "Hound Dog." A year later, Blades had his first public performance as a guest singer for his brother's rock band, for which he became a regular performer.

Young Blades's love affair with rock and roll came to an abrupt end in 1964 as a result of an incident in the Panamanian Canal Zone. U.S. troops stationed in the zone killed, wounded, and jailed 250 Panamanians protesting a refusal by U.S. students of the Canal Zone Balboa High School to fly the Panamanian flag. The incident propelled Blades into political consciousness and the embrace of his Panamanian identity. He ceased singing in English and turned away from the North American rock music that had been his standard repertoire. Instead he began to devote his talent and energy to the increasingly popular traditional Latin American styles. These included the Afro-Puerto Rican *bomba* and *plena*, and the Cuban *son* and *congas*. Another significant influence on Blades during this period was the Argentine balladeer of the *nueva canción* movement, Piero, who fueled the young Panamanian's growing interest in making music to support and promote social change.

Blades studied law at the University of Panama. He continued in the local music scene, mainly with the Afro-Cuban band, Bush y su Nuevo Sonido, with whom he first recorded an album. Student unrest following the 1968 military coup of Omar Torrijos led to the closure of the university, which Blades took as an opportunity to travel to New York, where he pursued an offer to sing in the band of the legendary *conguero*, Joe Cuba. During his short visit in 1969, Blades realized the challenges and opportunities presented by the upheaval of 1960s New York. The energy of the civil rights and antiwar movements had spawned parallel and intersecting movements, most notably the Chicano and Latino renaissance. In New York, communal self-awareness, pride, and celebration in the Latina and Latino community was expressed musically through the salsa. This hybrid musical form with Afro-Caribbean roots originating in New York had become identified with barrio culture. Blades, always a keen observer, saw a gap between the narrow thematic range of the genre and the day-to-day reality of Latinas and Latinos that the music sought to celebrate and represent. A commitment to broaden the genre's thematic range—and hence, its social impact and audience—became his life-long project.

Upon hearing that his university had reopened in Panama, Blades returned and completed his law degree. But in 1974, after two years practicing law in a bank and counseling prisoners during his free time, he decided to return to New York City. Initially, he worked as a law clerk at the Panamanian Consulate but soon realized that he wanted to devote himself to music. He obtained a low-wage job as a mailroom clerk at Fania Records, a leading producer and distributor of salsa, and began frequenting salsa clubs as he continued to write lyrics and compose on his guitar. His first big break came when Ray Barretto (bandleader of the Fania All-Stars), contacted him to do vocals for a major concert in Madison Square Garden. His debut was a success and earned him a permanent place with Barretto's All-Stars. When Barretto left Fania to pursue his interests in jazz, the remaining band members, including Blades, created a new group, Guarare, with whom Blades performed for two years.

Collaboration with Willie Colón

In 1977, when Blades began working with Willie Colón, he was finally able to perform his own compositions. The Colón-Blades collaboration, which lasted until 1982, was extremely productive for both musicians. But most important, it constituted a revolutionary coming of age for salsa, as their work combined innovative arrangements with topics of unprecedented seriousness, depth, and implication. The reception of *Metiendo Mano* (Butting In) was lukewarm, but their 1978 *Siembra* (Planting), which contained eight Blades compositions—among them his signature song, "Pedro Navaja"—sold a record three million copies for Fania Records, as a growing audience raved about the combination of highly literate and socially relevant lyrics with an Afro-Caribbean beat. The 1980 two-part *Maestra Vida* (Life the Teacher), an opera inspired by the writings of Gabriel García Márquez, sold poorly but was acclaimed for its ambitious narrative breadth. Their 1980 controversial hit, "Tiburón" (Shark), which critiqued the impact of superpower dominance of the cold war era, sealed the commercial and artistic success of the Blades-Colón collaboration and proved to the music industry that there was a market for the heady lyrics and innovative arrangements that Blades's compositions brought to salsa.

Reaching Out to Anglo-Americans

Following his cordial parting of ways with Colón in 1982, Blades shifted his attention to reaching out to the Anglo-American audience, seeking to educate them about the poverty, dictatorship, and repression that characterized the Latin American political scene in the mid-1980s. The undertaking again stretched the expectations of his growing audiences worldwide. Blades formed his own group, Seis del Solar (The Six from the Tenement), broke with Fania Records, and signed on as the first Latino performer with Warner Communications' Elektra/Asylum Records.

In Seis del Solar's first recording with Elektra, the 1984 *Buscando América* (In Search of America), Blades substituted the trumpets with vibraphones to allow for the foregrounding of his compelling lyrics. He also incorporated jazz and rock elements to represent the cultural complexity and tensions of modern day Latin America. And finally, for the first time on a mainstream record label, he insisted on having his English translations of his Spanish lyrics appear on the record album, a practice he has maintained throughout his career. *Buscando América* was an unprecedented success. It sold over 400,000 copies, received Blades's first Grammy nomination, and made several top ten lists in 1984. The album paved the way for future collaborations with U.S. rock and pop stars such as Joe Jackson and Linda Rondstadt, who appear on his 1985 album, *Escenas*, and with Lou Reed, Elvis Costello, and Sting, who appear on the English language album, *Nothing but the Truth* (1988). The latter of these two albums further explores the dramatic juxtaposition of musical styles and soul-searching topics related to love and violence, the Iran-Contra scandal, the AIDS epidemic, and the ongoing civil war in El Salvador. Blades's 2002 Grammy Award-winning album, *Mundo*, pursued the eclectic convergence of world musical forms, its lyrics focusing on global harmony and the possibility of human understanding.

Blades's success in mainstream circles had its detractors among salsa purists and those who perceived his "crossing over" as an abandonment of his Latino roots. The Panamanian-born artist was steadfast in responding to his critics, insisting that his goal was never to cross over, but to explore, musically, the possibilities of "convergence," as music, language, and cultures, meet in the middle.

The issue of "crossing over" is central to Blades's first successful film part as Rudy Veloz, an East Harlem *salsero* attempting to break into the mainstream music scene in *Crossover Dreams* (1985). The film had limited distribution but gained Blades recognition as a screen natural and yielded him subsequent film acting offers, many of which he refused because they would have required him to portray drug dealers, gang members, or other stereotypical characterizations of Latinos. His most notable performances are in the film version of *The Milagro Beanfield War* (1988); as a death-row inmate in *Dead Man Out* (1989), which won him an ACE Award; and as a nervous rookie in Spike Lee's *Mo' Better Blues* (1990).

Public Service

At no point did Blades's multiple talents and indefatigable energies become more apparent than between 1982 and 1985. While completing *Buscando América*, touring to support the album, and acting in *Crossover Dreams*, he completed a master's degree in international law at Harvard University. The degree brought to light Blades's commitment to public service, a career path he first pursued as a presidential candidate in the 1994 Panamanian elections, running as a candidate for the Papa Egoro Movement, which he had founded. He received 17 percent of the national vote with a platform focused on the renewal of civic life, a reduction of Panama's national debt, the need to overhaul the Panamanian social and medical security systems, and to defeat poverty, corruption, and excessive bureaucracy. Undeterred by defeat, Blades sought other opportunities for public service in his native Panama. In 2004 was named minister of tourism by Panamanian president, Martín Torrijos.

See also Central Americans; Colón, Willie; Fania All-Stars; Music, Popular; Nueva Canción; *and* Salsa.

BIBLIOGRAPHY

Cruz, Barbara C. *Rubén Blades: Salsa Singer and Activist.* Springfield, N.J.: Enslow, 1997.

Marton, Betty A. *Ruben Blades.* New York and Philadelphia: Chelsea House, 1992.

Randel, Don Michael. "Crossing Over with Rubén Blades." *Journal of the American Musicological Society*, 44 (1991): 301–323.

Rodríguez, Ana Patricia. "Rubén Blades at the Transnational Crossroads." In *Latino/a Popular Culture*, edited by Habell-Pallán, Michelle, and Mary Romero, 85–101. New York: New York University Press, 2002.

Schnabel, Tom. "Rubén Blades." In *Rhythm Planet: The Great World Music Makers*, 18–22. New York: Universe, 1998.

TAMARA R. WILLIAMS

BLANQUEAMIENTO. The concept of *blanqueamiento* refers to ethnic, cultural, and racial "whitening." Blanqueamiento, an ideology as well as a social practice, is a major form of racism in the United States. It is a racist way of thinking that places value on white Anglo culture while implicitly devaluing nonwhite cultures. In turn, blanqueamiento works to recreate a social hierarchy based on race and to perpetuate white supremacy. Yet, because such racist beliefs are so pervasive in society and its institutions, they often remain invisible or are ignored.

Cultural Colonialism

The notion of blanqueamiento relates to what can be called cultural colonialism. It is a way of privileging white culture and associating it with superiority and refinement. Blanqueamiento accepts Anglo-American whiteness as developed and advanced. In referring to "race" in cultural terms, blanqueamiento links whiteness to high status, wealth, power, national culture, civilization, Christianity, modernity, and development. Thus "whitening" in the cultural sense is "becoming" more modern, more civilized, and more superior in terms of national standards. These notions simultaneously associate blackness and

indigenousness with the lack of cultural refinement, ambition, and civilization. Nonwhite cultural expressions are in turn considered barbaric, vulgar, unself-reflective and stupid. These principles of blanqueamiento indirectly reject and devalue black and indigenous culture.

Persons who consciously or unconsciously pursue a course of becoming "whiter" and consider themselves superior in "cultural" terms to darker nonwhite people ascribe to principles of blanqueamiento. Given the negative cultural ascriptions that blanqueamiento associates with blackness and indigenousness, it purports the view that upward mobility cannot be achieved if a nonwhite identity is maintained. It suggests that nonwhites are the potential equals to whites in physical terms, but that their traditions and modes of behavior are heavily influenced by an earlier, lesser state of cultural development. Therefore blanqueamiento promotes a system of beliefs that places socioeconomic advancement and success in relation to racial "development."

This ideology of blanqueamiento has been utilized by nonwhites for purposes of social advancement. Blanqueamiento links whiteness with success and blackness with poverty on the level of social relations of class society and the cultural space of the nation. It is a continuing legacy of a time when society was modeled on a race-based caste system. Slavery produced a social order that assigned people of color the lowest rank in the social hierarchy. It became legally and socially beneficial for people of color to mix with whites to "whiten" their blood and lineage. Nonwhites could improve their social status by "whitening" themselves through marriage or informal affairs with lighter if not white people. Thus blanqueamiento adheres to notions of *adelantar la familia*, advancing the family socially through "whitening."

Internalized Racism

Given the context of a racially based social system, people of color who adhered to notions of blanqueamiento aspired to "become" light and to get as far away from slavery as possible. Instead of developing a consciousness of their own worth, they absorbed the discriminating beliefs imposed on them from above. Intermarrying with people of lighter skin color was a mechanism for people of color to integrate themselves better into society and establish their social distance from slavery. Racial mixture blurred the visible boundaries between racial groups. Yet for nonwhites, being accepted into larger society was also conditional on cultural "lightening" as well. Under the rationale of blanqueamiento, white social attributes help to offset nonwhite racial attributes, making conformity to white social norms necessary.

In this light, nonwhites come to perpetuate the racial hierarchy and racism that oppresses them. "Successful" nonwhites end up being dependent on and/or associating with whites-blacks, even if there is no personal motive to "whiten" themselves or their children. The same disdain with which they were regarded by most whites they often applied to their peers. "Whitening," physically or culturally, was a precursor for upward mobility. In turn social, economic, and political advancement was conditional on engaging in adaptive strategies that promoted racist ideas and practices. Success and acceptance entail acting like and purporting the racist values of those in power. This conditional acceptance of people of color by placing a premium on white strategies and practices that promote blanqueamiento is sometimes termed today as "passing."

Blanqueamiento specifically encourages Latinos and Latinas to identify or orient themselves toward whiteness. Ideas of blanqueamiento sustain eugenic notions that white blood is stronger than other types and would dominate the mixture. Under this principle the process of mixing, both racially and culturally, is seen as a progressive whitening of the population that would eventually bring about the elimination of blacks and Indians. Mixture would orient society toward a distinctively whiter end of the spectrum. The ideology of blanqueamiento presumes that the best means of integrating minorities into society is suppression of African and nonwhite derived expressions. Thus nonwhites should assimilate and adhere to "superior" Western norms and values. In this way blanqueamiento works to reiterate the hierarchies of a racial order and to perpetuate racism.

Blanqueamiento is also an unstated physical and cultural goal of the United States. Symbols of nationhood such as the "melting pot" and diversity are coupled with ideologies of blanqueamiento. A pernicious pluralism exists when diversity is embraced, because the essence of such beliefs is still rooted in Euro or Anglo whiteness. Legal and government discourses of "nondiscriminatory color blindness" imply blanqueamiento and result not in equity but in a subtle form of racism.

Such discourses can lead to the self-discrimination of Latinos and Latinas. The assimilating elements of heterogeneity devalue or deny the contributions of people of color to the nation. Latinos and Latinas are denied agency in claiming status as real producers of elements of national culture. If people cannot honor their own culture and history both privately and publicly, they are essentially giving in to the oppression of forced assimilation in the dominant culture.

The U.S. population as a whole is not willing to accept the quality of nonwhite peoples as part of the cultural construct of the nation. Discourses on pluralism fail to understand how black people have engaged in cultural practices that have transformed the nation, its culture, and its people. Neglecting or minimizing the contribution of Latinos and Latinas and Afro-Latinos and Afro-Latinas to the culture and formation of the nation denies official recognition of the true racial composition of the population. In turn, such discourses of blanqueamiento harm nonwhite cultural identities that are defined both privately by the individual and publicly by the community and society.

Furthermore, such discourses seek not only to de-Africanize the nation but also to blame those classified as nonwhite for the worsening state of the nation. Thus blanqueamiento results in a struggle over the value of historical and cultural contributions made by Latinos and Latinas and other nonwhites to the emerging nation. Blanqueamiento purports positive values associated with whiteness and in turn plays a part in undermining the formation of a distinct Latino and Latina identity. The hegemony of blanqueamiento has become part of the natural order of society and the nation, so that it is not questioned and is unconsciously promoted.

See also Afro-Latinos; Black-Latino Relations; Internalized Racism; Mestizaje; Race and Racialization; *and* Whiteness.

BIBLIOGRAPHY

Helg, Aline. "Race in Argentina and Cuba, 1880–1930: Theory, Politics, and Popular Reaction." In *The Idea of Race in Latin America, 1870–1940*, edited by Richard Graham. Austin: University of Texas Press, 1990.

Martinez-Alier, Verena. *Marriage, Class, and Colour in Nineteenth-Century Cuba: A Study of Racial Attitudes and Sexual Values in a Slave Society*. Ann Arbor: University of Michigan Press, 1974.

McIntosh, Peggy. "White Privilege: Unpacking the Invisible Knapsack." *Peace and Freedom* (July/August 1989): 10–12.

Roediger, David. *Wages of Whiteness: Race and the Making of the American Working Class*. London and New York: Verso, 1991.

Torres, Arlene, and Norman E. Whitten Jr., eds. *Blackness in Latin America and the Caribbean*. 2 vols. Bloomington: Indiana University Press, 1998.

Wade, Peter. *Race and Ethnicity in Latin America*. London: Pluto, 1997.

ALYSSA GARCIA

BOMBA. *Bomba* is a musical and dance genre embedded in Afro–Puerto Rican traditions. The term also refers specifically to the drum, which is the genre's fundamental instrument. Bomba belongs to the Caribbean musical heritage and to its renewal through migrations. While maintaining its African roots, it has evolved, making an impact on contemporary Puerto Rican and Latino and Latina music and cultures.

Bomba lies at the heart of the legacy of African slaves brought to Puerto Rico from diverse nations along the West Coast of Africa by the Spaniards beginning in the sixteenth century. Musical traditions and rituals were crucial to the slaves' cultural and spiritual survival. Such rituals were rooted in the ethnic and religious diversity and in the experiences of plantation and fugitive slaves. The lack of early colonial historical records concerning slavery has made it difficult to study Afro-Caribbean musical traditions. However, scholars have pointed out that the Ashanti *mpintin* (from Ghana) and the Puerto Rican bomba are essentially the same musical composition. Bomba dances may also be traced to other ethnic groups in Africa, including those from western Congo. For slaves, isolated and harshly repressed, music and dance became symbols of the preservation of their spirituality and culture.

Many similarities remain between bomba and other African and Afro-Caribbean traditions. The historian and ethnomusicologist Héctor Vega-Drouet has stressed the persistence of percussion and movements characteristic of African music. The recurring rhythm is played by the second of two drums (the low-pitched *buleador*), while the first drum (the high-pitched primo or *requinto*) plays the variations. The bomba drums themselves are also called *cueros* (skins) or *barriles* (barrels). They are held between the legs and are beaten with four fingers of the bare hand. The other two traditional instruments in bomba are the *cuá* (two sticks) and the *maracas* (rattles).

Performances have a theatrical or ceremonial structure and are characterized by a joyful spirit. Usually held outdoors and traditionally in towns throughout the coastal cane fields, bomba performances begin with a song as the dancers keep a basic step in place. The dancers face the drums, and the vocalist and the chorus usually stand behind them. Songs are in call-and-response form, encouraging participation. The repetitive lyrics and rhythmic patterns suggest a ritual atmosphere with interaction among musicians, dancers, and a circle of spectators. The lyrics, often humorous, belong to oral traditions.

Inspired by lyrics and rhythm, one of the dancers abandons the circle, approaches the drums, and improvises a complex dialogue with the primo. The dancer becomes a sort of lead musician, spinning off variations of her or his own. In the *piquetes* the primo's beat mirrors the dancer's footwork, which is polyrhythmic and playful. The female dancer moves her hips in counterpoint with other parts of the body or keeps the upper body immobile. She can move and turn fast while waving her skirt. The male dancer flaunts intricate foot patterns while holding his arms close to his body. He can twist, quiver, or remain still for a few seconds. The intensity of the music and the dance grows until it reaches a heightened point. If the dancer outwits the drummer, she or he is sometimes called *bruja* or *brujo* (witch). When her or his dance comes to an end, the dancer regains the basic step back into the circle as a new performer approaches the primo. This can go on indefinitely. Usually the dancer is alone, but when dancing with a partner there is no physical con-

tact. During festivities, as in the patron saint celebrations at Loíza Aldea, bomba groups play for extended periods of time. Musicians have traditionally been male, but singers and dancers can be either men or women. Women have recently begun to play the drums.

Bomba has been passed on for generations. In *El elemento afronegroide en Puerto Rico* the linguist Manuel Álvarez-Nazario identified several bomba names with roots in Africa: *yubá, candungué, curiquingué, guateque, mariandá. Calinda, cunyá, grasimá, leró,* and *sicá* derived from Afro-French communities of the Antilles. Others, such as *bambulaé (holandés)*, came from Afro-Caribbeans of Curaçao in the Dutch Antilles. After the abolition of slavery in the nineteenth century, bomba continued to develop. Mixed with other influences, it presented diverse styles in each community and in the streets of the barrios (neighborhoods). The towns of Loíza Aldea and Santurce in the north especially contributed to its preservation and dissemination and have given birth to families of bomba musicians. The Cepeda family in Santurce and the Ayalas in Loíza have left a lasting mark.

Meanwhile the *plena*, a musical and dance rhythm related to bomba, originated in working-class neighborhoods in Ponce at the beginning of the twentieth century. Their music is similar, but the rhythms, the instruments, and the dance are different. During the 1950s and 1960s two Puerto Rican musicians, Ismael Rivera and Rafael Cortijo, quickly became influential in maintaining and transforming bomba and plena. They brought forms not usually heard or seen outside the barrio to television and performed them with a band that had added many new instruments.

In assessing music and dance, it is essential to underline the role of the massive migration of Puerto Ricans to the United States and the social and cultural transformations of Latinos and Latinas in the early-twenty-first-century United States. The Puerto Rican diaspora, which started at the beginning of the twentieth century, has been shaped to a large extent by the colonial relationship with the United States. In spite of the harsh environments of industrial cities, Puerto Ricans preserved their music in their homes or in dance clubs, where Hispanic bands have performed since the 1930s. Revered among migrants in the 1950s, the voice of Ismael Rivera and the orchestra of Rafael Cortijo successfully bridged the musical and dance forms of the Puerto Rican barrio and their transformation in migrant communities.

This long process culminated in the 1970s with the incorporation of bomba and plena rhythms within the singular New York–Caribbean phenomenon known as salsa. In the early twenty-first century bomba and plena are a continuing source of inspiration throughout Puerto Rico, as is apparent in the energy of young musicians and in the proliferation of festivals, recordings, and videos. In the United States a new generation of teachers and performers continues to grow. New names, such as "bombazo" and "bomplenazo," are further proof of their vitality. Puerto Ricans in the diaspora have discovered in this musical and dance tradition a vehicle for recognizing themselves as a distinct community and a body language that allows Latinos and Latinas and others from different backgrounds to connect with ancient rituals.

See also **Plena** *and* **Salsa.**

BIBLIOGRAPHY

Álvarez-Nazario, Manuel. *El elemento afronegroide en el español de Puerto Rico*. San Juan, P.R.: Instituto de Cultura Puertorriqueña, 1974.

Flores, Juan. *From Bomba to Hip-Hop: Puerto Rican Culture and Latino Identity*. New York: Columbia University Press, 2000.

Vega-Drouet, Héctor. "An Historical and Ethnological Survey on Probable African Origins of the Puerto Rican *Bomba*, Including a Description of Santiago Apóstol Festivities at Loíza Aldea." Ph.D. diss., Wesleyan University, 1979.

Vissepó, M., and Lydia M. González. *La herencia de un tambor: En homenaje a Rafael Cortijo*. Video documentary (color, 45 min.), San Juan, P.R.: CINETEL and Puerto Rican Foundation for the Humanities, 1985.

ALMA CONCEPCIÓN

BONILLA, FRANK

BONILLA, FRANK (b. 1925), founder of Latino Studies. In the early 2000s, Frank Bonilla was considered one of the most important intellectuals in the development of Latino Studies in the United States. Born in New York City in 1925 to Puerto Rican parents, Bonilla was, as he put it, "an elder among the second generation of Puerto Ricans here." Bonilla grew up in the largely Puerto Rican neighborhood of East Harlem in Manhattan, or "El Barrio," as it was called. At age eleven, he was sent to live with a friend of his parents, a professor at a black college in Memphis, Tennessee. It was then that Bonilla first felt the full force of Jim Crow institutionalized racism, learning quickly and fully "what mainstream United States thought of his people, his color and his ancestry."

Education and Academic Career

Bonilla served in World War II in the 65th Infantry Regiment's occupation of Germany. Following the war, Bonilla returned to New York City, married, and entered the City College of New York (CUNY). He earned a BBA (bachelor's of business administration) in 1949 and, in 1954, an MA in sociology from New York University. Bonilla then entered Harvard University, earning his PhD in sociology in 1959. During his time at Harvard, Bonilla held a John Hay Whitney Fellowship (1954–1955) and a Doherty Foundation Fellowship for Advanced Study in Latin America (1955–1957).

FRANK BONILLA. (Centro de Estudios Puertorriqueños)

It was not until the late 1960s, nearly ten years after Bonilla received his PhD and nearly twenty years after he first entered college, that radical civil rights movements that specifically addressed the concerns of Latinos and Latinas began to emerge. However, although they came too late to help Bonilla negotiate the higher education system as a minority student, these movements still greatly affected him. As an active academic and a person of color, Bonilla found himself, along with many others, at a decisive point in the struggles of marginalized people in the United States. Latinos and Latinas had come to realize that they needed to have their say in the struggle for self-determination. Much later, as director of El Centro de Estudios Puertorriqueños, Bonilla would say that the goal of El Centro was to reach out to young Puerto Ricans and other Latinos and Latinas grappling with harsh social conditions in communities all over the United States, and to help them "assemble the basic facts and necessary understandings of where we stand in relation to U.S. society so that we can act more effectively as individuals and as a group."

In 1960, the year after he completed his PhD, Bonilla joined the American Universities Field Staff on a special contract to collaborate on a research program to be carried out on behalf of UNESCO (United Nations Educational, Scientific, and Cultural Organization) and the Economic Commission for Latin America (ECLA). The research, encompassing a dozen small surveys in Argentina, Chile, Mexico, and Brazil, sought to investigate aspects of the relation between social development and education in Latin America. This was in preparation for a UNESCO–ECLA conference on Education and Economic and Social Development in Latin America that took place in March 1962 in Santiago, Chile. In 1961, Bonilla became a regular associate of Field Staff in Brazil, taking on responsibility for periodic reporting on social, economic, and political events. Between January and May of 1962, Bonilla lectured at seven U.S. university campuses.

Bonilla began publishing very soon after completing his education and remained a highly prolific scholar. In 1962, in conjunction with his research through the American Universities Field Staff, Bonilla coauthored the research monograph "Education and the Social Meaning of Development." Over the next nine years, he published four more research monographs. In 1963, Bonilla wrote the chapter "A National Ideology for Development: Brazil," which was published in the book *Expectant People*.

In 1963, Bonilla became an associate professor in the Political Science Department of the Massachusetts Institute of Technology, and a senior staff member for International Studies at MIT. From 1963 to 1967, he carried out an extensive program of research into Venezuelan politics in collaboration with the Center for Development Studies of the Central University of Venezuela. In 1967, Bonilla was made full professor at MIT and remained there until 1969. Also in 1967, he became the program advisor in Social Science to the Ford Foundation's Brazil site. He resided in Brazil from 1968 to 1970 as a visiting professor in the Department of Political Science at the Universidade Federal de Minas Gerais.

Center for Puerto Rican Studies

In 1969, Bonilla left MIT and became professor of political science at Stanford University, as well as the senior associate for the Institute of Political Studies at Stanford. By this time, Bonilla was becoming nationally known in academic circles as an authority on the subjects of political science and sociology, especially as they pertained to Latin America and to people of Latin American ancestry living in the United States. In 1973, he was finally able to combine these skills and areas of knowledge in an ideal

way: he was asked to become professor of political science and the first director of the Center for Puerto Rican Studies at Hunter College (part of the City University of New York). The center was the first research institution of Latino Studies of any kind in all of the City University of New York, and it was through his work at the center that Bonilla firmly established himself as one of the most influential intellectuals in this field.

During the first half of the twentieth century, there were very few research centers or institutes devoted to Latino Studies or schools where one could study in the field. The notable exception was the University of California, Berkeley. Following the Cuban Revolution in 1959, the cultural climate began to change as the U.S. government put money toward "National Resource Centers" to study Latin America. This federal interest and funding, combined with the forces of the civil rights movements, nurtured the proliferation of Latino Studies programs and centers. This proliferation was also due to the work of Bonilla and others, who took the established fields of sociology, political science, economics, and Latin American studies and applied them to Latin America and Latinos and Latinas living in the United States. Thus, Latino Studies emerged as a distinctive field of study in which scholars and practitioners combined knowledge of both Latin America and the United States to explain the conditions and struggles of people of Latin American ancestry living in the United States. By the early 2000s, there were around thirty research bodies in colleges and universities across the United States devoted to some form of Latino and Latina or Hispanic Studies. Furthermore, one could pursue a major or a concentration in Latino and Latina Studies at virtually any of the larger colleges throughout the United States.

In 1977, Bonilla also became a professor of sociology at Hunter College. During his tenure at Hunter, he was appointed Thomas Hunter Professor of Sociology (in 1986), and in 1996 he spent a semester as a visiting professor at Princeton University's Department of Politics. In 1983 he, along with several other scholars in the field of Latin American studies, founded the Inter-University Program for Latino Research (IUPLR). IUPLR is the only nationwide university-based research organization bringing together scholars from a wide variety of disciplines to conduct policy-relevant research on Latinos and Latinas. IUPLR creates links between scholars, policy experts, public officials, and community advocates. In 1988 Bonilla became the managing codirector of IUPLR.

Throughout his academic career, Bonilla continued to publish books and articles on the subjects of sociology, political science, Latin America, and Latino Studies. Bonilla's Marxist views and theories became well-known, particularly through *Labor Migration under Capitalism*

(1979). This text, officially published as a collaborative effort of the Center for Puerto Rican Studies, is often seen as Bonilla's most important work. It serves to explain the situation of Puerto Rican workers in the United States from a macro point of view, connecting the economic and political structures of the United States and Puerto Rico.

Bonilla retired in 1995. In the early 2000s, he served on the national advisory board of IUPLR and held the title of Thomas Hunter Professor of Sociology, Emeritus, of Hunter College. In 1997, he was named one of the "100 Most Influential Hispanics" by *Hispanic Business Magazine*. His academic achievements can, of course, be counted, but his overall influence on Latino Studies in the United States, and on the personal and educational development of thousands of students, both Latinos and Latinas and others, is so great as to be immeasurable.

See also **Centro de Estudios Puertorriqueños** *and* **Inter-University Program for Latino Research.**

BIBLIOGRAPHY
"100 Most Influential Hispanics." *Hispanic Business*, October 1997, 52.
Bonilla, Frank. Personal Interview by John Gutierrez. January 29, 2003.
Maldonado, Adál Alberto. *Portraits of the Puerto Rican Experience.* New York: IPRUS Institute, 1984.
New York Progressive Network. Frank Bonilla. http://www.nypn.org/htm/resources/frank-bonilla.html.

RAMÓNA HERNÁNDEZ

BORDER, THE. The United States–Mexico boundary has its roots in the sixteenth century, when European competition for control of North America began. In colonial days the British, and to some extent the French as well, constantly challenged the Spanish presence in the farthest reaches of northern New Spain, creating tension zones from Texas to Louisiana to Florida. In time the French and Spanish frontiers, thinly populated and weakly protected, receded, while the expanding British and European American population advanced southward and westward. Continuous confrontations over territory kept the borderlands in a chronic state of turmoil.

The controversy over the limits of the Louisiana Territory became one of the most contentious issues in the early nineteenth century. The United States, which had purchased Louisiana from France in 1803, claimed Texas as part of the deal, but Spain, which owned Louisiana from 1763 to 1800, disagreed. After years of acrimony, the United States and Spain signed a treaty in 1819 that established definite borders for Louisiana, transferred Florida to the United States, and recognized Texas as Spanish territory. American expansionists, however, remained adamant about the "legitimacy" of the U.S. claim to Texas.

Between the 1820s and the 1840s Texas figured prominently in the border conflicts between the United States, a country determined to expand its territorial domain, and Mexico, a newly created republic (1821) desperately struggling to hold on to all of its possessions. In 1836 European Americans, who had moved into Texas en masse in preceding years, led an insurrection against the Mexican government, and by 1845 that province became part of the United States through annexation. To Mexico, the U.S. absorption of Texas amounted to aggression, and that conflict constituted a major issue in the subsequent deterioration of relations between the two countries. In 1846 the United States, desirous of acquiring more land, provoked a war against its weaker neighbor, paving the way for Mexico's further loss of territories.

The signing of the Treaty of Guadalupe Hidalgo in 1848 ended the war and formally established the Rio Grande, from its mouth to the El Paso area, as half of a new border, with an irregular line running westward along the desert to the Pacific Ocean as the other half. Modification of that border took place in 1853, when the United States pressured Mexico to sell portions of Sonora and Chihuahua as part of the Gadsden Treaty. Thus, as a result of the aggressive expansionism practiced by European Americans from the 1830s to the 1850s, the United States acquired Mexico's far northern frontier, namely Texas, New Mexico, Arizona, California, Nevada, Utah, Colorado, and parts of Wyoming, Kansas, and Oklahoma.

Fate of Mexicans in the Borderlands, 1848–1910

In the aftermath of the United States–Mexico War, for the estimated 80,000 Mexicans residing north of the new boundary who desired to continue living in Mexican territory, the only alternative became to move southward. Thus approximately three thousand Mexicans from Texas and New Mexico migrated to points in Tamaulipas and Chihuahua, retaining their allegiance to the motherland. Others unable or unwilling to move remained in their homes, placing their futures in the hands of the U.S. government and those European Americans who migrated into the newly incorporated Southwest. The Treaty of Guadalupe Hidalgo guaranteed the citizenship, property, and religious rights of the Mexican population now living under U.S. jurisdiction, but violations of such assurances became commonplace.

In effect, Mexicans in the border region, as elsewhere in the Southwest, became a colonized group, having undergone foreign conquest and marginalization within the political, economic, and social system imposed by the United States. The degree of colonialism varied from place to place and among different social classes, but functionally all people of Mexican descent felt its sting. Untold numbers lost their land, suffered racial and ethnic discrimination, or ran afoul of an oppressive police apparatus. Mexican workers endured lower wages than their European American counterparts, substandard working conditions, and few opportunities for upward advancement. In short, segregation, poverty, poor education, and everyday discrimination relegated ordinary people of Mexican origin to a lower working class.

In U.S. communities adjacent or close to the border, recurring international incidents spawned exaggerated nationalism and nativism among European Americans, leading to chronic conflict. Three examples of violent confrontations illustrate the highly charged environment in the region, especially on the Texas-Mexico frontier. The first example is the "Cart War" of 1857, during which jealous European American businessmen attacked Mexican teamsters who dominated trade from San Antonio to the Texas coast. Seventy-five people died in these assaults. A second instance of conflict is the 1859–1860 raiding led by Juan Nepomucena Cortina on European American–controlled settlements in the Texas lower Rio Grande Valley. Cortina's attacks stemmed from abuses perpetrated on the Mexican-origin population by European Americans. Twenty-three persons died in these disturbances. Third, in the El Paso area in 1877, Mexican Americans joined with Mexican nationals in a rebellion against newly arrived, power-seeking European American politicians and profiteers intent on taking over communal salt mines. Several clashes produced numerous deaths, destruction of property, and tense international relations. Many Mexican Americans accused of perpetrating violence against European Americans found refuge in Mexico. Among historians, this incident is popularly known as the San Elizario "Salt War."

For people residing on the Mexican side of the border, the post-1848 years complicated already difficult frontier conditions. The new boundary encouraged more incursions on the part of U.S. Indians, who could now raid settlements in Mexico and evade capture by quickly returning to U.S. soil. Article 11 of the Treaty of Guadalupe Hidalgo obligated the United States to stop such incursions, but either lack of will or lack of resources prevented official compliance, and the problem persisted. Much to the dismay of frontier Mexicans, things got worse after 1853, when the Gadsden Treaty allowed the United States to absolve itself from the obligation of restraining Indian raiding. In the decades that followed, transborder Indian raiding constantly disrupted life along the border. In addition, numerous invasions of Mexico by French and European American filibusters, adventurers, and soldiers of fortune took a heavy toll.

One immediate economic effect of the establishment of the new border in 1848 was to convert Mexican frontier settlements into satellites of the United States. The competition provided by European American merchants who moved into the region in the 1850s devastated many Mexican businesspeople who had no access to capital or manufactured goods, both of which were more readily available to their counterparts north of the line. For ordinary *fronterizos* (borderlanders), the major effect of the new border was a higher cost of living, for now tariffs had to be paid on "foreign" commodities imported into Mexico. As a result of economic dislocation, scores of Mexicans emigrated to the United States, where more favorable conditions prevailed.

The Mexican government provided some relief by allowing a Free Zone (Zona Libre) to function in certain border areas beginning in the late 1850s. Under the Free Zone, fronterizos could import foreign products without having to pay the normal duties. That helped stimulate the economy of the Mexican border towns, but at the cost of increasing external dependence. In 1885 the Porfirio Díaz regime recognized the unique conditions at the frontier and extended the Free Zone along the length of the border. Local trade flourished, ushering in prosperity unseen in previous eras. Yet dependence on the U.S. economy continued to rise because the commercial stimulus in the region originated abroad. Then in 1905 the Mexican government eliminated the Free Zone following protests from U.S. merchants hurt by the diversion of commerce to the Mexican side and pressures from Mexican businesspeople and industrialists from the interior who resented the preferential tariff treatment given borderlanders. Once again the border communities saw their economic fortunes change for the worse.

In the larger Mexican borderlands, U.S. capitalists invested huge sums of money in states like Chihuahua and Sonora. By the 1880s foreign companies had built railroads along important routes that connected central Mexico with the northern states and with the United States. As the U.S.–financed railroads reached rich Mexican mining districts and productive agricultural and ranching areas, they came to symbolize U.S. dominance, for they facilitated the export of precious metals and raw materials to the United States. The railroads also transported Mexican workers to U.S. work sites throughout the borderlands.

As owners of Mexican mines, oil fields, farms, ranches, and sundry industries, European Americans exerted disproportionate influence in Mexico, engendering more resentment among Mexicans. That resentment played a pivotal role in the unrest that gripped Mexico in the early years of the twentieth century, an unrest that assumed nationwide proportions and eventually exploded into civil war.

The Mexican Revolution along the Border

After almost four decades of living under the Díaz dictatorship, the people of Mexico launched an insurrection in the 1910s that became one of the world's major revolutions of the twentieth century. Borderlanders felt firsthand the effects of the fighting, for their region held great importance for both *federales* (government troops) and *insurrectos* (insurgents).

Instability and intrigue touched the border even before the official start of the Revolution in November 1910. For example, a labor strike in Cananea, Sonora, in 1906 assumed national importance because of the collusion between Mexican government officials and foreigners in suppressing it. Workers directed their demands for better wages and working conditions at the copper magnate William Greene, who owned the Cananea mine as well as other properties. Greene became one of the great symbols of foreign domination in Mexico, inspiring nationalism among the people. On the U.S. side, the self-exiled Flores Magón brothers agitated for radical change in their homeland by publishing an anti-Díaz newspaper, raising funds, and recruiting volunteers for their ragtag army. Staying a step ahead of Díaz's agents, the brothers carried on their activities in San Antonio, El Paso, Saint Louis, Los Angeles, and San Diego.

With the onset of the Revolution, many important battles occurred along the border, including the capture of Ciudad Juárez in 1911 by the followers of Francisco Madero, the invasion of northern Baja California by the Flores Magón brothers the same year, the defeat of Pancho Villa at Agua Prieta, Sonora, in 1915 by the Venustiano Carranza government, and the raid of Columbus, New Mexico, by the Villistas in 1916. As control of the country, or portions thereof, shifted from one side to the other, prominent insurrectos as well as defenders of the Díaz regime frequently crossed into the U.S. border cities to find refuge or to plan their next campaigns in Mexico. For example, Francisco Madero, Pancho Villa, Pascual Orozco, Victoriano Huerta, and many other leaders spent extended periods in El Paso on various occasions.

From the perspective of Mexican American borderlanders, one of the most significant events during the years of instability on the border is the raiding that took place in the lower Rio Grande Valley of Texas in 1915–1916. The raids involved Mexican nationals and Chicanos and Chicanas who followed the ideology proclaimed in the Plan de San Diego, a revolutionary document that called for an uprising in the U.S. Southwest, the creation of an independent state that might later be annexed to Mexico, and the liberation of African Americans and Native Americans from European American domination. Although the origin of the plan is uncertain, there is no question that many border Tejanos who had grievances against the power structure in Texas capitalized on the raids to exact vengeance and to make their discontent felt. To be sure, the raiders included common bandits motivated by the

possibility of deriving personal gain. Tragically the raids engendered brutal repression by the Texas Rangers, sheriffs, and vigilantes in countless Mexican American communities, farms, and ranches. Perhaps the most positive result of the raids was the attention focused on problems in the border region, especially the abuses inflicted by rogue lawmen. In 1919 an investigation documented widespread unprofessional behavior on the part of the Texas Rangers, and much to the relief of Mexican Americans, state authorities subsequently curtailed the activities and power of that police force.

The instability wrought by the Revolution in Mexico drove hundreds of thousands of economic refugees into the United States, and many of them settled in cities like Laredo, San Antonio, El Paso, Tucson, San Diego, and Los Angeles. Most of the migrants were working-class people who sought jobs and a peaceful life. They entered the United States during a time of growth in the Southwest, and they found employment in agriculture, ranching, mining, railroads, urban industries, and the service sector. Without their presence, cities such as El Paso and San Antonio would not have grown as rapidly as they did during the period.

Immigrants from the middle and elite segments of Mexican society contributed to expansion of economic activity in the U.S. border region by buying properties, establishing businesses, and spending money on consumer goods. Significantly they and their descendants also provided additional resources and leadership in the Mexican American community, which at that time suffered from acute underdevelopment owing to decades of isolation, neglect, and racism at the hands of the dominant European American population.

Prior to World War I, Mexican immigrants crossed the border with relative ease. But that situation changed in 1917, when the U.S. Congress passed a law that required immigrants to pay a head tax, demonstrate their ability to read, and, in the case of those under contract with employers, limit their stay in the United States to six months. These new requirements, coupled with a fear felt by many Mexicans that they might be drafted into the U.S. military, resulted in a sudden downturn in immigration. When the United States entered World War I, the shortage of workers created by these developments led to an economic emergency, and the government quickly suspended the restrictive provisions of the law and assured Mexican nationals that they would not be drafted. The policy reversal had the desired effect, and the migration flow returned to normal. Immigration officials renewed the suspension of the restrictions several times in the next four years, bowing to pressure from employers who argued that serious labor shortages would recur otherwise. To give structure and order to the flow of workers, the

U.S. government established a guest worker program that dictated wages, working conditions, and length of stay in the United States. In effect the guest worker program of the late 1910s was a precursor to the bracero program of the post–World War II era.

Boom and Bust, 1920–1940

After the Mexican Revolution, a less-confrontational climate settled over the borderlands. Sovereignty violations and large-scale international violence became a thing of the past, leading to a decrease in nationalistic sentiments on both sides of the border. Mexico began the process of political, economic, and social reconstruction, slowly diminishing the conditions that had previously precipitated internal large-scale civil wars. Meanwhile, modernization and sustained economic growth became strongly institutionalized in the U.S. borderlands, engendering a closer relationship with northern Mexico, which, since the latter part of the nineteenth century, had in effect functioned as an extension of the U.S. economy. The more stable environment ushered in during the 1920s shaped the borderlands in ways that differed considerably from earlier periods when isolation, underdevelopment, and turmoil were the order of the day.

New industries in the Southwest, such as oil production, tourism, and urban manufacturing, experienced growth along with traditional sectors, such as agriculture, ranching, and mining. Expansion created new opportunities and drew capital and new residents, including immigrants, to the region. Brownsville increased its population from 12,000 in 1920 to 22,000 in 1930, Laredo from 23,000 to 33,000, El Paso from 78,000 to 102,000, and San Diego from 148,000 to 203,000. Meanwhile, the cities on the Mexican side also expanded, albeit more modestly. Matamoros grew from 9,000 residents in 1920 to 10,000 by 1930, Nuevo Laredo from 15,000 to 22,000, Ciudad Juárez from 19,000 to 40,000, and Tijuana from 1,000 to 8,000. Such statistics, however, did not include millions of Americans who visited the Mexican border cities when the Volstead Act of 1920 made it illegal to produce, transport, or consume liquor in the United States.

During the Prohibition years, from 1920 to 1933, communities such as Ciudad Juárez and Tijuana acquired infamy as centers of vice and moral abandon. Mexican fronterizos, while benefiting from the bonanza engendered by Prohibition in the United States, found themselves on the defensive, having to explain to their countrymen and foreigners why they tolerated so much drinking, gambling, and prostitution in their communities.

The tourism boom in the Mexican border cities, coupled with job opportunities in the U.S. Southwest, led to an increase of migration from the interior of Mexico to the border region, swelling the pool of cheap labor situated in close proximity to U.S. industries. Eventually large numbers of Mexicans settled in countless U.S. communities, where they found employment in agriculture, mining, the railroads, factories, or service occupations. Desperate need drove these immigrants to work long hours for low pay, making them ideal workers in the eyes of employers. Other sectors of U.S. society, however, saw the workers differently. Immigration restrictionists objected to the presence of "too many" Mexicans in the United States and sought to convince the government to curtail their entry. Thus the 1920s witnessed the first major U.S. debate on Mexican immigration.

The Great Depression reversed the migration flow from Mexico as massive unemployment in the United States created overwhelming pressures to deport and repatriate foreign workers. Mexicans became a prime target group for restrictionists. Thus during the 1930s from 500,000 to 1 million people of Mexican heritage, many of them actually U.S. citizens and legal immigrants, departed the United States both as "voluntary" and "involuntary" repatriates. For the Mexican border communities, the repatriates presented profound challenges. Many migrants on their way to the Mexican interior became stranded in cities like Ciudad Juárez, necessitating assistance from local government agencies and charitable organizations. Desperate repatriates often resorted to begging and some even to crime as they struggled to survive.

Having to care for large numbers of impoverished migrants severely tested the border towns, whose fortunes had changed drastically after the 1929 crash. Precipitous drops in commerce, industrial activity, and tourism spawned widespread unemployment and poverty from Tijuana to Ciudad Juárez and Matamoros. Conditions deteriorated further when Prohibition came to an end in the United States in 1933, driving many tourist establishments out of business. Clearly the Mexican side experienced harder times during the decade than the U.S. side because of the severity of the crisis in Mexico. Yet poor residents of U.S. cities like Laredo and El Paso endured plenty of suffering owing to economic circumstances not much better than those found in Mexican urban centers.

War-Driven Growth, 1940–1965

By the late 1930s signs pointed to recovery from the devastation of the Great Depression, and once the United States entered World War II in 1941, the trend upward became clear. Both sides of the border received an unprecedented impulse for new development as a result of the growth of defense-related industries in the U.S. Southwest. The U.S. government expanded existing military installations, created new ones, financed research facilities to develop modern weaponry, and awarded contracts to companies that produced armaments. New industries that served the needs of the military stimulated other economic activity, which in turn attracted increasing numbers of people to formerly slow-growing centers of population in desert areas. Large government expenditures also went for improvements in infrastructure, such as interstate highways and water projects, substantially raising the capacity of the region to sustain rapid urbanization. Growth was further stimulated by the Korean and Vietnam Wars and the increasing shift of economic activity from the industrial Snowbelt to the southern and western Sunbelt.

U.S. border cities benefited substantially from these trends, expanding and diversifying their economies beyond the traditional agricultural, ranching, mining, trade, and service-oriented activities. For example, by the 1960s El Paso had boosted its agricultural and tourist sectors and had developed substantial labor-intensive industries that employed large numbers of low-wage workers, many of them from Mexico. The need for Mexican domestics went up dramatically as European American women became wage earners in ever-increasing numbers and as a result needed help with housekeeping and child care. As the U.S. border cities became more integrated into the national economy, giant corporations established local operations. Soon modern commercial centers and shopping malls sprang up to serve the mushrooming middle-class suburbs.

The post–World War II boom affected the Mexican border cities just as forcefully, with the result that new waves of job-seeking migrants from the interior of Mexico began to make their way to the northern frontier. The economic growth along the border also reflected trends throughout Mexico because the postwar years constituted a period of great national economic expansion. *La frontera* (the border zone), with its dynamic, U.S.–driven economy, surpassed most other regions of Mexico in the expansion of trade, industry, and tourism. As military installations in the U.S. borderlands enlarged their populations during the war years, soldiers, sailors, and marines by the millions visited the Mexican border cities, stimulating local entertainment and other service-related activities. Tourism continued to rise as more and more European American families traveled in the U.S. Southwest and made short trips across the border and as more visitors spent time at the border in preparation for trips to the interior of Mexico. Commerce also grew rapidly as U.S. shoppers, particularly Mexican Americans, crossed the border in growing numbers to buy a wide variety of Mexican products.

The large-scale and steady flow of migrant workers northward across the boundary illustrates the strong symbiotic relationship between the U.S. and Mexican borderlands since the days of World War II. Starting in 1942 the bracero program, the bilateral labor-contract arrangement that supplied Mexican workers to U.S. agriculture well into the 1960s, created a stream of migration that swelled the population of the frontier communities. Initially workers merely used the border cities as way stations on the journey to the U.S. interior, but eventually large numbers of these migrants made la frontera their permanent home. With the termination of the bracero program in 1964, borderlanders once again faced a crisis because the displaced braceros expanded an already sizable local labor force that was firmly oriented toward the U.S. economy.

Migration from the interiors of the United States and Mexico accounted for much of the population growth experienced by the border cities in the post–World War II years. For example, Brownsville-Matamoros, Laredo–Nuevo Laredo, El Paso–Ciudad Juárez, and San Diego–Tijuana experienced dramatic gains from 1940 to 1960 (see Table 1).

TABLE 1. *Population Growth, Select Border Cities, 1940–2000*

	1940	1960	1980	2000
Brownsville	22,000	48,000	85,000	335,000
Matamoros	16,000	143,000	239,000	418,000
Laredo	39,000	61,000	92,000	193,000
Nuevo Laredo	29,000	96,000	203,000	311,000
El Paso	97,000	277,000	425,000	680,000
Ciudad Juárez	49,000	277,000	567,000	1,219,000
San Diego	203,341	573,000	876,000	2,814,000
Tijuana	16,000	166,000	461,000	1,212,000

SOURCES: U.S. Bureau of the Census, Census of Population, 1940, 1960, 1980, 2000. Washington, D.C.: Bureau of the Census; México, Dirección General de Estadística, Censo General de Población, 1940, 1960, 1980, 2000.

The Border Region since 1965

By the mid-1960s the border region had assumed a new character, having evolved from an economically marginal and underdeveloped area a few decades before into one of the most rapidly growing zones of North America. New opportunities opened up when the expanding global economy discovered low-cost labor and other attractions at the border, triggering an unprecedented boom that transformed select urban centers. The highly interdependent transnational economies found in vibrant twin-city complexes like El Paso–Ciudad Juárez and San Diego–Tijuana and the ties these communities developed with countries far beyond the boundaries of the United States and Mexico catapulted them to new heights in world manufacturing and trade. But rapid growth brought many new problems to a poverty-stricken region with limited natural resources to support a large population. As the border prospered, it also had to endure recurring crises.

Population growth and migration. The population growth trends recorded on the border in the post–World War II years continued during the period from 1960 to 2000. San Diego, the largest urban center, grew by almost 400 percent, recording 2.8 million residents in 2000, while its neighbor Tijuana swelled by 630 percent to 1.2 million. Brownsville grew by almost 600 percent to 335,000, Matamoros 192 percent to 418,000, Laredo 216 percent to 193,000, Nuevo Laredo 224 percent to 311,000, El Paso 145 percent to 680,000, and Ciudad Juárez 340 percent to 1.2 million (see Table 1).

Migration continued to be the main source of population growth on the border. As demand for low-wage workers picked up on both sides of the line, people from Mexico's interior moved northward in ever-increasing numbers. After 1965 foreign as well as domestic maquiladoras, or assembly plants, acted as a powerful magnet for workers, especially young women from rural areas or small towns. Other opportunity sectors in the Mexican border cities included tourism, commerce, construction, services, domestic manufacturing, and sundry jobs provided by the informal economy.

Once at la frontera, migrants quickly learned about higher-paying jobs in the United States, and many of them crossed the border, some only temporarily and others permanently, some with documents and others without them. When the U.S. immigration law of 1965 made it much more difficult for nonskilled workers to obtain legal residency in the United States, the undocumented traffic soared, triggering a heated debate in U.S. society. Lawmakers in Washington, D.C., introduced a number of restrictionist bills in the 1970s and early 1980s in repeated attempts to stop unregistered migration, but each proposal went down to defeat. Then in 1986 Congress passed the Immigration Reform and Control Act (IRCA), which increased border enforcement, enacted sanctions against employers of undocumented persons, and granted amnesty to undocumented individuals who had lived in the United States continuously since January 1, 1982. This landmark legislation promised to curtail international labor migration from Mexico once and for all, but it only diminished the flow temporarily. *Indocumentados* (people lacking immigration papers) continued to enter the United States because strong U.S demand for their services persisted and because employers found loopholes in the new law.

Along the border many indocumentados took advantage of the amnesty provision to legalize their status. Social agencies and community organizations assisted in the effort to identify people who qualified for amnesty and also helped with the required paperwork. Across the United States 2.7 million immigrants received amnesty, most of them Mexicans. Without a doubt border people constituted a sizable percentage of that number.

By the early 1990s the levels of apprehensions by the Border Patrol resembled those of the pre–IRCA period. Frustrated by the failure of the 1986 law to stem the flow of undocumented immigration, the U.S. government turned to other strategies. The Immigration and Naturalization Service (INS) strengthened the infamous "Tortilla Curtain," a much-publicized 1970s border fencing project intended to stop or at least slow down the crossing of undocumented migrants in key urban areas. The "Tortilla Curtain" had stirred controversy because officials originally proposed adding sharp blades on top of the fence that would cut off fingers and toes of people attempting to scale it. That design feature triggered angry demonstrations in the United States and in Mexico, forcing the INS to construct a fence simply meant to be a barrier and not a physical danger to intruders. By the 1980s, the "Tortilla Curtain" had so many holes that it had lost its effectiveness, and the INS made repairs and reinforced other extant walls on the border. New barriers also went up, including formidable corrugated steel walls along the San Diego–Tijuana sector and the Arizona-Sonora border. More television cameras and electronic sensors guarded strategic points in the border cities, while powerful stadium lights illuminated the all-important San Diego–Tijuana crossing. The INS also dramatically increased the size of the Border Patrol and assigned more helicopters, land vehicles, and other equipment to border duty. The militarization of the border was in full swing.

The greater presence and assertiveness of border law enforcement agents became evident in El Paso–Ciudad Juárez in 1993 with the implementation of Operation Blockade. Immigration officials sought to stop immigrants from crossing the Rio Grande with an overwhelming show of force, positioning personnel and vehicles along the riverbank at close proximity to each other around the clock. When critics spoke out against this military-style campaign, the authorities changed its name to Operation Hold the Line in an effort to soften the image of the new approach to halting unwanted immigration. Few immigrants could penetrate the line. In the first five months of the operation, Border Patrol apprehensions declined by 73 percent in comparison to the same period a year earlier. According to media accounts, most El Pasoans, including Mexican Americans, strongly supported the blockade, but residents of neighboring Ciudad Juárez made their outrage known in street demonstrations, international bridge shutdowns, and boycotts of U.S. stores.

The success of the blockade in El Paso prompted the INS to implement similar campaigns elsewhere.

Operation Gatekeeper and Operation Safeguard followed along the California–Baja California and Arizona-Sonora borders, respectively. Collectively the blockades proved highly successful in deterring illegal crossings in urban centers, forcing huge numbers of determined, would-be immigrants to head to unpopulated, remote, and increasingly dangerous areas to cross the border. Tragically, deaths became a common occurrence in desert zones, mountainous terrain, and treacherous stretches of the Rio Grande. Between 1993 and 2001 over 2,200 border crossers lost their lives as a result of drownings, accidents, exposure, and homicides.

The human catastrophe on the border prompted a variety of responses from concerned citizens. Human rights and religious organizations, especially in southern Arizona, provided assistance to at-risk immigrants by establishing water stations in the desert and conducting "Samaritan patrols" along trails used by the immigrants. On the other hand, some ranchers and anti-immigrant groups engaged in vigilante activity as they attempted to stop undocumented people from entering the United States.

The deteriorating conditions at the border caused the Mexican government to pressure the United States to consider the possibility of creating a new guest worker program as a way of channeling the undocumented immigrants into a legal, safer means of crossing the border. Unfortunately the terrorist attacks of September 11, 2001, and the subsequent acute U.S. concern for security on the border interrupted the immigration negotiations. In the absence of a formal binational agreement to handle undocumented immigration, the border in the early twenty-first century continued to be a dangerous place for many people seeking a better life.

Maquiladoras. One of the most significant developments in the borderlands in the last half of the twentieth century was the emergence of the border industrialization program, under which the Mexican government permitted foreign corporations to operate low-wage, export-oriented assembly plants in the border communities. Mexico City saw such factories as constituting a necessary first step on the road to eventual creation of large-scale border manufacturing under the control of domestic industrialists. The assembly plants became popularly known as maquiladoras, and within a short time they assumed great importance in the region's economy.

The high unemployment rate along the border caused by the U.S. termination of the bracero program in 1964 offered the perfect opportunity for Mexican border entrepreneurs to obtain the endorsement of Mexico City for the maquiladora initiative. Patterned after offshore industries in the Far East, the maquiladoras grew at a modest rate in the first few years of the program. By the mid-1970s,

however, the maquiladoras took off, achieving phenomenal expansion when recurring economic crises in Mexico and the attendant chronic devaluation of the Mexican peso reduced labor costs to rock-bottom levels. By 2001 over 3,700 maquiladoras employed close to 1.3 million workers, with hundreds of thousands of others employed in sectors of the border economy directly or indirectly related to the program. In a generation the maquiladoras became the principal economic activity along the Mexican border, providing striking evidence of the area's overwhelming ties to the U.S. economy. Mexico City's old goal of having industries on the border firmly under Mexican control and integrating other sectors of the border economy to the national system had not materialized.

Over the years the rapid growth of maquiladoras created nightmares for communities on the Mexican side that did not have the resources to provide infrastructure to support workers and others dependent on the industry. Hundreds of thousands of workers and their families lived in primitive conditions, many lacking even basic services like water and electricity. Overcrowding led to shortages of schools and attendant social problems. Air pollution and water contamination assumed alarming levels in the industrial centers, with some maquiladoras contributing directly to the problem by ignoring waste-disposal regulations. For example, it has been common for large numbers of slum dwellers to store drinking water in drums disposed of by maquiladoras, drums that formerly contained harmful chemicals. Not surprisingly the incidence of disease arising from water contamination is exceedingly high along the border.

In the United States the primary concern with maquiladoras has been loss of jobs, prompting U.S. labor unions to demand, without success, an end to the program. Many communities in the interior of the country, especially in the industrial Midwest, have complained of plant closures by companies that have relocated assembly operations in Mexico. In cities like El Paso manufacturers such as garment producers have shifted operations involving tens of thousands of labor-intensive jobs to the Mexican side. Such a loss has angered Chicana and Chicano workers but, lacking political clout, they have been unable to reverse the trend.

The acute vulnerability of the maquiladora industry to international wage competition and periodic global recessions was demonstrated repeatedly in the last several decades of the twentieth century but never so dramatically as during the crisis of 2001–2002. As a result of sluggishness in U.S., European, and Asian markets and the devastating impact of the terrorist attacks of 2001, droves of maquiladoras shut down operations or moved their factories to China, Thailand, and Vietnam, lured there by production costs much lower than those in Mexico.

Toward the end of 2002 the number of maquiladoras in Mexico had dropped by 500 to approximately 3,200, and jobs had dipped by 200,000 to slightly above 1 million. Wages topped the list of push factors that drove maquiladoras to relocate. In 2002 entry-level workers could be hired for as low as US$0.25 an hour in Asia, compared to US$1.50 to US$2.00 in Tijuana and Ciudad Juárez. The stability of the Mexican peso kept wages from dropping in Mexico, disappointing multinationals accustomed to periodic declines in their payroll as a result of devaluations. New taxes imposed by the Mexican government and the prospect of more regulation constituted two additional push factors influencing maquiladoras to leave the Mexican border region.

Globalization and NAFTA. The emergence of maquiladoras in the 1960s provided striking evidence of the rapidly growing integration of the border region into the global economy. Multinational corporations from the United States, Asia, and Europe saw the abundant low-cost labor pools in centers like Ciudad Juárez and Tijuana and the proximity of these cities to the lucrative U.S. market as ideal factors in addressing the problems of rising production costs and international competition. Before long, a who's who of leading global companies operated plants engaged in a wide variety of assembly operations, and in time some high-tech industries made their appearance as well. Routinely these companies established infrastructure on the U.S. side of the border to support the work in Mexico, including administrative, transportation, and warehousing centers. In that way both Mexican and U.S. border cities functioned as a single economic entity firmly linked to the world economy.

The 1960s also witnessed a renewed effort on the part of the Mexican government and domestic producers to stop, or at least slow down, the overwhelming consumption of U.S. and other foreign consumer goods by the booming Mexican border population. Through the Programa Nacional Fronterizo (PRONAF), the government sought to expand consumption of national products on the northern frontier. Although PRONAF achieved some success, Mexican fronterizos continued buying foreign goods in large quantities, with people shopping directly in the United States in ever-increasing numbers. The foreign-oriented consumption patterns on the border, along with extant acute job reliance on foreign companies and tourists, underscored the reality of firmly established external economic dependence in the region. Acceptance of that reality led Mexico City to allow more foreign products to enter the border communities without having to pay the usual duties. The practice of exempting fronterizos from tariffs has its origins in the Zonas Libre of the nineteenth century and various other free trade experiments during the first half of the twentieth century.

With this historical experience on the northern frontier as a backdrop, the extraordinary pressures wrought by the national economic crises in the 1970s and 1980s prompted the Mexican government to strongly embrace free trade as a major part of its economic development strategy for the whole country. Negotiations by Mexico, Canada, and the United States finally produced in 1993 a watershed pact known as the North American Free Trade Agreement (NAFTA), which provided for the elimination of tariffs, some under a short-term schedule and others over the long term. NAFTA also removed other traditional obstacles to cross-border trade and business, such as extant barriers to foreign investment. Responding to concerns by labor unions and environmentalists, NAFTA established two commissions and a development bank to deal with worker displacement and pollution problems. However, much to the disappointment of advocates of workers' rights, the agreement did not allow the free flow of labor across the international boundaries of North America.

While NAFTA supporters have proudly emphasized that, since the agreement took effect in 1994, a boom in international trade has stimulated growth and created many new jobs in the three countries, critics have focused on various perceived serious negative consequences. U.S. labor unions and their supporters have charged that NAFTA has encouraged more plant closures in the United States and the shift of assembly operations to Mexico. Environmentalists from the three countries have contended that the safeguards created by NAFTA have been insufficient to deal with the serious ecological problems that have plagued the overcrowded border cities. In Mexico, critics have bitterly complained that the increased influx of foreign capital and consumer products has harmed key national industries such as agriculture and has displaced large numbers of domestic workers.

The pronouncements on both sides of the free trade issue have validity, but the problem is usually that both defenders and detractors tell only part of the story, and in reality it is still too early to pass judgment on the NAFTA experiment. As predicted, in the period of adjustment to the new system of economic exchange, some sectors have derived great benefits from free trade, whereas others have been gravely injured by it. In the long run, if NAFTA indeed contributes to producing well-paying jobs and to upgrading the standard and quality of life of the population affected by the agreement, including borderlanders, then it will be a success. But if NAFTA is proved to be the cause of constant job disappearance in the United States or the cause of chronic worker displacement in key sectors of the Mexican economy or if free trade does not lead to genuine economic development in Mexico and creates only low-wage jobs there, then it must be judged a failure. In addition, any assessment of NAFTA must take into account progress toward elimination of environmental degradation on the border. A decade after the enactment of NAFTA much remained to be done on the environmental front.

Border lawlessness and insecurity. One of the constant features of border life from the nineteenth century to the age of NAFTA was lawlessness stemming from a variety of conflicts and illegal activities. In addition to undocumented migration, drug smuggling has been one of the main sources of crime and friction between the two countries in the late twentieth century and the early twenty-first century. On two occasions the United States has taken major steps to disrupt the flow of traffic on the border in an effort to ameliorate the problem. For nearly a month in 1969, U.S. authorities sustained a campaign known as Operation Intercept to curtail the entry of drugs into the United States. Rigid inspections at many crossing points caused tempers to flare and business on both sides to decline drastically. Mexican border communities in particular felt the impact in a severe way. Federal officials in Washington, D.C., received much criticism for their handling of the problem. Many border residents felt that the resulting negative economic and diplomatic effects far outweighed the seizure of limited amounts of drugs.

In 1985 the drug problem once again prompted the U.S. government to institute tight inspections at the border for several weeks, predictably causing havoc in the border communities. The kidnapping and murder of a U.S. drug agent and numerous assaults on U.S. tourists in Mexico ostensibly served as the motive for taking that drastic action. U.S. officials apparently hoped the interruption of trade and tourism at the border and in the interior of Mexico would put pressure on the Mexican government to become more aggressive in the fight against drugs. It also appears that the Ronald Reagan administration used the tightening of the border to accomplish broader policy objectives toward Mexico, that is, to pressure Mexicans to modify their positions on Central American conflicts and other foreign policy questions where significant differences existed between the two nations. Mexico, however, continued to maintain its independent policy toward Central America and severely criticized Washington for failing to effectively address the root cause of the drug problem—insatiable demand and consumption in the U.S. population.

As the two countries feuded, drug trafficking increased, and the border became more violent. The United States substantially beefed up the Border Patrol, the Drug Enforcement Agency, and the Customs Service in an effort to stop the flow of narcotics. Military personnel were also used selectively to patrol portions of the border and to help with inspections in the ports of entry. With the stepped-up militarization, more deadly confrontations erupted between enforcement personnel and smugglers.

Tragically, innocent people, including migrants and residents of border towns, sometimes perished as they were caught in the deadly crossfire between the two sides. For example, a widely publicized incident occurred in 1997, when a U.S. Marine mistakenly shot the young goatherder Esequiel Hernandez Jr. along the Texas border. On the Mexican side drugs have transformed cities like Tijuana and Ciudad Juárez into battlegrounds as cartels fight each other as well as law enforcement agents. Since the 1980s many shootings and massacres have occurred, with many innocent bystanders among the victims. In Ciudad Juárez over three hundred women have been brutally murdered since 1990. Whereas many people speculate that a serial killer is responsible for these gruesome crimes, others blame vicious criminals associated with the drug trade and even the police as the perpetrators.

Growth and the border ecology. A common sentiment in both countries is that the border region has paid a high human and ecological price for the economic expansion and urbanization that transformed the borderlands into a major player in the global economy. Overpopulation, overutilization of scarce resources, insufficient infrastructure, and poverty became common, overwhelming problems from Brownsville-Matamoros to San Diego–Tijuana. Lacking resources to address massive social needs, border municipalities, especially on the Mexican side, have had to cope with a multitude of problems, including wretched living conditions in mushrooming slums, disease, malnutrition, unemployment, shortages of schools, delinquency, and crime.

Unrestrained and rapid growth has occurred despite environmental disadvantages inherent in the region, especially the scarcity of water. New methods and advanced technology developed throughout the twentieth century allowed agricultural and population centers to claim large amounts of water from underground sources and to divert it from rivers and lakes situated nearby and far away. Energy-producing resources and raw materials for construction have been extracted from the landscape in appreciable quantities. Without a doubt the ability of desert cities to grow and prosper has been one of the most remarkable developments in the history of the borderlands.

Not surprisingly, the ever-increasing need for water in arid urban and rural zones has generated considerable interregional conflict within the U.S. Southwest and between the United States and Mexico. During the twentieth century California and Arizona contested the waters of the Colorado River in often-bitter legal battles. In the late twentieth century, El Paso, Texas, and the state of New Mexico feuded in the courts over whether El Paso has a right to water from underground wells just across the state boundary. The issue stirred such strong feelings that people from southern New Mexico promoted economic boycotts of El Paso. Water controversies also erupted in the international arena because of the designation of rivers as part of the boundary between the United States and Mexico and because of the spanning of the boundary by underground water deposits or aquifers. Treaties signed in the 1900s, 1940s, and 1970s over the use of water are indicative of recurring disagreements between the two countries. In the late twentieth century and early twenty-first century a prolonged drought in the borderlands generated considerable hostility in Texas toward Mexico because of insufficient flow into the Rio Grande via Mexican tributary streams. Mexican authorities defended the policy of diverting the water during the drought as necessary to meet the needs of desperate people from Mexico's northeast.

Water pollution is a related problem that triggered controversy in the late twentieth century. Residents of California's Imperial Valley complained about the waste materials dumped at Mexicali into the Rio Nuevo, which flows northward into the Salton Sea. Reportedly the polluted water presented a grave danger for the spread of diseases like hepatitis, typhoid, and encephalitis. At San Diego–Tijuana raw sewage flowed for decades into the United States via the Tijuana River, damaging the beaches and causing severe harm to agricultural lands and water wells. In the lower Rio Grande Valley of Texas, residents of *colonias* (poor rural neighborhoods) blamed polluted water as the cause of deformities in human embryos.

Apart from water contamination, some border communities have endured high levels of air pollution. Although natural phenomena, such as temperature inversion, that occur in the desert climate and topography that tends to trap polluted air in narrow spaces partly explain the problem, human activities have had a far more serious effect. Industrial waste, auto emissions, pesticide use, agricultural dust, open burning, and unpaved streets are some of the more significant contributors to the contamination of the air. Small communities such as Presidio-Ojinaga and Del Rio–Ciudad Acuña attribute their relatively mild problems to burning and dust, but at El Paso–Ciudad Juárez polluting practices of residents combine with natural causes to produce serious levels of pollution at various times during the year.

Transboundary networks. The pronounced interdependence along the border has made it essential that interruptions in the normal flow of people and trade across the boundary be avoided or at least kept to a minimum. More than any other sector, borderlanders themselves have sought to maintain an orderly and harmonious climate to prevent damage to the area's delicate economy and to existing neighborly relations. In response to many controversial issues and incidents that have arisen at the border and many disruptive policies implemented by government offi-

cials, for generations borderlanders from both countries have worked informally to minimize friction.

Efforts to maintain good neighborly relations have spanned a wide variety of arrangements, including the creation of binational border cities associations and the maintenance of international relations committees by municipal governments, chambers of commerce, and service clubs on both sides of the boundary. Additionally, health organizations, churches, and cultural, sports, and youth groups have maintained less formal but significant contact. Finally, the daily transborder contact stemming from the extensive routine movement of workers, businesspeople, students, shoppers, and tourists has fostered a wide network of positive relationships.

Initiatives at the state level have also helped lessen friction and promote harmony. For example, since the 1940s Texas has had a Good Neighbor Commission that has worked to smooth out problems between Texas and its bordering Mexican states. Similarly, Arizona and Sonora and California and Baja California for decades have had commissions to coordinate matters of mutual concern. The governors of the U.S. border states and the Mexican border states have held many meetings over the years to promote trade, cultural exchange, and friendship across the political line. Although these state and local initiatives have certainly not solved major problems, they have helped considerably to maintain calm, order, and a semblance of security along the border.

In the arena of personal transborder interaction, large numbers of Latinos and Latinas from California to Texas have incorporated as integral parts of their living and working spaces Mexican cities such as Tijuana, Mexicali, Nogales, Ciudad Juárez, Nuevo Laredo, Matamoros, and interior centers in the Mexican border states, such as Hermosillo, Chihuahua City, and Monterrey. Intense cross-border interaction has evolved in many forms, including job commuting, family visits, shopping, and tourism. Sustained contact with Mexico has kept Mexican culture vibrant in the United States and has given a powerful impetus to a binational identity among millions of people. The decision of the Mexican government in 1996 to allow Mexicans abroad to retain their citizenship even if they become naturalized U.S. citizens has further strengthened the extant transnational border. Previous apprehensions among immigrants to the United States about losing basic rights and privileges in Mexico, especially with respect to property ownership in coastal and border areas, have been eliminated.

See also **Amnesty Movement; Border Patrol; Bracero Program; Cortina, Juan; Immigration and Naturalization Service; Immigration Policy and Border Control: Post–September 11; Immigration Policy, Twentieth**

Century; Maquiladoras; Mexican Revolution; Mexican-Origin People in the United States; Militarization of the Border; North American Free Trade Agreement; Treaty of Guadalupe Hidalgo; *and* United States–Mexican War.

BIBLIOGRAPHY

Arreola, Daniel D., and James R. Curtis. *The Mexican Border Cities: Landscape Anatomy and Place Personality*. Tucson: University of Arizona Press, 1993.

Dunn, Timothy J. *The Militarization of the U.S.–Mexico Border, 1978–1992: Low-intensity Conflict Doctrine Comes Home*. Austin: CMAS Books, University of Texas at Austin, 1996.

Fernández, Raúl A. *The Mexican-American Border Region: Issues and Trends*. Notre Dame, Ind.: University of Notre Dame Press, 1989.

Fernández, Raúl A. *The United States–Mexico Border: A Politico-Economic Profile*. Notre Dame, Ind.: University of Notre Dame Press, 1977.

Fernández-Kelly, María Patricia. *For We Are Sold, I and My People: Women and Industry in Mexico's Frontier*. Albany: State University of New York, 1983.

Hall, Linda B., and Don M. Coerver. *Revolution on the Border: The United States and Mexico, 1910–1920*. Albuquerque: University of New Mexico Press, 1988.

Herzog, Lawrence A. *Where North Meets South: Cities, Space, and Politics on the U.S.-Mexico Border*. Austin: Center for Mexican-American Studies, University of Texas at Austin, 1990.

Lorey, David E. *The U.S.–Mexican Border in the Twentieth Century*. Wilmington, Del.: Scholarly Resources, 1999.

Martínez, Oscar J. *Border People: Life and Society in the U.S.-Mexico Borderlands*. Tucson: University of Arizona Press, 1994.

Martínez, Oscar J. *Troublesome Border*. Tucson: University of Arizona Press, 1988.

Nevins, Joseph. *Operation Gatekeeper: The Rise of the "Illegal Alien" and the Making of the U.S.-Mexico Boundary*. New York: Routledge, 2002.

Peña, Devon G. *The Terror of the Machine: Technology, Work, Gender, and Ecology on the U.S.-Mexico Border*. Austin: Center for Mexican-American Studies, University of Texas at Austin, 1997.

Rippy, J. Fred. *The United States and Mexico*. New York: Knopf, 1926.

Ruiz, Ramón Eduardo. *On the Rim of Mexico: Encounters of the Rich and Poor*. Boulder, Colo.: Westview Press, 1998.

Ruiz, Vicki L., and Susan Tiano, eds. *Women on the U.S.-Mexico Border: Responses to Change*. Boston: Allen and Unwin, 1987.

Vila, Pablo. *Crossing Borders, Reinforcing Borders: Social Categories, Metaphors, and Narrative Identities on the U.S.-Mexico Frontier*. Austin: University of Texas Press, 2000.

Weber, David J. *The Mexican Frontier, 1821–1846*. Albuquerque: University of New Mexico Press, 1982.

OSCAR J. MARTÍNEZ

BORDER ART. The concept of border art emerged in the early 1980s with the growing militarization of the United States–Mexico international border. The rise of this phenomenon coincided with a burgeoning of artistic activity around and within border cities and towns, such as San Diego–Tijuana and Juarez–El Paso. Border art is not necessarily defined by a particular medium or by any specific stylistic-formal conventions, though public performances, community engagement projects, and mixed media installations are recurrently used by various artists practicing it. Border art is more appropriately defined by its subject matter and content, which often focuses on the social, political, and cultural realities of life in the United States–Mexico border region. Common themes addressed by border artists may include the plight of undocumented workers in the United States, the violence suffered by immigrants as they attempt to cross this border, or the biculturalism and transnationalism that characterize life in this area. Though border art primarily focuses on how this national boundary affects the lives of Mexican, Chicana and Chicano, and Mexican-descended peoples, artists practicing it come from diverse ethnic, cultural, and national backgrounds.

Border art does not necessarily operate under the assumption that the United States–Mexico border is an impenetrable and aggressive barrier that divides families and clearly demarcates the economic inequities that exist between Mexico and the United States. Many artists have chosen to represent the border as a capricious and arbitrary international boundary inscribed in the collective imagination of dominant U.S. culture. These artists portray the border as the unfortunate result of a long, sustained history of colonization and expansion endured by populations on both sides of the line. Other artists have chosen to underscore the transculturation, heterogeneity, and cultural hybridity that still take place in the border region in spite of attempts on the part of U.S. agencies to curtail movement from Mexico to the United States. Thus border artists often prefer to engage the notion that this is necessarily a porous border and that the actual physical walls and fences put in place to prevent movement tend to have the reverse effect.

The practice of border art was deeply affected by the publication of the Chicana writer and theorist Gloria Anzaldúa's treatise on border theory titled *Borderlands/La Frontera: The New Mestiza* (1987). In this text Anzaldúa proposes that the borderlands are not only situated along the United States–Mexico border but are also located within the lives and experiences of those individuals who posses a marginalized position in society: "*Los atravesados* live here [in the borderlands]: the squint-eyed, the perverse, the queer, the troublesome, the mongrel, the mulatto, the half-breed, the half dead; in short, those who cross over, pass over, or go through the confines of the 'normal' " (p. 26).

Anzaldúa also made quite an impact by underscoring the experiences of women of color and insisting that they live a heightened bordered existence because of the marginalization and discrimination they face as a result of their gender, ethnicity, class, and, in the case of lesbians of color, sexuality. Though it is unclear whether artists were reacting to the ideas being formulated by Chicana

DONKEY CART ALTAR. Mixed media and paint on wood by David Avalos, 1985. (Courtesy of David Avalos)

thinkers like Anzaldúa or to the same sociopolitical phenomena as these writers, the introduction of a border "discourse" revolutionized the way border art was conceptualized. Now artists began to discuss both the physical and the symbolic borders that shape and define differential subjectivities.

Border Artwork

The members of the Border Arts Workshop/Taller de Arte Fronterizo (BAW/TAF), an artistic collective from the San Diego–Tijuana border region, are undoubtedly the pioneering and trailblazing figures in the history of border art. Established by Michael Schnorr, David Avalos, and Victor Ochoa in 1984, BAW/TAF became one of the first artist groups to make border issues a central component of their mission as an artistic collective. Perhaps one of BAW/TAF's most celebrated performances was *End of the Line*, which took place at Border Field Park–Playas de Tijuana in 1986. This is actually the site where the border fence extends all the way to the Pacific Ocean. The members of BAW/TAF set up a banquet table right on this borderline and proceeded to have a symbolic meal, where participants passed food items back and forth across the

border, thereby ignoring the "authority" of the line. Simultaneously, individuals dressed themselves in foam costumes, designed by Victor Ochoa, representing numerous border types: the Border Patrol officer, the coyote, the tourist, the bishop, and so forth. In the background the artists placed silhouettes of the three ships Columbus sailed to the Americas, the *Pinta*, the *Niña*, and the *Santa María*. The inclusion of the ships reminded spectators that contemporary issues regarding the United States–Mexico border are very much part of the history of colonization in the Americas.

BAW/TAF was influential not only because it forged a new aesthetic and art form in the history of both contemporary American and U.S. Latina and Latino art but also because of the individual talents that emerged from this collective. Though his partnership with BAW/TAF was relatively short-lived, David Avalos continued exploring border issues in collaboration with other artists as well as on his own. In 1988 he joined forces with fellow San Diego artists Elizabeth Sisco and Louis Hock in the project *America's Finest Tourist Plantation*. The artists designed a poster depicting three pairs of hands: the first washing dishes, the second in handcuffs, and the third handing out clean towels in a hotel. Above them the text reads "America's Finest Tourist Plantation." These posters were placed on one hundred city buses that happened to make stops at various tourist attractions during the 1988 Super Bowl in San Diego. While San Diego was actively fortifying its border with Mexico to curb and criminalize Mexican immigration, the tourist industry remained heavily dependent on the labor of undocumented workers. *America's Finest Tourist Plantation* exposed the unethical practices of dominant city politics while also revealing how the local economy benefited from abusive forms of labor.

Avalos joined forces with Sisco and Hock again in 1993 to create *Art Rebate/Arte Reembolso*. Like their previous project, *Art Rebate* put a public and uncomfortable lens on the reality of undocumented workers in the United States. During a span of several weeks in 1994, the artists distributed a total of $4,500 in $10 bills to undocumented workers in San Diego. Avalos, Sisco, and Hock sought out places where workers usually converge and where employers generally go to find inexpensive labor. Each worker who received money was asked to sign a "receipt" with his or her signature, name, date, and location where the "transaction" took place. The artists were hoping to call attention to the fact that undocumented workers are taxpayers in an economic system that denies them any benefits, such as health care, welfare, and social security. In a sense Avalos, Sisco, and Hock were symbolically reimbursing the workers for their unrecognized and disenfranchised labor. The project also sought to undermine the stereotypical image of Mexicans as lazy parasites on the U.S. economy. The project generated a public outcry primarily because of its funding. The artists had received grants from private sources and from the National Endowment for the Arts (NEA). Many residents in San Diego and local politicians felt it was outrageous that federal money should be used to give "handouts" to non–U.S. citizens who were residing illegally in this country. The controversy ultimately led to the withdrawal of the NEA money from the project.

In 1985 Avalos created his infamous mixed-media installation titled *Donkey Cart Altar*. Tapping into the modernist tradition of using found objects to create works of art, Avalos utilized one of the carts on which tourists usually pose for photographs in Tijuana to construct this installation. The artist transformed the cart into a Day of the Dead altar by including two votive candles and a skull. The individual commemorated in this cart-altar is not a Catholic saint or a deceased family member but rather a border-crossing immigrant who is being detained and searched by a Border Patrol agent. Avalos included a number of poignant elements within this installation that deeply inform his audience's reading of this work. Directly below the body of the immigrant one sees a dollar sign alluding to the dream of financial stability that motivates immigrants to cross the border but also to the financial benefits reaped by the U.S. economy in having the cheap and unregulated labor of undocumented workers. But the power of the *Donkey Cart Altar* also resided on its subsequent location, as critic Jo-Anne Berelowitz explained: "The piece became highly controversial when, in 1986, Avalos installed it in the San Diego Courthouse, a charged placement, for it is here where cases involving undocumented Mexican workers are tried" (p. 81).

Another important figure who emerged from the ranks of BAW/TAF is Guillermo Gómez-Peña, performance artist and art critic extraordinaire. A native of Mexico City with formal training in conceptual art media, Gómez-Peña brought a theatricality and drama to the practice of border art, thus making the performative element a critical component of the genre. The artist, however, soon left BAW/TAF to pursue a successful career as a solo performance artist and art critic that earned him the coveted MacArthur Fellowship in 1991. One of the first performances Gómez-Peña enacted after his break from BAW/TAF was *Border Brujo*, which the artist staged in various venues from 1988 to 1990. The set consisted of an altar heavily adorned with stereotypical objects and trinkets associated with Mexican culture. Taking on the persona of a shaman possessed by numerous spirits, Gómez-Peña acted out various characters associated with Mexican and U.S. culture on both sides of the border: the urban Chicano gang member, the undocumented immigrant, the Anglo-American tourist visiting Mexico, the Border Patrol agent, and so forth. The transition from one character to the other was signaled by a quick change in costume or accessory and by different props, like a ghetto blaster, a bullhorn, or a flashlight. These characters straddled the fine line between racial stereotypes and realistic social representations. From time to time Gómez-Peña's own critical voice surfaced as a Mexican-Chicano artist trying to survive the racism and discrimination of the contemporary art scene. Unlike in other examples of border art, here Gómez-Peña is not referring directly to the United States–Mexico border as a site of cultural and political contestation but is alluding to the bordered, bicultural, and hybrid identities typical of the border experience.

Gómez-Peña's contribution to the development of border art rests not only on his performance work but also on his prolific critical writing. In texts like *Warrior for Gringostroika* (1993) and *The New World Border* (1996), he describes the United States as a necessarily hybrid place where borders are continuously erected and destroyed. He sees that the cultural, political, and social structures in the United States once believed to be stable and absolute are indeed in a constant state of flux. As an artist he insists that for him "the border is no longer located at any fixed geopolitical site. I carry the border with me and I find new borders wherever I go" (1996, p. 5). He likens the figure of the border-crossing immigrant to that of the artist. He explains, "I am a migrant performance artist. I write in airplanes, trains and cafés. I travel from city to city, coast to coast, country to country, smuggling my work and ideas of my colleagues" (p. 5).

But perhaps one of the most important events that ushered in a new phase in the history of border art was the founding in 1992 of the triennial exhibitions *inSITE*, multimedia "exhibitions" of site-specific installations and community-engagement projects in various locations throughout the San Diego–Tijuana border region. Coordinated by Consejo Nacional para la Cultura y las Artes, Mexico (CONACULTA), and Installation, a nonprofit art organization in the United States, *inSITE* challenged the conventions of traditional exhibition practices by not constructing an enclosed and finite space (such as a gallery) to display artwork but rather providing means and resources for artists to carry out their various installations and projects within the spaces of their choosing. For example, Betsabeé Romero's piece *Ayate Car*, displayed during *inSITE97*, located on the Mexican side of the border, consisted of an elaborately decorated car filled with flower petals that ran aground when it encountered the border fence.

Another phenomenon that deeply affected the practice of border art was the onset of globalization. The economic inequities brought about by globalization became

AMERICA'S FINEST TOURIST PLANTATION. Silk-screened by David Avalos, Elzabeth Sisco, and Louis Hock, 1988. (Courtesy of David Avalos, Elizabeth Sisco, and Louis Hock)

a focus of critique for many artists practicing border art. The rise of the *maquiladora* industry along the Mexican side of the border as a result of the North American Free Trade Agreement (NAFTA) became the subject matter of much border art. Maquiladoras are foreign-owned factories and plants situated within this border region in Mexico. NAFTA and other free trade agreements ushered in by globalization significantly decrease the regulation and taxation of industrial and financial practices across international borders. These maquiladoras pose quite an opportunity for foreign business interests in Mexico. By keeping their plants and factories in Mexico, U.S. and foreign corporations can manufacture goods at a fraction of the cost, given that workers in these maquiladoras can be subjected to excessively long shifts and poor working conditions at a rate of anywhere between $0.85 to $1.25 an hour, all within Mexican labor laws.

Twentieth-century events surrounding the United States–Mexico border attracted much international attention to the region. Artists from various parts of the globe created artwork about the realities lived by those inhabiting the United States–Mexico border region. Much media attention has been directed at the city of Juárez in the Mexican state of Chihuahua, the site of more than three hundred murders of young women since 1993. Although theories have cited organ trafficking and religious cults as possible motives for the killings, most of the murder cases remain unsolved, and evidence of sexual abuse has been found on the bodies of many of the victims. These events

have generated myriad reactions around the globe by women artists horrified by these heinous crimes. Underlying their treatment of the subject is the realization that violence is a critical component of life along the United States–Mexico border and that this violence is often targeted at women's bodies. In 2002 the Chicana digital artist Alma López created a poster in conjunction with Alicia Gaspar de Alba's book *Desert Blood: A Novel on the Maquiladora Murders.* Intended to "raise awareness on Juarez murders in order to assist in finding missing women and girls," as López states in the poster itself, the various images in the composition were put together through the use of digital technology. A young woman stands clutching a dress as she directs her gaze toward the ground. On the ground a pile of garbage sits next to a fence, a reference to the United States–Mexico border. As the eye moves across the garbage pile, the spectator rather unexpectedly encounters the legs of a dead woman, half-buried in the sand. This gruesome detail operates as an indicator of the low regard with which women's bodies are treated. A transparent cross is superimposed in the center of the composition, making reference to the various crosses and makeshift altars that have appeared along the border as the result of these deaths. Aside from increasing awareness about these murders, López's poster also attempts to give a voice to the victims of these crimes. A Chicana-Mexicana artist who was born in Mexico but raised in Los Angeles, López was personally touched by the plight and suffering of the victims in Juárez.

Nevertheless, the violence directed at women on the United States–Mexico border also struck a chord with non-Mexican women artists. Such was the case of the Swiss artist Ursula Biemann, whose video essay *Performing the Border* (1999) focused on the lives of women working for the maquiladora industry in Juárez. This work reflects the research the artists carried out in Juárez in 1988 and 1998. *Performing the Border* includes footage of Juárez women being interviewed by the artist, documentary police clips about the murders, and images of the actual border fence among other sequences. The images are interspersed with voice-over narrations and running texts that provide a critical response to the imagery shown on the video. Biemann looks at the Juárez case as relevant to women across the globe, not just Mexicanas and Chicanas. Moreover, both López and Biemann created a type of border art that put the focus of critique on the gendered predicaments that surface as a result of this national boundary.

Border art ultimately emerged as a symptom of late-twentieth-century anxieties in the United States and elsewhere about the decline and ethical bankruptcy of time-honored institutions of power and longstanding notions about the existence of a center and margin within social relations. Border art took on the delicate task of exposing the underbelly of hegemonic empires and dominant cultural institutions. The history of border art, however, is still developing and undergoing constant transmutations. With twenty-first century crises like the September 11, 2001, terrorist attacks on the World Trade Center and the Pentagon, the so-called war on terror waged by the George W. Bush administration, and the increasing loss of civil liberties in the United States as a result of these tragedies, new symbolic and tangible borders have been emerging. The form border art will take in the near future will undoubtedly be affected by these new social, political, and cultural realities.

See also Anzaldúa, Gloria; Art, Chicano; Border, The; *and* Juárez Murders.

BIBLIOGRAPHY

Anzaldúa, Gloria. *Borderlands-La Frontera: The New Mestiza.* 2nd ed. San Francisco: Aunt Lute Books, 1999.

Berelowitz, Jo-Anne. "Conflict Over 'Border Art': Whose Subject, Whose Border, Whose Show?" *Third Text* 40 (Autumn 1997): 69–83.

Cockcroft, Eva. "Vidas Perdidas/Lost Lives." *New Art Examiner* 16, no. 10 (June 1989): 52–53.

Costello, Rose. "Art on the Borderline." *Artwork Magazine* 34 (Apr. 1997): 6–9.

Durant, Mark Alice. "Activist Art in the Shadow of Rebellion." *Art in America* 80, no. 7 (1992): 31–35.

Fox, Claire F. *The Fence and the River: Culture and Politics at the U.S.–Mexico Border.* Minneapolis: University of Minnesota Press, 1999.

Fusco, Coco, ed. *Corpus Delicti: Performance Art of the Americas.* London and New York: Routledge, 2000.

Gingeras, Alison M. "Border Realities VIII—Broken Promises: Cultural Value Is Non-Negotiable." *Art Papers* 19, no. 3 (Apr.–May 1995): 35–36.

Gómez-Peña, Guillermo. "Death on the Border: A Eulogy to Border Art." *High Performance* 14 (Spring 1991): 8–9.

Gómez-Peña, Guillermo. "Diálogos Fronterizos." *La Comunidad* 263 (Aug. 4, 1985): 2–3.

Gómez-Peña, Guillermo. *The New World Border: Prophecies, Poems, and Loqueras for the End of the Century.* San Francisco: City Lights Books, 1996.

Gómez-Peña, Guillermo. *Warrior for Gringostroika: Essays, Peformance Texts, and Poetry.* St. Paul, Minn.: Graywolf Press, 1993.

Joselit, David. "Living on the Border." *Art in America* 77, no. 12 (Dec. 1989): 120–128.

Kanjo, Kathryn, ed. *La Frontera = The Border: Art about the Mexico–United States Border Experience.* San Diego, Calif.: Centro Cultural de la Raza, 1993.

Kelley, Jeff. "Exits and Entrances: Jeff Kelley on Border Art." *Artforum* 28, no. 7 (Mar. 1990): 23–24.

Kelley, Jeff, ed. *The Border Art Workshop/Taller de Arte Fronterizo (BAW/TAF) 1984–1989.* San Diego, Calif.: Border Art Workshop/Taller de Arte Fronterizo, 1988.

Pérez, Emma. *The Decolonial Imaginary: Writing Chicanas into History.* Bloomington and Indianapolis: Indiana University Press, 1999.

Sánchez, Osvaldo, and Cecilia Garza, eds. *Fugitive Sites: inSITE 2000–2001 New Contemporary Art Projects for San Diego–Tijuana.* Curated by Susan Buck-Morss, et al. San Diego, Calif.: Installation Gallery, 2002.

Schneider Enriquez, Mary. "Beyond the Border." *ARTnews* 99, no. 1 (Jan. 2000): 80–84.

Simonds, Cylena. "Public Audit: An Interview with Elizabeth Sisco, Louis Hock, and David Avalos." *Afterimage* 22, no. 1 (Summer 1994): 8–11.

Volkart, Yvonne. "War Zone: Bodies, Identities, and Femininity in the Global High-Tech Industry." *N. Paradoxa* 4 (1999): 88–90.

Wagner, Sandra. "Artists Explore the Tijuana–San Diego Border." *Sculpture* 17, no. 2 (Feb. 1998): 32–37.

Wagner, Sandra. "Dossier: Border Art." *Sculpture* 15, no. 1 (Jan. 1996): 8–9.

Weiss, Rachel. "El reembolso que rugió: Arte y economía en la frontera." *Art Nexus*, no. 14 (Oct.–Dec. 1994): 62–65.

Yard, Sally, ed. *inSITE97 Catalogue.* San Diego, Calif.: Installation Gallery, 1998.

GUISELA M. LATORRE

BORDER INDUSTRIALIZATION PROGRAM.

The aim of the Border Industrialization Program (BIP), instituted in 1965, was to reduce unemployment in the northern border cities of Mexico. It resulted in the termination of the bracero program. The bracero program had been initiated in 1942. It permitted Mexican men to migrate into the United States in order to work temporarily in the agricultural sector, and then return to Mexico.

The Border Industrialization Program was initiated on May 20, 1965, and was formally introduced in October 1965. It was modeled on the Export Processing Zones (EPZ) already in existence in Hong Kong, Taiwan, Malaysia, Singapore, the Philippines, and other regions. The goal of the Mexican government was to diminish

MEXICAN WORKERS. An electronic parts factory in Tijuana, Mexico. (PhotoEdit)

unemployment by turning the isolated northern border of Mexico into a dynamic growth area with the installation of foreign companies to help local development. According to the BIP, the companies involved were to be located in the industrial parks that had been created on the border in 1962. The principal activity of these companies was assembly production, and the factories built under this program were called *maquiladoras*.

The BIP offered fiscal advantages to both Mexico and the United States. Mexican law allowed for temporary operation of foreign companies. U.S. law allowed U.S. companies to export components into other countries and then reimport the assembled products into the United States with no taxes upon re-entry. Therefore, machinery, vehicles, parts, and anything else needed for processing was imported into Mexico duty-free for assembly or processing. Taxes were assessed only on the increased value of the product and on any foreign components added to the production.

On April 14, 1966, a new provision was added to the BIP in order to make the importation of materials for the maquiladoras more efficient. In June 1966, the industry and commerce secretary of Mexico and the treasury secretary of the United States announced the operating terms for companies that were registered under the BIP. The rules were known as the Five Point Plan. BIP companies had to be located within twenty kilometers of the border, and they could temporarily import machinery, equipment, additional parts, and raw materials used in the production process tax-free. Exportation of the finished products was also tax-free. Foreign technicians were allowed to work in Mexico only if authorized by the Mexican government.

All the firms operating under this program had to comply with certain financial and labor requirements. They also had to rent their facilities from a Mexican citizen or company, because of a provision in the Mexican Constitution that prohibits foreign citizens from owning property within a hundred kilometers of the border. The companies were only authorized to operate in areas near cities with customs facilities, such as Palomas and Ciudad Juárez in Chihuahua, Piedras Negras and Ciudad Acuña in Coahuila, and Nuevo Laredo, Reynosa, and Matamoros in Tamaulipas. The first investments arrived in 1966. By the end of the 1960s the program included 147 enterprises and 17,000 workers, a majority of whom were women. Most of the earliest firms in the program were electrical and electronics companies.

The advantages for Mexico in this program were the creation of more employment in the region, giving people better incomes and standards of living; increase of foreign currency; the use of new techniques and methods of production; increase in consumption; and in certain cases an increase in the raw materials produced in Mexico. The chief advantage for the United States was the low cost of labor, which made American companies more competitive at home and abroad. A large percentage of the Mexican salaries returned to the United States because the workers spent their money on food, clothing, and other U.S.–made products. Other advantages included the opportunity to use American raw materials, reduced transportation costs, and the ability to keep their technological advances confidential because the companies could send their own technicians.

See also Border, The; Bracero Program; *and* Maquiladoras.

BIBLIOGRAPHY

Bermúdez, Antonio J. *El rescate del Mercado fronterizo: Una obra al servicio de México.* Mexico City: Ediciones Eufesa, 1966.

Farías, Jorge. *Industrialization Program for the Mexican Northern Border.* Mexico: Editorial Jus, 1969.

Programa Nacional Fronterizo. *National Border Program.* Mexico, 1961.

Secretaría de Industria y Comercio. *Programa de industrialización de la frontera norte de México.* Mexico, 1971.

CIRILA QUINTERO

BORDER PATROL. The United States Border Patrol is the mobile and uniformed law enforcement arm of the Department of Homeland Security. Its primary mission is the detection and apprehension of unauthorized entrants into the United States at the country's boundaries.

The Border Patrol was established in 1924. Its origins, however, are in the late 1800s. The U.S. government first appointed customs inspectors to patrol the boundary with Mexico in approximately 1870 to guard against the smuggling of tobacco, sugar, cattle, and other contraband. The passage of the Chinese Exclusion Act in 1882 resulted for the first time in the placement of agents along the boundary to prevent the entry of unauthorized immigrants—specifically from China. During World War I, in late 1917, the Immigration Service began requiring passports of all who wanted to cross from the United States into Mexico to limit the ability of individuals who were in the service of enemy governments to communicate with those governments. During this time Washington also stationed some troops along the boundary.

Although unauthorized entries dropped during the war, they picked up quickly following its end and intensified as Congress placed additional restrictions on immigration. As a result, pressures grew to increase efforts to stymie unauthorized boundary crossings. The bureau's commissioner general stressed in 1919 that such efforts were needed in the face of large numbers of apprehensions of unauthorized European and Chinese immigrants smuggled in from Canada, Mexico, and Cuba. In the aftermath of World War I, there was also widespread fear that huge numbers of emigrants from war-devastated Europe might try to enter the United States extralegally. Indeed from 1919 to 1920 the number of entries into the United States increased by 300 percent.

On May 28, 1914, the Department of Labor was granted $1 million for "additional land-border patrol," thus creating the U.S. Border Patrol out of the previous boundary policing unit and greatly strengthening boundary policing in the process. Through the Immigration Act of 1925 Congress expanded the Border Patrol's duties to the policing of the seacoasts in the face of large-scale immigrant smuggling from Cuba to Florida and the Gulf Coast.

The Border Patrol assigned 450 officers to the Mexican and Canadian borders and to the Florida and Gulf of Mexico coasts. Through the 1920s and 1930s the Border Patrol grew slowly. By the 1930s it used cars, trucks, motorboats, radios, and horses to patrol the country's boundaries. During this time roughly an equal number of agents worked in the Canadian and the Mexican border regions. The Border Patrol added autogiros and airplanes to their equipment in the 1940s. During Prohibition the Border Patrol concentrated most of its resources on preventing the smuggling of alcohol into the United States, and following the repeal of Prohibition in 1933 its efforts went toward preventing the entry of unauthorized immigrants from Mexico.

In the aftermath of a massive deportation and repatriation campaign of people of Mexican origin from the United States in the 1930s, the Border Patrol grew considerably. The outbreak of World War II caused great consternation within the federal government, which feared that foreign agents with nefarious intentions would attempt to enter the United States clandestinely. The administration played an important role in making immigration and border enforcement issues of national security and transferred the Immigration and Naturalization Service from the Department of Labor to the Department of Justice. (President Herbert Hoover had consolidated the Bureau of Immigration and the Bureau of Naturalization into the INS in 1933.) Congress appropriated funds to add

BORDER PATROL. An agent with undocumented Guatemalan immigrants in Calexico, Calif., 2003. (Jimmy Dorantes-Latin Focus.com)

BORDER PATROL. Members of the Border Patrol wait for illegal immigrants, 1951. (Time Life Pictures/Getty Images)

712 Border Patrol officers, almost doubling the authorized size of the force. The agency carried out many functions during the war, including guarding "enemy alien" detention camps and diplomats and helping the U.S. military guard the country's East Coast against the potential entry of agents from the Axis powers.

Though the Border Patrol grew, it was unable to realize its stated mission. The length of the boundaries for which the Border Patrol was responsible limited its effectiveness, especially in the face of the agency's relatively small size, the sophistication of smugglers, and the large numbers and sheer determination of migrants. As early as 1927, for example, reports stated that smugglers were operating at least fifteen airplanes in the Los Angeles district alone. Furthermore, the Border Patrol had to contend with the intense transboundary social networks of the border region, many of which long preceded the establishment of the international divide. In addition, farmers along the U.S. side of the boundary actively encouraged Mexican workers to step across the line and work on their farms. According to a 1934 INS report, this practice was difficult to stop given the Border Patrol's size and difficult to prosecute successfully because of the sympathy of juries to the needs of growers.

Economic factors—namely the need for domestic capital to have a highly exploitable labor force—served as the basis for what some referred to as the "revolving door" function of the Border Patrol and the INS generally. Through much of the twentieth century the Border Patrol often overtly served the needs of employers, allowing migrants to enter and remain in the country at times of high labor demand but preventing them from entering or deporting them when they were no longer needed or desired (for engaging in labor organizing, for example).

Powerful agricultural interests played a significant role in the gap between state rhetoric championing strong boundary policing and actual state practice. This gap characterized U.S. immigration enforcement efforts through most of the twentieth century. It appears that national political leaders, especially those from border states, had little political will to fund policing the border adequately. In 1952 and 1954, despite increasing numbers of unauthorized immigrants, many members of Congress from border states voted to cut monies for the Border Patrol. By 1954 the Border Patrol employed only two hundred guards at any one time.

Limited funding for boundary enforcement continued during the 1960s and 1970s. Although the number of apprehensions of unauthorized entrants rose from about 71,000 in 1960 to 345,000 in 1969, the number of permanent INS positions remained constant. The Border Patrol's 1980 budget was only $77 million, less than that of Baltimore's police department and far less than half that of Philadelphia's.

As public awareness and concern about a southern boundary "out of control" and increasing numbers of unauthorized immigrants grew in the 1970s, the Border Patrol was given more resources. In the 1980s the Border Patrol became increasingly involved in drug interdiction—part of the so-called war on drugs—and such activities came to significantly define the agency's work. The Border Patrol grew at a dramatic rate in the 1990s, when official and public anxiety reached a historic high. In 1994 the number of Border Patrol agents was about forty-two hundred. In the beginning years of the twenty-first century the number stands at approximately ninety-five hundred. Over 90 percent of the agents are stationed along the boundary with Mexico, and about 40 percent of the agents are now of Latino *and* Latina origin.

See also Border, The; Bracero Program; Immigration and Naturalization Service; *and* Militarization of the Border.

BIBLIOGRAPHY

Andreas, Peter. *Border Games: Policing the U.S.–Mexico Divide.* Ithaca, N.Y., and London: Cornell University Press, 2000.

Calavita, Kitty. *Inside the State: The Bracero Program, Immigration, and the I.N.S.* New York and London: Routledge, 1992.

Coppock, Donald R., INS Deputy Associate Commissioner, Domestic Control. "History: Border Patrol." Unpublished manuscript, available at the Immigration and Naturalization Historical Reference Library, Washington, D.C., ca. 1968.

Dunn, Timothy J. *The Militarization of the U.S.–Mexico Border, 1978–1992: Low-Intensity Conflict Doctrine Comes Home.* Austin: Center for Mexican American Studies, University of Texas at Austin, 1996.

Galarza, Ernesto. *Merchants of Labor: The Mexican Bracero Story.* Charlotte, N.C.: McNally and Loftin, 1964.

García, Juan Ramon. *Operation Wetback: The Mass Deportation of Mexican Undocumented Workers in 1954.* Westport, Conn., and London: Greenwood Press, 1980.

Lee, Erika. *At America's Gate: Chinese Immigration during the Exclusion Era, 1882–1943.* Chapel Hill: University of North Carolina Press, 2003.

Nevins, Joseph. *Operation Gatekeeper: The Rise of the "Illegal Alien" and the Making of the U.S.–Mexico Boundary.* New York: Routledge, 2002.

Wixon, I. F. "Immigration Border Patrol." Lecture no. 7. Immigration and Naturalization Service, U.S. Department of Labor, Washington, D.C., March 19, 1934.

JOSEPH NEVINS

BORICUA. *See* Puerto Ricans.

BORICUA COLLEGE. Boricua College in New York City is a postsecondary educational institution designed to meet the needs of the Puerto Rican and Latino and Latina community. The college's name is a reference to Borinquen, the Taino Indian name for Puerto Rico. It was founded in 1974 as a result of the efforts of the Puerto Rican Research and Resources Center. Convinced that the cause of the economic and social problems confronting the Puerto Rican and Latino and Latina communities in the United States was a crisis in education, the center set out to establish a college that would strengthen Boricua and Latino and Latina culture through bilingual and bicultural instruction and special course offerings in Puerto Rican and Latino and Latina history and art. The college also focuses on understanding and finding solutions to the problems confronting Puerto Rican and other Spanish-speaking people in the United States.

The college's program of study seeks to develop the students' intellectual skills and commitment to humanistic values and their capacity to assimilate knowledge for subsequent specialized training. It is the particular mission of the college to address the need for bilingual professionals for the human service institutions of New York City and the need for bilingual early-childhood-education teachers in the city's public schools. The college's program of study also examines the relationships of the peoples and countries of North, Central, and South America, and of the Caribbean region, in regard to politics, economics, and culture.

The college seeks to respond to the special needs of nontraditional students: adults returning to school after years of employment or homemaking and students with work or family responsibilities. Students design programs of individualized instruction, meeting one on one with faculty members to plan and evaluate them, and working at their own pace toward their intellectual and career goals. Throughout the semester, small groups of students meet with faculty in a weekly colloquium to discuss and evaluate issues and problems related to their studies.

Boricua College enrolls some 1,200 full-time students in its associate in arts, bachelor of science, bachelor of arts, master of arts, and master of science degree programs. The college operates three learning centers; two are located in Brooklyn and the third on Manhattan's Upper West Side. Boricua College is a member of the Middle States Association of Colleges and Schools, the Commission on Independent Colleges and Universities, the Association of Governing Boards of Colleges and Universities, and the Hispanic Association of Colleges and Universities.

See also Higher Education, *sidebar on* Hispanic Serving Institutions; Hispanic Association of Colleges and Universities; Hostos Community College; New York; *and* Puerto Ricans.

BIBLIOGRAPHY
Torres, Ida Nilda. "Boricua College: An Academic Response to the Socioeconomic Needs of Puerto Ricans in New York City." PhD diss., Teachers College, Columbia University, 2000.

CARLOS SANABRIA

BOTÁNICAS. *Botánicas* are specialty stores that cater to the health and spiritual needs of customers in Latina and Latino neighborhoods. These specialty stores offer herbs and botanical by-products for use in both religion and folk medical traditions. Customers use botánicas to obtain herbs, teas, salves, ointments, and homeopathic products that are used for therapeutic purposes. Botanically based remedies are grounded in ancestral values towards health. For religious or spiritual purposes, customers can purchase articles that pertain primarily to the Roman Catholic Church and its sacraments. Believers in Espiritismo and Santería worshippers can find articles used in rituals and ceremonies. In addition to religious articles and health remedies, some botánicas stock more conventional merchandise, such as commercially produced vitamins, over-the-counter medications, natural foods, and other products that are more commonly associated with health-food stores or pharmacies. Botánicas are also known in different geographic regions as *yierberías* (literally, "herbal stores") or *boticas* (literally, "drugstores").

Botánicas provide several important social functions in Latina and Latino communities. Principally, their role pertains to healing and spirituality. However, they also serve as places where community members can find acceptance and even mediation in negotiating social services outside their immediate environment. Botánicas are usually low-profile businesses that rely on word-of-mouth advertisement. Despite that, their location and services are well known to the immediate community.

In most Latina and Latino cultures, the practice of traditional medical lore is a culturally accepted norm. In some Latina and Latino enclaves, medical lore is used exclusively. This is especially the case for recently arrived immigrants, the poor who cannot afford standard medical care, those without health insurance, and Latinas and Latinos who find conventional medicine ineffective or impersonal. However, recent studies indicate that Latinas and Latinos, regardless of birthplace or socioeconomic status, who incorporate some form of alternative medicine do so to supplement standard medical care. Once labeled as catering to the superstitious or to those interested in the occult, botánicas are increasingly respected by the medical profession as attitudes towards patient care change.

Among Mexicans and Mexican Americans, the practice of alternative medicine is known as *curanderismo*; many Cubanas and Cubanos and Afro-Latino communities follow the therapeutic beliefs of the Santería faith. In Puerto Rican communities, the practice of Espiritismo is espoused. The common trait of these traditional medical practices is their holistic approach to well-being. Health remedies incorporate both physical and spiritual therapeutic measures in the belief that good health results from an equilibrium between the two. Unlike conventional medicine, traditional medical practices recognize that illnesses of the psyche (envy, bad luck, stress, and so on) are unhealthy conditions that require treatment. Thus healing involves the total person, not just the body.

In addition to a holistic approach to healing, Latina and Latino medical lore typically incorporates a belief that supernatural forces affect health. In clusters that maintain Christian practices, prayer is the intercession required for God to bestow good health or heal sickness. Botánicas located in these clusters tend to carry more merchandise whose origins lie in European religious traditions. Such merchandise includes rosaries, crucifixes, *veladoras* (candles), prayer cards, incense, oils, and religious icons. Among the most popular icons are images of the Virgin Mary, the Sacred Heart of Jesus, Saint Jude (patron saint of hopeless causes), and Saint Anthony (patron saint of lost items). Along with articles associated with the Christian tradition, these botánicas also sell items linked to secular spiritual powers, such as amulets,

BOTÁNICA. Oils, candles, and statues of saints to cure physical and spiritual ills. (Photograph by Socorro Castañeda-Liles)

milagros (charms portraying an afflicted anatomical part), perfumes, hennas, healing stones, and potions.

Spiritual powers are associated with an amalgam of Spanish colonial and indigenous health beliefs. In traditional Mexican cultures, curanderismo retains the remnants of the ethnobotanical practices among original native inhabitants. Curanderismo adheres to a belief that the patient, the patient's family, and the *curandero* (the healer) are jointly responsible for nursing the patient back to health. The natural world is intertwined with the supernatural, thus requiring the intervention of the curandero. The curandero, with his or her gift of healing, can communicate with the spiritual realm and dispel the spirits that are causing disharmony in the body and soul of afflicted individuals. In Puerto Rican Espiritismo, a spiritual medium exorcises evil spirits that are at the root of a client's emotional or physical malady.

Botánicas that serve customers of the Santería religion offer articles pertaining to ceremonial rituals. Santería traces its beginning to the Yoruba people of precolonial Nigeria and Benin who were brought as slaves to Cuba, Puerto Rico, and Brazil. During their settlement in the Caribbean, the practitioners of Santería incorporated Catholicism for survival, as the open expression of native religious practices was prohibited. In the Yoruba belief system, the traditional *orishas* (gods) were associated with a specific health condition. For example, the orish

Chango is associated with violent death. In the New World, Chango became Saint Barbara, the patron saint of those who died violently. Santeria botánicas tend to carry items of the orish and the clothing worn by practitioners during services. Other ritual merchandise includes ceremonial masks, *elekes* (beaded necklaces), drums, and other traditional musical instruments.

Most botánicas are owned and managed by individuals knowledgeable about the holistic and supernatural approaches to health maintenance. Some even offer space in a nonpublic area where healers can administer treatments or provide personal consultations. Most proprietors are not healers themselves but rather provide referrals, healing tools, and a safe area for practicing traditional healing methods.

Alternative medicine is increasingly accepted by conventional American health care providers. Evidence of this acceptance is the scholarly investigations on the effectiveness of home remedies that are prevalent in many societies and on the importance of spiritual issues in health care. The National Institutes of Health has even established the National Center for Complementary and Alternative Medicine. Appropriately, the center's first director was an American Indian pediatrician who had training in North American indigenous healing practices. Medical school programs now offer courses that include cultural sensitivity, spirituality, and medical lore in patient care. As botánicas continue to flourish throughout Latina and Latino communities in the United States, their social stigma is diminishing.

See also Curanderismo; Environmental Knowledge, Traditional; Espiritismo; Health; Medicine, Traditional; *and* Santería.

BIBLIOGRAPHY
Gomez-Beloz, Alfredo, and Noel Chavel. "The Botánica as a Culturally Appropriate Health Care Option for Latinos." *Journal of Alternative and Complementary Medicine* 7, no. 5 (2001): 537–546.
Spector, Rachel E. *Cultural Diversity in Health and Illness.* Upper Saddle River, N.J.: Prentice Hall, 2000.

GILDA BAEZA ORTEGO

BRACERO PROGRAM. As early as 1940, farmers had been warning the U.S. government about farm labor shortages in the Southwest. When the United States entered World War II in December 1941, farm labor shortages became acute as the workforce went off to war or to higher-paying defense industry jobs. The farm labor supply was further eroded when thousands of Japanese American farmers were sent to internment camps. According to U.S. agribusiness, the labor supply was not sufficient to harvest the crops, which would result in food shortages unless the government procured an outside labor force. On July 23, 1942, soon after Mexico declared war on the Axis powers, the "Agreement between the United States of America and Mexico Respecting the Temporary Migration of Mexican Workers" was signed. It went into effect on August 4, 1942, and later became known as the bracero program.

Mexican Farm Laborer Immigration Prior to World War II

The World War II bracero program was not the first time the United States had looked to Mexico for help with labor shortages. During implementation of the Chinese Exclusion Acts (1882–1943), Mexican immigration was encouraged to replace Chinese railroad workers. During World War I, the United States responded to an agricultural labor shortage by allowing temporary workers from Mexico into the country for the duration of the war.

The Mexican immigrants were mostly welcomed in their new communities during World War I, as long as those communities had labor shortages. During the Great Depression, the dismal U.S. economy and shrinking job market caused many Americans to resent the influx of immigrants, who they believed were depressing wages and taking away scarce jobs. The situation worsened after the Dust Bowl in the midwestern and southern states sent many farm workers west looking for work. The competition for agricultural jobs increased the anger toward Mexican farmworkers. As a result, more than 400,000

Mexican nationals and Mexican Americans were removed to Mexico without deportation hearings between 1929 and 1934, although thousands were U.S. citizens.

The World War II Agreement

Many government agencies, including the Departments of State, Agriculture, Labor, and Justice and the War Manpower Commission, helped to develop the wartime farm labor program. U.S. officials knew they would have to assure the Mexican government that its citizens would not be subjected to the racial hostilities of the previous decades. The Department of Agriculture, represented by officials from the Farm Security Administration (FSA) and the Office of Agricultural War Relations, along with a U.S. ambassador, met with representatives from Mexico.

One of Mexico's greatest concerns was the treatment of its citizens after their work was no longer needed. During the Great Depression, Mexico had to pay transportation costs for repatriated Mexican workers, and those who were not repatriated remained in the United States without support from either government. To prevent this from happening again, the agreement explicitly stated that the contracts would comply with Mexico's labor law in providing the workers with transportation, living expenses, and repatriation. In addition, the United States would cover all transportation costs of the workers, including their living and any other expenses incurred while traveling between the place of origin in Mexico and the U.S. farm.

Under the bracero agreement, Mexico would permit its citizens to work in the United States for temporary, renewable periods under agreed-upon conditions. The conditions stipulated methods of recruitment, transportation, standards of health care, wages, housing, food, and the number of hours that braceros (farmhands) were allowed to work. The agreement also required the contracts to be written in Spanish, under the supervision of the Mexican government, and the wage would be the same as wages paid to similar workers, but never less than thirty cents an hour. The workers were also to receive three dollars a day if they were unemployed for 75 percent of the contract period, excluding Sundays. The Agreement barred Mexican citizens from U.S. military service and stated that they would be protected from discrimination during their stay in the United States. Additionally, to protect the workers' rights, the workers would elect a representative to deal with the employer, and the Mexican consuls would make efforts to protect the workers.

Violation of these protections was supposed to result in the suspension of braceros' availability for the violating area. However, the terms were, for the most part, ignored by both the growers and the U.S. government.

Although the chief purpose of the agreement was to protect the Mexican workers, the United States was assured

LABOR CENTER. Mexican farmworkers being processed in Hidalgo, Tex., 1959. (Associated Press)

that the Mexican workers would not displace domestic workers or depress wages. The agreement also provided that the United States could treat as illegal the stay of workers after the expiration of their contracts. Another provision ordered the withholding of a percentage of the braceros' pay, which they would receive upon their return to Mexico. This provided for a mandatory savings account for the bracero and an assurance to the U.S. government that the bracero had an incentive to return home at the end of the contract.

The Operation of the World War II Agreement

On September 29, 1942, the first 1,500 braceros came to the United States to work in sugar beet fields in California. Later that year, over 2,700 more braceros arrived.

The U.S. government was to act as intermediary between the farm owners and the immigrants to ensure that the farm owners abided by the agreement. Thus, the original agreement named the U.S. government, represented by the Farm Security Administration, as the employer. The U.S. Employment Services (USES) reviewed requests for workers after confirming that alternative local labor sources did not exist, and then USES notified the Mexican government of the number of workers needed. The resulting employment contracts were between the U.S. government, through the FSA, and the Mexican workers. Farm owners subcontracted with the federal government

for the employees. This provided central oversight of the number of recruitments and the implementation of the program. However, farm owners were used to regulating their workers on their own terms and objected to this regulation of labor relations by the federal government.

Braceros across the country endured poor food, excessive charges for board, substandard housing, discrimination, physical mistreatment, inappropriate deductions from their wages, and exposure to pesticides and other dangerous chemicals. Many states violated the conditions of the agreement, and Texas lost its privilege to utilize bracero labor altogether until after the war because of severe discrimination.

In 1943, Congress adopted a joint resolution, Public Law 45, which changed the agreement and explicitly mentioned Mexico's labor law. However, it also appeared to allow direct recruitment of Mexican workers at the border, as had been permitted during World War I. As soon as they learned of this change, farm owners in Texas, banned from the bracero program, immediately began to recruit workers directly from Mexico. This interpretation of the resolution was short-lived, however, and the direct recruiting was soon stopped.

The railroad bracero labor program began in 1943. Although not as long-lived as the agricultural bracero program, it was heavily utilized during the war. The railroad program was effected through an exchange of letters between the U.S. and Mexican ambassadors. It was similar to the farm labor agreement, with provisions that the braceros would not be subjected to discriminatory treatment, that they would not be enrolled in U.S. military service, and that the agreement would otherwise comply with Article 29 of Mexico's labor law.

The Bracero Program after the War

The bracero program was extended for two years after the end of the war because farm owners claimed that the domestic labor force would not perform the "stoop labor" that was done by the braceros. In 1947, Congress enacted Public Law 40, which allowed for the continuation of the program until December 31 of that year. After that date, however, immigration was allowed to continue because farm owners warned that the labor shortage still existed.

In 1948, Congress turned over the administration of the program to the U.S. Employment Services by enacting Public Law 893. This law allowed the administrator of the Federal Security Agency, in carrying out his USES responsibilities, to recruit workers in the Western Hemisphere for "temporary agricultural employment." Even though the law gave USES responsibility for direct supervision of the program, the Immigration and Naturalization Service retained control over the immigration aspects of the program.

Public Law 78, enacted in 1951, was a major codification of the agreement that was due to expire that year. The Mexican government warned that it would not renew the agreement unless the United States passed a law that provided additional guarantees to the Mexican workers. After the war, the U.S. government was largely out of the picture, and farm owners were subject to fewer restraints in the recruitment of workers. Mexico hoped that codification of the agreement would answer concerns about low wages and other abuses of the program.

Mexico also demanded that the United States address the problem of illegal immigration. Not only was Mexico concerned about the appalling conditions suffered by these workers, it also wanted to stop immigration to the United States because workers were needed in Mexico to facilitate economic expansion there. A proposal in the 1951 bill that would have penalized farmers who knowingly hired Mexicans who were illegally in the United States was rejected, however, because of the farmers' adamant opposition to it.

The U.S. involvement in the Korean War in 1951 had increased Mexico's bargaining power. Similar to what had occurred during World War II, there was additional need for foreign workers to replace those who went abroad to fight the war. When the conference report on Public Law 78 was submitted, Senator Allen J. Ellender of Louisiana remarked that the government might have gone too far in giving Mexico so many protections for its workers, but that the provisions were necessary because it was the "only way by which we can obtain these workers."

Mexico found that its bargaining power drastically declined in the years after the Korean War. Eventually, Mexico lost two of its most important battles: ensuring tougher protections against illegal immigration and keeping recruitment centers away from the border. The latter was important to Mexico because it feared that recruitment centers at the border would bring thousands of Mexican citizens to border towns that could not support them.

The Reality of the Farmworker Agreement

The protective provisions of the agreement were often not followed after workers arrived at the farms. The decentralized nature of the farm labor program at the local level meant that farm owners treated the workers as they pleased, with little threat of government sanction. The agreement did provide for a complaint process, but the braceros knew this would do little good, as the farm owner could simply hire another worker and list the complaining bracero as an unfit worker.

The most common complaints about the program concerned housing and food. Across the nation, farmworker housing was inadequate and sanitation was lacking. This was especially true in California, where many workers were housed in old army barracks or in the temporary housing used for interned Japanese before more permanent quarters were built. The Department of Labor had established standards but had no real enforcement power, except for withholding braceros, and there were too few resources to conduct routine inspections. The standards themselves were not clearly defined, and when the department attempted to make them more specific, farm owners protested. The department abandoned efforts to establish more stringent housing standards, and instead issued even more ambiguous ones, which favored the farm owners.

The bracero program had effects beyond the Mexican citizens involved in it. Prior to their internment during World War II, Japanese Americans either owned or worked on many acres of California's farmland. The bracero program enabled Anglo farmers to take this land. The program thus translated to a sort of farm subsidy for Anglo farmers, serving as a further disincentive to release the Japanese from internment.

The problems with the program did not end at the border. There were many reports of Mexican officials taking advantage of the intense competition for contracts by charging a commission for procuring them. In addition, both countries were concerned about the number of Mexican citizens who entered the United States illegally in hopes of obtaining work. Farm owners in Texas were able to get around the ban on braceros in their state by hiring these undocumented workers. Other farm owners simply chose to hire such workers instead of braceros because it was cheaper and it was not necessary to comply with any of the governmental protections regarding wages, housing, and sanitary conditions. During a Senate debate in 1951, Senator Dennis Chávez of New Mexico noted that the wages paid to undocumented workers were often as low as 15 or 25 cents a day, and some farmers refused to pay any wages, but instead "paid" the workers with food. Both countries tried to deal with the problem but were afraid that abolishing the bracero program would only increase illegal immigration and the subsequent exploitation of these workers. This concern, as well as the firm position of agribusiness that the braceros were essential to their harvest, kept the program alive for years after the war.

The Final Years of the Program

Farm owners did not want the bracero program to end, but complaints persisted about the treatment of workers. More and more people charged that the program was nothing more than a farm subsidy that was being used to depress wages. Further, despite congressional hopes to the contrary, continuation of the program did not stem illegal immigration. Impoverished Mexican citizens were eager to obtain a bracero contract. Many of these men gathered at the border towns' recruitment centers, and if they were unable to secure a contract, there was not much to stop them from crossing the border illegally.

By the 1960s it became apparent that the program was falling out of favor. A major contention of its opponents was that it worked to the detriment of U.S. citizens. At the Western Interstate Conference on Migratory Labor in 1960, William H. Metzler, agricultural economist with the U.S. Department of Agriculture, noted that factors such as the increasing mechanization of farm crops like sugar beets and cotton and the injection of immigrant farm labor were decreasing the opportunity for U.S. citizens to find agricultural work. Louis Krainock of the AFL-CIO echoed Metzler's concern and argued that there were enough U.S. workers to fill the farm labor jobs and that braceros were not needed.

During the next few years, the competing concerns caused battles in the House and Senate. Some people wanted more protections for the braceros, while others wanted to protect the domestic workforce. In the end both sides compromised and the program was extended, without amendment, in 1961 and 1963. By 1964, however, the controversy associated with the bracero program was too great to overcome, and it was allowed to expire.

After the Bracero Program

Albeit at great human expense, during its operation the bracero program provided many benefits to U.S. agriculture. Farmers were able to produce enough food during World War II to keep up with increased demand. After the war, continuation of the program assured farmers that they would have an adequate workforce, and it led to expansion of farms and improved farming methods. In recognition of the contributions of the bracero workers, Congress passed House Resolution 522 in 2002 to honor the memory of the braceros on the sixtieth anniversary of the program.

Although the braceros wanted an opportunity to earn wages that allowed them to help their families who remained in Mexico, many workers reported that they did not see promised wages or, if they did, they were required to spend much of it for essentials such as food or even tools needed to perform their jobs. For example, a bracero contract referred to in a Senate debate showed that the worker was charged $3.25 as a mandatory 10 percent savings deduction, $15.75 for board, and $10 for an advance, after which his total pay was $3.35. Such reports are so typical that the program is often cited as an embarrassing example of exploitive legislation.

The problems of the bracero program were again exposed when a class action lawsuit was filed in 2001. The lawsuit alleged that the mandatory deduction from the braceros' paychecks was not returned to the workers, as promised, upon their return to Mexico. The lawsuit was later dismissed, but not before the story of the apparent mismanagement of the braceros' money was made public.

The United States often still looks to foreign countries to supply labor, and when such bills are being considered in Congress, heated debates ensue over the fear that the country will create a new bracero program. Nevertheless, the McCarran-Walter Act of 1952 established a fallback bracero regime, the "H-2 Program," which revived all the worst features of its predecessors. Under this program, the U.S. Department of Labor has power to admit foreign labor for temporary jobs if able, willing, and qualified domestic workers cannot be found at the time and place where they are needed. Like workers in the bracero program, these migrants are totally dependent on the farm owners for employment. If the worker proves himself to be hard working and faithful, he might be asked to return the following year; if not, he can be removed from the country with no appeal.

To the extent that the bracero program was a substitute for legal (permanent) immigration, it contributed to depressed wages and to a disregard for standard working conditions. This, in turn, led agribusiness to come to expect a workforce that could be exploited. Undocumented workers, therefore, have become the braceros' successors. Predictably, this caused difficulty in forming unions that could oversee the conditions of the farmworkers, because the farm owners could easily report complaining workers to the immigration authorities or simply hire other workers in their place.

The United States will continue to use foreign labor, particularly during labor shortages. The bracero program was an early answer to this need for labor and, although the program has died, the dependence on cheap labor has not. In his 1969 testimony before the Senate Subcommittee of Labor, César Chávez noted that the bracero program "lives on in the annual parade of thousands" of undocumented workers and workers with green cards (resident aliens) on their way to U.S. farms. Chávez's leadership of the United Farm Workers led to the establishment of protections for farm workers provided by unionization and stemmed much of the exploitation that had been spawned by the longstanding reliance of the United States on the bracero program.

See also Border, The; Deportation of Chicanos and Chicanas; Immigration; *and* Immigration Policy, Twentieth Century.

BIBLIOGRAPHY

An Act to Amend the Agricultural Act of 1949. U.S. Statutes at Large 65 (1951): 119–121.

Acuña, Rodolfo. *Occupied America: A History of Chicanos.* 2nd ed. New York: Harper and Row, 1981.

Agreement between the United States of America and Mexico Respecting the Recruiting of Mexican Non-Agricultural Workers. U.S. Statutes at Large 57 (1943): 1353–1365.

Agreement between the United States of America and Mexico Respecting the Temporary Migration of Mexican Workers, Treaty with Mexico. U.S. Statutes at Large 56 (1942): 1759–1769.

Anderson, Henry P. *The Bracero Program in California.* New York: Arno Press, 1976.

Calavita, Kitty. *Inside the State: The Bracero Program, Immigration, and the I.N.S.* New York: Routledge, 1992.

Carrasco, Gilbert Paul. "Latinos in the United States: Invitation and Exile." In *Immigrants Out! The New Nativism and the Anti-Immigrant Impulse in the United States,* edited by Juan F. Perea. New York: New York University Press, 1997.

Congressional Record. 82nd Cong., 1st sess., 1951. Vol. 97, pts. 4–6.

Congressional Record. 87th Cong., 1st sess., 1961. Vol. 107, pts. 6, 15.

Craig, Richard B. *The Bracero Program: Interest Groups and Foreign Policy.* Austin: University of Texas Press, 1971.

Driscoll, Barbara A. *The Tracks North: The Railroad Bracero Program of World War II.* Austin: University of Texas Press, 1999.

Galarza, Ernesto. *Farm Workers and Agri-Business in California, 1947–1960.* Notre Dame, Ind.: University of Notre Dame Press, 1977.

Galarza, Ernesto. *Merchants of Labor: The Mexican Bracero Story, An Account of the Managed Migration of Mexican Farm Workers in California.* Charlotte, N.C.: McNally and Loftin, 1964.

Gamboa, Erasmo. *Mexican Labor and World War II: Braceros in the Pacific Northwest, 1942–1947.* Austin: University of Texas Press, 1990.

Jensen, Richard J., and John C. Hammerback, eds. *The Words of César Chávez.* College Station: Texas A&M University Press, 2002.

Kirstein, Peter N. *Anglo over Bracero: A History of the Mexican Worker in the United States from Roosevelt to Nixon.* San Francisco: R&E Research Associates, 1977.

Making an Appropriation to Assist in Providing a Supply and Distribution of Farm Labor for Calendar Year 1943. U.S. Statutes at Large 62 (1948): 1238–1239.

President's Commission on Migratory Labor, U.S. Dept. of Labor. *Migratory Labor in American Agriculture.* Washington, D.C.: GPO, 1951.

President's Committee on Migratory Labor. U.S. Dept of Labor. *Proceedings: Western Interstate Conference on Migratory Labor, April 10–13, 1960, Hotel Westward Ho, Phoenix, Arizona.* Washington, D.C.: GPO, 1960.

To Provide Assistance in the Recruitment and Distribution of Farm Labor for the Increased Production, Harvesting, and Preparation for Market of Agricultural Commodities to Meet Domestic Needs and Foreign Commitment. U.S. Statutes at Large 62 (1948): 1238–1239.

U.S. Dept of Agriculture. *Backgrounds of the War Farm Labor Program.* Prepared by the Bureau of Agricultural Economics and the Farm Security Administration. Washington, D.C.: GPO, 1942.

U.S. Dept. of Agriculture, Bureau of Agricultural Economics. *The Hired Farm Working Force of 1952 with Special Information on Migratory Workers.* Washington, D.C.: GPO, 1953.

U.S. Dept. of Agriculture, Economic Research Service. *Termination of the Bracero Program: Some Effects on Farm Labor and Migrant Housing Needs.* Agricultural Economic Report No. 77. Washington, D.C.: GPO, 1962.

GILBERT PAUL CARRASCO

BRAZILIANS. In the mid-1980s, significant numbers of Brazilians began emigrating for the first time in the nation's history. There had previously been a substantial amount of migration among different regions inside the country, and in the late nineteenth and early twentieth centuries Brazil had been a destination for major flows of immigrants from Europe and Asia. These immigrants went mostly to rural areas in response to an immigration policy that derived from an alliance between the state and coffee growers to solve a labor shortage. Plantation labor became scarce after the slave trade was banned in 1850, and the problem worsened with the abolition of slavery in 1888. Italian, Portuguese, and Spanish immigrants formed the majority in the first wave. Later, they were joined by Japanese agricultural laborers. Immigrants to Brazil included relatively few skilled workers, or professionals such as physicians and lawyers, or even builders or foremen. The few skilled workers and professionals who did go to Brazil from other countries went directly to the cities, particularly São Paulo, an important commercial and financial center for coffee export through the nearby port of Santos.

The data available on recent Brazilian emigration are limited, but the Foreign Ministry estimates that out of a total population of some 170 million, around 1.9 million Brazilians live abroad. An estimated 800,000 are in the United States: Most Brazilians residing in the United States are of working age, white, and middle-class in origin. They usually emigrated in search of work in nonspecialized services. This is typical of emigrants who left

FAUSTO MENDES DE ROCHA. Executive Director of the Brazilian Immigrant Center. (Bizuayehu Tesfaye/AP)

during the 1980s, which Brazilians often call the "lost decade" in allusion to both economic crisis and frustration over unfulfilled promises of political liberalization. Most young Brazilian emigrants during that period were in pursuit of the social and economic advancement that they felt was denied them in their own country.

The occupational profile of Brazilian immigrants in the United States shows a decline in status compared with the jobs they held at home. There they were elementary and high-school teachers, bank workers, students, and even highly qualified professionals. In North America, they usually end up in the so-called secondary labor market as house and office cleaners, dishwashers, busboys or busgirls, construction workers, and hotel chambermaids. Some set up their own small businesses, usually providing cleaning services or running ethnic arts and crafts stores. Social and economic advancement is chiefly represented by the opportunity to consume, thanks to the substantially higher wages paid in the United States.

Family strategies for improving the quality of life and achieving social mobility through emigration in a globalized world tend to be strongly influenced by social networks, which provide information about destinations, serve as a home base for new immigrants, and facilitate entry into the labor market. Such networks help explain why certain cities are preferred destinations for immigrants. For Brazilians who immigrate to the United States, those cities are New York, Boston, and Miami. In the Boston and Miami areas, Brazilians have constructed different forms of sociability with Latinos and Latinas.

Brazilian-Latino Relations in Boston

In Framingham, Massachusetts, there is a significant presence of Brazilian immigrants. In parts of metropolitan Boston where many Brazilians live (Somerville,

Cambridge, East Boston, Allston-Brighton), they share with Latinos and Latinas not only a place of residence but also a focus on ethnic trading in the town center. Brazilian immigrants have benefited from the experience of their Latino and Latina neighbors in some respects, but have consciously kept their distance in other ways.

In the 1990s, the Brazilian community's emerging leadership was building ties with Latinos and Latinas and learning from their experience. A good example was the Brazilian Immigrant Center in Allston-Brighton, which focused on defending the rights of Brazilians under U.S. labor laws. The same did not apply, however, to Brazilian immigrants in general: they had not built significant bridges with Latinos and Latinas, and, in fact, the Brazilian community kept mostly to itself. Moreover, Brazilians in the United States tended to entertain the old stereotype of the "lazy Hispanic" in order to affirm their own identity as hardworking people.

There was nothing accidental about their adoption of this stereotype. The media contributed to it by disseminating an image of Brazilians as hard workers. They had carved out a niche for themselves in the unskilled-labor market, taking advantage of the many employment opportunities available in Massachusetts during the boom years of the 1980s. They did work hard—as many hours a day as a typical factory worker at the start of the Industrial Revolution—usually in two or more part-time jobs concurrently.

When Brazilian immigrants strive to make their mark as hard workers, to some extent they are echoing the situation found in Brazil in the early twentieth century. Native Brazilians were then regarded as lazy by immigrants to Brazil, who saw themselves as the hard workers. Brazilian immigrants to the United States have similarly found a lazy alter ego: not the U.S.–born white, but the Hispanic.

The stereotypes about Hispanics most often voiced by Brazilian immigrants are that they do not work, they live off welfare, and they deal in drugs. The Brazilians frequently point out that, unlike Hispanics, they never resort to welfare (usually meaning unemployment benefits). Such stereotypes in fact already existed in U.S. society before the arrival of Brazilian immigrants, who latched on to them as a means of self-affirmation and to reinforce their image of themselves as hardworking people.

Brazilian-Latino Relations in Miami

Relations between Brazilians and Latinos and Latinas in Miami are quite different from those in Boston. Brazilians in Miami, who in Brazil had always felt remote from their neighbors in other South American countries, enter into close relations with Latinos and Latinas and discover a common identity with them. The differences are due to two factors: the nature of "mainstream" ethnicity in Boston and Miami, and class relations in these two localities.

In Boston, they are all immigrants at the bottom of the social pyramid. They are all in the same boat in the sense that all start by doing the menial jobs that are reserved for immigrants and do not require the qualifications or skills they brought with them from Brazil.

Brazilians in Miami, on the other hand, many of whom first immigrated to other cities such as Boston or New York, on moving to Florida come up against a distinct social segmentation between workers and entrepreneurs in the Brazilian community. A Brazilian entrepreneurial class was already well established in Miami before the main influx of working-class immigrants. The newcomers found that they had more in common, in socioeconomic terms, with working-class Latinos and Latinas than with their middle-class countrymen. This tendency is reinforced by the demographic characteristics of the city:

> Unwittingly, Miami had become the nation's first full-fledged experiment in bicultural living in the contemporary era. Other U.S. cities, such as New York and Los Angeles, also have large Spanish-speaking and immigrant populations, but nowhere has the social and economic weight of the newcomers or their political significance been greater than in South Florida
> (Portes and Stepick, pp. xi–xii)

In other words, it can be said that there is no ethnic mainstream in Miami; social divisions fall along socioeconomic rather than ethnic lines.

Boston and Miami Compared

Brazilian immigrants are at the bottom of the social pyramid in both Boston and Miami. In Boston, they have to deal with the weight of an Anglo mainstream that takes a negative view of Latinos and Latinas, but in Miami the Latinos and Latinas themselves are part of the prevailing biculturalism. As a result, Brazilians in each city have developed different identity strategies. In Boston, they focus on inward-looking solidarity, largely effacing the class differences that separated them back in Brazil ("we're all in the same boat here"). They also reinforce the image of themselves as hard workers by adopting the stereotype of the "lazy Hispanic." In Miami, however, working-class Brazilian immigrants find themselves disowned by relatively affluent Brazilian entrepreneurs who make a point of keeping separate, and they therefore build closer ties to working-class Latinos and Latinas as a strategy of identity formation and social self-affirmation.

The Brazilians build relations with Latinos and Latinas mainly in the workplace, as coworkers or subordinates. These relations eventually extend beyond work to friendship, community associations, and religious affiliation. In this context, a specific feature of Brazilian Protestant churches in the two regions is worth noting. Whereas in Boston these churches limit their activities to the Brazilian community, in Miami they reach out to the entire Latino and Latina community. This outreach reinforces Brazilian-Latino relations through the considerable influence of these churches in the lives of Brazilian immigrants.

Miami is similar to other places in which large numbers of Brazilian immigrants are found in terms of socioeconomic profile. In every area researched they all have jobs, although most are manual laborers or semiskilled workers. They tend to occupy a specific niche in the labor market, with variations from place to place: a great many are shoeshiners in New York, cleaners in Boston, pizza deliverers in San Francisco, and valet parking attendants for the big hotels in Miami Beach.

Trends for the Future

Despite their relatively recent arrival in the United States in significant numbers, Brazilian immigrants have swiftly built social networks and are already forming a second generation that will bring significant changes to their community profile. Their relations with Latinos and Latinas, and with the Brazilian immigrant community itself, are changing. The Miami paradigm may eventually predominate in other parts of the United States.

See also Socio-Economic Profile *and* South Americans.

BIBLIOGRAPHY
Halter, Marilyn, ed. *New Migrants in the Marketplace: Boston's Ethnic Entrepreneurs*. Amherst: University of Massachusetts Press, 1995.
Light, Ivan, and Carolyn Rosenstein. "Expanding the Interaction Theory of Entrepreneurship." In *The Economic Sociology of Immigration: Essays on Networks, Ethnicity, and Entrepreneurship*, edited by Alejandro Portes. New York: Russell Sage Foundation, 1995.
Oboler, Suzanne. *Ethnic Labels, Latino Lives: Identity and the Politics of (Re)Presentation in the United States*. Minneapolis: University of Minnesota Press, 1995.
Portes, Alejandro. "Economic Sociology and the Sociology of Immigration: A Conceptual Overview." In *The Economic Sociology of Immigration: Essays on Networks, Ethnicity, and Entrepreneurship*, edited by Alejandro Portes. New York: Russell Sage Foundation, 1995.
Portes, Alejandro, and Alex Stepick. *City on the Edge: The Transformation of Miami*. Berkeley: University of California Press, 1993.
Sales, Teresa. *Brazilians away from Home*. New York: Center for Migration Studies, 2003.
Winnick, Louis. *New People in Old Neighborhoods: The Role of New Immigrants in Rejuvenating New York's Communities*. New York: Russell Sage Foundation, 1990.

TERESA SALES

BREAK DANCING. Break dancing is the expression of hip-hop culture through bodily movements, or as Raquel Rivera has written, its "kinesthetic expression."

This practice emerged in the 1970s and 1980s, primarily among black, Latina and Latino youth (a majority of whom were Puerto Rican) in the New York neighborhoods of the South Bronx, Harlem, Brooklyn, and Queens. Break dancing is sometimes also referred to as breaking, rocking, b-boying, and b-girling (though it is dominated mostly by males). According to Tina Mata and Mimi McKay, while break dancing is performed to hip-hop music, it also incorporates "other urban arts, such as scratching, rap and graffiti painting." In fact, Sally Banes has called break dancing "physical graffiti."

Though break dancing, or breaking, technically refers only to the floor movements (such as the spins performed on the head, hand, or back, and the footwork), it has become a "generic term that refers to a variety of originally independent dances or dance steps: the 'electric boogie,' which involves wavelike movements that start at one part of the body and move to another; 'popping,' which refers to jerky movements in which the bones seem to pop out of their joints; the 'robot,' in which dancers move parts of the body in isolation from one another; 'locking,' which involves collapsing parts of the body, then snapping them back into position; and the 'moonwalk,' a mime movement [made popular by Michael Jackson] in which the dancer appears to walk while actually standing still (Mata and McKay, p. 347). Breaking also involves acrobatic feats, mime, and martial arts motions, especially jabbing and thrusting gestures, and some ballet and jazz movements.

This form of urban bodily expression represents a continuity with African, African American, and Afro-Caribbean dance traditions, comprising its Afro-diasporic roots. This is evident in its format of a solo performer inside a ring, its syncopated rhythmic structure, its movement vocabulary, its rhetorical modes of boasts and insults, and its function as a competition and exhibition among males. It has been compared to martial arts such as *capoeira* in Brazil and combat dances historically practiced by communities of African descent in the Americas, and to the *cocobalé*, "an African-derived musical/martial arts form" practiced in Puerto Rico.

While break dancing has been associated mostly with black urban youth culture, it is important to remember that Puerto Rican and Afro-Caribbean youth in New York City also participated in its historical development, particularly in the development of the combat dance style called "rocking" or "uprocking." Among the better-known Puerto Rican dancers are Crazy Legs, Ken Swift, PopMaster Fable, Honey Rockwell, and Mr. Wiggles. Also notable are Rockafella and Kwikstep (Rivera, p. 101), a husband and wife team and directors of Full Circle Productions, a contemporary break dancing and hip-hop performance group whose appearances include the yearly Harlem Jazz Dance Festival. Of course, African American dancers have also led the break dancing movement, including D.J. Afrika Bambaata, organizer of the Zulu Nation in the Bronx and founder of Soul Sonic Force. Kurtis Blow was the first to cross over into the pop market.

It is equally important to note that despite the male domination of break dancing, young women have also contributed to its development. Key female figures have included Mamma Maribel, Sunkist Evie, Bunny Lee, Headspin Janet, Lazy Doze, and Baby Love.

Break dancing became mainstreamed and popularized during the early 1980s through the *Graffiti Rock* television show with Michael Holman and the New York City Breakers, who also performed for President Ronald Reagan. The documentary film *Style Wars* appeared on PBS in 1983, and the Hollywood film *Flashdance* with the Rock Steady Crew was released the same year, giving the dance form national visibility. Other films that were instrumental in popularizing the dance form included *Wild Style* (1982) and *Beat Street* (1984). Breaking made something of a comeback in the media during the late 1990s, yet after the breaking and graffiti craze of the first half of the 1980s, these art forms, as mainstream commodities, were relegated to history. However, performers such as Rockafella and Kwikstep have kept the dance form alive, and at the local level it is still actively cultivated in many circles. As Raquel Rivera has written, "breaking is still passed on from generation to generation in New York nightclubs, schools, community centers and parties." Rivera points to the importance of The Point, a center of activism and arts for young people in the South Bronx. There, breaking workshops and classes continue to train young men and women in this art form. In other words, while mainstreaming made break dancing a national commodity only temporarily, it has remained a meaningful art form for young blacks and Latinas and Latinos in the urban centers of the United States.

See also Afro-Latinos; Graffiti; Hip-Hop; Latina Musicians; Music, Popular; *and* Youth Culture.

BIBLIOGRAPHY

Banes, Sally. "Breakdancing: A Reporter's Story." In *Folklife Annual 1986*, edited by Alan Jabbour and James Hardin, 9–21. Washington, D.C.: American Folklife Center at the Library of Congress, 1987.

Flores, Juan. *From Bomba to Hip Hop: Puerto Rican Culture and Latino Identity*. New York: Columbia University Press, 2000.

Fresh, Mr., and the Supreme Rockers. *Breakdancing*. New York: Avon Books, 1984.

Marlow, Curtis. *Break Dancing*. Cresskill, N.J.: Sharon Publications, 1984.

Mata, Tina, and Mimi M. McKay. "Breakdancing." Black Dance in America: A Symposium. Symposium sponsored by the Department of Theater and Dance, University of Texas at Austin, 1991.

Rivera, Raquel Z. *New York Ricans from the Hip Hop Zone*. New York: Palgrave Macmillan, 2003.

PRISCILLA RENTA AND FRANCES APARICIO

BREAST CANCER. Breast cancer, which afflicts both women and men, involves malignant tumors in the breast. (In general types of cancer—malignant carcinoma—are named after the part of the body where the cancer starts.) The breast is comprised of lobules (milk-producing glands), ducts (tubes that carry milk to the nipple), fatty tissue, and lymphatic tissue (carrying lymph, a clear fluid comprised of immune system cells and tissue waste). The lymphatic vessels of the breast lead to the lymph nodes under the arms, called axillary nodes. The most common types of breast cancer follow: (1) ductal carcinoma in situ, a breast cancer of early stage, is usually confined to the ducts but sometimes has an invasive component as well; (2) infiltrating (invasive) ductal carcinoma, which represents 80 percent of breast cancer cases, starts in the ducts, then breaks through the wall of the ducts to invade the fatty tissue of the breast, from where it can spread to other parts of the body; (3) infiltrating lobular carcinoma, which represents 10 to 15 percent of breast cancer cases, starts in the lobules (milk glands) and spreads to other organs in the body; and (4) lobular carcinoma in situ remains confined to the lobular area. The most common symptoms of breast cancer are lumps (painful or painless) and spontaneous, persistent, and unilateral (on one side) nipple discharge, each of which is cause to visit a physician.

Breast Cancer and Minorities

According to the 2000 census, Latinas are the largest female minority population in the United States. Research on breast cancer demonstrates a correlation between race and ethnicity and mortality rates. Latinas and African American women with breast cancer, because they tend to have more advanced stages of the disease when diagnosed, have higher mortality rates compared to white women. Jennifer Campbell's reviews of the research suggest that socioeconomic status, race, and demographics are significant factors predicting advanced stages of breast cancer at diagnosis. For example, the National Council of La Raza in 2000 reported that 34 percent of Latinos and Latinas were uninsured and delayed visits to physicians for lack of resources, cultural restrictions, or lack of education. A study of the barriers Latinas with breast cancer face regarding compliance with treatments noted that 91 percent reported they were afraid because they lack health insurance. Studies have demonstrated that routine breast cancer screening leads to improvements across racial and ethnic groups. However, public campaigns providing free screening and distribution of guidelines and community outreach programs for low-income, uninsured, and undocumented Latinas remain insufficient. Also breast cancer programs for Latinas should take into account that Latinas are not a homogenous group in terms of social class, language (Spanish, Creole, French, and Portuguese), culture, and education. Screening campaigns should address Latina multiplicities.

A study in San Diego comparing non-Hispanics and Hispanics showed that lower income is related to later diagnosis. Economic barriers force some Latinas of low socioeconomic status to get medical services from community health centers and hospital outpatient programs. Research shows that these establishments lack outreach programs to address screening guidelines and that they operate under the assumption of literacy in English. There is a lack of bicultural programs that take language and place of origin (the Caribbean, South America, Central America) into consideration. Also research on undocumented and immigrant Latinas with breast cancer has been neglected. In general undocumented Latinas are reluctant to get screening and treatment for fear of arrest and deportation.

Some scholars hold that breast cancer is the leading cause of death among Latinas and that the number of cancer-related deaths is larger that generally reported because Latina or Hispanic as an ethnic category tends to include only white Latinas, excluding women of African descent. Aggressive early detection screening programs are necessary to reduce the high mortality and mastectomy rates. Racial and class disparities are part of the history of cancer diagnosis, treatments, and trials; mammography screening rates; and public education campaigns. Physicians' perceptions of low-income women contributes to disparities in breast cancer diagnosis. Research at the University of North Carolina measured the impact of the categories of race and ethnicity and socioeconomic status on physician recommendations for mammographies and revealed that physicians are less likely to recommend procedures to some patients because of the cost or the perceived likelihood of noncompliance. Spanish-language television also advertises the need for self-exams. But these campaigns assume the woman has medical insurance and is prepared to seek care, and they do not take into account low socioeconomic status, disparities in the health care system that lead to the high mastectomy rate among Latinas, or the death rate caused by lack of health insurance.

Herbert W. Nickens concluded that socioeconomic status is a significant variable for studying health and behavior patterns. Because of the correlation between race and ethnicity and socioeconomic status, the category of low socioeconomic status needs to be analyzed in terms of the multiplicity of races and ethnicities. This multiplicity is part of the cultural system that governs the formation and flow of knowledge and power. Frantz Fanon's analysis sheds light on the racialized construction of gender. The "racialized gaze" implies that the bodies of minorities are "surrounded by an atmosphere . . . of uncertainty" (Fanon, p. 110). The medical gaze inscribes those with particular race and ethnicity and low socio-economic status within a racial web of power or within a set of defects, making a negative judgment of the patient's ability to comply, her responsibility toward her body, and her ability to understand information. This signals the existence of racism that impacts Latina women receiving health services and recommendations for mammography. In institutional settings, racism can take multiple forms, manifesting itself in discontinuous or systematic practices. The racialized gaze has manifested itself in late diagnosis, lack of medical access, and lack of mammography recommendations for minorities. This disparity in access reveals a "politics of racism" and a practice of exclusion.

These practices create different realities of breast cancer for different groups, influenced by levels of economic privilege and the politics of race and affecting the choice of treatment options. Medical practitioners and social movement activists are working to eliminate the disparities in diagnoses, treatments, and services. For minorities these disparities lead to: (1) delays in the diagnosis of cancer, as a consequence of which the cancer is more advanced at diagnosis; (2) reduced chances of surviving treatment as the necessity of undergoing more extensive toxic treatment increases; (3) higher mastectomy rates; (4) reduced chances of cure as the risk of recurrence and death increases; and (5) possibly increased chances of occupational exposure to carcinogenic substances, for example, to DDT and organochlorine pesticides for Latinas working in agriculture, factories, and other occupations (more research is needed in this area).

The mortality rate for Latinas and other minority women with breast cancer is higher than for white women. A technology of power inscribes the bodies of women along racial and class lines and politics. Joe Feagin and Hernán Vera's analyses map out medical institutions as "embedded in a shaped social context." The authors define white racism as "the socially organized set of attitudes, ideas and practices that deny African American and other people of color the dignity, opportunities, freedoms, and rewards that this nation offers to white Americans" (Feagin and Vera, p. 7). Hence the breasts of Latina, African American, and Native American women manifest a racialized politics. In 2004 the Minority Women's Health Summit called attention to legislation that encourages health workers to serve undocumented and immigrants less. In addition, for many Latinas of low socioeconomic status, the body is constructed as taboo, which produces a reluctance to perform self-examinations or to undergo medical examinations of the breasts.

Diagnosis and Treatment

In general, diagnosis of breast cancer is made via mammogram with the help of ultrasound or other imaging techniques. Diagnosis is also made via biopsy, including fine-needle biopsy, core-needle biopsy, and surgical biopsy, all of which require general or local anesthesia. Biopsies study tissue and return the following possible results: benign, malignant, atypical hyperplasia (excess production of cells), or clear. Another piece of pathology information important for determining treatment is whether the cancer cells have receptors for estrogen and progesterone. To provide conceptual categories to aid with prognosis and choice of treatments, the American Joint Committee on Cancer developed the TNM system, which describes the progressive stages of a cancer: the T stage (cancer confined to the primary tumor), the N stage (cancer spread to nearby lymph nodes), and the M stage (cancer metastasized to distant lymph nodes, bones, or other body organs). The TNM system takes into account lymph node status, estrogen, and progesterone receptor levels in the tumor tissue and other information. Each patient with breast cancer has a different treatment, as indicated by the results of tumor biopsy, lymph status, and so forth. The TNM system has been subdivided further to represent the tumor's size, progression, and lymph status.

Breast cancer has two general types of treatment: local (surgery, radiation therapy) and systemic (hormone therapy, adjuvant chemotherapy). Types of breast cancer surgeries include lumpectomy (removal of cancerous tissue and margins); partial mastectomy (removal of 1 to 50 percent of the breast tissue); simple mastectomy; total mastectomy; and radical mastectomy, which is rarely performed. In a lumpectomy the surgeon removes as much of the cancer as possible (tumor or non-palpable cancer) as well as margins (tissue around the tumor), but it is crucial to know whether or not the cancer has spread to the lymph nodes under the arms (known as sentinel nodes). If the pathology of the lymph nodes shows that cancer cells have metastasized (spread through lymph vessels to other parts of the body), more aggressive chemotherapy is indicated.

Systemic treatments used to kill cancer cells remaining elsewhere in the body include chemotherapy (drugs given in a cycle) and hormonal therapy. Systemic treatments are used pre- or postsurgery, depending on the patient's diagnosis. The most common chemotherapies are: (1) a cocktail containing Cytoxan, methotrexate, 5 fluorouracil; (2) Adriamycin; and (3) Taxol or new drugs. During chemotherapies Latinas of higher socioeconomic status combine alternative treatments (visualizations, Chinese medicine) with conventional treatments. Those Latina women with medical insurance have the possibility of reconstructions. (Women must be aware of the effects of silicone on the body and the search for alternatives, such as saline and flap procedures using the patient's own body tissue, blood vessels, and fat and muscle from the

TABLE 1: *Resources, Advocacy, and Support*

ORGANIZATION/AGENCY	DESCRIPTION OF SERVICE	TELEPHONE /WEB
Avoncares Program for Medically Underserved Women	For women in need of diagnostic services or treatment of breast, cervical, ovarian, and other cancers.	(800) 813-HOPE
American Cancer Society	Information, education, brochures for patients and health care professionals.	(800) ACS-2345 www.americancancer.org
Medicine Program	For a $5 fee per prescription, will explore whether a patient qualifies for a pharmaceutical company patient assistance program.	(573) 996-7300 www.themedicineprogram.com
Las Isabelas	Support, education, and transportation for screening.	(408) 287-4890 www.lasisabelas.org
Corporate Angel Network	Provides cancer patients with free transportation to and from distant treatment centers.	(914) 328-1313 www.corpangelnetwork.org
Patient Advocate Foundation	Advocacy and information (insurance and financial advice).	(800) 532-5274 www.patientadvocate.org
National Breast Cancer Coalition	Grassroots advocacy and social movement organization.	(202) 296-7477 www.natlbcc.org
Susan G. Komen	Support education, screening, and treatments.	(800) I'M Aware www.komen.org
White Memorial Medical Center	Support group, early screening, and bilingual education programs.	(323) 268-5000 www.whitememorial.com
Y-Me National Breast Cancer Organization	Support, education, and free screenings.	(312) 986-8338 (800) 221-2141 (English hotline) (800) 986-9505 (Spanish hotline) www.y-me.org (bilingual site)
Entre Mujeres	Support and education.	(760) 344-5019 www.cancerlinks.com/mujeres
Gilda's Club Worldwide	Support group and education (bilingual).	(888) GILDA-4-U www.gildasclub.org
Wellness Community	Support groups, education, and other services (bilingual).	(888) 793-WELL www.thewellnesscommunity.org

gluteal, abdominal, or hip areas.) After local treatment and systemic therapy, the patient is followed for five years for continued remission (absence of cancer) or recurrence of cancer (in the soft tissue of the breast, scars, or other parts of the body).

Research on breast cancer treatment practices raises questions about medical conduct and legislation policies. A number of studies report little difference in survival rates between those undergoing lumpectomies and those undergoing mastectomies. However, women of lower socioeconomic status are more often advised to have mastectomies (breast removal) than women of higher status. Such recommendations are not based solely on medical judgment but, depending on the doctor's training and perceptions, may also be based on the woman's socioeconomic status and place of residence. These recommendations need to be correlated with Latinas' lack of medical insurance and immigration status in the United States.

Advocacy

Celebrities and artists have become public advocates to promote both early detection and organizations that help uninsured Latinas. Celia Cruz became an activist to help uninsured Latinas access early intervention programs. The award-winning Latina singer-songwriter Soraya advocates for Latinas to break their fears about breast cancer and has been creating music about the journey. Mayte Prida, a producer of children's television programs, reveals in a journal narrative (*Una etapa difícil*) her personal experience with breast cancer. In addition Prida produced a video to educate low-income Latinas. Furthermore, in their own artwork, the artists Diana Solís and Sonia Báez-Hernández and the poet Juana Goergen, among others, have imprinted testimonies of a new subjectivity and of body modification after their experiences with breast cancer. The works of Solís and Báez-Hernández address the body's transformation, mutilation, and deformities caused by surgery and treatments. Latina artists explore through art and literature their experiences with breast cancer as raw material. Literature and art are testimonies on how they reconstitute their bodies through dissimilar personal interpretations, management of normality, aesthetic and subjective choices of treatments, surgeries, and reconstruction.

Latinas in literature and artwork trace their anguish, self-interrogation, memories, and gender crisis. Báez-Hernández, Jean-Réne Rinvil, and Diego Perez's documentary *Territories of the Breasts* reveals social inequality in medical service for uninsured Latinas, gender crises, support systems, and medical knowledge of seven Latinas and their artistic expression.

See also Health *and* Health Care Access.

BIBLIOGRAPHY

Báez-Hernández, Sonia. "Breast Cancer: New Aesthetic of the Subject and Body's Inscription." Paper presented at Body Modification: Changing Bodies, Changing Selves, Sydney, Australia, April 2003.

Báez-Hernández, Sonia, Jean-Réne Rinvil, and Diego Perez, dirs. *Territories of the Breasts*. Independent documentary. 2005.

Bentley, J. R., R. J. Delfino, T. H. Taylor, et al. "Differences in Breast Cancer Stage at Diagnosis between Non-Hispanic White and Hispanic Populations, San Diego County 1988–1993." *Breast Cancer Research and Treatment* 50 (1988): 1–9.

Campbell, Jennifer B. "Breast Cancer—Race, Ethnicity, and Survival: A Literature Review." In *Breast Cancer Research and Treatment* 74, no. 2 (July 2002): 187–192.

Eisenstein, Zillah. *Manmade Breast Cancers*. Ithaca, N.Y.: Cornell University Press, 2001.

Fanon, Frantz. *Black Skin White Masks*. New York: Grove Press, 1967.

Feagin, Joe, and Hernán Vera. *White Racism: The Basics*. New York: Routledge, 1995.

Greaves, Mel. *Cancer: The Evolutionary Legacy*. New York: Oxford University Press, 2000.

Hedeen, Ashley, and Emily White. "Breast Cancer Size in Hispanic Women, by Birthplace: 1992–1995." *American Journal of Public Health* 91 (January 2001): 122–125.

Hubbell, A., L. Chavez, S. Mishara, et al. "Differing Beliefs about Breast Cancer among Latinas and Anglo Women." *Western Journal of Medicine* 164 (May 1996): 405–408.

Jacobellis, Jillian, and Gary Cutler. "Mammography Screening and Differences in Stage of Disease by Race/Ethnicity." *American Journal of Public Health* 92 (July 2002): 1144–1150.

Langlands, A. O., V. Gebski, D. Hirsch, et al. "Delay in the Clinical Diagnosis of Breast Cancer: Estimating Its Effect on Prognosis, with Particular Reference to Medical Litigation." *Breast* 11, no. 5 (October 2002): 386–393.

Leopold, Ellen. *A Darker Ribbon: Breast Cancer, Women, and Their Doctors in the Twentieth Century*. Boston: Beacon Press, 1999.

Lorde, Audre. *The Cancer Journals*. San Francisco: Aunt Lute Books, 1997.

O'Malley, Michael S. et al. "The Association of Race/Ethnicity, Socioeconomic Status, and Physician Recommendation for Mammography: Who Gets the Message about Breast Screening?" *American Journal of Public Health* 91 (January 2001): 49–54.

O'Malley, Ann S. et al. "Acculturation and Breast Cancer Screening among Hispanic Women in New York City." *American Journal of Public Health* 89 (February 1999): 219–227.

Prida, Mayte. *Una etapa difícil*. Los Angeles: Terra Entertainment, 2002.

Morris, David. *Illness and Culture in the Postmodern Age*. Berkeley: University of California Press, 1998.

Nickens, Herbert W. "The Health Status of Minority Populations in the United States." *Western Journal of Medicine* 155, no. 1 (July 1991): 27–36.

SONIA BÁEZ-HERNÁNDEZ

BRIGADA ANTONIO MACEO. Sometime around noon on December 22, 1977, a group of fifty-five young Cuban exiles—the vast majority of them U.S. residents—milled around the airport in Kingston, Jamaica. They stood around a huge pile of luggage chatting excitedly. To the casual eye, these young men and women, most in their early and late twenties, were students and young professionals on holiday. In truth they were embarking on a historic voyage. These seemingly ordinary travelers were making their first return trip home since Cuba's 1959 socialist revolution. They were the members of the Antonio Maceo Brigade (Brigada Antonio Maceo, BAM). This trip by the *brigadistas* (members of the Antonio Maceo Brigade) constituted a significant turning point in the relationship of the Cuban government to its diaspora of exiles and emigrants.

For eighteen years the Cuban American members of the group had been barred by both the United States and Cuba from visiting their homeland. Cuban exiles residing in Spain and Mexico were prevented from returning by the Cuban government. But in 1977 U.S. president Jimmy Carter did not renew the sixteen-year-old U.S. ban on travel to Cuba. In a conciliatory gesture the Cuban government reciprocated by extending an invitation to young Cuban professionals and intellectuals to visit their homeland. Cuba's gesture had also been prodded by a request a year earlier for a return visit from the members of the editorial board of *Aríeto*, a now defunct magazine then published in New York City by young Cuban American intellectuals who favored a rapprochement with Cuba. Cuba's Instituto Cubano de Amistad con los Pueblos (Cuban Institute of Friendship with the Peoples) extended the invitation directly to *Areíto*. Upon its receipt, the members of *Areíto* initiated a search for young Cuban exiles both in the United States and abroad who were willing to challenge the more vocal and organized anti-Castro leadership in the Cuban exile community.

In a matter of months a group of fifty-five young men and women was assembled. Its members called themselves the Antonio Maceo Brigade after a black Cuban military general of the nineteenth century known for his fierce fighting against Spain in defense of his homeland. According to the group's declaration of principles, the name was chosen, among other reasons, to convey the group's intention to maintain a historical link to the homeland and to express the members' rebellion against their involuntary departure as children.

For the most part, the members of the first group to visit Cuba since the 1959 socialist revolution had been friends and supporters of *Areíto*, activists in student movements against the Vietnam War, participants in progressive movements in Puerto Rico and in the Puerto Rican or Chicano and Chicana communities in the United

States, or members of *Jóven Cuba*, another U.S.-based progressive magazine led by young Cuban Americans. While the first group of BAM members included a range of political beliefs, it was generally true that the majority admired the political and social changes in the new Cuba. There were three important criteria for inclusion in the first and subsequent trips to Cuba by BAM members: (1) participants had left Cuba involuntary as a result of parental decision; (2) they had not engaged in acts of organized violence against the Cuban government; and (3) they supported the normalization of relations between the United States and Cuba and the lifting of the U.S. trade embargo against the island.

Experiences in Cuba

On the night of December 12, 1977, BAM members landed at Jose Martí Airport in Cuba. They were greeted by a group of Cuban hosts similarly matched in age and educational level and by a large group of representatives of the Cuban media. Many of the Cuban hosts accompanied the brigadistas throughout the three-week tour of their homeland, visiting hospitals, schools, cultural centers, museums, and farms. There were meetings with well-known political personalities; celebrities, such as the world-renowned Cuban ballerina Alicia Alonso; and musicians and singers from Cuba's young socialist troubadours of Nueva Trova, such as Sara González and Silvio Rodriquez.

The brigadistas toured the entire length of Cuba in three dazzling Japanese buses. Their home base was on the outskirts of Havana Province in Camp Julio Antonio Mella, named after a young Cuban student leader of the 1920s who was reportedly assassinated while in exile in Mexico by orders of Cuban president Gerardo Machado. The camp, in the utilitarian style of most summer recreational facilities, was made up of a group of wooden, one-story buildings with cement floors, cold-water showers, a dining hall, separate dormitories for males and females, and a large open-air stage for cultural events. Luscious vegetation and an abundance of *palmas reales*, the royal palms that characterize the Cuban landscape, surrounded Camp Julio Antonio Mella.

When in the camp, BAM members awoke each morning at 6:00 A.M. to Nueva Trova music blasting from the camp's loudspeakers, followed by cold showers under Cuba's chilly December sky and a shot of strong Cuban espresso. Their first day in Cuba, Friday, December 23, 1977, set the tone for a tour that repeatedly contrasted the past left behind with the changes taking place in the rediscovered homeland. On day one, the Cuban hosts showcased a psychiatric hospital and a vocational school. The Hospital Psiquiátrico had been transformed from a postrevolution, prison-style mental hospital named Mazorra, complete with shackled patients, into a model mental health facility. At La Escuela Vocacional Lenin (Lenin Vocational School) secondary school students from both the city and the countryside engaged in a rigorous academic curriculum and worked an hour and a half each day assembling batteries to be sold through government-owned enterprises. In both these visits, as in the ones to come, animated and intense conversations took place between *los de aquí* (Cubans living on the island) and *los de allá* (the exiled visitors). The nomenclature was in itself significant since all exiles were up until then commonly dubbed *gusanos* (worms) to denote their reduced status as traitors to their homeland. On their first day in Cuba, Antonio Maceo Brigade members also visited the tomb of the brigade's namesake, the Cuban national hero Antonio Maceo. Placing a wreath on his tomb, the brigadistas honored the common patriotic history that linked all Cubans.

But for many BAM members the most memorable moments occurred when they reconnected with family and friends. Their tales, filled with emotion and childhood memories recovered, were documented in a special issue of *Areíto* magazine in 1978.

One young woman recounted that while working to help build apartments for Cuban workers in the town of Ariguanabo, she realized that her stepfather had been the former owner of the local textile mill, now government owned. She was struck by the irony that eighteen years after her departure, she was helping to build homes for the same workers who had once been her stepfather's employees. Another told of visiting family in the city of Santiago de Cuba and accidentally discovering a letter dated 1897 written to Captain Nicolas Sauvanell, a deceased grandfather. In the letter the grandfather was being commissioned to lead one of the military regiments under the command of General Antonio Maceo.

One young man recalled that his new Cuban friends cried with him when he knelt by the grave of a mother he had not seen since he was nine years old. Another brigadista told how her past seemed to have frozen in time. Upon entering her mother's former sewing room in her grandparents' home in Havana, she found an old and yellowed calendar with its first page dated October 15, 1961—ten days after her family had left Cuba. The essence of these evocative experiences was summarized by one of the first BAM members in an interview with the *New York Times* upon his return home: "The country is the people and the family we still have there. While we were there with our families, we were true Cubans, revolution or not, and there was an instant rapport" (Smothers).

But there was more to come. On Friday, January 13, 1978, a day before the brigadistas were scheduled to return to their respective homes abroad, the dazzling Japanese buses unexpectedly headed for La Plaza de la

Revolución (Plaza of the Revolution) in Havana—the epicenter of the Cuban government. In the early evening BAM members found themselves face-to-face with Cuban president Fidel Castro. Dressed in his signature olive-green military uniform, smoking a cigar, and accompanied by bodyguards and stenographers, Castro walked into the room and shook each and every hand. He spoke about the economic crisis of the time and its impact on the Cuban economy, about Cuban history and culture, about domestic policy, about terrorism, and about the Cuban exile community. Castro also asked the brigadistas many questions: Where did they come from? What was their average age? What did they think about various issues of the day? The young people queried back and finally posed the ultimate question by asking Castro to evaluate the impact of their visit. The Cuban president noted that it had been well received and that it opened up the possibility of resolving the historical divide between Cubans. Four hours later Castro stood up and uttered the most famous line of the encounter: *La Patria ha crecido* ("Our homeland has grown").

Impact of the Trip

Upon their return home, a core group of the fifty-five brigadistas, most of them residents of New York City, began the task of formally organizing the Antonio Maceo Brigade. In the declaration issued by the BAM National Committee, the group recognized that the first brigade had been composed largely of members who, because of their participation in the anti–Vietnam War and civil rights movements in the United States, were drawn to the romanticized Cuban Revolution embraced by intellectuals and political activists of the late 1960s and early 1970s. They predicted that as the political landscape changed, future brigadistas and visitors to Cuba would reflect more diverse political beliefs. Recognizing that the majority of Cuban exiles did not sympathize with the Cuban Revolution, they suggested that a majority would be in favor of a political rapprochement between the United States and Cuba if it encouraged family reunification and the possibility of pleasure visits to the island by exiles. In their statement they challenged the staunch and well-financed anti-Castro opposition in Miami, characterizing it as a "minority" that used intimidation tactics to silence those with dissimilar views. By 1977 several Cuban American groups, including the editorial board of the magazine *Areíto*, the Institute of Cuban Studies, and religious groups such as Christians for Justice and Liberty and the Church of the Good Pastor in Miami, Florida, had also taken a public stance in support of improved United States–Cuba relations.

The goodwill left behind in Cuba prompted the Cuban government to lessen its distrust of Cuban exiles. Less than a year later, on September 6, 1978, at a press conference with Cuban American journalists who had traveled to Cuba, Castro proposed a dialogue between the leaders of the Cuban Revolution and Cubans representing a broad spectrum of those living abroad. Seventy-five individuals were invited to participate in El Diálogo (The Dialogue) held in Havana during two sessions conducted in November and December 1978. The Committee of Seventy-five, as the group was called, negotiated the release of numerous Cuban political prisoners, discussed ways to reunite separated families, and proposed the implementation of new regulations that would allow Cubans abroad to visit relatives in Cuba. Up to this time the Cuban government had only allowed "exceptional" visits by exiles. El Diálogo led the way for the development of regular channels of communication and travel regulations that would address the needs of Cuba's exile community.

In February 1979 three members of the first Antonio Maceo Brigade opened up Marazul Tours in New York City, the first U.S.–based travel agency to arrange routine trips to Cuba, and another BAM member opened up a similar agency in Puerto Rico. In 1980 the first Marazul charter flight from the United States arrived in Cuba. In its first year of operation the agency recorded sending 100,000 Cuban Americans to visit family in Cuba. The agency later expanded its services, sending study tours of Americans permitted by U.S. law to travel to Cuba for educational or religious purposes or people-to-people exchanges. It eventually opened up four permanent offices in Miami, Florida, and in New Jersey.

But over the years, the number of Cuban Americans allowed to travel to Cuba varied as the U.S. and Cuban governments held travel hostage to their political wrangling. In May 1982 the administration of President Ronald Reagan reinstituted the U.S. ban on travel to Cuba lifted by President Carter, denying U.S. citizens the right to travel but exempting family visits by Cuban Americans. In 1984 the U.S. Treasury Department served two subpoenas on Marazul Tours demanding the names and addresses of all individuals who had traveled to Cuba since the U.S. travel ban had been reinforced. In May 1985 Cuba suspended all travel by Cuban Americans to visit relatives when the U.S. government launched Radio Martí, a radio station broadcasting news from the United States to Cuba under the direction of anti-Castro groups. Cuba ended the suspension of visits home by exiles in 1986, first limiting and later increasing the number of visits per year. In June 2004 the U.S. government, under the administration of President George W. Bush, again restrained travel to Cuba, limiting travel by Cuban Americans to once every three years and only to visit immediate family members. Under this new policy many former brigadistas were barred from returning home, since the vast majority no longer had immediate family members still living in Cuba.

As the members of the first Antonio Maceo Brigade had feared, their visit to Cuba angered the anti-Castro leadership in the Cuban exile community. The media attacks in the form of virulent editorials and articles attacking them as "communist agents" were expected, as was the predictable pressure from displeased family and friends. Brigadistas who lived in the large Cuban American communities in Florida and New Jersey were particularly vigilant. A member of an anti-Castro student group called Abdala told the *New York Times* that the Antonio Maceo Brigade would probably become "a Castro fifth column here." In the same article a husband and wife who had gone on the first BAM visit told a reporter that the anticommunist feeling in their New Jersey neighborhood was so strong they feared it would lead to violence.

The dangers proved even more ominous than anticipated. In December 1979 Omega 7, a self-proclaimed Cuban terrorist group, bombed the Cuban mission to the United Nations and New York City's Lincoln Center, where a performance of Cuba's Orchestra Aragón was scheduled to take place. In December 1980 Omega 7 bombed Viajes Varadero, a travel agency in San Juan, Puerto Rico, that organized travel to Cuba under the direction of Carlos Muñiz Varela, a member of the first Brigada Antonio Maceo and the Committee of Seventy-five. Three months later Muñiz Varela was assassinated in Puerto Rico. In November 1980 Omega 7 claimed responsibility for the assassination of Eulalio Negrín, another member of the Committee of Seventy-five. Negrín, to the astonishment of many observers, was killed in front of his son, outside his home in Union City, New Jersey.

For more than a decade the Antonio Maceo Brigade continued to help young Cuban exiles make that first return trip home. It also organized a brigade of *maceitos*, groups of U.S.–born children of former brigadistas. But over time the need for these memorable group visits back home organized by the Antonio Maceo Brigade ceased to exist. In 2004 regular channels, albeit limited and hostage to the state of United States–Cuba relations, allowed Cuban Americans to visit immediate relatives (parents, children, spouses) on the island. And some without immediate relatives there (perhaps driven by the same spirit to reconnect with the homeland that had moved the first brigadistas) even risked U.S. government fines by traveling through third countries in defiance of new U.S. travel restrictions.

For over a quarter of a century the Antonio Maceo Brigade continued to exist in the midst of political and demographic changes unimagined in 1977. BAM's national coordinator, a member of the first brigade, publicly supported Cuba's politics and ideology. The brigade's offices were relocated from New York City to Miami,

Florida, where its national coordinator regularly participated in demonstrations to protest limitations on travel and commerce to Cuba. While not in agreement with BAM's pro-Cuban stance, other Cuban Americans in Miami at times joined the protests to demonstrate their support for family reunification.

The demographics of the Cuban American population of Miami had also unexpectedly shifted. The 2000 U.S. census showed that approximately half of all Cuban Americans living in Miami left Cuba after 1980. And it was generally accepted that, unlike their pre-1980 counterparts, their departures were not due to political reasons. Like immigrants everywhere, the vast majority left their country of origin in search of improved living conditions.

Finally, the members of the first Antonio Maceo Brigade were also dramatically different. With age, time, and experience, the vast majority were no longer mesmerized by the romance of the Cuban Revolution. As founders of other Cuban American organizations or recognized academics, writers, and other professionals, these former brigadistas now held openly divergent views on the politics of their country of origin—ones that were increasingly nuanced and more critical.

Still, the members of the first Antonio Maceo Brigade might all agree on one thing: that first return visit home had a profound personal impact, reconnecting them to the involuntarily abandoned homeland and forever bridging the seemingly insurmountable divide that separated Cuban exiles from the people and memories left behind.

See also **Areíto**; **Cuban Americans**; *and* **Terrorism**.

BIBLIOGRAPHY

Grupo Areito. "Contra Viento y Marea: Havana, Cuba; Casa de las Americas, 1978." Special Issue, *Areito* 4 (Spring 1978). Special edition entirely dedicated to the Antonio Maceo Brigade.

Pérez-Stable, Marifeli. "Young Cuban Exiles Visit Homeland." *Guardian* (New York), March 8, 1978, 24.

Smothers, Ronald. "Cuban Exiles Visiting Home Find Identity." *New York Times*, February 14, 1978, 37.

DAGMARIS CABEZAS

BROWN BERETS. The Brown Beret National Organization emerged initially from the progressive politicization of a group of East Los Angeles high-school and college students during the Chicano/a movement of the 1960s and 1970s. This group, first organized as Young Citizens for Community Action (YCCA), sought to improve its community through civic involvement. During 1967, YCCA was renamed Young Chicanos for Community Action to acknowledge the climate of social change and positive ethnic identification. But a growing list of incidents of police abuse and harassment, the gathering power of the Chicano/a movement, and the development of a militant consciousness among various ethnic groups influenced another shift in YCCA's purpose and ideology. Members of the group no longer identified as "young citizens" conforming to the self-help paradigm of assimilation or as "young Chicanos" who blended into the community. Rather, after a change in leadership and membership, the group advocated social change through radical political action and heightened visibility. It reflected a cadre approach to social change centering on a smaller grouping of well-trained and disciplined militant individuals who would serve as community guardians and leaders in collective actions.

Philosophy and Influences

The beret served as a multilayered symbol of solidarity with third world peoples while also distinguishing a Chicano and Chicana identity. Brown Berets were most visible when they participated in marches and military formations where, in their signature brown uniform, they displayed unity, pride, and self-assertion. As a disciplined group of "soldiers," members had to participate in military drills and training. For many individuals, these disciplinary drills and the overall orientation toward cultural nationalism and self-determination enabled the flourishing of individual self-esteem and, for some, a turn away from self-destructive behavior and toward constructive social change.

Several historic developments and movements influenced the philosophy and language of the organization, including the third world revolutions and the rise of the Black Power movement. Ernesto "Che" Guevara was espoused as a symbol of Latin American self-determination that resonated with militant Chicano and Chicana youth. Images of Che Guevara could be found in the Brown Berets' Los Angeles newspaper *La Causa*. The Texas-based Beret newspapers *La Conciencia* and *Regeneración II* featured the Flores Magón brothers, early advocates of the Mexican Revolution. The founding of the Black Panther Party for Self Defense in Oakland by Huey Newton and Bobby Seale also influenced the development of the Brown Berets, to whom they are often compared.

In general, the Brown Berets did not necessarily emphasize a specific theory of social change; rather, they focused broadly on group unity, self-defense, and militant challenges to social injustice. The Brown Berets expressed a belief in the necessity for revolutionary activity while embracing the philosophy of cultural nationalism, which emphasized cultural pride and self-determination rather than the revolutionary nationalism that guided the Black Panther's philosophy. This perspective eventually led to conflicts among Brown Beret chapters, some of which espoused more specific theories such as revolutionary Marxism or communist internationalism.

Development

The development of the organization in Los Angeles quickly sparked the creation of Brown Beret chapters not only in the southwestern United States and Texas, but across the United States to places as remote as Kansas City, Seattle, and Minnesota. While some common understandings of the group's goals and practices existed as well as a national structure, the actual composition and goals of the individual chapters were not uniform. Members of the Brown Beret chapters included high school students, college students, workers, as well as individuals identified as *vatos locos* or *cholos* who had been pushed out of the schools. In fact, the organization sought to recruit these marginalized young men and women as "revolutionaries" who would defend and advocate for Chicano communities in the United States. Patterns of Chicano political participation in particular regions or other immediate issues facing a community also shaped the demographics of the organization. For example, in San Antonio, Texas, a majority of the Westside chapter members were veterans of the war in Vietnam. In Pittsburgh, California, the chapter membership included American Indians and Filipinos. Regional identities were also expressed in the adoption of a particular chapter slogan. While the founding chapter adopted the slogan "La Causa," chapters in south Texas, some affiliated with the Mexican American Youth Organization and La Raza Unida Party, adopted the slogan "Carnalismo."

Other organizations during the 1970s, such as La Junta, several of which grew out of the Berets, also espoused a cadre approach. In some regions, Chicano and Chicana activists created organizations similar in orientation to the Brown Berets, but with different names or political philosophies, such as the Black Berets in San Jose, California, and Los Comancheros (Followers of the Comanches) in New Mexico. These groups often coexisted with the Brown Berets. In Chicago and New York, the Puerto Rican Young Lords Party similarly adopted the beret as a symbol of self-determination.

Police brutality served as a fundamental concern and spearheading issue for Brown Berets, as they organized numerous protest marches and called for community review of local police officers throughout the Southwest. Indeed, several Brown Beret activists were arrested or were casualties of the era's turmoil and the authorities' use of force to subdue militant activities. In addition to their focus on police brutality, Brown Berets supported and participated in numerous movement struggles such as the United Farm Worker's grape boycott and the Poor People's March on Washington in June 1968. They offered resources and served as security monitors in the student walkouts taking place throughout the Southwest. Brown Berets, through a joint effort with Rosalio Muñoz, a UCLA

BROWN BERETS. Protest in Sacramento, Calif., 1971. (© Bettmann/CORBIS)

student, established the National Chicano Moratorium Committee. The NCMC protested U.S. involvement in the Vietnam War through a series of marches, which culminated in the National Chicano Moratorium of August 29, 1970, the largest march by a minority group protesting U.S. foreign policy and the war in Vietnam. Some chapters funded, organized, and staffed successful free clinics and free breakfast programs largely through the organizing skills of the group's women members. In the late 1970s and early 1980s, Brown Berets in Austin, Texas, organized community protests against drag boat races near East Austin because the races disrupted residents' lives and polluted the area. They also raised awareness of conditions in the prison system and opposed urban development plans that did not include community input.

A misconception of the Brown Berets is that the organization was composed only of men. This may be a result of the identification of militancy with masculinity and male power. Despite the predominance of male members and male-dominated leadership in chapters, women asserted a presence in the organization and were often crucial to the effectiveness of organizing activities. One area in which women were visible was as the editorial staff of Brown Beret newspapers in Los Angeles and Texas. Women's participation in the militant display of drilling and marching and work on the newspaper, a major outlet for promoting the organization, suggested equal treatment. However, the division of labor in the day-to-day working of the organization often followed the same pattern as that of women in other Chicano/a movement organizations, where they were expected to fulfill the "domestic" work rather than participate in political debates or leadership. The original East Los Angeles chapter included at least a dozen women, many of whom had completed high school and were in the workforce. One of these women did hold a leadership role as a minister. This group of Chicana Brown Berets chose to leave the organization and to maintain their involvement in the Chicano antiwar effort on their own terms. In some cases, individual women who joined the organization during the flourishing of a Chicana feminist movement, were able to be more visible as leaders and spokespersons.

After the National Chicano Moratorium, the Chicano/a movement went into a period of decline precipitated by internal divisions over political ideology, infiltration by law enforcement agencies, and heightened police violence at rallies. Nevertheless, the Brown Berets in California continued their activities in early 1972 by launching the Caravana de la Reconquista (Caravan of Reconquest), a march throughout the southwestern United States to raise consciousness about persistent social injustice, particularly the issues of territorial dispossession and police brutality. The Caravana ended with the symbolic reconquest of Catalina Island. Setting up camp on the island, the Berets occupied Camp Tecolote for a month and attracted media attention until they were asked to leave. Despite the "official" ending of the organization by pronouncement of Prime Minister David Sanchez in 1972, the Brown Beret organization persisted in various regions, often maintaining the symbol of the beret, but with diverse political goals and orientations. In Texas, several Beret chapters continued to organize against police brutality, protest environmental degradation, and support political campaigns. While many chapters disbanded or shifted direction, the Brown Berets continue to symbolize militant protest politics, a challenge to the status quo, and intense cultural pride.

See also **Chicano/a Movement.**

BIBLIOGRAPHY

Chávez, Ernesto. *¡Mi Raza Primero! (My People First!): Nationalism, Identity, and Insurgency in the Chicano Movement in Los Angeles, 1966–1978.* Berkeley: University of California Press, 2002.

"Chicano Militants: Assertions and Aims." In *The Chicanos in America 1540–1974: A Chronology and Fact Book*, edited by Richard A. Garcia. Dobbs Ferry, N.Y.: Oceana, 1977.

Espinoza, Dionne. " 'Revolutionary Sisters': Women's Solidarity and Collective Identification among Chicana Brown Berets in East Los Angeles, 1967–1970." *Aztlán: A Journal of Chicano Studies* 26, no. 1 (Spring 2001).

Marin, Marguerite. *Social Protest in an Urban Barrio: A Study of the Chicano Movement, 1966–1974*. Lanham, Md.: University Press of America, 1991.

DIONNE ESPINOZA

BRUJERÍA. *Brujería* (broo-heh-REE-ah), or Spanish witchcraft, originated in medieval Spain where it was identified with witchcraft, an earth religion practiced by the ancient Celts. The Spanish painter Francisco de Goya y Lucientes immortalized the practices of Spanish witchcraft in the etchings he called *Caprichos*. In the same drawings he also condemned the persecution of the *brujos*—practitioners of brujería—by the Spanish Inquisition. This caused the Grand Inquisitor to suspect Goya of being a sympathizer and perhaps a practitioner of brujería. Goya, however, had powerful contacts at the court of Carlos IV who saved him from being another victim of the Inquisition.

The beliefs and practices of brujería were brought to Latin America by the Spanish conquistadores. As a religion it did not win many adherents among the indigenous populations of the various Latin American countries, who had their own magico-religious beliefs and practices. The word "brujería" soon became associated with common sorcery, in which magic rites and spells were used in an attempt to overcome the forces of nature, as well as personal problems, such as illness. This early meaning of brujería still survives in Latin America and in U.S. Latino and Latina communities. A brujería is a magic spell that is cast with the intention of creating changes in a person's life, for good or evil; a *brujo* or *bruja* (witch) is a person who specializes in casting these spells.

The Spanish sought to convert the Indians, and later the African slaves, to Catholicism, forbidding them the worship of their natural deities. In an effort to conceal their beliefs and magico-religious practices from their Spanish masters, the Indians identified their deities with some of the saints of Catholicism. The result was the various syncretic religions of Latin America. In Cuba the beliefs of Yoruba slaves engendered *santería*, which identifies Yoruba deities with Catholic saints. The syncretism between Catholic saints and African or native deities is widespread in Latin America, and it is very much a part of the practice of brujería.

In Mexico the Virgin of Guadalupe, identified with the Aztec goddess Tonantzin, is at the core of the country's flourishing brujería business. Commonly known as "La

BRUJERÍA. (Paul Rodriguez/Latin Focus)

Guadalupe," the Virgin is used in many magical spells and rituals. La Guadalupe is a matriarchal system; most of its rites and magical practices are conducted by women known as brujas or *curanderas*. In Mexico City's open markets, the brujas sell herbs, potions, and amulets, and they cast spells for their many clients, mostly with the aid of La Guadalupe.

In Venezuela, the cult of María Lionza is practiced throughout the entire country. María Lionza is a sylvan deity who is said to live in the mountainous regions of Venezuela. She is also identified with the Virgin Mary, and some of her rites are wild and deeply disturbing. Like Mexico's brujas, the priests and priestesses of María Lionza use herbs, potions, and amulets in their magical practices.

The Dominican Republic also has a popular deity identified with the Virgin Mary. Her name is Metresili and her image shows her surrounded by jewels and flowers. There are also priests and priestesses who heal illnesses and cast spells in her name.

In Central America, especially Guatemala, the descendants of the Mayas still worship the ancient deities of their ancestors under the guise of Catholic saints. In Guatemala, the cult of Saint Simon is so widespread that the Catholic Church accepts his worship by the *indígenas*, or natives, even though he is secretly identified with Judas Iscariot. The image of Saint Simon, affectionately called "Shimon" by the populace, has an open mouth where a cigarette is placed daily to ensure his protection and his help with everyday problems.

There are specific rites and magic spells used by shamans or brujos throughout Latin America to help their clients, and they all invoke the aid of a saint or a spiritual entity. For example, a common brujería used to attract a reluctant lover invokes the aid of Saint Martha. A small dish of olive oil is placed in front of an image of the saint. A piece of cotton is rolled between the fingers to form a wick. The cotton wick is placed in the oil until it soaks up enough oil. The wick is then lit and a special prayer is said in honor of Saint Martha, asking her to bring the desired individual to the feet of the petitioner, debased and humiliated. A similar brujería is conducted invoking the aid of the Archangel Michael to overcome an enemy. In this rite, a glass of water is overturned over a small dish that prevents the water from spilling outside the glass. A white candle is also turned upside down and lit on the bottom of the glass. The Archangel Michael is then asked that in the same manner that the glass of water is overturned so will the evil intentions of the enemy be likewise overturned against him, bringing him or her the archangel's ire in the form of mayhem and destruction.

Brujería in all of its many forms is also practiced in the United States by U.S. Latinos and Latinas. The ingredients used in the practices and magic spells of brujería may be found in stores known as *botánicas* or *yerberías*. These shops, found in U.S. cities with a substantial Latino and Latina population, are classified as "religious good stores" and offer herbs and roots, incenses, oils, colored candles, amulets, religious images and other magical objects. Some even offer the services of resident brujos or brujas who prognosticate the future, cast spells and practice folk healing, usually for a hefty fee. This makes the botánica—and brujería—a very profitable business. Transplanted from its original Latin American soil, brujería seems to be doing well in the United States, where it serves the needs of immigrant and U.S.-based Latinas and Latinos.

See also Botánicas *and* Curanderismo.

BIBLIOGRAPHY
Devine, Mary Virginia. *Brujeria: A Study of Mexican-American Folk Magic; and A Chicano Book of Shadows, Excerpts from the Libreta de brujería*. St. Paul, Minn.: Llewellyn Publications, 1982.
Frazer, James George, Sir. *The Golden Bough: A Study in Magic and Religion* (1890). New York: Dover Publications, 1997.
Frazer, James George, Sir, comp. *The Native Races of America; a Copious Selection of Passages for the Study of Social Anthropology.* Edited by Robert Angus Downie. London: P. Lund, Humphries, 1939.
Gonzalez-Wippler, Migene. *Santeria: The Religion.* St. Paul, Minn.: Llewellyn Publications, 1989.
Murray, Margaret. *God of the Witches.* New York: Oxford University Press, 1952.
Scot, Reginald. *The Discoverie of Witchcraft* (1584). Edited by Brinsley Nicholson. Totowa, N.J.: Rowman and Littlefield, 1973.
Wedeck, Harry E. *Treasury of Witchcraft.* New York: Crown Publishers, 1961.

MIGENE GONZALEZ-WIPPLER

BURCIAGA, JOSÉ ANTONIO (1940–1996), Chicano writer and artist. José Antonio "Tony" Burciaga was a pioneering and inspirational Mexican American author, humorist, artist, and community activist. His creative work continues to provide Chicana and Chicano communities with sustenance and affirmation, as well as offering inspiration to young artists, writers, and cultural workers.

Burciaga was born in El Paso, Texas. As a child, he lived with his family in the basement of an El Paso synagogue, where his father, José Cruz Burciaga, worked as a caretaker (although the Burciagas were Catholic). Burciaga later noted in his writings that he inherited his sense of humor from his father, while his mother, a teacher who had stood firm in her beliefs while teaching in Mexico, taught him to never compromise on the truth.

After his high school graduation, Burciaga enlisted in the air force. His tour of duty took him to Iceland and to Zarazoga, Spain. He began to produce creative writing and artwork during this time. Upon his return to the United States, Burciaga attended college at the University of Texas at El Paso, earning a bachelor's degree in fine arts in 1968. He then worked as an illustrator, first for the air force in Wells Branch, Texas, and later for the Central Intelligence Agency in Washington, D.C. During this time, he fell in love with Cecilia Preciado, and they married in 1974. The couple later moved to California when his wife was offered a job as an administrator at Stanford University. Over the years, they had two children, Rebeca and Toño.

In California, Burciaga threw himself into his writing and art. He wrote a column for several newspapers, focusing on his musings as a Chicano in California. In his later prose and poetry, he merged cultural perspectives, literary traditions, and languages (including Spanish, English, Nahautl, and the Mexican American street dialect *caló*) to present a unique and uniquely Mexican American voice. Over the years, he published several books, including the prose collections *Spilling the Beans* (1995) and *Drink Cultura: Chicanismo* (1993), the poetry collection *Undocumented Love/Amor Indocumentado: A Personal Anthology of Poetry* (1992), and a book of essays, *Weedee Peepo* (1988, 1992). The latter's title was a loving mispronunciation of "We, the people" as expressed by his parents and an affirmation of his parents and other Chicanas' and Chicanos' right to inclusion in U.S. social life.

Burciaga's writing was buoyed by a playful sense of humor, even while he never backed away from describing the cultural prejudice and personal struggles that Mexican Americans often face. Such subjects as California's Proposition 187, NAFTA, and his own battles with cancer were fodder for his writing. As the author Arturo Islas noted in an introductory quote to *Drink Cultura*, "[He] knows we laugh the hardest when we are in pain." Much of Burciaga's writing aimed to teach readers about the history and perspective of Chicanas and Chicanos in the United States, so often left out of traditional histories. The ephemera of daily life and its importance in the cultural lives of Chicanas and Chicanos was one of Burciaga's favorite themes. His topics ranged from his love of the jalapeño and of pinto beans, to his weekly childhood trips across the border with his brother to get a haircut, to the challenges of the "Tex-Cal" Latina and Latino marriage.

Burciaga was known for presenting his writing in the style of a performance artist. He might dress like a priest, pretend to bake a cake, or throw tortillas, Frisbee-style, into the audience if he felt the writing called for it. In relation to this comedic style, in 1984 Burciaga was invited to be one of the founding performers of Culture Clash, a comedy troupe known for skewering life's foibles from a Latina and Latino perspective. Initially called Comedy Fiesta, in its early years the group performed standup comedy for enthusiastic audiences in cafés and community centers throughout Northern California. Burciaga later left the group in order to focus on other pursuits.

As an artist, Burciaga was known primarily as a muralist while also working in other art forms. His best-known mural is *The Last Supper of Chicano Heroes*. It is one of several he painted at Casa Zapata, the Chicana- and Chicano-themed dormitory at Stanford University, where he served as resident fellow from 1985 to 1994. After polling Chicana and Chicano students and activists, Burciaga created *The Last Supper of Chicano Heroes*, which depicts such inspirational figures as César Chávez, Emiliano Zapata, Dolores Huerta, Martin Luther King Jr., Che Guevara, and Luis Valdez. Burciaga's murals at Casa Zapata also include *Mythology of Maize* and *The Cycle of Life*, inspired by the historical mythology of corn and Chicana and Chicano history in the Southwest.

Some of Burciaga's other works were turned into greeting cards, such as *Drink Cultura*, a parody of a soft-drink logo in Coca-Cola red set against a background of Mexican-flag green. This painting eventually became the cover

art for his collection of essays of the same title. The cover of *Undocumented Love* also features artwork by Burciaga, a painting of a Mexican Christ figure attempting to run across a border of barbed wire. This figure is positioned, crosslike, atop a heart dripping blood onto an already blood-spattered American flag.

Aside from serving as an artistic role model, Burciaga also mentored Chicana and Chicano and other students at Stanford University throughout his years as resident fellow. He was known as an enthusiastic community activist, taking part in numerous marches, rallies, and meetings over the years.

In his lifetime, Burciaga received many awards in recognition of his contributions to the arts. Among them was the 1992 American Book Award from the Before Columbus Foundation for *Undocumented Love*. He also received the 1995 National Hispanic Heritage Award for Literature. In 1997, he posthumously was declared a Texas Treasure for his contributions to the state's history and culture.

In 1994, while he and his wife were living in Carmel, California, Burciaga began a battle against stomach and liver cancer. He continued to write until his death on October 7, 1996.

See also Art, Chicano; Culture Clash; *and* Murals.

BIBLIOGRAPHY
Burciaga, José Antonio. *Drink Cultura: Chicanismo*. Santa Barbara, Calif.: Joshua Odell Editions, 1993.
Burciaga, José Antonio. *Spilling the Beans: Lotería Chicana*. Santa Barbara, Calif.: Joshua Odell Editions, 1995.
Burciaga, José Antonio. *Undocumented Love/Amor Indocumentado: A Personal Anthology of Poetry*. San Jose, Calif.: Chusma House, 1992.
Vélez-Ibañez, Carlos G. "The Humanity of the Literature and Art of José Antonio Burciaga." *Aztlán* 22, no. 2 (Fall 1997): 207–227.

MARY C. BELTRÁN

BURGOS, JULIA DE (1914–1953), poet, journalist, and schoolteacher. Julia de Burgos is considered one of the finest voices of Puerto Rican poetry. With a determined character, she lived life intensely at the margin of social conventions and ardently embraced the independence movement in her country, which made her a symbol not only of national resistance but also of the feminist movement. Her turbulent life, torn between deep existential conflict and amorous deceptions in the midst of permanent economic penury, as well as her final tragic undoing, inspired numerous legends about her persona. Moreover, her tormented biography in conjunction with the elevated quality of her verses has made her a revered author.

A Life of Struggle

Julia Constancia Burgos García was born in rural Carolina, Puerto Rico. Her childhood was marked by two

JULIA DE BURGOS. (Jose Garcia Betances, University of Puerto Rico)

opposing factors that molded her view of the world in a decisive manner, both regarding her way of understanding life and her poetic universe. On the one hand, she was reared in extreme poverty, in part because of the famine that decimated the island during the early years of the twentieth century. On the other hand, as a child her spiritual identification with the natural surroundings turned her homeland into an idyllic refuge, a symbol of innocence and purity to which her memory would return when the vicissitudes of life suffocated her. Thus, early in her childhood a life of bittersweet oppositions was formed: "This is my fate: the shadow next to the light, pain along with happiness," Julia wrote to her sister Consuelo (Jiménez de Báez, p. 10). Still, with the support of family and friends, the hard-working adolescent was able to finish her studies and became a teacher in 1933.

In 1934, she married Rubén Rodríguez Beauchamp, whom she divorced in 1937. Also in 1937, de Burgos published her first book of poetry, *Poemas exactos a mí misma* (Poems Exact to Myself), in a typed edition from which only a few poems have been saved. By publishing *Poema en veinte surcos* (Poem in Twenty Furrows) in 1938, she began to forge her own path as an author; she later traveled throughout Puerto Rico trying to sell the book herself, in order to defray the costs of caring for her dying mother.

That same year, de Burgos met the true love of her life, Juan Isidro Jimenes Grullón, a Dominican doctor and sociologist, when he was in Puerto Rico to give a speech. Her *Canción de la verdad sencilla* (Song of the Simple Truth, 1939), a book of poetry that received a prize from the Institute of Puerto Rican Literature, is the testament of the intimate spiritual communion with her beloved, in which the poet encounters the redemption of a life marked by deception, even though her sadness lingers.

In January 1940, de Burgos embarked with Juan Isidro on a trip to New York, from which she would never return to Puerto Rico. Their stay in the city was marked by economic hardship, but also by cultural activities where she was celebrated. Similarly, the fulfillment of their shared love contrasted with the acute discomfort from the solitude of the metropolis. Juan Isidro left for Cuba, but Julia stayed in New York until she managed to gather enough money for the trip; those months alone when she was struggling to survive in an inhospitable environment broke her spirit, and she began to contemplate suicide.

Her arrival in Havana in the middle of 1940 was an immense relief. She rejoined her love and at once felt at home because the landscape and the human environment reminded her of her homeland. They lived by the Atlantic Coast. There, toward the end of 1940, the inspiration for her third and final book of poetry, *El mar y tú* (The Sea and You), was born. The book reflected in verse the emotional processes that were operating on her life, beginning with the abundance of love, "Velas sobre un recuerdo" (Sails over a Memory). But the joy of this period soon waned. Juan Isidro's parents, from a privileged position in the upper class, were opposed to the marriage because they viewed de Burgos as a woman who rejected their traditional values, to say nothing of her humble origins. That the secure relationship she had imagined was crumbling is captured in the poem that closes the book, "Naufragio" (Poems for a Shipwreck). De Burgos suffered periods of serious emotional distress. In the middle of 1942, when Juan Isidro definitively told her that as long as his parents were alive he could not marry her, she decided to leave. Soon thereafter, Juan Isidro arrived unexpectedly with a ticket to New York for her. She had to pack her bags and leave with five pesos in her pocket. This rupture marked a progressive spiritual deterioration that she could not contain.

De Burgos arrived desolate in New York in July 1942, and she was obliged to go out in the street to look for housing and employment. She undertook many odd jobs and lived from house to house. In November, Juan Isidro passed by New York and proposed that she return with him. She wrote to her sister: "Juan Isidro returned to Cuba without me, as for me only one dignity exists" (Jiménez de Báez, p. 61). De Burgos met a musician, Armando Marín, whom she married and with whom she lived for a few years.

From that point on, de Burgos's life consisted of an interminable battle against depression and poverty. All of her attempts to publish her book *El mar y tú* (The Sea and You) were fruitless. The circumstances did not foster literary creation. She increasingly turned to drinking and developed cirrhosis of the liver. The final years of her life witnessed successive crises of mental and physical deterioration, numerous hospitalizations and occasional escapes. The few poems that she wrote during these years are full of lacerating anguish and a "desperate solitude." Shortly before her death, she wrote the poem "Farewell in Welfare Island" in English:

> It has to come from here,
> right this instance,
> . . . .
> my cry into the world.
> My cry that is no more mine,
> but hers and his forever,
> the comrades of my silence,
> the phantoms of my grave.

(Burgos 1997)

It was the year 1953. Released from the hospital in May, de Burgos went to live with relatives in Brooklyn. In July, she fell unconscious in the middle of a street in Harlem; she was transported to a hospital but was pronounced dead on arrival. The cause was determined to be pneumonia. The unidentified corpse was buried in a common plot. A forensic photograph led friends and family to find her a month later. They requested the unearthing of her casket, and she was transported to Puerto Rico, where she was received with great honors. Her remains were reburied in Carolina Cemetery, in the land that she adored. Her unedited book was published the following year, in 1954, under the title *El mar y tú, otros poemas*.

Poetry

De Burgos's poetic work is composed, on one hand, of profoundly intimate poems filled with an exalted anguish, and dominated by existential worries, love, and death. On the other hand, there are poems of the patriotic sort, in which she feverishly defends the Puerto Rican independence movement, and social poems, in which she fearlessly denounces political oppression and social injustice. *Poema en veinte surcos* describes the search for self and the definition of her being. This book also includes her most anthologized poem, dedicated to a river from her childhood, "Río Grande de Loíza":

> Río Grande de Loíza! . . .
> My wellspring, my river,
> . . . .
> my childhood was all a poem in the river,
> and a river in the poem of my first dreams.

(Burgos 1997)

The next book, *Canción de la verdad sencilla*, exalts the amorous fusion, which represents for her a return to the innocence and purity of her childhood through the union of spirit and nature. This is evident in "El encuentro del hombre y el río" ("The Encounter of the Man and the River"): "The two, clear with strength, loved each other in my spirit, / at once kissed my emotion which cried" (Burgos 1997).

Leaving behind a solid poetic legacy that sparked a transcendental renovation and enrichment of Puerto Rican poetry, de Burgos's shipwreck at the age of thirty-nine drowned the verses that were yet to be written by this exceptional poet and woman of the Americas.

See also Literature; Nuyorican Theater and Poetry; Poetry; *and* Puerto Rican Independence Movement.

BIBLIOGRAPHY

Burgos, Julia de. *Song of the Simple Truth: The Complete Poems.* Compiled and translated with an introduction by Jack Agüeros. Willimantic, Conn.: Curbstone, 1997.

Burgos, Julia de. *Homenaje a Julia de Burgos.* Revista mairena (Edición especial). Puerto Rico: Universidad de Piedras Negras, 1985.

Jiménez de Báez, Yvette. *Julia de Burgos: Vida y poesía.* San Juan, P.R.: Editorial Coquí, 1966.

MARÍA DEL CARMEN VICENTE

BUSINESS. To study the growth of Latino and Latina businesses in the United States, it is necessary to understand how immigrants of diverse nations, arriving in a country of business opportunity, can successfully organize a firm and succeed economically. The most difficult stumbling block is limited English-language proficiency. For this reason, many Latino and Latina businesses buy and sell in Spanish or Portuguese. Eventually many of them overcome this obstacle and enter the mainstream of American business. The will to succeed, mostly through hard work, and the presence in the United States of social, economic, and political conditions nonexistent in countries of origin are the main factors that determine accomplishment among Latino and Latina businesses.

Even though they find obstacles such as discrimination, Latino and Latina immigrants are met with peaceful conditions and social stability to compensate for these limitations. Almost as important to Latino and Latina immigrants are the sources of affordable financing as well as access to technical and commercial training and education at relatively low costs. Another stumbling block for Latino and Latina entrepreneurs is planning, organizing, and establishing an enterprise without adequate knowledge of a competitive market where initiative, risk-taking, and appropriate financing are paramount. Without the organizational drive to overcome these conditions, the neophyte businessperson will meet obstacles despite the experience he or she gained in his or her country of origin. The fact that a businessperson operates in an ethnic enclave mitigates but does not eliminate these obstacles.

Nevertheless, studies spanning the thirty years between 1967 and 1997 indicate, perhaps surprisingly, the ascent of Latino and Latina enterprises. In fact, the rapid growth of this population has been accompanied by the expansion of Latino and Latina businesses, a fact borne out by the figures presented here. However, it must be recognized that Latino-owned and Latina-owned businesses still represent a small part of overall U.S. business activity. Within the immigrant enclaves that exist in many American cities, Latino-owned and Latina-owned companies nevertheless do have a major presence.

In Houston, San Antonio, Miami, Los Angeles, New York, and other U.S. cities, Latino and Latina entrepreneurs constitute a fundamental segment of their local economies. They organize businesses that create jobs and stimulate demand, particularly in the enclaves where Latinos and Latinas predominate. A key ingredient of this is the continued growth of Latino and Latina immigrants, feeding into the labor force, forming new households, and allowing Latino and Latina entrepreneurs to thrive in the retail, service, and manufacturing sectors.

The numbers clearly demonstrate the business volume and sales income of Latino and Latina firms operating in the United States. The numbers analyzed here focus on benchmark years over an extended period, beginning in 1967 and ending in 1997. (A new survey for 2002 will be published in the year 2006.) However, prior to an analysis of these numbers, it is important to first look at the reasons for the success of firms, as some of them have achieved advanced stages of development.

Determinants of Success

A common denominator present among the preeminent Latino and Latina companies is the entrepreneur. Personal factors motivated the individual to establish the firm and subsequently to lead it toward success. The following personal factors appear most important:

1. A need for achievement, or the drive to fulfill an objective or a goal.
2. Acceptance of responsibility for the actions taken and the work accomplished.
3. Determination and constancy in the work. This means putting in long hours daily and overcoming a multitude of obstacles while retaining a positive attitude.
4. The willingness to face risk in the affairs of the enterprise, but ensuring that such risks are tolerable.
5. The need for quick and continuous information, as well as feedback on management performance.
6. Creativity with respect to ideas and methods.

These entrepreneurial characteristics, or personal factors, translate into positive behavior when technical expertise is adequate, and human relations with the staff are well conducted through motivation, direction, and communication.

Management theory is replete with studies and models with respect to the above matters. The contributions of John Atkins, David McClelland, Frederick Herzberg, Victor Vroom, and others repeatedly emphasize the psychological and personal factors in entrepreneurship.

During the early part of the life cycle of the business concern, it is impossible to separate its performance from that of its captain and his or her entrepreneurial accomplishments. It is only later that a hierarchical structure of command emerges. That happens when the firm has already matured and its advisers and intermediary levels of management make for a defined separation from the entrepreneur.

On the other hand, there are alternative studies that cannot be easily dismissed. They suggest that a successful business leader is one who knows how to choose a capable staff and can delegate early in the life of the enterprise. When a business leader can disengage from the day-to-day management by placing authority in subordinates, he or she can concentrate on the long-term planning of the business concern, setting goals and objectives.

Finally there are the external factors that facilitate the growth of an initially small firm into a larger successful company. These include the presence of a real opportunity, a dynamic industrial sector that pays a good labor income, a sufficient population with a satisfactory level of income, and a good communications infrastructure.

TABLE 1. *Minority-Owned Business Censuses: Year of Reference and Publication Date*

REFERENCE YEAR	PUBLISHED
1967	1971
1972	1975
1977	1982
1982	1986
1987	1990
1992	1996
1997	2001

TABLE 2. *Latino Firms: Number, Total Sales, and Average Sales per Firm, 1982–1997*

	NUMBER	SALES ($1,000)	AVERAGE SALES
1982	248,141	14,976,337	60,354
1987	422,373	24,731,600	58,554
1992	771,708	72,824,270	94,368
1997	1,199,896	186,274,582	155,242

SOURCES: U.S. Department of Commerce, Bureau of the Census, 1982 Survey of Minority-Owned Business Enterprises, Minority-Owned Businesses, Hispanic; 1987 Economic Census, Survey of Minority-Owned Business Enterprises, Hispanic; 1992 Minority Business 92-2; 1997 Minority Business EC 97 CS-4.

Number and Traits of Latino and Latina Firms

The first time that a census of minority firms was conducted by the Bureau of the Census of the Department of Commerce was in 1967. This early effort is part of the overall business censuses undertaken by the U.S. government every five years. Businesses belonging to Latinos and Latinas were counted in numbers, sales income, and number of employees. The time span for publishing such data has been as wide as seven years (between 1975 and 1982, for example) and as short as four (see Table 1).

Table 2, which examines the most recent years, when the Latino and Latina experience became significant, shows how Latino and Latina companies tripled between 1982 and 1992. In the 1992 to 1997 period, the number of Latino and Latina companies increased 55 percent. The value of sales expanded even more dramatically. Between 1982 and 1987 it grew by $10 billion; it tripled in the next five-year period and expanded 156 percent from 1992 to 1997. The average income per company, however, remained nearly stagnant between 1982 and 1987. It grew by 61 percent from 1987 to 1992 and grew again by 65 percent between 1992 and 1997. During this same ten-year period, the consumer price index for urban

TABLE 3. *Latino Firms with Employees: Number, Sales and Employment, 1982–1997*

	NUMBER	SALES	EMPLOYEES
1982	39,917	10,652,868	189,636
1987	82,908	17,729,432	264,846
1992	115,364	57,187,370	691,056
1997	211,884	158,674,537	1,388,746

SOURCES: U.S. Department of Commerce, Bureau of the Census, 1982 Survey of Minority-Owned Business Enterprises, Minority-Owned Businesses, Hispanic; 1987 Economic Census, Survey of Minority-Owned Business Enterprises, Hispanic; 1992 Minority Business 92-2; 1997 Minority Business EC 97 CS-4.

consumers rose 40 percent. Thus, there was real growth in the incomes of Latino and Latina firms.

The data presented in Table 3 identify an important variation with respect to the earlier data, since the figures in Table 3 include only companies with employees. In contrast to Table 2, which factors a trend with regard to the number of firms, Table 3 not only charts growth in family-based businesses, but analyzes the first growth phase in light of a business's ability to hire from outside the family.

The following conclusions can be drawn from the larger (second phase) business concerns. Their growth was particularly rapid after 1987, with many businesses attaining an intermediate size. The data show that from 1987 to 1997 that the number of businesses with employees enlarged by 156 percent, and their total sales grew nine-fold, with their employment increasing by a factor of five.

Such high growth in the number, and especially the size, of Latino and Latina firms was partly fostered by the expansion of the U.S. economy during the decade under examination. There was only one recession to interrupt what otherwise was a period of above-average growth in the U.S. economy, drawing a new pattern of economic cycles characterized by short contractions and long recoveries. This period of growth contrasts largely with the 1982 to 1987 period.

TABLE 4. *Latino Firms with Employees: Average Sales and Employment per Firm, 1982–1997*

	AVERAGE SALES	AVERAGE NUMBER OF EMPLOYEES
1982	266,876	4.75
1987	213,845	3.19
1992	495,712	6.00
1997	748,875	6.55

SOURCES: U.S. Department of Commerce, Bureau of the Census, 1982 Survey of Minority-Owned Business Enterprises, Minority-Owned Businesses, Hispanic; 1987 Economic Census, Survey of Minority-Owned Business Enterprises, Hispanic; 1992 Minority Business 92-2; 1997 Minority Business EC 97 CS-4.

Yet an even more telling indicator of how firms owned by Latinos and Latinas have come of age is depicted in Table 4. Table 4 shows that the average sales revenue of these firms reached almost $750,000 in the year 1997, while mean employment per firm was calculated at six and a half workers.

Ethnic Groupings

There are salient variations in degree of entrepreneurship among different Latino and Latina populations. Table 5 provides the most up-to-date picture of Latino and Latina firms, according to ethnicity, cross classified with sales revenues, and irrespective of whether the companies had employees.

These firms are usually concentrated in areas where different Latino and Latina groups have a concentration of population. Therefore, a notable characteristic of Latino and Latina entrepreneurship is the constitution of economic enclaves, where different groups buy from each other and support the business ventures of the same national origin grouping.

Thus Mexican American firms tend to be concentrated in the West and Southwest of the United States. Among the fifty states, the most recent census shows California with 191,765 companies of Mexican American origin, followed by Texas with 160,689, Arizona with 19,491, and New Mexico with 11,164. In 1997 the state of Illinois, with Chicago as the epicenter, boasted 15,584 Mexican American business firms.

Firms owned and operated by Cubans are concentrated in Florida, owing to the state's large population of Cuban Americans and its proximity to the island-nation. With its concentration of Cuban Americans, Florida is home to 72 percent of the total number of Cuban American companies (125,273 in 1997).

The third-largest distinct group is firms established by Puerto Ricans, which are almost evenly divided between Florida (15,421 firms) and New York (17,124 firms), the latter a traditional destination for the group. There are substantial population concentrations of Puerto Ricans in both states.

These demographic concentrations and the resulting economic power of such ethnic enclaves have yielded substantial political power for these populations. This is especially the case in places like Miami-Dade County, where many Cuban exiles have become American citizens and have exercised their right to vote. This explains why both Miami-Dade County and Miami proper have elected mayors of Cuban origin. The majority of the county and city commissioners are also aligned with Cubans. Furthermore, a number of Cubans have also been elected to Congress, although it should be emphasized that other Latinos and Latinas have supported Cuban American candidates. In the West, similar examples can be provided from other Latino and Latina enclaves, where numerous mayors of Mexican origin hold office. There are also congresspersons of Mexican origin in the West who have been elected to represent in Washington, D.C. In the state of Colorado, citizens elected a Mexican American to serve in the U.S. Senate. And finally, beyond the West and Florida, Puerto Ricans have been elected to numerous offices in New York state.

TABLE 5. *Latino Firms Subclassified by Ethnicity and Sales, 1997*

ETHNIC GROUPS	NUMBER OF FIRMS	SHARE (%)	SALES	SHARE OF SALES (%)
Cubans	125,273	10	26,492,208	14
Mexicans	472,033	39	73,706,753	40
Puerto Ricans	69,658	6	7,461,069	4
Spanish	57,160	5	16,922,913	9
Latin Americans	287,314	24	40,997,923	22
Other	188,458	16	20,693,715	11

SOURCES: U.S. Department of Commerce, Bureau of the Census, 1982 Survey of Minority-Owned Business Enterprises, Minority-Owned Businesses, Hispanic; 1987 Economic Census, Survey of Minority-Owned Business Enterprises, Hispanic; 1992 Minority Business 92-2; 1997 Minority Business EC 97 CS-4.

Type and Size of Latino Firms

In 1997, 85 percent of the firms owned by Latinos and Latinas operated as sole proprietorships, which meant they were wholly owned by their operators. However, even though large in numbers, these companies accounted for but 22.6 percent of total sales income. Only 6.5 percent of the Latino and Latina business concerns were corporations. However, since their size was typically larger, they accounted for 38.6 percent of the total revenues of Latino and Latina businesses. More recently, Subchapter S corporations—which accounted for 5.4 percent of the number of enterprises—had revenues representing 33.4 percent of the total. Finally, the least common business organization, partnerships, constituted 2.3 percent of the total number, accounting for 4.5 percent of the sales of Latino and Latina firms.

Another attribute of size is whether companies are large enough to have employees; that is, they are not simply "mom and pop" type stores. Companies with employees made up only 17.7 percent of the total number of Latino and Latina businesses. However, these companies represented 85.2 percent of the total sales income of Latino and Latina businesses.

Finally, how were the Latino and Latina companies distributed across the industrial classifications in place in 1997? Table 6 details their distribution.

Share of Latino Firms in the U.S. Total

The 1997 census reports that there are 20,821,934 companies in the United States, which generated revenues of $18,553,243,047,000, equivalent to an average income of $891,000. Companies of Latino and Latina origin totaled 1,199,896, generating sales of $187,274,582,000, for mean sales of $155,000. This means that Latino and Latina firms generated 5.8 percent of the total, but accounted for only 1 percent of total sales revenues. The above notwithstanding, the same census figures indicate that between 1992 and 1997 Latino and Latina businesses grew 30 percent, while overall U.S. business expanded by 7 percent. During the same period, the incomes of Latino and Latina businesses expanded by 49 percent while revenues of all U.S. companies grew 40 percent.

Reasons for Growth and Survival of the Firms

Several university studies have concluded that three factors usually stimulate and later facilitate the establishment of an enterprise by an immigrant.

The first is the psychological factor arising from a personal trauma affecting the potential entrepreneur. In the case of Latinos and Latinas, this psychological factor arises from the geographical displacement of having to leave their homeland because of economic or political reasons. Facing a lack of opportunities, Argentines, Mexicans, Dominicans, or Puerto Ricans arrive in the United States willing to change occupations or professions in order to improve their lot. In the case of Cubans, the political system of their country of origin does not allow them to become entrepreneurs, a fate once shared by Nicaraguans in the recent past. Colombians emigrate because of social instability and insecurity, while Venezuelans are wary of the direction in which governmental policies are moving in that country.

The second factor is the climate of social stability and security provided in the United States.

The third factor impacting potential entrepreneurs in the United States is the availability of credit at low interest rates, as well as technical advice and public support for those willing to establish a business concern.

The synergistic interaction of these three factors facilitates enterprise creation or an "entrepreneurial event." The process that results in the establishment of a firm was originally developed in theoretical form by Professor Albert Shapero at the Department of Management of the University of Texas at Austin. Further study and research by Shapero and others involving entrepreneurs of Filipino,

TABLE 6. *Distribution of Latino Companies across Industrial Classifications in 1997*

Agriculture, Forestry, Fishing, and Mining	3 percent
Construction	13 percent
Manufacturing	2 percent
Transport, Communications, Water, and Public Services	7 percent
Wholesalers	3 percent
Retailers	13 percent
Finance, Insurance, and Real Estate	5 percent
Services	42 percent
Other Not Classified	13 percent

Pakistani, Italian, and British origin confirm the validity of this theory.

In addition to these "objective" factors, several "subjective" or qualitative factors have been identified. They include ambition among younger immigrants for education and a willingness to work hard at establishing a business concern; the desire of older, experienced professionals to achieve a middle-class lifestyle; and, more generally, attributes such as persistence, unflagging energy, and a willingness to confront risk.

Economic Weaknesses of Latinos and Latinas

Latino and Latina businesses, like other segments of the U.S. business sector, were vulnerable to the vacillations of the American economy at the dawn of the twenty-first century. The 2001 recession, which was complicated by the economic shock of the terrorist attacks of September 11, 2001, impacted Latino and Latina entrepreneurs. These setbacks, however, were gradually reversed by 2004.

In a study published in January 2002, the Pew Hispanic Center found that the Latino and Latina community, and particularly its entrepreneurial sector, suffered relatively large damages during the economic contractions subsequent to September 11, 2001. The recession resulted in high rates of Latino and Latina unemployment and overall weakness in ethnic enclaves as business reflected the downturn in the markets.

Conclusion

According to the U.S. census of 2000, the Latino and Latina population in the United States is the fastest growing large ethnic group, having expanded by 57.9 percent between 1990 and 2000. The U.S. population as a whole grew by only 13.2 percent during the same period. Yet, Latino and Latina firms have not shown expansion in proportion to its population growth. The 1.2 million businesses belonging to Latinos and Latinas, employing 1.3 million workers, and drawing revenues of $186.3 billion, represent only a small fraction of the U.S. business universe. The latter comprises 20.8 million concerns, generating an income of $18.3 trillion. Thus in 1997, Latino and Latina firms accounted for only 6 percent of the total number of businesses and just 1 percent of total sales.

Nevertheless, hundreds of thousands of Latino and Latina entrepreneurs have been able to establish more than 1 million firms, employing more than 1 million workers. This has been a result of hard work and sacrifice. Cities such as Miami, Albuquerque, Santa Fe, Los Angeles, New York, San Antonio, and El Paso have been transformed into metropolitan centers in which Latino and Latina economic enclaves have spawned a widespread variety of Latino and Latina firms, strongly contributing, not only to their local economies, but also to the improvement of the quality of life in those communities.

See also Philanthropy.

BIBLIOGRAPHY

Caudill, William, and George DeVos. "Achievement, Culture, and Personality: The Case of Japanese Americans." In *Minority Responses: Comparative Views of Reactions to Subordination*, edited by Minako Kurokawa. New York: Random House, 1970.

Danco, Léon A. *Beyond Survival: A Guide for Business Owners and Their Families*. Cleveland, Ohio: The Center for Family Business, University Press, 1982.

De Alonso, Irma T., and Jorge Salazar-Carrillo. "Cuban-Owned Enterprises in the United States." Proceedings to the Association for the Study of the Cuban Economy (ASCE), Miami, Florida, 1992.

Greiner, L. E. "Evolution and Revolutions as Organizations Grow," *Harvard Business Review* (July–August 1972): 37–46.

Kroeger, C. V. "Managerial Development in the Small Firm," *California Management Review*, 27, no. 1 (1974): 41–47.

Longenecker, Justin G., Carlos W. Moore, and J. Williams Petty. *Small Business Management: An Entrepreneurial Emphasis*, 13th ed. Mason, Ohio: Thomson South-Western, 2004.

Rodriguez, Leonardo. "The Cuban Entrepreneur of South Florida." Selected Papers of the National Association of Hispanic Professors of Business and Economics. Proceedings, University of Phoenix, 1984.

Rodriguez, Leonardo. "Here Comes the Latin Market." *Nuestro Business Review*, June 1991.

Rodriguez, Leonardo. "El Plan de negocios: Piedra angular en la creación de una empresa," *Empreciencias*. Boletín de Investigación, Universidad Mariano Egaña, Santiago de Chile, Octubre 2000.

Rodriguez, Leonardo. "The Role of the University in Development of the Hispanic Entrepreneur in the Twenty-first Century." Monograph Series, no. 2. DePaul University, Chicago, 1985.

Salazar-Carrillo, Jorge. "Recent Business Outcomes of Hispanic Immigrants." *Greater Miami Economic Report 1997*. Greater Miami Chamber of Commerce, May 1997.

Shapero, Albert. "The Displaced, Uncomfortable Entrepreneur." *Psychology Today* 7, no. 1 (November 1975): 83–89.

United States Department of Commerce, Economics and Statistics Administration, U.S. Census Bureau. *Hispanic 1997*. EC97CS-4.

Ward, J. L. *Keeping the Family Business Healthy: How to Plan for Continued Growth, Profitability, and Family Leadership*. San Francisco: Jossey-Bass, 1988.

LEONARDO RODRÍGUEZ AND JORGE SALAZAR-CARRILLO

BUZIO, LIDYA (b. 1948), artist. Born in Montevideo, Uruguay, in 1948, the ceramicist Lidya Buzio was raised in close proximity to one of the most significant avant-garde movements in South America. Buzio's sister, a jeweler, is married to the son of Joaquín Torres-García, the pioneering modernist painter. Buzio's oeuvre is considered to be directly influenced by the legacy of Torres-García. The vibrant artistic community in Montevideo in which Buzio was raised began with Torres-García's founding of the Asociación de Arte Constructivo (Association of Constructivist Art; AAC) a group of artists inspired by Torres-García's articulation of a constructivist universalist aesthetic, and its proposal to formulate a new artistic language for the Americas. The workshop school El Taller Torres-García (the Torres-García Factory; TTG) in Montevideo functioned for several decades as a laboratory for the creation of constructivist and abstract art using new materials and methods. The AAC and TTG focused upon the study of indigenous cultures and symbols as well as modernist constructivist sensibilities to formulate a multimedia South Americanist aesthetic. After Torres-García's death in 1949, the TTG remained a prominent center of cultural activity for a decade under the direction of some of its earlier members, including the painter Julio Alpuy. By the 1950s, however, the activities of the group had shifted to other locales.

As a developing artist, Buzio studied privately with several notable Uruguayan artists. She studied painting with Guillermo Fernández and José Montes from 1964 to 1966 and ceramics with José Collell from 1967 to 1968. In 1972, a Torres-García retrospective at the Guggenheim Museum brought Buzio to New York City with her sister and brother-in-law. There, Buzio began to study with Alpuy. Synthesizing Collell's techniques of painting figures on pots with the AAC and TTG's interest in the art and images of Amerindian, African, and Oceanic cultures and classical art history, Buzio began to produce ceramic work incorporating pre-Columbian and ancient Greek designs in friezelike bands. Buzio then began to paint still lifes on clay, and in the mid-1970s incorporated images of the New York cityscape into her ceramic work.

Buzio is best known for these ceramic engagements of flat, geometric architectural images similar to the ones produced by Torres-García in the 1920s. This stylization of her architectural imagery owes a great deal to her investigation during numerous trips to Italy of early and pre-Renaissance frescos. The pervasive imagery and perspective of Buzio's work plays with the conventions of fourteenth-century and early-fifteenth-century Italian artists in the process of developing the conventions of both atmospheric and linear perspective through the study of architectural exteriors. Technically, Buzio's interest in fresco greatly informs the production of her ceramics. The technique of fresco, taken from the Italian word for "fresh," involves painting on fields of wet plaster with a combination of pigment and water. The paint is absorbed by the wet plaster, becoming part of the wall or surface itself. In a similar respect, Buzio's imagery is inseparable from its ceramic surface. Beginning with earthenware slabs, Buzio draws directly on the unfired clay that she shapes into graceful curvilinear vessels. She then gradually fills in her colorful details on the surface with the use of pigmented slips (colored liquid clay). The vessels are burnished, fired, and waxed with mineral oil or lard.

Thematically, Buzio's work eliminates the human body in favor of a metaphysical investigation of space. The presence of the human body was integral to the production of perspective in the work of Renaissance artists. Their scenes teem with human activity, and human narratives often function as the central vanishing point of their compositions. Buzio's ceramic works remove the human element from their rendering of architecture and, with their three-dimensionality, eliminate the existence of a "central vanishing point." Instead of architectural imagery functioning as a mere backdrop to human activity, Buzio foregrounds the scenery, often zooming in on horizon lines defined solely by the intersection of rooftops with the sky, as in *Dark Blue Roofscape* (1986). In this way, Buzio works with many of the same strategies as did the Italian artist Giorgio de Chirico (1888–1978). De Chirico also played with conventions of a somewhat tilted perspective and the simulation of fresco coloration and style, creating works that reflect a Romantic concern with melancholy and emptiness, such as his *Mystery and Melancholy of a Street* (1914). De Chirico's influence upon Buzio is evident in the gradated coloration of the passages of sky in her vessels and in her thematic concerns, such as the man-made delineation of empty space. Buzio's slightly skewed architectural perspective, as in *Corner Building* (1998); chiaroscuro shadowing; and seemingly incongruous placement of objects all help to create the somewhat ominous atmosphere in her work. Buzio's interest in containers, be they vessels or buildings, is not limited to two-dimensional images "drawn" on her ceramics. Rather, many of her works have inner dividers and structural details, cutouts resembling architecture, or planes that jut out from the surface of the vessel with the imagery.

While most famous for her architectural ceramic vessels, Buzio's concern with structure, volume, and classical imagery is also reflected in her still life collages and wood constructions. Works such as *Still Life Construction with Pears* (1998) integrate imagery of ancient Greek statuary, prototypical objects of the still life tradition like fruits and vegetables, and Buzio's distinctive architectural forms in playful constructivist compositions. Indeed, the constructivist legacy is evident in both the impersonality and the transparency of method and material in Buzio's still life constructions and pottery.

Buzio has exhibited extensively in the United States and abroad. Her work is in many notable permanent collections, including those of the Los Angeles County Museum of Art, Los Angeles; the Metropolitan Museum of Art, New York; the Smithsonian Institute, Washington, D.C.; and the Victoria and Albert Museum, London. In 1984, Buzio married Dan Pollock, the director of the Cecilia de Torres Gallery, an art space focused on the work and legacy of the artists of El Taller Torres-García. Buzio and Pollock live in New York City.

See also South Americans.

BIBLIOGRAPHY

Beardsley, John, and Jane Livingston, with Octavio Paz. *Hispanic Art in the United States: Thirty Contemporary Painters and Sculptors.* Houston, Tex.: Museum of Fine Arts, 1987.
Clark, Garth, ed. *Ceramic Echoes: Historical References in Contemporary Ceramics.* Kansas City, Mo.: Contemporary Art Society, 1983.
Clark, Garth, and Oliver Watson. *American Potters Today.* London: Victoria and Albert Museum, 1986.
Lynn, Martha Drexler. *Clay Today: Contemporary Ceramists and Their Work.* Los Angeles: Los Angeles County Museum of Art, 1990.

TAMARA BEAUCHAMP

C

CABRERA, LYDIA (1899–1991), ethnologist. Lydia Cabrera was a Cuban ethnologist, writer, and folklorist, and the author of twenty-three volumes about Afro-Cuban myths, languages, and cultures. She was the youngest of eight children of Raimundo Cabrera, a prominent writer and publisher, and Elisa Bilbao Marcaida. She received most of her elementary education at home, a common practice for upper-class Cuban families. Another type of education that strongly influenced Cabrera's work came from her contact with her family's black servants. Her interest in Afro-Cuban themes grew from what she called "a re-encounter with the world of fantasy of my early childhood" and the influences of avant-garde movements such as French Surrealism and Picasso's Primitivism.

In 1927, Cabrera left for Paris to study painting, earning her degree at L'École du Louvre. Her first work, a collection of short stories entitled *Cuentos negros de Cuba* (1936), was published in French. It received mixed reviews in Cuba but opened the path to her research on Afro-Cuban cultures. Fernando Ortiz, the leading ethnologist and founder of the field of Afro-Cuban studies, who was also Cabrera's brother-in-law, understood the importance of her work to the burgeoning field of Afro-Cuban ethnology. In the Cuban edition of *Cuentos negros* (1940), Ortiz described her short stories as a "collaboration between Negro folklore and its white translator."

Although the practice of slavery was abolished in 1886, Cuba was still a racist society. Public spaces were segregated, and prejudice was strong. The descendants of slaves in Cuba belonged predominantly to two groups who came from West Africa as part of the transatlantic slave trade: the Yoruba or *lucumí*, and the Congo or *bantú*. Two of their religions survived in Cuba, Santería and Palo Monte.

Cabrera was particularly interested in these Afro-Cuban religions and visited Pogolotti, a poor black neighborhood in Havana, during a brief visit to Cuba from Paris in 1930. Her serious ethnographic work started in 1938, after her final return to the island. Cabrera's numerous trips to black neighborhoods in Havana and Matanzas broke taboos of race, class, and gender relations in Cuban society. By using personal memories, literature, and storytelling, she inaugurated a new method of writing ethnographic research. This method consisted of connecting with her informants in long conversations, sharing personal details and stories instead of asking direct questions. With these conversations, Cabrera abolished the "scientific detachment" of ethnographic research, and looked at her informants as subjects who had valuable memories to share. *El monte* (1954), Cabrera's best-known work, is an account of Santería, Palo Monte, and herbal medicine. It remains the main manual for practitioners of these religions.

In June 1960, a year after the Cuban Revolution, Cabrera went into exile. After a brief stop in Madrid, she settled in Miami. Thus, Cabrera could be considered part of the first generation of post-Revolutionary Cuban writers in exile (1960–1970). After a silence of twelve years, she started writing again in 1970. Scholars consulted her as an authority on Afro-Cuban studies. For many Cubans and Cuban-Americans, as well as for people from the Caribbean diaspora in the United States who practice Santería, Cabrera's writings constitute a type of initiation into a world of magic and poetry. Her works remain popular, occupying a special place at the border between literature and ethnography. Her personalized, subjective method of research has become a model for many contemporary Latino and Latina scholars. Since her death in 1991, her papers, photographs, and memorabilia have been in the Otto G. Richter Cuban Heritage Collection at the University of Miami.

See also Afro-Latinos; Cuban American Writers; Exilio; Folklore; Religion and Spirituality; *and* Santería.

BIBLIOGRAPHY

Castellanos, Isabel, and Josefina Inclán, eds. *En torno a Lydia Cabrera. Cincuentenario de "Cuentos negros de Cuba" (1936–1986)*. Miami: E. Universal, 1987.

Quiroga, José. "Queer Desires in Lydia Cabrera." In *Tropics of Desire: Interventions from Queer Latino America*, 76–100. New York: New York University Press, 2000.

Rodríguez-Mangual, Edna M. *Lydia Cabrera and the Construction of an Afro-Cuban Identity*. North Carolina: University of North Carolina Press, 2004.

Simo, Ana María. *Lydia Cabrera: An Intimate Portrait*. New York: Intar Latin American Gallery, 1984.

JOSSIANNA ARROYO

CALIFANO V. TORRES (1978). In *Califano v. Torres*, the Supreme Court denied Supplemental Security Income (SSI) benefits to people who moved to Puerto Rico from other states. Established in 1972, the SSI program grants benefits to blind, aged (over sixty-five), and disabled persons. It is a "welfare" type of program that, unlike traditional Social Security benefits, is available to people who did not work or who have not earned enough to qualify for traditional Social Security benefits (old age, survivors, and disability insurance). For individuals whose traditional Social Security benefits under the disability and retirement programs are below the SSI benefit amount, SSI supplements those benefits and guarantees a minimum level.

Congress, in creating the SSI program, made it available only to residents of the United States, which it defined as the fifty states and the District of Columbia. The plaintiffs in *Califano v. Torres* challenged that provision of the statute, claiming it was unconstitutional because it applied to persons who, by moving to Puerto Rico, had lost the benefits to which they were entitled when they lived in the states. The district court found that the limitation interfered with the constitutional right to travel and that there was no compelling governmental interest to justify such interference.

The Supreme Court first determined that the fundamental right to travel was not implicated in this case. It explained that right as one that ensured newly arrived residents the right to the same governmental benefits and privileges as other residents of a given state. The district court's reading of that right would give a person who moved to Puerto Rico from another state greater benefits than those enjoyed by other residents of Puerto Rico.

The Supreme Court found that a law providing for governmental payments of monetary benefits is entitled to a strong presumption of constitutionality. The standard is whether the legislature's judgments are rational, and not invidious. The Court justified the exclusion of persons from Puerto Rico from the SSI program on three grounds: first, that Puerto Rico's tax status was unique; second, that the cost of including Puerto Rico would be great (approximately $300 million per year); and third, that the inclusion of the SSI program might seriously disrupt the Puerto Rican economy. What is not clear from the Court's opinion, however, is whether this was Congress's rationale in excluding Puerto Rico from the program or the government's explanation after the fact.

The plaintiff's complaint also challenged the statute based on the equal protection component of the due process clause of the Fifth Amendment. The district court did not reach a decision on this claim. *In dicta*—a legal term describing a statement in a judicial opinion that is not necessary for the decision of the case and is thus not binding on courts in subsequent cases—the Supreme Court stated that "[a]cceptance of that claim would have meant that all otherwise qualified persons in Puerto Rico are entitled to SSI benefits, not just those who received such benefits before moving to Puerto Rico."

This opinion represented a summary disposition of the case, as the Court did not receive briefs on the merits of the case or hear oral arguments. Justice William Brennan would have affirmed the district court's decision. Justice Thurgood Marshall would have granted oral argument.

As a result of Congress's actions and this decision, any elderly, blind, or disabled SSI recipient living in the states who moved to Puerto Rico would lose those benefits. Since SSI benefits in most cases represent a higher benefit amount than most states provide under their own programs, the consequences are rather grave—greater impoverishment. Low-income elderly, blind, and disabled persons living in Puerto Rico are thus relegated to living in greater poverty than are their counterparts in the states. Puerto Rican SSI recipients living in the states have to choose between going back to the place where perhaps they were born or have family and other support networks—necessary when one is disabled or elderly—and greater economic stability. When *Califano v. Torres* is read together with *Harris v. Rosario*, it becomes clear that Puerto Ricans in Puerto Rico hold second-class citizenship under U.S. law. This is because they are not entitled to the same civil and political rights as are those living in the states, and are subject to the almost total discretion of the U.S. Congress in construing their legal rights.

See also **Harris v. Rosario; Insular Cases; Puerto Ricans;** *and* **Puerto Rico, Colonialism in.**

BIBLIOGRAPHY

Malavet, Pedro. "Puerto Rico: Cultural Nation, American Colony." *Michigan Journal of Race and Law* 6 (2000): 1–106.

Rivera Ramos, Efrén. *The Legal Construction of Identity*. Washington, D.C.: American Psychological Association, 2001.

Roman, Ediberto. "The Alien-Citizen Paradox and Other Consequences of U.S. Colonialism." *Florida State University Law Review* 26 (1998): 1–47.

ALICIA ALVAREZ

CALIFORNIA. It is estimated that approximately 300,000 Native Americans inhabited the area now know as California before Spanish explorers arrived in search of wealth. On September 28, 1542, an expedition led by Juan Rodríguez Cabrillo sailed into the San Diego Bay, beginning the era of Spanish colonization. The Spanish empire governed the area from 1769 to 1821, decimating the Native American population. The Spanish established three major institutions in California: Franciscan missions, presidios, and pueblos. The pueblos were small civilian centers, and the presidios provided limited military protection. However, the most significant of the Spanish colonial institutions were the missions.

Missions

There were twenty-one missions located between present-day San Diego and San Francisco. They had two primary goals: to advance the Spanish empire and to convert the Native American population to Roman Catholicism. California Indians were recruited to the missions, where they were given religious instruction and taught practical skills. They were also acculturated into Spanish cultural norms because the missions were considered temporary institutions, to be disbanded once the Native Americans were ready to take their place as productive members of the Spanish empire. Because of this forced acculturation process, many California Indians would come to identify themselves as Chicanos and Chicanas or Mexican Americans.

Converted Indians, known as neophytes, were required to stay at the missions after they had been baptized. They were not allowed to return to their former way of life. However, Mission Indians had numerous strategies to resist the oppressive forces of the missions. Some ultimately escaped, but soldiers were often used to recapture the runaways. After Mexico won its independence in 1821, the secularization of the missions gradually began to take place. By 1836 the social structure of Mexican California had been largely transformed from the mission system to a pastoral economy. The missions lost their lands as well as most of their power. The church lands were redistributed primarily to Mexican administrators and military officials. Secularization was supposed to have been accompanied by the emancipation of the missions' indigenous populations. However, most Mission Native Americans did not receive any lands. Few of those who did receive lands, were able to keep them, so that the majority of Native Americans became landless tenants.

Increased Immigration

During the 1840s, visitors and settlers from the United States began arriving in California in greater numbers. The U.S. government became increasingly interested in acquiring California. Adhering to principles of Manifest Destiny, the United States declared war on Mexico in 1846 and seized California. The war ended on February 2, 1848, with the signing of the Treaty of Guadalupe Hidalgo. California, Nevada, Utah, Arizona, New Mexico, and parts of Colorado and Wyoming were ceded to the United States.

In 1848, gold was discovered in California, and the subsequent gold rush transformed the state. During the summer of 1848, gold fever brought people from Hawaii,

Oregon, Utah, Mexico, Peru, Chile, China, and Europe. Hundreds of new towns came into being. San Francisco, for example, grew from six hundred people in 1848 to twenty-five thousand just one year later. These increases in population allowed California to acquire statehood in the fall of 1850.

Because of the migration spurred by the gold rush, California became the most ethnically diverse region in the country. However, with increased diversity came ethnic conflict. Many Native Americans were victims of genocidal campaigns. The rancho elite lost their lands to natural disasters and to legal and extralegal maneuvers. Latino miners experienced violent repression and discriminatory taxes. In 1850 there were fifteen thousand Mexican miners working in the southern mines. Two-thirds of them left the region after the passage of the Foreign Miners License Tax. Most went back to Mexico.

Economic Growth

The transcontinental railroad was completed in 1869, making California much less isolated. The railroad hurt many merchants as eastern products flooded California markets; however, it also opened eastern markets to California's agricultural industries, making them more prosperous.

The 1880s ushered in tremendous growth. Easier access via rail, along with publicity extolling the beauty, climate, and health benefits of living in California, brought 200,000 new inhabitants to southern California in 1887 alone. As the population grew, so did the economy. Agriculture was central to this expansion. Wheat grown in the Central Valley became the most important farm product in California. In southern California, citrus production became dominant. Huge oil deposits also contributed to the state's economic growth. Oil was discovered in the San Joaquín Valley, Santa Barbara County, Ventura County, and the Los Angeles basin. The early 1920s brought a massive oil boom with the tapping of oil fields near Huntington Beach, Whittier, and Long Beach. Apart from agriculture and oil production, California also saw the development of a fledgling motion-picture industry. It began just southeast of Oakland, but eventually relocated to Hollywood.

Racial Discrimination

With the growth of the cities, Latinos and Latinas in California, the majority of whom were of Mexican descent, were segregated into barrios. This process was well underway throughout California by the mid-1800s and complete by 1870. Between 1900 and 1930, new barrios were established within central cities across California. They sprang up from agricultural and railroad labor camps and colonies. The formation of these segregated neighborhoods was reinforced by the exclusion of Latinos and

Latinas from white neighborhoods through racially restrictive covenants and other legal and extralegal forms of exclusion, including violence and harassment. The suburbanization of many Los Angeles industries also influenced the establishment of segregated Mexican suburbs.

This segregation was further exacerbated by increasing immigration from Mexico in the 1910s, as large numbers of refugees fled the violence of the Mexican Revolution. The increasing Mexican population in Los Angeles County—5,000 in 1900, 50,000 in 1920, almost quadrupling to 190,000 by 1930—put enormous pressure on Mexican ethnic enclaves. Mexican workers were concentrated in blue-collar, unskilled work and were rarely able to move up from the lowest economic rungs.

In the 1930s, California felt the impact of the Great Depression. Thousands of Dust Bowl migrants came to California in search of a better life, often displacing Latino and Latina workers in agriculture and other industries. Xenophobia and nativism flourished. The federal government responded to the perception that Mexican immigrants were taking jobs from American citizens by resorting to mass repatriation. Estimates of the number of people deported range from 250,000 to 2 million but most scholars estimate that at least 500,000 Mexicans and Mexican Americans—including many U.S. citizens—were deported during the 1930s.

In the 1930s and 1940s, anger and resentment toward Mexican American communities continued to grow. This anger often manifested itself in harassment and violence. The violence culminated in the summer of 1943 with the so-called zoot suit riots.

The labor shortage caused by World War II led to federal legislation establishing the Bracero Program, a guest worker program, in 1942. During its 22 years of existence, 5 million temporary contract laborers from Mexico were brought to the United States as farmworkers. One-third of the braceros came to work in California's citrus and other agricultural fields.

The Post–World War II Era

During the 1940s and 1950s, segregation was challenged and began breaking down. In 1946, *Mendez v. Westminster School District* banned separate schools. In the 1950s, California began to see the initial stages of residential desegregation. Mexican American businessmen and veterans played a central role in the desegregation process. The 1944 G.I. Bill of Rights made Mexican American veterans eligible for government loans that allowed them to start businesses, attend college, and buy homes. Some of these veterans were able to buy homes in previously all-white neighborhoods through the G.I. Bill, which provided further impetus for desegregation. The bill also created opportunities for Mexican veterans to leave farm work. Thus, the number of Mexican property owners began to increase steadily.

The Chicano/a Movement of the 1960s and 1970s encompassed various movements and goals throughout the country. Its most important manifestations in California included the economic activism of the United Farm Workers led by César Chávez and Dolores Huerta; the youth and student activism of groups such as the Movimiento Estudiantil Chicano de Aztlán (MEChA) and the Brown Berets; and activism in the visual arts, theater, and literature.

During the late 1970s and early 1980s, the Latino and Latina population in California became increasingly diversified, as new immigrants from Central American countries migrated north to escape brutal, U.S.–supported civil wars in their countries. In the early 2000s, according to the U.S. census, there were approximately 35.5 million people in the state of California, about one-third of whom were Latinos and Latinas. Eight and a half million of the approximately 11 million Latinos and Latinas in the state are Mexican Americans. Central Americans comprise the second largest group of Latinos in the state. In the early twenty-first century, Los Angeles has the second largest urban concentration of Mexican-origin people after Mexico City and a population of Salvadorans that is equal to or greater than that of San Salvador.

See also **Barrios; Bracero Program; Brown Berets; Catholicism; Census; Central Americans; Chávez, César; Chicanos and Chicanas; Demographics; Deportations of Mexican-Origin People in the United States; Education; Employment Discrimination; Huerta, Dolores; Méndez v. Westminster; Mexican-Origin People in the United States; Mexican Revolution; Migrant Workers; Missions and Other Colonial Churches; Movimiento Estudiantil Chicano de Aztlán; Native Americans/Mexicanos; Pueblos; Treaty of Guadalupe Hidalgo; United Farm Workers; United States–Mexican War;** *and* **Zoot Suit.**

BIBLIOGRAPHY

Camarillo, Albert. *Chicanos in a Changing Society: From Mexican Pueblos to American Barrios in Santa Barbara and Southern California, 1848–1930.* Cambridge, Mass.: Harvard University Press, 1979.

Gutiérrez, David G. *Walls and Mirrors: Mexican Americans, Mexican Immigrants, and the Politics of Ethnicity.* Berkeley: University of California Press, 1995.

Haas, Lisbeth. *Conquests and Historical Identities in California, 1769–1936.* Berkeley: University of California Press, 1995.

Monroy, Douglas. *Thrown among Strangers: The Making of Mexican Culture in Frontier California.* Berkeley: University of California Press, 1990.

Pitt, Leonard. *The Decline of the Californios: A Social History of the Spanish-Speaking Californians, 1846–1890.* Berkeley: University of California Press, 1966.

Romo, Ricardo. *East Los Angeles: History of a Barrio.* Austin: University of Texas Press, 1983.

Sánchez, George J. *Becoming Mexican American: Ethnicity, Culture, and Identity in Chicano Los Angeles, 1900–1945*. New York: Oxford University Press, 1993.

GABRIELA SANDOVAL

CALLE OCHO.

Calle Ocho is a long thoroughfare that changes name and character several times as it crosses the state of Florida connecting the cities of Tampa on the northwest coast to Miami on the southeast coast. As it leaves Miami to the west and heads through the Everglades, across the Florida peninsula and up the West Coast to Tampa, it is called Highway 41. This roughly 350-mile stretch of highway is also referred to as the Tamiami Trail, which is a combination of the names of the two cities it connects: Tampa and Miami. Only the relatively small portion of the street that runs through Miami's Little Havana neighborhood is referred to as Calle Ocho. But Calle Ocho is the name that locals and outsiders alike are most familiar with.

Symbolically, the portion of Calle Ocho that passes through the neighborhood of Little Havana constitutes sacred space in the geographic imagination of, and about, Miami's Cuban community. In the early 1960s, the first wave of Cuban refugees came to the United States on the heels of Castro's communist revolution on the island. Many came directly, or eventually relocated, to Miami. Once a predominantly Jewish neighborhood called Riverside, this neighborhood became the heart of early Cuban immigration and was renamed Little Havana. Shops along Calle Ocho reflect the Cuban origins of the residents: grocers such as Sedanos and La Roca cater to the Spanish-inspired culinary traditions of Cuba; cafés selling small cups of strong, sweet *café cubano* inhabit every block; and famed restaurants like Versailles are social gathering points for Cuban Americans. Other landmarks along Calle Ocho include the Moderna Poesía bookstore, the hair salon of Marisleysis González (Elián González's self-proclaimed surrogate mother), Máximo Gómez/Domino Park, and the Tower Theater. Calle Ocho is also the venue for the Calle Ocho Festival, a Latino-oriented marketing extravaganza that marks the end of Carnival in February.

Changes in the commercial and residential landscape of Calle Ocho reflect the current demographic changes underway in Little Havana. Little Havana has become a target of gentrification by relatively affluent Miamians wishing to live closer to the booming downtown financial district. YUCAS (Young Upwardly Mobile Cuban Americans) are a significant segment of those gentrifying Little Havana, arriving as much for reasons of nostalgia as for the housing stock. While the neighborhood is still a Latina and Latino enclave at over 95 percent Hispanic, not even half of its population identified as "Cuban" in the 2000 census. Over one quarter of Little Havana's residents are recent arrivals from Central American countries, particularly Nicaragua and Honduras, while more and more Argentineans and Colombians—like the Cubans before them—are arriving on the heels of political and economic chaos in their home countries. Today, one is just as likely to see a Nicaraguan *fritanga* restaurant as a Cuban establishment along Calle Ocho. This has prompted some to suggest that the neighborhood's name be changed from Little Havana to The Latin Quarter. In response, tourists to Miami are encouraged to visit Calle Ocho for an authentic Cuban experience with no passport needed.

See also Cuban Americans; Florida; González, Elián; *and* Little Havana.

BIBLIOGRAPHY
Orihuela, María Luisa. *Calle Ocho* Miami, Fla.: Ediciones Universal, 1998.
Stepick, Alex, Guillermo Grenier, Max Castro, et al, eds. *This Land Is Our Land: Immigrants and Power in Miami*. Berkeley and Los Angeles: University of California Press, 2003.

PATRICIA PRICE

CALÓ.

Caló as used in Mexican American communities and in Chicano literature refers to a speech style that mixes words and phrases from a variety of sources as a special, in-group slang. Its origin lies with the *gitanos*, or gypsies, of Spain. The word itself means "dark" or "black," referring to the exotic coloring of the nomads, who claimed to be from Egypt. The slang, a mixture of the Romany and Spanish created by the gypsies of the nineteenth century, was transported to the New World in the early twentieth century through Mexico City and subsequently spread to El Paso, Texas. In that border city it was adopted by young men, who gave it their own stamp by incorporating English into what was by then a Spanish-based argot. These speakers, predominantly underprivileged bilingual Chicano youths, became known as "pachucos," resulting from wordplay on the name of their home city. When they rode the rails westward through the Southwest on their way to Los Angeles in the 1930s, the slang they spoke became known as pachuco talk. In fact, in some communities caló is more commonly known as pachuco.

This speech style did not remain restricted to these young men, who were associated with gangs and criminal activity, although they played a big role in creating its bilingual flavor. The individuals who could create new words in a clever fashion by blending English with Spanish were admired and respected by their peers. In the late 1930s and the 1940s Chicano and Chicana teenagers listened to swing music in their leisure time; dressed in zoot suits, platform shoes, and short skirts; and spoke of "the drape shape" and the "reet pleat." As with subsequent

TABLE 1. *Examples of Pachuco Caló*

WORD/PHRASE	TYPE	FUNCTION	CURRENT MEANING
bato/vato	Romany	"old, important"	young man, guy
buti/bute	Romany	intensifier	much, many, very
chota	gypsy slang	"informer"	the police, the law
nel/Nelson	neologism	negative (*n-*)	no, no way
Simón	neologism	affirmative (*sí-*)	yes, sure
Mexicles	neologism	play on words	Mexico
mi ruca	meaning extension of "old person"		my ol' lady, my girl
mi jefa	meaning extension of "boss"		my mom, my wife
ya estufas	wordplay	*ya estuvo*	it's all over
ay te wacho	Spanish/English mixed phrase	see you later	

teenage slang, the pachuco caló sounded hip and cool to friends and acquaintances. It was a small step for these teens to display their bilingual ability and bicultural identity by incorporating this unique slang into their everyday speech. Adolescents, teens, and young adults in the Southwest adopted this speech style as they came into contact with it in the 1940s and 1950s. Soon their parents and the community in general tuned in to the kids's slang and even began to understand it themselves. As a result some words and phrases became fairly widespread, and many are still known and used in the early twenty-first century.

One individual who contributed to the popularity of pachuco caló in the 1940s and 1950s was Lalo Guerrero, a Chicano singer-songwriter from Tucson, Arizona. Having met and socialized with the original pachucos when they stopped to work in Tucson on their way west, he learned their slang and later incorporated it into several songs, including "El Pachuco y el Tarzán," "Marijuana Boogie," and "Los Chucos Suaves." Some of this slang was incorporated into the 1978 play and subsequent movie *Zoot Suit* by Luis Valdez, which featured the charismatic figure of "El Pachuco" as a main character. A similar slang emerged from the barrios of poor, marginalized youths in Mexico City in the early-to mid-twentieth century. The Mexican film star Cantinflas was the best-known embodiment of this figure in Mexico.

The pachuco caló of Mexican Americans shares some general linguistic features with the original Romany-based slang dialect of the *gitanos*, just as its speakers share some social characteristics with that group. Considered by scholars to be a secret language used primarily by those whose activities skirted the law, the slang shares many of the characteristics of secret languages around the world, such as metaphor, wordplay, taboo language, and word creation (neologisms) to make meanings obscure to the uninitiated. This argot also uses some of the traditional caló words—with origins in Sanskrit—originally used by the *gitanos*. Table 1 gives some examples of these categories.

However, not all of the mixed English-Spanish expressions used in these communities are truly caló or pachuco. Some are merely part of a more general dialect of Chicano Spanish. This dialect, part of a widespread dialect of Spanish spoken by Mexican-heritage speakers in the United States, routinely incorporates word borrowings, calques (translations), code-switching between the two languages, and English-influenced Spanish. It also incorporates general Mexican slang. Table 2 gives some examples of these different types.

Although pachuco caló has been used in the southwestern United States for many decades, other populations continue to use a Spanish slang to keep their meanings secret. In this type of caló, reported to be used in U.S. prison populations where Spanish is spoken, the words and phrases are kept fresh by speakers motivated to creatively hide their true meanings, much like the original gypsies and pachucos are said to have done. Although this prison slang might not popularly be known as caló, its continued life as a criminal argot is part of a long tradition of secret dialects in Europe and in the New World.

In sum, caló has a long tradition that began in Spain and was transported to Mexico and the southwestern United States. What started out as a street slang has been adopted into everyday speech in many Mexican American

TABLE 2. *Examples of Chicano Spanish*

WORD/PHRASE	TYPE	CURRENT MEANING
muy "nice"	code-switch	very nice
hacer un "party"	code-switch	to have a party
mopear/mapear	borrowed word	to mop
chainear	borrowed word	to shine (shoes)
llamar patrás	calque	to call back
¡quiúbole!	general Mexican slang	what's up? (greeting)
¡qué suave!	general Mexican slang	how cool

communities that want to give a distinct bilingual and bi-cultural flavor to their speech.

See also **Bilingualism and Biculturalism; Cantinflas; Guerrero, Lalo; Pachucos and Pachucas; Sleepy Lagoon Trial;** *and* **Spanglish.**

BIBLIOGRAPHY

Fuentes, Dagoberto, and José A. López. *Barrio Language Dictionary: First Dictionary of Caló.* Los Angeles: Southland Press, 1974.

Galván, Roberto A., and Richard V. Teschner, comps. *El Diccionario del español chicano/The Dictionary of Chicano Spanish.* Lincoln-wood, Ill.: National Textbook, 1995.

Guerrero, Lalo, and Sherilyn Meece Mentes. *Lalo: My Life and Music.* Tucson: University of Arizona Press, 2002. The chapter "The Pachuco Years," 96–102, discusses "El Pachuco y el Tarzán" and "Marijuana Boogie," and an appendix presents Guerrero's compre-hensive discography.

Ornstein-Galicia, Jacob. "Chicano Caló: Description and Review of a Border Variety." *Hispanic Journal of Behavioral Sciences* 9 no. 4 (1987): 359–373.

Robinson, Linton H. *Mexican Slang: A Guide.* Campo, Calif.: Bueno Books, 1992.

Webb, John Terrence. "Mexican-American Caló and Standard Mexi-can Spanish." In *Spanish in the United States: Sociolinguistic As-pects*, edited by Jon Amastae and Lucía Elías-Olivares. New York: Cambridge University Press, 1982.

MaryEllen Garcia

CAMNITZER, LUIS (b. 1937), artist and writer. Luis Camnitzer is a visual artist and writer who was born in Lübeck, Germany, on November 6, 1937. His Jewish fam-ily fled to Uruguay in 1939. Camnitzer has identified as Uruguayan but also as "a citizen of memory," as he says in a footnote to his essay "Wonderbread and Spanglish" (1991), because he has lived in the United States since 1964 but does not consider himself an American. He has written of the alienation and familiarity he feels while straddling two cultures imperfectly and observing each with the eyes of an expatriate, a visitor, and a local. It is not surprising that Camnitzer's art often deals with the ambiguities of identity, language, exile, imprisonment, and the experience of reality. His art also exhibits a keen interest in politics (particularly Latin American politics) in conjunction with ethics and resistance to injustice. He prefers to work with installations that encourage the viewer's participation, as in his *Untitled Installation for Documenta XI* (2001–2002), in which a doorway leading to a blue sky with clouds becomes a cement wall as the viewer walks from one side to another. Most of his art is deliberately evocative rather than didactic; he believes that which is inexplicable and mysterious in a work of art is the magical thing that makes it art.

Camnitzer began his career as a printmaker after study-ing at the Escuela Nacional de Bellas Artes (National School of Fine Arts) in the Universidad de la Republica in Montevideo, Uruguay, where he earned a degree in sculp-ture. As he states in "Chronology" (1991), he chose to cre-ate prints because they could reach a wide audience, which adhered to his belief that art should be made ac-cessible to everyone. He explored expressionism (the at-tempt to represent the subjective emotional response the artist has to an object or event) with his prints. His work became unsatisfying for him because expressionism was too result-oriented, while his prints were not being as democratically distributed as he had hoped.

Camnitzer realized that he was searching for a way to evoke unpredictable interpretations of his art and that he was not successfully meeting that challenge. He became fascinated by the concept of creating art that could not be owned by a single person, art that was based on ideas as opposed to physical images. The viewer's perception of an idea, as represented by text, could lead to the viewer's own mental imagery. The viewer would thus create the final product in his or her own mind, and then all viewers would be able to walk away "owning" the art they had produced. In this way, Camnitzer could intellectually de-mocratize the distribution of his art and also evoke unique, unpredictable understandings of it. This began with text-based art such as *This is a mirror. You are a writ-ten sentence* (1966). He also created stickers with text that were "exhibited" in public places like restrooms and ele-vators because he could not get them into a formal art ex-hibition at the time; this method of display was in keeping with his belief that art should be publicly acces-sible.

Camnitzer's work with text expanded into large instal-lations such as *Living Room* (1969), a model of a living and dining room constructed entirely with words, which was exhibited at the Museum of Fine Arts in Caracas, Venezuela, in 1969. He considered it a success when he witnessed viewers walking around the words that de-scribed the dining table while treading on the words de-scribing the rug. His work with text soon included imagery. An example is *Envelope* (1967), in which the drawing could also represent a chimney or a tunnel and merely needs a change in title for an entirely different in-terpretation. He was beginning to explore the arbitrari-ness of meaning. Camnitzer also began to include objects in his text-image combinations, as he did in *Leftovers* (1970), an exhibit of eighty numbered boxes wrapped in blood-stained gauze that construct a wall covered with written inventories of weapons. This piece alludes to po-litical repression in Latin America and was exhibited at the Paula Cooper Gallery in New York in 1970.

Camnitzer chose to work less on political art while at-tempting to produce a method by which he could com-municate through imagery and text without allowing the text to literally describe the imagery in any way. It was an evolution of his earlier ideas, culminating in the installation *Arbitrary Objects and Their Titles* (1979), which consists of twenty prewritten titles and twenty random objects that the viewer organizes into an intelligible narrative in his or her mind despite their lack of obvious connection. Camnitzer continued to explore this kind of evocative art in *The Archaeology of a Spell* (1979) and *Fragments of a Novel* (1980).

Now that he had developed his art such that it could evoke the viewer's own entirely personal interpretation, Camnitzer felt ready to return to political art. His more political work is sensitively suggestive rather than exploitatively propagandistic. The series of photo-etchings *From the Uruguayan Torture* (1983–1984) depicts images such as a finger with a wire tied around it, a glass of water, and an empty bottle, each accompanied by objective, handwritten text, such as "The instrument was explained in detail." Each piece calls to mind an awareness of the physical and psychological abuse that prisoners undergo during and after torture. The viewer is made painfully aware of the intimately annihilative relationship between a torturer and his or her victim without having to look at graphic, bloody images of human abuse. Like most of Camnitzer's art, it allows the viewer to have a thoughtful and sensorially perceptive experience that informs the art instead of forcing the viewer to be the placid recipient of a didactic message. Other examples of his political work are *Massacre of Puerto Montt* (1969), *Common Grave* (1970), *The Agent Orange Series* (1985), and *The Books of the Walls* (1993).

Camnitzer is also known for his writing on art theory and history, particularly that which pertains to Latin America. His writings grapple with such issues as political oppression, cultural identity, the commercialization of art, and ethics in art. Although he is a respected art writer, he has stated that if the experience of perceiving a work of art could be perfectly explained through words alone, then it could no longer be considered art. This statement has informed his body of work and makes him an important conceptual artist of the twentieth and twenty-first centuries.

See also **South Americans.**

BIBLIOGRAPHY
Binder, Pat, and Gerhard Haupt. "Luis Camnitzer: Interview, Details." Universes in Universe, 2002. universes-in-universe.de/car/documenta/11/bhf/e-camnitzer-2.htm.
Camnitzer, Luis. "Chronology." In *Luis Camnitzer: Retrospective Exhibition 1966–1990*, organized by Jane Farver, 52–53. Bronx, N.Y.: Lehman College Art Gallery, 1991.
Camnitzer, Luis. *New Art of Cuba*. Austin: University of Texas Press, 1994.
Camnitzer, Luis. "Wonderbread and Spanglish." In *Luis Camnitzer: Retrospective Exhibition 1966–1990*, organized by Jane Farver, 44–47, 64. Bronx, N.Y.: Lehman College Art Gallery, 1991.
Mosquera, Gerardo. "Politics and Ethnicity in the Work of Luis Camnitzer." In *Luis Camnitzer: Retrospective Exhibition 1966–1990*, organized by Jane Farver, 27–28. Bronx, N.Y.: Lehman College Art Gallery, 1991.
Ramírez, Mari Carmen. "Moral Imperatives: Politics as Art in Luis Camnitzer." In *Luis Camnitzer: Retrospective Exhibition 1966–1990*, organized by Jane Farver, 4–13. Bronx, N.Y.: Lehman College Art Gallery, 1991.
Riggs, Thomas, ed. *St. James Guide to Hispanic Artists: Profiles of Latino and Latina American Artists*. Detroit, Mich.: St. James Press, 2002.

ELIZABETH LIANG

CAMPAIGN FOR A JUST TRANSITION.

The Campaign for a Just Transition is a process by which labor unions and environmental and environmental-justice groups seek to work with industry to move "communities and workers from unsafe workplaces and environments to healthy, viable communities with a sustainable economy" (Just Transition Alliance). This campaign began gaining strength in the early 1990s, when labor groups and environmental-justice organizations began organizing to oppose the North American Free Trade Agreement (NAFTA), which lacked strong protections for labor and the environment. In the late 1990s, these groups gathered again to oppose President Bill Clinton's bid to fast-track new global economic agreements that would extend NAFTA's labor and environmental pitfalls to countries beyond the United States, Mexico, and Canada.

Background

Although global trade agreements became a catalyst for the Campaign for a Just Transition, leaders and members of the Oil, Chemical and Atomic Workers (OCAW), which later merged with the Paper, Allied-Industrial, Chemical and Energy Workers (PACE), had been dealing with environmentally hazardous substances in their workplaces since the 1950s. Workers in these industries had a heightened consciousness of the ecological effect of their work on human and environmental health and, as a result, had been active on a number of environmental fronts for decades. The concept of a "just transition," as it would later be dubbed, began emerging during the 1980s, when jobs were being lost because of the scaling back of nuclear industries and the banning of some highly toxic pesticides. Union members were aware that workers and their communities bear the primary economic brunt of job losses. They observed that a new federal Superfund law provided millions of dollars to clean up some of the contaminated sites on which they had formerly worked and noted that nothing was being provided for worker compensation or retraining.

The situation prompted one prominent OCAW leader, Anthony Mazzocchi, to quip, "They were going to treat dirt better than workers" (Moberg). Mazzocchi, credited with starting the debate about a "just transition," envisioned a government-established fund that would provide full wages and benefits plus tuition costs, much like the World War II–era G.I. Bill. The fund would be used to facilitate worker transition to more environmentally friendly industries. The notion of a "just transition" was enthusiastically embraced by PACE, the American Federation of Labor-Congress of Industrial Organizations (AFL-CIO), and environmental-justice groups such as the Southwest Network for Environmental and Economic Justice (SNEEJ), the Farm Worker Network for Economic and Environmental Justice (FNEEJ), and the Indigenous Environmental Network. While such a fund has not been successfully established, an OCAW proposal to generate the monies for the fund called for the federal government to collect corporate contributions through a surcharge. This surcharge would be on substances that are either to be banned or phased out because of their harmful effects on the environment.

By drawing connections between labor and environmental issues, alliances that have formed around interconnected labor and environmental problems have helped to build connections between unions and the environmental-justice movement that seek to redress the harms done to minority and low-income communities, where polluting industries are frequently sited. As an organizing concept, a "just transition" confronts corporations that pit workers against environmentalists by threatening to cut jobs, downsize, shut down, or locate to another country if they are forced to be environmentally responsible.

Throughout the 1980s, corporate union-busting, automation, lockouts, concession demands, and job flight overseas were common responses to pressures from environmental activists and legislation aimed at enforcing environmental regulations, but a series of disastrous refinery and chemical-plant explosions in the United States and the devastating Union Carbide gas release in Bhopal, India, in the early 1980s urged labor leaders and environmentalists to find common ground on which to fight for workplace safety and environmental responsibility. The chemical plant disasters had been caused by corporate downsizing, which resulted in more reliance on poorly trained nonunion subcontractors for maintenance work. If a company was willing to use less-skilled labor or move out of the United States to cut costs and escape environmental regulation and union demands for more safety, argued OCAW organizing director Richard Leonard, "then it's probably just as inclined to treat other elements in society in the same fashion—neighbors, taxpayers, consumers, and regulators acting on behalf of society" (Moberg). Such corporate irresponsibility led to greater interest in the goals and aims of a "just transition."

The Alliance

Consequently, the concept of a "just transition" has not been confined to the workplace. Supported by the U.S. union-backed Public Health Institute, the Just Transition Alliance (JTA) has been a key player in promoting a "just transition" as a way to embrace the whole community when it suffers from both economic losses and environmental degradation. Since 1996, the JTA has brokered alliances between unions, community groups, and environmental-justice groups seeking to protect human and environmental health by eliminating, substituting, or reducing the chemicals used in production; championing safer methods of production; and improving the safety systems inside and outside production facilities. The Alliance has also been concerned with preserving and expanding job opportunities, income, and the tax base in communities where toxic-related industries are being phased out or eliminated. The JTA also addresses the health and safety of people living in the communities surrounding polluting industries who may have been exposed to the toxins produced by those industries. In addition, the Alliance participates in national and international policy processes that advocate for labor-friendly climate-change policies, support legislation to hold the U.S. military responsible for environmental hazards, and seek to insert Just Transition language into documents produced at gatherings such as the United Nations World Conference Against Racism and the Earth Justice Summit.

The JTA is currently at work in several U.S. communities with large Latina and Latino populations. For example, in Rillito, Arizona, a predominantly African American and Latina and Latino community, 107 workers at Arizona Portland Cement—who are represented by PACE, and Tucsonians for a Clean Environment, a SNEEJ affiliate—have come together to fight the state of Arizona's worst air pollution (releases of nickel and cobalt into the air, which is causing lung cancer, asthma, and other health complaints among workers and community members). As result, workers have won a new union contract and focused attention on the contaminants being released from the plant into the surrounding communities.

The JTA has also been at work in San Antonio, Texas, where Kelly Air Force Base was closed in 2001. Because of the closure, sixteen thousand workers lost their jobs. The surrounding community (primarily Latina and Latino and working class) suffered both economically and environmentally because of toxins that had been dumped on the base and that had contaminated the local water supply. Many in the community argued that the U.S. Department of Defense was shirking its responsibility to clean up the site. Local Just Transition organizers helped make sure that all interested community stakeholders were included in discussions on how the community might move from one type of economy to another and addressed its claims about the Department of Defense. In Los Angeles, the JTA brought together PACE members who worked at the Chevron/Texaco refinery in El Segundo, California, and low-income Latina and Latino members of the community who were associated with La Causa and were concerned about toxic air and water emissions. With the help of JTA organizers, a pollution-prevention strategy was designed.

Both labor unions and environmental-justice activists see the enormous potential of alliances working to address interrelated labor and environmental problems. However, labor and environmental activists do not always agree on every issue. Joint efforts between labor unions, environmental-justice organizations, environmental regulators, and corporate managers, such as those facilitated by the JTA, help stakeholders see their shared interests and think collectively about ideas for joint action.

See also Environmental Justice; Environmental Justice and Latinas; Environmental Justice Networks; Environmental Protection Agency; Environmental Racism; Farm Worker Network for Economic and Environmental Justice; Southwest Network for Environmental and Economic Justice; *and* Tucsonians for a Clean Environment.

BIBLIOGRAPHY
Just Transition Alliance. www.jtalliance.org
Moberg, David. "Greens and Labor: It's a Coalition That Gives Corporate Polluter Fits." *Sierra*, January/February 1999. www. sierraclub.org/sierra/199901/unions.asp
Public Health and Labor Institutes. *Just Transition Movement: For Jobs and the Environment*. May 1998, Draft 7.1. An educational resource/manual for teachers produced for Title IV workshop by OCAW Local 8-149.

JONI ADAMSON

CANANEA MINERS' STRIKE. The history of Cananea remains tied to its role in a changing world economy. Although indigenous peoples such as the Pima and the Tohono O'odham inhabited the area, Cananea first appeared in Spanish records in the 1760s when Jesuit missionaries operated mines in the area. Throughout the nineteenth century, Sonoran miners, known as *gambusinos*, engaged in sporadic mining in the area. By the 1860s, Sonoran strongman Ignacio Pesqueira had acquired control of the mines and initiated limited operations.

After many failed attempts, the railroad was at last brought to Sonora in 1882, an event that set the stage for a dramatic expansion in mining. The railroad connected the northern border city of Nogales with the port city of Guaymas. Eventually, an additional line connected Cananea to the border communities of Naco and Nogales, ensuring the development of the region. With transportation secured, large-scale mining became possible, and foreign investors flocked to Sonora. By 1896, William C. Greene had acquired the mines in the district and launched the Cananea Copper Company. Cananea's population skyrocketed as the town attracted Mexicans and foreigners alike, including people from Asia, Europe, the Middle East, and the United States. In 1891, the town had fewer than one hundred inhabitants. By the early 1900s, its population numbered over twenty thousand surpassing Guaymas and rivaling Hermosillo, the state capital. Cananea's city officials complained about their inability to coalesce the "constant wave of humanity from all over the world that flocks to this place."

With Greene at the helm, American interests monopolized all major economic activity in Cananea. With the acquiescence of Sonoran authorities, company officials kept tight control of activity in the mining town. Besides the mines, Greene owned surrounding haciendas, controlled cattle and agricultural production and lumber supplies, and dominated most businesses in the town. Several thousand U.S. miners, engineers, and speculators left their stamp on the culture of the town. Besides the usual Mexican festivities, U.S. citizens in Cananea held public celebrations for the Fourth of July, Thanksgiving, and other holidays. Mexicans of all social classes, including miners, merchants, and landowners, resented Greene's dominant position and contemptuously referred to the American company as the "Octopus of Cananea." Other critics referred to the foreign mining enclaves as "Yanquilandia."

United States operators of the mine instituted a policy of social and racial labor segmentation. Foreigners held the skilled positions, receiving five dollars a day. Mexicans performed the majority of labor-intensive jobs, including the most dangerous tasks, and received substantially less pay than did the foreigners, the equivalent of three pesos a day. Accidents, including dismemberments and fatalities, were common. For protection, Mexicans erected shrines with images of the Virgin of Guadalupe and burned ceremonial candles throughout the mine. Those who survived such hazardous work were forced to contend with respiratory illnesses for the remainder of their lives.

Housing arrangements also reflected a policy of racial and social segmentation. The United States selected the area of La Mesa, a flat plain separated from the Mexican community by a series of ravines and gulches, as their private enclave. At La Mesa, the foreigners erected an impressive assortment of buildings, including businesses, hotels, municipal offices, and personal residences. Mexicans lived in a series of hillside neighborhoods where most homes were constructed of cheap and often discarded lumber and other building materials. Besides the

CANANEA MINERS' STRIKE. Interior of El Ronquillo Mechanical Workshop, c. 1904. (Cananea Information, Mexico)

crowded and unsanitary conditions, miners and their families faced bitter cold during the winter and the constant smoke from the mine smelters that blew over the community.

The operation of the mine quickly took a toll on the countryside, fundamentally altering the local environment. The mines' constant need for lumber led to the deforestation of the surrounding region. The chemicals used in the processing of the ores contaminated most water sources in the area, affecting people throughout the state.

Faced with these conditions, workers and their families began to organize. Their initial efforts reveal the existence of the trans border relations between Cananea's laborers and mining communities in neighboring Arizona. Activists from the Partido Liberal Mexicano (Mexican Liberal Party), an anarchist party led by the Flores Magon brothers, and members of the U.S. Western Federation of Miners helped organize Cananea's workers. By the spring of 1906, Mexican workers were preparing to confront the U.S. company, demanding 5.00 pesos a day for an eight-hour shift and an end to the unequal treatment between foreigners and Mexicans. One flyer distributed at the mine proclaimed that at Cananea, "Yankees, Blacks and Chinese are valued more than Mexicans." The company refused the workers' demands and instead, with the support of the Mexican government, used both local troops and 275 Arizona rangers, who crossed the border illegally, to crush the strike, resulting in several deaths and multiple arrests. The strike at Cananea became a symbol of the growing dissatisfaction with the government of Mexican president Porfirio Díaz as well as the economic and cultural presence of the United States in Mexico.

The U.S.–owned Anaconda Company acquired the mine in 1917 to become the Compañia Minera de Cananea. Under its direction, Cananea became one of the largest copper mines in the world. As the mine expanded, workers' demands and environmental concerns persisted through much of the twentieth century. In 1971, the Mexican government finalized the nationalization of foreign holdings and acquired a controlling interest in the mine. By 1990, it had shifted its strategy, adopting neo liberal economic policies and privatizing state-owned enterprises. Cananea was sold to Grupo Mexico, a private company. Although the new company managed to increase production, it also dramatically reduced the labor force, leading to a series of labor disputes that eventually culminated in a strike in November 1998. As in 1906, the 1998 strike garnered international support, especially from miners across the border in Arizona. During the course of the strike, Cananea became a symbol of the absence of worker and environmental protections and the disparities between Mexico and the United States in the North American Free Trade Agreement.

See also **Labor and Labor Strikes.**

BIBLIOGRAPHY

Cuevas Arámburu, Mario, comp. *Sonora: Textos de su historia.* Hermosillo, Mexico: Instituto de Investigaciónes Mora, 1989.

Ruiz, Ramón Eduardo. *The People of Sonora and Yankee Capitalists.* Tucson: University of Arizona Press, 1988.

Sariego Rodríguez, Juan Luis. *Enclaves y minerales en el norte de México: Historia social de los mineros de Cananea y Nueva Rosita, 1900–1970.* Mexico City: Centro de Investigaciones y Estudios Superiores en Antropología Social, Ediciones de la Casa Chata, 1988.

Tinker Salas, Miguel. *In the Shadow of the Eagles: Sonora and the Transformation of the Border during the Porfiriato.* Berkeley: University of California Press, 1997.

Valencia Ortega, Ismael. *Cananea.* Hermosillo, Mexico: INAH-SEP, 1984.

MIGUEL TINKER SALAS

CANNERY WORKERS. Since the 1940s, the sorting, grading, washing, peeling, trimming, coring, slicing, cooking, and packing of canned and frozen food has been handled primarily by Mexican American women. Chicanas are especially prevalent in the heart of cannery production, California, where the number of cannery workers peaked around 1960 before tapering off as a result of automation and runaway capital. Cannery work is poorly paid and tiresome, involving long hours, great noise, and injurious hazards. But in periodic struggles, Latina and Latino cannery operatives have transformed pain, poverty, and vulnerability into solidarity and power.

Early Twentieth Century

By the twentieth century, food processing was already a full-fledged industry, as population growth and mass advertising created a national market for fruits, vegetables, and meat. Processors packed a wide variety of foodstuffs, including apricots, blueberries, peaches, corn, beans, pickles, olives, walnuts, tuna, clams, and sardines. During World War I, disruption of foreign product lines like Italian tomato paste and the need to feed faraway troops prompted building of new canneries in urban areas near railway lines. Conveyor belts, filling machines, and automatic labeling introduced a new speed of production. Piece-rate pay in some job classifications gave way to hourly wages.

Expansion of production bred concentration of capital. Many individually owned canning sheds were absorbed into centralized concerns typified by corporate organization, larger workforces, and a more elaborate division of labor. Small canneries survived too, but by 1917, the California Packing Corporation (Cal Pak) with its Del Monte label controlled 50 percent of the canned goods market.

Eager to obtain the cheapest labor available, canneries employed successive waves of immigrants, including Chinese, Italians, Portuguese, Russian Jews, Armenians, Japanese, and Filipinos. Female and child labor was the rule. New immigrants were young, productive, and easily exploited, increasing profit margins. Mexican workers were never a majority of the cannery workforce before 1939, but they roamed as far north as Alaska, where nearly 1,500 worked in 1917. In Los Angeles, 23.5 percent of the cannery labor force was Mexican by 1928.

Xenophobia in the 1920s, combined with the Depression of the 1930s, sharply reduced opportunities for Latina and Latino cannery workers. A revival came about with the shortage of domestic labor during World War II. Chicanos and Chicanas were hired in large numbers, and by the mid-1940s California canneries had established a structure that would endure: women, overwhelmingly Mexican Americans, occupied the low-level, seasonal jobs, while men, almost wholly Anglos, occupied the permanent, skilled, supervisory positions (with white floorladies in between). Chicanos were paid less than Anglos; women less than men; Chicanas least of all.

Outside of the Southwest, cannery workers had different profiles. In Wisconsin, the typical pea or cherry cannery worker was a male Latino migrant laborer, either single or with family left temporarily behind in Mexico or British Honduras. In Alaska and Hawaii, salmon and pineapple canneries drew primarily on Native American and Asian labor, and in Delaware cannery labor was migratory and overwhelmingly African American. From the 1940s on, however, most national cannery output was produced by people of Mexican birth or descent who were long resident in California communities.

Between 1930 and 1950, the typical Mexican cannery worker was a single young daughter living at home and contributing to the household income. Sometimes whole extended families worked in a plant together. By the late twentieth century, wives and single mothers came to predominate, juggling household tasks and work.

Organized Labor

Labor organizing among vegetable, fruit, and fish cannery workers has had three basic aims: winning company recognition of unions; obtaining better pay, benefits, and conditions; and seeking rank-and-file union control. In this quest, cannery workers have received support from anticapitalist movements of the left and have been opposed by companies and the state.

The first great strike of California cannery workers came in 1917, led by the Toilers of the World, a variant of the Industrial Workers of the World. Suppressed, it did not achieve union representation. Equally unsuccessful—disbanded with fire hoses and vigilante clubs—was the 1931 San José strike mobilized by the Cannery and Agricultural Workers Industrial Union (CAWIU), led by Communist Party members.

Nonetheless, the rising labor movement of the 1930s persuaded California's food-processing industry of unionism's inevitability. Canners started to recognize tame conservative union locals of the American Federation of Labor (AFL) and International Brotherhood of Teamsters

(IBT). Cannery workers themselves preferred the militant United Cannery, Agricultural, Packing, and Allied Workers of America (UCAPAWA), affiliated with the Congress of Industrial Organizations (CIO). UCAPAWA called the AFL locals bogus "company unions," a view partly sustained by a National Labor Review Board (NLRB) ruling in 1940.

UCAPAWA was interracial, with many Chicana and Chicano shop stewards and executive board members, a number of Communist leaders, and 124,000 members by 1938. In 1944, the union was renamed the Food, Tobacco, Agricultural, and Allied Workers Union of America (FTA) to better reflect its total composition. When the AFL handed over its cannery locals to the IBT in 1945, an FTA-IBT fight to the death broke out. Northern California cannery workers voted for the left-wing FTA in 1945, but the NLRB, pressured by business, ordered a new election. The Teamsters, using bullying and red-baiting, aided by employers and Catholic clerics, won the next election by a slight margin in 1946. When the NLRB upheld the election results in 1949, the FTA disbanded its cannery locals, and the CIO expelled the FTA in the anticommunist purge of 1949–1950. California's cannery unions were under Teamster jurisdiction ever after.

In 1969, San José cannery workers—angered by Anglo local officials' excessive salaries, coziness with employers, cronyism, and Mafia corruption—formed the Mexican American Workers Educational Committee. Soon a statewide network formed: the Comité de Trabajadores de Canería, or Cannery Workers Committee (CWC). Infused with Chicano nationalism, inspired by the United Farm Workers (UFW) of César Chávez, the CWC defended rank-and-file cannery worker interests in the plants and Teamsters union. The core CWC initiators were Chicano men, primarily year-round engineers.

The CWC brought claims of gender and racial discrimination against canners before the Equal Employment Opportunity Commission (EEOC), saw that contracts were printed in Spanish, pushed grievance processes, established service centers for workers, and elected reformers to midlevel union posts. When the UFW was threatened by a thuggish raid from the IBT in 1973, cannery workers wore "Teamsters for Chávez" buttons, picketed for the grape boycott, and hoped for UFW takeover of cannery locals. Many were bitterly disappointed by a 1977 truce that included a UFW promise not to organize canneries, even though ethnic-familial bonds suggested a potential alliance between Mexican farmworkers and Mexican food processing workers against growers and processors (a strategy explored earlier by UCAPAWA).

From the 1980s onward, cannery workers played a significant part in the nationwide union reform caucus Teamsters for a Democratic Union, but management pushed hard in the 1980s and 1990s for concessions and weaker contracts. In 1985 to 1987, one thousand Watsonville Canning and Shaw frozen food workers, three-fourths of them women, with socialist and radical backing, carried out an eighteen-month strike and four-day wildcat in rejection of a weak contract. Without a single defector crossing the picket lines, the Watsonville strikers retained their union and benefits while defying a collaborationist leadership. Over the next decade, however, five of the eight canneries that had made Watsonville "The Frozen Food Capital of the World" relocated, most to Mexico, seeking cheaper labor.

Other worker campaigns have met with more success. Beginning in 1999, 750 mostly Latina workers with an average salary of $14,000 a year went on strike for twenty-five months against Basic Vegetable Products of King City, California, in opposition to management's demand for a wage freeze and the downgrading of full-time jobs to part-time status. Although the company hired permanent replacement workers in a bid to break the union, a Teamsters-organized boycott of Basic's institutional purchasers reduced sales so severely that its owners sold the company to a ConAgra subsidiary, Gilroy Foods. The new company recognized IBT Local 890 as the plant's bargaining unit and, in 2001, granted a contract providing an 8 percent wage increase over two years, seniority rights, and health and pension benefits.

See also Labor and Labor Strikes.

BIBLIOGRAPHY

Bardacke, Frank. "Watsonville: A Mexican Community on Strike." In *Reshaping the U.S. Left: Popular Struggles in the 1980s*, edited by Mike Davis and Michael Sprinker. New York: Verso, 1987.

Cecil, Kathy, and Kathleen Connell, eds. *Groundswell: Farmers, Farmworkers, Cannery Workers, Cooperativa Members and Native Americans Speak Out*. San Francisco: Center for Rural Studies, 1979.

Guerrero, Julio Cesar. "Latino Activism Could Change the Teamsters." *Labor Notes*, no. 218 (May 1997): 3.

Ruiz, Vicki L. *Cannery Women, Cannery Lives: Mexican Women, Unionization, and the California Food Processing Industry, 1930–1950*. Albuquerque: University of New Mexico, 1987.

Zavella, Patricia. *Women's Work and Chicano Families: Cannery Workers of the Santa Clara Valley*. Ithaca, N.Y.: Cornell University Press, 1987.

CHRISTOPHER PHELPS

CANTINFLAS (1911–1993), comic actor. In 1956, American movie audiences were introduced to Mario Moreno in Michael Anderson's Hollywood extravaganza, *Around the World in 80 Days*. But aside from Mexican immigrants, U.S.–born Chicanas and Chicanos, and other Latin Americans familiar with popular culture from south of the border, few were aware that Moreno, who played Passepartout, the valet sidekick to David Niven's Phileas Fogg, was the international celebrity known as

CANTINFLAS. (John Dominis/Time Life Pictures/Getty Images)

Cantinflas. The irony of Cantinflas's meager Hollywood roles, including that of Passepartout, who was nothing more than a stereotypical Mexican, is that they ran counter to what many critics saw as the "subversive" nature of his previous work in Mexican cinema while also constituting the unceremonious apex of a successful career that took him from poverty to wealth. Thus, Cantinflas's significance to U.S. Latina and Latino comedy is not predicated on his American appearances but on the transnational influence of his earlier Mexican films, which endeared him to audiences familiar with what his original *pelado* (peasant) character signified—the comedic ingenuity of a Latin American underclass struggling with both racial and class subordination and what Mexican scholars refer to as "the chaos of modernity."

Early Career

Born Mario Alonso Moreno Reyes on August 12, 1911, Cantinflas was raised with his twelve siblings in a poor neighborhood in Mexico City. The son of a mailman, he grew up working at a variety of menial jobs, including

stints as a bullfighter and a boxer, before becoming a member of a *carpa*, a traveling tent-theater show that featured circus acts and slapstick humor. As the legend goes, Moreno's first appearance as a master of ceremonies so wracked him with stage fright that he soiled his pants in front of a live audience. In order to recover his wits and dignity before the crowd, which, typical of such a venue, consisted primarily of Mexico City's underclass of peasants and the working poor, he began spouting a rapid-fire stream of gibberish, mixing nonsense and obscenities, which became his primary shtick. When the audience heckled him with accusations that he had been drinking (*inflear*, meaning "to fill up") in the local cantina, his stage name of Cantinflas was born.

Dressed in patched trousers that sagged below his waist, a dirty long-sleeved undershirt, a torn scarf for his neck, a hat two sizes too small, and sporting a sparse yet shaggy mustache, Cantinflas personified the pelado, a term that literally means "hairless" but that came to signify the penniless urban vagabond of rural origin. Coming on the heels of the Mexican Revolution, the pelado figure spoke volumes about Mexico's drive towards industrialization and modernity and the dislocating effects both had on rural mestizo (mixed-blood) peasants. Being displaced from their lands and desperate to escape the poverty of their provincial villages, destitute rural peasants discovered that their only salvation was the obligatory migration to the nation's capital. Miles outside of the Federal District to the north were the city's most desolate barrios, consisting of underdeveloped brick and stucco dwellings that covered steep, rocky hillsides. Here, rural peasants have historically been kept at bay by civic policies intended to prevent saturation of the city's inner quarters. It is from within the rural underclass of this suburban environment that the pelado type represented by Cantinflas actually emerged. But whereas the pelado actually represented a negotiation between rural peasantry and the disorienting effects of the modernizing big city, Mexican elites preferred to focus on the uncouth and "primitive" aspects of the figure, perceiving it as threatening and driven by primal and carnal instincts. But this was not to be the case with Cantinflas, who, as the Mexican cultural critic Carlos Monsiváis suggested, was co-opted by the Mexican culture industry as a *peladito*; with the diminutive "-ito" diluting the figure's connotations of social chaos.

By the age of twenty-six, Cantinflas was already working as a supporting actor in Mexican features such as *No te engañes, corazón* (Don't deceive yourself, my heart, 1936) and ¡*Así es mi tierra!* (That's how my land is! 1937) while holding down a gig in Mexico City's Follies Bergéres theater. By appearing in a succession of commercials for American products made in Mexico, Moreno accrued enough capital to establish his own production company, Posa Films, whose primary product was motion pictures featuring himself. Hence, in 1939 he embarked on a series of short films featuring Cantinflas in a variety of situations that reflected his earlier professions (*Cantinflas the Bullfighter*, *Cantinflas the Boxer*, *Cantinflas the Cabbie*, and so on). More significantly, his screen persona downplayed the obscenities that were familiar to his carpa audiences but that would have been unacceptable to the middle-class spectators of Mexican cinema and sharpened the social and political content of what scholars have referred to as his "verbal pyrotechnics."

Political Satirist

As suggested by Monsiváis, the politicized aspects of Cantinflas's brand of comedy that were too destabilizing for carpa audiences—and that could possibly have brought him trouble from local authorities—became more acceptable for film spectators. Specifically, by the middle 1930s he tailored his carpa act of nonsensical speech into a parody of the demagogic style of public speaking practiced by politicians and union leaders during the leftist administration of Lázaro Cárdenas. Thus, the Cárdenas government's Marxist inclination to proselytize the Mexican masses through public speeches that went on forever but said nothing became grist for Cantinflas's brand of satire. The irony was that his act endeared him to both the lower class, who wearied of government promises of a social egalitarianism that never transpired, and the upper class, who detested the government's leftist designs to equally distribute Mexico's abundant resources. Although his popularity amongst bourgeois intellectuals fluctuated, alternating between amusement at his subversion and condescension toward his working-class humor, Cantinflas eventually became firmly established as a symbol of national identity. Thus, by the golden age of Mexican cinema in the 1940s, the pelado, as represented by Mario Moreno's Cantinflas, had been instituted and critically received as the ideal representation of the urban Mexican of rural origins, who justifiably ridicules and usurps the pettiness of the bourgeoisie and authorities while comically navigating the various spheres and castes of Mexican society.

Legacy

In *Cantinflas and the Chaos of Mexican Modernity*, the most authoritative biography on Mario Moreno to date, the author Jeffrey Pilcher outlines three phases of the comedian's career: (1) his formative years leading up to the 1940s, during which his subversive nature was most intact; (2) the peak of his popularity from the mid-1940s to the mid-1950s, in which he became co-opted and incorporated into Mexico's ruling elite; and finally (3) from the 1950s onward, during which he essentially became a spokesman for Mexico's industrialization program and was firmly established as part of the nation's authoritarian

regime. For Chicanas and Chicanos and other U.S. Latinas and Latinos, the Cantinflas that is best remembered and remains pervasive is the one of the first phase, in films such as *Ahí está el detalle* (That's the detail, 1940) and *El gendarme desconocido* (The undercover cop, 1941), whose subversion of class stratification and authority was an inspiration to Mexican immigrants and working-class Mexican Americans. Whether expressed in the immigrant adapting to American hegemony and sociocultural displacement, or in the Chicana and Chicano negotiating cultural hybridity with meager resources in a materialistic society, the legacy of Cantinflas remains intact as a model for negotiating migration, modernity, and class subordination, albeit in a comedic manner.

See also Actors and Actresses; Comedy and Humor; *and* Film.

BIBLIOGRAPHY

Hershfield, Joanne, and David R. Maciel, eds. *Mexico's Cinema: A Century of Film and Filmmakers*. Wilmington, Del.: Scholarly Resources, 1999.

Monsiváis, Carlos. *Mexican Postcards*. Translated by John Kraniauskas. London, New York: Verso, 1997.

Mora, Carl J. *Mexican Cinema: Reflections of a Society, 1896–1988*. Revised Edition. Berkeley: University of California Press, 1989.

Paranaguá, Antonio Paulo, ed. *Mexican Cinema*. London: British Film Institute, 1995.

Pilcher, Jeffrey M. *Cantinflas and the Chaos of Mexican Modernity*. Wilmington, Del.: Scholarly Resources, 2001.

Stavans, Ilan. *The Riddle of Cantinflas: Essays on Hispanic Popular Culture*. Albuquerque: University of New Mexico Press, 1998.

SONNY RICHARD E. ESPINOZA

CANTÚ, NORMA V. (b. 1954), lawyer and educator. Norma V. Cantú is a third-generation Mexican American who was born in 1954 and raised in Brownsville, Texas. The oldest of six children, she was an academically outstanding student and avid reader. Growing up in a segregated community, Cantú saw signs in restaurants that said "No Mexicans or Dogs Allowed," and she remembered her parents' vivid description of riots in Lubbock, Texas, that took place when black and Latino soldiers tried to sit in the whites-only section of a movie theater. Despite these palpable reminders of everyday inequality, Cantú pursued her educational aspirations. Out of 2,000 students in her high school class, she was among only 750 who graduated. She entered an even more select group when at age nineteen she earned her bachelor's degree summa cum laude from the University of Texas–Pan American. Returning to the classroom, she taught high school English before obtaining her law degree from Harvard at the age of twenty-two.

After her graduation from law school, Cantú returned to Texas to become regional counsel and education director

NORMA V. CANTÚ. (Courtesy of Norma V. Cantú)

for the Mexican American Legal Defense and Educational Fund (MALDEF), a post she held for fourteen years. During her tenure there she became something of an institution, renowned for her skills as a litigator and widely regarded as an effective and worthy adversary. Cantú liked to joke that "some of my best friends are people I've sued: my high school principal, college president"—not to mention her home state of Texas. At MALDEF, Cantú litigated some of the leading cases in the quest for equal educational opportunity, challenging school districts to desegregate their student bodies, provide high-quality bilingual education programs to children with limited English proficiency, and offer equivalent resources to students regardless of race, ethnicity, or class. One of her landmark victories came in *Edgewood v. Kirby*, when she successfully challenged gross disparities in the funding of public schools in Texas during the 1980s.

Cantú left MALDEF to become assistant secretary of education for civil rights from 1993 to 2001 during the Clinton administration. A gifted litigator, Cantú nevertheless understood the unique obligations of her role as an administrator. She was committed to resolving as many disputes as possible by mutual agreement rather than resorting to adversarial proceedings. To that end her office disposed of about one-third of its caseload through voluntary corrective action. The results were impressive. During her first two years on the job, she resolved 20 percent more complaints than were resolved in the year preceding her tenure. Defying the view that government bureaucrats cannot be efficient, she increased the annual rate of resolution another 20 percent by the end of her term in Washington, D.C. Cantú clearly understood that doing justice means remedies are prompt as well as fair.

Although Cantú sought amicable resolutions whenever possible, she was not averse to taking some political heat to uphold principles of nondiscrimination. She faced intense criticism from conservatives for her stances on affirmative action, bilingual education, and gender equity in athletics. For instance, in 1996 a federal court of appeals declared the admissions program at the University of Texas Law School unconstitutional because it relied on racial preferences. The following year Cantú wrote a letter to state officials reminding them that the federal government could cut off aid to higher education if the state failed to use affirmative action when necessary to remedy the vestiges of past discrimination. Although consistent with the court's ruling that preferential treatment could be used only to rectify intentional wrongdoing, Cantú's letter prompted Senator Phil Gramm of Texas to threaten to block funding to the Department of Education. Although Cantú had to mollify Gramm, she emerged bloodied but unbowed. Afterward she continued to introduce herself cheerfully as "a product of affirmative action and proud of it."

When partisan critics alleged that Cantú had used her office to promote bilingual programs rather than intensive English instruction, a General Accounting Office (GAO) report concluded that the charges were unfounded. After surveying 245 school districts that entered into compliance agreements with the Office for Civil Rights, the GAO found that 77 percent did not feel pressured to adopt a particular instructional approach. In a letter that accompanied the report, Cantú said her staff sought to "work cooperatively with school districts to ensure that appropriate services are provided to English-language learners" and was "gratified" by the results of the GAO investigation. Despite the intense conflicts she encountered, Cantú kept her overall mission and philosophy uppermost in her mind. She worked tirelessly to ensure that remedies are "educationally sound, do no harm to the improvement of education, and make civil rights law a reality, not just a promise."

After completing her service with the Clinton administration, Cantú returned to her home state. She holds a joint appointment in law and education at the University of Texas at Austin. She is sharing her wealth of experience and legacy of dedicated advocacy with a new generation of students. Her courses and seminars on education law and the Americans with Disabilities Act offer a new way for her to advance both her faith in education and her commitment to equality.

See also Mexican American Legal Defeuse and Education Fund.

BIBLIOGRAPHY
Celis, Willam. "An Impatient Advocate Stirs Up the Education Department's Civil Rights Office." *New York Times*, August 3, 1994, p. B6, col. 1.

Healy, Patrick. "A Lightning Rod on Civil Rights." *Chronicle of Higher Education* 46, no. 4 (September 17, 1999): A42.

Henry, Tamara. "Civil Rights Crusader Begins New Mission." *USA Today*, June 17, 1993, p. 4D.

Jaschik, Scott. "Clinton Chooses Hispanic Activist from Texas to Head Education Department's Office for Civil Rights." *Chronicle of Higher Education* 39, no. 28 (March 17, 1993): A27.

Jaschik, Scott. "A New Philosophy and New Style at the Office for Civil Rights." *Chronicle of Higher Education* 39, no. 45 (July 14, 1993): A19.

"Panel Discussion: Contemporary Challenges in Race Relations." *New York Law School Law Review* 43 (1999): 129.

RACHEL F. MORAN

CAPETILLO, LUISA

CAPETILLO, LUISA (1879–1922), free thinker, feminist, anarchist, labor organizer, and novelist. Luisa Capetillo was born in Arecibo, Puerto Rico, on October 28, 1879. Her mother, Luisa Margarita Perone, was a French immigrant who came to Puerto Rico to become a governess for the children of a prominent, local family in Arecibo. Instead, she was employed as a domestic. Luisa's father, Luis Capetillo Echevarria, arrived from Spain with hopes of making his fortune in Puerto Rico. Instead, he was hired as a worker in various trades.

Luisa Capetillo's parents were of like minds in their philosophical and political ideology. Both came to Puerto Rico imbued with post–French Revolution ideas about the rights of citizens and workers. They lived together with their only child but never wed. They educated their daughter at home and provided a very liberal education for her. Capetillo was encouraged to keep an open mind and to debate contradicting ideas of the day. Capetillo embraced the anarchist philosophy that emerged from Arecibo and other neighboring tobacco towns. She was a baptized Catholic but did not believe in the rigid dogmas and rituals of the Catholic Church. However, she considered herself a good Christian who believed in justice and equality.

At age nineteen, Capetillo met and fell in love with Manuel Ledesma, who was from a prominent family in her hometown of Arecibo. In 1898, Capetillo and Ledesma had their first child, Manuela. Two years later, they had a son, Gregorio, but during the following year their relationship ended. Now a single mother, Capetillo went to work in the fledgling textile industry while her mother took care of the children. She became a reader in a local tobacco factory. Traditionally, a reader (*lector*) sat or stood at a podium on the factory floor and read aloud to the workers stemming leaves and rolling cigars. Often, passages were repeated so the workers could commit them to memory. In the afternoon, discussion and debate about the passages ensued without interruption of work. Workers listened to the latest news on labor strife and global anticolonial rebellion as well as to works by Zola, LeBon, Darwin, Engels, and Bakunin. Workers paid for the reader from their daily wages and selected the passages to be read. While working in this factory, Capetillo was exposed to La Federacion de Torcedores de Tabaco (Federation of Tobacco Rollers), which was affiliated with La Federacion Libre de Trabajadores (Free Federation of Labor, FLT). The first union in Puerto Rico, La Federacion Regional de Trabajadores (Regional Federation of Workers), had been formed in 1898 during the occupation by the United States. The FLT subsequently affiliated with the American Federation of Labor (AFL).

Capetillo's union involvement began in 1901 during a farmworkers' strike led by the FLT. An extraordinary labor leader, she raised the consciousness of the workers through her activities and challenges to social conventions of the day. She was so talented in organizing that her hometown of Arecibo became the most unionized town in the country. In 1908, she urged the FLT to adopt a policy to fight for women's suffrage. She insisted that all women, not just the wealthy and literate, should have the right to vote. A proletarian feminist movement thus developed as an integral component of the organized labor movement, and the vanguard of the women's emancipation movement existed within the ranks of the FLT. This union waged legal battles in favor of universal suffrage and better working conditions and against economic exploitation of all workers.

In 1909, as part of the FLT's ambitious campaign "la cruzada del ideal" (crusade of the idea), Capetillo and other labor unionists traveled on foot or horseback throughout Puerto Rico to organize and train workers. The same year, Capetillo published a collection of essays, *Ensayos Libertarios*. She was the first Puerto Rican woman to commit her feminist ideas and theories on women's rights to print. Also in 1909, she wrote and published *Mi opinión sobre las libertades, derechos y deberes de la mujer* (My opinion about the Liberties, Rights, and Responsibilities of Women), the first feminist thesis written in Puerto Rico. Although an ardent feminist, Capetillo did not belong to any of the emerging feminist organizations of the day. Instead, she focused her energies on labor movements, believing that the union was the vehicle for poor women to obtain justice and equality.

Capetillo is known as the first woman to wear pants in public, which she did as a challenge to social conformity. Yet her most controversial notion was that of "free love," which many have mistaken for promiscuity. Capetillo's essays explain clearly that women should have the right to choose whom they wish to love freely without legal interference, including matrimony.

Most of Capetillo's work projected her views into the future by addressing and instructing subsequent generations about an alternative lifestyle. She took pride in having become an activist, journalist, and writer without receiving a formal education. In a play she wrote, *Influencias de las ideas modernas* (Influences of Modern Ideas), she speaks about her self-made education and career. Ivette Romero-Cesareo states that Capetillo presents to the reader a celebration of self-legitimization. As she established experience as authority, she proposed alternatives to the social norms of the day.

In 1912, Capetillo traveled to New York City, where she established ties with the Puerto Rican and Cuban tobacco workers. A year later, she moved to Tampa, where she again became a lectora in the tobacco factories. She then published the second edition of *Mi opinión*. Her next stop was Cuba, where she joined the sugar-cane workers strike that had been organized by La Federación Anarquista (The Anarchist Federation of Cuba). She circulated a manifesto that advocated violence, for which she was ordered to leave Cuba. However, before leaving Cuba she was arrested for wearing men's clothing (pants) in public. News of her arrest was printed in all of the Puerto Rican and Cuban newspapers.

She returned to Puerto Rico, where she organized and participated in various strikes including the Sugar Cane Strike of 1916. More than forty thousand workers from thirty-two municipalities participated in that strike. It resulted in an average increase in salaries of 13 percent. Between 1916 and 1918, a period of many hard-fought strikes in Puerto Rico, Capetillo traveled often to New York City. She established a boarding house and café on 22nd Street and 8th Avenue. She worked long hours but she loved to cook and took the opportunity to feed any who were hungry despite their inability to pay for the room or their food.

In 1919 Capetillo traveled to the Dominican Republic in support of striking workers. At this time, the Socialist Workers Party became the political arm of the FLT. She participated in a political campaign for the Socialist Workers Party, even though they opposed Capetillo's anarchist ideology.

In 1922 Capetillo was overcome by tuberculosis. She died on October 10, 1922. Capetillo remained lively and active in her causes until her death. It is difficult to measure her influence in labor movements and in women's suffrage, since her name is not among those in historic documents.

See also **Latina Labor and Community Organizers; Performing Arts and Theater;** *and* **Transgender.**

BIBLIOGRAPHY
Duany, Jorge. *The Puerto Rican Nation on the Move: Identities on the Island and in the United States*. Chapel Hill: University of North Carolina Press, 2002.
Ortiz, Altagracia, ed. "Introduction." *Puerto Rican Women and Work: Bridges in Transnational Labor*. Philadelphia: Temple University Press, 1996.
Romero-Cesareo, Ivette. "Whose Legacy?: Voicing Women's Rights from 1870s to 1930s." *Callaloo* 17, no. 3 (1994).
Valle Ferrer, Norma. "Feminism and Its Influence on Women's Organizations in Puerto Rico." In *The Puerto Rican Woman: Perspectives on Culture, History and Society*, 2nd ed., edited by Edna Acosta-Belén, 75–87. New York: Praeger, 1986.
Valle Ferrer, Norma. *The Story of Luisa Capetillo: A Pioneer Puerto Rican Feminist*. Volume 4 of *Nuestra Voz*. New York: Lang, 2004.

LINDA C. DELGADO

CARA EXHIBITION. The Chicano Art: Resistance and Affirmation Exhibition (1965–1985), better known as CARA, which means "face" in Spanish, toured the mainstream art world between 1990 and 1993. CARA was organized over a period of seven years by a national advisory board of Chicano and Chicana artists, art administrators, art historians, and other Chicano and Chicana activists and scholars in collaboration with the museum staff of the University of California, Los Angeles (UCLA) Wight Art Gallery. Its three-year national touring schedule included the art museums of cities as diverse as San Francisco, Fresno, Tucson, Denver, Albuquerque, Washington, D.C., New York, El Paso, and San Antonio. Not only were its size and scope monumental, but CARA was a tribute to the artistic production of El Movimiento, the Chicano and Chicana civil rights movement that arose in the sixties along with the Black Power Movement, the women's movement, and the American Indian Movement. With a bottom line of over a million dollars, the show was funded in part by the Rockefeller Foundation, the National Endowment for the Arts, the Andy Warhol Foundation for the Arts, the California Arts Council, and the Lila Wallace–Reader's Digest Fund. A Getty Grant made publication of the nearly four-hundred-page exhibition catalog possible.

CARA was the first major national exhibition of artwork that politically and aesthetically allied itself with the goals, visions, struggles, and ideologies of the Chicano/a movement. As articulated in its mission statement, the exhibition had an overtly political purpose to represent, educate, and empower *la plebe*, the working-class community of Mexican descent in the United States, which had never seen itself addressed or represented in a mainstream museum. But CARA had a second, equally political purpose. In its insistence on being recognized as an art exhibit rather than an ethnographic display of cultural "Others," CARA demonstrated that the Chicano and Chicana artists exhibited in the show, most trained in U.S. schools of art, constituted a distinct school of American art known as the Chicano and Chicana art movement.

Although it was not the first Chicano and Chicana art show to grace the halls of mainstream venues, it was certainly the largest, the one with the most extensive traveling schedule, the most expensive, and the most controversial of the twenty-odd exhibitions of specifically Chicano and Chicana art in California and the Southwest during the twenty years prior to and including CARA. CARA's emergence onto the mainstream art scene occurred in the heyday of the so-called diversity movement, a time when three other national shows of Hispanic-, Latino- and Latina-, and Mexican-themed art were already traversing the master's house. Organized at approximately the same time were exhibitions marking the five-hundred-year anniversary of Christopher Columbus's voyage to the New World, such as the National Museum of American History's stationery *Seeds of Change* and the Florida Museum of Natural History's traveling *First Encounters: Spanish Explorations in the Caribbean and the United States, 1492–1570.* Seen together, all of these shows created a "discovery" context wherein the art and cultural production of primarily Hispanic and Native American cultures were highlighted to promote the symbolic politics of diversity programming in mainstream museums. In 1987 *Hispanic Art in the United States* opened at the Museum of Fine Arts in Houston, and in 1988 *The Latin American Spirit* opened at the Bronx Museum. The mammoth exhibit *Mexico: Splendors of Thirty Centuries*, which opened at New York's Metropolitan Museum of Art in 1990, coincided with CARA.

The Exhibition

A retrospective of the first twenty years of the Chicano and Chicana art movement, CARA included 128 pieces of art— paintings, lithographs, drawings, sculptures, photographs, installations—and 54 mural images and represented the work of some 180 artists. Among them were such prominent artists as Carmen Lomas Garza, Rupert García, Carlos Almaraz, Malaquías Montoya, Frank Romero, Judith Baca, David Avalos, Patssi Valdéz, Gronk, César Martínez, Luis Jiménez, Ester Hernández, Yolanda López, Melesio Casas, and Santa Barraza. The exhibit also included such lesser known but likewise important artists as Delilah

LAS TRES MARIAS. Colored pencil on paper mounted on panel with upholstery backing and mirror, by Judy Baca, 1976. (Smithsonian American Art Museum, Washington, D.C./ Art Resource, NY)

Montoya, Harry Gamboa Jr., Juana Alicia, Cecilia Concepción Alvarez, Carlos Fresquez, Kathy Vargas, Richard Duardo, Celia Muñoz, Yreina Cervantes, Charles "Chaz" Bojórquez, Barbara Carrasco, and Rene Yañez. The art ranged from the figurative to the abstract, expressionism to realism, and minimalism to *rasquachismo* (a working-class style with vivid colors, vernacular forms, and recycled materials), but the content of the work had a coherent purpose: to raise the consciousness of the viewer about Chicano and Chicana life and culture.

The show was arranged into nine sections, beginning with La Causa, a small homage to the farmworker struggle spearheaded by César Chávez and Dolores Huerta that is said to have galvanized the Chicano/a Movement in 1965. Following were Cultural Icons, Civil Liberties, Urban Images, Regional Expressions, Reclaiming the Past, Feminist Visions, and three "casitas," or the freestanding structures of three California-based Chicano and Chicana art collectives, Los Four, the Royal Chicano Air Force, and ASCOAU (or Nausea). The section Mural Arts was displayed in rear-projected slides and accompanied by a closed-circuit video on some of the muralists whose work was displayed. Another closed-circuit video documented the selection process of the exhibition which, along with the content of the casitas, added a self-reflexive element to the exhibition, presenting the histories of these collectives and the aesthetic and ideological discussions involved in selecting artwork for CARA. The exhibit ended with Redefining American Art, featuring the work of eight Chicano and six Chicana artists whose work is in both private and public collections of American art.

Because historical memory constitutes such a critical part of Chicano and Chicana political consciousness, CARA was as much a retrospective of Chicano and Chicana art as a visual representation of Chicano and Chicana history. The exhibition proper was preceded by the Historical Timeline etched onto Plexiglas panels that placed the artwork within national, international, and regional events related to the emergence of the Chicano and Chicana community in the United States. Although Chicano and Chicana art per se did not officially come into being until the 1960s, the political and historical issues depicted by the Chicano and Chicana art movement went all the way back to the two conquests of Mexico that form a foundational identity for people of Mexican descent (be they Mexican or U.S. nationals).

The first was the Spanish conquest of the Aztec nation of Tenochtitlán in the sixteenth century when Spanish missionaries and conquistadores claimed a sovereign land and people in the name of the Catholic Church and the Spanish Crown. For all of its destructive and genocidal actions, Spanish colonialism resulted in an Indo-Hispanic *mestizaje*, or racial, religious, and cultural hybridity—a new racial construct upon which the Mexican character is based. In the early twentieth century, Mexican philosopher José Vasconcelos would term this fifth race born of European interbreeding with Indian, African, and Asian strains *"la raza cósmica,"* or the cosmic race. Borrowing from Vasconcelos, Chicano and Chicana activists used the idea of "la Raza" and "mestizaje" as core concepts of Chicano and Chicana political identity. Thus, the image of the mestizo head—a tripartite head showing a Caucasian profile, an indigenous profile, and the product of their mixture in between—was considered a cultural icon of the Chicano/a Movement and found multiple expressions in Chicano and Chicana art, as is seen in Amado Peña's 1974 silkscreen, *Mestizo*, which appeared in CARA's Cultural Icons room.

The Anglo-American imperial takeover of the Mexican north in the nineteenth century began with the battle of the Alamo in 1836, five years after the hordes of illegal Anglo immigrants that had invaded the Mexican province of Texas claimed it to be an independent republic. Ten years later, the United States–Mexico War (1846–1848) culminated in the binational Treaty of Guadalupe Hidalgo and the loss of over 50 percent of Mexico's northern territories to the United States, with the annexation not only of Texas, but also New Mexico, Arizona, Nevada, Colorado, Utah, California, and parts of Wyoming and Idaho. Overnight, the Mexican citizens of these northern provinces became second-class residents of occupied territory, and therein the roots to Chicano/Chicana or Mexican American identity are found. This loss of land would eventually lead to the loss of culture, language, and identity that characterizes the colonized condition.

Dispossessed descendants of that treaty, Mexicans Americans for over 150 years have been engaged in the dual process of adapting to and resisting the effects of Anglo-American colonization, and at the same time retaining and practicing their Mexican cultural traditions. It can be said then that two central themes have occupied the Chicano and Chicana aesthetic consciousness for over thirty years, themes which are underscored in the title of the CARA exhibition: resistance and affirmation. Thus, issues of conquest, colonization, land usurpation, racial and linguistic discrimination, political disenfranchisement, poverty, and labor exploitation were prominently displayed in the show, alongside images of community survival, political mobilization, and cultural pride through the representation of Mexican American beliefs, traditions, rituals, heroes, and family.

In addition, a panel of bilingual quotations discussed the main signifier of the exhibit, the word "Chicano." A popular definition during the 1970s was the one given by a Chicano journalist of the *Los Angeles Times*, Rubén Salazar, considered the first martyr of the Chicano/a Movement when the Los Angeles Police Department riot police killed him during the Chicano Moratorium of 1970. The Chicano Moratorium was an anti–Vietnam War demonstration in protest of the disproportionate number of Mexican American soldiers being killed in combat. Although it was a peaceful demonstration, sheriff's deputies attacked the protestors and dispersed the crowd with tear gas. Salazar, who covered the march for the *Los Angeles Times*, was killed by a tear-gas projectile. Salazar defined a Chicano as a "Mexican American with a non-Anglo image of himself" (Salazar, p. 7). One of the quotations on the panel was Chicana artist Carlota Cárdenas' assertion—dated 1977—that naming oneself Chicano or Chicana was a political act: "It was an act of cultural identification with one's Mexican-Spanish-Indio heritage. One who becomes

THE DEATH OF RUBEN SALAZAR. (© 1986, Frank Romero/Smithsonian American Art Museum, Washington, D.C./Art Resource, NY)

assimilated in the Anglo-American society would not use 'Chicano' as a label." Indeed the political consciousness of Chicanismo rejects outwardly imposed labels of identity and consciously claims the name Chicano or Chicana, a term that signifies identification with one's mestizo and mestiza race, awareness of the colonized history of Mexico, and resistance to the American melting pot ideologies like assimilation and English only. The rallying cry of "Chicano power" implies this multifaceted awareness and pride in the racial, cultural, and linguistic differences inherent in Chicano and Chicana identity.

Cultural Icons, the section with objects and symbols that represent the community's core beliefs and values, included the Virgin of Guadalupe, considered the brown-skinned spiritual empress and protector of the indigenous peoples of the Americas; Emiliano Zapata, the Mexican revolutionary champion of land rights struggles; Frida Kahlo, incarnate expression of the feminist motto, "the personal is political," and symbol of Mexican indigenous pride and socialist politics; the black eagle of the United Farm Workers; and the zoot suit, the 1940s uniform of pachuco and pachuca (inner-city youth of Mexican-descent) resistance to

Anglo hegemony. Indeed eight of the fourteen pieces in the Urban Images room depicted the stylized pants, wide-brimmed hat, and dapper coat of the zoot suit, signifier of pachuco culture, and three other pieces represented the pachuca style and stance adopted by Chicanas.

Regional Expressions, the section of the exhibition that showed the diversity of Chicano and Chicana experiences in different parts of the United States, featured Carlos Fresquez's three-dimensional *Zoot Suit en los Rockies*, suggesting that pachuco and pachuca culture indeed flourished outside of Los Angeles. This regional representation of Chicano and Chicana experience was the aspect of the show most criticized by artists and viewers, who found the West Coast overrepresented. Though not completely effective, this section meant to show that the borders of Chicano and Chicana life and culture have expanded beyond California and the Southwest, taking root in the Midwest, the Pacific Northwest, the South, and on the East Coast. From the rural experience of faith healing with the local *curandero* in South Texas to hanging with the homeboys in East Los Angeles, mowing the suburban lawn in San Antonio, graduating from high school in small-town Illinois, or carving a new identity for the Statue of Liberty, the regional expressions in the exhibit showed Chicanos and Chicanas as an integral part of the national American landscape.

Reclaiming the Past, devoted entirely to representations of family and religious traditions, was dominated by mixed-media installations, such as Amalia Mesa-Bains's rose-strewn altar memorializing the Mexican actress Dolores del Rio and *nicho*, or box art, related to the Mexican Day of the Dead celebration. Civil Liberties and Feminist Visions had more politicized themes. Feminist Visions illustrated issues that directly impacted women's lives, such as involuntary sterilization, abortion rights, the women's movement, and liberation from the sexual stereotypes of patriarchy as rendered by artists who claimed both Chicana and feminist identity politics. Civil Liberties depicted abuses of civil and human rights, particularly deportations and police brutality. The separation of these two sections, along with the fact that all but one of the pieces in the Civil Liberties, Urban Images, Cultural Icons, and La Causa rooms were by men while all of the pieces in Feminist Visions were by women, suggests that for all of the good intentions of the CARA organizers to effect an "awareness of gender issues in all aspects of the exhibition, in both process and product" (CARA Selection Committee), the gender standpoint was not one of the strongest or most respected positions in the Chicano/a Movement. Despite the fact that most of the Chicanas included in CARA outwardly defined themselves as artists with a feminist vision, they constituted a political minority within the movement that constantly had to defend itself against insider attacks from both men and women in El Movimiento. This gender marginalization was reflected in CARA, as only about 40 of the 180 artists in the show were women.

The intention of the last room in the show, Redefining American Art, was to emphasize the idea that although Chicano and Chicana art is rooted in the artistic traditions of Chicano and Chicana and Mexicano and Mexicana culture and history, it must also be seen within the pop, modern, conceptual, and feminist repertoires of mainstream art. In other words, because Chicano and Chicana artists like Carmen Lomas Garza, Frank Romero, Ester Hernández, Gronk, César Martinez, and Rupert García are collected in museums alongside Andy Warhol, Georgia O'Keefe, and Jackson Pollock, CARA argued that Chicano and Chicana art was in fact browning the face of American art.

Reception

Because it was rendered from the politicized perspectives of artists who identified as Chicano or Chicana (rather than Mexican, Latino or Latina, or Hispanic) and who af-

filiated with El Movimiento, the work in CARA was a politically charged art of pride and protest that also defied mainstream aesthetic conventions, particularly the "art for art's sake" philosophy that privileged form over content and economic value over community empowerment. Even the process of conceptualizing and developing the exhibition challenged the institutional culture of mainstream art museums wherein a single curator determines the vision and the artwork for an exhibition. Practicing the politics of self-determination and insider representation, the CARA organizers insisted on a democratic process and created a multitiered organizational structure that involved, aside from the advisory board and the Wight Gallery staff, the participation of twelve committees, six national task forces, a design team, and an editorial board. This process of intercultural collaboration was one of the distinguishing (and most problematic) features of the exhibition.

Indeed the problems of this consensus approach to organizing a mainstream art exhibition were made manifest at the ten venues CARA visited, each of which, by contractual agreement, had to negotiate with the CARA organizers if it wanted to implement any changes to the show. This aspect of the contract, however, was not always honored. At least three museums, for example, substituted an "ethnic" or "welcoming" image in place of the exhibition logo—a pair of disembodied eyes staring out from between the letters of the acronym—without the written permission of the CARA organizers. The San Francisco Museum of Modern Art, capitalizing on the "diversity" fever of the day, used Amado Peña's *Mestizo Head*, and the National Museum of American Art used Carmen Lomas Garza's more serene and domestic *Camas para Sueños* for the show's titular image. The El Paso Museum of Art not only changed the logo to a coiled pink snake with a paintbrush for a tail (a graphic not found among the exhibition pieces) but also altered the name of the show, calling it Interpretations of Hispanic Reality, with the actual title of the show in footnote font on the exhibition brochure distributed at the site.

El Paso was not the only venue that had problems with the race and class connotations of the word "Chicano" in the show's title. The same issue came up in Albuquerque, Tucson, and Denver, all cities with large Mexican American populations, but only El Paso actually renamed the show. In Fresno the show was criticized for appearing in a "white museum" ("Chicano Art on Display," p. F1). The San Antonio Museum of Art added an extra room featuring the work of emerging Tejano artists to show the work of a new generation of Chicano and Chicana artists and to help correct CARA's regional underrepresentation of Texas. This decision was made unilaterally by the Chicano art historian Jacinto Quirarte, who had been invited by the San Antonio Museum of Art to guest curate the show. Such were the concessions the CARA organizers had to make for the sake of bringing la plebe's art to mainstream museums across the country.

In its three-year tour CARA was seen by over 300,000 people, many of whom were exposed to Chicano and Chicana art and identity politics for the first time. CARA received multiple, often contradictory responses. But in the main, viewer comments in the books offered at some venues expressed examples of what Stephen Greenblatt calls "resonance and wonder" (Greenblatt, p. 42), two powerful emotions of both personal and collective identification that a strong work of art should evoke in the viewer.

In Albuquerque viewer responses ranged from "the exhibit touched my heart. I saw myself, my parents, and grandparents in the art," to "We didn't force them to come here and yet they complain. They could have stayed in Mexico" (Gaspar de Alba, pp. 225–226). In El Paso, CARA drew four thousand people on the first day. One viewer gleaned from the cultural politics of the show the idea that a public museum should represent its constituency, and a staff member at the El Paso Museum noted that because of CARA many of the residents of El Paso actually discovered the city had an art museum. At the National Museum of American Art in Washington, D.C., some viewers were disturbed or threatened by the unequivocal sense of ethnic and racial pride generated by the art, and others were offended by the use of Spanish-English wall text. But there too CARA received high praise not only from other Latinos and Latinas but also from European visitors and Asian Americans, African Americans, and Anglo-Americans, who expressed solidarity with La Causa and congratulated the Smithsonian on its commitment to multiculturalism.

The show was covered extensively in local newspapers, national periodicals, and arts magazines, totaling 151 reviews between its opening in Los Angeles in September 1990 and its closing in San Antonio in August 1993. Harsh critiques of the art's political agenda, in the *Los Angeles Times*, *Washington Post*, *Texas Monthly*, *New Art Examiner*, and *Wall Street Journal*, for example, were balanced by page after page of positive commentary and thoughtful analysis of the entire exhibition package, including the artwork, the catalog, the educational K–12 packets distributed at local schools in preparation for museum visits, and the cultural programming scheduled at each venue. This outreach programming included screenings of Chicano and Chicana films, presentations of *floricanto*, or poetry and music, theatrical performances, workshops, lectures, panels, and guided tours.

CARA was much more than an art exhibit. It was a historical, cultural, and political event. As its acronym and the reverse gaze of the exhibition logo suggest, CARA gave a face to the social, historical, and cultural realities of Mexican-descended people in the United States at the same time that it flew in the face of mainstream exhibition conventions and changed the face of "American" art.

See also Art, Chicano; Chávez, César; Chicano/a Movement; Curanderismo; Huerta, Dolores; Mestizaje; Pachucos and Pachucas; *and* Virgen de Guadalupe.

BIBLIOGRAPHY
CARA Selection Committee, CARA Archives, University of California, Los Angeles, Chicano Studies Research Center. See the minutes to the first meeting, November 1986.
"Chicano Art on Display." *Bakersfield Californian*, November 3, 1991, F1.
Gaspar de Alba, Alicia. *Chicano Art Inside/Outside the Master's House: Cultural Politics and the CARA Exhibition.* Austin: University of Texas Press, 1998.
Greenblatt, Stephen. "Resonance and Wonder." In *Exhibiting Cultures: The Poetics and Politics of Museum Display*, edited by Ivan Karp and Steven D. Lavine, 42–56. Washington, D.C.: Smithsonian Institution Press, 1991.
Griswold del Castillo, Richard, Teresa McKenna, and Yvonne Yarbro-Bejarano, eds. *Chicano Art: Resistance and Affirmation, 1965–1985.* Los Angeles: Wight Art Gallery, University of California, Los Angeles, 1991. Exhibition catalog.
Memmi, Albert. *The Colonizer and the Colonized.* Translated by Howard Greenfield. Boston: Beacon Press, 1991. Originally published in 1965.
Salazar, Rubén. "Who Is a Chicano? And What Is It the Chicanos Want?" Pt. 2. *Los Angeles Times*, February 6, 1970, 7.
Ybarra-Frausto, Tomás. "*Rasquachismo*: A Chicano Sensibility." In *Chicano Aesthetics: Rasquachismo*, 5–8. Phoenix, Ariz.: MARS (Movimiento Artístico del Río Salado), 1989. Exhibition catalog.

ALICIA GASPAR DE ALBA

CARRASCOLENDAS. *Carrascolendas*, originally broadcast in 1970 on the Public Broadcasting Service (PBS), was the first bilingual educational program on network television in the United States to address the needs of Latina and Latino children. The production was part of the thrust by the U.S. Office of Education (which later became the U.S. Department of Education) to fund bilingual educational programs following the civil rights legislation of the 1960s, which included the War on Poverty initiatives. The series was made possible by funding efforts stemming from Title VII (the Bilingual Education Act) of the Elementary and Secondary Education Act, which advocated bilingual education as part of school curricula. It received further funding from the Emergency School Assistance Act, which supported efforts to assist with school desegregation by promoting an atmosphere of ethnic and racial harmony.

The program was initiated as a regional production with a focus on Chicana and Chicano culture, broadcast on KLRN-TV, the community PBS station for Austin and San Antonio in Texas. By the time the series aired nationwide on PBS in 1972, it incorporated Puerto Rican and Cuban American themes and actors as well. At the end of the original network run in 1978, *Carrascolendas* was carried by over two hundred public broadcasting stations. Reruns aired on commercial and cable channels throughout the United States, Latin America, and Canada, with portions of the series still in reruns in isolated broadcast access venues in 2003. Begun with an initial grant of $200,000 for 30 black-and-white programs, *Carrascolendas* eventually received funding for budgets of nearly $6 million. Production staffs and actors together numbered as many as one hundred full-time and part-time participants, recruited from all over the United States and Latin America. The programs incorporated multicamera studio video sequences, filmed-on-location inserts, and animated vignettes, reflecting the diversity of Latina and Latino culture. The series won top broadcast industry awards from a variety of organizations, including the New York International Film Festival, the German Prix Jeunesse, and the Japan Prize Festival.

Originally conceptualized, written, and produced by Aida Barrera, the majority of the 220 programs featured a single storyline designed within the musical-comedy genre. Inspired by the stories of Barrera's own childhood growing up on the Texas-Mexico border, the programs, intended for children three to nine years old, were set in the mythical town of Carrascolendas. The dramatic televised stories revolved around fully scored and choreographed musical numbers interwoven with slapstick sequences featuring a host of broadly drawn characters, such as the bilingual lion Agapito and the living dolls Dyana and Berta, who lived in their own human-size toy world. The picaresque comics Caracoles and Campamocha were styled after the antiheroes of the *carpas* (tents) shows that toured South Texas during the 1920s and 1930s, as well as the classic Mexican Golden Age comedies of the 1950s and 1960s featuring performers such as Cantínflas, Tin Tan, Resortes, and Mantequilla. The dialogues were scripted in a mixture of Spanish and English, echoing the natural and easy style of bilinguals. Although the scripts did not resort to direct translations, the conversations nonetheless acknowledged a heterogeneous multicultural and multilingual audience of Latinas and Latinos and non-Latinas and non-Latinos having different language capabilities and experiences.

The goal of the pan-ethnic program was to reawaken Latina and Latino children, and by extension their parents and families, to the possibilities encompassed in their cultural and linguistic heritage, regardless of where in the ethnic and racial spectrum they happened to be. The objective was to reestablish a sense of community with a commonality of ideas, participating in American mainstream cultural values while at the same time celebrating

Carrascolendas. The PBS program was first broadcast in 1970. (Courtesy of Aida Barrera and University of Texas Press)

Latina and Latino cultural and linguistic differences. A television series was a way to provide an audience of children with a semblance of mythological instruction, a way to bring the group back to its central unifying core of Latina and Latino culture. *Carrascolendas* was intended to create a new mythological paradigm, one that spoke directly to Latina and Latino children in a way that they understood.

The goal of the series was exemplified by the title of the program, which served as a symbol of both the validation of Latina and Latino culture, and the informal transmission and sometimes fanciful playfulness inherent in language. The title *Carrascolendas* represents an oral transmutation of Carnestolendas, which means "carnival" and which was the historical name of a town founded in 1752 on the Texas-Mexico border. The name, transmitted through the generations, eventually became known as Carrascolendas. In choosing the name of the series, Barrera wanted to validate the linguistic oral transmutations common to the Chicana and Chicano and Latina and Latino experience, which are the source of many of the cultural contradictions facing

Latinas and Latinos. She also wanted to capture the linguistic playfulness of a word like "Carrascolendas," which would appeal to children.

Basing a television program on the strong currents of Latina and Latino culture had its drawbacks. Chief among these was the organizational structure and corporate culture within the institution of public broadcasting itself. Because programs like *Carrascolendas* had originated with federal initiatives identified with the compensatory issues of the War on Poverty aimed at "disadvantaged," low-income children, these productions were not believed to have the appeal that network television programs, especially public broadcasting productions, were supposed to have. When government funding ended, as it did for *Carrascolendas* in 1976, the impetus for the public broadcasting community to continue producing bilingual programming ended with it. The end of government funding frequently also meant the end of employment for minority producers and staff members trained in productions such as *Carrascolendas*. When the money ran out, KLRN-TV dismissed most of the *Carrascolendas* minority staff. These staff members was considered too inexperienced in television production, despite the fact that many of them had been associated for six years with an award-winning national series, whose multimillion-dollar budgets had exceeded the local budgets for the community station.

See also Barrera, Aída; Bilingual Education; Bilingual Education Act; Bilingualism and Biculturalism; *and* Television, Spanish-Language.

AÍDA BARRERA

CASA HGT. CASA HGT (Centro de Acción Social Autónoma) grew from the Hermandad General de Trabajadores (HGT), which was founded in 1951 by Bert Corona. In the 1970s, in conjunction with the Casa de Carnalismo, a community youth organization in the Boyle Heights barrio of East Los Angeles, it developed into a militant nationalist organization.

Bert Corona was one of the most influential Mexican American political and community leaders from the late 1930s to the 1990s. Corona, president of a longshore and warehousemen's union local, played a key role in the 1940s and 1950s in Los Angeles organizations such as the Mexican Congress, Sleepy Lagoon Defense Committee, and ANMA (Asociación Nacional Mexico Americano). Corona survived Red-baiting in the 1950s to found MAPA, the Mexican American Political Association, and the Hermandad General de Trabajadores, a community-based immigrant rights organization. He also became an advisor to Chicano movement organizations such as La Raza Unida Party and the Casa del Carnalismo.

Young Chicanos founded the Casa del Carnalismo in the 1970s to defend themselves from police brutality arising from a grassroots effort to confront drug dealers in the area. The police, who felt threatened by neighborhood action against drugs, chose to view anti-drug activists as drug dealers. A shootout led to arrests, a trial, and the Committee to Free Los Tres, organized by attorney Antonio Rodriguez. Many of the Comite por Los Tres activists, who were supported and advised by Corona, came under his political influence. They thus gained experience in operating a community legal aid clinic and providing information about immigrant rights. The political perspective and objectives of their organization broadened into a larger political organization to defend the civil and political rights of both Mexican immigrants and Mexican Americans. Uniting with CASA HGT, the group evolved into a Mexican nationalist party in the United States.

CASA HGT began to view itself as a political party representing a national liberation movement. In 1975 it adopted the name CASA (Centro de Acción Social Autónoma). Corona continued to advise the group, but Rodriguez and other younger people took over its leadership. Corona stated that he disagreed with their strategy because he felt that they first needed to build a grassroots base before a political party could succeed. According to Corona, CASA followed an erroneous strategy in believing that a militant vanguard could attract a broad membership.

CASA sought to unite with activists from labor, immigrant rights, and Chicano and Chicana student groups to work with other militant nationalist and Marxist groups, including the Crusade for Justice and La Raza Unida Party. It established connections with, and was influenced by, the Puerto Rican Socialist Party. Although East Los Angeles remained its base, the organization expanded to include groups in Chicago, San Antonio, Colorado, and other areas of California, where regional CASA HGTs were established. In some areas, such as Chicago, the HGT had a stronger organizational base that allowed them to survive the breakup of CASA after 1971.

Membership in Los Angeles reached several hundred members, and total national membership ranged from three hundred to five hundred members by 1977. Organizationally, CASA's work was divided into labor, immigrant rights, student, legal defense, and newspaper (*Sin Fronteras*) committees. CASA members were active in the ILGWU in Los Angeles, Texas, and Chicago, and had members in other unions such the United Electrical Workers and the Steelworkers. Attorney Antonio Rodriguez directed La Clínica de la Raza, which counseled undocumented workers. CASA formed the National Coalition for Immigration Rights, which conducted a national campaign in cooperation with other immigration-rights organizations. *Sin Fronteras*, a newspaper edited by Carlos

Vasquez, was published by CASA. It adopted a militant position of unity of Latino and Latina people without borders, rights of Latinas, and solidarity with Puerto Rico, Cuba, and other national liberation struggles.

CASA came to regard Mexicans and Mexican Americans (or Chicanos and Chicanas) as two segments of the Mexican people divided by imperialism and possessing the right of national self-determination as a single nation. By 1977 CASA was engaged in discussion of the National Question and whether and when it should declare itself a party of the Mexican people in the United States.

CASA participated in the 1977 National Immigration Conference in San Antonio, one of the last major efforts of the National Coalition for Fair Immigration Laws and Practices. Conflict with other organizations involved in the conference weakened CASA and damaged its effectiveness. By the end of 1977, internal strains and conflicts caused a leadership crisis. Eventually the decision was made to dissolve the organization.

Following the demise of the national CASA, some of its activists continued as political activists and labor organizers—for example, CASA Chicago and the Hermandad Mexicana Latinoamericana, which was derived from the CASA HGT. CASA Chicago continued to exist and to exercise a important influence on community organization and politics in the Pilsen neighborhood. Pilsen's Rudy Lozano Library is named after a murdered CASA Chicago leader. The Hermandad Mexicana Latinoamericana, led by Bert Corona's protégé Nativo Lopez, plays an important role in Latino politics. Some CASA members and sympathizers have been elected to office, such as Antonio Villaraigoza and Gilbert Cedillo to the California state legislature. Many former CASA members have continued to work in legal defense, immigration rights, community organization, and education.

See also Chicago; Corona, Bert; Chicanos and Chicanas; Crusade for Justice; East Los Angeles; Immigration; La Raza Unida Party; Mexican American Political Association; Mexican-Origin People in the United States; *and* Sin Fronteras.

BIBLIOGRAPHY

Acuña, Rodolfo. *Occupied America: A History of Chicanos*. 4th ed. New York: Longman, 2000.

Chávez, Ernesto. "Creating Aztlán: The Chicano Movement in Los Angeles, 1966–1978." PhD diss., University of California, Los Angeles, 1994.

Chávez, Ernesto. *Mi Raza Primero! (My People First!): Nationalism, Identity, and Insurgency in the Chicano Movement in Los Angeles, 1966–1978*. Berkeley: University of California Press, 2002.

García, Mario T. *Memories of Chicano History: The Life and Narrative of Bert Corona*. Berkeley: University of California Press, 1994.

Gómez-Quiñones, Juan. *Chicano Politics: Reality and Promise, 1940–1990*. Albuquerque: University of New Mexico Press, 1990.

Gómez-Quiñones, Juan. *Mexican American Labor, 1790–1990*. Albuquerque: University of New Mexico Press, 1994.

Navarro, Armando. *La Raza Unida Party: A Chicano Challenge to the U.S. Two-Party Dictatorship*. Philadelphia: Temple University Press, 2000.

ANTONIO RIOS-BUSTAMANTE

CASAL, LOURDES (1938–1981), poet and activist. The founder of the Institute for Cuban Studies, Lourdes Casal studied at the Universidad de Santo Tomás de Villanueva (a private Catholic University in a plush neighborhood in Havana, Cuba.

Education and Activism

Casal had a diverse intellectual and professional training. At the university, she initially registered in the school of engineering, then switched to psychology. A voracious reader, she became versed in literature (prose and poetry), political science, and social psychology, among other disciplines.

Casal's passion for knowledge and truth led to sharp twists and turns in her political, religious, and personal life. She was an active opponent of the Cuban revolutionary government when she left Cuba in 1961 to join many others in the U.S. Cuban exile community, and she journeyed to Africa in 1962 under CIA sponsorship. Her long years in New York living with other Latinos and Latinas (Dominicans and Puerto Ricans) in the 1960s and 1970s sharpened her awareness of social and racial inequities as never before and led her to sympathize with the revolutionary government. She cofounded the Institute for Cuban Studies in 1969 as well as the journals *Nueva Generación* (1972) and *Areíto* (1974).

Her political turning point—from opponent to sympathizer of revolutionary Cuba—was marked by the publication of *El Caso Padilla* (1972), a critical review of the famous purging and recanting of Heberto Padilla in 1971. In May 1973 Casal became the first Cuban exile to return to Cuba; she stayed until mid September. Upon her return to the United States she said to this author, "After the Pinochet Coup in Chile, . . . and beyond some real problems within the Cuban national process, . . . I choose to support Cuba . . . as I fail to see the feasibility of democracy as we know it in Latin America."

When the Cuban revolutionary leadership decided—with the consent of President Jimmy Carter—to plan a gathering of selected Cuban exiles in Havana in late 1978, Casal was instrumental in making the list of invitees. This gathering became known as El Diálogo (The Dialogue), in which the "Group of 75"—Cubans from abroad who came to Havana in November and December 1978—discussed points of interest with Fidel Castro and other Cuban officials. This encounter brought about the liberation of 3,600 political prisoners from Cuban jails. Together with their families, these prisoners and several thousand former political prisoners, also with their families, came to the United States on charter flights. Multiple commercial and cultural projects were developed in the aftermath of El Diálogo. Certainly, Cuba and Cubans on the island were never again the same. In the summer of 1980, Casal was part of an Institute for Cuban Studies conference on Cuban soil, in the midst of the last stages of the Mariel boatlift. It was a difficult, tense, and poignant experience for everyone attending.

Reflections

As time passed, Casal's health rapidly deteriorated. She died prematurely in Havana at age forty-three on February 1, 1981, after a long and painful struggle with various and serious diseases. Her powerful, clear mind and spirit had dragged her aching body through her latter earthly years. Those who cherish the gift of her friendship and who walked with her through the journey and challenge of life appreciate her blend of brains, wits, and tenderness. She would argue strongly without hurting others in their views or feelings. She showed an ability to lubricate debates while also enriching them. The following texts illustrate the colors and flavors in the fascinating pilgrimage of this extraordinary Cuban woman. They come from María Cristina Herrera's *Itinerario Ideológico: Antología de Lourdes Casal*, a collection of writings by and about Casal. The first comes from Herrera's dedication (all translations by Herrera):

> Within this diversity of commitments underscoring her earthly years, the love of Cuba and an inalterable, admirable honesty were paramount in Lourdes. Many times she agonized before challenging alternatives. To choose was not always easy, but for her it was always clear, beyond risks, even of life itself.
>
> (Herrera, p. 1)

The essayist Leonel Antonio de la Cuesta writes that "the best characterization of her life is that of a woman in an agonizing search of the absolute, while that of a person dominated by Unamuno's yearning of not being classified by one of many labels of the times" (Herrera, p. 8). José Prince, asserting the role of truth in Casal's life, writes, "The Lourdes I met in 1970 was a woman in search of alternatives for the Cuban situation. . . . What mattered was the reopening of contacts between all Cubans, irrespective of where they lived and their ideologies."

Casal explained her own trajectory in this way:

> And how and why one returns to Cuba? And what happens to us upon coming back? In my case, I returned to Cuba in an attempt to face a number of questions which through years had become an obsession. What was, after all, the Cuban Revolution? Was it possible for me to experience a living reencounter with the most radical and convulsing event in the history of my country? Could I reencounter Cuba, not already at the physical level, but at another level . . .?
>
> (Herrera, p. 101)

Perhaps Casal's poem "Siempre he vivido en Cuba" (I've always lived in Cuba) best summarizes the difficulty of her rapport with her homeland and the United States:

> I live in Cuba.
> I've always lived in Cuba,
> even when I believed to dwell
> faraway from the alligator of agony
> I've always lived in Cuba …

Finally, this poem by Eliseo Diego, laureate Cuban Catholic poet and a valued friend of Casal, appeared in a memorial to Casal. It expresses the value she embodied for others:

> Lourdes, my child, it's worth the bother, the others deserve all bothers.
> I'm with them now, in your now of before, and how
> All love you, how they love you.
> They are going to live for you, I swear. Now, calmly sleep on my shoulder,
> That you don't see, that you don't feel, but that was made for you from the beginning of the world.

See also Cuban Americans; Exilio; *and* Institute for Cuban Studies.

BIBLIOGRAPHY

Casal, Lourdes. "Africa Ante el Problema Cubano." *Itinerario Ideológico: Antología de Lourdes Casal.* Miami: Ediciones Diáspora, 1982.

Diego, Eliseo. *A la memoria de Lourdes Casal: Palabras Escritas UN TRECE DE OCTUBRE.* Havana, Cuba: ICAP-CASA, 1986.

Domínguez, Jorge I. "Las reuniones del Instituto de Estudios Cubanos." *Treinta Años de Instituto de Estudios Cubanos.* Miami: Alexandria Library Inc., Electronic Publishing House, 2000.

Herrera, María Cristina, ed. *Itinerario Ideológico: Antología de Lourdes Casal.* Miami: Ediciones Diáspora, 1982.

María Cristina Herrera

CASTILLO, ANA (b. 1953), writer. Born in Chicago on June 15, 1953, Ana Castillo is a prominent and prolific Chicana novelist, poet, and theorist. Regarded as one of the central writers in creating a body of work that speaks to the experiences of Chicanas, she has often been credited with helping create and legitimate the corpus of Chicana literature as a distinct field. Castillo attended Chicago City College then earned a bachelor of arts in art from Northwestern Illinois University in 1975. She earned a master of arts in Latin American and Caribbean studies at the University of Chicago in 1979 and followed with a PhD in American Studies at the University of Bremen in Germany.

Since 1977, Castillo has authored, edited, and translated more than fifteen books focused on Chicana archetype, history, myth, sexuality, magical realism, Third World feminism, and indigenism. Among her poetry collections are *Otro canto* (1977), *The Invitation* (1979), *Women Are Not Roses* (1984), *My Father Was a Toltec: Poems* (1988), *My Father Was a Toltec and Selected Poems, 1973–1988* (1995), and *I Ask the Impossible: Poems* (2001). In addition, she has authored four novels, *The Mixquiahuala Letters* (1986), *Sapogonia: An Anti-Romance in 3/8 Meter* (1990; an uncut version was released in 1994), *So Far from God* (1993), and *Peel My Love Like an Onion: A Novel* (1999). Castillo authored a book of short stories, *Loverboys* (1996), and edited two volumes of essays, *The Sexuality of Latinas*, with Norma Alarcón and Cherríe Moraga (1993), and *Goddess of the Americas/La diosa de las Américas* (1996). She and Norma Alarcón translated the groundbreaking anthology *This Bridge Called My Back, Writings by Radical Women of Color*, originally edited by Cherríe Moraga and Gloria Anzaldúa, into Spanish as *Esta puente, mi espalda: Voces de mujeres tercermundistas en los Estados Unidos* (1988). Castillo's other works include the children's book *My Daughter, My Son, the Eagle, the Dove: An Aztec Chant* (2000) and the collection of original essays *Massacre of the Dreamers: Essays on Xicanisma* (1994). Castillo's work has been included in numerous anthologies, newspapers, Web sites, and magazines. Along with Norma Alarcón, Castillo founded the literary journal *Third Woman*.

Castillo has garnered much recognition, including the American Book Award from the Before Columbus Foundation, a Carl Sandburg Award, a Mountains and Plains Booksellers Award, a Sor Juana Achievement Award, and fellowships from the National Endowment for the Arts. Her private and public papers have been preserved in the California Ethnic and Multicultural Archives at the University of California, Santa Barbara. She was a writer in residence in English and Latin American and Latino and Latina studies at DePaul University. She has one son, Marcel Ramon Herrera.

Castillo's writings are central to furthering Chicana feminist epistemology and more specifically Xicanisma or Third World feminist stances that disrupt black and white binaries and erase Chicanas from mainstream discussions of race and ethnicity. This "Mexic Amerindian" feminism further builds upon projects begun by the Chicana feminists Moraga and Gloria Anzaldúa, whose works disrupt static notions of race and identity. Castillo, like these other Chicana feminist writers, has sought to move toward a transnational feminist politics that displaces the human-made Mexico–United States border by focusing on the borderlands or third space and the experiences of what Castillo has terms brown, indigenous, or

ANA CASTILLO. (Photo by Antonio Perez)

countryless women. Castillo argued that indigenous women have largely been ignored and historically and socially disenfranchised both by the dominant culture and by white feminist movements and the masculine-driven Chicano movement. Castillo's Xicanisma or transnational feminism transcends borders and nationalities as it focuses on experiences and the effects of difference and marginalization resulting from colonialism, *mestizaje* (mixed-race identity), racism, classism, and sexism. These effects or feelings of difference allow communities to move beyond demarcations bound by nationality, race, class, and culture to larger transcultural identifications and communities. Castillo's work largely centers on empowering the voices, history, and experiences of third world indigenous women, whose creativity has been silenced and appropriated by sexist cultures through racism, oppression, and psychic oppression.

Similar to work by other feminists of color, such as the black feminist and scholar Patricia Hill Collins, who wrote about black women's history of intellectualizing in the everyday, Castillo's work through the reclamation of indigenism seeks to disrupt and subvert dominant paradigms of theorizing in academia by placing theory and practice within the realm of everyday women's lives and experiences rather than in the ivory tower. The Chicana literary scholar Tey Diana Rebolledo (1995) observes that Castillo's novels not only challenge theory and practice but also act as forms of autoethnography or personal narrative through their privileging of the stories of Chicanas as told by Chicanas. Laura Gillman and Stacey Floyd-Thomas, in their essay "Con un pie a cada lado/With a Foot in Each Place: Mestizaje as Transnational Feminisms in Ana Castillo's *So Far from God*" (2001), observe that the novels are political acts because they write into existence silenced narratives. This Chicana-centered narrative told through the voices and experiences of Chicanas led academics such as Rebolledo and Alvina Quintana to call Castillo an ethnographer or interpreter of Chicana culture.

In reclaiming indigenism, Castillo focuses on recovering Chicana spirituality and power through the reexamination and reinterpretation of lineages of historical archetypes and matriarchy in Chicana and Chicano cultures. In chapter three of *Massacre of the Dreamers: Essays on Xicanisma*, Castillo examines what she terms the ancient roots of machismo by linking Islamic beliefs or heritages with the Spanish Catholicism brought to Mexico during its colonization. In addition to tracing these lineages, Castillo examines the subordination of women's power and sexuality through the manipulation of religious icons, mythologies, and histories. Castillo analyzes precolonial belief systems to unearth histories of matriarchy and mother goddess worship that were transformed into patriarchal structures of power via colonialism and the Catholic Church, specifically through the use of the patron saint of Mexico, the Virgen de Guadalupe, and the Mexican Eve figure, Malintzin Tenépal, translator and lover of Hernán Cortés. Castillo rejects the images of these women as passive or submissive, as reinforced by Mexican intellectuals such as Octavio Paz and further cemented in the rhetoric of the Chicano movement, instead seeing them as active agents of change and empowerment. Furthermore, in celebrating these figures Castillo calls for the larger embracing of Chicana sexuality historically regulated by them as symbolic virgin and whore. The reclaiming of female creativity, power, and matriarchy begins with the embracing of Chicana sexuality as a way to remove the vestiges of colonialism. As Alarcón, Castillo, and Moraga note in the introduction to *The Sexuality of Latinas*, Latina sexuality has often been hidden or distorted within the rhetoric of the family, and for many women, understandings of sexuality come through experiences of sexual violence. The family, accountable to the larger rhetoric of the church, is the point for socialization of female sexuality. Castillo argues that the family reflects larger patriarchal tendencies that place women in the role of serving men in their desire to serve God. As a result of these patriarchal practices within religious rituals, Castillo argues, women are spiritually and sexually oppressed. She contens that replacing the image or guiding principle of the Father with the Mother or a matriarchal center would create a more nurturing society.

Castillo's creative works and her essays are well regarded for her strong feminist or woman-centered politics and her imaginative writings that reflect the various experiences and political identifications of Chicanas in the United States. The critic Elisabeth Mermann-Jozwiak argues that Castillo's novels, often characterized as using elements of magical realism popularized by the Latin American writers Gabriel García Márquez and Isabel Allende, has helped to create a unique Chicana literary style that decenters patriarchal biases inherent in literary forms such as the family saga. Using postmodern theories and methods, Castillo has enacted and enabled a third space that negotiates cultures while simultaneously challenging Eurocentric assumptions about the writing of fiction. Thus, Castillo has been a driving force for Chicana feminists through the political themes in her writings and in her cultural and political activism.

See also Alarcón, Norma; Anzaldúa, Gloria; Catholicism; Literature; Moraga, Cherríe; Poetry; *and* Sexuality.

BIBLIOGRAPHY

Ana Castillo. Web site www.anacastillo.com

Castillo, Ana. *I Ask the Impossible: Poems*. New York: Anchor Books, 2001.

Castillo, Ana. *The Invitation*. San Francisco: A. Castillo, 1979.

Castillo, Ana. *Loverboys: Stories*. New York: Norton, 1996.

Castillo, Ana. *Massacre of the Dreamers: Essays on Xicanisma*. Albuquerque: University of New Mexico Press, 1994.

Castillo, Ana. *The Mixquiahuala Letters*. Binghamton, N.Y.: Bilingual Press/Editorial Bilingüe, 1986.

Castillo, Ana. *My Daughter, My Son, the Eagle, the Dove: An Aztec Chant*. New York: Dutton Books, 2000.

Castillo, Ana. *My Father Was a Toltec: Poems*. Albuquerque, N.Mex.: West End Press, 1988.

Castillo, Ana. *My Father Was a Toltec and Selected Poems, 1973–1988*. New York: Norton, 1995.

Castillo, Ana. *Peel My Love Like an Onion: A Novel*. New York: Doubleday, 1999.

Castillo, Ana. *Sapogonia: An Anti-Romance in 3/8 Meter*. Tempe, Ariz.: Bilingual Press/Editorial Bilingüe, 1990.

Castillo, Ana. *So Far from God*. New York: Norton, 1993.

Castillo, Ana. *Women Are Not Roses*. Houston, Tex.: Arte Público Press, 1984.

Castillo, Ana, ed. *Goddess of the Americas/La diosa de las Americas*. New York: Riverhead Books, 1996.

Gillman, Laura, and Stacey M. Floyd-Thomas. "Con un pie a cada lado/With a Foot in Each Place: Mestizaje as Transnational Feminisms in Ana Castillo's *So Far from God.*" *Meridians* 2 (2001): 158–175.

Merman-Jozwiak, Elisabeth. "Gritos desde la frontera: Ana Castillo, Sandra Cisneros, and Postmodernism." *Melus* 25 (2000): 101–118.

Paz, Octavio. *The Labyrinth of Solitude: Life and Thought in Mexico.* Translated by Lysander Kemp. New York: Grove, 1962.

Quintana, Alvina E. "Ana Castillo's *The Mixquiahuala Letters*: The Novelist as Ethnographer." In *Criticism in the Borderlands: Studies in Chicano Literature, Culture, and Ideology*, edited by Héctor Calderón and José David Saldívar. Durham, N.C.: Duke University Press, 1991.

Rebolledo, Tey Diana. *Women Singing in the Snow: A Cultural Analysis of Chicana Literature.* Tucson: University of Arizona Press, 1995.

Trujillo, Carla, ed., *Chicana Lesbians.* Berkeley, Calif.: Third Woman Press, 1991.

BERNADETTE MARIE CALAFELL

CASTILLO, AURORA (1914–1998), community activist. Aurora Castillo cofounded Madres del Este de Los Angeles (Mothers of East Los Angeles), a grassroots environmental justice organization that successfully opposed the proposed building of a toxic waste incinerator and state prison in Eastside Los Angeles. Castillo proudly called herself the great-great-granddaughter of Augustine Pedro Olvera, one of the original settlers of Los Angeles. She was born and raised in East Los Angeles with a brother and two sisters and chose not to marry or to have children. She attended community college and worked as a secretary until she retired.

Castillo often spoke of the discrimination she experienced in school and at work and how she overcame it. In high school she argued with her counselor, who wanted her to take courses in millinery (hat making) rather than classes in business. Convincing the counselor to allow her into the business courses, she developed accounting and secretarial skills. In the 1930s counselors typically advised Mexican American women to take home economics—sewing and cooking classes—instead of business courses "for their own welfare." Castillo contended that counselors perceived Mexican girls as low achievers. In the 1930s she was among the few Mexican Americans who graduated from Garfield High School in Eastside Los Angeles.

Castillo's father, Joaquin Pedro Castillo, who had served in the U.S. Navy during World War I and later belonged to labor unions, reminded her that she had the right to take whatever courses she wanted. Her mother, Frances Castillo, hoped her daughters would find white-collar work. During the Great Depression, Castillo's parents worked in a laundry, but they always instilled pride in the family's Mexican heritage. After Castillo graduated from high school, she took a job in the Douglas Aircraft clerical sector, where she worked for three years during World War II, and her sister, Henrietta, found work in the factory. The World War II defense industry provided new employment opportunities for women.

As a full-time worker, Castillo had little time for political or community activities other than voting. She attended mass regularly and decided to become more active in church activities shortly after the passing of her father in 1959. When she expressed her feelings of great loss to the priest, he suggested she might ease her grief through volunteer work with the youth. Following his advice, Castillo volunteered for various church-based groups, events, and fund-raisers, including the Guadalupanas, a group that organized the procession for Our Lady of Guadalupe. In addition, she volunteered as a counselor for teen girls. One of her last places of employment was with the archdiocese of Los Angeles. When she retired in 1982, she resumed a closer working relationship with the church and began keeping the accounts for the annual weeklong fiesta aimed at raising funds for the church.

In 1986, after Sunday mass, Father John Moretta, the priest at Resurrection Parish, informed women about the state prison proposed for the densely populated Eastside neighborhood where Castillo had lived all her life. He asked them to organize a women's group called the Madres del Este de Los Angeles or Mothers of East Los Angeles (MELA) in opposition. Castillo took a lead position, helping to inform and mobilize other community members. Although she was not a mother, she perceived her role as one of protecting the community for the children and asserted that mothers promote children's interests, unlike some public officials who promote self-interests. She insisted that if a child's safety is jeopardized, the mother turns into a lioness.

As a core activist in MELA, Castillo acted as a spokesperson for English media and provided a clearinghouse for numerous petitions and letters to the governor. She testified regularly at public hearings and before elected officials. Using a manual typewriter in her living room, she often typed copies of letters for the group's records. Her home became a center for organizing demonstrations, and she maintained a "phone tree" to notify hundreds of women about meetings, marches, and hearings, often on short notice.

Over the course of several months, Castillo observed much personal growth in the women of the group. At first women were timid when they spoke at public hearings, but gradually they learned how to make themselves heard. She worked closely with Father Moretta and Frank Villalobos, a landscape architect and urban planner who helped arrange and fund bus trips so MELA members could travel to Sacramento, and she conveyed travel plans to the members. Sometimes three busloads of MELA women made the grueling twelve-hour trip from Los Angeles to Sacramento, where half of them demonstrated on the steps of the capitol and the other half lobbied the legislators. Because travel funds were scarce, the women packed lunches, and on some visits they got back on the bus immediately after the demonstration.

Castillo was proud of the efforts of the Eastside community, comparing it to the political strategies of the more affluent areas of Los Angeles: "You know that Pacific Palisades group asked for our backing. But what they did, they sent their powerful lobbyist that they pay thousands of dollars to get our support against the drilling in Pacific Palisades. So what we did was tell them to send their grassroots people, not their lobbyist" (Pardo, p. 4).

In 1995, for her role in the organization, Castillo was named North American winner of the Emma Goldman Environmental Prize for her unflagging efforts to oppose the toxic waste incinerator and prison planned for Eastside Los Angeles and for promoting environmental and political awareness. The prize is awarded to one person from each continent. Castillo was the first person from Los Angeles and the first Latina to win the prestigious award, often called the Nobel Prize for environmentalists. Upon receiving the award, she reflected on MELA's collective efforts and "asserted that all people, regardless of ethnicity, race, education and income, have a right to a clean environment." (Quintanilla, p. E1). MELA members recognized Castillo for her organizational skills, tenacity, and commitment to bettering the quality of life in East Los Angeles.

See also East Los Angeles *and* Madres del Este de Los Angeles.

BIBLIOGRAPHY

Pardo, Mary. "Mexican American Women Grassroots Community Activists: Mothers of East Los Angeles." *Frontiers* 1, no. 1 (1990): 1–7.
Quintanilla, Michael. "The Earth Mother." *Los Angeles Times*, April 24, 1995: E1.
Russell, Dick. "Environmental Racism." *Amicus Journal* 11, no. 23 (Spring 1988): 22–32.

MARY PARDO

CASTRO, FIDEL

CASTRO, FIDEL (b. 1926), Cuban leader. Fidel Castro was born in Biran, Cuba, on August 13, 1926, the third of seven children of Ángel Castro y Argiz, a Spanish immigrant and wealthy landowner and entrepreneur, and Lina Ruz González. He attended Belén High School in Havana, and law school at the University of Havana, where he became a student leader and political activist. A gifted orator, Castro became a rising political star in the left-of-center, reformist Party of the Cuban People (*Ortodoxos*) and was a candidate for the Cuban House of Representatives in the 1952 elections that were abruptly suspended by Fulgencio Batista's coup d'etat and subsequent dictatorship.

Convinced that direct action through armed struggle and revolution were the only solutions to Cuba's turbulent and corrupt political system, on July 26, 1953, Castro and a group of 150 men and women attacked the Cuartel Moncada, Cuba's second-largest military base. The plan was to take over the city of Santiago de Cuba and spark an insurrection to overthrow Batista's dictatorship. Although the attack failed badly, and more than half of the group was captured or killed, Castro had launched a movement that would grow stronger and more rapidly than anyone could have imagined.

Castro and his comrades were tried and charged with conspiracy to overthrow the government, and he was sentenced to fifteen years in prison. At the trial, Castro, acting in his own defense, accused Batista of usurping power, violating the Cuban constitution, and committing gross violations of human rights. He concluded his defense speech with the now immortalized words, "Condemn me if you will, history will absolve me." He was released from prison in May 1955, as part of a general amnesty for political prisoners, and went into self-imposed exiled in Mexico to organize the next phase of the struggle against Batista.

On December 2, 1956, Fidel Castro and a group of eighty-one other men invaded Cuba from Mexico and launched a guerrilla war that culminated on January 1, 1959, with Batista's rushed departure into exile and Castro's triumphant entrance into Santiago de Cuba. Almost immediately after the triumph, Castro announced a series of revolutionary measures that included governmental reorganization, agrarian reform, urban reform, the elimination of gambling and prostitution, and the nationalization of Cuba's natural resources and basic industries. During its first year, the Revolutionary Government passed more than 1,500 laws, many of which affected the business and political interests of the United States in Cuba. These reforms resulted in the breaking of diplomatic relations between the two governments on January 3, 1961. In April 1961, a force 1,500 Cuban exiles, trained and armed by the United Sates, attempted to overthrow the Cuban government. Their invasion was soundly defeated within seventy-two hours, and Castro's prestige and admiration increased significantly in Cuba and throughout Latin America, Asia, and Africa. In the early twenty-first century the United States and Cuba do not have full diplomatic relations, and since 1962 the United States has maintained an international trade blockade against Cuba.

Many Cubans, especially business and property owners, reacted to the Revolutionary Government's social transformation by going into exile in the United States. Others became disaffected as Castro's Revolutionary Government consolidated its power after the invasion's defeat, and also opted for exile in Miami, Florida, from where they conspired and organized armed missions against Castro. The Cuban exile community grew rapidly in numbers (1.3 million in 2004) and prospered economically and politically in the United States, but it has failed to achieve its main objective: the overthrow of Fidel Castro and the Cuban Revolution. The Cuban community's collective and generalized hatred of Fidel Castro has shaped its political character and identity as extremely conservative, single-issue oriented, and blindly aligned with the Republican Party. Demonizing Castro, however, has paid high political dividends for some, as Cubans have dominated electoral politics in Florida and have elected five Cuban Americans to the U.S. Congress. Together, these elected officials, with the support of powerful lobbying organizations like the Cuban American National Foundation, have been able to persuade both the Democratic Party and the Republican Party to maintain a hard-line policy toward Castro and the Cuban Revolution. During the last decade of the twentieth century and at the beginning of the twenty-first, Castro's popularity has declined with Cubans. Even though social services have been provided, civil liberties have not. Today, most Cubans in Miami and in Cuba voice critical views of Castro's forty-five-year hold on power. Indeed, not only have Cuban elites been leaving the island, but poor and rural Cubans, as well as Afro-Cubans, have also now joined the exodus.

See also **Bay of Pigs; Cuban Americans;** *and* **Guevara, Ernesto "Che."**

BIBLIOGRAPHY

Balfour, Sebastian. *Castro.* 2nd ed. London: Longman, 1995.

Blanco, Katiuska. *Todo el tiempo de los cedros: Paisaje familiar de Fidel Castro Ruz.* Havana, Cuba: Casa Editora Abril, 2003.

Borge, Tomás. *Face to Face with Fidel Castro: A Conversation with Tomás Borge.* Translated by Mary Todd. Melbourne, Australia: Ocean Press, 1993.

Dubois, Jules. *Fidel Castro: Rebel, Liberator, or Dictator?* Indianapolis, Ind.: Bobbs-Merrill, 1959.

Liss, Sheldon B. *Fidel!: Castro's Political and Social Thought.* Boulder, Colo.: Westview Press, 1994.

Quirk, Robert. *Fidel Castro: The Full Story of His Rise to Power, His Allies, and His Adversaries.* New York: Norton, 1993.

Szulc, Tad. *Fidel: A Critical Portrait.* New York: Morrow, 1986.

FÉLIX MASUD-PILOTO

CATHOLICISM. Catholics have been present within what is now the United States for five centuries. Spanish Catholic colonial foundations between 1565 and 1821 established Christianity in Florida and what is now the U.S. Southwest. Political and military events in the 1800s brought these territories, as well as French Louisiana, which was temporarily ruled by Spain from 1766 until 1803, into the United States and extended U.S. domination at the end of that century to Puerto Rico, Cuba, and

CATHOLIC DEVOTION. Procession to the shrine of the Virgin of Guadalupe. (Associated Press)

the Philippines, longtime Catholic colonies of Spain. In the nineteenth and twentieth centuries the Latino and Latina Catholic presence gradually expanded throughout the United States and became increasingly diversified in terms of national origins.

Spanish Colonial Period, 1565–1821

Spain was the European defender and promoter of Catholicism, which was its state religion with no other allowed. By 1508, when Europeans still thought the newly discovered Americas were Asiatic islands rather than continents, the pope in Rome had made a series of agreements establishing the *patronato real* (royal patronage) of the Spanish crown over the church in these territories. The Spanish monarchy committed itself to supporting the exclusive establishment of the Catholic Church and to financing the missionary effort among the native peoples. In return the papacy conceded to Spain major control over church life in the new territories, a control expanded by the Spanish crown in succeeding centuries to matters never intended by the church.

During the Spanish colonial period, the Spanish, their converted Indian allies from central Mexico, African slaves and free persons, and mestizo and mulatto off-spring established themselves permanently in Florida and the northern frontier of New Spain (New Mexico, Texas, Arizona, and California). In these areas the Catholic faith was locally administered in three principal ways. Missions were established for the evangelization of the Native Americans; chaplains were assigned to the military garrisons; and parishes were established for the Hispanic civilians.

In most places the Franciscans (or Jesuits briefly in Florida in 1566–1572 and in Arizona in 1701–1767) served in all three capacities, as missionaries, military chaplains, and pastors. An exception to this general pattern was St. Augustine, Florida, where, since its founding in 1565 as the first Christian settlement in the future continental United States, diocesan clergy (clergy belonging to a diocese, led by a bishop) served as pastors and chaplains to the Hispanics, while Franciscans tended to the missions. In Texas also, diocesan clergy began ministering in San Antonio in 1731 and other communities such as Laredo and Goliad in later decades. But it was not until 1816 that diocesan clergy began to be permanently established as pastors in any of the New Mexican towns, and not until the 1840s in California.

Religious brothers worked alongside the missionary priests in some places. But given the remote, generally dangerous and poor conditions of the Catholic communities on the northern frontier, no convents of religious sisters were established under Spain or Mexico. However, at the Ursuline convent founded by the French in New Orleans in 1727, two Hispanic women made their religious profession in 1781.

Churches apart from the missions were usually built for the Hispanic communities. These churches and the plazas upon which they were situated were the center of community life. The vast majority of the increasingly mestizo and mulatto population was truly and devotedly Catholic in belief and practice, not "nominal" or solely "veneer" Christians, as is sometimes alleged. Although often described as ignorant in doctrine by visiting church dignitaries, their faith and devotion were invariably praised. Colonial Hispanic Catholicism permeated every aspect of life, both private and public: Sunday worship, feast-day celebrations, political ritual, roadside monuments, interrelational bonds through *compadrazgo* (especially through sponsorship of someone's child in baptism), everyday language (for example, *si Dios quiere*: if God so wills; *buenos dias le de Dios*: may God grant you a fine day), and other types of communal and private devotion.

For some there was also recourse to practices frowned upon by the church, and as in every age, there were also the less pious and the anticlerical. In certain cases, persons would be denounced to the church-run Inquisition.

In New Spain, however, and even more so on its northern frontier, the Inquisition was a much more limited institution than is usually alleged. As Solange Alberro affirms for all of Mexico in *Inquisición y sociedad en México*, "the number of cases of repression are ridiculously small in face of an apparently unalterable legend" (Alberro, p. 592).

By the late 1700s, as the missionary effort among Native Americans was just beginning in California, it had ended in Florida and was on the decline in Texas and Arizona. Still remaining, however, and indeed oftentimes growing, were the Hispanic parishes with their priests. In Texas, local Hispanic vocations to the priesthood were emerging by the 1780s, and native sons would serve several communities in the first half of the 1800s. In New Mexico the Hispanic population began extending in all directions with the establishment of new parishes and chapels. In Arizona, Tucson was founded, and Hispanic settlement was increasing, while in California seven military and/or civilian towns were established with their chapels.

With the growth of the English colonies on the Atlantic Coast, the issue of Anglo-Protestant immigrants, legal and illegal, into the Spanish frontier colonies began to emerge in the later 1700s. In Florida unchecked immigration from the southern United States made the northern country outside of St. Augustine and Pensacola mostly unchurched or Protestant without clergy. By the time the United States annexed Florida in 1821, Hispanic Catholics were already a submerged minority in Pensacola and an isolated ethnic island in St. Augustine. In Louisiana, Spanish officials continued the laissez-faire approach toward non-Catholics established by the French, since they too wanted to encourage foreign merchants and immigrants. Protestants were solely required to refrain from public Protestant worship. When the United States took over Louisiana in 1803, east Texas became the next Spanish area to experience the strong pressure of religiously indifferent, skeptical, and Protestant foreign immigration. There once again local officials including clergy adopted a generally tolerant attitude.

The United States and Mexico, 1821–1850

Mexico achieved its independence from Spain in 1821, the same year the United States annexed Florida. Since the United States had already governed Louisiana since 1803, after 1821 only northern Mexico (today's southwestern United States) remained under Hispanic, and more precisely Mexican, direction. Outside the continental United States, Puerto Rico, Cuba, and the Philippines remained part of the Spanish Catholic empire until the end of the 1800s.

In the transition from Spanish to U.S. rule, Hispanic Catholics who had already become an ethnic minority in Louisiana and Florida under Spain suddenly became a religious minority in a Protestant United States. As a consequence of the political change in sovereignty, they were also transferred to the jurisdiction of the U.S. Catholic Church. Intent on protecting their own ways, leaders in both Assumption Parish (Valenzuela) in Louisiana and St. Augustine in Florida quickly seized upon U.S. democratic and congregational notions to form church lay boards that claimed total control over parish affairs. In St. Augustine this led to a brief schism within the community, but a new bishop in distant Mobile gradually asserted control. These Hispanic Catholic communities in the South evolved in predictable patterns for minorities within a dominant culture that often frowned upon them. For a good part of the 1800s they preserved their ethnic identity and much of their culture, including their loyal Catholicism. With changing cultural dynamics by the 1900s, however, their descendants became mostly assimilated into the larger culture. Small groups in both St. Augustine and Louisiana continue to proudly promote their respective Minorcan and Isleño (Canary Island) cultural heritages.

Meanwhile, in newly independent Mexico after 1821, Catholicism was maintained as the nation's exclusive religion. In actual practice, however, local officials in Mexican Texas continued their previous tolerant attitude toward non-Catholic immigrants, as long as they did not make a public demonstration of Protestantism. Foreign "Catholic" immigration was encouraged, and within a decade the land rush in Texas made the eastern third of today's state (to the east of the Guadalupe River) a heavily Southern Protestant or religiously indifferent region. To the west, Mexican Catholics remained the overwhelming population in the vicinity of the San Antonio River, where they were joined by Irish Catholic colonists, and along the Rio Grande. New Mexico, Arizona, and California, protected by immense land and ocean barriers and alerted to Anglo-American tendencies by the Texas experience, received relatively few foreigners before 1848 and retained their strong Hispanic/Mexican Catholicism.

Up to the 1820s almost all the Hispanic settlements on the northern frontier had their own resident priests or were regularly visited by clergy from nearby locations. During that decade, however, a clergy crisis began to manifest itself in Mexico and especially on its northern frontier. In New Mexico, where at least four friars were expelled as Spaniards, there were only half as many priests in 1829 as there had been three years earlier, and yet the Hispanic population was steadily growing. Thanks largely to the ordination of native sons of New Mexico, the twelve priests in 1829 gradually increased to eighteen by the later 1840s, and all the larger Hispanic towns had their own resident priest. In southern Arizona, however, there was a single resident Franciscan for only four of the

years between the expulsion of the two friars as Spaniards in 1828 and the end of Mexican church jurisdiction in 1859. Otherwise the Mexican population of less than one thousand received a visit only about once a year from a priest in Sonora.

In the territory of today's Texas, mostly diocesan clergy continued regular priestly ministry for all the centers of Catholic population up through 1834. Left mostly unattended, however, often to their satisfaction, were the settlements composed of mostly non-Catholic Anglo-Americans. During the Texas Revolution against Mexico in 1835–1836, the Catholic communities in the vicinity of the San Antonio River, being the principal theater of war, were devastated, and most were temporarily abandoned. Upon the formation of the independent Republic of Texas, only San Antonio remained with a pastor. Along the future Texas side of the Rio Grande, however, Mexico still retained control, and the Mexican church continued to provide resident pastors for almost all of the settlements into the 1850s.

In California the secularization and despoliation of the California missions after 1834 destroyed church finances. Since some former missions were practically depopulated and the rest, taken over by Mexicans, no longer required two priests for their operation, the seventeen friars in late 1841, although only about half the number twenty years earlier, were still able to staff all but three places. The Mexican bishop who arrived that year for the newly established California diocese experienced mounting frustration with the nonexistent finances and the continuing clergy shortage. After his death in 1846, the administrator he left in charge provided critical leadership for the California church during the U.S. conquest of California several months later and during the 1849 gold rush and its aftermath. With the gold rush the Mexicans in northern California became a highly marginalized minority, while those in southern California temporarily remained a numerical majority under hostile Anglo pressure. The diocesan administrator, no longer bound by the Mexican government's refusal to allow foreign missionaries after California was officially annexed to the United States in 1848, successfully recruited or incorporated new foreign clergy. As a result, there were twenty-eight priests serving in California when a new bishop from the United States arrived in late 1850.

Thus the Catholic Church on the northern Mexican frontier, far from abandoning or neglecting the people as has often been alleged, demonstrated its perseverance and resiliency in very difficult times of epochal political and religious change. In view of these realities, the standard assertion that Hispanic and Mexican Catholic popular religiosity emerged to fill a religious void caused by the absence of clergy during the late colonial and the Mexican periods is not sustainable. Rather in most cases, with the notable exceptions of Arizona after the 1830s and some mountain villages in northern New Mexico, clergy and laity regularly celebrated together a shared spirituality. In some cases priests introduced new devotions that became popular, while in others laity were the innovators. In northern New Mexico lay confraternities such as the Penitentes played an important role, while in Texas and California they did not. The Hispanic Catholic religiosity of the northern frontier was a rich and complex reality that deserves much more investigation, extending beyond the typical focus on the Penitentes and Our Lady of Guadalupe.

U.S. Southwest, 1850–1880

The U.S. Southwest was created between 1845 and 1856 through the annexation of the Republic of Texas and the conquest or purchase of the other portions of northern Mexico. With the change in national sovereignty, the U.S. Catholic Church took over the official direction of Catholic life from the Mexican church and established the first local dioceses (except for the already existing diocese of California). This usually occurred within a few years of the political transfer. Just as had been the case earlier in Florida and Louisiana, the U.S. church called upon European clerics working in the United States to be its first bishops in all these new areas. Successful local vocations to the priesthood had already ceased in Texas during the Mexican period, and had never become established in Arizona nor California. In New Mexico there were several more native Hispanos ordained before 1880, but in decreasing frequency. To help serve the growing Mexican and Hispanic communities in the Southwest, the new bishops recruited European clergy from their homelands.

Even though the new southwestern dioceses were eventually able to provide clergy to the Mexican-era parishes and start new parishes in other settlements both old and new, many smaller communities remained without resident priests for long periods. Circuit-riding clergy would visit these settlements and ranches at varying intervals or make special trips for marriages or the dying. The regular religious life of these communities was sustained by their traditional piety and practices. In New Mexico the Penitentes often provided Catholic leadership in such cases.

In many new southwestern towns to which Hispanics migrated during this period, they were the great majority of Catholics and thus strongly shaped the initial Catholic base. In some, however, such as Trinidad, Colorado, European and American Catholics, even when a small minority, dominated local church affairs and public worship. In San Francisco, multinational Hispanics were outnumbered by other Catholics and soon had no church to consider their own. They were at first allotted a Mass in Spanish in the city's new multinational parish and later entrusted to a citywide vicar for Hispanics. In the 1870s they successfully petitioned with the help of several South and Central American consuls for their own Spanish-language parish.

Relations between the new church leadership and the Hispanics and their remaining Hispanic clergy varied from place to place and person to person. The new clergy were from a reforming European church, whose stricter moral views influenced by Jansenism were more in line with Calvinistic Protestantism than with Mexican Catholicism. They frowned upon drinking, dancing, and gambling, which were regular pastimes among Hispanics and which were variously participated in by many Hispano and Mexican priests. The new European clergy, trained to fight both Protestantism and secularizing governments on the "old" continent, emphasized regular preaching, something often lacking among the clergy of the Mexican regime. A few Hispanic clergy apparently had more or less clandestine mistresses and children, but others were accused of sexual impropriety simply by suspicion and innuendo. Unfortunately, different moral sensibilities, the undeniable failings of some Hispanic/ Mexican clergy of this period, and cultural and racial prejudice too often led to slanderous accusations about other or even all Hispanic clergy. In certain cases—such as the famous ones of Fathers Martínez, Gallegos, and Ortiz in New Mexico and the Mexican Franciscans in California—disputes over church finances, properties, and discipline played a major role.

Consequently, several priests of the former Mexican regime were suspended or dismissed from ministry by the new bishops, often without proper investigation. A few priests in New Mexico and California chose on their own to return to their former Mexican dioceses. But these controversies should not be overgeneralized. Bishop Alemany in California retained all the Mexican priests there and was a staunch supporter of the Mexican Franciscans at Santa Barbara in their dispute with Bishop Amat. Even Bishop Lamy in New Mexico continued the majority of the Hispanic priests and ordained several new ones. Nevertheless, due to several factors—dismissals, infirmity, and the lack of new ordinations due to societal transitions and the skeptical attitude of the new foreign clergy—Mexican/Hispano clergy disappeared sooner or later from the new southwestern dioceses during these decades.

On the other hand, the European and American religious sisters who arrived for the first time in the Southwest to begin schools, orphanages, and hospitals in strongly Hispanic or Mexican communities attracted vocations from the beginning. Only rarely, however, as in the case of the Sisters of Loretto in New Mexico, did the internal culture of these religious groups intentionally adopt Hispanic traits. Apparently very few Hispanas, such as Dolores Perea (Sister Lucía) in Santa Fe and Rosa

Solis (Sister Teresa) in Brownsville rose to positions of key leadership within their congregations.

As Hispanos and Mexicans lost power in many places, their Hispanic/Mexican Catholic parishes, societies, and religiosity became accentuated as central expressions of their enduring communal identity, their founding role in the settlements, and their resistance to total subjugation and assimilation. Contrary to recently fashionable historiography, the U.S. Catholic Church personnel during this period were not primarily concerned with the rich elite while neglecting Hispanics, nor was their ministry among Hispanics during this period intent on "Americanizing" them. The new multinational clergy and religious sisters and brothers generally admired the people's faith, religious piety, hospitality, and great respect for priests and religious. Bishops insisted that the new church personnel learn Spanish, and learn they did. Most of the foreign clergy encouraged and participated in the people's traditional religious celebrations, while they also introduced and popularized new devotions and practices.

At the same time, the new clergy had a stricter sense of proper decorum in religious observances, frowned on associated dances, and, in deference to Protestant Sabbath sensitivities, avoided Sunday revelries. The new clergy generally found the people lacking in their understanding of church doctrine and in the reception of certain sacraments (confession and communion, as well as marriage in South Texas). Some faulted the people as lax morally. Rarely were the new clergy openly racist, but several were condescending. Most were paternalistic and culturally biased, trying to inculcate their own variant of European Catholicism on the Hispanic Catholic base.

The bishops, aware of the church's losing battle over public education in Europe and often reacting to Protestant initiatives among their Catholic flocks, emphasized Catholic education. In turn, Hispanics strongly supported these initiatives, aided by European Catholic funding agencies and sometimes public funds, which provided education consonant with their Hispanic Catholic faith and culture. Most schools and certainly all charitable institutions in significantly Hispanic towns served the more affluent (boarders) and those of lesser means (day students), with the latter usually being the great majority. The use of Spanish in the Catholic schools varied depending on local conditions, from instruction in Spanish, to bilingual education, to English instruction with classes teaching Spanish, to insistence on English.

Mexicans in the "American" Southwest and Midwest, 1880–1940

In the Southwest, the great Anglo tide of immigration with the arrival of the railroads relegated most Hispanics and Mexicans to a segregated numerical minority. Even in the stronger Hispanic homelands—northern New Mexico, South Texas, and the El Paso district—Anglos made deep inroads. Only where Hispanics remained a large majority of the population, such as in Santa Fe, Laredo, and certain rural ranching districts, did the former more accommodationist interracial patterns survive. Everywhere else divisions were sharply drawn, Spanish was eliminated as a common language, and the newcomer Anglos gained almost complete political control. Hispanics with long residency in the United States began to protest being perceived and classified by racist Anglo newcomers as indistinct from new Mexican immigrants, and started identifying themselves as Hispanic Americans or similar titles.

With such greatly altered social dynamics, the formerly pervasive Hispanic Catholicism became limited to the barrios and often became less public in its expression. Not only was a duality introduced into the communities' Catholicism with the establishment of English-speaking Catholic parishes, but also Protestants started competitive Hispanic churches, schools, and immigrant centers. Many people also expressed faith in folk healers and shrines not officially recognized by the Catholic Church, such as Pedro Jaramillo in South Texas, Teresa Urrea in Arizona, la Capilla de los Milagros in San Antonio, and, somewhat later, el Tiradito in Tucson. In most places the Catholic Church, while maintaining its schools and starting new ones, lost its dominance in the education of Hispanics, due more to the rise of public education than to Protestant denominational efforts. In response to the increasingly widespread poverty among Mexicans and Hispanics, new local Catholic social-welfare societies began to appear.

The surge in Mexican immigration after 1910 did not reverse these basic trends. While the vast majority of Mexican immigrants were located in the Southwest, some also began to establish notable communities in the Midwest and New York. Among the exiles from revolutionary Mexico were Mexican and Spanish clergy and religious sisters and brothers who provided invaluable help in starting new parishes and religious institutions for the rapidly increasing Mexican population. Most of the Mexican clergy and religious eventually returned, but several of the Spanish religious groups remained and were joined by others directly from Spain in succeeding decades. In the Southwest the Mexican immigrants reinvigorated old faith practices, introduced others, and brought about a resurgence of public ritual. In the Midwest they developed national parishes, which became centers of community and identity for large surrounding areas. New pious societies of both Mexican and American provenance appeared, such as the Guadalupanas, the Caballeros de Colón (Knights of Columbus), the Vasallos de Cristo Rey (Servants of Christ the King), and the Santo Nombre (Holy Name).

In both the Southwest and the Midwest racial and ethnic tensions became evident among Catholics, as Mexicans were often made to feel unwelcome by pastors or parishioners in Anglo or European churches. On the other hand, there are numerous examples of non-Mexican Catholics who aided Mexicans in significant ways. Although more parish schools were constructed, they were never able to cater to the majority of the population. Many immigrants, intending to return to Mexico, did not establish strong parish connections in the new unfamiliar surroundings. Many men especially did not attend church regularly because of the demands of work. The growing need for catechists who could respond to these new conditions led to the founding of the important Confraternity of Christian Doctrine and new religious societies of Hispanics and other women to train lay catechists. Church social-welfare efforts also increased significantly with community centers and health clinics, and became more organized on the diocesan level.

During the 1920s a national policy of assimilation to the Anglo-American way of life triumphed in the United States. The Catholic Church joined in the effort to make good English-speaking American citizens out of the Mexican immigrants, while most of the clergy during this period continued to respect and value their culture and language. During a national period of "Americanization," the Mexican-barrio and Hispanic Catholic parishes served as the major social institutions beyond the family in supporting the people's community life and identity.

With the deportations accompanying the Great Depression, the number of Mexicans in the United States dramatically declined for a decade, but not in certain cities like San Antonio, which became urban refuges marked by even greater poverty. Southwestern bishops appealed to the national church to help them address "the Mexican problem" as something beyond their limited local means. But attitudes toward promoting systemic change that would bring about greater social justice varied among church leaders and the faithful themselves, because of fears of communism among labor organizations and ties with the rising Catholic middle and upper classes. Thus, some bishops and priests denounced labor protests, while others supported unions and other social action.

Cubans on the Atlantic Coast

Outside the Southwest, by 1880 the "ethnic-island" Hispanic Catholic communities in St. Augustine and certain places in Louisiana were entering a stage of major assimilation to the dominant local culture. But along the Atlantic Coast a small number of Cuban and Puerto Rican political exiles and businessmen had begun to emigrate to New York after 1820, including the famous Father Félix Varela. In 1868 a stronger immigration of Cubans began

to New York and Key West and, two decades later, to the Tampa area. Tampa quickly became the largest center of Cuban American life until the 1950s. By 1914, 15,600 Cubans and 4,000 Spaniards formed half of the multiracial Catholics of the St. Augustine diocese, which included most of Florida.

In Cuba itself most people were poorly educated in the Catholic faith and little involved in the institutional church, if not actually alienated from it and anticlerical. This was due to several historical factors: long-standing and increasing secularizing influences in Cuba, the refusal of sugar-mill owners to provide for the Christianization of their massive number of African slaves, the growing lack of clergy outside Havana, and the support of continued Spanish rule by the mostly Spanish clergy. In Key West and Tampa the radical ideologies of the Cuban labor movement were also very strong. Nevertheless, the great majority of Cubans professed Catholicism (even if the Santería of many Afro-Cubans was only nominally Catholic), baptized their children, and had a personal and family-based faith life.

The non-Hispanic clergy and sisters who were sent to Key West and Tampa were confronted for decades with a very low level of Cuban participation in parish life, although the schools (taught in English) did have an impact on some of the youth. After 1914, Cuban immigration to the United States was quite low, until a gradual increase in the 1950s briefly made New York the largest U.S. Cuban community. But the extensive neocolonial connections that developed after the United States helped Cuba achieve independence from Spain in 1898 brought about a continual stream of travelers between the two nations.

Puerto Ricans in the Northeast

When the United States took control of Puerto Rico after the Spanish-American War in 1898, Anglo-Protestant Manifest Destiny was at its height. The great majority of the people outside San Juan had become accustomed to a Catholicism that was home and family based, with participation in official church services only on a few important feast days annually. The people's faith was basically orthodox but with very little doctrinal education. Children were always baptized, but church marriages were usually practiced only among the upper class and the emerging middle class. The principally Spanish elite, especially the males, had strong secularizing tendencies and were mostly indifferent to the institutional church or even hostile. Peasants in the interior mountain region would usually have their illegal marital unions "fixed" afterward by the church, but the coastal laborers and, in the twentieth century, the urban proletariat became accustomed to concubinage and impermanent unions. Native-born Puerto

Rican priests had greatly decreased in the later nineteenth century, making Spaniards the principal clergy.

After 1898 the mostly Spanish clergy and sisters on the island left in great numbers. As U.S. Protestant missionaries and educators entered, the Catholic bishops and the bulk of the sisters and clergy (mostly from religious orders) were also imported from the northeastern United States. There were only twelve native-born priests by 1925. These quadrupled by 1960, but practically the only religious congregations to have Puerto Rican recruits were Spanish and later Puerto Rican female ones. The Catholic clergy on the island quadrupled from 1910 to 1960, many more parishes and rural chapels were established, devotions and pious societies were fostered, and much energy was put into Catholic schools, but the proportion of priests to people was still quite low, so that many areas remained with church services biweekly or monthly. American clergy remained perturbed by the noninstitutional character of Puerto Rican Catholicism and the marriage situation and sought mostly without success to alter both. While Puerto Rico continued to have a basically Catholic ethos, by the 1950s Pentecostalism had become the largest Protestant group on the island and helped make it one of the most Protestant of all Latin American countries.

Puerto Ricans began to come in larger numbers to the Northeast after 1917, the year in which they were made U.S. citizens. In the previous two decades the New York dioceses had established one or the other Spanish-speaking parish to care for the small pan-Hispanic population. As Harlem developed into a major lower-class Puerto Rican barrio, Puerto Rican national parishes and a settlement house were founded. The parishes were not very successful for many reasons: the disorientation and racism experienced by the immigrants in the Northeast, the growing appeal of Pentecostalism, the constant flux of people between the mainland and the island, and perhaps most of all the religious history of Puerto Rico itself.

The Second Generation and the Second Wave, 1940–1965

The period from World War II to the Second Vatican Council (1962–1965) witnessed both the coming to adulthood of a large U.S.–born generation of Latinos and Latinas and the beginning of a strong second wave of immigrants from Puerto Rico, immigrants from Mexico, and refugees from Cuba. This was the Great Migration epoch for Puerto Ricans, impacting first the Northeast and spreading to the Midwest, Florida, and other parts of the country. It was also the first massive exodus of Cubans to Florida after the Castro revolution in 1959. This made Miami the new center of U.S. Cuban Catholicism. The first wave of Cuban refugees were disproportionately middle- to upper-class laity, priests, and religious who introduced a culturally untypical more institutional Catholic element into Cuban Catholicism in the United States. For twentieth-century Mexican immigrants, this was the period of the second great wave, establishing communities in the Northwest and Southeast and increasing their presence throughout the country.

During the 1940s a trend in the U.S. Catholic Church away from national parishes began to impact ministry among Latinos and Latinas. It was argued that national parishes did not respond adequately to the needs of the increasingly numerous second and third generations of immigrants, that fostering old-country nationalisms impeded the acceptance of Catholics by other Americans, that national parishes too often abetted racial discrimination, that since integration would eventually occur it was best to begin with it right away, that by the third generation national parishes were in a decline and became economic burdens, and that there were insufficient personnel to continue to provide for separate national parishes within the same territory.

In New York in the 1940s, the archbishop refused to create new national parishes for the mushrooming population of Puerto Rican immigrants, calling instead for bilingual or multilingual integrated parishes with definite territorial limits for membership. In the Southwest, some church officials began to change Mexican national parishes into territorial ones and to refuse requests to establish new national parishes. In what in hindsight was often an excess of reforming zeal, some bishops mandated that in smaller towns the "Mexican" and "Anglo" parishes be combined into one congregation. These actions often deprived the new Latino and Latina immigrants of the valuable spiritual and cultural center in their own neighborhood, which had proven so beneficial to previous generations.

In the Southwest it was often possible for the new immigrants to turn in phenomenal numbers to those Mexican "territorial" parishes that already existed, at times quite distant from their own homes, and thus make them unofficial national parishes. In some cases, such as with the colonial-era "La Placita" in Los Angeles, churches remained officially "national" for all the Spanish speaking without territorial restrictions. But the Puerto Ricans were more seriously handicapped by having relatively few preexisting Puerto Rican parishes to which to turn.

The same zeal for social justice that helped to motivate these bishops toward integrating parishes and schools also prompted the first national church organizations on behalf of the Spanish speaking. Archbishop Lucey of San Antonio was instrumental in the organization of the first Southwestern Catholic conferences on the Spanish speaking in 1943 and 1944, which led in turn to the formation of the Bishops' Committee for the Spanish Speaking in 1945. The latter group became an advocate for social action and promoted the development of local diocesan councils and diocesan offices for the Spanish speaking.

One of the principal concerns of these groups was the growing number of Latino and Latina seasonal migrant workers throughout the nation, with their oftentimes unmet pastoral and social needs. In several places church personnel sought to alleviate those needs, but they were often lagging in supporting the migrants' efforts to organize to demand better conditions. In California a few priests helped direct César Chávez into community organizing and began to speak out against injustice to the farmworkers. Such actions were not typical among the clergy and caused great tension within the Anglo-Catholic community.

As a large second generation of Mexican descent grew up, an internal church dispute developed over whether clergy from Mexico, who thoroughly knew and promoted Mexican culture and spirituality, should be the ministers of choice among immigrant families, or whether suitably trained bilingual American clergy, who could better respond to the Americanizing second generation, were preferable. This debate took place among clergy and within the ambivalent Mexican-descent communities themselves.

By this time the great majority of Mexican priests had returned to Mexico, and there seemed to be more instances when bishops assigned priests not sufficiently familiar with the Spanish language and Mexican religious practices. Some aggressively autocratic bishops, no longer coming from the ranks of clergy who had worked for decades among Hispanics or Mexicans, did not think highly of nor relate well to the Mexican population, even when in some ways they promoted their welfare. Several dioceses, which had previously relied heavily on religious orders for Hispanic ministry, mandated that all of their own seminarians and/or clergy learn Spanish. Also during this time some Hispanics and Mexican Americans began once again to be ordained to the priesthood, whereas previously there appears to have been very little vocational recruiting among them.

The Struggle for a Latino and Latina Church, 1965–2005

The year 1965 was a watershed in many ways for the U.S. Latino and Latina community. The major changes in U.S. immigration law that year greatly improved the possibilities for Latin American immigrants from other countries besides Mexico. Differing internal factors in those countries themselves and the ever-present U.S. involvement explain the subsequent immigration history of each national group. The first to massively immigrate were the

Dominicans, followed by the various Central American nations, and finally those of South America. Each of these nations has its particular Catholic history and practices. Indeed, there are significantly varying proportions of Catholics among these nationalities in the United States. A 2002 survey estimated that in the United States, 76 percent of Mexicans were Catholic, 70 percent of South Americans, 64 percent of Cubans, 55 percent of Puerto Ricans, and 51 percent of Central Americans. The people from these various nations bring their own expectations and gifts into the U.S. Catholic Church.

The Second Vatican Council, concluded in 1965, ushering in major changes in church life. These developments in long-held traditions profoundly affected all Latino and Latina Catholics and were variously received by them, with either joy or confusion or anger. The liturgical reforms of the council opened up the way for church services entirely in Spanish, the introduction of popular Latino and Latina music and traditional dances into the Mass, married lay deacons, and a greater role for the laity within the official liturgy. But in practice they also often led to the removal of traditional imagery from the churches and the loss of many devotions in official church life. These changes were symptomatic of many others affecting every dimension of the Catholicism that had been so formative in shaping the Latino and Latina experience.

It was in 1965 also that César Chávez and Dolores Huerta organized the National Farmworkers strike in Delano, which catalyzed many Mexican American Catholics into demanding social justice. For two decades there had been a gradually increasing if still small number of Mexican American and Puerto Rican priests on the mainland. But Latinos and Latinas had remained virtually absent from important church leadership positions. A group of Chicano priests formed Padres Asociados para Derechos Religiosos, Educativos y Sociales (PADRES) while Hispanic sisters formed Las Hermanas, as activist organizations to work for the improvement of conditions in both church and society for Latinos and Latinas. Besides advocating for various social causes, they demanded that Latino bishops, up to that time nonexistent, be appointed and that seminaries become more sensitive to their culture. In 1970 Patricio Flores became the first U.S. Latino bishop, soon followed by others. That same year the church's national office for the Spanish speaking was moved to the headquarters of the Bishops' Conference and later upgraded to a secretariat to provide it more influence in national church decisions.

The first broad-based national Encuentro (meeting) of representatives of the Latino and Latina church was held in 1972, followed by others in 1977 and 1985. It was also in 1972 that the Mexican American Cultural Center opened in San Antonio as a pastoral center for research and training in Hispanic culture and ministry, and other such centers followed in the Southeast, the Northeast, and other areas. Realizing that leadership in church and society calls for serious theological research and publication, the Academy of Catholic Hispanic Theologians of the United States (ACHTUS) was organized in 1989, and from this group has issued a steadily increasing amount of research and writing.

These have been important steps, but the full integration of Latinos and Latinas within the U.S. Catholic Church's life and mission remains an ongoing challenge. The perennial problems remain, as Latinos and Latinas become much more present in many places where formerly they were not part of the local church. There is still a great lack of native U.S. Latino and Latina vocations to the priesthood and religious life. Many would hold that the Catholic Church has not responded effectively enough to the world of the post-immigrant Latino and Latina generations. The increasing multi-nationality of Latino and Latina Catholics challenges the traditional self-concept and practice of more and more local church communities, including Latinos and Latinas themselves, as well as national organizations. Although the great majority of Latino and Latina Catholics in the United States remain lower class, the growing upper and middle classes often have different political and religious perspectives.

As Latinos and Latinas become a majority in the Catholic Church in this country, the questions of leadership training, still far from satisfactorily answered, become more important than ever. And their dialogue with others—African Americans, Asians, Indians, Anglos—both within and beyond the Catholic Church becomes critical. The growing numbers of recent immigrants from practically all of the Latin American nations and instant electronic communications bind and obligate the U.S. Latino and Latina community and the U.S. Catholic Church with Latin America in an unprecedented way. It is no longer possible for Latino and Latina Catholics to ignore or ostracize Latino and Latina Protestants. In the early twenty-first century, U.S. Latino and Latina Catholicism is youthful, increasingly variegated, and faced with a leadership responsibility for which many have not yet been offered adequate training.

See also Barrios; Central Americans; Chicanos and Chicanas; Cuban Americans; Dominicans; First Nations and Mexican-Origin People; Liberation Theology; Marianismo; Mexican-Origin People in the United States; Missions and Other Colonial Churches; Native Americans/Mexicanos; Penitentes; Protestantism; Puerto Ricans; Santería; South Americans; Theology; *and* Virgen de Guadalupe.

BIBLIOGRAPHY

Alberro, Solange. *Inquisición y sociedad en México, 1571–1700*. Mexico: Fondo de Cultura Económica, 1988.

Davis, Kenneth G., and Yolanda Tarango, eds. *Bridging Boundaries: The Pastoral Care of U.S. Hispanics*. Scranton, Pa.: University of Scranton Press, 2000.

Díaz-Stevens, Ana María. *Oxcart Catholicism on Fifth Avenue: The Impact of the Puerto Rican Migration upon the Archdiocese of New York*. Notre Dame, Ind.: University of Notre Dame Press, 1993.

Dolan, Jay P., and Allan Figueroa Deck, eds. *Hispanic Catholic Culture in the U.S.: Issues and Concerns*. Notre Dame, Ind.: University of Notre Dame Press, 1994.

Dolan, Jay P., and Gilberto M. Hinojosa, eds. *Mexican Americans and the Catholic Church, 1900–1965*. Notre Dame, Ind.: University of Notre Dame Press, 1994.

Dolan, Jay P., and Jaime R. Vidal, eds. *Puerto Rican and Cuban Catholics in the U.S., 1900–1965*. Notre Dame, Ind.: University of Notre Dame Press, 1994.

Matovina, Timothy, and Gerald E. Poyo, eds. *Presente! U.S. Latino Catholics from Colonial Origins to the Present*. Maryknoll, N.Y.: Orbis Books, 2000.

Matovina, Timothy, and Gerald E. Poyo, eds. *Recovering the U.S. Hispanic Catholic Heritage*. U.S. Catholic Historian 20 (Fall 2002), 21 (Winter 2003).

Neri, Michael Charles. *Hispanic Catholicism in Transitional California: The Life of José González Rubio, O. F. M. (1804–1875)*. Berkeley, Calif.: Academy of American Franciscan History, 1997.

Privett, Stephen A. *The U.S. Catholic Church and Its Hispanic Members: The Pastoral Vision of Archbishop Robert E. Lucey*. San Antonio, Tex.: Trinity University Press, 1988.

Sandoval, Moises, ed. *Hispanic Catholics: Historical Explorations and Cultural Analysis*. U.S. Catholic Historian 9 (Winter/Spring 1990).

Sandoval, Moises. *On the Move: A History of the Hispanic Church in the United States*. Maryknoll, N.Y.: Orbis Books, 1990.

Steele, Thomas J., Paul Rhetts, and Barbe Awalt, eds. *Seeds of Struggle/Harvest of Faith: The Papers of the Archdiocese of Santa Fe Catholic Cuarto Centennial Conference: The History of the Catholic Church in New Mexico*. Albuquerque, N.Mex.: LPD Press, 1998.

Stevens Arroyo, Antonio M. *Prophets Denied Honor: An Anthology of the Hispano Church in the United States*. Maryknoll, N.Y.: Orbis Books, 1980.

Treviño, Roberto. *The Church in the Barrio: Ethno-Catholicism in Houston*. Chapel Hill: University of North Carolina Press, forthcoming.

Tweed, Thomas A. *Our Lady of the Exile: Diasporic Religion at a Cuban Catholic Shrine in Miami*. New York: Oxford University Press, 1997.

ROBERT E. WRIGHT

CENSUS. How many Latinas and Latinos are in the United States in the early twenty-first century, and where did they come from? In the year 2000 the U.S. census indicated that 35.3 million residents of the United States reported they were Spanish, Hispanic, or Latina or Latino. (Brazilians were not included in this count because they are Portuguese-speaking.) This meant that 12.5 percent of the total United States population, or one out of every eight United States residents, was "some kind of" Latina or Latino. If one added the 3.8 million Puerto Ricans resident in Puerto Rico to the above total, it would become 39.1 million Latinas and Latinos in 2000. Of the 35.3 million, 58 percent checked a box indicating they were Mexican, 10 percent Puerto Rican, 3 percent Cuban, and 2 percent Dominican, and 28 percent said they were some other type of Hispanic or Latina/Latino. This last category was called "All Other Hispanic or Latino" (AOHL) in the census. In this last category were people who came from (or whose ancestors had come from) the remaining Spanish-speaking countries, for example, 655,165 Salvadorans, 470,684 Colombians, 260,559 Ecuadorians, 233,926 Peruvians, and 217,589 Hondurans. There were also smaller groups from other countries in Latin America in this category plus 100,135 Spaniards and a large group (686,004) who indicated they were "Spanish," "Hispanic," or some other generic Latina/Latino term but did not give their country of origin. (A substantial number of Latinas and Latinos [5,349,889] was "not elsewhere classified," meaning those individuals did not indicate they were Hispanic or Latina/Latino. However, other aspects of their census forms indicated that they were, such as a record indicating that a relative in a household was headed by one or more Latinas or Latinos.)

These numbers indicate that the Latina/Latino pot in the United States is quite diverse when it comes to Latina/Latino national origins. There are also some fairly clear patterns. Because of history and migration, this Latina/Latino pot is more Mexican and Central American in the West and Southwest, more Caribbean in the Northeast and the South, and a mixture of both in the Midwest. However, the census shows that the Latina/ Latino populations are becoming larger and more heterogeneous in each region. For example, in the area historically known as "Little Havana" in Miami, non-Cuban Latinas and Latinos outnumber Cubans. In all areas of the country, towns that previously never had Spanish-speaking communities now have shops, restaurants, and schools that service (predominantly) Spanish-speaking communities. Some states have seen their Latina/Latino populations increase over 200 to 300 percent, for example, Alabama, Georgia, Nevada, North Carolina, and Tennessee. Although in 2000, 75 percent of Latinas/Latinos were still concentrated in seven states (California, Texas, New York,

Florida, Illinois, Arizona, and New Jersey), there were substantial concentrations in all states. According to the census, the growth of Latina/Latino populations is also fueling the growth of the U.S. population as a whole. Between 1990 and 2000 Latinas and Latinos accounted for 40 percent of U.S. population growth, leading to the increasing Latinization of the United States.

How Does the Census Arrive at These Numbers?

Data on Latinas and Latinos is collected by many agencies, but the U.S. Census Bureau collects the most comprehensive, most extensively used data on Latinas and Latinos. They do so by asking the whole population whether or not they are Latinas/Latinos. In the year 2000 the census question read as shown in Figure 1.

The data on the number of Colombians, for example, comes from write-in responses to this question. The U.S. Constitution requires that, in order for the people of the United States to be accurately represented within their politically elected bodies, a count of the population, that is, a census, must be taken every ten years. Over the years the census has expanded to count not just individuals but a multitude of other characteristics, such as gender, age, and housing conditions.

Latino and Latina Responses to the Race Question

The census also asks everyone in the country what his or her race is. The race question in the 2000 census is shown in Figure 2.

The census does not include Latinas/Latinos as a race category because the census position is that Hispanics can be of any race.

When one looks at how Latinas and Latinos answered this question, one sees some interesting results. Latinas and Latinos did not answer the question the same way non-Latinos and non-Latinas did. For example, whereas less than 1 percent of the non-Latino and non-Latina population reported they were of "Some other race," 42 percent of Latinas and Latinos chose this category. (In fact Latinas and Latinos constitute the overwhelming majority in this category, between 95 and 97 percent.) Of Latinas and Latinos, 47.9 percent said they were "White," 2 percent reported they were "Black, African Am., or Negro," 1.2 percent said "American Indian or Alaska Native," 0.5 percent indicated they were in one of the Asian

FIGURE 1

7. **Is Person 1 Spanish/Hispanic/Latino?** *Mark the "No"* box if *not* Spanish/Hispanic/Latino

[The following check-off categories were provided:]

No, not Spanish/Hispanic/Latino   Yes, Puerto Rican
Yes, Mexican, Mexican Am., Chicano   Yes, Cuban
Yes, other Spanish/Hispanic/Latino – print group

8. What is Person 1's race? Mark X one or more races to indicate what this person considers himself/herself to be.

FIGURE 2

[The check-off categories provided were as follows:]

White
Black, African Am., or Negro
American Indian or Alaska Native – Print name of enrolled or principal tribe

Asian Indian	Japanese	Native Hawaiian
Chinese	Korean	Guamanian or Chamorro
Filipino	Vietnamese	Samoan
Other Asian – print race		

Some other race – print race

or Pacific Islander categories, and another 6.3 percent chose two or more groups. Data from the 2000 census for each Latina/Latino national origin group is not yet publicly available; however, analysis of the 1990 figures indicates that Latina/Latino national origin groups differed with regard to their racial self-classification patterns. For example, of the largest groups, only 12 percent of the Cuban group chose the "other race" category, whereas 47 percent of Mexicans, 46 percent of Puerto Ricans, and 38 percent of the "other Spanish/Hispanic/Latino" group did. However, whereas the different Latina/Latino groups varied in the extent to which they chose the "other race" category, all of them chose this category to a greater degree than did non-Latinos (less than 2 percent).

The different Latina/Latino national origin groups also varied in the extent to which they chose the other racial categories in 1990, when the Census Bureau restricted respondents to selecting only one racial category. Again focusing first on the largest groups, 84 percent of Cubans chose the "White" category as compared with 51 percent of Mexicans, 46 percent of Puerto Ricans, and 52 percent of the AOHL group. Self-classification as "Black" varied from 0.9 percent in the Mexican group to 7 percent in the Puerto Rican group, with 6.5 percent of the AOHL group and 3.7 percent of the Cuban group reporting they were "Black." Among the smaller groups, the Panamanian group reported the highest percentage "Black" (36 percent), Colombians the highest percentage "White" (64 percent), Panamanians the highest percentage "American Indian" (2.94 percent), and Salvadorans the highest percentage "other race" (59 percent).

Large numbers of Latinas and Latinos also chose the "Some other race" category for the last three censuses. Moreover many Latinas and Latinos, when they checked off the "Some other race" category, wrote in the box that explicitly asked for race the name of a Latina/Latino country or group to "explain" their race or their "otherness." For example, they wrote in that they were "Dominican," "Honduran," or "Boricua" (Puerto Rican). The fact that these Latina/Latino referents were, in the main, cultural or national-origin terms suggests that many Latinas and Latinos

viewed the question of race as a question of culture, national origin, and socialization rather than simply biological or genetic ancestry or color. Indeed, studies have found that for many Latinas and Latinos "race" is understood to be national origin, nationality, ethnicity, culture, or a combination of these and skin color. When many (but not all) Latinas and Latinos use the term "race" or *raza*, they tend to consider it a reflection of these understandings. Studies have also found that Latinas and Latinos tend to see "race" as a continuum, not as a dichotomous variable in which individuals are either white or black. Although Latinas and Latinos tend to utilize cultural frames of reference when discussing race, "race" as understood by Latinas and Latinos is not without its implications of power and privilege in Latin America or in the United States.

What determines how Latinas and Latinos respond to questions of race? There are a lot of variables that influence how Latinas and Latinos respond. For example, there are contextual variables, such as who asks the question, who answers the question, and how and where the question is asked. In other words, is there an Anglo interviewer, a Latina/Latino category as a possible choice, or the presence of other cultural groups as categories? What is the purpose of the question? How is the question phrased, structured, formatted, and where is the question placed, that is, after a question about national origin or before? There is a host of other variables that also appear to exert an influence on how Latinas and Latinos respond to questions of race. Some examples include a person's phenotype or how others classify him or her; the physical variation within the person's family, such as being the lightest or the darkest one within the family; the family's class status; and the person's age, generational status in the United States, or educational attainment. Also important are whether the person speaks only English; significant experiences in schools, jobs, and social settings; neighborhood socialization; experiences of racial discrimination; the racial structure in different regions of the United States; and the racial formation process in his or her country of origin and the extent of antiblack racism therein. All of these influence how Latinas and Latinos respond to questions of race.

How Have Latinos Been Counted in the Past?

If one reviews the classification history of Spanish-origin or Spanish-speaking peoples in the United States census, one finds, first, that classifying Latinas and Latinos has been highly variable. Second, one finds that this fluctuation has involved not just "racial" classification changes but also the use of cultural criteria, such as language, surname, and "origin." Both types of criteria have been used to determine whether or not a person is what one might call a Latina/Latino in the early twenty-first century. In many ways the history and experience of Latinas and Latinos with census enumeration highlights how multidimensional and fluid the concepts of race and ethnicity have been over time. In part because of these changing criteria, the experience of Latinas and Latinos in the United States illustrates the social constructedness of race.

With regard to the history of racial classification, one finds the following set of changes. Perhaps in response to increasing numbers of Mexican immigrants at the time, the first time Latinas and Latinos were specifically counted in the national decennial census was in 1930, when a separate category for "Mexicans" appeared in the race question. The data gathered as a result of this "Mexican" category was reported subsequently with the "other races" data. As the census report indicated at the time, "Persons of Mexican birth or parentage who were not definitely reported as White or Indian were designated Mexican" and included with "other races" (U.S. Bureau of the Census 1932, p.1). Thus in 1930 Mexicans were placed in a "Mexican race" category unless interviewers determined they were white or Indian. (No other Latinas and Latinos were separately counted.) At the time census takers were instructed, "In order to obtain separate figures for Mexicans, it was decided that all persons born in Mexico, or having parents born in Mexico, who were not definitely White, Negro, Indian, Chinese, or Japanese, would be returned as Mexicans (Mex)" (U.S. Bureau of the Census 1989, p. 60). One can only imagine the difficulty census takers, who in all likelihood were predominantly non-Latino whites, must have had in excluding in this highly physically heterogeneous Mexican population those who were "definitely White, Negro, Indian, Chinese, or Japanese" from the "Mexicans."

In 1930 there was also apparently some concern that Mexicans who were "definitely not white" might have been counted previously with the white population. In the 1930 census there was a table that estimated the number of Mexicans that had been included in the white population in the 1920 census. The intent of this table was to provide an estimate of the number of Mexicans who had been miscounted as "Whites" in the previous census. A

chart of the number of Mexicans in selected states accompanied this table. It also included the nativity status of Mexicans and whether they were of foreign or mixed parentage. In essence, since there had been no Mexican racial category in the previous 1920 census, the concern was that some Mexicans might have been counted in the white category, and this was a belated attempt to determine how many had been placed in this category.

The subsequent 1940 census dropped this Mexican racial category. The census did not indicate why this change occurred, but the 1940 census noted, "Persons of Mexican birth or ancestry who were not definitely Indian or of other nonwhite race" were to be counted as white in 1940 (U.S. Bureau of the Census 1943, p. 6). Thus in the space of a decade Mexicans went from having a separate race category into which they were placed—unless of course it could be proved they were white, Indian, or of another nonwhite race—to being included in the white category—unless determined to be Indian or another nonwhite race. Moreover whereas in the 1930 census "Mexicans" were counted as part of a generic "other races" category, in 1940 Mexicans were counted as "White"—unless they had been classified into another nonwhite category.

The criterion established in 1940 was used to classify Mexicans racially for the next two censuses. This definition of Mexicans was explicitly stated in the introductions to the decennial censuses of 1950 and 1960. The same criterion was also applied to other Latinas and Latinos who came in greater numbers after World War II, for example, Puerto Ricans in the late forties and fifties, Cubans during the sixties, and Dominicans and Central and South Americans in the late sixties and seventies. In the 1960 census the instructions given to census takers for determining race or color by observation directed that "Puerto Ricans, Mexicans, or other persons of Latin descent would be classified as 'White' unless they were definitely Negro, Indian, or some other race" (U.S. Bureau of the Census 1989, p. 78). Prior to 1970 a census enumerator visited people in their homes and recorded their race and other census information. However, it was in a sample of the 1970 census that enumerators first asked Latinas and Latinos to choose a category for race from standard race categories (such as those in Figure 2). However, if respondents chose a response, such as "Mexican" or "Puerto Rican," they were reclassified, depending on their appearance, by the census enumerators into the racial categories that were listed, that is, white, black, and so forth. As a result of this practice, most Latinas and Latinos were classified as "White" prior to 1980. Indeed, in 1970, 93.3 percent of Latinas and Latinos were classified as "White."

The U.S. census first used mail-back questionnaires in 1980. In this and subsequent censuses everyone (including Latinas and Latinos) determined his or her own race from the categories listed. This was the beginning of self-reporting for the whole population. Also in 1980 the U.S. census first introduced what it called the "Hispanic identifier," that is, a question that specifically counted people of Spanish language or origin. A generic term was sought to count the various Spanish-origin populations, and the term "Hispanic" was created for this purpose.

Cultural criteria have also been used to define and classify Latinas and Latinos in the U.S. census. As in the case of racial classification, the cultural markers and categories used to classify Latinas and Latinos have changed over time. In 1940 the census used a linguistic definition to determine who was Latina/Latino, and "Persons of Spanish mother tongue" were reported. In 1950 and 1960 the census's language criterion was dropped and "persons of Spanish surname" were reported. In the 1970 census individuals were asked about their general "come from," or, as the census put it, "about their 'origin,'" and respondents could choose among several Latina/Latino origins listed on the questionnaire. Thus between 1940 and 1970 Latinas and Latinos were enumerated according to three different cultural criteria, that is, linguistic (1940), surname (1950 and 1960), and "origin" (1970). In sum, the classification of Latinas and Latinos in the U.S. census has involved major variation and flux, including varying cultural and racial criteria over time.

Race and Citizenship Rights

Latinas and Latinos have not been the only group to experience shifts in racial placement and labeling both in the census and in the legal realm. The classification and legal experiences of Asian Indians, Native American Indians, African Americans, and Pacific Islanders, for example, illuminate the historical difficulty the United States has had dealing with mixture and with groups who have not folded neatly into discrete categories of color. These groups' experiences also underscore the extent to which classifications have been influenced by and in turn have influenced political considerations. In the past one's racial classification often determined citizenship and other rights. For example, because of legislation passed in 1790 and in existence until 1952, nonwhites were not allowed to become naturalized citizens. In some states, for example, noncitizens were not allowed to own land at certain points. Also under Jim Crow laws native-born persons of color were routinely relegated or channeled into segregated, generally inferior facilities or denied (through formal and informal means) the basic rights of citizenship, such as voting. Consequently many individuals went to court in an attempt to be classified as "white" so as to be entitled to all the rights and privileges of "white" citizens in the United States.

The Latina/Latino experience has been less legally contentious than that of other groups because Latinas and Latinos were not generally denied citizenship. Citizenship issues for Latinas and Latinos have been more a matter of defining what citizenship means rather than securing it. Citizenship was granted to many Spanish-speaking persons as a result of the treaties signed after United States conquests of Florida, the Southwest, and Puerto Rico. However, many questions about this citizenship have been and are still raised, such as whether this citizenship by conquest was an equivalent or a second-class citizenship; the extent to which citizenship rights were denied after conquest; and whether this citizenship included cultural citizenship, that is, the right to speak Spanish and maintain one's culture.

It is difficult to say to what extent census classifications have influenced the racial identity of Latinas and Latinos; more research is needed in this area. Clearly Latina and Latino responses influenced the census's new policy of allowing people to choose more than one race, which parents of biracial children and multiracial individuals had lobbied for. This was a significant departure from the census's previous 200-year policy. It is also clear that historically Latinas and Latinos have confounded and continue to confound the basic bipolar (white or nonwhite) racial structure that evolved in the United States. In part this is because they are not easily accommodated into the bipolar structure—nor in some cases do they wish to be—because of their varying phenotypes, mixtures, and perspectives on race. This group, perhaps more than other groups, illustrates the permeability and shifting lines of the bipolar structure.

Increasingly the research from all fields argues against the existence of biologically based race groups and for the concept of socially constructed races. What the experience of Latinas and Latinos in the census shows most clearly is the extent to which concepts of race and ethnicity overlap, just as they do in real life.

See also Asian Latinos; Central Americans; Chicanos and Chicanas; Citizenship; Mexican-Origin People in the United States; Native Americans/Mexicanos; Puerto Ricans; Race and Racialization; South Americans; *and* Whiteness.

BIBLIOGRAPHY

REFERENCES

Acuña, Rodolfo. *Occupied America: A History of Chicanos*. 3rd ed. New York: Harper and Row, 1988.

Cabranes, José A. *Citizenship and the American Empire: Notes on the Legislative History of the United States Citizenship of Puerto Ricans*. New Haven, Conn.: Yale University Press, 1979.

Denton, Nancy A., and Douglas S. Massey. "Racial Identity among Caribbean Hispanics: The Effect of Double Minority Status on Residential Segregation." *American Sociological Review* 54 (1989): 790–808.

Flores, William V., and Rina Benmayor, eds. *Latino Cultural Citizenship: Claiming Identity, Space, and Rights*. Boston: Beacon Press, 1997.

Haney López, Ian F. *White by Law: The Legal Construction of Race.* New York: New York University Press, 1996.

Hernández, José. *Conquered Peoples in America.* Dubuque, Iowa: Kendall/Hunt Publishing, 1994.

Kissam, Edward, Enrique Herrera, and Jorge M. Nakamoto. "Hispanic Response to Census Enumeration Forms and Procedures." Task Order No. 46-YABC-2-0001, Contract No. 50-YABC-2-66027 submitted by Aguirre International, 411 Borel Ave, Suite 402, San Mateo, Calif., 94402 to U. S. Bureau of the Census, Center for Survey Methods Research (March 1993).

Martin, Elizabeth, T. J. DeMaio, and P. C. Campanelli. "Context Effects for Census Measures of Race and Hispanic Origin." *Public Opinion Quarterly* 54 (1990): 551–566.

Oboler, Suzanne. *Ethnic Labels, Latino Lives: Identity and the Politics of (Re)Presentation in the United States.* Minneapolis: University of Minnesota Press, 1995.

Rodríguez, Clara E. *Changing Race: Latinos, the Census, and the History of Ethnicity in the United States.* New York: New York University Press, 2000. Much of the material in this entry is drawn from this book; readers are referred to it for more in-depth analysis of contemporary and historical issues concerning census classifications in the 2000 census.

Tienda, Marta, and Vilma Ortiz. " 'Hispanicity' and the 1980 Census." *Social Science Quarterly* 67 (March 1986): 3–20.

CENSUS REPORTS

U.S. Bureau of the Census. *200 Years of U.S. Census Taking: Population and Housing Questions, 1790–1990.* Washington, D.C.: U.S. Department of Commerce, Bureau of the Census, 1989. This report provides a good overview of the changes in census questions over time.

U.S. Bureau of the Census. *Overview of Race and Hispanic Origin: Census 2000 Brief.* This report provides a summary of major items on the Latina/Latino population from the 2000 decennial census data.

U.S. Bureau of the Census. *We, the American . . . Hispanics.* Ethnic and Hispanic Statistics Branch, Population Division, November 1993. Washington, D.C.: U.S. Government Printing Office, 1993. This report presents the major results of the *1990 Census of Population: Social and Economic Characteristics* for the Hispanic population in the United States.

U.S. Department of Commerce. Economics and Statistics Administration. "Results of the 1996 Race and Ethnic Targeted Test," Population Division Working Paper No. 18, U.S. Bureau of the Census, Washington, D.C. 20233-8800, May 1997. This is an interesting analysis of how Latinas and Latinos and other groups responded to various versions of the race question, including choosing more than one option, adding a multiracial category, and including "Hispanics" as a race category.

CLARA E. RODRÍGUEZ

CENTER FOR LATINO INITIATIVES.

The inclusion of Latinas and Latinos at the Smithsonian Institution coincides with the 1992 publication of a landmark report, *Excellence and Equity: Education and the Public Dimensions of Museums*, by the American Association of Museums. The key idea in the report is that "museums must become more inclusive places that welcome diverse audiences, but first they should reflect our Society's pluralism in every aspect of their operations and programs" (p. 3).

CENTER FOR LATINO INITIATIVES. (Smithsonian Center for Latino Initiatives)

In 1994 the Smithsonian Institution published a report entitled *Willful Neglect: The Smithsonian Institution and U. S. Latinos*. The report gives a thorough account of the lack of Latina and Latino representation institution-wide. In 1995, as result of *Willful Neglect*, Congress voted to allocate a special fund to the institution to stimulate Latino programming, exhibitions, and collections. Two years later, on May 5, 1997, the Board of Regents of the Smithsonian approved the creation of the Center for Latino Initiatives, which opened in August 1998. The center is charged with the administration of the fund, and with the task of fostering a vision for Latinas and Latinos at the institution.

The center's main purpose is to create a Latina and Latino presence at the nation's museum. The center's goals are: (1) to support research in the social sciences, arts/culture, and the humanities; (2) to bridge the gap between the Smithsonian Institution and the growing field of Latina and Latino studies; (3) to provide coordination of Latina and Latino programs and events throughout the Smithsonian Institution to enlarge audiences; (4) to provide access to Smithsonian collections, exhibitions, and programs as a venue for cross-cultural understanding, self-expression, community dialogue, and development.

The programs, exhibitions, on-line presentations, and educational activities developed by the Center for Latino Initiatives are targeted for a general U.S. audience, with particular emphasis on the Latina and Latino community. Bilingual presentations provide cultural accessibility to the programs and educational activities. The center reaches out nationally by offering information on activities of the Smithsonian, employment opportunities, public programs, and Latino collections on its website. The website offers important content information, photographic history, and interpretation of the collections at the Smithsonian Institution, and artistic works created by United States Latina and Latino visual and performing artists. The Latino Virtual Gallery, part of the center's website, provides electronic means for the viewer to explore and discover the contributions of Latinas and Latinos to fine arts, culture, and science.

Since its creation in 1998 the center has organized and presented several exhibitions (Rhythms of Identity, 2000; and Young Americanos, 2001), conferences (The Interpretation and Representation of Latino Cultures, First National Conference at the Smithsonian Institution, 2002; and Boleros: Romantic Songs of the Americas, 2002), public programs (Yomo Toro, 2002; Ruth Fernandez, 2002; Annamer Castrello, 2002; Arturo Sandoval, 2001 among others), and educational programs (The Latino Graduate Training Seminar, 1995–2001; music workshops, 2000–2003; and Kids Art, 1999–2002).

See also Museums.

BIBLIOGRAPHY

Excellence and Equity: Education and the Public Dimension of Museums. Washington, D.C.: American Association of Museums, 1992.

Willful Neglect: The Smithsonian and U.S. Latinos. Report of the Smithsonian Institution Task Force on Latino Issues. Washington, D.C.: 1994.

Ybarra-Frausto, Tomás, and Ana Sol Gutiérrez, chairs. *Towards a Shared Vision: U.S. Latinos and the Smithsonian Institution.* Final Report of the Latino Oversight Committee. Washington, D.C.: Smithsonian Institution, 1997.

MAGDALENA MIERI

CENTRAL AMERICANS. Central Americans have been migrating to the United States since the nineteenth century, but until the 1980s they had constituted a relatively small group and had remained relatively invisible, "passing," or being mistaken, for Mexicans. Although around two-thirds of Central Americans are foreign-born and have arrived in the United States since the mid-1980s,

Salvadoran and Nicaraguan coffee growers were already traveling regularly to the United States for business and pleasure in the early 1900s. Through the commercial ships that transported bananas from Honduras to the United States, Hondurans became acquainted with new opportunities and then traveled north in search of work. These early contacts led to the establishment of different Central American communities that continue to receive immigrants today. Notable among these are New Orleans and San Francisco, cities with some of the longest histories of Central American migration.

The presence of Central Americans (Guatemalans, Hondurans, Salvadorans, Nicaraguans, Costa Ricans, and Panamanians) in the United States has only been noticed since the 1980s, when a political and economic crisis destabilized several countries in that region and many of their citizens were forced to abandon their homes. Many (mostly Guatemalans, Nicaraguans, and Salvadorans) went to adjacent Central American countries, others (mostly the Maya Guatemalans) settled in refugee camps in southern Mexico, and many have since returned to their homelands. Others made their way farther north to the United States and Canada, where they have established vibrant communities. Some of those who initially landed in refugee camps in Mexico also continued to travel north and have settled in the United States. Central Americans now constitute one of the fastest-growing Latino and Latina groups in the United States. As the majority of Central Americans in the United States are foreign born, their immigrant experience affects their lives and those of their children, helping to shape who they are, how they relate to others, and the kinds of communities they are creating.

The political crises in Central America can be linked to the massive increase of Central American migration to the United States since the 1980s. A civil war from 1980 to 1992 in El Salvador, an armed conflict in Guatemala that flared for over thirty years, and another one in Nicaragua that began in the mid-1970s when Anastasio Somoza was in power and continued for a decade after he was deposed in 1979, contributed to tripling and sometimes more than quintupling (as in the case of the Salvadorans) the number of immigrants from these countries in the United States. These immigrants set out for the United States, often crossing several international borders in the process, because of existing links with family and friends who were already established there. These ties had been forged over a long history of U.S. political, military, economic, and cultural influence in Central America. Therefore, when the conditions in Central America deteriorated to the point where many sought refuge elsewhere, the United States emerged as the destination of choice. Many emigrated in the midst of a civil war, leaving their countries at a moment's notice

CASA GUATEMALA

Casa Guatemala was founded in Chicago in 1983 as the Otto Rene Castillo Solidarity Committee. Its goal was to inform the growing refugee community about the situation in Guatemala and to build solidarity to oppose the war there. During the 1980s, the committee published a bimonthly newsletter, organized community forums, served as a clearinghouse for information and referrals, and arranged public speaking engagements for Guatemalan church, university, and indigenous leaders. As the community established roots in Chicago, the organization changed its name to reflect its wider array of services, including preparation courses and testing for the GED (general equivalency diploma), courses in English as a Second Language (ESL), and workshops on immigration, health, and arts.

MARICELA GARCIA

CASA GUATEMALA, CHICAGO. (Courtesy of Casa Guatemala)

or in situations of extreme danger. Often they had to travel by land, which made their journeys costly and dangerous. Their numbers increased exponentially, the class composition of these flows changed dramatically, and U.S. immigration policies stiffened during the period they arrived.

This initial reception has shaped their incorporation in the United States in multiple ways.

The increase in Central American migration has added a different component to the Latino and Latina population. In contrast to the Mexican migrants who have dominated Latin American migration into the United States, Central Americans come from dissimilar contexts, comprise groups that are socioculturally and economically different, and have been received dissimilarly by the U.S. government as well. As Nestor Rodríguez and Jacqueline Hagan (1999) observe, the U.S. Latin American population now includes well-educated and unskilled immigrants, political refugees, wealthy landowners and peasants, as well as a variety of ethnic groups such as Garifuna (Black Caribs) from Belize and Honduras, and Maya groups from Guatemala. Thus, Central Americans present a new facet in the Latina and Latino mosaic, complete with new family forms, community alliances, relations with societal institutions, and forms of cultural expression that will further enrich the Latino and Latina experience in the United States.

Demographic Profile

According to the 2000 U.S. census, there are over 1.5 million foreign-born, plus almost 1 million U.S.–born, Central Americans in the United States, although several groups argue that these figures are much higher, as census undercounting has been a notorious problem among Latinas and Latinos. The largest group of Central Americans is the Salvadorans, who account for 41 percent of all Central Americans, followed by Guatemalans with 24 percent, Hondurans with 14 percent, and Nicaraguans with 11 percent. It is worth noting that in 1990 Salvadorans made up roughly the same proportion, but Guatemalans constituted 20 percent, Nicaraguans 15 percent, and Hondurans an even smaller percentage. Thus, from 1990 to 2000, the composition of the Central American population in the United States has changed, mostly because of increased migration from Honduras as a result of devastating natural disasters and also because of a steady increase of migration from Guatemala.

Age and Sex Although often lumped into a single category, Central Americans are richly diverse culturally, socially, and demographically. For instance, the sex ratios among the different groups are dissimilar. According to the 2000 U.S. census, women comprise slightly more than half of the immigrants from Costa Rica and Nicaragua, and almost 60 percent of those from Panama, but they represent 49 percent among Hondurans, 47 percent among Salvadorans, and only 43 percent among Guatemalans. Again, these ratios have changed since 1990 when, except for Guatemalans and Salvadorans, slightly more than half of all Central Americans were women, and the sex ratios were closer than they were in 2000. With respect to age, Central Americans fall somewhere in between the two other large Latin American immigrant groups: they are slightly older than the Mexicans but younger than the Cubans. The 2000 census indicates that close to three-fourths of the different Central American groups are between the ages of eighteen and sixty-five. However, the proportion of young and old members varies by group. Over one-third of Panamanian and Costa Rican households do not have anyone under eighteen years of age, but this proportion is lower among the other groups, and only one-fifth of Salvadoran households do not have anyone under eighteen. At the other end of the age spectrum, approximately 10 percent of Nicaraguan, Panamanian, and Costa Rican households have at least one person who is sixty-five or over, but this proportion hovers around 6 percent for Hondurans, Guatemalans, and Salvadorans. These household compositions reflect the particular migration history of each group, and they affect a host of social relations among these groups both in the United States and in the origin countries, where many Central Americans still have close relatives.

Education In terms of education, the 2000 census indicates that Panamanians and Costa Ricans are the most educated, with approximately one-fourth having a high-school diploma, one-quarter some college education, and around 15 percent a bachelor's degree. Among Guatemalans and Salvadorans 40 percent have completed eighth grade or less, about 18 percent have a high-school diploma, approximately 11 percent have some college, and approximately 4 percent have a bachelor's degree. Over 40 percent of Guatemalans and Salvadorans do not speak English well or do not speak it at all, whereas close to three-fourths of Panamanians are native speakers or speak English very well. Costa Ricans, Hondurans, and Nicaraguans fall somewhere in between.

Languages Even if they do not speak English well or at all, this group is by no means Spanish monolingual. Although Spanish is the first (and sometimes only) language for the majority of Central Americans, it is not the only language represented. Guatemalans who are of Maya descent may also speak K'anjob'al, Kaqchikel, K'iche, or any of twenty-one Maya languages. Hondurans who originate on the Caribbean coast of their country and some Belizeans also speak Garifuna. Nicaraguans from the Atlantic coast of Nicaragua may speak English or Mesquito at home instead of Spanish. In fact, many Maya Guatemalans may be fluent in at least one Maya language but not in Spanish, an issue to which the teachers in U.S. schools where these immigrants concentrate are beginning to attend. Local churches are also sensitive to this issue, and in cities like Los Angeles there are now Masses said in different Maya languages as well as in Garifuna.

Race and ethnicity Central Americans are not homogeneous with respect to race and ethnicity. For instance, whereas 60 percent of Costa Ricans self-identified as "white only" in the 2000 census, this proportion was slightly over one-third among Salvadorans and Guatemalans, about half among Nicaraguans, 40 percent among Hondurans, and fewer than 30 percent among Panamanians. This self-identity affects not only the manner in which they participate in societal institutions, but also how they relate to one another within the larger Latina and Latino group.

Household composition Central Americans are diverse in terms of family composition and living arrangements as well. Whereas in 1990 fewer than 10 percent of Panamanian households included people who are not related, more than one-fourth of Honduran and Guatemalan and almost one-third of Salvadoran households included nonfamily members. The average household size ranged from three members among Costa Ricans and Panamanians to over four members among Guatemalans, Salvadorans, and Hondurans. According to the 2000 census, except among Hondurans, approximately 60 percent of Central American households consisted of married couples, with women heading between 15 and 20 percent of Central American households. The proportion of female-headed households was slightly above 20 percent among Panamanians and below 15 percent among Hondurans. In 2000 more than half of all Central Americans lived in renter-occupied housing, from a low of approximately 50 percent among Panamanians to a high of almost 70 percent among Hondurans, with many living in households of five or more members. Many of these immigrants, particularly Guatemalans, Salvadorans, and Hondurans, live in poor neighborhoods; thus, their rents are high in relation to their earnings. A survey in San Francisco found that 75 percent of Salvadorans there spent more than one-half of their incomes on rent.

Household income Even though Central American households usually have several family members in the labor force, and their labor force participation rates are high (ranging from 70.5 percent among Panamanians to 76 percent among Salvadorans in 1990), their family incomes are not high. In 2000 the median family income for Guatemalans, Salvadorans, and Hondurans was $34,000. It was $40,200 for Nicaraguans, $38,500 for Costa Ricans, and $45,000 for Panamanians. Individual (per capita) incomes were about $16,000 for Guatemalans, Hondurans, Salvadorans, and $19,000 for Nicaraguans, $22,000 for Costa Ricans, and $27,800 for Panamanians. Approximately one-fifth of Guatemalan, Salvadoran, and Nicaraguan families live below the poverty line. The poverty level is slightly over 10 percent among Costa Ricans and under 10 percent among Panamanians. It is important to keep in mind that the Central Americans' income is not only low, but is stretched substantially in different directions, as many regularly send money to family members still living in their countries of origin.

Places of residence Central Americans have settled in different destinations in the United States, mostly in cities and metropolitan areas, but there are some salient concentrations. With the exception of Panamanians (only half of whom live in urban conglomerates), the overwhelming majority of these immigrants have concentrated in large metropolitan areas. California receives more than half of them, followed by Florida, Texas, New York, New Jersey, and the Washington, D.C./Virginia area. Within these states, there are some important concentrations. Los Angeles, for instance, is home to half of all Central Americans in the United States, with more than half of the two largest groups (Salvadorans and Guatemalans) residing there. Whereas Los Angeles is home to the largest concentration of Salvadorans and Guatemalans, Salvadorans comprise the majority of the Latina and Latino population in Washington, D.C., and San Francisco has the longest continued history of Salvadoran migration to the United States. More than half of all Nicaraguans in the country call Miami their home, and New York is the most popular destination for Panamanians. There are now sizable Central American communities in the Midwest, in the Northeast, and in the South as well.

Community life Central American immigrants have created bustling communities and neighborhoods that recreate important aspects of their cultures. Existing institutions, such as churches, have expanded and created new institutions. Central Americans have opened hundreds of small businesses to serve a growing number of fellow immigrants. These immigrants build communities in their daily lives through a host of activities, including cultural expression. Central American writers, painters, and poets are actively contributing to the ever-growing diversity of Latino and Latina cultural expressions in the United States. Undoubtedly their presence will alter the sociocultural landscape of those communities.

An important aspect of the Central Americans' experience is their secondary migration patterns. For instance, a recent study of Latina and Latino immigration to the Phoenix metropolitan area revealed that although the majority of these immigrants had initially settled in other areas of the United States—mainly in California—they had relocated to the Phoenix area because they had either a relative or a friend who informed them of the different opportunities that Phoenix had to offer. In some cases the relatives or friends put a job within reach of the newcomer even before the person physically moved to Phoenix. Similar experiences are being reproduced all over the United States.

U.S. reception and legal status The majority of Central American immigrants have faced not only stiff U.S. immigration policies, but also profound uncertainty, as immigration law has been applied unevenly not only across groups, but also at different points in time within the same group, creating discrepancies among Central Americans. The web of legal obstacles and often undecipherable and intractable immigration laws have made legality paramount in the Central Americans' lives. Moreover, increasingly rigid immigration laws make obtaining even a simple U.S. tourist visa in their home countries difficult. Thus, many Central Americans have traveled north without a visa, which means that they have had to enter the United States clandestinely and travel by land at least part of the way. Traveling by land from Central America to the United States often involves complicated arrangements with *coyotes* (one who smuggles immigrants), as well as robberies, assaults, and extortion by local authorities along the way.

Many Central American immigrants left their countries for reasons that are directly linked to the political and economic conflicts in that region. Upon arrival in the United States, most were not officially recognized as refugees by the U.S. government. The reason for this situation can be found in U.S. foreign policy in the region. During the civil conflicts in Guatemala and El Salvador, for instance, the Salvadoran and Guatemalan governments fought the opposition with substantial U.S. support. Thus, the U.S. government could not legally recognize the refugees generated by the conflict. Notwithstanding legal barriers, however, many Central Americans have continued to enter the United States. Once on U.S. soil, Central Americans could apply for political asylum, but Salvadorans and Guatemalans did not fare well; throughout the 1980s fewer than 3 percent of these applicants were granted asylum.

Immigrants' rights groups lobbied on the Guatemalans' and Salvadorans' behalf, and eventually Congress granted Temporary Protected Status (TPS) from deportation to all Salvadorans who arrived prior to September 19, 1990. This temporary amnesty was not extended to Guatemalans. It allowed Salvadorans to live and work in the United States for a period of eighteen months. It was extended a few times and finally expired in December 1994. Close to 200,000 Salvadorans applied for this dispensation. Fewer submitted applications for the successive extensions, as some became permanent residents, and others found the application procedure confusing and reliable information hard to obtain. TPS was neither asylum nor refugee status, and the only privilege bestowed was the conferral of a work permit. In 1990, as a result of a settlement of a class action suit (*American Baptist Churches v. Thornburgh* [ABC] legislation) that alleged discrimination against Guatemalans and Salvadorans on the part of the

GRUPO MAYA

Grupo Maya was founded in Florida in 1983 under the auspices of Holy Cross Services Center to help the thousands of indigenous people fleeing the violence in their villages in Guatemala. Providing assistance was difficult because the refugees were from the Kanjobal ethnic group and most did not speak Spanish, but a Maya language. This attracted the attention and solidarity of Native American organizations and leaders. Grupo Maya assisted the community with political asylum applications and protested against deporting Guatemalans to a war-torn society. As the needs of the community changed, Grupo Maya evolved into a social service organization.

MARICELA GARCIA

Immigration and Naturalization Service, immigrants from these countries were allowed to resubmit asylum applications. Initially the success rate of Salvadoran applications increased to 28 percent and those of Guatemalans to 18 percent in fiscal year 1992, but it leveled off and then declined.

The 1997 Nicaraguan Adjustment and Central American Relief Act (NACARA) provided that undocumented Nicaraguans could, under certain circumstances, be granted a "cancellation of removal" (cancellation of deportation). Some Salvadorans and Guatemalans were also included as beneficiaries of the act. Salvadorans who entered the country before September 19, 1990, and Guatemalans who entered on or before October 1, 1990, and registered under the ABC settlement, or who had filed an asylum application before April 1, 1990, could be granted a cancellation of removal. Under the terms of this legislation, Salvadorans already placed in deportation procedures are required to appear before an immigration judge to request a cancellation of removal, and his or her immigration status will then be changed to permanent resident. Nicaraguans, by contrast, are not required to appear before an immigration judge in order to be granted the benefit. Immigrants' rights groups have lobbied on behalf of Salvadorans so that the benefits that NACARA confers upon Nicaraguans and certain other nationals—permanent residence without a hearing on a case-by-case basis—would also be extended to Salvadorans. However, in October 1998, Congress denied Salvadorans (and Guatemalans) this benefit. After the devastating earthquakes in El Salvador in early 2001 the United States granted TPS once to those who arrived following the disaster, for a period of nine months, a protection that has been extended several times.

Nicaraguan asylum seekers during the 1980s were given an ambivalent reception. During this decade about one-quarter of the Nicaraguan applicants were successful. The U.S. government had been reluctant to grant Nicaraguans any special dispensation, but under pressure from the Cuban American constituency in Miami—where the majority of the Nicaraguans live—it stopped deporting Nicaraguans for a short period of time between 1987 and 1988. Nicaraguans could apply for asylum; they were given work permits but not access to the resettlement aid similar to that given to lawfully recognized refugees. When Congress froze military support for the Contras in 1988, the number of Nicaraguans entering the United States increased substantially. To stem this flow, the U.S. government reversed its policy, and Nicaraguans—now without work permits or protection from deportation—were treated as undocumented immigrants again. However, Nicaraguans who can prove that they have resided in the United States continuously since December 1, 1995, can be considered for adjustment of status to permanent residency and granted "green cards."

Hondurans also have been granted a temporary special dispensation. After Hurricane Mitch devastated many towns in Honduras and left thousands of people homeless in 1998, many Hondurans made their way to the United States to join relatives and friends already here. To alleviate their plight, Hondurans were granted Temporary Protected Status for a period of nine months; they had until July 1999 to submit their applications, a dispensation that was extended several times.

Central Americans who arrived in the United States prior to January 1, 1982—the cutoff point to apply for amnesty under the Immigration Reform and Control Act (IRCA)—applied for this benefit. However, the thousands who arrived at the height of the political upheaval in their countries in the 1980s were ineligible for this provision. All of this means that a large proportion of these immigrants have been and remain in the country undocumented. The Immigration and Naturalization Service (now called the U.S. Citizenship and Immigration Services) has estimated that close to 60 percent of Salvadorans and Guatemalans and approximately 40 percent of Nicaraguans in the country are undocumented, and similar estimates probably now apply for Hondurans.

The civil conflicts in Central America officially ended in 1990 in Nicaragua, in 1992 in El Salvador, and in 1996 in Guatemala, but migration from the region to the United States has continued. The political and economic forces behind the massive migration of recent decades are still in place, and many Central Americans now face high levels of violence associated with common crime, as some of these countries have the highest homicide rates in the Western Hemisphere. In spite of improved economic growth rates, some of these countries have very high levels of unemployment and underemployment. All of these factors continue to create structural and social conditions conducive to continued migration to the United States.

Labor Force Participation of Men and Women

Central Americans have high rates of labor force participation, but they are likely to be concentrated in a few occupations and industries. Those with relatively higher levels of education and English-language skills (Costa Ricans, Panamanians, and Nicaraguans) tend to concentrate in technical and administrative support occupations, whereas those with lower educational levels and English-language proficiency (Guatemalans, Salvadorans, and Hondurans) are more likely to work in service occupations and in manufacturing, as operators and laborers. Central American men with skills find white-collar jobs; those with fewer skills work in construction, landscaping, restaurants, hotels, and janitorial services. Skilled Central American women work in clerical and administrative jobs; those with fewer skills work as housekeepers, babysitters, hotel chambermaids, or janitors. It is important to note that these are not clear-cut distinctions, as the legal status of Central American men and women greatly affects their options in the labor force. Persons with higher educational levels (even college graduates) and work experience are forced to accept lower-skilled work when they are undocumented. Some Central Americans have opened businesses that cater to compatriots and other Latina and Latino clienteles, and there is a growing proportion who are self-employed, many as street vendors. Many Central Americans have organized to improve their working conditions in the different industries in which they work. One example is the street vendors in Los Angeles (who are mainly Central Americans), who have formed the Association of Street Vendors to lobby for the legalization of the activity in that city.

The concentration of Central American immigrants in certain employment sectors does not depend solely on their legal status, individual characteristics, or human capital levels, but also on what jobs are available at the time and place of their arrival in the United States. During recessionary times, jobs—even low-paid—in the occupations and industries where Central Americans concentrate are scarce, so new immigrants accept whatever work may be available. This was the case in California during the recession of the early 1990s. Many undocumented as well as documented Guatemalan and Salvadoran men were unable to find work in the usual niches and had to resort to day labor, congregating on street corners waiting for potential employers to hire them. As the economy improved, these work sites did not go away; men now find day work in this manner not only in California but elsewhere in the country, including suburbia. The recession also forced many Central Americans (men and women) into the "informal economy," selling products and services out of their homes or in the streets, a practice that persists in spite of economic recovery. Thus niches created during harsh economic times have endured and become some of these immigrants' most important avenues for employment.

Central Americans have different experiences in the labor market depending upon where they live in the United States. Terry Repak found that jobs in construction for Central Americans were plentiful and better paid in Washington, D.C., than elsewhere, particularly in Los Angeles, where the majority of these immigrants live. In fact, Repak reports that one immigrant traveled to the District of Columbia every spring for the construction season and then returned to Los Angeles during the winter. Central American men also labor in restaurants as dishwashers and busboys in Washington, a pattern also found among Salvadoran men in New Jersey and in San Francisco.

Central Americans' labor force participation differs by gender in important ways. The jobs that women perform, such as babysitting, tend to be available even during harsh economic times, and these jobs tend to be unregulated and away from the public eye. For these reasons women, even when undocumented, often are able to find jobs more easily than men, and in some cities, like Los Angeles, Salvadoran and Guatemalan women seem to have taken over the housekeeping niche. Salvadoran women in Los Angeles are twelve times and Guatemalans thirteen times more likely than the general population to work as private servants, as cleaners and childcare workers; for Mexican women this factor is only 2.3. But in spite of the relative ease with which these immigrant women find jobs (a situation observed from San Francisco to Los Angeles to New Jersey), when men and women both work, men earn more than women do, and Central American women have been found to experience less "success" and occupational mobility than their male counterparts.

Women, Men, and Gender Relations

Central American women have been pioneers in immigration. Repak found that it was women who initiated Central American (mostly Salvadoran) migration to Washington, D.C. U.S. diplomats working in El Salvador and other Central American regions in the 1960s brought their housekeepers back to the United States. Once in the United States, these women petitioned for their relatives, who in turn brought other family members, thus initiating a pattern of chain migration. In the 1980s, when Central Americans were fleeing their countries, there was already a Central American community established in Washington, D.C., and migration to that city increased exponentially; women took part in this migration in great numbers. Some moved to reunite with or accompany husbands, parents, or other relatives, but many migrated on their own. In fact, Repak found that two-thirds of the

Central American women in her sample had made the decision to migrate on their own, without the collaboration or assistance of male partners or fathers, demonstrating an "unusual degree of autonomy."

Often Central Americans have established new families in the United States, rearrangements that do not always work out smoothly. These new family arrangements, coupled with the economic contributions of the women (sometimes as sole or main breadwinners), have affected gender relations in important ways among this group. Although Central American women have had a long history of labor-force participation, and most worked outside the home prior to migration, their economic contributions in the United States confer on them increased status within their families. Gains in status sometimes translate into more egalitarian gender relations, but other times the result is comparatively more unbalanced gender relations in favor of men because the women do not want to upset delicate arrangements in the home that would threaten the men's position. In other cases, most notably among groups with relatively more egalitarian gender relations prior to migration (as in the case of Maya Guatemalans) there is not much change in gender relations with women's increased economic participation.

Outside of the household Central American women have been found to forge community networks that benefit them and their families. These informal ties tend to be contingent on the types of jobs that these women perform (as is the case for the men, too). For instance, Jacqueline Hagan found that Guatemalan women who worked as live-in domestics had smaller and weaker social networks than their male counterparts, who had more extensive contacts in the community. In another study, Salvadorans and Guatemalans who worked as domestics but did not live in their employers' homes were found to have wide-reaching networks in the community. In fact, this study found that because women actively sought resources in community organizations—as they were in charge of those family needs for which these organizations could provide assistance—their networks ended up being broader than those of men. The women who spent time at community organizations were able to establish networks independent of those of men, learning (and later on sharing with other women) crucial information about their rights and other important aspects of life, such as U.S. laws that protect women against domestic violence.

Family and Intergenerational Relations

Some Central Americans come to the United States single and establish families here; others arrive alone, having left their families back home. Many come undocumented, meaning that their journeys have to be undertaken by land, which would put accompanying children in much danger. Some bring their children, but given the high crime rates and ubiquity of drugs in some of the neighborhoods where they live, the parents send the children back to their countries to shield them from these dangers. These children remain in the care of other relatives, while their parents (or parent) labor in the United States to send them money for the necessities of life. Although the material and financial lot of these children (and their relatives) improves when the parents (or parent) send money and gifts from the United States, this improvement does not come without a price. Many of these parents and children live in "transnational families," separated by distance but remaining closely in touch through various forms of modern technology. The unstable legal status of many of these families and their still precarious financial situation makes it difficult for them to see each other regularly, as they cannot travel back and forth if they are undocumented or in the process of regularizing their status.

Parents in the United States eventually send for the children left behind. But the often lengthy separations create tension when the family is reunited, as the parents and children feel like strangers and ultimately find little to share as a family. Leigh Leslie observes that family reunification for Central Americans can be problematic because of the unrealistic expectations that the parents and the children have of each other. Sometimes the children reproach the parents for having "abandoned" them for too long. Other times the children, accustomed to the material goods financed by the parents' labor in the United States, demand the same when they join the parents, although the parents are usually unable to provide these material goods because having the children in the United States creates significant additional expenses. Other times, family reunifications do not work out smoothly because new families have been formed in the United States, particularly when step- and half-sibling combinations have been created. These problems are sometimes exacerbated when newcomers have to join relatives in overcrowded homes, living conditions that are common among many poor Central Americans. In these cases family separations cannot simply be celebrated as part of these immigrants' enduring links with their communities of origin, but must be tempered by the numerous costs and the anxiety, dislocation, and alienation that such separations often produce.

In the United States, Central American children usually face the triple burden of entering adolescence, a new society, and reconstituted families with little resemblance to those they knew before, which puts great pressure on them and on the rest of their family members. Many of these children have been exposed to the ravages of war, witnessing the abduction or murder of family members, tortured bodies in the streets, bombings, crossfires, and

other instances of adult-sized violence. In addition, many of them, some as young as twelve years old, were forcibly recruited by combatant groups. The considerable trauma with which many of these children have arrived in the United States sometimes has been manifested in learning problems and difficult behavior during adolescence. Many Central American children can be diagnosed with post–traumatic stress disorder, which leads to educational delays that curtail their capacity to adapt. Others have not been witnesses, but have heard their family members recount such experiences. For many Salvadoran children such memories have shaped who they are and how they relate to their country of origin.

This issue is compounded because once in the United States, these children become overburdened with adult duties that sometimes interfere with their development. They often acquire English-language skills before others in their families, and they also become more familiar with the culture of their new environment. They often translate for their parents and interpret the new culture for them. The children thereby acquire nearly adult authority and status within their families—a situation that can spur intergenerational conflict. However, in spite of these many adversities, these youngsters show remarkable resilience, and many are contributing meaningfully and in diverse forms to their communities, schools, and families.

At the other end of the age spectrum, older Central Americans also go through substantial change in the United States. They are not able to find jobs like the younger immigrants and seldom master the English language. Thus they depend almost entirely on their relatives for everything they need. And even though among this group it is generally expected that the children will support their parents in old age, in the United States time and financial constraints make it difficult for the children to fulfill these cultural expectations. Thus, on the one hand, older immigrants must depend on their children for financial, material, informational, and emotional assistance, but on the other, the children cannot always provide such support. The situation is exacerbated by the fact that older immigrants also expect higher status and a measure of respect that is generally absent in the contexts where they now reside. Moreover, the high cost of health care becomes an added concern for older Central American immigrants who lack access to health benefits and other means to treat themselves. Even if they labored hard in their home countries, they are not guaranteed old age security either there or in the United States.

In spite of the challenges they face, older Central Americans contribute in many important ways to their communities and families. They often care for their children's children, a welcome relief for the often financially overburdened adult immigrants. They are also important transmitters of culture, and provide key emotional and moral support, advising and comforting the younger members of their families. Though their children and grandchildren sometimes reject their admonishments and rebel against them, these older immigrants' presence in the families and communities is vital. In a study of Nicaraguan elderly in San Francisco, Stephen Wallace identified them as making important contributions to their families and to the creation of community.

Community: The Church and Other Organizations

Central Americans left their places of residence for reasons that often are linked directly or indirectly to the conflicts in that region in the 1980s and 1990s. But they arrive in the United States because of the dense networks of family and friends that most have here. Even if the relatives who await the newcomers do not always have the resources to assist them, the newly arrived manage to procure assistance from others around them—family, friends, or compatriots. One of the most important places for Central Americans to connect with others and to obtain varied forms of assistance is the church. They frequently attend Catholic, mainline Protestant, evangelical, or Pentecostal churches, often traveling long distances to get to their places of worship. Importantly, the church provides a space for them to connect with others and facilitates the exchange of assistance among them. The Catholic Church and mainline Protestant churches have provided a range of services that help the immigrants with their settlement. Although the smaller evangelical churches do not have the wide-ranging infrastructure to provide services to the immigrants, their role in the newcomers' lives has been central. In some cases, newcomers themselves have established churches and have opened up their new temples to welcome their brothers and sisters in need. Additionally, through the church these immigrants are often able to remain connected to their communities of origin, as churches create institutional spaces that connect the immigrants with people back home. Thus for many Central American immigrants their church-based networks are vital, as they help them establish important links in their new communities that are crucial for their physical and emotional survival.

Conditions for Central Americans in the United States have been adverse, but it would be a mistake to portray these immigrants as simply passively accepting whatever fate befalls them. To meet the challenges they have faced in the United States, Central Americans—especially the Salvadorans, Guatemalans, and Nicaraguans who have arrived since the mid-1980s—have organized in different ways to help their compatriots. These Central Americans set up community organizations that target the needs of the newly arrived, providing a wide range of services, from legal defense and services for asylum applicants to job referrals, free health clinics, shelters and other emergency services, and psychological counseling. These organizations often work in conjunction with churches, particularly established denominations such as the Catholic, Lutheran, and Presbyterian churches. However, these organizations are not government funded, and consequently, their budgets are always very constrained.

Central Americans have joined forces with local residents with whom they share political ideologies to lobby on behalf of their compatriots. For Salvadorans and Guatemalans this has meant local residents—Anglos, Chicanos and Chicanas, and others—who were also ideologically opposed to the U.S. involvement in Central America and who in turn recognized the plight of the Central Americans in the United States as victims of U.S. foreign policy. For Nicaraguans, many of whom live in Miami, it was the powerful Cuban community that joined forces with them. Many Nicaraguans and Cubans shared important political affinities, as their resettlement in the United States was linked to the establishment of Marxist regimes in their respective countries. The alliance with the Cubans produced an important victory for the Nicaraguans, as they were able to temporarily revert the practice of deportation of Nicaraguan nationals in the mid-1980s.

An important objective of these community organizations was to provide legal assistance, but also to organize and coordinate support for the rights of these immigrants, particularly Salvadorans and Guatemalans, and they actively pursued cases for Central Americans. For example, it was because of the mounting pressure from solidarity and immigrants' rights groups that the Justice Department agreed to provide Temporary Protected Status to Salvadorans. In this and similar cases, it was the community organizations set up by the Central American newcomers themselves that were behind these victories. As Central Americans have become established in the United States and their objectives have shifted from the transitory and specific conditions of refugee flight to a more permanent situation, these organizations have also changed their programs and objectives. They are now advocating for longer-term projects, rights, and approaches reflecting the increasing settlement of this population, as well as for the end of the armed conflicts in Central America. Central Americans have also organized to advocate for their rights as workers and as members of the communities in which they live. They have lobbied city councils to legalize street vending, organized janitors to fight for more just working conditions and pay, and worked assiduously to make their neighborhoods safer.

The Central Americans' contributions to their new home extend beyond community work and religious participation. Many Central American writers, musicians, painters, and poets—some born and raised in their countries of origin, some in the United States, and others having arrived at young ages—are actively contributing to the ever-growing diversity of Latino and Latina cultural expressions. The work of these artists captures the Central Americans' experience of living in a legal limbo, of lengthy family separations, of having lost their homes and sometimes relatives in armed conflict, of memories of violence, and of a harsh settlement in the United States. For instance, the musical production of the group Lilo González y los de la Mt. Pleasant recounts the experiences of Central American immigrants in the Washington, D.C., area in songs such as "Amor sin Papeles" (Love without Documents) and "La Mount Pleasant." The painter Karla Rodas also captures the liminal state in which many Central Americans find themselves, as she poetically inscribes onto the canvas the endless legal entanglements that govern their lives. This new artistic production will undoubtedly enrich the Latino and Latina cultural landscape by adding the singular experiences of this newer group.

See also Census; Immigrant Children; Immigration; *and* Indocumentados.

BIBLIOGRAPHY

Calderón, Ricardo. *Situación socio-económica de la comunidad salvadoreña en el área de la Bahía de San Francisco.* San Francisco: Centro para Refugiados Centroamericanos/Asociación de Salvadoreños, 1992.

Census of Population. *Persons of Hispanic Origin in the United States.* Bureau of the Census: U.S. Department of Commerce, Economics and Statistics Administration. CP-3-3, 1990.

Chinchilla, Norma Stoltz, and Nora Hamilton. "Seeking Refuge in the City of Angels." In *City of Angels*, edited by Gerry Riposa and Carolyn Dersch, 84–100. Dubuque, Iowa: Kendall/Hunt, 1992.

Chinchilla, Norma, Nora Hamilton, and James Loucky. "Central Americans in Los Angeles: An Immigrant Community in Transition." In *In the Barrios: Latinos and the Underclass Debate*, edited by Joan Moore and Raquel Pinderhughes, 51–78. New York: Russell Sage Foundation, 1993.

Espino, Conchita M. "Trauma and Adaptation: The Case of Central American Children." In *Refugee Children: Theory, Research, and Services*, edited by Frederick L. Ahearn Jr. and Jean L. Athey, 106–124. Baltimore: Johns Hopkins University Press, 1991.

Fink, Leon. *The Maya of Morganton: Work and Community in the Nuevo New South.* Chapel Hill: University of North Carolina Press, 2003.

Hagan, Jacqueline Maria. *Deciding to Be Legal: A Maya Community in Houston.* Philadelphia: Temple University Press, 1994.

Hagan, Jacqueline Maria. "Social Networks, Gender, and Immigrant Incorporation: Resources and Constraints." *American Sociological Review* 63 (1998): 55–67.

Hondagneu-Sotelo, Pierrette, and Ernestine Avila. "I'm Here, but I'm There: The Meanings of Latina Transnational Motherhood." *Gender and Society* 11 (1997): 548–571.

Ignatius, Sarah. "An Interim Assessment of the Asylum Process of the Immigration and Naturalization Service." National Asylum Study Project. Immigration and Refugee Program, Program on the Legal Profession, Harvard Law School. Cambridge, Mass: Harvard University, 1992.

Immigration and Naturalization Service. *INS Releases Updated Estimates of U.S. Illegal Population.* U.S. Department of Justice. News Release, February 7, 1997.

Leslie, Leigh A. "Families Fleeing War: The Case of Central Americans." *Marriage and Family Review* 19 (1993): 193–205.

López, David E., Eric Popkin, and Edward Telles. "Central Americans: At the Bottom, Struggling to Get Ahead." In *Ethnic Los Angeles*, edited by Roger Waldinger and Mehdi Bozorgmehr, 279–304. New York: Russell Sage Foundation, 1996.

Mahler, Sarah J. *Salvadorans in Suburbia: Symbiosis and Conflict.* Boston: Allyn and Bacon, 1995.

Menjívar, Cecilia. "Salvadorans and Nicaraguans: Refugees Become Workers." In *Illegal Immigration in America: A Reference Handbook*, edited by David W. Haines and Karen E. Rosenblum, 232–253. Westport, Conn.: Greenwood Press, 1999a.

Menjívar, Cecilia. "The Intersection of Work and Gender: Central American Immigrant Women and Employment in California." *American Behavioral Scientist* 42 (1999b): 595–621.

Menjívar, Cecilia. "Religious Institutions and Transnationalism: A Case Study of Catholic and Evangelical Salvadoran Immigrants." *International Journal of Politics, Culture and Society* 12 (1999c): 589–612.

Menjívar, Cecilia. *Fragmented Ties: Salvadoran Immigrant Networks in America.* Berkeley: University of California Press, 2000.

Menjívar, Cecilia. "Living in Two Worlds? Guatemalan-Origin Children in the United States and Emerging Transnationalism." *Journal of Ethnic and Migration Studies* 28 (2002): 531–552.

Menjívar, Cecilia. "Religion and Immigration in Comparative Perspective: Salvadorans in Catholic and Evangelical Communities in San Francisco, Phoenix, and Washington D.C." *Sociology of Religion* 64 (2003): 21–45.

Menjívar, Cecilia, Eugenio Arene, Cindy Bejarano et al. "Contemporary Latino Migration to the Phoenix Metropolitan Area." Report presented to the Center for Urban Inquiry. Tempe: Arizona State University, May 1999.

Miller Matthei, Linda, and David A. Smith. "Belizean 'Boyz 'n the 'Hood'? Garifuna Labor Migration and Transnational Identity." In *Transnationalism from Below*, edited by Michael Peter Smith and Luis Eduardo Guarnizo, 270–290. Comparative Urban and Community Research, vol. 6. New Brunswick, N.J.: Transaction Press, 1998.

Popkin, Eric. "Guatemalan Mayan Migration to Los Angeles: Constructing Transnational Linkages in the Context of the Settlement Process." *Ethnic and Racial Studies* 22 (1999): 267–289.

Portes, Alejandro, and Alex Stepick. *City on the Edge: The Transformation of Miami.* Berkeley: University of California Press, 1993.

Repak, Terry A. *Waiting on Washington: Central American Workers in the Nation's Capital.* Philadelphia: Temple University Press, 1995.

Rodríguez, Ana Patricia. "Fronteras centroamericanas, Centroamericanos fronterizos." A quien corresponda: Literatura virtual. http://www.angelfire.com/va3/literatura/ANAPATRICIA.htm.

Rodríguez, Nestor P., and Jacqueline Hagan. "Central Americans." In *The Minority Report: An Introduction to Racial, Ethnic, and Gender Relations*, edited by Anthony Gary Dworkin and Rosalind J. Dworkin, 278–296. 3rd ed. Dallas, Tex.: Harcourt Brace Jovanovich, 1999.

Sanford, Victoria. *Buried Secrets: Truth and Human Rights in Guatemala.* New York: Palgrave Press, 2003.

Urrutia-Rojas, Ximena, and Néstor P. Rodríguez. "Unaccompanied Migrant Children from Central America: Sociodemographic Characteristics and Experiences with Potentially Traumatic Events." In *Health and Social Services Among International Labor Migrants: A Comparative Perspective*, edited by Antonio Ugalde and Gilberto Cárdenas, 151–166. Center for Mexican American Studies. Austin: University of Texas Press, 1997.

Wallace, Stephen P. "Community Formation as an Activity of Daily Living: The Case of Nicaraguan Elderly in San Francisco." *Journal of Aging Studies* 6 (1992): 365–383.

CECILIA MENJÍVAR

CENTRO CULTURAL DE LA RAZA. The Chicano/a rights movement of the 1960s and 1970s marks a significant change in the collective experience and identity of the Mexican American community in the United States. It is a moment in history in which students, community activists, educators, artists, and community members organized together to create and demand institutional changes for the betterment of the Chicano and Mexicano communities. The Chicano/a rights movement saw a flourishing of work produced in the arts, in education, and in politics that honored the experience and knowledge of Chicanas and Chicanos. Institutions like Centro Cultural de la Raza were founded in an attempt to create an alternative space for the education and cultural nourishment of the Chicana and Chicano community.

Established in 1970 at the height of the Chicano/a movement in California, the Centro is San Diego's first and only arts-education center dedicated exclusively to the study, preservation, teaching, and dissemination of Chicana and Chicano, Mexicana and Mexicano, and Indigenous arts. Over the course of its thirty years, the institution has become a regional, national, and international resource for information on the cultural art forms of the United States–Mexico border region. Its strategic location in Balboa Park allows easy access to tourists and residents interested in cultural and educational events.

The Centro's circular building is the home of several historical murals that were painted at the height of the Chicano/a rights movement in the 1970s. As of this writing, the performance space accommodates some 150 audience members, and the art gallery features the work of local, regional, national, and international artists. In addition, the building holds several offices and classroom or workshop spaces equipped with computer and video technology designed for use in community educational activities.

The core of the Centro's programming has four major artistic and educational components: performing arts, literary arts, visual arts, and education. The performing arts program is linked to the local, national, and international performance scene through its relationships and collaborations with numerous artists and organizations representing all disciplines. It is a belief of the Centro that the performing arts are an accessible expression of cultural awareness that is available to a wide range of audiences and that "it has the power to project humanity's innermost metaphors and innate concepts." In this vein, the Centro utilizes both traditional forms and new technologies to promote the development of a Chicana and Chicano, Mexicana and Mexicano, and Indigenous cultural experience that reflects its past, present, and future. Among the various artistic forms presented or taught at the Centro are Danza Azteca, ballet folklórico, ballet clásico, expressive movement, theater, music, storytelling, film and video, performance art, spoken word, and Indigenous performance traditions.

A driving force of the Centro's mission is its educational component. Thus, one of its more important goals is the establishment of an on-site charter school. In an effort to reach this goal, the organization has developed a strategic plan that includes the following:

- Teacher-training workshops that help instructors use the exhibitions and presentations as part of their curricula;
- A youth summer arts camp that combines the visual, performing, and literary arts; and
- An educational summit to develop specific strategies for using the arts to teach all subject areas (Centro's website)

The Centro visual arts department's programmatic goal is to give voice to contemporary culture as well as to preserve connections to an artistic past by advocating a "cross-disciplinary approach to art-making that encourages innovative ways of examining such global ideas as culture, identity, history, religion, gender, sexuality, labor, science, social justice and technology." It presents a wide range of work that explores and comments upon the experience of Chicana and Chicano, Mexicana and Mexicano, and Indigenous peoples in the Americas. The Centro's exhibitions feature local, regional, national, and international artists and are housed in one of San Diego's premier exhibition spaces. The visual arts department also administers the Centro's permanent collection, some pieces of which are housed at the University of California, Santa Barbara, as part of the Davidson Library's Collection of Ethnic and Multicultural Art (CEMA).

The Literary Arts Program also promotes the exploration of Chicana and Chicano, Mexicana and Mexicano, and Indigenous experience through the medium of the written word. The Centro "views creative writing as one of the most democratic and readily-available forms of art-making" that "has the power to give voice to persons and groups of people who have historically been silenced, and to transform the realities of community history and daily life into a tangible reality." In the same way that the performing arts are taught within a historical, social, and political context, the literary arts are located within the literary history of Chicana and Chicano, Mexicana and Mexicano, and Indigenous literary history. A major focus of this program is the preservation and collection of primary sources and community history.

See also Chicano/a Movement *and* Murals.

BIBLIOGRAPHY
Web site of Centro Cultural de la Raza. www.centroraza.com.

Marissa Ramirez

CENTRO DE ESTUDIOS PUERTORRIQUEÑOS.

Centro de Estudios Puertorriqueños (Center for Puerto Rican Studies) at Hunter College, City University of New York, is the only university-based research institute in the United States devoted to the interdisciplinary study of the Puerto Rican experience. A corollary goal is to study the experience of Latinos and Latinas and other contemporary diaspora communities in the United States.

The Centro is also the oldest Latino and Latina research and archival institution in the northeastern United States. It was founded in 1973 by a coalition of faculty, students, and community activists with the explicit purpose of linking scholarly inquiry to policy debates and social action. In its first decade the Centro articulated a model of knowledge production based on several core principles. The organization's mission and methods should: (1) delineate a systematic critique of modern capitalism, (2) construct a critical approach to understanding the problematic condition of Puerto Ricans, (3) exemplify collaborative styles of work and operate under democratic forms of governance, (4) defend the existence of Puerto Rican studies departments from efforts to dismantle or co-opt them, and (5) provide an autonomous space for the training and self-production of Puerto Rican scholars independent of traditional graduate programs.

The Centro has grown into a major research and educational resource center noted for its alternative approaches to research and policy analysis, its faculty and student exchange programs in Puerto Rico and the Caribbean, and its ties to academic, advocacy, and community-based constituencies. Outreach activities have made its resources available to a wide range of institutions, including schools, churches, senior citizen centers, and prisons. Over the years Centro researchers have produced a steady stream of articles, books, documentaries, and other materials. The *Centro Journal*, a refereed multidisciplinary and bilingual publication, has been issued since 1987.

The Centro's library and archives are home to the largest collection of Puerto Rican Studies research materials in the United States. The library holds and provides access to books, serials, microforms, audiotapes, and videotapes containing information by and about Puerto Ricans. Holdings are acquired in English and Spanish and in all areas of the humanities, the social sciences, and the arts. A major strength of the library is its works on the history of Puerto Ricans in the United States and particularly in New York and the Northeast. In 2002 it received the Debra E. Bernhardt Annual Archives Award for Excellence in documenting New York's history. The library was credited for its strong outreach program that has made previously unknown archival records accessible to students, teachers, scholars, genealogists, and the community at large. With its five thousand linear feet of archival materials and forty thousand vintage photographs, it is the world's only repository dedicated exclusively to the Puerto Rican diaspora. It is also the third largest Latino and Latina repository in the country, following collections based at Stanford University and the University of Texas at Austin.

The Centro emerged from the community and student activism of the 1960s. By the late 1960s several universities had established Puerto Rican studies departments in response to student demands for a curriculum that would address the origins and evolution of the Puerto Rican migration. Previously the study of Puerto Rico was centered on two themes: (1) Operation Bootstrap as a successful model of economic development and (2) the "culture of poverty" thesis as the explanation for social pathology and family dysfunction in the Puerto Rican community. Centro researchers, along with other academics and intellectuals of the day, challenged these assumptions about the Puerto Rican condition. A new perspective, influenced by Marxian and other radical traditions, argued for a different perspective.

According to this alternative thinking, the continuing poverty that characterizes much of the diaspora results neither from cultural inadequacies of the population nor from the unfortunate timing of migration to U.S. urban centers. Rather, the Puerto Rican dilemma is the result of a political-economic system (capitalism) that deprives significant strata of the population (especially those subject to racism and colonialism) of the wherewithal to achieve a decent standard of living. Therefore the social processes and institutional mechanisms by which groups of people are so deprived should be the prime subjects of analysis.

During the 1970s and 1980s the Centro issued a series of publications based on these propositions. Some of the key studies are assembled in *Labor Migration under Capitalism* by the History and Migration Task Force, Centro de Estudios Puertorriqueños (1979); *Industry and Idleness* by Frank Bonilla and Ricardo Campos (1986); and *Divided Borders* by Juan Flores (1993).

The Centro was a founding member and a host institution of the Inter-University Program for Latino Research (IUPLR), a national consortium of Latino and Latina research centers created in 1983. The IUPLR has sponsored collaborative teams to examine various issues affecting Latinos and Latinas. The Centro contribution to this body of work is represented in several publications, among them *Latinos in a Changing U.S. Economy*, edited by Rebecca Morales and Frank Bonilla (1993); *Latino Cultural Citizenship* by William V. Flores and Rina Benmayor (1997); and *Borderless Borders*, edited by Frank Bonilla et al. (1998).

Over the years researchers have conducted inquiries on many topics, including history and migration, language policy, oral histories, education, cultural studies, politics, and health policy. A steady stream of studies has been issued along these lines, and the *CENTRO Journal* has become a principal forum for many writers to expand on these analyses. The journal has published special issues on topics such as youth culture, the AIDS crisis, race and identity, and regional Puerto Rican history (New York, Chicago, and Hawaii). Other works of the research staff that reflect greater attention to the topics of racial identity and local history are *Taíno Revival*, edited by Gabriel Haslip-Viera

(2001) and *Pioneros* by Felix V. Matos-Rodríguez and Pedro Juan Hernández (2001).

The founding director and driving force behind the Centro in its first two decades was Frank Bonilla. His retirement in 1993 ushered in a period of transition and strategic planning for the future. The organization continues its unique work in the spirit of its motto, *Aprender a luchar, Luchar es aprender* (To learn is to struggle, to struggle is to learn).

See also **Bonilla, Frank** *and* **Puerto Ricans.**

BIBLIOGRAPHY

Bonilla, Frank, and Ricardo Campos. *Industry and Idleness*. New York: Centro de Estudios Puertorriqueños, 1986.

Bonilla, Frank, et al., eds. *Borderless Borders*. Philadelphia: Temple University Press, 1998.

Flores, Juan. *Divided Borders*. Houston, Tex.: Arte Público Press, 1993.

Flores, William V., and Rina Benmayor. *Latino Cultural Citizenship*. Boston: Beacon, 1997.

Haslip-Viera, Gabriel, ed. *Taíno Revival*. Princeton, N.J.: Markus Wiener, 1999.

History and Migration Task Force, Centro de Estudios Puertorriqueños. *Labor Migration under Capitalism*. New York: Monthly Review Press, 1979.

Matos-Rodríguez, Felix V., and Pedro Juan Hernández. *Pioneros*. Charleston, S.C.: Arcadia, 2001.

Morales, Rebecca, and Frank Bonilla, eds. *Latinos in a Changing U.S. Economy*. Newbury Park, Calif.: Sage, 1993.

ANDRÉS TORRES

CERVANTES, LORNA DEE (b. 1954), Chicana poet. An internationally acclaimed Chicana poet, Lorna Dee Cervantes is the author of two award-winning volumes of poetry, *Emplumada* (1981) and *From the Cables of Genocide* (1991). Her work has appeared in more than 150 anthologies, including *The Norton Anthology of American Literature* and *The Heath Anthology of American Literature*. She is the winner of the Peterson Prize for Poetry, the Latino Literature Award, and the American Book Award, and she has received two fellowships from the National Endowment for the Arts as well as a Lila Wallace–Reader's Digest Award. Since 1974 Cervantes has presented at more than one thousand poetry readings, lectures, performances, and panel presentations in such places as the Library of Congress, the White House, the Walker Art Center, and major university campuses. Her work has been translated into German, Italian, French, Spanish, and Czechoslovakian. She directs the creative writing program at the University of Colorado, Boulder.

Cervantes began her publishing career not only as a writer but also as a literary activist. She founded Mango Publications in 1974, a time when Chicano and Chicana writing was dominated by men. She published the famous Chicano Chapbook series and *Mango*, a cross-cultural literary and art magazine. Cervantes coedited and copublished a broadside series of women's art and literature, and during the early 1990s she founded and edited *Red Dirt*, a biannual, cross-cultural poetry journal. She also coordinates an annual writing retreat for women of color, providing space, time, and intensive writing workshops dedicated to developing emerging literary voices.

Cervantes's evolving poetics are significant in American letters because they form connections across a range of literary traditions and canons. Her work has the potential to revitalize models of political and social solidarity and action while offering important models for reading poetry and cultural texts. Most importantly Cervantes is a masterful poet, as aware of literary form and traditions as she is of history and the work poets have done and can do.

Cervantes's first collection, *Emplumada* (1981), was well received. Critics thought it marked the "threshold of a new phase for Chicano literature" (Madrigal, p. 137), while describing a "world simply built by feminine ancestors" (Saldívar, p. 87). Her work was groundbreaking because of its multiplicity and specificity of voice as female, Chicana, and working class. Cervantes's themes centers primarily on questions of ethnic and gender identity as well as her search for a poetic voice as a Chicana and as a woman. Her second collection, *From the Cables of Genocide: Poems on Love and Hunger* (1991), was not so widely reviewed. Perhaps one reason for the relative quiet surrounding the collection had to do with its departure in style from *Emplumada*. Where her first collection is introspective and overtly political, her second is, in contrast, slippery. Its range is broader and more self-consciously literary, showing greater emphasis on the positioning of poetic voice. Cervantes carefully develops deferral as a poetic strategy, most explicit in her manipulation of enjambed lines. In these poems, she reveals a prevalent deferral of meaning, desire, and certainty and creates productive tensions and multiplicities of meaning. Consequently the connections between the personal, mythic, and historical are deeply intertwined.

Throughout her work Cervantes develops an expanding frame of reference for Chicana poetry. She moves from a pride in the indigenous roots of Mexican and Chicana and Chicano culture that is characteristic of classic Chicano and Chicana literature to a broad engagement with global cultural and political influences. Cervantes's references—which range from the traditional Chicana and Chicano tropes of Nahuatl and Mesoamerican images to Hispanophone modernist poetry, from Celtic folklore to Greek myth—indicate a shifting of consciousness. Not only is it important, as Cervantes has stressed, to participate in a "cultural break" that disrupts monological versions of history and culture, but it is also important to extend the scope of struggle and the alliances that can be imagined in poetry and formed in the world.

From the Cables of Genocide consists of dense, lyrical poems that, rather than speak directly to the issue of genocide, assume it as an underlying fact. The term "genocide" is important because of its historical and political uses. The losses occasioned by genocide shapes this poetry in nuanced imagery, linking poems thematically and formally throughout the sections of the volume. The title significantly echoes *Cables to Rage* by African American poet Audre Lorde, shifting the reader's understanding of where Chicana poetry might locate itself. This affinity with African American feminism, embedded here in the allusion to one of its preeminent figures, is not overtly expressed in the poems, yet it shapes Cervantes's poetic sensibility as surely as the history of genocide. In this collection and in her subsequent work Cervantes extends a Chicana and Chicano poetic tradition across cultural lines to connect explicitly with third world feminist concerns.

Cervantes's poem "Coffee" stands as the culmination and expression of her poetics. It is a long poem of six sections. Evoking the military-ordered massacre in Acteal in December 1997, "Coffee" travels across space and time. From Guatemala it connects to the Jewish poet Hans Sahl fleeing Nazi persecution in Germany and to events in France and the United States. The poem moves back to Acteal to describe the massacre, then it shifts to a young woman protesting in Denver. It ends in the first-person voice of the poet, whose final words are *"con safos,"* a signature of protection and defiance ever present in urban *placas*, or Chicana and Chicano graffiti markings. "Coffee" is at once an epic and a personal poem in scope and tone, detailing the horrors of the massacre in the context of global capitalism and neocolonialism as well as the role of poetry in the world.

Questions of aesthetics and history and of literary and cultural tradition are deeply interlinked in Cervantes's work. She does not engage in consolation or in monumentalizing the dead; instead, she identifies with them. Cervantes creates a way of understanding devastating cultural and historic losses, specifically a way of understanding the ways women experience grief. Pushing those connections, she engages difficult questions about the meanings of historical loss and the possibilities of connection across cultural differences and oppositional worldviews.

Cervantes writes poems about Chicanas in gangs, connecting them to Chumash and Greek myths while describing the realities of their lives. She writes of poverty, combining dignity with righteous anger. She writes about families and their histories and how she is connected to families on the other side of the globe. The scope of her poetic vision is vast, intimately connective, and deeply democratic. Cervantes is part of a generation of Latina and Latino poets who, along with Martín Espada and Francisco Alarcón, write powerfully about love and beauty and its importance to struggles for social justice.

See also Chicanos and Chicanas; Literature; Mexican-Origin People in the United States; *and* Poetry.

BIBLIOGRAPHY
Arteaga, Alfred. *Chicano Poetics: Heterotexts and Hybridities*. New York: Cambridge University Press, 1997.
Cervantes, Lorna Dee. *Emplumada*. Pittsburgh, Pa.: University of Pittsburgh Press, 1981.
Cervantes, Lorna Dee. *From the Cables of Genocide: Poems on Love and Hunger*. Houston, Tex.: Arte Público Press, 1991.
Chávez Candelaria, Cordelia. "Rethinking the 'Eyes' of Chicano Poetry; or, Reading the Multiple Centers of Chicana Poetics." In *Women Poets of the Americas: Toward a Pan-American Gathering*, edited by Jacqueline Vaught Brogan and Cordelia Chávez Candelaria. Notre Dame, Ind.: University of Notre Dame Press, 1999.
Madrigal, Sylvia. "Book Review of *Emplumada*." *Imagine* 1, no. 1 (Summer 1984): 137–140.
Pérez-Torres, Rafael. *Movements in Chicano Poetry: Against Myths, against Margins*. New York and Cambridge, UK: Cambridge University Press, 1995.
Saldívar, Jose David. "Book Review of *Emplumada*." *Revista Chicano-Riqueña* 12, no. 2 (Summer 1984): 87–89.

ELIZA RODRIGUEZ Y GIBSON

CHACÓN, JUAN (?–1985), labor organizer. In 1954, at the end of the McCarthy era, a cabal of politicians, Hollywood studio executives, and big labor leaders—including the film industry's own International Alliance of Theatrical Stage Employees and Moving Picture Machine Operators—suppressed the release of Herbert Biberman's socially conscious melodrama *Salt of the Earth*, making it the first motion picture to be banned in the United States. The film was suppressed primarily because the director, Biberman; his producer, Paul Jarrico; and the film's screenwriter, Michael Wilson, were blacklisted by Hollywood because of their lack of cooperation with Joseph McCarthy and his Senate subcommittee, which had conducted a witch-hunt of the motion picture industry in order to root out what it perceived as "Communist subversives." Despite being blacklisted, Biberman and his associates were able to finance and complete the film—despite numerous attempts by Hollywood, local politicians, the state department, and vigilantes to obstruct its making—by creating their own production company, which set a new precedent for independent motion picture production.

Importance to Latinos

But for U.S. Latinos at the time, what was most significant about the suppression of *Salt of the Earth* was the film's subject matter. It was a fictionalized account of the Local 890 chapter of the International Union of Mine, Mill, and Smelter Workers' struggle against Empire Zinc in Grant County, New Mexico. As a union of predominantly

Mexican and Mexican American mine workers, Local 890 had embarked on a lengthy and grueling campaign against the corporate giant of the copper industry, demanding better wages and racial-economic equality. Among the Chicano and Anglo leadership of Local 890 was its president, Juan Chacón, the son of an immigrant Mexican mine worker. Chacón had entered the mines at the age of eighteen and had also served during World War II as a merchant marine and afterward became a welder and a civil servant before returning to his father's profession. A militant and unabashed member of the American Communist Party, Chacón was the inspiration for *Salt of the Earth*'s Mexican American protagonist, Ramón Quintero, and rose to the occasion when the film's producers basically asked him to "play himself" in the male lead. Although Chacón had no acting experience, his performance displayed an uncanny sensitivity and verisimilitude that was later praised by film critics and scholars.

Despite being a nonprofessional actor, Chacón held his own with veteran Mexican actress Rosaura Revueltas, who played the role of Esperanza Quintero, the film's female protagonist and narrator, whose character suggested his own wife, Virginia Chacón, herself a passionate union activist and member of the Communist Party. Adhering to the classical Soviet cinema convention of integrating actual working people into a film's cast, the producers of *Salt of the Earth* hired several members of Local 890 to play extras or supporting roles in the film, including Anglo union leader Clinton Jencks and his wife Virginia Jencks, both also avowed activists and passionate leftists. This sense of

gender parity in the film's casting was integral to its narrative, which recounted how a court injunction prevented union members from picketing, with the result that their wives—Local 890's Ladies Auxiliary—walked in place of them on the picket lines. As depicted in the film, for a period during the strike at Empire Zinc the women achieved gender equality and set a feminist precedent that, to their later dismay, would not be repeated for years. Although Chacón was at first leery—partly because of his traditional patriarchal beliefs—of the protofeminist ideals and developments that the strike generated, he later conceded his disappointment that after the strike the union's Ladies Auxiliary regressed to its former role and did not maintain the advances it temporarily achieved.

After the film's suppression, Chacón became one of its most passionate defenders, disregarding the controversy over the film and the red-baiting that permeated big labor. He returned to his position as president of Local 890 and for a period in the late 1960s rejoined the rank-and-file when his bids for reelection were hampered by the union's upper bureaucracy, which was often influenced by a company management that was uncomfortable with his reputation for militancy. Although he was fired from his job with Kennecott in 1974 and again joined the rank and file after a later stint as union president, Chacón maintained his militancy well into his retirement and upheld his firm belief in workers' rights until his death in 1985.

Legacy

Juan Chacón remains an inspiration for Chicanas and Chicanos, other Latinas and Latinos, and all those engaged in the struggle for workers' rights, gender equality, and the dignified representation of Latina and Latino culture and social realities. Indeed, the multidimensional representation of the Chicano male that Chacón brought to the screen in *Salt of the Earth* was far ahead of its time and arguably has yet to be matched by any contemporary representation that Hollywood has offered. Although his onscreen legacy is small—and has been too often ignored—his embodiment of art, politics, and social reality will remain a testament to the resilience of Latinos and Latinas in the face of exploitation and injustice.

See also **Labor and Labor Strikes.**

BIBLIOGRAPHY

Lorence, James J. *The Suppression of* Salt of the Earth: *How Hollywood, Big Labor, and Politicians Blacklisted a Movie in Cold War America.* Albuquerque: University of New Mexico Press, 1999.

Wilson, Michael, and Deborah Rosenfelt. *Salt of the Earth.* New York: Feminist Press, 1978.

SONNY RICHARD E. ESPINOZA

JUAN CHÁCON. With Rosaura Revueltas in *Salt of the Earth*, 1954. (Photofest)

CHARREADA. *See* Jaripeo.

CHÁVEZ, ANGÉLICO (1910–1996), priest, poet, and historian. Fray (Friar) Angélico Chávez was born on April 10, 1910, in Wagon Mound, New Mexico, as Manuel Ezequiel Chávez to Fabián Chávez, a professional carpenter, active politician, and avid supporter of statehood, and Nicolasa Roybal de Chávez, a schoolteacher. Both parents were civic leaders who ensured the education of their ten children by supporting New Mexico statehood and U.S. expansion at the turn of the twentieth century. Chávez grew up in Mora, New Mexico, and was educated in Midwestern seminaries, where he began to paint and write poetry. His teachers christened him with his pen name Fray Angélico after the Florentine painter Fra Angelico. In 1937, Chávez returned to New Mexico as the first native Franciscan priest, and he served as pastor of several towns until he retired in 1972. Chávez died on March 18, 1996 and left behind a corpus of literary, historical, and cultural production that befits his status as New Mexico's Renaissance man.

Several prominent Anglo-American poets, including Witter Bynner and Alice Corbin Henderson, the founder of *Poetry* magazine, helped publish Chávez's first book of poetry, *Clothed with the Sun*, in 1939. *New Mexico Triptych*, a collection of short stories, followed in 1940. After serving as a chaplain in the Army during World War II and the Korean War, Chavez began compiling, translating, and republishing the church's Spanish colonial archives and became New Mexico's official archivist. In 1948, the Santa Fe Historical Society published *Our Lady of the Conquest*, three essays about La Conquistadora, Santa Fe's beloved statue, and brought Chávez into the foray of historical scholarship. His 1954 text *La Conquistadora*, which retells the history of the lady statue in its own voice, was published alongside *Origins of New Mexico Families*, a two-part genealogical study that remains the authoritative text on New Mexican surnames, and in 1959 Chávez wrote *The Virgin of Port Lligat*, a poem inspired by Salvador Dalí's painting of the virgin. Chávez's 1974 autobiographical text, *My Penitente Land*, followed his retirement from the ministry, and he returned to historical recovery with *But Time and Chance* (1981), *Tres Macho He Said* (1985), and *Wake for a Fat Vicar* (2004), a biographical trilogy about three of New Mexico's leading priests—Antonio José Martínez, José Manuel Gallegos, and Juan Felipe Ortiz. The last was published posthumously.

As early as his seminarian days, Chávez began hybridizing his creative work, combining Old English literary styles with New Mexican themes in his poetry and mixing sacred and profane images in his art. His later writings likewise blend poetry and prose, autobiography and history, and genealogy and fiction. While Chicano and Chicana literary scholarship remains cool to Chávez's ostensibly simple and quaint literature, his writings span the 1930s to the 1990s and shape New Mexico's Spanish

ANGÉLICO CHÁVEZ. (Photo courtesy of *New Mexico Historical Review*)

colonial history through narratives that reveal the complex and contradictory formation of the state's regional and national identity; for this reason Fray Angélico is remembered as New Mexico's leading man of letters.

See also Conquistadora La *and* New Mexico.

BIBLIOGRAPHY

Chávez, Fray Angélico. *My Penitente Land: Reflections on Spanish New Mexico*. Albuquerque: University of New Mexico Press, 1974.

McCracken, Ellen. *Fray Angélico Chávez: Poet, Priest and Artist*. Albuquerque: University of New Mexico Press, 2000.

MELINA V. VIZCAÍNO

CHÁVEZ, CÉSAR (1927–1993), labor union organizer. César Estrada Chávez was born in Yuma, Arizona, to Librado Chávez and Juana Chávez. He was the second of five children. The Chávez family had a small farm and ran a country store. As the Depression intensified, and years of drought forced thousands off the land, the Chávez family lost both their farm and store in 1937. César was ten years old when the family packed up and headed for California. These were difficult years, sleeping by the side of the road, moving from farm to farm, from harvest to harvest. César attended thirty-eight different schools before he finally gave up after finishing the eighth grade.

As Chávez learned the hard lessons of life, he absorbed important values from his parents. His father, Librado, taught him the importance of hard work and opened his eyes to the inequities of the farm-labor system. His mother, Juana, a deeply religious and compassionate woman, emphasized the importance of caring for the less fortunate and the power of love.

In the early 1940s the Chávez family settled in Delano, a small farm town in California's San Joaquin Valley, where César would spend his teenage years. In 1946, César Chávez enlisted, and spent what he later described as "the two worst years of my life," in the navy. When he got out of the service, he returned to Delano and married his high school sweetheart, Helen Favela. Their relationship, and the support that Helen gave him throughout his life, provided Chávez with the solid base that allowed him to devote his life to helping others. Chávez and Helen moved to San Jose, where their first child, Fernando, was born. Over the years the family grew to include seven children—Fernando, Linda, Paul, Eloise, Sylvia, Anthony, and Anna.

Nonviolence

In San Jose, Chávez met a local priest, Father Donald McDonnell, who introduced him to the writings of Saint Francis and Mahatma Gandhi, and the idea that nonviolence could be an active force for positive change. But Chávez needed to learn how to put these principles into action.

The man who taught Chávez how to do that arrived in San Jose in 1953. Fred Ross was an organizer. He was in San Jose to recruit members for the Community Service Organization (CSO). CSO helped its members with immigration and tax problems and taught them how to organize to deal with problems like police violence and discrimination. To Chávez, Ross's simple rules for organizing were nothing short of revolutionary. Their meeting was the beginning of a lifelong friendship.

Chávez rapidly developed as an organizer and eventually became president of CSO. When the organization turned down his request to organize farmworkers in 1962, he resigned and returned to Delano. From 1962 to 1965 he crisscrossed the state, talking to farmworkers. His new organization, the National Farm Workers Association (NFWA), used the model of community service that Chávez had learned in CSO. Chávez did not want to call it a union, because of the long history of failed attempts to create agricultural unions, and the bitter memories of those who had been promised justice and then been abandoned. But in 1965 the union issue finally exploded. The Agricultural Workers Organizing Committee (AWOC), a mostly Filipino union, went on strike when the Delano table-grape growers cut the pay rates during the harvest. Chávez asked his organization to join the strike and quickly became its leader.

The strikers faced odds that could not be overcome by traditional labor tactics. Under Chávez's leadership, the struggle became defined in new terms. They would do battle nonviolently since they could never match the growers in physical force. They were a poor movement so they would emphasize their poverty. For many years all organizers and volunteers from Chávez down were paid room and board and $5 a week. Although there were picket lines in the fields, the real focus moved to the cities, where grapes were sold. Hundreds of students, religious workers, and labor activists talked to consumers in front of markets, asking them to do a simple thing: "Help the farmworkers by not buying grapes." At its height, over 13 million Americans supported the Delano grape boycott. The pressure was irresistible, and in 1969 the Delano growers signed historic contracts with the United Farm Workers Organizing Committee (UFWOC), which later became the United Farm Workers of America (UFW).

Chávez had inspired an organization that did not look like a labor union. His vision did not include just the traditional bread-and-butter issues of unionism; it was about reclaiming dignity for people who were marginalized by society. What had started as the Delano grape strike came to be known as La Causa, The Cause. Whether they were farmworkers fighting for a better life, or middle-class students trying to change the world, those who were drawn to the farmworkers' movement were inspired by Chávez's example to put aside their normal lives and make exceptional sacrifices.

Chávez placed harsher demands on himself than on anyone else in the movement. In 1968 he fasted (the first of several fasts over his lifetime) to recommit the movement to nonviolence. In many ways the fast epitomized Chávez's approach to social change. On one level it represented his spiritual values, his willingness to sacrifice and do penance. At the same time, he and his lieutenants were extremely aware of the political ramifications of his actions, using the fast as a way of both publicizing and organizing for their movement. Fasting was also an expression of his deep spirituality. Like most farmworkers, Chávez was a devout Catholic. His vision of religion was a progressive one that prefigured the "preferential option for the poor" of liberation theology. In the UFW, the mass was a call to action as well as a rededication of the spirit.

CÉSAR CHÁVEZ. Chávez leading striking workers near Delano, Calif. (©TakeStock Photos)

Organizing

The 1968 fast marked the beginning of Chávez's emergence on the national political scene. The presidential candidate Robert Kennedy came to Delano to break bread with Chávez at the end of his fast. Chávez responded by committing UFWOC to campaign for Kennedy in the California primary. Their voter registration and get-out-the-vote efforts provided Kennedy's margin of victory in California.

Over the years, the UFW became a significant political force, demonstrating that Mexican Americans could and would participate in electoral politics when their concerns were at stake. Chávez's understanding of the relationship between economic issues and political participation was the starting point for a growing wave of Latino and Latina activism and electoral activity, which eventually led to the election of thousands of Latino and Latina officials and a major shift in the American political landscape.

Chávez had never expected that victory in the battle for farmworkers' rights would be achieved during his lifetime. In fact, the first stunning victories with the grape growers were followed by major setbacks. First in the lettuce industry, and then when the grape contracts expired in 1972, growers sought out the powerful Teamsters union and signed contracts with them that rolled back the UFW's hard-fought gains. The UFW responded with strikes that left thousands in jail and, eventually, two of its members dead. But the "interunion" battle had left the public confused and made a new boycott against lettuce and grape growers difficult.

Chávez looked for a political solution to the impasse. He supported Jerry Brown's bid to become governor of California, and in return he was able to engineer the nation's first law giving farmworkers the right to union elections. The passage of California's Agricultural Labor Relations Act in 1975 led to an overwhelming series of UFW election victories, and it seemed that Chávez had finally achieved his goal of organizing farmworkers.

The UFW had given up the boycott in exchange for the right to union elections. But relying on the law became less effective, as growers learned to use it to delay signing contracts. After early successes under the farm labor law, Chávez pulled back from organizing, although he continued to travel extensively to promote awareness of the farmworkers' struggle. The election of a Republican governor in 1982 made enforcing the law even more difficult.

Other Efforts

Chávez's goals and vision were changing as well. He began to focus on the dangers of pesticides, which had always been a major source of illness among farmworkers. It was a subject that drew a positive response from an environmentally conscious public. Instead of using volunteers, he relied more and more on direct mail. He built low-cost housing for farmworkers and considered starting an urban organizing campaign in Mexican American communities. He became interested in modern management techniques and group dynamics, including the group therapy techniques of Synanon, a drug rehabilitation program.

Although questions were raised about his effectiveness in later years and about some of his political positions, such as supporting the Marcos regime in the Philippines and prioritizing California over other states, Chávez had become a remarkable symbol—for Latinos and Latinas, community activists, the labor movement, young people, and all who valued his values and commitment. He had accomplished something that no one else had ever been able to do: build a union for farmworkers. In the process he trained a generation of activists who would apply their skills in other communities and struggles.

César Chávez died in Yuma, Arizona, close to the place where he was born, on April 23, 1993. He was sixty-six years old. His funeral in Delano attracted thousands of Americans from all walks of life. Years before his death, Chávez had been asked by a union member if he wanted to be remembered by statues and other public memorials. Chávez replied, "If you want to remember me, organize!"

See also **United Farm Workers.**

BIBLIOGRAPHY
Allen, Gary. *Communist Revolution in the Streets*. Boston and Los Angeles: Western Islands, 1967.

Ballis, George. *Basta!: The Tale of Our Struggle*. Delano, Calif.: Farm Workers Press, 1966.

Brill, Steven. *The Teamsters*. New York: Simon and Schuster, 1978.

Day, Mark. *Forty Acres: Cesar Chavez and the Farm Workers*. New York: Praeger Publishers, 1971.

Dunne, John Gregory. *Delano: The Story of the California Grape Strike*. New York: Farrar, Straus, and Giroux, 1967.

Ferriss, Susan, and Ricardo Sandoval. *The Fight in the Fields: César Chávez and the Farmworkers' Movement*. New York: Harcourt Brace, 1997.

Fusco, Paul, and George D. Horowitz. *La Causa: The California Grape Strike*. New York: Collier, 1970.

Galarza, Ernesto. *Merchants of Labor: The Mexican Bracero Story*. Charlotte, N.C., and Santa Barbara, Calif.: McNally and Loftin, 1964.

Kushner, Sam. *Long Road to Delano*. New York: International Publishers, 1975.

Levy, Jacques E. *Cesar Chavez: Autobiography of La Causa*. New York: Norton, 1975.

London, Joan, and Henry Anderson. *So Shall Ye Reap: The Story of Cesar Chavez and the Farm Workers' Movement*. New York: Crowell, 1970.

Matthiessen, Peter. *Sal Si Puedes: Cesar Chavez and the New American Revolution*. New York: Random House, 1969.

McWilliams, Carey. *Factories in the Field*. (1935) Santa Barbara, Calif., and Salt Lake City, Utah: Peregrine, 1971.

McWilliams, Carey. *North from Mexico: The Spanish-Speaking People of the United States*. (1948) New York: Greenwood Press, 1968.

Meister, Dick, and Anne Loftis. *A Long Time Coming: The Struggle to Unionize America's Farm Workers*. New York: Macmillan, 1977.

Rose, Margaret Eleanor. "Women in the United Farm Workers: A Study of Chicana and Mexicana Participation in a Labor Union, 1950–1980." PhD diss., University of California at Los Angeles, 1988.

Ross, Fred. *Conquering Goliath: Cesar Chavez at the Beginning*. Keene, Calif.: El Taller Grafico Press/United Farm Workers, 1989.

Scharlin, Craig, and Lilia V. Villanueva. *Philip Vera Cruz: A Personal History of Filipino Immigrants and the Farmworkers' Movement*. Los Angeles: UCLA Labor Center, Institute of Industrial Relations and UCLA Asian American Studies Center, 1992.

Taylor, Ronald. *Chavez and the Farm Workers*. Boston: Beacon Press, 1975.

Tejada-Flores, Rick, and Ray Telles, dirs. *The Fight in the Fields: Cesar Chavez and the Farmworkers Struggle*. Documentary film. San Francisco: Paradigm Productions, 1997. Distributed by Cinema Guild New York.

RICK TEJADA-FLORES

CHÁVEZ, DENISE (b. 1948), writer. Born in Las Cruces, New Mexico, Denise Chávez is considered a foundational figure in the development of the woman-centered Chicana literary movement that followed the largely male-dominated Chicano renaissance of the sixties. Other notable figures are Ana Castillo, Lorna Dee Cervantes, Sandra Cisneros, and Helena María Viramontes. A prolific playwright, fiction author, and sometimes poet, Chávez has earned praise for giving voice to the personal and private lives of southwestern Mexican American women as these evolve, resist, and intersect with the broader collective struggle for equality and justice in the United States–Mexico borderland communities. A self-described "cultural warrior," Chávez gives voice to the untold secrets related to the search for self-identity, agency, and desire through a frank and complicating exploration of gender and class issues viewed from a feminist and Chicana perspective.

Chávez's focus on women and the struggles of her community has roots in her childhood and family ties. She was raised primarily by her Mexican mother, Delfina Rede Faber Chávez, a Spanish teacher, devout Catholic, and one-time student of Diego Rivera. Chávez, her mother, and her two sisters were abandoned early on by her father, E. E. "Chano" Chávez, a Georgetown-educated lawyer and an alcoholic. Chávez attributes her success to her mother's modeling of a life with a career and a love of education and reading. Chávez also traces to her mother's family her activist strain, the origins of her commitment to speaking out on human rights and for the equality of all people and of the Latino and Latina community in particular. Although her parents were separated, Chávez had constant contact with both sides of her family. In her *testimonio* (testimony) "Heat and Rain" she states that this experience of navigating separation and extension, of "growing up solitary in the midst of noise," ultimately evolved into the essential qualities of her work as a writer.

But acting, not writing, was Chávez's first passion. She became, in the words of the critic Martha Heard, "the most formally trained of all the New Mexican Hispanic Playwrights" (Heard, p. 83). This passion was nurtured while Chávez attended the all-girls, Catholic Madonna High School, where she was encouraged to participate in all areas of theater production. Chávez further pursued her interest in drama at New Mexico State University,

DENISE CHÁVEZ. (Daniel Zolinsky)

where she earned a B.A. in drama and wrote her first play, *The Wait*, which won the New Mexico State University Best Play Award in 1970. She earned an M.F.A. in drama at Trinity University in San Antonio, Texas, in 1974 and an M.A. in creative writing at the University of New Mexico at Albuquerque in 1984. Chávez has written approximately fifteen plays (most of them prior to 1985) and has participated actively as both a writer and an actress in theatrical productions and projects in the Southwest. She has worked with the Dallas Theater Center, the New Mexico Artists-in-the-Schools Program, the New Mexico Free Theater (dedicated to bilingual street theater geared toward substance abusers), the Compañía de Teatro de Albuquerque, and the Theater in the Red in Santa Fe, among other institutions. Chávez has also taught drama and writing at the University of Houston, the American School in Paris, and the College of Santa Fe, and she has worked extensively in community outreach programs as a teacher, most notably at the Radium Springs for Women, a medium security prison in the Las Cruces area.

Chávez's plays take place in and evoke the diverse landscapes of New Mexico—deserts, rocky outcrops, plazas, barrio streets, public landmarks, and intimate domestic spaces. Action and suspense in Chávez's work, in a manner reminiscent of Eugene O'Neill (to whom Chávez repeatedly expresses her great debt), deeply probe human character and motives, human transformation, and stasis. While these central actions have compelling universal appeal, the struggles, defeats, and triumphs experienced by individual characters are plotted to underscore the specific and multiple challenges encountered by the Latino or Latina protagonists, whose wills, or lack thereof, are mediated or hindered by cultural practices, class and ethnic determinism, and gender inequities.

Chávez draws on a wide variety of theater traditions and styles to dramatize her stories. Her one-act play *Plaza* (1984) explores the character of Iris, an unhappily married storekeeper, who observes, gossips, and judges her friends and community through her store window. Through Iris's conversations with her friend, the audience comes to understand that the glass window that separates Iris from the street and the people who inhabit it is a metaphor for the isolation and transparency of the rigid social boundaries and cultural practices that have shaped her life. One learns that Iris had painfully controlling parents who told her "what to do, who to talk to, and who to marry." She identifies the controlling nature of her too "Spanish" parents as an inherently ethnic trait and ultimately rejects her heritage and community—and the hope of love and intimacy embodied in the budding relationship between her friend and Benito—in favor of the loneliness and isolation of life behind the glass. In striking contrast to the realism of *Plaza*, Chávez's play *El camino* uses masks, dance, and popular festivals to evoke the existentialist drama of the Guatemalan Carlos Solórzano.

Inspired and nurtured by members of the male Chicano renaissance, such as Rudolfo Anaya, Chávez made her debut as a fiction writer with the award-winning *The Last of the Menu Girls* (1986). In a distinct departure from her male predecessors, Chávez wrote seven interrelated stories that feature the strikingly unremarkable (at first)—some have said formless—adolescent hospital "menu girl" Rocío Esquibel. As the stories unfold, so does the life of the maturing protagonist, who intuitively confronts the ties that bind her: gender; class; ethnic stereotyping; dependence; repressed sexuality; and fear of death, dying, and bodily decay. In another striking departure, *Menu Girls* experiments with a distinctively innovative and eclectic form. Chávez draws on many genres—literary and nonliterary—to construct her stories. She plays freely with conventions of time and space for effective dramatic impact, and she does not hesitate to populate her texts with Spanish and bilingual speakers. *Menu Girls* sheds narrative conventions in favor of structures and techniques more readily identified with theater, such as shifting scenes, gaps in temporal and spatial unity, and dramatic monologue and dialogue, to compellingly mirror the complexity of the cross-cultural, intergenerational, and feminine Southwest border.

In 1994 Chávez published her first novel, *Face of an Angel*, which focuses on the coming to consciousness of

Zoveida Dosamantes, head waitress at El Farol Restaurant in Agua Oscura. The novel garnered instant acclaim and won several awards, most notably the American Book Award in 1995. It was cited for its compelling narrator, its rich and diverse narrative texture, and its frank treatment of private and often untold stories dealing with extramarital affairs, divorce, incest, parental abuse, domestic violence, sexual desire, self-exploration, and menstruation. Zoveida, the narrator, is precociously endowed with an urgency and desire to tell the story and proceeds with a remarkable intergenerational and matrilineal account of the Dosamantes family. A thematic exploration of the idea of service underscored through Zoveida's ongoing effort to complete a project, *The Book of Service: A Handbook for Service*, ties the story together. Ultimately service, in particular the service of women, as a concept and as a practice, is complicated and edified in a nuanced critique and revision of the stereotypical and ethnocentric view of the Latina as the mindless and impoverished woman and employee in the service industry. A persistent search for and encounter with spiritual meaning in life complements this revised notion of service. Zoveida's spiritual journey, rooted in an explicitly womanist devotion to the Virgen de Guadalupe, is open, evolving, and ultimately a reflection of the synchronism of faiths—Catholicism, Native American spirituality, and New Mexico faith rituals—that characterizes the New Mexican faith communities. The rich narrative texture of *Face of an Angel* is characterized by what Douglas Anderson has identified as Chávez's "exuberant inclusiveness." Indeed, Chávez's novel reflects the increasingly distinctive practice among borderland writers of redrawing the borders of discourse to blur the boundaries between oral and written texts and between popular culture and canonical culture. *Face of an Angel* reflects a keen interest and humorous curiosity in the interplay—the gaps, the duplications, and the intersections—of a wide array of texts ranging from oral history and folklore passed down to her by the women in her family to soap operas, tabloids, and movie magazines and to literary discourses more conventionally understood.

With *Loving Pedro Infante* (2001) Chávez moved into another area of popular culture, this time focusing on the popular Mexican icon, singer, and idol Pedro Infante. In this lighthearted but heartrending story, Tere and her friend Irma turn to active membership in the Pedro Infante Club #256 in an attempt to transcend their disillusionment and frustrations with the vicissitudes of love.

Chávez is a consummate writer and activist working tirelessly on behalf of her craft and her community. In addition to writing, she is a founding member of the National Institute of Chicana Writers and the founder and artistic director of the Border Book Festival. Chávez, like many other writers of her community and generation, entered the twenty-first century with a renewed conviction of the power of words to speak the truth about her community and to continue the legacy of her mother's family by speaking out for things that matter: justice, peace, and equality for all human beings.

See also Literature; New Mexico *and* Testimonios.

BIBLIOGRAPHY

Chávez, Denise. *Face of an Angel*. New York: Farrar, Straus, and Giroux, 1994.

Delgadillo, Teresa. "Denise Chávez: *Face of an Angel*." In *Reading U.S. Latina Writers: Remapping American Literature*, edited by Alvina E. Quintana, 37–50. New York: Palgrave MacMillan, 2003.

Heard, Martha E. "The Theatre of Denise Chávez: Interior Landscapes with *Sabor Nuevomexicano*." *Americas Review* 16, no. 2 (Summer 1988): 83–91.

Keating, AnaLouise. "Towards a New Politics of Representation? Absence and Desire in Denise Chávez's *The Last of the Menu Girls*." In *We Who Love to Be Astonished: Experimental Women's Writing and Performance Poetics*, edited by Laura Hinton and Cynthia Hogue, 71–80. Tuscaloosa: University of Alabama Press, 2002.

Mehaffy, Marilyn, and AnaLouise Keating. "'Carrying the Message': Denise Chávez on the Politics of Chicana Becoming." *Aztlan* 26, no. 1 (Spring 2001): 127–155.

Quintana, Alvina E. "Orality, Tradition, and Culture: Denise Chávez's *Novena Narratives* and *The Last of the Menu Girls*." In *Home Girls: Chicana Literary Voices*, 93–111. Philadelphia: Temple University Press, 1996.

TAMARA R. WILLIAMS

CHÁVEZ, HELEN (b. 1928), labor activist. Helen Fabela Chávez is a labor activist and the widow of César Estrada Chávez, the Chicano labor leader who cofounded the United Farm Workers of America (UFW). A first-generation Chicana with a traditional upbringing and limited education, Helen has played an instrumental role in the movement for farm workers' rights, yet describes her vocation as caring for the family (Rose, p. 209). Helen did the bulk of her union work in her home, often after working long days as a field laborer. Perhaps because Helen herself has emphasized her roles of wife and mother, studies of the Chicano and Chicana labor movement, with rare exceptions, have primarily focused on César and UFW cofounder Dolores Huerta. Information about Helen tends to be inconsistent and expressed in relation to her husband's life.

Early Life

Helen Fabela was born in Brawley, California, on January 21, 1928. Her father or her grandfather, depending on the source, fought in the Mexican Revolution. This revolutionary history is generally invoked as the source of Helen's commitment to social change. Her mother and father—from Sombrete and San Jacinto, respectively—emigrated

HELEN CHÁVEZ. Helen Chávez (in polka-dot blouse, third from right) with her family, 2000. (Gary Kazanjian/AP)

separately from Mexico and married in California. Both worked as migrant laborers, first in the Imperial Valley and later in the San Joaquín Valley. The Fabela family eventually settled south of Delano.

Helen first met César in 1942 while she was a student at Delano High School. Her father's death forced Helen to quit school. She went from working after school in a grocery store to working full time in the fields so she could help her widowed mother, two sisters, and four brothers. Helen and César married on October 22, 1948, in Reno, Nevada, and returned to Delano. They unsuccessfully tried sharecropping strawberries in Greenfield and lived in Crescent City while César worked in a lumber mill. In 1952, they rented a house in a San José barrio called *Sal Si Puedes* ("Get out if you can.") By 1959, they had eight children.

The couple soon became involved in labor organizing. Their local Catholic priest gave César's name to Fred Ross, an organizer looking for local leaders to participate in the Community Service Organization (CSO) and its agenda of constructive political action. César distrusted Ross as an unwanted Anglo outsider and avoided him for days. Helen, however, felt Ross might have "something positive" to offer and revealed where her husband was hiding. Ross's commitment to help the disenfranchised won over César, who became a full-time CSO organizer and then national director in 1958.

Helen also became politicized through CSO activities. During voter registration drives, she taught literacy classes for migrant workers seeking to pass the U.S. citizenship test and vote. While César was organizing, Helen cared for the children, worked ten hours a day to support the family, and assisted with CSO business. Since César often came home exhausted, Helen would handwrite the CSO daily activity reports that he dictated. Historian Margaret Rose suggests that the uncompensated auxiliary efforts of women like Helen helped the CSO become one of the most successful Mexican American associations in California at this time.

Later Political and Organizing Activities

Along with fellow organizer Dolores Huerta, César resigned from the CSO in 1962 to start the Farm Workers Association, later known as the National Farm Workers Association (NFWA). The family moved back to Delano where Helen took a job picking grapes at $1.25 an hour while César traveled to build the new union. During one meeting, the NFWA board members voted Helen into the post of accountant despite her protests. Helen learned quickly and soon became the full-time administrator of the NFWA credit union, keeping faultless financial records for more than twenty years.

In 1965, the NFWA merged with the mostly Filipino Agricultural Workers Organizing Committee (AWOC) to become the United Farm Workers Organizing Committee (UFWOC), a truly multiethnic union under the AFL-CIO, the American Federation of Labor–Congress of Industrial Organizations. They dubbed their shared efforts *La Causa* (the Cause). Despite brutal opposition, the UFWOC adhered to nonviolent principles, protesting unfair labor practices through strikes, boycotts, pickets, fasts, and marches. Helen joined the picket lines to demand union recognition and was arrested in 1966 for shouting *"Huelga!"* ("Strike!") at the W. B. Camp ranch.

In 1971, the Chávez family moved to Keene, California. An abandoned preventorium, a treatment facility for children liable to develop tuberculosis, became the new UFWOC headquarters, dubbed *La Paz* (peace). Helen moved to this location "with great reluctance" since she had unpleasant childhood memories of being a lonely, isolated patient there. In 1973, the UFWOC became the United Farm Workers (UFW).

Helen has maintained that a woman's proper place is in the home, but she never shied away from work or from organizing. While managing the credit union, Helen worked in the onion fields and grape vineyards to support her family. In 1974, she joined César in spreading word of the grape boycott to Europe. Helen was arrested a total of four times for acts of civil disobedience. In 1975, hostile growers had Helen and her daughter Linda jailed for speaking with workers at Jack Pandol & Sons grape ranch. They were released when the courts upheld a state regulation allowing union organizers to meet with workers in the fields during nonworking hours. Helen's other highly publicized arrest occurred in 1978 when she and César tested the constitutionality of an Arizona ban against picketing. Helen's example inspired other Mexicanas and Chicanas to support union efforts.

Helen devoted her life to her family, wielded considerable influence over her husband, and contributed significantly to the UFW. César said that Helen's unwavering support and willingness to sacrifice for the greater good allowed him a sense of freedom and clarity in his activism. The Chávez family continued to work toward social justice. Seven of the children have joined the struggle for migrants' rights. In 1993, César died in his sleep. The next year, Helen accepted the Presidential Medal of Freedom in César's honor.

See also Chávez, César; Huerta, Dolores; Latina Labor and Community Organizers; Migrant Workers; *and* United Farm Workers.

BIBLIOGRAPHY
California Dept of Education. *César E. Chávez Research Site*. chavez.cde.ca.gov/researchcenter/

Cesar E. Chavez Foundation. http://www.cesarechavezfoundation.org/.

Day, Dorothy. "On Pilgrimage—June 1971." *The Catholic Worker*, June 1971. (DOC #510). The Catholic Worker Movement. www.catholicworker.org/dorothyday/daytext.cfm?TextID=510 and www.catholicworker.org/dorothyday/daytext.cfm?TextID=576

Dunne, John Gregory. "Helen . . . César . . . and the $100 Prize." Source: "Delano" by Noonday Press, 1967. *Viva César E. Chávez!* César E. Chávez Institute, San Francisco State University. www.sfsu.edu/~cecipp/cesar_chavez/helencesar100.htm

Garcia, Lucio (Tony). "A Man is Born: The Beginning." *Cesar Chavez: Viva La Causa!* projects.edtech.sandi.net/brooklyn/chavez/Links/thebeginning.htm

Griswold del Castillo, Richard, and Richard A. Garcia. *César Chávez: A Triumph of Spirit*. Norman: University of Oklahoma Press, 1995.

Levy, Jacques E. *César Chávez: Autobiography of La Causa*. New York: Norton, 1975.

"Linda Chavez Rodriguez, daughter of Cesar Chavez, obituary." *Las Culturas.com*. www.lasculturas.com/lib/newsUFWLindaChavez.php

"A Page from the Life of Cesar Chavez." Originally appeared in *El Malcriado*, April 15, 1970. *Viva César E. Chávez!* César E. Chávez Institute, San Francisco State University. www.sfsu.edu/~cecipp/cesar_chavez/life.htm

Rose, Margaret. "Traditional and Nontraditional Patterns of Female Activism in the United Farm Workers of America, 1962 to 1980." In *Chicana Leadership: The Frontiers Reader*, edited by Yolanda Flores Niemann, Susan H. Armitage, Patricia Hart, et al., 202–220. Lincoln: University of Nebraska Press, 2002.

"The Story of Cesar Chavez: The Beginning." July 16, 2004. *UFW: The Official Web Page of the United Farm Workers of America, AFL—CIO*. www.ufw.org/cecstory.htm

Young, Jan. "Small Man With a Big Dream" from "Cesar Chavez and the Migrant Farmworkers," 1967. *Viva César E. Chávez!* César E. Chávez Institute, San Francisco State University. www.sfsu.edu/~cecipp/cesar_chavez/smallmanbigdream.htm

TAMARA C. HO

CHAVEZ, LINDA (b. 1947), political advocate. In her 2002 autobiography, Linda Chavez calls herself the "the most hated Hispanic in America." Since the 1980s, Chavez has challenged the Latino lobby on immigration, affirmative action, and bilingual education. Though controversial, she is an important voice on topics concerning Latinos and Latinas in the United States.

Chavez was born on June 17, 1947, in Albuquerque, New Mexico. Her mother, Velma McKenna, married Rudy Chavez shortly after World War II. Chavez's upbringing was humble, and she notes three principal factors that shaped her childhood: her father's alcoholism, the death of her sister, and the Catholic faith. The family eventually moved to Denver and there she met her future husband, Christopher Gersten, while attending the University of Colorado. The couple married in June 1967, and Chavez graduated with a degree in literature in 1970. Gersten, who considered himself both an atheist and socialist, influenced Chavez's politics, although she always expressed some trepidation.

Chavez became distressed over the result of the radicalism she witnessed while attending graduate school at UCLA. She was most disheartened by what she considered lax entry standards for minorities and also grew increasingly concerned about the implementation of racial quotas.

In late 1971, the couple moved to Washington, D.C., where Chavez found a job writing grant proposals for a Latino advocacy firm. It was while working at the American Federation of Teachers, however, that she refined her neoconservative thought. As the editor of *American Educator*, Chavez challenged what she saw as the negative impact of quotas and bilingual education. In the 1980s, her political transformation complete, she accepted a post in

LINDA CHAVEZ. Chavez with President Ronald Reagan in 1986. (Dirck Halstead/Time Life Pictures/Getty Images)

See also Bilingual Education; New Mexico; Political Participation; *and* Public Policy.

BIBLIOGRAPHY

Chavez, Linda. "The Battle over Bilingual Education." October 23, 2002. www.townhall.com/columnists/lindachavez/lc20021023.shtml

Chavez, Linda. "The Bush Proposal." January 8, 2004. www. town-hall.com/columnists/lindachavez/lc20040108.shtml

Chavez, Linda. "Learning the Truth about Bilingual Education." *Jewish World Review*, October 15, 1999. www.jewishworldreview.com/cols/chavez101599.asp

Chavez, Linda. *Out of the Barrio: Toward a New Politics of Hispanic Assimilation*. New York: Basic Books, 1991.

Chavez, Linda. *An Unlikely Conservative: The Transformation of an Ex-Liberal, or, How I Became the Most Hated Hispanic in America.* New York: Basic Books, 2002.

Nuñez-Janes, Mariela. "Bilingual Education and Identity Debates in New Mexico: Constructing and Contesting Nationalism and Identity." *Journal of the Southwest* 44, no. 1 (2002): 61–78.

Ross, Alfred, and Lee Cokorinos. "Assault on Diversity." March 31, 2003. www.thenation.com/doc.mhtml?i=20030414&s=ross.

Scheer, Robert. "Her Compassion for One Is Deserved by Many." January 11, 2000. www.thenation.com/doc.mhtml?i=20010122 &s=20010111

JORGE IBER

the Reagan administration (as staff director of the U.S. Commission on Civil Rights), ran unsuccessfully for the U.S. Senate from Maryland in 1986, and moved on to work for a conservative think tank, the Manhattan Institute. She established her own conservative policy group, the Center for Equal Opportunity, in 1995. Chavez continues to speak out against bilingual education and current immigration policies. Although she argues for amnesty for the undocumented, she also advises newly arrived Latinos and Latinas to learn English and to assimilate and accept "American" culture.

During the 1990s, Chavez became a noted contributor to newspapers and magazines, writing extensively on Latino and Latina topics and on what she perceived as the negative outcome of various governmental programs. She also wrote on labor issues, set-aside programs, and the minimum wage. In 2001, her expertise attracted the attention of President George W. Bush, who nominated her for secretary of labor. The selection drew loud protests from unions and Latino and Latina advocates. Their organizations were prepared to challenge the nomination in the Senate, but it never came to a vote. Chavez had neglected to mention to officials that she had provided lodging and money to an individual who had lived in the United States illegally. This oversight brought on even more criticism and charges of a double standard from Chavez's opponents, and she was forced to withdraw her nomination in early January 2002.

CHAVEZ RAVINE. Chavez Ravine was a thriving, multigenerational Chicano barrio from the early twentieth century through the 1950s. Named for Julian Chávez, who obtained the land in the mid-1840s, Chavez Ravine was located in the hills just to the north and east of downtown Los Angeles. In 1911, the land was developed for housing and sold to Mexican families on affordable terms. The new residents built a thriving community with two public schools, El Santo Niño Catholic Chapel, San Conrado Mission, and various barbershops, clinics, and stores. What the community lacked in services it made up for with its quiet, small-town atmosphere and distance from the discriminatory treatment its residents faced in other communities.

After World War II, returning veterans became civic leaders, petitioning the city for improved city services, expanded sewers, paving of roads, and street lights. Bus service was expanded to the Chavez Ravine area. Then, in 1950 the people learned their community had been designated "blighted" by the housing authority and had been chosen for a major public housing program. From 1950 through 1953, most of the residents were forced out through threats, persuasion, deception, eminent domain, and finally, eviction.

The community resisted displacement. Allying themselves with the conservative Small Property Owners Association, they declared that they would organize according to American principles. Well-dressed Chavez Ravine residents packed public hearings, but the decision to build the project was upheld. Property was seized through eminent domain, with the promise that the land be designated for "public use only." Still, many refused to leave.

After sustained opposition from powerful real estate interests, led by the *Los Angeles Times*, who called public housing "creeping socialism," the citywide program was reduced in size. The Chavez Ravine project was cancelled. Ultimately, the city decided to sell the Chavez Ravine land to the Brooklyn Dodgers for one dollar and the exchange of Wrigley Field, a small Pacific League baseball field already owned by the Dodgers. The city also agreed to spend millions of dollars paying for leveling canyons and building access roads.

On May 8, 1959, in front of television and newspaper cameras, Los Angeles County Sheriffs forcibly evicted the Aréchiga family from their Chavez Ravine home of thirty-six years. Immediately afterward, the house was bulldozed. The Aréchigas protested that their land had been taken for "public use," not for a privately owned baseball stadium. Aurora Vargas, a daughter of the Aréchigas, displayed her husband's uniform with a sign reading "My husband died in World War II to defend our Home." Many others were evicted, with less fanfare.

The eviction caused anger and resentment in the Mexican American community. It became symbolic of the discrimination faced by Chicano and Chicana communities nationwide, and it showed that resistance was legitimate if policies were not.

Even in the early 2000s, the remaining residents protested traffic conditions caused by baseball games, and stopped the Dodgers from expanding access roads. The Dodgers tried on three occasions and under three owners to build a football stadium on adjacent land owned by the team. Each time, the remaining area residents prevented the plans from going forward. Each summer, former residents' families gather in Elysian Park for a community barbeque, where they share photographs, stories, and reunite with old friends.

The struggle of the people of Chavez Ravine to preserve their homes has become part of the collective memory of Los Angeles Chicanos and Chicanas as a story of resistance, and is seen as emblematic of the larger struggle against displacement. As others resist displacement, they declare, "Remember Chavez Ravine."

See also California; Chicanos and Chicanas; *and* **Mexican Origin People in the United States.**

BIBLIOGRAPHY

Acuña, Rodolfo F. *A Community under Siege: A Chronicle of Chicanos East of the Los Angeles River, 1945–1975.* Monograph Series, no. 11. Los Angeles: Chicano Studies Research Center, Publications, University of California at Los Angeles, 1984.

Normark, Don. *Chavez Ravine, 1949: A Los Angeles Story.* San Francisco: Chronicle Books, 1999.

Sullivan, Neil J. *The Dodgers Move West: The Transfer of the Brooklyn Baseball Franchise to Los Angeles.* Reprint. New York: Oxford University Press, 1989.

RONALD W. LÓPEZ II

CHICAGO. According to the 2000 census, Chicago is home to more than three-quarters of a million Latina and Latino residents. It ranks behind New York and Los Angeles with the third largest Latina and Latino population in the United States. Mexicans and Mexican Americans are by far the largest of Chicago's Latina and Latino population, comprising slightly more than 70 percent, with Puerto Ricans constituting 15 percent. With large numbers of Cuban, Guatemalan, Ecuadoran, and Colombian residents, Chicago's Latina and Latino communities are some of the most diverse, albeit under-studied, populations in the United States.

Although Mexicans and Puerto Ricans have very different migration histories and hail from nations with distinctive political, economic, and social relationships to the United States, the ways in which both groups arrived in Chicago and the larger Midwest region are strikingly similar. Both groups were actively recruited by employers seeking new sources of labor for Chicago's expanding industrial economy. Both groups engaged in agricultural work throughout the Midwest. Both groups were an important source of low-wage labor in both sectors of the economy. Mexican workers, however, arrived much earlier than Puerto Rican contract laborers, first arriving in large numbers between 1916 and 1929. They filled an important vacuum in the wartime economy that witnessed the sudden decline of European immigration as a result of new restrictions based on literacy requirements. Mexican workers were exempt from the literacy and other punitive requirements of the Immigration Acts of 1917, 1921, and 1924 and were, instead, actively recruited to work for railroad companies as track and maintenance laborers, as well as for Chicago's thriving steel mills and meatpacking industries. Mexican laborers also were engaged in seasonal agricultural work in Ohio, Michigan, Indiana, and Iowa. As in the West and Southwest, however, Mexican workers recruited to Chicago were legally granted only temporary residence and suffered nativist hostilities that eventually resulted in the repatriation of thousands of Mexicans during the Great Depression.

World War II and the postwar era witnessed renewed Mexican immigration and internal migration from the Southwest to Chicago and surrounding areas. This was also the beginning of large-scale Puerto Rican labor migration, expanding the city's small Puerto Rican population that had existed since the interwar period. The Bracero Program, beginning in 1942, met the need, once again, for wartime labor in both the agricultural and industrial sectors of the economy, drawing on Mexican workers to supply Chicago industries. Beginning in 1946, Puerto Rican migrants joined the expanding pool of contract laborers as they were actively recruited to work in Chicago factories and homes. Originally, private employment agencies were key to this process, recruiting Puerto Rican men to work in

CHICAGO NEIGHBORHOOD. Children playing in Pilsen-Little Village, Chicago, 1991. (© Ralf-Finn Hestoft/CORBIS)

the steel industry and young Puerto Rican women to work as domestics throughout the area. By 1949, the island government had established a Migration Division Office in Chicago in order to facilitate the continued migration of Puerto Ricans to the city. It also provided services to migrants and collaborated with government officials and community organizations in assimilating Puerto Rican migrants to their new urban context. This city-island collaboration contributed to the steady growth of Puerto Ricans in Chicago in the postwar era. By 1960, the Latina and Latino population of Chicago's metropolitan area included more than thirty-two thousand Puerto Ricans and nearly fifty-six thousand Mexicans.

In Chicago, both groups had very similar residential settlement patterns, determined largely by residential discrimination and by proximity to employment. In the 1940s and 1950s, for example, they settled in Back of the Yards (near Chicago's meatpacking plants) as well as the neighborhoods just west of the Loop. Puerto Rican migrants also lived in Chicago's "Black Belt" and in the East and West Garfield Park neighborhoods. They moved farther north into the Lincoln Park area in the 1960s, establishing an identifiable Puerto Rican barrio along Division Street in the West Town and Humboldt Park communities. Mexicans tended to reside farther south and west in the areas of Pilsen and La Villita, establishing a strong ethnic enclave. Although Chicago continues to be defined as a "city of neighborhoods," with clear ethnic and racial geographies, the city's Latina and Latino residents have shown a more flexible residential pattern as a result of shared language and marginalization in the housing market.

Chicago's Cuban, Central American, and South American populations have decidedly different migration histories, although they share important similarities with Mexican and Puerto Rican residents. As throughout the United States, Cuban immigrants settled in Chicago in large numbers in the early 1960s in the wake of the Cuban Revolution of 1959, although small numbers of Cubans did reside in the city before that time. The first substantial wave of Cuban immigrants came primarily from the business and professional classes. Their settlement was facilitated in Chicago and other U.S. cities by federal programs and financial assistance, such as aid for establishing local businesses. Some scholars have noted that Cuban professionals and businesses benefited from the growing Latina and Latina population in need of specialized services and were actively recruited to work in Chicago businesses. By the 1970s more than fifteen thousand Cubans lived in Chicago, although since that time their numbers, like Chicago's population in general, have diminished.

Central and South American immigrants from Guatemala, El Salvador, Honduras, Nicaragua, Colombia, and Ecuador are Chicago's most recent arrivals, coming in large numbers since the 1970s. They, too, have contributed to the city's growing Latina and Latino communities. Although these groups did not arrive as contract labor like the Mexican and Puerto Rican migrants before them, the incorporation of many of the Central Americans into Chicago's economy has been similar to theirs, while the economic position of South Americans has tended to resemble that of Chicago's Cuban community. Puerto Ricans, Mexicans, and Central Americans, for example, tend to be concentrated in the low-wage manufacturing, service, and labor sectors of the economy, while South Americans and Cubans show higher employment rates in the city's retail, finance, and real estate industries. Despite increased gentrification throughout Chicago neighborhoods—most notably in those with large numbers of Latina and Latino residents in the North and Near Northwest areas—the city continues to have vibrant Latina and Latino neighborhoods. It is precisely this diversity, as well as the unique experiences of long-standing Puerto Rican and Mexican communities living side by side, that makes Chicago's Latina and Latino communities rich, distinctive, and an important window into understanding the complexities of Latina and Latino life in the United States.

See also **Central Americans; Chicanos and Chicanas; Mexican-Origin People in the United States; Puerto Ricans;** *and* **South Americans.**

BIBLIOGRAPHY

Betancur, John J., Teresa Córdova, and María de los Angeles Torres. "Economic Restructuring and the Process of Incorporation of Latinos into the Chicago Economy." In *Latinos in a Changing U.S. Economy: Comparative Perspectives on Growing Inequality*, edited by Rebecca Morales and Frank Bonilla. Newbury Park, Calif.: Sage, 1993.

Padilla, Elena. "Puerto Rican Immigrants in New York and Chicago: A Study in Comparative Assimilation." PhD diss., University of Chicago, 1947.

Padilla, Felix M. *Puerto Rican Chicago*. Notre Dame, Ind.: University of Notre Dame Press, 1987.

Pérez, Gina. *The Near Northwest Side Story: Migration, Displacement, and Puerto Rican Families*. Berkeley: University of California Press, 2004.

Suttles, Gerald D. *The Social Order of the Slum: Ethnicity and Territory in the Inner City*. Chicago: University of Chicago Press, 1968.

GINA PÉREZ

CHICANO/A MOVEMENT. "Chicano/a movement" is the comprehensive term for multiple forms of militant activism enacted by Mexican Americans during the Vietnam War era. The achievements of every Chicano/a movement organization, from the United Farm Workers union to the Alianza Federal de Pueblos Libres to the Crusade for Justice to MEChA (Movimiento Estudiantil Chicano de Aztlán), emanated from the idea that working-class Mexican Americans could demand and win progressive change. By acting upon this belief, activists broke with earlier identities based on traditional assimilation and the tacit acceptance of second-class citizenship in order to launch a sustained attack against racial and economic injustice.

The term "cultural nationalism" can be understood as the strategic use of key features of Mexican and Mexican American history and culture in order to develop individuals and groups capable of asserting themselves and demanding self-determination. Otherwise known as "Brown Pride" or "Brown Power," cultural nationalism was at work to varying degrees within all Chicano/a movement organizations. It was a necessary precondition for empowering communities that previously had been unsuccessful in mobilizing on a mass scale.

At the center of Chicano/a movement projects was an understanding that the majority of Mexican Americans had been denied access to the promised rewards of liberal democracy and the American Dream. Despite the efforts of advocacy groups such as LULAC (League of United Latin American Citizens), the G. I. Forum, and the Alianza Hispano Americana, only minimal progress had been made on the most important civil rights fronts. From the late 1920s until the late 1960s, these groups appealed to an emerging but tiny middle class through traditional pathways of assimilation. In Los Angeles, for example, the Mexican American Movement (MAM) mobilized ethnic Mexican students in order to promote education and military service as keys to success. MAM and other groups used ethnic pride as an organizing tool, but did not engage in the pointed critique of liberalism or the outright rejection of assimilation that characterized the more radical organizations that began to appear in the mid-1960s.

The Chicano/a movement can be described as the expansion and acceleration of earlier forms of activism as the collective demands for social justice became more intense and more radical strategies were employed. During the Vietnam War period, the gap between the expectations generated by U.S. ideologies of upward mobility ("Horatio Alger" or "bootstraps" philosophy) and the actual material conditions faced by the Chicano and Chicana working class was simply too great. The Chicano/a movement also participated directly in the Third World critique of Eurocentrism and white supremacy that had its roots in the early twentieth century and exploded in the anticolonial struggles that followed World War II.

The Chicano/a movement shared a number of features with anticolonial projects around the world. The ideologues of Manifest Destiny had declared that the United States was an extension, indeed an exceptional form, of northern European civilization and, according to "scientific racism," a creation of the superior Anglo-Saxon or Nordic races. Within this mythology, Mexicans in the United States were viewed as a mixture of "inferior" southern European (Spanish) and "primitive" Amerindian stock. They were represented by traditional historiography and sociology as a people without history.

Ethnic Mexicans in the southwestern United States during the late 1960s and early 1970s challenged the myths of Anglo-Saxon superiority and the inevitable march of civilization from east to west. Chicano and Chicana activists and intellectuals reinterpreted the U.S. military takeover of northern Mexico in 1848 and began to rewrite their community's history, to demand self-determination, and to investigate their relationship to the histories of other disenfranchised populations. Drawing inspiration from pre-Columbian indigenous cultures, the 1910 Mexican Revolution, the 1959 Cuban Revolution, the anti-war movement, and African American radicalism, Chicano and Chicana militancy became an impressive example of the global insurgencies known as the Sixties.

Despite the influence of African American politics and culture on Chicano and Chicana youth during this period, it would be inaccurate to claim that the Chicano/a movement took black activism as its primary inspiration. The activism of many young Chicanos and Chicanas owed just as much to the "Venceremos" of revolutionary Cuba as it did to "We Shall Overcome." Figures such as Malcolm X, Martin Luther King Jr., and the Black Panthers certainly played important roles in the radicalization of some sectors of the Chicano/a movement, but the political agendas and styles of Chicano and Chicana organizations cannot be explained exclusively through the model of black activism.

It is important to remember, however, that Chicano and Chicana activists did participate in a variety of black civil rights struggles and built black/brown coalitions wherever possible. The work of Maria Varela and Elizabeth "Betita" Martinez in SNCC (Student Nonviolent Coordinating Committee), Reies López Tijerina's early contacts with the Nation of Islam and the Black Panther party, and the involvement of Crusade for Justice, Brown Beret, and Alianza members in the 1968 Poor Peoples' Campaign (originally led by Dr. King) all demonstrated an understanding that the situation of their communities was linked to that of African Americans. Pan-Latino alliances with Puerto Rican and Mexican groups were also common among student sectors of the Chicano/a movement, the National Chicano Moratorium Committee, and La Raza Unida Party.

Because of the variety of organizations and agendas that fall under the general heading "Chicano/a movement," it is difficult to reduce Chicano and Chicana activism to one ideological position. It has been argued that the Chicano/a movement was "nationalist" at its core. This view fails to take into account the Raza activists who participated in the Communist Labor Party, the Socialist Workers Party, and other organizations in which the primary concern was not the "nation" or "race" but rather the issues of class struggle, imperialism, and international solidarity. Courageous Chicana feminists mounted a powerful critique of sexism and patriarchal oppression inside the Chicano/a movement, yet many of them gained a sense of empowerment through their association with Chicano/a movement organizations. When the entire *Movimiento* is too hastily reduced to the worst features of "nationalism," its rich complexity is oversimplified.

See also American G. I. Forum; Brown Berets; Chicanos and Chicanas; Crusade for Justice; Guevara, Ernesto "Che"; League of United Latin American Citizens; Manifest Destiny; Movimiento Estudiantil Chicano de Aztlán; Military; Political Thought; *and* United Farm Workers.

BIBLIOGRAPHY

Espinoza, Dionne. "Pedagogies of Nationalism and Gender: Cultural Resistance in Selected Representational Practices of Chicana/o Movement Activists, 1967–1972." PhD diss., Cornell University, 1996.

García, Ignacio M. *Chicanismo: The Forging of a Militant Ethos among Mexican Americans*. Tucson: University of Arizona Press, 1997.

Mariscal, George. *Brown-Eyed Children of the Sun: Lessons from the Chicano Movement, 1965–1975*. Albuquerque: University of New Mexico Press, 2005.

Muñoz, Carlos, Jr. *Youth, Identity, Power: The Chicano Movement*. London and New York: Verso, 1989.

Rosales, F. Arturo. *Chicano!: The History of the Mexican American Civil Rights Movement*. Houston, Tex.: Arte Público Press, 1996.

JORGE MARISCAL

CHICANO PARK, SAN DIEGO. San Diego's Chicano Park was created as the result of a dramatic community takeover of a parcel of urban land in 1970. Today it is the site of what many consider the most impressive collection of outdoor murals in the United States.

Mexican Americans began to settle in this particular section of San Diego in the late nineteenth century. By 1905 this barrio, close to downtown, had come to be known as Logan Heights. The pace of settlement picked up after 1910 as revolution broke out in Mexico and large numbers of Mexicans began to emigrate to the United States. Population growth continued during the 1940s, with defense plants and naval shipyards sprouting up along the Logan Heights waterfront, providing a new source of employment for local residents.

During the 1950s, changes in the zoning of Logan Heights allowed an influx of automobile junkyards, referred to as "yonkes" by local residents. The disruption of barrio residences accelerated in the 1960s as the new Interstate 5 freeway cut through the heart of the barrio, effectively bisecting the Logan area. Then in 1969 the Coronado Bay Bridge opened, with the approach to the bridge passing over Logan Heights. All of these changes, with their attendant loss of residences and local businesses, took place without significant community input.

As a result, by the late 1960s a number of developments had had a strongly negative impact on what had once been a thriving ethnic community. No one could have foreseen at that time that this area would soon become a focal point for the Chicano movement, which had been building strength throughout the Southwest and Midwest since the mid-1960s. However, conditions in Logan Heights were ripe. All that was needed was a spark.

That spark was struck in April 1970, when bulldozers began clearing land under the Coronado Bridge pylons. Barrio residents as first assumed that work had commenced on a promised city park, only to find that the area had been designated for a California Highway Patrol station. Infuriated, local residents and students physically occupied the site and began working it themselves, manually removing brush and planting trees.

After a protracted period of negotiation, an agreement was reached among the city, the state, and local residents, laying the groundwork for the creation of an official city park now universally know as Chicano Park. While the takeover and creation of the park was a local event carried out by community people, it was powerfully informed by the broader Chicano movement, which was then reaching its peak.

A central tenet of that movement was self-determination, which generally took one of two forms: community control or alternative institutions. In the case of Logan Heights, community control was expressed in the collective occupation of a piece of barrio land. The process of forming alternative institutions followed with the creation of a community center on that land, and a community health facility adjacent to it.

The other major effect of the Chicano movement on Chicano Park lay in the realm of culture and history. With its emphasis on ethnic affirmation and cultural nationalism, the movement had produced a strong interest in history on the part of its adherents. Chicano activists shared the perception that much of their history as a people had been buried, and what remained had been distorted. Their collective voyage to historical rediscovery led them first to U.S. southwestern history, then to Mexican and Spanish colonial history, and finally to the pre-Columbian era. In their quest for historical roots, many traveled to Mexico, often for the first time.

Among the Chicano artists who undertook this voyage of discovery were Salvador "Queso" Torres, a Barrio Logan resident and graduate of Oakland's College of Arts and Crafts. Torres had conceived of a project to paint murals on the supporting towers of the Coronado Bridge and Interstate 5. In 1971 he journeyed to Mexico City, where he studied firsthand the monumental murals of artists such as David Alfaro Siqueiros. Upon his return he continued working with other local artists on a plan to translate their historical and artistic visions into a series of giant murals. The takeover of Chicano Park provided the opportunity, and the first murals appeared on the site in 1973. More murals were added in 1974 and 1975, now with the involvement of invited artists from such urban centers as Los Angeles and Sacramento.

The Chicano Park murals can be grouped into two broad categories. One takes a spiritual and mystical direction, drawing heavily on Aztec, Mayan, and Toltec symbols and mythology. Among the specific symbols are the Aztec plumed serpent Quetzalcoatl, Olmec stone heads, pyramids, indigenous warriors, and the earth goddess Coatlicue. The Mexican icon, the Virgin of Guadalupe, represents another spiritual thread.

A second, more secular mural category focuses on political events, movements, and historical figures. Mexican revolutionaries Miguel Hidalgo, Emiliano Zapata, and Pancho Villa are joined by international figures "Che" Guevara and Salvador Allende. César Chávez, rank-and-file farmworkers, and the Brown Berets represent the Chicano movement.

The years 1977 and 1978 saw several new murals, including one commemorating the struggle against the junkyards ("¡Varrio Sí, Yonkes No!"), one dedicated to a Chicano prisoners' union, and another depicting the Mexican artists David Alfaro Siqueiros, José Clemente Orozco, Diego Rivera, and Frida Kahlo. Additional murals have been added in the 1980s and 1990s, often with the participation of non-Chicano artists. Some of the later murals have memorialized the park takeover itself, as well as park activists such as José Gómez and Laura Rodríguez.

In 1980 Chicano Park was officially recognized as a historic site by the city of San Diego. In the words of artist/writer Eva Cockcroft:

> In a certain sense, Chicano Park serves a function similar to that of a Medieval Cathedral. At the center of the community, its majestic piers retell to the people of the community the stories common to their collective history and culture—a history and culture that they have only begun to re-appropriate. Out of the most alienating of twentieth century America landscapes, the freeway interchange, and without outside aid, the artists and people of Logan have created a place of beauty (p. 99).

See also **Chicano/a Movement.**

BIBLIOGRAPHY

Chicano Park. Produced by Mario Barrera and Marilyn Mulford. Directed by Marilyn Mulford. New York: Cinema Guild. Documentary. 1989.

Cockcroft, Eva. "The Story of Chicano Park." *Aztlan* 15, no. 1 (Spring 1984): 79–102.

The History of Chicano Park. San Diego State University. Instructional Technology Services. www.chicanoparksandiego.com.

Muñoz, Carlos, Jr. *Youth, Identity, Power: The Chicano Movement*. London: Verso Press, 1989.

MARIO BARRERA

CHICANOS AND CHICANAS.

The Spanish conquest (1521) and the subsequent colonization of the indigenous peoples of Mexico and the rest of the Americas led to the creation of a Spanish Indian hybrid race. In modern

Mexico the new race would be named "mexicanos." In the United States, people of Mexican origin have referred to themselves in a variety of ways, depending upon their historical era. Prior to what became known as the Mexican American generation (1930s and 1940s), the majority of Mexican-origin people in the United States referred to themselves as Mexican if they were recent immigrants from Mexico. Those who were born in the United States referred to themselves according to the state or region in which they were born, for example Tejanos, Nuevo Mexicanos, or Californianos.

"Chicana" or "Chicano" as a term of self-identification is riddled with historical, political, and cultural meanings. Although the origin is unknown, one of the more popular myths claims the term originates from Azteca roots. Chicano is possibly the abbreviated form of mexicano, pronounced "mechicano," derived from Mexica, the name for the Aztecas of the Central Valley of Mexico before the arrival of the Spanish in the sixteenth century. Self-identified Chicanos and Chicanas in the 1960s were keenly aware that the name had pejorative meaning in the 1940s and 1950s throughout the southwestern United States, most often referring to working-class or poor fieldworkers. In an effort to reclaim the "indigenous" share of Spanish and Indian ancestry, many Mexican-origin people in the United States began to use Chicana or Chicano as a politicized term of self-identification, in much the same way that "Negroes" of the 1960s and 1970s took up "black." In fact, similar to the way in which many black people challenged "Negro" as a conciliatory impulse, Chicanos and Chicanas also challenged "Mexican American." The self-identifying name Mexican American has roots in the repatriation and deportation campaigns against Mexicans in the 1930s, and the name became widespread after World War II. However, Mexican American is still used by contemporary people of Mexican origin who consider Chicana or Chicano too militant a term. In the 1970s many agreed that despite its militancy, the Chicano/a Movement, similar to the larger civil rights movement, compelled the government to acknowledge the problems that Mexican Americans faced. In the early twenty-first century many people of Mexican-origin background, both native- and foreign-born, are comfortable with more than one identity label, and it is common to see members of families use several terms, including Chicana and Chicano, Mexican American, Mexican, mexicana and mexicano, *raza*, and Latina and Latino, depending on the social context.

Numerous indigenous peoples inhabited the Americas before the arrival of Columbus and other Spanish explorers, and they developed spectacular civilizations defined by their own artistic, architectural, scientific, and philosophical achievements. What is clear is that Mesoamericans, the indigenous peoples of Mexico, had a thriving influence upon other indigenous inhabitants from the Guatemalan Petén in the south all the way north to the Colorado Plateau. Therefore to begin with the Aztecas is not altogether inappropriate, but Native American populations in the Greater Mexican North (now considered the southwestern United States) were already thriving. These indigenous cultures have endured in the cultural practices and worldviews of present-day Mexican-origin peoples.

Chicano and Chicana history, that is, the historical study of Mexican-origin people in the United States, has been constructed around four pivotal events. The events are as much a part of Mexican history as they are a part of U.S. history. That is precisely where one finds Chicano and Chicana history, in between these two nations. This is not to say that other events were not as important to Chicanos and Chicanas but that, for the most part, historians have relied heavily upon these four great events as prime markers of Chicano and Chicana history. They are: (1) the Spanish Conquest, 1519–1521; (2) the United States–Mexican War, 1846–1848; (3) the Mexican Revolution, 1910–1920; and (4) the Chicano/a Movement, 1960s and 1970s. These events are interconnected across time and space as vital moments in Chicano and Chicana history.

Spanish Conquest

Prior to the arrival of Hernán Cortés, the Aztecas lived in the Central Valley of Mexico and ruled over the other indigenous peoples of the region. Estimates of the precontact indigenous population in the Central Valley of Mexico run as high as two million. By the time the Spanish entered Tenochtitlán in 1519, the Mexica (as they referred to themselves) had begun to make enemies of other indigenous communities, including the Tlaxcaltecas, who are often blamed for the downfall of Tenochtitlán because they allied themselves with Cortés against the Mexica. The invading conquistadors and their native allies were expelled from Tenochtitlán in 1519, but when Cortés returned in 1521, he found the population had been decimated by smallpox and measles epidemics and was less able to resist the conquest. Accidental germ warfare led to the fall of the Azteca Empire.

Despite the biological catastrophe underlying the conquest, the person most often blamed for the fall of Mexico in the popular Mexican discourse is Malintzin Tenepal, or La Malinche, her syncretic name. The Spanish and their chronicler Bernal Diaz called her Doña Marina. For many Chicana scholars, La Malinche is the mother of the hybrid Spanish Indian race, often referred to as mestizas and mestizos. The story of La Malinche is one of the most important stories of Mexican and Chicano and Chicana history. On the one hand, there are those who blame her and say that Mexicans are all "hijos de la malinche," sons of a fallen woman. Then there are those who defend her as a woman who survived her historical circumstances. Robbed of her birthright, Malintzin was sold to Maya merchants, who in turn sold her to Tabascans. At the age of fourteen, she became both slave and cultural translator to Cortés. She spoke several dialects and languages and therefore became indispensable to Cortés and his soldiers; hence the conquest could not have occurred without her assistance. Some scholars claim that, like other Aztecas of the period, Malintzin believed that Cortés was Quetzalcoatl, their former ruler who declared that he would return in the year 1-Reed. It is unknown when or where Malintzin died; however, she disappeared at age twenty-two.

The appearance of the Virgen de Guadalupe also dates to the Spanish conquest of 1521. Not until the appearance of the brown-skinned Virgen de Guadalupe at Tepeyec in 1531 to the Indian man Juan Diego did Mexicans embrace Catholicism. The historical legacy of La Malinche and La Virgen de Guadalupe exemplify the way the conquest dictated specific gender roles for women, gender roles that continue to plague modern women. A woman is often placed in one of two categories: she is either "bad" like La Malinche or "good" like the Virgin. Chicano and mexicano culture continues to exploit the two icons to characterize women, whether in art, literature, or film.

While the Aztecas fought for survival in the Central Valley of Mexico, three agriculturally advanced societies had already emerged and ruled over the region that would become Spain's far northern frontier. The Hohokam of southern Arizona and Sonora, the Mogollon of Casas Grandes, Chihuahua, and southern New Mexico, and the Anasazi of Chaco Canyon and the Four Corners persisted at the time of conquest and into contemporary times. By the early sixteenth century, when the Spanish had already begun to explore the northern frontier, the Pueblo and other indigenous civilizations had their own advanced centers of trade and agriculture with loose federations that had inhabited the region for thousands of years, particularly around the Rio Grande valley where towns flourished, using the river for irrigation.

From the sixteenth century to the eighteenth century, the Spanish continued exploration, conquest, colonization, and settlement throughout the Greater Mexican North, or what came to be known as the Spanish borderlands, a term coined by the historian Herbert Eugene Bolton in the early twentieth century. The mixture of Spanish and Indian assured the rise of mestiza and mestizo culture, a culture that would be neither Spanish nor Indian but rather an amalgam of both. *Mestizaje* is the term applied to the racial mixing in the already mixed race of Indian and Spanish mestizas and mestizos as well as to the interbreeding with blacks and other Indians in the borderlands. Racial distinctions also became markers for class and caste systems in the North.

The Spanish entered present-day New Mexico and settled the town of Santa Fe in 1608. The soldiers were accompanied by Franciscans, who built the first missions to help "settle" the area. The friars were to "Hispanicize" the indigenous population, which meant converting the Pueblo Indians to Christianity. Towns tied to missions rose up throughout the Greater Mexican North. Arizona was settled in 1691, Texas in 1718, and Alta California in 1769. The Spanish had three main motivations for their settlement of the region: (1) to safeguard the frontier from other European powers who might move in, particularly France and England; (2) to convert Indians to Christianity; and (3) to find rich minerals, especially gold. The Spanish Crown encouraged the settlements in the so-called New World, hoping for riches that would support the economic ambitions of empire.

The missions in Arizona, California, and Texas served similar purposes and grew in size and number throughout the colonial period. They were located in the interior of New Mexico, in the Santa Cruz River watershed of Arizona, along the Río Bravo del Norte or Rio Grande in Texas, and along the coast of Alta California. In Texas the missions surrounded San Antonio de Bexar, with the Alamo being the first mission in the area, built shortly after the French colonists built a fort in Matagorda Bay in 1684. By the seventeenth and eighteenth centuries, the Spanish were replaced by a majority of mestizas and mestizos, often referred to as Spanish Mexicans, that is, people ruled over by the Spanish Crown yet already mestiza and mestizo by interbreeding and culture. The centuries that followed the Spanish conquest were centuries of colonization and settlement. The mestiza and mestizo population became the majority, while the indigenous population died in large numbers from disease and massacre. The Franciscans and Jesuits who established the missions extracted labor from Indians in an *encomienda* system that was in many ways a form of slave labor. In the Pueblo Revolt of 1680, the Indians resisted conquest and colonization by the Spanish. The Pueblo launched a revolt that forced the Spanish to flee southward to El Paso del Norte; however, by 1694, the Spanish regained control of present-day New Mexico.

After the Pueblo Revolt, other indigenous groups defied Spanish and Spanish Mexican authority. In 1693 the Tejas Indians revolted, and in 1751 the Pimas revolted in Arizona and Sonora, leading many to point out that the mission systems were a failure, given the harsh exploitation of the indigenous. Nor did the Indians convert as easily as the Franciscans would have liked. In California, for example, the politics and policies of the Spanish Crown permitted the ongoing rape of Amerindian women in the

1770s. While the father president of the California missions, Junipero Serra, protested the rapes by writing letter after letter to Viceroy Bucareli, the sexual assaults against the women did not cease. Although the viceroy seemed to listen, the result shows that the Indian women were merely perceived as the objects of the Spanish Crown. Rather than stop the assaults, the Crown offered to Spanish Mexican soldiers a plot of land and two cows and a mule if they married an Indian woman, helping to "Hispanicize" her, that is, convert her to Catholicism by marrying her despite having raped her. Such were the colonial policies that shaped California's frontier in the eighteenth century.

Along with racialized gender oppression, caste and class derivations constructed the hierarchy in the Spanish borderlands. Spanish, criolla or criollo (of Spanish parents yet born in the New World), *color quebrado* (designated social status instead of race, usually skilled artisans), mestiza or mestizo (Indian and Spanish), mulatta or mulatto (black and Spanish or black and mestiza or mestizo), *genízara* or *genízaro* (Hispanicized Indian captives), *india or indio* (non-Hispanicized Indians), and coyote (black and Indian) were all examples of class, caste, ethnic, and racial designations in the 1790 census of Santa Fe. However, this hierarchy obscured another process that involved transculturation. It has been noted that over time the mestiza and mestizo and indigenous populations intermixed. But there was also an important spatial dimension that resulted from multigenerational co-inhabitation of shared watersheds settled by indigenous and mestiza and mestizo peoples in the Greater Mexican North. This "presence of place" yielded a substantial exchange of cultural, ecological, and political knowledge.

In the beginning of the nineteenth century, Mexico fought its war for independence from Spain. With independence in 1821, the far northern frontier, or Spanish borderlands, came under the rule of Mexico, a nation that had been a region of loose provincial federations in the sixteenth century. The cultural and political conflicts among the indigenous populations of the north, the Mexican inhabitants, and the incoming Euro-American immigrants intensified throughout the nineteenth century and set the stage for the next great event of Chicano and Chicana history, the United States–Mexican War of 1846–1848.

The United States–Mexican War

From 1821 to 1848 New Mexico, Arizona, California, Utah, Nevada, and Colorado were under Mexican national rule. By 1836 Texas became the exception. The population of Euro-Americans in the region was only twenty-five hundred in 1820; however, after 1824, the year Mexico passed a colonization law that encouraged Euro-Americans to immigrate to their provinces, that number increased considerably. At that time the Comanche Indians roamed the area from the northern Llano Estacado to the southern part of Tejas below San Antonio de Bexar. In an effort to hold onto their right and custom of traveling and inhabiting the state beyond its political or national boundaries, the Comanche often raided Mexican settlements. The Mexican government invited foreigners to Tejas so their new settlements would act as a buffer zone between Mexico and the expansionist United States as well as help protect Mexican settlements from Comanche raids.

With the Louisiana Purchase of 1803, the United States had nearly doubled its territory on the North American continent. The Euro-American immigrant population of the nineteenth century did not stop in Louisiana but rather moved farther west across the borders of Mexico. What occurred was not what Mexico planned. U.S. immigrants flocked into Coahuila and Tejas, soon outnumbering the population of Mexicans. By 1830 there were twenty thousand Euro-American settlers with their two thousand slaves. Mexicans were fewer than five thousand. In 1829, just five years after the colonization law was passed, the native Tejano Manuel Mier y Terán wrote a letter to the Mexican minister of war warning him of the foreigners who were taking over the province. He wrote that incoming immigrants had little or no respect for Mexicans living in the province of Tejas and that they considered Indians and blacks inferior to white Americans. The native Tejano saw that his home, the home of his ancestors, was being taken over. The government of Mexico attempted to repeal the colonization law, but it was too late. Anglo-Texans became the majority in the region, and they already resented Mexican rule.

By 1835 Anglo-Texans were preparing to revolt against Mexico. The Battle of the Alamo on March 6, 1836, and the Battle of San Jacinto on April 21, 1836, settled the conflict, if only politically. At the Alamo, Davy Crockett, James Bowie, and William Travis (none of whom was a native Texan) gave their lives in the name of the new republic and became its mythic heroes. Although there is no evidence to prove that Travis ever drew "the line in the sand" to separate the heroes willing to fight to their deaths from the cowards who refused to fight, the metaphor of the line in the sand has become part of the popular history associated with the rise of the Texas Republic and its presumed heroes. At San Jacinto, where Sam Houston and his troops defeated Santa Anna, the battle cries "Remember the Alamo" and "Remember Goliad" were heard as the Anglo-Texans and Mexican Tejanos massacred the Mexican army in retaliation for the defeats at the Alamo and Goliad. Juan Sequín was one of the Tejano heroes of San Jacinto who fought for independence from Mexico alongside Anglo-Texans. For the next ten years Texas would be its own republic, independent from Mexico and the United States.

The nineteenth-century United States was already plagued by racial injustice against black slaves and the ongoing horrific treatment of Native Americans. The ideology of Manifest Destiny buttressed racist beliefs that the white race was superior to all others. Manifest Destiny also provided Euro-Americans with the "God-given" right to move westward into Mexican provinces to civilize the land and its people. After Texas became a republic, the United States debated whether it should be allowed to enter the Union. Given that the majority of Anglo-Texans were from the south and were slave owners who had brought their slaves, some argued that admitting Texas into the Union would result in an imbalance of powers between the North and the South. In the North, the Whig Party included opponents of slavery and therefore opposed the annexation of Texas. In the South, Democrats who were slave owners wanted to annex Texas into the Union. Not until James K. Polk ran for president did anyone dare to bring the debate to the forefront of American politics. Polk garnered support for his election in 1844, and many suspected the support meant that the majority of the U.S. population favored annexation. Before Polk entered office, President John Tyler passed legislation through Congress, and Texas was a republic no more by December 1845. In February 1846 the Texas Republic flag came down.

Alarmed about the consolidation of U.S. territories, the Mexican government believed that U.S. expansion into Mexico had only just begun and that colonization efforts would continue into Mexico's northern provinces. President Polk had his sights set on California and sent the U.S. diplomat John Slidell from Tennessee to offer Mexico $25 million for California. The Mexican government refused to receive him, claiming Slidell was actually seeking to negotiate the Rio Grande as the political boundary between the United States and Mexico instead of the Nueces River as recognized by Mexico. The Mexican government was fully aware of Manifest Destiny and its role in the rationalization of Anglo-American expansionist aims. American racism toward Mexican citizens, especially those who lived in the far northern provinces of New Mexico, Arizona, and California, intensified. From 1821 to 1846 the U.S. diplomats to Mexico were mostly from the southern slave states, and they viewed Mexicans as childlike, irresponsible, mentally and physically inferior, incapable of managing their own affairs, and cowardly in defense of their honor. While U.S. diplomats did little to improve relations between the two nations, Polk plotted his dream for an "empire on the Pacific."

Polk received news in April 1846 that he used to instigate war against Mexico. Earlier that year Polk had sent a small army under General Zachary Taylor to occupy the land south of Corpus Christi on the Rio Bravo del Norte. Mexicans considered this an aggressive measure against them since they recognized the Nueces River, which was 150 miles north of the Rio Bravo, as the established boundary between the two countries. When the Mexican army crossed the river to the northern bank and fired the first shot against Taylor's army, Polk declared that "American blood had been shed on American soil."

Some claimed that Polk instigated a war with Mexico for no other reason than to expand slavery into the northern Mexican states of Arizona, New Mexico, and Colorado. Still other opponents to "Polk's little war" claimed that the presidential administration merely wanted to expand its territories, believing that just as Texas had been colonized and settled by Euro-Americans, the rest of northern Mexico could be colonized as well. Ultimately Polk got his war.

On February 2, 1848, the opposing nations signed the Treaty of Guadalupe Hidalgo to end the United States–Mexican War. According to the treaty, the United States obtained the state of California, the territories of New Mexico, Arizona, Nevada, and Utah, and parts of Colorado and Wyoming. Overall the United States added 1,000,200 square miles to its territory and managed to pay Mexico a mere $15 million for the entire region.

The aftermath of the war bred more bloodshed and violence, solidifying racial divisions. Throughout the newly annexed territories, Mexicans lost ownership of most of their land, and many resisted the second-class status they experienced after the war. In retaliation Euro-Americans lynched Mexican men and women. In 1851 the first Mexican woman to be lynched in California was a woman named Josefa who lived in Downieville. Evidently an Anglo man insulted Josefa, calling her a whore after he threatened the Mexican man with whom she lived. When the Anglo man entered Josefa's home and continued to revile her, she killed him with a knife. After a brief trial, she was condemned to hang despite the fact that she acted in self-defense. Between 1821 and 1940 over five hundred Mexicans were lynched, leading to more resistance.

Although the Treaty of Guadalupe Hidalgo guaranteed certain rights for Mexicans who became U.S. citizens after the United States–Mexican War, many of those rights were systematically violated or ignored by local, state, and federal governments. Hundreds of Mexicans joined Josefa as victims of systematic violence by Anglo-Americans. They defended themselves through so-called social banditry by such people as Juan Cortina in Texas and Tiburcio Vasquez in California. By the 1870s Vasquez was known as a "desperado" who robbed stagecoaches and attempted to raise an army against the Euro-Americans. He was caught and hanged after an all-white male jury found him guilty of his exploits. Juan Cortina was raising his own army against the U.S. colonizers in Texas. Cortina had already gained notoriety throughout Texas in the 1850s. In 1861 he escaped to Mexico, where he fought against French occupation, then continued to live in Mexico along the South Texas border, where many believed he would send rustlers to the Anglo ranches on the U.S. side. Although Cortina was never apprehended, Anglo-Texans seized on his mythic stature to rationalize the harsh and unjust mistreatment of Tejanos.

While armed resistance against Euro-American colonization was seemingly unsuccessful, there were other, more subtle forms of cultural resistance that continue to exert influence on U.S. culture in the early twenty-first century. For example, before and during the United States–Mexican War, Gertrudis Barceló, "La Tules," of Santa Fe, New Mexico, accommodated Euro-Americans in her gambling saloon, where she gained profits from U.S. soldiers' losses. In some ways she helped to "Hispanicize" the men who stayed behind in New Mexico after the war. She supported the Catholic Church and social organizations in Santa Fe, where she lived until her death in 1852. La Tules was a businesswoman who grew wealthy as a result of the war yet shared that wealth with her community. She was certainly not the norm for the era. Most Spanish Mexican women became impoverished after the war; however, La Tules represents women who survived and resisted in their own way, by acclimating outsiders to New Mexican culture and society and thereby sustaining the influence of that culture in particular communities and regions.

During the nineteenth century, racial ideology continued to dominate the American imagination, rendering people of color unrecognized as citizens. Mexicans, who became Americans when a political boundary was etched across North America separating the northern provinces from Mexico, were treated the same as any colonized group whose land boundaries shift as the result of a war. With second-class citizen status, Mexican Americans entered the twentieth century as a people miscast as immigrants, their long colonial past erased.

The Mexican Revolution

Migration patterns from the northern states of Mexico continued in a back-and-forth movement to and from the Greater Southwest, particularly Texas and California. No other event created more massive migration north than the third great event of Chicano and Chicana history—the Mexican Revolution of 1910. By the late nineteenth century, immigration into the United States intensified due to the political and economic policies of the Porfiriato. Porfirio Díaz ruled as president and dictator of Mexico during its Iron Age, from 1876 to 1911. The hundreds of miles of railway built during the Porfiriato moved lead, copper, and iron from the mines of Mexico into the United States, but the other commodity valuable to the United States was Mexican labor, and immigrants boarded trains and reached the United States–Mexico border, where they entered the United States in cities like El Paso del Norte, Texas; Laredo, Texas; Brownsville, Texas; Nogales, Arizona; and Tijuana, California. In 1910 over 70 percent of Mexican immigrants settled in Texas. In Porfirio Díaz's Mexico, 97 percent of rural families owned no land at all, while the remaining *hacendados* offered semifeudal conditions to the five million Indian and mestiza and mestizo peasants living in central Mexico.

Although Díaz's administration modernized Mexico, modernization came at a high price. Díaz sold Mexico's resources cheaply to foreign investors. Indigenous and peasant communities were uprooted and dispossessed of their lands. Employment dropped dramatically, and many were forced to leave their own country to eke out a living. By 1900 Mexico was an economic colony of the United States and Europe. U.S. investors owned three-quarters of the mines, more than half of the oil fields, and sugar, coffee, maguey, cotton, and rubber plantations. These resources did not stay in Mexico for Mexican consumption but were exported, draining the home market and leaving Mexican workers without jobs. As a result many jumped on the railroad that carried Mexico's minerals to the United States. In 1900 only 237 immigrants entered the United States; however, ten years later that number approached 18,000. By the end of the Mexican Revolution in 1920, many more thousands had fled the violence to the United States, but many also left in search of economic stability.

In the United States the 1920s were a decade of economic prosperity and "nativist" restriction of immigration of southern, central, and eastern Europeans. By the 1920s the "nativists" had stirred the U.S. Congress to pass restrictive measures against the darker races that they feared would make their own Nordic stock impure. The eugenicists, many of whom were scientists, provided the country with the intellectual theories that promoted the purity of the white race. Interestingly the eugenics movement also gained support in Mexico for those scientists and physicians who claimed that the European race was superior to the Indian. As a result mestizas and mestizos were encouraged to downplay the Indian part of Mexican identity.

Eugenicists joined nativists and contributed to the debate that helped push through the 1917 Immigration Act, the Quota Act of 1921, and the Johnson-Reed Immigration Act of 1924. Nativists also wanted to close the borders to Mexicans and the southern and eastern Europeans who were entering the United States by the thousands during the early decades of the twentieth century. The 1917 Immigration Act was the first measure restricting the entry of eastern Europeans, Asians, and southern Europeans as well as Mexicans. An $8 head tax was imposed, and each immigrant had to be able to read in one language before he or she could cross the border from Mexico into the United States. Nearly seven thousand Mexicans were turned back at the border because they could not meet the requirements of the act. Cotton growers, however, needed laborers whom they could pay less than their states' assigned minimum wage. They lobbied the U.S. government to allow Mexicans to enter and work in the fields of the Southwest. Therefore the act was not enforced as rigorously against Mexicans. The restrictive measures of 1921 and 1924, however, were enforced, and illegal entry into the United States increased as a result. Moreover in 1924 Congress appropriated $1 million for the establishment of a 450-man patrol stationed along the United States–Mexico border.

Despite these restrictive acts, the economic demand for Mexican laborers lured them into the midwestern towns of Chicago; Detroit, Michigan; and Gary, Indiana. The steel industry sent representatives to Mexico to recruit laborers, who eventually brought families to settle in cities like Chicago.

In October 1929 the stock market crash changed the lives of Mexicans living in the United States. As a result of the Great Depression, many Mexicans now faced deportation from the United States back to Mexico. Scholars have argued that the first crucial phase of Mexican immigration began with the influx of immigrants from Mexico during the violent phase of the revolution. The 1920s brought more immigrants, and the numbers of those arriving from Mexico rose to over fifty thousand per year. By the crash of 1929 that number had dropped to fewer than forty thousand per year. The following year fewer than eleven thousand Mexicans crossed the border into the United States. When the deportation trials of the 1930s began to threaten Mexican-origin people in the United States, the number of Mexican immigrants who attempted to enter the United States dropped dramatically to two thousand or fewer from 1932 to 1939. Repatriation and deportation were costly measures, and for the most part it became difficult to prove that someone could or should be deported. But many Mexicans were encouraged to return to Mexico under the pretense that they had land waiting for them. The Mexican government made an agreement with the U.S. government and even set up campsites in secluded regions of Mexico where there was no water or resources for those who were deported.

The most aggressive deportation trials occurred in Los Angeles, where a large population of Mexicans lived. In effect welfare officials were dismayed at the dramatic rise of those on welfare rolls. The Great Depression had left many unemployed, and they sought aid from the municipality. To discourage Mexicans from applying for welfare, city officials pressured the federal government to allow them to deport unemployed Mexicans. Although the government agreed initially, a legal obstacle prevented the city of Los Angeles from deporting Mexicans. If a Mexican had worked for five years in the city, then she or he was eligible for relief. The deportation was unsuccessful until the next strategy was developed. Welfare officials decided to promise temporary relief to Mexicans if they in turn promised to leave the United States at public expense.

Railroads carried Mexicans from Chicago; Detroit, Michigan; and Gary, Indiana back to Mexico. The very companies from the Midwest that had recruited Mexican labor were now paying to send them back to Mexico. As a result of these deportations, many Mexicans left on their own; others were either encouraged or coerced into leaving. In fact, because so many feared deportation, they did not turn to the federal government for assistance, nor did they seek medical attention. Estimates of the number of Mexicans deported during the Great Depression run as high as 500,000, including many U.S.-born citizens. However, it is important to note that records were not kept by the federal government.

As a result of the repatriation and deportation trials, many Mexicans turned to mutual aid societies, or *mutualistas*, to help them survive in their communities in the United States. Because many had lived in the United States for a few decades and others for generations before the United States–Mexican War, they stayed in their homes throughout the Southwest and the Midwest, helping each other through societies such as the Sociedad Mutualista Obrera Mexicana (Mutual Aid Society for Mexican Workers), established in Houston, Texas, in the mid-1930s, which provided money to families who wanted to give family members decent funerals. Mutual aid societies operated under the principle of trust among the Mexican and Mexican American communities. Family members contributed funds to a neighborhood pool of money. When a member of the society lost a job or needed health care, the society would assist them financially until they were able to work again.

It is false to assume that all Mexicans were victims of deportation in the 1930s. Although many were deported, many also stayed in the United States. Some were fortunate enough to have jobs, while others became involved in the labor strike activity that swept the country during the Great Depression. In California over 140 strikes occurred among agricultural laborers, whose ranks included many Mexicans. All of the strikes contested wages. Unions, such as the United Cannery, Agricultural, Packing, and Allied Workers of America (UCAPAWA), responded to Mexican American women's demands for better conditions in the workplace from 1939 to 1951. In San Antonio, Texas, Mexican women and men who worked as pecan shellers held a strike in 1938 to contest lowered wages. The activist Emma Tenayuca was one of the strike's important leaders.

World War II created dramatic changes in Mexican American communities in the 1940s. To begin with, the war created a shortage of laborers on the home front. As a result the United States ushered in a war emergency measure to allow Mexican nationals into the country to work in agriculture. The Bracero Program was initiated in 1942 and lasted beyond the war until 1964. Although it was not of, for, or about Mexican Americans—as the United States–Mexican War and the Mexican Revolution of 1910 had been—World War II is significant precisely because during it a disproportionate number of Mexican Americans served and died in the U.S. armed forces. Over half a million Mexican American men and many women served during World War II, and there were many casualties as well as many veterans who received Purple Hearts. There were others, however, who fought a race war at home.

Labeled "zoot suiters" by the press, many young men expressed cultural pride by donning elegant, long suit jackets with baggy dress pants and parading through their neighborhood streets in the 1940s. In 1943 a group of white American sailors entered a Mexican American neighborhood in Los Angeles, where, they claimed, they were attacked by zoot suiters. The police raided the neighborhood but found no one to blame. As a result about two hundred sailors rode in twenty taxicabs through the Mexican American areas of Los Angeles. When they saw Mexican American young men in zoot suits, the sailors jumped out of the taxis, beat and stripped the young men, and left them on the curb, injured and bleeding. For the next week in June 1943 similar attacks occurred when other servicemen joined the sailors. The police became involved only by arresting the zoot suiters who had been beaten and stripped. Mexican American women who dressed like "pachucas" were also targeted during the riots. Similar riots spread to other cities, such as Philadelphia; New York; San Diego, California; and Detroit, Michigan. For many the Zoot Suit Riots represented a legitimate race war at home. Filipino Americans and black Americans who donned zoot suits also engaged in the riots. They too had grievances about racism in the United States, along with Mexican Americans who felt betrayed by a government that disproportionately drafted them for war while offering them little in the way of social services, education, housing, or decent employment with living wages.

The Chicano/a Movement

In many ways the Zoot Suit Riots set the stage for the upcoming battles for civil rights in the 1950s and the subsequent Chicano/a movement of the 1960s and 1970s, which is the fourth great event of Chicano and Chicana history. Like the Spanish conquest of 1521, the United States–Mexican War of 1846–1848, and the Mexican Revolution of 1910, the Chicano/a movement of the mid- to late twentieth century marks a pivotal moment in the history of Chicanos and Chicanas. Without the Chicano/a movement, the history of Mexican-origin people in the United States would still be silenced and nonexistent in university classrooms.

Mexican-origin people in the United States had called themselves Mexicans during the early twentieth century; however, after the repatriation and deportation campaigns of the 1930s and after World War II, many began to emphasize that they too were Americans. Hence Mexican American became the most common term of self-identification. By the 1960s the Mexican American population could document the racial discrimination they had experienced in jobs, schools, and courts. A militant faction of the population began to protest the discrimination. Eager to confront an America that was denying the Mexican-origin population its civil rights, they rallied around a term that honored working-class origins as well as indigenous influence. They called themselves Chicanos and Chicanas. The movement erupted in the 1960s after the Zoot Suit Riots and after World War II, when young Mexican American men returned from the war as heroes yet still faced racial discrimination in low-paying jobs. If they approached the Equal Employment Opportunity Commission (EEOC) to voice grievances, the federal commission ignored them. Moreover, their children were segregated despite the fact that *Brown v. Board of Education* had desegregated schools as early as 1954. In schools throughout the Southwest, segregation was still practiced. In classrooms the history of Mexicans in the United States was only noted when the mythic heroes of the Alamo were invoked. Those who attended the university began to demand the history and study of Chicanos and Chicanas. Many walkouts, or "blowouts," occurred in high schools and colleges as students protested the negation of their history. The Chicano/Chicana student movement emerged in 1967 and 1968, when students marched out of their classrooms in Colorado, Texas, New Mexico, and California.

As early as 1962 César Chávez and Dolores Huerta envisioned a union for all farmworkers in the United States and eventually organized the United Farm Workers of America (UFW). By the mid-1960s their spirited effort to unionize farmworkers throughout the country advanced with strikes, boycotts, and protest marches. For many, Chávez became the national leader of the movement after the successful strike against the grape growers in Delano, California, in 1965. His strategy included incorporating Mexican field hands, many of whom had no rights in the

United States. After Delano, Chávez traveled throughout California urging the boycott of grapes. In 1966 he attempted to unionize workers in Texas but faced right-to-work laws and other obstacles. By the late 1960s, however, his vision had spread throughout the Southwest and into the Midwest to Wisconsin, Michigan, Ohio, and Indiana. Often marching with a banner depicting La Virgen de Guadalupe, the UFW won support from the Catholic contingent.

As early as 1963 Reies López Tijerina founded La Alianza Federal de Mercedes (the Federal Alliance of Autonomous Land Grants), and for the next seven years he fought to restore lands he argued the United States had stolen from New Mexicans in 1848. To rectify the injustice Tijerina staged marches and protests, including twice occupying the Kit Carson National Forest. Arrested a number of times for his protests, he often stood trial, and in 1968 he defended himself and was found not guilty. He was convicted in 1969 and went to prison until 1971.

In 1969 the First National Chicano Youth Liberation Conference was held in Denver, Colorado, where Rodolfo "Corky" Gonzáles had already organized the Crusade for Justice. The meeting was significant because the famous manifesto "El Plan Espiritual de Aztlán" was drawn up. For the first time the mythical Aztlán was invoked, symbolically referring to the territories that the United States had taken from Mexico after 1848. Also in 1969 José Angel Gutiérrez and his wife Luz Gutiérrez led La Raza Unida Party (LRUP) and won elections in Crystal City, Texas, where Chicanos and Chicanas comprised 85 percent of the population in a district run by an Anglo-American minority.

The Chicano/a movement came to its apex in 1970, when the National Chicano Moratorium was organized to protest the war in Vietnam. Thousands of Chicanos and Chicanas from the Southwest and the Midwest traveled to Los Angeles in August 1970 in one of the largest demonstrations against the war. Many activists had pointed out that although Chicanos and Chicanas comprised only 10 percent of the U.S. population, they constituted more than 20 percent of the war's casualties, while in the college classrooms of the University of California, Los Angeles (UCLA), Chicanos and Chicanas made up only 1 percent of the student population. The contradictions were obvious to Chicano and Chicana activists. The events that ensued at the Chicano Moratorium in 1970 are memorable precisely because the behavior of the police demonstrated the manner in which Chicanos and Chicanas had been mistreated for over a century. What began as a quiet, organized protest turned into a riot, with many Chicanos and Chicanas injured and one killed. The news reporter Rubén Salazar, originally from El Paso, Texas, was sent to report on the moratorium for a local Los Angeles television station. When a teenager stole a soda pop from a convenience store, riot police stormed the park where the moratorium was being held. Salazar was on the scene with a crew, and when Salazar and the crew entered the Silver Dollar Bar for a drink, the police threw gas projectiles into the bar, one of which hit Salazar on the head and killed him. Salazar became one of many symbols for the Chicano/a movement, and his death represented yet another affront against Chicanos and Chicanas in the twentieth century. Disillusioned because they were relegated to the worst jobs in the country, with few opportunities for education and no apparent economic advancement in the 122 years since the signing of the Treaty of Guadalupe Hidalgo, Chicanos and Chicanas had nothing to lose and continued to protest in the streets, in college classrooms, and in the courtrooms.

The movement also spawned a literary and art explosion among Chicanos and Chicanas in the 1960s and 1970s. Many small book presses like Arte Público Press and journals like *Quinto Sol* published poetry, short stories, and novels by writers who described injustices experienced by Mexicans in the United States. Artists described inequality in their work but also conveyed the promise of the future. Although it did not open at the UCLA Wight Art Gallery until 1990, the Chicano Art: Resistance and Affirmation, 1965–1985 (CARA) exhibition was the culmination of two decades of creative work by Chicano and Chicana artists. The CARA exhibition excluded the murals of Las Mujeres Muralistas (The Women Muralists), but it did include artwork by Chicana feminist artists such as Yolanda López and Ester Hernández.

One of the most vital nonprofit organizations established during the movement was the Mexican American Legal Defense and Education Fund (MALDEF). With the lawyer and activist Vilma Martinez as its president in 1975, MALDEF redressed grievances filed by Chicanos and Chicanas who experienced discrimination in employment, education, and the courts. Between 1970 and 1980 MALDEF filed desegregation suits, voting rights suits, suits on behalf of bilingual education advocates, and other suits for Chicano and Chicana civil rights.

Legacy

In the late twentieth century many of the organizations founded during the Chicano/a movement, such as MALDEF and the UFW, continued to thrive as new issues came to the forefront of Chicano and Chicana politics. Immigration rights for Latinos and Latinas, who continued to enter the United States from Mexico and Latin America, received national attention as anti-immigration laws were passed, just as they had been in the early twentieth century. Proposition 187 in California gave U.S. citizens permission to scapegoat immigrants once again. In the early twenty-first century battles over affirmative action also persist as notions of "reverse racism" gain popularity for the white majority that negates history and denies the colonization of Chicanos and Chicanas. English-only campaigns challenge Latinos and Latinas' right to bilingual education, a right that was guaranteed by the Treaty of Guadalupe Hidalgo yet never enforced.

The Zapatistas of southern Mexico have spurred transnational activism and compelled Mexicans in the United States to look south to the indigenous movement that contests notions of hybridity. Moreover the North American Free Trade Agreement (NAFTA) of 1993 opened the doors to more U.S. industry along the border in Mexico, where maquiladoras hired mostly young, unskilled female workers. The environmental toxicity perpetuated by the maquiladora industry continues to pollute the United States–Mexico border. Environmental racism throughout the Southwest has had detrimental effects upon those living in regions and cities that are dumping sites for the nation's waste and for the by-products of hazardous industries. In places as remote as Sierra Blanca, Texas, and in regions that have been stripped of their resources, such as rural Colorado and New Mexico, excessive mining and timbering have led to social displacement and economic decline for Chicana and Chicano communities.

Chicanas and Chicanos, that is, Mexican-origin people in the United States, are quickly becoming a major demographic and political force. It is estimated that by the year 2050 one out of every six persons in the United States will be from a Mexican-origin background. Chicanas and Chicanos face numerous political and economic challenges. These challenges are compounded by the persistence of poverty, discrimination, hostility, and fear from the dominant culture and by the implications of the rise of a "national security state" in the aftermath of the September 11, 2001, terrorist attacks. Mexican-origin people face a second term for the most conservative and dangerous presidential administration in history.

Through the course of their history—from conquest and colonization to the rise of the Chicano/a Movement—Mexican-origin people have not just been "oppressed victims" of Anglo racism and capitalism. They have also been agents of their own history, actively creating social movements to transform the dominant structures of society by challenging the underlying levers of political and economic power. A century and a half of labor strikes and other workers' struggles; the campaigns by the GI generation to attain equality and acceptance; the student movements for the establishment of Chicano studies and against the Vietnam War; the movement for an independent third-party electoral strategy (La Raza Unida); the land rights movement in search of restored commons; the

movement for women's rights and equality within the Chicano/a Movement and community; the struggle for legal and educational equality led by MALDEF; the rise of queer and lesbian civil rights struggles; the perennial struggles against the militarization of the border and the criminalization of immigrants; and the rise of environmental justice struggles—all these are the by-products of the historical and cultural agency of the Mexican-origin people in the United States as they struggle to achieve a sustainable and just society that provides all people with quality of life through education, housing, medical care, living wages, and safe workplace and living environments.

See also Arizona; Ballot Propositions 187, 209, and 227; Border, The; Bracero Program; California; Census; Chicano/a Movement; Demographics; Deportations of Mexican-Origin People in the United States; Education; Employment Discrimination; First Nations and Mexican-Origin People; Immigration; Immigration and Naturalization Service; Immigration Policy, Twentieth Century; Labor and Labor Strikes; Language Rights; Latino Identities and Ethnicities; Malinche, La; Maquiladoras; Mexican-Origin People in the United States; Native Americans/Mexicanos; New Mexico; Race and Racialization; Texas; United States–Mexican War; *and* Zoot Suit.

BIBLIOGRAPHY

Acuña, Rodolfo. *Occupied America: A History of Chicanos*. 3rd ed. New York: Harper and Row, 1988.

Castañeda, Antonia I. "Sexual Violence in the Politics and Policies of Conquest: Amerindian Women and the Spanish Conquest of Alta California." In *Building with Our Hands: New Directions in Chicana Studies*, edited by Adela de la Torre and Beatríz M. Pesquera, 15–33. Berkeley: University of California Press, 1993.

Cypess, Sandra Messinger. *La Malinche in Mexican Literature: From History to Myth*. Austin: University of Texas Press, 1991.

Faulk, Odie B. "The Presidio: Fortress or Farce?" In *New Spain's Far Northern Frontier: Essays on Spain in the American West, 1540–1821*, edited by David J. Weber. Dallas, Tex.: Southern Methodist University Press, 1988.

García, Mario. "Americans All: The Mexican American Generation and the Politics of Wartime Los Angeles, 1941–45." In *The Mexican American Experience: An Interdisciplinary Anthology*, edited by Rodolfo O. de la Garza et al., 210–212. Austin: University of Texas Press, 1985.

Gaspar de Alba, Alicia. *Chicano Art: Inside/Outside the Master's House: Cultural Politics and the CARA Exhibition*. Austin: University of Texas Press, 1998.

Gómez-Quiñones, Juan. *Roots of Chicano Politics, 1600–1940*. Albuquerque: University of New Mexico Press, 1994.

González, Deena. *Refusing the Favor: The Spanish-Mexican Women of Santa Fe, 1820–1880*. New York: Oxford University Press, 1999.

Graebner, Norman A. *Empire on the Pacific: A Study in American Continental Expansion*. Santa Barbara, Calif.: ABC-Clio, 1983. Originally published 1955.

Gutiérrez, David G. *Walls and Mirrors: Mexican Americans, Mexican Immigrants, and the Politics of Ethnicity*. Berkeley: University of California Press, 1995.

Gutiérrez, Ramón A. *When Jesus Came, the Corn Mothers Went Away: Marriage, Sexuality, and Power in New Mexico, 1500–1846*. Stanford, Calif.: Stanford University Press, 1991.

Limerick, Patricia Nelson. *The Legacy of Conquest: The Unbroken Past of the American West*. New York: Norton, 1987.

MacLachlan, Colin M., and Jaime E. Rodríguez O. *The Forging of the Cosmic Race: A Reinterpretation of Colonial Mexico*. Berkeley: University of California Press, 1980.

Martínez, Vilma S. "Vilma S. Martínez Testifies before the U.S. Commission on Civil Rights about the Mexican American Legal Defense and Educational Fund (MALDEF), 1975." In *Major Problems in Mexican American History: Documents and Essays*, edited by Zaragosa Vargas, 419–421. New York: Houghton Mifflin, 1999.

McWilliams, Carey. *North from Mexico: The Spanish-Speaking People of the United States*. New York: Greenwood Press, 1968.

Peña, Devon, and Joseph Gallegos. "Nature and Chicanos in Southern Colorado." In *Confronting Environmental Racism: Voices from the Grassroots*, edited by Robert D. Bullard, 141–160. Boston: South End Press, 1993.

Pérez, Emma. *The Decolonial Imaginary: Writing Chicanas into History*. Bloomington: Indiana University Press, 1999.

Reisler, Mark. *By the Sweat of Their Brow: Mexican Immigrant Labor in the United States, 1900–1940*. Westport, Conn.: Greenwood Press, 1976.

Riley, Carroll L. "The Indians of the Southwest in 1492." In *Major Problems in Mexican American History: Documents and Essays*, edited by Zaragosa Vargas, 48–53. New York: Houghton Mifflin, 1999.

Rodriguez, Jeanette. *Our Lady of Guadalupe: Faith and Empowerment among Mexican-American Women*. Austin: University of Texas Press, 1994.

Rosales, F. Arturo. *Chicano! The History of the Mexican American Civil Rights Movement*. Houston, Tex.: Arte Público Press, 1997.

Ruiz, Vicki L. *Cannery Women, Cannery Lives: Mexican Women, Unionization, and the California Food Processing Industry, 1930–1950*. Albuquerque: University of New Mexico Press, 1987.

Sánchez, George J. *Becoming Mexican American: Ethnicity, Culture, and Identity in Chicano Los Angeles, 1900–1945*. New York: Oxford University Press, 1993.

Stern, Alexandra Minna. "Responsible Mothers and Normal Children: Eugenics, Nationalism, and Welfare in Post-Revolutionary Mexico, 1920–1940." *Journal of Historical Sociology* (1999): 369–397.

U.S. Census Bureau. *Historical Statistics of the United States, Colonial Times to 1957: A Statistical Abstract Supplement*. Washington, D.C.: U.S. Government Printing Office, 1960.

U.S. Department of Labor. *Annual Reports of the Commissioner-General of Immigration, 1900–1939*. Washington, D.C.: U.S. Government Printing Office, 1900–1939.

Vélez-Ibáñez, Carlos G. "Cultural Roots of Ancient Southwest Indians." In *Major Problems in Mexican American History: Documents and Essays*, edited by Zaragosa Vargas, 39–48. New York: Houghton Mifflin, 1999.

Weber, David J., ed. *Foreigners in Their Native Land: Historical Roots of the Mexican Americans*. Albuquerque: University of New Mexico Press, 1973.

Ybarra, Lea, and Nina Genera. "Lea Ybarra and Nina Genera Report on Chicano Mobilization against the Vietnam War, 1972." In *Major Problems in Mexican American History: Documents and Essays*, edited by Zaragosa Vargas, 389–391. New York: Houghton Mifflin, 1999.

Emma Pérez with Devon Peña

CHICO AND THE MAN. *Chico and the Man* is notable as the second most successful television series to date with a Latino lead character (the most successful being *I Love Lucy*, starring Desi Arnaz). A situation comedy, *Chico and the Man* was broadcast on NBC from 1974 through 1978. The storyline focused on a surrogate father-son relationship between a young, brash Mexican American, Chico Rodriguez (Freddie Prinze), and Ed Brown, an older, cantankerous Anglo-American (Jack Albertson), who learn to overcome cultural differences as they work and live together in Ed's run-down garage in East Los Angeles. The series was created by James Komack.

The show's clear star was Freddie Prinze, one of the most successful Puerto Rican comedians in U.S. history. Born Frederick Karl Pruetzel to a Puerto Rican mother and a Hungarian father, Prinze grew up in the Washington Heights neighborhood of New York City. He attended the New York High School of Performing Arts, but dropped out after he began working as a comedian at the age of sixteen. This led to appearances on television talk shows, such as *The Tonight Show with Johnny Carson*. After a breakthrough appearance on *The Tonight Show*, he was invited to audition for the pilot of a new series. When Prinze was cast in *Chico and the Man*, he was only nineteen years old.

The show premiered on September 13, 1974, with a theme song scored by José Feliciano. It was a quick hit, earning a number three spot in the ratings and making a national star of Prinze. However, Los Angeles Chicanas and Chicanos picketed NBC's Burbank studios and wrote letters of complaint to protest the casting of Prinze in a Mexican American role and Chico's inaccurate accent and dialect. Complaints prompted show producers to retool the character as half Puerto Rican who had been raised in New York City.

The series storylines tended to capitalize in a humorous way on the theme of ethnic conflict. Ed drove business away with his cantankerous demeanor, while Chico cleaned up the garage and brought business in with his positive attitude. Prinze's irreverent comedy was also worked into the show. The series earned an Emmy Award for Albertson in 1976, while Prinze was nominated for a Golden Globe in 1977. The show also was consistently among the top six shows in the ratings while Prinze starred. While there were no Latina and Latino producers or directors, and virtually no Latina and Latino writers on the series, Latina and Latino guest stars included Carmen Zapata, Cesar Romero, Alma Beltrán, Julio Medina, Rose Portillo, Danny Mora, Jerry Velasco, and Rodolfo Hoyos Jr.

The show suffered a severe blow in January 1977, when Prinze committed suicide. The series continued for another season, however. Prinze's character was written out of the show, while child actor Gabriel Melgar was brought in to play Raul Garcia, who is eventually adopted by Ed. Charo also had a recurring role as Raul's aunt. Audiences did not respond favorably, however, and the show was cancelled in 1978.

See also Comedy and Humor.

BIBLIOGRAPHY
Alpern, David M. "Chico's Last Act." *Newsweek*, February 7, 1977.
"Chico and The Man." Television Heaven. www.television heaven.co.uk/chico.htm.
Kasindorf, Jeanie. "If I Was Bitter, I Wouldn't Have Chosen Comedy." *New York Times*, February 9, 1975.
Pruetzel, Maria. *The Freddie Prinze Story*. Kalamazoo, Mich.: Master's Press, 1978.

MARY C. BELTRÁN

CHILDREN IN THE JUVENILE JUSTICE SYSTEM.

The juvenile justice system generally addresses a wide array of issues including parental rights and responsibilities, statutory offenses, delinquent acts, and the transfer of juveniles accused of committing adult crimes. The juvenile justice system in the United States is plagued by a number of structural problems. Chief among them are the lack of resources, the ambiguous application of the Bill of Rights, and the lack of court personnel culturally competent in Latino cultural issues. Latino and Latina children and juveniles tend to experience a second-class justice in the criminal justice system, and the system itself tends to exacerbate this experience.

Although there are some developmental differences between children and juveniles and some clear differences between juveniles and adults, the juvenile justice system has a tendency to regard children older than seven as competent and therefore capable of assuming responsibility over their delinquent or criminal actions. However, unless children and juveniles are involved in either a statutory offense or delinquent activity, it is not likely that they will interact with the juvenile justice system. For the most part children come into contact with other state institutions, such as a department of social services (DSS). Adjudicated juveniles are generally institutionalized in a department of youth services (DYS) facility. Nonetheless, juveniles accused of criminal activity are increasingly treated like adults.

One of the major problems facing research on the experiences of Latino and Latina youth and the juvenile justice system is the lack of standardized methods for the collection of data or information. Thus, whereas it is possible to make some generalizations, it should be clear that the experience of Latino and Latina youth is contingent on a wide array of factors, including the local implementation of national laws and standards, the composition of the court personnel, and other local demographic factors. Notwithstanding, there is some available research that can offer important information regarding this topic.

The Development of the Juvenile Justice System

Prior to the creation of the juvenile courts in 1899, children were routinely treated as little adults and could be subject to the same penalties as adult offenders. Children under the age of seven were presumed to be incapable of formulating criminal intent. In contrast, the law could submit children between the ages of seven and fourteen to special inquiries in order to determine their capacity to formulate criminal intent. Those over the age of fourteen could be treated as adults on the basis of their crimes. While the juvenile courts continued to embrace these age categories, the courts began to adopt a rehabilitative ideal as an alternative to adult punishment.

The early juvenile courts were conceived as civil institutions designed to rehabilitate delinquents and to Americanize young immigrants. By the mid-1930s most states had created juvenile courts. However, because judges were given virtually unlimited discretion, these courts routinely handed out disproportionate adjudications or punishments that were disproportionate to the offenses committed by juvenile offenders. This unchecked judicial discretion was legitimated on the grounds that judges needed unrestrained power in order to rehabilitate the delinquent offender.

The Supreme Court began to regulate the juvenile courts during the 1960s. The Court established first that juvenile court judges were required to conduct a "full investigation" and hold a legal "ceremony" before they could waive juveniles to criminal courts in *Kent v. United States* (1966). However, the court neglected to define the criteria of this "ceremony." As a result there is no uniform national standard in place to determine whether a child or a youthful offender should be transferred from a juvenile court to an adult criminal court. The court's silence on this question has led to the disproportionate transfer of Latino and Latina juveniles to adult jurisdictions.

The Supreme Court next established in *In re: Gault* (1967) that juveniles were entitled to certain due process rights, such as the right to counsel, in juvenile proceedings. In a third ruling, *In re: Winship* (1970), the Court further established that judges needed "proof beyond a reasonable doubt" in order to adjudicate a juvenile delinquent. Together these opinions suggested that the juvenile courts, and by extension the juvenile justice system, would be governed not by the full Bill of Rights but by certain constitutional provisions. The Court has continuously argued that children and juveniles are different from adults and that legal actors need as much latitude as possible to make the most effective intervention. The Court's ambiguity has resulted in the creation of a juvenile justice system that is inherently unfair to juveniles because of its institutionalized and legalized subjectivity.

In 1974 Congress sought to regulate the penal aspects of the juvenile justice system by adopting the Juvenile Justice and Delinquency Prevention Act (JJDPA). The basic goals of the JJDPA were to separate juveniles from adults by providing financial incentives to states that complied with the act. Despite subsequent congressional efforts to transform the JJDPA, this law provides for the removal of juveniles from jails, the sight and sound separation of juveniles from adults in correctional facilities, the collection of data on minority confinement, and the deinstitutionalization of status offenders or offenders who violate local ordinances that would not constitute a crime for legal purposes. This law is undergoing revisions for its reauthorization in the early twenty-first century. One of the most contentious issues has been the proposal to eliminate the requirement that states collect information on the disproportionate confinement of minorities.

Finally, it should be noted that there are few national or federal juvenile justice standards. Thus each state has developed its particular juvenile justice system. Research has demonstrated that most states are expanding the number of laws for which juveniles can be tried as adults while simultaneously lowering the age at which a child can be considered an adult. In 1998 twenty-three states could try a child or juvenile of any age in an adult court. Oklahoma established the lowest age of criminal responsibility at seven years of age, in contrast with the average state's ascription of criminal responsibility at the age of fourteen.

While most states rely on judicial discretion determining whether a juvenile can formulate criminal intent, some states, like California, allow prosecutors to determine which court should have jurisdiction over a juvenile accused of committing a crime. Most research demonstrates that while Latino and Latina youth are not waived to adult courts at the same rates as black offenders, they are generally transferred at higher rates than their white peers accused of committing the same offenses.

Latina and Latino Youth and the Juvenile Justice System

¿Dónde está la justicia?, a report by Francisco A. Villaruel, Nancy E. Walker, Pamela Minifee, Omara Rivera-Vázquez, Susan Peterson, and Kristen Perry, provides a comprehensive analysis of the relationship between Latino and Latina juveniles and the legal system in the United States. The authors suggest that, like black youthful offenders, Latinos and Latinas are overrepresented at each stage of the juvenile justice system and generally receive harsher treatment than their white counterparts. Legal actors in the juvenile justice system tend to stereotype Latino and Latina youth as members of gangs.

Children generally come into contact with the juvenile justice system in two ways: because of non–law enforcement petitions from and as a result of contact with police officers and other legal actors. Juvenile courts generally address status offenses and other noncriminal delinquent behavior. Parents can petition the court to declare their children incorrigible, school administrators can seek help in enforcing school attendance, or other state actors can request the courts' intervention. Latinos and Latinas may often find themselves in an embattled relationship with the juvenile justice system.

On the one hand, Latino cultural norms tend to place emphasis on the role of the community in curbing delinquent behavior. It is quite common for Latino parents to send their children to their home countries or to depend on community members to help them correct their children's behavior. The problem, however, is that Latino communities often lack the necessary economic, political, and social resources to counteract the influence of gangs and other criminal activities. At the same time, relying on the juvenile justice system is often dangerous, because the juvenile courts are often understaffed, lack culturally competent personnel, and lack institutional resources to address issues in a nonpunitive manner. More important, however, is the fact that once a juvenile enters into contact with the juvenile justice system, he or she may have a juvenile record that follows him or her until adulthood.

There are no national standards regulating police interventions with juveniles. Police often stop and search juveniles without probable cause or even reasonable suspicion and often rely on the spirit of anti-gang laws to justify their interventions. When they treat juveniles like adults, they often neglect to consider the juveniles' maturity or capacity to understand the context of a stop. Latino and Latina juveniles are generally profiled as gang members and drug dealers. A 2000 study of the California juvenile justice system conducted by Mike Males and Dan Macallair demonstrates that in Los Angeles Latino and Latina youth are twice as likely to be arrested as white juveniles suspected of committing the same offenses. Latino and Latina juveniles are also more likely to be coerced by the police during interrogations. Moreover, Latino and Latina juveniles are twice as likely to be detained in a pretrial facility as their white counterparts. These experiences can be exacerbated by the immigrant status of the parents. Non-English-speaking Latino parents are regularly misled by police officers into waiving their rights. Additionally some parents may be reluctant to intercede on behalf of their children if their intervention could affect their status as immigrants.

Unlike adults, juveniles are not entitled to a speedy trial. The juvenile justice system may not necessarily intervene on behalf of a juvenile until he or she has committed a serious offense, and then the system generally seeks to impose a punitive disposition. Generally once the young offender enters the juvenile system, the prosecutor can choose either to bring charges against the offender or to divert the offender to a community program or state institution. Some research suggests that prosecutors are less likely to divert Latino and Latina youth and are more likely to push a case through the punitive system. Because prosecutors are often elected, it is not uncommon to see white district attorneys taking harsher stances toward Latino youthful offenders. Prosecutors tend to seek adjudication of Latino youth in jurisdictions with a high percentage of Latin American immigrants.

Latino and Latina juveniles who lack financial resources and face adjudicatory proceedings often find themselves without competent legal representation. This has dire consequences for them given the general lack of defense attorneys competent in juvenile proceedings. In addition, the Villaruel et al. report suggests that juvenile courts may often neglect to provide translators, interpreters, or personnel with the appropriate language skills to communicate with non-English-speaking offenders. This is exacerbated by the fact that defense attorneys may not possess the relevant cultural competency to contextualize the offender's experience and his or her potential for rehabilitation. Thus whereas the juvenile justice system may offer diversionary alternatives to formal adjudication, Latino and Latina youth and their parents or guardians may often not be aware of treatments, counseling services, after-school care programs, and other alternatives to detention or institutionalization.

If there is a statutory provision excluding certain juveniles from being adjudicated in a juvenile court and in the event that the prosecutor lacks the appropriate discretionary power, then the judge has the power to decide whether a child should be subject to adjudication proceedings or to a criminal trial. As Males and Macallair have demonstrated, Latino and Latina juveniles in Los Angeles are six times more likely to be waived to an adult court than their white counterparts. National data collected in the report prepared by Villaruel et al. demonstrates that Latino and Latina youth are adjudicated in juvenile courts and convicted in criminal courts at disproportionate rates throughout the nation.

Latinos and Latinas are generally at least three times more likely to be confined and incarcerated than their white counterparts. In addition, adjudicated Latino and Latina youth are more likely to serve longer sentences than adjudicated and convicted white offenders. Villaruel et al. document that the admission rates for Latino and Latina youth to state facilities in the United States ranges from 1.3 to 13 times the rate for white youth charged with the same offenses. In other words, Latino and Latina youth are disproportionately represented in state facilities. In addition, research demonstrates that Latino and Latina youth receive longer sentences than any other

racial or ethnic group. It is possible to argue that court personnel, including judges, often label Latino and Latina youth as gang members and, by extension, as drug users and dealers.

Departments of youth services and correctional facilities generally lack personnel with multilingual skills and relevant cultural competence. Moreover given the trend to cut social services and rehabilitative programs from state facilities, Latinos and Latinas accused of participating in delinquent or criminal activity are more likely to face adult sentences. When sentenced as adults, Latino and Latina youth often find themselves in a no-win situation. When incarcerated with adults, Latino and Latina youth may find themselves caged for twenty-three hours a day, seven days a week. They are more likely to be abused by both adult inmates and correctional officers and thus are more likely to commit suicide. At the same time, when placed in juvenile facilities, Latino and Latina youth may find themselves forced to join juvenile gangs or in some cases may find themselves detained with juveniles who are members of rival gangs.

Issues in the Juvenile Justice System

There are specific areas in which the juvenile justice system fails the Latino community. Officials in schools, judges and juries involving the death penalty for juveniles, and problems in the immigration system all pose serious issues for Latino and Latina juveniles.

Schools. The Supreme Court has repeatedly held that school settings are special places where the Bill of Rights may be modified in the interest of aiding school officials in achieving their educational goals. School officials have often taken advantage of the law's ambiguity to affirm their power over students and to adopt punitive policies. Latino and Latina youth are often detained, rounded up, and subjected to special interrogations seeking to demonstrate their gang membership, regardless of whether they have any prior delinquent or criminal records. Latino and Latina juveniles are often subject to heightened levels of supervision and discipline in schools, sometimes leading to the external intervention of legal actors such as the police.

Death penalty. On March 1, 2005, the U.S. Supreme Court held in *Roper v. Simmons*, 543 U.S. (2005) that it was unconstitutional to impose the death penalty on juveniles who were under the age of 18 when their crimes were committed. This ruling overturned a long practice of executing juveniles in the U.S. that dates back to the year 1642. According to Victor L. Streib, the leading expert in juveniles and the death penalty, since then at least 366 juvenile offenders have been executed. Twenty-two of these executions occurred between January 1, 1973, and April 30, 2004, when the death penalty was still applicable to juvenile offenders in the U.S.

Of the twenty-two executive juveniles, Ruben Cantu of Texas became the first and only Latino male to be executed. He was executed in 1993, and he had committed his crime at the age of 17. However, between 1973 and 2004, out of 227 juveniles sentenced to death, 27 were Latino males. They were sentence in Texas (17), Arizona (4), Florida (3), Nevada (2), and North Carolina (1). While Latinos were less likely to receive the death penalty than their white or black peers, they were still more likely to be sentenced to death than juveniles of Asian or Native American heritage. As of April 30, 2004, there were fifteen Latino juveniles in death row, and they accounted for 21 percent of juveniles awaiting executions will be commuted.

Immigration. Children of immigrant parents, whether born in the United States or abroad, have often found themselves undergoing Immigration and Naturalization Service (INS) proceedings. Villaruel et al. note that the INS has detained an average of five thousand immigrant youths per year, and most of these are Latino and Latina. These youths are often separated from their parents, regardless of their citizenship status, and they may often languish in an INS facility without any advocates or any intervention. Latino and Latina youths facing INS deportation proceedings are often treated like adults yet are denied basic due process rights, such as access to counsel. Villaruel et al. also document some instances in which Latino and Latina youths of South and Central American heritage have often been dropped off at the United States–Mexico border, where they are left to fend for themselves. In these cases, where the juvenile justice system could perhaps provide more progressive solutions, the INS has neglected the juvenile justice system as an alternative.

Assessment

Latino and Latina juveniles are generally subject to a second-class justice in both the adult legal system and the juvenile justice system. This is because different actors within the juvenile justice system tend to profile Latino and Latina youth as either gang members or drug dealers. Research suggests that tough antigang laws and drug laws are generally drafted with the profile of a Latino or Latina criminal in mind. In addition, media and other sources of information tend to stereotype Latino and Latina youth as members of gangs and drug dealers. There is further evidence to suggest that legal actors assume young Latinos and Latinas will be involved in some gang- or drug-related activity.

See also **Criminal Justice System** *and* **Immigrant Children.**

BIBLIOGRAPHY

Males, Mike, and Dan Macallair. *The Color of Justice: An Analysis of Juvenile Adult Court Transfers in California.* Washington, D.C.: United States Department of Justice: Building Blocks for Youth, 2000.

Streib, Victor L. "The Juvenile Death Penalty Today: Death Sentences and Executions for Juvenile Crimes, January 1, 1973–December 31, 2002." www.law.onu.edu/faculty/streib/juvdeath.pdf

Villaruel, Francisco A., Nancy E. Walker, Pamela Minifee, Omara Rivera-Vázquez, Susan Peterson, and Kristen Perry. *¿Dónde está la justicia?* Michigan State University, Institute for Children, Youth and Families: Building Blocks for Youth, 2002. www.buildingblocksforyouth.org/Full%20Report%20English.pdf

CHARLES R. VENATOR SANTIAGO

CHILDREN'S BOOKS. Critics have often made a distinction between "children's books" and "children's literature" based on the absence or presence of such literary qualities as a compelling plot, the psychology of characters, accurate representation of cultural reality, creative use of language, and the text's ability to appeal to the reader at an emotional level. Such characteristics elevate the goals of children's books beyond didacticism and entertainment and expand their definition beyond the mere use of age-appropriate language and illustrations.

Books for Latino and Latina Children

The history of books written and published for Latino and Latina children in the United States dates back to 1889, when the Cuban writer José Martí wrote and published *La edad de oro* (The Golden Age) while in exile in New York City. Intended as a monthly literary magazine for Spanish-speaking children, *La edad de oro* was distributed from New York to Latin America with the hope of educating, entertaining, and inspiring readers, "niños y niñas," with stories, poems, and essays written in "clear words" and accompanied by "fine illustrations." Although only four issues were published, *La edad de oro*—later republished as a book—captivated the imagination of Spanish-speaking children and inspired many generations of writers with its high standards for children's literature.

Among the new expectations set by *La edad de oro* was an emphasis on clear language, on truth—factual or emotional—and on uncompromising literary quality. Children's literature, as practiced by Martí, comprised all genres and explored a variety of perspectives and themes. The twenty-three pieces that make up *La edad de oro* encompass almost every theme present in Latino and Latina children's literature in the early twenty-first century: reflections on history and historical figures, inventions, adventure and travel, legends, folktales and traditions, and also explorations of poverty, and racial and social discrimination. These texts present a subtle but strong denunciation of oppression and intolerance, while together they celebrate the ideals of equality, freedom, justice, and hope championed by Martí.

Authors

The early appearance of *La edad de oro* did not, however, bring about a long and rich tradition of publishing for

Latino and Latina children in the United States. For most of the twentieth century, while children's literature as a whole was experiencing a great boom with such writers as L. M. Montgomery, A. A. Milne, Margaret Wise Brown, and C. S. Lewis, books for Latino and Latina children remained almost nonexistent until the 1980s and 1990s.

The few notable exceptions were such writers as Pura Belpré, Ernesto Galarza, Rudolfo Anaya, Nicholasa Mohr, and Alma Flor Ada, who recognized the need for children's books that addressed the linguistic, social, and cultural realities of Latino and Latina children, while retaining the high literary standards that Martí had set forth in his groundbreaking work.

Pura Belpré. Pura Belpré was born in Cidra, Puerto Rico, in 1909, and after immigrating to the United States she became the first Puerto Rican librarian in the New York public library system. Through her work, she became a relentless advocate for the development and acquisition of culturally relevant library materials for Latino and Latina readers, especially children. A renowned storyteller and puppeteer, Belpré wrote and compiled numerous Puerto Rican folktales, among which is *Pérez and Martina* (1932), her famous retelling of the love story between a cockroach and a mouse, and *The Tiger and the Rabbit and Other Tales* (1946), the first English-language collection of Puerto Rican folktales published in the United States. During the 1960s, Belpré continued her reinterpretations of Puerto Rican folktales with *Juan Bobo and the Queen's Necklace* (1962) and *Oté, A Puerto Rican Folk Tale* (1969). Her most influential text also comes from this period. *Santiago* (1961) is the story of a young boy whose family leaves Puerto Rico for New York City and whose days are spent reminiscing about his old life on the island and how his pet hen must have fared since he left. Critics see in Belpré's publication of Santiago a progression characteristic of the work of Latino and Latina children's writers: after the celebration of traditions and re-creation of family roots, their texts tend to move toward a representation of present-day reality and its challenges.

Ernesto Galarza. In writing for Latino and Latina children, Ernesto Galarza drew heavily from his life stories to explore the Mexican American experience. While very young, Galarza and his family migrated to the United States, displaced by the Mexican Revolution. In *Barrio Boy* (1971), he chronicles his journey from a mountain village in Mexico to Sacramento's barrio. A devoted teacher and advocate for Latino and Latina literacy, Galarza responded to the lack of culturally appropriate bilingual materials in the public school system by writing and self-publishing a series of bilingual Mini Libros, featuring riddles and poems, which he illustrated with his own photography.

Rudolfo Anaya. Rudolfo Anaya's first work of fiction, *Bless Me, Ultima* (1972), is a coming-of-age novel steeped in the land and folklore of his native Southwest. Set in the 1940s, this highly autobiographical text has been praised for its realistic portrayal of the aspirations and challenges of a Mexican American family in rural New Mexico, the courageous struggle of its young protagonist to come to terms with his family's expectations and his own goals, and the text's seamless integration of such folk elements as the legend of La Llorona, the "Crying Woman" who drowned her children and is said to come back to haunt waterways, and traditional remedies of folk medicine. The novel helped define Chicano and Chicana identity as built upon family, tradition, and myth and outlined its challenges from the often-conflicting ideals of this three-cornered foundation.

For younger children, Anaya focused on compiling and retelling folktales, legends, and traditions of his native Southwest, among which are *The Farolitos of Christmas* (1985) about the tradition of placing luminarias on Christmas Eve and welcoming the *pastores* for a treat of *posole*, *tamales*, and *biscochitos*. Its sequel, *Farolitos for Abuelo*, is a heartwarming story about a girl who, looking for a way to honor her departed grandfather, starts a tradition of placing luminarias on the graves of loved ones. Anaya also revisits the often-told legend of La Llorona in *Maya's Children: The Story of La Llorona* (1984) in a version set in ancient Mexico with a less frightening plot in which the children are left in the hands of *Señor Tiempo* instead of being drowned. In 2001, Anaya published *My Land Sings: Stories from the Rio Grande*, which includes the retelling of five traditional tales of New Mexico and five original stories steeped in Mexican and Native American folklore.

Nicholasa Mohr. Nicholasa Mohr's first novel, *Nilda* (1974), is a semiautobiographical tale told through the eyes of a ten-year-old girl who relies on her imagination to endure the cultural and economic challenges of growing up Puerto Rican in the Bronx. The search for identity and the struggle to find a balance between family roots and her surroundings became a mainstay in Mohr's fiction. Aimed at a young-adult audience, *Felita* (1979) and *Going Home* (1986) expose the difficulty of growing up between two cultures, never finding comfort exclusively in one or the other.

Alma Flor Ada. Among the precursors to the editorial boom of Latino and Latina children's books is the Cuban-born writer Alma Flor Ada. Like Anaya and Mohr, Ada addressed her writing to this audience before there was an established market. A steadfast researcher, educator, and advocate for Latino and Latina children's literature, Ada is also undoubtedly the most prolific writer for this readership, having published over 150 titles in Spanish,

English, and bilingual editions. In her critical writings, Ada has expressed a concern with the quality of children's publishing, especially for the Latino and Latina market. While she concedes that non-Latino and non-Latina writers who have had a long-term exposure to the Latino and Latina culture could potentially write valuable texts for this readership, she also insists on the importance of producing texts that are culturally and linguistically accurate and that portray the Latino and Latina culture with respect, responsibility, and authenticity without compromising literary and artistic quality.

Increased Demand

In response to the demographic expansion of the Latino and Latina population, the U.S. market for Latino and Latina children's books experienced a dramatic increase during the 1990s. The publishing industry responded to the pressing demand for Spanish-language and bilingual children's books with an indiscriminate editorial approach, which often favored the translation into Spanish of popular English-language titles without regard to the cultural representation of its intended readership.

Independent presses. Several independent publishing houses battled against this trend by publishing children's texts whose plots and illustrations echoed the cultural realities of Latino and Latina communities. Among these are Piñata Books, an imprint of Houston's Arte Público Press, San Francisco's Children's Books Press, and El Paso's Cinco Puntos Press.

Established in 1994, Piñata Books has flourished as an independent publisher of children's and young-adult titles dedicated exclusively to Latino and Latina readers. While it publishes an average of only ten titles a year, the quality of its books has been recognized with many prestigious awards, such as the Paterson Prize for Young Adult Literature and the Skipping Stones Award. Its list of published writers boasts such names as Ofelia Dumas Lachtman, Diane Gonzalez Bertrand, and Pat Mora. Committed to cultural and linguistic accuracy, titles published under this imprint explore issues, themes, and traditions that pertain specifically to Latino and Latina youth. Its illustrated books are published in a bilingual format—favored by elementary educators and parents—while young-adult novels are generally published in English.

The children's division of Cinco Puntos Press is another example of a successful independent press that specializes in the literature of the United States–Mexico border, Mexico, and the Southwest. Its efforts to represent a distinct border Latino and Latina culture in its literature fill a void that has been left largely untouched by larger publishers.

Commercial presses. The response from commercial publishing to the demand for Spanish-language and bilingual children's books has been mixed, as has the quality of the titles they have released. While some publishers have made an effort to seek Latino and Latina writers, most have been content with publishing translations of popular English-language titles or importing Spanish-language books from Latin America and Spain. Lectorum, an imprint of children's megapublisher Scholastic, illustrates this trend. Founded in 1960 as an importer of Spanish-language books, it touts itself as the largest and oldest importer of Spanish-language children's titles, being the exclusive distributor of works published by Beascoa, Edebé, Edelvives, Everest, Kókinos, Litexsa, Noguer, and Serres, and of the Harry Potter books in Spanish. As a publisher, Lectorum has released several titles by Colombian writer and illustrator Ivar da Coll, yet the bulk of its publications remains Spanish-language translations of such children's series as Arthur, Franklin, and the Dr. Seuss books. While popular and entertaining, these books reflect a cultural reality that does not correspond directly to that of most Latino and Latina children. Similarly, the children's publications of Rayo, an imprint of HarperCollins Publishers, while featuring several Latino and Latina writers such as Alma Flor Ada and Juan Felipe Herrera, remain largely Spanish-language translations of such popular titles as *Harold and the Purple Crayon*, *Goodnight Moon*, and *Ramona the Pest*.

In the late 1990s, the Children's Book Council (CBC), a nonprofit trade organization dedicated to encouraging literacy and promoting children's books, initiated a campaign to encourage publishers of English-language children's books to produce Spanish-language titles. The CBC defined the market for Spanish-language children's books based mainly on demographic changes, citing the increasing demand for bilingual materials for the classroom—and, specifically, the "Limited English Proficiency" of many Spanish-speaking children in the United States. As a secondary consideration, it added the desire of many Latino and Latina parents to maintain their Spanish-language skills and pass them on to their children, and the growing popularity of Spanish-as-a-second-language courses in elementary schools throughout the country. While the CBC campaign recognized the importance of stories that feature "Hispanic protagonists" or that "deal with aspects of Hispanic culture," its recommendations did not distinguish texts written by and about Spanish-speakers in the United States from those originating in Latin America and Spain. With such a broad definition of what is culturally appropriate—clearly privileging language over ethnicity—it is not surprising that the CBC advocated for the translation of popular titles from other languages under the premise that "good literature is universal." The campaign, however, insisted on the importance of hiring native speakers of Spanish as translators, especially those with an extensive understanding of the cultures exposed in the texts, so as to produce translations that are linguistically and somewhat culturally accurate.

Organizations and awards. In spite of the editorial trend of favoring Spanish-language translations of established titles over autochthonous texts, many Latino and Latina writers participated in the children's literature publishing boom of the 1990s and beyond. One organization responsible for the drive behind publishing culturally appropriate titles for Latino and Latina children is RE-FORMA, an affiliate of the American Library Association. Established in 1971, REFORMA has advocated actively for the development of library collections to include Spanish-language and Latino and Latina–centered materials. In their efforts to advance Latino and Latina children's literature, REFORMA established in 1996 the Pura Belpré Award, presented to a Latino and Latina writer and illustrator for the children and young-adult market whose work best portrays, affirms, and celebrates the Latino and Latina cultural experience in its diversity while maintaining the highest literary and artistic standards. Cosponsored by the Association for Library Service to Children, this biennial award has been an important incentive to publishing high-quality children's literature by Latino and Latina writers in the United States and Puerto Rico.

Another REFORMA initiative that has provided a tremendous boost to Latino and Latina children's publishing and awareness is the Día de los Niños/Día de los Libros campaign. Introduced in 1997 as a collaborative effort between schools, libraries, and community organizations to celebrate childhood and promote bilingual literacy, the initiative has become an annual event celebrated on April 30—the traditional date for the celebration of *El día del niño* in Mexico.

Other literary prizes that have fostered excellence in Latino and Latina children's literature are the Américas Award for Children's and Young Adult Literature and the Latino Literary Hall of Fame Book Awards. In 1993, the Consortium of Latin American Studies Programs established the Américas Award to recognize U.S. children's books, in English and/or Spanish, for presenting a culturally authentic and engaging representation of Latin America, the Caribbean, or Latinos and Latinas in the United States. This multicultural award has recognized the work of many Latino and Latina writers, from its first winner Lulu Delacre for *Vejigante/Masquerader* to Judith Ortiz Cofer for her young-adult novel *The Meaning of Consuelo*.

The Latino Literary Hall of Fame, founded in 1999 to promote literacy and literary excellence in Latino and Latina communities, hosts annual book awards that recognize the work of publishers and authors serving the growing Latino and Latina market. Among past winners in children's literature are *Uncle Chente's Picnic/El picnic de tío Chente* by Diane Gonzales-Bertrand, *César Chávez:*

La lucha por la justicia by Richard Griswold del Castillo, and *Mi gorrita/My Cap* by Georgina Lázaro.

Genres and Themes

While all genres, from poetry to drama, are represented in recent Latino and Latina children's literature, the illustrated short story remains the indisputable leader. The format correlates directly to the needs of bilingual educators for early-grades material, and responds to the desire of many Latino and Latina families to preserve their linguistic and cultural heritage by using reading materials for their children that reflect these goals. However, as Latino and Latina children become accustomed to reading books that reflect their cultural and linguistic reality, it is likely that they will look to other genres for representation. As this readership matures, so will their stories, a trend that some publishers have already anticipated by encouraging Latino and Latina writers to produce young-adult novels for Latino and Latina readers.

The themes of contemporary Latino and Latina children's literature have not changed dramatically from those explored by Martí in *La edad de oro* over a century ago. Family relations and traditions are one of the main themes of this literature, especially for illustrated early-reader books. The close-knit families they depict emphasize the importance of interpersonal relations (*Cuadros de familia/Family Pictures* by Carmen Lomas Garza, *Hairs/Pelitos* by Sandra Cisneros), strong ties to the extended family (*A Birthday Basket for Tía* by Pat Mora, *Familia/Family* by Diane Gonzales Bertrand), and adherence to family traditions, especially culinary ones (*Las empanadas que hacía la abuela/The Empanadas that Abuela Made* by Diane Gonzales Bertrand, *Too Many Tamales* by Gary Soto, *Kikirikí/Quiquiriquí* by Diane de Anda). Numerous titles focus on grandparents as role models and sources of inspiration for their grandchildren (*Abuelita's Paradise* by Carmen Santiago Nodar, *Remembering Grandma/Recordando a abuela* by Teresa Armas, *My Tata's Guitar/La guitarra de mi tata* by Ethriam Cash Brammer).

Holidays (*Pablo Remembers: The Fiesta of the Day of the Dead* by George Anacona, *Arbol de navidad* by Alma Flor Ada) and traditional crafts (*The Piñata Maker/El piñatero* by George Ancona, *Lupita's Papalote/El papalote de Lupita* by Lupe Ruiz-Flores) are also featured prominently, highlighting children's creativity and resourcefulness.

Young-adult novels have been the preferred genre for exploring such issues as poverty (*Buried Onions* by Gary Soto), prejudice (*Felita* by Nicholasa Mohr), the hardships of migrant farmworkers (*Breaking Through* and *The Circuit: Stories from the Life of a Migrant Child* by Francisco Jiménez), and tales of culture clash and adjustment (*My Diary from Here to There/Mi diario de aquí hasta allá* by Amada Irma Pérez and Maya Christina González, *The*

Upside-Down Boy/El niño de cabeza by Juan Felipe Herrera). However, some of these issues have been addressed successfully in illustrated children's books by employing a subtle and humorous approach, as is the case of Gary Soto's *The Pool Party*, which explores prejudice and social differences, Ofelia Dumas Lachtman's *Pepita Talks Twice/Pepita habla dos veces* on biculturalism, depicting a girl who resents acting as an interpreter for her family and neighbors, and Juan Felipe Herrera's memoir of his migrant-farmworker childhood in *Calling the Doves/El canto de las palomas*.

While history and historical fiction have been published primarily for Latino and Latina young-adult readers (*Before We Were Free* by Julia Alvarez, about life during the dictatorship of Rafael Trujillo in the Dominican Republic), the lives of historical and contemporary figures as role models have fared better in illustrated children's books. Latino and Latina activists such as César Chávez (*Elegy on the Death of César Chávez: A Poem* by Rudolfo Anaya, *César Chávez a Hero for Everyone* by Gary Soto, and *César Chávez* by Consuelo Rodriguez, among many others) and Jessie de la Cruz (*Jessie de la Cruz: A Profile of a United Farm Worker* by Gary Soto) and writers such as Isabel Allende (*Isabel Allende: Memories for a Story/Recuerdos para un cuento* by Raquel Benatar) and Sor Juana Inés de la Cruz (*A Library for Juana* by Pat Mora) are the subject of a considerable number of early-reader titles.

Latino athletes, particularly baseball players, are another mainstay of children's books (*Home Is Everything: The Latino Baseball Story from the Barrio to the Major Leagues* by José Luis Villegas, and *Beisbol*: *Pioneros y leyendas del beisbol Latino* by Jonah Winter and Bruce Markusen Rodriguez), but these tend to be addressed to an older readership.

Retellings of legends and folktales are another mainstay in illustrated early-reader books, perhaps as an acceptable vehicle for moralizing stories, which would otherwise not be well-received by young readers. Among the best-known are Rosalma Zubizarreta's *La mujer que brillaba aún más que el sol/The Woman Who Outshone the Sun*, Julia Alvarez's *The Secret Footprints*, and Alma Flor Ada's *The Lizard and the Sun/La lagartija y el sol*.

See also Anaya, Rudolfo; Galarza, Ernesto; Literature; Mohr, Nicholasa; Publishers; Publishing; *and* Soto, Gary.

BIBLIOGRAPHY

Ada, Alma Flor. *A Magical Encounter: Latino Children's Literature in the Classroom*. Boston: Allyn and Bacon, 2003.

Day, Frances Ann. *Latina and Latino Voices in Literature: Lives and Works*. Westport, Conn.: Greenwood, 2003.

Moller, Sharon Chickering. *Library Service to Spanish-Speaking Patrons: A Practical Guide*. Englewood, Colo.: Libraries Unlimited, 2001.

Norton, Donna E. *Through the Eyes of a Child: An Introduction to Children's Literature*. Columbus, Ohio: Merrill, 1987.

LYDIA GIL

CHIMAYÓ. Chimayó is the name of several related entities: Tsi Mayoh, a 7,056-foot hill in the upper Santa Cruz River Valley some thirty miles north of Santa Fe, New Mexico, sacred to the Tewa Pueblo Indians; a dozen or more neighboring Spanish *placitas* (small clusters of houses), sparsely settled in the 1600s before the 1680 Pueblo Revolt and resettled soon after the 1692–1693 Reconquest; a post-1870 Hispanic weaving tradition; and *El Santuario*, a nineteenth-century healing shrine in the southeastern placita El Potrero, destination of the largest religious pilgrimage in the United States. Earlier known for trade in chili, apples, and weavings, in the 1900s Chimayó became a center for tourism in northern New Mexico.

Tsi Mayoh ("Hill of the East" in Tewa) is one of four sacred hills or mesas (*Tsin*) with powerful Pueblo shrines. Archaeology indicates longstanding nomadic Indian presence, with the first dwellings dating from circa 1000 C.E. and abandoned before Spanish settlement.

The enclosed, defensive Plaza del Cerro (Tsi Mayoh), dedicated to San Buenaventura, developed during the 1700s, when it was home to pioneer weaver Nicolás Gabriel Ortega, whose descendants gained prominence among northern New Mexico Hispanic weavers and later vendors of weavings. Early traders distinguished "Indian" from "Mexican" blankets. After 1870, Santa Fe curio merchants and Santa Fe Railway/Fred Harvey Company dealers used "Chimayó" for the latter, which developed a characteristic regional style. Entered on the National Register of Historic Places in 1972, Plaza del Cerro has been since 1994 a concern of the community-directed Chimayó Cultural Preservation Association and its history museum.

The nearby Plaza del Potrero was a site of healing hot mud springs long recognized by Pueblo Indians, traditionally the spot (*El Pozito*) where Don Bernardo Abeyta (1771–1856) was miraculously healed, unearthed a crucifix of Nuestro Señor de Esquípulas, and built a small chapel (1814–1816) for its veneration. Abeyta probably learned about the Esquípulas devotion during trading trips to northern Mexico. It originated in Guatemala in the sixteenth century as a Mayan-Spanish devotion involving healing geophagy (earth-eating) and a miraculous crucifix called El Cristo Negro. Miracles here at El Santuario were rivaled by a family chapel on Potrero plaza dedicated to Santo Niño de Atocha, brought from Mexico by Abeyta's neighbor, Blas Severiano Medina, around 1857. The Abeyta family later installed a Santo Niño in El Santuario, but by the 1920s pilgrimages and family resources had declined, forcing them to sell. The Spanish Colonial Arts Society (a Santa Fe preservation group founded in 1925) arranged for its purchase and transfer to the Archdiocese of Santa Fe on October 15, 1929, as a "religious museum" and church mission. Designated a National

Сhimayó. Santuario de Chimayó. (Ernesto Burciaga/Rainbow)

Historic Landmark in 1970, it draws pilgrims from North and Latin America throughout the year, with thousands walking during Holy Week.

First called "A New Mexico Lourdes" in January 1916, Chimayó has since figured in numerous tourist promotions. A March 1992 Department of Tourism national advertising campaign linked Easter pilgrimages to the "Lourdes of America" with the "famed Ortega weavings" as "just one of the many wonders of New Mexico waiting for you," provoking outcry (as, for example, in *Time Magazine*'s April 13, 1992, business notes) against marketing a religious experience as a tourist attraction.

See also New Mexico.

BIBLIOGRAPHY
Howarth, Sam, and Enrique R. Lamadrid. *Pilgrimage to Chimayó: Contemporary Portrait of a Living Tradition*. Santa Fe: Museum of New Mexico Press, 1999.

Lucero, Helen R., and Suzanne Baizermann. *Chimayó Weaving: The Transformation of a Tradition*. Albuquerque: University of New Mexico Press, 1999.
Usner, Don J. *Sabino's Map: Life in Chimayó's Old Plaza*. Santa Fe: Museum of New Mexico Press, 1995.

Marta Weigle

CHISTES. The word *chiste* can have various meanings, such as joke, jest, or trick. Joking and jokes within Latina and Latino communities may have a social function and reveal political and social positions of participants. In any number of Latina and Latino gathering places, one can find *chistes de Pepito* or *de Jaimito* or *chistes colorados* as well as joking sessions where everyone joins in telling jokes and engaging in *relajo*, or poking fun. Joking sessions are popular in Central America, the Caribbean, and Mexico, so immigrant communities from these areas carry on the practice in the United States. Américo Paredes noted that in Chicana and Chicano communities as well as in immigrant Mexican communities, joking persists as a form of subversive opposition to the hegemony of the United States. Joking can be an act of resistance and contestation. Wordplay and punning occur in daily exchanges in the workplace, in bars, and on the streets, wherever people can take the opportunity to gather and have a good time. In the United States, bilingual joking, that is, joking that relies on linguistic confusion caused by translation or false cognates, proliferates.

In Latina and Latino folk tradition, the salacious adventures of Pepito and sometimes his brother Jaimito provide ample material as these child protagonists' wordplay often results in humorous predicaments replete with misogynist and sexist overtones, invariably involving sexual innuendo. Pepito, a young boy, sometimes appears as a comical trickster figure; at other times he is a sly and devious underdog—but always the joke is gender specific. There are also a number of salacious gender-specific female jokes replete with double entendres that are said only among females. In-group joking is a common phenomenon and runs rampant during bridal showers or bachelor parties. In one of the least offensive of the Pepito jokes, a variant of one that focuses on the skin color of Latinas and Latinos, Pepito has died and gone to heaven. Since everyone who goes to heaven has to work, God goes up to Pepito and says, "Pepito, you are going to make babies. Here is this wheel, and every time you turn it, a baby will come out." For hours, Pepito spins the wheel at full speed; then he starts to get tired. As he slows down, a black baby comes out. Pepito exclaims, "Damn! I better hurry because they are burning!"

Political jokes featuring Pepito or Jaimito also dominate Cuban joke cycles, as exemplified in this Pepito joke, posted as an example of typical Cuban humor.

A schoolteacher in Havana asked her class, "If the sea between Cuba and Miami were to dry up, how long would it take to walk across?" When she got no response, she asked Pepito to give an answer.

After a moment of thought, he said, "Forty days."

The teacher was naturally surprised. "Pepito," she said, "the distance from Havana to Miami is only about ninety miles. Maybe I didn't make the question clear. Pretend that it's all smooth and level ground. NOW how long would it take?"

Pepito insisted however on his answer of forty days.

"But why?" asked the teacher.

"Well, because you would constantly have to say, 'Excuse me,' 'Pardon me please,' 'Excuse me, sir,' 'Pardon me Miss,' 'Excuse me . . .' "

("Miami or Bust . . .")

Pepito's answer, of course, implies there would be a multitude of Cubans trying to get to Miami.

The anonymous voices that share similar patterns of expression for the sake of conversation and laughter exist in all communities. In Latina and Latino communities in the United States they also function as the purveyors of a cultural practice that constitutes cultural memory. Most communities have a joke teller and storyteller who may also have in her or his repertoire the inside jokes of the group. In typical traditional fashion, the jokester and storyteller, or *cuentista*, is a member of the community who assumes the role and whom everyone recognizes as a master. At weddings, wakes, and other family gatherings, it is that person who is expected to initiate the joke- or story-telling event. One of the highest compliments that the community can bestow is that someone is "muy bueno pa contar chistes"—very good at telling jokes.

Noting that the second or third generation of Chicanas and Chicanos may lose the connection of popular speech forms such as jokes and *dichos*, Chuck Tatum optimistically cites the "influx of Mexican and other Latin American immigrants together with family visits to Mexico" as factors that will reinforce proficiency in Spanish and thereby assure the persistence of these popular speech forms (Tatum, pp. 188–189).

See also Chicanos and Chicanas; Cuban Americans; Dichos; Folklore; Mexican-Origin People in the United States; *and* Paredes, Américo.

BIBLIOGRAPHY
"Cesaretto Humor" Spazio Web site. xoomer.virgilio.it/cesaretto/che/cubanos.htm

Chistes.centramerica.com Web site. chistes.centramerica.com

"Miami or Bust . . ." Rec.Humor.Funny Jokes Web site. www.netfunny.com/rhf/jokes/90q2/cuban.html

Paredes, Américo. *Uncle Remus con Chile*. Houston, Tex.: Arte Público Press, 1993.

"Pepito Jokes." Welcome to Miami Web site. www.welcometomiami.com/jokes/pepito

Schmidt, Samuel. *Humor en serio. Análisis del chiste político en México*. México D.F.: Aguilar, 1996.

Tatum, Charles M. *Chicano Popular Culture: Que Hable el Pueblo*. Tucson: University of Arizona Press, 2001.

Toelken, Barre. *The Dynamics of Folklore*. Logan: Utah State University Press, 1996.

ROSE RODRIGUEZ RABIN AND NORMA E. CANTÚ

CHOLOS AND CHOLAS. The word *cholo* has a variety of meanings. The term has been traced to Spanish colonial times, when it was used as a derogatory label for Indians who assimilated into the culture of the Spanish elite. In Peru, "cholo" is still used to describe an indigenous person. After 1848 in the United States, the word was a pejorative label for laboring-class Mexicans, or for *mestizos* or half-breeds.

The term shifted in meaning in the urban setting of early twentieth-century America. It became connected to working-class Chicano gangs. The cholo label could be applied to individuals who were affiliated with a gang, but also to those who just copied the style without joining a gang. In the early 2000s, the term can even be found in mainstream American popular culture with a variety of definitions: a gang member, any urban youth of Hispanic origin, or a style or aesthetics of dress, language, or images, such as tattoos or graffiti.

The cholo in the 1960s represented the evolution of the *pachuco* of the 1940s and 1950s, who also possessed a particular urban style of dress that blended elements of Mexican and American culture. Whereas the original use of the term "cholo" during Spanish colonial times implied an acculturation to the dominant culture's values, the use of the term in the mid–twentieth century implied a refusal to assimilate. Cholos of the 1960s, like pachucos, retained certain aspects of their Mexican culture, such as the emphasis on family ties, male bravado, and the use of *caló* (a Mexican American barrio dialect).

The cholo style was based on class as well as ethnicity. Working-class cholos wore the clothing they could afford, transformed it into a "style," and flaunted it. The cholo style is functional as well as culturally connected. Its basic elements are baggy khaki pants (heavily starched and impeccably pressed), a white T-shirt, a plaid Pendleton shirt worn as a jacket, and a bandanna. Other elements can include fedora hats and watch chains, like the pachucos, and also shaved heads and tattoos (with Old English lettering and blue India ink). James Diego Vigil traces the khaki pants to the popularity of military clothing among barrio youth in southern California after World War II and the Korean War. Later, the blue jeans that were worn in California prisons became part of the "choloization" of dress for Chicano and Chicana youth. For the cholas, the style is similar, typically including perfectly coiffed hair, tank tops or blouses, and heavy makeup, especially around the eyes and lips. Working-class youth made this affordable style into a statement of cultural pride and respect for one's community or neighborhood. The cholo style allowed them, like the pachucos before them, to assert a distinct Chicano or Chicana identity that used fashion, language, and body movements to represent their refusal to be assimilated or *engabacheado* (anglicized). The fact that cholo style was connected to prison and gang styles was the main reason that, within the dominant American culture and even among some Latinos and Latinas, it carried a negative image.

Cholo style merged with the lowrider culture of the 1960s and 1970s, and the dress and language became a defining characteristic of barrio youth. Lowriders were often labeled as "cholos on wheels" or "gangs on wheels" by popular media outlets and law enforcement agencies. Hollywood movies about Chicanos and Chicanas in the late 1970s, such as *Walk Proud* (1979), *Up in Smoke* (1978), and *Boulevard Nights* (1979), featured cholos and lowriders as symbols of barrio life, and further led to their characterization as criminal elements in society. A perfect example of how the dominant media portrayed Chicano and Chicana culture negatively during the late 1970s can be found in *The New Yorker* magazine, which published an article on lowrider and cholo culture in East Los Angeles. The article painted a picture of a violent, gang-infested locale. This is not to say that cholos cannot be violent or own lowriders, but any Chicano or Chicana youth growing up in East Los Angeles could adopt the cholo look, gang-affiliated or not.

Because of the image of cholos as criminals, many in the Chicano and Chicana community worked to distance themselves from this style. For instance, the inclusion of cholos within the pages of *Lowrider Magazine* in the late 1970s generated debate and offended some of its readers. Many lowriders saw themselves as role models, not gang members. Some readers thought that linking the cholo with the lowrider in the magazine might produce a harmful effect, since the police often viewed lowriders and cholos as the same. Yet in November 1980, *Lowrider Magazine* included a whole fashion layout on "The Cholo Look" and asserted that it was a "fashion of resistance" toward the dominant American culture, not always a style worn by gang members. The goal of the short article was to shed a more positive light on the cholo style.

Despite its origins as a symbol of cultural resistance, the cholo style has found its way into American popular culture. Its influences can be found in punk music, the skateboard scene, and hip-hop culture. It is no longer only for Chicanos and Chicanas living in the barrio. For instance, Gwen Stefani of the rock group No Doubt, who grew up in Orange County, California, has claimed to be influenced by the chola fashion style. Mr. Cartoon, of Los Angeles, specializes in cholo-style tattoos—classic blue, black, or gray India ink and Old English lettering—that emerged out of East Los Angeles and prison cultures. He has inked such celebrities as the rapper Eminem and the pop singer Justin Timberlake.

Cholo style can still be a way for Chicanos and Chicanas to assert cultural pride, or even a representation of gangster culture. Yet it has also become fashionable within the dominant American culture. It continues the barrio tradition of using one's body and style of dress to create a cultural identity that represents not only individuality but also a connection to a community or neighborhood.

See also **Chicanos and Chicanas; Gangs; Lowriders; Mexican-Origin People in the United States; Pachucos and Pachucas; Youth Culture;** *and* **Zoot Suit.**

BIBLIOGRAPHY
"The Cholo Look." *Lowrider Magazine*, November 1980.
Fregoso, Rosa Linda. "Homegirls, Cholas, and Pachucas in Cinema." *California History Magazine*, Fall 1995, 317–327.
Harris, Mary G. *Cholas: Latino Girls and Gangs*. New York: AMS Press, 1988.
Sandoval, Denise Michelle. "Bajito y Suavecito/Low and Slow: Cruising through Lowrider Culture." PhD diss., Claremont Graduate University, 2003.
Trillin, Calvin, and Edward Koren. "Our Far-Flung Correspondents: Low and Slow, Mean and Clean." *New Yorker*, 54.21, July 10, 1978, 70–74.
Vigil, James Diego. *Barrio Gangs: Street Life and Identity in Southern California*. Austin: University of Texas Press, 1988.

DENISE M. SANDOVAL

CHOTEO. According to the authoritative *Diccionario de la lengua Española* of the Royal Academy of Spain, the word *choteo*, derived from the verb *chotear*, means "to make fun of something or someone." The *Diccionario* suggests that the word is found in Latin American but not Peninsular Spanish. As a popular term, "choteo" may be thought of as an umbrella expression covering a range of word and body play shared to some degree by different Latino groups, although the literature on the subject is skewed considerably toward males of Puerto Rican and Mexican origin. Sexual and scatological language tends to characterize such play, but less charged language may be used as well.

Almost without exception, *choteando* is a practice of ritualized insult, that is, an artful manipulation of words and body to seemingly insult another party. Scholarly attention has focused on the question of whether or not a real insult is intended, on the propensity toward sexuality and scatology, and on the predominantly working-class locus of this kind of play. (A parallel practice in African American culture is known as "signifying.") Several styles of this distinctive speech play are found in Latina and

CHOTEO. Gathering at the Rincon Criollo Community garden in the Morisania section of the Bronx, New York, June 1998. (© Andrew Lichtenstein/The Image Works)

Latino cultures, and there is a certain amount of scholarly debate concerning its social interpretation.

Choteo can cover a number of often overlapping practices. It can signify any generalized bantering or teasing, free from sexuality and scatology: a group of friends teasing a member about a new hairstyle, for example. However, it also covers more specific forms such as *relajando*, a form found in both Puerto Rican and Mexican culture, including those cultures in the United States. The verb *relajar* literally means "to cut," or more precisely, "to disembowel," a term that expresses the verbal and physical interactions included in the term *relajando* or *relaje*. The event itself can be called *un relaje* (a cutting-up), and a practitioner may also be referred to as *un relaje*, someone who cuts up. According to Anthony Lauria, among Puerto Ricans relajando generally refers to "insult, banter and so forth," but it can also cover "the telling of jokes, obscene or otherwise, the use of obscenity . . . friendly grappling, punching, slapping and the expressive use of images and metaphors of sexual intercourse" (Lauria, pp. 58–59). In Mexican culture such sexually charged and witty double entendres are also called *albures*, *puntadas* (literally, "pointed" remarks), *pendejadas* (seemingly silly but actually witty commentary and physical actions), and *ocurrencias* (literally, "occurrences," but actually bizarre verbal and physical acts).

These interactions tend to occur among men. There is also some association with working-class or lower socioeconomic status. These gender and class associations have given rise to scholarly debate as to the social and psychological significance of choteo. Samuel Ramos, in *Profile of Man and Culture in Mexico* (1934), characterizes such verbal and physical practices among lower-class Mexican men as threatening to the social order. Their "crude and suggestive language," their "diction, which abounds in ordinary words . . . but . . . with a new meaning" makes such a man "an animal" whose practices "are illusory reactions against his real position in life which is a nullity" (Ramos, p. 61). Other Mexican intellectuals, such as Octavio Paz, Roger Bartra, and Jorge Portilla, have followed Ramos in viewing choteo or *relajo* as socially and politically dysfunctional, especially in the context of Mexico's continuing socioeconomic plight.

On the other side of the debate are U.S. Latino commentators, such as Lauria, Miguel Diaz-Barriga, and José Limón, who have collectively fashioned a much more affirmative and generous interpretation of this practice. Lauria notes that "to engage in *relajos* of any sort is to engage in a relation of *confianza*—of trust and familiarity with that person" (Lauria, p. 62). The clear suggestion here is that, notwithstanding the seeming aggression of such practices, they are paradoxically rituals that build community. They can be said to be an eroticized, playful projection of freedom in a world of oppression. Diaz-Barriga describes an interview with one informant as a relajo that is deeply ironic and playfully critical of both the dominant Mexican society and the anthropologist conducting the study.

Choteo and its subsidiary forms are a group of expressive practices that engage Latinos (and sometimes Latinas) of the working class in particular. They have also attracted and engaged anthropologists and other social commentators. This dual interest speaks of a powerful cultural presence in Latina and Latino communities and one that no doubt will continue to engage practitioners and analysts alike.

See also Comedy and Humor.

BIBLIOGRAPHY

Bartra, Roger. *The Cage of Melancholy: Identity and Metamorphosis in the Mexican Character.* Translated by Christopher J. Hall. New Brunswick, N.J.: Rutgers University Press, 1992.

Castro, Rafaela. "Mexican Women's Sexual Jokes." *Aztlán, a Journal of Chicano Studies* 13 (1982): 275–294.

Diaz-Barriga, Miguel. "The Culture of Poverty as Relajo." *Aztlán, a Journal of Chicano Studies* 22 (1997): 43–66.

Lauria, Anthony J. " 'Respeto,' 'Relajo' and Inter-Personal Relations in Puerto Rico." *Anthropological Quarterly* 37 (1964): 53–67.

Limón, José E. *Dancing with the Devil: Society and Cultural Poetics in Mexican-American South Texas.* Madison: University of Wisconsin Press, 1994.

Paz, Octavio. *The Labyrinth of Solitude: Life and Thought in Mexico.* Translated by Lysander Kemp. New York: Grove Press, 1961.

Ramos, Samuel. *Profile of Man and Culture in Mexico.* Translated by Peter G. Earle. Austin: University of Texas Press, 1962.

Speilberg, Joseph. "Humor in a Mexican-American Palomilla: Some Historical, Social, and Psychological Implications." *Revista Chicano-Riqueña* 2 (1974): 41–50.

JOSÉ E. LIMÓN

CINCO DE MAYO. On May 5, 1862, a French army approached the city of Puebla, Mexico, with intentions of overcoming its defenders and ultimately colonizing Mexico for the emperor Napoleon III of France. An army of *guerrilleros* under the command of Ignacio Zaragoza, a native of Goliad, Texas, stood between the invaders and their plans. Using proven European tactics of artillery barrages and frontal assaults, the French launched repeated attacks on the fortified city. But the Mexicans held their ground, and the French retreated. Thenceforth, the day of this epic showdown came to be observed as the *Cinco de Mayo*, both in Mexico and in Greater Mexico, the area in the United States where people of Mexican origin reside.

Up until about the 1920s, the Cinco de Mayo celebrations served Mexican-origin residents with a private space and time wherein they reaffirmed their identity as *Mexicanos*. People recalled their years in the homeland and exalted Mexico for its valiant men and women. The revelers genuinely celebrated their affinity to Cinco de Mayo patriots such as Ignacio Zaragoza and to other heroes like

CINCO DE MAYO. Celebration of Cinco de Mayo in San Antonio, Texas. (©Bob Daemmrich/The Image Works)

Miguel Hidalgo and Benito Juárez. In segregated zones they proclaimed their pride via open-air oratory, declamations, and recitation of poetry. They dressed up in the native fashions of the homeland, played Mexican music, and sold and bought Mexican foods and delicacies.

Historically, the Cinco de Mayo observations have served other functions in Latina and Latino communities across the United States. As a leisure activity, the Cinco de Mayo commemoration offered a respite, or at least a distraction, from the onus of everyday life. As a group spectacle, it became a force for community solidarity. It rallied folks behind shared goals such as financing, with scant nickels and dimes, the cost of the celebration. The Cinco de Mayo anniversary further acted to reinforce the leadership roles of the fiesta coordinators. Common people anointed these organizers as community spokespersons and endorsed them as intermediaries to bring colonial problems to the attention of city hall bureaucrats. Up until the mid-twentieth century, for instance, it was men and women closely identified with Cinco de Mayo and other community affairs who succeeded, however modestly, in getting school boards to attend to special needs of students or local companies to donate to one barrio cause or another.

The celebrations became more culturally inclusive during the early decades of the twentieth century. Anglo municipal leaders recognized their potential for serving a larger purpose: the fiestas generated revenue for the city through hall rental fees, and they presented the opportunity for a bit of political campaigning. Young Latinas and Latinos undergoing increasing Americanization by then demanded modernization as well. By the 1920s, some of the new American dance crazes had infiltrated the ceremonies. By World War II the Cinco de Mayo celebrations provided the occasion for selling war bonds, and by the 1950s they had become ideal times for raising scholarship monies. In the early twenty-first century the Cinco de Mayo celebrations serve the original purpose of accentuating the celebrants' dual culture, while inculcating lessons of the past to an increasingly Americanized generation.

See also Festivals.

BIBLIOGRAPHY

Alamillo, José M. "More Than a Fiesta: Ethnic Identity, Cultural Politics, and the Cinco de Mayo Festivals in Corona, California, 1930–1950." *Aztlán: A Journal of Chicano Studies* 28 (Fall 2003), 57–85.

De León, Arnoldo. *Ethnicity in the Sunbelt: Mexican Americans in Houston.* College Station: Texas A&M University Press, 2001.

De León, Arnoldo. *Las Fiestas Patrias: Biographic Notes on the Hispanic Presence in San Angelo, Texas.* San Antonio, Tex.: Caravel, 1978.

ARNOLDO DE LEÓN

CISNEROS, HENRY G. (b. 1947), politician. The political trajectory of Henry G. Cisneros, former Secretary of Housing and Urban Development (HUD) in the Clinton administration and former mayor of San Antonio, Texas, can be traced back to a paper that Cisneros wrote as a student at MIT; in it, he outlined what it would take to be elected mayor. By 1985 he was being hailed by local political observers in San Antonio as a "New American" whose charisma as well as political astuteness seemed to be without rival in contemporary San Antonio's political history. In 1993 an article proclaimed him the "Prince of the City." In San Antonio, Anglos, Chicanas and Chicanos, and African Americans alike proudly claimed him as the star that brought fame and fortune to their hometown. His stature cast him as a Chicano political leader who represented the elusive promise of political inclusion. Cisneros was in a position to lead a community that had been excluded for most of the first half of the twentieth century in taking its rightful political place not only in San Antonio but also in state and national politics.

Cisneros was born into a political family. His maternal grandfather, Jose Romulo Munguia, was an immigrant fleeing from the vicissitudes of the Mexican Revolution. Once in San Antonio, Munguia established a print shop in the 1920s that is still operating in the early 2000s in the Westside barrio of San Antonio. His sons, Ruben and Romulo, continued his legacy through the print shop and involvement in local politics. Cisneros's maternal grandmother as well as his mother were also very active in civic activities, adding to the Munguia legacy. In that environment, his father, George Cisneros, a colonel in the army, and his mother, Elvira, provided young Henry Cisneros a middle-class life in the midst of the poverty faced by most Chicano families.

Like many middle-class post–World War II Chicano children, Cisneros attended and graduated from Central Catholic High School. From there he attended Texas A&M, where he was the first Chicano commander of the combined Texas A&M band, and graduated in 1969. After first serving at the age of twenty-one as assistant director of the Model Cities Program in San Antonio, his graduate studies took him to Harvard and MIT. He finished his doctorate in metropolitan administration at George Washington University. While there he also served as a White House intern in the Nixon administration with Elliot Richardson, Secretary of Housing, Education, and Welfare (HEW).

One of Cisneros's most profound attributes is his practical approach to politics. Upon returning to San Antonio in 1974, he aligned himself with the Good Government League (GGL), a nonpartisan slating group established by the economic elite of San Antonio. His climb toward the top of the political ladder began. The GGL, which had since its establishment in 1954 included Chicanos in their successful slates for city council, recruited Cisneros for their

HENRY G. CISNEROS (Paul Buck/EPA Photo/EFE/AP)

election bid in 1975. Despite the setbacks that the GGL faced that year, Cisneros was elected to the city council.

As a city council member, Cisneros took various populist positions on the side of the community on issues dealing with labor, water, education, and housing, among others, endearing himself to the Chicano community. Significantly, in a split vote on the city council on whether to accept a Justice Department order to establish an election plan that would provide more access to the Chicano community or challenge the order in court, Cisneros voted to accept the order. San Antonio thus moved to single-member districts in 1977.

At the same time, Cisneros supported economic development, the sole objective of the conservative GGL and its main constituents, the Greater Chamber of Commerce of San Antonio. Astutely avoiding disastrous confrontations with the economic elite in his various populist positionings, he was able to gain the financial and political support of the economic elite in his first bid for mayor in 1981. He won with over 60 percent of the votes cast, becoming the first Chicano mayor of San Antonio since Juan Seguin was Alcalde of San Antonio in the 1860s. In 1983 he won re-election with over 90 percent of the vote. He remained as mayor until 1989, when he chose not to run again.

As mayor, Cisneros gained national visibility. President Ronald Reagan appointed him in 1983 to the Bipartisan Commission on Central America chaired by Henry Kissinger. Walter Mondale considered him for his running mate in his 1984 bid for president. Cisneros was consistently touted as senatorial and/or gubernatorial material throughout his tenure as mayor. Indeed, Cisneros was identified positively by both conservatives and liberals, depending on where one was observing. But regardless of the position one took, Cisneros was a rising star in the marketplace of politics. Cisneros had, one could argue, astutely maneuvered his political trajectory so that he presented no threat to either the Right or the Left.

As mayor, Cisneros provided a legacy of growth and expansion that is unmatched in San Antonio's history. His leadership brought federal monies to San Antonio that further developed the downtown business district. His efforts brought investments to San Antonio, including a major tourist attraction, Sea World. In addition, his charismatic leadership convinced the voters to vote for the city-financed construction of a major sports arena, the Alamo Dome.

At the same time Cisneros did not forget his electoral base. He took populist positions on issues that favored the poor and the working class. Cisneros's ties to business also helped him establish an education partnership that brought together the city, the local colleges and universities, local business, and various community organizations. This partnership provided financial aid for college to young people in the poorest school districts of San Antonio.

After retiring from public office in 1989, Cisneros dove into private business. With the election of Bill Clinton as president, true to his potential, Cisneros accepted a position as Secretary of Housing and Urban Development (HUD). While there, Cisneros seemed more at ease in taking liberal positions because of the more narrow focus of his department. Cisneros's political rise to the top seemed set until an investigation by the federal government. The investigation centered on his failure to report taxable income and the complications of a love affair, which forced him into retirement from public political life.

An eloquent and passionate speaker, Cisneros continued to be solicited for public speaking engagements in the early 2000s. Whatever view one may take of him, he continues to cast his shadow over the political world.

See also **Political Participation and Political Representation.**

BIBLIOGRAPHY

Cisneros, Henry. "A New Minority Voting Trend—Its Causes and Impact: San Antonio, Texas." Unpublished student paper. Cambridge, Mass., ca. 1972/1973.

Diehl, Kemper, and Jan Jarboe. *Cisneros: Portrait of a New American.* San Antonio, Tex.: Corona, 1985.

Rosales, Rodolfo. *The Illusion of Inclusion: The Untold Political Story of San Antonio.* Austin: University of Texas Press, 2000.

Tolson, Mike. "The Prince of the City." *Hispanic Business*, April 1983, 52–61.

Wolff, Nelson W. *Mayor: An Inside View of San Antonio Politics, 1981–1995*. San Antonio. Tex.: San Antonio Express News, 1997.
                                                    RODOLFO ROSALES

CISNEROS, SANDRA (b. 1954), poet, novelist, and short-story writer. Sandra Cisneros was born in Chicago in 1954 to a Mexican father and a Chicana mother. The only girl among seven children, Cisneros grew up in poverty. Because many of her childhood years were spent moving back and forth between Mexico City and Chicago, she was unable to establish a stable sense of home in either country. The family's frequent relocations were also upsetting for Cisneros because they did not provide her with the opportunity to develop close relationships with other children and contributed to feelings of isolation, shyness, and introversion. She has noted on more than one occasion that her childhood loneliness contributed to her love of reading and that most of her childhood was spent buried in books. She found comfort in such books as Virginia Lee Burton's *The Little House* and Lewis Carroll's *The Adventures of Alice in Wonderland*.

In 1966, when Cisneros was eleven years old, the family's frequent migrations to Mexico ended. Her parents purchased a home in one of Chicago's run-down Puerto Rican communities. Despite their limited formal training, Cisneros's parents instilled the value of education in all their children, encouraging them to study hard. This family value sustained Cisneros and consequently enabled her to move beyond the expectations of the nuns and her less-than-adequate education in one of Chicago's Catholic schools. In high school Cisneros began to express her creativity, writing poetry and working as the editor of the school's literary magazine. After her graduation, she attended Loyola University, where she majored in English and earned a bachelor of arts degree in 1976.

Although she wrote poetry and short stories in high school, Cisneros has suggested that her writing actually started at Loyola University, when she began her formal training in a creative writing class in 1974. Cisneros earned her master of fine arts at the Iowa Writers' Workshop in 1978. She subsequently described the turning point in her writing. While she was in graduate school, her sense of literary alienation was exacerbated by a discussion of Gaston Bachelard's *Poetics of Space*. Her classmates responded instinctively to the text, using their childhood homes as examples, summoned by their memories of homes with attics, stairways, and cellars—dwellings unlike anything Cisneros had ever experienced. Initially the discussion made her doubt her ability and self-worth because it forced her to recall the poverty of her childhood, but later it led her to reconsider her classmates' observations and the class assumptions upon which they were based. Ultimately Cisneros's frustration and awareness of difference fueled an onslaught of anger that led to the discovery of her distinctive literary opportunity and the production of *The House on Mango Street* (1983), a lyrical novel portraying the life of Esperanza, an adolescent growing up in a working-class Puerto Rican neighborhood in Chicago.

Cisneros's experiences in graduate school proved empowering because they inspired her efforts to develop a literary voice capable of representing memories of her inner-city Latino home in Chicago. The creation of the down-to-earth, "nonacademic" voice of a poor Chicana has enabled Cisneros to represent vivid, compelling vignettes about the lives of Latinas from a distinctly female-oriented perspective. *The House on Mango Street*, replete with its nonscholarly voice, has been widely celebrated by critics, teachers, adults, and adolescents alike, apart from earning her the Before Columbus Book Award. This initial recognition of her work was later underscored by international acclaim for her writing and numerous other awards, which include the Lannan Literary Award and the American Book Award and fellowships from the National Endowment for the Arts and the prestigious MacArthur Foundation Fellowship. In addition to writing, Cisneros has worked as a high school teacher, a college recruiter, a counselor for university students, a literature director for the Guadalupe Cultural Arts Center in San Antonio, Texas, and a writer-in-residence at the Foundation Michael Karolyi in Vence, France. She has worked as a visiting professor at California State University, the University of California, the University of Michigan, and the University of New Mexico.

Although in the early twenty-first century Cisneros is noted primarily for her fiction, her poetry has also garnered critical attention. *Bad Boys*, her first collection of poetry, was published in 1980 by Mango Publications, an alternative press in San Jose, California, and *My Wicked, Wicked Ways*, a second volume of verse, was published in 1987 by Third Woman, another independent press in California. Whereas Cisneros once described *The House on Mango Street* as a collection of lazy poems, the sixty poems in *My Wicked, Wicked Ways* resemble short stories that revisit her childhood in Chicago, survey her European travels, and portray the sexual repression and guilt brought about by her strict Mexican and Catholic upbringing. Both books exemplify Cisneros's gift for successfully crossing generic boundaries. The success of these publications caught the attention of the mainstream publishing world, and in 1991 Cisneros signed a contract with Random House to publish her first collection of short stories, *Woman Hollering Creek*, and to reissue *Mango Street* in a Vintage paperback edition.

Sandra Cisneros. (Gene Blevins/CORBIS)

Woman Hollering Creek is unlike her earlier works in that it broadens her geographic focus representing the United States–Mexico borderlands. The region's historic connections to the First and Third Worlds have provided fertile ground for Cisneros to explore and highlight the migration, poverty, discrimination, and cultural vitality of people at the border. The stories in this collection are divided into three sections that are thematically distinct. The first, "My Friend Lucy Who Smells Like Corn," portrays young girls struggling with issues related to indifferent family members, confining cultural traditions, and gender roles. Like *The House on Mango Street*, this section features the voices of inexperienced and somewhat naive little girls shaped by the powerful forces of media and advertising industries on both sides of the Mexico–United States border. The second section, "One Holy Night," features a series of adolescent protagonists confronted with issues of identity and sexuality, again weaving the interconnections and contradictions that characterize the borderland experience. The final section, "There Was a Man, There Was a Woman," features the experiences of adult women protagonists who seek autonomy from patriarchal control and confining cultural

traditions. Overall the tales in this collection feature strong female characters from both sides of the Texas-Mexico border. The success of *Woman Hollering Creek* was followed by Knopf's publication of Cisneros's bilingual picture book *Hairs/Pelitos* (1994), with illustrations by the artist Terry Ybáñez; her third volume of poetry, *Loose Woman* (1994), and a hard-cover edition of *My Wicked, Wicked Ways* (1995).

The MacArthur Foundation Fellowship provided Cisneros with the resources and time to produce her long-awaited second novel, *Caramelo*, published simultaneously in Spanish and English by Knopf in 2002. It is an extraordinary work, bursting with originality and literary flare. In many ways this multigenerational saga of a Mexican Chicano/a family's travels from Mexico to Chicago that culminates with LaLa Reyes's coming of age in San Antonio, Texas, fills in the blank spaces left in all of Cisneros's previous books. Although it is not an autobiography proper, Cisneros has said it is based on truth and on real people, a comment that can probably be made about her complete works thus far.

See also **Chicago; Chicanos and Chicanas; Literature; Mexican-Origin People in the United States** *and* **Poetry.**

BIBLIOGRAPHY

Cisneros, Sandra. "Do You Know Me? I Wrote *The House on Mango Street*." *Americas Review* 15 (Spring 1987): 77–79.

Cisneros, Sandra. "Ghosts and Voices: Writing from Obsession." *Americas Review* 15 (Spring 1987): 69–73.

Madsen, Deborah L. *Understanding Contemporary Chicana Literature*. Columbia: University of South Carolina Press, 2000.

Quintana, Alvina E. *Home Girls: Chicana Literary Voices*. Philadelphia: Temple University Press, 1996.

Saldívar-Hull, Sonia. *Feminism on the Border: Chicana Gender Politics and Literature*. Berkeley: University of California Press, 2000.

Yarborough-Bejarano, Yvonne. "Chicana Literature from a Chicana Feminist Perspective." In *Chicana Creativity and Criticism: Charting New Frontiers in American Literature*, edited by María Herrera-Sobek and Helena María Viramontes. Houston, Tex.: Arte Público Press, 1988.

ALVINA E. QUINTANA

CISPES. *See* **Committee in Solidarity with the People of El Salvador.**

CITIZENSHIP. The development of citizenship in industrial democratic societies, in particular the United States, represents the application of a rule of law that universalized the relationship of the individual to the state. For the average citizen, citizenship represents access to the rights of membership in a society—civil, political, and social—on an equal footing with everyone else. The extension of social rights, which did not come about until the twentieth century, places citizenship at the center of a conflict over the shape and content of society. Moreover, citizenship

CITIZENSHIP. A mass oath of citizenship in Los Angeles, California. (© Jimmy Dorantes/LatinFocus.com)

must be seen from both an immigrant and a native perspective. That is to say, the Latino community represents one of the most transnational communities in the United States—a large part of its demographic growth is in the flow of immigrants, documented and undocumented.

Latina and Latino citizenship in the United States must be considered in the context of a political struggle not only for inclusion, not only in the critical area of social claims, not only in terms of cultural and political identity, but also in the broader global economic context that engulfs the Americas today. How to go about defining who is a citizen is contested. But just as important is how to define what citizenship is about.

Strangers in One's Own Land

War and annexation rather than immigration brought about citizenship for the first Mexicano communities in the southwestern United States. When Texas was annexed in 1845, several thousand residents of Mexican/Texan descent were made citizens. Then in 1848, with the conclusion of the one-sided United States–Mexican War, the signing of the Treaty of Guadalupe Hidalgo conferred citizenship, through Article VIII, to Mexicans who were residents in the Southwest and who so chose. However, Article IX explicitly discusses the remaining Mexicans and their property rights as residents of the ceded territories. It was not until 1912 that New Mexicans gained citizenship.

Moreover, property rights and claims to citizenship were consistently denied through a combination of legislative and judicial decisions. Further complicating the

process was the historic "race war" that pitted the Mexicano landowners, vaqueros, and laborers against the claims made by white settlers. The reality was that citizenship was a negotiable issue and depended on where one found oneself. Throughout the Southwest, Mexicano families with land and power managed to maintain some semblance of citizenship, while Mexicanas and Mexicanos who were landless and poor exercised very little power over their rights to citizenship.

While the common experience of most Tejanos, Nuevo Mexicanos, Arizonanos, and Californios has been one of victims of racial domination and labor exploitation (to the point of genocide in some areas), access to citizenship rights for these various southwestern communities varied from place to place. In some regions, citizens voted; in others they had no access to voting except in controlled settings. In still other areas they were in political power, particularly in some counties of south Texas and in New Mexico.

This mosaic of experiences represents the beginning of a politics in the Chicano community, and it would largely shape the nature of citizenship for Chicanas and Chicanos in the twentieth century. That is to say, while the legal order specified a citizenship that encompassed the rights of Mexicanas and Mexicanos, as for any other group in the United States, the historical process of accumulation, land conflicts, and labor conflicts defined citizenship from place to place.

Given this persistent rejection of them as Americans, Mexicanas and Mexicanos generally found that they were denied any political presence. Indeed, this historical situation led to the coining of the phrase "strangers in one's own land." Further compounding this lack of power over their political and social life was the impact of a closing border, which gradually increased the distance from the Mexican experience.

Another aspect of the experience of Mexicanos and Chicanos that has figured into the definition of citizenship for the Latino community in the United States can be traced to the pervasive transnational political and cultural environment at the beginning of the twentieth century. Regardless of what term was used to describe the community—whether Mexicana Americanas and Mexicano Americanos, Mexican Americans, or Chicanas and Chicanos—the reality was that they found themselves in a transnational situation where their history and, in most cases, their families were connected to Mexico while at the same time their social and cultural reality was rooted in the United States. During that historical period, the border, which had been superimposed on existing communities and economic systems, was still a porous dividing line between the two nations. Along the United States–Mexico border, Mexicanas and Mexicanos from both sides came and went as families, as workers, and, most important as organizations.

As a consequence, to this day the local and community nature of Latina and Latino politics remains a profound legacy. From the beginning of the twentieth century up to and during the World War II period a stark anti-Mexican environment prevailed. In this context, citizenship in its fullest sense of the word, including political rights at the national and state levels as well as property rights in some areas, would not become a practical reality for most Latinas and Latinos until after World War II. In the period leading to World War II, citizenship was less than a reality for most Mexicano families. Poll taxes were imposed in Texas and California until the 1964 Supreme Court ruled them unconstitutional. In some counties in Texas, literacy tests were given to Mexican American voters. On the other hand, in New Mexico a legislative mandate provided ballots, explanations for voting, and other voting-related materials in both English and Spanish upon demand. Thus, whereas New Mexicans (Nuevo Mexicanas and Mexicanos) have enjoyed political representation since the signing of the Treaty of Guadalupe Hidalgo, national political representation for Mexican Americans was not to be a reality for the first two-thirds of the twentieth century. There was no Hispanic caucus in Congress nor, obviously, was there any Latina and Latino agenda.

Indeed, a mosaic of rights and lack of rights existed throughout the Southwest. As a result, in the stead of any clear citizenship rights and the participation that this would normally entail, labor organizations became a major means by which Mexicanas and Mexicanos expressed their political views, claimed their rights, and maintained their cultural and historical integrity. The *mutualista* societies were another important venue through which Mexicano families organized to protect themselves and most important to ensure education for their children and to maintain their history and culture. All told, the venues where citizenship rights and the struggle for those rights occurred continued to be local.

The claim for citizenship, most especially for the right to participate in mainstream politics, came from an emerging urban middle class. Because of the racially exclusive political parties of the time, both Democratic and Republican, the venues they used were civic organizations, the longest lasting being the League of United Latin American Citizens (established in 1929) and the American G.I. Forum (established in 1948), representing veterans. Through these organizations, Mexicanas and Mexicanos mobilized their communities around gaining their civil rights, including the right to an education and the right to vote. The thread that connected all of these groups—labor, mutualista, and middle class—was the anti-Mexican environment in which they found themselves. The struggle for cultural integrity was part of the struggle for citizenship. That is to say, the struggle for political rights was at the same time a struggle for cultural and community rights.

The end result is what could be called a hybrid experience, following W. E. B. DuBois's observation concerning African Americans—both experiences being born out of rejection and absolute marginalization. A "color line" existed inside America's soul, shaping a reality with no real escape or possibility for any kind of real legitimate citizenship until after World War II.

For most Mexicanas and Mexicanos in the United States, the dividing line took a different turn, with the Indian base in northern Mexico becoming the dominant historical and cultural referent point. Also, while most of the Native American tribes were in conflict with both the white settlers and the earlier Spanish settlers along with the mestizo population (mixed Indian and European), the mestizo legacy also contributes to the vicissitudes in the development of citizenship and socioeconomic inclusion for Mexicanas and Mexicanos.

Thus, hybridity emerges from a cultural and racial conflict that has long and deep political roots. For the Mexicano and Mexicana, the "color line" was a border that separated two nations and at the same time imposed on the community a cultural divide that exists into the early twenty-first century. Politics thus has remained local because of the varied experience of resistance and/or accommodation in different places throughout the Southwest. This has profoundly shaped what citizenship has come to mean. In the end it is culture more than race that has shaped that "color line," not only for the Mexicano and Mexicana community but also for most Latino and Latina communities in the United States. And it is that "color line" that has contained Latina and Latino politics at a local level.

As a consequence, the Mexicano and Mexicana community has consistently taken its claims for rights into the arena of culture, including language. Thus, culture has played a profound role in shaping the politics of the community, which in turn has shaped citizenship.

En las Entrañas del Monstro/In the Belly of the Beast

The other major Latino community whose history in the United States was also determined by war and annexation and whose politics has been shaped by this "color line" is the Puerto Rican community. The United States' war with Spain in 1898 led to the annexation of Puerto Rico as a possession and later as a "commonwealth." In a more profound and alienating manner, Puerto Ricans would also become strangers in their own land but for different historical reasons.

The Puerto Rican community's alienation is reflected in the three choices—commonwealth, statehood, and independence—presented to it in past elections. As a commonwealth, which describes their status for most of the twentieth century, it has its own governing institutions but no political representation in Congress or the Electoral College. As a state, it would gain congressional representation and a voice in the Electoral College. But what many Puerto Ricans fear is that the English language would become a political issue. As it is, English is already taught throughout the island. Indeed, efforts to make English the main language in the schools are perceived as tantamount to Americanization and are well under way. Independence, which was a very strong political movement through World War II and into the 1960s, is not a feasible option unless the United States provides the necessary conditions for a transition to that status. In the end, commonwealth has been the hapless choice, since statehood would represent further Americanization of a proud island.

In this context, the "color line" for Puerto Ricans is clearly complicated by two factors that interact to define their American experience. First, the roots of Puerto Rican identity have never been severed from the island. Culture and politics are intimately woven into their political makeup. Thus, the "color line" represents a political reality that persistently maintains an island community in limbo, without the rights and powers of a state and without the self-determination of a sovereign people. Second, the roots of the Puerto Rican community lie in the Caribbean Afro-Latino experience. As a consequence,

Puerto Ricans have been racialized over time. This has compounded the "color line" in ways not always present in the Mexicano and Mexicana experience. That is to say, Puerto Ricans in the United States have faced a "color line" that is both actual and cultural. In the end, because of the close relationship between culture and community, Puerto Rican politics have also been defined at the local level. Citizenship is defined through community.

Consolidation of an American Empire and Its Consequences

Not until the Cuban Revolution in 1959 did any other Latino groups enter the United States in significant numbers. A large Cuban community fleeing Fidel Castro's revolution arrived in and eventually dominated politics and community media in Miami. The propertied, professional class was overrepresented in the first wave of Cuban refugees. Contrary to the migration experiences of both Mexicans and Puerto Ricans, the initial landing of Cubans in Miami was sponsored by the United States in keeping with its anti-Communist policies. However, the size of the Cuban community, like its language and culture, ensured that its political influence remained at the local level. Not unlike Mexican refugees from the Mexican Revolution, the Cubans' initial objective was to return, in this case after successfully overthrowing the Fidel Castro regime. Eventually, Miami, under the economic leadership of a Cuban elite class, became a regional "global city," directing a large share of the financial investment going to Latin America.

The main political impact of the Cuban refugees was in Florida, in particular Miami. Eventually, Cubans did gain a political presence in the federal government. The point, however, is that their politics have for all practical purposes remained local. While class has certainly intervened in their quest for citizenship, one can argue that Cubans also face a "color line" in the sense that their ties to Latin America and the Caribbean have made culture a politically contested site, albeit for different historical reasons than for Puerto Ricans and Mexicans. Nevertheless, this has not altered the local character of the evolving political empowerment in the Cuban community. Cubans entered the United States with a parolee status, since they believed that they would be returning to the island. In 1965, when it became evident that they were here to stay, the U.S. government agreed to adjust their status, resulting in the Cuban Adjustment Act of 1966, which makes every Cuban who lands on U.S. soil immediately eligible for residency status after one year.

Following the ousting of the Arbenz regime in Guatemala in 1954, the landing of U.S. Marines in Santo Domingo (1965), the U.S.–supported coup against Salvador Allende's socialist regime in Chile (1973), the support for a brutal right-wing government in El Salvador, and the funding of the Contras against the Nicaraguan Sandinista regime during the 1980s, identity has loomed paramount in the Latina and Latino experience, especially in the 1990s. This post–World War period, especially the 1970s and 1980s, brought about profound changes in the political experiences of Latinas and Latinos in the United States. First, the military incursions into Latin America during these periods brought in refugees in numbers that have not been seen since the Mexican Revolution at the beginning of the twentieth century. Second, each of these groups reflected different class experiences as well as racial/ethnic experiences. The extreme contrast consists of the Chileans, who came with professional experience, were generally more European, and saw themselves as exiles, and the Guatemalans, who were mainly Indian, working class and poor, and generally part of the undocumented immigration into the United States across the United States–Mexico border.

The Cultural Is Political, the Political Is Cultural

Since 1921, the Mexican American middle class has defined its stake in citizenship from a cultural perspective. In the establishment of the League of United Latin American Citizens in Corpus Christi, Texas, in 1929, their philosophy was that as U.S. citizens Mexicanos and Mexicanas had a right to participate in the political process while at the same time maintaining the right to their cultural heritage. To this day, both goals dominate the organization's mission. They continue to emphasize education as the answer to the problems they face as a community, and they continue to emphasize civic participation as a higher goal than individual self-interest. But more important, they continue to claim cultural space as citizens.

The statement "the cultural is political and the political is cultural" describes the material basis (the social, political, and economic reality) for the local nature of citizenship and the historical struggle to claim rights as well as the political struggle to defend the community from harmful policies instigated at the state and national levels. As to the local nature of citizenship, the political struggle over and defense of cultural space has not been abstract but is anchored in a community. The local became the terrain on which the Mexicano community struggles to maintain its cultural space and at the same time participate as citizens in the political process.

The notion that the political is cultural emerges from a process in which the Mexicano and Mexicana community has had to constantly engage a political and cultural reality that has no knowledge of, nor the sensitivity or political will to address, issues that it faces. The issues that have shaped politics for most Latina and Latino communities include civil rights, political exclusion, union exclusion, and racial discrimination and domination. In the early twenty-first century, these issues have expanded to policy areas that address, among other areas, education (including curriculum content, bilingual education, testing, and so on) and health (diabetes is the most prominent disease, which is seen to be exacerbated by what is referred to as the New World Syndrome). Thus, the political process itself has "culturalized" the politics of citizenship as the community struggles to confront issues from a collective perspective.

Immigration, and the xenophobic reaction to it, has both "culturalized" politics and "politicized" culture. The economic reality of Latina and Latino immigrants does not recognize borders, instead requiring more transnational labor than is legally allowed. The transnational job market created by the global economic activity, while historically a reality that has its roots in the beginning of the twentieth century, clashes directly with the more traditional and provincial view of citizenship defined narrowly from a legal perspective without considering other significant aspects of "citizens" as workers and members of communities. More important, unlike other immigrants Latinas' and Latinos' ties to this land were already rooted in established communities. Another major difference is that while immigration represents economic opportunity for the majority of the Latina and Latino immigrant population, it also represents a continuing cultural and language connection across the Americas. The question today is whether the United States can address the issue of immigration with the seemingly anachronistic laws that govern immigration and legally define citizenship.

The "browning" of America, then, is not simply about skin color; it is about a massive cultural impact on all of its institutions, especially that of citizenship. It is still a major concern for those who see the United States in static, or Anglo Saxon, individualistic, terms. As such, the citizenship of Latinas and Latinos is a contested terrain not simply in legal terms, that is, naturalization, but in cultural terms as well. It remains to be seen how citizenship will evolve in a globalized twenty-first century.

See also **Central Americans; Chicanos and Chicanas; Cuban Americans; League of United Latin American Citizens; Mexican-Origin People in the United States; Puerto Ricans; Treaty of Guadalupe Hidalgo;** *and* **United States–Mexican War.**

RODOLFO ROSALES

CIVIL RIGHTS ACT (1964). The Civil Rights Act of 1964 was aimed at reinforcing constitutional provisions. Decades of de jure (legal) and de facto (custom and practice) discriminatory treatment facilitated segregation in public educational institutions and housing, interfered with the right to vote, maintained unequal employment practices, and in general materially injured the socioeconomic well-being of Latinos and Latinas and other minorities.

Civil rights legislation did not result from an isolated and independent legal thrust but rather stemmed from decades of civil unrest, the deaths of activists, and protests against Jim Crow policies, laws, and traditions. The failure of a state to prosecute civil rights infractions not only benefited perpetrators but also disenfranchised African Americans and Latinos and Latinas. While a few beneficial educational opinions emerged, they highlighted the need to address inequality on the federal level. The impetus behind the act thus highlights societal and legal barriers to the citizenship rights of Latinas and Latinos and other communities of color.

Continuing the course President John F. Kennedy had established, President Lyndon B. Johnson introduced civil rights legislation. But heated debates and an aggressive filibuster by southern representatives derailed its immediate passage. Congress eventually passed the law on July 2, 1964, making it the first major civil rights legislation since Reconstruction. The act established the Commission on Civil Rights and the Equal Employment Opportunity Commission. Subsequent legislation, such as the Equal Employment Opportunity Act of 1972, the Pregnancy Discrimination Act of 1978, and the Civil Rights Act of 1991, enlarged its framework. Several of the legislation's antidiscrimination provisions enabled Latinas and Latinos to challenge discriminatory practices, such as the lynching of African Americans and Chicanas and Chicanos, other forms of brutality, and poll taxes or literacy requirements that precluded minorities from exercising their franchise rights.

Title I of the act prohibits attempts to impede voting rights. It rendered literacy tests illegal and authorized federal officials to monitor elections. To buttress its provisions, the act provides injunctive relief against discriminatory conduct in federal district courts and authorizes the U.S. attorney general to initiate litigation where necessary. Although the act succeeded initially, Latinos and Latinas have confronted increasingly sophisticated legal challenges to their franchise rights.

The act also addresses substantial harm stemming from societal norms and Jim Crow traditions. In many locations Latinos and Latinas could not access railway cars, theaters, restaurants, hotels, or public swimming pools. Title II of the act prohibits discrimination or segregation based on race, color, religion, or national origin that would hinder the "full and equal enjoyment" of the public sphere. Although Title II is crucial in prohibiting discrimination, it nonetheless creates an exemption that protects private clubs or other establishments not open to the public. This provision authorizes the attorney general to institute actions that allow "the orderly progress of desegregation in public facilities."

Segregation practices in the nation's educational institutions also materially injured Latinas and Latinos. Spanish-speaking youth were often tracked into "special education" courses for their linguistic skills or were discouraged from completing their high school educations. Desegregation of public facilities under Title III thus enables Latino and Latina legal challenges against segregation and inequality, but it does not provide for busing or the mechanisms required to expedite desegregation. Efforts to desegregate public schools consequently have failed to match the stated goals of the act, and Latinos and Latinas therefore are more concentrated in segregated school systems than in 1964.

The lack of access to federal programs or federal funding has generated Latina and Latino protests. Title VI of the act prohibits discrimination on the basis of race, color, sex, national origin, or religion in programs receiving federal funds. Title VI, however, fails to provide a basic framework to promote diversity in the disbursal of federal benefits. Accordingly affirmative action plans and policies have sought to increase the diversity of recipients in education, business, government, and other areas supported by federal funds. Yet efforts to diversify the workplace continue to face reactionary legal challenges. Several key legal opinions, moreover, have narrowly redefined and limited the structures of remedies available. Court opinions have introduced restrictive legal standards that redefine discrimination outside the scope and purpose of the legislation. Aggressive legal challenges thereby render diversity programs vulnerable to sustained, concerted, and coordinated legal challenges.

Latinos and Latinas also faced disparate and unequal treatment in urban and rural employment. The promotion of nonminority workers with lesser qualifications over Latinos and Latinas left the latter with little recourse and without the means to challenge discriminatory hiring or hostile employment practices. In contrast, Title VII provides for equal employment opportunities but also encompasses the terms and conditions of employment. Title VII nonetheless excludes employers with fewer than fifteen employees, and narrow legal rulings have eroded gains by requiring increasing degrees of proof of discriminatory treatment in the workplace.

Although they do not constitute a homogenous group, Latinos and Latinas have long employed the act in education, in challenging hostile employment practices, and in addressing the lack of diversity among federal funding recipients. Costly litigation and reactionary challenges to class action suits, however, render group-based remedies vulnerable and have caused a shift to individually addressed litigation.

The act's sections, moreover, retain their own independent and individualized legal tests in determining whether discrimination has taken place and generate further demands of proof for party litigants. Affirmative action and minority set-aside programs that seek to promote diversity in federal policies remain highly contentious issues that succumb to retrenchment policies. Finally, immigration law is facing restrictionist policies that further hinder the enforcement of civil rights laws in Latino and Latina immigrant communities.

In sum, violent action prevented Latinas and Latinos from enjoying all the attributes of U.S. citizenship. The increasingly contested legal terrain demonstrates the need for renewed mobilization of a wide spectrum of the population to enforce the goals of the act. A redirected focus on justice and racial equality for Latinos and Latinas and the nation's other ethnic communities would encourage equal treatment.

See also Affirmative Action; Citizenship; Employment Discrimination; *and* Jim Crow.

BIBLIOGRAPHY

PRIMARY WORKS

Adarand Constructors, Inc. v. Pena, 515 U.S. U.S. 200 (1995).

Civil Rights Act of 1964, Public Law 88-352, 78 Stat 241, codified as amended at 42 U.S.C. § 2000 (2004).

Garza v. County of Los Angeles, 918 F.2d 763 (9th Cir. 1990), cert. denied, 498 U.S. 1028 (1991).

Hopwood v. State of Texas, 78 F.3d 932, cert. denied, 518 U.S. 1033 (1996).

Regents of California v. Bakke, 438 U.S. 265 (1978).

Serna v. Portales Municipal Schools, 499 F.2d 1147 (1974).

Soria v. Oxnard School District Board of Trustees, C.D. Cal. 1974, 396 F. Supp. 539 (1974).

Thornburg v. Gingles, 478 U.S. 30 (1986).

Villanueva v. Carere, 83 F.3d 481 (1996), 85 F.3d 481 (1996).

SECONDARY WORKS

Cameron, Christopher David Ruiz. "How the Garcia Cousins Lost Their Accents: Understanding the Language of Title VII Decisions Approving English-Only Rules as a Product of Racial Dualism, Latino Invisibility, and Legal Indeterminacy." *California Law Review* 85 (1997): 1347–1393.

Johnson, Kevin R. "The End of 'Civil Rights' as We Know It? Immigration and Civil Rights in the New Millennium." *University of California Los Angeles Law Review* 49 (2002): 1481–1511.

Ontiveros, Maria. "To Help Those Most in Need: Undocumented Workers' Rights and Remedies under Title VII." *New York University Review of Law and Social Change* 20 (1992–1994): 607–640.

"The Ties That Bind: Coalitions and Governance under Section 2 of the Voting Rights Act." *Harvard Latino Law Review* 117 (2004): 2621–2642.

GUADALUPE T. LUNA

CLASS. *See* Demographics *and* Census.

CLEMENTE, ROBERTO (1934–1972), Puerto Rican baseball player. With a career that lasted eighteen seasons with the Pittsburgh Pirates and led him to baseball's Hall of Fame, Roberto Clemente's stellar play and fierce pride inspired generations of players from Puerto Rico and other communities in Latin America and the United States. The proud and generous Puerto Rican used the fame and recognition he acquired as a professional ballplayer as a platform from which he aided a number of charitable causes in Pittsburgh, in his native Puerto Rico, and in other Latina and Latino communities. His tragic death while embarking on a humanitarian relief mission to earthquake victims in Nicaragua on December 31, 1972, revealed the depth of his commitment to people regardless of national origin and made him a hero to countless Latinas and Latinos.

The son of Melchor Clemente, a foreman on a sugarcane plantation, and Luisa Walker de Clemente, a homemaker, Roberto Clemente was born on August 18, 1934, in the town of Carolina. The youngest child in the Clemente household, he demonstrated an affinity for baseball at an early age. Developing quickly as a ballplayer, by the age of fifteen he had attracted the attention of teams within Puerto Rico's "Doble A" league, a developmental league for the island's professional league. After a year in the developmental circuit, Clemente signed with Santurce in the Puerto Rican Winter League at the age of eighteen. Although unable to crack Santurce's vaunted starting outfield, which included the future Hall-of-Famer Willie Mays and Negro League star Willard Brown, the young outfielder nonetheless caught the eye of Brooklyn Dodgers scouts. Brooklyn signed Clemente as a "bonus baby," and he spent his first professional year (1954) with Brooklyn's minor-league affiliate in Montreal. Following the 1954 season, the Pittsburgh Pirates drafted away the talented Puerto Rican when the Dodgers failed to elevate him to the big-league squad.

Clemente's prolific hitting (he was the first Latin American to accumulate 3,000 hits), his outstanding fielding, and his powerful throwing arm left their mark on baseball history. He was at his best on baseball's grandest stage, the World Series. Clemente made base hits in all fourteen World Series games in which he appeared, in 1960 and 1971. Pittsburgh's 1971 series against the favored Baltimore Orioles served as a showcase. His clutch hitting, his smart base running, and his fielding electrified fans. After the Pirates won the series, Clemente finally garnered the acknowledgement he had long sought from the North American press, which named him the series' Most Valuable Player.

Clemente's years in the majors were not always smooth. He and other players encountered a new set of challenges that distinguished them from the previous

ROBERTO CLEMENTE. (Bettmann/CORBIS)

generations of Afro-Latinos, whose sole opportunity to play professionally in the United States was in the Negro Leagues. When Clemente made his debut in 1955, Major League baseball was only eight years removed from the start of racial integration and was still dealing with the residue of its segregated past—one quarter of major league teams still had not fielded a black player. During this initial phase of integration, the entry of darker-skinned players like Clemente made the project all the more complex. Dark-skinned Hispanic ballplayers, especially foreign-born ones, also embodied cultural differences that unsettled the expectations of those who only saw them as black.

Although he understood the power the press wielded, Clemente nevertheless spoke frankly with the media, whether it was about his injuries, his views on race relations, or the patriarchal beliefs held by some of those he encountered while playing America's favorite sport. His status among the game's elite did not prevent sportswriters from referring to him as "the dusky flyer," the "lashing Latin," or the "chocolate-covered islander," as journalist Steve Wulf observes in his 1992 retrospective *Sports Illustrated* article. Fiercely proud of being both black and Puerto Rican, as biographer Kal Wagenheim notes, Clemente at times told others that the press treatment made him feel like "a double nigger," accosted for being black and also for being Puerto Rican. In the end, Clemente believed that ultimately he did not play for the approval of the press but rather for the fans. A personal sense of responsibility to the fans and as a black Puerto Rican motivated how he played and guided his off-the-field activities. The Puerto Rican outfielder was not embarrassed by having to sit out a game if he felt physical ailments prevented him from performing at full capacity. Many sportswriters believed Clemente took this to extremes. Some even labeled him a hypochondriac; others questioned his work ethic. The accusations worked to further strain the relationship between the Puerto Rican all-star and the English-language press.

Off the playing field, Clemente worked hard to help the less fortunate, setting a model for all his fellow players in charitable activities and generosity. His tragic death on New Years Eve in 1972 while en route to Nicaragua with relief supplies for earthquake victims marked a significant transition in Hispanic baseball history. Clemente's death signaled the end of a pioneering generation of Latin American–descended players who integrated different leagues and teams throughout the United States. Ironically, his 3,000 career hits became the benchmark of hitting excellence, widely viewed as the standard that virtually guarantees a player enshrinement in the Hall of Fame. Whenever a major leaguer approaches 3,000 hits, fans are reminded of Clemente's legacy, introducing a newer generation of fans to the Puerto Rican star that shone in the constellation of America's homegrown game. In 1972, major league baseball renamed its Commissioner Award, given to the player who best exemplifies sportsmanship, community involvement, and contribution to his team, the Roberto Clemente Award. Just as significant, Puerto Rican and Latina and Latino communities throughout the United States have also commemorated Clemente's legacy by renaming educational and recreational facilities in his honor.

See also **Baseball** *and* **Puerto Ricans.**

BIBLIOGRAPHY

Official Roberto Clemente Web site. www.robertoclemente21.com/
Wagenheim, Kal. *Clemente!* Chicago: Olmstead Press, 1973.
Wulf, Steve. "Arriba Roberto." *Sports Illustrated* 77, issue 27, December 28, 1992, 114–128.

ADRIAN BURGOS

COALITION FOR JUSTICE IN THE MAQUILADO-RAS.

The Coalition for Justice in the Maquiladoras (CJM) is a trinational, nonprofit, nongovernmental coalition based in San Antonio, Texas, composed of organizations from religious, labor, environmental, community, and women's groups in Mexico, the United States, and Canada. Fundamental to the coalition's mission is a commitment to improve working conditions and living standards for workers in the maquiladora industries in Mexico. CJM is committed to democratic processes and coordinated action and strives for a better quality of life, sustainable development, social justice, human rights, and environmental stability in the communities where maquiladora workers live. CJM's actions are carried out wherever transnational corporations violate workers' rights and have a negative effect on the environment by polluting their communities.

Maquiladoras are factories with predominantly U.S. but some Canadian, Asian, and European ownership that produce goods for export, largely to the United States. Over one million Mexican workers are employed in maquiladoras and live in *colonias* (shantytowns) that surround them. They earn on average $45 to $50 per week working on the assembly lines of profitable multinational corporations. Most workers are between the ages of sixteen and twenty-five, although it is not uncommon for girls as young as thirteen to be employed. Workers are forced to meet high productivity quotas with long hours and illegal mandatory overtime. Those who try to stand up for their rights often face intimidation, harassment, and physical violence from the companies and corrupt unions.

The passage of the North American Free Trade Agreement (NAFTA) in 1994 opened the door for multinational corporations to extend their factories from Mexico's northern border into the entire country. A lack of enforcement of labor and environmental regulations on the part of the Mexican government further encourages companies to violate workers rights.

CJM was born in 1989 during the debate over NAFTA from the conviction that a strong coalition of cross-border forces was needed to address the devastating effects of free trade on maquiladora workers. In addition to targeting low wages, CJM has mobilized around health and safety violations and their harmful effects, among them repetitive stress injuries and neurological damage to newborn children due to a lack of protective equipment and to toxic working conditions. CJM places special emphasis on defending the rights of women in the maquiladoras who suffer discrimination, humiliation, and sexual harassment in the workplace.

CJM's programs are premised on the belief that the key to social change lies in empowering workers from all social sectors to educate one another, claim their rights, and organize within and beyond their local communities.

CJM's activities include developing worker-to-worker contacts and bridges among the three countries; holding U.S. corporations accountable for living wages and improved working conditions; supporting shareholder activism in major corporations that operate maquiladoras; and holding workshops and producing educational materials to increase maquiladora workers' knowledge about their rights and giving them the information they need to advocate on their own behalf.

Fundamental to CJM's work has been the Maquiladora Worker Empowerment Project, which holds workshops at the national, regional, and local levels. The workshops, which use popular education techniques, are an important means of raising consciousness and promoting self-sufficiency. Their aim is to "train the trainers," who can then share their knowledge and strategies directly with their grassroots organizations and raise awareness in their own communities, thereby becoming more effective agents for social change. Since its beginning CJM has published pamphlets, among them *The Maquiladora Code of Conduct*—a model for ensuing codes of conduct—*The Issue Is Health, The Market Basket Survey*, and *The Purchasing Power Index*. In 1999 CJM published two volumes of the *Federal Labor Law* manual, written in popular language, that has been an important resource in empowering maquiladora workers to defend their rights.

In 1996 CJM hired its first executive director, a former maquiladora worker, and it became tri national with members from Mexico, the United States, and Canada. CJM has been a pioneer in international multisectoral coalition building, serving in 1997 as a model for the Hemispheric Social Alliance, a coalition of organizations that came together to fight against the Free Trade Area of the Americas. Implicit in the coalition's structure is the conviction that cross-border work is a necessary tool to confront a multinational social problem. CJM has used the coalition's strength to educate Congress and to launch a number of important campaigns. In the early 1990s CJM worked with local leadership in Matamoros, Tamaulipas, Mexico, to carry out a national campaign against chemical corporations, such as the Stepan Company and the Dupont Corporation, that were contaminating local neighborhoods. The prize-winning video *Stepan Chemical: The Poisoning of a Mexican Community* (1992) was produced as a part of this campaign.

CJM also has participated in extensive public education in the United States on the effects of NAFTA and has consistently mobilized members against fast-track legislation. In 1994 CJM joined with other organizations in filing one of the first complaints accepted for consideration before the National Administrative Office (NAO) under the NAFTA labor-side agreements against the Sony Corporation for violations of workers's right to organize. In 2000 the coalition sought justice for the Custom-Trim/Auto-Trim workers in Matamoros and Valle Hermoso, Tamaulipas, with another NAO complaint that addressed health and safety violations. In 1996 a concerted effort among ALCOA workers and CJM members led to higher salaries and concrete improvements in the working conditions inside ALCOA plants. Through the proxy rights of CJM member religious groups, maquiladora workers attended the annual shareholders meeting of ALCOA and denounced the poisoning of workers, unsanitary conditions, and marginal wages. In 2001 CJM committed its support to the Duro Bag workers in Rio Bravo, Tamaulipas, in their struggle for better wages, improved working conditions, and a union of their own choice. On their behalf CJM mobilized twenty-five cities and educated consumers about NAFTA's impact. As the maquiladoras move south in Mexico, CJM joins forces with other groups in the south working to educate workers and create more sustainable economic models.

See also **Border, The; Colonias; Juarez Murders; Maquiladoras;** *and* **North American Free Trade Agreement (NAFTA).**

BIBLIOGRAPHY

Coalition for Justice in the Maquiladoras. www.coalitionfor justice.net/

ROSEMARY HENNESSY AND MARTHA OJEDA

COALITION OF GUATEMALAN IMMIGRANTS IN THE U.S. The Coalition of Guatemalan Immigrants in the U.S. (CONGUATE) was founded in 1998 by a group of community leaders to promote the advancement of Guatemalans in the United States and to support the social and economic development of Guatemala. Historically, the most widespread networks of Guatemalan organizations in the United States emerged during the 1980s and 1990s to organize the community against the war in Guatemala and to support the newly arriving

CENTRO TECUN UMAN

The *Centro Guatemalteco Tecun Uman* was founded in 1998 by a group of Guatemalan immigrants living in New York City. Its mission is to build the leadership capacity of the Guatemalan community and to advocate for changes in immigration policy. The Center offers leadership development programs with information on Guatemalan and U.S. history, political analysis, public policy development, and advocacy and organizing. The Center seeks to engage the community in civic activities that include meeting with members of Congress and other elected officials to advocate for reforms in the immigration system and for immigrant and human rights.

MARICELA GARCIA

FRATERNIDADES GUATEMALTECAS

There are hundreds of Guatemalan Fraternities or hometown associations across the United States, primarily in cities with large concentrations of Guatemalan immigrants such as Los Angeles, Chicago, and Houston. The purpose of these groups is twofold: to maintain a sense of community where members can find support and preserve their culture and traditions, and to raise funds for social development projects in their towns of origin. They support clinics, churches, sport facilities, orphanages, and other projects that benefit the community. In cities where the Guatemalan community has reached a sophisticated level of organizational maturity, the hometown associations are clustered under broader organizations to coordinate their work more effectively. In Los Angeles, the Guatemalan Fraternities Association is an umbrella for twenty-four organizations.

MARICELA GARCIA

refugees. These organizations were critical of the Guatemalan government for launching a war against its own people in order to maintain an economic system that kept the majority of the population impoverished. They also opposed the U.S. policies, including military aid to Guatemala, that contributed to intensifying the war.

The purpose of these organizations ended with the signing of the Peace Agreement in December 1996. While a few redefined their mission, many ceased to exist. Nonetheless there was a vacuum of political power in the community and a need for something new to emerge. The polarization of the various sectors as a result of the war made it difficult for Guatemalans to come together. CONGUATE emerged with a multi-issue and multi-sector agenda attempting to bridge the various expressions and interests of the community. It is important to note that immigrant rights and immigration reform are the most unifying issues among Guatemalans and CONGUATE's priority.

CONGUATE is a membership-based organization. In 2004, the membership consisted of twenty-five organizations working on behalf of the community for legal, charity, cultural, civic, and advocacy purposes. The organizations represent the cultural, ethnic, and socioeconomic diversity of the Guatemalan society. They include social service agencies, hometown associations, chambers of commerce, community-based organizations, and policy and advocacy groups. CONGUATE's member organizations are located in the major U.S. cities where Guatemalans have established roots, including Los Angeles, New York, Miami, Houston, Chicago, and Washington, D.C. The goals of CONGUATE are to strengthen the leadership and organizational capacity of the community, to advocate for federal and local policies that benefit Guatemalans, to support social and economic development in Guatemala, and to build alliances with other sectors that work on similar issues.

GUATEMALAN UNITY INFORMATION ASSOCIATION

The Guatemalan Unity Information Agency (GUIA) is a nonprofit organization based in Los Angeles, California. It was founded in 1997 through the joint efforts of community leaders and the Guatemalan consulate in Los Angeles. Its mission is to empower the Guatemalan and Latina and Latino communities by providing legal, educational, and health-related information and services. The main programs are immigration services, GED (general equivalency diploma) classes, English as a Second Language (ESL) classes, assistance to obtain affordable health care, food distribution, and workshops on topics relevant to the community.

GUIA assists thousands of families with immigration petitions and participates in advocacy activities to pass pro-immigrant policies at the state and federal levels. In 2002, GUIA opened a second office in Miami, Florida.

MARICELA GARCIA

Structurally, CONGUATE has a general assembly composed of all member organizations that annually elects a board of directors. The volunteer board of directors is responsible for the governance and execution of the plans of the organization. The structure includes special interest committees such as Immigration, Commerce, Indigenous, and Youth. Funding to support CONGUATE comes primarily from membership fees.

According to the Organization for International Migration, in 2002 there were approximately 1.2 million Guatemalans living in the United States. The flow of immigrants has been constant and increasing since the 1980s. In 2000, 177,757 Guatemalans entered the United States, legally or without authorization.

Therefore, working on immigrant rights and immigration policy is an essential component of CONGUATE's work. Through coordinated efforts, CONGUATE advocates for immigration reform policies to support family reunification and to allow undocumented immigrants to legalize their status. It encourages policy makers to develop a new generation of immigration policies that take into consideration that the flow of immigrants is inevitable in a global economy, and that the best strategy to decrease migration is to invest in the economic development of the sending countries.

Other important issues in CONGUATE's policy and advocacy agenda are education and health. In order to advance its immigration and civil rights agenda, CONGUATE joins other Latino and Latina groups, dialogues with members of Congress and other policy makers, and organizes community actions. Through its membership base, CONGUATE engages the community in civic participation, including running for local boards, registering to vote, and becoming U.S. citizens.

The transnational experience of the Guatemalan community is reflected in CONGUATE's binational agenda. Ten percent of the Guatemalan population lives in the United States, and their remittances constitute the largest source of income for Guatemala. In addition to family remittances, immigrants send collective donations to support social development projects such as clinics, schools, and orphanages that benefit their towns of origin.

CONGUATE promotes the participation of Guatemalan immigrants in the political discourse in Guatemala. The role of immigrants has become essential for the Guatemalan economy, and their political influence is increasing. Guatemalan immigrants in the United States are financially backing candidates, running for local elections in Guatemala, and demanding the right to vote abroad. The level of political influence that Guatemalan immigrants have reached is reflected in policy changes in Guatemala. Through their advocacy efforts, immigrants have engaged the government in a process to develop an immigration policy agenda that includes the creation of a high level office responsible for developing and implementing immigration policies and programs. For the first time, the Guatemalan Congress introduced a legislative proposal that would authorize Guatemalans the right to vote while living abroad. In addition, President Oscar Berger formed the Vice Ministry of Immigration Affairs, allocated funds to repatriate the corpses of immigrants who die in the United States, and agreed to give immigrants a key role in evaluating the services of the Guatemala consulates.

Furthermore, CONGUATE supports the efforts of community members to establish businesses in the United States. The secretary of commerce assists Guatemalans in organizing chambers of commerce in major cities in order to provide information, offer technical assistance, and develop business networks. Through the secretary of commerce and the chambers of commerce, CONGUATE supports small and medium-size business in Guatemala by finding markets for their products in the United States and promoting investment in Guatemala.

The broad representation of sectors makes CONGUATE a powerful organization, but it also constitutes its greatest challenge. Maintaining the diversity of interests and sustaining the growth of the coalition will depend on the ability of the leadership to negotiate and find agreement among its members to move forward an agenda that benefits the majority of the people in the United States and Guatemala.

See also **Central Americans.**

BIBLIOGRAPHY

Galeano, Eduardo. *The Open Veins of Latin America: Five Centuries of the Pillage of a Continent*. New York: Monthly Review Press, 1973.

Handy, Jim. *Gift of the Devil: A History of Guatemala*. Ontario, Canada: Between the Lines, 1984.

Jonas, Susanne. *Of Centaurs and Doves: Guatemala's Peace Process*. Boulder, Colo.: Westview Press, 2000.

Schlesinger, Stephen, and Stephen Kinzer. *Bitter Fruit: The Untold Story of the American Coup in Guatemala*. Garden City, N.Y.: Doubleday, 1982.

MARICELA GARCIA

CODE-SWITCHING. Estimates indicate that roughly half the world's population is bilingual. Stated differently, "Bilinguals already outnumber monolinguals, [and] it can be expected that this trend will continue in the twenty-first century" (Hamers and Blanc, p. 1). According to Rita Franceschini, "There seems to be more and more evidence that [code-switching] is a language universal in the behaviour of multilingual speakers" (Franceschini, p. 51). "Code-switching" is typically defined as the "alternating use of two or more 'codes' within one conversational episode" (Auer 1998, p. 1), where "codes" refers to distinct language varieties or dialects. Although code-switching is a common linguistic outcome in situations of language contact, prevailing ideologies of linguistic purity make it a disparaged practice in most bilingual communities. Considered a chaotic practice, code-switching is seen by most nonspecialists as a sign of lack of mastery of either or both languages. Even a leading researcher on bilingualism has claimed that the ideal bilingual is someone who is able to switch between languages when required to do so by changes in the situation but who does not switch when the speech situation is unchanged and "certainly not within a single sentence" (Weinreich, p. 73). Specialists, however, recognize code-switching as a functional practice and as a sign of bilingual competence. The results of a groundbreaking study of the phenomenon, for example, provided "strong evidence that code-switching is a verbal skill requiring a large degree of linguistic competence in more than one language, rather than a defect arising from insufficient knowledge of one or the other. The rule governed nature of code-switching is upheld by even the non-fluent bilinguals in the sample" (Poplack, p. 255).

Shana Poplack distinguished three types of code-switching: extrasentential, intersentential, and intrasentential. Extrasentential switching is the insertion of tag elements from one language into an otherwise monolingual discourse in another language. Examples of extrasentential code-switching include the addition of "pues," "tú sabes," or "¿no?" to otherwise monolingual English discourse or "well," "you know," or "okay?" to otherwise monolingual Spanish discourse. Intersentential switching refers to switching at the sentence or utterance boundary, whereas intrasentential switching is characterized by a switch from one language variety to another within a single utterance. The following sentences from Ana Celia Zentella's *Growing up Bilingual* (1997) exemplify these three types of code-switching:

1. *Porque estamos en huelga de gasolina*, right? (Zentella, p. 94).
2. *Vicky me cuida*. She's my babysitter (Zentella, p. 133).
3. Give me a kiss *o te pego* (Zentella, p. 112).
4. Uuuu! an' *en mi casa*, when I was—*cuando yo estaba durmiendo*, to me I saw *unos ojo(-s) pega(d)o/h/ en la pared haciendo así*. Uuuu my God when I saw that, *lo/h/ pelo(-s) se me pararon así* (Zentella, p. 129).

Sentence (1) is an example of extrasentential code-switching, (2) and (3) are both examples of intersentential code-switching, and (4) contains both inter- and intrasentential code-switching. Poplack points out that tag items and single nouns are the easiest elements to switch; they tend to be used emblematically in bilingual contexts, and they are used even by speakers with low levels of bilingual proficiency.

Many theoretical approaches to code-switching have found it necessary to distinguish between code-switching and borrowing. There is great variability in the literature, however, in the definition of borrowings, their distinction from loanwords on the one hand and code-switches on the other, and even in whether a distinction needs to be made. Generally, a borrowing is a single word in one language that is inserted into talk in a second language. Two main criteria have been used to distinguish between code-switching and borrowing and between borrowings and loanwords: distribution of the word throughout the community and integration of the item into the host language's systems of sounds (phonology) and structure (morphosyntax). Loanwords, for example, are generally integrated phonologically and morphosyntactically into the host language, and they may be used by monolingual speakers of the host language with no recognition of their other-language origins. Borrowings, in contrast, may or may not be integrated into the host language; they may be used by proficient bilingual speakers or by incipient bilinguals with only marginal exposure to the other language. Indeed, even in the speech of an individual there may be variation in the integration of lexical items from one usage to the next. Josiane F. Hamers and Michel H. A. Blanc explain that researchers such as Poplack distinguish between code-switching (in which other-language lexical items retain their other-language inflections) and borrowing (in which the lexical items are integrated syntactically, morphologically and—usually but not always—phonologically). They further distinguish nonce borrowing, in which words are spontaneously borrowed on the spot and not widely distributed in the corpus or the community. Hamers and Blanc sum up this problematic terrain by suggesting the following position:

> Borrowing and code-switching are phenomena at either end of a continuum: an established loan-word is a historically transmitted word that has been integrated with the recipient language, while code-switching is a more or less spontaneous, bounded switch from sentences of one language to sentences of another, affecting all levels of linguistic structure simultaneously. Borrowings may look like code-switches in that they retain a foreign status (especially in phonology), while code-switches often resemble borrowings in brevity and in being fitted into the syntax of another language.
>
> (Hamers and Blanc, p. 259)

While some may quarrel with parts of this statement, it is a stance around which some consensus likely exists.

As the preceding discussion may have demonstrated, the terminology used to describe the use of more than one language variety in a single interaction is often confusing and contradictory. Suzanne Romaine, for example, states that "in the study of language contact there has been little agreement on the appropriate definitions of various effects of language contact" (Romaine, p. 124). While the variety of terminological difficulties in the field of code-switching research is beyond the scope of this overview, it is necessary to briefly examine two terms sometimes used in lieu of code-switching—language alternation and code-mixing. Peter Auer uses the term "language alternation" in lieu of code-switching as a "cover term for all instances of locally functional usage of two languages in an interactional episode" (Auer 1984, p. 7). Under the umbrella of language alternation, Auer distinguishes between transfer—the insertion of a discrete conversational structure such as a word, phrase, or sentence—and code-switching—the switch from one language variety to another "tied to a particular point in conversation" (Auer 1984, p. 12). Similarly the term "code-mixing" is sometimes used as an umbrella term to include code-switching and borrowing, but others use the term in opposition to code-switching to describe "a deviation from the norm in each language due to familiarity with two languages" (Hamers and Blanc, p. 58). This concept of code-mixing is similar to the concept of interference or transfer used in discussions of second-language acquisition to describe the practice, sometimes successful and sometimes not, of applying the rules of one's native language to the production of speech in the second language.

Researchers have also problematized the notion of code in code-switching. Susan Gal and Kathryn Woolard explain that "cultural categories of communication, such as named languages, dialects, standards, speech communities and genres, are constructed out of the messy variability of spoken interaction" (Gal and Woolard, p. 129). It has been demonstrated, for example, that whereas one might speak of Spanish-English code-switching, use of the labels "Spanish and English" masks a great deal of heterogeneity. Zentella attempts to make this heterogeneity explicit by specifying the many language varieties that make up the linguistic repertoire of the New York Puerto Rican community she researched. She identifies three varieties of Spanish (Popular Puerto Rican Spanish, Standard Puerto Rican Spanish, and English-dominant Spanish) and four varieties of English (Puerto Rican English, African American Vernacular English, Hispanized English, and Standard New York City English) in the community's linguistic repertoire. Another critique is introduced by Celso Alvarez-Cáccamo, who finds that the conceptualization of the term "code" in code-switching has become synonymous with "language variety" to the detriment of the investigation of the phenomenon; he argues that a clear distinction needs to be made between "code" and "language variety." He prefers to define code as it was originally conceived by Roman Jakobson and others, as an associative mechanism that underlies the production and interpretation of linguistic material. By equating code with language variety, Alvarez-Cáccamo suggests, researchers of the phenomenon have included in their analyses examples of "meaningless codemixing" (that is, speakers are not aware of two separate varieties) and excluded from consideration monolingual data in which switching of codes is found. He argues for keeping the notions of "communicative code" and "language variety" separate, although the equation of these two concepts is still generally accepted in the field.

Approaches to Understanding Code-Switching

There are three basic approaches to examining code-switching: grammatical, sociolinguistic, and interactional. All three approaches in their own ways endeavor to demonstrate the ordered, rule-governed, or patterned nature of what is popularly considered to be a random practice.

The grammatical approach to research on code-switching has focused on the constraints imposed on code-switching by the structure (morphosyntax) of the two language varieties involved. Poplack proposed two central constraints on code-switching. First, the Free Morpheme Constraint states that code-switching may occur after any linguistic unit (morpheme) provided that it is a morpheme that may occur independently or not attached to other morphemes. Second, the Equivalence Constraint states that code-switching may occur at any point where the two language varieties involved are structurally equivalent so that the switch does not violate the grammar of either language. Although these two constraints have generally been supported by subsequent research, they are considered tendencies rather than unbreakable rules. Furthermore, code-switching between two language varieties with few points of structural equivalence may result in a greater tendency to violate the equivalence constraint.

Another approach that has been influential in the study of code-switching from the grammatical perspective is Carol Myers-Scotton's Matrix Language Frame Model (MLF). The MLF Model aims to explain the structure of intrasentential code-switches by positing that, in any code-switched interaction, one language, the matrix language, dominates. Given this assumption, Myers-Scotton proposed two principles: the Morpheme Order principle (the order of morphemes will be that of the matrix language) and the System Morpheme principle (system morphemes, or linguistic units that contain grammatical as opposed to lexical meaning, in intrasentential switching will be from the matrix language). Jeff MacSwan applied the approach of Noam Chomsky's minimalist program to the study of intrasentential code-switching. Put briefly, the minimalist program is a universal theory of language structure in which the structural rules are limited to the lexicon or the inventory of words in the language. The minimalist approach to code-switching therefore views code-switching as the "mixing of two lexicons" during interaction (MacSwan 2000, p. 45). MacSwan argues that there are no specific constraints that govern code-switching (such as those proposed by Poplack or Myers-Scotton) because the same lexical constraints come into play in combining words in bilingual conversation as in monolingual conversation.

Finally, Pieter Muysken differentiates between three types of code-switching (although he prefers the term "code-mixing"): insertion (basically borrowing), language alternation (basically code-switching), and congruent lexicalization (single- and multiword code-switching of lexical and grammatical elements). He relates the use of the three different types of code-switching to speakers' proficiency (for example, speakers who mainly use insertion are likely dominant in one language) and sociolinguistic profile of the bilingual community (for example, communities in which insertion code-switching dominates are likely to have a shorter duration of language contact).

The sociolinguistic approach to code-switching attempts to answer the question of "which bilingual communities show language alternation in which situations and why" (Auer 1984, p. 1). Jan-Petter Blom and John J. Gumperz's "Social Meaning in Linguistic Structure" (1972), the classic study of code-switching practices from a sociolinguistic perspective, examines the phenomenon in a Norwegian town whose linguistic repertoire includes a national language, Bokmål, and a regional dialect, Ranamål. Blom and Gumperz found that each of the language varieties in the community's linguistic repertoire had social significance: the standard variety was associated with education and power, whereas the dialect was

tied to involvement with a local network and association with local norms. This observation led to the proposal of a distinction in bilingual language minority communities between a "we code" used by in-group members with other in-group members to express solidarity in informal situations and a "they code" used by in-group members with both in- and out-group members to signify distance and prestige in more formal situations.

A second sociolinguistic approach is associated with Joshua Fishman, who proposed the concepts of domains and role-relations as a means of connecting individuals' language choices and their communities' patterns of language choices. Domains are centers of social interaction, such as work, family-home, school, or religion-ceremony. Role-relations differentiate within domains (such as the family) between individual speakers (such as grandparents, parents, siblings, and children). By identifying the language varieties used by speakers in different domains and with different role-relations within those domains, one is able to observe, for example, if the bilingual situation appears to be stable (that is, generations using the same language varieties in the same domains) or if a shift in language choice is under way (that is, younger generations using one language variety in more domains and with more role-relations than older generations). According to Fishman, domains and role-relations "reveal the links that exist between micro- and macrosociolinguistics" (Fishman 1986, p. 451).

The interactional approach examines the use of code-switching in conversational interaction. Blom and Gumperz distinguished between two types of code-switching: situational, in which speakers switch due to change of topic, participants, or setting; and metaphorical, in which speakers use a switch to "achieve special communicative effects, while participant and setting remain the same" (Li Wei, p. 15). According to Blom and Gumperz, speakers may use metaphorical code-switching to enact or highlight certain types of social relationships within a conversational interaction. Gumperz points out, for example, that two Chicano or Chicana professionals interacting in English may switch to Spanish at the end of the conversation to highlight their shared ethnic heritage:

A: Well, I'm glad I met you.
B: *Andale pues.*

(Gumperz, p. 59)

The concept of metaphorical code-switching relies on a community's shared association of certain language varieties with certain social groups and places great importance on the direction of the switch (that is, from English to Spanish versus from Spanish to English). Gumperz also described several common discourse strategies bilingual speakers accomplish through code-switching, including highlighting quotations, interjections, reiterations, and message qualification. In this case, the direction of the switch is not as important as the switch itself, which is used as a contextualization cue or a signal to interactants that a change or shift in the ongoing interaction is indicated.

Another interactional approach is the Markedness Model proposed by Myers-Scotton. In this model, Myers-Scotton focused on what she calls the "negotiation principle" underlying all choices of codes in conversational interaction: the speakers' choice of code in every conversational interaction references or indexes the community's language norms (for example, a preestablished set of speakers' rights and obligations) that the speaker wants to "be in force" during the interaction. The unmarked choice in a given situation is the one that is expected, whereas the marked choice is unusual or unexpected and therefore socially and interactionally significant. The interactional significance of unexpected utterances is interpreted by the analyst in light of the sociolinguistic context of the conversation.

Zentella proposed a typology different from that of Myers-Scotton. Zentella examined the impact of factors on code-switches by the five girls and their interlocutors in her corpus of over one hundred hours of spontaneous conversation in three categories that she refers to as on the spot variables, those that could be observed, such as physical setting and linguistic and social identities of the participants; in the head variables, those that include "the shared knowledge of how to manage conversations, how to achieve intentions in verbal interaction, and how to show respect for the social values of the community, the status of the interactants, and the symbolic value of the languages" (Zentella, pp. 82–83); and out of mouth variables, those that relate to the morphosyntactic constraints that impact where intrasentential code-switches tend to occur or not occur. Zentella recognized that these three types of variables do not act independently but rather work together to influence the code-switching practices of the children in El Bloque, a New York Puerto Rican community. Therefore, on the spot variables, such as age and language proficiency, interact with out of mouth variables, such as grammatical acceptability of intrasentential switch points.

Finally, Auer's interactional approach builds on Gumperz's notion of contextualization cue and examines the details of everyday, bilingual conversational interaction (the conversation analysis approach). Auer claims that the sequential, interactional approach (that is, analyzing each utterance in a conversation turn by turn) to the examination of code-switching has the potential to answer a question he considers of primary importance: "If the number of types of language alternation isn't finite, then *how* do participants agree on one interpretation or the other *in loco*?" (Auer 1984, p. 3). This approach represents a departure from the others in two basic ways: it recognizes the conversational dimension of code-switching (rather than studying individual utterances out of their dialogic context), and it reconstructs the procedures that participants in conversation use to interpret code-switching in context. Auer proposed two basic category pairs (code-switching versus transfer and participant-related versus discourse-related) that, he argues, form participants' basic procedural apparatus for interpreting the meaning of instances of language alternation in conversation. These four types of signaling are not meant to be understood as merely a new set of functions, similar to Gumperz's or Zentella's. Rather, they are meant to reflect the participants' procedure for attributing meaning to individual instances of code-switching. Importantly, the four types are not mutually exclusive. Although Auer presented prototypical cases of each type for the purpose of defining them, he explained that in conversation individual instances of code-switching may have multiple meanings.

Spanish-English Code-Switching

While the above discussion outlines the theoretical approaches to code-switching, the focus will now shift to Spanish-English code-switching in U.S. Latina and Latino communities. Code-switching and borrowing have become, for better or worse, a defining characteristic of the U.S. Latino and Latina language varieties popularly referred to as Spanglish. Spanish-English code-switching in the United States is not a monolithic language variety or linguistic practice. Code-switching is sensitive to the norms of different communities and the proficiency of individual speakers. Rene Gingras noted, for example, that particular community norms exist in the evaluation of the grammatical form of code-switched utterances. Particular community norms can develop due to a variety of factors, including the language varieties in contact (for example, the presence or absence of another language variety such as African American English), the length of contact between Spanish and English in the community, the relative prestige of the variety of Spanish and its speakers, and speakers' attitudes toward the majority language and linguistic assimilation.

As seems to be the case in most if not all language contact situations, attitudes toward code-switching tend to be negative. This negative evaluation is not new. Doris Meyer cited the criticism of code-switching in an editorial from *El Tiempo*, a Las Cruces, New Mexico, newspaper from 1894. Monolingual Spanish speakers, for example, tend to disparage contact varieties of Spanish, pointing out their impurity or their lack of intelligibility. Gloria Anzaldúa explained, "Chicanas feel uncomfortable talking in Spanish to Latinas, afraid of their censure. Their language was not outlawed in their countries. They had a whole lifetime of being immersed in their native tongue; generations, centuries in which Spanish was a first language, taught in school, heard on radio and TV, and read in the newspaper" (Anzaldúa, p. 58).

Spanish monolingual speakers are not alone in their criticism of code-switching. Bilingual U.S. Latinas and Latinos also report negative attitudes toward the linguistic practice despite the fact that they themselves may code-switch. Rosa Fernández reported that a young, professional Mexican American woman in her study code-switched frequently during a sociolinguistic interview although she had declared that code-switching was bad, that it was not appropriate in formal settings, and that it was only permissible if a speaker was not proficient in both languages. Eva Mendieta reported that an overwhelming majority of Mexican and Puerto Rican speakers in her sample (from northwest Indiana) felt that there was a difference between the variety of Spanish they spoke and those spoken in Mexico or Puerto Rico, respectively, and half of those who perceived a difference attributed it to interference from English. Roughly half of speakers in her sample described their U.S. variety of Spanish as inferior to or less correct than Mexican or Puerto Rican Spanish. When the local varieties are considered on their own merits, however, and not compared with a distant, monolingual norm, the evaluation tends to be positive. Almeida Jacqueline Toribio, in an examination of the code-switching practices and an evaluation of four bilingual speakers of Mexican heritage from Santa Barbara County, California, found that "despite the low prestige associated with code-switching, covert norms value the duality conveyed by the linguistic alternations. In other words, code-switching is foregrounded in the speech of Latinos such as [one of the participants] because it serves the important function of signaling social identity" (Toribio, p. 115). Carmen Fought found that speakers in her study also evaluated code-switching positively for its potential as a bridge between Spanish speakers and passive bilinguals.

While considered primarily an oral phenomenon, code-switching is also found in a variety of written genres, including literature. According to Yvette Burki, intersentential and intrasentential code-switches are found in the Nuyorican literature she examined. She found that authors use code-switching as a linguistic resource to carry out a variety of pragmatic-discursive functions, agreeing with Gumperz, and poetic functions. In "El sonavabitche," for example, Anzaldúa uses code-switching for both pragmatic-discursive and poetic functions:

Mojados, he says again,
leaning on his chipped Chevy station wagon
Been here two weeks
about a dozen of them.

The *sonavabitche* works them
from sunup to dark—15 hours sometimes.
Como mulas los trabaja
no saben como hacer la perra.
Last Sunday they asked for a day off
wanted to pray and rest,
write letters to their *familias.*
¿Y sabes lo que hizo el sonavabitche?
He turns away and spits.
Says he has to hold back half their wages.

(Anzaldúa, p. 125)

Code-switching is also used in less-formal written genres. For example, the editorial in *Latina* frequently makes use of tag switches and single-noun switches. In a 2003 issue, however, the editorial director Betty Cortina wrote: "The *Latina* staff had just gathered to drink rioja wine, munch on *pastelitos de guayaba con queso* and celebrate the close of this issue, when the sad news arrived. '*Se murió Celia*,' the mother of a staffer tearfully reported when she called to make sure we had heard (Cortina, p. 42). Here Cortina uses both borrowings and code-switches. This language choice serves to direct her discourse to a bilingual (if English-dominant) audience.

Examples of code-switching can be found in theater, such as in the work of Luis Valdez (for example, *Los vendidos*) and Dolores Prida (for example, *Coser y cantar*); in performance art, such as that of Guillermo Gómez Peña (for example, *Border brujo*); in stand-up comedy, such as that of George López (for example, *The Original Latin Kings of Comedy*); and in films from diverse U.S. Latina and Latino communities. For example, in the opening scene of the film *Real Women Have Curves*, Estela, the sister of the protagonist, Ana, leads Ana into a conversation with her mother:

Estela:	Ay, Ana something happened to amá.
Ana:	What happened?
Estela:	I don't know. Come and talk to her.
Ana:	Estela, I always have to do it. You go.
Estela:	She wants you, not me (entering bedroom)
Estela:	Ana's here, amá.
Abuelo:	Buenos días.
Ana:	Buenos días abuelito.
Mamá:	Ayyyy.
Estela:	Say something.
Ana:	Mamá.
Mamá:	What is it?
Ana:	It's Ana.
Mamá:	Ay m'ija, come closer . . . I'm really sick . . . You'll have to make breakfast for the men.
Ana:	Breakfast? Mamá, can't Estela do that?
Mamá:	Estela has a lot of work at the factory . . . Ay, m'ija, I woke up in the middle of the night soaking wet. It was like I was on fire. Aay. . .
Ana:	Okay, mama . . . What's wrong? Is it your legs?

Mamá:	Ay, sí.
Ana:	What about your back?
Mamá:	Ay, sí.
Ana:	And your head?
Mamá:	¡Qué va!
Ana:	And how's your hearing?
Mamá:	¿Qué?
Ana:	Today's my last day of high school, mamá. I'm not going to miss that.
Mamá:	Malagradecida.
Ana:	Ah, so the pain is gone!
Mamá:	I struggle with it just like I struggled to give birth. And raise you. And take care of this family. Sí me duele.
Ana:	I didn't ask you to give birth to me, okay?
Papá:	Ya ya ya ya. Ya estuvo ¿eh?
Mamá:	Estela, what is wrong with your sister? Ándale, ayúdame.

(Cardoso)

In this interaction, English and Spanish are used to construct the characters' identities and personalities. Ana, the teenager, is bilingual, but she prefers English. Although she switches to Spanish to address her grandfather (to indicate respect), she refuses to follow her mother's switch to Spanish and maintains a nonmutual language choice (to indicate rebellion). This interaction includes both participant-related code-switching (for example, Ana's switch to Spanish to address her grandfather) and discourse-related switching (for example, Papá's use of a contrasting language to shift the interaction away from the conflict or Mamá's switch from English to Spanish accompanying a shift from asking Estela's opinion to ordering her to help). The nonmutual language choices of the mother and daughter highlight the conflict between the two.

Code-switching as a linguistic resource is also exploited in a variety of music genres from salsa to hip-hop to regional Mexican music. For example, code-switching is employed in "Estoy enamorada," a song by the Mexican American singer-songwriter Yolanda Pérez in a duet with Don Cheto, a Los Angeles radio personality. Early in the song, Yolanda's boyfriend calls the house, and her father, who doesn't know she has a boyfriend, answers:

Papá:	¿Bueno?
Novio:	Yo, is Yo there?
Papá:	¿Quién?
Novio:	Yolanda, su hija.
Papá:	No no este wrong number. No no ande hablando a esta casa por favor.
Yolanda:	Dad?
Papá:	¿Qué pasó hija?
Yolanda:	Did somebody call?
Papá:	No nadien. Un cholo pero era wrong number.
Yolanda:	What? Pero ¿porqué le colgaste a mi boy friend?

(Pérez)

Again, the nonmutual language choice of the two generations highlights the conflict between father and daughter.

In addition to being used as a resource for constructing characters' identities and relationships, code-switching is also used in a variety of genres for bilingual wordplay directed at a bilingual audience. Whereas this is common in poetry, it is also found in oral discourse, both planned and unplanned. For example, Cheech Marín hosting *The Original Latin Kings of Comedy* opens the show by asking "Aaay ¿qué pasó, El Paso? What's happening?"

Research on code-switching from grammatical, sociolinguistic, and interactional perspectives indicates that it is a rule-governed practice that bilingual speakers use to index identities and relationships, manage conversational interactions, and otherwise respond to the sociolinguistic demands on them as members of bilingual communities. Despite the criticism of code-switching by members of bilingual communities and outsiders alike, it also seems to enjoy a covert prestige as an in-group language practice. Although code-switching is generally considered a spontaneous, conversational phenomenon, it is also used in a variety of planned discourses from music lyrics to stand-up comedy and in written form, both formal and informal.

See also **Anzaldúa, Gloria; Bilingual Education; Bilingualism and Biculturalism; Chicanos and Chicanas; Language and Identity; Mexican-Origin People in the United States; Nuyorican Theater and Poetry; Prida, Dolores;** *and* **Valdez, Luis.**

BIBLIOGRAPHY

Alvarez-Cáccamo, Celso. "From 'Switching Code' to 'Code-switching': Towards a Reconceptualization of Communicative Codes." In *Code-switching in Conversation: Language, Interaction, and Identity*, edited by Peter Auer. London: Routledge, 1998.

Anzaldúa, Gloria. *Borderlands/La frontera*. San Francisco: Aunt Lute Books, 1987.

Auer, J. C. P. *Bilingual Conversation*. Amsterdam: John Benjamins, 1984.

Auer, Peter, ed. *Code-switching in Conversation: Language, Interaction, and Identity*. London: Routledge, 1998.

Blom, Jan-Petter, and John J. Gumperz. "Social Meaning in Linguistic Structure: Code-switching in Norway." In *Directions in Sociolinguistics*, edited by John J. Gumperz and Dell Hymes, 407–434. New York: Holt, Rinehart, and Winston, 1972.

Burki, Yvette. "La alternancia de códigos en la literatura neorriqueña." *Revista internacional de lingüística iberoamericana* 2 (2003): 79–96.

Cardoso, Patricia, dir. *Real Women Have Curves*. HBO/Newmarket Films, screenplay by George Lavado and Josefina López, 2003.

Cortina, Betty. "*Entre nos . . .* : A Few Words from the *Editoras*." *Latina*, September 2003.

Fernández, Rosa. "Actitudes hacia los cambios de códigos en Nuevo México: Reacciones de un sujeto a ejemplos de su habla." In *Spanish in the United States: Sociolinguistic Issues*, edited by John J. Bergen, 49–58. Washington, D.C.: Georgetown University Press, 1990.

Fishman, Joshua. "Domains and the Relationship between Micro- and Macrosociolinguistics." In *Directions in Sociolinguistics: The*

Ethnography of Communication, edited by John J. Gumperz and Dell Hymes, 435–453. Oxford, U.K.: Blackwell, 1986.

Fishman, Joshua. "Language Maintenance and Language Shift As a Field of Inquiry: A Definition of the Field and Suggestions for Its Further Development." *Linguistics* 9 (1964): 32–70.

Fought, Carmen. *Chicano English in Context*. New York: Palgrave, 2003.

Franceschini, Rita. "Code-switching and the Notion of Code in Linguistics: Proposals for a Dual Focus Model." In *Code-switching in Conversation: Language, Interaction, and Identity*, edited by Peter Auer, 51–72. London: Routledge, 1998.

Gal, Susan, and Kathryn A. Woolard. "Constructing Languages and Publics: Authority and Representation." *Pragmatics* 5 (1995): 129–138.

Gingras, Rene. "Problems in the Description of Spanish-English Intra-sentential Code-switching." In *Southwest Areal Linguistics*, edited by Garland Bills. San Diego, Calif.: Institute for Cultural Pluralism, 1974.

Gumperz, John J. *Discourse Strategies*. Cambridge, U.K.: Cambridge University Press, 1982.

Gumperz, John J., and Eduardo Hernández-Chávez. "Cognitive Aspects of Bilingual Communication." In *El Lenguaje de los Chicanos: Regional and Social Characteristics Used by Mexican Americans*, edited by Eduardo Hernández-Chávez, Andrew D. Cohen, and Anthony F. Beltramo, 154–163. Arlington, Va.: Center for Applied Linguistics, 1975.

Hamers, Josiane F., and Michel H. A. Blanc. *Bilinguality and Bilingualism*. 2nd ed. Cambridge, U.K.: Cambridge University Press, 2000.

Li Wei. *Three Generations, Two Languages, One Family: Language Choice and Language Shift in a Chinese Community in Britain*. Clevedon, U.K.: Multilingual Matters, 1994.

MacSwan, Jeff. "The Architecture of the Bilingual Language Faculty: Evidence from Intrasentential Code-switching." *Bilingualism: Language and Cognition* 3 (2000): 37–54.

MacSwan, Jeff. *A Minimalist Approach to Intrasentential Code Switching*. New York and London: Garland, 1999.

Mendieta, Eva. "Actitudes y creencias linguisticas en la comunidad Hispana del noroeste de Indiana." *Hispanic Linguistics* 9 (1997): 257–300.

Meyer, Doris. *Speaking for Themselves: Neomexicano Cultural Identity and the Spanish-Language Press, 1880–1920*. Albuquerque: University of New Mexico Press, 1996.

Muysken, Pieter. *Bilingual Speech: A Typology of Code-Mixing*. Cambridge, U.K.: Cambridge University Press, 2000.

Myers-Scotton, Carol. *Duelling Languages: Grammatical Structures in Codeswitching*. Oxford: Clarendon Press, 1993.

Myers-Scotton, Carol. *Social Motivations for Codeswitching: Evidence from Africa*. Oxford: Clarendon Press, 1993.

Pérez, Yolanda. "Estoy enamorada." *Déjenme llorar*. Compact disc. Los Angeles: Fonovisa, 2003.

Poplack, Shana. "Sometimes I'll Start a Sentence in Spanish y Termino en Español: Toward a Typology of Code-Switching." In *The Bilingualism Reader*, edited by Li Wei, 221–256. London and New York: Routledge, 2000.

Romaine, Suzanne. *Bilingualism*. 2nd ed. Oxford: Blackwell, 1995.

Toribio, Almeida Jacqueline. "Spanish-English Code-switching among U.S. Latinos." *International Journal of the Sociology of Language* 158 (2002): 89–119.

Weinreich, Uriel. *Languages in Contact: Findings and Problems*. New York: Linguistic Circle of New York, 1953.

Zentella, Ana Celia. *Growing up Bilingual*. Malden, Mass.: Blackwell, 1997.

HOLLY R. CASHMAN

COINTELPRO. COINTELPRO is the acronym for a domestic counterintelligence program operated from 1956 to 1971 by the Federal Bureau of Investigation (FBI) and coordinated by the Domestic Intelligence Division. This program was initially devised to disrupt and neutralize the Communist Party of the United States through an aggressive campaign of covert operations. Beginning in the mid-1960s the FBI director, J. Edgar Hoover, expanded the scope of COINTELPRO to "counteract domestic terrorism and conduct investigations of individuals and organizations who threatened terroristic violence" (Federal Bureau of Investigation). The FBI justified the deployment of the draconian COINTELPRO operations to prevent Communist infiltration of "legal mass organizations" but primarily of domestic groups that dissented from government policy. COINTELPRO employed illegal and legal covert measures to "neutralize" and destroy organizations that the FBI identified as a threat to national security. A Senate committee that investigated COINTELPRO reached a radically different conclusion regarding the targets and tactics of the FBI. The committee found that "covert action programs have been used to disrupt the lawful political activities of individual Americans and groups and to discredit them, using dangerous and degrading tactics which are abhorrent in a free and decent society" (U.S. Senate). Over two thousand known COINTELPRO operations were launched against Communists and an array of domestic political organizations and social movements created and led by African Americans, Native Americans, and Latinas and Latinos. A small number of these operations were launched against white supremacists (primarily the Ku Klux Klan). The FBI unilaterally determined whether any domestic political organizations posed a threat to national security and if so whether to authorize COINTELPRO operations.

COINTELPRO, the FBI, and the Chicano/a Movement

The black liberation movement, the Puerto Rican independence movement, and the American Indian Movement (AIM) were singled out for particularly aggressive intrusion. The FBI records that have been released do not indicate the extent to which official COINTELPRO operations were deployed against Chicano and Chicana organizations. Yet the history of the most prominent and militant groups of the Chicano/a movement of the 1960s and 1970s is marked by a systematic campaign of intimidation and disruption by FBI operatives. In fact the vast majority of if not all prominent Chicano and Chicana civil rights and political organizations were subject to FBI surveillance. COINTELPRO operations were directed primarily against those organizations that advocated militant cultural nationalism and national liberation. All the Chicano/a associations targeted by the FBI were legitimate political organizations. Some were committed to social-justice goals through community-building campaigns, others to anti–Vietnam War activities, and others to non-electoral paramilitary but legal political protest to affect public policy. The Chicano/a groups targeted by the FBI included but were not limited to La Raza Unida Party, Centro de Acción Social Autónoma, the Brown Berets, the Crusade for Social Justice, the Chicano National Moratorium, and the United Farm Workers (UFW). The FBI identified some of these legitimate organizations as potential threats to national security and applied the draconian, unconstitutional methods it used in its domestic counterinsurgency operations against the Communists.

One of the earliest targets of particularly aggressive COINTELPRO and police disruption was the Colorado-based Crusade for Social Justice, founded by Rodolfo "Corky" Gonzáles, a charismatic and unusually effective political leader. According to Ernesto Vigil, one of the organization's leaders and its chronicler, the crusade's "rejection of mainstream politics . . . opened the way for a strategy of militant grassroots organizing and independent political action in which Chicanos would decide their destiny independent of institutions controlled by others" (Vigil, p. 26). The FBI became alarmed at the crusade's increasingly successful organizing efforts and its growing notoriety as an effective Chicano/a liberation movement as well as at indications that it was assuming a national leadership role as a dissident organization. The FBI was ever-vigilant about the crusade's international connections to Mexican radical and Communist organizations and to domestic dissident groups, especially AIM. In order to discredit the crusade, the FBI tried to link it to Fuerzas Armadas de Liberación Nacional (FALN), the clandestine Puerto Rican revolutionary organization that was responsible for a series of bombings. The FBI organized a disinformation campaign that spread rumors that the crusade and AIM had acquired weapons and conspired to use them to "kill a cop a day." Attorneys who sought to quash subpoenas served on two crusade members to appear before a federal grand jury investigating FALN argued that the FBI had a "documented history . . . to generally dissipate and discredit efforts of minority groups and civil rights organizations as part of their COINTELPRO program" and that the FBI had "practiced this program against the Crusade for Justice" (Vigil, p. 354). The crusade was infiltrated by FBI operatives and subjected to a relentless campaign of intimidation, which included fabricated charges and the misuse of the judicial process to obtain convictions of the organization's leadership, including Corky Gonzáles. The destruction of the crusade's facilities and continuing legal battles depleted the organization's resources. FBI-perpetrated factionalism and incarceration of its leadership demoralized and ultimately undermined the crusade.

The Brown Berets organization (originally the Young Chicanos for Community Action) was a nonstudent youth organization at the center of the Chicano/a movement. The paramilitary Brown Berets were established in 1967 and like the Black Panthers formulated a radical nationalist cultural perspective. The Berets called for Chicano and Chicana self-reliance and militant opposition to the public authorities that were the source of Chicano and Chicana poverty and oppression. Brown Berets chapters were established nationally, and the organization was pivotal in establishing the National Chicano Moratorium Committee, which organized marches and activities against the Vietnam War. Its history was marked by confrontation with police authorities and the deaths, injuries, and incarceration of many of its members. FBI agents infiltrated many of the local Brown Beret chapters and fomented factionalism and internal discord, which debilitated the organization. In 1972 David Sánchez, the founder and leader of the Brown Berets, announced the dissolution of the movement (which claimed a membership of five thousand in ninety chapters). He faulted the government for "police harassment and infiltration, internal squabbles . . . which ruined discipline" and could lead to bloodshed (Chávez, p. 57).

Chicano and Chicana organizations that did not adopt militant cultural nationalism and avoided confrontation with public authorities were not immune from FBI surveillance and disruption. La Raza Unida Party (RUP) was another important Chicano and Chicana political organization victimized by FBI counterinsurgency operations, including infiltration, harassment, burglaries, and so on. RUP was a legitimate political party that promoted Chicano and Chicana cultural pride and was highly critical of conservative Mexican American organizations (such as the League of United Latin American Citizens (LULAC) and the American G.I. Forum). Although it rejected the relevance of the existing two-party system, RUP was the first ethnic-based political party that fielded candidates for elective office. From the organization's inception in 1970 through its demise in 1981, RUP's leadership was closely monitored by the FBI.

The Centro de Acción Social Autónoma (CASA) was founded by the community activists Bert Corona and Soledad Alatorre in Los Angeles as "a voluntary, democratic mutual assistance social welfare organization" to provide service to undocumented Mexican workers (Gutiérrez, p. 190). By 1975, with a membership in the thousands, it adopted a Marxist-Leninist philosophy and called for international labor unity among the Chicano and Chicana working class and workers in Mexico to organize against multinational corporations. The corporations, CASA told its followers, were responsible for the impoverishment of Latina and Latino workers throughout the hemisphere. The FBI viewed CASA with increased concern, given its growing membership, militant internationalism, and radical critique of capitalism. CASA was infiltrated on the grounds that its activities could violate federal statutes prohibiting seditious conspiracy and advocating the overthrow of the government.

COINTELPRO also initiated illegal infiltration and surveillance of the United Farm Workers Union and its founder, César Chávez, beginning in 1965. The UFW, which was locked in a battle for survival with California growers, was infiltrated by FBI agents, who generated field reports to discredit the organization and sought to link it with Mexican Communist organizations. The FBI shared information with the growers and purposefully failed to investigate the criminal actions of the growers against the union and its impoverished members. The aggressive and extensive covert actions of the FBI and police authorities against dissident Chicano/a organizations severely weakened the vibrant Chicano/a Movement and made its dream of achieving social justice for this portion of the American population elusive.

The FBI and Puerto Rican Independence and New Left Organizations

The FBI has monitored the political activities of Puerto Rican communities in New York and Chicago, ever-vigilant to possible links between independence organizations in Puerto Rico and their sympathizers in the United States. After the 1954 Nationalist Party attack on the U.S. House of Representatives, 250 FBI agents arrested 91 Nationalists in New York. The San Juan FBI office was ordered in 1960 to "exchange ideas relative to tactics and techniques" with the New York bureau "because of the large number of Puerto Ricans residing in New York" and "the fact that" independence organizations were active in the city (Churchill and Wall, p. 71). COINTELPRO targeted the Young Lords and effectively infiltrated the organization and destroyed it by promoting irreconcilable factionalism. The Young Lords member Irís Morales wrote: "Police agents within the organization worked to intensify the differences and natural contradictions that existed among us. Intimidation tactics and beatings silenced opposition." In Chicago, FBI agents blocked and destabilized alliances that were developing between the Black Panther Party and the Young Lords. The Chicago COINTELPRO agent monitored the emerging coalition between the Panthers and the Lords and "would submit appropriate counterintelligence suggestions" (Wolf).

Although the FBI had been involved in Puerto Rico since at least 1936, when it investigated the Nationalist Party, in 1960 Hoover expressed alarm that a resurgent independence movement on the island would establish links with the socialist Cuban government. Speaking before the General

Assembly of the United Nations on September 28, 1960, both Fidel Castro, president of Cuba, and Nikita Khrushchev, leader of the Soviet Union, condemned the United States for the "crime of colonialism" and listed Puerto Rico among the colonized nations of the world. The resurgence in the mid- to late 1950s of organizations committed to Puerto Rican independence was of particular concern to the FBI. Among the most prominent of these organizations, all built in the wake of the virtual eradication of the radical Nationalist Party, were the Puerto Rican Pro-Independence Movement (MPI); the Federation of Pro-Independence University Students (FUPI), a renewed militant Puerto Rican Socialist Party; and Acción Patriotica Unitaria. The FBI seemed convinced that these organizations, which subscribed variously to socialist or Marxist-Leninist philosophies and were avowedly critical of U.S. colonialism or were sympathetic to the Cuban socialist regime, would resurrect the militant Nationalist Party campaign for Puerto Rican independence.

It is in the context of the rapid consolidation of the Cuban Revolution, the growing internationalization of Puerto Rico's political status, and what Socialist Party president Juan Mari Bras called the "dawn of new struggle for independence" (Silén, p. 429) that the FBI began COINTELPRO operations in Puerto Rico to wage an aggressive campaign to eviscerate and render ineffective these independence organizations. In August 1960 Hoover authorized agents in Puerto Rico to undertake a clandestine campaign to "disrupt the activities" of organizations seeking independence "through other than lawful, peaceful means" and informed them that he was "not interested in mere harassment" (Churchill and Wall, p. 68). Puerto Rico was a high priority arena for COINTELPRO operations. The FBI either worked closely or shared information with the Puerto Rican police (which had its own Intelligence Division), U.S. military intelligence, and the Central Intelligence Agency.

By the end of 1962 the FBI expanded its covert action campaign to infiltrate and disrupt the operations of virtually all groups advocating independence, irrespective of whether they advocated peaceful means to achieve this goal. The MPI and FUPI, neither of which advocated the use of violence to attain independence, were the first organizations targeted by COINTELPRO operatives. In 1966 Hoover testified that at least nine proindependence organizations that were seen as a continuous problem for U.S. internal security "were under investigation" (Merrill-Ramírez, p. 260). Mari Bras was a frequent target of harassment and persecution given his centrality to the independence cause and his international stature as an opponent of U.S. colonialism. The COINTELPRO goal was to destroy the independence organizations because their actions were drawing world attention to Puerto Rico's colonial situation and in the process eroding the legitimacy of the U.S.–supported Popular Democratic Party that governed the island.

The FBI planted informers and agent provocateurs in a number of organizations to create discord and confusion among *independentistas*. FBI operatives tried to discredit the movement by linking it with "Communist Cuba," hoping that this would encourage defections. FBI operatives employed blatant tactics of intimidation and misused the police and judicial powers of the Puerto Rican government. According to Rubén Berríos, president of the Puerto Rican Independence Party, COINTELPRO waged "a frontal attack on an entire movement and an entire set of ideals. It is virtually an act of war upon our people's will, determination and rights" (Churchill and Wall, p. 88).

The FBI's long history of violating the civil rights of Puerto Ricans came to light in congressional testimony by Director Louis Freeh, who conceded that the agency had undertaken "egregious illegal action, maybe criminal action. . . . Particularly in the 1960s, the FBI did operate a program that did tremendous destruction to many people" (González). After the suspension of COINTELPRO, the FBI remained deeply involved in combating legitimate independence organizations, which, despite evidence to the contrary, were portrayed as potentially violent revolutionary groups. Throughout the 1970s the independence movement was subjected to a virtual campaign of terrorism that included bombings of Independence Party and Socialist Party headquarters. Mari Bras's son was murdered in 1976. Two young independentistas were murdered in Cerro Maravilla in 1978, provoking a legislative inquiry and accusations that the FBI attempted to obstruct the investigations. According to the reporter and writer Alfred López, during a fifteen-year period (1971 to 1986) over 170 attacks of various types committed against independence movement organizations were documented. The FBI and local police were singularly incapable of investigating the cases and arresting any suspects. In December 1999 Puerto Rican governor Pedro Rosselló revealed that the Police Intelligence Division in a "corrupt practice" had compiled secret dossiers (*carpetas*) on scores of thousands of Puerto Ricans, the vast majority of whom were independence sympathizers. The FBI provided assistance and, reportedly, actual training to local police authorities on surveillance techniques and directed police agents in conducting these clandestine operations.

A long-standing campaign of state-sponsored repression against proindependence organizations and the virtual criminalization of individuals sympathetic to independence help explain the dramatic decline in popular support for self-determination in Puerto Rico during the last half of the twentieth century. Proponents of Puerto Rican independence have paid a high price for their belief that their country is a colony.

See also Brown Berets; Chicano/a Movement; Gonzáles, Rodolfo Corky; Mari Bras, Juan; Puerto Ricans; *and* Young Lords Party.

BIBLIOGRAPHY

Bosque Pérez, Ramón, and José Javier Colón-Morera, eds. *Las carpetas: Persecución política y derechos civiles en Puerto Rico*. Río Piedras, P.R.: CIPDC, 1997.

Chávez, Ernesto. *"Mi raza primero!" (My People First!)*. Berkeley: University of California Press, 2002.

Churchill, Ward, and Jim Vander Wall. *The COINTELPRO Papers*. Boston: South End Press, 1990.

Federal Bureau of Investigation (FBI). *History of the FBI: Vietnam War Era: 1960s–1970s*. www.fbi.gov/libref/historic/history/ vietnam.htm

González, Juan. "FBI Campaign in Puerto Rico Lasted More than 4 Decades." *New York Daily News*, May 24, 2000.

Gutiérrez, David G. *Walls and Mirrors*. Los Angeles: University of California Press, 1995.

López, Alfred. *Doña Licha's Island: Modern Colonialism in Puerto Rico*. Boston: South End Press, 1987.

Merrill-Ramírez, Marie Antoinette. "The Other Side of Colonialism: COINTELPRO Activities in Puerto Rico in the 1960s." PhD diss. University of Texas at Austin, 1990.

"91 Puerto Ricans Rounded Up Here." *New York Times*, March 9, 1954, 1.

Ring, Harry. "FBI Aided Growers in Fight against Farm Workers." *Militant* 59, no. 24 (1995). themilitant.com/1995/5924/ 5924_23.html.

Silén, Juan Angel. *Historia de la Nación Puertorriqueña*. Río Piedras, P.R.: Editorial Edil, 1980.

U.S. Senate, Select Committee to Study Government Operations with Respect to Intelligence Activities. *Final Report: Book II*. April 26, 1976. www.icdc.com/~paulwolf/cointelpro/churchfinalreportIIcd.htm

Vigil, Ernesto B. *The Crusade for Justice: Chicano Militancy and the Government's War on Dissent*. Madison: University of Wisconsin Press, 1999.

Wolf, Paul. COINTELPRO.org. www.icdc.com/~paulwolf/cointelpro/newleft.htm#bpsplit

PEDRO CABÁN

COLÓN, JESÚS

COLÓN, JESÚS (1901–1974), writer. Jesús Colón was born into a working-class family in Cayey, Puerto Rico. At age sixteen he moved to New York, where he worked in a variety of jobs, including "washing dishes, working on the docks, or at the many odd jobs in innumerable factories and shops" (Colón 1993, p. 37). His wide range of jobs allowed him to witness the exploitation and abuse suffered by lower-class and unskilled laborers. Although Colón finished high school in New York and attended two years of college, he was primarily a self-taught individual, a tireless reader, and a collector of books and other written material, such as pamphlets, invitations, newsletters, leaflets, and periodical articles. He became increasingly aware of social, political, and economic issues as he ventured deeper into Anglo-American society.

In 1923 Colón began to publish articles in several New York newspapers, such as *Justicia*, *Gráfico*, *Pueblos*

Hispanos, Liberación, Daily Worker, Worker, Daily World, and *Mainstream.* In 1927 and 1928 he published in *Gráfico* a series of chronicles and some humoristic poems signed with pseudonyms like Miquis Tiquis and Pericles Espada as well as his own name. In these first chronicles, written in Spanish, Colón maintained a position that separated him from the workers and members of his community and that was more in line with the Hispanic journalist elite.

The chronicles Colón signed with the pseudonym of Miquis Tiquis contained strong criticisms of the Hispanic community and its members' behaviors. It is difficult to reconcile the author of those chronicles with the person who later wrote in support of workers and against discrimination and racism toward Hispanics and all people. Edwin Karli Padilla interprets this early period in Colón's work, when his style was close to casual speaking, as his attempt to establish a dialogue with the migrant masses arriving in the United States. But Colón had a limited vision of the lives of Latinos and Latinas in New York, and his point of view changed as he became conscious of the realities immigrants and minorities faced.

The chronicles' main character, Miquis Tiquis, ridicules Latino and Latina immigrants. Padilla mentions that Miquis Tiquis wanted to present the interests of the "collective we." However, Colón did not identify with the audience but judged it with sarcasm. For Colón, Latinos and Latinas were "bullanga latina (a la que) le gusta el brillo. El brillo chillón y bullanguero de los nombres sonoros, los títulos rimbombantes y las modas exageradas [a noisy Latin crowd, fond of glaring names, overstated titles and exaggerated fashions]" (Colón 2001, p. 9). Likewise, Miquis Tiquis exhibits a misogynistic attitude toward Latina women that was shared by several other Hispanic writers of the time, such as Alberto O'Farrill and Julio G. Arce, the latter publishing under the pseudonym Jorge Ulica. Colón, O'Farrill, and Arce held women responsible for Hispanic moral and cultural values, but in actuality these male writers were protecting the privileges they brought from their homelands. Those privileges would be threatened if Latina women patterned their behavior after that of more liberated American women.

While Colón published the Miquis Tiquis chronicles, he also wrote for the same newspaper other chronicles titled "Cartas inmorales a mi novia" and signed them Pericles Espada. These chronicles were a first step toward a writing style intended to create a more serious social awareness. These chronicles, using the fiancée as a metaphor for the homeland, addressed religion, culture, the proletariat, and capitalism. Although Colón stated in the first letter that he intended to produce a dozen, publishing stopped with the fifth letter. In the third letter, which discussed religion, Colón stated that as people evolve and become educated they stop believing in God. His readers,

who were mostly Catholic, were offended and apparently stopped reading these chronicles, causing the letters to suddenly disappear from *Gráfico.*

As Colón became aware of the racism, discrimination, and exploitation suffered by workers in New York City, his writing reflected that awareness, and he became one of the most politically active Puerto Ricans in the city. Typically Puerto Rican writers on the island belonged to an intellectual elite and wrote for a select audience. However, Colón came from humble origins and had joined the workers' cause early in his life in his native Cayey, where he had seen traditional readers in the cigar factories, whose job it was to read to the workers. After 1943 his political awareness reinforced his solidarity with workers, and he wrote about the perils they suffered in New York City. During this second phase Colón published articles in Spanish in *Pueblos Hispanos* and *Liberación* and in English in the *Daily Worker, Worker, Daily World,* and *Mainstream.* English collections of his writings are *A Puerto Rican in New York* (1961) and *The Way It Was and Other Writings* (1993).

The articles published in *Pueblos Hispanos* and *Liberación* addressed the post–World War I social context. Colón radicalized his anticapitalism, his anti-imperialism, and his internationalist stance. Later he changed the language but continued his commitment. Writing in English for the *Daily Worker,* he declared himself an active, militant member of New York's Communist Party, and he continued this involvement until he passed away in 1974.

In 1961 Colón published *A Puerto Rican in New York,* a collection of autobiographical sketches previously published in newspapers. This work has great literary and historic value insofar as it arguably gives birth to a social and literary awareness among Puerto Ricans. As a black Puerto Rican, Colón created an enlightening document about the political status of minorities in the United States not only for his ethnic group but for the whole country. He advocated political awareness among the entire American society. Colón presented the cultural contributions of Puerto Ricans in an attempt to change American perceptions of them.

Published almost twenty years after his death, *The Way It Was and Other Writings* brings together Colón's sketches, chronicles, and other writings. Edna Acosta-Belén and Virginia Sánchez Korrol, as they indicate in the preface, selected the book's contents from the author's archives to stress Colón's relevance for subsequent generations. Colón had indicated that his career could be summarized by four activities, which were reading, studying, organizing, and fighting.

Colón's writings, activism, and leadership made him a role model for future generations. His work is considered a starting point in the development of Puerto Rican literature in the continental United States. He was among the first widely known writers to publish in English about the experiences of the working class and racial discrimination. Colón's writings during the 1940s and 1950s place him among the pioneers of Latino literature. Acosta-Belén's view that "Colón represents the voice of those Puerto Ricans who have made their lives in the United States metropolis" could be expanded to include other Hispanics and even other immigrants who have built communities in the United States (Colón 1993, p. 23).

See also Literature; New York; *and* Puerto Ricans.

BIBLIOGRAPHY

Balestra, Alejandra. "Alberto O'Farrill y Jesús Colón: Dos cronistas en Nueva York." In *Recovering the U.S. Hispanic Literary Heritage*, edited by Ramón Gutiérrez and Genaro Padilla, vol. 4, 133–144. Houston, Tex.: Arte Público Press, 1993–2002.

Barradas, Efraín. *Partes de un todo: Ensayos y notas sobre literatura puertorriqueña en los Estados Unidos*. San Juan, P.R.: Editorial de la Universidad de Puerto Rico, 1998.

Colón, Jesús. *Lo que el pueblo me dice:Crónicas de la colonia puertorriqueña en Nueva York*. Edited by Edwin Karli Padilla Aponte. Houston, Tex.: Arte Público Press, 2001.

Colón, Jesús. *A Puerto Rican in New York and Other Sketches*. New York: Mainstream Publishers, 1961.

Colón, Jesús. *The Way It Was and Other Writings*. Edited by Edna Acosta-Belén and Virginia Sánchez Korrol. Houston, Tex.: Arte Público Press, 1993.

Flores, Juan. *Divided Borders*. Houston, Tex.: Arte Público Press, 1993.

Kanellos, Nicolás. *The Hispanic Almanac: From Columbus to Corporate America*. Detroit, Mich.; London; and Washington, D.C.: Visible Ink Press, 1994.

Padilla, Edwin Karli. "Jesús Colón: Relación entre la crónica periodística, lenguaje, y público." In *Recovering the U.S. Hispanic Literary Heritage*, edited by Ramón Gutiérrez and Genaro Padillo, vol. 3, 371–382. Houston, Tex.: Arte Público Press, 1993–2000.

Sánchez Korrol, Virginia. *From Colonia to Community: The History of Puerto Ricans in New York City*. Berkeley: University of California Press, 1983.

Alejandra Balestra

COLÓN, MIRIAM (b. 1936), actress, director, and producer. Born in Ponce, Puerto Rico, on August 20, 1936, Miriam Colón has been called a legendary pioneer and the grand lady of Hispanic and Latino and Latina theater in the United States. A socially conscious, passionate, and devoted artist, she has attained success not only as a multifaceted performer (stage and film actress) but also as a founding director and producer. Decades of acting and efforts to promote Hispanic theater have made her a powerful presence in both Puerto Rican and U.S. performing and artistic groups. Colón has also been a crusader for the arts and artistic space and opportunities for the Hispanic and Latino/Latina communities. She established herself as a productive film and theater artist, performing fluently in both Spanish and English, while simultaneously founding a theater company and securing a permanent location and

funding for the Puerto Rican, Spanish, and Latin American theater in New York City.

Colón was raised and educated in Puerto Rico. From her working-class parents, who instilled in her an admiration and love for culture, she learned strength and confidence in herself and her work. She discovered her vocation early on, when she first attended a performance. While in high school she began acting in university productions and auditing drama courses. When admitted to the University of Puerto Rico, she had already completed with distinction most of the required courses for the drama curriculum. Her experience with the University of Puerto Rico's Teatro Rodante Puertorriqueño or Puerto Rican Mobile Theater (mirrored in Federico García Lorca's mobile unit La Barraca); the mentorship of pioneering Puerto Rican directors such as Leopoldo Santiago Lavandero, Nilda Martínez, and Victoria Espinoza; her artistic relationship with actors such as Rafael Enrique Saldaña and Lucy Boscana; and her important acting participation with Ramón "Diplo" Rivera in Jack Delano's *Los peloteros* (1953), considered among the best in Puerto Rican film history, were foundational as she began her artistic journey toward reaching traditionally neglected audiences and advancing the opportunities of Hispanics in the United States.

A scholarship from the University of Puerto Rico allowed Colón to study with Erwin Piscator at his Dramatic Workshop and at the Technical Institute in New York. In 1953 she joined the Actors Studio, becoming the first Puerto Rican accepted as a member. That year also marked her debut in New York in two different cultural spheres. First, for the Spanish-language community, on May 7 she performed in the first production in the city of the Puerto Rican writer René Marqués's play *La carreta* (*The Oxcart*). The play, directed by Roberto Rodríguez Suárez and staged at a church, was an immediate success. Second, in December, Colón made her debut on Broadway in *In the Summer House* with Judith Anderson, under the direction of José Quintero.

The success of *The Oxcart*, an emblematic play about the hopes and frustrations of a Puerto Rican family journeying from the countryside to the urban ghetto in San Juan and from there to New York, called for more performances, and the play became popular among the Spanish-speaking audiences until its English debut at the Greenwich Mews Theater in 1966. This experience contributed to Colón's realization of the need for a Spanish-language theater company, and Colón and Rodríguez Suárez founded the Nuevo Círculo Dramático, considered the first company in New York devoted to presenting works in Spanish. Also known as Teatro Arenal, from 1956 to 1958 it staged texts by Ramón Ferreira, García Lorca, Rodríguez Suárez, and Victor Ruiz Iriarte.

As an accomplished film actress, Colón has appeared in *The Blue Diner, All the Pretty Horses, Gloria, Lone Star,*

MIRIAM COLÓN. (CORBIS)

Sabrina, The House of the Spirits, City of Hope, Scarface, Backroads, Isabel La Negra, The Profession of Joel Delaney, One-Eyed Jacks, and *The Appaloosa* (the last two with Marlon Brando). In addition to her impressive film appearances, Colón has over 250 television credits, including *Alfred Hitchcock Presents, Gunsmoke, The Virginian, Bonanza, Dr. Kildare, Ben Casey, The Dick Van Dyke Show, Sanford and Son, Murder, She Wrote, NYPD Blue, Third Watch, Highway to Heaven, America's Most Wanted, L.A. Law, The Bill Cosby Show*, and many others. As a stage actress Colón has performed in *The Boiler Room, Julius Caesar* at the New York Shakespeare Festival, *Simpson Street*, Bertolt Brecht's *Señora Carrar's Rifles*, and others.

However, her most gratifying achievement has been the establishment and successful maintenance of the Puerto Rican Traveling Theater (PRTT). Created in 1967, this company has fulfilled, thanks to Colón's professional leadership, the objectives she originally envisioned: to fill a cultural space in the city by promoting self-awareness and esteem of the targeted Hispanic and Latino/Latina minority audiences; to increase tolerance and understanding among the diverse ethnic components of the city; and to provide free or affordable artistic entertainment to poor communities, expanding their cultural horizons, achieved through its Annual Summer Tour and its touring programs. The theater also has provided artistic vocational training to Latinos and Latinas through the Training Unit of Youth and the Raúl Julia Training Unit. The creation of the Playwrights Unit in 1977 fostered training for actors and provided space for new Latino and Latina authors to stage their texts.

Consistent with Colón's philosophy, the PRTT has presented its productions both in Spanish and in English. The Puerto Rican Traveling Theater, the first Spanish mobile theater in New York, while maintaining its touring commitment, also became the first Hispanic theater to open a space in an Off-Broadway location (Eighteenth Street) and to be reviewed as an Off-Broadway theater. When it moved to Forty-seventh Street, it became the first Hispanic theater in the Broadway district. These locations contributed significantly to Colón's other goals, to reach new Spanish- and English-speaking audiences and to premiere with success plays not only from Puerto Rico but also from Spain, France, the United States, and Latin America.

Colón was the first Hispanic to receive the New York City Mayor's Award of Honor for Arts and Culture (1982) and the Athena Award from the New York Commission on the Status of Women (1985). Other recognitions include an honorary doctor of letters from Montclair State College (1989), the White House Hispanic Heritage Award (1990), the Obie Award for Lifetime Achievement in the Theater (1993), and the Dramalogue Award for Outstanding Achievement in Theatre (1994). She was an ALMA Awards Nominee for the category of Outstanding Actress in a Daytime Drama in 2002.

See also Actors and Actresses; Performing Arts and Theater *and* Puerto Rican Traveling Theatre.

BIBLIOGRAPHY

De la Roche, Elisa. *¡Teatro Hispano! Three Major New York Companies*. New York: Garland, 1995.

Kanellos, Nicolás. *Hispanic Firsts: 500 Years of Extraordinary Achievement*. Detroit, Mich.: Gale, 1997.

Kanellos, Nicolás, ed. *The Hispanic-American Almanac: A Reference Work on Hispanics in the United States*. Detroit, Mich.: Gale Research, 1993.

Maldonado, Adál Alberto. *Portraits of the Puerto Rican Experience*. Edited by Louis Reyes Rivera and Julio Rodríguez. Bronx, N.Y.: IPRUS, 1984. 43–44.

Puleo, Gus. "Living and Working in the Border Town." *Latin American Review* 54 (Spring 1997): 11–18.

Santiago, Hermenegildo. "Miriam Colón-Valle and the Puerto Rican Traveling Theater: A Lifelong Fascination with the Dramatic Arts." *Matices* (New Jersey Department of Community Affairs) 3, no. 2 (Fall 1998): 1, 8–10.

ASELA R. LAGUNA

COLÓN, WILLIE (b. 1950), salsa musician and activist. William Anthony Colón Román, better known in the Latin music world as Willie Colón, was born on April 28, 1950, in Bronx, New York. A second-generation Puerto Rican musician, Willie Colón is a pioneering and founding figure of New York–style salsa music. His early experimentations in the late 1960s and numerous productions as singer, trombonist, composer, and producer for the last forty years have earned him an important place in the history and development of Latino music in the United States and worldwide. Willie Colón has also been an engaged social activist, a television actor and producer, and has run for political office. Indeed, he is most renowned for the unique ways in which he has integrated the expression of social concerns in his musical compositions and arrangements. While he is a common household name among Puerto Ricans on the Island and in the diaspora, and among many U.S. Latinos and Latinas, he has not gained the mainstream visibility among Anglo audiences that other Latino and Latina pop music figures, such as Marc Anthony, Gloria Estefan, and Ricky Martin, have enjoyed. Willie Colón, however, has resisted being part of the music industry's efforts to mainstream salsa music. While he believes that salsa music is a vehicle that unifies Latinos and Latinas throughout the hemisphere and the world, he has also continued to insist that music should speak to the historical experiences and social struggles of local and national Latino and Latina communities in the United States. In his own words, "I guess I'm one of America's best-kept secrets."

Early Career and Influences

Willie Colón's early experiences growing up in the Bronx were far from the fame and glitter of the mainstream Latin music industry. He used to shine shoes on the corner of 138th Street and St. Ann's Avenue in the Bronx. Although he dropped out of high school, most of his musical formation came from the influences at home and in his neighborhood. He has written about the experience of listening to the Latin sounds on the street as he lay in bed at night; that "the night had rhythm." He refers to those outside, neighborhood rhythms coming from the car radios or from the corner jamming sessions as his "rhythmic security force." "The rhythms protected us," he writes, foregrounding the profound psychological and communal meaning that Latin music had for him as a young boy in the Bronx (Collazo, p. 10). He has also credited his grandmother for playing traditional Puerto Rican music at home and for giving him a trumpet at the age of twelve. By age fourteen, Willie Colón had started his first band and by 1967, at age sixteen, he had signed his first contract with the Fania label and produced his first album, *El malo.* Since then, he has recorded more than forty albums and

WILLIE COLÓN. (Scott Gries/Getty Images)

has sold nearly ten million records. In this way, Colón embodied the collective experience of many Latino and Latina artists and writers who were self-taught and became important voices in their respective artistic fields despite their exclusion from educational institutions. Precisely because of this social marginality, they powerfully integrated political and social critiques during their heyday in the 1960s and 1970s while they experimented formally by fusing different genres and forms into a new aesthetic.

Willie Colón's early experimentation with Puerto Rican music exemplifies the fusion and hybrid aesthetic that led to the pan-Latino musical sound that is known as "salsa." By combining traditional Puerto Rican forms, such as *bomba, plena,* and *jíbaro* music, with the sounds of New York jazz, and with an instrumental configuration led by the trombones that created an aggressive, harsh, urban sound, Colón became one of the pioneers, an iconic figure of early salsa music in New York. By age nineteen, he was the third trombonist in the Fania All Stars Orchestra and had become the most important idol in the Fania family. By then, as César Miguel Rondón writes, "the trombones represented salsa" (Collazo, pp. 54–55). While Colón credits his style of trombone playing to the influence of Barry Rogers, the trombonist for Eddie Palmieri's La Perfecta orchestra, and to Mon Rivera, it is important to underscore that New York–produced salsa music differed significantly from traditional Cuban music because of the use of the trombones on the frontline, an instrumental arrangement that gave New York salsa music an urban slant. It is precisely this harsh, urban, aggressive sound, coupled with the self-representation of many of the musicians as brawlers, delinquents, or outlaws, that made this early salsa unacceptable to middle-class, mainstream audiences.

Growth and Stages of Career

Indeed, Willie Colón's persona in the world of salsa music was precisely that of *"El malo"* (The Bad Guy), the title of his first record in 1967. The lyrics of the song—*"el malo de aquí soy yo porque tengo corazón"* (the bad guy here is me because I have a heart)—encapsulate the poetics and politics of this constructed identity. On the one hand, "el malo" was an epithet referring to Willie's reputation as a brawler, but also referring to his interpretive style on the trombone. Thus, the rebelliousness, fueled by his social marginality, was translated into the aesthetic of the trombone, and deemed by many veterans of Latin music as being "unharmonic." The strategy of constructing a violent, aggressive masculinity among Latino musicians and writers—Héctor Lavoe, Pedro Pietri, Miguel Pineiro, and Ismael Rivera, among others—could be seen as an aesthetic that contested the colonial and economic dispossession of the Latino male in the political economy of the inner city, a discourse that preceded the gangsta rap discourse. The titles of Willie Colón's records of the period are indicative of this collective, decolonizing effort: *The Good, the Bad, and the Ugly, The Hustler,* and *Lo Mato.* Yet the foregrounding of this masculinity also had an impact on gender politics, for aggression was also directed at women, as Héctor Lavoe's song, "Bandolera" (produced by Willie Colón) makes disturbingly explicit. César Miguel Rondón, a historian of salsa music, explains that Willie Colón's musical style—rooted in the local—became the style associated worldwide with salsa. His characteristic connection to the barrio and a musical style that was always *"propio, auténtico y efectivo"* (his own, authentic, and effective) (Rondón, p. 79) ironically led to the increasing popularity of salsa music, particularly in the larger Latin American and Caribbean urban centers as well as in New York and other urban Latino cities in the United States. Rondón defines three musical stages in Colón's career:

1. From 1967 to 1971, with the production of *El Malo* and the beginning of his productions with the Fania label;
2. From 1971 to 1973, with the release of *Asalto Navideño* (Christmas Parties), which was one of the best-selling albums produced by Fania, and includes the hit "La Murga" (song from Panama);
3. Willie Colón's band breaks up in 1973, and from 1975 on, Willie Colón initiates more systematic experimentations with Latin American rhythms, including the Puerto Rican bomba and plena, rock, *danzón,* folkloric music, Arabic melodies, Brazilian bossa nova, and with symphonic salsa (*Baquiné de los angelitos negros*). He also develops oppositional salsa, known as "salsa consciente" (salsa with a consciousness). During this period, Colón collaborates with Rubén Blades in the production of *Siembra,* one of the classics of *salsa consciente.*

Collaborations

Some of Colón's most significant achievements were his collaborations with leading singers, such as Puerto Rican Héctor Lavoe during the early stages of his career, Cuban Celia Cruz in the 1980s, and Panamanian composer and singer Rubén Blades during the late 1970s. These recordings exemplify the importance of collective work as a means of contesting the capitalist mandates of individual fame. They also foreground the best of Willie Colón as an instrumentalist, arranger, and producer. With Héctor Lavoe as lead singer, Colón's productions of hits such as "Che Che Colé," "Calle Luna, Calle Sol," "La Murga," and "El Todopoderoso," co-authored by Lavoe and Colón, became hits in their time and, later, salsa classics. Yet the Blades-Colón collaboration has been perhaps the most visible in the history of salsa music. Known as the "Salsa music dynamic duo," Blades and Colón created the *"salsa consciente"* style in the late 1970s. The 1977 *Metiendo Mano* and 1978 *Siembra* include major cuts that articulate strong social, political, and class critiques of Latin American society, as well as anti-imperialist songs such as "Tiburón." Cuts such as "Plástico," "Buscando Guayaba," "Ojos," and "Pablo Pueblo" include lyrics that have undoubtedly become part of the collective unconscious of numerous Latino and Latina listeners in Latin America and the United States. In 1982 Blades and Colón parted ways; in 1995 they collaborated on the production of "Tras la Tormenta" (in reference to their breakup), and on May 3, 2003, they joined forces in a reunion concert in Puerto Rico attended by 27,000 fans.

Since then, Willie Colón has continued to produce records and to arrange music, and remained involved in television acting and media productions. In 1990 Colón released the song "El Gran Varón," which addresses the reality of AIDS and gay sexuality in the Latino community. Other releases, such as *Honra y Cultura, Color Americano,* and *Hecho en Puerto Rico,* offer critical perspectives on the various social, historical, political, and racial experiences of Puerto Ricans in the United States and on the Island within arrangements that continue to fuse diverse Latin American, Hispanic, and international rhythms and styles. In addition, Willie Colón's long-term residency in Mexico City, where he acted in the soap opera *Demasiado corazón* on which he managed a salsa club, has also had an impact on the ways in which his music articulates the intersections between Puerto Rican and Mexican experiences. Songs such as "Lowrider" and "Cumbia Bomba" in *Demasiado corazón* attest to this Puerto Rican–Mexican and inter-Latino space.

Social Activism

The social and political critiques of Colón's music are not just rhetoric or symbolic language. He has been a steadfast and tireless social activist who has advocated for diverse causes, such as banning the use of pesticides, for Vieques during the demilitarization campaign, for Hispanic artists in the United States, as a spokesperson for CARE in Latin America, and on behalf of Puerto Ricans in New York. He ran for a seat in Congress in 1994 and, although defeated, made a point of reaffirming the need for Puerto Ricans and Latinos to become involved in official politics and in voting.

Colón has received numerous awards and recognitions for both his musical achievements and his activist efforts. In addition to the ten gold albums and eleven Grammy nominations, he has been awarded the Chubb Fellowship at Yale University in 1991, a Recognition by the Puerto Rican House of Representatives in 1999, an honorary doctorate from Trinity College in 1999, the EPA Environmental Quality Award for his work on the illegal PSA pesticides in 2001, the Entrepreneur of the Year Award by the Long Island Hispanic Chamber of Commerce in 2002, and the Military Order of the Hawk by the Secretary of the Armed Forces of the Dominican Republic in 2002. Perhaps because of his public criticism against the Miami salsa industry and against Anglo incursions into Latino music, Willie Colón has not been embraced by many in the music industry. However, his focus on the needs and realities of the Puerto Rican and Latino and Latina working-class communities in the United States and in Latin America have gained a place for him as one of the most important voices worldwide in Latin music and as one of the few musicians who have successfully integrated social concerns and critiques with innovative music making.

See also **Blades, Rubén; Bomba; Plena; Puerto Ricans;** *and* **Salsa.**

BIBLIOGRAPHY

Collazo, Roberto G. "The Colón Connection." *The Village Voice* (New York), April 4–10, 2000.
Colón, Willie. "The Rhythms." *The Portable Lower East Side* (New York) (1988): 9–12.
Rondón, César Miguel. *El libro de la salsa: Crónica de la música del Caribe urbano*. Caracas, Venezuela: Editorial Arte, 2000.

FRANCES R. APARICIO

COLONIAS. Colonias generally are subdivisions in unincorporated areas with inadequate infrastructure that are inhabited and built by residents with low incomes. They demonstrate one or more of the following characteristics: unpaved streets, no numbered street addresses, no sidewalks, no storm drainage, no sewers, no or little electricity, no potable water, and no telephone services. Often, colonias are not in compliance with local building codes and regulations. Most colonias are found along the United States–Mexico border and are a result of a lack of land use regulation. At the beginning of the twenty-first century, border states face a critical period. Inadequate infrastructure resulting from unregulated property development has resulted in the creation of over fifteen hundred colonias nationwide. Texas alone has over fourteen hundred colonias. In 1995, the Texas Water Development Board estimated that over 340,000 Texas residents lived in some 1,436 colonias.

Many colonia residents are U.S. citizens or legal permanent residents. They are predominantly Hispanic, young, and unskilled. In general, the educational level of colonia residents is low, and illiteracy is high. The primary language is usually Spanish, which often impedes the understanding of policies, procedures, and legal documents and access to programs to which they are legally entitled. It is estimated that 43 percent of all colonia residents live in poverty.

History of Unregulated Colonia Developments

The development of colonias occurred as early as the 1800s in areas of Doña Ana County, New Mexico, and continues along and beyond the borders of Texas, New Mexico, Arizona, and California. Colonias formed when rural landowners began to divide their land into parcels and to sell those parcels to buyers who received a contract for deed in lieu of a property title. Colonias were often built as the winter homes of migrant agricultural workers. Generally, the land is within a 150-mile radius of the border and is undesirable for agricultural or business development. These lots are sold cheaply because the land is often located outside a municipality where platting is required. This poses a major problem; counties have seen hundreds of unregulated colonias develop over the years.

Arizona Colonias

Arizona denies the existence of colonias. However, the manager of the State Office of Water Quality does acknowledge that some rural housing areas in the state have inadequate water supplies because developers have found a way to circumvent state regulations governing the provision of water services. In many instances, these colonias differ from colonias in Texas and New Mexico since the state has sewage standards that apply to all housing units. Arizona colonias also have adequate housing and roads compared with those in other border states. The main problem that does exist among these subdivisions is unsuitable water systems. The Pima County Community Development Coordinator estimates that about seventeen rural subdivisions and developments in the county have no public water system, and some have no water system at all. Most are located in the eastern part of Pima County around the city of Tucson.

California Colonias

Colonias have been deemed illegal in California, which refers to colonia residents as squatters. The state's "temporary" colonias are a nuisance to those residents who live in expensive areas along the California-Mexico border. Their neighbors have often demanded that the temporary tenements be bulldozed, but usually the residents just rebuild the houses. Unlike colonias in other states, California's colonias are not centered near urban concentrations.

The greatest concentration of colonias is in the southeastern tip of Imperial County, which borders Baja California and Arizona. These colonias have been in existence since the 1930s, when migrants came to work in the fields. According to Rosalind Guerrero of the Calexico Department of Public Works, there are nine colonias in the county. These colonias lack proper sewage and potable water. Since their existence stems from the 1930s and 1940s, the developers cannot be prosecuted as the laws during that time did not require the installation of sewage or drinking lines for subdivisions. Moreover, these areas were platted. In the early twenty-first century, the significant issues of the colonias stem from the environmentally unsafe canals where the residents bathe and draw water for cooking.

New Mexico Colonias

Much of New Mexico's colonia population lives in Dona Ana County, thirty-five miles from the Mexican border. Plots of land platted for subdivision prior to 1990 were exempted from strict waste disposal requirements. In 1997, a loophole in state law that allowed developers to sell unplatted lots without water or utilities was closed. However, mobile homes do not have to meet the same utility standards that built housing does. So stricter housing laws resulted in an increase in the number of mobile homes in the area. As has happened in many other cases, colonia developers found ways to skirt laws intended to put them out of business.

Water and Health Problems in the Colonias

Colonia residents usually experience serious health and water problems. A 1990 General Accounting Office (GAO) study found that out of 842 colonias identified in 6 Texas counties, 503 had access to water systems, and only 3 had access to sewer systems. Additionally, between 4 and 13 percent of households used untreated water for drinking, washing, bathing, and cooking. The 1990 census indicates that incomplete plumbing facilities were found in approximately 50 percent of colonia houses in rural counties and 20 percent of houses in urban counties. Furthermore, incomplete kitchen facilities were found in 40 percent of colonia households in rural counties and 15 percent in urban counties.

As expected given these conditions, the health of colonia residents is quite poor. Frequently, colonia residents have no health insurance. They have a higher incidence of disease and a host of health problems, including gastroenteritis, skin disease, and other water-related problems. Other health studies have found high rates of hepatitis A, salmonellosis, shigellosis, and tuberculosis among colonia residents. Thus, the colonias' living conditions pose a serious threat to the health of their residents.

Colonia Housing

A lack of affordable housing along the border is the primary reason for the proliferation of colonias. Although the price of land within border cities may not be much higher than in rural areas, the purchase of land within a city generally requires the use of traditional financing for which a low-income person may not qualify. Individuals searching for affordable housing alternatives have turned to rural land "developers" who offer financing through what is referred to as a "contract for sale" or "contract for deed."

Under a contract for sale, the purchaser typically enters into a contract to buy a small residential lot (for example, 60 feet by 100 feet) at a low down payment (for example, $100) and a low monthly payment (for example, $100), usually for a total cost of $3,000 to $12,000. However, the purchaser does not obtain the deed of ownership of the property until the contract has been paid in full. The finance rates for these contracts are often as high as 12 to 14 percent. This type of arrangement can lead to abuses. A late payment may be subject to exorbitant penalties or be grounds for foreclosure. Developers have often entered into contracts to sell land with only the promise of basic infrastructure such as paved roads and access to water and sewer. The poor infrastructure in many colonias is the result of broken promises.

Due to the uncertainty of actual ownership of property, financial institutions have been reluctant to finance housing in colonias, and insurance companies have been reluctant to offer coverage. Also, the traditional method of home finance (for example, payments on a monthly basis) is not usually feasible for colonia residents because many are migrant farmworkers with seasonal employment. Colonia residents must often pay for the construction of their homes on a cash basis. For this reason, many residents are only able to finance the construction of their homes on a piecemeal basis, a fact that results in piecemeal electrical connections, indoor plumbing, and heating or habitation in a partially constructed home until completion. For families struggling along the border, the colonias provide a viable option for affordable housing and home ownership.

Colonias as a Form of Affordable Housing

The economy of the border region is a contradictory picture of prosperity and poverty. The jobs created have been in the wholesale and retail trade, service, and manufacturing sectors with typically low wages. Additionally, this region has one of the fastest-growing populations in the country, and although the number of jobs has increased, the unemployment rate remains in the double digits. Together, these factors create a powerful demand for affordable housing. Unfortunately, the market has failed to respond with an adequate supply, thus thousands of low-income families are in a precarious position. For those with extremely low incomes, colonias provide an affordable housing option.

Housing quality. Colonia proliferation has led to some of the worst housing conditions in the nation, often likened to third world living conditions. The Housing Assistance Council estimates that residents of Texas border counties are three times more likely to live in substandard housing than are people in either rural or urban areas nationwide. Most colonia homes are designed and built by the residents, who buy a plot of land from a developer and proceed to build as they are able to afford it. Under a contract for deed, the owners have no equity in their property; therefore, they are not able to take out loans against their property to build or make improvements. As a consequence, they pay cash for materials and often use cheap or scavenged substandard materials, such as old billboards or torn down fences. Rooms are built piece by piece over a period of time, and the families are often forced to live in the completed rooms without bathrooms or kitchens.

Most residents build their homes without input from professionals such as structural engineers, carpenters, or masons. Homes may lack a proper foundation, adequate roofing, or structural support. As a result, colonia houses generally are not built to code or according to any standard. Since most colonias are not constructed within incorporated areas, their builders are not forced to comply with model subdivision rules and building regulations. Colonia homeowners therefore are limited as to any future home improvement loans they might attain.

Water, wastewater, and plumbing. According to the 1990 census, 65 percent of the households in colonia areas do not have public sewage. According to that census, 19 percent do not have public water, more than twice the proportion of households statewide. Additionally, areas with colonias are ten times more likely to lack comprehensive plumbing than are other areas throughout the state.

Affordable Housing Alternatives

Cheap housing alone will not alleviate the complex economic situation of households in colonias. However, without the introduction of effective affordable housing programs, colonias will continue to grow, regardless of laws prohibiting them. Families along the border with a regional median household income of $15,998 and a poverty concentration of 38 percent are forced to find whatever accommodations they can afford.

Federal Programs to Assist Colonias

The 1990 Cranston-Gonzales National Affordable Housing Act required Texas to set aside 10 percent of its annual Community Development Block Grant (CDBG) allocation for colonia-related projects. In 1995, the Texas legislature allocated an additional 2.5 percent of CDBG money to fund five self-help centers to be established in border counties.

Initiatives such as the self-help centers are a big step in a positive direction. The centers provide items such as tools, materials, blueprints, and housing plans and services such as seminars on building techniques and counseling on how to get low-interest loans. Enabling families to contribute toward solving their need for housing can dramatically cut costs and gives them the skills to build their homes correctly, reducing the proliferation of substandard housing. Such a program alone, however, will fail to meet the needs for border families. With the decline in federal housing funding, states will have to create additional methods for providing affordable options for border households.

CDBG is one program of the Department of Housing and Urban Development (HUD). Another major HUD initiative was the promulgation of Colonia Housing Standards. In cooperation with the Federal Housing Administration (FHA), Colonia Housing Standards made many colonia homes eligible for federally insured home loans. Prior to the adoption of the Colonia Housing Standards, most colonia home owners could not get home loans because federal regulations prevented the insuring of loans that bankers might have made to build or improve substandard housing. The HUD Colonia Housing Standards are a waiver that relaxed this regulation and made federally insured loans available to the owners of the better homes in colonias.

The U.S. Department of Agriculture (USDA) had programs in place to improve rural homes. However, many colonias are in the rural outskirts of counties that have metropolitan areas, so they are deemed ineligible for this assistance.

Manufactured Homes Alternative

Another possible solution is manufactured housing. According to the Manufactured Housing Institute, owning a manufactured home is actually less expensive than renting a house or apartment. In 1990, the average manufactured home cost $27,800. By contrast, the average price of a new site-built house was $149,000, and an existing site-built house was $118,000. Whereas the price of site-built homes has increased 7.7 percent annually since 1980, manufactured home prices have increased only 3.8 percent. The median income of mobile home households is $20,026, compared with $30,531 for other households. Manufactured homes appear to be an affordable option for lower-income families.

Community Organizing as a Factor in Improving Colonia Services

Community organizations have been an important factor in improvements in the infrastructure and living conditions of many colonias. At the south end of the Texas-Mexico border, Valley Interfaith organized colonia residents to pressure elected officials to improve colonia housing and water. At the north end of the Texas-Mexico border, a sister organization, El Paso Interreligious Sponsoring Organization (EPISO), worked toward the same end. Both organizations are part of the Texas Industrial Areas Foundation Network, an alliance of organizations that teaches people to help themselves.

These two organizations rallied community members to organize and lobby for water rights. They organized large gatherings of colonia residents to demand that political candidates promise to improve colonia conditions. These organizations directed media attention to colonias, which sometimes shamed local officials into action. This type of media exposure has determined the way the state of Texas responds to the larger issue of colonias across the state.

Proyecto Azteca is another influential community organization. In Spanish, "Azteca" is an acronym for Assembly of Zones of Workers Working in Friendship for Equality in Housing. Many colonia residences are built by the people who live in them. Proyecto Azteca seeks to improve the skills of the residents and to facilitate access to funding and materials with the goal of increasing the quality of the housing and the labor force skills of the residents.

The Future of Colonias

Although the colonias may be an affordable housing option for low-income families along the border, they are by no means a solution to the problem. One out of five border households still faces excessive housing costs. And whereas colonias have provided housing for low-income families, the Texas legislature has enacted laws that stifle the growth of new colonias. Passed in 1995, House Bill 1001 forbids the sale of undeveloped lots. Developers must certify that the water quality and connections, sewer connections or septic tank, and electric and gas connections all meet minimum state standards. In addition, lots already purchased cannot be situated with new gas or electric services unless there are adequate water and sewer services.

The issue of enforcement in Texas and the other states is vital to stopping the proliferation of substandard housing. The Texas Office of the Attorney General has taken bold steps to end the growth of colonias and leads the border states in enforcement. Clearly, Texas has the largest colonia problem, but it also has many innovative solutions. The adoption of strict laws, the development of colonia agencies, state and federal funding, and the prosecution tactics of the attorney general have led to an emphasis on stopping the proliferation of colonias.

In New Mexico, the efforts of local community leaders show that political influence matters. The building of colonia coalitions is increasing the amount of funding and improvement occurring in these communities. Their political force is probably the strongest among the colonia groups in the border states.

Both Arizona and California have similar restrictions in subdivision laws. Nevertheless, colonias exist in these states as well. Clearly, the small numbers of colonias indicate that to a great extent their laws are stopping the proliferation of these substandard settlements. To completely end the existence of colonias or colonia-like housing, however, the nation must recognize the problem and establish national policy to eliminate substandard housing.

Learning More about Colonias

The Forgotten Americans, a documentary about colonia life filmed in the late 1990s, touches on the issues of housing, water, infrastructure, community organizations, self-help initiatives, education, and political jurisdictions. The film premiered at the Smithsonian Institution in March 2000 and was broadcast on PBS in December 2000 and October 2001. The PBS Internet link presents material related to the film.

See also **Arizona; California; Chicanos and Chicanas; Mexican-Origin People in the United States; New Mexico; Poverty;** *and* **Texas.**

BIBLIOGRAPHY

Axel-Lute, Miriam. "In Their Own Hands: Colonias Organize." Shelterforce Online 82, July–August 1995. http://racerelations.about.com/gi/dynamic/offsite.htm?site=http%3A%2F%2Fwww.nhi.org%2Fonline%2Fissues%2F82%2Fcolonias.html.

Battle, Stafford L. "Manufactured Homes: An Affordable Alternative." *Journal of Housing* 47 (November–December 1990): 303–307.

Chahin, Jaime. Children of the Colonias. W. W. Kellogg Foundation. Las Colonias, 2000. http://www.lascolonias.org.

Chapa, Jorge, Jorge del Pinal, and Jesus Garcia. "Enumeration, Housing Characteristics, and Sampling Rates in the Colonias of the Texas Border Area: A Perspective on Census Data." In *1993 Research Conference on Undercounted Ethnic Populations: Proceedings; May 5–7, 1993*, 247–274. Washington, D.C.: Bureau of the Census, 1993.

General Accounting Office. *Rural Development: Problems and Progress of Colonias Subdivisions near Mexico Border*. Washington, D.C.: GAO.RCED-91-37, November 5, 1990.

Holtz, Robert K., and C. Shane Davies. *Third World Colonias: Lower Rio Grande Valley, Texas*. Policy Research Project Report Series no. 72. Austin: Lyndon B. Johnson School of Public Affairs, University of Texas, 1993.

Lyndon B. Johnson School of Public Affairs. *The Health of Mexican-Americans in South Texas*. Austin: University of Texas, 1979.

Lyndon B. Johnson School of Public Affairs, Lower Rio Grand Valley Policy Research Project. *Colonias in the Lower Rio Grande Valley of South Texas: A Summary Report*. Austin: University of Texas, 1977.

O'Hare, William, and Barbara Clark O'Hare. "Upward Mobility." *American Demographics* 15, no. 1 (January 1993): 26–32.

Public Broadcasting Service (PBS). *The Forgotten Americans*. 2000. http://www.pbs.org/klru/forgottenamericans/colonias.htm.

Rosell, Ellen. "New Mexico's Colonias: The Roadrunners Are Coming Home to Roost." Report presented at the Twenty-fifth Annual Meeting of the Urban Affairs Association, Portland, Oregon, May 3–6, 1995. See p. 6.

Selwyn, B. J., et al. "Epidemiological Issues in Family Health along the U.S.–Mexico Border." Report prepared for the Pan-American Health Organization Symposium, "Foundations for the Future: The Health of the Family along the U.S.–Mexico Border," El Paso, Texas, February 17–19, 1993.

Texas Department of Housing and Community Affairs. *1996 State of Texas Consolidated Plan*. 1995.

Texas Department of Housing and Community Affairs. *Texas Colonias: Creating Real Solutions to Poverty*. September 17, 1993.

JORGE CHAPA AND BELINDA DE LA ROSA

COLORADO. In 2000, Colorado had a population of 4,301,261, of whom 17.1 percent, or 735,601, were Hispanic. Between 1990 and 2002 the Hispanic population grew by 73 percent. The 2000 census registers 421,670 speakers of Spanish in the state. Of these, 61 percent are Mexican, less than 2 percent are Puerto Rican, 0.5 percent Cuban, and 36 percent "Other Hispanic." Most of the "Other Hispanic" group probably represents descendants of the Spanish-speaking population that lived in greater New Mexico when the area was forcibly joined to the United States. Supporting this theory is the fact that only about 28 percent of the total Hispanic population is foreign born, while 40 percent of the Mexican population is foreign born.

San Luis Valley

The first permanent European settlement in Colorado is attributed to Spanish American settlers who moved north from New Mexico into the expansive San Luis Valley in 1851 on the basis of land grants. Prior to this, Spanish explorers and merchants had traversed the state, and its indigenous population of Utes was drawn into the economy and society of the northern Spanish frontier. Francisco Vásquez de Coronado and his company crossed the southeastern portion of the state on their trek into the plains. Along his route, trade networks were established with Plains Indians and later with the Anglo Americans of the Mississippi valley along what became known as the Santa Fe Trail. In the early nineteenth century another highway crossed southwestern Colorado, connecting Santa Fe with the Spanish city of Los Angeles, California. As a result, what is now Colorado was part of Spanish, then Mexican, New Mexico, and completely integrated into the economy of the Spanish frontier. The Louisiana Purchase and the United States–Mexican War brought Colorado into the United States by 1848.

The Spanish-speaking population of the San Luis Valley, with its close historical and cultural ties to neighboring northern New Mexico, has been one of the main sources of Colorado's Latino and Latina communities. As the economy of other parts of Colorado grew in part because of mining and agriculture, this population provided migrant labor. It has established communities in the cities of Colorado as well as in many other areas of the Mountain West. Although this migration was caused partly by population growth, it was also due to the alienation of the land from the Hispanic community's farmers, either by private individuals or by the U.S. government. In the latter case, the common lands of the grantees, the shared property of the Hispanic communities, were taken by the federal government for other uses. Conflicts over the disposition of the land grants have served as a focus of organization and social solidarity for the local Spanish American population.

Immigrant Contribution

The railroads that facilitated the export of minerals and agricultural produce from the state also brought in immigrants from Mexico, who established another Latino/Latina community. At one time Colorado produced more than a quarter of the total national production of sugar beets, largely as a result of the presence of Mexican labor. The importance of this agricultural labor force is illustrated by the distribution of Colorado's Latino and Latina population in the early twenty-first century. Although the largest concentrations of Hispanics are found near New Mexico (for example, Conejos county has the highest percentage, at 58.9 percent Hispanic), the other cores of Latino and Latina settlement are in metropolitan Denver and in the plains counties where agriculture dominates the economy. Another significant Hispanic population is found near the resorts of Colorado's mountains, where Latinos and Latinas have become a major work force. Mexican immigrants, as well as other Hispanics, have also provided an important source of labor in Colorado's mines.

Cultural and Political Significance

As the largest city in the state, Denver has long had a significant Latino and Latina population. During the 1960s, the social inequality faced by Latinos and Latinas in Denver served as a springboard for the development of national Chicano consciousness and the Chicano a Movement. In 1967, Denver activist and writer Rodolfo "Corky" Gonzáles wrote the seminal epic poem *Yo Soy Joaquín/I am Joaquin*. It has become part of the canon of Chicano and Chicana literature. The demand for recognition and identity that animates Gonzáles's verse is often credited with creating a social and political movement. Gonzáles hosted the Youth Liberation Conference in Denver in 1969, drawing student leaders from throughout the Southwest. His "Spiritual Plan of Aztlán" claimed that the Southwest was the mythical homeland of the Aztecs, Aztlán. He gave a territory, a history, and an identity to what had before been only a group of hyphenated minorities.

One result of Gonzáles's Crusade for Justice was that Denver became a center for the creation of important Chicano and Chicana art, particularly of the muralist style. The first Chicano and Chicana art gallery in Denver, El Grito de Aztlán Gallery, was located in the Crusade for Justice's headquarters. It produced muralists such as Carlota Espinoza, Emanuel Martinez, Jerry Jaramillo, and Leo Tanguma.

Colorado has also produced other Latino and Latina writers. Poet, educator, and Denver poet laureate Abelardo "Lalo" Delgado is known for many books, including *Chicano: 25 Pieces of a Chicano Mind*. Poet and novelist Gloria L. Velásquez is the author of *I Used to Be a Superwoman*.

Colorado continues to produce Latinos and Latinas of national importance. Federico Peña, who was mayor of Denver from 1983 to 1991, served as U.S. Secretary of Transportation (1993–1997) and as Secretary of Energy (1997–1998) in the cabinet of President Bill Clinton. Democrat Ken Salazar was elected to the U.S. Senate in the 2004 elections, becoming only the fourth Hispanic to serve in that body in the nation's history.

See also Aztlán; Census; Chicanos and Chicanas; Colorado Acequia Association; Crusade for Justice; Demographics; Education; Gonzáles, Rodolfo Corky; Land Grants; Land Rights Council, San Luis, Colorado; Mexican-Origin People in the United States; Murals; New Mexico; San Luis People's Ditch; *and* United States–Mexican War.

BIBLIOGRAPHY

Delgado, Abelardo B. *Chicano: 25 Pieces of a Chicano Mind*. Denver, Colo.: Barrio Publications, 1969.

Deutsch, Sarah. *No Separate Refuge: Culture, Class, and Gender on an Anglo-Hispanic Frontier in the American Southwest, 1880–1940*. New York: Oxford University Press, 1987.

Gonzáles, Rodolfo. *I Am Joaquín/Yo soy Joaquín*. New York: Bantam, 1972.

Kutsche, Paul, ed. *The Survival of Spanish American Villages*. Colorado Springs, Colo.: Colorado College, 1979.

Quintana, Frances Leon. *Pobladores: Hispanic Americans of the Ute Frontier*. Aztec, N.M.: F. L. Quintana, 1991.

Van Ness, John R., and Christine M. Van Ness, eds. *Spanish and Mexican Land Grants in New Mexico and Colorado*. Manhattan, Kans.: Sunflower University Press, 1980.

Velasquez, Gloria L. *I Used to be a Superwoman*. Houston, Tex.: Arte Público Press, 1997.

Weber, David J. *The Mexican Frontier, 1821–1846: The American Southwest under Mexico*. Albuquerque: University of New Mexico Press, 1982.

DAVID CLARK KNOWLTON

COLORADO ACEQUIA ASSOCIATION. The Colorado Acequia Association (CAA) is a grassroots organization that was legally formed in 1998 when the leaders of the individual *acequias* in southern Colorado's Culebra watershed gathered to address the legal and social battles that many acequias were facing individually. The CAA was formed because the acequias can fight the onslaught of modern industrialism more effectively as a group. The organization focuses on protecting the watershed and preserving the historic acequia family farms that are a natural and cultural heritage. The CAA works to prevent speculators and other outsiders from confiscating, buying, or grabbing water that has kept the acequia farms from perishing.

The acequias in the Culebra watershed represent about 280 family farms, and most of these have been in the same families for more than 100 years. These acequia farmers and small ranchers have attained a legacy as sustainable practitioners with a long history of stewardship of land and water. They are also known for their seed-saving traditions and the incredible variety of native crops (including corn, bean, and squash), many of which are now marketed to the organic niche.

However, acequia farmers have to adapt to change, including the influence of agricultural markets, and the CAA seeks to address this as well. For example, between roughly 1910 and 1940 the trend for many farmers in the area was to grow not only traditional crops like corn, beans, and squash but also commercial row crops such as cabbage, lettuce, broccoli, and other cool-weather crops. In the early twenty-first century most of the Culebra watershed ranchers are in the cattle market; there are no great riches, but cows have kept the ranches alive.

Many *dichos* (aphorisms) abound when it comes to describing the values that inform the farmers' lifestyles and the situation the acequias have had to endure with little apparent technology and virtually no money. The double jeopardy occurs when the new technologies overtake the proven old ones that have served the acequias so well. The acequias have adapted to the capitalist society, but there are many legal loopholes and situations that pose harm and difficult dilemmas for them. For example, in the old days when cash was in short supply and families were huge, the labor required to make the waterways run was provided by the *parciantes* (water rights stakeholder and user). Now the ditch fees or assessments involve the hiring of labor, with money being paid to contractors who use modern-day backhoes to dredge and clean the ditches. The bad part is that involving the community of all parciantes in the maintenance and operation of acequias is becoming rarer. The *mayordomo* and the contractor begin to be the only two people that are involved with crucial acequia projects, and the basic democracy of the system begins to falter. The community is no longer involved. The checks and balances system is lost where the capitalist economy corrupts the acequia system and its governance structures. The CAA thus works to preserve and revive the customary practices and traditional law of the acequia institution as a form of local democratic self-government.

A sense of community works, and that is why the acequia system has been around for such a long time. Whether one preaches a capitalist voice or that of a more socialized society, the workability of the acequias has been protected by the community of the parciantes. One cannot underestimate the power of money, but to keep a well-managed acequia, money must play a minor role and community a much larger one, with maintenance accomplished by each parciante taking care of his or her own section of the ditch. Money has a tendency to separate the parciantes from the acequia. There is an old adage, "El pastor sabe mas de las borregas que el dueño" (The shepherd knows more about the sheep than the owner). In a similar way, the acequia system works best when one maintains these forms of mutual aid and cooperative labor, and this is another important mission of the CAA.

Finally, the acequias are renowned for the ecological benefits they provide, such as wildlife habitats, including wetlands and woodlands; riparian corridors that prevent wind erosion and protect water quality; and the provisioning of wild edible and medicinal plants. Thus an important objective of the CAA is to promote the restoration and protection of the watershed and its ecological integrity. Acequia farmers recognize that "Sin agua no hay vida" (Without water there is no life) and therefore support the work of the CAA to protect and restore the ecology of the watershed. Consequently the CAA considers itself an organization dedicated to environmental justice but with a bioregional or place-based vision in its philosophy of land and water ethics.

See also Acequias; Agroecology; Culebra Coalition; New Mexico Acequia Association; *and* San Luis People's Ditch.

BIBLIOGRAPHY

Peña, Devon G., and Joseph C. Gallegos. "Local Knowledge and Collaborative Environmental Action Research." In *Building Community: Social Science in Action*, edited by Philip Nyden et al. Thousand Oaks, Calif.: Pine Forge Press, 1997.

Peña, Devon G., and Joseph C. Gallegos. "Nature and Chicanos in Southern Colorado." In *Confronting Environmental Racism: Voices from the Grassroots*, edited by Robert D. Bullard. Boston: South End Press, 1993.

JOSEPH C. GALLEGOS

COMEDY AND HUMOR. Like many aspects of the Latino and Latina experience in the United States, the development of comedy and humor reflects the dual cultural consciousness that characterizes Latino and Latina identity. While most contemporary Latino and Latina humorists poke fun at life in the United States, many of the elements in their comedic repertoires derive from Latin American and Hispanic Caribbean traditions. Many artists, particularly those who work in film, television, and stand-up comedy, have integrated their Latino and Latina perspectives into mainstream comedic genres, thus appealing to a broad, multicultural audience. However, comedy and humor remain viable means of representing a distinct Latino and Latina identity and often serve to raise political awareness as well as articulate social protest.

Theories and Definitions

There is an infinite number of reasons why people laugh, from the involuntary physical excitement of tickling to the self-conscious laughter of embarrassment. Although claims are often made that this or that person lacks a sense of humor because he or she rarely laughs, contemporary biologists argue that humor is a genetic characteristic of humankind necessary for health and survival. One's sense of humor develops in response to social and cultural influences, such as family, community, and nation. The ability to laugh at others and at oneself also depends on the particular context in which an object or event is perceived as humorous. For these reasons, two people may perceive the same object in completely different ways. Similarly, what may cause a roomful of people to laugh on one particular occasion may not produce the same results at another time. Because humor is so subjective and so dependent on context, what may cause one person to double over in laughter may cause another to turn away in disgust or indifference.

Despite the near impossibility of establishing a standard for what is funny, philosophers, psychologists, anthropologists, and literary critics have for centuries attempted to discover the common element in comedy and humor. In

Plato's *Philebus*, Socrates argues in a dialog with one of his students that laughter arises from a mixture of malice and pleasure, since one enjoys seeing the misfortune of the weak and ignorant. Aristotle reaffirms this notion in his *Poetics* when he describes comedy as the "imitation of people who are worse than average." These early philosophers contributed to what is known as the Superiority Theory of laughter, the "sudden glory" of which Thomas Hobbes wrote in his *Leviathan* (1651). This theory contends that people are in constant struggle and that they take joy in the follies of others as a way to confirm their own moral superiority.

Much ethnic humor operates in this way, and Desi Arnaz's character on the *I Love Lucy* show epitomizes the laughable Latin who mixes up popular sayings and provokes laughter with his heavy accent. A more recent comedic performer, John Leguizamo, has exploited ethnic humor to undermine the Latino and Latina inferiority complex in his one-man shows *Mambo Mouth* and *Spic-O-Rama*. He parades onstage ethnic stereotypes of Latinos and Latinas and performs an exorcism of their power to shame the community into invisibility. His characters unapologetically display their shortcomings to the audience so that those who laugh at them do so not from a sense of moral superiority but from the shock of self-recognition in the characters' follies.

Henri Bergson, in his famous philosophical study *Laughter: An Essay on the Meaning of the Comic* (1900) ascribes a social function to the Superiority Theory, arguing that laughter acts as a form of corrective against "mechanical inelasticity" that is encrusted onto living things. In other words, people laugh at others who have taken on the mechanical characteristics of a puppet or an automaton in their deeds or ways of thinking. This version of the Superiority Theory sheds light on Luis Valdez's play *Los Vendidos* (1967), which satirizes various Chicano and Chicana stereotypes by portraying them as inanimate puppets that come to life when their owner and salesman, Honest Sancho, snaps his fingers for his potential client, Miss Jimenez. The play subverts the assimilated Mexican American's sense of superiority over the Chicano and Chicana stereotypes when it is revealed that the puppets are really the masters of their owner and their own fates. The audience laughs at the mechanized behavior of the stereotypes but also laughs at the folly of Honest Sancho and Miss Jimenez, who attempt to barter in human lives. As a social corrective, *Los Vendidos* exposes the inferiority of those who think themselves superior.

The Superiority Theory fails to explain many instances of comedy and humor, particularly those that derive from language games, such as puns or the "sense in nonsense" that characterizes absurd humor. These types of humor operate through double meanings and contradictory logic and thus incite laughter at an incongruity. The German philosopher Arthur Schopenhauer firmly established the source of all laughter as the perception of incongruity between a concept and a real object. For example, in Miguel de Cervantes's *Don Quijote* (1605–1615), much of the humor arises from the incongruity between what Don Quijote believes he sees and what is really there. The Incongruity Theory also helps explain the humor behind the nonsensical diatribes of the Mexican comic genius Cantinflas (Mario Moreno), known as *cantinfladas*. In films such as *Ahí está el detalle* (Here is the point) (1940), Cantinflas's underdog character—the *pelado*, or poor rascal—subverts authority figures by answering questions with evasive nonsense that has a logic of its own. Audiences laugh at the authority figures as they struggle to comprehend the incongruities in Cantinflas's speeches.

In the case of Latinos and Latinas, the incongruities between Spanish and English or between Hispanic and Anglo-American ways of life offer many opportunities to produce humor. The Puerto Rican poet Tato Laviera has used the humorous incongruities of Spanglish to recast bilingualism as a legitimate form of communication rather than as a degenerate hybrid of two "pure" languages. The title of Laviera's 1985 collection of poetry, *AmeRícan*, uses homophonic and orthographic devices to create a pun; "AmeRícan" sounds like "I'm a Rican" but looks like "American," thus articulating a Puerto Rican identity in the United States through the fusion of Spanish and English. Latino and Latina humorists also provoke laughter by highlighting the incongruities of their dual cultural consciousness, particularly when second-generation Latinos and Latinas negotiate the cultural divide between their traditional Spanish American parents and their modern Anglo-American environment. The comedic film *Tortilla Soup* (2001) offers a good example of how a family of Chicanas straddles cultural and linguistic incongruities to affirm their bicultural identity. The female characters' attempts to introduce new cultural practices and ideas into their household conflict with their father's traditionalism, but by the film's end he accepts their new ways of thinking and their Spanglish as vibrant expressions of pride and independence.

In addition to its social functions, laughter also plays a role in physical and psychological health. The British philosopher and sociologist Herbert Spencer, in "The Physiology of Laughter" (1860), argues that not all incongruities lead to laughter, but those that do constitute a "descending incongruity," for the consciousness goes from great things to small. This cognitive shift results in an overflow of nervous excitement, which then leads to laughter's stimulation of the muscular system and internal organs that benefits physical health. Spencer's notion helped to establish the Relief Theory of laughter, which

considers humor and all forms of the comic to be socially acceptable means of releasing pent-up tension. Perhaps the most well-known proponent of the Relief Theory is Sigmund Freud, whose seminal work *Jokes and Their Relation to the Unconscious* (1905) modifies Spencer's theory to argue that laughter arises when a quota of "psychical energy," which has previously been channeled toward a taboo or inhibition, is suddenly released by a joke toward a lifting of that taboo. For Freud, the joke teller produces the means by which the inhibition is lifted and thus experiences pleasure when the recipient of the joke laughs, even though the teller does not laugh while delivering the joke. In the context of Latino and Latina comedy and humor, the Relief Theory helps explain how a stand-up comedian like Carlos Mencia can take the most taboo of subjects—race, sex, religion, or politics—and find ways to make an audience laugh at its own unwillingness to discuss these topics. In performances like *Take a Joke America!* (2000), Mencia utters what many would consider virulent racial slurs. According to the Relief Theory, Mencia's jokes allow the audience to release the tension that builds up from avoiding any discussion of race relations for fear of offending others. Mencia lifts that inhibition by offending every racial and ethnic identity in the audience.

Transcultural Humor

While most theories of humor fit under one of the three categories just described, Latino and Latina humor draws from a wide array of cultural traditions. Luis Valdez and the Teatro Campesino that he helped establish incorporated many of the elements of the Mexican *carpas*, or tent circuses, that traveled extensively throughout the Southwest and were popular with the working classes. These carpas offered entertainments such as jugglers, acrobats, singers, and dancers as well as the comedic performances of the *pelado*, an underdog character who acted out satirical sketches and delivered witty commentaries on the struggles of everyday life. (Cantinflas also got his start in Mexican carpas.) Teatro Campesino combined this Mexican tradition with the Italian commedia dell'arte and the agitprop theater of the 1960s in its efforts to promote a politically engaged humor. By deflating the seriousness of authority figures, the company's *actos*, or short sketches, engaged its audience of farmworkers with the familiar Mexican form of humor known as *relajo*, which the philosopher Jorge Portilla describes as a communal suspension of seriousness before a perceived social value. Although Portilla contends that the Mexican relajo is purely negative because it offers no value to take the place of that which it denies, in the hands of politically engaged groups such as Teatro Campesino, relajo provokes communal laughter in order to raise awareness and expose social injustice.

A close relative to the Mexican relajo is the Cuban *choteo*, a form of derisive humor that undermines the seriousness of situations and authority figures. Jorge Mañach, in his essay *Indagación del choteo* (1928), describes the choteo as a relaxation of mores, a celebration of disorder, and a leveling of hierarchies. Like the relajo, the choteo results in communal laughter, but its instigator deflates seriousness in order to assert an individual identity in the face of social control. One of the most well-known practitioners of choteo was the radio legend Leopoldo Fernández, better known as Trespatines. Trespatines's misadventures in *La tremenda corte* (The Tremendous Court) pitted this roguish character against a judge and the plaintiffs, who accused him of all sorts of trickery and misdeeds. Much like Cantinflas, Trespatines used illogical arguments to defend himself against his accusers. Although originally taped in Cuba, these radio programs have aired in the United States since the 1960s and have influenced many Latino and Latina humorists. In the work of Cuban Americans, like the fiction writer Achy Obejas and the playwright Eduardo Machado, the second-generation characters display the sneering disdain for authority that resonates with the older choteo, but their difficulty in reconciling their Cuban heritage with a United States reality often tinges their choteo with a more Anglo-American ironic detachment. Although these characters laugh at authority and social conformity, their laughter betrays a solitary cynicism and insecurity uncharacteristic of the more playful, communal Cuban choteo.

In Puerto Rico, Venezuela, and Colombia the term *guachafita* can refer to noisy disorder as well as to a festive atmosphere of joking and buffoonery. Puerto Rican humorists have drawn from this tradition as a means of cultural survival and as an alternative to "melting-pot" assimilation. In "La guagua aérea" (1983), by the Puerto Rican novelist Luis Rafael Sánchez, the narrator describes an instance of collective guachafita that occurs on one of the regular flights shuttling Puerto Ricans between the island and the mainland. The passengers laugh uproariously when a crab escapes from someone's luggage and frightens the white American flight attendant. Once their laughter undermines the authority of the crew, the Puerto Rican passengers enjoy a rowdy guachafita, in which they share food, liquor, stories, and jokes. The destabilizing effect of the guachafita allows popular Puerto Rican culture to infiltrate the highly regimented North American space.

This infusion of popular culture has also characterized the humorous works of several U.S. Puerto Rican writers, including Tato Laviera, Víctor Hernández Cruz, and Pedro Pietri. Both Laviera and Hernández Cruz incorporate the rhythms of Afro-Caribbean music in their bilingual poetry, while Pietri combines surrealism and absurd humor with the guachafita's irreverent, festive sensibility. In his play *The Living Room* (1975) Pietri depicts the absurd foibles of a family whose only son has secluded himself in a tent in the middle of the living room, vowing to remain there until he can fix the record player. Without their source of music, the family engages in nonsensical arguments about whether or not the son has lost his mind. When he emerges at the end of the play, like a Nuyorican Godot who finally arrives, he puts the record player in its proper place, and the entire cast dances to the music that fills the stage. Pietri's play demonstrates that at the core of Puerto Rican identity lies the festive spirit of the guachafita and that without this source of pleasure the Puerto Rican family falls into disarray and discord. The communal laughter and gaiety of the guachafita embody what Mikhail Bakhtin, in *Rabelais and His World* (1965), calls the carnival spirit, which overturns social hierarchies through mockery but also revives and renews the feelings of community and freedom. This spirit, expressed in music, poetry, and performance, has been a crucial component in establishing a Puerto Rican identity in the United States.

Latinos and Latinas and Ethnic Humor in the United States

On the darker side of humor, jokes about racial and ethnic minorities convey aggression toward those groups that retain their cultural differences and resist assimilation to the American melting-pot ideology. Aggressive ethnic humor has long been a part of the immigrant experience in the United States, particularly at the beginning of the twentieth century, when a great influx of Europeans came to American shores and competed for space and resources. Ethnic humor is much more prevalent in heterogeneous societies like the United States, yet its level of aggressiveness tends to correspond to historical moments of political or economic tension. Christie Davies, in *Ethnic Humor around the World* (1990), argues that ethnic jokes display the feelings of superiority one group holds in regard to another and that those who share such jokes do so as a way to project unwanted traits onto the outsiders. For instance, despite the fact that many Mexicans crossed the border in search of labor during the bracero program of 1942–1964 and that even in the early twenty-first century they continue to provide cheap labor for the agricultural industry, "lazy Mexicans" remains one of the ethnic slurs leveled against these hardworking people. Those who make jokes about "lazy Mexicans" appear to project their own aversion to hard work onto an immigrant group whose presence in the United States is motivated by the search for labor.

Ethnic humor functions quite differently when a minority group makes jokes about itself. Jews have a long tradition of self-deprecating humor that has served as a way to deal with the oppression from which they have historically suffered. Lenny Bruce, considered one of the pioneers of modern stand-up comedy, was a master of redirecting the aggression of self-deprecating Jewish jokes away from himself and onto the audience. Lois Leveen, in "Only When I Laugh: Textual Dynamics of Ethnic Humor" (1996), writes that ethnic jokes about one's own group acknowledge existing stereotypes while exposing their limitations in an effort to move beyond them. One example she cites comes from the Puerto Rican comedian Joey Vega, who says: "Yeah, make a joke about how Puerto Ricans steal your hub-caps, everybody laughs. C'mon, that's not true. We'll steal your whole car" (Leveen, p. 36). Vega's self-deprecating joke takes the risk of perpetuating a negative stereotype, but by making fun of the very culture in which these ethnic jokes circulate, he subverts their aggression away from the Puerto Ricans they ridicule. Other comedians and comedic performers, such as John Leguizamo, Paul Rodriguez, Cheech Marín, George Lopez, and Carlos Mencia, have also appropriated the negative stereotypes of Latinos and Latinas and used them in their stand-up routines to expose the audience's biases and misperceptions. The African American comedians Richard Pryor, Eddie Murphy, and Chris Rock have similarly exploited the racist stereotypes of blacks, and their comedy routines have had great appeal across the entrenched racial and ethnic divides that give the lie to the American melting-pot dream.

Humor as Social Critique

Often a Latino or Latina humorist's most effective means of social critique is the direct attack that satire offers. Originally conceived as a mixture of prose and poetry that ridiculed Roman society (such as Petronius's *Satyricon*), satire can appear in almost any artistic medium, from song to film, painting to fiction. Satire positions the reader or audience in unequivocal opposition to the objects it holds up for ridicule. A satirist exposes society's vices and follies with the aim of promoting their correction. For example, Sor Juana Inés de la Cruz, in her well-known poem "Hombres necios que acusáis," censures misogynist men who seduce women passionately but scorn them if they fall into temptation. Modern-day Latino and Latina satirists take aim at the problems that plague contemporary society, as in the case of Lalo Alcaraz, the political cartoonist whose comic strip *La cucaracha* lambastes everything from racial profiling to the commercialization of Latino and Latina identity. The San Francisco–based performance troupe Culture Clash, in their 1988 show *The Mission*, deftly combined critiques of colonialism, religious hypocrisy, and the singer Julio Iglesias, whom they represent as one of the entertainment industry's exoticized, whitened Latinos. The New York performance artist Reno, in her one-woman show *Rebel without a Pause*, found humor in the horrific terrorist attacks of September 11, 2001, which she witnessed personally. She ridiculed the absurd behavior of Manhattanites who fled the city like refugees with matching sets of luggage, and she excoriated the Bush administration for its assault on civil liberties.

Because political satire often targets current events, the laughter it provokes can be transitory. Satire's topical nature underscores one of the requirements for humor to succeed: the humorist and his or her audience must share a set of cultural codes. Because Latino and Latina humorists can draw from multiple cultural traditions, they are finding that their social critiques resonate with wider audiences. Alcaraz's cartoons have gone into national syndication, Culture Clash's performances have been televised on PBS, and Reno has taken the film version of her show as far as Toronto and Havana.

When Latino and Latina artists direct their humorous critiques at other works of art, they often employ the imitative power of parody. Parody can imitate a specific work or an entire genre, exaggerating the most recognizable features of the original in order to lay bare its artistic devices. Asco, the conceptual art and performance group from Los Angeles, consistently used parody to push the limits of what could be considered acceptable Chicano and Chicana art. In their 1972 street performance *Walking Mural*, Harry Gamboa Jr. filmed Asco members Patssi Valdez, Willie Herrón, and Gronk dressed as parodies of Chicano mural figures parading down Whittier Boulevard. The critic Chon A. Noriega writes that this performance offered a critique of Chicano and Chicana muralism and its emphasis on cultural authenticity. While Asco's parodic performance functioned as a satire of complacency in contemporary art, other forms of Chicano and Chicana parody do not necessarily deride the original works they imitate. In some cases parodic art pays homage to the work on which it is based while still using humorous incongruity to make the original address new issues. The Chicana painter Yolanda Lopez's 1978 piece *Portrait of the Artist as the Virgin of Guadalupe* depicts one of the most revered figures in Chicano/Chicana and Mexican cultures as a young woman in running shoes boldly striding forward, snake in one hand and a red-white-and-blue cherub trampled underfoot. Lopez's parody invokes the spirituality associated with the Virgin as a way to validate the challenges that contemporary Chicanas face in the United States. While Lopez's painting forgoes the satiric critique of Asco's performance, both of these parodies engage traditional elements of Chicano/Chicana culture and rework them to convey new meanings.

Border Humor

Latinos and Latinas in the United States negotiate the contradictions of their dual cultural consciousness, and in many cases their presence has transformed the geopolitical landscape to create a borderland of cultural hybridity. For writers like Gloria Anzaldúa, the border is a physical space as well as a mestiza consciousness. The incongruities that arise when the Third World infuses the First World with its languages and cultural practices can be the source of conflict and misunderstanding, but because humor depends so heavily on just such incongruity, the border can also accommodate laughter. Cheech Marín, in his 1987 film *Born in East L.A.*, exposes the U.S. xenophobia toward Mexican immigrants and the way racial and ethnic prejudice turn a blind eye on difference. His character, a Chicano mistaken for an illegal alien and deported back to Mexico by the Immigration and Naturalization Service (INS), draws heavily from Cantinflas's pelado, but in this case the underdog outsmarts the border patrol and returns home accompanied by a teeming mass of brown-skinned illegals. Marín's film confronts head-on America's worst fears of a brown invasion, but its comedy celebrates those who not only cross and occupy the border but who have survived oppression and exclusion by cultivating a border consciousness.

The avant-garde performance artist Guillermo Gómez Peña, a self-described "Border Brujo" and "Cyber Vato," has also explored the humorous possibilities of life on the border. His performances challenge the boundaries between languages and cultures and the institutionally imposed limits that separate and categorize different artistic media. His installation event *Orozco MEXotica* (May 17–18, 2002), performed in front of Dartmouth College Library's Orozco murals, epitomized multimedia art and its ability to bring together sight, sound, movement, and hypertext. The performers wore incongruous combinations of different national costumes and, without scripted dialogue, engaged the audience through gestures and dance, using the Mexican muralist José Clemente Orozco's *Epic of American Civilization* as a backdrop. Gómez Peña developed a Web site in conjunction with this performance so an interactive investigation into cultural hybridity could continue in cyberspace. *Orozco MEXotica*, along with many of Gómez Peña's other performances and installations, resonates with the French artist Antonin Artaud's notion of a "Theater of Cruelty," which uses humor as "destruction"; that is, the destruction of limits on reality and of complacency in art.

Gender, Sex, and Sexuality

Humor's aggression sometimes serves as a form of sexual titillation, particularly in the obscene jokes shared between members of the same sex. When Freud discusses obscene jokes and sexual innuendo, he emphasizes the role these forms of the comic play in exposing human bodily needs through degradation and unmasking. However, many Latino and Latina artists use sexual comedy and humor to expose the patriarchal structures that define gender and sexuality. The Chicana author Ana Castillo's *So Far from God* (1993) casts a family of women in a plot that parodies the hyperbolic sentimentalism of Mexican melodrama, but the novel's subtle irony mainly serves a Chicana feminist satire of machismo's misogyny and sexual exploitation. The Cuban American Alina Troyano, aka Carmelita Tropicana, has used performance art as a means to aggressively challenge sexism and homophobia. Her piece *Your Kunst*

Is Your Waffen (subsequently filmed by her sister Ela Troyano), is a parodic send-up of women-in-prison films and musical comedy. Its characters take on different gender and sexual identities, thus blurring the lines between "normal" and "deviant" sexual behavior. Ela Troyano has also questioned the stability of categories such as "straight" and "gay" in her film *Latin Boys Go to Hell* (1997). The comedic performance artist Marga Gómez, of Puerto Rican and Cuban heritage, addresses the issue of homophobia in Latino and Latina families by saying: "Latino families are not more homophobic than other families. They are uniquely homophobic." These artists use humor not only to expose machismo and to break the silence of homophobia in the Latino and Latina community, they also push the limits of what constitutes feminism and queerness in America, since these discourses on gender and sexuality tend to be dominated by a white, middle-class sensibility.

The Latino Family Comedy

One of the most popular forms of entertainment in the United States that perpetuates middle-class sensibility is the television sitcom, and although Latinos and Latinas have only recently made inroads in this medium, Desi Arnaz in *I Love Lucy* remains one of the most influential actors in its development. Much of the humor in this show revolves around Lucy's madcap schemes to star in one of Ricky's nightclub acts, but Ricky's accent, his frequent emotional outbursts in Spanish, and his status as a "hot-blooded Latin" also contribute to the show's comedy. Despite its stereotypical depiction of Cuban culture, the show broke ground by showing American audiences one of the first interethnic families on television. Decades passed before another Latino, Freddie Prinze Sr., was given a starring role in a network sitcom, but by the 1970s, particularly after the huge success of shows like *All in the Family*, *Good Times*, and *The Jeffersons*, the humor in Prinze's *Chico and the Man* focused on race relations, cultural difference, and the urban working class from a more enlightened perspective. Nevertheless these shows targeted a mainstream audience and often attempted to educate the Anglo-American viewer about minorities with whom they might not have direct familiarity.

Not until the low-budget PBS production *¿Que Pasa USA?* first appeared in the late seventies did a sitcom speak the language of Latinos and Latinas to Latinos and Latinas. The Miami Cuban family in this show spoke a mixture of English, Spanish, and Spanglish, and it accurately represented the intergenerational conflicts between the traditionalist parents and grandparents, on one side, and the bicultural children, on the other. The show's humor mostly centered on situations in which the English-speaking, public realm infiltrated the highly guarded private space of the Cuban American home. More recently Telemundo has produced *Los Beltrán*, one of the first bilingual comedies on a Spanish-language network. Like its predecessor, *Los Beltrán* comically depicts a Cuban American family dealing with the challenges of modern life in the United States, but it also finds humor in the conflicts that arise between Latino and Latina groups, especially between the conservative Cuban American patriarch and his radical Chicano son-in-law.

In this way *Los Beltrán* resembles another sitcom, *The George Lopez Show*, in which the title character, a Chicano from a humble background, marries a Cuban American princess. Much of the show's comedy arises when George, who works hard to establish a stable, middle-class family, continually runs up against his past life on the mean streets. Even the character of his acerbic mother, who was forced to drop out of school and raise George on her own, represents the harsher realities of the Chicano and Chicana experience in which George struggles to negotiate. The stable, hardworking family appears in yet another Latino-themed sitcom aimed at a younger audience: Nickelodeon's *The Brothers Garcia*. These shows exemplify both Latinos and Latinas' increased visibility in mainstream American media outlets and the ways such media are reshaping Latino and Latina identity. To a certain degree the families depicted on these sitcoms avoid cultural assimilation and sustain their Latino and Latina heritage, but by following the sitcom formula they also present Latinos and Latinas with idealized images of middle-class success and social conformity. Sitcoms are well known for their quick resolutions to conflicts and their uncritical representation of the American dream. Family-friendly sitcoms smooth over the critical, subversive edges of Latino and Latina humor, which may lead to more visibility on network television but to fewer original voices.

The Latino and Latina Sense of Humor: Honor and Self-Reflection

The notion that all humans—regardless of race, gender, or nationality—can have a "sense of humor" is relatively new. For centuries laughter was associated solely with aggression toward others, particularly among primitive societies and the lower classes. The term "humor," which originally referred to a person's disposition or mood, developed as a way to identify a particular type of sympathetic, self-reflexive laughter and was mainly associated with a cultivated British temperament. Other national traditions often denied themselves capable of having a "sense of humor." The Spanish critic Wenceslao Fernández-Flóres once wrote that Spaniards abhorred humor because their obsession with protecting their code of honor prevented them from ever laughing at themselves and predisposed them to laugh derisively at others. As inheritors of the culture and language of *La Madre Patria*, Latinos and Latinas also value a code of

honor, and although it often manifests itself negatively as machismo and paternalism, it also sustains strong ties to family and community and a sense of pride and dignity in Latino and Latina cultural heritage. Yet this pride has not prevented Latinos and Latinas from using comedy and humor to scrutinize their own foibles and weaknesses. Comedy and humor have served Latinos and Latinas as weapons against injustice and oppression, but Latino and Latina humorists have demonstrated a great capacity to hold up a mirror to their own communities. This unique combination of honor and self-reflection adds a new texture to the American cultural fabric and will provide ample material for Latino and Latina comedy and humor for years to come.

See also **Anzaldúa, Gloria; Arnaz, Desi; Cantinflas; Castillo, Ana; Culture Clash; Gamboa, Harry, Jr.; Gómez Peña, Guillermo; Gronk; Laviera, Tato; Leguizamo, John; López, Yolanda; Marín, Cheech; Obejas, Achy; Pietri, Pedro; *¿Que Pasa USA?*; Valdez, Luis;** *and* **Valdez, Patssi.**

BIBLIOGRAPHY

Aparicio, Frances R. "Salsa, Maracas, and Baile: Latin Popular Music in the Poetry of Víctor Hernández Cruz. *MELUS* 16, no. 1 (Spring 1989–1990): 43–58.

Bakhtin, Mikhail. *Rabelais and His World*. Translated by Hélène Iswolsky. Bloomington: Indiana University Press, 1984. Original Russian published in 1965.

Bergson, Henri Louis. *Laughter: An Essay on the Meaning of the Comic*. Translated by Cloudesley Brereton and Fred Rothwell. New York: Macmillan, 1911. Original French published in 1900.

Broyles-González, Yolanda. *El Teatro Campesino: Theater in the Chicano Movement*. Austin: University of Texas Press, 1994.

Davies, Christie. *Ethnic Humor around the World: A Comparative Analysis*. Bloomington: Indiana University Press, 1990.

Fernández-Flóres, Wenceslao. *El humor en la literatura Española: Discurso leído ante la Real Academia Española en la reception del Excmo*. Madrid: Impr. Saez, 1945.

Fregoso, Rosa Linda. *The Bronze Screen: Chicana and Chicano Film Culture*. Minneapolis: University of Minnesota Press, 1993.

Freud, Sigmund. *Jokes and Their Relation to the Unconscious*. Translated and edited by James Strachey. New York: Norton, 1960. Original German published in 1905.

Gamboa, Harry, Jr. *Urban Exile: Collected Writings of Harry Gamboa Jr*. Edited by Chon A. Noriega. Minneapolis: University of Minnesota Press, 1998.

Gómez Peña, Guillermo. *The New World Border: Prophecies, Poems, and Loqueras for the End of the Century*. San Francisco: City Lights, 1996.

Leveen, Lois. "Only When I Laugh: Textual Dynamics of Ethnic Humor." *MELUS* 21, no. 4 (Winter 1996): 29–55.

Mañach, Jorge. *La crisis de la alta cultura en Cuba, indagación del choteo*. Edited by Rosario Rexach. Miami, Fla.: Ediciones Universal, 1991. Originally published 1925–1928.

Morreall, John, ed. *The Philosophy of Laughter and Humor*. Albany: State University of New York Press, 1987.

Muñoz, José Esteban. *Disidentifications: Queers of Color and the Performance of Politics*. Minneapolis: University of Minnesota Press, 1999.

Pilcher, Jeffrey M. *Cantinflas and the Chaos of Mexican Modernity*. Wilmington, Del.: Scholarly Resources, 2001.

Portilla, Jorge. *Fenomenología del relajo, y otros ensayos*. Mexico City: Fondo de Cultura Económica, 1997. Originally published in 1966.

Rœckelein, Jon E. *The Psychology of Humor: A Reference Guide and Annotated Bibliography*. Westport, Conn.: Greenwood Press, 2002.

Rose, Margaret A. *Parody: Ancient, Modern, and Post-Modern*. Cambridge, U.K.: Cambridge University Press, 1993.

ISRAEL REYES

COMISIÓN FEMENIL MEXICANA NACIONAL. The founding and growth of the Comisión Femenil Mexicana Nacional (CFMN) were the result of several developments, most of them associated with the leadership and vision of Francisca Flores. Born in San Diego on December 3, 1913, Flores was already in her late fifties when she turned her attention to the fostering of Chicana leadership in Los Angeles. Undaunted and indefatigable, Flores was a seasoned community organizer by the time she initiated the first steps toward the founding of CFMN. She had worked on the Sleepy Lagoon case (1942–1944), become involved in community organizing through the Community Service Organization (CSO) of the early 1950s, participated in the founding of the Mexican American Political Association (MAPA) in 1959, and worked on Edward Roybal's successful 1962 electoral campaign for the U.S. House of Representatives from California.

In 1970, in the wake of the National Chicano Issues Conference, Grace Montañez Davis, who became deputy mayor under Los Angeles mayor Tom Bradley (1973–1993), arranged a meeting between her former MAPA colleague, Francisca Flores, and Ed Aguirre, then Regional Director of the U.S. Department of Labor. Flores—accompanied by Frances Bojorquez, Amelia Camacho, Vi Muñoz, and Evelyn Velarde Benson—wanted to speak to Aguirre about the employment training, childcare, and educational needs of Chicanas. She proposed the establishment of a center to meet these needs for women in Los Angeles. Aguirre wanted to see a plan on paper. Flores promptly handed him a proposal for a federally funded training, employment-referral, and counseling center for women in Los Angeles, to be called the Chicana Service Action Center (CSAC). The Comisión Femenil Mexicana National was created on paper as a nonprofit corporation, enabling the women to receive a grant of $50,000 from the U.S. Department of Labor. CSAC headquarters was established on Olympic Boulevard in East Los Angeles, with Lilia Aceves as its first executive director. Flores eventually began two newsletters associated with both organizations: *Comisión Femenil Mexicana* and the *Chicana Service Action Center Newsletter*. The former provided statistical surveys of Chicana employment patterns, legislation relevant to women, and information on women's publications. The CSAC newsletter focused on employment and the status of Chicanas in the labor market.

In 1971, Flores called a series of preliminary CFMN meetings, inviting a cross-section of women from around the county who represented potential leadership among a younger generation of Chicana activists. Among those who attended were Alicia Escalante, founder of the East Los Angeles Welfare Rights Organization; Gloria Molina, who would go on to become California's first elected Chicana assemblyperson and the first female and person of color elected to the Los Angeles Board of Supervisors; Yolanda Nava, a counselor and later director of the United Way's Neighborhood Youth Core Program who became a broadcaster and author; and Anna Nieto Gomez, counselor and lecturer in the California State University system.

In 1972, Flores encouraged five young women, including Nava, Molina, and Ana Maria Peña, to found a local Los Angeles chapter of the Comisión Femenil Mexicana. The activities of the Los Angeles chapter were closely associated with those of the national chapter, since key activists were involved at both the local and the national level and were subject to the control of Flores. The Los Angeles chapter worked against the Talmadge Amendment, a congressional bill requiring those in need of public assistance to register for work. The chapter also joined the Mexican American Legal Defense Fund (MALDEF) as plaintiffs in a class action suit against the sterilization of Mexican women in state hospitals; MALDEF's Antonia Hernandez successfully litigated the case. The Los Angeles chapter also established the Centro de Niños, a bilingual, bicultural childcare center for the working poor and women who were training for work or completing their formal education. Funding for the Centro was made possible with the help of California state legislator Richard Alatorre, who assisted Yolanda Nava in securing a state grant. During this time, Flores encouraged Nava, Molina, and Aceves to testify before the California Commission on the Status of Women. They became the first Chicanas ever to testify before the Commission. The women expressed concern over its lack of Mexican American representation. Subsequently, the Los Angeles chapter worked with Assemblyman Richard Alatorre and the western regional director for the U.S. Commission on Civil Rights, Phil Montes to appoint the first Mexican American woman, Carolyn Orona, to the Commission.

The final step in the development of CFMN took place in June 1973, when the Los Angeles chapter hosted the CFMN's first organizational conference in Goleta, California, a small community north of Santa Barbara. By this time, CFMN had grown in visibility and political importance in California. The meeting was run strictly by Robert's Rules of Order to prevent its takeover by outside interests. The conference drafted a constitution for CFMN and identified organizational goals, including Chicana leadership development, the dissemination of information on Chicana women and their achievements, the promotion of programs seeking solutions to women's issues, and the identification of issues lending themselves to coalition work with other women's groups and movements. Although CFMN is no longer operational as a national body, local chapters throughout southern California continue to be active. Francisca Flores died in 1996. She was 82.

The University of California, Santa Barbara, now houses the archives of the Comisión Femenil Mexicana Nacional. Those of the Los Angeles chapter are housed at the University of California, Los Angeles. In addition to these papers, photojournalist Rosemary Quesada Weiner possesses a personal archive that visually documents the political careers of Comisión leaders as well as the activities of the Comisión Femenil Mexicana at the local and national levels.

See also Mexican American Legal Defense Fund; Mexican American Political Association; Roybal, Edward; *and* Sleepy Lagoon Trial.

BIBLIOGRAPHY

Comisión Femenil Mexicana Nacional. Papers. California Ethnic and Multicultural Archives (CEMA), Special Collections Department of the University Libraries. Santa Barbara: University of California, Santa Barbara.

Flores, Bill. "Francisca Flores, 1913–1996." clnet.sscnet.ucla.edu./research/francisca.html

ADELAIDA R. DEL CASTILLO

COMMITTEE IN SOLIDARITY WITH THE PEOPLE OF EL SALVADOR.

CISPES, the Committee in Solidarity with the People of El Salvador, was formed in 1980 following conventions in Los Angeles and Washington, D.C. CISPES emerged out of a broad movement to end U.S. support for the Salvadoran armed forces during its twelve-year war against Marxist insurgents. CISPES advocated an end to the war and to U.S. involvement in the war, but CISPES activists developed an agenda that went beyond simple anti-interventionism, embracing the struggle of poor Salvadorans for a more just social order and supporting an insurrectionist and revolutionary guerrilla organization—the Farabundo Martí National Liberation Front (FMLN).

CISPES began as a network of local chapters, but by 1985 it had developed a structure based on local chapters that coordinated their work through a national executive committee. CISPES held its first national conference in 1985 in Washington, D.C., and held one every two years after. Representatives from 120 CISPES chapters attended that first conference. By the mid-1980s, as many as three hundred local chapters had been established, many on college campuses. Before each conference, members circulated position papers and strategy papers among the local chapters. During the conferences, participants broke into

smaller groups to review the position and strategy papers. Those papers that received support in the small work groups were later voted upon by the larger conference. Proposals that garnered a simple majority vote won approval. Local chapters could send as many participants to the conferences as they wished, but each chapter had only two votes. Leadership positions were also filled by voting. Local chapters were organized into regions, with each region electing a regional coordinator. At the national conferences, a three-member executive committee was elected for a two-year term. The executive committee and the regional coordinators constituted the decision-making body in between the conferences.

The War in El Salvador

CISPES was established in response to the civil war in El Salvador and as a repudiation of U.S. support for the Salvadoran government. The war lasted approximately twelve years (1980–1992), but its roots lie in the decades of economic inequality and military dictatorship that preceded it. In 1931, General Maximiliano Hernández Martínez seized power in a military coup. He became the first in a series of military dictators aligned with a small class of landowning elite. Communist organizers and union activists, led by Agustín Farabundo Martí, were organizing a general strike in the major cities, while peasants were rebelling against the continual loss of land and rural unemployment, particularly in the coffee-growing regions in western El Salvador. But Hernández Martínez crushed the rebellion before it took place, killing as many as 30,000 people in the space of just a few weeks. Fear of renewed repression discouraged any display of open political resistance for the next several decades.

In the 1970s, things began to change. Peasants began organizing agricultural cooperatives and rural workers' unions in the countryside. Progressive elements of the Catholic Church were instrumental in transforming peasant attitudes and mobilizing popular resistance to government repression and economic exploitation (Binford, p. 106; Byrne, pp. 27–28). In 1968, the bishops of Latin America held a conference in Colombia to discuss how to implement Vatican II, including the adoption of a "preferential option for the poor." This approach to ministry meant that priests and nuns committed themselves to serving the needs of their poor parishioners and to using religious teachings to help them understand their poverty and disenfranchisement as unjust. Priests trained lay catechists who went to rural communities and helped popularize a critique of economic exploitation and political repression that was articulated through religious discourse. Their teachings appealed to those who feared open political resistance but nonetheless struggled to defy their own subjugation. This new critique of poverty paved the way for the more pointed political discourse of the rebel groups who began to organize soon after.

At the same time, intellectuals and radicals, inspired by the Cuban revolution of 1959, began to organize Marxist political groups. Some of the radicals formed small guerrilla armies, while others organized mass popular social movements that led public protests and educational campaigns. The Salvadoran government reacted with repression and violence, including indiscriminate killings of peasants, priests, labor organizers, students, and activists. Right-wing death squads tortured and killed suspected political activists with impunity. The military and police forces detained suspected activists and their family members, many of whom were never seen again. In 1980 alone, military and paramilitary groups killed approximately 10,000 civilians.

Besides a rise in state-sponsored violence, several other events in 1980 intensified the war and inspired international concern over the situation in El Salvador. The five main guerrilla armies—the Ejército Revolucionario del Pueblo (ERP), Fuerzas Populares de Liberación (FPL), Fuerzas Armadas de Resistencia Nacional (FARN), Partido Revolucionario de Trabajadores Centroamericanos (PRTC), and the Fuerzas Armadas de Liberación (FAL)—united to form the FMLN. Each group maintained its individual political identity, but they now coordinated their military actions. In March of that year, members of the Salvadoran military shot and killed Archbishop Oscar Arnulfo Romero, an outspoken critic of the violence and state repression. The killing of Archbishop Romero shocked the world and brought the struggle in El Salvador to the front pages of newspapers around the world. In December, four U.S. nuns were raped and killed by members of the Salvadoran military. These high-profile assassinations brought increased international attention to the war in El Salvador and horrified antiwar activists and religious leaders in the United States.

As the violence intensified in El Salvador, thousands of people fled the country, most of them to the United States. From 1977 to 1979, the official rate of emigration from El Salvador to the United States remained close to 20,000 per year, but in 1980 it jumped to 104,628 and in 1981 to 214,128. Most migrants settled in San Francisco, Los Angeles, Houston, New York, and Washington, D.C. There, they mobilized to support newly arriving refugees, to educate the U.S. public about the war in El Salvador, to lobby U.S. officials to end their support of the Salvadoran government, and to aid in the postwar reconstruction of El Salvador. It is no accident that the founding conferences of CISPES took place in Los Angeles and Washington, D.C., cities where antiwar activists and religious groups were coming into contact with refugees eager to share their stories of persecution and violence.

Many local CISPES activists first learned about the war in El Salvador from Salvadorans who fled to the United States. In particular, members of CISPES established close relations with activists from the Frente Democrático Revolucionario (FDR) and the FPL, one of the five guerrilla groups that constituted the FMLN. Though CISPES formally supported the FMLN as a whole, it historically identified more closely with the FPL and its key political figures. Local activists in the United States set the priorities of the national organization through the conferences, but CISPES received political analysis and news from the FPL. During the war, relations between the five member organizations of the FMLN were troubled and, although CISPES was associated with the FPL, it formally refused to take positions on the power struggles within the FMLN.

The war ended in 1992 following the signing of the Chapultepec Peace Accord. The accord disbanded the Salvadoran military and police forces, which were reconstituted to include former combatants of the FMLN and the armed forces as well as civilians. The FMLN was converted into a political party and subsequently became the main opposition party. The governing party, the National Republican Alliance (ARENA), was formed during the war. Despite its implication in death squad activity, it continued to win presidential elections. During the course of the war, approximately 75,000 people died. The United Nations attributed most of those deaths to government forces and the associated death squads.

U.S. Involvement in the War in El Salvador

During the 1980s, the U.S. government became increasingly entangled in the war in El Salvador. President Jimmy Carter first sent military advisors in 1980. President Ronald Reagan was more stridently anticommunist and feared that the revolution in Nicaragua would produce a domino effect in Central America, leading to communist takeovers throughout the region. He saw the FMLN as a Soviet-sponsored organization even though the Soviet Union gave almost no support to the Salvadoran rebels. He manipulated and lied to Congress, sending more military advisors than were authorized and covering up human-rights abuses by the Salvadoran military. The U.S. government pressured Salvadoran wartime leaders such as Napoleon Duarte not to enter into peace talks with the FMLN, preferring an all-out victory, but in the end this strategy only prolonged the war. By the late 1980s, U.S. aid to the Salvadoran government was almost one hundred percent of the country's budget. President George H. W. Bush continued propping up the Salvadoran government, despite ample evidence of rampant human-rights abuses. Over the course of twelve years, the U.S. government sent over $6 billion to the Salvadoran government for direct military assistance and training and even more in nonmilitary aid. Were it not for the efforts of organizations like CISPES, the U.S. government probably would have invested much more in the Salvadoran government than it did.

The Antiwar Movement in the United States

CISPES was part of a broader solidarity movement that sought to end U.S. support for the governments of El Salvador and Guatemala and for the Contras, a guerrilla army fighting the Sandinista government in Nicaragua. A variety of religious communities became involved, offering sanctuary to Central Americans fleeing the wars in their countries and protesting U.S. intervention in those countries. Local chapters of CISPES often worked with activists from the sanctuary movement, but CISPES was unique on several counts. Unlike the sanctuary movement, CISPES was not motivated by religious faith but rather by political commitment. Although many of the members of CISPES were veteran activists from the antiwar movements of the 1960s, CISPES sought to go farther than those anti-interventionist organizations by declaring itself in solidarity with the people of El Salvador and by identifying with their struggle against military dictatorship, violence, and repression.

Solidarity meant more than opposition to U.S. intervention abroad. In the case of CISPES, solidarity meant providing support for the disenfranchised of El Salvador as they struggled against foreign intervention as well as the repressive measures of their own government. Although many sanctuary groups sympathized with the refugees fleeing violence in Central America, they did not become involved in the political struggles occurring there; their primary focus was to end U.S. support for the wars and to provide a haven for those fleeing them. In contrast, CISPES declared its support for the FMLN. The sanctuary movement was organized at a local level, and individual sanctuary groups were interconnected in a loose and unofficial network. CISPES created a democratic national structure in which local chapters coordinated their work and voted on policies and priorities. Finally, sanctuary groups lent their support to people fleeing the violence in El Salvador, Guatemala, and Nicaragua. CISPES identified primarily with the struggle in El Salvador, though it supported the work of organizations tied to groups in Nicaragua and Guatemala as well.

Like other solidarity and sanctuary groups, CISPES worked to educate the U.S. public about its own government's involvement in the war in El Salvador and lobbied government officials to push for an end to the war. These groups also advocated for the rights of thousands of Salvadoran refugees in the United States. But CISPES extended its work into El Salvador, supporting those who suffered the effects of the war. For example, during the war CISPES funded radio stations affiliated with the FMLN, medical brigades in FMLN-controlled territories, and the creation of new communities for civilians affected by the violence. In addition, CISPES utilized more innovative and confrontational tactics than did other solidarity groups. Local CISPES chapters blocked freeways, organized militant sit-ins, and even shut down the Pentagon in 1988. They performed a mock fashion show in Seattle's shopping district and added a "bomb" balloon to Macy's Thanksgiving Day Parade in 1989.

CISPES organized delegations of people from the United States who went to El Salvador to learn about the reality of the war, and it brought Salvadorans to the United States to speak to groups there. CISPES marches and rallies regularly attracted thousands of supporters. A 1982 march to the White House brought 70,000 people to the capital.

Many of the individuals who founded CISPES chapters were veteran antiwar activists who had developed a critique of U.S. foreign policy during the Vietnam War. Like the broader solidarity and sanctuary movements, CISPES members were predominantly Euro-Americans, though this varied according to region. Some chapters, such as those in southern California, had a larger percentage of Salvadorans and U.S.-born Latinas and Latinos. Chapters in the southern United States had a larger proportion of African Americans. Throughout the country, Salvadoran activists supported CISPES, but many preferred to organize among Salvadorans, establishing organizations such as the Committee of Central American Refugees (CRECE), the Central American Refugee Center (CARECEN), and El Rescate.

FBI Investigations of CISPES

Between 1981 and 1985, the FBI conducted two investigations of CISPES, which it suspected of being a foreign agent of the FMLN and of supporting their military actions in defiance of U.S. policy. In the context of the cold war, the FBI saw CISPES as a Soviet front and set out to prove that it was directly controlled by the FMLN. The FBI closely watched CISPES activists, tapped their phones, photographed and followed them, illegally broke into CISPES offices, and infiltrated local chapters. As part of its investigation, the FBI established close relations with the Salvadoran National Guard, a security force closely related to death squads (Sandweiss, p. 92). The FBI fed the Salvadoran National Guard information about CISPES activists, potentially endangering their lives.

The FBI was unable to find proof that CISPES was directly controlled by the FMLN. Meanwhile, CISPES activists learned of the FBI investigation. Ironically, an FBI informant who had infiltrated the Dallas chapter of CISPES sued the FBI in small claims court for withholding payment for his services. A local journalist happened to hear the story and reported it. With the help of the Center for Constitutional Rights, CISPES filed a lawsuit against the FBI. As a result, FBI Director William Sessions publicly apologized to CISPES in 1988 and disciplined three of the agents involved. CISPES activists had ended up confronting political repression in the United States that mirrored the persecution of activists in El Salvador. Several CISPES activists received death threats in the United States, and in one case a Salvadoran CISPES activist was kidnapped, raped, and tortured by a Salvadoran death squad in Los Angeles.

Main Achievements of the Solidarity and Sanctuary Movements

CISPES, along with many other solidarity and sanctuary groups, played a key role in educating the U.S. public about its government's involvement in the war in El Salvador. In galvanizing public opinion against the war, CISPES played an important role in pressuring Congress to limit U.S. funds to the government of El Salvador. Sanctuary groups were particularly effective at providing support for Central American refugees in the United States, including transporting them across the United States–Mexico border, securing safe havens for them, and forcing the U.S. government to provide them with appropriate legalization programs that recognize the unique circumstances that propelled them to flee their homelands. CISPES was unique in providing support to Salvadoran civilians affected by the war. And CISPES and other solidarity organizations gave hope to the people of El Salvador who opposed U.S intervention there. CISPES perpetuated the U.S. antiwar movement and helped produce a generation of activists, some of whom took up other struggles after the war in El Salvador ended.

CISPES in the Twenty-first Century

After the conclusion of the war in El Salvador, CISPES redefined its priorities and strategies. It devoted considerable energy to monitoring elections in El Salvador and to ensuring that the Salvadoran government implemented all of the provisions of the peace accord. CISPES continued to support the FMLN as it transformed itself from a guerrilla organization into a political party. In addition, CISPES mobilized support in the United States for labor struggles in El Salvador, including those of *maquiladora* workers and government employees facing the relentless privatization of public services. CISPES came out against the Central American Free Trade Agreement (CAFTA) and the Free Trade Agreement of the Americas (FTAA), seeing them as a new avenue for the imposition of U.S. priorities on the region.

See also Central Americans; Sanctuary Movement; *and* United States Interventions in Latin America.

BIBLIOGRAPHY

Baker-Cristales, Beth. *Salvadoran Migration to Southern California: Redefining El Hermano Lejano*. Gainesville: University Press of Florida, 2004.

Berryman, Phillip. *Inside Central America*. New York: Pantheon Books, 1985.

Berryman, Phillip. *Liberation Theology*. New York: Pantheon Books, 1987.

Binford, Leigh. "Peasants, Catechists, Revolutionaries: Organic Intellectuals in the Salvadoran Revolution, 1980–1992." In *Landscapes of Struggle: Politics, Society, and Community in El Salvador*, edited by Aldo Lauria-Santiago and Leigh Binford. Pittsburgh: University of Pittsburgh Press, 2004.

Byrne, Hugh. *El Salvador's Civil War: A Study of Revolution*. Boulder, Colo.: Lynne Rienner Publishers, 1996.

Coutin, Susan. *The Culture of Protest: Religious Activism and the U.S. Sanctuary Movement*. Boulder, Colo.: Westview Press, 1993.

La Feber, Walter. *Inevitable Revolutions: The United States in Central America*. 2nd ed. New York: Norton, 1993.

Sanbrano, Angela. Interview with the author. June 17, 2004.

Sandweiss, Stephen. "Spying on Solidarity: The FBI's Investigations of the Venceremos Brigade and CISPES." Master's thesis, San Francisco State University, 1990.

United Nations. Comisión de la Verdad para El Salvador. *De la locura a la esperanza: la guerra de 12 años en El Salvador*. San Salvador: Editorial Arcoiris, 1993.

BETH BAKER CRISTALES

COMMON LAND LAW (LEY DEL EJIDO). *See* Land Grants.

COMMUNITIES ORGANIZED FOR PUBLIC SERVICE. Ernesto Cortéz Jr. and other activists in San Antonio, Texas, founded Communities Organized for Public Service (COPS) in 1974. Cortés was trained in community activism by Saul Alinsky's Chicago-based Industrial Areas Foundation, which advocated a pragmatic approach to organizing. Given its Alinsky-inspired approach, COPS harkened back to an older style of organizing, similar to the Community Service Organization, rather than the more militant groups that emerged during the Chicano/a Movement.

COPS is an association of twenty-six Catholic parishes with the predominantly Latino West Side and South Side of San Antonio as the main organizing unit. These parishes became the organization's building blocks and their leaders became its leaders. The first four presidents of the organization were Andres Sarabia (1974–1976), Beatrice Gallegos (1976–1978), Carmen Badillo (1978–1980), and Beatrice Cortez (1980–1982). COPS avoided issues that were not of immediate concern to its members. Surveying the communities, COPS discovered that drainage, utility rates, traffic problems, and other everyday issues were of major concern to San Antonio residents. This popular approach to determining issues was also reflected in the governing structure of the organization.

True to its name, COPS was first and foremost concerned with communities and their interests. Families and neighborhoods were the most important entities for COPS, and its work sought to protect and preserve these institutions in inner-city San Antonio. To that end, in 1977 COPS pressured the city of San Antonio to end the proliferation of empty lots that had become dumping grounds for waste and stopped the spread of junkyards. COPS also successfully opposed the construction of the proposed Bandera freeway.

Electoral politics also received COPS's attention, although in Alinsky fashion the organization did not participate in partisan politics; instead, it sponsored voter registration drives to ensure that San Antonio's ethnic Mexicans had a voice in government. Because of pressure from COPS as well as other organizations, San Antonio adopted a district-based city council system in 1977. This structural change ensured that there were never fewer than four ethnic Mexicans on the San Antonio city council in the period from 1977 to 1999. With the help of COPS, Henry Cisneros became the first Latino mayor of a major American city in 1981. In addition, from 1977 to 1979 COPS fought the city of San Antonio's master plan for development, its opposition stemming from the amount of development that would be given to suburban areas rather than the inner city. COPS's protest ensured that the plan was tabled and eventually abandoned.

Into the late 1980s, COPS continued to win important victories for San Antonio residents. In 1989, COPS devised a plan for a $10 million housing trust fund that financed affordable housing in inner-city neighborhoods. Its get-out-the-vote drive in that same year provided the margin of victory necessary for the passage of a $46 million bond issue for library improvement and neighborhood literacy centers. Another bond issue COPS supported provided $140 million for continued street and drainage improvements. COPS also worked with the San Antonio police chief to create a community policing strategy, resulting in the establishment of three neighborhood storefront police stations and the development of a foot patrol program.

See also **Chicano/a Movement; Cisneros, Henry G.;** *and* **Cortéz, Ernesto, Jr.**

BIBLIOGRAPHY

Acuña, Rodolfo. *Occupied America: A History of Chicanos*. New York: Longman, 2004.

Rosales, Rodolfo. *The Illusion of Inclusion: The Untold Political Story of San Antonio*. Austin: University of Texas Press, 2000.

Sekel, Joseph D. "Communities Organized for Public Service: Citizen Power and Public Policy in San Antonio." In *Latinos and the Political System*, edited by F. Chris García. Notre Dame, Ind.: University of Notre Dame Press, 1988.

ERNESTO CHÁVEZ

COMMUTER NATION. "Commuter Nation" is a metaphor for the back-and-forth migration of Puerto Ricans between the island of Puerto Rico and U.S. mainland communities. It is one of many literary representations of Puerto Rican migration—such as "revolving door migration," "swallow migration," and "nation on the move"—used to capture the pendulum motion of Puerto Rican migrants. This pattern challenges the conventional understanding of migration that assumes unidirectional movement and entails, instead, circular travel between island and mainland destinations. Because they are U.S. citizens, Puerto Ricans moving between the island and U.S. destinations do not cross geopolitical borders as do immigrants from other countries such as Mexico, hence the ease with which Puerto Ricans can commute between the United States and Puerto Rico. As members of a "commuter nation," Puerto Ricans exist, move, raise families, and fashion cultural and national identities in a state of fluidity.

This idea of Puerto Rico as a "commuter nation" has seriously challenged a number of previously unquestioned notions regarding nation, identity, peoplehood, and belonging. It questions, for example, the assumption of a geographically delimited notion of nation and identity, and advances instead a vision of nation that is geographically dispersed, dynamic, and constructed in ways similar to Benedict Anderson's (1991) idea of an imagined community. The "commuter nation" also undermines the idea of national identity that often rests on homogenized, stable, and coherent assumptions and proposes a heterogeneous and fluid idea of national identity. Describing Puerto Rico as a "commuter nation" is one way for the Puerto Rican diaspora—those living on the mainland—to lay claim to a national identity that is more inclusive, complicated, and representative of the experiences of colonization, migration, and displacement that have characterized Puerto Ricans' lives since the United States' occupation of the island in 1898. In short, conceptualizing the Puerto Ricans as members of a commuter nation acknowledges that membership in a nation entails more than geographic location. It is about imagining oneself connected to a larger national community often separated by space.

Extent of Circular Migration

Although the idea of Puerto Rico as a commuter nation was originally meant as a metaphorical device for understanding Puerto Ricans' experiences of mobility and capturing the ebb and flow of people, ideas, capital, and information, there has been much debate among academics, policy analysts, and government officials about the extent to which Puerto Ricans are engaged in high levels of mobility as well as the consequences of an allegedly transient lifestyle. On the one hand, some policy analysts like

COMMUTER NATION. Airport in Puerto Rico. (Latin Focus.com)

Linda Chávez (1991) have blamed the tendency of Puerto Ricans to engage in circular migration for their poor economic standing in United States mainland communities. Because Puerto Ricans move frequently between the island and the United States, she argues, they fail to create sufficient attachments to local labor markets and community organizations, which contributes to their economic distress. Many Puerto Rican scholars have countered these claims, explaining that Puerto Rican circular migration does not contribute to Puerto Rican poverty but is, in fact, one of many ways in which Puerto Ricans attempt to address problems of poverty and unemployment in their households and local communities. Still other writers have called for more research to investigate the degree to which Puerto Ricans actually engage in circular migration. Although some studies suggest that only a small percentage of Puerto Ricans show high levels of back-and-forth movement but tend instead to live rooted lives in particular communities, the idea of Puerto Ricans as a transient people making up a commuter nation continues to animate Puerto Rican literature and cultural production.

Identity and Place

One notable example of this is Luis Rafael Sánchez's short story "La guagua aérea" (1994) or "The Airbus," an ironic account of the conversations, dramas, and thoughts of passengers on a routine flight from San Juan to New York City. The idea of an airbus succinctly captures the ease with which Puerto Ricans move between the island and the mainland as if they were merely taking a local bus ride. It is also an allegory for a Puerto Rican imaginary of place and identity that is fluid, not fixed, and floating between "two ports" (Sánchez, p. 22). By locating his story between two geographical spaces, Sánchez explores how Puerto Ricans' identities are constructed not solely on the island or on the mainland, but rather in a creative space in between nations, cultures, and places, creating a hybrid place and identity. This fusion of intersecting identities and places is best captured in the words of a passenger who, when asked where she comes from in Puerto Rico, responds by saying, "New York, Puerto Rico." This observation underscores the ways in which Puerto Rican national and cultural identity rests less on where one resides than on how one chooses to define oneself.

Like the idea of the commuter nation, the metaphor of the airbus begins with the reality of an island that has experienced high levels of back-and-forth movement that have come to define Puerto Rican life. In this regard, Puerto Rico is not unlike its Caribbean neighbors. Both in the past and at the present moment, the Caribbean is characterized by the movement of people, capital, goods, and information. It is a place where, as the anthropologist Sidney Mintz notes, soon after the conquest "people began coming from somewhere else," and where ethnic, racial, and national identities were forged, contested, and reconfigured (p. 296). Certainly, travel has made it easier for people to move between destinations and has allowed distant places to remain socially connected. However, the practices giving rise to the idea of a commuter nation have deeper roots, reaching down to the beginning of colonialism in the Caribbean region and enduring in contemporary Puerto Rican life both on the island and in mainland communities.

See also **Puerto Ricans.**

BIBLIOGRAPHY

Chávez, Linda. *Out of the Barrio: Toward a New Politics of Hispanic Assimilation.* New York: Basic Books, 1991.

Duany, Jorge. *The Puerto Rican Nation on the Move: Identities on the Island and in the United States.* Chapel Hill: University of North Carolina Press, 2002.

Mintz, Sidney. "Enduring Substances, Trying Theories: The Caribbean Region as *Oikoumene.*" *Journal of the Royal Anthropological Institute* 2 (1996): 289–310.

Sánchez, Luis Rafael. "La guagua aérea." In *Selections.* San Juan: Editorial Cultura, 1994.

Sandoval Sánchez, Alberto. "Puerto Rican Identity Up in the Air: Air Migration, Its Cultural Representations, and 'Cruzando el Charco.'"

In *Puerto Rican Jam: Rethinking Colonialism and Nationalism*, edited by Frances Negrón-Muntaner and Ramón Grosfoguel. Minneapolis: University of Minnesota Press, 1997.

GINA M. PÉREZ

CONGRESO MEXICANISTA.

By the first decade of the twentieth century, Anglo-American aggression against Texas Mexicans was such that Mexican civil and social rights, economic stability, and land ownership were fast deteriorating, contributing to a growing landless Mexican workforce. Racism and the unfair application of the law gave way to alarming acts of violence involving the lynching and burning alive of Mexicans, with impunity to transgressors. Anglo newcomers to Texas and their farming projects were intent on displacing Mexican cattle raising by dispossessing Mexicans of their ancestral land. In response to this crisis, four hundred Texas-Mexicans and residents of Mexican borderland towns gathered in Laredo, Texas, in 1911 to voice their grievances and develop a plan of action. There were some twenty-four official representatives of mutual-aid societies and Masonic lodges, labor and community leaders, journalists, and teachers from south Texas towns and cities. Nuevo Laredo, Ciudad Camargo, and Mendez sent Mexican representatives.

Unlike the violent insurrection proposed four years later by the Plan de San Diego—also originating in south Texas—El Congreso Mexicanista (the Mexicanist Congress) sought to explore moral, nonviolent alternatives of redress. Nicasio Idar, a Texas-Mexican by birth and the force behind the organization of El Congreso, was a Mason and a prominent member of the Laredo community, having served as an officer of the Benito Juárez Lodge; he had also participated in the highly regarded mutual-aid society Sociedad Mutualista Hijos de Juárez, and served as assistant city marshal and as justice of the peace. Nicasio Idar was also known as a defender of the Mexican working class. Before his move to Laredo, he had been involved in efforts to unionize railroad workers in northern Mexico; he continued to support the unionization of Laredo railroad workers. In 1904, when leaders of the revolutionary Partido Liberal Mexicano sought refuge in Laredo from Mexican persecution, Idar offered his support. As editor and publisher of *La Crónica*, Idar, together with his son Clemente and daughter Jovita, denounced class and racial prejudice and called for the convocation of El Congreso Mexicanista.

Although El Congreso was forced to address the practical reality of alarming acts of violence against the Texas-Mexican community and Anglo patterns of justice, the loss of ancestral land, the exploitation and growing poverty of Mexican laborers, and the exclusion of Mexican children from American schools, Congreso participants articulated their strategies of action in florid, idealistic terms. Indeed, Nicasio Idar welcomed Congreso participants as if they had been chosen for a transcendental mission: "You are the apostles of goodness, the propagandists of unity, the workers of culture, the soldiers of progress and the defenders of the right and justice of our people" (Zamora, p. 98). Pedro Grado, who delivered El Congreso's farewell address, appealed to the wealthy members of the Mexican community, to its mutual-aid societies and charities, and to secret Masonic societies, frankly to any group "that simply has altruism as their ideal." They were to provide resources, social networks, and access to political power as a possible solution to the growing marginalization and segregation of Mexicans. Ultimately, this may have proved to be "ineffectual rhetoric" (Montejano, p. 117), too romantic a response for the crisis at hand, but not all agree with this assessment. The historian Emilio Zamora describes these values and sentiments as evocative of the meaning and spirit of mutualism. Texas-Mexican mutual-aid societies tried to enhance the material well-being of the Mexican working class by providing for the needy through services, special funds, and charities, but they also aspired to build character through proper moral comportment and the exaltation of ideals such as humanitarianism, fraternity, civic mindedness, reciprocity, responsibility, and altruism. Together, these helped sustain south Texan Mexicanism during a period when Mexicans were forced to protect themselves from physical, socioeconomic, and ideological onslaughts.

During the early part of the twentieth century, south Texas had the highest percentage of Mexicans in the state, and inhabitants of Laredo, including the Idars, were proud Mexicans who spoke and wrote in Spanish and looked to the heroes and ideals of Mexican nationalism as a response to Anglo-American racial and socioeconomic oppression. The term "Mexicanista" used by the print media and mutual-aid societies of the day conveyed sentiments of cultural nationalism and collective efforts of self-help. Although American-born, south Texas Mexicans self-identified as "Mexican" or as subscribing to "Mexicanist" sentiments because of a profound love and cultural affinity to the mother country. To be sure, the term "Mexican" was the "English equivalent of the most popular self-referent used at the time by Mexicans in Texas" (Zamora, p. xi).

El Congreso Mexicanista's cultural nationalism and project of defense for Mexican people would resonate in the United States's sociocultural and political struggles of the mid 1960s and early 1970s. The anthropologist José E. Limón identifies common themes in the mobilization efforts of El Congreso and Chicanismo. El Congreso's attempts at political unification on a broad scale, its rejection of cultural loss, its support for the establishment of alternative educational institutions for school children, and the teaching of Spanish, Mexican history, and Mexican culture, Limón argues, anticipate the moral, political, and cultural goals of the Chicana and Chicano civil rights movement. Chicanas and Chicanos, too, would borrow the motto "Por la Raza y para la Raza" (By the Race and for the Race) of La Gran Liga Mexicanista de Beneficencia y Protección, the only federation that convened as a result of El Congreso. Lastly, attention to the organization of women and the defense of their rights predated Chicana feminism when La Liga Femenil Mexicanista, a women's auxiliary group of the Gran Liga, with Jovita Idar as president, was established on October 15, 1911.

El Congreso Mexicanista appears to have had a short life, as did its offspring La Gran Liga Mexicanista de Beneficencia y Protección. As Limón informs us, no mention is made of either after 1911. Their presence, nonetheless, attests to what Emilio Zamora identifies as an early twentieth-century effort by Mexican workers in the United States to establish a federation of community organizations.

See also Chicano/a Movement; Mutualista Organizations; *and* Texas.

BIBLIOGRAPHY

Gómez-Quiñones, Juan. "Plan de San Diego Reviewed." *Aztlán* 1, no. 1 (spring 1970): 124–132.

Limón, José E. "El Primer Congreso Mexicanista de 1911: A Precursor to Contemporary Chicanismo." *Aztlán* 5, nos. 1 & 2 (spring, fall 1974): 85–117.

Montejano. David. *Anglos and Mexicans in the Making of Texas, 1836–1986*. Austin: University of Texas Press, 1987.

Weber, David J., ed. *Foreigners in Their Native Land: Historical Roots of the Mexican Americans*. Albuquerque: University of New Mexico Press, 2003.

Zamora, Emilio. *The World of the Mexican Worker in Texas*. College Station: Texas A&M University Press, 1993.

ADELAIDA R. DEL CASTILLO

CONGRESSIONAL HISPANIC CAUCUS. The Congressional Hispanic Caucus (CHC) is an informal group of approximately eighteen members of Congress. The stated purpose of the organization is to advocate and express, through the legislative process, concerns and issues that affect the Latino and Latina community and Spanish-speaking territories (Puerto Rico and Guam, among others). The CHC was founded in 1976 as a legislative service organization of the U.S. House of Representatives. In the early twenty-first century, it was structured as a congressional member organization, governed by the rules of Congress.

Five Hispanic congresspersons (Herman Badillo, Baltasar Corrada, Henry B. Gonzalez, Kika de la Garza, and Edward Roybal) were the founding members of the CHC. Their primary purpose was to monitor legislative and other governmental activities that affect Latinas and Latinos. They also examined executive and judicial actions and worked with other groups inside and outside of Congress. Another important focus of the CHC is to educate Latinas and Latinos to become more involved in the political system. To this end, Roybal, de la Garza, and Corrada established the Congressional Hispanic Caucus Institute (CHCI), a nonprofit 501(c)(3) organization, in 1978 to serve as the educational arm of the CHC.

The CHCI extends the reach of the CHC beyond the walls of Congress and seeks to prepare future generations of leaders. The CHCI's Annual Gala during Hispanic Heritage Month was initiated as a fund-raising activity for the organization. Over the years, the CHCI has held legislative seminars throughout the year on important Latina and Latino issues.

The standing task forces reflect the breadth of issues addressed by the caucus: telecommunications and technology, health, immigration, education, business and economic development, civil rights and census, livable communities, international relations, arts and entertainment, labor, and veterans' affairs. Although these issues affect every constituency, some of them are particularly important to Latinas and Latinos—the Census 2000 procedures and possible undercounting of Latinas and Latinos; lack of medical insurance and access to health services; civil rights protections for immigrants; access to and representation of Latinas and Latinos in mass media programming; small business support and loan programs; the digital divide for Latinas and Latinos; U.S. foreign policy in Latin America, especially Cuba; and NAFTA. Public policy on these issues particularly affects the Latina and Latino community and its key segments (immigrants, undocumented workers, limited English speakers, refugees, central city dwellers, among others). The CHC provides a focus for individuals and groups to seek action on issues that are important to them.

The CHC has not always shown unanimity in the wide range of policy areas. Rather, it sees itself as a policy forum to promote exchange among its members. For example, Congressman José Serrano (D-NY), while serving as CHC chair, noted the following: "Although we have our divisions, we do have common grounds on what we feel are the key issues, including education, health care, welfare and immigration." He went on to add, "We have members who are conservative and members who are liberal. . . . But somehow on the principal issues, we've found common ground."

Similarly, Rep. Diaz-Balart (R-FL) expressed the view that regionalism and partisanship rarely interfere with the caucus agenda. "We will have our differences of opinion, but that rarely gets in the way of what we come together to do—represent our Hispanic communities." The continuing development of the CHC serves both to broaden this common ground and to expand the Caucus's

CONGRESSIONAL HISPANIC CAUCUS. Governor Bill Richardson of New Mexico speaks after receiving the Medallion of Excellence for Leadership at the Congressional Hispanic Caucus Institute's 26th Annual Gala September 24, 2003, in Washington, D.C. (Getty Images)

working base. The latter goal involves working collaboratively with other caucuses and increasing the number of associate members.

Since the inception of the CHC, its leadership has been the result of shared responsibilities and individual specialized skills. The chair of the caucus rotates from year to year. Each member takes an active role as head of a specific task force, as well as multiple memberships in other task forces. Given the breadth of concerns and issues, and the relatively small size of the caucus, shared responsibilities and a collective leadership have been the norm. Over time, especially following each reapportionment process, the number of Latina and Latino congresspersons has experienced a modest jump. Initially, its membership, other than Corrada (representative for Puerto Rico), consisted primarily of Mexican American Democrats from the Southwest. By the early 1980s, it had grown to eleven, including more Latinas and Latinos from California, Texas, and New Mexico. Manuel Lujan (R-NM) was in Congress at the time of the CHC formation and was a part of the organization.

The CHC membership has shown diversity in both party affiliation and ethnic origin. There have been more Democrats than Republicans, but the commonality of Latino and Latina issues and concerns has bridged partisanship, for the most part. It was not until the 105th Congress that there was no Republican Latino or Latina representation in the CHC. More Latino and Latina subgroups were represented in the late 1980s and early 1990s. The election of Ileana Ros-Lehtinen (R-FL), Lincoln Diaz-Balart (R-FL), Nydia Velásquez (D-NY), and José Serrano (D-NY) expanded the Cuban, Puerto Rican,

and Dominican participation in the caucus. The schism was created within the CHC as its members (Becerra, D-CA and Torres, D-CA) were part of a delegation to Cuba to explore alternative policies from the isolation of Cuba and the lack of formal diplomatic relations between the United States and Cuba. Differences over U.S. policies toward Cuba influenced the decision of Representatives Ros-Lehtinen and Diaz-Balart to formally disassociate themselves from the CHC. However, at the same time, Rep. Robert Menendez (D-NJ), another Cuban congressperson, stayed in the caucus.

Finally, a comprehensive overview of the CHCI needs to include the range of activities dealing with leadership development and fund raising. In 1985, the CHCI expanded its board membership to include influential members of the private sector and community leaders nationwide. Its fellowship and internship programs provide opportunities for young Latinos and Latinas to learn first-hand about the policy-making process. In addition, the CHCI hosts regional conferences to encourage networking and dialogues about issues and concerns. Fund-raising activities include the Fiesta de Golf Tournament, the Annual Gala, Reyes de Comedy Night, the Alumni Association, and corporate support. The caucus continues to develop as a legislative and policy advocate and leader for the Hispanic community.

See also **Political Participation; Political Representation;** *and* **Public Policy.**

BIBLIOGRAPHY

Garcia, F. Chris, ed. *Pursuing Power: Latinos and the Political System.* Notre Dame, Ind.: University of Notre Dame Press, 1997.

Garcia, John A. *Latino Politics in America: Community, Culture, and Interests*. Lanham, Md.: Rowman and Littlefield, 2003.

Maciel, David R., and Isidro D. Ortiz, eds. *Chicanas/Chicanos at the Crossroads: Social, Economic and Political Change*. Tucson: University of Arizona Press, 1996.

McClain, Paula D., and Joseph Stewart. *"Can We All Get Along?": Racial and Ethnic Minorities in American Politics*. Boulder, Colo.: Westview Press, 1998.

Sierra, Christine. "Latino Organizational Strategies on Immigration Reform: Success and Limits in Public Policy Making." In *Latinos and Political Coalitions: Political Empowerment for the 1990s*, edited by Roberto E. Villareal and Norma G. Hernandez, 61–80. New York: Greenwood Press, 1991.

Skerry, Peter. *Mexican Americans: The Ambivalent Minority*. New York: The Free Press, 1993.

JOHN A. GARCIA

CONJUNTO. Texas-Mexican *conjunto* music has its historical roots at the end of the nineteenth century. Most music scholars credit the fusion that today represents Tex-Mex conjunto music to the interaction between German immigrants and Mexicanas and Mexicanos in Central Texas. The conjunto pioneer accordionist Santiago Jiménez Sr. said that Mexicanos adopted the *acordeón*—the conjunto's core instrument—from German and Czech immigrants who settled in Central Texas towns near San Antonio like Fredericksburg and New Braunfels. The accordion, the lead melody instrument, is in fact what gives conjunto music its unique sound and therefore is often referred to as the heartbeat of Tex-Mex music.

During the late nineteenth century, the accordion emerged as a popular instrument in a variety of sociomusical events and dances. The accordion of the late 1890s was combined with a homemade goatskin drum called *tambora de rancho* (ranch drum) and later with instruments such as the violin and various woodwinds. Along with the accordion, another instrument that has remained part of the traditional conjunto evolution is the *bajo sexto*, or twelve-string guitar. The traditional conjunto ensemble, then, consists of a button accordion, a bajo sexto, drums, and a guitar.

The recording history of conjunto music dates back to the 1920s, when major recording labels such as Victor and Bluebird traveled throughout southern states recording African American–derived music that came to be referred to as "race records." During this era, Mexican artists in Texas were among the first to record. Lydia Mendoza, in fact, was one of these. Among accordionists, the first to record with these large American companies was Bruno Villareal, in 1928. Villareal, who began playing the two-row button accordion as a youngster, later took up the piano accordion and by 1935 had recorded at least fifty-five records. During the 1930s, three accordionists contributed unique stylization to the music: Pedro Ayala, Santiago

Jiménez Sr., and Narciso ("el Huracán del Valle"; the Hurricane of the Valley) Martínez. Martínez, often referred to as the father of conjunto music, recorded his first *polca*, "la chicharronera," in 1936. Santiago Jiménez Sr. is credited with having added a *tololoche* (contrabass) to the conjunto; in the 1940s, it became a standard feature of the ensemble.

Music historians assert that the drum did not always have a central place within the ensemble. In fact, drums were not common in conjunto music until the late 1940s and early 1950s. Originally, drums were used mainly in live performance and left off recordings because they were considered a musical nuisance. Pedro Ayala recorded around 1948 and was arguably the first to integrate the saxophone, merging conjunto and *orquesta* (Tex-Mex version of the American orchestra) styles of music. Another key conjunto accordionist, Valerio Longoria, entered the recording scene around 1945. Longoria is attributed with having combined singing with accordion playing. Specifically, Longoria integrated *canciones rancheras* (ranchera songs) and the velvet sound of the bolero with the conjunto repertoire. Longoria was also among the first to play the instrument in the standing position. He was also known for adjusting the reeds on the instrument, giving a hoarse sound to the accordion. Longoria's integration of the modern drums also established a different format of conjunto music that became widely accepted, including the accordion, bajo sexto, electric bass, and drums. Contemporaries of Longoria included Tony de la Rosa, best known for having slowed down the tempo of the music to a choppier pace. This slower tempo caught on and soon became a standard in conjunto music.

The most significant result of de la Rosa's novel conjunto beat was a popular new dance called *el taquachito* (the possum). Eventually, it became the most recognized style of dance associated with Tex-Mex conjunto music. Numerous other conjuntos and accordionists emerged during the 1960s. Among the most-recognized and most widely recorded accordionists were Paulino Bernal, Rubén Vela, Flaco Jiménez, Oscar Hernández, and Esteban Jordán. Bernal was among the first to more fully integrate vocal harmonies into conjunto music. His playing of the four- or five-row chromatic button accordion widened the possibilities for harmony and became his unique signature. Jordán, often referred to as the Jimi Hendrix of conjunto accordion music, moved the music through sonic spaces of rock, jazz, and blues to place an electrifying performative mark on conjunto music never before imagined. In similar fashion, Mingo Saldivar—best known for swinging his accordion around his waist—has gained a huge following, especially among contemporary accordionists. Saldivar has introduced the use of the instrument beyond its original purpose and towards a function as performance partner.

As the twentieth century came to a close, Flaco Jiménez, son of Santiago Jiménez Sr., was recognized for having taken conjunto music far beyond its geographic locality of South Texas, from New York to Tokyo.

Numerous women have accomplished significant strides within the male-dominated, patrilineal tradition of conjunto accordion music. Chavela Ortiz and Lupita Rodela had extremely successful careers in the 1980s. Eva Ybarra, arguably among the most-skilled accordionists in contemporary conjunto, has carved out a successful career since the 1990s. In recognition of her superb skills, Ybarra has been commissioned for various accordion apprentice programs in Austin and San Antonio. One major result of this has been the number of young women accordionists, like Victoria Galvan and Cecilia Saenz, who now represent yet another evolution in this dynamic music tradition. In 1980, the Guadalupe Cultural Arts Center in San Antonio initiated the first Tejano Conjunto Festival, thereby reinstitutionalizing the music within a broader public culture that extends from South Texas to Japan to Mexico. As the annual festival continues to grow, it will stand as a testament to the transformations of a century-old musical tradition that for working-class Texas-Mexicans has consistently been a soundscape of "home," ever-changing and always rhythmically turning like the counterclockwise dance of el taquachito.

See also Chicanos and Chicanas Jiménez, Flaco; Jiménez, Santiago; Latina Musicians; Mendoza, Lydia; Mexican-Origin People in the United States; Music Industry; *and* Tex-Mex Music.

BIBLIOGRAPHY

Accordion Dreams, produced and directed by Hector Galán. 60 mins. Distributed by Galán Productions, 2001, VHS.

Chulas Fronteras/Del Mero Corazón, produced and directed by Chris Strachwitz and Les Blank. 86 mins. Distributed by Arhoolie Productions, 1976/1979, VHS.

Peña, Manuel M. *The Texas-Mexican Conjunto: History of a Working-Class Music.* Austin: University of Texas Press, 1985.

San Miguel, Guadalupe. *Tejano Proud: Tex-Mex Music in the Twentieth Century.* College Station: Texas A&M University Press, 2002.

Tejeda, Juan, ed. *Puro Conjunto: An Album in Words and Pictures.* Austin, Tex.: Center for Mexican American Studies, 2001.

DEBORAH R. VARGAS

CONNECTICUT. Between 1992 and 2000, the Latino and Latina population of Connecticut increased by 40 percent, from 228,000 to 320,000 residents. The overall growth in the state's population during this period was only 6 percent, from 3.2 million to 3.4 million. By 2000, Latinos were 9 percent of the total and outnumbered blacks by more than 10,000 residents.

The majority of Latinos and Latinas in Connecticut in 2000 were Puerto Rican, accounting for 61 percent of the total. The second-largest Latino and Latina group was "Other Hispanics," at 30 percent, consisting of a mixture of Central and South American nationals. The second- and third-largest national subgroups were Mexicans (7 percent) and Colombians (3 percent). Three cities had the largest concentrations of Latinos and Latinas in the state: Bridgeport, Hartford, and New Haven. Together these cities accounted for 38 percent of the state's Latino and Latina residents.

In 2000, the median age in Connecticut was thirty-seven years. For whites it was forty, and for African Americans it was thirty. The median age for Latinos and Latinas was twenty-five years.

Further population statistics reflect the difficult socioeconomic situation of Latinos and Latinas in Connecticut. The state's unemployment rate was 4 percent in 2000. For whites it was 3 percent, compared to 7 percent for Latinos/Latinas and blacks. The state's median household income in 1999 was $54,000. For whites it was $58,000 and for Latinos and Latinas only $32,000; African Americans earned $35,000. Only 7.9 percent of persons were below the poverty level in 1999. The rate for whites was 5 percent, but for Latinos and Latinas and blacks it was 25 percent and 19 percent respectively.

Of persons twenty-five years old and over, 84 percent were high-school graduates and 31.4 percent had a bachelor's degree or higher. Only 57 percent of Latinos and Latinas in Connecticut had a high-school diploma, and 13 percent had a bachelor's degree or higher, compared to 86 and 39 percent respectively for whites and 69 and 17 percent for African Americans.

According to the 2001 edition of the *National Directory of Latino Elected Officials*, 26 Latinos were elected officials in Connecticut—5 state representatives, 17 municipal officials, and 4 school board members. By 2004 there were 27 with the addition of one state representative from Waterbury as a result of the 2001 redistricting process. This represents 13 percent of statewide and congressional officials, which relative to the Latino proportion of the state population constitutes a robust index of political representation. In 2003, at the congressional level, parity in representation would have meant one Latino elected official but there were none. Similarly, parity in the state legislature required 17 Latino members but only 6 held seats in 2004. In 1999, in the state's 203 boards, commissions, committees, and councils, Latino representation was 2.7 percent—a mere 54 members out of 1,997 throughout the state. In 1994, the state had established the Latino and Puerto Rican Affairs Commission to review the impact of state legislation on the Latino community and to encourage the political participation of Latinos.

In 2001, the city of Hartford elected Puerto Rican Eddie Pérez as its mayor, making him the first Latino mayor in the state's history. Pérez pushed for the creation of a statewide Latino and Latina advisory group within the Democratic party. In 2004 this group became the Hispanic Democratic Caucus, with a mandate to pursue a Latino-centered public policy agenda in the state.

See also Census; Central Americans; Chicanos and Chicanas; Demographics; Education; Mexican-Origin People in the United States; Political Participation; Puerto Ricans; *and* South Americans.

BIBLIOGRAPHY

Connecticut Office of Legislative Management. *Legislative Guide: Office of the Secretary of the State of Connecticut. Gender and Racial Diversity on Connecticut State Appointive Bodies, 1999.* March, 2000.

Sembor, Edward C. *An Introduction to Connecticut State and Local Government.* Lanham, Md.: University Press of America, 2003.

U. S. Census Bureau. quickfacts.census.gov/qfd/states/09000. html

U. S. Census Bureau, American FactFinder. factfinder.census.gov/home/saff/main.html?_lang=en

JOSÉ E. CRUZ

CONQUISTADORA, LA. La Conquistadora is a small wooden statue brought to Santa Fe, New Mexico, by Fray Alonso de Benavides in 1625. The Spanish colonists removed the statue from her throne in the *Parroquia* (parish church) during the Pueblo Revolt of 1680, when the indigenous insurgency forced the evacuation of the Spanish to the El Paso–Juarez area, or Guadalupe de el Paso. Don Diego De Vargas credited the statue with protecting the exiles against their enemies at the time, *los indios bárbaros* (wild Indians), and he referred to it as *Nuestra Señora de la Conquista* (Our Lady of the Conquest) in his military journals. In 1693, the statue returned to Santa Fe with De Vargas, as his conquistadors wrested the capital from the occupying Tanos: the retaking was not bloodless, for the Tanos defended Santa Fe from the conquistadors and their *mestizo* (mixed), *genízaro* (detribalized Indians), and Pueblo Indian allies. In the end, La Conquistadora reigned in the governor's palace until 1717, when the Saint Francis Cathedral became the icon's permanent home. The statue survived many harsh years of frontier life and became integral to New Mexico's modern, twentieth-century development in the United States.

Confraternity of La Conquistadora

In 1776, alongside the founding of the California missions and contemporaneous with the American Revolution, Fray Francisco Atanasio Dominguez visited New Mexico and reported to Mexico City the existence of a confraternity devoted to La Conquistadora. Members honored the statue by paying dues, embellishing the lady with an extensive wardrobe, and dressing her for a traditional pilgrimage from the Saint Francis Cathedral to commemorate De Vargas's 1693 Reconquest. Throughout the nineteenth and early twentieth centuries, the confraternity was virtually nonexistent and the statue neglected, but in 1933, as part of the Spanish revival initiated by Anglo-American artists residing in Santa Fe, the local artist Gustave Baumann restored the statue's queenly appearance. In 1956, Edwin V. Byrne, the archbishop of Santa Fe, reestablished the Confraternity of La Conquistadora, and it continued to dress and prepare the statue for its annual fiesta pilgrimage even into the twenty-first century.

La Conquistadora is a regional icon that highlights crucial moments in New Mexican history, from the Spanish colonial era through the twentieth century. For instance, in 1954 Fray Angélico Chávez, a New Mexican priest and prolific writer, penned La Conquistadora's autobiography, in which the statue speaks in the first person and ostensibly tells its own narrative as the oldest Madonna in North America. Clearly a product of the revival movement, the autobiography recounts the intimate details of New Mexico's Spanish colonial history and warns against the threat of (nuclear) modernity in the future. Twenty years later, the narrative was republished during the Chicano and American Indian movements and in response to the statue's 1973 theft. The theft generated public mayhem and made national headlines between stories of Vietnam and civil rights in the early 1970s. The statue was a hostage in a southern New Mexican mineshaft until state police rescued it, held it as state evidence, and returned it to the Saint Francis Cathedral in time for La Conquistadora's 350th anniversary in New Mexico.

Competing Marian Images

La Conquistadora's twentieth-century popularity coincides with the emergence of Our Lady of Guadalupe as a popular icon for Chicana and Chicano activists and artists. In terms of spirituality, Our Lady of Guadalupe and La Conquistadora are similar, but culturally they are different. In some ways, La Conquistadora competes with the Guadalupe image and the working-class mestizo population that it represents, for Our Lady of Guadalupe appeared to Juan Diego in Mexico in 1531 and imprinted the image of a dark-skinned virgin on his *tilma* (apron) to represent a fusion of indigenous mythology and Catholicism. La Conquistadora, on the other hand, heralded Spain's military colonization of the Americas and the myth of *limpieza de sangre* (pure blood) in the New World. Though often characterized as "Our Lady of Peace," La Conquistadora functions as a reminder of New Mexico's colonial legacies: while the statue inspired De Vargas's 1693 Reconquest, it also figured significantly in the Anglo-inspired Spanish revival movement and, somewhat later, in Santa Fe's tourist industry.

La Conquistadora. (Latin Focus Photo Agency)

La Conquistadora's 1930s restoration invigorated the statue's Spanish regality, but the icon has changed with New Mexico's historical currents. Originally, the statue represented the Assumption of Our Lady and was never meant to be dressed, but her seventeenth-century devotees transformed her wooden body into the image of a Spanish queen. The transformation occurred contemporaneously with the Pueblo Revolt and the emergence of Our Lady of Guadalupe as a popular New Mexican icon. However, La Guadalupana is not the only Marian image that competed with La Conquistadora; there were several virgins the statue contended with throughout her reign in New Mexico. The images of Our Lady of Remedies and Our Lady of Light in the sixteenth and seventeenth centuries and Our Lady of Lourdes in the nineteenth century made their appearance in New Mexico, but none are as old as the New Mexico lady statue. Indeed, during Santa Fe's fiesta, which is the largest civic event in the city and the oldest Marian festival in North America, La Conquistadora continues to parade annually through the streets for tourists and locals alike as the First Lady of Santa Fe.

See also Chávez, Angélico; Festivals; Inditas, Las; Native Americans/Mexicanos; New Mexico; Parades; *and* Virgen de Guadalupe.

BIBLIOGRAPHY

Chávez, Fray Angélico. *La Conquistadora: The Autobiography of an Ancient Statue*. 3d ed. Santa Fe: Sunstone, 1983.

Chávez, Fray Angélico. *Our Lady of the Conquest*. Santa Fe: Historical Society of New Mexico, 1948.

Grimes, Ronald L. *Symbol and Conquest: Public Ritual and Drama in Santa Fe*. 2d ed. Albuquerque: University of New Mexico Press, 1992.

MELINA V. VIZCAÍNO

CONVERSOS. *See* Jewish Latinos and Latinas.

COORS BOYCOTT. Provoked by a University of Colorado regent named Joseph Coors, who placed himself in the forefront of opposition to the formation of Chicana and Chicano Studies and Black Studies Departments and even asserted that the presence of minority students on

COORS BOYCOTT. Broadside handed out during the boycott. (Coors Boycott and Strike Coalition Collection, Auraria Library, Denver, Colo.)

campus cheapened the university experience, in 1968 Rodolfo "Corky" Gonzales from the Crusade for Justice and Paul Gonzales from a local American G.I. Forum chapter called for a boycott of the Colorado-based Adolph Coors Brewery. They were soon joined by a broad-based multicultural coalition that included the United Farm Workers, the League of United Latin American Citizens (LULAC), the National Council of La Raza, the National Student Association, the AFL-CIO and affiliated unions, women's groups, and several gay and lesbian organizations. Boycotters addressed a range of issues, including the company's discriminatory hiring practices; its funding of ultraconservative political candidates, far-right-wing organizations including the Heritage Foundation, and antigay hate groups; and its bitter drive to remove unions from its breweries, which landed it on the AFL-CIO "Do Not Patronize" list. It became one of the longest and most successful boycotts of the late twentieth century, as notable for its broadly based coalition as for its long and effective life.

Also notable was Coors's ability to devise innovative strategies to weaken and divide the opposition, which included paying organizations to withdraw their support for the boycott. Through its deep pockets, Coors convinced many groups, including the LULAC in 1974 and the American G.I. Forum in 1977, to pull out of the coalition. But a number of supporters found other reasons not to succumb to payoffs, and the boycott intensified as Coors's reactionary politics continued during the Reagan administration. In the early 1980s, Coors associates continued many openly racist and homophobic policies; engaged in illegal dumping of contaminated waste; provided illegal support for the Nicaraguan Contras and the Iran-Contragate affair; opposed the Equal Rights Amendment; and continued to engage in union busting. In this second stage of the boycott, Coors's counterboycott became even more creative, as the corporation increased its spending to quiet civil rights organizations while it engaged in new public relations, advertising, and marketing initiatives. By the mid-1980s the company reached critical accords with major Latina and Latino organizations including the American G.I. Forum, the National Council of La Raza, National Image, Inc., the Hispanic Chamber of Commerce, the Cuban National Planning Council, and LULAC, as well as African American groups including the National Association for the Advancement of Colored People, Operation PUSH, and the organizers of Black History Month. The agreements generally called for organizations to withhold support for the boycott in exchange for Coors funds. These included millions of dollars for advertising, sponsorship of music and cultural events to support businesses owned by Latinas and Latinos and African Americans, and money for scholarships and direct employment to people of color. Simultaneously, Coors intensified its advertising aimed at minority consumers in both English- and Spanish-language news media.

While Coors's investments after the agreements of the late 1970s failed to halt a downward trend in sales, its advertising became increasingly sophisticated. The corporation simultaneously made direct infusions of advertising money linked to the agreements of 1984, and Coors sales in Latina and Latino and African American communities skyrocketed. Meanwhile, the company's vicious and costly antiunion campaign continued to wear down organized labor, which in 1987 decided to call off its own boycott. A handful of organizations, including groups promoting the rights of women, gays, and lesbians, continued to exert pressure to continue the boycott, until finally the company accepted some of their most basic demands. Yet ongoing threats and short-lived calls for boycotts continued through the 1990s. Furthermore, after briefly succumbing to pressures from feminist critics, the corporation resumed its longstanding media strategy aimed at increasing sales by advertising via openly sexist messages. Through the years several organizations, including the United Farm Workers, refused all monetary offers from Coors and continued to criticize civil rights organizations for accepting what they considered blood money, but corporate efforts had produced a split in the boycott alliance.

In response to decades of pressure, Coors did institute several changes. It adopted a multicultural and nonracist façade and antidiscrimination policies aimed at hiring minority employees; it also began to provide same-sex partner benefits. Meanwhile, the corporation continued to fund ultraconservative organizations, legislation, and projects as well as the campaigns of right-wing politicians. This was only slightly offset by much smaller contributions to charities and moderate and conservative Latina and Latino and African American organizations and enterprises, mostly representing upper- and middle-class business interests. Coors's vast contributions to and maneuvering on behalf of ultrareactionary and conservative interests while offering token sums to minorities became a widely copied model among conservative corporate interests to defuse the militancy of the Chicana and Chicano movement and other progressive political organizations. Little of this funding ever reached the poorest and most needy within Latina and Latino, African American, and Native American communities, whose more progressive elements consistently refused to accept funds, the effect of which was to disengage politically moderate middle-class civil rights organizations. Meanwhile, Coors took advantage of the sharp rightward turn in labor politics nationwide. It hired antiunion consultants, conducted costly and time-consuming antiunion campaigns, and promoted decertification elections whose ultimate effect was to place unions with Coors contracts on the defensive. Organized labor and the unions in Coors plants largely collapsed under the pressure and were often unable to prevent the frequently blatant illegal actions recommended by corporation consultants. As a result, the number of unionized workers in its plants throughout the nation plummeted.

See also American G.I. Forum; Galarza, Ernesto; González, Rodolfo Corky; Labor and Labor Strikes; League of United Latin American Citizens; *and* National Council of La Raza.

BIBLIOGRAPHY

Acuña, Rodolfo. *Occupied America: A History of Chicanos*. 4th ed. New York: Longman, 2000.

Baum, Dan. *Citizen Coors: An American Dynasty*. New York: Morrow, 2000.

Bellant, Russ. *The Coors Connection: How Coors Family Philanthropy Undermines Democratic Pluralism*. Boston: South End Press, 1991.

Burgess, Robert J. *Silver Bullets: A Soldier's Story of How Coors Bombed in the Beer Wars*. New York: St. Martin's, 1993.

Márquez, Benjamin. *LULAC: The Evolution of a Mexican American Political Organization*. Austin: University of Texas Press, 1993.

DIONICIO VALDÉS

CORONA, BERT (1918–2001), civil rights and labor leader. Although less well known than César Chávez, Bert Corona is equally important in U.S. and Chicano/Chicana history. Chávez did what no one had done before when he successfully organized farmworkers. Corona did what no one else had done before when he organized undocumented workers.

Corona's life spanned the major periods of Chicano and Chicana, or Mexican American, history of the twentieth century. Corona's parents came out of the Mexican Revolution of 1910. His father, Noe Corona, was a follower of Pancho Villa and a member of his elite fighting unit Los Dorados. Noe Corona was assassinated in 1921 while attempting to resurrect the Villa movement. Bert Corona never knew his father, but the stories of his father as a fighter for social justice instilled the same values in him. In addition his mother and his grandmother instructed Corona and his siblings to care for the poor and the oppressed. These principles became the center of Corona's life.

Corona was born in El Paso, Texas, on May 29, 1918. After he graduated from high school, he migrated to Los

HUMBERTO "BERT" CORONA. (Dave LaBelle/*Ventura County Star*/AP)

Angeles and obtained a job at a downtown warehouse in the late 1930s, when the militant Longshoreman's Union was organizing the warehouse industry. Corona joined the union and quickly became one of its major leaders, organizing the unskilled and largely immigrant workforce.

It was in the union movement that Corona was introduced to the responsibilities of an organizer. The lessons he learned there and never forgot included the importance of building coalitions among different ethnic groups and building organizations at the grassroots level to include not only workers but their entire families.

After serving in World War II, Corona returned to Los Angeles to resume his community work. In the late 1940s he became one of the principal organizers for the Community Service Organization (CSO) in California. He traveled the state to register Mexican American voters, leading to the election of Edward Roybal to the Los Angeles City Council in 1949. Roybal was the first Mexican American elected to the city council in the twentieth century.

In the 1950s Corona also became a key organizer for the Asociación Nacional México-Americana (ANMA). ANMA was an offshoot of the Mine, Mill, and Smelter Workers, one of the most progressive unions at the time, which was influential among Mexican American workers in the Southwest. In California, Corona assisted in the unionization of Latina and Latino workers and provided civil rights support. Part of his work consisted of supporting the strikes organized by braceros, the contract workers from Mexico imported into the United States at that time.

In 1960 Corona and Roybal started the Mexican American Political Association (MAPA). MAPA became the principal Latina and Latino political and electoral group in the country during that decade. It sought to attract attention to civil rights issues of Mexican Americans concerning education, housing, jobs, health, and police brutality. At the same time MAPA became the first national Latina and Latino electoral organization to participate actively in U.S. presidential politics. Corona, for example, was one of the key organizers of President Lyndon B. Johnson's campaign in California in 1964. Four years later Corona was a national codirector of Robert F. Kennedy's presidential campaign, which ended in tragedy with Kennedy's assassination following his victory in the June primary in California.

The death of Robert Kennedy, a close friend of Corona's, shifted Corona's attention away from electoral politics and back toward community organization. He joined and soon led the Hermandad Mexicana Nacional, which became the largest self-help organization for undocumented workers in the United States. For more than thirty years—until his death—Corona served as its executive director, organizing thousands of Latina and Latino undocumented workers and their families in struggles to protect themselves against repressive anti-immigrant legislation and movements such as California's anti-immigrant Proposition 187 in 1994.

No one has done more to call attention to the problems of the undocumented and to protect them than Corona. Through his values and his work, he inspired and educated numerous Latinas and Latinos who have become labor, community, and political leaders in their own right. Even in the months before his death, when he was confined to a wheelchair, Corona traveled to Sacramento, California, to lobby for immigrant rights. When he entered a room, he became the center of attention because people respected him so much. He was a giant of a leader.

One of the last things Corona was asked was whether he would ever retire. He said, "No, because we still have so many struggles ahead of us." He died working for social justice and striving to make his country fully live up to its ideals, especially for its more marginalized people.

See also Chávez, César; Gonzáles, Rodolfo Corky; Mexican American Political Association; *and* Roybal, Edward.

Mario T. García

CORPI, LUCHA (b. 1945), poet and novelist. Lucha Corpi, best known for her mystery novels, is one of the earliest of the successful Chicana or Chicano novelists. Now living in the San Francisco Bay area, she was born in Jáltipan, Veracruz, Mexico, in 1945, spent her teen years in San Luís Potosí, and moved to the United States in 1964. While living in northern California during the socially disruptive period of the sixties, she witnessed and participated in the turbulent social movements that would provide historical contexts for her novels, enabling her to document the rise of the Chicano/a movement.

Corpi's first collection of poetry appeared in *Fireflight: Three Latin American Poets* (1976). Like all her future books of poetry, this one was written in Spanish and translated by Catherine Rodríguez-Nieto. As Corpi says, "I have come to realize that the language of my poetry is and will always be Spanish, perhaps because this is the language in which I learned from my mother and grandmother to feel the world and express those feelings" (personal communication, 2003). In 1980, Corpi's *Palabras de mediodía/Noon Words* was published, a book of poetry that would identify her as a major figure in Chicana and Chicano literature. (It was republished by Arte Público in 2001.) Corpi was hailed as an important voice, a poet who was lyrical, personal, and yet willing to engage political issues. A child of the political movement of the 1960s and a member of the Chicano/a movement of the 1970s, Corpi addressed issues beyond love and death.

LUCHA CORPI. (Arte Público Press)

She was one of the first poets to articulate a feminist Chicana identity apart from a Chicano identity. Her transnational identity gave voice to the woman who leaves one country to embrace another that does not necessarily embrace her, enduring the agony born of the tension between a Mexican tradition and an alien but inviting contemporary American culture.

Ten years later, Third Woman Press, a small feminist press dedicated to producing works by women of color, published Corpi's award-winning *Variaciones sobre una tempestad/Variations on a Storm* (1990). Lyrical and personal, this book returns to many of Corpi's earlier themes, foregrounding the conflicts a traditional patriarchal society creates for the individual who tries to be culturally loyal while exerting the right to forge an identity beyond traditional roles.

In 1984, Corpi produced her first novel, *Delia's Song*, a coming-of-age tale and a thinly veiled autobiographical description of her years at Berkeley. The book takes place in the early 1970s at an elite northern California university and narrates the conflicts experienced by a young Mexican girl as she tries to assimilate into an Anglo academic culture at the same time that she is energized by the excitement of the early Chicano/a movement. Marking a radical shift in prose style, Corpi's second novel, *Eulogy for a Brown Angel: A Mystery Novel* (1992), signals her move into the mystery genre. The novel features the first Chicana detective in American literature; Gloria Damasco, besides being a member of the Mexican American community, is a feminist and a political activist. Damasco challenges the reader's traditional concepts of how a detective looks and thinks. Corpi also redefines the mystery novel by incorporating as part of the background the political atmosphere of the Chicano/a civil rights movement. The melding of genres and the introduction of the Chicana and Chicano culture show Corpi as an innovative writer.

Eulogy for a Brown Angel, which won the PEN Oakland Josephine Miles Prize in fiction and the Multicultural Publishers Exchange Book Award of Excellence in Adult Fiction, was followed by other Gloria Damasco mysteries: *Cactus Blood* (1995) and *Black Widow's Wardrobe* (1999).

The ethnic-American detective, such as Gloria Damasco, is no longer a curiosity, but in 1992 it was new to both Chicana and Chicano literature and the mystery genre. In her portrayal of a feminist political activist who also happens to solve mysteries, Corpi also depicts a strong Chicana active in the day-to-day political and personal life of her community. Detective Damasco confronts the conflicts inherent in the relationship between two strong and competitive cultures, and, because she is intimately aware of her Mexican culture, she has among her tools for solving mysteries access to the culture's belief in the nonphysical aspects of existence. Corpi is able to incorporate Mexican myths and legends into her stories, giving the reader information on specific cultural histories. This allows her to describe specific Mexican cultural traditions and Chicana and Chicano practices, from celebrating the Day of the Dead to participating in Mexican family gatherings. From the Chicano Moratorium to the United Farm Workers strike, Corpi keeps Chicana and Chicano political history alive in the literary imagination. Because of Corpi's own transnational experiences and history, the settings of her mystery novels include more than just northern California. Gloria Damasco moves about San Francisco, Los Angeles, and Cuernavaca, Mexico, as well as Native American communities. Corpi's skill at weaving intricate mysteries in the panoramic experience of a transnational identity brings a fairly recognizable mass genre to a whole new level.

Critics acknowledge that Corpi has expanded the field of the mystery novel by her introduction of a Chicana detective. She has also expanded the field of Chicana and

Chicano literature by moving the mystery novel into a place of literary importance.

See also Chicano/a Movement; Chicanos and Chicanas; Día de los Muertos; Literature; Mexicans in the United States; National Chicano Moratorium; *and* United Farm Workers.

BIBLIOGRAPHY

PRIMARY WORKS

Corpi, Lucha. *Black Widow's Wardrobe*. Houston: Arte Público Press, 1999.

Corpi, Lucha. *Cactus Blood*. Houston: Arte Público Press, 1995.

Corpi, Lucha. *Crimson Moon*. Houston: Arte Público Press, 2004.

Corpi, Lucha. *Delia's Song*. Houston: Arte Público Press, 1984.

Corpi, Lucha. *Eulogy for a Brown Angel: A Mystery Novel*. Houston: Arte Público Press, 1992.

Corpi, Lucha. *Fireflight: Three Latin American Poets*. Translated by Catherine Rodríguez-Nieto. Berkeley, Calif.: Oyes, 1976.

Corpi, Lucha. *Palabras de mediodía/Noon Words*. Translated by Catherine Rodríguez-Nieto. Berkeley, Calif.: Fuego de Aztlán, 1980.

Corpi, Lucha. *Variaciones sobre una tempestad/Variations on a Storm*. Translated by Catherine Rodríguez-Nieto. Berkeley, Calif.: Third Woman Press, 1990.

Corpi, Lucha. *Where Fireflies Dance/Ahí, donde bailan las luciérnagas*. San Francisco: Children's Book Press, 1997.

Corpi, Lucha, ed. *Máscaras*. Berkeley, Calif.: Third Woman Press, 1997.

SECONDARY WORKS

Carabi, Angels. "*Belles Lettres* Interview: Lucha Corpi." *Belles Lettres* 7.2 (1991–92): 48–52.

González, Maria C. *Contemporary Mexican-American Women Novelists: Toward a Feminist Identity*. New York: Peter Lang, 1996.

Ikas, Karin Rosa, ed. *Chicana Ways: Conversations with Ten Chicana Writers*. Reno, Nev.: University of Nevada Press, 2002.

Pearson, Carol. "Writing from the Outside In: Constructs of Memory and Chicanas as Private Eyes in Three Detective Novels by Lucha Corpi." *Interdisciplinary Literary Studies: A Journal of Criticism and Theory* 4 (2002): 38–51.

Rodriguez, Ralph E. "Cultural Memory and Chicanidad: Detecting History, Past and Present, in Lucha Corpi's Gloria Damasco Series." *Contemporary Literature* 43 (2002): 138–170.

MARÍA C. GONZÁLEZ

CORRETJER, JUAN ANTONIO (1908–1985), Puerto Rican poet and political activist. Juan Antonio Corretjer was the son of Diego Corretjer Hernández, a Catalan descendant, and María Brígida Montes González, the daughter of farmers from Lares, Puerto Rico. He was born in 1908 in Ciales, a mountain village known for the bravura its inhabitants demonstrated in 1898, when they resisted the occupation of the U.S. Army in the aftermath of the Spanish-American War.

Corretjer was affiliated from early adolescence with the Juventud Nacionalista (Young Nationalists), a subgroup of the separatist political organization Partido Nacionalista Puertorriqueño (Puerto Rican Nationalist Party). Also a precocious writer, at age eighteen he began studying

JUAN ANTONIO CORRETJER. (Nacion y Patria)

journalism in San Juan and published poems in local newspapers. One of his most notorious poetic texts from that period, titled "*Canción multitudinaria*" (Song for the Masses) and published in *La Democracia*, is held by Puerto Rican writer José Luis González as proof of the existence of a *nacionalismo socialista* (socialist nationalism) in Puerto Rico as early as 1928. Gonzalez's appraisal proves important not only because it underscores Corretjer's Marxist-oriented political ideology, a preference he defended all his life, but also in that it dispels the general opinion among historians and critics that Corretjer became a Marxist only after being incarcerated in Atlanta, Georgia during the 1940s.

Political Activism

Corretjer briefly established himself in New York City toward the end of the 1920s before returning to Puerto Rico to become a member of the Partido Nacionalista in 1930. In New York, the Puerto Rican poet collaborated with Augusto César Sandino, a Nicaraguan rebel who fought a long guerrilla war against several presidents who were supported by U.S. marines. Corretjer also joined the Liga Antiimperialista de las Américas (Anti-imperialist League of the Americas), a leftist organization opposed to U.S. military interventions in Latin America. The Liga was presided over by the Mexican artist Diego Rivera, and included among its members the Cuban Juan Antonio Mella, the Venezuelan Salvador de la Plaza, the Salvadorian Agustín Farabundo Martí, and Sandino himself.

Under the tutelage of Pedro Albizu Campos, the charismatic young leader of the Partido Nacionalista and graduate of the Harvard School of Law, Corretjer increased his political activism in the push toward Puerto Rican independence. During the first part of the 1930s, he traveled to the Dominican Republic, Haiti, and Cuba, lobbying for support. Corretjer helped Albizu Campos lead the famous sugar cane workers' strike of 1934, which resulted in the concession to all of the union's demands. This event marked the period of greatest strength for the nacionalistas but also gave way to the worst outburst of political repression in Puerto Rico's modern history. Corretjer, together with Albizu Campos, poet Clemente Soto Vélez, and other prominent members of the Partido Nacionalista were incarcerated, first in San Juan in 1936 and then in Atlanta from 1937 to 1942.

Since Corretjer was forbidden to return to Puerto Rico until 1946, upon his release from prison he returned to New York to resume his political activism. This second stay in New York gave rise to significant ideological differences with the Partido Nacionalista, especially with regard to the strategy for achieving Puerto Rican independence and the plans for what to do after reaching such a goal. Corretjer was, above all, a socialist. As such, his ideas for founding a republic were interwoven with his beliefs in a socially egalitarian state. He eventually returned to San Juan and continued to plead for a noncolonial political status for Puerto Rico.

Literary Works

Corretjer's active political life was matched by a prolific literary oeuvre that includes prose fiction, nonfiction, and, particularly, poetry. Agüeybaná, his first collection of poems, already contained one key motif that came to characterize Corretjer's poetry: the exaltation of the myths and traditions of the Taíno (Arawak) Native Americans, who were exterminated in the sixteenth century by the combination of European diseases brought to the islands of the Caribbean and by the cruelty of the Spanish colonial enterprise. In Juan Antonio Corretjer o la poesía inebitable (Juan Antonio Corretjer or the Inevitable Poetry), probably the most original critical account of Corretjer's poetry, Puerto Rican poet and literary critic Joserramón Melendes affirms that the publication of Agüeybaná in 1932 sparked

an unprecedented interest in the Taíno heritage. According to Melendes, the indigenous population acts as a historical paradigm for early 2000s Puerto Ricans in the sense that, in Corretjer's depiction, precolonial peoples were truly free political subjects. Without a doubt, Corretjer's poetry is deeply marked by his political convictions. In his most critically acclaimed book of poetry, Yerba bruja (1957), or Bewitching Grass, for instance, the allusions to the independent nature of the native populations as an entity not subject to European cultural rule became more explicit, acquiring the tone of a maxim. In the very prologue of Yerba bruja, Corretjer states:

No he pretendido desenterrar una momia. He deseado hacer visible el resplandor de la imaginación india presente en la nuestra (It was not my intent to dig up a mummy. I wanted to bring to light the splendor of the indigenous imagination that lives on in our own).

(Alabanzas, p. 77)

Other widely commented volumes of Corretjer's poetry include El Leñero: Poema de la revolución de Lares (Leñero: Poem of the Lares Revolt, 1944) and Distancias (Distances, 1957). El Leñero is an epic poem on the life of Manuel Rosado, leader of the failed insurrection that proclaimed the independence of Puerto Rico from Spain in 1868. Written while Corretjer was imprisoned in Atlanta, the poem is composed entirely in décimas, a fixed verse form of Spanish origin consisting of ten lines. Distancias was the product of another period of incarceration in San Juan's La Princesa prison, the result of the 1950 nationalist revolt in the mountain village of Jayuya against U.S. rule. Corretjer continued to publish poetry and works of political thought until his death in San Juan in 1985.

See also Albizu Campos, Pedro; Literature; Nuyorican Theater and Poetry; Puerto Rican Independence Movement; Puerto Ricans; *and* United States Interventions in Latin America.

BIBLIOGRAPHY

Corretjer, Juan Antonio. *Alabanzas/Antología*. Edited by Marisa Rosado and María Gisela Rosado. La Habana, Cuba: Centro Cultural Pablo de la Torriente Brau, 2000.

Corretjer, Juan Antonio. *Obras completas*. Edited by José Luis Vega. San Juan, P.R.: Instituto de Cultura Puertorriqueña, 1977.

Medina, Ramón Felipe. "Juan Antonio Corretjer: Homenaje a la figura total." *Sin Nombre* 5 (1975): 49–61.

Melendes, Joserramón. *Juan Antonio Corretjer o la poesía inebitable*. Río Piedras, P.R.: QeAse, 1996.

NÉSTOR E. RODRÍGUEZ

CORRIDOS. The *corrido* is a verse narrative, a story sung to a musical accompaniment, portraying characters engaged in heroic, often tragic, struggles in real or realistic episodes that reflect the language, experiences, and values of common folk. For approximately two hundred years, corridos have been a cherished part of a traditional heritage in various regions of Mexico and the United States. In contemporary times, new generations with roots and interests in traditional culture have helped to further promote the study, preservation, and dissemination of the corrido.

Conventional Themes and Episodes

The corrido is often based on a historical incident, or whenever it is a fictional composition, the tale must be considered a believable account. Realistic aspects include the mention of dates and locations, a language that conforms to familiar dialectal forms, most often a variation of Mexican rural Spanish. The tempo of the melodies accompanying the corridos may vary from the waltz to the polka but they must provide an appropriate emotional resonance to the narrative themes, metrics, and cadences considered appropriate by the audience. The instruments employed in the performance will vary according to the musical conventions of the region where the corrido is sung. A guitar is the foundational instrument; the accordion and a twelve-string guitar (*bajo-sexto*) have become traditional in southwestern United States and northern Mexico. But in the state of Guerrero, for example, the harp is still used, as well as musical ensembles such as the mariachi in both the United States and Mexico, and the large brass groups known as *banda* in California and Sinaloa.

Corridos are characterized by a series of conventional scenes, including foreshadowing of events that occur in the narrative, a journey portraying pursuers and the pursued, and a verbal defiance launched by a protagonist to the antagonist and their inevitable clash followed by victory or defeat. The narrative voice may pass a moral judgment on a significant aspect of the events and may commemorate the protagonist and his deeds or the event that has occurred. Not all of these factors need to appear in a narrative to be considered a corrido, but it must contain a sufficient number of these elements to be judged as part of the genre and its tradition.

A fundamental factor in the corrido is a clash of opposing forces: without such open confrontation between opponents a composition cannot be considered a corrido. Protagonists are individuals who demonstrate positive community values: respectful to elders, loyal to their families and friends, generous with the weak, courageous before danger, and not intimidated by the abuses of the powerful. Knowledgeable corrido audiences are sensitive to subtle narrative points: showing disapproval to those opponents considered abusive, disloyal, demeaning, or cowardly, and demonstrating admiration for examples of courage, compassion, loyalty, and strength.

Origins and Evolution

Spanish ballad narratives or romances arrived to the New World in the sixteenth century and disseminated throughout Latin America. These ballads share a number of similarities with the corrido in language, metrics, and narrative conventions. Such evidence provides support to the thesis that the origin of the corrido must be found in the Spanish romance tradition. Scholars have pointed out that, while there may be a romance-corrido relationship, corridos have deep roots in local history, social conventions, and values, advancing the theory that the genre may have originated in the Texas-Mexico border area.

The collection and study of corridos did not begin until the 1920s. Heroes in early narratives—"Jesús Leal" (1873), "Heraclio Bernal" (1880s), and "Gregorio Cortez" (1901)—generally represent rebels, often accused or labeled as bandits, who confront figures of social or political authority:

Corrido de Jesús Leal

El día veintiocho de enero,	On the 28th of January,
no me quisiera acordar,	I wish I could forget,
cuando Don Félix venía	when Don Felix came to
A aprehender a Jesús Leal.	arrest Jesús Leal.

At some point, the bandit or outlaw evolves into a fuller figure fighting powerful enemies from a position of equality:

Gregorio Cortez

Decía Gregorio Cortez	Gregorio Cortez would say,
con su pistola en la mano:	with his pistol in his hand,
—No corran, rinches cobardes,	"Don't run, you cowardly rangers,
con un solo mexicano.—	from one lone Mexican."

Such equality among rivals continued during the Mexican Revolution (1910–1920) in the portrayal of corrido heroes: Francisco Villa, Emiliano Zapata, Benito Canales.

La batalla de Zacatecas	The Battle of Zacatecas
Ahora sí borracho Huerta	Now, drunkard Huerta,
harás las patas más chuecas	You'll really get bow-legged
al saber que Pancho Villa	when you find out that Pancho Villa
ha tomado Zacatecas.	has captured Zacatecas.

In the years following the Mexican Revolution, local figures and incidents were, again, the subject of corridos: "Alonso" (1923), "La inundación de California" (a flood in 1928), "Simón Blanco" (1937), and "El Moro de Cumpas" (a horse race in 1957). Commercially successful corridos from this period also include fictional stories, such as "Juan Charrasqueado" or "El caballo blanco." In recent years the theme of drug trafficking has been prominent in a great number of narrative songs labeled "narcocorridos," though not all of these can be considered part of the genre as they lack the conventional features of the corrido tradition. A few genuine corridos from this period have continued to be sung after more than two decades. Among the most popular are "Lamberto Quintero," "Se les peló Baltazar," and "El corrido de Gerardo."

Camelia la texana (contrabando y traición)	
Una hembra, si quiere a un hombre,	When a woman loves a man,
por él puede dar la vida,	she will give up her life for him,
pero hay que tener cuidado	but watch out
si esa hembra se siente herida,	if the woman feels wounded:
la traición y el contrabando	betrayal and drug smuggling
son cosas incompartidas.	just don't mix!

Transmission and the Corrido Tradition

In earlier years corridos were transmitted primarily through oral networks. The oral corrido circulated in local, informal performances, generating versions as the composition traveled by word of mouth. The evolving oral tradition adapted from region to region and has helped to preserve the corrido in the memories of succeeding generations.

An important factor in the evolution of the corrido has been its shift from oral transmission to literary or commercial consumption: in printed form via broadsides, songbooks, or cited in literary works. It also was recorded in mechanical or electronic media: wax cylinders, pianola rolls, phonographic discs, cassettes, compact discs, films, and videos. In spite of this substantial transformation from folklore to popular culture, corridos maintain a sufficient number of conventional and familiar characteristics that conform to a solid genre tradition. Perhaps the most important factor in determining the quality of a corrido is (a) the length of time it has been in circulation and (b) the number of regions where it is known. That is, the longer it is remembered among diverse audiences and locations, the higher is the likelihood that a corrido may be considered a classic, as it embodies the identity and cultural history of the folk community. Indeed, these historical, linguistic, musical and technical adaptations often result in corridos whose apparent artistic simplicity underlies great beauty and complexity.

See also Chicanos and Chicanas; Literature; Mexican-Origin People in the United States; *and* Poetry.

BIBLIOGRAPHY

Hernández, Guillermo E. "What is a Corrido? Thematic Representation and Narrative Discourse." *Studies in Latin American Popular Culture* 18 (1999).

Mendoza, Vicente T. *Lirica narrativa de Mexico: El corrido*. México: Instituto de Investigaciones Estéticas. Universidad Nacional Autónoma de México, 1964.

Paredes, Americo. *"With His Pistol in His Hand": A Border Ballad and Its Hero*. Austin: University of Texas Press, 1958. Reprint, 1990.

Strachwitz, Chris, Philip Sonnichsen, and James Nicolopulus. *Corridos and Tragedias de la Frontera. First Recordings of Historic Mexican-American Ballads (1928–1937)*. Folklyric Records 7019-7020. 1994.

GUILLERMO E. HERNÁNDEZ

CORTEZ, ERNESTO, JR., community activist. A native of San Antonio, Texas, Ernesto Cortez Jr. graduated from Texas A&M with a degree in English and economics and attended graduate school at the University of Texas. During the 1960s, while he was a student, Cortez was involved with the lettuce and grape boycotts initiated by the United Farm Workers union in California and with the South Texas Valley citrus and melon strikes in 1967 and 1968. He was also one of the founders of the Mexican American Youth Organization (MAYO), which eventually led to the establishment of La Raza Unida Party in Texas in the 1970s. In 1969 he became the director of economic development for the Mexican American Unity Council, a community development organization in the Westside barrios of San Antonio.

By 1970 Cortez was developing a strategy to organize the Westside barrios of San Antonio. His vision was to establish a quasi-governmental structure in response to the continuing efforts by the city elite to exclude the barrios from the decision-making process. He made initial contact with Saul Alinsky, who gained national prominence as a "radical community organizer" (Finks). After various sojourns into communities throughout the nation, the most prominent among them Rochester, New York, and Oakland, California, Alinsky established the Industrial Areas Foundation (IAF) in Chicago to support efforts by communities to organize across the United States. Cortez went to Chicago to train as a community organizer. With a grant from the Church of Christ, Cortez recruited various community activists to the IAF training program in Chicago. By 1973 he established a sponsoring committee to help coordinate the organizing activities, which led to the founding in 1974 of Communities Organized for Public Service (COPS) in the barrios of San Antonio.

Closely following the Alinsky community organization tactics and methods, Cortez developed the leadership from the communities themselves. Then several important rules were established. First, no leader of COPS would use her or his position to run for public office. Second, COPS itself would not get directly involved in electoral politics. The organization's leaders invited politicians to address the COPS membership in what they called accountability nights with the stipulation that the politicians would answer the questions fielded with a yes or a no.

The one variation to the Alinsky method was the use of Catholic Church parishes as an organizational base. Cortez organized on the premise that the parish halls were where residents maintained some kind of control of their lives in the midst of an historic neglect by the political and economic institutions of San Antonio. Following this premise, Cortez organized through the parishes, putting them together to form a quasi-governmental structure where communities could speak to the power structure in their environment. Utilizing the Alinsky tactics, COPS took on winnable issues. Because of COPS, the Westside and Southside barrios of San Antonio enjoyed a renewed investment in public services, including sidewalks, curbs, and drainage systems. Addressing the lack of access to economic resources for home improvements and expansions, COPS led actions to choke up the lobbies of the one major bank in San Antonio, the Frost National Bank, bringing business to a stop. This action eventually gained concessions from the bank's management. In summary, COPS played a major role in establishing basic justice in the distribution of public services and in the economic development of the city.

In addition COPS coalesced with the Conservation Society from the North Side (as pointed out by a local pundit, Chicana *viejitas* [little old ladies] from the Westside formed a most unlikely coalition with the blue-haired Anglo middle-class viejitas) to successfully oppose construction over the recharge zone for the sole water source for San Antonio. In 1978 COPS publicly announced its opposition to any business coming to San Antonio unless it offered a minimum salary of $15,000 for every employee. After national attention focused on the action, the economic and financial elite met with COPS and agreed to greater investment in public services for the barrios in exchange for COPS rescinding its challenge. In the 1980s, recruiting young Chicana and Chicano students to do the research, COPS documented the lack of libraries and health facilities throughout the barrios of San Antonio. Consequently the city built new libraries and health clinics throughout its barrios.

Cortez went on to organize a network of Chicana and Chicano community organizations in Texas, including El Paso Interreligious Sponsoring Organization (EPISO) in El Paso, Valley Interfaith in the Rio Grande valley of south Texas, the Metropolitan Organization in Houston, Allied Communities of Tarrant (ACT) in Fort Worth, and Austin Interfaith in Austin. This network successfully addressed statewide issues such as education, health, and housing. The network eventually expanded to other organizations, including Metro Alliance in San Antonio; Fort Bend Interfaith in Fort Bend, Indiana; the Border Organization of Eagle Pass and Del Rio, Texas; Dallas Area Interfaith; Pima County Interfaith Council (PCIC) in Tucson, Arizona; Valley Interfaith Project in Phoenix, Arizona; East Valley Interfaith Organizing Effort in Tempe, Arizona; Albuquerque Interfaith in Albuquerque, New Mexico; Omaha Together One Community (OTOC) in Omaha, Nebraska; Triangle Interfaith Project in southeast Texas; and the West Texas Organizing Project. As the Southwest regional director of the IAF, Cortez established a network of twenty-three community organizations from the Jeremiah Group in New Orleans to A Metropolitan Organizing Strategy (AMOS) in Des Moines, Iowa, to the One La IAF in California, which extends from Los Angeles to Sacramento to Pasadena.

By the 1990s an infrastructure of community organizations dotted San Antonio. Not all of these organizations belong to the IAF. However, the two most prominent, COPS and the Metropolitan Alliance, a network of non–Catholic church organizations, did, and together they became a major influence in the decision-making processes in city hall.

Cortez has received several honors and awards for his community involvement. In 1984 he received the MacArthur Award for his work as a community organizer and director of the Los Angeles Metro Organizing Strategy in Los Angeles. In 1997 he received the Heinz Award in the public policy category for his work training organizers in the Southwest. Both awards included a $250,000 individual prize.

See also **Communities Organized for Public Service; La Raza Unida Party;** *and* **Mexican American Youth Organization.**

BIBLIOGRAPHY

Finks, P. David. *The Radical Vision of Saul Alinsky*. New York: Paulist Press, 1984.

RODOLFO ROSALES

CORTEZ, GREGÓRIO (1875–1916), Mexican American folk hero. Born on June 22, 1875, near the present-day towns of Reynosa and Matamoros, Mexico, Gregório Cortez and his family crossed into Texas sometime during his childhood years and found a society where race prejudice defined the social position of Mexicans. In South Texas, Anglos prevailed over people of Mexican heritage by monopolizing the more influential political offices, through election, appointment, or patronage. Anglos enforced the Mexicans' submission through violence, lynching, or reliance on law authorities, among them the Texas Rangers, known as the *rinches*. Segregationist customs further acted to enforce the understanding that Mexicans were not the Anglos' equals.

Occupational restrictions increased the subordination of Mexicans. As a rule, Anglos controlled the more lucrative openings in the economy, among them the professions, the manufacturing sector, and ranching and farming, as well as trade and commerce. What remained for the majority of Mexicans to earn a livelihood was thus unskilled employment in the cities, sunup-to-sundown work on the farms or ranches, or clearing land or working the railroad lines with pick and shovel. About the time that Gregório Cortez and his family arrived on the Texas border, moreover, South Texas was undergoing a farm revolution wherein old ranches were being broken up and turned into new farmlands. For many Mexican families that had previously lived year-round on a ranch, seasonal farm laborer migrant work became the only option. Some of the more adventurous headed for the interior of the state where they might find better options. Such were the circumstances that brought Gregório Cortez and his brother Romaldo to Karnes, Gonzales, and surrounding counties in 1889.

Encounters with Law Enforcement

In 1901, Gregório and Romaldo Cortez rented land near Kenedy (Karnes County, Texas). On June 12 of that year, the local sheriff appeared unexpectedly at their home, inquiring about a stolen horse that Gregório had allegedly acquired recently. The sheriff's translator misinterpreted Cortez's responses and alerted the sheriff that Cortez was resisting the order to surrender. Both men then drew pistols, and in the exchange of fire the sheriff fell to the ground, mortally wounded. Romaldo also received a wound (which turned out to be fatal), and the translator fled for his life in the melee.

Aware that killing a white man was an egregious transgression, Cortez quickly told his family where to take refuge, mounted his wounded brother on horseback, and marched toward Kenedy to seek medical assistance. Gregório left Romaldo in Kenedy, then took off on foot in a northward direction, hoping to deceive the posse, which presumably would figure that Cortez would trek toward the border. But a search detail determined Cortez's whereabouts at a friend's home in Belton (Gonzales County, Texas), and upon reaching it, rushed the household with women and children inside. In the fusillade that followed, Cortez killed another sheriff before escaping into the brush and eluding the posse altogether.

Certain of facing lynch law, Cortez struck for the border, receiving help from friends along the way. But no matter his adroitness at horseback riding or his knack for dodging his pursuers, he could not foil them as they relied on the telegraph, the telephone, and the railroad lines to stay hot on his trail. Yet Cortez rode and walked, zigzagging and falsifying his tracks along the way, doing without food, water, and sleep for long stretches of time. On June 22, 1901, he reached a ranch in the vicinity of Laredo, but there an acquaintance he trusted notified the law and Texas Rangers arrested him.

There followed a series of trials to determine Cortez's guilt on the charge of killing the two sheriffs as well as the constable who had been killed in another encounter with Cortez. Not until four years later, in 1905, did the courts find Cortez guilty of killing the sheriff in the shootout of June 12, 1901. Cortez went to prison until July 1913, when the governor pardoned him. Cortez died in 1916.

Popular and Political Interpretations

The Gregório Cortez incident evolved immediately into more than a simple face-off between a man and some peace officers. According to Américo Paredes, author of *"With His Pistol in His Hand": A Border Ballad and Its Hero*, the story took on legendary proportions as Mexicans in towns and rural areas throughout Texas recounted the exploits of Gregório Cortez. Oral tales depicted Cortez as possessing superhuman abilities and accomplishing Herculean feats. Stories had him persevering in the face of hunger, thirst, and fatigue and outwitting the rinches and eluding posses with superior horsemanship. *Corridos* (ballads) further extolled Cortez's courage in face of superior odds. Over the years, singers would give slightly different renditions of events, but they universally praised Cortez for his actions while denigrating that of his pursuers, not the least of which were the hated rinches, who for Mexican Americans represented the less savory elements of the Texas constabulary. Corridos depicted the rinches as cowardly villains outsmarted by the fortitude, resourcefulness, and manliness of Gregório Cortez.

The Gregório Cortez affair also turned into a political issue for the Latina and Latino community. For many, Cortez's response to the sheriff's conduct symbolized an act of daring defiance and resistance long overdue against oppressors who persecuted Mexicans and demanded servility at every turn. Cortez's fate also worried the Mexican American populace, for if lynch law remained as retaliation against insolent Mexicans, could the political system grant him a fair trial? His defense became a topic of much public concern. Common people familiar with the case sympathized with the accused, and groups with the facility to do so undertook a fundraising effort. The Miguel Hidalgo workers' society of San Antonio launched a letter-writing drive to collect the needed money for legal fees. Groups in the many Texas *colonias* further sponsored benefit events. Two newspaper editors from San Antonio (Pablo Cruz of *El Regidor* and F. A. Chapa of *El Imparcial*) used their newspaper columns to keep people abreast of the case, and they looked after the money raised to ensure that Cortez got adequate legal protection.

The Gregório Cortez legend was integrated into the politics of the Chicano Movement long after the man had died. In the 1960s and 1970s students, who made up the bulk of the *movimiento*, saw in Cortez a historical example of a Chicano just like themselves challenging a racial order that insisted on quiescence. Cortez retains a place in Chicano history as a person having turned to one of several possible alternatives in response to political discrimination.

See also Corridos; Criminal Justice System; Migrant Workers; Paredes, Américo; Texas; *and* Texas Rangers.

BIBLIOGRAPHY

The Ballad of Gregorio Cortez. Directed by Robert M. Young. Los Angeles: Moctesuma Esparza Productions, Inc., 1982.

Limón, José E. "Healing the Wounds: Folk Symbols and Historical Crisis." *The Texas Humanist: Ideas, History, and Culture* 6 (March/April 1984): 21–23.

Limón, José E. *The Return of the Mexican Ballad: Américo Paredes and His Anthropolitical Text as Persuasive Political Performance.* Stanford, Calif.: Stanford Center for Chicano Research, 1986.

Paredes, Américo. *"With His Pistol in His Hand": A Border Ballad and Its Hero.* Austin: University of Texas Press, 1971.

ARNOLDO DE LEÓN

CORTINA, JUAN (1824–1894), Mexican American folk hero. Born in Camargo, Tamaulipas, in 1824, Juan Nepomuceno ("Cheno") Cortina is known in Texas for a rebellion he led there in 1859 and 1860.

Cortina moved with his widowed mother to the U.S. side of the Rio Grande sometime during the 1840s. Working on his mother's property during the 1850s, Cortina watched as Anglo-Americans—who had arrived in the wake of the United States–Mexico War (1846–1848)—displaced Mexicans from positions in the legal and political systems, defrauded grantees of lands, and rapidly established economic dominance by virtue of their imported wealth. As Cortina saw it, Anglos committed crimes against Mexicans with impunity and often escaped punishment by virtue of their connections to the Anglo-controlled judicial system.

JUAN CORTINA. (Library of Congress Prints and Photographs Division)

The Cortina Wars, 1859–1860

Cortina's pent-up resentment against the newcomers exploded following an incident at a local café one morning in July 1859. Going there for morning coffee, Cortina came upon the city marshal berating a drunken Mexican whom Cortina knew as a hard-working ranch hand. Cortina sought to reason with the peace officer, but was greeted with a racial epithet. Gunfire followed. Cortina left the sheriff prostrate and fled with the vaquero (cowboy).

On September 28, in an effort to avenge personal injustices inflicted upon him by local Anglos, Cortina and some seventy-five followers stormed into Brownsville and in an ensuing encounter killed four men. Cortina retreated to his ranch and from there issued a proclamation dated September 30 explaining his actions. In it he accused an Anglo clique in Brownsville and surrounding communities of complicity in mistreating the Mexican population. Because Anglos had gone unpunished for crimes they committed against innocent Mexicans, Cortina explained, he had taken it upon himself to ensure that they met justice.

Anglos reacted to Cortina's effrontery by sending a company of volunteers to capture him. Cortina proved elusive but, on October 24, a military skirmish took place between Cortina's columns and a detachment of Anglo recruits named the Brownsville Tigers. Cortina defeated them along with a Mexican force from Matamoros, which had joined up with the Americans. The next month he waylaid a small ranger force searching for him. After that, his fame spread throughout the valley, and his victories won over more believers to his cause.

Cortina issued a second proclamation (dated November 23, 1859). In it, he reiterated his complaints against the Anglos of South Texas. He proposed creating a secret society that would avenge committed wrongs or perhaps punish those responsible for persecuting Mexicans. He further appealed to governor-elect Sam Houston to employ the legal system to safeguard Mexican rights. In late 1859 and winter of 1860, however, a combined force of Texas Rangers and the federal military under Major Samuel Heintzelman defeated Cortina and pushed him and his troops across the Rio Grande into Mexico. With his retreat, Cortina's major role in Texas history ended, but he remained active in the region during the Civil War years and the rest of the decade. He died in Mexico in 1894.

Ramifications

Though a localized affair, the Cortina Wars had national ramifications. For one thing, they occurred almost simultaneously with John Brown's raid on Harper's Ferry, thus deepening the sense among Southerners that forces hostile to their way of life besieged them. Further, it diluted the confidence that Anglo Southerners (and especially Texans) had in the Union's ability to defend them against threats on the frontier, whether the threats were caused by Indians or by Mexicans from south of the border. Moreover, Cortina's actions necessitated the deployment of federal troops at a time of approaching civil war. Having been reassigned elsewhere just a few months earlier, the military had to return to the Rio Grande and contend with something wholly unconnected to the national crisis. Also inflicted on the national consciousness was a question surfacing for the first time following the war with Mexico: How was government (or Anglo society) going to deal with the discontented Mexican population indigenous to the conquered territories?

At the regional level, indeed, Juan Cortina's dispute highlighted the many problems that the native Tejano and Tejana population had with American rule. Tejanos and Tejanas felt bitter toward the colonial system that favored Anglos at their expense. Cortina's challenge also brought to center stage the sensitive issue of race relations, which shaped interaction between the two communities in Texas long after. Land conflicts and economic differences also lay behind Cortina's action, as he had seen firsthand the way Anglo lawyers and speculators questioned the legitimacy of old land grants or simply acquired Mexican lands by paying delinquent taxes.

Beyond these several implications, the Cortina Wars of 1859–1860 became literally the stuff of legends. For decades after, common people in South Texas spoke of Juan Cortina as the very embodiment of a community fancying an uprising against the insensitive rule of callous Anglos. For many, "Cheno" possessed the bold courage and temerity to do what others only dared to scheme about. No wonder that he became the central figure in *corridos* sung by those in Mexican American communities wont to extol the heroic exploits of great men.

The Juan Cortina episode has also intrigued modern scholars. For almost a century after 1859, Texas historiography tended to see Cortina as had his Anglo contemporaries in 1859–1860: as a Mexican opportunist, bandit, and cattle rustler who issued proclamations to justify his lawlessness. Not until the late 1940s did the first scholarly defense of Cortina appear, and since then several other historians have advanced interpretations favorable to the man. During the 1970s revisionists portrayed him as a "social bandit" representing the discontented community of Mexicans challenging an oppressive social order. Other writings, while acknowledging his defense of Mexicans, portray him as a product of the Rio Grande region during midcentury, where similar Anglo figures intrigued to amass power and fortune. The full story of Juan "Cheno" Cortina no doubt will fascinate future generations of Texans, for controversial figures seldom fade from history's pages.

See also **Criminal Justice System.**

BIBLIOGRAPHY
Goldfinch, Charles W. "Juan N. Cortina, 1824–1892: A Re-Appraisal." In *Furia y Muerte: Los Bandidos Chicanos,* edited by Pedro Castillo and Albert Camarillo, 85–112. Los Angeles: Aztlán Publications, UCLA, 1973.
Larralde, Carlos, and José Rodolfo Jacobo. *Juan N. Cortina and the Struggle for Justice in Texas.* Dubuque, Iowa: Kendall/Hunt, 2000.
Thompson, Jerry D., ed. *Juan Cortina and the Texas-Mexico Frontier, 1859–1877.* El Paso: Texas Western Press, 1994.

ARNOLDO DE LEÓN

COSTURERAS AND SASTRES. The *costurera* (seamstress) in the Latina and Latino community has been a figure both familiar and unacknowledged, whether she or he sews for a limited clientele or works in a mill or sweat shop. In this brief essay, we will look at the role of the costurera and the *sastre* (tailor) in the community and how these traditional occupations have changed in the last fifty years.

The community costurera whose clientele is often limited to her immediate neighborhood or circle of friends and neighbors and the textile worker who labors in a factory or does piecework at home share some common concerns. In the 1920s and 30s and even into the post–World War II era, Latinas were predominantly employed in such occupations, especially in Los Angeles and the Southwest, where companies like Levi Strauss and manufacturers of children's clothing found cheap labor. But with the advent of the North Atlantic Free Trade Act (NAFTA), multinational companies began seeking ever-cheaper *mano de obra* (labor force), and these operations moved elsewhere. In the 1950s and 1960s, store-bought clothing began to be more readily available. But it was expensive, so costureras and sastres remained busy, as did *zapateros* and *zapaterías* (shoemakers and shoe repair stores) and *barberos* and *peluqueros* (barbers and hair stylists). More recently, the availability of less-expensive off-the rack clothes resulted in the waning of the tradition of turning to a sastre or a costurera for hand-sewn clothes. But while ready-made clothing for special occasions can be bought from Wal-Mart or department stores, sastres and costureras remain popular in the Southwest and in Greater Mexico, where seamstresses and tailors carry on the traditional occupations. Every Puerto Rican, Central American, and Chicana and Chicano community has a costurera who will concoct elaborate *quinceañera* (fifteenth-birthday) dresses and bridal gowns. Often, she will also sew or crochet the traditional baptismal gown, or

COSTURERAS AND SASTRES. Seamstresses in a factory in El Paso, Tex. (© Nic Paget-Clarke)

ropón. So the life markers of baptism, first communion, quinceañera, and marriage that are observed with special feasts are also made festive with special clothing.

While the role of the costurera and the sastre seem pivotal to the community's sense of self, the textile worker and the labor organizations associated with them have also had an effect on the fabric of U.S. Latina and Latino communities. In San Antonio, Texas, for example, the Levi Strauss company's displaced workers formed *Mujer Obrera* to resist antilabor tactics and later to oppose the outsourcing of the work to the developing world. While the plant ultimately closed, the group was successful in organizing and in providing for themselves and other displaced workers; the oppressive conditions under which they worked and their awareness of the even harsher conditions for people in the developing world made them all the more determined. Costureras and sastres continue to work in the textile industry in California and in New York for low wages and in less than ideal working conditions while the lone seamstress or tailor working from home or from a small storefront continues to be a regular feature of the barrios of Greater Mexico and Puerto Rico.

See also **North American Free Trade Agreement.**

NORMA E. CANTÚ

COTERA, MARTHA (b. 1938), activist. Martha Cotera was born Martha Piña in 1938 in Nuevo Casas Grandes, Chihuahua, Mexico. In the late 1940s, she migrated to El Paso, Texas, with her family. A strong mother, grandparents with a lively interest in Mexican politics, and a love of education shaped her early years in El Paso. She received a bachelor's degree from the University of Texas, El Paso, in 1962 and married Juan Cotera, a fellow student, a year later. In 1971, she obtained a master's degree in education from Antioch College.

During the 1960s, an era of Mexican American organization for social justice and civil rights, Martha P. Cotera emerged as a leading activist, writer, and feminist in the Chicano/a and women's movements in Texas and across the Southwest. Martha and her husband had been involved in the Political Association of Spanish-Speaking Organizations (PASSO) and soon became supporters of the burgeoning farmworkers' movement in the mid-1960s. But the pivotal moment of Cotera's involvement in the Chicano/a movement came in 1969, when she participated in the educational struggle of students who were walking out to protest racial discrimination in the schools of Crystal City. After the Crystal City walkouts, the Coteras moved briefly to Mercedes, Texas, where she worked as a librarian at the Colegio Jacinto Treviño, an educational pilot program sponsored by Antioch College.

Cotera was part of a network of activists including José Angel Gutiérrez, a key figure in the walkouts and head of La Raza Unida Party. This group was founded in 1970 by Chicano/a movement activists, who were critical of the existing two-party system and of the lack of Latino and Latina elected officials in districts heavily populated by Mexican Americans. Cotera's involvement in the RUP was a major development in her evolution as a leading woman activist in the Chicano/a movement. Cotera, along with the veteran activist Virginia Muzquiz and Luz Gutiérrez (then-wife of RUP Chairman José Angel Gutiérrez), were leaders in party activities. As an RUP member, Cotera worked on political campaigns and ran as a candidate for the State Board of Education in 1972. In order to ensure that women would continue to be represented in the RUP leadership and agenda, Cotera and others formed Mujeres por La Raza Unida, a women's caucus within the party that advocated the recruitment of women as members, their candidacy for political office, and the representation of women's issues within the party's platform.

This founding signified Cotera's conviction that the formation of separate women's caucuses and organizations served as an important strategy for advancing women's issues, which could exist alongside involvement in the generally male-dominated organizations of the Chicano/a movement. In addition to her RUP involvement, Cotera was a key figure in several statewide organizing efforts by women that reflected her concern with improving the status of Chicanas at the state and national levels. In 1972, Cotera and several of her Mujeres Pro-Raza Unida colleagues, including Evey Chapa, a political scientist, created a presence within the meetings of the Texas Women's Political Caucus (held in preparation for the National Women's Political Caucus meetings held in 1972 in Houston) by creating a Chicana Caucus within the TWPC and drafting several resolutions for the TWPC's consideration. Cotera was also among the early organizers of the Mexican American Business and Professional Women's Association (MABPWA), "the first major Texas-based professional club exclusively for Mexican-American women," according to the *Handbook of Texas Online*. In 1977, she participated in statewide advisory meetings as a follow-up to the 1976 International Women's Year Conference. Through these activities, she insisted upon Chicana visibility in state and national conversations about public policy on Mexican-American women.

Drawing upon her background as an educator and a librarian, Cotera founded Information Systems Development, an independent research and publishing company, with which she hoped to address the few outlets for publications by, for, or about Mexican Americans. Information Systems Development not only responded to the lack of resource materials on Chicanos but also, perhaps more importantly, to the lack of materials on Chicanas. Arguably, her most important publication was *Diosa y Hembra* (1976), a reprint of *Profile of the Mexican American Woman*, which she had written to provide a broad overview of Chicana history. *Diosa y Hembra* produced a tidal wave of interest and excitement among Chicana student activists and within the women's movement. She then compiled and published *The Chicana Feminist* (1977), a series of essays and speeches reflecting her experiences and observations of

the dynamics of feminism within the Chicano/a Movement and of race within the American women's movement. Essays such as "Our Feminist Heritage" (1973) documented historical Mexican and Mexican American women activists to challenge the notion that feminism was foreign to Mexican American culture. Another essay, "Feminism as We See It" (1972), inspired by the difficulties she faced working with the largely white, middle-class Texas Women's Political Caucus, outlined the differences between Anglo feminists and Chicana feminists while also highlighting their similar political goals. Cotera's critical, politically astute, and often humorous commentary on the topics of feminism, gender roles, coalition politics, and public policy have been germane to contemporary Chicana feminist thought.

See also Chicano/a Movement; Chicanos and Chicanas; *and* Mexican-Origin People in the United States.

BIBLIOGRAPHY

Cotera, Martha P. *The Chicana Feminist*. Austin, Tex.: Information Systems Development, 1977.

Cotera, Martha P. *Diosa y Hembra*. Austin, Tex.: Information Systems Development, 1976.

Garcia, Alma M., ed. *Chicana Feminist Thought: The Basic Historical Writings*. London: Routledge, 1997.

Villareal, Mary Ann. "The Synapses of Struggle: Martha Cotera and Tejana Activism." In *Las Obreras: Chicana Politics of Work and Family*, edited by Vicki L. Ruiz, 273–295. Los Angeles: UCLA Chicano Studies Research Center, 2000.

DIONNE ESPINOZA

COWBOYS. *See* Vaqueros.

CRIMINAL JUSTICE SYSTEM. In *Miranda v. Arizona* (1966), a case involving a Mexican immigrant accused of murder, the Supreme Court held that police officers must give certain warnings to a suspect before his or her statements made during custodial interrogation can be admitted as evidence. On June 26, 2000, the Court held in *Dickerson v. United States* that Miranda warnings have "become embedded in routine police practice to the point where the warnings have become part of our national culture." As these Supreme Court rulings suggest, Latinos and Latinas have played a central role in shaping the historical development of the criminal justice system in the United States. The relationship between Latinos and Latinas and the criminal justice system extends from the founding of the nation to the twenty-first-century legal arguments for the recognition of the "enemy combatant" and the legitimacy of "Camp X-Ray."

The study of the criminal justice system traditionally encompasses the relationship between crime, victims and survivors, society, and the legal actors who handle criminal offenses. These legal actors include law enforcement

CRIMINAL JUSTICE SYSTEM. Police officer reading rights to a suspect. (© Bob Daemmrich/The Image Works)

(police), which arrests individuals; the courts (court personnel such as judges, prosecutors, defense attorneys, and juries), which participate in the sentencing process; and the correctional system (prisons and parole, among other entities), which is in charge of imprisonment. Crimes generally fall into three major categories: crimes against persons, property crimes, and public order crimes. Latinos and Latinas have historically experienced a second-class justice in the criminal justice system.

Categorizing Crime

One of the key problems in studying the relationship between Latinos and Latinas and crime lies in the ways Latinos and Latinas have been categorized. Most of the national data or information available has tended to focus on race and particularly on black-white differences. In addition, whereas Latinos and Latinas have had racialized experiences with legal actors, the criminal justice system has traditionally described Latinos and Latinas in ethnic terms, namely as Hispanics. Historically, Latinos and Latinas were generally categorized as either white or black, often inflating local and federal crime statistics. In 1997, however, the Office of Management and Budget revised its standards for classifying federal data on race and ethnicity, defining the Hispanic, Latino, or Latina as a person of Cuban, Mexican, Puerto Rican, South or Central American, or other Spanish culture or origin, regardless of race. The definition also includes the possibility of using the term "Spanish origin" to describe the Latino and Latina. These new standards also provided for the identification of combined race and ethnicity. However, legal actors who lack cultural competency generally categorize Latino and Latina suspects as exclusively either white or black, resulting in the distortion and underreporting of data or information on ethnicity. In other words, Latinos and Latinas may experience higher percentages of crime and victimization than are reported.

In contrast, some commentators have suggested that the experience of Latinos and Latinas in the United States should be understood within the context of the Irish experience. This argument suggests that Latinos and Latinas, like the Irish immigrants arriving at the dawn of the twentieth century, have experienced various forms of discrimination but have also managed to work their way into the criminal justice field in increasing numbers. While interesting, this argument has a tendency to focus on legal actors and not on offenders. Moreover, Latinos and Latinas as a group, unlike the Irish, comprise a plurality of people of different racial, ethnic, and national origins. Like most conservative rhetoric, this argument is based upon the homogenization of Latinos and Latinas into one ethnic and racial group.

Research on the relationship between Latinos and Latinas and crime has a tendency to focus on the experience of citizens of Latino and Latina heritage and Latin American immigrants residing in the continental United States or on its borders and to neglect the experience of Latinos and Latinas with the criminal justice system in Puerto Rico. This neglect is important because the research in Puerto Rico challenges most of the general findings on the experience of Latinos and Latinas with the criminal justice system. For example, research suggests that strong neighborhood and community relations tend to reduce crime among Latinos and Latinas in the United States. However, Puerto Rico, a community populated by U.S. citizens of Latino and Latina and Latin American heritage, has the second highest murder rate in the nation. Moreover, whereas Latinos and Latinas have a tendency to experience discrimination on the part of white legal actors, Puerto Ricans often experience even more repression at the hands of Puerto Rican legal actors on the island, as do immigrants of Dominican Republic and Haitian heritage. To be sure, it is common knowledge that Puerto Rican lawmakers have historically embraced more reactionary criminal justice policies on the island than those adopted on the mainland. U.S. citizens and Latin American immigrants residing in Puerto Rico have become invisible in the research on Latinos and Latinas and crime. More work needs to be done to compare and contrast the experience of U.S. citizens and immigrants residing in Puerto Rico and experiencing the U.S. criminal justice system on the island with that of Latinos and Latinas on the mainland.

Measuring Crime

At least four official reports offer information or data on crime and violence in the United States, namely the Uniform Crime Reports (UCR), the National Incident Based

Reporting System (NIBRS), the National Crime Victimization Surveys (NCVS), and the National Assessment Program (NAP). In addition, various agencies throughout the nation regularly compile reports on specific issues relating to crime. These reports can be misleading and problematic for numerous reasons, including the fact that Latino and Latina victims may not report a crime; the victim may inform a police officer, but the officer may neglect to report the incident; incidents may be reported, but police departments may manipulate the information for strategic purposes; and police officers may lack cultural competency, or they may be biased. Notwithstanding these problems, these federal reports represent the main source of information on national trends on crime.

The UCR was developed during the 1920s by the International Association of Chiefs of Police (IACP) to develop a uniform system of reporting criminal statistics. Managed by the Federal Bureau of Investigation (FBI), the UCR program compiles statistics on nearly 1,700 city, county, and state law enforcement agencies that convey information on reported crimes. Some research suggests that the available information on Latinos and Latinas may be inaccurate because police officers who lack cultural competency tend to homogenize or racialize Latinos and Latinas as Anglo-blacks or Anglo-whites and thus end up misreporting crimes in which Latinos and Latinas are participants. In addition, some research suggests that Latino and Latina victims may not report crimes because they feel police officers do not care, are racist, are inefficient, and generally are not sensitive to the problems faced by Latinos and Latinas.

The UCR data do not reveal much regarding the experiences of Latinos and Latinas with crime and the criminal justice system. Despite this shortcoming, the Index of Crime Statistics for Murder and Non-Negligent Manslaughter, perhaps the most reliable index of the UCR, provides important data that are often neglected by academics in the mainland United States. When comparing state-by-state indexes for the year 2001, It is interesting to note that next to the District of Columbia, which reported 40.6 murders per 100,000 inhabitants, Puerto Rico had a rate of 19.6 homicides, followed by Louisiana with a rate of 11.2. These statistics are important because they challenge the findings of scholars who study the relationship between Latinos and Latinas and crime. Most of this research suggests that Latinos and Latinas have a lower incidence of murder because Latino and Latina neighborhoods and communities help reduce criminal behavior among Latinos and Latinas and Latino and Latina immigrants. Yet this data would suggest that a predominantly Latino and Latina community may have little if any impact in deterring criminal behavior.

The NIBRS was developed in an effort to address the shortcomings of the UCR and to expand its database with more information, including questions of ethnicity. In 1990, Congress passed the Hate Crime Statistics Act of 1990 (HCSA), which further amended the UCR by requiring the collection of statistics on crimes motivated by racial, religious, ethnic, and national origin, sexual orientation, and disability bias. The HCSA draws its information from both the Summary Reporting System (SRS) and the NIBRS. According to a 2002 report, 44.9 percent of the hate crimes reported in 2001 were racially motivated, while 21.6 percent were driven by bias toward an ethnicity or national origin. The data on ethnic or national origin crimes showed that anti-Latino and anti-Latina bias accounted for 30.1 percent, the highest group percentage in this category. To be sure, the majority of hate crimes victims based on ethnic or national origin were experienced by Latinos and Latinas, who experienced various forms of discrimination by white offenders, ranging from intimidation to murder.

The NCVS reports also address some of the limitations of the UCR program by collecting information based on direct interviews and incident reports by citizens. Notwithstanding the inherent problems arising from nonreporting or underreporting of crimes by Latinos and Latinas, a special report by the Bureau of Justice Statistics using NCVS data on Latino and Latina victims of violent crimes between 1993 and 2000 provides important information. According to the findings of this report, the rate of violent victimization of Latinos and Latinas fell from sixty-three victimizations per one thousand to twenty-eight. In 2000, for example, most of the violence experienced by Latinos and Latinas often took the form of simple assault (59 percent); about 20 percent were robbed; 19 percent were victims of aggravated assault; and about 2 percent survived a rape or a sexual assault. In general, unmarried males and juveniles were most likely to experience violent victimization during this period. For the most part, the rate of violent victimization of Latinos and Latinas was lower than that of blacks yet higher than that of whites between 1993 and 2000.

Latinos and Latinas and the Criminal Justice System

The lack of standardized reporting throughout the United States makes research on Latinos and Latinas and crime difficult to conduct. More important, however, is the fact that the United States provides for a dual system (federal and state) of criminal justice. In addition, localities respond to Latino and Latina offenders and victims in different and disparate ways. Thus, the experience of the Chicano and Chicana in a southwestern criminal justice system may be radically different from that of the Cuban residing in Miami or the Puerto Rican residing in either New York City or Puerto Rico. Likewise, the experience of black Latinos and Latinas is generally quite different from that of white Latinos and Latinas, even in places like Puerto Rico, where the majority of the population is Puerto Rican. These challenges are compounded with often inefficient, bureaucratic systems that neglect to prioritize the pursuit of justice. In general, research suggests that Latinos receive second-class justice in the U.S. criminal justice system.

Law Enforcement

Police officers are traditionally in charge of local law enforcement, investigative follow-up, and other forms of initial intervention. Police officers are generally responsible for preventing criminal activity, arresting suspects, and recovering stolen property. Law enforcement at a federal level includes legal actors like agents from the Drug Enforcement Administration (DEA), the Federal Bureau of Investigation (FBI), the former Immigration and Naturalization Services (INS), now the U.S. Citizenship and Immigration Services (USCIS), the U.S. Customs Service, and the U.S. marshals. Whereas police powers have been traditionally relegated to the states, federal law enforcement plays an important role with respect to Latinos and Latinas as a result of the communal bonds with Latin American immigrants.

Most of the available research on the experiences of Latino and Latina interaction with the police suggests that Latinos and Latinas feel less protected by the police and experience disproportionate vigilance and overpolicing, harassment, arrests, and discrimination. In some places, Latino and Latina suspects are more likely to be shot by police officers than are other groups. Some research suggests that Latinos and Latinas are often harassed and verbally abused by police officers. It is important to note that police officers who lack cultural competence often escalate situations that could otherwise be addressed in a nonviolent manner. For example, police officers who attempt to shame Latino males in front of significant members of their communities may often find themselves having to use force to make an intervention. In contrast, some research also suggests that community-policing programs (COP) that encourage direct contact between Latinos and Latinas and police officers can improve Latino and Latina perceptions of law enforcement in significant ways. This research has been reinforced by the fact that Latinos and Latinas experience high rates of violent and property crimes.

There is, however, ample evidence that federal law enforcement agents have a tendency to abuse and harass Latino and Latina suspects. Customs officials and Border Patrol agents are regularly accused of civil rights violations against Latino and Latina immigrants. These experiences are exacerbated by the increasingly punitive nature of federal laws.

The Criminal Courts

Perhaps the greatest difficulty in assessing the relationship between the experiences of Latinos and Latinas with the criminal justice system lies in the fact that the U.S. criminal court system is federal in nature. This not only means that there are two criminal court systems, namely a federal system and a state system, but also that courts either have separate jurisdiction or in some cases joint or concurrent jurisdiction. This has been especially evident in the prosecution of drug cases. Thus, it is important to note that the criminal court responses to Latino and Latina offenders and victims may often be guided by national ideologies. Nevertheless, approximately 95 percent of criminal prosecutions occur in state criminal courts.

The prosecution is generally charged with deciding whether to try a case, pursue a plea bargain, or dismiss the case for lack of evidence. Most prosecutors are elected and tend to be politically vulnerable. It is not likely that the average district attorney or assistant district attorney will admit that he or she discriminates against Latino and Latina victims and offenders. Some ongoing research suggests that prosecutors, with the noted exception of domestic violence (DV) court prosecutors, have a tendency to not pursue cases where non-English-speaking victims are involved. This research further suggests that prosecutors often lack the cultural competence, the language skills, and the commitment to provide justice to Latino and Latina victims. This lack of commitment often results in the dismissal of cases in which Latinos and Latinas are victims. These problems have been compounded by the lack of financial resources to hire Spanish-speaking interpreters and court investigators. In contrast, when Latino and Latina offenders are charged with committing a crime against a white victim, it is more likely that the prosecutor will try the case expediently.

The Sixth Amendment to the U.S. Constitution provides that all defendants facing criminal charges shall be entitled to the assistance of counsel for their defense. But a number of factors compromise the quality of legal representation Latinos and Latinas receive. According to Caroline Wolf Harlow during the 1998 fiscal year, 73 percent of Latinos and Latinas in state prisons were represented by public defenders, in contrast to 69 percent of white and 77 percent of black inmates. At a federal level, however, 56 percent of Latinos and Latinas were likely to rely on public defenders, in comparision with 57 percent of whites and 65 percent of blacks. This research further suggests that defendants with publicly financed attorneys generally have the same conviction rates. For obvious reasons Latinos and Latinas who do not speak English are more likely to receive poor representation by public defenders who cannot speak Spanish. This problem is especially heightened by the absence of competent court translators. Judges are responsible for the management and governance of a court and the ensuing trials. Traditionally, judges are responsible for supervising the conduct of the court personnel; they determine what evidence, motions, and objections are admissible; they determine what instructions should be given to a jury; they answer any questions of law; and generally they decide what sentences to impose.

There is a significant body of literature available on the selection of minority judges that includes various discussions on judicial politics. Judges at both state and federal levels tend to be white and male. Minority judges tend to be black, followed by Latino and Latina, Asian, and Native American judges. Some research suggests that in states where judges are elected, Latino and Latina judges do not fare as well because of gerrymandering practices that make it difficult for Latino and Latina voters to elect them. For example, a study conducted by Robert C. Luskin, Christopher N. Bratcher, Christopher G. Jordan, Tracy K. Renner, and Kris S. Seago demonstrated that as of 1991 blacks and Latinos and Latinas constituted one-third of the population of Texas, but only 45 of the 396 district judges and 3 of the 80 appellate court judges were black and Latino and Latina. This study also found that Latino and Latina judges who were not reelected tended to take liberal stances. To be sure, in the case of California it has been widely noted that California Supreme Court Justice Cruz Reynoso was not reelected because of his liberal stance on the death penalty. He had voted against imposing the death penalty in forty-six out of forty-seven death penalty cases.

According to the research conducted by Sheldon Goldman and Elliot Slotnick, Latinos and Latinas constitute the third-largest number of appointees at the federal level, anteceded by blacks and a disproportionate amount of white judges. While the Jimmy Carter and Bill Clinton administrations appointed more Latino and Latina judges to the U.S. Court of Appeals than did the Ronald Reagan and George H. W. Bush administrations, the numbers remain abysmally low. For example, while 97.4 percent (76) of Reagan's appointments of appellate judges were white and only 1.3 percent (1) was Latino, Clinton appointed 77.1 percent (37) white judges and 10.4 percent (5) Latino and Latina judges. In general, the federal courts remain overwhelmingly staffed by white judges and personnel. It should further be noted that whereas there has been one U.S. Supreme Court justice of Hispanic heritage, Benjamin N. Cardozo (1932–1938), whose parents were born in Spain, no president has appointed a Latino or Latina Supreme Court justice.

Regarding the question of sentencing, some early research on the experiences of judges with the criminal justice system in Texas suggests that Latinos and Latinas felt the criminal courts were generally fair. Subsequent research demonstrates that race and ethnicity play important roles in contemporary sentencing decisions. Statistics clearly indicate that blacks and Latinos and Latinas tend to receive more punitive sentences than do their white counterparts. Cassia C. Spohn suggests that there are several possible explanations, including that blacks and Latinos and Latinas commit more serious crimes and have more serious prior criminal records, that they generally lack the financial resources to hire private attorneys, and that judges may base their decisions on personal biases and discrimination. By contrast, some research in the Pennsylvania court system suggests that Latino and Latina defendants are more at risk to receive harsh penalties than is any other ethnic or racial group. Darrell Steffensmeier and Stephen Demuth further suggest that judges may often situate Latinos and Latinas within the context of the drug wars. Other research on federal sentencing by the same authors demonstrates that ethnicity had a small to modest effect on sentence outcomes favoring white defendants and penalizing Latinos and Latinas, with blacks placing in the middle. This is quite important given that the federal government has adopted a number of sentencing guidelines that presumably address sentencing disparities.

The key case defining the relationship between Latinos and Latinas and the juries is *Hernandez v. Texas*, 347 U.S. 475 (1954). This Supreme Court opinion addressed the systematic exclusion of persons of Mexican decent from service in juries in Texas, and held that the equal protection clause of the Fourteenth Amendment was not directed solely against discrimination between blacks and whites. More importantly, the court reasoned that Latinos could be treated as a different and distinct class for the purpose of the Fourteenth Amendment.

Corrections

After an individual has been convicted of a crime, a judge typically may choose among a plurality of options to exact a proportional punishment. In the absence of clear sentencing guidelines mandating a particular form of punishment and depending on a number of additional factors, such as prior record of convictions and the nature and seriousness of the crime, a judge may choose to incarcerate an individual and or suspend his or her sentence and place the individual on probation. An offender can also be released prior to the expiration of his or her sentence and be placed on parole.

Perhaps the major challenge of the correctional system lies in the lack of trained correctional personnel with cultural competence and sufficient language skills. Correctional facilities generally lack trained staff members fluent in Spanish. According to information available for 2002, in the Federal Bureau of Prisons the Latino and Latina staff make up only 10.9 percent of the total correctional staff in federal facilities, compared to whites (64.5 percent) and blacks (21.1 percent). The federal Latino and Latina prison population is estimated to be 31.7 percent.

According to the 1999 state parole statistics, black inmates were more likely to be released on parole (47.3 percent) than were whites (35.4 percent) or Latinos and Latinas (16.1 percent). However, black offenders tended to serve longer prison sentences than did white and Latino and Latina offenders. Black offenders released by discretionary parole in 1999 served thirty-seven months, in comparison to white offenders (thirty-four) and Latinos and Latinas (thirty-three). Black offenders also served an average of seven more months than did white (thirty-one) and Latino (thirty) offenders released by mandatory parole. It is important to note that, according to the Bureau of Justice statistics, between 1990 and 1999 the success rates among state parole discharges increased from 31 percent to 51 percent among Latinos and Latinas and from 33 percent to 39 percent among blacks, in contrast to a drop among whites (44 percent to 41 percent).

Twenty-first Century Issues

There are several issues that shape the contours of policy debates affecting the experience of Latinos and Latinas in the criminal justice system. The following section, while not exhaustive, provides some information for further research.

Drugs and Latinos. A majority of offenders (55.1 percent) under the Federal Bureau of Prisons has been convicted of drug offenses, compared to the next highest types of convictions, namely firearm, explosive, and arson offences (9.6 percent) and immigration violations (9.1 percent). Research suggests that a disproportionate number of Latinos is likely to be convicted because judges associate the "War on Drugs" with Latino offenders and Latin American immigrants owing to the Latino and Latina media stereotypes detailed in the conclusion of this essay.

Immigration and criminal aliens. In the year 2000, 87.1 percent of all defendants charged with federal offenses were Latin American immigrants. Approximately 75 percent of immigration offenders were charged with unlawful entry (25 percent) or reentry (50 percent) into the United States, 20 percent were charged with alien smuggling, and 5 percent were charged with misuse of visas and other immigration offenses. In May 2002, the federal prison population consisted of U.S. citizens (70.6 percent), Mexican citizens (16 percent), Colombians (2.4 percent), Dominicans (2 percent), Cubans (1.7 percent), and unknown or other citizens (7.3 percent). The Department of Homeland Security (DHS) and the INS are especially prone to detain Latin American immigrants without access to basic due-process rights and without

being charged. Latin American immigrants are often detained in camps without being charged, and in some cases they are deported without any formal investigation. For example, there are many documented cases of Latinos and Latinas, U.S. residents, and Central and South American immigrants released in Mexico without access to any form of legal counsel. By contrast, there have been some debates over the DHS/INS policy of deporting convicted immigrants to their countries of origin. Immigrants of Latin American heritage generally have little or no access to the criminal justice system and indeed are processed in arbitrary and unjust ways The deportation of Latinos and Latinas has also become a major problem in Latin America. In some cases U.S Latinos who have grown up in the United States have little or no connection to their countries of birth, and are often alienated and treated as undesirable foreigners. Deportees are also often scapegoated for the increase in local crime and in some cases they are subject to extrajudicial persecution. The debates over the Mara Salvatrucha in El Salvador provide a clear example of some of the polemics surrounding the deportation of Latinos and Latinas.

Gender violence. Domestic violence (DV) courts generally offer more effective forms of justice because the court personnel tend to have higher degrees of commitment. Despite this commitment, Latinas often have poor recourse to justice when court officers lack cultural competency and language skills. More importantly, cultural norms and neighborhood traditions may often discourage Latinas from seeking help from the courts when facing multiple forms of gender violence. Yet some research also suggests that Latin American immigrant women are more likely to seek help from the criminal justice system in the United States than in their native countries, where resources and attitudes toward gender violence may not be as conducive.

Homicide. Ramiro Martinez Jr. has published a comprehensive book-length discussion of the relationship between Latinos and Latinas and homicide. Among other things, Martinez contends that despite an increase in Latin American immigration, Latino and Latina crime has not risen as expected. He further suggests that this could be explained as the result of the strength of Latino and Latina communities and their buffering effect on crime. More interestingly, he also argues, research shows that, contrary to popular opinion, Latin American immigrants exhibit lower crime rates than do native Latinos and Latinas. Yet, Martinez contends, whereas Latinos and Latinas have lower crime rates than do blacks, because of higher degrees of social integration, they exhibit higher rates than do whites.

The death penalty. The Supreme Court reinstated the death penalty in 1976. Since then thirty-eight states and the federal government have adopted this form of punishment. By the end of the year 2000, 37 states and the federal government held 3,593 prisoners on death row. Latino and Latina inmates composed 11 percent or 339 of the inmates with a known ethnicity. This was less than black and white inmates but more than American Indians and Asians. Research demonstrates that offenders who murder white victims are more likely to receive the death penalty than are those who murder nonwhite victims. This could account for the lower numbers of Latinos and Latinas on death row. The federal government has executed at least two Latinos since 1927. In 1948, Carlos Ochoa Romero was executed in California as a result of a murder conviction, and in 2001 Juan Raul Garza was executed after being convicted as a serial killer.

The government of Mexico has raised a polemic regarding the death penalty against the United States over the latter's violations of the Vienna Convention on Consular Relations. In the World Court case *United Mexican States v. United States of America* (2003), the Mexican government urged the United States to stay the executions of fifty-four Mexican nationals awaiting execution in ten states. The Mexican government argued that the United States violated the Mexicans' rights by failing to tell them that they were entitled to consular assistance after arrest in violation of the language of the convention. Like most cases involving the death penalty, this case argues that Latinos and Latinas are generally given poor or inadequate access to effective legal representation.

Terrorism and the state. Latinos and Latinas who have challenged U.S. imperialism have historically been treated as terrorists by the U.S. government. Accordingly, a number of Latinos and Latinas have been imprisoned as political prisoners with little or no access to basic human rights or due-process rights. Chicanos and Chicanas and Puerto Rican nationalists have been the most notable victims of state violence. Historically, Puerto Rican Nationalists affiliated with the Nationalist Party, and other groups like the Macheteros (machete wielders) who advocated for the island's independence have been treated as terrorists by both the FBI and the Department of Justice. During the 1960s, the FBI, through organizations such as COINTELPRO, also identified Chicano and Chicana activists as terrorists.

Most recently, the U.S. Government deemed Jose Padilla, a U.S. citizen of Puerto Rican heritage, as a member of Al Quaeda and has classified him as an "enemy combatant." Although the category of enemy combatants has usually been reserved for individuals captured in combat situations who are at the time not wearing a uniform, in the case of Mr. Padilla, the government detained him on the U.S. mainland, holding him for more than two years without charging him with any crime, and denying him access to his basic due-process rights.

Final Thoughts

The representations of Latino and Latina criminals and victims and survivors can influence the ways lawmakers and policy makers draft pertinent legislation, the ways legal actors respond to crimes involving Latinos and Latinas, and more generally how society perceives Latinos and Latinas. The traditional ways of representing Latinos and Latinas, namely by relying on racial categories, have often led to their disappearance from official statistics. The media has played a central role in the representation of Latinos and Latinas as criminals. Diego O. Castro contends that Hollywood filmmakers have historically portrayed the Latino as a hot-blooded, vicious killer and the Latina as a sexy and submissive woman of easy virtue. He argues that since 1898 more than seven thousand films have negatively stereotyped Latinos and Latinas. He notes that by 1932, Hollywood had produced more than eighteen hundred films that depicted Latinos as Mexican villains and bandits who murdered, lied, robbed, plundered, gambled, and raped innocent Americans. Moreover, whereas the film industry generated more than 2,100 films that portrayed Latinos and Latinas as fun-loving people, between 1956 and 1993 most of the 3,100 films produced portrayed Latinos as vicious urban gang leaders and sociopaths who prey on American victims.

Similarly, Juan F. Perea suggests that the media coverage of the 1992 Los Angeles riots emphasized images of Latino-looking people looting stores and carrying large amounts of stolen merchandise. But citing the work of David Hayes-Bautista et al., Perea notes that most of the early victims of crowd violence were Latinos and Latinas, one-third of the dead were Latino and Latina, between 20 and 40 percent of the stores damaged were owned by Latinos and Latinas, and one-half of those arrested were of Latino and Latina heritage. However, while the Los Angeles riots had a tremendous affect on Latinos and Latinas, Latinos and Latinas were largely excluded from the debate that took place afterwards. Thus, whereas Latinos and Latinas were portrayed as robbers and looters, the media also excluded Latino and Latina voices from participating in the public debates on the implications of police brutality in Los Angeles.

In sum, it is important to note that the media has shaped the perception of Latinos and Latinas as criminals while simultaneously marginalizing Latinos and Latinas from participating in public debates regarding crime and society. These media images have influenced every aspect of the criminal justice process and have resulted in the second-class justice Latinos and Latinas receive.

See also Children in the Juvenile Justice System; Gonzales, Alberto; Police; Prisons; *and* Racial Profiling.

BIBLIOGRAPHY

Castro, Diego O. " 'Hot Blood and Easy Virtue': Mass Media and the Making of Racist Latino/a Stereotypes." In *Images of Color, Images of Crime*, edited by Coramae Richey Mann and Marjorie S. Zatz. Los Angeles: Roxbury Publishing, 1998.

Cheurprakobkit, Sutham. "Police-Citizen Contact and Police Performance: Attitudinal Differences between Hispanics and Non-Hispanics." *Journal of Criminal Justice* 28 (2000): 325–336.

Federal Bureau of Investigation. *Hate Crimes Statistics, 2001*. Uniform Crime Reports. Clarksburg, W.Va.: Criminal Justice Information Services Division, 2001.

Goldman, Sheldon, and Elliot Slotnick. "Clinton's Second Term Judiciary: Picking Judges under Fire." *Judicature* 82 (1999): 264–284.

Haney-Lopez, Ian F. *Racism on Trial: The Chicano Fight for Justice*. Cambridge, Mass: Belknap Press of Harvard University, 2003.

Hayes-Bautista, David E., Werner Schink, and Maria Hayers-Bautista. "Latinos and the 1992 Los Angeles Riots: A Behavioral Sciences Perspective." *Hispanic Journal of Behavioral Sciences* 15 (1993): 427.

Luskin, Robert C., Christopher N. Bratcher, Christopher G. Jordan, Tracy K. Renner, and Kris S. Seago. "How Minority Judges Fare in Retention Elections." In *Judicial Politics, Readings from "Judicature,"* edited by Elliot Slotnick. Chicago: American Judicature Society, 1999.

Martinez, Ramiro, Jr. *Latino Homicide: Immigration, Violence, and Community*. New York: Routledge, 2002.

Nevares-Muñiz, Dora. *El crimen en Puerto Rico: Tapando el cielo con la mano*. Hato Rey, P.R.: Instituto para el Desarrollo del Derecho, 1996.

Perea, Juan F. "*Los Olvidados*: On the Making of Invisible People." *New York University Law Review* 70 (1995): 965–991.

Rennison, Callie M. *Hispanic Victims of Violent Crime, 1993–2000*. Bureau of Justice Statistics, Special Report NCJ 191208. Washington, D.C.: U.S. Department of Justice, 2002.

Spohn, Cassia C. "Thirty Years of Sentencing Reform: The Quest for a Racially Neutral Sentencing Process." *Criminal Justice* 3 (2000): 427–501.

Steffensmeier, Darrell, and Stephen Demuth. "Ethnicity and Judges' Sentencing Decisions: Hispanic-Black-White Comparisons." *Criminology* 39 (2001): 145–178.

Steffensmeier, Darrell, and Stephen Demuth. "Ethnicity and Sentencing Outcomes in U.S. Federal Courts: Who Is Punished More Harshly—White, Black, White-Hispanic, or Black-Hispanic Defendants?" *American Sociological Review* 65 (2000): 705–729.

Tarver, Marsha, Steve Walker, and P. Harvey Wallace. *Multicultural Issues in the Criminal Justice System*. Boston: Allyn and Bacon, 2002.

Wolf Harlow, Caroline. *Defense Council in Criminal Cases*. Bureau of Justice Statistics, Special Report NCJ 179023. Washington, D.C.: U.S. Department of Justice, 2000.

CHARLES R. VENATOR SANTIAGO

CRITICAL RACE THEORY AND LAT CRIT THEORY.

Critical Race Theory (CRT) and Latino and Latina Critical Theory (Lat Crit) are progressive movements in the law and in legal education that seek to secure the rights of people of color generally (CRT) and of Latina and Latino people in particular (Lat Crit). They also seek to transform American society and law in humane, nonracist directions.

The earlier and broader movement, Critical Race Theory, sprang up in the mid-1970s when progressive lawyers and legal scholars across the nation realized that the heady gains of the civil rights era had stalled and were even being reversed. New approaches and theories were needed to cope with the veiled, subtle, or institutional forms of racism that were developing and an American public that increasingly seemed tired of hearing about race.

These new approaches were brought forth by a number of scholars. Derrick Bell, an African American teaching at New York University School of Law, wrote about "interest convergence"—the notion that it is white self-interest, not altruism, that determines the course of civil rights and African American fortunes. The late Alan Freeman, a white scholar who taught at SUNY–Buffalo School of Law, described how cautious, incrementalist Supreme Court jurisprudence, even when impeccably liberal in aspiration, ended up legitimizing racial discrimination. Girardeau Spann, an African American scholar at Georgetown Law Center, urged that race reformers quit the habit of reflexively taking grievances to the courts and instead engage in "ordinary politics"—voter-registration campaigns, street marches, and mass protests. Charles Lawrence, also of Georgetown Law Center, posited a new theory of unconscious discrimination, aimed at circumventing the Supreme Court's increasing insistence that racial discrimination, to be redressed, must be shown to have been intentional.

Building on the insights of forerunner movements, such as critical legal studies and radical feminism, and borrowing insights from American radical figures such as Frederick Douglass, W. E. B. Du Bois, Martin Luther King, and César Chávez, as well as contemporary continental writers such as Antonio Gramsci and Jacques Derrida, the school quickly produced a body of distinctive scholarship. It also began to hold a series of annual workshops and occasional public conferences. Today, scholars in many disciplines, including education, sociology, and American studies, consider themselves Critical Race Theorists, or at least fellow travelers. Educators, for example, use CRT's ideas to analyze hierarchy and tracking in the schools, IQ and standardized testing, and controversies over the curriculum and Western canon. Unlike some academic movements, CRT contains an activist dimension: it seeks not only to understand society but also to change it for the better.

Recently, CRT has spun off a number of sister movements, including QueerCrit (which analyzes issues of sexual orientation), radical Asian American jurisprudence, and Latina and Latino Critical jurisprudence, or Lat Crit. Most of these successor movements hold separate annual or regional meetings and produce their own distinctive scholarship while continuing to maintain friendly relations with the umbrella, or parent, movement, Critical Race Theory.

Lat Crit began as a caucus, or special interest group, within CRT and a general sense that the black-themed writing that was characteristic of that movement's early days devoted scant attention to the issues and problems confronting Latinas and Latinos. A series of law-review articles by Juan Perea, professor of law at the University of Florida, and Richard Delgado of the University of Colorado, critiquing the deficiencies of a black/white binary paradigm of race and tracing their implications for Latina and Latino litigators, gave impetus to the early movement. Scholars soon began to address distinctly Latina and Latino issues in the law, including language rights (Perea) and the role of color identification in Latina and Latino civil rights strategies (George Martinez, Southern Methodist University School of Law). Ian Haney Lopez, of the University of California–Berkeley School of Law, analyzed the role of courts in constructing the white race and devised a new theory of institutional racism to account for the exclusion of Latina and Latino jurors. Kevin Johnson, a Latino professor at the University of California–Davis School of Law, contributed several studies of the role of race in U.S. immigration law and two books on racial mixture.

Other Lat Crit scholars analyze bilingual education, media and popular stereotypes of Latinas and Latinos, sanctuary for Latin American refugees, and the role of conquest in shaping U.S.–Latina and Latino relations. Still others examine historical documents, such as the Treaty of Guadalupe Hidalgo, in an effort to understand those relations and redress historical grievances. Another group of scholars focuses on issues of Latina and Latino identity, examining, for example, Latina and Latino panethnicity, strategies for multiracial coalition, and the history of census categories for Latinos and Latinas.

Somewhat more ecumenical than the founding movement, Critical Race Theory, the Lat Crit organization consciously welcomes all comers. Its annual conferences attract whites, feminists of every description, and many African American and Asian scholars and activists. Students, representatives from other countries, and members of many academic disciplines attend as well. Although Critical Race Theory's scholarship has slowed somewhat in recent years and exhibited a preoccupation with issues of identity rather than power, Lat Crit writing is in full flower. Each of the eight annual conferences has spawned a hefty law-review symposium containing the leading papers presented at the conference, and a classroom course book, or reader, introduces students to the main themes of this fast-growing body of scholarship.

What does the future hold for these two movements? As the population of color—Latinas and Latinos in particular—grows, the need for progressive analyses of problems of race can only increase. The United States considers itself a nation under law; accordingly, the role of legal institutions in regulating relations among the races is apt to remain both central and contested. Both considerations suggest that Critical Race Theory and Lat Crit Theory are likely to remain significant forces on the national scene in the years ahead.

See also **Race and Racialization.**

BIBLIOGRAPHY

Crenshaw, Kimberlé, ed. *Critical Race Theory: The Writings that Formed the Movement*. New York: New Press, 1995.

Delgado, Richard, and Jean Stefancic. *Critical Race Theory: An Introduction*. New York: New York University Press, 2001.

Delgado, Richard, and Jean Stefancic. *The Latino/a Condition: A Critical Reader*. New York: New York University Press, 1998.

Perea, Juan. "The Black/White Binary Paradigm of Race." *California Law Review* 85 (1997): 1213.

RICHARD DELGADO

CRUSADE FOR JUSTICE. The Chicano/a movement of the 1960s and 1970s transformed the Mexican American people beyond the intentions and expectations of the leaders who inspired it. While the long-range impact wrought by leaders such as Reies Lopez Tijerina on land-grant issues, César Chávez on the plight of the farm workers, and José Angel Gutiérrez on efforts to form a national Chicano and Chicana political party have all been questioned, few people doubt that the Chicano/a movement inspired a cultural reawakening of the Mexican American people in the United States.

Of the leaders and organizations associated with the Chicano/a movement, those who contributed most to the "Chicano cultural renaissance" were Rodolfo "Corky" Gonzáles and the organization he formed, the Crusade for Justice. Gonzáles was the founder (in 1965) of the crusade and the heart and soul of the organization during its most active years. Because of his literary skills, Gonzáles came to be identified as the "poet laureate" of the Chicano/a movement and its most capable philosopher and interpreter.

As a youth in the urban barrios of Denver, Colorado, Gonzáles personally experienced the vicious cycle of gangs, drugs, and crime that swallowed up so many young Chicanos and Chicanas. In his own case, his youthful energy found expression in the boxing ring. Gonzáles first earned fame as a scrappy young professional fighter who won enough fights to be ranked third in the world in the featherweight division.

Yet in the midst of it all, he abruptly quit the ring and opened an insurance agency to support a wife and a growing family that eventually included eight children. The insurance agency afforded Gonzáles time to pursue his growing interest in urban civic action. He became active in youth programs, including the opening of a free boxing gym for barrio kids. He also became active in Democratic Party politics, becoming at age twenty-nine the youngest ward captain. He also became head of Los Voluntarios, a Chicano political action group involved in representing barrio residents in conflicts with municipal government. Under Gonzáles's leadership, Los Voluntarios uncovered police brutality in Denver. His party involvement and his popularity with local residents made Gonzáles an important rising leader for Denver's Democratic Party. His part in the successful 1960 John Kennedy presidential campaign led to other important positions, including leadership of Denver's War on Poverty programs. His involvement with these programs, however, grew into disenchantment as he coped with bureaucratic ineptitude, red tape, waste, and inefficiency. Gonzáles grew weary of attending conferences that repeated the familiar rhetoric of promises and projects while little was being done to change the barrios.

In 1965, Gonzáles resigned all his positions in the party and in poverty programs and formed La Crusada Para Justicia, the Crusade for Justice, declaring it a "movement born out of frustration and determination to secure equality with dignity." He insisted that the crusade be separate and independent of private or government agencies.

The crusade became Gonzáles's base for expressing Chicano and Chicana demands for better housing, equal educational opportunities, jobs, and land reform as well as the medium for articulating his own philosophical pronouncements on the Chicano/a movement. The crusade published a newspaper, *El Gallo*.

Gonzáles and the crusade presented a new interpretation of Chicano and Chicana history and articulated a new vision of Chicanos and Chicanas in the United States. Gonzáles promoted a growing cultural awareness and pride that provided a basis for cohesion and drove a unified effort toward political and social empowerment. The crusade's message was conveyed in three main forms and forums: community activism, literary expression, and a new political party.

From the beginning, the crusade was a multifaceted urban barrio organization representing Denver's Chicanos and Chicanas in their struggles with city hall. Among its stated goals were demands for better and equal housing, economic and educational opportunity, and agricultural and welfare reform. Although the crusade eschewed violence, it supported a peaceful student walkout and mass demonstration that led to a violent confrontation in Denver in early 1969.

A one-stop, self-help Chicano and Chicana community center served as the headquarters for the crusade. In *La Raza*, Stan Steiner described it as a place

> with a school of "Liberation classes," a nursery, gymnasium, Mayan ballroom, Chicano art gallery, Mexican shops, library, community dining room and community center, job skill bank, legal aid service, Barrio Police Review Board, health and housing social workers, athletic leagues, a barrio newspaper [*El Gallo*], a bail bond service, a kitchen and a "Revolutionary Theatre." (p. 385)

As the most prominent Chicano and Chicana organization in Denver and all of Colorado and the only one primarily concerned with urban civic action, the crusade became involved in an endless array of causes, local and national, that expanded its influence and notoriety. Gonzáles was in constant demand throughout the country as a speaker at rallies, forums, and other gatherings. Nationally, Gonzáles and the crusade received and gave support to other Chicano and Chicana leaders and organizations, black and Native American leaders, and anti–Vietnam War activists.

In the spring of 1969, the crusade sponsored the first of a series of National Chicano Youth Liberation Conferences. More than a conference, it was a "fiesta," a celebration of Chicano and Chicana art, history, music, and culture. The five-day event brought together over fifteen hundred young Chicanos and Chicanas from all over the country and from all walks of life to attend the workshops on philosophy, history, art, poetry, music, and self-identity.

These conferences, along with the crusade's school of art and culture, known as La Escuela Tlatelolco, encouraged young Chicanos and Chicanas to learn about their history and cultural heritage, to embrace their culture, and to creatively express their pride in being Chicano and Chicana. The language and message of the conference eventually became the language and message of the Chicano/a movement as manifested by frequent utterances by community leaders about "Chicano and Chicana nationalism" and Aztlán, which were popularized by Gonzáles and the crusade.

The artistic expression encouraged by the crusade gave rise to a "renaissance" of Chicano art, music, and writing. Emanuel Martinez, whose murals celebrate Mexican history and Chicano and Chicana identity, began his work at the crusade. Carlota Espinoza, whose murals focused on Chicanas, designed an outstanding mural for the altar at Our Lady of Guadalupe Church in Denver. Leo Tanguma became known for his mobile murals, assembled and disassembled for indoor and outdoor exhibitions, that depict events in the Chicano and Chicana movement. The crusade inspired the work of Teatro Campesino, a traveling theater group that presented a theatrical variation of Gonzáles poem "I Am Joaquin." Also produced on film, the presentation was a popular attraction in demonstrations and other events of the Chicano/a movement.

Gonzáles's epic poem; his play *A Cross for Maclovio*, a literary self-portrait of his youthful days as a boxer; and his other writings inspired a renaissance in Chicano and Chicana literature. George Hartley suggests that "I Am Joaquin" was the inaugural work of the Chicano and Chicana literary renaissance. It was the first literary work that identified a Chicano and Chicana literature and thus retroactively provided a common label for all of the Chicano and Chicana literature dating back several centuries.

CRUSADE FOR JUSTICE. Corky Gonzalez being arrested during a protest at Denver West High School, March 1969. (Duane E. Howell, Denver)

By fusing the various elements—justice, civil rights, Spanish and Indian historical heritage, farm labor laws, land, cultural pride, and recognition—that had been of concern to Mexican Americans under the label "Chicano and Chicana," "I Am Joaquin" created a literary and philosophical foundation for the concept of Chicanismo that was the rallying cry for the Chicano/a movement.

"I Am Joaquin" is a literary masterpiece that reflects an effort to capture the unity and diversity of Chicano and Chicana identity. The poem depicts the conflicting historical diversity (Spanish versus Indian and elites versus masses) that merged in the formation of La Raza as well as the main themes—repression and confrontation—that have characterized the Chicano and Chicana experience.

Gonzáles's ideas also found expression in various forms as he and the crusade sponsored and participated in events associated with the Chicano/a movement. To Gonzáles, nationalism was the key to the liberation of Chicanos and Chicanas. At the symposium "Chicano Liberation" at Hayward College in California, Gonzáles outlined his concept of nationalism and elaborated on how nationalism was to serve as a tool for Chicanos and Chicanas.

Part of Gonzáles's and the crusade's success in conveying their joint ideals and philosophy was in engaging young people in the movement. They convinced young people that the Southwest was their homeland of Aztlán (the legendary Aztec homeland).

Accordingly, at the end of the first Chicano Youth Liberation Conference, the conferees adopted El Plan Espiritual de Aztlán, which bore the indelible literary and philosophical imprint of Gonzáles. The plan encompassed the spirit of Chicano and Chicana nationalism based on common language, culture, history, and tradition and a rejection of the dominant Anglo-American culture.

All of the crusade's early activities pointed ultimately to a broader strategy for national political change. The implementation of the strategy to bring about Chicano and Chicana nationalism was begun by the crusade in its sponsorship of the Second National Chicano Youth Liberation Conference in March 1970, which launched Colorado's version of La Raza Unida Party (LRUP).

Gonzáles had envisioned that La Raza Unida Party would educate Chicanos and Chicanas and forge a national Chicano and Chicana consciousness as a means for liberation and self-determination. Accordingly, he advocated a national LRUP convention to nominate a presidential candidate (perhaps himself) in time for the 1972 presidential election. As a counterpoint to Gonzáles, José Angel Gutiérrez, who had led the creation of the LRUP in Texas and had already experienced some electoral success in local elections, saw the call for a national convention as premature. His vision was that LRUP would compete with the major parties by electing Chicanos and Chicanas at the local and state levels. Suspicious that Gonzáles would succeed in his call for a national convention and thus gain control of the party, Gutiérrez eventually agreed, and the first national LRUP convention met in El Paso, Texas, in September 1972.

It was not surprising that the two main candidates for the position of national chairman were Gonzáles and Gutiérrez, the leaders of the two largest state delegations, those from Colorado and Texas, respectively. Representatives from most other states were split in their loyalties to the two candidates. Ultimately, Gutiérrez was elected chairman, and Gonzáles averted a walkout by his supporters by graciously endorsing his election. The convention ended on a harmonious note, but the harmony was short-lived as the basic differences between the two main leaders resurfaced and tore the party asunder. In the end, the party never realized the expectations of either Gonzáles or Gutiérrez, nor did it ever reconcile the divergent philosophies of its two primary leaders.

The radical activism of Gonzáles and the Crusade for Justice attracted the suspicions of local and federal police agencies, already vigilant in view of the anti–Vietnam War sentiment and the confrontations of the black civil rights movement, the Chicano/a movement, and the Native American activism of the 1960s and 1970s.

On election day in November 1970, Denver police staged a predawn raid on the crusade's headquarters. Ostensibly searching for weapons, the police held several crusade volunteers for several hours, and when they left they took several tapes and a copy of the *I Am Joaquin* film. This was only the first in a series of efforts by law enforcement authorities to suppress activities of the crusade. Almost from the beginning, the activities of Gonzáles and the crusade attracted the interest of investigative agencies, particularly the Federal Bureau of Investigation (FBI).

The circumstances that brought the decline of the Crusade for Justice are related to the organization itself and to external circumstances. Like other Chicano and Chicana, black, and Native American organizations, the crusade reached its peak of influence in the 1960s and 1970s then declined as the intensity of the movement dwindled.

Internally, the sheer weight of carrying the crusade on his shoulders for so many years along with the demands of so many controversial and confrontational causes took its toll on Gonzáles. The constant pressure, threat, and scrutiny of investigative agencies and the setbacks encountered with the struggle must have been frustrating and discouraging. The seemingly boundless energy that carried the crusade in the early days through every form of challenge and obstacle was no longer there.

In 1987, Gonzáles was involved in an automobile accident that resulted in serious head injuries and some memory loss. This certainly affected his ability to lead the crusade. But even before Gonzáles's accident, the crusade faced financial difficulties that forced it to curtail some of its programs and sell its headquarters building. While in the early twenty-first century it still exists as a nonprofit corporation with a more limited membership and still operates its school, the crusade is largely a shell of the former organization.

See also Chicano/a Movement; Chicanos and Chicanas; González, Rodolfo Corky; La Raza Unida Party; *and* Plan de Aztlán.

BIBLIOGRAPHY

Garciá, Ignacio M. *United We Win: The Rise and Fall of La Raza Unida Party.* Tucson: MASRC, University of Arizona, 1989.

González, Rodolfo. "I Am Joaquin." In *Minority Group Politics: A Reader,* compiled by Stephen J. Herzog. New York: Holt, Rinehart, and Winston, 1971.

Hartley, George. "I Am Joaquin: Rodolfo 'Corky' Gonzales and the Retroactive Construction of Chicanismo." epc.buffalo.edu/authors/ hartley/pubs/corky.html.

El Plan Espiritual de Aztlán. Documents of the Chicano Struggle. A Pathfinder Merit Pamphlet. New York: Pathfinder Press, 1971.

La Raza: Why a Chicano Party. A Merit Pamphlet. New York: Pathfinder Press, 1970.

Rivera, George. "Chicano Art in Colorado: An Overview." latinoart-community.org/community/EducationalRes/Vistas/Rivera-ChicArt-InCO.html

Steiner, Stan. "Epilogue: The Poet in the Boxing Ring." In *La Raza: The Mexican Americans.* New York: Harper and Row, 1970.

Vigil, Ernesto B. *The Crusade for Justice: Chicano Militancy and the Government's War on Dissent.* Madison: University of Wisconsin Press, 1999.

Vigil, Maurilio E. *Chicano Politics.* Washington, D.C.: University Press of America, 1978.

MAURILIO E. VIGIL

CRUZ, CELIA

CRUZ, CELIA (ca. 1924–2003), Cuban singer. No other performer is so closely identified with the sound of salsa music as Cuban diva Celia Cruz. Over an artistic career that spanned several decades, she popularized first modern Cuban dance music and later the salsa sound throughout Latin America and the United States. Many contemporary Latina and Latino musicians in the United States and elsewhere first became familiar with the foundations of the music they play today through the recordings of Celia Cruz.

Celia Cruz was born to working-class parents in Havana on October 21, probably around 1924, although the exact year of her birth is unknown. Family members noticed her performing talents when she was very young and encouraged her to become a singer. During the 1930s Celia took part in amateur hours in radio stations and other contests where young artists sought to jump-start their careers. By the early 1940s she had become a known name in Havana. She sang on the radio, in small theaters, for private parties, and in towns outside Havana.

In the late 1940s her star began to rise rapidly. She traveled to Mexico and Venezuela for several months, her first trip outside Cuba, as the singer in a dance review. The visit

CELIA CRUZ. Celia Cruz holding Latin Grammy award, October 30, 2001. (Nick Ut/AP)

New York–based salsa boom. Beginning in the early 1970s she recorded a number of LPs in succession with band leaders Johnny Pacheco, Willie Colón, La Sonora Ponceña, and Ray Barretto, which catapulted her into a lead role in the salsa phenomenon. A fourteen-year period culminated in 1988 with her recording of *Ritmo en el corazón* (Rhythm in the Heart) with Ray Barretto, for which she received a Grammy Award.

The 1980s and 1990s were excellent for Celia Cruz: along with winning the Grammy, she was awarded a star on Hollywood's Walk of Fame, received honorary doctorates at Florida International University and Yale University, and won numerous other awards and recognitions. She also appeared briefly in two films, *The Mambo Kings* and *The Perez Family*. After the 1980s she was in constant demand, performing in Japan, Germany, Finland, France, Spain, Portugal, Brazil, Argentina, Venezuela, Colombia, Peru, Ecuador, Costa Rica, and Santo Domingo, among other places. Musical releases such as *Azucar negra* (Black Sugar), *Irrepetible* (Unrepeatable), and *La negra tiene tumbao* (The Black Woman Has a Drum) met with continued success. As the twenty-first century began, Celia Cruz, although afflicted with serious ailments, continued to ride a crest of popularity and carry a busy schedule. She passed away on July 16, 2003. Over the course of decades, Celia Cruz maintained a most varied career during which she sang in Spanish and in English, Cuban mambos and Argentine tangos, boogaloo tunes and Mexican *rancheras*, Puerto Rican *bombas* and Cuban boleros. She became an international star easily recognized because of her flamboyant performance attire and wigs. But it was in the area of Cuban dance music and salsa, a musical idiom dominated by male singers, that she made her voice and her inimitable "¡Azúcar!" synonymous with the entire genre.

See also **Barretto, Ray; Colón, Willie; Puente, Tito;** *and* **Salsa.**

BIBLIOGRAPHY

Betancur Alvarez, Fabio. *Sin clave y bongó no hay son.* Medellín, Colombia: Editorial Universidad de Antioquia, 1993.

Cruz, Celia. Interview in Smithsonian Institution Jazz Oral History Program, September 25–26, 1996, Hollywood, Calif.

Díaz Ayala, Cristóbal. *Música Cubana del areyto a la nueva trova.* San Juan, Puerto Rico: Editorial Cubanacán, 1981.

Fernández, Raul. "Celia Cruz: Artista de América Latina." *Deslinde* 21 (Bogotá, Colombia), July–September 1997.

Valverde, Umberto. *Celia Cruz: Reina rumba.* Bogotá, Colombia: Editorial La Oveja Negra, 1981.

RAUL FERNÁNDEZ

to Venezuela afforded her the opportunity to record for the first time. Back in Havana she got her first major break when she was asked to sing with the well-established and increasingly popular Cuban *conjunto* La Sonora Matancera. For the next nine years Celia recorded hit tune after hit tune with the group. Their music was broadcast to the whole island five days a week. She was featured at all of Havana's famous nightclubs: Tropicana, Montmartre, Sans Souci, and others. With La Sonora Matancera or on her own, she traveled to Haiti, Puerto Rico, Venezuela, Colombia, Peru, the United States, and other countries. She traveled to the United States for the first time in 1957 to receive a music award in New York City.

Shortly after the Cuban revolution of 1959, Celia Cruz moved to Mexico with La Sonora Matancera. The period from the early 1960s to the early 1970s was slow for her compared to the 1950s and compared to what would follow. Celia continued to record and travel with La Sonora Matancera, and she began her association with New York *timbalero* Tito Puente. In the 1960s and 1970s, she recorded a number of LPs with Puente that went largely unnoticed. Then came her association with the incipient

CRUZ, MIGDALIA (b. 1958), writer. Born and raised in the South Bronx, Migdalia Cruz is one of the most prominent Latina or Latino playwrights in the United States. Her plays have been produced and commissioned in esteemed venues across the United States and abroad. The recipient of numerous awards that have fostered her development as a playwright, Cruz has gained recognition as an National Endowment for the Arts (NEA) and McKnight playwriting fellow and as a Theatre Communications Group/Pew Charitable Trust (TCG/PEW) national artist in residence. In 1995 and 1996 the Latino Chicago Theater Company produced an entire season of Cruz's work, a rare honor for modern playwrights. Cruz writes in a wide range of genres, including realist dramas, musicals, operas, and collections of monologues. Her dramatic work is perhaps best known for its densely rich poetic language and its unflinching treatment of female sexuality and embodiment.

The social and political climate of the South Bronx in the 1960s, wherein working-class and impoverished African American and Latino and Latina communities struggled for civic services and resources, informs the artistic vision and subject matter of much of Cruz's work. In an interview with the performance scholar Tiffany Ana López, Cruz stated, "I write about poverty from a woman's point of view" ("Black Opium," p. 202). Throughout her childhood Cruz was nurtured by her parents, Pedro and Gloria Cruz, who emigrated from Puerto Rico to the South Bronx, where Migdalia was born on November 8, 1958. She regards her father's poetic soul as one of the influences on her artistic sensibilities. Cruz has said: "People always think I've had this tragic childhood, and that all of these horrible things I write about have happened. In real life, I had a great childhood; I just had a bad neighborhood" ("Black Opium," p. 202). Cruz has often drawn upon this autobiographical context in her depiction of characters struggling for redemptive moments while caught within violent surroundings. Much of her work engages with characters' struggles to create a sense of home. As such, her plays also speak to the experiences of dislocation and dynamic creation among Nuyorican communities, for whom New York City is often a hostile site of struggle and the Puerto Rican "homeland" is but an imagined memory.

Educated at Stuyvesant High School, a competitive-admission school in Manhattan, Cruz initially envisioned a career as a scientist. After graduating at age sixteen, she entered City College in Queens to pursue a math major until she encountered the dramatic and linguistic innovations of Samuel Beckett. In 1980 she earned a BFA in playwriting at Lake Erie College in Ohio, and in 1984 she earned an MFA in playwriting at Columbia University. But according to Cruz, her most influential education as a playwright occurred during her five years of study at the International Arts Relations (INTAR) Hispanic Playwrights-in-Residence Laboratory in New York under the tutelage of Maria Irene Fornés. The workshop, launched by Fornés in 1981, is largely responsible for mentoring and training a generation of Latina and Latino playwrights, including Cherríe Moraga and Edward Gallardo. Cruz attended the lab from 1984 through 1988 and again in 1990, during which time she crafted her signature style of poetic realism.

Among her other influences, Cruz acknowledges the Spanish playwrights Federico García Lorca and Miguel de Cervantes and the American novelist Toni Morrison. These authors' sweeping lyricism provides a model for Cruz's striking poetic language. Cruz also builds on the American realist traditions of Eugene O'Neill and Tennessee Williams and on the cinematic style of the experimental playwright Adrienne Kennedy, all of whom are Cruz's stylistic models. Aside from Fornés, whom Cruz credits with crafting her voice as a playwright, Cruz also notes the impact of Piri Thomas, whose autobiography, *Down These Mean Streets*, marked her first encounter with a compelling and honest portrayal of Nuyorican communities and offered an affirmation of the subjects she sought to depict in her plays.

Cruz has written more than thirty dramatic works. Her most widely produced play, *Miriam's Flowers* (first produced in 1990, published in 1991), explores the contours of mourning within a Nuyorican family in the South Bronx. The title character, Miriam, negotiates her grief over her young brother's death through acts of sexual exploration and self-mutilation. The play's episodic montage and lyrical diction captures both the grotesque and the sublime moments of Miriam's suffering and redemption. Like *Miriam's Flowers*, *The Have-Little* (produced in 1991, published in 1996) draws from events of Cruz's childhood and centers on a young female protagonist who negotiates conflict through her sexuality. *The Have-Little*, which takes its title from a reference in Cervantes's *Don Quixote de la Mancha*, was a finalist for the Susan Smith Blackburn Playwriting Prize in 1991. In *Telling Tales* (produced in 1990, published in 1993), a collection of monologues, Cruz reveals her mastery of the monologue form, wherein the densely poetic and pain-stricken psyches of her characters are vividly portrayed. Cruz's attentiveness to the interplay between displaced desire and violence permeates the trinity of characters that occupy *Lucy Loves Me* (produced in 1991, published in 2000) and *Fur* (produced in 1995, published in 2000).

In *Lolita de Lares* (produced in 1995) and in *Che-Che-Che!* (produced in 1997), Cruz re-envisions two iconic Latina and Latino revolutionary leaders. *Lolita* recounts the story of Dolores "Lolita" Lebrón, who struggled for Puerto Rican independence, while *Che* combines music and choreography to depict the revolutionary Ernesto "Che" Guevara as a young man, as a dead man, and as the old man he never became. Cruz's historical focus on revolution also informs her reinterpretation of Lorca's *The House of Bernarda Alba* in *Another Part of the House* (produced in 1996), which relocates Lorca's story in Cuba on the cusp of its independence from Spain in the 1890s. Cruz reinterprets another dramatic classic, John Ford's *'Tis a Pity She's a Whore*, in her play *Salt* (produced in 1998), which reveals Cruz's continuing concern about the ways young people navigate devastating surroundings. *Salt* was a finalist for the Blackburn Prize in 1997. In addition to dramas of poetic realism, Cruz has written three radio plays, the libretto for the musical *Street Sense* (produced in 1991), and the book and lyrics for *Rushing Waters* (produced in 1993) and *Frida: The Story of Frida Kahlo* (produced in 1991, published in 1998). *Rushing Waters* was commissioned by Cornerstone Theater in Los Angeles, a community-based theater that casts local citizens in plays staged to address and resolve community conflicts. In *Frida*, as in *Lolita de Lares*, Cruz conducts the important act of staging Latina history.

Through her work Cruz renders visible the frequently overlooked, particularly the often-censured depictions of Latina sexuality. Like all artists, Cruz writes from her place of origin. For Cruz this process is also a politicized act, as she not only gives voice to the silenced but movingly reveals the heartbreaking lyricism and poetic sensibilities that permeate the lives of many Latina and Latino communities. Cruz succinctly described her dedication to this artistic vision: "You can take the girl out of the South Bronx—but you would have to cut my heart out to make me forget" (Perkins and Uno, p. 107).

See also **Fornes, Maria Irene; INTAR; Nuyorican Theater and Poetry; Puerto Ricans;** *and* **Thomas, Piri.**

BIBLIOGRAPHY

PRIMARY SOURCES

Frida: The Story of Frida Kahlo, with Hilary Blecher. In *Here to Stay: Five Plays from the Women's Project*, edited by Julia Miles. New York: Applause, 1998.

Fur: A Play in Nineteen Scenes. In *Out of the Fringe: Contemporary Latina/Latino Theatre and Performance*, edited by Caridad Svich and María Teresa Marrero, 71–114. New York: Theatre Communications Group, 2000.

The Have-Little. In *Contemporary Plays by Women of Color*, edited by Kathy A. Perkins and Roberta Uno, 106–126. New York: Routledge, 1996.

Lucy Loves Me. In *Latinas on Stage: Criticism and Practice*, edited by Alicia Arrizón and Lillian Manzor. Berkeley, Calif.: Third Woman Press, 2000.

Miriam's Flowers. In *Shattering the Myth: Plays by Hispanic Women*, edited by Linda Feyder, 51–84. Houston, Tex.: Arte Público Press, 1992.

Telling Tales. In *Telling Tales: New One-Act Plays*, edited by Eric Lane, 1–17. New York: Penguin, 1993.

SECONDARY SOURCES

López, Tiffany Ana. "Black Opium: An Interview with Migdalia Cruz." In *Latinas on Stage: Criticism and Practice*, edited by Alicia Arrizón and Lillian Manzor, 201–215. Berkeley, Calif.: Third Woman Press, 2000.

López, Tiffany Ana. "Violent Inscriptions: Writing the Body and Making Community in Four Plays by Migdalia Cruz." *Theatre Journal* 52 (2000): 51–66.

Marrero, María Teresa. "Out of the Fringe? Out of the Closet: Latina/Latino Theatre and Performance in the 1990s." *TDR: The Drama Review* 44 (Fall 2000): 131–153.

DEBORAH PAREDEZ

CRUZ, NILO (b. 1960), playwright. Nilo Domingo Cruz, winner of the 2003 Pulitzer Prize for drama, was born on October 10, 1960, in Matanzas, Cuba. He came to the United States on a Freedom Flight shortly before his tenth birthday. He grew up in Miami and attended Miami-Dade Community College's Wolfson Campus. Later, Cruz earned an MFA in playwriting at Brown University (1993). Cruz has held numerous teaching posts, including at Yale University, New York University, Brown University, and the University of Iowa.

Cruz won the 2003 Pulitzer Prize for drama for *Anna in the Tropics* (2002). The play was commissioned by Coral Gables's New Theatre and had its world premiere in October 2002, directed by Cuban American Rafael de Acha. Cruz is the first Latino playwright to win the coveted award in drama. For the same work he also won the American Theatre Critics's Association/Steinberg New Play Award. Other plays of his have won the Alton Jones Award, Kesselring Prize, AT&T Award, Kennedy Center Fund for New American Plays, Rockefeller Grant, and Theatre Communications Group Artist in Residence Grant.

Anna is one of two plays in Pulitzer history to have won without a previous Broadway production (the other was Robert Schenkkan's *The Kentucky Cycle* in 1992). *Anna* was selected not only for its theatrical qualities but also for its poetic and evocative language, two trademarks of Cruz's work. The piece takes place in a 1929 Cuban tobacco factory in Ybor City, near Tampa, Florida. It draws on the Cuban tradition of hiring *lectors* (readers) for the tobacco workers, a tradition that lasted until 1933. The play centers on the power of fiction over the ordinary lives of the factory workers, particularly the women. The novel that the lector reads is Leo Tolstoy's masterpiece of feminine emotional emancipation, *Anna Karenina*. *Anna in the Tropics* later enjoyed a New York stage production at the Royale Theatre, starring the Latino actor Jimmy Smits as the lector and Daphne Rubin-Vega.

Cruz's creative writing career was encouraged by two other Cuban Americans: Teresa María Rojas, the actress, director, teacher, and founder of Prometo theater troupe at Miami Dade College; and Maria Irene Fornes, the Obie Award–winning playwright and founder of the INTAR (Interamerican Arts Relations) Playwrights-in-Residence Laboratory in New York. INTAR is the hothouse creation of many Latino and Latina talents such as Migdalia Cruz,

NILO CRUZ (© David Bergman/CORBIS)

Eduardo Machado, Cherríe Moraga, José Rivera, Caridad Svich, and Edwin Sanchez, among others. The Laboratory nurtured these artists and many others.

Cruz's works include *Night Train to Bolina* (1994), *A Park in Our House* (1995), *Dancing on Her Knees* (1996), *Two Sisters and a Piano* (1998), *A Bicycle Country* (1999), *Hortensia and the Museum of Dreams* (2001), *A Very Old Man With Enormous Wings* (2002), *Anna in the Tropics* (2002), *Lorca in a Green Dress* (2003), and *Beauty of the Father* (2004).

See also Cuban American Writers; Cuban Americans; INTAR; *and* Playwrights.

BIBLIOGRAPHY

Corces, Laureano. "Más allá de la isla: La identidad cubana en el teatro del exilio." In *De las dos orillas: Teatro cubano*, edited by Heidrun Adler and Adrián Herr, 659–664. Madrid, Spain, and Frankfurt, Germany: Vervuert Iberoamericana, 1999.

Cruz, Nilo. *Anna in the Tropics*. New York: Theatre Communications Group, 2003.

Cruz, Nilo. *Lorca in a Green Dress*. Oregon: The Oregon Shakespeare Festival, 2003 Production.

Cruz, Nilo. "Night Train to Bolina." In *Out of the Fringe: Contemporary Latina/Latino Theatre and Performance*, edited by Maria Teresa Marrero and Caridad Svich. New York: Theatre Communications Group, 2000.

González, Mirza. "Persistencia y resistencia: Visión de "lo cubano" en el teatro del exilio en inglés." In *De las dos orillas: Teatro cubano*, edited by Heidrun Adler and Adrián Herr, 65–75. Madrid, Spain, and Frankfurt, Germany: Vervuert Iberoamericana, 1999.

Mann, Emily. "Nilo Cruz." *Bomb* 86 (2003–2004): 70–75.

Munk, Erika. "The Children Are Angels Here." *Theater* 33 (2003): 62–63.

Muñoz, Jose Esteban. "The Onus of Seeing Cuba: Nilo Cruz's Cubanía." *South Atlantic Quarterly* 99 (2000): 455–459.

McAuliffe, Jody. "Interview with Nilo Cruz." *South Atlantic Quarterly* 99 (2000): 461–470.

TERESA MARRERO

CRUZ AZACETA, LUIS. *See* Azaceta, Luis Cruz.

CUBAN AMERICAN COMMITTEE. In 1979 the U.S. State Department, for the first time in the twenty-year history of the Cuban exile community in the United States, received a petition signed by more than ten thousand Cuban Americans supporting normalization of relations with Cuba. The Cuban American Committee Research and Education Fund (CACREF), established in 1976, organized the petition campaign. CACREF was the first Cuban exile group to openly pressure the U.S. Congress and government officials for changes in U.S. policy toward Cuba.

Two years after Cuba's 1959 revolution, the United States severed diplomatic relations with Cuba. In 1962 President John F. Kennedy announced a total trade embargo. Later the United States banned travel to Cuba. Cuba's socialist government for its part banned all Cuban exiles from returning home. But by the late 1970s the U.S. government had lifted the ban on travel to Cuba, and Cuba permitted thousands of Cuban exiles to visit family on the island. Further changes appeared imminent. From the late 1970s to the early 1980s the Cuban American Committee founder Manolo Gomez focused on working through the media and other public forums to put pressure on U.S. government officials to fully normalize relations with Cuba. But by 1985 retaliatory actions by both the U.S. government and the Cuban government forced CACREF to shift focus and pursue a strategy that would allow it to influence changes in policy by both governments more directly.

In May 1982 President Ronald Reagan reinstituted the travel ban to Cuba except for visits home by Cuban Americans with relatives on the island. In 1985, responding to pressure from the well-financed anti-Castro Cuban American National Foundation, the Reagan administration launched Radio Martí. The radio station, staffed by supporters of the Cuban American National Foundation, transmitted news and programs from the United States to Cuba on a 24-hour basis. Cuba responded by suspending all visits by Cuban Americans to relatives in Cuba. The Cuban government lifted the ban a year later but intermittently curtailed the number of annual visits. The Cuban American Committee replied by regrouping and expanding its board of directors as it prepared to counter the influence of the right-wing Cuban American National Foundation on the U.S. Congress. The committee officially opened an office in Washington, D.C., named Alicia

Torres as its executive director, and received increased financial support from the Arca Foundation, which in the late 1980s was interested in improving the U.S. foreign policy toward Cuba.

During the 1988 U.S. presidential campaign, the expanded Cuban American Committee convinced the Hispanic caucus of the Democratic Party in Illinois to approve a resolution favoring normalization of relations with Cuba. That year CACREF members and supporters presented the Democratic Party with a resolution to include normalization of relations with Cuba in their national platform. A year later the Cuban American Committee was instrumental in convincing U.S. congressional leaders to include a hearing, in an ongoing congressional review of U.S.–Cuba policy, that would invite testimony from moderate groups in the Cuban American community. This marked the first time U.S. legislators officially gathered testimony from Cuban American groups favoring a rapprochement with Cuba and expressing concern over the intimidation and terrorist tactics used by Cuban exile groups to silence dissension in their community. In response to these hearings, Claiborne Pell proposed an expansion of family reunification efforts, George Crocket proposed a resumption of direct mail service to the island, and Stephen Solarz proposed an investigation into the humanitarian impact of the trade embargo.

In the late 1980s the Cuban American Committee cosponsored academic conferences at Harvard University and at the School for Advanced International Studies of Johns Hopkins University that, for the first time, included the views of moderate Cuban Americans. In the 1980s and the early 1990s CACREF members were routinely interviewed by both the English-language and the Spanish-language media, appearing for the first time as a countervoice to the anti-Castro Cuban American National Foundation. At the time CACREF's executive director organized the Cuba Working Group, a coalition of representatives of diverse groups that joined the Cuban American Committee in its efforts. In 1989 the CACREF board of directors sent Cuban government officials a document making the case that, by virtue of the innumerable trips back and forth to the island by Cuban Americans, an "immigration" agenda was emerging in opposition to the "exile" agenda of the anti-Castro leadership. The Cuban government, it argued, needed to take the humanitarian needs of its immigrant community into consideration when making future policy decisions. In 1991, in pursuit of its "immigrant" agenda with Cuba, CACREF hosted a conference on Saint Simon's Island in Georgia that attracted a diverse group of second-generation young intellectuals and professionals from Cuba as well as second-generation Cuban Americans. Together they began the task of identifying potential changes in Cuba's policies that would benefit all second-generation Cubans.

Despite the sustained efforts of the Cuban American Committee, the U.S. Congress passed the 1992 Cuban Democracy Act, which prohibited foreign-based subsidiaries of U.S. companies from trading with Cuba and prohibited travel to Cuba by U.S. citizens and family remittances to Cuba. Its supporters predicted that the new law heralded the immediate fall of the Cuban government. It did not, and later legislation ameliorated its impact. But it did begin the decline of the Cuban American Committee Research and Education Fund. Support from major donors, including the Arca Foundation, declined, and by 1994 CACREF had ceased to exist. But like all seminal movements, its ripple effect continued, and a decade later various other organizations of moderate Cuban Americans had sprung into existence. CACREF had opened the way. Its efforts openly challenged the authority of the Cuban American National Foundation in the U.S. Congress and the national media and called attention both in the United States and in Cuba to the emergence of a moderate Cuban American immigrant agenda.

See also **Cuban Americans; Cuban Democracy Act of 1992;** *and* **Cuban Embargo.**

BIBLIOGRAPHY

Glasgow, Kathy. "The Cuban Connection." *Miami New Times*. June 9, 1993. www.miaminewtimes.com

Torres, Alicia M. "The Cuban Democracy Act and Humanitarian Issues: Peaceful Transition of Another Sarajevo Next Door?" Written testimony presented to the U.S. Senate Subcommittee on Western Hemisphere and Peace Corps Affairs of the Committee on Foreign Relations. August 5, 1991.

Torres, Alicia M. "H.R. 4168—Humanitarian Impact of the Bill and Politics behind Its Drafting." Written testimony presented to House Foreign Affairs Committee. April 8, 1992.

DAGMARIS CABEZAS

CUBAN AMERICAN NATIONAL FOUNDATION/PAC.

The Cuban American National Foundation (CANF) has been the most influential Cuban American and perhaps Latino and Latina lobby organization in the United States, particularly in the foreign policy arena. Established in 1981 by a group of Cuban American businesspeople, including its founder and director until 1997 Jorge Más Canosa (1939–1997), the foundation has imprinted U.S. foreign policy toward Cuba since then. The CANF was molded after the successful Jewish lobby. Its main objective has been to influence Washington's policy toward Havana; its secondary goals have included the promotion of Cuban American interests (in areas such as migration and family reunification) and the advocacy of several other foreign policy concerns, some of which were far removed from Florida and Cuba (for instance, the support for anticommunist rebels in Angola during the 1980s).

On both fronts the CANF has been remarkably capable. It has been one of the pillars sustaining the United States'

CUBAN AMERICAN NATIONAL FOUNDATION. CANF march in Miami, April 29, 2000, in protest against the Immigration Naturalization Service raid that took Elián González from his Miami relatives and returned him to his father. (Getty Images)

embargo toward Cuba, even in a post–cold war world, and influenced U.S. policy toward Nicaragua and Angola in the 1980s. The success of the organization, which has offices in Miami, Florida; Washington, D.C.; and Union City, New Jersey, and chapters in a number of other states and Puerto Rico, has been the result of several factors: good timing, dedicated leadership, effective mobilization of an electoral constituency, pragmatic political strategy, and considerable financial resources.

At the time of its founding, the CANF encountered little competition in the lobby arena. Few organizations were interested in United States–Cuba policy. Indeed, with the exception of smaller groups that did not have the deep pockets of the foundation, no other organization was solely focused on Cuban affairs. Its inception in 1981 coincided with the advent of the Reagan administration, which supported the foundation. President Ronald Reagan shared with the foundation a remarkably compatible worldview that regarded communist regimes as nefarious; Fidel Castro's in Cuba was no exception. Reagan ushered in a rebirth of the cold war, especially in the Caribbean Basin. The White House saw Castro's Cuba as the source of instability in the region and as such a threat to U.S. national interests. Ideological convergence between the CANF and the executive branch opened the doors of the halls of power and influence to Más Canosa and the foundation.

The Reagan administration relied on the CANF to support key initiatives (such as aid to the Nicaraguan Contras), and in turn the president endorsed the CANF's pet projects. At the same time, the Republican Party sought to attract Cuban Americans to its fold, and the Reagan embrace of the foundation played into this partisan strategy perfectly. Since the 1980s, the CANF has been tightly associated with the Republican Party. Convergence with the executive branch does not explain totally the reasons behind the ability of the organization to become a major political player in Washington. Auspicious timing and the close connection with the executive was parlayed successfully by effective institutional leadership at the hands of Más Canosa.

Más Canosa not only attracted tens of thousands of followers among his Cuban American compatriots but also mustered political clout in Congress and in the White House. That he could influence the voting of a highly concentrated electoral community in key states (for example, Florida and New Jersey, where the majority of Cuban Americans is concentrated) and could make generous contributions to electoral campaigns on both sides of the political spectrum cemented his political standing locally and nationally. Moreover, Más Canosa could be both an ardent ideologue and a convincing pragmatist when the situation required it. The strategy of lobbying and contributing to both Democrats and Republicans even though the organization was clearly identified with the Republican Party paid off. The CANF eventually counted on steadfast supporters on both sides of the aisle in Congress. The strategy also facilitated the emergence of a bipartisan consensus on Cuba, a consensus that has held, despite challenges and erosion, well into the beginning of the twenty-first century. Even under Democratic administrations, the CANF wielded what could be considered a veto power over U.S. policy toward the island. Democrats (including President Bill Clinton) have attempted to garner the goodwill of the CANF in the hope of making inroads into the Republican stronghold in the Cuban American community.

After the early 1980s, the foundation's influence extended from the White House into Congress, which has guaranteed the organization's place in the political debate over Cuba policy. CANF lobby efforts have translated into specific policies, including the establishment of Radio Martí (funded by the U.S. government to transmit radio and television programming to Cubans on the island) and later T.V. Martí, which has been blocked by the Cuban government. CANF influence has reached well beyond Cuba policy. As mentioned, the foundation became an important actor in the making of U.S. policy toward Nicaragua and Angola in the 1980s. In both cases, the CANF endorsed support for armed groups fighting the governments of the nations.

The CANF also tackled other issues, for which it won the respect of thousands of Cuban Americans. For example, the CANF took charge of resettling Cuban refugees who had immigrated to other countries after the Mariel boatlift in 1980. The CANF has provided a host of services to the community and has even supported sending humanitarian aid to the island after natural disasters. The CANF also courted supporters throughout the world and among leaders of governments. After Más Canosa's death in 1997, the organization experienced a leadership crisis that resulted in a split. A major policy redirection took place under the successor to Más Canosa, his son Jorge Más Santos. The younger Más has charted a more moderate course of action based on a peaceful transition toward democracy and capitalism in Cuba. One of the most dramatic shifts has been the CANF's engagement with and support for human rights activists (once perceived as suspect) and for the nascent civil society on the island.

With this change in direction, the CANF has placed Cuban politics in the hands of Cubans and has moved the center of gravity away from Washington and the United States. The new policy came at a cost, though, as the organization lost a group of its founders and longtime supporters. The disaffected argued that the foundation had betrayed its initial mandate for a totally new Cuba, a vision that does not allow any compromise with the current government or with those who advocate a piecemeal reform movement (such as the Proyecto Varela, which attempts to use the Cuban legal provisions to change the constitution and move to a democratic political system).

Since the late 1990s, the CANF has promoted a number of activities in support of human rights on the island. It has also financed reconstruction efforts after natural disasters in Florida and Central America. The CANF has been the target of criticism from a number of quarters. Under Más Canosa, the CANF was perceived as an authoritarian and personalistic institution that responded to the personality of Más Canosa. Yet this seems a simplistic characterization. Opponents also charged that the hard line vis-à-vis Cuba (what some referred to as the pressure-cooker approach) would lead to a social explosion that would not only cause turmoil and suffering for the Cuban people but would also backfire on U.S. interests.

In the early twenty-first century, the CANF is not the organization it was in its zenith. Although still influential and even predominant among Cuban American organizations, the foundation has to deal with the challenge of other players in the field, including one established after the Elián González affair, the Cuba Study Group, composed of wealthy Cuban exiles who advocate a shift in U.S. policy. Without a doubt, the CANF is an example of a Latino and Latina lobby group that has the resources and the know-how to compete in the U.S. lobby arena and to do so with remarkable success. The CANF also illustrates two relevant lessons: first, that local and national politics are intimately entwined with international affairs and, second, that ethnic groups are a factor of import in foreign policy making in the United States. Especially in the latter, the CANF is exemplary and a likely harbinger of what is to come in terms of Latino and Latina influence on U.S. policy toward Latin America. However, it is not a foregone conclusion that the experience of the CANF can be replicated with its degree of efficacy.

See also Cuban Americans; Cuban Embargo; González, Elián; *and* Más Canosa, Jorge.

BIBLIOGRAPHY
Fernandez, Damian J. "From Little Havana to Washington, D.C.: Cuban-Americans and U.S. Foreign Policy." In *Ethnic Groups and U.S. Foreign Policy*, edited by Mohammed E. Ahrari. New York: Greenwood, 1987.
Torres, María de los Angeles. *In the Land of Mirrors: Cuban Exile Politics in the United States.* Ann Arbor: University of Michigan Press, 1999.

DAMIAN FERNANDEZ

CUBAN AMERICAN WRITERS. Given the waves of immigrants that have come from Cuba to the United States for almost two centuries, it is useful to approach the cultural production of Cuban American writers and artists through the critical lens provided by a theme-and-variations compositional form. From this standpoint, exile, a catalyst for thousands of Cuban nationals to leave the island since the early nineteenth century, is the larger theme into which sub-movements among immigrants and their descendants introduce variations that change the mood, texture, and complexity of the overall theme while sustaining its core structure.

Critics have suggested it is an exile consciousness that makes Cuban Americans distinctive within the Latina and Latino community. Mexican Americans and Chicanos and Chicanas have always populated the Southwest, even after the border between the United States and Mexico was redrawn in the mid-nineteenth century. Puerto Ricans now enjoy citizenship status as a result of the neocolonial links between the island and the mainland. And a majority of Dominicans and other nationals enter the United States as immigrants seeking a better life. On the other hand, it has largely been political events in Cuba that have forced Cubans to enter the United States, a country that for the last forty years or so has refused to grant full diplomatic relations to Cuba and that enforces an economic embargo against the island. At the same time, the vastly different historical circumstances that have given rise to distinct waves of immigration and the personal experiences of exiles both before leaving the island and once in the United States preclude unifying all exiles in one seamless homogenizing category. No single category could accommodate the many ways in which Cubans have engaged with their surrounding realities once in exile. Moreover, some of the ways used to give expression to that engagement provide points of contact with other Latina and Latino groups, whereas others do not.

The Nineteenth Century

A foundational period in Cuban history, the early nineteenth century saw an ideological rift develop between those favoring the perpetuation of the colonial system of power (or its reform) and those advocating independence from Spain, while another sector backed annexation by the United States. Clearly abetted by colonial contradictions and the rise of nationalism throughout Latin America, the drive for independence gained strength as the century unfolded, but those who embraced it risked reprisal. Hence, a few noted Cuban writers who supported self-determination were banished from the island. Among these was Félix Varela (1788–1853), a Catholic priest who spent twenty-five of his thirty years of exile in New York championing humanitarian causes. Highly regarded by his contemporaries as an independent, progressive thinker, Varela wrote *Cartas a Elpidio* (Letters to Elpidio, 1835) and in 1824 founded the newspaper *El Habanero*. Authorship of the historical novel *Xicoténcatl*, long anonymous, has been attributed to him also. Varela was the founder of the Church of the Transfiguration in Lower Manhattan in the 1830s and was named Vicar General of the New York diocese in 1837. He died in St. Augustine, Florida, in 1853, the year José Martí was born. In 1997 he was honored in New York with a commemorative stamp.

Fleeing from an accusation of conspiring against the Spanish colonial authorities, José María Heredia (1803–1839) lived in New York and Philadelphia from 1823 to 1825. In addition to numerous articles on literary topics, Heredia wrote several epistolary essays on the United States. One of these, dated December 4, 1823, and published in Cuba in Domingo del Monte's journal *La Moda o Recreo Semanal del Bello Sexo* (Fashion or Weekly Entertainment for the Fair Sex), focused on Boston, where Heredia disembarked in 1823. The regularity of the urban grid, the dense population yet lack of destitution, the beauty of the women, and above all the orderly functioning of the city appealed to Heredia, whose positive image of Boston stood as a symbol of the United States. "Carta de Filadelfia" (Letter from Philadelphia, 1824) bespeaks the similar effect Philadelphia had on the poet. Finally, in a third letter written on November 31, 1826, entitled "Carta sobre los Estados Unidos" (Letter about the United States), he confessed his admiration for this "land of liberty" that offered refuge to the oppressed. In New York, Heredia published a collection of poetry, *Poesías* (Poems), which included one of his most anthologized works, the "Oda al Niágara" (Ode to the Niagara). It is said that Heredia wrote "Himno del desterrado" (Hymn of the uprooted), another celebrated poem, in 1825 on his way to Mexico.

Cirilo Villaverde (1812–1894) sought political asylum in New York in 1849 after being arrested in Cuba for his separatist ideas. It was here that he revised most of the manuscript of *Cecilia Valdés o la Loma del Angel*, the first edition of which appeared in 1839, and he published the definitive edition of this antislavery novel in the United States in 1882. During the long period Villaverde spent in exile, he wrote numerous political essays such as "El señor Saco con respecto a la Revolución de Cuba" (Mr. Saco with regard to the Cuban Revolution, 1852) and "La revolución de Cuba vista desde Nueva York" (The Cuban Revolution seen from New York, 1869). He was director and editor of several magazines and newspapers.

José Martí (1853–1895) wrote after Villaverde's death that he considered him a gifted novelist. The two had met in New York where Martí, preeminent writer, patriot, and standard-bearer for Cuba's independence, spent the last fourteen years of his life in a thriving Hispanic community. Hailed as a precursor of *modernismo*, the literary movement that transformed Latin American literature at the end of the nineteenth century by endowing it with an indigenous voice, Martí was only seventeen years old when he was forced to abandon Cuba for his political activities. After living in Spain, Mexico, Guatemala, and Venezuela, Martí arrived in the United States in 1881 and remained in this country until 1895. It was in the United States that he organized the Cuban Revolutionary Party in 1892 and edited *Patria*, the party's newspaper. It was here also that he wrote the greater part of his works. In early 1895, Martí returned to Cuba to take up arms against the Spanish authorities, and he died on the battlefield that same year.

Martí's vast oeuvre includes extraordinary poetry, collected in such books as *Versos sencillos* (Simple verses, 1891), *Ismaelillo* (Little Ishmael, 1882), *Versos libres* (Free verses, written in the 1880s and published posthumously in 1913), and *Flores del destierro* (Flowers of exile, published for the first time in 1933). He also wrote plays, a novel, a collection of writings for children titled *La edad de oro* (The golden age), and numerous chronicles and journalistic articles on a wide array of topics. An admirer and critic of the United States, he focused in his chronicles on a variety of American figures, including Edgar Allan Poe, Mark Twain, Henry David Thoreau, Walt Whitman, and Ulysses S. Grant, as well as on sites of special significance such as the Statue of Liberty and the Brooklyn Bridge. "Our America" (1891), Martí's most famous essay, calls for a unified view of Latin America. "A Vindication of Cuba," published on March 25, 1889, in the *New York Post*, stands as Martí's courageous response to a scathing attack on Cuban national character written by several U.S. congressmen, published in the *Philadelphia Manufacturer* on March 6, 1889 and endorsed by the *New York Evening Post*.

The Early Twentieth Century

Between 1899 and 1938, over 95,000 Cubans joined the ranks of émigrés in the United States. Much remains to be documented concerning the communities made up of expatriates in Key West, Tampa, and New York, and to a lesser extent in Philadelphia and Baltimore, in the first half of the twentieth century. Recently, Evelio Grillo (b. 1920) chronicled his life as an Afro-Cuban in Tampa during the early to mid-twentieth century in *Black Cuban, Black American: A Memoir* (2000). Foremost among his concerns is racial discrimination, which led black Cubans to forge alliances with the African-American community rather than commingle with white fellow Cubans.

José Yglesias (1919–1995), the son of immigrant cigar makers from Cuba and Spain, wrote a number of novels that draw on his own life in Tampa and New York. In *The Truth about Them* (1971) and other novels, Yglesias delves into his ethnic and working-class background to offer a portrait of Cuban émigré life in the United States. Desi Arnaz's memoir, *A Book* (1976), focuses on his rise to fame and his marriage to Lucille Ball, his partner in the television sitcom *I Love Lucy*. Arnaz (1917–1986) escaped from Cuba in the 1930s during the Machado dictatorship and, using his wits, quickly made his way up in the entertainment industry. Another Cuban who left the island before 1959 and achieved recognition is María Irene Fornés (b. 1930), a playwright known for her treatment of feminist themes in such plays as *Fefu and Her Friends* (1977), as well as for her experimental theater. *La vida real* (1986), a testimonial novel by island-based Cuban writer Miguel Barnet, provides a window into the life of working-class émigrés who supported the 1959 socialist revolution from afar.

The 1959 Revolution and Its Aftermath

A majority of the many renowned writers and artists who fled the island after the socialist takeover, as part of the largest exodus in Cuban history, chose to settle in the United States. They did so for a number of reasons, including proximity of the United States to the homeland, their relative familiarity with U.S. culture and society, and the warm reception extended to individuals fleeing a socialist regime at the apogee of the cold war. Lydia Cabrera (1900–1991) and Enrique Labrador Ruiz (1902–1991) as well as the visual artists Rafael Soriano (b. 1920) and José María Mijares (b. 1921) settled in Miami, Florida, where a large Cuban enclave would take root in the 1960s. Eugenio Florit (1903–1999), who left Cuba in 1940 and served on the faculty of Barnard College, and Lino Novás Calvo (1905–1983), who taught at Syracuse University, made New York their place of residence. Despite the real constraints stemming from a linguistic environment alien to them, many of the exiled writers continued to publish works that reflected a nostalgic attitude toward the world left behind, an attitude bolstered by undying expectations of an eventual return to the island. Given that they have remained, culturally at least, close to the Cuba they knew, and given their exclusive use of Spanish, this generation of exiles can be considered Cubans in the United States rather than Cuban Americans. For them change in location did not bring about a parallel change in worldview.

After leaving Cuba in 1960, Lydia Cabrera carried on her work on Afro-Cuban legends and published several works, among them *Ayapá, cuentos de jicotea* (Ayapá, Hicotee stories, 1971). Novás Calvo's *Maneras de contar* (Ways of telling, 1970) includes both previously published and unpublished stories, some of which are set in the United States. Jorge Mañach (1898–1961), a prominent Cuban thinker of his generation, wrote *Teoría de la frontera* (Theory of the border, 1971) and *El espíritu de Martí* (The spirit of Martí, 1973) in Puerto Rico.

The implicit or explicit denunciation of the Cuban government one would expect from dissident writers can be found in such novels as *Cruzados de la aurora* (Crusaders of dawn, 1972) by the prolific exiled writer José Sánchez Boudy (b. 1927), and in two novels by Hilda Perera (b. 1926), *El sitio de nadie* (Nobody's place, 1972) and *Plantado* (Planted, 1981), as well as in some of Novás Calvo's short stories. Lorenzo García Vega (b. 1926), has remained active as a poet. Women writers Amelia del Castillo (1925), Ana Rosa Núñez (1926–1999), and Pura del Prado (1931–1996) published several poetry collections in exile.

A highly heterogeneous group of Cuban poets, playwrights, essayists, and fiction writers spanning generations has continued to write in Spanish despite permanent residence in the United States. These include Angel Cuadra (b. 1931), Rita Geada (b. 1937), Sonia Rivera Valdés (b. 1937), José Corrales (1937–2002), Lourdes Casal (1938–1981), José Antonio Arcocha (1938–1998), Orlando Rossardi (b. 1938), Juana Rosa Pita (b. 1939), José Kozer (b. 1940), Eliana Rivero (b. 1940), Isel Rivero (b. 1941), Manuel Cachán (b. 1942), Uva Clavijo (now Uva de Aragón, b. 1944), Emilio Bejel (b. 1944), Julio E. Miranda (1945–1998), Magali Alabau (b. 1945), Omar Torres (b. 1945), Guillermo Rosales (1946–1993), Maya Islas (b. 1947), Amando Fernández (1949–1994), Alina Galliano (b. 1950), Carlota Caulfield (b. 1953), Iraida Iturralde (b. 1954), and Lourdes Gil (b. 1955). Lourdes Casal received the Casa de las Américas Award for *Palabras juntan Revolución* (Words gather Revolution, 1981), a book of poems. Other recipients of the award were Rivera Valdés for *Las historias prohibidas de Marta Veneranda* (The prohibited stories of Marta Veneranda, 1997), and the Areíto group for *Contra viento y marea* (Against all odds, 1978), a book of testimonies. Casal was one of the first to build bridges between young exiled Cubans and Cubans on the island, through the journal *Areíto* (1974–1984) and other ventures. Years later, Ruth Behar (b. 1956) would claim Casal's legacy of dialogue in an anthology she edited, *Bridges to Cuba/Puentes a Cuba* (1995), in which Cubans on both shores collaborated. José Kozer is regarded as one of the best poets writing in Spanish today. A professor of literature at the City University of New York for many years until his retirement, Kozer has written over ten books of poetry in Spanish since 1972. Others who continue to write in their native language include Matías Montes Huidobro (b. 1931), a well-known playwright teaching in Hawaii; Mireya Robles (b. 1934), author of an acclaimed feminist novel, *Hagiografía de Narcisa la Bella* (Hagiography of Narcisa the Beautiful, 1985), and a resident of South Africa for some time; Octavio Armand (b. 1946), poet and editor of the journal *Escandalar* (1978–1984) and a long-time resident of New York who now lives in Caracas, Venezuela; and novelist Mayra Montero (b. 1952), who resides in Puerto Rico. All of the accomplishments of these writers, too numerous to record here, are evaluated in Espinosa Domínguez's panoramic study of Cuban exile literature. Required reading for anyone interested in Cuban literary history, this all-encompassing study serves as a testament to the exceptional literary output of Cubans beyond the borders of the island, as well as to the vitality of a literature in Spanish on U.S. soil.

Departing from the socioeconomic and aesthetic makeup of the first waves of post-1959 immigrants, if not from their ideology, the writers who abandoned Cuba during the Mariel boatlift of 1980 gave a different twist to the exile theme, leaving their distinctive mark on Cuban exile literature. The boatlift was a mass exodus of Cubans through the Mariel harbor triggered by deteriorating socioeconomic conditions on the island. Nearly 25,000 Cubans headed for the United States in a six-month period. Having spent part of their adult lives under a socialist regime, the Mariel writers had experiences noticeably different from earlier exiles. Furthermore, some of these writers identified themselves as homosexuals and as such openly defied the entrenched homophobia of the conservative Cuban exile community. Despite the initial rejection of the so-called "marielitos" by the established Cuban community in Miami, Cuban letters went through a renaissance of sorts after their arrival. The Mariel writers actively pursued their literary interests, publishing and founding several journals, and they assumed a leading role in the condemnation of repression.

An eminent writer who left the island at this time, following a tormented period of persecution and even imprisonment, Reinaldo Arenas (1943–1990) had written some important novels in Cuba but had been allowed to publish little. Arenas founded *Mariel* (1983–1985), a noted if short-

lived cultural journal that promoted many of the new talents, and published numerous works of fiction, among them *El portero* (The doorman, 1989) and *Viaje a La Habana* (Trip to Havana, 1990), both of which take place, at least in part, in the United States. The film adaptation of Arenas's agonizing autobiographical narrative, *Antes que anochezca* (Before night falls), which was published posthumously in 1992, brought his tragic life to the attention of the general public. Other writers in the Mariel group include René Ariza (1940–1994), Reinaldo García Ramos (b. 1944), Ismael Lorenzo (b. 1945), Carlos Victoria (b. 1950), Rafael Bordao (b. 1951), and Roberto Valero (1955–1993). The visual artists Eduardo Michaelsen (b.1920), Juan Boza (b.1941), and Carlos Alfonzo (1950-1991) also left Cuba via Mariel. Jesús J. Barquet (b. 1953), himself a fine poet, has written an insightful account of the Mariel writers.

Although they did not leave Cuba in the boatlift, Heberto Padilla (1932–2000) and Antonio Benítez Rojo (b. 1931), both prominent writers, settled abroad at about the time of the Mariel exodus. Padilla, whose falling-out with the Cuban regime in 1971 and subsequent *mea culpa* had made him a *cause célèbre* among Western intellectuals, cofounded *Linden Lane Magazine* in 1982 with the poet Belkis Cuza Malé (b. 1944). Padilla also published a novel, *En mi jardín pastan los héroes* (Heroes grazing in my garden, 1981) and his memoirs, *La mala memoria* (translated into English as *Self-Portrait of the Other*, 1989). A professor of Latin American literature at Amherst College in Massachusetts, Benítez Rojo has continued to evolve as an outstanding novelist, short story writer, essayist, and literary critic. Two of his best-known works are the historical novel *El mar de las lentejas* (Sea of lentils, 1984) and the essay *La isla que se repite* (The repeating island: The Caribbean and the postmodern perspective, 1989), a study of Caribbean culture inspired in part by chaos theory.

Cuban American Writers, the Sons and Daughters of Exile

Cuban American as a rubric has been applied to the sons and daughters of Cuban exiles in the context of a multicultural United States. Critical reflections on Cuban Americans, as opposed to Cubans in the United States, took off in the 1980s. With their articles, anthologies, and book-length studies, several critics, including Pérez Firmat, Rivero, Alvarez Borland, and Hospital, have made noteworthy contributions to the understanding of writers such as Pablo Medina (b. 1948), Gustavo Pérez Firmat (b. 1949), Roberto G. Fernández (b. 1951), Eduardo Machado (b. 1953), Ricardo Pau Llosa (b. 1954), Elías Miguel Muñoz (b. 1954), Achy Obejas (b. 1956), and Virgil Suárez (b. 1962), among others. Most of these writers are novelists, but there are accomplished poets and playwrights in their midst. Although a diverse group writing mostly in

English or in a bilingual mode, these authors nevertheless share a sense of hybridity and cultural duality resulting from their first-hand knowledge of both Cuban and American cultures. Having arrived in the United States as children or young adults, these writers have been fractionally labeled the "one-and-a-half" generation, a term coined by the sociologist Rubén G. Rumbaut and popularized by the critic Gustavo Pérez Firmat (b. 1949), also a novelist and poet, in his study of the bicultural location of the offspring of Cuban exiles. The generation has also been dubbed *los atrevidos* (the daring ones) by Carolina Hospital. While most critics reserve the term Cuban American specifically for this cohort living "on the hyphen," others, such as Burunat, García, and Cortina, apply it indiscriminately to all Cubans residing in the United States regardless of their generation or sensibility. Although most of these writers have not returned to Cuba, they re-create their native land through memory and imagination.

The staying power of images etched in memory during childhood, images that embody a part of the Cuban American equation, comes to life in some of the paintings and installations by Cuban American visual artists. The work of Humberto Calzada (b. 1944) evokes Cuban colonial architecture while the mixed medium of old family photographs and text chosen by Tony Mendoza (b. 1941) recalls his affluent Cuban past. Ana Mendieta (1948–1985), whose early death truncated a promising career, returned to her native land to trace in its soil, in Jaruco, the silhouette of pre-Columbian earth goddesses. Luis Cruz Azaceta's (b. 1942) poignant expressionist canvases depict the violence sensed both in Cuba and New York. Other artists of this generation are Julio Larraz (b. 1944), Paul Sierra (b. 1944), María Brito (b. 1947), Emilio Falero (b. 1947), Mario Algaze (b. 1947), Tony Labat (b. 1951), Mario Bencomo (b. 1953), Félix González Torres (1957–1996), Miguel Padura (b. 1957), and Ernesto Pujol (b. 1957).

Some writers in this group share commonalities with Chicano and Chicana and Puerto Rican writers. Achy Obejas's collection of short stories *We Came All the Way from Cuba So You Could Dress Like This?* (1994) and her novel *Memory Mambo* (1996), both deeply rooted in the Latina and Latino community of Chicago, grapple with the subject of ethnic and sexual identity in ways reminiscent of other Latina writers. The Puerto Rican barrio in East Harlem, New York, serves as locale for the play *Botánica* (Botanical store, 1990) by Dolores Prida (b. 1943), while the musical *4 Guys Named José . . . And Una Mujer Named María* (2001) distills a more Latina and Latino flavor. Other plays by Prida, such as *Beautiful Señoritas* (1977) and *Coser y cantar* (Sewing and singing, 1981), ponder the fate of Latinas in a bilingual and bicultural milieu.

Given their stress on gender and ethnicity, autobiographical essays by Eliana Rivero (b. 1940) and Ruth Behar (b. 1956) reveal a shared terrain with Latina writers (as Latinas in an Anglo society and as women in a patriarchal social order) with whom these authors have occasionally collaborated (see *Telling to Live: Latina Feminist Testimonies*, 2001). The work of Alina Troyano, a successful performance artist also known as Carmelita Tropicana, explores what it means to be Latina and lesbian. Some of these writers have been more likely than others to maintain ties with Cuba at a professional and personal level.

Cuban ethnic writers who left the island as infants or who were born in the United States have introduced still another variation on the theme of exile. Oscar Hijuelos (b. 1951), the first Latino or Latina to win the Pulitzer Prize, and Cristina García (b. 1958), a finalist for the National Book Award, but have been labeled ethnic writers have been widely acknowledged by the literary mainstream. These writers are more grounded in U.S. culture—although their work continues to seek inspiration in Cuban-related topics. Hijuelos's and García's best-known novels, *The Mambo Kings Play Songs of Love* (1989) and *Dreaming in Cuban* (1992), respectively, attest to the incidence of motifs related to the island. Nilo Cruz (b. 1961), a playwright who came from Cuba as a young boy, sets his play *Anna in the Tropics*, winner of the Pulitzer Prize for drama in 2003, in Tampa's Cuban enclave of Ybor City. The artist María Martínez Cañas (b. 1960), who, like García, left Cuba as an infant, has used maps, stamps, and old passports to construct a sense of place and identity. Another Cuban writer, the younger Ana Menéndez (b. 1970), author of a well-received short story collection, *In Cuba I Was a German Shepherd* (2001), seeks inspiration in Cuban exile culture. Only through their embrace of an imagined Cuba can these writers claim a connection to the culture of exile.

The Cuban Diaspora

Finally, any consideration of Cuban exile literature and art would have to include some mention of its diasporic dimensions. Post-1959 Cuban exile writers and artists have settled in such varied places as Spain (Gastón Baquero, Carlos Alberto Montaner, Jesús Díaz), France (Severo Sarduy, Eduardo Manet, Zoe Valdés), Sweden (René Vázquez Díaz), Mexico (Eliseo Alberto, Rafael Rojas), the United Kingdom (Guillermo Cabrera Infante), and Italy (Calvert Casey). Cuban American writers and artists are certainly implicated in this larger reality—still another variation to gauge on the theme of exile. This truism no doubt has an effect on how ethnicities are lived and perceived, for the notion of a diaspora aids in the construction of more fluid identities not tied to a single territory. Despite the increasing consciousness of a diaspora, however, the preferred destination for exiled Cuban intellectuals continues to be the United States. The recent arrival here of several well-known writers, including Daína Chaviano, signals both continuity and renewal. It augurs well for the future of Cuban American literature.

See also Arnaz, Desi; Cabrera, Lydia; Casal, Lourdes; García, Cristina; Hijuelos, Oscar; Marielitos; Martí, José; Obejas, Achy; Suárez, Virgil; *and* Varela, Félix.

BIBLIOGRAPHY

Alvarez Borland, Isabel. *Cuban-American Literature of Exile: From Person to Persona.* Charlottesville: University Press of Virginia, 1998.

Barquet, Jesús J. "La generación del Mariel." *Encuentro de la cultura cubana* 8, no. 9 (1998): 110–125.

Burunat, Silvia, and Ofelia García, eds. *Veinte años de literatura cubanoamericana: antología 1962–1982.* Tempe, Ariz.: Bilingual Press, 1988.

Cortina, Rodolfo J. "History and Development of Cuban American Literature: A Survey." In *Handbook of Hispanic Cultures in the United States: Literature and Art,* edited by Nicolás Kanellos and Claudio Esteva-Fabregat. Houston, Tex.: Arte Público Press, 1993.

Duany, Jorge. "Reconstructing Cubanness: Changing Discourses of National Identity on the Island and in the Diaspora during the Twentieth Century." In *Cuba, the Elusive Nation: Interpretations of National Identity,* edited by Damián J. Fernández and Madeline Cámara Betancourt, 17–42. Gainesville: University Press of Florida, 2000.

Espinosa Domínguez, Carlos. *El peregrino en comarca ajena. Panorama crítico de la literatura cubana del exilio.* Boulder, Colo.: Society of Spanish and Spanish-American Studies, 2001.

Fuentes-Pérez, Ileana, Graciella Cruz-Taura, and Ricardo Pau-Llosa, eds. *Outside Cuba: Contemporary Cuban Visual Artists = Fuera de Cuba: Artistas cubanos contemporáneos.* New Jersey and Miami: Office of Hispanic Arts (Rutgers University) and Research Institute for Cuban Studies, 1988.

Heredia, José María. *Revisiones literarias: Selección y prólogo de José Ma. Chacón y Calvo.* Havana, Cuba: Publicaciones del Ministerio de Educación, 1947.

Hospital, Carolina, ed. *Cuban-American Writers: Los atrevidos.* Princeton, N.J.: Ediciones Ellas/Linden Lane Press, 1988.

Maratos, Daniel C., and Marnesba D. Hill. *Cuban Exile Writers: A Bio-bibliographic Handbook.* Metuchen, N.J.: Scarecrow Press, 1986.

Pérez Firmat, Gustavo. *Life on the Hyphen: The Cuban-American Way.* Austin: University of Texas Press, 1994.

Rivero, Eliana. "From Immigrants to Ethnics: Cuban-American Women Writers in the U.S." In *Breaking Boundaries: Latina Writing and Critical Readings,* edited by Asunción Horno-Delgado et al. Amherst: University of Massachusetts Press, 1989.

Rivero, Eliana. "(Re)Writing Sugarcane Memories: Cuban Americans and Literature." In *Paradise Lost or Gained? The Literature of Hispanic Exile,* edited by Fernando Alegría and Jorge Rufinelli. Houston, Tex.: Arte Público Press, 1990.

IRAIDA H. LÓPEZ

CUBAN AMERICANS. Cubans have resided in the United States for almost two centuries. Their experience is characterized by a great deal of diversity but also by common elements that provide the basis for a cohesive approach to the Cuban American story. Cuban migration patterns to the United States changed often, and Cuban American communities faced significantly different political and socioeconomic realities. Nevertheless, whatever the class and racial origins of these communities, the turbulence of Cuban history produced certain themes that offer a unifying approach to the subject.

In the nineteenth century, Cuban communities in the United States promoted insurgencies in Cuba to achieve freedom from Spain. In the first half of the twentieth century, they struggled to defend their communal integrity in the face of political and economic change in the United States. In the second half, Cuban efforts to overthrow the Communist regime in their homeland shaped community formation and identity. Throughout these two centuries, nationalism influenced Cuban community integration into North American society, informing an exile identity dedicated to affecting political and socioeconomic change in their homeland and an ethnic identity that often guided the realities of daily life in the United States. But whether advancing nationalist, exile, or ethnic concerns, which were often difficult to separate, Cubans integrated into their new country of residence, eventually becoming citizens, accommodating their political culture, individual and family values, economic aspirations, and cultural expressions.

Immigration and Settlement

During a ten-month British occupation of Havana in 1762 during the Seven Years' War, Cubans discovered the benefits of commercial relationships outside the Spanish Empire. Merchants from the English colonies along the Atlantic Coast visited the Spanish colonial city, initiating a relationship of critical importance for Cubans. After that time, many citizens of the now independent republic of the United States visited and resided in Cuba, but many more Cubans moved north. They traveled to cities like New Orleans, Philadelphia, and New York, where they worked and, increasingly, pursued their education, taking advantage of opportunities opened by the expanding economic ties between Cuba and the United States.

Among the most visible immigrants were the political exiles who arrived in considerable numbers during the 1820s through the 1850s, seeking ways to free Cuba from Spanish rule. Their numbers increased during the final half of the nineteenth century, as a thirty-year struggle to break from Spain commenced in 1868 with the Ten Years' War. These exiles were joined throughout the century by economic immigrants, most of whom worked in a cigar industry that appeared in Florida, Louisiana, and New York during the final third of the century. Though no reliable estimates exist, perhaps some twenty to thirty thousand Cubans lived in the United States during these years. In the new century, migration continued, with some sixteen thousand arriving in the 1920s alone; most were connected with the cigar industry labor markets, but change was under way. Mechanization of the North American cigar industry, shifts in fundamental market demand for cigars as a result of the popularity of cigarettes, and the onset of the Great Depression in 1929 slowed Cuban immigration to about nine thousand during the next decade.

The immediate post-Depression era brought a migratory resurgence from Cuba. Not connected with cigar markets, this migration resulted from the generally evolving economic and political relationship between Cuba and the United States set in motion by the North American occupation of Cuba in 1898 as a result of the Cuban insurrection of 1895 and the subsequent Cuban-Spanish-American War. The occupation ensured almost unlimited access to Cuba for U.S. citizens, who gained a dominant foothold in the island's economy, a trend that became even stronger in the 1940s and 1950s. Despite one of the highest per capita incomes in Latin America, Cuba suffered from a poor distribution of resources, a relatively high cost of living, and a large underemployed labor force. These economic difficulties, aggravated by political corruption and violence, paved the way for a military coup in 1952, led by former president General Fulgencio Batista, that created an even deeper political crisis and revolution. Throughout these years, Cubans left the island in increasing numbers. Twenty-six thousand arrived in the United States during the 1940s and almost eighty thousand during the next decade.

What seemed to be an increasing but rather stable migratory stream across the Straits of Florida in the 1950s became a flood with the tumultuous events of a Communist revolution that shook Cuba in the early 1960s. On January 1, 1959, Batista fled Cuba, leaving a power vacuum filled by guerrilla leader Fidel Castro Ruz, who by the end of 1961 declared Cuba a Marxist-Leninist State. Radical socioeconomic transformations and a repressive political system drove over a million Cubans to leave home by 2000. Cubans in some way associated with the Batista government left first. Cuba's socioeconomic elite followed, as a wholesale nationalization of the Cuban economy proceeded throughout the 1960s. In 1965, the Cuban Adjustment Act gave Cubans unprecedented and special preference in U.S. immigration law, virtually guaranteeing their access to the United States. Under this law, the United States facilitated the arrival by air and boat of some 300,000 Cubans beginning in 1965 and continuing through 1973, when the Cuban government prohibited further departures.

In the 1970s, the Cuban government turned away from its haphazard economic policies and embraced the Soviet Union's centralized planning model, improving economic conditions considerably. Nevertheless, pressures to emigrate continued unabated, and thousands, tired of continual shortages and political intolerance, sought ways to leave. Frustrations finally came to a head during April 1980 when over ten thousand people sought asylum in the Peruvian embassy in Havana. U.S. government criticisms of Castro's handling of the grave affair provoked the government to open the Cuban port of Mariel for all who wanted to leave. During the next five months, Cuban Americans manning a flotilla of boats, yachts, and other vessels transported some 125,000 Cubans to U.S. shores. This exodus temporarily relieved the migration pressures in Cuba, but they became even stronger during the 1990s after the Soviet Communist Bloc collapsed, leaving the Cuban government politically and economically isolated. As the Cuban economy spiraled downward, consumer and food shortages caused panic and desperation among the many who departed on small boats, rafts, and even inner tubes.

During the summer of 1994, the exodus increased dramatically, and tens of thousands, encouraged by the Cuban government, now set out across the Straits of Florida, forcing the U.S. government to change its open-door policy to Cuban immigration. Under the new policy, the U.S. government returned to Cuba immigrants intercepted in the Florida Straits, but increased the annual quota for Cubans seeking legal entrance to the United States. While U.S. government policy sought to return as many Cubans as possible caught on the high seas, political pressures from the Cuban community resulted in a compromise that gave those Cubans successfully reaching U.S. territory the right to remain.

Communities and Economy

The earliest visible Cuban communities in the United States formed in the nineteenth century. Prior to the Civil War, Cubans did not generally reside in distinct communities but rather scattered in neighborhoods in numerous cities, especially New York, New Orleans, and Philadelphia. Beginning in the 1870s, with the rebellion in Cuba and the growth of the cigar industry in the United States, migration increased, and cohesive Cuban communities appeared in New York and Key West, where people resided in close proximity, often creating distinct neighborhoods. They developed political and social institutions, published newspapers, created economic traditions, and offered public expressions of their cultural traditions, reflecting Cuba's class and racial composition. By the middle of that decade, an estimated twelve thousand Cubans lived in the United States, the largest concentration in New York. Among them were members of Havana's sugar and landholding elite, middle-class entrepreneurs and professionals, and a significant multiracial working class mostly employed in the cigar factories. At the end of the conflict in Cuba in 1880, many middle-class Cubans returned home, while tobacco workers continued to arrive, mostly in Florida, in even greater numbers. By 1885, about five thousand Cubans resided in Key West, and they quickly gave the town a national reputation for its anti-Spanish political agitation and high-quality Cuban cigars. That year, almost one hundred Key West cigar factories of various sizes employed some three thousand workers.

Beginning in 1886, Cubans also established cigar factories in the Tampa Bay area, which eventually supplanted Key West as the primary producer of Cuban cigars in the United States. By 1927, Tampa's 159 cigar factories employed some 13,000 workers and produced 504 million cigars annually. Besides the cigar trade, Cubans in these towns worked as innkeepers, teachers, bakers, sailors, journalists, factory managers, clerks, pastors, bankers, storekeepers—indeed, the entire gamut of activities necessary to provide goods and services to the mass of workers laboring in the factories. Though the various Cuban communities in the United States developed separate identities, leaders, and institutions, until the end of the 1920s many operated within the context of the cigar industry labor market. Cuban families usually had economic and social ties in more than one community, and connections with Havana were often strong, since political disturbances, strikes, and economic cycles produced considerable movement in both directions across the Strait of Florida.

During the 1930s, the Florida cigar industry fell on hard times. Some Cuban workers returned to Cuba, but many went north, especially to New York, which again became the most important Cuban center in the United States during the 1940s and 1950s. In 1943, for example, out of a total of about twenty-two thousand Cubans registered as resident aliens, just over eleven thousand lived in New York, New Jersey, Massachusetts, and Pennsylvania, while a little more than seven thousand settled in Florida. While the largest U.S.–born Cuban population still resided in Florida, the majority of Cuban immigrants now arrived in the northeast of the United States. Most came in search of work, fleeing the economic and political difficulties facing Cuba during these decades. Though precise statistics are not available, employment opportunities in U.S. industries, such as shoe and leather factories, along with the great demand for Cuban music and baseball players during the 1940s and 1950s, attracted working-class migrants. This post–World War II generation of immigrants involved in entertainment and sports, particularly music, dance, and baseball, gave Cubans a national visibility for the first time. Television exposure, particularly through the personality of Desi Arnaz, the Cuban husband in *I Love Lucy*, made North Americans more aware than ever before of the Cuban presence.

Cuban residential patterns in the United States shifted again with the radical political transformations in Cuba and the mass exodus after 1959. Florida again emerged as the most important settlement area for Cubans, although Miami now displaced Key West and Tampa as the primary destination. By 1980, Cubans in the Dade County metropolitan area, which included cities such as Miami, Hialeah, Sweetwater, and Miami Beach, contained almost 600,000 Cubans, producing an entrepreneurial and dynamic enclave economy that transformed the region.

Cubans in south Florida created a diverse and ethnically integrated economy that provided considerable opportunities for exiles. Many of the Cubans of the first exile wave in the 1960s brought with them an educational background, economic skills, and experience with capitalism, although most Cubans did not achieve economic stability and advancement without considerable personal and family sacrifice.

Initially, Cuban exiles experienced clear downward social mobility. In Miami, many took any available jobs to maintain their families, while others became self-employed in an emergent Cuban-supported informal economy composed of a variety of professional, technical, and personal services. Many eventually established small businesses that required little initial capital, while others took nonunionized garment and construction jobs.

The ever-increasing number of Cuban arrivals, as well as the North American market, provided a customer base that allowed for the emergence of a diverse set of economic enterprises that expanded rapidly. Cubans established restaurants and cafeterias, gas stations, grocery stores and eventually supermarkets, book and record stores, hardware, appliance and furniture stores, funeral homes, radio stations and newspapers, theaters, pharmacies and clinics, and the whole range of businesses that a community requires. The enclave became an entrepreneurial community that relied on personal relationships, Cuban business networks, and ethnic solidarity for its prosperity.

In addition to the profits and savings generated by these activities, Cubans acquired private capital and federal loans and established larger enterprises, including banks, car dealerships, large companies, corporations, and the like. These enterprises established markets outside of Miami, in other parts of the United States, and in Latin America, creating tremendous economic possibilities for the enterprising Cuban business community. As Cubans continued to arrive during the next decades, they also found jobs in this community, further expanding the economic enclave.

Cubans also reproduced their professional classes. At first, many professionals could not practice their vocations, which many abandoned, but with the support of the Cuban Refugee Program (1961–1975), others learned English and underwent professional relicensing to work in the United States. These professionals and others in

CUBAN AMERICAN PROTEST. Thousands of Cuban protestors fill the streets of Little Havana in Miami in 1995 to protest the repatriation of Cuban rafters. (Doug Mills/AP)

the community emphasized education and invested a great deal in sending their children to colleges and universities, another factor that in time strengthened the enclave and allowed it to grow.

Large numbers of Cubans also settled in the Northeast, mostly in New Jersey and New York, establishing communities in Union City and the city of West New York, two New Jersey towns on the Hudson River. By 1970, a little more than one-third of West New York's total population of 40,666 was Cuban, and by 1980 the Union City–West New York area had incorporated about 100,000 Cubans. As with Miami, most Cubans in these communities who arrived during the 1960s experienced a substantial decline in their occupational status. During the 1970s, almost half improved their occupational position, especially those who had worked in higher status jobs in Cuba before emigrating. During the decade, the proportion of Cuban migrants holding white-collar jobs doubled.

Besides the Miami and New Jersey enclaves, Cubans settled in cities across the United States. As the influx of Cubans began to overwhelm south Florida, the Cuban Refugee Program sponsored the relocation of immigrants to other areas. By 1980, some thirty thousand Cubans lived in Los Angeles; twenty-four thousand in Chicago; thirteen thousand in Boston; ten thousand in Atlanta; eight thousand in Washington, D.C.; five thousand in Dallas–Fort Worth; and two thousand in New Orleans.

As a whole, the Cuban communities that formed as a result of the post-1959 migrations fared relatively well economically. Median family incomes surpassed other Latina and Latino groups, although they did not reach the income

levels of Anglo-American society. This higher income resulted from several factors, including their peculiar demographic characteristics, U.S. government support of the refugees, the benefits of Miami's enclave economy, and the successes of Cuban women entering the labor market who contributed substantially to family incomes.

The Exile Tradition

Nationalism and its expression of exile identity dominated Cuban worldviews and their communities for most of two centuries. For exiles, steeped in Cuban nationalism, the homeland defined it all, and in their communities they cultivated an environment defined by their expatriate condition. Nostalgia, nationalist political discourses, and the latest news from home in the local Cuban media all contributed to an exile perspective. At home, dinner conversations expressed and transmitted values and aspirations for a future that included Cuba. In the late nineteenth century, readers (*lectores*) in the Florida cigar factories, who literally read novels, newspapers, and plays to workers as they rolled cigars, constantly reminded the workers of the communities' primary obligation to the homeland. With the end of the war of independence, these communities ceased being primarily exile, but they retained deep nationalist sentiments, steeped in their historical traditions, that contributed to a strong ethnic identity as the communities reshaped themselves.

After the Cuban Revolution of 1959, in Miami, Union City, and other cities, Cubans in bodegas, restaurants, and other Cuban-run enterprises kept their radios tuned to the numerous talk-radio shows that obsessively dealt with *el tema* (the topic). When not listening to Spanish-language talk radio or television, people gathered in parks, malls, coffee shops, and a variety of places and talked about the latest issues relating to Cuba. Historically, the "Cuban question," whether defined as evicting the Spanish, ridding the island of one dictatorship or another, or overthrowing Communism, shaped identity wherever Cubans gathered and formed communal bonds within the United Sates. Cubans maintained their claim on the identity and culture of their land of origin and much of what they did in exile affirmed their *cubanidad*, or sense of being Cuban.

Generations of exiled political leaders of varied backgrounds and motivations took the lead forming exile communities. From Father Felix Varela, in the late 1820s, to José Martí sixty years later, to Jorge Más Canosa in Miami a century after that, Cuban exile leaders in the United States reflected tremendous diversity of personalities, political perspectives and visions, and talents. Despite their differences, what they had in common was an unyielding commitment to constructing communities with an exile character dedicated to changing affairs in Cuba. They worked not primarily to facilitate integration into a new society, but to perpetuate an exile perspective that would even win over Cubans who did not arrive predisposed to participate in exile activity.

Many of these leaders spoke to their communities through newspapers and other print media, and later, radio, television, and eventually even the Internet. *El Habanero* (1824–1826) in Philadelphia and New York, *El Porvenir* (1890s) in New York, *El Yara* (1878–1898) in Key West, and *Réplica* (1960s–1970s) and *El Nuevo Herald* in Miami (beginning in 1987), to name just a few newspapers, had the same goal of maintaining a constant exile discourse among a highly nationalistic Cuban population. Political organizations and clubs also provided leaders with the vehicles to mobilize their communities. For a century and a half, beginning in the 1840s, hundreds of Cuban nationalist organizations appeared, reflecting differing political perspectives, strategic considerations, personality preferences, and levels of militancy. Communities also promoted national symbols, and each historical era adopted nationalist heroes and observed patriotic annual commemorations. Linked to this were public monuments that offered a visual reminder of the exile imperative. Education also often promoted exile culture, values, and political perspectives among the young, aimed at creating a new exile generation. In 1871, Cubans in Key West established Instituto San Carlos, which among other things provided schooling in a totally Cuban environment for the community's children. This same instinct for using education to instill exile values appeared much later in the Cuban community of Miami, where after-school programs kept children fluent in Spanish and in touch with Cuban culture and history.

The exile tradition also included constant efforts by armed militants to invade Cuba or otherwise overthrow the regimes their opposed. From the 1870s to the 1890s, exiles on many occasions purchased weapons for insurgents or attempted to infiltrate the island to initiate or support guerrilla operations against Spanish authorities. Similar activities occurred in the 1960s and 1970s when armed groups—often trained by the U.S. government—attempted to land in Cuba and join already active resistance movements against the Castro government. Exiles during this era often disagreed about tactics and accused each other of being "reactionaries" or "Communists," leading sometimes to violence among themselves.

Whether speaking of the late nineteenth or late twentieth centuries, the innumerable ways exiles promoted awareness of the Cuban question within their communities played a critical role in maintaining loyalty to the homeland and an exile consciousness that became a central feature of community life. Cubans shared their exile perspectives at home, at work, and in social contexts, ensuring the establishment and continuation of an enthusiastic and lasting commitment to their vision of Cuba.

Ethnic Identity and Acculturation

The deep commitment of Cubans to their homeland did not of course mean they stood unaffected by the reality of their residence in the United States. Cubans existed within exile and emergent ethnic identities and could not avoid the inevitable integrative processes that drew them into North American political, socioeconomic, and cultural life. In some ways, their nationalist instincts and exile experiences informed and provided useful experiences and resources for engaging their lives as permanent residents and citizens of the United States.

At the end of the Cuban war of independence in 1898, community exile perspectives faded as a Cuban republic emerged. The separatist press ceased to exist, patriot clubs disbanded, and exile activism disappeared, although nationalism remained central to the historical memory of the communities themselves. Books, memoirs, and accounts of the exile ordeal of the nineteenth century that gave birth to their communities, and the devotion expressed to such leaders as José Martí and others who had actually walked their streets, succeeded in transmitting nationalist feelings to the next generations and contributing to an emergent ethnic identity. Though sporadic political activities of exiles agitating against one regime or another in Cuba over the years remained, community activities shifted away from exile politics to ethnic solidarity as they sought livelihood and security in the United States.

This ethnic identity proved important at a time when Cubans found themselves facing the increasingly powerful assimilative forces of society as their own communities became less isolated and drawn more into mainstream life in the United States. One Cuban American writer from Tampa, José Yglesias, in his autobiographical novel *The Truth about Them* (1971), remembered his elders' descriptions of Martí as a great man but lamented that the Cuban martyr's life and contributions were never even mentioned in his junior high and high school classes. North American society expected U.S. Cubans to dispense with their historical memory and embrace the "American" story. In Key West, Cubans faced similar challenges to their identity. In the 1930s, a Works Progress Administration report on the San Carlos Institute noted that:

> The most significant thing about San Carlos at the present is that its students are taught to be good Cuban-Americans—to become Americanized and yet to maintain their cultural identity as Cubans and Spanish-speaking people. They are taught to be proud of their race, language, and culture. . . . [But] San Carlos cannot compete with the public schools in moulding [sic] the present generation of Cuban children in Key West. For the public schools are intent upon a program of complete Americanization; their only concern with Cuban culture is to obliterate it entirely.
>
> (Works Progress Administration)

In Tampa and Key West, perhaps the most powerful factor undermining a strong nationalist and ethnic identity was the decline of the cigar industry. Changing tastes and mechanization eliminated jobs, forcing tobacco workers to return to Cuba, move to New York, or find employment in workplaces where class and ethnic solidarity was of little consequence. The educating and unifying role of the practice of *lectura* (reading) in the factories disappeared in 1931, banned by the owners. Disruption of traditional employment patterns, processes of ideological socialization, and the effects of public-school education on longstanding value systems contributed to dissipating the working-class communities in Key West and Tampa.

These forces of assimilation constantly chipped away at Cuban nationalist and ethnic identities even after the 1950s, when the massive immigration of Cubans provoked by the Cuban Revolution reinforced and reinvigorated the Cuban presence in the United States. Though these new communities altered the overall class and social composition and political ideology of Cuban communities, they, like the previous centers, also expressed a strong nationalism, a resurgent exile identity, and a sense of ethnic solidarity. The immigrant generation of 1960 maintained their exile identity without much difficulty, almost always referring to themselves as *Cubanos*, but their children faced forces of assimilation perhaps even more quickly than Cubans had before. Never as isolated from the mainstream North American society as Key West and Tampa, Cubans in Miami came into contact with the U.S. public school system, television, and popular culture. They learned to speak English quickly, and Spanish often became their second language. Second- and third-generation Cubans in Miami readily acknowledged their Cuban American reality, which represented an adjustment to U.S. society, but this ethnic culture also remained distinctive and self-perpetuating. As the Cuban American writer Gustavo Pérez Firmat suggested, Cubans lived on the "hyphen," between two realities, two cultures, two worlds. Nevertheless, whether identifying as Cubanos or "Cuban-Americans," Miami Cubans usually maintained a deep emotional and psychological connection with their country of origin.

Women

For women, moving from Cuba to the United States and confronting change and accommodation consciously or unconsciously inspired them to challenge traditional gender roles. As exiles, women participated as political leaders, promoted cultural traditions, and advocated change in Cuba, while as ethnic women they advanced their socioeconomic interests and generally defended their communities. From the 1870s to the 1920s, most Cuban women in Florida remained in the home, although over time they increased their participation in the labor market, especially in the tobacco trades. Women arriving after World War II, and perhaps more so after the Cuban Revolution, entered labor markets in even higher percentages and worked in a much wider scope of employment that gave them greater influence in their communities than their sisters had enjoyed earlier in the century.

Whether from home or the workplace, women always played a critical role in the exile arena. Throughout the final third of the nineteenth century, they became a mainstay of local revolutionary activities, working in clubs and dedicating countless hours to the nationalist cause. Besides contributing time, they hosted visiting political leaders, organized parades, banquets, raffles, and picnics, and collected contributions for nationalist projects. This was reenacted after 1959, and, despite the more conservative context, women maintained a spirit similar to their predecessors' in building a new exile identity. Among other things, they participated in demonstrations, organized letter-writing campaigns, produced anti-Castro literature, and led boycotts against British and Spanish goods to protest trade agreements with Cuba.

In addition to their deep commitment to exile politics, women played an important role in helping their communities adjust to the new society. In the late nineteenth and early twentieth centuries, working-class women offered a great deal of moral and material support for labor movements that defended the rights of their heavily working-class communities. During labor strikes women opened their homes to displaced families, providing solidarity and sharing resources. Women also left their homes to raise money, serve on strike committees, organize soup kitchens, and participate in protest demonstrations, promoting a nationalist consciousness and an immigrant ethic of defense of family and community.

Two generations later, women departing Cuba for the United States, this time from middle-class backgrounds, also confronted new values and attitudes that changed them and their families. Greater participation in the labor market and civil society led to political and social activism directly linked to issues of adjustment within North American society. Bilingual education, politics and voting, women's rights, salaries, and workplace issues became common topics of concern and discussion. Younger women, particularly the college educated, challenged the traditional values of Cuban society as barriers to effective involvement in their new society. Many embraced the values of the civil rights movement and feminism, joined political groups on the right and left, and let their positions be known. In general, Cuban women in the United States participated actively in advancing their community's exile agenda as well as involving themselves in the daily concerns of adaptation to life in the United States. Dade County Congresswoman Ileana Ros and social activist Lourdes Casal, for example, had very different visions on a number of issues, but both women challenged traditional gender expectations within their communities as they struggled to keep their families and traditions intact during times of displacement and adjustment.

Labor Organizing

As with women, the Cuban workers also promoted their exile and ethnic interests through the specific lens of class and the vehicle of labor movements. Cuban communities have always reflected the class diversity of their homeland, though not always in the same proportions. Throughout the nineteenth and early twentieth centuries, migrations tended to be heavily working class. During the first twenty years of the Cuban Revolution, arrivals to the United States were mostly of the middle and upper classes, reflecting societal responses to the radical and socialist transformations in Cuba's economy and society. This changed considerably after 1980, when migrant flows again included significant numbers of the island's working classes. It is not surprising, then, that class-conscious Cubans struggled to defend their socioeconomic rights and their livelihoods in the United States at the same time that they embraced Cuban nationalism and worked to change conditions in their homeland.

Cuban workers arriving to the United States during the late nineteenth century brought with them clearly expressed political and socioeconomic activist traditions. By the end of the 1870s, workers in Key West had organized a tobacco workers' union, and workers in Tampa and New York followed suit in the 1880s. Anarchist leaders such as Enrique Messioner, Enrique Creci, and Guillermo Sorondo influenced these unions by the late 1880s, resulting in increased militancy and confrontations, as well as challenged nationalist leaders who attempted to maintain worker attention exclusively on matters relating to Cuban independence. During the early 1890s, in order to calm the factories and ensure worker support for the nationalist movement, political leader José Martí developed a political discourse advocating a social order "with all, and for the good of all." For the most part, Cuban workers accepted Martí's formula and supported the war to defeat Spain in Cuba, but they never abandoned their commitment to their social and economic rights. Indeed, with the end of the war, working-class leaders filled the political vacuum left by nationalist exiles returning to Cuba and shifted attention to the socioeconomic problems in their communities. Cuban workers in Tampa, Key West, and New York participated in reorganizing their communities, leading resistance and strikes in defense of their labor rights through the 1930s. In Tampa especially, this activism produced a highly conscious radical working-class community with a strong sense of class and ethnic solidarity.

This activism reflected developments in Cuba itself, where during the first half of the twentieth century workers formed labor movements of many ideological persuasions. Influential labor confederations pressed for workers' rights and achieved the passage of some of the most progressive labor legislation in the Western Hemisphere, institutionalized in the Cuban Constitution of 1940. Important political actors in Cuban politics during the 1940s and 1950s, Cuban labor generally supported the revolutionary movement led by Fidel Castro. The Cuban Revolution's unanticipated Communist trajectory, however, caused most of Cuba's labor leadership to leave the island for Miami. Cuba's former labor bosses focused their energy on overthrowing the regime in Cuba and initially paid little attention to labor matters in south Florida, although they later encouraged the emergence of a Cuban labor movement associated with the AFL-CIO. By 1990, Dade County Latinas and Latinos, mostly Cuban, represented about 26 percent of union membership. In 1988, a Cuban became head of the AFL-CIO central labor council, and an AFL-CIO affiliated Labor Council for Latin American Advancement (LCLAA) attracted to its ranks twenty-seven Cuban labor leaders representing twenty-one local unions. LCLAA's primary task was not only to encourage Cuban membership but also to increase their numbers in the ranks of administration and leadership. Like their compatriots a century earlier, Cuban workers who brought with them a legacy of labor activism and class concerns had to confront a suspicious exile community who thought these activists took the focus off the community's primary concerns with Cuba. While certainly as anti-Castro as the rest of their compatriots, Cuban labor activists nevertheless resented the excessive concern with foreign policy and neglect of local domestic class concerns of importance to organized labor in south Florida. Cuban workers in the United States worked hard for 150 years to balance their socioeconomic needs as ethnic workers in the United States with their exile concerns about the fate of their homeland.

Cubans of Color

For many Cubans, race was important to how they thought about nationalism and adjusted to North American society. Blacks and mulattos have always been represented within the Cuban communities in the United States. During the late nineteenth century, Cubans of color probably accounted for between 15 and 20 percent of the immigrant population, a proportion that fluctuated but that remained significant up until 1959, when it declined precipitously as a result of the Cuban Revolution. One estimate is that blacks and mulattos constituted only about 6 percent of Cubans in the United States several years after the Cuban Revolution, a proportion, however, that increased with the Mariel boat lift and subsequent migrations. This migration experience reflected the initial belief among Cubans of color that the Cuban Revolution would benefit them and the later sense of disillusionment with the course of the revolutionary process.

Race was often a source of considerable tension within the Cuban communities, both as exiles and as people attempting to accommodate to U.S. society. The first identifiable Cuban community of color in Key West during the final third of the nineteenth century included its own leaders and institutions. Others appeared later in Tampa and New York. Though blacks and mulattos in these communities certainly shared a strong sense of Cuban identity with their white compatriots and supported nationalist initiatives, they also felt a need to articulate their own identity and agenda, demanding that whites become more conscious of the debilitating impact of their racist attitudes. Within exile and nationalist communities, race was a source of considerable concern and debate. Indeed, José Martí, in an attempt to unify the nationalist cause, spoke of race often, urging his white compatriots to overcome prejudices in order to establish an independent nation free of racial hatreds and discriminations. On the basis of this, for example, in New York Afro-Cuban newspaper editor Rafael Serra encouraged Cubans of color in all the exile communities to support the independence movement in the mid-1890s.

The extent of racial divisions in the Cuban communities became especially clear after the end of the independence war when Cuban and North American race politics deepened and hardened already existing tensions and divisions. In the clearest example, the initially integrated El Club Nacional Cubano, Octubre 10 in Tampa in 1900 suffered a racial split leading to the formation of Afro-Cuban club Los Pensadores de Martí y Maceo. This formal segregation of the Cuban community reflected not only the deepening divisions associated with Florida's Jim Crow laws but also race tensions among Cubans in Cuba over postindependence politics and social policy. This development in Tampa confirmed Afro-Cubans' worst fears about their white compatriots and launched them on a divergent process of acculturation that connected them with the African American community of the United States.

Facing similar prejudices, those who resided in the Northeast, especially New York, often interacted with other Caribbean people of African descent including Puerto Ricans and Dominicans. While Afro-Cubans tended to maintain their Cuban identity and cultures, they also contributed to the beginnings of "Hispanic" neighborhoods in New York City. Though studies did not yet exist in the early 2000s, racial dynamics within Cuban communities did not seem to change significantly after 1959. While often engaged in exile activities supporting the anti-Castro initiatives of their white compatriots, many Cubans of color who settled in Miami also faced racism and, like those earlier in the twentieth century, partially escaped these attitudes by establishing interactions with African Americans and other Hispanics of color from the Caribbean. Like those before them, they established their own institutions as a way of preserving their distinct identity. Also, in Dade County from the 1970s to the 1990s many Cubans of color found themselves caught between Cuban American and African American disagreements over political and socioeconomic interests, frequently leading to violence.

U.S. Politics

Cuban participation in U.S. politics involved an ethnic as well as exile logic. Cubans voted for local leaders who influenced domestic policy concerns but at the same time maneuvered to affect U.S. foreign policy toward Cuba. The first community experience in formal party politics began in Key West during the 1870s, when thousands of tobacco workers and political exiles formed an important voting block within the Republican Party. White Republicans recruited Cubans and, with African Americans and black immigrants from Barbados, created an alliance that offset the majority Democratic Party controlled by the town's traditional southern white population. Cuban goals initially focused on their homeland, and they offered to exchange their vote for Republican support of their war of independence. Republican politicians agreed and sealed their coalition by giving Cubans positions as justices of the peace, as county clerks, and in other public offices. In 1876, for example, Carlos Manuel de Céspedes, son of the Cuban insurgent leader, became mayor of Key West and thus the first Cuban elected to public office in the United States. During the next twenty years, numerous Cubans held offices as city aldermen and state legislators, as well as other local positions in Key West and, later, Tampa. Beginning in 1876, the Democratic Party reemerged to control Florida politics as Reconstruction came to an end, slowly drawing Cubans into its ranks. During the late nineteenth century, mostly Cuban cigar manufacturers and businessmen joined the Democrats hoping to stem the growing tide of labor activism but, after the 1920s, working-class Cubans also joined, supporting President Franklin Roosevelt's New Deal policies.

Cubans arriving in the United States with the onset of the Cuban Revolution also expressed interest in domestic politics throughout the 1960s and 1970s, but only slowly became citizens and gained the right to vote. Not until the late 1970s did Cubans mobilize behind their own candidates, generally under the auspices of the Republicans. They gravitated to the Republican Party in reaction to Communism, but also probably because the thousands of small entrepreneurs within the Cuban American communities felt more comfortable with free enterprise Republicans than with southern Democrats. Also, Democrats did not initially provide Cubans with much opportunity to run for office. In the 1980s, Cuban enthusiasm for elective office increased as a result of a combination of exile and ethnic political considerations. Specifically, the Mariel boat lift increased frustrations regarding U.S. policy toward Cuba, and an increase in xenophobic expressions in the United States and Dade County presented a threat to ethnic identity. In the 1980s and 1990s, Cubans elected their own as councilpersons, mayors, and judges to municipal and county governments in south Florida and New Jersey. They also occupied ten Florida legislative and three congressional seats, including one in New Jersey. In the 2002 election, Cubans gained an additional congressional seat in Florida. Cubans also achieved national prominence by learning the finer points of political lobbying. In 1980s, a hard-line exile group, the Cuban American National Foundation (CANF), lobbied the U.S. government and promoted anti-Castro exile perspectives on the international scene with considerable success. Other older Cuban organizations, like the Cuban American Committee and the Cuban Committee for Democracy, used similar means to offer a more liberal and flexible approach to the Cuban question.

Cuban involvement in U.S. politics certainly did not signal an abandonment of exile consciousness but did alter its expression. Indeed, Cubans used their newly formulated, ethnically defined political power to promote local and state interests but also advocated agendas related directly to Cuba. Their emergence nationally as influential actors on Cuba issues during the 1980s and 1990s reflected how ethnic and exile concerns operated together quite comfortably.

Religion

Always present in Cuban communities, though at different levels of intensity, religious life too reflected exile and ethnic dynamics. In the nineteenth century, Cuban Catholics and Protestants organized in exile, though for a number of reasons their influence on community life was much less than would be the case a century later. In general, Catholicism developed a bad reputation among Cubans because of the Church's support for Spain during the wars of independence. Earlier in the century, Father Felix Varela had called on the Church to change this stance but to no avail, and, by the 1870s to the 1890s, many Cubans in the United States had abandoned the Catholic Church altogether. Protestants profited from this and established active communities led by pastors deeply committed to Cuban nationalism and independence. At the same time, they took advantage of the situation to preach against the Catholic Church and its values, suggesting that an independent Cuba could not rely on Catholic values if it expected to prosper. Despite the activism of Protestants, most Cubans at the time turned for inspiration to a variety of nonreligious philosophical traditions including masonry, socialism, and anarchism, or to African-based religions like Santería. Though present in the heavily working-class Cuban centers of Key West and Tampa during the first half of the twentieth century, religious traditions did not displace the dominant working-class ideologies or even masonry.

Cuba itself remained a highly secular society throughout the twentieth century, though religions did prosper. Protestantism grew on the island after independence from Spain, as did Catholicism, which managed to reestablish its credibility as the largest Christian tradition, especially during the 1940s and 1950s. As a result, thousands of Cuban Protestants and Catholics were among the exiles who organized communities in the United States in the 1960s and 1970s in the wake of Castro's Revolution. Cuban Jews (whose numbers had grown on the island with the influx of eastern European Jews in the 1920s to the 1940s) and adherents of the African-based religious traditions like Santería, still the largest of Cuba's religious traditions, also participated in establishing religious communities. Though all of these traditions had a different take on the Cuban Revolution, they all agreed that the government's aggressive atheism inhibited their freedom of religious devotion and practice.

These various religious groups played an important role within the exile communities, bringing a diversity of thought and action to bear on the Cuban question, but they also focused on helping Cubans adjust to their new place of residence. In the post-1959 era, for example, Catholics participated actively in Miami's anti-Castro activism. In churches all over the exile communities, Cuban Catholics prayed for their homeland's deliverance from Communism, and they established numerous lay organizations that not only focused religious concerns but also emphasized "the evils of atheistic communism." Cuban priests and the Church hierarchy in Cuban communities continually urged their parishioners to maintain a hard stance against the Castro regime. Perhaps the most revealing example of this highly politicized religiosity was expressed through their patroness, the Virgen de la Caridad del Cobre. For centuries, Cubans had prayed to their patron saint for protection of their families and their country during times of difficulty, and they did the same in exile by building a shrine in Miami, overlooking Biscayne Bay and facing Cuba. In December 1973, the shrine, Ermita de la Caridad del Cobre, was completed and dedicated and became the destination of pilgrimages for Cubans from all over the United States. Celebrations at the shrine included special masses, processions, observances of Cuban holidays, and a variety of other events that linked Cuba's religious heritage to the exile political traditions of the Cubans in the United States.

Besides participating with an exile agenda, Cuban Catholics also sought to participate fully with the North American Church but—on the advice of the exiled auxiliary bishop of Havana, Msgr. Eduardo Boza Masvidal (who resided in Venezuela)—to do so in the spirit of "integration without assimilation." Boza Masvidal, considered by Catholics their spiritual leader in exile, advised them to embrace their new home economically and politically but not at the expense of their identity as Cuban Catholics. Within the archdiocese of Miami, Cuban Catholics advocated for their culture and language, asking for Hispanic pastors, Spanish masses and confessions, bilingual Catholic schools, senior appointments for Cubans, and other cultural rights. What was a heavily Irish American Church in Miami during the 1960s became one that reflected the dramatic influence and impact of Cubans in the region. As with other aspects of life explored in this essay, Cuban Catholicism in south Florida revealed the community's commitment to their homeland but also their intention to adjust to their new life as ethnic Americans.

Epilogue

This overview of Cubans in the United States has emphasized the experience in relation to their exile and ethnic identities, but Cubans certainly did not live in isolation from others. They established daily relationships, some more cordial than others, with Anglo-Americans, African Americans, the Jewish community of south Florida, and Latinas and Latinos of other national origins. Historically, many thousands of Cubans settled across the United States in communities where they constituted just a few families within Anglo-American or African American majorities. In these cases, the forces of assimilation were very powerful, and many altogether lost their sense of being Cuban, embracing the worldviews and cultures of those among whom they lived. Those who resided in the enclaves also necessarily engaged others, but they naturally had greater flexibility in defining the nature of the relationships, which rarely focused on assimilation. Perhaps the most affirmative relations were with others of Latin heritage who shared numerous cultural characteristics, socioeconomic interests, or political perspectives.

During the late nineteenth century in New York, Cubans engaged a vibrant Hispanic community composed of immigrants from many places in Latin America, including the Caribbean, Mexico, and Central and South America. Until the end of the century, Cubans and Puerto Ricans, along with supporters from other Hispanic communities, collaborated in their struggle to free their homelands from Spain. Antillean solidarity in New York continued even after the war of independence against Spain, as they worked together in cigar and garment factories and organized unions and other community activities. In the early twentieth century, Cubans in Ybor City, Florida, also created a community and shared economic interests, geographical space, and political ideas with immigrants from Spain and Italy. Drawn together by the cigar industry, these groups identified with each other as Latins and used Spanish as their common tongue. Looked down upon by the dominant white Tampa population, Ybor City became a tight-knit working-class community dedicated to defending their cultural and political ideals.

Even the post-1959 Cuban community in Miami inevitably, though slowly and perhaps reluctantly, entered into relationships with other Latina and Latino groups. Throughout the forty years during which Cubans arrived in huge numbers, immigration from other Latin American regions also grew. In Dade County, Mexicans, Puerto Ricans, Dominicans, Central Americans, and South Americans joined Cubans in "Latinizing" the south Florida region. Many Latinas and Latinos participated in what was initially an exclusively Cuban economic enclave, and relationships among the groups grew, including intermarriage. Certainly, Cuban nationalist perspectives remained, often causing stresses with their Latina and Latino neighbors, who sometimes viewed them as arrogant and overbearing, but Cuban leaders responded to the demographic reality, especially on a number of domestic political issues.

Though Cuban identity remained, the need to "think Latina and Latino" also emerged as a growing imperative.

Cuban integration into North American society cannot be understood as a linear trajectory of assimilation, but rather as a complex, multidimensional process influenced by nationalism, an exile dimension, ethnic consciousness, and solidarity with other Latina and Latino and Hispanic groups. This guaranteed an ongoing and distinct Cuban presence in the United States for almost two centuries.

See also Art, Cuban American; Bay of Pigs; Cuban American Committee; Cuban American National Foundation/PAC; Cuban American Writers; Cuban Communities Abroad Project; Cuban Democracy Act of 1992; Cuban Embargo; Cuban Political Prisoners; Cuban Research Institute; Florida; Labor and Labor Strikes; Little Havana; Marielitos; *and* Ybor City.

BIBLIOGRAPHY

Antón, Alex, and Roger E. Hernández. *Cubans in America: A Vibrant History of a People in Exile*. New York: Kensington, 2002.

Dixon, Heriberto. "The Cuban-American Counterpoint: Black Cubans in the United Sates." *Dialectical Anthropology* (1988): 227–239.

Dolan, Jay P., and Jaime R. Vidal. *Puerto Rican and Cuban Catholics in the U.S., 1900–1965*. Notre Dame, Ind.: University of Notre Dame Press, 1994.

García, María Cristina. *Havana USA: Cuban Exiles and Cuban Americans in South Florida, 1959–1994*. Berkeley: University of California Press, 1996.

González-Pando, Miguel. *The Cuban Americans*. Westport, Conn.: Greenwood, 1998.

Greenbaum, Susan D. *More than Black: Afro-Cubans in Tampa*. Gainesville: University Press of Florida, 2002.

Grenier, Guillermo J., and Alex Stepick. *Miami Now!: Immigration, Ethnicity, and Social Change*. Gainesville: University Press of Florida, 1992.

Grillo, Evelio. *Black Cuban/Black American: A Memoir*. Houston, Tex.: Arte Público, 2000.

Hewitt, Nancy. *Southern Discomfort: Women's Activism in Tampa, Florida, 1880s–1920s*. Urbana: University of Illinois Press, 2001.

Hijuelos, Oscar. *Our House in the Last World*. New York: Persea, 1983.

Ingalls, Robert P. *Urban Vigilantes in the New South. Tampa, 1882–1936*. Knoxville: University of Tennessee Press, 1988.

Jorge, Antonio, Jaime Suchlicki, and Adolfo Leyva de Varona, eds. *Cuban Exiles in Florida: Their Presence and Contribution*. Coral Gables, Fla.: University of Miami Research Institute for Cuban Studies, 1991.

Masud-Piloto, Félix. *From Welcomed Exiles to Illegal Immigrants: Cuban Migration to the U.S., 1959–1995*. Lanham, Md.: Rowman and Littlefield, 1996.

Matovina, Timothy, and Gerald E. Poyo, eds. *Presente! U.S. Latino Catholics from Colonial Origins to the Present*. Maryknoll, N.Y.: Orbis, 2000.

Mirabal, Nancy Raquel. "'No Country but the One We Must Fight For': The Emergence of an Antillean Nation and Community in New York City, 1860–1901." In *Mambo Montage: The Latinization of New York*, edited by Agustín Laó-Montes and Arlene Davila. New York: Columbia University Press, 2001.

Mormino, Gary, and George E. Pozzetta. *The Immigrant World of Ybor City: Italians and Their Latin Neighbors in Tampa, 1885–1985*. Urbana: University of Illinois Press, 1987.

Olson, James S., and Judith E. Olson. *Cuban Americans: From Trauma to Triumph*. New York: Twayne, 1995.

Pedraza-Bailey, Silvia. *Political and Economic Migrants in America: Cubans and Mexicans*. Austin: University of Texas Press, 1985.

Pérez, Louis A., Jr. *Cuba and the United States: Ties of Singular Intimacy*. Athens: University of Georgia Press, 1990.

Pérez, Louis A., Jr. *On Becoming Cuban: Identity, Nationality, and Culture*. Chapel Hill: University of North Carolina Press, 1999.

Pérez Firmat, Gustavo. *Life on the Hyphen: The Cuban-American Way*. Austin: University of Texas Press, 1994.

Pérez-Stable, Marifeli. *The Cuban Revolution: Origins, Course, and Legacy*. New York: Oxford University Press, 1993.

Portes, Alejandro, and Robert L. Bach. *Latin Journey: Cuban and Mexican Immigrants in the United States*. Berkeley: University of California Press, 1985.

Portes, Alejandro, and Alex Stepick. *City on the Edge: The Transformation of Miami*. Berkeley: University of California Press, 1993.

Poyo, Gerald E. *"With All, and for the Good of All": The Emergence of Popular Nationalism in the Cuban Communities of the United States, 1848–1898*. Durham, N.C.: Duke University Press, 1989.

Rogg, Eleanor Meyer, and Rosemary Santana Cooney. *Adaptation and Adjustment of Cubans: West New York, New Jersey*. New York: Fordham University Hispanic Research Center, 1980.

Stubbs, Jean. *Tobacco on the Periphery: A Case Study in Cuban Labour History, 1860–1958*. Cambridge, U.K.: Cambridge University Press, 1985.

Torres, Maria de los Angeles. *In the Land of Mirrors: Cuban-American Politics in the United States*. Ann Arbor: University of Michigan Press, 1999.

Tweed, Thomas A. *Our Lady of Exile: Diasporic Religion at a Cuban Catholic Shrine in Miami*. New York: Oxford University Press, 1997.

Works Progress Administration. "San Carlos Institute." Yonge Library, University of Florida.

Yglesias, José. *The Truth about Them*. New York: World, 1971.

GERALD E. POYO

CUBAN COMMITTEE FOR DEMOCRACY.

Established in 1993, the Cuban Committee for Democracy (CCD) was envisioned by its founders as an alternative to the existing political Cuban American organizations of the time. It was no coincidence that the CCD was created at a critical moment in post–cold war history in which Cuba was experiencing a dramatic economic crisis and the possibility of political change on the island seemed proximate. The nonprofit group, led by Cuban American professionals and academics who were at odds with the Cuban American National Foundation, the main political institution of the community, had an overarching purpose: to demonstrate to the U.S. government and to Cubans on the island that the Cuban American community was not composed exclusively of conservatives who advocated a pro-embargo line vis-à-vis the Cuban government. From that point of departure, the CCD attempted, with little success, to provide financial support for politicians, activists, and initiatives that endorsed moderate policies toward Cuba. What the CCD accomplished with modest results was to bring together, support, and represent a sector of

Cuban Americans (who favored a policy of normalization toward Cuba) who lacked an effective voice in politics and wanted to lobby for change in United States–Cuba policy.

The CCD had two other important goals: (1) to contribute to the process of reconciliation of Cuban society both on the island and in the diaspora and (2) to defend (at least conceptually) the sovereignty of Cuba by endorsing national solutions to the political problems of the nation. The principal policy initiatives that the CCD pursued to achieve its ends and that differentiated the committee from other exile organizations included advocacy against the continuation of the United States' embargo on Cuba and engagement with officials and counterparts on the island. Although the CCD supported a transition from one-party rule to democracy, it abstained from drafting a blueprint for such. Rather, it proposed guidelines in three broad areas: (1) democratization in Cuba (i.e., emphasizing the need for a regime that would respect the rule of law and guarantee civil liberties), (2) U.S. policy (i.e., opposing the continuation of economic sanctions that, according to the organization, hurt the Cuban population by eroding their standard of living instead of eroding government control), and (3) the Cuban American community (i.e., promoting policies that would bring social and cultural reconnection between Cubans and Cuban Americans, such as travel, aid, remittances, and exchanges, and expanding political space for freedom of expression and civil debate among Cuban Americans concerning Cuban matters). The CCD initiated a number of media projects, namely a radio program (*Radio Transición*), a newsletter (*Transition News*), and a short-lived journal (*Cuban Affairs/Asuntos Cubanos*). In the early twenty-first century, the CCD is a moribund organization due to the inability to secure major sources of funding, the lack of positive response from the Cuban government to CCD initiatives, the failure to muster popular support and secure a strong constituency, and the divisions within the leadership.

See also **Cuban American National Foundation/PAC** *and* **Cuban Americans.**

BIBLIOGRAPHY

Fernández, Damián J. *From Little Havana to Washington, D.C.: Cuban-Americans and U.S. Foreign Policy.* Edited by Mohammed E. Ahrair. New York: Greenwood, 1987.

Torres, María de los Angeles. *In the Land of Mirrors: Cuban Exile Politics in the United States.* Ann Arbor: University of Michigan Press, 1999.

DAMIÁN FERNÁNDEZ

CUBAN COMMUNITIES ABROAD PROJECT.

Even before Cuba became an independent island nation, its colonial Spanish government kept tabs on exiles who had fled the island. In the mid-1800s they successfully lobbied the Vatican not to name Felix Varela, a Cuban priest living in the United States, as archbishop of New York. They feared that this would give his anticolonial stance too much visibility. Instead, he was named to the Philadelphia archdiocese. In the 1950s, as exiles fleeing the Batista regime came to Miami, the mayor of Havana periodically issued travel warnings to other Cubans vacationing in Florida that they may be harassed by the revolutionaries. But it was not until after the 1959 revolution that the Cuban government became institutionally active in regard to exiles. This interest has had intelligence, political, and economic goals. This essay will trace the evolution of the Cuban government's interest in its communities abroad.

Policies toward communities abroad are closely linked to a country's emigration policy, and in the case of the Cuban government since the revolution, this has vacillated between an open door policy, to anyone who wants to leave can but cannot return, to completely shutting the doors. Emigration became a trump card to use in its confrontations with the U.S. government as it also provided an escape valve for discontent during moments of domestic crisis.

Cuban Governmental Activism and Exiles

But governmental activism in this realm has also included a host of political and economic interests. After the 1959 revolution, the Cuban government had great interest in finding out what was going on in the exile community. Many exiles fled a regime they had initially supported and teamed up with the United States, which had vowed to overthrow the Cuban government. The Cuban government made systematic efforts to infiltrate the military, political, and even social service organizations in the Cuban community in the United States. This project was housed within Cuba's Ministry of the Interior, specifically its counterintelligence offices. Exiles were enemies of the revolution, and their activities were closely monitored. They were called *gusanos*, "worms," literally denoting the one duffle bag they were allowed to take with them but also a double entendre suggesting that they were low-life.

In the early 1970s a debate in the exile community ensued as to whether Cuban exiles should engage in dialogue with the government from which many of them had fled. Two groups led the discussion: radical Catholics organized by the Instituto de Estudios Cubanos and young exiles in search of identity and alternative politics clustered around publications such as *Areito* and *Joven Cuba*. Lourdes Casal, a sociologist and poet, forged a link between the two groups and built the bridge that finally allowed the exiles to return.

At first the Cuban government reacted negatively to the exiles' desire to return. Officials feared that returning visitors might be infiltrators or could be used by the exile opposition to gather information about contemporary life on the island. They were also wary of the potential impact on the Cubans who remained on the island. But after intense lobbying, the Cuban government authorized the visit of a select number of exiles. Two or three individuals, usually from different organizations, were allowed to enter at any one time. They were told by government officials not to tell anyone that they were Cuban. Official policy, after all, defined all who had left as traitors, and they were not allowed to return.

By 1977 the number of young exiles wanting to return to the island was increasing. With the blessing of Cuban government officials, a group was formed called the Antonio Maceo Brigade. Their first trip was filmed in a documentary called *55 Hermanos* that caused a great sensation all over the island.

The young exiles wanted better relations between the community abroad and the Cuban government and successfully advocated for a meeting between the Cuban government and exiles. The historic meeting, held in two sessions in November and December 1977, resulted in the release of thirty-five hundred political prisoners and permission for another fifteen thousand political prisoners and their families to leave the island, and it succeeded in establishing regular visits of exiles to the island. The Cuban government was asked to set up a governmental institution to deal with the many issues of communities abroad, but by then the Ministry of the Interior and some offices in the Ministry of Foreign Relations were in charge of the community project colloquially known as the COCU EX (*comunidad cubana en el exterior*).

The changing political climate in the United States under the Carter administration and the reversal in Cuban policy resulted in more than 100,000 exiles returning to the island in 1979 to visit relatives. The trips became an important source of hard currency for the Cuban government and a sore spot for exiles, who felt exploited by the amount of money charged by the Cuban government and charter agencies in Miami.

In 1980 another exodus erupted, and more than 120,000 Cubans hurriedly left through the port of Mariel. The Cuban government reversed its policies toward its communities abroad and halted all visits, citing them as the main cause of public discontent on the island. The exiles, who had been dubbed "mariposas" (transformed gusanos), were turned back into materialistic, uncaring counterrevolutionaries, and the doors in and out of Cuba were once again shut until the late eighties.

Policy Shifts

All along there were different factions in the Cuban government; some advocated for better relations with the exile community and others for maintaining a hard-line policy, a haunting symmetry to exile organizations. After the fall of the Soviet Union, Cuba entered into a severe economic crisis and began looking for sources of cash. The exiles were let back in and were encouraged to send remittances to their relatives. By the mid-1990s remittances had become Cuba's largest contributor to its GNP, surpassing sugar and tourism. One popular joke in Cuba says, "We didn't call you a traitor, we said traidolares" (bring dollars).

In the mid-1990s a conference called the Nation and Its Emigrants was organized by the Ministry of the Interior and the Ministry of Foreign Relations. The conference was held on the island, and several hundred Cubans from every continent in the world attended. During the conference many of the participants complained about the bureaucratic difficulties they faced in traveling to Cuba, including the expense of passports, reentry visas, and lodging and the prohibitions against bringing relatives to hotels because the Cuban government restricts island Cubans from entering tourist hotels. Bigger questions about political prisoners and the political participation of emigrants in home country politics were evaded. Repatriation was once again ruled out.

During a reception at the Palace of the Revolution hosted by Fidel Castro, participants' private conversations were filmed and subsequently were sold to the Miami press, thus setting off a major scandal. One participant, Magda Montiel, who had run for Congress in Florida, was filmed flirting with Castro over a conversation about political prisoners. In the background, however, a factional fight was being waged between those who had been in charge of the Cuba community project and the new generation of party bureaucrats wanting to get a piece of the lucrative exile policies.

Several more meetings have been held in Havana, some resulting in minor modifications in the paperwork required for exiles to travel to the island. A government publication called *Correo de Cuba* is published and distributed on the Internet. While it does provide some practical information for travel from time to time, it is filled with political tirades against Miami Cubans and is heavily laced with nostalgia as a means of reaching out to those who have left.

The Elián González incident again created a major confrontation between the government and the exile community. This time island officials portrayed exiles as the "Miami Mafia."

Legacy

In general the policy toward the communities abroad has been characterized by a tension between the government's need to confront exiles and its desire to lure them back to the island.

These debates have created echoes in academic circles. Explanations about why people leave, how much money they will bring back, and the impact they have on the island are battled in the confines of government-controlled think tanks. In the cultural realm, there have been debates about whether or not to publish writers who have left. In the late twentieth century this policy was somewhat loosened. But many exile writers are now published without their consent, and their works are carefully edited.

Debates about exiles have also found their way into the literary and film imaginations. One of Cuba's earliest film successes, *Memorias de subdesarrollo* (Memories of Underdevelopment, 1968), traces the disaffection of a middle-class man as many of his friends and family leave the island. *Lejania*, shot in the 1980s, and *Miel Para Oshun*, produced in the 1990s, both depict returning exiles as hopelessly nostalgic and tragic characters, lost and looking for their motherland. In contrast, *Vigia*, an alternative cultural project, has tried to work collaboratively with many exiles and has published writers such as Gaston Baquero, Jose Kozer, and Ruth Behar.

Despite the good intentions of many of these cultural officials and activists, the policies toward the community are carefully crafted in the halls of national security offices and are jealously guarded. They not only belong to the revolutionary rhetoric of historic struggles against traitors, but they have become the most important cash-producing policy for the island government.

See also **Brigada Antonio Maceo; Cuban Americans;** *and* **González, Elián.**

BIBLIOGRAPHY

Masud-Piloto, Felix. *From Welcomed Exiles to Illegal Immigrants: Cuban Migration to the U.S., 1959–1995.* Lanham, Md.: Rowman and Littlefield, 1996.

Torres, María de los Angeles. *In the Land of Mirrors: Cuban Exile Politics in the United States.* Ann Arbor: University of Michigan Press, 1999.

MARÍA DE LOS ANGELES TORRES

CUBAN DEMOCRACY ACT OF 1992.

On February 5, 1992, U.S. Congressman Robert Torricelli introduced the Cuban Democracy Act (CDA) with the expressed intent of "wreak[ing] havoc on the island." The bill was passed by Congress on October 15, 1992, and signed into law by President George H. W. Bush on October 23. This marked not only the tightening of U.S. economic policy towards Cuba but also the shifting of primary authority over Cuban policy from the Executive to Congress. This latter change severely restricted the president's discretion and was a derogation of executive primacy in a matter of foreign relations.

By the time the CDA was enacted, less than a year after the breakup of the Soviet Union, when many believed Castro's fall was imminent, the Cuban trade embargo was over thirty years old. In 2003, over forty years after the embargo began, U.S.–Cuban policy, even as strengthened by the CDA (and in 1996 by the Helms-Burton Law, "The Cuban Liberty and Democratic Solidarity Act") has still failed to achieve its objective of destabilizing the Castro regime.

Antecedents

On July 6, 1960, immediately pursuant to Congress's amendment of the Sugar Act of 1948, President Dwight D. Eisenhower unilaterally reduced the quota of sugar imported from Cuba. Castro reacted by nationalizing by forced appropriation enterprises and property of U.S. citizens. In turn, President Eisenhower broke off relations with Cuba. In an attempt to achieve destabilization of the Castro regime, an economic embargo was imposed on exports in 1960 and on imports in 1962. These actions, by Executive fiat, were possible under the Trading with the Enemy Act of 1917 (TWEA). In 1977, the TWEA was amended prospectively to apply only in wartime, but any emergency previously declared could be extended on a year-by-year basis. Every year since, U.S. presidents have extended the Cuban embargo in the national interest.

Provisions

The CDA's provisions further the aim to bring down the Castro regime. Section 6001 ("Findings") provides that Castro's government has consistently disregarded "internationally accepted standards of human rights and . . . democratic values [by] restrict[ing] the Cuban people's exercise of freedom of speech, press, assembly, and other rights recognized by the Universal Declaration of Human Rights." The section claims that the Cuban people desire freedom and oppose the Castro government as well as condemns Cuba's military-dominated economy and its "military interventions and subversive activities throughout the world." These findings also recognize that the breakup of the Soviet Union and Eastern Europe "dramatically reduced Cuba's external support and threatened Cuba's food and oil supplies . . . provid[ing] the United States and the international democratic community with an unprecedented opportunity to promote a peaceful transition to democracy in Cuba."

Section 6002 ("Statement of Policy") provides that U.S. sanctions will continue until Castro moves toward democratization and shows greater respect for human rights. Section 6003 ("International cooperation") instructs the president to encourage other countries to restrict their trade with Cuba and imposes sanctions against countries that assist Cuba, including rendering them ineligible for assistance under the Foreign Assistance Act of 1961, the Arms Export Control Act, and "any program for forgiveness or reduction of debt owed to the United States Government."

Section 6004 ("Support for the Cuban people") allows for private donations of food by nongovernmental organizations to Cuba and the export of medicines and medical supplies. Section 6005 ("Sanctions") prohibits certain transactions between U.S. firms and Cuba by prohibiting the issuance of required licenses. It also prohibits a vessel

that enters a port in Cuba in order to engage in trade of goods or services from loading and unloading cargo in U.S. ports within 180 days after departure from a Cuban port. Similarly, "a vessel carrying goods or passengers to or from Cuba or carrying goods in which Cuba or a Cuban national has any interest" cannot enter a U.S. port. Finally, this section instructs the president to establish strict limits on remittances to Cuba by persons in the United States to ensure that remittances are used only in connection with travel of Cubans to the United States and not used by the Cuban government as a source of U.S. currency.

Section 6006 provides that food, medicines, and medical supplies for humanitarian purposes will be made available to Cuba if Castro's regime publicly commits to holding "free and fair elections for a new government within six months and is proceeding to implement that decision" or has made a public commitment to respect internationally recognized human rights and basic democratic freedoms and is not providing weapons or funds to any group in any other country that seeks violent overthrow of the government of that country.

Section 6007 allows the president to waive Section 6005 sanctions upon the determination and the reports to Congress that the Cuban government has held free and fair elections, has permitted opposition parties time to organize and access to the media to all candidates, has shown respect for basic civil liberties and human rights of Cuban citizens, has moved towards the free-market economy, and has made commitments to constitutional change that ensures free and fair elections. Once those conditions are met, the president is to encourage the admission or reentry of the new democratically elected Cuban government to international organizations and international financial institutions, to provide emergency relief during Cuba's transition to a market economy, and to take steps to end the Cuban embargo.

Legacy

In sum, the CDA codified the existing travel ban, extended the embargo to prohibit foreign-based U.S. subsidiary companies from trading with Cuba, prohibited family remittances to Cuba, and strengthened the embargo by prohibiting ships from loading or unloading cargo in U.S. ports for 180 days after delivering goods to Cuba. This last prohibition strongly discourages shippers from delivering goods to Cuba, including medical equipment and medicines. Although Section 6004 permits private groups to deliver food and medicines to Cuba, it is significant that, at the time of the CDA's passage, 70 percent of Cuba's trade with foreign-based U.S. subsidiary companies was in food and medicines. These provisions have resulted in claims that the CDA violates international law as well as U.N. resolutions that food and medicines cannot be used as weapons in international conflicts.

The most controversial of the CDA's provisions, which also raises the claim of the CDA effecting international law violations, is the restoration of the provision of the 1962 embargo that had been repealed in 1975—the prohibition against foreign-based U.S. subsidiary companies from doing business with Cuba. Significantly, because under international law a subsidiary is a citizen of the state of incorporation, other states have claimed that the

CDA illegally seeks to extraterritorially extend U.S. laws. Since 1992, when the CDA was still pending in Congress, the European community has objected in the U.N. General Assembly to this provision's prohibition. Every year since then, the General Assembly has adopted resolutions that call upon "States to refrain from promulgating and applying laws and measures" whose "extraterritorial effects affect the sovereignty of other states and the legitimate interests of entities or persons under their jurisdiction, as well as the freedom of trade and navigation" and also urge the repeal of such laws—a thinly veiled reference to the CDA. The United States, on the other hand, explains its vote against these yearly resolutions by echoing the sentiments expressed in the CDA's findings, policy, and sanction provisions. Specifically, the United States asserts its political and economic rights to exclude as trading partners those who fail to embrace democratic forms of government, violate fundamental human rights, and demonstrate little respect for human dignity, freedom, and the worth of the individual. These peacetime justifications for the embargo are replete with dated cold war rhetoric. In the words of a *New York Times* editorial, "This misnamed act [the Cuban Democracy Act] is dubious in theory, cruel in its potential practice and ignoble in its election-year expediency."

See also Cuban Embargo *and* Helms-Burton Act.

BIBLIOGRAPHY

Bell, Jason S. "Violation of International Law and Doomed U.S. Policy: An Analysis of the Cuban Democracy Act." *University of Miami Inter-American Law Review* 25 (1993): 77–129.

Cameron, Joanna R. "The Cuban Democracy Act of 1992: The International Implications." *Fletcher Forum of World Affairs* 20 (1996): 137–147.

Carayiannis, Peter P. "The Cuban Democracy Act: Success or Failure?" *Journal of International Law and Practice* 3 (1994): 195–204.

Cuban Democracy Act of 1992, Pub. L. 102-484, 22 U.S.C. § 6001 *et seq.*

Exec. Order No. 12,854, 58 Fed. Reg. 36,587 (July 7, 1993) (President Clinton, Implementation of the Cuban Democracy Act).

Erikson, Daniel P. "The New Cuba Divide." *The National Interest* 67 (Spring 2002): 65–71.

Herd, Julia P. "The Cuban Democracy Act: Another Extraterritorial Act That Won't Work." *Brooklyn Journal of International Law* 20 (1994): 397–442.

Jeffries, Trevor R. "The Cuban Democracy Act of 1992: A Rotten Carrot and a Broken Stick?" *Houston Journal of International Law* 16 (1993): 75–100.

Nova, Michael A. "Cuba Sí, Castro No! The Cuban Democracy Act of 1992 and Its Impact on the United States' Foreign Policy Initiatives towards Establishing a Free and Democratic Cuba." *Journal of Transnational Law and Policy* 3 (1994): 265–282.

U.S. Economic and Trade Policy Toward Cuba, Hearing Before the Subcommittee on Trade of the House Committee on Ways and Means, May 7, 1998 (statement of David J. Cibrian, Esq.). waysandmeans.house.gov/legacy.asp?file=legacy/trade/105cong/5-7-98/5-7cibr.htm.

BERTA HERNÁNDEZ-TRUYOL

CUBAN EMBARGO. Reacting to social, economic, and political reforms enacted by the Cuban Revolution of 1959 that affected U.S. interests in Cuba, the Eisenhower administration broke diplomatic relations with the Cuban Revolutionary Government on January 3, 1961, two weeks prior to the inauguration of John F. Kennedy. The latter inherited plans for an invasion of Cuba by Cuban exiles, organized and financed by the United States, and when the invasion at the Bay of Pigs failed, the administration resorted to stronger economic sanctions against Cuba, imposing a total trade embargo on February 7, 1962.

The main goal of the U.S. trade embargo against Cuba is to economically strangulate the Cuban Revolution and return Cuba to the U.S. sphere of influence as a dependent client state. Although the embargo has failed to achieve its main goal, it has certainly made the lives of most Cubans extremely difficult, and through its influence, it has blocked the Cuban government's ability to qualify for and receive economic aid and loans from international organizations and governments controlled or influenced by the United States. The economic hardships generated by the embargo have been largely responsible for the emigration of more than one million Cubans to the United States and for Cuba's loss of more than $80 billion in international trade during the past four decades.

In order to resist and survive the United States' economic war against the country, the Cuban government, after declaring the revolution socialist in April 1961, came to rely heavily on trade with and aid from the former Soviet Union and Eastern European socialist governments. Within a few years, Cuba radically transformed its economy from a capitalist, market-dependent system to a socialist, centrally planned one. Trade and aid from the socialist nations—which averaged $6 billion a year from 1961 to 1991—allowed the Cuban government to survive the United States' economic war against it and helped advance the revolution's ambitious domestic social agenda. By 1975, Cuba was universally recognized as an exemplary developing nation for the high-quality free medical care and education provided to all of its citizens.

In 1991, when the Soviet socialist system was dismantled and most socialist governments in Eastern Europe fell, the Cuban government was again forced to restructure its economy by opening it to foreign investments, mainly from Western Europe, Canada, Latin America, and Asia. The U.S. Congress, expecting that the Cuban government would also collapse, and pressured by the powerful Cuban American lobby based in Miami, Florida, passed the Cuban Democracy Act (also known as the Torricelli Act) in October 1992. According to its author, the act was designed to "wreak havoc on that island," by tightening and internationalizing the embargo, and punishing foreign companies and individuals doing business and investing in Cuba. In 1996, the U.S. Congress passed a second law designed to discourage and intimidate foreign investors doing business in Cuba. The Cuban Liberty and Democratic Solidarity Act (also known as the Helms-Burton Act), sought, among other things: (1) to punish foreign companies operating in Cuba by denying U.S. visas to their employees, officers, and their families; (2) to allow filing of claims for lands and property nationalized by the Cuban Revolutionary Government in U.S. courts; and (3) to prohibit U.S. citizens and corporations from extending financing to any foreign person who uses property in Cuba formerly owned by U.S. entities. Although the United States did not have any jurisdiction to pass these laws, and both laws were clearly extraterritorial in nature and counter to international law, they are both still in effect.

Except for the vocal and economically powerful Cuban American community in South Florida, the U.S. economic embargo against Cuba has almost no popular support in the United States. Internationally, the unilateral sanctions have even less support. The Cuban government has consistently received overwhelming and unflinching support from the international community every time it has presented its case in favor of lifting the sanctions in the United Nations. Every year since 1992, the Cuban government has argued that according to Article II of the Geneva Convention on the Prevention and Punishment of the Crime of Genocide, "the United States blockade qualifies as an act of genocide, and is therefore, a crime under international law." The vote has always resulted in a resounding moral victory for Cuba. In the 2004 United Nations general session, 179 nations voted in favor of lifting the sanctions and four against. As usual, the United States refused to abide by international law and exercised its powerful veto.

For more than four decades, the U.S.'s international boycott of the Cuban economy has failed to achieve its goal of strangulating the Cuban economy. Nevertheless, encouraged and supported by the conservative Cuban American community in South Florida, in May 2004, the second Bush administration unveiled the United States latest plan to destroy the Cuban Revolution. The administration's "Commission for Assistance to a Free Cuba," presided over by Secretary of State Colin Powell, calls not only for a continuation of the embargo but also for regime change and the occupation of Cuba by the United States in a "post-Castro" era.

The Cuban Revolution has been able to survive the United States aggression by decentralizing its economy, attracting foreign investors, developing tourism, and resorting to import substitution. It has, however, paid an enormous price. Cuban government sources report that U.S. hostility and attacks against the revolutionary process have claimed the lives of 3,500 Cuban citizens and caused $200 million in damages during the past forty-two years.

See also Castro, Fidel; Cuban Americans; Cuban Democracy Act of 1992; *and* Helms-Burton Act.

BIBLIOGRAPHY

Domínguez, Jorge I., Omar Everleny Pérez Villanueva, and Lorena Barberia, eds. *The Cuban Economy at the Start of the Twenty-first Century*. Cambridge, Mass.: Harvard University Press, 2004.

Morley, Morris, and Chris McGillion. *Unfinished Business: America and Cuba after the Cold War, 1989–2001*. Cambridge, UK: Cambridge University Press, 2002.

Murray, Mary. *Cruel and Unusual Punishment: The U.S. Blockade against Cuba*. Melbourne, Australia: Ocean Press, 1993.

Roy, Joaquín. *Cuba, the United States, and the Helms-Burton Doctrine: International Reactions*. Gainesville: University Press of Florida, 2000.

Schwab, Peter. *Cuba: Confronting the U.S. Embargo*. New York: St. Martin's Press, 1999.

FÉLIX MASUD-PILOTO

CUBAN POLITICAL PRISONERS. From 1960 to 2000, over 827,550 Cubans emigrated to the United States, mostly as political refugees. From the very beginning of this large exodus, political imprisonment on the island has shaped—even defined—the Cuban American experience. Most families have a relative or are in some way acquainted with someone who has endured or is still trapped inside Cuba's "tropical gulag." Many will always grieve for those who paid the ultimate price. Dr. Armando Lago's comprehensive review of existing reports reveals that at least 885 political prisoners have died of medical negligence, assassination by guards, or, in despondency, by their own hand. In addition, he has documented more than 5,500 Cubans executed mostly by firing squad inside the walls or nearby fields of Castro's dungeons—close to four thousand were killed just in the first three years of the Cuban Revolution.

Cuban leader Fidel Castro has occasionally released political prisoners to maximize political capital abroad. Over time, foreign dignitaries have secured the release of hundreds of political prisoners prior to the conclusion of their sentence, generally conditioned on their exile. As a result, many have come to live in the United States—mostly in Miami and Bergen County, New Jersey, where they have organized into associations and meet regularly to share experiences and create public awareness. Some former prisoners, such as Ela Bravo and Luisa Pérez, are engaged in projects documenting their ordeals. Over four decades, the steady exile of former political prisoners has contributed poignant first-hand testimonies that have forged a strong sense of common struggle within the exile community and garnered support in U.S. political circles to continue exerting pressure on the Cuban regime.

Castro's Rule

The story of how Fidel Castro has trounced opposition through political imprisonment for four decades begins right after his rise to power on January 1, 1959. As head of a broad-based coalition and leader of the rebel guerrilla army, Castro took over when dictator Fulgencio Batista fled the country. Many Batista supporters and members of the armed forces were swiftly detained and, without fair trials, executed or sentenced to long prison terms. These were just the first victims.

Rather than hold promised democratic elections and restore constitutional rule, Castro began to concentrate all political and economic power in the state, fueled a social struggle based on class hatred and atheism, and embarked on what soon became totalitarian Communist rule supported by the Soviet Union. Civil liberties were abolished, land and businesses confiscated, and the free press, private schools, and most churches were shut down. Feeling betrayed, thousands of men and women instrumental in Batista's fall organized an underground opposition. "Counterrevolutionaries" caught conspiring or "worms" thought to threaten the new order—from student leaders and priests to prominent members of Castro's Rebel Army—were put to death, sent to prison, or driven into exile.

The historic group of political prisoners—several thousand men and over a thousand women—served very long sentences. Many, known as *plantados*, refused "re-education" (political indoctrination). To hold their growing numbers, numerous prisons were built all over the country. In the mid-1960s concentration camps known as the UMAP (Military Units to Assist Production) were also erected to "reform" young political dissenters, religious people, gays, and exit applicants through forced labor.

Over time, the number of political prisoners diminished as repression became institutionalized and many Cubans fled to exile or simply felt too afraid or impotent to oppose the all-powerful state. International pressure helped shorten their sentences to an average of three or four years in the 1990s compared with over twenty to thirty years in the 1960s. Arbitrary arrests and short detentions also became commonplace. However, in March of 2003, seventy-five dissidents were sentenced to an average of eighteen years in prison after the government cracked down on small openings that Cuba's growing, but unauthorized, dissident movement and independent press had gained in recent years.

The number of prisoners at any given time or on a cumulative basis is unknown. Cuba does not allow the International Red Cross, the United Nations, or international human rights groups to monitor or inspect prisons. Dr. Efrén Córdoba reports that at the end of the 1960s over sixty thousand political prisoners were believed to be in

jail, but by 1998 the pope requested pardon for only approximately five hundred known cases, of which the government freed around half on the condition of their leaving the country. At the end of 2004, betweeen three hundred and four hundred prisoners of conscience were thought to exist. They serve time for such acts as "disrespecting" authority, creating or distributing "enemy propaganda," attempting to leave Cuba without government authorization, and displaying "dangerousness" or "antisocial behavior."

Unique about Cuba is how many inmates not generally defined as political prisoners are serving time for "criminal" activities that are ordinary in free societies—buying or selling anything privately, engaging in informal market activities, or possessing certain food not authorized by the government. As a result, countless Cubans have, at one time or another, been imprisoned for direct or indirect political reasons. A local human rights group—Comisión Cubana de Derechos Humanos y Reconciliación Nacional—conservatively calculates the current prison population at around 100,000. With an island population of over eleven million, this represents one of the world's highest rates of imprisonment. The group also notes that when Castro took power, Cuba had fourteen prisons; today there are two hundred, of which forty-five are high-security facilities.

Prison Conditions and Punishment

There is extensive documentation of the terrible prison conditions Cuban inmates face—whether serving time for political or criminal causes. Psychological torture, beatings, long periods of solitary confinement, denial of medical attention, squalid living conditions, overcrowding, malnutrition, putrid food, contaminated water, an abundance of contagious diseases, rats and bugs, and many other hardships are common fare. The treatment of political prisoners is particularly harsh. A consistent and long litany of such horrors is available in daily reports from the island at www.CubaNet.org and is regularly described by international human rights organizations.

Numerous and compelling prison memoirs have been published—most in Spanish—that constitute a damning testimony of these horrors. Armando Valladares authored the most widely known such account, now translated into several languages. He was arrested in the early days of the Cuban Revolution for not placing on his office desk a Marxist slogan that denied his Christian faith. In prison, he became a poet and gained worldwide attention, which prompted his release after twenty-two years. After coming to the United States, he was named Ambassador to the Human Rights Commission of the United Nations by Presidents Reagan and George H. W. Bush. Ana Rodríguez co-authored a memoir in English of the nineteen years she served of a thirty-year sentence for "counterrevolutionary acts of sabotage." Her moving description of the distinct torments faced by women political prisoners is a remarkable tale of human fortitude. Both currently live in Miami.

Castro has typically dealt very harshly with former comrades in arms who refused him blind loyalty. Mario Chanes de Armas, one of his first and most loyal lieutenants, served a thirty-year sentence—longer than any other known political prisoner anywhere in the world—for retiring from the armed forces in opposition to Castro. Today, he lives in Miami blind from damage to his eyes suffered in confinement. Also in Miami is Huber Matos, one of the Revolutionary Army's highest-ranking commanders in the fight against Batista. He served twenty years for challenging Castro's power grab.

These shocking testimonies, delivered consistently and over four decades, have served to illustrate the repressive and violent nature of the Castro regime. Direct knowledge of this wanton imprisonment and brutality has fueled the Cuban exile community's passionate opposition to Castro, its rebellion against injustice, and its clamor for human rights. It has solidified the commitment of Cubans in America, as well as their descendants, to see Cuba free and democratic. Mercifully, many prison accounts also speak of extraordinary courage and unshakable conviction in the face of horrific abuses. By demonstrating how faith, valor, and dignity can overcome terror, they have rendered evil powerless and inspired a hope that one day may help heal the deep wounds afflicting the Cuban nation, today spilled into America and most corners of the world.

See also Cuban American Committee *and* Cuban Americans.

BIBLIOGRAPHY

Asís, Moisés. "Judaism in Cuba 1959–1999: A Personal Account." Presented at the Third Annual South Florida Symposium on Cuba Faith and Power: Religion in Contemporary Cuba. University of Miami, September 12–13, 1998. www.juedisches-archiv-chfrank.de/kehilot/cuba/cuba-hist.htm.

Boswell, Thomas. "A Demographic Profile of Cuban Americans." *Miami*, September 2002, Table 11, p. 32.

Bureau of Customs and Immigration Services. "2002 Yearbook of Immigration Statistics." uscis.gov/graphics/shared/aboutus/statistics/index.htm.

Bureau of Democracy, Human Rights, and Labor, U.S. Department of State. "Country Reports on Human Rights Practices—2003." www.state.gov/g/drl/rls/hrrpt/2003/27893.htm

Chanes de Armas, Mario. "Life Goes On—For Men and Country." Editorial. *The Miami Herald*, August 4, 1993, p. 13A.

Commission on Human Rights. "Representative on Situation of Human Rights in Cuba Cites 'Unprecedented Wave of Oppression' in the Country." Press Document, March 24, 2004. www. unog.ch/news2/documents/newsen/cn04021e.htm.

Córdova, Efrén. "Represión e intolerancia." Cuban Center for Cultural Social and Strategic Studies, Inc., 1999. www. cubancenter.org/uploads/40years09.html.

"Cuba's Prisons: A Devil's Island." Editorial. *The Miami Herald*, September 24, 2003.

Human Rights Watch. "Cuba's Repressive Machinery: Human Rights Forty Years after the Revolution." June 1999. hrw.org/reports/1999/cuba/.

Lago, Armando. "Cuba: The Human Cost of Social Revolution." Manuscript for publication, 2004. Some data available at website "Cuba Archives-Research Reports." www.cubaarchive.org/downloads/CA14_2003_07_26_update.pdf

Lescot, Patrick. "Dissident Study Calls Cuban Prisons 'Tropical Gulag.'" Associated Free Press, Havana, May 11, 2004.

Matos, Huber. *Cómo llegó la noche*. Barcelona: Tusquets, 2002.

Snow, Anita. "Activists: Cuban Prisons Are Worse." Associated Press, Havana, January 26, 1998.

Snow, Anita. "Cuba Won't Let Human Rights Monitor In." Associated Press, March 14, 1993.

Rodríguez, Ana, and Glenn Garvin. *Diary of a Survivor: Nineteen Years in a Cuban Women's Prison*. New York: St. Martin's Press, 1995.

Sánchez, Elizardo. Informe de la Comisión Cubana de Derechos Humanos y Reconciliación Nacional, La Habana, 11 de mayo de 2004. www.cubanuestra.nu/web/article.asp?artID=1949.

Valladares, Armando. *Against All Hope: A Memoir of Life in Castro's Gulag*. Translated by Andrew Hurley. New York: Knopf, 1986.

                                                MARIA C. WERLAU

CUBAN RESEARCH INSTITUTE. The Cuban Research Institute, known by its initials, CRI, was established in 1991 by the provost of Florida International University (FIU) so as to fulfill, in the area of Cuban and Cuban American studies, the university's threefold mission: research, teaching, and service. As the largest institution of public higher education in southern Florida, FIU (a part of the State University System of Florida) has unique obligations and opportunities in developing Cuba-related programs because of the following conditions: (1) the university's location in the largest concentration of the Cuban diaspora, a community with more than seven hundred thousand persons of Cuban origin, geographically situated at the limited gateway between Cuba and the United States; (2) the largest nucleus of faculty experts on Cuba and the Cuban American community of any university in the United States; and (3) the largest undergraduate student body of Cuban origin of any university (including the University of Havana).

Mission

Given FIU's unique situation with respect to Cuba, the mission of the CRI is to develop quality programs intended to place the university in a leadership position in the field of Cuban and Cuban American Studies. To accomplish its mission, the CRI develops academic programs in three main areas: faculty support, research activities, and dissemination of research; organization of conferences, seminars, and lectures; and outreach through the sponsorship of events of special interest to the community. It is the mission of the CRI to facilitate the participation of faculty experts in public discussion, media coverage, and public-policy formulation on issues regarding Cuba and Cuban Americans; to expand the courses on Cuba and Cuban Americans offered to undergraduate and graduate students; to increase the number of faculty at the university with expertise in Cuban and Cuban American studies; to produce publications; to make FIU an important international and national hub of scholarly activity in relation to Cuba and its diaspora; and to assist in the development of the Cuba-related holdings of the university library.

Organization and Personnel

The Cuban Research Institute is administratively located in the Latin American and Caribbean Center (LACC) of Florida International University, a nationally recognized center for the study of Latin America. The CRI, however, has its own separate budget and staff and is administratively accountable to both the director of LACC and the provost.

In the early 2000s, the director of the CRI is Lisandro Pérez, professor of sociology and the founder of the institute. His published work has focused primarily on the Cuban American community and also social change in Cuba. The assistant director is Uva de Aragón, a poet, writer, and scholar in the humanities.

The CRI advisory board is composed of FIU faculty members with an interest in the study of Cuba and/or the Cuban American community. The board meets every semester to hear a report from the director, review accomplishments, suggest new initiatives and projects, and approve goals and plans for the future. It represents the formal mechanism for faculty input and participation in the work of the CRI.

Major Accomplishments

The CRI has secured more than 1.5 million dollars in external funds. It was awarded a Resident Fellowship Program in the Humanities by the Rockefeller Foundation for the period from 1994 to 1998. The program brought fourteen scholars from throughout the world, including Cuba, to FIU for one-semester fellowships on the program theme "Island and Diaspora: National Identity, Sovereignty, and Reconciliation in the Twenty-First Century." The CRI also obtained, through a national competitive process, the editorship, from 1999 to 2004, of *Cuban Studies*. Published by the University of Pittsburgh Press, *Cuban Studies* has been the leading journal in the field for more than twenty-five years. Lisandro Pérez has served as the editor and Uva de Aragón as the associate editor.

The CRI has established a tradition for hosting, every eighteen months, the most important national and international conference in the field, attracting nearly two hundred scholars in a wide range of fields and scholarly interests. The first CRI conference was held in October of 1997.

Academic Contact with Cuba

Since its establishment in 1991, the CRI has operated under the principle that, despite the difficulties involved, a leading university center focused on Cuba could not be developed without establishing extensive contacts with Cuba, facilitating communication between scholars in the United States (and especially at FIU) and academics and academic institutions in the island. Given the state of United States–Cuba relations, and especially the highly politicized character of the Cuban American community, following that principle has not always been easy. But the CRI has garnered a significant record in facilitating and developing reciprocal academic contacts with the island. Such success would not have been possible without the support of the Ford Foundation, Rockefeller Foundation, John D. and Catherine T. MacArthur Foundation, and Christopher Reynolds Foundation.

Inter-University Program for Latino Research

The CRI has long been a member of the Inter-University Program for Latino Research (IUPLR), a consortium of university-based research centers dedicated to the study of Latina and Latino communities. The CRI is the only IUPLR-affiliated center located in the southeastern United States and the only one with a focus on Cuban Americans. The IUPLR has enabled the CRI to take part in the national Latina and Latino research agenda, integrating FIU faculty and students into nationally based projects and programs involving the Latina and Latino presence in the United States.

See also Inter-University Program for Latino Research *and* Research Centers.

LISANDRO PÉREZ

CUBAN WAR OF INDEPENDENCE. The Cuban War of Independence was fought in three contiguous stages. During "La Guerra Grande" or Ten Years War (1868–1878), the Cuban insurgents fought the Spanish forces to a stalemate, but refused the empire's offer of autonomy and pledged to continue fighting until full independence was won. From 1879 to 1880, a smaller and weaker rebel army continued fighting in "La Guerra Chiquita" or Small War, while the movement's political leadership in exile secured the necessary funds to open the final phase of the war under the unifying banner of the Cuban Revolutionary Party.

The final phase of the war began on February 24, 1895. Although Cuba had lost many of its key military leaders during the first phases of the protracted war, veteran fighters like Antonio Maceo and Máximo Gómez returned from exile to lead the final push for independence. Equally important to the war effort was José Martí, founder and president of the Cuban Revolutionary Party, who unified all separatist factions, and led an international diplomatic campaign to raise funds and recruit fighters for the war. In May 1895, the independence forces suffered a major blow when Martí was killed in battle, leaving behind his vision of a Cuba "With all and for the good of all" as a challenge for those who would govern the independent nation.

On February 15, 1898, the war took an unexpected and fateful turn when the USS *Maine* exploded and sank in Havana Harbor, killing 266 American sailors. Although the United Sates had remained neutral in the conflict, it had clear interests in Cuba, as demonstrated by its attempts to purchase the island from Spain on three different occasions. In response to the sinking of the *Maine*, President William McKinley formally declared war on Spain on April 25, and within six months the war that had been fought by Cubans for thirty years was over. The United States then proceeded to militarily occupy and rule Cuba, and to dominate the negotiations that led to the Treaty of Paris of December 10, 1898. The terms of Spain's surrender gave the United Sates control over four new territories: Cuba, Puerto Rico, the Philippines, and Guam. By taking over the remnants of the Spanish Empire, the United States entered the twentieth century as a world power and the most powerful nation in the Americas, roles it continues to play today.

When the United States ended its military occupation of Cuba on May 20, 1902, it left the door open to control Cuban affairs. The Platt Amendment, which the United States forced Cuba to include in its constitution of 1901, gave the new world power the right to land troops and occupy the country if necessary to protect American lives and property, veto power over Cuban foreign policy, and the right to build American military bases in Cuba. The Platt Amendment was abrogated in 1934, but the military base at Guantánamo Bay remains under United States control.

See also **Cuban Americans; Guantánamo Bay; Martí, José;** *and* **Platt Amendment.**

BIBLIOGRAPHY

Foner, Philip S. *The Spanish-Cuban-American War and the Birth of American Imperialism, 1895–1902.* 2 vols. New York: Monthly Review Press, 1972.

Healy, David. *Drive to Hegemony: The United States in the Caribbean, 1898–1917.* Madison: University of Wisconsin Press, 1988.

LaFeber, Walter. *The New Empire: An Interpretation of American Expansion, 1860–1898.* Ithaca, N.Y.: Cornell University Press, 1963.

Offner, John L. *An Unwanted War: The Diplomacy of the United States and Spain over Cuba, 1895–1898.* Chapel Hill: University of North Carolina Press, 1992.

Pérez, Louis A., Jr. *Cuba Between Empires, 1878–1902.* Pittsburgh, Penn.: University of Pittsburgh Press, 1983.

FÉLIX MASUD-PILOTO

CUISINE. Cooking is a cultural act, an infinite series of instants that manifest what one is and whence one comes. Cuisines are also the most enduring elements of the collective memory. The United States is a surprisingly vast, multicultural cauldron in which the ingredient that grows most in importance is of Hispanic origin, or better yet, of Iberian origin, with its variety of flavors, its profound odors, its colorful dishes, and its culinary memories that resist not only the impact of time but the cultural and geographic remoteness of its origins.

One must keep in mind that any given cuisine depends on resources and taste; that is, what the marketplace has to offer and the inherited and reinforced culture. Take, for example, the dishes prepared for the saints in Afro-Latino cooking or the singularity of specific seasonings: chili in dishes of Latinos and Latinas of Mexican origin and *sofrito* in those of Puerto Rican origin. Each represents an indelible milestone of the past, the invisible heritage so proudly carried as active memory that can become burdensome if carried as passive nostalgia.

Kitchen Recipes Bridge Different Cultures

Culture is a symbolic world one is all too often unable to translate, and the art of cooking is part of that world. It is practiced incessantly, day after day. This perhaps is the reason one rarely stops to think of all the implications enclosed in its lengthy process, a practice that mixes various ingredients in a determined manner to obtain a dish that will be shared collectively, that is, culturally.

Each person interprets differently the word "cuisine," which in Spanish, *cocina*, is synonymous with kitchen. Some may hark back to the place where they always ate, others to their dream kitchens, yet others to their favorite dishes. The word "cuisine" is a sort of verbal idea that shifts constantly, rarely conceived as frozen in time like a still photograph. Cooking is language. Each person knows at least one recipe that has been with him or her throughout life, even though he or she may have never actually tried to make it. And each recipe has its own story, continually retold in a particular manner.

When speaking of food, as of love or faith, people recollect their own histories. This includes family roots, the past and the places that marked it, the feast days that modeled one, such as christenings, weddings, funerals, the Day of the Dead, the Day of the Three Magi (January 6), and the Day of the Virgin of the Candelaria or Yemanja (February 2). It includes as well the personal circumstances that set each person apart, even within families; one's ability to prepare something one likes, for better or for worse; one's moods, which are essential to any task; the family's cookbook (that trusty memory trunk); the sadness suffered by the loss of links, such as the recipe that vanished when one last moved or that was lost for

MAKING BURRITOS. Making burrito sauce in the kitchen of Las Juanitas Restaurant, Kalamazoo, Mich., September 2003. (John A. Lacko/*Kalamazoo Gazette*/AP)

good with the death of an aunt. When this happens one feels it in a most personal manner, because love, faith, and food are personal commitments that sustain the community. They all hinge on one's good taste and capabilities, one's daring and tolerance.

Recipes are merely attempts to avert defeat. This is why outsiders perceive them as incomplete truths. It is the reason one says, when the results are not what was expected, that something must be hidden, some important ingredient was omitted. The older the recipe, the farther back one searches for oneself, the harder it is to decipher it. Whoever was inventive enough to set it on paper left out the obvious, that which anyone could know. What else, one asks, can "bake as usual" mean? Recipes, though, endure. Behind each one, behind every one of its words, are legions that carried the habits of their native lands to their new country, all so often without perceiving it, forced to adapt, to merge and work in new ways. Their recipes (that is, their cuisines) remain as a gesture of resistance in the face of the possibility of the total loss of cultural identity.

In letters sent to the author Laura Esquivel, mostly handwritten, Latino and Latina high school kids expressed their feelings after reading *Like Water for Chocolate* (1992). Besides their interest in the love story itself, what was most surprising was how strongly they identified with the elaboration of major meals, with the festive air that surrounds cooking in that culture. It was not rare for them to include a detailed description of a major celebration at home or a unique family recipe as a gift to the author who had made them look at their reflections in the mirror.

The Symbolic Pantry

The lexicon of Latino and Latina arts, images, colors, sounds, and words preserved and incorporated into English celebrates its enormous indebtedness to food. The visual arts often depict the fruits of tropical paradises lost. Music is an unending banquet of delectable dishes. Novels such as *Caramelo* (2002) by Sandra Cisneros (of Mexican origin) or *When I Was Puerto Rican* (1993) by Esmeralda Santiago (born in Puerto Rico), whether describing a Mexican delicacy or the pungent perfume of a guava whiffed just before leaving San Juan, enlarge the unconquerable arsenal of an identity that travels not to dissolve but to add itself to another one.

In that passage toward "otherness," probably the most prominent form of art is music, which may explain the edible power contained in its references to food, beckoning one to share melodiously in endless banquets of dishes to be savored with all one's senses. "Los pasillos de tía Conga," by Conjunto Céspedes, the African Cuban combo based in San Francisco, is a good example of how everyday life is celebrated in food: "Let's go to tía Conga's to eat fried yucca / White rice an' a little fried meat." The song, written by Gladis "Bobi" Céspedes, Guillermo Céspedes, and Wayne Wallace, is by no coincidence included in an album called *Una sola casa* (One single home), whose recurrent theme is to keep the promise, no matter when or where, of maintaining ties with folk and kin.

The book of recipes in Cuban songs is endless, including "Bacalao sin espinas" (Cod without fish bones) and "Arroz con leche" (Rice and milk). Cuban cooking, though, is not

GUACAMOLE (AVOCADO DIP)

In many homes of Mexican extraction, guacamole is still prepared using the traditional *molcajete* and *tejolote* (mortar and pestle). A fork and a bowl may be substituted, but never a blender. It is wonderful with tacos and snacks.

2 large avocados

2 tablespoons onion, finely chopped

1 clove garlic, finely chopped

1 or 2 chilies serranos, sliced

10 sprigs cilantro (coriander), chopped

lime juice

salt

pomegranate, to decorate

Cut avocados in half, remove pits, and scoop out flesh. Mash the flesh with a fork.

In a bowl (or *molcajete*), combine avocado, onion, garlic, chilies, and cilantro, and mix thoroughly. Take care not to turn it into a meal.

Add lime juice and salt to taste.

Serve immediately.

alone in the larger songfest. Another trait that links Latinos and Latinas is that just about anyone can sing a complete menu to whatever rhythm pulses in the neighborhood.

Mexico's National Council for Culture and the Arts published, in its series of Lecturas Mexicanas (1999), *El que come y canta* (He who eats and sings), a gastronomic songbook that consists of two tomes compiled and introduced by Aline Desentis Otálora.

From the onset one sees that not all the songs included are of Mexican origin, but all of Mexico grew up with them and traveled with them. A good number of Mexican musicians born on either side of the United States–Mexico border moved back and forth between both countries (Germán Tin Tan Valdéz and Lalo Guerrero, for example), sweetening the lives of several generations of children and grown-ups with their music-making. One needs only to read one of the songbook's indexes to start salivating.

Ageless verses spring straight from the tilled earth to the kitchen, such as "La milpa" (The cornfield), "La nopalera" (The cactus field), "El camotal" (The sweet potato field), every song a double entendre. Peddlers' and hawkers' melodic cries include "El pregón de los azucarillos" (The sweets caller) and "El turronero" (The nougat vendor). Other songs hark back to kitchen tasks, like "El bodeguero" (The pantryman) and "La mesera" (The waitress), and to kitchen utensils, like "El comal y la olla" (The skillet and the pan). Some songs include recipes and condiments, such as "En toda la extensión de la palabra amor" (To the full extension of the word love) and "La rajita de canela" (Cinnamon sliver). Other songs contain complete menus, especially for

breakfast and dinner, and sing endless parades of fruits, "Naranaja dulce" (Sweet orange); eggs, "La gallina ponedora" (The hatching hen); "El Colás 2," horn-goat tamales (which refers to those an unfaithful person prepares for the spouse); bread, "Tons qué mi reina, ¿a qué hora sales al pan?" (So, my dear, what time will you go fetch the bread?); tortillas, "La mula maicera" (The corn mule); poetic beans, "Los frijoles de Anastasia" (Anastasia's beans); butters and cheeses, "La pastora" (The shepherdess); and hors d'oeuvres, "Todos tienen tortita menos yo" (Everyone's got their snack but me). As for lunchtime, one can sing the hardy quick meal, "La panza es primero" (The belly's first), or order à la carte: first, the soup, "Sabor al caldo" (Add flavor to the broth); then vegetables, "Te crees muy salsa" (You think you're the dressing); tacos, "De tripas, cuajo, y corazón" (Guts, rennet, 'n' heart); meats, "Picadillo" (Minced meat); poultry, "Pollito con papas" (Chicken 'n' taters); and seafood, "Camarón pela'o" (Peeled shrimp). The list is endless, a potpourri of regional and international dishes, and finally come the inevitable sweets and desserts.

The act of cooking is undoubtedly where one can best appreciate the profound and concentric roots of cultural crossbreeding in its widest sense. One is, literally and metaphorically, what one eats; people have combined their ways, rhythms, and tastes with the aromas, tastes, and textures of ancient lore.

The pantry is based on several clearly identifiable ingredients that have become emblems of Latin American and Latino cuisines: maize or sweet corn, beans, chilies or *ajíes*, yams, rice, sugarcane, sweet potatoes, and manioc or mandioca (especially among people from the Caribbean and the Gulf of Mexico and those who learned from their African forebears how to prepare tuberous roots). Most important in the face of lack and need is the power of the imagination, which transforms the inedible into a delicacy.

Latino and Latina cuisine has various unique histories. However interesting the fusion of cuisines may be to contemporary gastronomy, as its fame grows and gathers

MARGARITA

4 cups or more crushed ice

½ cup white tequila

¼ cup Cointreau

3 tablespoons sugar syrup

juice of 4 limes

1½ teaspoons salt

In a blender blend the ice, tequila, Cointreau, syrup, and lime juice for 30 seconds.

Moisten the rims of 6 glasses with lime juice and invert on a saucer of salt to lightly coat the rims. Divide the margarita mixture among the glasses and serve.

QUIMBOMBÓ CON POLLO (OKRA WITH CHICKEN)

1 pound *quimbombó* (okra)	½ cup oil
1 chicken (about 1 kilogram), quartered	3 cups water
1 green pepper	juice of 3 lemons
2 or 3 unripe bananas (not too hard)	Lightly cook the quartered chicken in oil with the garlic and onion.
2 garlic cloves, chopped	Add the salt, pepper, tomato puree, vinegar, chicken stock, and wine.
1 big onion, chopped	Wash whole okra (*quimbombó*), cut ends off, and slice 1 centimeter
2 teaspoons salt	thick. Soak in water and lemon juice.
½ teaspoon black pepper	When chicken is half cooked, add the *quimbombó* with the water and
1 cup tomato puree	lemon juice. Cook until soft.
1 cup chicken stock	Mash bananas and roll into balls. Add to mixture.
1 cup vinegar	For a thicker stew, add less lemon and cook until most of the water
1 cup dry white wine	evaporates. Take care to avoid stirring the mixture too much while cooking.

adepts in the United States, one cannot risk being impressed merely by veneer or lose sight of the specific origins of Latino and Latina tastes and needs. An honest cuisine takes pride in its ingredients and saves its influences.

Of Origins and the Global Market

Products and cooking habits were shared between the First Nations of the American continent and the incoming European societies and included a brisk trade with the Orient. Italian cuisine would be inconceivable without the Mexican tomato, the Spanish *tortilla de patata* (Spanish potato pancake) without the Peruvian potato. It is equally hard for Latin Americans to think of cooking without oil or milk.

A gastronomic culture develops through the exchange of discoveries and inventions, be they machines, tools, food research, or work habits. Probably no other nation has welcomed so many ways of cooking as the United States, where the need to supply small barrio stores with specific foodstuffs is acknowledged and where large supermarket chains stock the unique products that grace many different cuisines.

In order to interest large communities in exotic flavors, the food industry has developed all manner of strategies, demonstrations, and tasting sessions of products, ingredients, and recipes for dishes considered local glories somewhere in the world. On the Internet hundreds of links offer "authentic," "original," "truly home" cooking, dishes, and recipes. Every site created by restaurants, specialized stores, and community service groups treasures its claim to authenticity, as if food were a relic rather than an active element in culture.

It is said that great cuisines travel poorly, though it would be unfair to pass judgment on any of the world's cuisines. The fact remains that tastes are indissolubly linked to the soils where they originate; they depend on the seasons and the care of humans to protect the environment. For example, *escamoles* (ant eggs known as the caviar of the Mexicans) are edible for a brief period of thirty to forty days just prior to the rainy season. They can certainly be frozen, stored, transported, and sold during the rest of the year, but they are not readily available in any large quantity. Importing *escamoles* is not profitable, and once defrosted they taste nothing like those freshly harvested from the nest. Nevertheless ant eggs are available in several cities in the United States, as are *chapulines* (grasshoppers), blue maize tortillas, and the worms of the maguey, the century plant.

Living far from the gastronomic homeland stimulates talent, ingenuity, and patience. Neither idleness nor prosperity nor excess has generated great cuisines. These are linked to the working classes, the hungry, those who have defied obstacles and convention, and those who have invented and reinvented dishes that smell of tender sweet corn and of steaming potatoes, dishes that contrast white rice and black beans.

Want is a demanding mistress. It tests the imagination severely and sharpens intuition; it shuns primness but maintains a spark of rebellion and the shadow of that battered dignity that leads one to find bits of onion, garlic, tomato, cilantro, and parsley that produce the ferocious air of immediate cooking, the cooking barred from recipe books until someone garnishes it with words such as "exquisite," "sublime," or "delicate."

In education the storyteller nourishes, as does food. Storytellers help children and adults approach cultures different from their own, acquire a notion of ethics, and learn about the world. Mothers, aunts, and grandmothers tell of meals as they were prepared at home. The first thing one gets used to is the flavor of those tales at the table, bread's smoky odor permeating the kitchen, Aunt Toña's punch that got one tipsy for the first time. Two or three generations of women may gather to cook tamales, and the party begins. One first participates by watching, listening to their laughter, hearing their timeworn tales

TAMALES

"Tamale" is the Spanish version of the Nahuatl *tamalli*. A tamale is a stuffed bun or roll made of freshly ground or sieved maize dough. There are virtually thousands of variations, simple to extraordinarily sophisticated. They are commonly classified according to the way they are wrapped, their contents, the types of salsas or gravies (or the lack of these), and their places or countries of origin. Tamales are in fact the foremost traditional nourishment in most of Latin America and are well known in most of the United States. Chef John Rivera Sadler has dedicated enormous efforts to erecting a museum to the tamale on the property of the Mission of San Juan Capistrano in Los Angeles, California. The following tamale *de hoja* "in leaves" is a simple recipe.

10 ripe tomatoes
10 fresh corncobs
3 onions, chopped
1 cup pork meat, chopped
6 cloves of garlic, chopped
6 green peppers, chopped
1 teaspoon ground pepper
1 lime
1 sprig fresh coriander
2 teaspoons ground oregano
2 laurel leaves
salt to taste

Remove maize leaves from cobs and put aside.

Grind the maize, adding drops of water until creamy. Strain in medium-sized sieve.

Prepare a seasoning with the chopped garlic, onion, peppers, coriander, tomatoes, and the juice of half a lime.

Cook the cleaned and chopped meat in a little water, add the oregano, salt, pepper, and the rest of the lime juice. Use bitter orange instead of lime if you like. Mix with the ground maize.

Choose the best leaves and make as many "beds" as possible, using two or three leaves for each one, making sure the tamale mix on each bed does not spill out. Bundle each with a string and tie a knot.

Boil tamales in water with the salt and laurel leaves.

Drain and serve with chili sauce.

---

that seem new. The stories are told in broken Spanish, peppered with *sofrito, adobo, guanajo,* or shredded turkey meat (it all depends on the kitchen whence the seasoning originated). The cooks knead the flour, exorcizing drudge by beating the dough into a resilient, porous softness. The tales shape a person and, depending on the filling, add taste and color to the future.

Faced by such an inherited abundance, instant food has barely any meaning, for all its precooked claims of speed ("merely add water") with their promise of a more hygienic, efficient, and cosmopolitan world. Parallel phenomena engendered by globalization often incorporate elements that seek to reproduce "the ways of yore," a whole range of foodstuffs "typical" of certain places (tacos, empanadas, *arepas, adobos,* moles, dressings, sauces, gravies). Yet a border taco is different from those eaten elsewhere in Mexico, beginning with the type of flour, maize or wheat; its size; the filling; and whether it is served hot or cold.

Traditional or local peculiarities are transformed regardless. The Taiwanese movie *Eat Drink Man Woman* (1994) was quickly adapted by a Latino filmmaker into *Tortilla Soup* (2001), a recipe claimed by millions of Mexicans as their very "own original" formula. The movie proves that what is considered "own original" is at best a registered inventory of elements, textures, smells, colors, and forms that constitute a language of sensations.

A cuisine allows for re-creations and is nourished by intuition. Any number of recipes for enchiladas exist. In New Mexico they are flat and topped with an egg, in southern Texas the tortillas are filled with white cheese and rolled, and elsewhere in Texas they are covered with chili con carne sauce.

Family Recipe Books: An Enriching Heritage

On a given morning, one leafs through that notebook in which one's mother wrote recipes and glued clippings from papers and magazines and bits torn from letters, all vestiges of a personal appetite. For the first time one discovers one's mother's desire for permanency: a toothache remedy, a recipe for flour tortillas, an oak leaf infusion, how best to clean wine stains, a snippet of a phrase that seems meaningless for the moment.

One mentions this to a friend, hoping to awe her with such maternal manias. She is not surprised at all. In fact she is passionately moved by her own grandmother's calligraphy, which spreads across several notebooks, smudged by hurried readings, yellowed by time and flour, patient, sad, resigned scrawls scribbled with different inks, an improvised script, kitchen notebooks on the brink of completion. Another friend will swear her home stores more such notebooks. They exist in all Latina homes. Many a mother saved hers—almost secretly, not daring to hope anyone could cherish them—among old gas bills and unanswered letters. She understood them to be, somehow, sinful writing, particularly suspicious because of their uselessness. Such cookbooks, surely an inherited custom, are like a caress, mostly a pleasure. Their careful texts are coarse whispers contained in the scratching on a page.

Family cookbooks are built day by day, spontaneously, informally. They are almost autobiographical, as intimate as to be nearly confessional. They are written during secret,

RAW MOJO

6 tablespoons pork fat

mashed onion, cut into rings

1 clove of garlic

6 tablespoons bitter orange juice

salt

Heat the fat and when it starts to boil, remove from heat.

Add salt, onion, garlic, and orange juice.

Pour over vegetables and serve.

cloistered hours, when one defiantly saves a daring new mincemeat formula, dreaming of the smiles it will bring to one's best beloved, anticipating the praise it will elicit hours later from the people sitting around the table. Homemade cookbooks collect desires, aspirations, wishes to improve and to be loved more; they serve to guard, through broth, sweat, and spoons, one's own and proper place.

Lighting Hearth Stoves

The kitchen at home is still the anchor of cultures, the port where one wishes to dock. It does not demand definitions or definitive answers; it is a good kettle that has boiled for centuries and that holds ingredients, which have three, deeply influential sources.

There is no avoiding the similarities between Latino and Latina dishes and Spanish cooking, possibly the source that most homogenizes Latino and Latina cuisines. Spaniards certainly contributed their cuisine from the conquest to colonial times. But interestingly the produce of the Americas impacted Spain and then came back as a characteristic gastronomy of that country. Exchange and appropriation make it difficult to distinguish or even recognize origins.

Techniques, products, and language were constantly adopted and naturalized, crossbreeding in the processes, which are the mark of every healthy society.

The truly Mexican tomato has become an emblematic symbol of the Catalan cuisine. Potatoes and coconut ice cream are natural in any Spanish menu, as natural as the *tostón* (fried banana), the *lechón* (piglet), the *cabrito asado* (roast kid) and the *sopa de migas* (dried bread soup) served in Latino restaurants in the United States.

Frying, roasting, baking, and stewing (*estofado*) took root in the Americas during colonial times, according to Esther Sánchez Botero. It is difficult to confirm which peoples exactly bestowed them on U.S. cuisine. Andalusians claim their recipe for fried fish as their own. Galicians traditionally claim to be the inventors of the empanada, though communities of Bolivian origin claim the authentic empanada in opposition to those of Chilean origin, who in turn vie against the Peruvians as originators of the authentic seviche (raw fish cocktail).

Techniques traveled hither and yonder, back and forth. Among those peculiar to the New World, Sánchez Botero lists grilling, stick roasting, and smoking. The latter consists of using the heat of smoke to extract water from short-term nonperishable products and adding salt to preserve them. One could conceivably accept a Pacific Islands origin. Claudio Vadillo López quotes privateer William Dampier as writing that:

> During a good part of the 17th century until the beginning of the 18th century, pirates learnt from the Arahuacs how to sun dry their meat and smoke it by burning green wood. The Arahuac called this meat bucan, a word which then described as buccaneers those pirates who used the technique and who spread this form of conserving meat to different settlements along the Mexican coasts in the Gulf of Mexico.
>
> (López)

PICADILLO

Picadillo (minced meat) has no precise translation, but it describes a domestic dish. It is usually prepared with beef and pork in equal measures, though in striving for a lighter diet, turkey may be used.

4 tablespoons olive oil

1 pound ground round (sirloin)

1 large onion, peeled and chopped

1 large green bell pepper, cored, seeded, and coarsely chopped

1 or 2 chilies serranos, chopped

3 medium potatoes (Idaho or Maine), peeled and cut into half-inch cubes

1 8-ounce can tomato sauce

salt and ground black pepper to taste

2 teaspoons *sofrito* (Combine in blender chopped cilantro; 6 whole leaves *recao*, chopped; 1 medium onion, chopped; and 1 clove garlic, crushed. Puree until it acquires a smooth saucelike consistency.)

10 pimento-stuffed olives

2 plantains, peeled and cut into half-inch cubes

Heat 2 tablespoons of the olive oil in a large kettle or skillet and add beef. Cook on high heat until meat loses its red color.

Drain excess pan drippings and reduce heat to medium. Add onion and bell pepper and sauté until meat is brown and onion is transparent (some 3 minutes). Remove from heat and set aside.

In a separate frying pan, heat the remaining olive oil and stir-fry the plantains and potato cubes until golden (some 5 to 7 minutes). Remove and drain on paper towels.

Return beef to stove and, cooking on low heat, add tomato sauce, *sofrito*, salt, pepper, potatoes, olives, and plantains. Stir to combine. Cover and let simmer for 10 minutes.

SANCOCHO

This treasure, prepared for special occasions, is of Dominican origin, though Latinos and Latinas of Puerto Rican, Cuban, and Caribbean origin all claim it as their own. Since it requires many ingredients, patience, and lots of time, it is best to prepare it with the help of good friends, small shots of rum, and cold beer. Traditionally it is made with beef, but the "seven meats" recipe is the deluxe version.

Before beginning, clean all the meat except the pork sausage or *longaniza*, chop into small squares, and varnish with lime.

1 pound goat meat

1 pound *longaniza* (pork sausage)

1 pound pork

2 pounds beef with bone

1½ pound chicken or hen (hen requires more time to soften)

2 pounds pork ribs

1 pound smoked ham bones

2 limes, cut in half

1 tablespoon ground garlic

3 tablespoons oil

2 large green chilies, sliced thick

1 pound yams, chopped into 2-centimeter squares

2 large onions

½ pound ham, chopped into 2-centimeter squares

2 tablespoons chopped celery

1 pound orange pumpkin

½ pound malanga or yautia (types of yam), chopped into 2-centimeter squares

½ pound potatoes, chopped into 2-centimeter squares

3 unripe bananas, two of them chopped into 2-centimeter squares

2 cups meat stock

2 cups chicken stock

½ cup olives and capers

2 cups corn cobs, chopped into 2-centimeter squares (if desired)

½ teaspoon powdered oregano

½ teaspoon powdered *sazón*

½ teaspoon cilantro (coriander)

2 teaspoons vinegar

1 teaspoon Tabasco sauce

Boil beef in a casserole with herbs, garlic, vinegar, capers, *sazón*, and salt. Stir to distribute evenly.

Heat oil in iron pan. Add the beef and carefully baste (the oil is hot) beef while stirring. Cover and wait one minute, then stir again. Add a little water if mixture sticks to pan. Continue cooking another 20 minutes.

Add pork and cook 15 minutes more, adding water if necessary.

Add the rest of the meat and both stocks and allow to cook for 10 more minutes.

Add one quart water and wait for it to boil. Add yautia or malanga and the chopped green bananas. Allow to cook for 10 minutes.

Grate the third green banana and add to pan. Add the rest of the ingredients, adding water if needed. Stir regularly so nothing sticks to the bottom. Allow to cook until all ingredients are done.

Take 2 cups of vegetables from pan, grind, and pour back in. Allow to cook until stew thickens.

Add salt to taste. Serve steaming hot with white rice and slices of avocado.

Latino cuisines' second heritage is in ingredients of Caribbean origin influenced by Africa. These include all types of banana, coconut, yucca and *ñame* roots, *quimbombó* (okra), an enormous variety of tropical fruits, deliciously sweet coffee, fermented sugarcane drinks, and a refreshing drink made of molasses with a touch of cinnamon or aromatic herbs, to mention but a few.

Santería arrived hand in hand with the act of cooking. Like most religions, its dogma is based on mystery. Profoundly rooted in Africa, as errant as its peoples, and carrying the stigma of slavery, it sustains itself cloaked in a mantle of clandestine airs. Even so, in Santería cooking is equal to maintaining, preserving, initiating, communicating, and strengthening individual and collective ties. In this religion everything begins and ends in the kitchen; nothing can be compared to the energy emanated by offerings made to the orishas. The kitchen is the great sacred laboratory where knowing how to cook to delight the gods foremost, then the community, and seasoning the food with faith and beauty meets with the approval of the deities.

The third root is that of the First Nations, of home, and includes all the various elements that originated in the American continent. Rooted in a millennial past that condenses myths, legends, theories, and reflections, the pre-Hispanic cuisines stand out as America's own domestic reflection of mature cultures that were already, long before the arrival of Europeans, a fertile menu of multicultural seasonings. To follow the tracks that lead back to the five major zones where pre-Hispanic cuisines developed (present-day Mexico and Guatemala, Ecuador, Bolivia, Peru, and Paraguay) requires facing the memory of a reiterated, irreplaceable appetite for all sorts of chilies, a great variety of techniques, the use of all types of maize, and the capacity to feed off anything, beginning with tiny insects and the humblest wild herbs, the famous *quelites*. Upon their arrival in the Americas the Europeans actually believed God had created more than one world. All those animal and vegetable species, beans, pumpkins, tomatoes, chilies, turkeys, and the splendid cocoa, were unlike anything they had known.

Since then Latino and Latina cuisine has been touched and enveloped by new flavors, specifically those that many call "the Anglo culture." Latinos and Latinas celebrate Thanksgiving Day, stuffing turkeys *à l'americaine*. Puerto Ricans would never miss their Spaghetti Day (they are not the only ones). Everyone occasionally fancies a hamburger, a pizza, a cola drink. But be warned, in adventures of any sort, personal tastes have a way of imposing themselves. "Latino and Latina food" is characteristically hot and spicy, exhibiting an addiction to spices, to the heavy, phosphorus-laden flavors and tremendously sweet desserts. It is a cuisine of contradictions in which dozens of spices and herbs mix to flavor one single dish. This is why Latino and Latina kitchens are never without that stone, wooden, or porcelain tool, the mortar and pestle, known as *pilón*, *mortero*, or *molcajete* (or as the *comadre* is wont to say, "Where do you keep your wireless blender?").

Latinos and Latinas have never been ungrateful or puerile; they move and travel on, taking even the parrot along. They like a generous table and pay close attention to innovative cooking programs on TV that share new techniques, showcase fusion food, or celebrate a healthy haute cuisine. They are not naive. But when at home, they still slurp soup up and dip morsels of bread in it. They preserve common recipes and interpret them to suit individual tastes. They treasure advice they someday will pass on to the children and prefer to eat among friends. And though at times they may forget to lay the tablecloth, they never find it hard to add an extra place, for where two can eat, four can eat, and where four sit, six may be seated.

Everyone's Home: Latino and Latina Cuisine

Latino and Latina cuisine is an invitation to travel in other latitudes and experience other customs on an imaginary map that recognizes language and common histories. It is a cuisine built on links, exchanges, and combinations with ingredients and techniques rescued and inherited from many manners of life and ways of eating. It is a great casserole in which the past is blended: family roots, places passed through, social life, curiosity, celebrations and feast days, personal circumstances, cooking skills, willingness, family recipes, even the loss and errors that lead to a new recipe, a discovery, an experience.

What stands out in the various Latino and Latina cuisines is their vocabulary, their domestic accent, which mutates constantly. Each and every one of these cuisines lives a creative moment, each looks to define itself and mark its presence. This is why they so frequently coincide and meet to appraise each other, and of course, to adapt. There is no sense in conceiving of Latino and Latina cuisines as fixed gastronomic formulas. They certainly do not allow themselves to "open up." They would vanish if they did. But the key to their freedom can be summed up in one single recipe, one that all great cuisines have followed, that is, practicing all the old recipes and then disregarding them, breaking their rules, adapting them to the moment, to family needs, to what the market has to offer, to what the body demands.

It is not a question of "transferring" local, traditional ways of preparing emblematic dishes to other social and cultural contexts. Certain cuisines do not travel well, and one has to respect this fact. In this sense, learning more about Latino and Latina cuisines allows one to adapt them better while safeguarding their origins, to appreciate an ability to interpret the places one came from.

Traditional history rarely mentions the art of cooking, including it only when it comes via the back door of universities or academia. This is why it is so important to celebrate the invisible heritage that one builds on a daily basis. One can scarcely conceive of contemporary culture without citing references and parameters as established by commonplace, day-by-day cooking, including its many grammatical and culinary doubts. The table one eats at is a communication space par excellence, where one nourishes what one is, discloses cultural patterns and thought patterns. The kitchen is the core of the dream home. It holds all the memories one listened to and repeats to those one loves.

A recipe is nothing but the evidence of one's personal history. Potentially each recipe is a mystery waiting to be unraveled. Its ingredients are precise facts one can deal with. As one manipulates the ingredients, one transforms the recipe into a concrete proposal. Cooking is the ability to make sense of oral and written words made of smells, flavors, and textures as understood by the intelligence of the senses. Because when all is said and done, identity is something that has no ending, one is simply cooking it.

See also Beans *and* Food and Literature.

BIBLIOGRAPHY

Cabieses, Fernando. *Cien Siglos de Pan.* 2nd ed. Lima, Peru: Escuela Profesional de Turismo y Hotelería, Universidad de San Martín de Porres, 1996.

Castelló Yturbide, Teresa. *Presencia de la Comida Prehispánica.* Researched by biologist Ignacio Piña Luján. Mexico City: Fomento Cultural Banamex, 1986.

Cocina indígena y popular. Mexico City: Dirección General de Culturas Populares of CONACULTA, 2000.

Colín, Salvador Miranda. *Identificación de las especies mexicanas y cultivadas del género Phaseolus.* Mexico City: ENA, Colegio de Posgraduados, 1996.

Crosby, Alfred W. *El intercambio transoceánico: Consecuencias biológicas y culturales a partir de 1492.* Mexico City: UNAM, 1991.

de Cárcer y Disdier, Mariano. *Apuntes para la historia de la trasculturización indoespañola.* México City: UNAM, 1995.

Iturriaga, José N. *La cultura del antojito.* 2nd ed. Mexico City: Editorial Diana, 1993.

Kennedy, Diana. *The Essential Cuisines of Mexico.* New York: Clarkson Potter, 2000.

López, Claudio Vadillo, and Lourdes Hernández Fuentes. *Sabores de América y el Caribe.* Mexico City: Editorial Clío, 2001. From the Las cocinas del mundo en México collection.

Muñoz Surita, Ricardo. *Diccionario Enciclopédico de Gastronomía Mexicana.* México City: Editorial Clío, 2000.

Otálora, Aline Desentis, ed. *El que come y canta . . . Cancionero gastronómico de México.* Two vols., part of Colección Lecturas Mexicanas. Mexico City: Consejo Nacional para la Cultura y las Artes, 1999.

Pilcher, Jeffrey M. ¡*Vivan los tamales! La comida y la construcción de la identidad mexicana.* Mexico City: Ediciones de la Reina Roja, SA de CV, in partnership with the Consejo Nacional para la Cultura y las Artes and Centro de Investigaciones y Estudios Superiores en Antropología Social, 2001.

Rivera, Oswald. *Puerto Rican Cuisine in América: Nuyorican and Bodega Recipes.* New York: Four Walls Eight Windows, 1993.

Sánchez Botero, Esther. *Recetas de la abundancia.* Bogotá, Colombia: Convenio Andrés Bello, 2001.

Torres Yzábal, María Dolores, Shelton Wiseman, and José N. Iturriaga. *El Gourmet Mexicano: Ingredientes auténticos y recetas tradicionales de las cocinas de México.* Singapore: Grijalbo, 2001.

Villegas, Liliana. *Delicious Tropical Fruits.* Bogotá, Colombia: Villegas Editores, 1990.

Zarvos, Nick, and Carlos Augusto Silva Ditadi, Pesquisa e Text. *Multissabores: A formação da gastronomia brasileira.* Brazil: SENAC, 2000.

Lourdes Hernández Fuentes
Translated from the Spanish by Felipe Ehrenberg

CULEBRA COALITION. The Culebra Coalition is a multiracial, grassroots organization working to protect the land and natural resources of the Rio Culebra watershed, located in the San Luis Valley of the Sangre de Cristo Mountain Range in Costilla County, Colorado, as well as the livelihoods, culture, and economic and environmental rights of San Luis area residents. The Culebra Coalition was initially organized in the early 1990s in response to the historic Taylor Ranch controversy, one of the most significant environmental justice struggles in the Southwest. The coalition coordinated the efforts of several environmental, cultural, social justice, and land grant activists and organizations that had been involved in the forty-year fight to regain access for heirs to the Sangre de Cristo Land Grant, of which Taylor Ranch is part, and to stop destructive logging practices in the highlands (colloquially known as La Sierra), which were damaging the watershed and irrigation systems downstream. The struggle resulted in a legal battle that persisted in appeals for twenty-one years, from 1981 until the landmark resolution in 2003.

The Taylor Ranch is a 77,500-acre tract that was historically part of the Sangre de Cristo Land Grant, settled in the 1850s by Indo-Hispano settlers. The ranch was sold in 1960 to Jack Taylor, a North Carolina lumberman and former Golden Gloves champion. Although his deed confirmed that descendants of the original Hispano settlers would continue to have access to the land and resources on the property as per previous terms, Taylor proceeded to fence the property and forcibly prevented the land grant heirs from entering, sometimes having them beaten or arrested. He further acquired a "fee simple" title to the property, that is, a title without any communal easements, by filing a Torrens action (No. 6904 [D. Colo. Oct 5, 1965]), which heirs began disputing in court in 1967. District and appeals courts ruled against the plaintiffs in a series of subsequent

lawsuits. However, in 1981, *Rael v. Taylor* began a twenty-one-year dispute regarding the legality of the notice given for Taylor's Torrens action, and the Colorado Supreme Court ultimately ruled in favor of the land grant heirs in 2002 and 2003 (*Lobato v. Taylor*). The court found that Taylor's deed granting access to the ranch for timber harvesting, firewood gathering, and grazing was binding, but that the heirs' claims to fishing, hunting, and recreation rights would not be upheld. Despite this latter finding, the decision was a landmark victory for the land grant heirs.

During the first twenty-five years of the four-decade-long legal battle, however, Jack Taylor carried on with harvesting timber in La Sierra's spruce and fir forests, often clear-cutting the land. After Taylor's death in 1988, his son, Zack Taylor, took over his estate. Faced with mounting debt and excessive legal and estate bills, the younger Taylor continued to harvest timber in La Sierra, before finally selling the ranch in the late 1990s to Lou Pai, a former Enron executive, and other parties. Access roads and intensive logging caused significant sedimentation in Rio Culebra's natural waterways and irrigation systems, directly threatening the ecological health of the watershed and impeding the ability of Indo-Hispano farmers to irrigate downstream. Thus, while a victory was achieved on the front of recognizing historic communal access rights to the resources of La Sierra, the threats to the livelihoods of the people of San Luis and to the ecological integrity of the Rio Culebra watershed worsened.

The Taylor Ranch controversy represents a quintessential environmental justice struggle in which social justice and environmental and economic rights are inextricably bound, and in which efforts that focus on one aspect of the situation inevitably run up against obstacles related to other aspects. In addition to involving activists and residents from San Luis, the struggle attracted the attention of national and international environmental groups, including Ancient Forest Rescue, Greenpeace, and Earth First!; local land grant organizations such as the Land Rights Council; social justice organizations including the American Civil Liberties Union and International Center for Human Rights Litigation; and regional environmental justice networks such as the SouthWest Organizing Project. In the early 1990s, the separate players on the plaintiff side of the Taylor Ranch struggle began collaborating under the umbrella of the Culebra Coalition.

The Culebra Coalition has been involved in developing a management plan to protect the resources in La Sierra. It has also worked with the Colorado Acequia Association and other watershed organizations. Finally, the Culebra Coalition has continued to work for the rights and livelihoods of the descendants of the original settlers of the Sangre de Cristo Land Grant and of the residents of San Luis.

See also Colorado; Colorado Acequia Association; Land Grants; Land Rights Council, San Luis, Colorado; Lobato v. Taylor; *and* Rael, Apolinar.

VANESSA MAZAL

CULTURAL LANDSCAPES. The cultural landscape is what geographers and others call the human-constructed environment as opposed to nature. Cultural landscape study is an established subfield of professional geography with a scholarly tradition that dates to the late nineteenth century in Europe and to the 1930s in the United States. Its conventions and standards of analysis have been declared and generally accepted by geographers and by researchers in cognate fields like landscape architecture, planning, and anthropology.

The theory of cultural landscape is predicated on the understanding that all societies and cultural groups occupy space, but how the space is defined, built upon, utilized, and transformed into place will vary by cultural group tradition. Cultural geographers, therefore, accept the basic principle that all human landscape has cultural meaning no matter how ordinary that landscape may be. Cultural geographers also assert that the landscape is a clue to culture. That axiom is applied by cultural geographers when they study the cultural landscapes of groups at many different scales, whether local, regional, national, or global.

Cultural geographers ask questions about landscapes created by specific groups as a material means to understand and reveal cultural behaviors and practices that are distinctive to those groups. Geographers typically employ qualitative methods to assess landscapes and meanings, and often conduct field studies to document cultural landscape patterns. The study approach is diachronic or historical because an assumption in landscape interpretation is that understanding the present is often rooted in past conditions. More recent cultural landscape studies have deconstructed landscapes represented in texts and as visual images. In all cultural landscape studies, researchers typically accept that landscapes are social constructions and that their meanings will vary with interpretations and contexts.

The 1980s saw the emergence of cultural landscape studies as a theme of research by geographers writing about Latinas and Latinos in the United States. These studies examine the relationships between specific Latina and Latino subgroups (for example, Cuban, Puerto Rican, and Mexican) and their ways of shaping distinctive places through cultural traditions and adaptive strategies. Field studies have documented Cuban yard shrines, Puerto Rican yard spaces, and Mexican "housescapes." Other studies have documented the cultural landscapes of Chicana and Chicano murals and public spaces such as plazas. Still other landscape studies concern specific place identities, such as Mexican cultural landscapes in San Francisco compared to similar but different Mexican cultural landscapes in San Antonio, Texas; Chicago; and San Diego, California. More recent writings have observed Latina and Latino shopping streets and transnational immigrant communities as themes of Latina and Latino cultural landscape study. Overwhelmingly, these place-based geographical writings have explored Mexican subgroup cultural landscapes with only a handful of investigations about other Latina and Latino subgroup landscapes. Several selected works by geographers exemplify the diversity and range of Latina and Latino cultural landscape study.

As part of their research in Miami's Little Havana, geographers Thomas D. Boswell and James R. Curtis pioneered urban cultural landscape study among Latinas and Latinos in the United States. They characterized Little Havana as an amalgam of both Cuban and American cultures, yet recognized that in this district, a Cuban who so chooses and speaks only Spanish can shop, eat, attend religious services and theaters, and be cared for medically without a word of English being spoken. Perhaps the most emblematic cultural landscape in Little Havana is Antonio Maceo Mini Park, a focal point for men who engage daily in playing dominoes. A small fifty-by-ninety-foot property in the heart of the commercial district called Calle Ocho, the park is separated from the street by a decorative iron fence. The tight space is covered by shade trees, below which are set several tile-roofed pavilions that protect tables where games of nine-dot dominoes, and sometimes chess and checkers, are played throughout the day and evening. A crowd, chiefly composed of men, gathers to play dominoes, but also to discuss politics, smoke cigars, and engage one another in a spirit that is very much male and Latin American. Perhaps more so than any other public space in the city, this small park evokes the essence of the old Cuba in Miami. In fact, the park is a symbolic space that is now represented in tourist souvenirs sold in the Little Havana curio store next door to the park.

Another cultural landscape, one increasingly common as Latinas and Latinos spread across the country to small towns and even to large cities where they have not traditionally been present, is the banner street or Latina and Latino shopping street. This cultural landscape has been studied in south Texas by the geographer Daniel Arreola, and in New York City by the geographer Inés Miyares. The types of businesses present, their names, and the varieties of advertising and storefront decoration are all clues to the character of the street. In Los Angeles, the old downtown shopping street of Broadway is called the new "Latinoway" of the city. The street has been marked by new cultural uses for spaces and buildings that include eating, shopping, entertainment, and a vital street culture of vendors. Today, "Latinoway" in Los Angeles mirrors the open-air market of Aztec times in ancient Mexico, called a *tianguis*.

Finally, a third example of a common Latina and Latino cultural landscape is what Arreola has called the Mexican American "housescape," found in residential areas of cities and small towns populated by Chicanas and Chicanos. Typically, the housescape comprises a detached single-family dwelling and its immediate surroundings in an urban barrio in the Southwest. This cultural landscape is a complex of elements that includes front property enclosure, exterior house color, and yard shrines. The housescape pattern indicates the most recent evolution of a historic landscape code that has linkages to pre-Columbian Mexico and Spain. This cultural landscape has been studied in various communities, and its persistence is explained by the ease of accommodation of the housescape to similar cultural circumstances over many generations.

Cultural landscape is a critical concept in the study of Latina and Latino cultures in the United States. Because landscape is a clue to cultural difference as well as similarity, it allows researchers to evaluate and differentiate how the plurality of Latina and Latino subcultures in the United States brings similar yet different traditions to the organization of space and the shaping of place.

See also Acequias; Calle Ocho; Little Havana; *and* Plazas.

BIBLIOGRAPHY

Arreola, Daniel D., ed. *Hispanic Spaces, Latino Places: Community and Cultural Diversity in Contemporary America*. Austin: University of Texas Press, 2004.

Arreola, Daniel D. *Tejano South Texas: A Mexican American Cultural Province*. Austin: University of Texas Press, 2002.

Boswell, Thomas D., and James R. Curtis. *The Cuban-American Experience: Culture, Images, and Perspectives*. Totowa, N.J.: Rowman and Allanheld, 1984.

Nostrand, Richard L. *El Cerrito, New Mexico: Eight Generations in a Spanish Village*. Norman: University of Oklahoma Press, 2003.

Suisman, Douglas R. "Plaza, Parque, Calle." *Places: A Quarterly Journal of Environmental Design* 8 (Spring 1993): 1–94.

Wilson, Chris, and Paul Groth, eds. *Everyday America: Cultural Landscape Studies after J. B. Jackson*. Berkeley: University of California Press, 2003.

DANIEL D. ARREOLA

CULTURE CLASH. Culture Clash is the most prominent Chicano and Latino performance troupe in the United States. The trio (Richard Montoya, Ric Salinas, and Herbert Siguenza) writes and performs its own material and has crafted a unique theatrical style that remains recognizable through a series of productions, ranging from sketch comedy to adaptations of Aristophanes. The work of Culture Clash is characterized by its timeliness and topicality; throughout the run of a production, the trio continues to hone its text, incorporating references to the day's news. The artists' style is performance collage; they weave together vignettes, comedy routines, character sketches, spoken word, song, and dance. Culture Clash represents the New Vaudeville, and its work is influenced by Cantinflas, Charlie Chaplin, Mexican *carpas* (tent circuses), and the *teatros* (theaters) of the Chicano and Chicana theater movement.

Throughout their long collaboration, Montoya, Salinas, and Siguenza have played the role of clown-as-critic in creating activist art. As comedians, they engage in sharp social criticism and overtly political statements, what they call in the title of one of their plays "comedy for these urgent times." Their work has influenced generations of Latino and Latina and Chicano and Chicana comedians and performers, including such groups as ChUSMA and the Taco Shop Poets. Demonstrating a commitment to multicultural performance, Culture Clash has also shared the stage with Asian American comedy troupes such as 18 Mighty Mountain Warriors.

Culture Clash was founded at San Francisco's Galeria de la Raza on Cinco de Mayo (May 5) 1984. Originally called Comedy Fiesta, the troupe was conceived by the visual artist Rene Yañez as a collective of actors, comedians, and poets. Comedy Fiesta was made up of Jose Antonio Burciaga, Marga Gomez, Richard Montoya, Monica Palacios, Ric Salinas, and Herbert Siguenza. Their early work with El Teatro Campesino brought them national attention. Eventually, the group fragmented, with Gomez and Palacios each pursuing solo performance and Burciaga, Montoya, Salinas, and Siguenza forming Culture Clash.

On Burciaga's departure, the remaining trio scripted its first full-length show. The writer/performers channeled their frustration over the lack of opportunities for Chicanos and Chicanas and Latinos and Latinas in theater and film into the script of *The Mission* (1988). The play tells the story of three unemployed Chicano actors who kidnap Julio Iglesias and hold him hostage until they are allowed to perform on television. Bookending this central plot is a satirical depiction of Father Junipero Serra's mission to convert the Indios of Mexico and California in the eighteenth century.

The Mission was a tremendous success in performances throughout the country. It was followed by a series of sketch shows: *A Bowl of Beings* (1991), *S.O.S.—Comedy for These Urgent Times* (1992), *Carpa Clash* (1993), and *Culture Clash Unplugged* (1994).

A Bowl of Beings features a series of highly charged comedy sketches: Che Guevara returns from the dead to find an apathetic Chicano activist getting stoned and waiting for a pizza; the First Chicano discovers he is the illegitimate son of Christopher Columbus (the father) and America (the mother). The production was filmed for *Great Performances* on PBS.

CULTURE CLASH. *Culture Clash in AmeriCCa*, Berkeley Repertory Theatre, 2003. Left to right: Ric Salinas, Herbert Siguenza, and Richard Montoya. (Courtesy Culture Clash/Photo by Tom Berne)

Next came an offer to executive produce and star in their own sketch comedy show. *Culture Clash*, the series, played for thirty episodes on FOX and featured guest appearances by Edward James Olmos, Jimmy Smits, Maria Conchita Alonso, and Dolores Huerta.

In 1994, the Miami Light Project commissioned a play from Culture Clash based on Miami residents. The trio was invited to make an extended stay in Miami and conduct interviews with local people. They then transcribed, edited, and interpreted the interviews, ultimately performing them as *Radio Mambo: Culture Clash Invades Miami*. It was the first play they wrote based on the narratives of others, launching Culture Clash's community-based work. *Radio Mambo* was followed by a series of commissions, including *Bordertown* (1998) for San Diego Repertory Theatre, *Nuyorican Stories* (1999) for INTAR in New York, and *Mission Magic Mystery Tour* (2001) for Brava! Women in the Arts in San Francisco.

In 1998, Culture Clash accepted a joint commission from South Coast Repertory in Costa Mesa, California, and Berkeley Repertory Theatre to do an adaptation of Aristophanes' *The Birds*. This was the first time the trio applied its theatrical process to a previously existing dramatic work. The members of the troupe filled the play with contemporary references and incorporated performance elements from vaudeville and the carpas. In 1998, Theatre Communications Group published *Culture Clash: Life, Death, and Revolutionary Comedy*, which contained the texts of *The Mission, Bowl of Beings*, and *Radio Mambo*. In 2001, *Culture Clash in AmeriCCa*, a compilation of community-based work featuring highlights from *Nuyorican Stories, Radio Mambo, Bordertown*, and *Mission Magic Mystery Tour*, premiered.

Culture Clash created *Anthems: Culture Clash in the District* for Arena Stage in Washington, D.C., in 2002. The trio was underway on interviews for this community-based work at the time of the September 11, 2001, attacks. The show took on a new resonance to respond to a city and country in crisis. This was the first production that did not feature all three Culture Clash members in the cast. While *Anthems* was performing in the District of Columbia, Herbert Siguenza was premiering his own show in California. *Yo Soy Cantinflas* (I am Cantinflas), based on the life and art of the Mexican comedian, debuted at the Yerba Buena Center in San Francisco. Siguenza wrote the script and played the title role.

Chavez Ravine, a commission from the Mark Taper Forum in Los Angeles, premiered in 2003. Based on two years of research and development, the play explores the 1950s relocation of a primarily Chicano and Chicana community from near downtown Los Angeles. The land was claimed for an ambitious public housing project, but development was stalled by political maneuvering. Instead, Dodger Stadium was built on top of Chavez Ravine. Returning to the narrative structure of *The Mission*, Culture Clash bookended the period drama with the depiction of Fernando Valenzuela pitching in Dodger Stadium in 1981.

Culture Clash continues to maintain a unique presence in the American theater, creating their own brand of theatricality at venues across the country. They hold an urgent and unwavering commitment to the political possibilities of theater. Culture Clash uses performance collage, community-based work, clowning, and comedy to make contemporary, movable, activist art.

See also **Performing Arts and Theater** *and* **Teatro Campesino.**

BIBLIOGRAPHY

Glenn, Antonia Grace. "Comedy for These Urgent Times: Culture Clash as Chroniclers in America." *Theatre Forum* 20 (Winter-Spring 2002): 62–68.

Glenn, Antonia Nakano. "Breaking Ground: Culture Clash Unearths Stories Long Buried in Chavez Ravine." *LA Alternative Press* 2, no. 3 (May 14–27 2003): 20–21.

Kondo, Dorinne. "(Re)Visions of Race: Contemporary Race Theory and the Cultural Politics of Racial Crossover in Documentary Theatre." *Theatre Journal* 52, no. 1 (Mar. 2000): 81–107.

Monaghan, Constance. "Mambo Combo." *American Theatre* 15, no. 3 (Mar. 1998): 10–14.

Montoya, Richard, Ricardo Salina, and Herbert Siguenza. *Culture Clash in AmeriCCa*. New York: Theatre Communications Group, 2003.

Montoya, Richard, Ricardo Salina, and Herbert Siguenza. *Culture Clash: Life, Death, and Revolutionary Comedy*. New York: Theatre Communications Group, 1998.

ANTONIA NAKANO GLENN

CUMBIA. Every Latin American culture has a sound it calls its own. Cubans and Puerto Ricans identify with salsa, although the Miami Cuban style is quite different from the Nuyoriquen version. Mexicans in California own the *ranchera*, just as the samba belongs to Brazilians wherever their numbers are large enough to make a community. Merengue and Dominican Americans go together hand in hand. So do Argentina and tango. The *cumbia* is an exception. Though its origins are in Colombia (Panama, Cuba, Guinea, and Ethiopia have also been cited as source points), the cumbia has transcended nationalities to function as a pan-Latin music, assimilated and embraced by almost every Latin culture in the United States. A dance, a style, and musical genre rolled into one, the cumbia is the soundtrack for twenty-first-century Latin Americans, regardless of ethnicity—ubiquitous on albums, on the radio, in clubs, in the streets, at festivals, and between innings at *beisbol* games.

A Caribbean rhythm with strong West African traits, cumbia is characterized by a two-part tempo that is neither too fast nor too slow with an accented backbeat traditionally carried by conga and guitar. The straightforward, strutting cadence of the 4/4 meter is tailored to sway hips and move feet.

Cumbia emerged from an obscure regional music called *costeño* that was popular along the Atlantic and Caribbean coasts of Colombia in the late nineteenth century. Costeño's own roots have been traced back to a seventeenth-century dance called the *cumbe* (a term derived from the African Yoruba tongue), which was performed by African slaves holding candles. The sexually charged courtship ritual in which a male dancer attempts to woo a seemingly unapproachable female dancer through seductive dance movements initially involved singing. When slaves were forbidden to sing in their own tongue, instruments were introduced, primarily *tambores* (drums from the African tradition), maracas, and *las gaitas*—indigenous flutes including *flautas de millo* made from cane or milo. Other instruments common to other musical styles were eventually introduced, including guitars, accordions, and horns. Meanwhile, cumbia the dance evolved into a folkloric style in Colombia in which both male and female dancers wore white.

During the early twentieth century, the sound spread inland as Colombia urbanized, though proper society scorned *el porro*, the popular cumbia rhythm, as immoral, lascivious, and too African. At the same time, access to the sea simultaneously established cumbia as an international music, the sound carried throughout Latin America by the shipping trade and immigration.

By the 1930s, cross-cultural influences from Cuba had infused big-band elements into cumbia, although the musicologist Ned Sublette contends cumbia may have been Cuban to begin with.

> In the 1940s [Cubanos] changed chords squarely on the downbeat, not the beat before, and in the early days rarely even syncopated the bass in the middle of the bar, typically preferring bass notes on one, three, and four, with a piano chunk in the space on two. . . . Before a nationalistic music movement took hold, Colombia's music was dominated by imports from Cuba—records, radio broadcasts and live shows by touring artists. This simple, unsyncopated, style of playing the *son* can be heard in many recordings of the 30s and 40s; Sonora Matancera, who used that groove extensively, were very popular in Colombia.
>
> (Sublette, pp. 2–3)

By the 1950s, the cumbia had swept across the plains and mountains of South and Central America and worked its way as far north as the borderlands of the United States, where it arrived in two forms. The simple, folkloric style of cumbia popularized by Conjunto Típico Vallenato was quickly embraced by the *norteño* groups of northern Mexico and south Texas, both of whom featured simple ensembles with the accordion as the centerpiece, like the Colombians did. A subgenre of Texas *conjunto* known as *grupos tropicales* further popularized the sound by playing cumbias exclusively.

The *combo*, or big-band version of cumbia, was distinguished by a large brass section. It was epitomized by the big-band interpretation by Mexico's Carmen Rivero Orquesta of the Colombian cumbia "La Pollera Colora," (The Chicken Farmer Colora), composed and performed by Wilson Choperena in 1962. This type of cumbia attracted a more sophisticated following, including Fito Olivares, a native of Ciudad Camargo in northern Tamaulipas, Mexico, five miles from the Mexico–United States border, who describes the Rivero version as a

CUMBIA. Cumia dancing in Washington, D.C. (© Jimmy Dorantes/LatinFocus.com)

defining moment in cumbia's evolution. The rhythms he heard were familiar—a slower, more purposeful variation of the Perez Prado mambos he grew up with—and, as Olivares quickly discovered, eminently danceable. Olivares's subsequent cumbia recordings, specifically "Juana la Cubana" and "La gallina" (The Chicken), million-selling international hits in the 1980s, helped spread the popularity of the sound across the United States. "La gallina" was subsequently licensed to help sell Burger King chicken sandwiches to Hispanics in the United States, and "Juana la Cubana" has been featured in the film *Lone Star* and on television's *X-Files*.

Cumbias eclipsed polkas in the early 1990s as the most popular dance in tejano, the mainstream sound of Texas Mexicans, in no small part because of hits by Selena y los Dinos, who enlisted Olivares to play the "authentic" cumbia sound on his saxophone on their recordings, and the *grupo internacional* La Mafia.

Colombia purists deride the various Mexican-influenced mutations of cumbia as *cumbia mariachi*, inferior and untrue to the original with the infusion of so many foreign elements. In truth, the cumbia has been appropriated by all Latin musics, to the point that salsa, merengue, and other styles are sometimes described as cumbias even when they are not.

Such history has little significance for contemporary Latin American cumbia aficionados, for whom the cumbia functions as an all-purpose dance sound meant to be moved to, not intellectualized. Cumbia has evolved into an all-purpose definition for rhythm, beat, instrumentation, and sound, inspiring a hundred subgenres, among them grunge-rock cumbia as popularized by Los Falcons and Los Black Stars, the cumbia dub of Celso Piña, and technocumbia, the highly polished electronica style articulated by A. B. Quintanilla and The Kumbia Kings. By and large, though, cumbia is pure pop, playful and unpretentious, pan-Latin rather than emblematic of a single nation or region, and rhythmically infectious enough to leap cultures and transcend social strata.

Olivares, who has carved out an impressive career spanning five decades and dozens of albums featuring cumbia, offers this rationale for cumbia's enduring qualities and universal Latin appeal: "It's never gone out of style because people have always enjoyed going out to dance."

See also Afro-Latinos; Dance and Dance Forms; Music, Popular; *and* Selena.

BIBLIOGRAPHY

Gibbs, Rodney. "The Rough Guide to Cumbia." World Music Network, Splendid E-zine, January 1, 2001. www.splendidezine.com/reviews/jan-1-01/rough.html

Peña, Manuel. *The Texas-Mexican Conjunto: History of a Working-Class Music*. Austin: University of Texas Press, 1985.

Sattley, Melissa. "Cumbre sobre el río." *Austin Chronicle*, Volume 22, Number 7, October 18, 2002.

Sublette, Ned. *Cuba and Its Music: From the First Drums to the Mambo*. Chicago: Chicago Review Press, 2004.

Varón, Jimena. "The Essence of Colombia." *Music Cultures of Latin America*, 1998. www.vallesounds.com/valle/jvessay1.html

Wade, Peter. *Music, Race and Nation: Música Tropical in Colombia*. Chicago: University of Chicago Press, 2000.

JOE NICK PATOSKI

CURANDERISMO. *Curanderismo* is a traditional medicine system found in Latin America and in the United States and practiced by some segments of the Mexican and Mexican American population. Curanderismo is a tradition that draws on many influences. It combines the indigenous spiritual, medical, and botanical knowledge present in the Americas prior to the conquest with comparable systems held and practiced by the invading Spaniards. The result was a practice that reflected the influences of both groups and established a dynamic tradition that continues to evolve and reflect current cultural practices. The evolution of curanderismo parallels the process of change in the indigenous populations that came into contact with the Spanish, just as the religious and medical traditions that came to the Americas were changed by contact with the indigenous population.

As well, curanderismo shares commonalities with other traditional medicine systems found throughout the world. Annemarie de Waal Malefijt notes that, cross-culturally, shamans are often called upon to diagnose and cure illnesses of natural or supernatural origin. Curanderismo fits into this paradigm. The shamanic elements normally associated with magico-religious/medicinal practices by other cultures are present: it has a central cultural/spiritual authority (the healer) and objects filled with mana. It is a system based on a holistic worldview recognizing that: (1) the supernatural and the "real" world occupy the same sphere of being; and, (2) human beings are intrinsically tied to the world around them.

The Mechanics of Curanderismo

While curanderismo is infused with Catholicism, it is not an organized religious practice, unlike Santería or Vodou, with which outwardly it may share some resemblance. Its appeal goes beyond religiosity. It is difficult at times to discern which elements are Catholic and which are indigenous or borrowed from some other tradition. It is not the dogma of the Catholic Church that drives curanderismo but rather a holistic view of the world, which is part of its philosophical foundation. However, Catholic/ Christian dogma is part of its practice. A healer will say that a person has to have faith in the healing process; she must choose to be active in her healing. And so, free will is an important component in a person's cure; it is demonstrative of the connection human beings have with God.

A spiritual rather than a religious practice grounded in local cultural intervention, curanderismo is communal and individualistic at the same time, in the sense that the healer and the individual are in a relationship to better the condition of that person. It is communal in that the healing of the individual is based on community values and cultural beliefs. However, there is no communal gathering for the worship of a divinity. Inasmuch as religious practice may be involved, these are not premised on organized religious practices. There is a hierarchy based on knowledge and expertise, but it is open to anyone wishing to participate, even those not of the culture, if they recognize their potential to heal and work on its development.

CURANDERIA MARKET. (Photograph by Socorro Castañeda-Liles)

As well, curanderismo is subject to the prevailing social, political, and economic conditions found within the community. A run of bad luck can manifest itself by job loss or money problems. A physical illness can be a result of anxieties over domestic problems. The healer will work with the client to resolve the underlying causes of an illness as well as its physical manifestation. In this fashion, curanderismo is greatly shaped and influenced by the local environment.

Healers

The practitioners of curanderismo are called *curanderas*, or *curanderos*. Healers are acknowledged by the community where they live as having a divine gift of healing. This gift of healing is called a *don*, and it is sometimes revealed to the healer in the form of a dream or some type of divine visitation. Healers believe that everyone is born with the ability to heal themselves or others (usually relatives). What distinguishes a person born with the don is their pronounced belief in their own abilities, which prefigures a supernatural revelation.

The calling to heal that separates the curandera and curandero from everyone else is not necessarily revealed early in life. Power is not transferred from one person to another; but there can be a guide, a teacher to instruct the possessor about the use of power. Once curanderas and curanderos recognize their don, they can learn to manipulate extrinsic power. Power exists everywhere but in unequal amounts, and those who know how can manipulate it. In many traditions, the possession of power carries an obligation to pursue an activist approach to life. Lack of power, lack of an activist mentality, leads to illness. Once a healer's power or ability is recognized as superordinary, the person must be trained in order to care for the gift and herself or himself properly. The curanderas and curanderos are quick to recognize the ultimate source, which for them is essentially their interpretation of a Christian God. But this is not a god that is separate from them, an anthropomorphic god, but rather a spirit without boundaries.

Central to curanderismo is the belief that the human body is in spiritual, physical, mental, and emotional harmony when in good health. Illness is the result of some type of disjuncture in this balance. These areas reflect the conceptualization of categories within curanderismo that define the *niveles* (realms of operation). There is a *nivel material*, the material realm in which healers cure by use of ritual objects, plants, and prayer; the *nivel espiritual* is healing conducted with the intercession of spiritual beings; and the *nivel mental* is healing conducted by the curandero/curandera manipulating his or her mental energy and healing through the laying on of hands.

A healer does not often work out of one realm exclusively but will combine techniques to better address the

CURANDERISMO. Applying a remedy for a blocked ear, Natalie, Texas, 1990. (Dore Gardner)

problem at hand. Healers will sometimes develop a specialty or are trained in one particular area. Examples of this are *parteras* (midwives), *sobadoras/sobadoros* (masseuses/masseurs), *hueseras/hueseros* (bone-setters), or *yerberas/yerberos* (herbalists). In practice, though, it is common for healers to use various materials to enact a cure.

Healers essentially "belong" to the community; they have a public persona that outweighs their private lives. How they conduct themselves and how they operate are dictated by tradition. They are "allowed" to alter performance and style in their healing practices but are bound by cultural definitions of what are acceptable behaviors and attitudes and what are not. However, they have the authority to regulate the behavior of other individuals by the diagnosis of illness, which often reflects a spiritual or mental conflict or a deviation from the cultural norms. Thus, they regulate behavior in their communities.

The goal of a healer is twofold, to help heal a person and for the person to learn to heal the self. The healer in her or his practice guides the client toward establishing a sense of living in harmony. To be in harmony means to stay healthy, to be whole. There is a concept of harmony at the core of the healers' philosophy. This idea is akin to that described as balance by other researchers. The concept of balance is one that stems from the Hippocratian doctrine of the "four humors," blood, phlegm, black bile, and yellow bile. This aspect of curanderismo is well documented by Trotter and Chavira as well as other social scientists, but George Foster was among the first to write about its origin.

Addressing Illness in a Cultural Manner

Arthur Kleinman defines illness as a culturally constructed occurrence with culturally defined parameters and solutions. As such, we can say that there are illness idioms pertinent to particular cultures, and that individuals can access these idioms to express somatized emotional distress. The culture thus defining illness also determines the cure. What this further means is that the bodily experience (of illness) cannot be separated from the cultural engagement of the individual with the world. Illness can be a way for an individual to express fear, suffering, and vulnerability in a culturally accepted manner. Traditional healers are, in a sense, translators of somatized distress. They can "read" the meaning of a person's illness in a way that goes beyond the physical. When a curandero or curandera determines that a client's illness stems from a sense of loss of control, the patient is encouraged to become an active agent in the curing process.

Within Arthur Kleinman's model of illness as a culturally constructed occurrence with culturally defined parameters and solutions, we can say that particular types of illnesses need a curandero's attention because they cannot be healed with conventional medicine. Individuals may tend to gloss over the pressures to acculturate, to deal with economics, labor issues, and social agencies—indeed, all the malevolent forces that people feel coming at them from outside the body, but embodiment of those forces manifests as illness.

This is not to say that all illnesses coming before a healer are free of a biomedical component, but what the healer is frequently concerned with is the underlying spiritual and emotional state of the person as well as the physical. The healing of the client is dependent on the "correct" interpretation of what the client is experiencing. Before any healing ritual occurs, the curandera will interview the individual, asking about marital problems; conflicts with neighbors, friends, or family; and money or legal problems. The healer takes all of this into account in determining the cause of a person's illness, then recommends an appropriate remedy.

People within the Mexican American community generally do not use curanderismo as a substitute for conventional medical services. Rather, many augment a program of Western medical care with visits to a healer. There is a general sentiment that Anglo-American doctors cannot cure "Mexican" illnesses like *susto* (fright), *mal de ojo* (evil eye), *caida de mollera* (sunken fontanel), and *empacho* (surfeit). The healing of these afflictions ties people to the culture and to the values held by the community.

Research and Writing on Curanderismo

The research in curanderismo has changed little over the years. Writings of the 1950s and 1960s describe curanderismo as a folk tradition that would disappear as the Southwest became more urbanized and Chicanas and Chicanos assimilated into the larger dominant Euro-

American society. Often studies of curanderismo were and continue to be clinical in nature and do not describe a legitimate belief system with its own history and systematics. If anything, the focus is to legitimize this folk tradition in accentuating its parallels with European scientific medicine.

Ari Kiev's book, *Curanderismo: Mexican-American Folk Psychiatry*, feeds a stereotypical view of Mexican American culture. William Madsen in 1964 wrote *The Mexican-Americans of South Texas* and is credited with being one of the first to use social class as a variable in understanding curanderismo. But his writing depicts Mexicans and Mexican Americans as superstitious and unsophisticated in their health beliefs and practices. Trotter and Chavira's 1981 book *Curanderismo* is the one most often cited in the literature. It is the first well-structured social science study examining curanderismo in its cultural context by interviewing numerous healers and their clients.

Access by health care providers into the Chicano community continues to be a motivating factor in studies of curanderismo. Topics are often concerned with dual-system access and delivery of medical services and mental-health care to those most likely to use the services of a curandera or curandero.

As a literary device or evocative tool, the curandera is common in literature. The figure lends itself to nostalgia, a cultural constant, and is the epitome of the virgin/whore binary, as Jose Limón demonstrates in his book *Dancing with the Devil* (1994). However, for feminists the curandera is a powerful figure closely aligned with the reworking of the Guadalupe/Tontantzin icon in feminist spirituality. Ann Castillo, in *Massacre of the Dreamers* (1995), references the curandera and ritual practices of healing as a tool of empowerment. The spirituality of curanderismo is appealing in its transformative aspect. Politically and culturally, it can prove an ordered approach for Chicana feminists to heal themselves and their community. It is also one manner in which to make real the differences between white feminist ideology and that expressed by Chicana feminists, in that embedded in curanderismo is the claim to an indigenous past.

Inés Hernández Avila, Yolanda Leyva, Ana Castillo, Gloria Anzaldua, and others have written about women reclaiming their *India* identity, moving toward a new concept of self. The work of Pat Mora, Rudolfo Anaya, Tomas Rivera, and others evoke the motif of the curandera in a positive and powerful manner in their writings.

However, in the social sciences, little work links curanderismo with the acculturation process of individuals as an avenue for identity formation, with issues of gender, or with other variables that define cultural orientation. For example, curanderas and curanderos describe the circumstances by which they became aware of their don, or gift of healing, as periods of chaos and personal turmoil. By accepting their don they consciously adopt a new identity; they become healers and bring to a close this particular traumatic period of their lives. This transition is not part of the standard literature on curanderismo. Yet, it has a direct correlation to the effectiveness of the healer in the community, because the healer, having been healed, can then stand as an affirmation of the tradition's capabilities. For women, becoming a curandera can also mean a change in status. Mexican and Mexican American culture has deep patriarchal roots in which women often hold secondary social and economic positions reinforced by like-minded values in the dominant U.S. society. Curanderas hold an elevated social status within their communities; when a woman becomes a curandera, she leaves that secondary positioning.

In adopting a new identity, the curandera/curandero becomes more a person of the community than a private self. The memory of her or his own healing episode is recreated every time she or he guides an individual through the process of healing. In this fashion, curanderismo seeks not only to heal but also to assist in the creation of a new "self." This new self is grounded in a shared traditional worldview, yet it is simultaneously better able to deal with the multiple and sometimes conflicting cultural and societal systems that are part of life for many Mexicans and Mexican Americans.

See also Botánicas; Health Care Access; *and* Medicine, Traditional.

BIBLIOGRAPHY

Alegria, D., E. Guerra, M. Cervando, et al. "El Hospital Invisible: A Study of Curanderismo." *Archives of General Psychiatry* 34 (1977): 1354–1367.

Castillo, Ana. *Massacre of the Dreamers*. New York: Plume, 1995.

de la Portilla, Elizabeth. "San Antonio as a Magical Crossroads: Healing and Spirituality in the Borderlands." PhD diss., University of Michigan, 2003.

Edgerton, Robert, et al. "Curanderismo in the Metropolis: The Diminished Role of Folk Psychiatry among Los Angeles Mexican-Americans." *American Journal of Psychotherapy*. 24 (1970): 124–134.

Foster, George. "Relationships between Spanish and Spanish-American Folk Medicine." *Journal of Amercian Folklore* 66 (1953): 202–203.

Gaines, Atwood, ed. *Ethnopsychiatry: The Cultural Construction of Professional and Folk Psychiatries*. Albany: State University of New York Press, 1992.

Graham, J. S. "The Role of Curanderismo in the Mexican-American Folk Medicine System in West Texas." In *American Folk Medicine: A Symposium*, edited by Wayland D. Hand. Berkeley: University of California Press, 1976.

Kiev, Ari. *Curanderismo: Mexican-American Folk Psychiatry*. New York: Free Press, 1968.

Kleinman, Arthur. *Patients and Healers in the Context of Culture: An Exploration of the Borderland between Anthropology, Medicine, and Psychiatry*. Berkeley: University of California Press, 1980.

Limón, Jose. *Dancing with the Devil*. Madison: University of Wisconsin Press, 1994.

Madsen, William. *The Mexican-Americans of South Texas*. New York: Holt, Rhinehart, and Winston, 1964.

Malefijt, Annemarie de Waal. *Religion and Culture: An Introduction to the Anthropology of Religion*. (1968) Prospect Heights, Ill.: Waveland, 1989.

Mayers, Raymond S. "Folk Medicine among Elderly Mexican American Women." *Journal of Drug Issues* 19, no. 2 (1989): 283–295.

Rivera, George, Jr. "AIDS and Mexican Folk Medicine." *Sociology and Social Research* 75 (October 1990): 3–7.

Trotter, Robert. "Contrasting Models of the Healer's Role: South Texas Case Examples." *Hispanic Journal of Behavioral Sciences* 4 (1982): 315–317.

Trotter, Robert, and Juan Chavira. *Curanderismo*. Athens: University of Georgia Press, 1981.

Urdaneta Maria, Delia Saldaña, and Ame Winkler. "Mexican-American Perceptions of Severe Mental Illness." *Human Organization* 54, no. 1 (1995): 70–77.

ELIZABETH DE LA PORTILLA

CUSTOMARY LAW. *See* Land Grants.

D

DANCE AND DANCE FORMS. Historically, dance and music have played an important role in Latina and Latino communities. They are perhaps the most visible expressions of the vast Latina and Latino and Caribbean presence in the United States. The rhythms that move Latinas and Latinos are danced and listened to across the country. Caribbean forms such as salsa and merengue, Mexican *quebradita*, and Argentinean tango enjoy national popularity. Mainstream entertainment industries frequently market these cultural forms under a generic "Latin" category. The sensuality inherent in many of these dance forms has often led to superficial conceptions of Latin dance as a purely entertaining and highly sexualized activity. A closer look, however, reveals that dance has played a key role in the forging of cultural, social, and political identities as part of an ongoing struggle to represent Latina and Latino communities.

Latina and Latino dance forms, like Latinas and Latinos themselves, have a long and complex history. Throughout the continuous waves of migration from Latin America and the Caribbean that began in the twentieth century, Latinas and Latinos have cultivated the many folk and popular dance forms they practiced in their countries of origin. Like all migrants, they brought with them their traditional social structures and cultural practices. But new cultural contexts call for different forms of social and political interactions and new self-definitions, so Latinas and Latinos have adapted their cultural forms, transformed existing structures, and created new forms.

Movement as ritual has been an important component of the migration experience. It has served as a practice by which people maintain ties with their past, assert their physical presence in a new environment, negotiate relationships in new social contexts, connect to their spirituality and religiosity, and construct positive alternatives despite conditions of discrimination, racism, and poverty. Africa-derived traditions in particular have been paramount in the creation of collective identities through music and dance.

Latina and Latino dance is not only a fixed representation of the past but also part of the embodied experiences of people creating a new culture, using modern technologies and engaging in transcultural dialogues. How one learns to move and dance is tied to broader cultural practices and to notions of gender, race, and class. The fluidity of dance allows for practices where traditions may be questioned and notions of masculinity and femininity reinforced or negotiated.

A survey of dances practiced in the United States demands that we first recognize the diversity within Latina and Latino communities. It is necessary to take into account history, geography, international economics, and politics. In the early twenty-first century, there were 37 million Latinas and Latinos in the United States, making them the largest minority group in the nation. Cities like New York, Miami, Los Angeles, Phoenix, Chicago, Houston, Springfield (Mass.), and Hartford (Conn.) show a strong Latina and Latino presence with growing political visibility and power. Although Latinas and Latinos are frequently categorized as a homogeneous ethnic group, based largely on their shared Spanish language, Latinas and Latinos in the United States include immigrants from all of the countries of Latin America and the Spanish-speaking Caribbean, as well as their offspring born and raised in the United States. (Those living south of the Mexican border are referred to as Latin Americans.)

Latinas and Latinos encompass a wide range of nationalities with distinct historical trajectories, deeply connected to U.S. economic and political policies. The country of origin, the time and circumstances of migration, race, social class, and where migrants settle in the United States decidedly mark the specifics of each community. Many migrants have come to the United States as political refugees, as migrant workers, as undocumented labor immigrants, or as a direct result of North American expansionism and colonialism. Following is a brief summary of the main characteristics of Latina and Latino migration and some of the dances that have traveled with them.

Mexicans who lived in what are now California, Arizona, New Mexico, and Texas became Mexican Americans when the United States annexed half of Mexico's land after the 1846–1848 United States–Mexican War and the Treaty of Guadalupe Hidalgo. The Mexico–United States border has been an area of social and political tensions ever since. Mexican workers continuously cross the border, legally and illegally, in search of work and better opportunities in the United States, where they are hired as cheap labor and take on service jobs. As a result, the border has been increasingly militarized throughout the years. There are large Mexican American and Chicana and Chicano communities in California, the Southwest, Michigan, and New York, where they dance Mexican versions of *danzón*, *cumbia*, and *son*, including mariachi. They also dance to Tex-Mex, *rancheras*, and Mexican rock. New dance forms, such as the popular quebradita, a fusion of *lambada*, rock, hip-hop, and cumbia, have been created to the sound of *banda* music.

Puerto Rico became a colony of the United States after the 1898 Spanish–American War. The Jones Act of 1917 granted Puerto Ricans U.S. citizenship but did not give them political representation. Millions of Puerto Ricans have migrated to the United States, satisfying the labor demands of U.S. industries, particularly at the height of Operation Bootstrap during the 1940s and 1950s. Many have worked in the needle industry, nurseries, and factories. At the beginning of the twenty-first century, a million Puerto Ricans lived in the New York area, and there were large numbers in Chicago, New Jersey, and Florida. The Puerto Rican migration brought with it Afro–Puerto Rican music and dance traditions, such as the *bomba*, *plena*, and *seis*. Puerto Ricans were key players in the development of salsa and hip-hop in the United States.

Although the Cuban presence in the United States dates back to the nineteenth century, the 1960s saw a massive migration of predominantly professional, upper- to middle-class Cubans who left the island after the 1959 Cuban Revolution. In its fight against Communism, the U.S. government granted automatic political asylum and subsidies to all Cubans who sought them. The 1980 Mariel boatlift brought a second wave of migration, this time made up mostly of black working-class Cubans known as *Marielitos*. In 1994, yet another substantial exodus of Cubans took to the ocean in rafts hoping to reach U.S. soil, where they expected to be granted political asylum. The largest concentration of Cubans is in Miami, but there are also many Cubans in New York and New Jersey. Afro-Cuban rhythms, dance forms, and religious rituals have been of great importance in Latina and Latino dance and culture. The Afro-Cuban religion *santería*, with its numerous dances in honor of each of the *orishas* (deities), is widely practiced by Cubans and other Latinas and Latinos in the United States. The Cuban rumba, son, *cha-cha-chá*, and mambo have strongly influenced other music and dance forms.

Thousands of Colombians have fled the decades-long civil war in that country. Panamanians and Dominicans, who have also experienced American military invasions, have migrated in great numbers, largely for economic reasons. There are vibrant Colombian, Panamanian, and Dominican communities in the New York area. The Colombian music and dance form cumbia with its many regional variations is widespread in the United States, as are the Colombian salsa and *vallenato*. Panamanians dance the *mejorana*, the *tamborito*, the Panamanian cumbia, and the *punto*. Dominicans dance *bachata* and merengue. Merengue is one of the best-known music and dance forms among Latinas and Latinos, and its simple, even step makes it accessible to dancers of different backgrounds.

Fleeing long, bloody wars in Central America, in the 1980s Salvadorans, Nicaraguans, Guatemalans, and Hondurans arrived in the United States in great numbers. With the United States deeply involved in these wars, many were granted political asylum as a means of accomplishing a broader foreign-policy objective. Others who were escaping prosecution and torture by U.S.–backed military juntas or paramilitary forces, such as the Nicaraguan Contras, were assisted by the Sanctuary Movement, a grassroots organization in the United States. Many Central Americans have established communities in California, Texas, Florida, and throughout the Northeast, where they dance son, *punta rock*, and other popular forms.

Cultural Encounters

Although Latin American dance forms are frequently referred to in national terms—the Dominican merengue or the Colombian cumbia, for example—they are often the result of cultural encounters, creolization, and transculturation, whereby different influences have merged to create new sounds and body expressions. These forms in turn "travel" and are consumed and reproduced in other places. As music and dance cross national borders, they are claimed and appropriated by people who share similar histories and life conditions. This may explain, for example, why Ismael Rivera, the Afro–Puerto Rican singer who popularized bomba and plena in the 1950s, was revered in Peru, Panama, and the United States, where there are significant Afro populations.

As dance forms migrate with Latin American and Caribbean dancers and musicians, they are transformed and developed in the United States. They are also consumed by U.S. culture, thus influencing North American society. Cuban rumba, for example, entered U.S. mass culture in the 1930s. It was the first of a vast range of Latin American and Caribbean dance forms that became popular with both Latinas and Latinos and non-Latinas and non-Latinos. In the 1940s, the Argentinean tango and the Colombian *bambuco* were danced alongside the swing, the foxtrot, the waltz, the calypso from Trinidad, and the bunny hop. The Puerto Rican plena and the Argentinean *milonga* were introduced during the 1960s.

One decisive factor in the evolution of Latina and Latino music and dance in the United States is the long, creative relationship between Latinas and Latinos and African Americans. Mexican Americans and African Americans in California, for example, shared, negotiated, and transformed music, dance, and other cultural forms during the 1940s and 1950s. The Mexican American *pachuco* culture of postwar Los Angeles was in close dialogue with the African American hipsters of Los Angeles. In the 1950s, Mexican Americans and African Americans created new cultural styles for America's youth, including car clubs, fashion trends, and dances such as the pachuco hop, the hully gully, and the *corrido rock*.

Puerto Ricans and African Americans in New York City have enjoyed ongoing cultural collaborations since the beginning of the twentieth century. James Reese Europe, an African American musician and bandleader, recruited black Puerto Rican musicians during World War I to join what came to be known as the 369th Infantry "Harlem Hellfighters" band. The group is credited with introducing American jazz to European audiences. Among the Puerto Ricans recruited by Europe was Rafael Hernández. One of Puerto Rico's most important composers, he wrote the quintessential Puerto Rican tune "Preciosa" in New York City.

Throughout the second half of the twentieth century, Cubans, Puerto Ricans, and other Latinas and Latinos and African Americans in New York City continued to influence and enrich each other's cultural forms. Their collaboration was vital for the emergence of important music and dance forms such as Latin jazz in the 1950s, a synthesis of Afro-Cuban rhythms and African American jazz; Latin boogaloo in the 1960s, which mixed mambo rhythms with black rock and roll; the hustle with its Latin variation known for its cha-cha flavor; salsa, which in the 1970s combined existing rhythms into something new; and hip-hop in the 1980s. These transcultural dialogues have allowed marginalized Latina and Latino communities to participate in the development of new dance forms that have influenced American culture and challenged notions of blackness and *latinidad*.

Salsa is a particularly interesting Latina and Latino dance form. Its music and dance elements date back to slavery and colonialism in the Caribbean. Its polyrhythms, as well as its vocal and instrumental call-and-response format, place it squarely among Afro-Caribbean sacred and secular cultural traditions. It is the result of a long history of migrations, including those of plantation slaves who were forced to relocate from island to island, of agricultural workers displaced from the countryside to urban centers, and of the many Caribbean people who journeyed

to the United States. Music and dance traveled with these migrations, bringing to New York City the sounds of the Cuban rumba and son, the Puerto Rican bomba, plena, and seis, and the Dominican merengue, among others. As these rhythms interacted with each other and with groups of musicians from other cultures, particularly African American jazz bands and theater orchestras, a new sound emerged. This sound integrated already existing rhythms into a new musical configuration. When salsa emerged in the 1970s, the overwhelming majority of Latinas and Latinos in New York City were Puerto Ricans. But Cubans, Dominicans, and other Latinas and Latinos who frequented dance clubs featuring salsa bands recognized these rhythms and forms and took to the dance floor in a frenzy. The internationalization of salsa has been massive. At the beginning of the twenty-first century, there are Puerto Rican, Cuban, Colombian, Venezuelan, African, and Japanese salsa bands with distinct styles and sounds.

In the late 1970s and 1980s, Puerto Ricans, African Americans, and West Indians living in the Bronx developed musical, visual, and dance forms that came to be known as hip-hop. Further study of the history of some of the hip-hop dances, such as breaking, uprocking, and electric boogie, as well as its dancers, known as b-boys and b-girls, allows us to closely examine how cultural and political identities are constructed and negotiated in dialogue with other American cultural forms and pan-Latino experiences.

Roots

Latina and Latino dance forms reveal a complex trajectory of international economics, politics, cultural encounters, and hybridization. Contemporary forms have their roots in preconquest indigenous traditions in Central and South America; African music, dance, and religious forms practiced throughout the Americas; and European cultural forms brought by the Spanish, British, Portuguese, Dutch, and French to the American continent and the Caribbean region. In many instances, these dance forms were themselves the result of earlier cultural hybridization. Spaniards, for example, had close cultural contact with Africans throughout the eight centuries that Moors occupied the Iberian Peninsula.

The mixing of indigenous peoples, African slaves, and Europeans created a wide range of racial categories throughout the Americas. For example, the mixing of Spanish and indigenous peoples in Central and South America resulted in mestizos. The mixing of Europeans and Africans found in the Caribbean, as well as along the Atlantic and Pacific coasts of Central and South America, resulted in mulattoes. The history of the conquest of the Americas and the exchanges between Europeans, indigenous peoples, and African slaves and their descendants is full of violence, conflict, and oppression. However, this history is also one of great cultural creativity and production, which was perhaps even a means of survival. As a result, communities throughout the immense geographical territory that encompasses Latin America and the Caribbean have developed a vast quantity of distinct dance forms and practices. Noted below are some of the many folk and popular dances transplanted to Latina and Latino contexts in the United States.

The people and cultural traditions of Cuba, Puerto Rico, the Dominican Republic, and the Caribbean coast running from the Yucatán in Mexico to Venezuela have a pronounced African quality. Many of the African slaves brought by force to the Americas came from West Africa, particularly the Kongo-Angola region. They worked in mines, on plantations, and in domestic service. Whenever possible, slaves practiced their religious ceremonies, in which music and dance were vital. Because of the heavy flow of slave migration, the music and dance forms found throughout the Americas share basic qualities while maintaining distinct variations. Some of the most salient characteristics of Africa-derived forms are the prominence of the drum; the use of polyrhythms; the isolation of body parts, which respond to the multilayered rhythms with sharp, staccato gestures or slow, sensual movements; vocal and instrumental call-and-response; improvisation of both music and dance; and circular formation of dancers and musicians. These forms have historically provided cultural spaces where bodies can assert cultural, religious, and political alternatives difficult to claim in

political terms. As a result, the transgressive elements of Afro-Latino dance forms such as the Puerto Rican bomba, the Cuban rumba, the Dominican *palo*, and hip-hop's b-boying (commercially known as break dance) have been met with suspicion, fear, and repression from the dominant society.

Many of the dances of the Garifuna in Belize have African traits, such as *punta*, which is danced at wakes and festivities, as well as the religious dance *duga*. The cumbia, of Bantu origin, is a couple-dance with a fast beat performed in the Caribbean regions of Colombia and Panama. Although cumbia originated in Colombia, its orchestra music had tremendous success in Mexico, and over time Mexican cumbia developed a distinct style. The tamborito is danced in Panama; the *tambor*, an improvised couple-dance, is performed in Venezuela. Cuban music and dance, which has been so influential in the dissemination of Caribbean genres, include son, rumba, mambo, *guaracha*, and cha-cha-chá. In Cuban and other Caribbean music, the *clave* (key), the rhythm pattern to which other rhythms relate, is recognized and danced to all over the world. The Dominican merengue, similar to the Haitian *mereng*, is a syncretic form fusing African and European influences. Bachata, associated with barrio and street culture, is popular among working-class Dominicans. The Afro–Puerto Rican bomba is characterized by the dialogue between the dance and the drum. The dancer challenges the drummer with steps and gestures that require specific drum sounds. The plena is a Puerto Rican urban music and dance form. Its instrumentation

MAMBO DANCE CONTEST. (© Monika Graff/The Image Works)

allows it to be mobile. It came to be known as the people's newspaper because the lyrics speak of current events.

The Pacific coast along Colombia, Ecuador, and Peru is also characterized by African influences and traditions. Afro-Peruvian dance and music, for example, developed in communities of slaves brought to work in the coastal mines of Peru. One of the Africa-derived dances practiced in that country is the *festejo*. The *cajón*, a box on which the percussionist sits astride, leaning down to play, accompanies many of these dances. Some of Bolivia's African-influenced dances, such as the *saya*, danced during carnival, date back to African slavery in the seventeenth and eighteenth centuries. Punta rock is a contemporary version of punta, the traditional Afro-Belizean dance and music form. The music has been transformed, but the dance steps remain the same. In the early twentieth century, Afro-Brazilian samba emerged as a commercialized carnival dance form; it is now danced all over the world. The lambada developed in the 1980s out of northeastern Brazilian dances such as the *puladinho, debocle,* and *gafieria*. Its worldwide popularity as an elaborate club dance lasted until the mid-1990s.

Mestizo and indigenous traditions are found in many Latin American dances. One of the most popular couple-dances in Guatemala is the son, which is played on the marimba. *El carbonero*, danced in El Salvador to lyrics depicting indigenous coal miners of the Teisalco volcano area, is similar to Mexican folkloric dances in the way women move their skirts. The *punto Guanacaste* is Costa Rica's national dance. Bambuco is a Colombian Andean dance that developed out of *mestizaje*. The plains of Colombia and Venezuela have large areas devoted to cattle ranching, with its distinct way of life. Here the *joropo* is popular. The dancers pair up but do not embrace while they perform intricate footwork based on the Spanish *zapateo*. The *currulao* is a Colombian dance that uses handkerchiefs in a way similar to the Andean *cueca*, even though the two are not directly related. *Chicha*, a fusion of urban cumbia, traditional highland *huayno*, and rock, emerged in Peru in the early 1960s. It was popular in the 1980s and became an expression of social frustration for Peruvian youth and those suffering from racial discrimination in Peruvian society. Vallenato is the most popular regional music and dance form in Colombia's Atlantic Coast region. In this dance, the partners hold their bodies close together while moving to five different rhythms: *paseo*, cumbia, son, *puya*, and merengue. The *pindín* emerged in the mid-twentieth century in Panama as a new music and dance form based on folk rhythms such as the tamborito. It is similar to the Colombian vallenato in its dance steps and use of the accordion. In the nineteenth century, the Argentinean and Uruguayan tango developed from the merging of African, European, and native Argentinean forms. Its early development took place in brothels, cafes, and dance halls in poor and working-class neighborhoods. The dancers display intricate step patterns and partnering skills while tightly embracing.

Mexican indigenous dances draw their traditions from the Olmec, Maya, Toltec, and Aztec. These ceremonial dances, known as *danzas*, commemorate secular and religious activities, such as the birth of the sun, harvest, hunting, fishing, combat, victory, marriage, childbirth, and death. Another secular indigenous dance is *el volador*, the dance of the flying pole. The dance takes place on a small platform atop a thirty-foot pole, which the dancers reach by means of a rope ladder. The *sandunga*, originally performed at funerals, is a solemn religious dance.

The intricate heelwork of the Mexican zapateo is clearly Spanish in origin. The *jarabe* became the national dance of Mexico in 1920. The native version of the dance is practiced at feasts and weddings. The Spanish version is a courtship dance widely known as the *jarabe tapatío* (Mexican hat dance). At the beginning of the dance, the man throws his hat in front of the feet of the woman. She puts it on, and they dance together. There are other versions, such as the jarabe of the bottle, the jarabe of the knot, the *jarabe tlaxcalteca*, and the *jarabe michoacano*. *Los moros y los cristianos*, performed by four men, is an historical dance that traces the conflict between the Moors and the Christians. The *huapango* has local variations from Hidalgo to Veracruz. Huapango is the Aztec name for the platform on which the dance takes place. As a rule, to begin the dance the man approaches the woman and offers his hat. The dancers perform a *zapateado*, tapping with their feet to create a counter-rhythm to the instrumental pattern.

In the Andean regions of Ecuador, Peru, Bolivia, northern Argentina, and northern Chile, music and dance are prominent features of life-cycle fiestas. Although Andean music is heard all over the world, the dances that accompany it are seldom performed outside the Andean region. Summer and winter solstices are marked with rituals in Peru, Bolivia, and Ecuador. Other rituals include *Pachama* (Mother Earth), *Danza de la Culebra* (Serpent Dance), and the Festival of Yucca for San Juan. In the improvisational *Punchay Kashwa* (Circle Dance) of southern Peru, groups of men and women face each other in separate semicircles. While the men play *charangos* (mandolins), both groups dance and sing in a rhythmic pattern. The cueca, a courtship dance in which dancers swing handkerchiefs in small circles over their heads, is found throughout Peru, Bolivia, Chile, Argentina, and Paraguay. Huayno is the most widely known dance of Inca origin, though it has undergone transformations since the Spanish conquest. This Quechua dance rhythm suggests a hopped-up waltz. The music is uplifting, although the lyrics may be sad or contain double meanings.

Internationalization

In the mid-twentieth century, numerous folk-dance groups were established throughout Latin America. Latinas and Latinos have formed similar groups and perform the same dances in the United States. In theory, folk dances are still practiced in their original forms, as the dance is taught from generation to generation. In reality, however, numerous changes may occur over time, and liberties are taken for the sake of formal stage and commercial presentations. Theatrical performances include complex choreographies, costumes, and artistic innovations. These formal presentations play an important role in community festivities and representations of culture.

The radio and record industries have been instrumental in disseminating dance music. They enable people to relate to music in a different way. People can collect favorite dance tunes, play them at their discretion, learn the lyrics by heart, and dance to the music at will. The boom box also has been important because of the mobility it grants dancers, allowing people to play music in the street and organize community events around music and dance. The boom box has played a key role in spreading hip-hop from the block parties in the Bronx, New York, where it was developed, to the informal dance stages created by b-boys in streets, parks, and subway stations across the nation, where the dancers perform for money. Parks and beaches also provide public spaces where families and friends gather around radios and boom boxes to dance and listen to music, even bringing their own instruments to play along.

The dissemination of national rhythms and musical forms—from *Tejano* music in the 1940s; tango, plena, and mambo in the 1950s; salsa in the 1970s; merengue in the 1980s; and hip-hop in the 1980s and 1990s—gave rise to ongoing musical dialogues that have influenced and shaped the dance forms they accompany. As entertainment industries like film and theater take interest in what are deemed marketable forms, Latina and Latino dances are adapted for mainstream mass consumption by both Latinas and Latinos and non-Latinas and non-Latinos. The tango, for example, is taught in ballroom-dance classes across the United States and performed in Broadway musical productions, such as *Forever Tango*. The musical *West Side Story* (1957), which depicts Puerto Ricans in New York City, both reinforced stereotypes and brought visibility to the Puerto Rican community and Puerto Rican artists such as Rita Moreno.

The migration experience incites the transformation and adaptation of familiar cultural forms. The new contexts in which these forms are practiced call for negotia-

tions as people incorporate new ways of behaving, seeing the world, and moving and experiencing the body. The migration experience can deepen ties with some traditions and cause a total break from others. Communities forge cultural identities that respond to the specificities of both their individual and collective experiences.

The Day of the Dead (October 31–November 2) is one of the religious holidays celebrated by Mexican American and other Latina and Latino communities. Festivities include picnics, music, and dancing. The Fiesta of Our Lady of Guadalupe (December 12) is celebrated in communities in California, New Mexico, and Kansas, among other places. Puerto Ricans in Florida hold a three-day celebration for the Fiesta de San Juan Bautista (June 24). Folk dancers with their bright, colorful costumes perform at patriotic celebrations of independence and at events like the festivities in Miami's Calle Oche, which is massively attended by Cubans as well as Nicaraguans, Salvadorans, Hondurans, and Guatemalans. The Puerto Rican Day parades in New York City and Chicago's Humboldt Park and the Dominican Day parades in Manhattan and the Bronx have become traditions where people literally take over the streets as they dance to popular rhythms.

As a consequence of migration, Latinas and Latinos who may not otherwise have contact with each other find themselves practicing their separate cultural forms in shared neighborhoods, creating pan–Latina and Latino experiences. They also practice these forms alongside those of other racial and ethnic groups. For example, Central Americans may dance punta rock alongside Jamaican *soca*, Dominican merengue, and Afro-beat rhythms like *soukous* from Zaire. In the midst of mixtures and transformations, the public presentation of traditional folk dances holds symbolic meaning. As immigrants struggle to claim a space within U.S. society, with its particular social and racial structures, folk dance offers a cohesive representation of their own cultures.

The process by which dance, like language, food, or music, becomes part of a collective identity is complex and persistent. In the United States, dance has facilitated pan–Latina and Latino experiences and endeavors that transcend geographical and national identities. For example, the military dictator Rafael Trujillo, who ruled the Dominican Republic either as president or as unelected military dictator from 1930 to 1961, instituted merengue as the country's official music and dance. Although he prohibited migration during his rule, some *merengueros* made it to New York City, where they became hits in popular Manhattan dance halls like the Palladium, which were frequented by Puerto Ricans and other Latinas and Latinos. This is the same dance club where the legendary Cuban musician Beny Moré and the Puerto Rican band

Cortijo y Su Combo played together for crowds of over-joyed Latina and Latino dancers in the 1950s. Today, a Guatemalan man might dance the Dominican bachata with a Puerto Rican woman in Trenton, New Jersey. Or Mexicans and Central Americans in the Southwest might dance a version of cumbia that has been so transformed that it hardly resembles the original dance from Colombia. The cultural and political processes by which individuals and communities adopt the rhythms and movements of other groups are complex. It may be that through this act, Latinas and Latinos negotiate collective identities within a society that clumps them together under one large umbrella called "Latin."

See also **Bachata; Banda; Black-Latino Relations; Bomba; Break Dancing; Cumbia; Latin Jazz; Mambo; Merengue; Music, Afro-Caribbean; Plena, La;** *and* **Salsa.**

BIBLIOGRAPHY

Aparicio, Frances, and Cándida Jáquez, eds. *Musical Migrations: Transnationalism and Cultural Hybridity in Latin/o America*. New York: Palgrave Macmillan, 2003.

Aparicio, Frances, and Susana Chávez-Silverman, eds. *Tropicalizations: Transcultural Representations of Latinindad*. Hanover, N.H.: University Press of New England, 1997.

Austerlitz, Paul. *Merengue: Dominican Music and Dominican Identity*. Philadelphia: Temple University Press, 1997.

Broughton, Simon, and Mark Ellingham, eds. *World Music: The Rough Guide*. Volume 2, *Latin and North America, Caribbean, India, Asia, and Pacific*. London: Rough Guides, 2000.

Delgado, Celeste Fraser, and José Esteban Muñoz, eds. *Everynight Life: Culture and Dance in Latin/o America*. Durham, N.C.: Duke University Press, 1997.

Flores, Juan. *From Bomba to Hip-Hop: Puerto Rican Culture and Latino Identity*. New York: Columbia University Press, 2000.

Gilroy, Paul. *The Black Atlantic: Modernity and Double Consciousness*. Cambridge, Mass.: Harvard University Press, 1993.

Glasser, Ruth. *My Music Is My Flag: Puerto Rican Musicians and Their New York Communities, 1917–1940*. Berkeley, Los Angeles, London: University of California Press, 1995.

González, Juan. *Harvest of Empire: A History of Latinos in America*. New York: Viking Penguin, 2000.

Perkins, William Eric, ed. *Droppin' Science: Critical Essays on Rap Music and Hip-Hop Culture*. Philadelphia: Temple University Press, 1996.

Quintero Rivera, Angel G. *¡Salsa, sabor, y control! Sociología de la música "tropical."* Mexico and Spain: Siglo Veintiuno Editores, 1998.

Rivera, Raquel. *New York Ricans from the Hip-Hop Zone*. New York: Palgrave Macmillan, 2003.

Roberts, John Storm. *The Latin Tinge: The Impact of Latin American Music on the United States*. New York: Oxford University Press, 1979.

Sloat, Susana, ed. *Caribbean Dance from Abakuá to Zouk: How Movement Shapes Identity*. Gainesville: University Press of Florida, 2002.

ALICIA DÍAZ

DAY OF THE DEAD. *See* **Dia de los Muertos.**

DE ARGÜELLO V. THE UNITED STATES. When California was still under Mexican rule, José de Argüello, the commandant of the Presidio of San Francisco, occupied the ranch known as "Las Pulgas" as early as 1795 based on a license from the governor of the province, Governor Diego de Borica, who awarded him Rancho de las Pulgas, an area of 35,260 acres, in 1795. The Ohlone, whom the Spaniards called *Coastanoans*, or coast dwellers, originally inhabited the area that included most of the land now known as the City of Menlo Park. As early as 1797, soldiers pastured and herded the king's horses on this rancho. In 1804, soldiers under the command of José de Argüello resided in huts on the land. The neighboring mission of Santa Clara sometimes pastured sheep on the Argüello ranch. Upon Argüello's death circa 1820, the rancho passed to his son, Luis Argüello. Meanwhile, the crown pastured its cattle on the ranch until about 1821, when the governor removed the king's cattle and permitted Luis Argüello to remain in sole possession of the rancho. In practice, Argüello's cattle wandered to the mountains and the adjacent valley, known as the Canada de Raymundo. The site was on the San Francisco Bay, and its occupancy followed the Spanish colonial custom of the presidio commanders appropriating the best property around the presidios.

When Luis Argüello succeeded his father in ownership, apparently the original proof of title was lost, something that was not uncommon at the time. In 1820 or 1821, Governor Pablo Vincente de Sola made a new title to Luis Argüello. After the death of Luis Argüello in 1830, his family remained in possession of the rancho.

In August 1835, a man by the name of Alvisu petitioned the Mexican governor for a grant of the Canada de Raymundo. The governor notified Argüello's widow and heirs of Alvisu's petition. The Argüellos responded, and their attorney appeared before the governor to protest against the grant to Alvisu. On November 26, 1835, the governor of California ordered that the petitioner should have a tract of land without specifying the boundaries and issued an order the next day, which had the formalities of a definitive title. At this point, the Rancho de las Pulgas allegedly composed twelve square leagues of land, one-third of which fronted the bay of San Francisco, was bordered by San Francisquito Creek to the south and San Mateo to the north, and extended back from the bay some three leagues to the sierra or range of mountains, and included the valley, or Canada de Raymundo. The alcalde made a report in which three witnesses testified as to what composed the Argüello grant. There was no dispute as to the Argüellos occupying Rancho of Las Pulgas, and the testimony suggests that the Argüellos also occupied the Canada de Raymundo. The first witness definitely included the land west of Monte Redondo and Canada "Raymundo," which would encompass the valley. The other two essentially corroborated the testimony of the first witness. This report seemingly confirmed the findings of the governor, who refused to cede the valley to Alvizu.

Meanwhile, the United States–Mexican War of 1846–1848 brought a change and established U.S. rule over California and the rest of the Southwest, beginning an assault on the property rights of Mexicans left behind. *De Argüello v. United States* (1855) was one of a series of cases ignoring the Treaty of Guadalupe (1848) and its letter of Protocol of Queretaro, which guaranteed former Mexican citizens equal protection of their property rights. The California Land Act of 1851, which required each grantee to present his or her claim, relied on consistent and equal application of law to protect interests. However, the act specified that it would rely on archival evidence and exclude oral evidence. Accordingly, the Argüellos filed their claim and expected to prevail. But the commissioners and the court only confirmed the Argüellos' legal title to the Las Pulgas grant and not to the valley. The question on the Argüellos' appeal was whether they proved title to the Valley of Raymundo or any land west of the boundary adjudged to by the Mexican authorities. The U.S. Supreme Court upheld the lower court and found that there was no trace or evidence of a grant from the Mexican governor. The Court held that the Argüellos' occupancy of the land was not evidence of ownership. The Supreme Court found:

> There is no sufficient evidence to satisfy our minds that any grant was ever made by Governor Borrica, or by De Sola. The archives of government show no trace of evidence of such a grant from either of them. They have not proved the existence of it by the testimony of anyone who had seen it; they assume the existence and loss of the documents, from the fact that none can now be found.

The courts discounted oral evidence and insisted on archival proof, which was a strict standard considering the slowness of the Spanish and Mexican bureaucracies. It also was commonplace for documents to be lost through natural disasters or human error. The reader must take the case in context with other land grant cases and consider the courts' role in bringing about an economic, political, and social transference of power.

See also Land Grants *and* Treaty of Guadalupe Hidalgo.

BIBLIOGRAPHY

Alfieri, Anthony V. "Race and Races: Cases and Resources for a Diverse America." *California Law Review* 89, no. 5 (October 2001): 1605–1620.

Luna, Guadalupe. " 'This Land Belongs to Me': Chicanas, Land Grant Adjudication, and the Treaty of Guadalupe Hidalgo." *Harvard Latino Law Review* 3 (Fall 1999): 115.

Perea, Juan F., Richard Delgado, Angela P. Harris, and Stephanie M. Wildman, eds. *Race and Races: Cases and Resources for a Diverse America*. Saint Paul, Minn.: West Group, 2000.

Ruiz Cameron, Christopher David. "One Hundred Fifty Years of Solitude: Reflections on the End of the History Academy's Dominance of Scholarship on the Treaty of Guadalupe Hidalgo." *Southwestern Journal of Law & Trade in the Americas* 5 (Spring 1998): 83.

Solidad De Arguello, Maria De La, et al. *Claimants and Appellants v. The United States. The United States, Appellants* v. *Maria De La Solidad De Arguello et al.* Supreme Court of the United States 59 U.S. 539; 15 L. Ed. 478; 1855 U.S. LEXIS 730; 18 HOW 539.

RODOLFO F. ACUÑA

DECADE OF THE HISPANIC. "Decade of the Hispanic" is the phrase used to designate the 1980s as the period in which the growing Latina and Latino population first came to national prominence. It represented the first time that the Latino and Latina community was widely viewed as a national political, economic, and cultural force.

There are conflicting claims about the origin of the term. Its first use has been attributed to a quote from the Cuban American writer Maria Elena Torano in a 1978 article in *U.S. News & World Report* on Latina and Latino appointees in the Carter Administration. It was also a marketing theme used by the politically ultraconservative Adolph Coors Brewing Company in the Los Angeles area in 1983 on billboards proclaiming Coors "the beer of the Decade of the Hispanic." The term was also used in a cover story in *Time* magazine. *Hispanic Business* magazine, founded in 1980, declared in 1989 that the eighties had been the "Decade of the Hispanic Entrepreneur."

Within the Latino and Latina community, outside of the business sector, the declaration of the "Decade of the Hispanic" was viewed cynically as simply a marketing term that masked the many problems besetting this population. This sentiment prompted the Chicano comedy troupe Culture Clash to come up with the widely quoted one-liner, "The decade of the Hispanic turned out to be a weekend sponsored by Coors." The use of this term also generated much discussion about the appropriateness of the word "Hispanic" to describe this nationally diverse population and of whether they represented a monolithic voting bloc.

The new national attention that Latinas and Latinos began to attract in the 1980s stemmed largely from a dramatic population growth rate of 61 percent in the preceding decade, which actually slowed to a less dramatic but still impressive 53 percent in the 1980s. By 1990, the Latina and Latino population was conservatively numbered by the Census Bureau at 22.4 million, almost 9 percent of the total U.S. population.

However, the socioeconomic status of Latinas and Latinos was troubling to many during this period. By the end of the Decade of the Hispanic, 22.3 percent of Latino and Latina families lived in poverty, compared to less than 10 percent of non-Latino and non-Latina families. In 1990, the median family income of Latinas and Latinos was $25,064, compared to $35,225 for the total U.S. population. This was also the decade in which the AIDS epidemic began, which has taken a major toll on Latinas and Latinos to this day.

While Latinas and Latinos made many gains in that decade, the overall picture was mixed. The number of Latina and Latino elected officials between 1984 and 1989, for example, rose from 3,128 to 3,783, mostly at the local level, but this represented less than 1 percent of all elected positions in the United States, despite the fact that Latinas and Latinos made up 9 percent of the population. There were only ten Latinas and Latinos in the U.S. House of Representatives and none in the U.S. Senate. This political underrepresentation persisted throughout the decade, despite the fact that Latina and Latino voter registration increased ten times faster than the national average between 1984 and 1988.

Latinas and Latinos perhaps made the most gains in this decade in the cultural sphere. It was a period that was predated by major mainstream productions like Luis Valdéz's *Zoot Suit*, which began as a local play in Los Angeles in 1978, went to Broadway in 1979, and later became a movie. In the 1980s, movies like *Stand and Deliver*, *La Bamba*, *The Milagro Beanfield War*, and *Fort Apache: The Bronx* were released; Latina and Latino actors starred in popular television series like *L.A. Law* and *Miami Vice*; musical groups like Los Lobos crossed over to the Anglo market, and performers like Linda Ronstadt began recording in Spanish. But in reaction to these cultural inroads and the growth of the Spanish language, the 1980s was also the decade where English-only laws were passed in eighteen states.

Perhaps most symbolic of this decade was the trajectory of the political career of Henry Cisneros. He was elected mayor of San Antonio in 1981 and a few years later was a rising national star in the Democratic Party, with his name being mentioned frequently as that party's first Latino or Latina vice presidential candidate. However, in 1984, when he was mentioned as a possible running mate for presidential candidate Walter Mondale, he became entangled in a scandalous and high-profile extramarital affair that derailed his higher political aspirations for years, and in 1988 he dropped out of politics for a time after serving four terms as mayor.

But probably the most important factor in the Latina and Latino cynicism about the Decade of the Hispanic was that it coincided with the election of Ronald Reagan and the ascendance of Republican conservatism. That party's campaign to undo New Deal and civil rights reforms developed momentum nationally just as Latinas and Latinos were poised to benefit the most from them.

In 1986, the Congress passed the landmark Immigration Reform and Control Act, which offered amnesty to many undocumented immigrants and at the same time increased employment discrimination against Latinas and Latinos because of its provision of sanctions against employers.

The Decade of the Hispanic was significant in that it was the first national recognition of the potential influence of the Latina and Latino population, which took another decade and the next century to be most fully acknowledged and exerted. It has remained a symbol of this early unfulfilled potential, of the damage caused by a U.S. nativist backlash, and of the dangers of corporate marketing hype and manipulation of vulnerable populations.

See also Census; Coors Boycott; Culture Clash; *and* Demographics.

BIBLIOGRAPHY

"Hispanics Make Their Move." *U.S. News & World Report* (August 24, 1981): 60.

del Olmo, Frank. "Commentary: Latino "Decade" Moves into '90s." *Los Angeles Times* (Nuestro Tiempo Edition), December 14, 1989, p. 1.

Roberts, Katherine, and Richard Levine. "Ideas & Trends: Coors Extends a $300 Million Peace Offering." *New York Times*, November 4, 1984, p. 23.

United States Census Bureau. *We, The American . . . Hispanics.* Washington, D.C.: United States Census Bureau, September 1993.

ANGELO FALCÓN

DELAWARE. The most widely known fact about Delaware is encapsulated in its nickname: the First State. While it is true that in 1776 the colony of Delaware became the first to declare itself a state, it carries its First State designation because it was the first to ratify the new U.S. Constitution, in 1787. A less commonly known fact is that Delaware is also called the Diamond State because of its wealth relative to its size; only Rhode Island is smaller. From the late eighteenth through the mid-twentieth centuries, Delaware's economy was centered on agriculture and manufacturing industries. State legislative changes in the 1980s added to the state's economy by luring many large New York banks to establish subsidiaries in Delaware. New jobs and a solid economic infrastructure were thus created. When considering Latinos and Latinas of Delaware, the name Diamond State takes on added meaning. Delawarean Latinos and Latinas are integrally woven into every sector of the state's social and economic fabric, and the Latina and Latino communities, though small, are richly diverse. This diversity found among Latinas and Latinos living in Delaware comes from those generations of Latinas and Latinos—mainly from Puerto Rico, Mexico, and Cuba—whose histories constitute Delaware's Hispanic heritage and from the numbers of newly arriving

Latinas and Latinos from these and other Latin American countries whose fluency in Spanish and recent memories of "home" renew collective Latina and Latino identity.

Delaware's overall population currently ranks forty-sixth in the nation. U.S. census figures tally a little over thirty-seven thousand Latinas and Latinos living in Delaware. Not factoring in racial difference, Latinas and Latinos make up a mere 4.8 percent of Delaware's population. Despite these modest numbers, Delaware's Latina and Latino communities mirror national trends. The largest group, constituting 1.8 percent of the total Latina and Latino population, are of Puerto Rican origin, followed closely by Mexicans at 1.7 percent and Cubans at 0.1 percent. The remaining 1.2 percent comes from Central and South American countries. One way to begin to understand the historical presence of this increasingly diverse population is to look at organizations dedicated to Delawarean Latinas and Latinos.

The Latin American Community Center (LACC) in Wilmington was established by first-generation Latinas and Latinos in 1969, on the heels of the struggle for civil rights led by African Americans. At the time of its founding, the main directive of the LACC was to help Latinas and Latinos assimilate into the English-speaking mainstream. To that end, the LACC provided English-as-a-second-language instruction and developed programs to help families manage the opposing pressures of cultural preservation and cultural change. The LACC continues to serve a diverse community of Latinas and Latinos with close ties to Puerto Rico, Mexico, Cuba, Guatemala, the Dominican Republic, and other Central and South American countries.

Spanish-speaking Latinas and Latinos in Delaware's three counties of Kent, Sussex, and New Castle are well served by the Hispanic media. Spanish-language and bilingual television, radio, newspaper, and magazine coverage connects Delawarean Latinas and Latinos to each other, to Latinas and Latinos in the bordering states of New Jersey, Pennsylvania, and Maryland, and to Latin America. With the aim of preserving ties to Latin America and of archiving Delaware's Hispanic heritage, in September 2004, the Delaware Historical Society Museum launched what will be an annual exhibit displaying historical artifacts documenting Delaware's Latina and Latino experience.

Remarkably, Delaware has a third nickname also applicable to its Latina and Latino communities: Small Wonder. On a small scale, Latinos and Latinas in Delaware typify the U.S. Latina and Latino experience in terms of diversity, historical presence, and ties to Latin America.

See also **Census; Immigrant Incorporation into U.S. Society;** *and* **Immigration.**

BIBLIOGRAPHY

Borland, Katherine. *Creating Community: Hispanic Migration to Rural Delaware*. Wilmington: Delaware Heritage Press, 2001.

LAURA C. VALDEZ-PAGLIARO

DEMOGRAPHICS. Demography, the scientific study of populations, has been one of the most important and most common ways, in the broadest sense, that the Latino and Latina experience in the United States is discussed and understood. A recurring theme in this regard for Latinos and Latinas is the notion of "demography as destiny" and the role of other determinants of social, political, and economic policy.

Population growth and size have defined much of the discourse on the Latino and Latina community, particularly since the release of the Census 2000 numbers. At the opening of the new millennium, the Census Bureau reported a Latino and Latina population of 35.3 million, representing 12.5 percent of the U.S. population. But beyond the large size of this population group, most striking was its rate of growth: during the 1990s the Latino and Latina population had grown a dramatic 57.9 percent, compared to 13.2 percent for the entire U.S. population. In addition, these Latino and Latina population numbers did not include the close to 4 million Latinos and Latinas who are U.S. citizens residing in the U.S. territories of Puerto Rico and the U.S. Virgin Islands, a result of the Census Bureau's inconsistent treatment of U.S. colonial populations.

Impact of the New Data

Census 2000 reported that Latinos and Latinas had become the largest racial-ethnic minority group in the country, for the first time surpassing the country's black population in size. The large numbers and rapid growth of the Latino and Latina population also generated much discussion about the "Latinization" of the United States. These developments had both positive and negative aspects to them. While the Latino and Latina community could use these numbers to make greater social, political, and economic claims on U.S. society, there was also a backlash both in general terms, particularly in the area of immigration, and from Latinos' and Latinas' main historical allies in the civil rights movement, African-Americans, many of whom felt threatened by these demographic changes. After 2000, Latinos and Latinas went from being largely ignored to becoming the focus of attention of politicians and corporations, with all the benefits and liabilities associated with such a dramatic shift.

The growth of the Latino and Latina population was also an important contributor to the new phenomenon of the "majority minority" city in the United States, where nine of the ten largest cities had population majorities composed of people of color. This has increased the importance of the issue of group representation in policy-making positions in the public, nonprofit, and private sectors. The significant and persistent underrepresentation of Latinos and Latinas in public sector employment at the local and federal levels of government, for example,

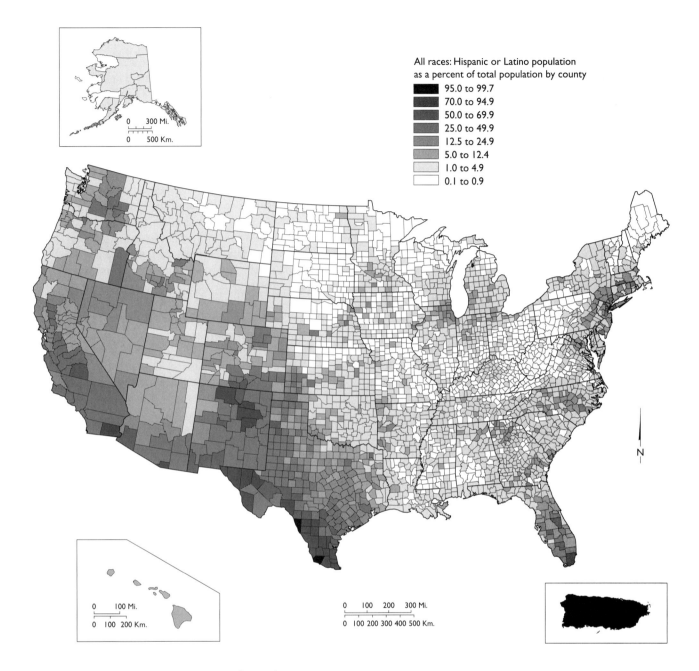

All races: Hispanic or Latino population
as a percent of total population by county

- 95.0 to 99.7
- 70.0 to 94.9
- 50.0 to 69.9
- 25.0 to 49.9
- 12.5 to 24.9
- 5.0 to 12.4
- 1.0 to 4.9
- 0.1 to 0.9

0   300 Mi.

0   500 Km.

0   100 Mi.

0   100 200 Km.

0   100   200   300 Mi.

0   100 200 300 400 500 Km.

PERCENT OF POPULATION. Latino population by county, 2000. (U.S. Census Bureau)

has become a recurring issue. Going beyond the affirmative action claims of the past, this movement for fair representation bases itself on broader diversity arguments as well as purely political and economic considerations.

The role of immigration in driving the demographic realities of Latinos and Latinas and the United States has become increasingly important. Besides fueling the national debate on immigration policy, the dramatic and continual growth of the Latino and Latina immigrant pop-

ulation has in many ways confounded the analysis of the realities and policy needs of the Latino and Latina community. Issues such as lower educational attainment, the relatively low rate of English language proficiency, high poverty rates, high labor force participation rates, and so on, while broadly attributed to Latinos and Latinas as a whole, may, in many circumstances, be the product of the new Latino and Latina immigrant flows into the country rather than the characteristics of Latino and Latina second and older generations. There are notions like the "Latino and Latina health paradox," in which Latinos and Latinas appear to exhibit health indicators superior to the general U.S. population, such as a longer life expectancy, that appears to be generation-specific but complicates the discussion of Latino and Latina health policy issues.

Difficulties in Defining Categories

A recurring and central problem in the discussion of Latino and Latina demographics is the definition of what is "Latino and Latina" or "Hispanic." This question includes debates over several issues: 1) Whether "Latino and Latina" or "Hispanic" is the best term to use and whether these pan-ethnic terms are meaningful at all for such a diverse national-origin population; 2) whether Latino and Latinas should be characterized as largely an immigrant population, along the lines of the older European immigrants, or a racial minority like African Americans; 3) the extent to which the Latino and Latina experience has been racialized in the United States; and 4) the pace and nature of Latino and Latina assimilation and acculturation into U.S. society and whether terms like "Latino and Latina" will have any significant social meaning in the future.

The role of the Census Bureau, which is a part of the United States Department of Commerce, has been central to the determination and discussion of the demographic realities of the Latino and Latina population. As the premiere statistical agency of the United States, the policies and practices of the Census Bureau have become critical concerns for the Latino and Latina community in a wide range of areas; demographic data and other information are also generated by a wide range of agencies and institutions ranging from other federal agencies, local planning commissions, universities, and state governments to marketing companies, international agencies, and many others.

In preparation for the 2010 census, the Census Bureau has begun the transition from its so-called "long form" to the ACS (American/Puerto Rico Community Survey), which would continually conduct sample surveys of the U.S. population as opposed to the current "snapshot" it takes every ten years. The more limited "short form" will continue to be administered to 100 percent of the U.S. population every ten years to obtain the population count and more limited demographic information.

As the Census Bureau makes this major change in the way it collects these statistics, concerns have been expressed in the Latino and Latina community that these changes could adversely affect the collection of accurate information on the nation's Latino and Latina population. These concerns include the loss of detailed demographic data on Latinos and Latinas at the small area level, the impact that the lack of Spanish-language interviewing could have, how the persistent undercounting of Latinos and Latinas will be addressed, and the basic question of how the Census Bureau will define the manner by which Latinos and Latinas identify themselves in these surveys.

Census 2000 resulted in perhaps the most accurate count of the Latino and Latina population ever undertaken, the result of better technologies and the active partnership of the Latino and Latina community at the grassroots level. However, following the release of the data from this count, there were a number of controversies that erupted concerning the counting of Latinos and Latinas. Probably the most

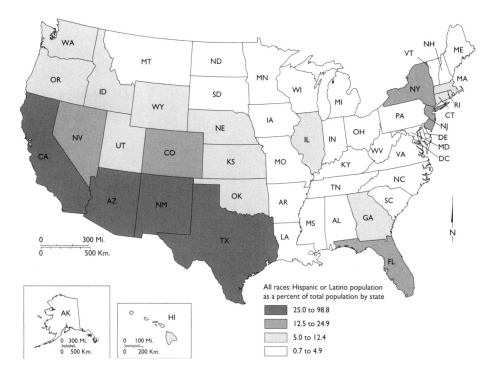

PERCENT OF POPULATION. Latinos by state, 2000. (U.S. Census Bureau)

All races: Hispanic or Latino population as a percent of total population by state

25.0 to 98.8
12.5 to 24.9
5.0 to 12.4
0.7 to 4.9

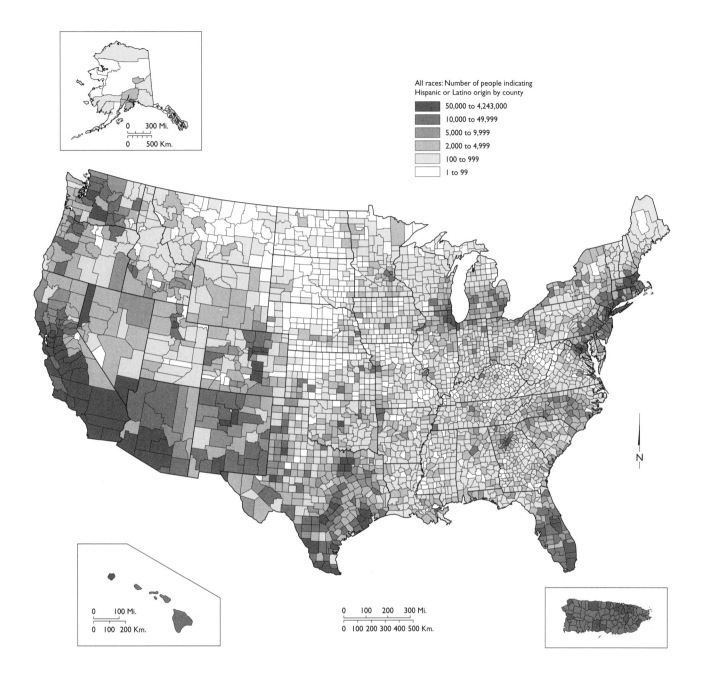

All races: Number of people indicating
Hispanic or Latino origin by county

50,000 to 4,243,000
10,000 to 49,999
5,000 to 9,999
2,000 to 4,999
100 to 999
1 to 99

NUMBER OF PEOPLE. Latinos by county, 2000. (U.S. Census Bureau)

discussed was what some have termed the "Other Hispanic Problem." This involved the misreporting of national-origin identifiers by those Latino and Latina subgroups that were forced to write-in their national origin in the census form (in contrast to the three largest Latino and Latina subgroups—Mexican, Puerto Rican, and Cuban—which are specifically listed in the census Hispanic question). This resulted in lower than actual numbers from groups like Dominicans, Colombians, and Salvadorians reporting their national origin and instead writing in broader categories like Hispanic, Latino and Latina, Spanish, and so on. It also resulted in artificially bloating the "all other Hispanic or Latino" category.

Issues for the Future Census

There are also many other issues facing the census on their treatment of Latinos and Latinas as they plan for the 2010 count. These include: 1) Their failure to accurately count Latinos and Latinas, primarily immigrants, who

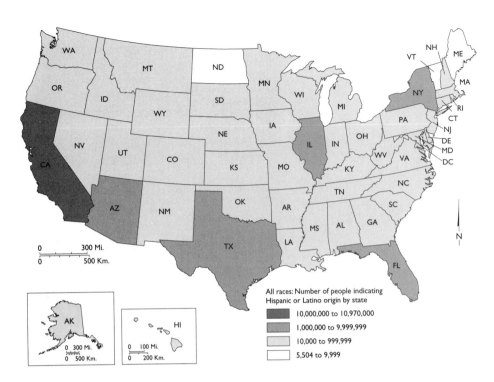

NUMBER OF PEOPLE. Latinos by state, 2000. (U.S. Census Bureau)

All races: Number of people indicating Hispanic or Latino origin by state

- 10,000,000 to 10,970,000
- 1,000,000 to 9,999,999
- 10,000 to 999,999
- 5,504 to 9,999

live in illegal housing units mainly in the larger urban centers; 2) the persistent undercount problem; 3) the disparate treatment of Latinos and Latinas in U.S. territories who are U.S. citizens, such as Puerto Rico and the U.S. Virgin Islands; 4) the Census Bureau's attempts to mechanically eliminate the "some other race" category in their race question that 40 percent of Latinos and Latinas checked off in 2000; 5) the Bureau's consideration of the proposal to collapse the Hispanic and race questions into one and, in effect, turning Latinos and Latinas into a racial group; 6) the use of confidential census data by the U.S. Department of Homeland Security in their anti-terrorism campaign and its potential violation of individual rights and negative impact on future census outreach into the Latino and Latina community; 7) how new enumeration technologies, such as personal digital assistants (PDAs), will affect the counting of the Latino and Latina population; and 8) the significant underrepresentation of Latinos and Latinas on the staff of the Census Bureau and its parent agency, the Commerce Department, which has the worst record of Latino and Latina employment among the major agencies of the federal government.

Because of the growing importance of the analysis of the demographics of the Latino and Latina population into the twenty-first century, especially with projections that non-Latino and non-Latina whites could become a minority of the U.S. population as early as mid-century, statistical policy issues will no doubt play a greater role in the agendas and priorities of the Latino and Latina community. While demography may or may not be destiny for Latinos and

Latinas, it is itself destined to remain an ongoing and central concern for their communities.

See also **Census** *and* **Race and Racialization.**

BIBLIOGRAPHY

Bean, Frank D., Jennifer Lee, Jeanne Batalova, et al., eds. *Immigration and the Fading Color Lines in America.* New York: Russell Sage Foundation, 2004.

Bean, Frank D., and Marta Tienda. *The Hispanic Population of the United States.* New York: Russell Sage Foundation, 1987.

Perlmann, Joel, and Mary C. Waters, eds. *The New Race Question: How the Census Counts Multiracial Individuals.* New York: Russell Sage Foundation, 2002.

Rodríguez, Clara E. *Changing Race: Latinos, the Census, and the History of Ethnicity in the United States.* New York: New York University Press, 2000.

Saenz, Rogelio. *Latino and Latinas and the Changing Face of America.* New York: Russell Sage Foundation, 2004.

United States Census Bureau. *Statistical Abstract of the United States: The National Data Book.* Washington, D.C.: Annual. www.census.gov/prod/www/statistical-abstract-04.html.

ANGELO FALCÓN

DEPORTATION CASES AND LEGISLATION.

Deportation involves the federal government's expulsion of a non–U.S. citizen from its territory for violating American immigration law. This is an important concept in understanding the difference between U.S. citizens and noncitizens. Under U.S. immigration law, only non–U.S. citizens may be deported; conversely, U.S. citizens are never subject to deportation.

Unlike a criminal proceeding, during which incarceration and punishment are often the law's ends, a deportation hearing is a civil matter whose sole purpose is to determine whether the noncitizen may lawfully remain in the United States or whether she must return to her home country. Notwithstanding this difference between civil and criminal proceedings, deportation may visit extreme physical and psychological hardships on noncitizens, depending on the political and socioeconomic conditions of their home countries as well as their kinship ties to relatives still living in the United States.

Just as it has the primary authority for deciding when noncitizens may enter the United States, Congress is also responsible for deciding when they must leave. While some states have on occasion sought to effect the deportation of noncitizens, individual states have no legal power to deport them. Thus, while a state may attempt to limit certain of its benefits to its citizens and residents, it may not do so if its sole purpose is to coerce non–U.S. citizens to leave the country. The power to deport resides exclusively in the federal government as defined by Congress.

Legislation

Congress's basic law on immigration and deportation, the Immigration and Nationality Act, divides deportable persons into two groups: those who entered the United States unlawfully, and those who, having entered lawfully, have violated the terms of their stay. Those who have entered unlawfully include undocumented migrants (or, pejoratively, "illegal aliens") who enter the United States without first being inspected by immigration officials, as well as those who have entered by using fraudulent documents. In contrast, those who have entered lawfully might be deported because they stayed longer than permitted, engaged in certain criminal activities, or aided terrorist activity, among other things.

For Latinas and Latinos in the United States, the most salient deportation cases and legislation have been those surrounding the issue of undocumented immigration. For many North Americans today, the morality of deporting undocumented immigrants is uncontroversial: If the law requires that one secure proper immigration documents to enter the United States and one fails to do so, one should be deported. To do otherwise would encourage lawlessness and be unfair to those noncitizens who abide by the process, so the argument goes. On the other hand, many forget that much of what is now the southwestern United States once belonged to Mexico, raising the question whether immigration rules created by a conquering nation may be ethically imposed upon the vanquished. Indeed, North American immigration and deportation policy vis-à-vis Mexico has reflected both of these philosophical extremes, sometimes encouraging

Mexican migration with few formal restrictions and at other times spending enormous amounts of capital and labor in a vain attempt to seal off the southern border.

Mexico and Central and Latin America. To illustrate, a brief review of the history of U.S. border policy toward Mexico and Central and Latin America might be useful. In the years before, during, and after the U.S. annexation of Mexican territory in what is now the American Southwest, many in the federal government wanted to ensure that Spain and other European nations no longer interfered with the Americas, leaving Mexico and its neighbors at the whim of the United States' imperial designs. This mindset was reflected in U.S. immigration and deportation policy during the late 1800s through the 1920s. While it was concerned about limiting southern and eastern European immigration, and it enacted laws barring Chinese migrants, Congress cared little about the United States–Mexico border during this period, exempting Western Hemisphere nations from any immigration quotas it chose to enact. In what may seem strange to modern readers, U.S. authorities at the time were more concerned with apprehending Chinese nationals entering surreptitiously from Canada than with Latinas and Latinos crossing the Rio Grande. Thus, Mexican migration before the 1920s was commonplace, especially during the period around the Mexican Revolution of 1909, when many traveled north to escape the war and to enjoy the economic prosperity of California and much of the American Southwest. Immigration from Central and Latin America was not as great, in part because of the greater distances between these regions and the United States, and in part because Mexicans were more likely to have family and social ties to the southwestern United States, it having once been Mexican territory.

Deportation movements. Two major deportation movements are worth noting following this otherwise unchecked period of immigration, both of which were prompted by poor U.S. economic prospects. The first came on the heels of the stock market crash of 1929, when the faltering economy led to the scapegoating of Mexican workers. Estimates run as high as one million Mexican deportees during the 1930s, tens of thousands of whom were U.S. citizens of Mexican descent who were wrongfully expelled.

This episode was followed by another high immigration period spurred by the war industry. Beginning in 1942, the United States was in dire need of agricultural workers, prompting negotiation of the bracero program, a treaty with Mexico for the supply of temporary farmhands. When, after the war, the U.S. government realized that it could not prevent domestic businesses from continuing to import cheaper, undocumented Mexican labor, it initiated the second major deportation initiative—"Operation Wetback"—in 1954, resulting in the removal of over one million undocumented Mexicans. It

DEPORTATION. Illegal Mexican migrant workers board a Flying Tiger airliner, near El Centro, California, in 1951 to be deported to their homes 1,200 miles away. (Associated Press)

was not until 1986 that Congress decided to curb not just the supply of Mexican workers but the demand as well by enacting employer sanctions for U.S. businesses that hired undocumented workers.

Even a brief survey of U.S. deportation policies reveals that these programs were responses to economic pressures that, during times of plenty, were less stringently enforced. Because the United States realizes that much of the labor-intensive agricultural and manufacturing work performed domestically is carried out by undocumented persons, many of whom happen to be Latina and Latino, its deportation policies against undocumented individuals will likely continue to reflect its economic fortunes, just as it did during the Depression and the post–World War II years.

Legal Cases

The debate regarding the deportation of Latinas and Latinos, however, moved beyond the ethics of expelling those unlawfully present to focus instead on whether racial profiling may be justified in the fight against undocumented immigration. Section 287(a)(1) of the Immigration and Nationality Act provides that immigration officials "shall have power without warrant to interrogate any alien or person believed to be an alien as to his right to be or to remain in the United States." As with any federal govern-

mental act, that power is limited by the Constitution, including the Fourth Amendment right to be free from unreasonable government searches and seizures, and the Fifth Amendment rights to due process and equal protection under the law. The key question, therefore, is whether a person's Latina or Latino appearance may be used by immigration officials as a factor in determining whether to inquire about that person's immigration status. On the one hand, law-and-order advocates contend that because many undocumented immigrants along the southern border are Mexican, a suspect's race may be used as one factor in determining whether the person is lawfully in the United States. Immigrant rights advocates, on the other hand, question whether such overbroad stereotyping is justified, considering that many of those who "look Mexican" are either U.S. citizens or noncitizens lawfully present, thereby implicating Fourteenth Amendment protections against racial discrimination.

In three seminal decisions regarding the constitutional Fourth Amendment right to be free from unreasonable government searches, the U.S. Supreme Court has sided with law enforcement officers, holding that one's "Mexican appearance" may be one factor among many in determining whether to question a suspected noncitizen, and, perhaps more important, ruling that the government may introduce illegally-seized evidence against noncitizens in deportation proceedings.

Brignoni-Ponce. First, in *United States v. Brignoni-Ponce* (1975), the Court stated that Border Patrol officers engaged in roving patrols along the United States–Mexico border may use race as a factor in determining whether to ask about a person's immigration status. To make sure their conduct complies with the Fourth Amendment's bar against unreasonable searches, Border Patrol agents are required to develop a "reasonable suspicion" that a person is not legally in the United States. *Brignoni-Ponce* concerned the actions of two Border Patrol agents who stopped a car based solely on the Mexican appearance of its three occupants, which was enough, in their minds, to create a "reasonable suspicion" that these persons were non–U.S. citizens. The Court disagreed, stating that the apparent Mexican ancestry of the car's occupants was by itself insufficient to meet the governing standard. It went on, however, to validate the use of race as a factor in immigration enforcement: "The likelihood that any given person of Mexican ancestry is an alien is high enough to make Mexican appearance a relevant factor, but standing alone it does not justify stopping all Mexican-Americans to ask if they are aliens."

Martinez-Fuerte. The following year, in *United States v. Martinez-Fuerte* (1976), the Court expanded on its holding in *Brignoni-Ponce*, finding that race may be a factor at permanent immigration checkpoints far removed from the border. *Martinez-Fuerte* concerned the actions of Border Patrol agents working at inland vehicle checkpoints many miles from Mexico. They admitted to referring certain drivers for further inspection by immigration authorities based largely on their Mexican appearance. Typically, secondary immigration inspections are reserved for those persons whose immigration status the Border Patrol is unsure of; here, the Border Patrol made it a practice to refer all those who looked Mexican for additional inspection. Just as it had in *Brignoni-Ponce*, the Court affirmed the idea that one's race may be used as a factor by the Border Patrol so long as it is not the exclusive criterion. And as in *Brignoni-Ponce*, the Court cited the government's estimate that 85 percent of the undocumented population in the United States was then of Mexican origin.

Lopez-Mendoza. Almost ten years after *Brignoni-Ponce*, the Supreme Court issued its ruling in *Immigration and Naturalization Service (INS) v. Lopez-Mendoza* (1984), arguably the most important deportation-related case issued by the Court, thereby warranting the extended discussion that follows. In *Lopez-Mendoza*, the Court held that the Fourth Amendment's exclusionary rule did not prevent the government from introducing illegally obtained evidence at a deportation proceeding.

Mexican citizens Adan Lopez-Mendoza and Elias Sandoval-Sanchez had entered the United States without proper immigration documentation and had worked at a transmission repair shop in San Mateo, California, and a potato processing plant in Pasco, Washington, respectively, at the time the INS arrested them in separate investigations of their workplaces.

Mr. Lopez-Mendoza was arrested when he revealed to an INS agent that "he was from Mexico with no close family ties to the United States." Of course, being from Mexico with no family in the United States does not, in itself, make one an undocumented immigrant. Mr. Sandoval-Sanchez's arrest was even more suspect. It was not clear who among the various INS agents arrested Mr. Sandoval-Sanchez, but the Court noted INS Agent Bower's testimony that "[t]he employee he thought he remembered as Sandoval-Sanchez had been 'very evasive,' and averted his head, turned around, and walked away when he saw Agent Bower." Evasiveness and flight, however, do not necessarily evidence guilt or illegal activity. As Justice John Paul Stevens noted in his *Illinois v. Wardlow* (1999) dissent,

> Among some citizens, particularly minorities and those residing in high crime areas, there is also the possibility that the fleeing person is entirely innocent, but, with or without justification, believes that contact with the police can itself be dangerous, apart from any criminal activity associated with the officer's sudden presence.

Despite these alternate explanations for their behavior, both Messrs. Lopez-Mendoza and Sandoval-Sanchez were arrested, interrogated about their immigration status, and were found to be undocumented persons. This information was then used to initiate deportation proceedings against them.

Both Messrs. Lopez-Mendoza and Sandoval-Sanchez challenged their arrests as unlawful under the Fourth Amendment's prohibition against unreasonable searches and seizures, arguing that any evidence of their undocumented status could not be used against them in the deportation proceedings, invoking the so-called "exclusionary rule." Four of the nine justices agreed with the respondents. As Justice William J. Brennan put it,

> The Government of the United States bears an obligation to obey the Fourth Amendment; that obligation is not lifted simply because the law enforcement officers were agents of the Immigration and Naturalization Service, nor because the evidence obtained by those officers was to be used in civil deportation proceedings.

The dissenters contended that the government should not be allowed to profit from its unconstitutional activity by introducing illegally obtained information against an alleged deportee. That the proceeding was not a criminal hearing was of no importance to Justice Brennan and his brethren; for them, the Fourth Amendment protections were designed primarily to ensure governmental compliance with the federal Constitution.

A slim majority of the Court, five justices led by Justice Sandra Day O'Connor, ruled otherwise:

> This litigation requires us to decide whether an admission of unlawful presence in this country made subsequent to an allegedly unlawful arrest must be excluded as evidence in a civil deportation hearing. We hold that the exclusionary rule need not be applied in such a proceeding.

The Court held that even if the INS had violated the Fourth Amendment by unlawfully arresting Messrs. Lopez-Mendoza and Sandoval-Sanchez, excluding these persons' admission of their undocumented status was not required by the exclusionary rule. The Court reasoned that the costs of excluding this probative evidence outweighed the harm to the noncitizens, especially since the Immigration and Nationality Act already provides much of the same protection against unreasonable government conduct that the Fourth Amendment does.

Criminal proceedings and deportation hearings. At the heart of the Court's decision, however, was the distinction the majority drew between criminal proceedings and deportation hearings. The Court distinguished between criminal trials intended to punish and civil deportation proceedings designed to determine one's eligibility to remain in the United States. Deportation hearings are held before immigration law judges, who, unlike criminal law judges, have no power to incarcerate or punitively fine deportees. "The judge's sole power is to order deportation; the judge cannot adjudicate guilt or punish the respondent for any crime related to unlawful entry into or presence in this country." Because criminal trials may result in incarceration, defendants are afforded more protections than are noncitizens in deportation proceedings. Standard criminal law protections such as the right to appointed counsel, to be present at trial, and to a jury trial are not required by the rules that govern deportations.

Assessment

Taken together, *Brignoni-Ponce*, *Martinez-Fuerte*, and *Lopez-Mendoza* represent the Supreme Court's support of stringent immigration law enforcement, particularly in pursuit of the undocumented immigrant. The Court has effectively curtailed the U.S. Constitution's Fourth Amendment prohibition against unreasonable government searches and seizures by allowing immigration law enforcement officers to engage in racial profiling (*Brignoni-Ponce*, *Martinez-Fuerte*) and, even if incriminating evidence were to have been obtained unlawfully,

to use that evidence in a deportation proceeding (*Lopez-Mendoza*). Perhaps not surprisingly, these rulings have contributed to the disproportionate deportation of Latina and Latino noncitizens. The immigration and race scholar Kevin Johnson has observed that despite the fact that they make up only about half of America's undocumented population, Latinas and Latinos constitute ninety percent of all deportees.

While it has yet to prove a successful strategy in the Supreme Court, "equal protection of the laws"—the idea that the law should treat all individuals equally—has been invoked by the Ninth Circuit Court of Appeals to challenge the validity of using race as a factor in immigration enforcement. In 2000, the federal intermediate appeals court held that the Border Patrol's use of race as a factor in enforcing immigration law along the United States–Mexico border in San Diego violated the Constitution's equal protection guarantee. In *United States v. Montero-Camargo* (2000), the Ninth Circuit distinguished *Brignoni-Ponce*, noting that demographic changes over the previous twenty years had led to a significant increase in the number of U.S. citizens and lawfully present persons of Latina and Latino descent in the San Diego, California, area. For the Border Patrol to continue to utilize race as a factor in its immigration enforcement efforts was, therefore, irrational. Put another way, the fact that a person in the San Diego–Tijuana border region looks Mexican was ruled an irrelevant criterion in trying to determine her lawful presence in the United States. The Circuit Court concluded that for the U.S. government to act otherwise was to treat individuals differently because of their race, something the equal protection guarantee of the federal Constitution generally does not allow.

See also **Americanization; Border, The; Bracero Program; Demographics; Immigration; Immigration and Naturalization Service; Indocumentados;** *and* **Race and Racialization.**

BIBLIOGRAPHY

Daniels, Roger. *Coming to America: A History of Immigration and Ethnicity in American Life*. New York: Harper Perennial, 1990.

Johnson, Kevin R. "The Case against Race Profiling in Immigration Enforcement." *Washington University Law Quarterly* 78 (2000): 675–736.

Legomsky, Stephen H. *Immigration and Refugee Law and Policy*. New York: Foundation, 2002.

Nevins, Joseph. *Operation Gatekeeper: The Rise of the "Illegal Alien" and the Making of the U.S.–Mexico Boundary*. New York: Routledge, 2002.

Romero, Victor C. "Whatever Happened to the Fourth Amendment?: Undocumented Immigrants' Fourth Amendment Rights after *INS v. Lopez-Mendoza* and *United States v. Verdugo-Urquidez*." *Southern California Law Review* 65 (1992): 999–1034.

VICTOR C. ROMERO

DEPORTATIONS OF MEXICAN-ORIGIN PEOPLE IN THE UNITED STATES.

One of the defining characteristics of modern territorial states is that they reserve the absolute right to control who enters, resides in, and leaves the space within their national boundaries. Associated with this claimed right is the power to expel or deport from national territory noncitizens who, for various reasons, are considered undesirable by government authorities. In the case of the United States, the history of deportations is inextricably tied to the collective experience of people of Mexican descent and, as the diversity of migrant-sending countries has grown, of Latinos and Latinas as a whole as well as to the growing power of the state to regulate immigration.

The first case of deportation in what became the United States seems to have occurred in 1639, when the Pilgrims in Massachusetts required the expulsion of paupers. The first piece of federal immigration legislation came in 1798, when Congress passed the Alien and Sedition Acts. The part known as the Alien Act empowered the president to arrest and deport any foreigner regarded as "a danger to the peace and security" of the United States. The intent of the law was to prevent the spread of radical ideas emanating from the French Revolution. (The law expired two years after its passage.)

In the following decades, anti-immigrant sentiment diminished significantly. At the same time growing concerns emerged about the arrival of poor immigrants from Europe, so much so that individual states began to implement attempts to regulate and deport immigrants. Congress put an end to such practices in 1876, when it outlawed immigration regulation by states and made it the exclusive purview of the federal government.

Through most of the nineteenth century, immigration into the United States was largely open. But beginning in 1875 Congress passed a series of laws barring the entry of would-be immigrants on the basis of qualitative characteristics, such as race and ethnicity, poverty, physical and mental health, political beliefs, and later quantitative characteristics that determined who could enter or not by reason of national origin. Perhaps the most infamous piece of legislation during this period was the Chinese Exclusion Act of 1882, the passage of which marked the first time since the Alien and Sedition Acts that the federal government had the authority to deport immigrants, specifically noncitizen Chinese, already in the country.

The right of the U.S. government to deport was enshrined in law in 1893, when the Supreme Court ruled that the government had the "the right to exclude or expel all aliens, or any class of aliens" in times of war or peace. Over the next forty years the number of deportations gradually increased, albeit in an uneven manner. Between 1892 and 1930 there was an average of 3,342 deportations annually—ranging from a low of 177 in 1895 to a high of 16,631 in 1930. By that time, there were twenty-six different reasons for immigration authorities to deport immigrants.

People of Mexican origin were largely immune from such practices through the nineteenth century, in part because of the low number of immigrants from Mexico. But as Congress passed legislation making it increasingly difficult to emigrate from Asia and eastern and southern

Europe, Mexican immigration increased significantly in the early decades of the twentieth century in large part due to active recruitment by American capital. And as the number of Mexican immigrants grew, so did the number of Mexican deportees.

Mass Deportations

The years around World War I and the aftermath of the 1917 Russian Revolution were a time of unprecedented attack by nativists—people opposed to sociocultural difference as embodied by "minorities" or foreigners— against organized labor, the Left, and immigrants. President Woodrow Wilson's Department of Justice alleged that there were large numbers of "Reds" or resident aliens of Russian origin in the United States who held Bolshevik principles and had the goal of overthrowing the federal government by force. An infamous incident took place on December 21, 1919, when U.S. authorities deported to Russia by ship 249 alien residents, including Emma Goldman, the famous anarchist and women's and labor rights activist. Such anti-Left scapegoating, combined with racism toward those from "south of the border," eventually resulted in the targeting of people of Mexican origin as well.

Whereas agricultural interests initially welcomed Mexican migrant workers, seeing them as hardworking and docile, nativists in California, where most of the immigrants lived, perceived them as a threat. During the 1913–1914 depression, nativists in Los Angeles made Mexicans their primary economic scapegoats, linking them to communism and other radical causes. And as Mexican workers became increasingly involved in militant unions and participated in strikes (typically violently repressed), growers and government authorities began to characterize them in a similar light, often colluding to deport union and political activists as a way of maintaining the labor-capital status quo.

The onset of the Great Depression in 1929 greatly changed the terms of the debate as restrictionist sentiment further intensified, with organizations ranging from the American Federation of Labor to the American Legion and the Veterans of Foreign Wars leading the charge. In the context of the Great Depression, Mexicans became convenient scapegoats once again, blamed for a variety of social ills. As one Los Angeles County supervisor stated, "If we were rid of the aliens who have entered this country illegally since 1931 our present unemployment problem would shrink to the proportions of a relatively unimportant flat spot in business" (Takaki, p. 333). It was in such a climate that the forced repatriation of tens of thousands of Mexicans took place in the 1930s, constituting the first time the federal government had carried out a mass expulsion of immigrants. The mass deportations

of people of Mexican origin often used methods that even a 1932 U.S. government commission characterized as "unconstitutional, tyrannic and oppressive" (Balderrama and Rodríguez, pp. 52–53). According to one study, U.S. authorities forcibly expelled an estimated 415,000 Mexicans between 1929 and 1935 with another 85,000 leaving "voluntarily," usually under intense pressure from local authorities. Some estimates of the deportations run as high as one million, including tens of thousands of U.S. citizens of Mexican descent.

Whereas many members of Los Angeles's business class supported the deportations, they were also confident that they could lure the Mexicans back to the area were the need to arise. But the position of the business community was not one of unanimity or consistency. The local chamber of commerce, for example, initially urged the government to ease up on the deportations for fear of the negative effect they might have on the labor supply. But this changed in 1933, when farmworkers staged the largest number of strikes in California agriculture's history, with Mexican workers participating in all of them.

Representatives of the Mexican government cooperated with local officials in carrying out the deportation and repatriation program throughout the Southwest in large part because they viewed the out-migration of Mexican workers in the early twentieth century as a threat to their country's efforts to industrialize and an embarrassment to the promise of the Mexican Revolution to eliminate socioeconomic inequalities. In numerous areas, Mexican consular officials helped identify and locate potential repatriates and paid for the costs of transporting them from the border region to their destinations in the Mexican interior.

The mass deportations slowed Mexican immigration into the United States to a negligible level. Not until 1942 did it pick up again in response to labor shortages brought about by World War II. That year also marked the beginning of a contract labor program, the so-called bracero program, which many expected would reduce unauthorized immigration from Mexico. Yet the opposite seems to have happened: unauthorized crossings appear to have significantly increased. This was in part due to the fact that many growers continued to prefer hiring "illegal" immigrants as it was less cumbersome and less expensive than hiring braceros. So grower practices significantly facilitated the rise in extralegal immigration. Moreover, through its actions the Immigration and Naturalization Service (INS) actually encouraged unauthorized immigration. The legalization of unauthorized migrants by U.S. authorities (popularly known as "drying out the wetbacks") served to increase extralegal immigration from Mexico as the news spread that the easiest manner to obtain a bracero contract was to enter the United States extralegally.

Operation Wetback

As unauthorized immigration grew, a number of state officials began to argue that uncontrolled immigration presented a threat to the stability of the agricultural economy and the larger society more generally. The 1951 report of the President's Commission on Migratory Labor was the first to sound the alarm, blaming "illegal" immigration for depressing wage rates in the Southwest and warning of its implications for public health and housing standards. Although growers and their congressional allies attacked the report, it focused critical attention on unauthorized immigration, linking the phenomenon to all sorts of social ills, including crime. Organized labor also fanned the flames.

Such critiques resonated with large segments of the public, especially given the severe recession of the early 1950s. Even most Chicano and Chicana organizations and the Mexican government called for fines against U.S. employers of unauthorized immigrants. Furthermore, the cold war and the prevailing anticommunism played a role in facilitating the rise of "anti-wetback," sentiment with some suggesting that "communists," other subversives, and spies were among those crossing into the United States from Mexico without authorization. Others, while stressing the national security dimensions of the perceived crisis, also emphasized the law and order aspect. One INS official, for example, proclaimed the increasing number of extralegal entrants from Mexico "the greatest peacetime invasion ever complacently suffered by another country under open, flagrant, contemptuous violations of its laws" (Dunn, p. 14).

The Eisenhower administration, however, was ambivalent in its response. While Eisenhower's attorney general Herbert Brownell helped incite public opposition to unauthorized immigration, his actions demonstrated the administration's uncertainty. Thus, after having reported to Congress that the "wetback problem" had never been so bad, Brownell recommended there be no increase in the Border Patrol's budget and there be a reduction in the INS's overall budget, suggesting it was premature to deport "illegal" workers. Nevertheless, in the face of growing pressure, the Eisenhower administration announced on June 9, 1954, the launch of a large-scale deportation strategy. What came to be known as "Operation Wetback" officially started eight days later.

Led by the INS commissioner general Joseph Swing, the operation involved the roundup and deportation of hundreds of thousands of suspected "wetbacks" working in both agriculture and industry in border states and those who were unemployed. According to the INS, the agency, with the cooperation and collaboration of local police authorities, apprehended and deported over a million migrants during fiscal year 1954, most of the apprehensions taking place during the operation. By means of high-visibility shows of force in restricted locales and highly sensationalized media coverage, the INS gave the impression of being far more powerful than it was, thus causing, according to the INS, many thousands of unauthorized migrants to leave the United States on their own.

Operation Wetback generated a good deal of adverse publicity and opposition in California among social welfare and immigration reform groups, which criticized the operation for violating the civil rights of undocumented workers and of U.S. citizens of Mexican descent. Chicano and Chicana groups for the most part, although deeply offended by the raids, were largely quiescent. A notable exception was La Asociación Nacional México-Americana, which had strong links to Left-leaning groups, such as the Independent Progressive Party and the National Committee for the Protection of the Foreign Born, and progressive labor unions such as the Mine, Mill, and Smelter Workers. All of them, along with some locals of the International Longshoremen's and Warehousemen's Union, strenuously protested the operation.

Although the operation resulted in a record number of deportations, the U.S. government compensated agricultural interests by greatly increasing the number of braceros admitted into the United States. Indeed, General Swing had met with growers and ranchers in the Southwest in the spring and summer of 1954 to enlist their support, promising them that the government would replace unauthorized workers with legal ones, or braceros. In this regard, the operation's most important outcome was to increase state and grower control over migrant labor.

Operation Wetback constituted the final mass deportation of immigrants from the United States on such a scale. Officials, however, continued to occasionally issue calls for large-scale deportations of "illegals." In the early 1970s, for example, when unauthorized immigration and control over the United States–Mexico boundary emerged as issues of significant national concern for the first time on both the official and the popular levels, William Saxbe, the U.S. attorney general under President Gerald Ford, called the presence of unauthorized immigrants "a severe national crisis" (Ostrow). Citing jobs, crime, and welfare costs, Saxbe called for the deportation of one million "illegal aliens," whom he described as mostly Mexicans. And in 1974, Leonard Chapman, President Ford's INS commissioner, wrote in *Reader's Digest*, "If we could locate and deport three to four million illegals who currently hold jobs in the United States . . . we could reduce our own unemployment dramatically—*as much as 50 percent*" ("Illegal Aliens," p. 190). Nevertheless such implicit threats never materialized.

There were still times when immigration authorities did engage in relatively large deportations. In October 1986, for instance, the Border Patrol responded to a significant increase in "anti-illegal" immigrant sentiment in northern San Diego County, California, by arresting and deporting three thousand unauthorized Mexican immigrants in the area. In 1992, during the Los Angeles riots, police arrested 1,044 unauthorized immigrants (10 percent of all riot-related arrests) within the first two weeks of the uprising. Authorities eventually handed all of them over to the INS for possible deportation back to Mexico and countries in Central America. Also, as before, the INS occasionally directly served the interests of capital by arresting and deporting unauthorized immigrants active in organizing fellow workers.

Criminal Aliens

Since the early to mid-1990s, as a result of increased anti-immigrant sentiment and the associated increase in the criminalization of immigrants, there has been a significant rise in deportations of unauthorized immigrants and of authorized immigrants who have broken the law. In fiscal years 1999 and 2001, the INS deported on average approximately 175,000 individuals, between 35 and 40 percent of whom were so-called criminal aliens. Mexican nationals were about 80 percent of the deportees, with the majority of the remaining 20 percent sent back to Latin American countries such as El Salvador, Colombia, and the Dominican Republic. (These numbers do not include the many tens of thousands of Mexican nationals apprehended annually by the Border Patrol while crossing into the United States without authorization. Mexican nationals have the option of "voluntarily" returning to their country instead of going before an immigration judge for a formal deportation hearing. Almost all of those apprehended exercise the first option and thus do not figure in the total of deportees.)

The 1996 Illegal Immigration Reform and Immigrant Responsibility Act had a dramatic effect on "criminal alien" deportations. The law now subjects noncitizen "aggravated felons" to deportation, regardless of how long ago their crimes occurred. It also greatly expanded the list of crimes for which "resident aliens" can lose their residency. Prior to 1996, the list was limited to murder, rape, and other major felonies. The list now includes selling marijuana, domestic violence, some cases of repeated drunk driving, and any conviction that carries a sentence of one year or more.

Undoubtedly, many of those deported as a result of the law have committed violent crimes. But assuming that the "criminal alien" population is similar to that which finds itself languishing in state and federal prisons in the United States, a large share of the deportees are most probably nonviolent drug law offenders. Often, they are married and have U.S.–born (thus citizen) children. The deportations thus typically take a large toll on the socio-economic security of the deportees' families, and paradoxically they most likely increase the demands immigrants place on the social security net.

For numerous reasons, including the growing number of domestic and international actors and institutions that influence the federal government's immigration regime, it is difficult to imagine the United States engaging in a mass deportation or expulsion of foreign nationals such as those that took place in the 1930s or in 1954. Indeed, U.S. authorities have promised their Mexican and Central American counterparts that they will not do so. But deportations of individual immigrants, at times in large numbers, will continue to occur as long as the state reserves the right to determine who can cross and remain within its territorial boundaries. And given that the unauthorized immigrant population is largely Latino and Latina, women and men from Latin American will continue to represent the vast majority of those targeted.

See also **Border Patrol; Bracero Program; Chicanos and Chicanas; Immigration; Immigration and Naturalization Service; Immigration Policy and Border Control: Post–September 11; Immigration Policy, Twentieth Century; Indocumentados;** *and* **Mexican-Origin People in the United States.**

BIBLIOGRAPHY

Acuña, Rodolfo. *Occupied America: A History of Chicanos.* New York: Harper and Row, 1988.

Balderrama, Francisco E., and Raymond Rodríguez. *Decade of Betrayal: Mexican Repatriation in the 1930s.* Albuquerque: University of New Mexico Press, 1995.

Calavita, Kitty. *Inside the State: The Bracero Program, Immigration, and the I.N.S.* New York and London: Routledge, 1992.

Chapman, Leonard F. "Illegal Aliens: Time to Call a Halt!" *Reader's Digest,* October 1976: 188–192.

Clark, Jane Perry. *Deportation of Aliens from the United States to Europe.* New York: Columbia University Press, 1931.

Dinwoodie, D. H. "Deportation: The Immigration Service and the Chicano Labor Movement in the 1930s." *New Mexico Historical Review* 52 (1977): 193–206.

Dunn, Timothy J. *The Militarization of the U.S.–Mexico Border, 1978–1992: Low-Intensity Conflict Doctrine Comes Home.* Austin, Tex.: Center for Mexican American Studies, University of Texas at Austin, 1996.

García, Juan Ramon. *Operation Wetback: The Mass Deportation of Mexican Undocumented Workers in 1954.* Westport, Conn., and London: Greenwood Press, 1980.

Guerin-Gonzales, Camille. *Mexican Workers and American Dreams: Immigration, Repatriation, and California Farm Labor, 1900–1939.* New Brunswick, N.J.: Rutgers University Press, 1994.

Lee, Erika. *At America's Gate: Chinese Immigration During the Exclusion Era, 1882–1943.* Chapel Hill: University of North Carolina Press, 2003.

Nevins, Joseph. *Operation Gatekeeper: The Rise of the "Illegal Alien" and the Making of the U.S.–Mexico Boundary.* New York: Routledge, 2002.

Nevins, Joseph. "Third World and 'Illegal' in the City of Angels." In *Unmasking Los Angeles: Third Worlds and the City,* edited by Deepak Narang Sawhney. New York: Palgrave, 2002.

Ostrow, Ronald J. "Saxbe Calls Illegal Aliens a U.S. Crisis," *Los Angeles Times*, October 31, 1974: 1.

Takaki, Ronald. *A Different Mirror: A History of Multicultural America*. Boston and New York: Little, Brown, 1993.

JOSEPH NEVINS

DETAINEES, CUBAN. During the Mariel boat lift of 1980, a group of 2,746 participants were classified as "excludable" by the U.S. Immigration and Naturalization Service (INS) and detained upon arrival in the United States. The main reason for their exclusion and detention was the fact that most had committed crimes in Cuba and therefore had to be kept in captivity until they completed their sentences in U.S. prisons and/or were deemed admissible to the country by a U.S. court. Their detention stirred a major controversy and created a legal dilemma for the U.S. government, since: (1) they had been invited to the United States by President Jimmy Carter, who allowed the boat lift to continue for five months; (2) they were imprisoned for crimes committed in a foreign country, and a country that the U.S. did not even recognize; (3) they were detained indefinitely and without specific charges; (4) prison conditions were considered "deplorable" and "shameful" by national and international human rights groups; and (5) they were denied a speedy trial by a jury of their peers.

The detention, exclusion, and treatment of this group represented a sharp reversal in the traditional "open arms" U.S. immigration policy of welcoming and admitting virtually all Cuban migrants as political refugees.

Cubans also had been—and still are—privileged by the Cuban Adjustment Act of 1966, which allows Cubans entering the United States, by any means, the right to permanent-resident status one year and one day after their arrival. The Mariel detainees, however, were the only Cubans not protected by the act, since they were never officially admitted to the United States.

The U.S. government justified the extreme measures taken against the detainees by claiming that it had been overwhelmed by the more than 125,000 Cubans who arrived during the Mariel boat lift, and because it feared that Castro had intentionally sent hardened criminals on the boat lift to export Cuba's crime problems to the United States. Although the latter was partly true, 98 percent of all boat lift entrants were hard-working, law-abiding citizens. The harsh treatment of the detainees and their detention without trial represented a gross violation of U.S. civil rights and universal human rights.

Political and civil rights groups like the American Civil Liberties Union (ACLU), the Coalition to Support Cuban Detainees (CSCD), and the Cuban American National Foundation (CANF), among others, advocated for the prisoners' rights through litigation and public pressure, but had little success. The failure of these efforts indicated that the Cuban exile community was losing political clout in Washington, at least on immigration issues, as the detainees lingered in prison without charge and without trial. It was not until 1984 that the U.S. and Cuban governments agreed on a plan to repatriate all Mariel entrants who had been detained since 1980. Unfortunately, the agreement was short lived—Cuba suspended the

MARIELITOS. The fishing boat *Mary Evelyn* arrives in Key West, Florida, crowded with Cuban refugees during the Mariel boatlift in April 1980. (Tim Chapman/MIAMI HERALD)

deportation to protest the Reagan administration's creation of Radio Martí, a U.S. government–funded radio station dedicated to transmitting propaganda programs to Cuba.

The Mariel boat lift and detainees controversy came at a time when the United States was besieged by more than 1 million asylum seekers from Haiti, Nicaragua, El Salvador, Honduras, and Guatemala. Although most of these people were trying to escape and survive political repression and war in their home countries, and had legitimate humanitarian cases, the INS ruled on their cases according to U.S. foreign policy priorities in the sending country, not the humanitarian merits of the case. More than 100,000 Haitians who sought political asylum in the United States from 1976 to 1980 were automatically categorized as economic refugees, detained, and deported back to Haiti, without any regard for the political situation they were trying to escape. Most Salvadorans were denied political asylum, since they were escaping the violence and repression of a government supported by the United States. On the other hand, Nicaraguans escaping the leftist Sandinista government (1979–1990), which the United States was trying to overthrow, were welcomed as political exiles.

The detention and exclusion of Mariel entrants and the double standard used by the INS to grant and deny asylum had significant political repercussions for both the Carter and Reagan administrations. Many analysts agree that the Mariel boat lift and the way it was handled was one of the main causes for Jimmy Carter's failure to win reelection in 1980. Faced with 125,000 asylum seekers from socialist Cuba and 50,000 Haitians fleeing from a pro–U.S. government, the Carter administration created a vague migratory status: "Cuban-Haitian Entrant: Status Pending." The new category helped cover the policy contradiction, but did not solve the status issue. Likewise, the Reagan administration faced a major crisis when the Cuban detainees rioted to protest the reactivation of the 1984 Cuba–U.S. immigration agreement. Frustrated by their seemingly endless prison terms and faced with the possibility of being deported to Cuba, the prisoners staged riots in the two prisons holding the largest number of Mariel detainees. The November 1987 riots in the Oakdale Detention Center in Louisiana and the Atlanta Penitentiary lasted ten days and left a toll of one detainee killed and more than a dozen injured. The rioters also burned five prison buildings and caused more than $20 million in property damages.

The detainees' situation was far from resolved in 2003, almost twenty-five years after their arrival in the United States aboard the "freedom flotilla"; more than one thousand Mariel "excludables" remained imprisoned in the United States without trial, and without any idea of when

and if they would be released. Haitian asylum seekers also remained in a state of limbo. Although they were still arriving in South Florida in large numbers in the early 2000s, most were almost immediately deported back to Haiti. Similarly, Central American political asylum seekers have been denied entry to the United States since the 1990s, when all the civil wars in that region ended.

See also Cuban Americans; Marielitos; *and* United States Interventions in Latin America.

BIBLIOGRAPHY

Grenier, Guillermo J., and Alex Stepick III, eds. *Miami Now: Immigration, Ethnicity, and Social Change*. Gainesville: University Press of Florida, 1992.

Hamn, Mark S. *The Abandoned Ones: The Imprisonment and Uprising of the Mariel Boat People*. Boston: Northeastern University Press, 1995.

Larzelere, Alex. *Castro's Ploy—America's Dilemma: The 1980 Cuban Boatlift*. Washington, D.C.: National Defense University Press, 1988.

Masud-Piloto, Félix. *From Welcomed Exiles to Illegal Immigrants: Cuban Migration to the U.S., 1959–1995*. Lanham, Md.: Rowman and Littlefield, 1996.

Portes, Alejandro, and Robert L. Bach. *Latin Journey: Cuban and Mexican Immigrants in the United States*. Berkeley: University of California Press, 1985.

FÉLIX MASUD PILOTO

DIABETES. Diabetes is caused by the body's failure to produce the hormone insulin or by its resistance to the actions of the insulin that is produced. Type I diabetes, or insulin-dependent diabetes mellitus, is an actual insulin deficiency caused by the destruction of pancreatic islet cells. Type II diabetes, or non-insulin-dependent diabetes mellitus (NIDDM), is characterized by high blood glucose in the presence of high insulin levels. Etiology of Type I diabetes is multiple factored and includes autoimmune, genetic, and environmental factors. Type II diabetes is associated with advanced age, obesity, family history of the disease, and physical inactivity. Warning signs of both types include fatigue, illness, frequent urination, excessive thirst, and blurred vision. Obesity is a characteristic of Type II diabetes while weight loss is associated with Type I.

Both forms of the disease have significant implications for Latinas and Latinos. Between 90 and 95 percent of Latina and Latino diabetics have Type II, and recent clinical observations indicate a parallel rate in newly diagnosed NIDDM in Latina and Latino children and adolescents. Further, the National Diabetes Information Clearinghouse (NDIC) estimates that about one-third of all Latinas and Latinos have undiagnosed diabetes. Thus, diabetes poses a major health threat to Latinas and Latinos.

To date, five major studies provide information on U.S. Latinas and Latinos and diabetes. Three focused on Latinas and Latinos, primarily on Chicanas and Chicanos (Mexican Americans) in the Southwest: the San Antonio Heart Study and the Starr County Study in Texas and the San Luis Valley Diabetes Study in Colorado. Only one survey, the Hispanic Health and Nutrition Examination Survey (HHANES 1982–1984), provided national data on the three major Latina and Latino subgroups—Chicanas and Chicanos, Puerto Ricans, and Cubans. More recently, the National Health and Nutrition Examination Survey (NHANES 1999–2000) included a national sample of Chicanas and Chicanos along with national samples of African Americans and whites. Most of the national population-based diabetes studies focus on Chicanas and Chicanos. According to Stern and Mitchell (1995), these studies discovered rates of diabetes two to three times higher for Chicanas and Chicanos than for non-Latina and non-Latino whites, and the HHANES found that Puerto Ricans in New York City have rates comparable to those of Chicanas and Chicanos.

These population studies and smaller clinical studies have examined genetic, behavioral, and sociocultural variables to determine the primary causes of the rapid growth of NIDDM among Latinas and Latinos. Most of this research has focused both on genetic links and on the relationship of the Native American genetic admixture to NIDDM prevalence. "Genetic admixture" means that contemporary Latinas and Latinos have genomes extensively composed of DNA inherited from Native Americans in the New World. The San Antonio study suggests that higher Native American genetic admixture results in higher Type II prevalence; however, the role of other variables is unclear. A major limitation of these genetic studies is the lack of national generalizability to the broader Latina and Latino population. Perhaps another major limitation is that "genetic studies" often resort to or favor "reductionist" models of genomic organization and function.

The impact of diabetes includes sequelae such as nephropathy (kidney disease); retinopathy (a disease of the eye's retina); poor circulation, which can lead to gangrene and loss of limbs; and gestational diabetes, which is associated with premature delivery. Related results of diabetes include higher rates of death from heart disease, strokes, high blood pressure, blindness, kidney disease, nervous system disease, amputations, and dental illnesses. Diabetes can also cause life-threatening biochemical imbalances. It has been thought that diabetics have weakened immune systems, and they are more susceptible to infection, though this may be due to poor circulation. They are more likely than nondiabetics to die of pneumonia or influenza. Guidelines for diabetic patient care created by the American Diabetes Association, the American Board of Family Practice, and the Centers for Disease Control and Prevention include annual foot examinations, an annual eye evaluation for retinopathy, and

urinalysis. Meticulous preventive measures can delay or halt some of the most severe complications; however, because many Latinas and Latinos are uninsured, they are often unlikely to get important preventive care.

There is some evidence of ethnic differences in the prevalence of complications linked to diabetes. The San Antonio Heart Study and NHANES found that the rate of diabetic retinopathy was twice as high in Mexican Americans, identified by a seven-question instrument, than in non-Hispanic white Americans. The San Antonio study also found evidence of higher prevalence of nephropathy among Mexican Americans. Conversely, the San Luis Study, in which ethnicity was self designated, found no difference between Hispanics and non-Hispanics in incidence of nephropathy and found a lower rate of retinopathy in Hispanics than in non-Hispanics.

Behavioral and sociocultural variables are critical in the growing epidemic of Type II diabetes in the Latina and Latino population. Like other groups, Latinas and Latinos in the United States are suffering from growing rates of obesity, a major risk factor associated with Type II diabetes mellitus. Table 1, "Obesity and Diabetes Prevalence Among U.S. Adults by Race," illustrates the correlation between diabetes and obesity.

Obesity results from lifestyle choices, income levels, diet choices, and lack of exercise. More Latina and Latino adults and children exercise little and consume more than other groups. For recent Latina and Latino immigrants, acculturative stress may result in poor diet and exercise choices, thereby increasing diabetes mellitus incidence and prevalence. The American Diabetes Association suggests that individuals limit caloric and fat intake, exercise regularly, reduce stress, and maintain a healthy weight. For diabetics, such behavior can help control blood glucose levels and improve health-related quality of life.

Although there is limited empirical evidence concerning diabetes rates in Latina and Latino subpopulations, it appears that certain Latina and Latino groups, such as Mexican Americans and Puerto Ricans, are experiencing rapid increases in obesity and Type II diabetes mellitus. Greater

TABLE 1. *Obesity and Diabetes Prevalence Among U.S. Adults by Race, BRFSS* 2001*

RACE	OBESITY %	DIABETES %
White	19.6	7.2
Black	31.1	11.2
Hispanic	23.7	9.0
Other	15.7	8.2

* Behavioral Risk Factor Surveillance System, 2001; Self-Reported Data

access to screening, health information, and appropriate care at varying disease stages is important to reduce morbidity and mortality rates associated with both forms of this disease; thus access to medical insurance is a life-and-death issue for Latinas and Latinos in the United States.

See also **Health; Health Care Access; Health, Children's; Hypertension;** *and* **Public Policy.**

BIBLIOGRAPHY

Behavioral Risk Factor Surveillance System. "2001 Obesity and Diabetes Prevalence Among U.S. Adults, by Selected Characteristics." Behavioral Risk Factor Surveillance System, 2001; Self-reported data. Data in table obtained from the Centers for Disease Control and Prevention website at www.cdc.gov/nccdphp/dnpa/obesity/trend/obesity_diabetes_characteristics.htm.

Centers for Disease Control and Prevention. "National Diabetes Fact Sheet." www.cdc.gov/diabetes/pubs/estimates.htm

National Diabetes Information Clearinghouse. "Diabetes in Hispanic Americans." National Diabetes Information Clearinghouse, 2002. diabetes.niddk.nih.gov/dm/pubs/hispanicamerican/index.htm. Links to many sites dealing with diabetes and kidney disease can be found at the main Internet site of the NDIC: http://diabetes.niddk.nih.gov/.

Stern, M. P., and B. D. Mitchell. "Diabetes in Hispanic Americans." In *Diabetes in America.* 2nd ed. Bethesda, Md.: National Diabetes Data Group, National Institutes of Health, NIH Publication No. 95–1468, 1995.

Zoorob, Roger J., and Michael D. Hagen. "Guidelines on the Care of Diabetic Nephropathy, Retinopathy, and Foot Disease." *American Family Physician* 56, no. 8 (15 November 1997). www.aafp.org/afp/971115ap/zoorob.html

ADELA DE LA TORRE AND TERENCE VALENZUELA

DIA DE LOS MUERTOS. *Día de los muertos* (Day of the Dead), November 2, is observed throughout Latin America, but the tradition is most auspiciously embraced in Mexico. It is a time when families visit the graves of their relatives, clean the graves, surround them with flowers, preferably marigolds, and light candles and incense. The practice, more accurately called *días de los muertos* or *días de finados* (Days of the Dead), is today a Catholic ritual with strong vestiges of Mesoamerican indigenous traditions.

This practice began as All Saints' Day (All Hallows' Day) on November 1 to commemorate all Christian saints and martyrs, and to replace a more ancient, non-Christian custom of ancestor worship. The Catholic Church sought to disassociate new Christians from this tradition, but the practice persisted. By the eleventh century, the liturgical calendar included a day to honor the dead, All Souls' Day on November 2, to follow All Saints' Day. Ancient customs fused with Christian rites and became a symbolic celebration that replaced such practices as feasting on graves. For Mexicans, special breads baked in memory of the dead are served during these days of remembrance.

Aztec-Mexican society and other Mesoamerican cultures already allowed days in their calendars for honoring the dead. Aztec observances included the Feast of the Little Dead, which commemorated infants and children (the innocents) and the Feast of the Dead, which remembered deceased adults. Sixteenth-century Spanish writings describe, and lament, how the Catholic tradition of All Saints' and All Souls' merged with indigenous beliefs and practices.

With a strong belief in the afterlife, the land of Míctlan, and the association of the continuum of life/death/rebirth, or resurrection, it is reasonable that Mesoamerican civilizations ascertained similarities and altered practices to coincide with Christian rituals. As the two cultures merged, alterations in both created a new syncretism. All Saints' Day became *día de los angelitos* or *día de los santos inocentes*, honoring the young and innocent deceased; All Souls' Day, *día de todos los muertos* or *día de los fieles difuntos*, commemorates deceased adults.

In pre-Hispanic times, celebrations included flowers, paper or bark images, foods such as tamales, fruits, pumpkin seeds, and beverages of chocolate and *pulque* (an alcoholic drink of the fermented sap of maguey). These traditions persist in Mexico, Central America, and other parts of the world.

The holiday is a lively and colorful event that may puzzle non-Latinos and non-Latinas. Western culture does not celebrate death; consequently, the extent of the Mexican observance may appear strange, even macabre. For Mexicans and other Latinas and Latinos, the ritual is a celebration of life, not death. In remembering deceased loved ones, Latinas and Latinos honor their ancestors in the hope that they too will one day be remembered just as reverently.

By the middle of the twentieth century, the observance seemed to wane outside of Mexico. However, a revival is evident in the early twenty-first century. In cities across the United States the celebration has taken on artistic dimensions. Altar tables with *ofrendas* (offerings) to the deceased are seen in museums and libraries.

Altars are shrines with photographs of the honored person decorated with flowers, *papel picado* (cut-paper images), fruits, special foods such as *moles* and *guisados* (meats in spicy sauces), candy skulls, chocolate, sugar cane, *pan de muerto* (skeleton-shaped pastries), the person's favorite beverage, cigars or cigarettes if appropriate, and related mementos.

In public exhibitions, photographs or images of famous or infamous personages are artistically and vividly displayed. Among popular personalities enshrined in artistic ofrenda expressions are Pancho Villa, César Chávez, Frida Kahlo, and Selena. Public displays of the last few years include altars honoring heroes of 9/11.

DIA DE LOS MUERTOS. A young girl prepares an altar in Sacramento, California. (Lawrence Migdale)

A universal practice on días de los muertos is the cleaning of graves. The practice is considered an obligation and shows great respect for the elderly, parents, and grandparents, and other family members who have passed on. Those remembered thus continue their cosmic journey to the heavens. Often, due to migration, some families may travel long distances, even across international boundaries, to perform this duty. Flowers and wreaths are placed on graves, prayers and memories are shared, and food and beverages may be consumed, but only after the deceased have first been invited to join in.

Even though most observances are private family events, they may take on a public or community aspect. Cemeteries decorated with ribbons and flowers, a celebration of a Catholic Mass, or blessing of graves by a priest are among public observances. At cemetery entrances vendors sell their wares for ofrendas for altars, and can become lively with riotous color, aroma, and sound. The cacophony of vendors peddling flowers, especially *cempasuchil* (marigolds), papier mâché figures, candles, pan de muerto, and molded sugar skulls, combined with the chattering of families and the inevitable singing of a remembered favorite melody creates an ambience of celebration.

A popular public observance in many Mexican venues is attending the Spanish play *Don Juan Tenorio*, the story of a libertine and seducer who cheats in life but cannot cheat death.

Whether public or private, elaborate or simple, in Mexico or elsewhere, día de los muertos is celebrated with artistry and flair. On the one hand, death is revered and, on the other, mocked. In Mexican folklore, *la muerte* (death) holds a special place because of its egalitarianism. Death takes everyone; it does not discriminate based on gender, class, creed, age, or color. For this reason, death is respected. Death is also mocked because of its inevitability. Death comes to all and, while not anticipated or welcomed, it is neither feared. It is an accepted consequence of life.

The best illustration of ridiculing death is seen in José Guadalupe Posada's (1852–1913) caricatures or *calaveras* (skeletons). Posada's illustrations of death are satirical characterizations of the ruling class and the Diaz dictatorship in Mexico. His political cartoons and illustrations appeared in newspapers, broadsides, and *papel picado* cutouts, and became popular images for the Day of the Dead. His works continue to inspire Latina and Latino artists and poets.

Calaveras are also poetic expressions that poke fun at the famous and infamous. These are written verses that mock those in high positions by reminding them of the inevitability of death, no matter how important or powerful they are. A custom practiced throughout Texas and the Southwest in the early twentieth century, calavera contests were held by local newspapers, in which entries were published and transmitted over the radio. This tradition of poetic calaveras has not fared well in recent years. Mexico maintains these written traditions, but not with the fervor of the last century. Still, the celebration of días de los muertos is not about to disappear. It carries the history of centuries and the shared values of diverse cultures. It offers a view of the past that is an amalgamation of indigenous American and European cultures. This union presents a unique and colorful way to celebrate life. At the same time, días de los muertos reminds us of the inevitability of death, for as the old adage goes: *El hombre encuentra la habilidad para todo menos para la muerte.* Humans can find a way to deal with anything except death.

See also Altares.

BIBLIOGRAPHY

Ancona, George. *Pablo Remembers: The Fiesta of the Day of the Dead.* New York: Lothrop, Lee & Shepard Books, 1993.

Carmichael, Elizabeth, and Chloe Sayer. *The Skeleton at the Feast: The Day of the Dead in Mexico.* Austin: University of Texas Press, 1991.

Hoyt-Goldsmith, Dian. *Day of the Dead: A Mexican-American Celebration.* New York: Holiday House, 1994.

Leon Portilla, Miguel. *Aztec Thought and Culture: A Study of the Ancient Nahuatl Mind.* Norman: Oklahoma University Press, 1963.

Posada, José Guadalupe. *José Guadalupe Posada, Ilustrador de la Vida Mexican.* Mexico City: Editorial de la Plástica Mexicana, 1963.

Toor, Frances. *A Treasury of Mexican Folkways.* New York: Crown, 1947.

Turner, Kay, and Pat Jasper. "Day of the Dead: The Tex-Mex Tradition." In *Halloween and Other Festivals of Death and Life,* edited by Jack Santino. Knoxville: University of Tennessee Press, 1994.

JUANITA ELIZONDO GARZA

DÍAZ, JUNOT (b. 1968), Dominican American author. Junot Díaz is the author of the best-selling short story collection *Drown* (1996), which has been translated into twelve languages. He has also edited one anthology, *The Beacon Best of 2001: Great Writing by Women and Men of All Colors and Cultures.* His fiction has appeared in *Story, The New Yorker, The Paris Review, Time Out, Glimmer Train, African Voices,* four annual volumes of *Best American Short Stories* between 1996 and 2000, and in 1999 the "The Future of American Fiction" issue of *The New Yorker.* Díaz was the only writer to be named one of *Newsweek* magazine's "New Faces of 1996," and *Drown* was nominated for the Quality Paperback Book Club's "New Voices" award in 1997. Most recently, Díaz has received a Pushcart Prize XXII, a Guggenheim Fellowship in 1999, a Lila Wallace–Reader's Digest Writers' Award, and the 2002 Pen/Malamud Award.

Born in 1968, Junot Díaz spent his early childhood in the Dominican Republic. After living several years separated from his father who had migrated to the United States, his family reunited in 1975 when they all moved to New Jersey. He pursued his education in New Jersey and obtained his bachelor's degree at Rutgers University. He later received a master of fine arts degree in Creative Writing at Cornell University. Díaz taught in the MFA program at Syracuse University from 1997 to 2002, and has taught in "Voices," a summer program for writers of color at the University of San Francisco, since 1996. In the early 2000s, he was an associate professor in the Writing and Humanistic Studies program at the Massachusetts Institute of Technology in Boston.

Visibly autobiographical, Díaz's collection of short stories, *Drown,* narrates several episodes in the life of Yunior, a boy who grows up in impoverished barrios of the Dominican Republic and later in the inner cities of industrial New Jersey. The stories "Ysrael," "Aguantando," and "No Face" are set in the Dominican Republic, where little Yunior, his brother Rafa, and their mother Virta struggle with poverty and separation from her husband, who has migrated to the United States. "Drown," "Edison, New Jersey," and the other stories are set in the United States and portray different stages of Yunior's coming of age in the claustrophobic atmosphere of an industrial neighborhood, where life seems doomed and hopeless.

According to his critics, it is Díaz's

> knack for language that ultimately enables him to achieve the visual richness of his work conferring tangibility to the experiences he captures in it. . . . Díaz causes words—and most notably the verbs—to show meaning plastically. Here is a fiction writer who draws on the robust lexical fund at his disposal to sculpt, to paint, to physically imprint the reality of his characters so as to make them seen.
>
> (Torres-Saillant)

Díaz's works reflect his Latino, Afro-American, and global literary experiences, and although critics have perceived various influences in his writing, many of them concede that his success resides in his crafting of a new voice in the American literary landscape. In other words, Díaz's writings capture the experience of the Dominican community in the United States in a style that exudes authenticity and transgresses established literary conventions on what is expected from minority writers. Although initially influenced by writers such as Ralph Ellison, Toni Morrison, Sandra Cisneros, and Piri Thomas, Díaz also distinguishes himself from minority writers of previous generations. Within the context of Dominican and other Latina and Latino writers, for instance, his work represents a generational shift in terms of his approach to the immigrant experience and his use of the language—particularly use of the Spanish language, which is interspersed throughout the English text and stands out for its absence of italics, quotation marks, or translations for an assumed English-speaking reader. For Díaz, Spanish is not different from English in terms of the quantity of people who speak it around the world. Consequently, there is no reason why it should be treated differently, as a "foreign" language:

> Why 'other' it? Why denormalize it? By keeping the Spanish as normative in a predominantly English text, I wanted to remind readers of the fluidity of languages, the mutability of languages. And to mark how steadily English is transforming Spanish and Spanish is transforming English. . . . When I learned English in the States, this was a violent enterprise. And by forcing Spanish back onto English, forcing it to deal with the language it tried to exterminate in me, I've tried to represent a mirror-image of that violence on the page. Call it my revenge on English.
>
> (quoted in Céspedes and Torres-Saillant, p. 904)

And while his writings portray the experience of characters growing up in poverty, Díaz is also careful not to become a "native informer," which in his words is

that historically familiar figure who writes about his/her own cultural/identity location for the consumption of primarily white outsider audiences, an act which by its very nature requires that the writer commit heavy-duty discursive violence on his/her cultural/identity site—simplifying, limiting, deforming it in the most brutal and familiar ways imaginable.

(quoted in Marsters)

Díaz's ethical position regarding the ways in which the experience of a minority community is represented is part of his critical stance against the conservative, white supremacist structures in American mainstream literature and publishing, which as he puts it, "only imagine Latino literature through magic-realism" (Díaz 2004). In other words, Díaz has committed himself to transgressing and subverting stereotypes that come from both mainstream and minority literary traditions. Now, as he converses with the works of international writers such as Edouard Glissant, Patrick Chamoiseau, Salman Rushdie, and W. G. Sebald, Díaz's commitment includes not only the Dominican community, but also the Caribbean, as he addresses the ways in which the literary tradition has guarded what he calls "the unimaginable silence of Caribbean history" (Díaz 2004).

See also Dominican Writers in the United States *and* Literature.

BIBLIOGRAPHY

Céspedes, Diógenes, and Silvio Torres-Saillant. "Fiction Is the Poor Man's Cinema: An Interview with Junot Díaz." *Callaloo* 23, no. 3 (Summer 2000): 892–907.

Díaz, Junot. 2004. Interview by Sophie Maríñez, November 11, 2004.

Marsters, Sarge. "Radical Alchemy: Junot Díaz on the Voices, Languages, and Structures behind His Fiction." In *Emerson College Newsletter* (Fall 2004).

Torres-Saillant, Silvio. "A Review of *Drown*." In *Urban Desires* 2 no. 5 (November-December 1996). Online. http://desires.com/.

SOPHIE MARÍÑEZ

DICHOS. *Dichos*, or *refranes*, are concise sayings popularized in Latina and Latino communities. In English, they are called proverbs, sayings, adages, maxims, and apothegms. These short, pithy comments are often repeated to illustrate a point or to give advice. Dichos reflect the community's wisdom, superstitions, and prejudices, which are based on life experiences. Traditionally, dichos were guides for conduct.

"The genius, wit and spirit of a country are discovered in its proverbs," said Francis Bacon. Dichos are the wisdom of many and as such are used widely in societies throughout human history through oral tradition. Dichos reflect generational experiences in rich ways with a predominantly popular and cultural flavor. Practical and simple, these philosophical sayings penetrate a society through the voices of speakers capable of concretizing daily events in accessible wording. Basically, a dicho is a brief, popular saying that has some truth, is usually symbolic, and poetically expresses a norm of conduct.

Dichos have been circulated by word of mouth for generations. They can be traced back to Spain under Muslim rule. Muslims ruled areas of Spain from 711 C.E. to 1492 C.E., and Spanish culture was shaped by this occupation. In the late sixteenth century, as the Spanish trekked northward from the interior of Mexico, the forces of colonization and acculturation spread the use of dichos. Although Native Americans had developed sophisticated cultures, with impressive traditions of folklore and literature, the Spaniards quickly imposed their own culture throughout the territory. It should be pointed out that the conquest occurred during Spain's greatest literary age, which gave rise to the works of Cervantes, Lope de Vega, and Góngora.

The origin of dichos is unknown but suggests the mingled Arabic, Christian, and Roman culture of the Latina and Latino peoples. An example of such a transcultural dicho is "Allá van leyes donde quieren reyes" (laws go the way kings direct). This dicho came from a popular reaction to the decision of King Alfonso VI of Spain in a twelfth-century dispute over whether the Mozarabic rite or the Roman rite should be practiced in the liturgy of the church of Toledo. The lesson from this dicho is that even if a king's decision is unpopular (Alfonso decided in favor of the Mozarabic rite), his word is final.

Dichos do not always come from life experiences. Some dichos have origins in popular stories, in apologues or moral fables. More often than not, dichos have roots in traditional Spanish poems called *romanceros*. Dichos derived from romanceros are usually the synthesis or conclusion of the narrative. The dicho "A buen capellán, mayor sacristán" comes from the following apologue:

A traveling chaplain stopped at a village inn to eat his lunch of roasted pigeon. Another traveler approached him and asked him to share his pigeon on promise of payment. The chaplain refused, and the traveler ate his lunch of dry bread next to him. When both finished eating the traveler told the chaplain, "Many thanks, Reverend, for we have both enjoyed the pigeon; you the taste of it, and I its aroma."

On hearing this, the chaplain insisted that the traveler pay for his part of the pigeon. A heated argument followed, the chaplain demanding payment and the traveler refusing to pay. The sacristan of the village was then summoned to settle the argument. "How much did you pay for the pigeon?" he asked the chaplain. "Half a dollar," he replied. Then the sacristan asked the traveler to produce a quarter, and making it bounce and tinkle on the table finally he pronounced, "Reverend, consider yourself paid by the sound of this coin for the traveler's enjoyment of the pigeon's aroma."

(Iscla Rovira, p. 5)

The dicho that summarizes this fable is, "Every smart chaplain needs a smarter sacristan."

When the Spanish brought dichos to different lands, the natives adopted some of them, altering the wording to meet their own philosophical needs. Still, dichos bear the stamp of Spanish philosophy and reflect a Spanish sense of values.

The origin of proverbs is in the observation of life's normal complexities and experiences. Because this observation is universal, the saying or dicho became accepted as a norm. Whenever a similar situation arose, the dicho was repeated, establishing itself in many cultures and societies. According to Francisco Caudet, sayings frequently point out "maxims of moral character . . . and their compilation constitute every culture's own collection of sayings." Along these lines, adds Caudet, "The existence of collected sayings is as old as our human identity and their genesis is lost in time at the same point that is ours."

Themes for dichos range from love and marriage to money, religion, superstitions, women and male chauvinism, and of course friendship. Lord Russell stated that proverbs are "the wisdom of many and the wit of one." This is because while dichos express the feelings of the community, only one person put them into words. Often times, dichos validate a standard for living and a way to conduct business or daily life. Most often, dicho*s* tells us about life in a particular community or culture. Dichos present a well-integrated, rational, and consistent picture of how a society views character and how it tries to conduct its social relationships and arrange its communities. Therefore, dichos have a dual function in society: they express and reaffirm normal views of character and suggest guidelines for the training of children and for personal conduct in general. An example of a dicho for child rearing is "A comer y a misa, a la primera llamada" (one comes to dinner and to Mass at the first call). Traditionally, there are three bell "calls" to Mass, and the obedient child gets under way at the sound of the first. Parents repeat this dicho to their children to remind them to obey.

The scholar and folklorist Américo Paredes counters this view of dichos by writing, "*Dichos* do not contain absolute truths; that is they are not a set of rules telling one exactly how to behave at all times." Instead, Paredes asserts, "They are a storehouse of good advice to be used in specific situations."

Another example of a dicho is "A buen hambre no hay mal pan" (no food is bad when you're good and hungry). Another is "A dios rogando y con el mazo dando" (Pray to God, but keep hammering away [at your problem]).

The proliferation of Web sites listing dichos shows the persistent interest in their use. Dichos are a product of life, and life continuously changes. The lessons we get from dichos will change as time and life move on. Dichos are transnational and transcultural. Oral tradition is vital to the existence of dichos. Acknowledging this, the Marques of Santillana titled his *refranero*, or collection of refranes, the first ever published, *Refranes que las viejas dicen tras el fuego* (Proverbs old women tell by the fireplace). Dichos will forever be passed down from generation to generation and from culture to culture.

See also Folklore *and* Literature.

BIBLIOGRAPHY

Abrahams, Roger D. "Proverbs and Proverbial Expressions." In *Folkore and Folklife: An Introduction*, edited by Richard M. Dorson. Chicago: University of Chicago Press, 1972.

Aranda, Charles. *Dichos: Proverbs and Sayings from the Spanish*. Rev. ed. Santa Fe, N.M.: Sunstone Press, 1977.

Arora, Shirley L. "Proverbs in Mexican American Tradition." *De Proverbio* 2 (1995). Available at DeProverbio.com

Ballesteros, Octavio A., and Maria del Carmen Ballesteros. *Mexican Sayings: The Treasure of a People*. Austin, Tex.: Eakin Press, 1992.

Caudet Yarza, Francisco. *Los mejores refranes Españoles*. Madrid: EDIMAT, 2000.

Iscla Rovira, Luis. *Spanish Proverbs: A Survey of Spanish Culture and Civilization*. Lanham, Md.: University Press of America, 1984.

Martínez Pérez, José. *Dichos, dicharachos y refranes Mexicanos*. México: Agata, 1998.

Paredes, Americo, and Raymund Paredes. *Mexican-American Authors*. Boston: Houghton Mifflin, 1972.

Ramírez, Dora Cecilia. "Más claro no canta un gallo." *Boletín Cultural y Bibliográfico* 28, no. 27, (1991).

West, John O. *Mexican-American Folklore: Legends, Songs, Festivals, Proverbs, Crafts, Tales of Saints, of Revolutionaries, and More*. Little Rock, Ark.: August House. 1988.

ROSE RODRIGUEZ-RABIN

DISEASE. *See* Alcoholism; Asthma; Birth Defects; Breast Cancer; Diabetes; HIV/AIDS; Hypertension; Reproduction and Health.

DISTRICT OF COLUMBIA. The establishment of Latin American embassies and international organizations in the nation's capital generated a small Spanish-speaking multiethnic population in Washington soon after World War II. This population grew along with the rest of the city as Washington became a world capital as well as a national one. Professional staff and domestic workers of the Spanish-speaking embassies and world organizations took up residence near present-day Adams Morgan and Mt. Pleasant. These neighborhoods were convenient to the many embassies situated around 16th Street and Massachusetts Avenue. Many domestic workers stayed after their host employers left the city. They settled in the area and persuaded family and friends from home to join them. This started the Latina and Latino community-building process in the city. Occasionally, individuals returned home for a while and then re-immigrated. They kept contact with the home country and encouraged family members to come to Washington. Latin American students at universities in the area added another significant segment to the growing Spanish-speaking population. Puerto Rican and Mexican American white-collar workers came to the area in great numbers for the federal jobs generated by the New Deal and World War II. For the most part, students and professional Mexican Americans kept themselves separate and aloof from the working-class Latina and Latino community.

Cuban exiles began to arrive to the area in the late 1950s and early 1960s, during and at the end of the Cuban revolution. In the 1960s, the Spanish-speaking population began to grow rapidly. The economic hardship and political turmoil in Latin America, combined with the alluring image of the United States as a place "where the streets are paved with gold," created a flow of legal and illegal immigration to the United States. In the 1960s and 1970s, South American immigrants came in large numbers, followed in the 1980s by major immigrations of Central Americans that continue through the early years of the twenty-first century. Of the latter, the leading country of origin has been El Salvador (in 2000, 26 percent of the population). The 1970s census estimate of Latinas and Latinos in the city was 15,671; in the 1980s it was 17,679; in the 1990s, 32,710; and in the 2000 census it was 44,954. It is the fastest-growing ethnic minority in the city and in the country.

In general, the majority of Latinas and Latinos in Washington, D.C., are immigrants. However, the 1.5 generation (born outside but growing up in the United States) and the growing number of Latinas and Latinos born in the city are having a significant influence on the social character of the local community and on society in general. These young people benefit from the cultural and social organizations established by earlier immigrant generations. Krishna Roy explains,

> While the City's population decreased, the Latino population increased. Latinos' population growth and the development of community infrastructure contributed to the stability of central city neighborhoods at a time when urban flight followed the 1968 riots, the city's subsequent neglect of the inner city, and the city's financial mismanagement of the 1990s (p. 5).

The city is divided into eight wards. Latinas and Latinos have tended to concentrate in Wards 1 and 4. The barrio, or oldest core of the Latino and Latina community, is located in the Mount Pleasant, Adams Morgan, and Columbia Heights neighborhoods in Ward 1. However, affordable housing has increasingly become a major problem for Latinas and Latinos, especially in these neighborhoods, and has forced them to move outside the city into the surrounding metropolitan area—the suburbs of Maryland and Virginia. Even as Latina and Latino business entrepreneurship has rapidly grown, most Latina and Latino workers have remained in lower-paying occupations, often working part-time with no employee benefits or job security.

See also Census; Central Americans; Immigration; Maryland; South Americans; *and* Virginia.

BIBLIOGRAPHY
Repak, Terry. *Waiting on Washington: Central American Workers in the Nation's Capital*. Philadelphia: Temple University Press, 1995.
Roy, Krishna. "Sociodemographic Profile." In *The State of Latinos in the District of Columbia: Trends, Consequences, and Recommendations*. Washington, D.C.: Council of Latino Agencies, 2002. www.consejo.org/publications.html. See Chapter 1.

OLIVIA CADAVAL

D'LEÓN, OSCAR (b. 1943), salsa singer. Born Oscar Emilio León, Venezuelan salsa singer Oscar D'León is also a bassist, bandleader, composer, and arranger. Known as "El León de la Salsa" (The Lion of Salsa) and "El Diablo de la Salsa" (The Devil of Salsa), he has become one of the most widely known salsa artists for his improvisational skills (*soneos*), his rich voice, and his dynamic stage performances. D'León embodies the best of Venezuelan salsa in his original arrangements and compositions, a repertoire that integrates the traditional Cuban influences of Beny Moré and la Sonora Matancera with the New York sound of Eddie Palmieri and the early *Nuyorican* salsa while imprinting his Venezuelan stamp on them. His music includes Venezuelan rhythms such as *la gaita* and the *joropo* and *cuatro* melodies in the brass arrangements.

Early Career

The son of a bricklayer, Oscar D'León was born on July 11, 1943, in the neighborhood of Antímano in Caracas, into a family that loved to listen to Cuban music on the radio. He was a self-taught bassist and singer and worked at various jobs during his youth in order to survive—he drove a taxi, worked at the General Motors factory in Caracas, and played in nightclubs—which has made him a role model of success through hard work.

In 1972, D'León created Dimensión Latina, a big band that functioned as a cooperative, since all the musicians

owned the profits of the band. During the next four years, D'León recorded six albums with Dimensión Latina; these were collected in *Una dimensión de éxitos* (A dimension of successes) and *Inolvidable* (Unforgettable, 1994). In 1976, when D'León decided to leave the band, the Puerto Rican vocalist Andy Montañez, lead singer for El Gran Combo de Puerto Rico, was invited to replace him. Montañez sang lead vocals with Wladimir Lozano and Rodrigo Mendoza. Montañez eventually left to form his own orchestra, but his participation in this Venezuelan band exemplifies the mutual exchanges and influences among the Puerto Rican and Venezuelan salsa artists. It is not surprising that Oscar D'León's performances and arrangements have been compared to those of Puerto Rico's iconic El Gran Combo in their big-band sound, choreography and showmanship, and repertoire that sings to the everyday lives of working-class men and women in the Caribbean. On November 11, 1980, Oscar D'León and Dimensión Latina held a reunion concert at the Poliedro Stadium in Caracas. The live album of the concert, *Dos colosos en concierto* (Two Giants in Concert), was released in 1981.

In 1976, D'León formed La Salsa Mayor, the orchestra that still backs him up during all his performances. By now, this orchestra has become an important training group for aspiring Venezuelan musicians. In a 2001 interview, D'León commented that it is important to give opportunities to young musicians because they have that "extra added energy." In fact, musicians such as Luisito Quintero, Raúl Agraz, and Robert Vilera started their careers with La Salsa Mayor.

D'León has recorded about sixty albums during his career, including *El más grande* (The Biggest, 1978), considered to be "one of his best albums ever"; *El rey de los soneros* (The King of Soneros, 1991), his first solo album under contract with Ralph Mercado Music (RMM); *Toitico tuyo* (I'm All Yours, 1994); *Sonero del mundo* (Sonero of the World, 1996), nominated for a Grammy Award; and *En Nueva York* (1997), which included the participation of Cuban trumpet player Arturo Sandoval and a duet with *Nuyorican* singer La India. His most recent CDs include *Doble play* (Double Play, 2000); *En vivo* (Live, 2000); *The Best of Oscar D'León* (2002); and *Infinito* (Infinite, 2003).

One of the keys to D'León's success is the popularity of many of his love songs, which combine dynamic arrangements and rhythms that are ideal for dancing with lyrics that reflect the gender politics between men and women in Latin American and Latina and Latino communities. His hits develop traditional motifs such as the woman who betrays the man ("Traicionera"), the *bandolera* (the golddigger), unrequited love ("Cuando ya no me quieras"—When You No Longer Love Me; "Lástima que seas ajena"—Too Bad You're Far Away), and carnal desire ("Matemática sexual"—Sexual Mathematics).

Varied Repertoire

D'León's repertoire, however, is not limited to love songs. As with many of the most important *soneros* and salsa interpreters, such as Rubén Blades, Celia Cruz, and Willie Colón, social issues, songs of resistance, and cultural reaffirmation are integral to his repertoire. The song "Hay que trabajar" (One Must Work), recorded with the late Tito Puente in 1991, motivates listeners to work and be productive in order to survive economically. "Casas de carton" (Cardboard Houses), which deals with poor housing and children living in poverty, is a strong statement against economic exploitation and social oppression. "Mi gente" (My People), which echoes Puerto Rican *sonero* Héctor Lavoe's "El cantante" (The Singer), pays tribute to Latin Americans' knowledge of, and authority in, dancing and producing music. By singing that "mi gente tiene conciencia/del ritmo y del timbal" (my people understand rhythm and the drum"), D'León recognizes the musical agency and rhythmic expertise of Latinas and Latinos and Latin Americans, making them collaborators in making music and dancing.

"Soy loco por ti, América" (I'm Crazy about You, America), a catchy melody that reminds us of Rubén Blades's hemispheric songs to Latin America, commemorates America's beauty through the topos of a love song. This composition, co-written with Brazilian Gilberto Gil, exemplifies D'León's pan-American vision, or sense of

Latinidad (a collectivity among Latinos) in his repertoire. Indeed, his great popularity stems from his versatility in both his singing and his performances. As he himself said, "We try to mix it all in. I even try to cover *rancheras*, *paso dobles*, boleros, merengues, jazz, jazz latino. My orchestra incorporates them all because we have fans all over the world and we try to please them as much as we can" (Rivera, p. 2).

While some critics have stated that D'León "exemplifies South America's acquisition of the Afro-Cuban legacy" (Agenzia Giornalistica Italia), it would be more accurate to recognize that Venezuela, culturally and musically, has been an historical part of a pan-Caribbean tradition and heritage. As such, it has played an important role in the multiple and hybrid musical influences that constitute Caribbean music. However, this said, we should not undermine D'León's strong connections to Cuban music. He revitalized Cuban classics such as Beny Moré's "Qué bueno baila Usted" (How Well You Dance), among others, and Celia Cruz has paid homage to him in the duet "El son de Celia y Oscar" (The Sound of Celia and Oscar). In this performance, Celia calls D'León "león que ruge en el mundo entero" (a lion that roars to the whole world), alluding to his international fame and influence. The refrain to the song, "son de los primeros," (they are the first, the *son* of the primary singers) plays with the word *son* (sound) as it refers both to the Cuban *son* and the improvisatory skills of both Celia and Oscar as pioneering *soneros*. In this context, Oscar D'León's importance as a *sonero* is also linked to the legacy of Ismael Rivera's improvisations, which marked the development of salsa music since the late 1960s.

D'León and La Salsa Mayor are known internationally. They have been invited to perform in more than 100 countries throughout Europe, Asia, Africa, and the Americas. D'León sang at the 1992 opening of the International Expo in Seville and has been invited to participate in most jazz festivals in Europe as well as in Japan, Turkey, and the Middle East.

On June 13, 2003, Oscar D'León suffered three heart attacks during a concert on the island of Martinique. After his recovery, he announced that he would resume performing in Rome, Italy, in July. Despite the challenge to his health, his motivation to continue performing on the world stage has not subsided. As he says in his song "Mi gente," he was born to bring happiness to his people through his music.

See also Salsa.

BIBLIOGRAPHY
Agenzia Giornalistica Italiana—News in English. "Oscar D'Leon to re-enter music scene at Rome's Fiesta." www.agi.it/english/news. July 11, 2003.
Berrios-Miranda, Marisol. Personal e-mail to author. July 21, 2003.
Child, John. "Profile: Oscar D'León." www.descarga.com. March 29, 1999.
Rivera, George. "A Conversation with Oscar D'León." www.jazzconclave.com. December 29, 2002.
Rondón, César Miguel. *El libro de la salsa: Crónica de la música del Caribe urbano*. Caracas, Venezuela: Editorial Arte, 1980.

FRANCES R. APARICIO

DLG. Featuring an eclectic blend of salsa, soul, hip-hop, and reggae, Dark Latin Groove (DLG) emerged from the New York Latin club scene in the late 1990s to produce some of the most influential Latin hybrids of the period. The group was the brainchild of the famed salsa producer Sergio George, who wanted to create a group that meshed the sounds of urban New York with Latin New York. George found a soulful Latin singer, Huey Dunbar, to represent the smooth, salsa-inspired piece of his idea, and James "Da Barba" de Jesus, a veteran ragga-influenced rapper who had worked as a backup singer with Tito Nieves and Sistah Souljah, to fill out the edgy part of the unlikely pairing.

The result was an infectious sound for the group that George labeled Dark Latin Groove. Unlike traditional salsa from the Caribbean, George's vision of his urban salsa was a more eclectic and refined styling that reflected the city of New York. It was nothing new for George, who had explored tropical and urban blends in his previous works with India and Marc Anthony. For the continuing evolution, George added in the spice of Jamaican dancehall. As veteran fans would recognize, this fusion was not really new either. Panamanian singer El General had explored the same territory with success in the early 1990s on such singles as "Te Ves Buena" and "Caramelo."

Of Puerto Rican and Jamaican descent, Dunbar was born and raised in New York. The only connection he had to his heritage was music. In fact, until he met George, Dunbar did not know how to speak or sing in Spanish. But within two years of meeting George, Dunbar was singing as a backup singer for other local Latin acts. By the time he was approached with the idea of DLG, he was nearly fluent in Spanish. His flexible voice range made him the perfect foil for de Jesus's hardnosed Jamaican rapping style.

George signed his project to his Sir George Entertainment record label in April of 1996 and began working on the group's debut. With George himself handling keyboard duties and several other noted musicians contributing to the album, *Dark Latin Groove* (1996) caught the ear of fans all over New York. Soon, the buzz created by the innovative urban hybrid began to catch on in other markets as well. Dunbar's strong, versatile tenor was perfectly complemented by de Jesus's gruff, rapid-fire rhythmic raps, making DLG an immediate crowd pleaser. A seasoned horn section gave extra energy to an already potent sound. The debut album eventually went gold and earned DLG a devoted following among fans and especially critics, who praised George's vision and innovativeness.

Having already tapped two of New York's largest minority groups (Puerto Ricans and Jamaicans) with Dunbar and de Jesus, George added another talented rapper to the DLG lineup for the group's sophomore effort, which reached another of the city's largest populations, Dominicans. With rapper Fragancia in the fold, DLG added another urban component to test the limits of the thumping fusion. The result was the 1997 release *Swing On*. Having a solid year of experience under its belt, DLG built upon the strengths of its debut and took more time on the production of *Swing On*. Fans loved the more refined, slickly produced album, which spawned hit singles like "La Quiero a Morir," "La Soledad," and "Magdalena, Mi Amor."

The album was another resounding success, reaching number two on *Billboard*'s tropical/salsa charts and selling over 300,000 copies in the United States alone, and thousands more around the world. This time, the group's powerful sound earned it a Grammy nomination and its first international tour. By the summer of 1998, DLG had performed sold-out shows in the United States, Colombia, Peru, and even Japan, including a crowd of sixty thousand in Cuzco, Peru. With new international recognition, Dunbar was frequently the focus of the group's media coverage. His good looks and fiery stage persona made him a natural for the spotlight.

Eager to continue DLG's success, George pulled the group back into the studio after its lengthy tour to start work on a third album. Hoping to capitalize on the band's rising popularity, George moved toward a more pop-oriented Latin sound for the follow-up to *Swing On*. *Gotcha* was released in 1999. Although the album sparked a few modest hits, such as "Volveré" and "Prisionero," it failed to reach the status of *Swing On*. However, Dunbar was becoming a bigger star than ever. After a tour supporting the album, Dunbar made the decision to leave the group to pursue a solo career.

Dunbar had become frustrated with the constraints of working with a group and wanted to pursue other types of music instead of being confined to the DLG sound. However, Dunbar didn't want to break with the producer who brought him up in the business, and he asked George to produce his solo debut. Released in 2001, *Yo Si Me Enamoré* attracted attention for Dunbar's passionate vocals and tropical beats. Behind the strength of the hit singles "Con Cada Beso" and "Yo Si Me Enamoré," the album reached number one on *Billboard*'s tropical/salsa charts and number fourteen on *Billboard*'s top Latin album charts. Dunbar's second solo album, *Music for My Peoples*, was released in 2003.

Although Dunbar's solo work is more reflective of traditional salsa music, the urban-infused DLG paved the way for a new crop of artists, many of them employing the same urban blueprint.

See also **Music, Popular** *and* **Salsa.**

BIBLIOGRAPHY

Jackson, Paul. "Latin Grooves." *Daily Yomiuri* (Tokyo, Japan), June 10, 1999.

McLane, Daisann. "Melting Pop." *Village Voice* (New York), August 19, 1997.

Mitchell, Gail. "Latin Music Mixes It Up with R&B." *Billboard*, October 2, 1999.

RAMIRO BURR

DOCUMENTARIES AND NONFICTION. Latin America has a distinguished documentary tradition: Santiago Alvarez in Cuba, Patricio Guzmán in Chile, Fernando Solanas in Argentina, and others developed the genre over the last fifty years, producing films that passionately documented the political and social struggles of the continent. Documentaries such as *The Battle of Chile* and *The Hour of the Furnaces* gained worldwide recognition. As early as the 1970s, Latina and Latino filmmakers in the United States became increasingly frustrated about the lack of Latina and Latino voices and representation in their own television and film screens, and turned to documentary film as an important expression to voice the creativity and social commitment of Latina and Latino communities in the United States.

From the early struggles to organize the farm workers in the vineyards of California, to the plight of Cuban and Haitian rafters arriving in Florida, Latina and Latino documentary makers have been recording the social and personal stories of the Latina and Latino experience. They have done so despite enormous challenges, few funds, and a lack of access to mainstream avenues for distribution and exhibition. Their main motivation was to portray their own version of a reality that was often distorted by Hollywood narrative films that stereotyped Latinos and Latinas as lazy villains or hot lovers.

Mexican Americans, the most established and numerous Latina and Latino immigrants, pioneered Latina and Latino documentary production. In 1969, Luis Valdez, the founder of the Teatro Campesino, directed *I Am Joaquín*, based on the poem by the Colorado-based activist Rodolfo "Corky" Gonzáles. Moctesuma Esparza, who has produced a dozen Latina and Latino–themed films during his career, became one of several activists-turned-filmmakers who were involved in the production of *Requiem 29* (1971), a documentary on the police riot that followed the killing of Chicano journalist Rubén Salazar during a street march. Defining themselves as

Chicanas and Chicanos, producers of Chicana and Chicano cinema created an awareness of a common identity and communicated a sense of pride to their audience. Latinas and Latinos gradually reached beyond that niche through documentaries that dealt with broader themes and were broadcast through mass-media outlets.

During the 1960s, Rick Tejada-Flores documented the first images of members of the United Farm Workers Union as they organized a grape boycott that brought national attention to the harsh working conditions, discrimination, and violence endured by the immigrant labor force. The farmworkers' strike, led by César Chávez, Dolores Huerta, and other Mexican American leaders in the California grape fields, brought the word *Huelga!* (strike) into the political discourse of the day, and those images helped strengthen the farmworkers' movement. In 1996, Tejada-Flores and Ray Telles incorporated that footage into a feature-length documentary, *The Fight in the Fields: César Chávez and the Farmworkers' Struggle*.

Other immigrant filmmakers expressed their vision and recorded their experiences through documentary film. Cuban Americans have also been active in filmmaking since the 1960s. The first documentary made in exile was Bebo Alonso's *La Cuba de Ayer* (1963), a compilation of newsreels interspersed with testimonies and performances by exiles. Orlando Jiménez-Leal directed *Improper Conduct* (with the cinematographer Nestor Almendros, 1984), an exploration of the discrimination towards homosexuals in Cuba and among exiles. Luis Argueta, who was born in Guatemala, made *The Cost of Cotton*, broadcast on PBS in 1978. More recently, Dominican-born filmmakers have produced documentaries; Yokasta Vázquez and Arsenio Rodríguez's *Dominicans in Florida: Three Decades of Immigration* (2004), had a screening at FIU in 2004. Dominicans living in New York feature in Alfredo de Villa's *Washington Heights* (2003).

Latina and Latino actors in Hollywood have moved beyond playing Latina and Latino characters in feature films and into documentary production. Cuban American actor Andy Garcia produced *Cachao* (1993), a documentary on the Cuban music legend. The Mexican American actor and director Edward James Olmos produced *Americanos: Latino Life in the U.S.* (2000), which was directed by Susan Todd and Andrew Young. It is significant that these established Hollywood actors invest their own resources in making documentaries that are usually much less profitable, in an effort to present more positive Latino and Latina role models than fiction films made by the big studios provide.

Women Documentary Producers

Latina filmmakers have made several landmark documentaries, such as the Oscar-winning *Agueda Martínez* (1977), directed by Esperanza Vásquez, and Sylvia Morales's *Chicana!* (1978). These films express themes related to the ethnic underclass developing in the United States and reflect on the complex web of values that subordinate women in society. Cuba-born, Puerto Rico–raised Ana María García, who is based in New York, made *La operación* (1982), about the forced mass sterilization of Puerto Rican women on the island.

Lourdes Portillo is the most prolific and best-known Latina filmmaker. Her documentary *Las Madres de la Plaza de Mayo* (with Susana Muñoz, 1986), about the struggle of the mothers of the disappeared in Argentina under the military dictatorship, received an Academy Award nomination. Portillo was born in Chihuahua, Mexico, and lives in San Francisco. She returned to Mexico to make other important documentaries, such as *La Ofrenda: The Days of the Dead* (1989), an examination of the relationship between cultural ritual and its transformations in the United States, and *Señorita Extraviada* (2002), investigating the murder of over three hundred women in Ciudad Juarez, on the United States–Mexico border. Her work is innovative and covers a range of issues, from an ironic, experimental look at the *Conquista* in *Columbus on Trial* to more personal explorations such as *The Devil Never Sleeps*.

Other Latina documentary makers are Nancy De Los Santos and Susan Rancho, who directed *The Bronze Screen: 100 Years of the Latino Image in Hollywood* (with Alberto Dominguez, 2002). Frances Negrón-Muntaner directed *Brincando el Charco* (1994), analyzing the intersection of race, class, and sexual identity as experienced by a Puerto Rican lesbian protagonist. Cuban American Ela Troyano made more experimental films mixing narrative and performance, such as *Carmelita Tropicana* (1994). Other, more personal documentaries include those made by Cuban Americans Ruth Behar and Rhonda Mitrani, who each returned to the island after growing up in the United States and chronicled their family's history in *Adio Kerida* and *Cuba Mia*.

Innovation

Latina and Latino documentaries became increasingly diverse in the 1980s, exploring issues such as art and literature, or countries and peoples beyond the U.S. borders. These documentaries are often narrated from a personal perspective and in a more intimate tone and are more willing to cross genre boundaries and experiment aesthetically.

Edín Vélez is a Puerto Rican experimental video artist who lives in New York. He has explored issues of cultural diversity in such documentaries as *Meta Mayan II* (1981), about indigenous Guatemalans, and *The Meaning of the Interval* (1987), about Japanese Buto performance.

Brazilian Korean American Iara Lee directed *Synthetic Pleasures* and *Modulations*, documenting avant-garde and electronic music.

The documentary *Ana Mendieta: Fuego de Tierra*, made in 1987 by the Cuba-born painter Nereyda Garcia-Ferraz with Kate Horsfeld, is a portrait of the life and work of the Cuban American artist Ana Mendieta, who until her tragic, untimely death in 1985 used her body, organic materials, and Afro-Cuban religious symbols to express her feminist political and poetic vision.

In the 1990s, this trend accelerated, with younger documentary filmmakers using experimental forms; mixing genres, styles, and narrative techniques with the conventions of the traditional documentary; and letting go of all constrictive aesthetic concerns. Carlos Marcovich shot parts of *Who the Hell Is Juliette* (1998) in New Jersey and the rest in Cuba and Mexico, using a dizzying range of visual, narrative, and editing techniques. Film directors working in fiction also began mixing genres and using documentary techniques. David Riker trained some of Manhattan's immigrant day laborers to act and re-enact their lives in his neo-realist narrative film, *La Ciudad*, in 1998, a scary and moving portrait of the difficulties faced by undocumented immigrants in New York.

Every Child Is Born a Poet: The Life and Work of Piri Thomas (2003), made by Jonathan Robinson in collaboration with the Puerto Rican, New York–based poet the film is named for, uses performance pieces and dramatic re-creation to explore what connects art and identity. *A Day without a Mexican* (2004), directed by Sergio Arau and Yareli Arizmendi and described by reviewers as a "mockumentary," is a fiction film that uses documentary techniques to imagine the paralysis overtaking California when one day the Mexican labor force mysteriously disappears.

Latina and Latino documentary makers have never abandoned social issues. The possibility of using film to instigate social change is a motivating force for filmmakers that transition from other professions, such as law or journalism. One of the most successful films in 2004 was *Farmingville*, directed by attorney Carlos Sandoval and Catherine Tambini. It won the Special Jury Prize at the Sundance Film Festival and has been exhibited as part of an effort to solve the problems created by the sudden influx of immigrant day laborers into suburban communities. *The Sixth Section*, directed by Alex Rivera, follows a group of Mexican immigrants from a small village in Puebla to their workplace in upstate New York, where they form a union to donate funds for improving their home village, such as building roads and a baseball stadium and funding water purification projects.

It is becoming difficult to categorize documentary films and filmmakers in an increasingly transnational, globalized world. Maisa Mendonca, a Brazil-born scholar based

at the time in San Francisco, made *Strong Roots*, a portrait of black Brazilian leader Benedita da Silva, and *Islands on Fire*, filmed in East Timor and Indonesia. Felix Zurita, a Spaniard living in Nicaragua, made *El Chogui*, which follows a Mexican who migrates to Los Angeles in search of a boxing career. Puerto Rican Frances Negrón-Muntaner, who is based in New York, has traveled as far as the Philippines and Guam to explore the impact of U.S. military interventions. Patricia Boero, a Cuban Uruguayan living in Florida, made *Paraguay: The Forgotten Dictatorship* and other documentaries on human rights in Australia and Uruguay. Mexican Carlos Bolado, who lives in California, turned his attention to the Middle East and co-directed *Promises* (with Justine Shapiro and BZ Goldberg), a documentary about Palestinian children growing up in the Israeli-occupied territories.

"Non-Latinas and non-Latinos" have also made a number of important documentary films about Latina and Latino issues and Latin America, often as a result of having lived there. Pamela Yates was one of the first American documentary makers to draw attention to human rights violations in Guatemala with her epic documentary *When the Mountains Tremble* (1984), which featured a then-unknown Rigoberta Menchú, who went on to win the Nobel Peace Prize. More recently, Yates and Paco de Onís have documented the atrocities committed in Peru in *State of Fear*. Patricia Flynn followed a midwestern immigrant to her native Guatemala to investigate the murders of her family in *Discovering Dominga*. Vicky Funari and Jennifer Maytorena Taylor documented a domestic worker's search for justice after suffering abuse as a child in *Paulina*. Laurie Collier directed *Nuyorican Dream*.

Economic Conditions

Documentary makers, especially minority filmmakers, often have to make their films on shoestring budgets, relying on meager resources, ingenuity, and dedication to bring their vision to the screen. Latino and Latina filmmakers have to search long and hard for financing from a limited number of sources that can cover only a fraction of the cost of producing a film.

Funders include the Corporation for Public Broadcasting (CPB), the Independent Television Service, the National Endowment for the Arts, and the National Endowment for the Humanities. Foundations and corporate donors provide the remaining funds. The private foundations that have contributed the most funds to producing documentaries include the John D. and Catherine T. MacArthur Foundation in Chicago, the Ford and Rockefeller foundations in New York, and the Open Society Institute, which created the Documentary Fund with funds from George Soros. This fund was transferred to the Sundance Institute in 2001. Other foundations that have a history of funding documentary productions include the Paul Robeson Fund and the Gerbode, Gund, Casey, Kellogg, and Mott foundations. Grant Makers in Film and Electronic Media, an affinity group of the Council on Foundations, has created a Web site with information about media funding strategies: www.fundfilm.org.

In an effort to increase the production of films made by minorities in the United States, CPB created the Minority Consortia in the 1970s, including a Latino consortium, later incorporated as the National Latino Communications Center (NLCC). In 1999, the NLCC closed down and was reconstituted as Latino Public Broadcasting (LPB). By 2004, LPB had funded some seventy-five documentaries, including works by Lillian Jiménez, Natatcha Estebañez, Ray Santisteban, and many others. Producers created the National Association of Latino Independent Producers (NALIP) in 1999 to promote the advancement, development, and funding of Latina and Latino film and media arts, including documentaries. NALIP has published a resource guide and holds an annual conference and workshops for its members.

Access to lower-cost video and digital technologies has made it possible for many Latino and Latina artists to express themselves more freely and record personal and social experiences more abundantly. They still face the challenge of reaching wider audiences through mainstream broadcasting and exhibition channels.

Exhibition and Distribution

Few Latina and Latino documentaries have been screened in theaters or on commercial television. Latina and Latino documentary makers were initially limited to showcasing their works in community screenings. Film festivals are a launching platform that offer Latina and Latino documentaries visibility, reviews, and in the best-case scenario, an interested distributor. If a theatrical venue cannot be found, the filmmakers seek a television broadcast. The Public Broadcasting Service (PBS) has been the most accessible outlet, as commercial stations, including Spanish-language stations, rarely broadcast independent documentaries. PBS has broadcast several television series that tell the history of Latina and Latino communities and are produced and directed by Latinas and Latinos. One example is *Chicano!*, a four-hour television series that follows the farmworkers' struggle but also focuses on the broader Latina/Latino movement. It was produced in 1996 by NLCC and Galán Productions and funded by several private foundations. This series was a collaboration between several Latino and Latina film producers, writers, and directors, including Jesús Treviño, Mylene Moreno, and Sylvia Morales. Another example is *The U.S.–Mexico War*, which aired in 1998. This four-hour series was produced by Paul Espinosa, Sylvia Komatsu,

and Rob Tranchin and directed by Ginny Martin of KERA-TV, a PBS station based in Dallas/Forth Worth, Texas. One interesting feature of this production is the producers' efforts to bring together scholars and historians and public television stations from both Mexico and the United States—a challenge that yielded a balanced and complex view of that war. The most prolific producers and writer-directors are Hector Galán and Paul Espinosa. They have brought many Latino and Latina stories to public television, collaborating on several PBS documentaries, including *Los Mineros* (1991), *The Border* (1999), and *Visiones: Latino Art in the U.S.*

Other immigrant voices are also being heard on PBS. For example, Ray Blanco, a Cuban American filmmaker based in New Jersey, produced and directed *Black and White in Exile*, a two-hour series that analyzes the conflicts between the Cuban and African American communities in Miami, Florida, and the different legal rights that apply to Haitians' and Cubans' immigrant and refugee status. PBS has also aired documentaries intended to recover the legacy of the 1960s, such as *Pa'lante, siempre pa'lante* by former Puerto Rican Young Lord Iris Morales and *Passin' It On*, about the Black Panther movement, by John Valadez (with Peter Miller).

In 2004, PBS broadcast *The New Americans*, a series that tracks the immigration process of several families from the moment they begin the visa application process in their home countries to their final transition to American society. Carlos Aparicio, Susana Aikin, Laura Simon, Renee Tajima-Peña, and Evangeline Griego participated in the production of the Dominican and Mexican stories in this series, which was produced by Kartemquin Films.

An important broadcasting venue within the PBS system is P.O.V. (Point of View), a showcase for independent documentaries that airs ten to sixteen films in each season. Founded in 1987, P.O.V. has helped launch over twenty Latina and Latino–made and Latina and Latino–focused documentaries, ranging from Helena Solberg's *Carmen Miranda: Bananas Is My Business*, to *90 Miles*, directed by Cuba-born Juan Carlos Zaldivar, a personal memoir that uses news clips, home movies, and personal narration to depict the emotional journey that shapes the identities of father and son as they arrive in the United States through the Mariel boat lift. Community exhibition venues remain important: Active Voice is a non profit team that creates documentary screening events and resource materials in collaboration with national and grassroots stakeholders, many of them Latinas and Latinos.

Distributors such as the Latin American Video Archives, Videoteca del Sur, Video Machete, and others mostly target the educational market or use community venues for their outreach. Many documentary makers are using the Internet to promote and distribute their works. As documentaries gain greater recognition and success at the box office, commercial distributors are becoming more interested in the works of Latino and Latina producers.

Academia is also incorporating Latina and Latino Studies into the curricula and highlighting the importance of Latina and Latino films in the study of social and cultural trends. Latina and Latino scholars such as Chon Noriega and Frances Negrón-Muntaner have written about issues of cultural identity and film. There is still a scarcity of representation of the Latina and Latino experience on small and large screens, but Latinas and Latinos are not as marginalized as they once were, and they have earned the right to make films about realities other than the narrow ethnic focus, beyond their own borders and cultures.

See also Chávez, César; Chicanos and Chicanas; Cuban Americans; Film; Film Producers; Immigration; Media and Latino Identity; Mexican-Origin People in the United States; Portillo, Lourdes; Puerto Ricans; Salazar, Rubén; Teatro Campesino; United Farm Workers; Valdez, Luis; *and* Young Lords Party.

BIBLIOGRAPHY

Abrash, Barbara, and Catherine Egan, eds. *Mediating History: The Map Guide to Independent Video by and about African American, Asian American, Latino, and Native American People*. New York: New York University Press, 1992.

Burton, Julianne, ed. *The Social Documentary in Latin America*. Pittsburgh, Pa.: University of Pittsburgh Press, 1990.

Ferris, Susan, and Ricardo Sandoval. *The Fight in the Fields: César Chávez and the Farmworkers Movement*. New York: Harcourt Brace, 1997.

Fregosos, Rosa Linda. *The Bronze Screen: Chicana and Chicano Film Culture*. Minneapolis: University of Minnesota Press, 1993.

King, John, Ana Maria Lopez, and Manuel Alvarado, eds. *Mediating Two Worlds: Cinematic Encounters in the Americas*. London: British Film Institute Publishing, 1993.

Noriega, Chon, ed. *Chicanos and Film: Representation and Resistance*. Minneapolis: University of Minnesota Press, 1992.

Noriega, Chon. *Ready for Prime Time: Minorities on Network Entertainment Television*, UCLA Chicano Studies Research Center, May 2002.

PATRICIA BOERO

DOMESTIC VIOLENCE. *See* Latinas and Intimate Partner Violence.

DOMESTIC WORKERS. Domestic work constitutes the largest female employment sector in the post-industrial world, yet it continues to be unregulated and invisible. At the turn of the twenty-first century, most of the women doing domestic work in the United States are from Latin America and the Caribbean. Domestic workers may be legal permanent residents, naturalized United States citizens, or undocumented. Regardless of their immigration status, Latina domestic workers in the United States and throughout the world have been among the most vulnerable workers in the global economy, subject to abuses, exploitation, and xenophobic attacks.

In the United States, paid domestic work includes several job categories: (1) live-in domestic; (2) live-out nanny-housekeeper; and (3) weekly cleaning jobs. It also includes a broader category of "human care providers" who provide live-in or live-out care for elderly people. Although the emotional and physical demands may be great, paid domestic work is frequently devalued as unskilled, easy, and "natural." Studies of paid domestic work paint a different picture.

For example, in 1997, housecleaners in Los Angeles earned an average of $9.46 per hour. Weekly housecleaners are frequently paid a flat fee, have some work autonomy and flexibility in terms of setting work hours, and tend to earn considerably higher hourly rates. The most difficult part of the job is to establish a group of houses to clean. It can also be difficult to get clients to respect the verbal agreements for payment. Housekeepers take great pride in their work, autonomy, flexibility, and wages. However, the job takes its toll on the body and, though satisfying, always carries the stigma associated with housework.

Live-in domestics are the most vulnerable workers in this occupation, working an average of sixty-four hours per week, and earning an average of $3.79 per hour. Their workdays are long, they have very little job flexibility or privacy, and they are frequently isolated from their families and communities. Often, there is no clear division between working time and time off.

Live-in domestics also have to submit to restrictions that increase their invisibility, exploitation, and vulnerability. For example, in Los Angeles they have encountered strict rules for telephone calls, seeing friends, and attending ESL classes, among other restrictions. Food is also a source of tension and indignity for them. Some employers rationed food, while others imposed strict rules about foods that they were allowed to eat. Women who have the opportunity usually leave this kind of work for other types of domestic work.

Live-out nanny-housekeepers are the most sought-after type of domestic worker in the United States. Latina live-out nanny-housekeepers report that they spend most of their time taking care of children, a source of both great satisfaction and frustration. In Los Angeles, they earned an average of $5.90 per hour and worked an average of thirty-five hours per week.

Gender shapes not only an immigrant woman's decision to leave home but also the obligations that keep her connected to her family in the country of origin. Many of the women who work as nannies and housekeepers are mothers who are trying to provide for their families. They

NANNIES. Beverly Hills, 1991. (Catherine Karnow/CORBIS)

have to leave their children behind because they cannot afford to bring them along, a disruption of traditional notions of family life.

In the arena of global capitalism, Latina domestics are vulnerable to exploitation and discrimination. In the United States, for example, although federal and state labor regulations protect domestic workers, most employers simply ignore these rules. Workers in Los Angeles have responded through formal organizations such as Domestic Workers' Association of the Coalition of Humane Immigrant Rights of Los Angeles (CHIRLA). Domestics in other parts of the country have been slower to respond. Race, class, gender, and immigration status tend to keep women from organizing politically for their working rights. Hondagneu-Sotelo (2001) adds that spatial and legal constraints also shape their ability to organize politically. Domestics tend to work segregated in homes in suburban neighborhoods and have little opportunity to interact with each other. But the most difficult barrier for domestics in the United States is that the state does not recognize them as workers.

Several socioeconomic processes underlie the domestic labor shortage of the early twenty-first century. In the industrial and postindustrial countries of the world, women have entered the workforce in unprecedented numbers, but they still have to meet their domestic responsibilities. Working mothers have developed a range of strategies for dealing with the double burden. The most common is to pass some of the work to other women in the family or to close friends. More affluent women are able to hire other women, mostly from developing countries, to do the domestic work. As more middle-class families seek to hire domestic help, the increasing demand has created a shortage of domestic workers.

At the other end of the global spectrum are poor and working-class women in countries that have been integrated into the global economy as exporters of labor. These are the women who seek to escape poverty and lack of opportunity in their own countries by filling in the domestic-labor gap in postindustrial economies like the United States, Canada, and Europe.

See also Global Cities and Processes; Globalization and Transnationalism; Immigration; North American Free Trade Agreement; Poverty; *and* Women and Migration.

BIBLIOGRAPHY

Anderson, Bridget. *Doing the Dirty Work? The Global Politics of Domestic Labour.* London: Zed Books, 2000.

Ehrenreich, Barbara, and Arlie Russell Hochschild. *Global Woman: Nannies, Maids, and Sex Workers in the New Economy.* New York: Metropolitan Books, 2002.

Hondagneu-Sotelo, Pierrette. *Doméstica: Immigrant Workers Cleaning and Caring in the Shadows of Affluence.* Berkeley: University of California Press, 2001.

Hondagneu-Sotelo, Pierrette, and Ernestine Avila. "I'm Here, but I'm There: The Meanings of Latina Transnational Motherhood." *Gender and Society* 11 (1997): 548–571.

Ibarra, María de la Luz. "Mexican Immigrant Women and the New Domestic Labor." *Human Organization* 59 (2000): 452–464.

Romero, Mary. *Maid in the U.S.A.* New York: Routledge, 1992.

MAURA I. TORO-MORN

DOMINICAN AMERICAN NATIONAL ROUNDTABLE. The Dominican American National Roundtable (DANR) was founded in December 1997 following a conference of two hundred Dominican leaders from around the United States. The conference was hosted by the Dominican American National Foundation in Miami, New York State Assemblyman Adriano Espaillat, and the Quisqueya in Action Youth Organization of Providence, Rhode Island. "The National Agenda," according to the conference theme, was the economic, political, educational, and socio-legal status of Dominicans and their communities in the United States, which were explored through talks, symposia, and workshops.

Although Dominicans had been visiting and settling in the United States since the nineteenth century, it was not until the 1961 assassination of the Dominican Republic's brutal dictator, Rafael Leonidas Trujillo, that a Dominican diaspora began to develop. The 1965 Dominican civil war and the subsequent U.S. invasion of the country, together with changes engendered by the 1965 United States Immigration and Naturalization Act, led to the establishment of a permanent community in the United States. New York City was the first and is still the largest Dominican settlement in the United States. By the 1990s, however, other Dominican settlements had developed in Providence, Rhode Island; Lawrence, Massachusetts;

Miami, Florida; and northern New Jersey. Although diverse in terms of local contexts and consequently their socio-economic experiences as racialized immigrants in each city, all of these Dominican communities shared political and economic marginalization to some degree. The formation of the DANR constituted an effort to organize in response to the thirty-year-old communities' local needs and to advocate for the global interests of Dominicans in the United States.

After that first conference in Miami, another meeting was organized at Alianza Dominicana in New York City, out of which a National Interim Steering Committee was created. The Steering Committee met in April 1998 at the City University of New York Dominican Studies Institute at City College, and planned a June 1998 conference in Washington, D.C. During that June meeting, DANR members introduced federal elected officials to the Roundtable's national agenda. The Roundtable's structure became more formalized, and in January 1999 the Steering Committee elected the first Board of Directors; its first president, Victor Capellan; and organization officers. A second conference, entitled "Toward the New Millennium—Strengthening Organizational Development for Dominican Communities in the United States," was organized for May 1999 in Providence, Rhode Island. Over six hundred attendees, including entrepreneurs, academics, students, artists, politicians, activists, and other interested parties, met in workshops and panel discussions to identify the community's needs and agenda.

In February 2000, the Roundtable was incorporated and obtained federal exempt status as a not-for-profit community advocacy organization. The Roundtable's administration consists of a Board of Directors, an Executive Committee, and an Executive Director. Assemblyman Espaillat was elected the Roundtable's second president at a third conference, "Dominicans in the United States: America's New Face," held October 6–8, 2000 at Columbia University. One year later, in October 2001, the Roundtable opened its headquarters in Washington, D.C. and elected its first Executive Director, José Ramon Bello. A fourth Annual Conference took place in Washington, December 7–9, 2001, and the Roundtable's third president, Ana I. García-Reyes, was elected. Three hundred participants attended the fifth Annual Conference held in Washington, D.C. in October 2002, organized around the theme "Our Local Empowerment Builds Our National Power." The Board of Directors elected founding member Margarita Cepeda-Leonardo president at that meeting.

The Board of Directors represents each of the major Dominican settlements and includes academics, entrepreneurs, professionals, and community leaders. After the 2002 election season, the DANR board happily reported the election of eighteen Dominican officials to city and state offices in New York, New Jersey, Rhode Island, Massachusetts, New Hampshire, Maryland, Michigan, and Puerto Rico.

The DANR runs several programs intended to introduce community members to political advocacy work: The Dominican American National Leadership Institute, the Dominican Internship Program, and the Dominican American Voter Registration and Participation Program. The Leadership Institute consists of residential retreats for the development of advocacy skills in emerging community leaders, particularly youth and women. The Dominican Internship Program is co-sponsored by the Grupo Dominicano de Profesionales–Washington, in collaboration with the Dominican Studies Institute. It was inaugurated in the summer of 2000 and is held in Washington, D.C. from June to August of each year. Promising Dominican college students are hosted by local families, are placed with federal agencies, congressional offices, and national and international advocacy organizations, and receive small stipends. Host organizations have included the World Bank, the Inter-American Development Bank, and the United States Senate Committee for International Relations.

During 2003, the Roundtable identified the census undercount of Dominicans, the deportation of lawful Dominicans, the legalization of undocumented Dominicans, the restoration of the 245(i) Family Reunification Act, and the reduction of the Affidavit of Support as key immigration policy issues affecting the Dominican community. In addition, the Dominican Business Impact Research pilot program was initiated to document and analyze the economic effect of corner grocery stores, 80 percent of which are owned and operated by Dominicans, in the Dominican communities of Washington Heights, New York City; Lawrence, Massachusetts; Providence, Rhode Island; and the Allapattah section of Miami. More information on these projects can be obtained from the organization's website, www.danr.org.

In the early years of the twenty-first century, the Roundtable had over three hundred individual members and nearly two dozen member organizations from Puerto Rico, New York, New Jersey, Massachusetts, Rhode Island, Maryland, Pennsylvania, Illinois, and Florida. The DANR is funded primarily by United States and Dominican corporate sponsors and by membership fees. This broad-based membership and support mirrors the transnational nature of the Dominican diaspora, which resides throughout the world and establishes vibrant communities abroad while continuing to sustain cultural, political, and economic ties to its country of origin.

See also **Dominicans** *and* **Dominican Studies Institute.**

BIBLIOGRAPHY

López, Nancy. *Hopeful Girls, Troubled Boys: Race and Gender Disparity in Urban Education*. New York: Routledge, 2002.

Pessar, Patricia R. *A Visa for a Dream: Dominicans in the United States*. Boston, Mass.: Allyn and Bacon, 1995.

Rodríguez de León, Francisco. *El furioso merengue del Norte: Una historia de la comunidad dominicana en los Estados Unidos*. New York: Editorial Sitel, 1998.

Torres-Saillant, Silvio, and Ramona Hernández. *The Dominican Americans*. Westport, Conn.: Greenwood Press, 1998.

GINETTA E. B. CANDELARIO

DOMINICAN DAY PARADE. After the assassination of the Dominican dictator Rafael Leónidas Trujillo in 1961, Dominican migration to New York City reached significant levels. The resulting concentrations of Dominicans, especially in the Washington Heights section of New York, led to the emergence of various Dominican cultural organizations. The Centro Cívico Cultural Dominicano was founded in 1962, followed by the Instituto Duartiano, the Centro Cultural Ballet Quisqueya, el Club Deportivo Dominicano, and Club Deportivo 30 de Marzo. Each of these organizations had the same objective: to unify and strengthen the growing Dominican community in Washington Heights. By 1982, there were approximately one hundred Dominican cultural organizations in New York City.

A young man of Dominican descent by the name of Miguel Guillermo Amaro felt that these organizations should be taken to a higher level, a plateau where everyone could share his ethnic pride. He wanted a Dominican Day Parade, similar to the parade his Puerto Rican friends had been enjoying for many years. There was much opposition and little support from politicians, community leaders, and fellow Dominicans. The idea of having a parade in a populated area such as Washington Heights seemed catastrophic at first. Disenchanted and defeated, Amaro encountered a longtime friend and community leader, Julio Cesar Rodriguez. Rodriguez had previously coordinated "El Desfile de la Hispanidad," a long-standing parade that takes place every October during Hispanic Heritage Month. He offered guidance and support to Amaro. In June of 1982, the first official meeting of new members of the Dominican Day Parade took place in "El Club Deportivo."

Amaro's dream came to fruition on Sunday, August 15, 1982, in the first Dominican Day Parade. The parade took place on Audubon Avenue from 165th Street to 191st Street, a span of over a mile. Thousands of spectators of all nationalities were in attendance. Because of this overwhelming response to the parade, its location was moved to accommodate its supporters, to longer, broader Amsterdam Avenue.

The parade took place on Amsterdam Avenue until 1985, when it again moved to a larger location, Avenue of the Americas in midtown Manhattan. Why not prestigious Fifth Avenue, some wondered. In an effort to be true to Dominican history, the founders decided that, since the Dominican Republic was the "cradle" of the New World of the Americas, the parade should take place on the Avenue of the Americas. The parade has been held on this street ever since.

Miguel Amaro's dream came true, but his young life ended on June 8, 1987, when he died in a car accident in New York. Other Dominican Day parades have developed since, including events in Paterson, New Jersey, and the Bronx, New York.

See also Dominicans.

BIBLIOGRAPHY

Encarnacion, Nelson. "Multitud Presencia Desfile Dominicano en Nueva York." *Listin Diario*, August 11, 2003.

"Los Organizadores del Desfile Dominicano Reclaman Apoyo." *Noticias del Mundo*, May 31, 1983, p. 2.

Tavares, Luis R. "Rechazar Declaraciones." *Noticias del Mundo*, December 6, 1982, p. 17.

JULIE RODRIGUEZ BENCOSME

DOMINICAN HOME COUNTRY PROJECT. When analyzing the efforts conducted by the government of the Dominican Republic to reach out to its diaspora community in the United States, one must keep in mind that the Dominican migration phenomenon is relatively recent. It was not until the 1970s that a significant flow of immigration to the United States occurred. Despite the recent incorporation of Dominicans into U.S. society, their accomplishments are many and reflect their proactive involvement in the receiving society. They have achieved these accomplishments mostly through their own merit and hard work, with little influence and support from the government back in the homeland.

Yet Dominicans' political activism in the receiving society, their active involvement in the everyday life of their home country, and their systematic insistence on having their political and civic rights recognized by the Dominican government have forced the homeland government to propose and adopt a number of laws that grant citizenship rights and services to Dominicans living abroad. Around the turn of the twenty-first century, the Dominican government undertook various initiatives to formally incorporate and acknowledge Dominicans who live outside the national territory.

It can be argued that the approval of dual citizenship and of the right to vote in the presidential elections from abroad are the most radical legal measures implemented by the Dominican government in favor of its diaspora.

TABLE 1. *Dominican Naturalized U.S. Citizens 1994–2003*

Country	1994	1995	1996	1997	1998	1999	2000	2001	2002	2003
Dominican Republic	11,390	9,999	29,459	21,092	11,916	23,089	25,176	15,010	15,591	12,627

SOURCE: U.S. Citizen and Immigration Services.

The right to dual citizenship is recognized in Paragraph IV, Item 4 of Article 11 of the Dominican Constitution. Electoral Law 275–97, ratified on December 21, 1997, in Articles 82 through 85 allows for Dominicans abroad to vote in the presidential elections. Because of the complicated and expensive process of setting elections in a foreign country, it was not until the elections of 2004 that Dominicans residing abroad were able to vote.

Prior to the approval of dual citizenship, many Dominicans were hesitant to become U.S. citizens for fear of being considered traitors to the *patria*, or motherland. Once rid of this emotional deterrent, many Dominicans became U.S. citizens as a means of enjoying the rights and benefits only conferred to U.S. citizens without sacrificing their Dominican heritage and loyalty to their native land. Table 1 shows that the number of Dominicans who have become U.S. citizens significantly increased after the laws were enacted.

Studies of other countries with similar practices indicate that in general voter registration and voter turnout are low among nationals living abroad. Data from the Dominican *Junta Central Electoral* show that in the presidential elections of 2004, voting abroad represented only 0.7 percent of total voting in the Dominican Republic (see table 2). It is interesting to note that turnout rates among Dominicans registered to vote abroad was very high, comparable to national levels in the Dominican Republic (73 percent).

With regard to institutional support, during President Hipólito Mejía's administration (2000–2004), there was an attempt to create a secretariat for Dominicans living abroad, but Congress never approved it. Consequently, President Mejía created through decree an Oficina de Ultramar (Overseas Office), which many argue neither functioned as designed nor produced the changes promised. Additionally, the long-established Dominicans Abroad Affairs Unit, under the Consular Department in the Secretariat of Foreign Affairs, has the objective of offering assistance and protection to Dominican citizens living abroad. For the most part, the work of this unit and the consulates abroad is limited to satisfying administrative needs. Even though the consulates generate significant amounts of revenue, few resources traditionally have been invested on behalf of the Dominican American community. The norm had been for the consulates to offer their services at very high costs, but in 2004 President

Leonel Fernández approved a 20 to 60 percent reduction of consular services fees.

Other laws and institutional support include temporary customs concessions, such as tax exemptions on up to $1,000 worth of gifts during the Christmas season (December 1– January 7), guaranteed by Law No. 9–96, ratified in 1996. In addition, Article 13 of Law 146–00, of December 27, 2000, facilitates the return of Dominican nationals and allows them to import their belongings without paying taxes. Likewise, Law 168, dating back to 1977, during Joaquín Balaguer's presidency, allows for returning Dominicans to import a car exempt from taxes. There have also been opportunities for Dominicans living abroad to access affordable and government-subsidized housing units.

According to Article 37 of Law 87–01, Dominican citizens living abroad retain the right to become part of the social security system in the Dominican Republic. Dominican migrants may transfer funds through the financial system, through a money-transfer agency, or through a branch of one of the Administradoras de Fondos de Pensiones, or pension-fund managers, linked to major banks. Besides remittances, nostalgic tourism, and political parties' campaign financing, this is another way the government mobilizes and encourages economic relations between the diaspora and the homeland. According to the Central Bank's estimates for 2004, remittances will be 12 percent of total Gross Domestic Product (GDP).

Another initiative taken by the Dominican government is the establishment of cultural institutions in the United States, such as la Casa de la Cultura Dominicana, located in New York since 1985. The Dominican government has also created the position of Commissioner for Cultural

TABLE 2. *Comparative Analysis of the Dominican 2004 Presidential Elections*

CITY/STATE	REGISTERED	VOTES CAST	PERCENT
Boston	4,202	3,536	84.15%
Miami	2,399	1,776	74.03%
New Jersey	6,418	4,502	70.15%
New York	24,343	16,608	68.22%
Total U.S.	37,362	26,422	70.7%
Total D.R.	5,020,703	3,656,850	72.85%

SOURCE: Junta Central Electoral.

Affairs, who is responsible for all cultural events and programs in the United States, including overseeing la Casa de la Cultura Dominicana.

A source for concern for many in the United States is the political activism of Dominicans in their homeland politics. Some fear that participating in politics at home prevents Dominicans from getting involved in politics in the United States. There is a significant and growing number of Dominicans elected to political posts in the United States. Yet many Dominicans still have strong ties with politics back home.

All major Dominican political parties have branches in the United States. U.S. cities with large Dominican populations serve as sites for political rallies, provide additional constituents, and are a viable source of campaign financing. This makes the United States more attractive to Dominican politicians.

The next major step on the political front would be for the Dominican diaspora to gain the right to congressional representation. President Leonel Fernández supports reforming the constitution to allow for this right of all Dominicans "to elect and be elected," contained in Article 13, to be extended to the legislative body.

The Dominican government's enthusiasm for empowering its people living in the United States by granting additional rights and safeguarding their interests has had its high and low points. Nonetheless, the government has recently created an Advisory Board of Dominicans Abroad and has with the objective of strengthening proposed a number of new initiatives its relationship with the diaspora in the United States as recognition of their great socioeconomic contributions to the Dominican Republic.

See also Cuban Communities Abroad Project *and* Dominicans.

BIBLIOGRAPHY
Banco Central de la República Dominicana. http://www.bancentral.gov.do/

Comisión Presidencial para la Reforma y Modernización del Estado. *Seminar el Voto de los Dominicanos en el Exterior* (Seminar on Voting Rights for Dominicans Living Abroad). Dominican Republic: Editora Buho, 2000.

Constitución Política de la República Dominicana, 2002 (Dominican Constitution). www.georgetown.edu/pdba/Constitutions/DomRep/domrep02.html

Dirección General de Aduanas (Customs Office). www.dga. gov.do/

Junta Central Electoral. http://www.jce.do/Boletines2004.asp

Ley Electoral 275–97 de la República Dominicana. www.jmarcano.com/mipais/politicos/leyelect5.html#titulo11

Rodríguez, María E., and Ramona Hernández, eds. *Building Strategic Partnerships for Development: Dominican Republic–New York State*. Fundación Global Democracia y Desarrollo. República Dominicana: Editora Corripio, 2004.

Secretaría de Estado de Relaciones Exteriores. *Las Normas y Prácticas Consulares*. República Dominicana: Editora Corripio, 2000.

Secretaría de Estado de Relaciones Exteriores (SEREX-Secretariat of Foreign Affairs). www.serex.gov.do/espanol/gestiones_consulares.htm

Superintendencia de Pensiones de la República Dominicana. www.sipen.gov.do/documentos/ley.pdf

United States Citizen and Immigration Services, Immigration Statistics on Naturalization. http://uscis.gov/graphics/shared/aboutus/statistics/NATZ2003yrbk/2003NATZ.pdf

Univision's Web site. "Buenas Noticias para los dominicanos en NY, Reducen coste de servicios consulares." www.univision. com:80/content/content.jhtml?cid=488549

Vega, Bernardo. *Diario de una misión en Washington*. Santo Domingo, República Dominicana: Fundación Cultural Dominicana, 2002.

MARÍA ELIZABETH RODRÍGUEZ

DOMINICAN INVASION OF 1965. In April 1965, the United States invaded the Dominican Republic with nearly twenty-three thousand U.S. Army and Marine troops. The invasion was in response to a revolt intended to restore the short-lived constitutional government of President Juan Bosch, who was overthrown by the Dominican military in September 1963 after less than eight months in office. The rebel leaders were Dominican civilians and some younger army officers, most notably Francisco Caamaño Deño; confronting them was the Dominican army, which sought to preserve the unelected and ineffective but conservative existing government. When the pro-Bosch "constitutionalists" appeared likely to defeat the Dominican military, which the United States relied upon to maintain control of the then-unstable republic, U.S. president Lyndon Johnson quickly sent in troops. The intervention was unilateral, although Washington soon pressured the Organization of American States (OAS) to create an Inter-American Defense Force, to which six Latin American countries, five of them controlled by their militaries, contributed token forces.

The intervention lasted for fifteen months. At the time, the U.S. State Department claimed to be acting as a neutral broker by separating the warring factions and arranging for elections. But widespread skepticism about U.S. claims, especially in Latin America, proved in the end correct. In the early twenty-first century, most scholars of these events have concluded that U.S. actions clearly favored the Dominican conservatives, both military and civilian. This group's triumph in the 1966 elections, followed by the complete withdrawal of foreign troops in September, led to stable but repressive civilian rule under Joaquín Balaguer, who had served as vice president under the former dictator Rafael Trujillo. After a long period of government under Balaguer, a more competitive democratic system gradually developed, producing governments that have seemed unable to solve the basic social and economic problems of the Dominican Republic, leading to massive Dominican immigration to the United States.

Why did the United States intervene in 1965? The original excuses offered by the State Department were that it had to protect the United States embassy and evacuate United States civilians, though neither was seriously threatened and a few marines could have solved the problem, and that there was danger of a Communist takeover. More to the point, Washington was acting to protect what U.S. leaders perceived to be U.S. strategic and economic interests. State Department officials had decided earlier that they disliked Bosch, who, though obviously democratic, they saw as too open to the political Left and an ineffective leader. Probably more important from the point of view of the U.S. government was the possible defeat of the U.S.-oriented Dominican military and the fact that some of those involved in the rebellion appeared to be leftists, including a few Communists.

The last factor assumed a special importance in the politics of that period. The Dominican rebellion occurred just four years after Fidel Castro declared Cuba a socialist state, an event that focused Washington's already intense cold war fear of Communism on Latin America. Thus, the Dominican rebellion immediately set off alarms in Washington and led President Johnson and his national security advisers to exaggerate the much-feared possibility of "a second Cuba." The result was a quick decision to launch a massive invasion.

Still another factor facilitated the sending of troops to the island nation. The intervention of 1965 was just the latest in a long history of U.S. invasions of Latin America and the Caribbean nations, all of them based on the U.S. belief that the country had the right, if not the obligation, to control the Western Hemisphere. The Dominican Republic itself had suffered a series of previous U.S. armed interventions, the most dramatic of which lasted from 1916 to 1924. For most of that eight-year period the Dominican constitution and elected government were suspended. In their place a U.S. admiral acted as military governor, making laws by decree that greatly affected the republic for decades to come and brought it more firmly under U.S. control. While the U.S. occupation did bring some benefits, such as a drastically improved road network, the results were on balance negative. Those who opposed the U.S. control endured severe military repression, the Dominican economy came more fully under U.S. domination, and thanks to the major role of the United States in facilitating the rise to power of General Rafael Trujillo, the republic suffered for thirty-one years under one of the worst dictatorships in twentieth-century Latin America.

Ironically, the unrest that proceeded the invasion in 1965 was also connected to U.S. insistence on control. Trujillo, in trying to manipulate Washington by flirting with Castro in the early 1960s, managed to anger the U.S.

government, which in any case found Trujillo's dictatorship an increasing embarrassment. Not long afterward, Trujillo was assassinated by members of the Dominican opposition aided by the Central Intelligence Agency (CIA). A period of great instability followed, during which a leading opponent of Trujillo, the long-exiled Bosch, was elected president and soon overthrown. The revolutionary effort to reestablish Bosch's constitutional government led directly to the 1965 U.S. invasion.

See also **Dominicans; Trujillo, Rafael; United States Foreign Policy;** *and* **United States Interventions in Latin America.**

BIBLIOGRAPHY

Calder, Bruce J. *The Impact of Intervention: The Dominican Republic during the U.S. Occupation of 1916–1924.* Austin: University of Texas Press, 1984.

Gleijeses, Piero. *The Dominican Crisis: The 1965 Constitutionalist Revolt and American Intervention.* Baltimore, Md.: Johns Hopkins University Press, 1978.

Lowenthal, Abraham F. *The Dominican Intervention.* Cambridge, Mass.: Harvard University Press, 1972.

BRUCE J. CALDER

DOMINICANS. In the 1990s, the Dominican Republic became one of the top five countries with immigrants to the United States, after Mexico, the Philippines, Vietnam, and China. Only Mexicans, Puerto Ricans, Cubans, and El Salvadorans constituted larger Hispanic populations in the United States than did Dominicans. According to the 2000 U.S. census, 764,945 persons of Dominican origin were living in the continental United States, a figure that represents nearly 9 percent of the population of the Dominican Republic (8.6 million). In addition, 56,146 Dominicans were counted in Puerto Rico, a U.S. territory that often serves as a springboard for migrants to the mainland. In addition, sizable Dominican communities have emerged in Europe, Latin America, and the Caribbean, particularly in Italy, Switzerland, the Netherlands, Canada, Panama, Aruba, Martinique, and St. Thomas. Although some scholars might contest this characterization, the Dominican Republic has arguably become the prototype of a transnational society that links people across many places scattered around the world.

Historical Overview

Before the 1960s, few Dominicans moved abroad; those who managed to do so were usually members of the white, urban, educated elite. During the dictatorship of Rafael Leónidas Trujillo (1930–1961), it was extremely difficult to obtain an exit visa from the Dominican government. Trujillo's restrictive policies reflected both a desire to prevent criticism of his regime and the promotion

DOMINICANS. The Dominican
Day parade in New York City.

of population growth in the Dominican Republic. Between 1931 and 1960, only 16,674 Dominicans were admitted to the United States. At this stage, Dominican migration consisted primarily of upper- and middle-class political exiles.

Nonetheless, small Dominican enclaves emerged in New York City during the first few decades of the twentieth century, especially on the Upper West Side of Manhattan, near the present location of Lincoln Center; in Morningside Heights, around Columbia University; and in El Barrio (Spanish Harlem). The first known Dominican-owned *bodega* (grocery store) in the city was established in 1933 on West 100th Street in Upper Manhattan. Another small community developed in the Corona section of Queens during the 1950s. Many of the first immigrants came from the village of Sabana Iglesia in the Cibao region of the Dominican Republic. In the early 1960s, Dominicans began to congregate on the Lower East Side (Loisaida) of Manhattan, in the Williamsburg section of Brooklyn, and, increasingly, in the Upper Manhattan neighborhoods of Washington Heights and Inwood.

During this period, prominent Dominican businessmen and diplomats formed social clubs and other voluntary associations that reflected the interests of their elitist membership. For instance, the Centro Cívico Cultural Dominicano (Dominican Civic and Cultural Center) was founded in 1962 and the Club Juan Pablo Duarte was founded in 1966. These groups tended to be politically conservative and geared toward preserving their Hispanic customs in the United States. In the beginning, working-class Dominicans lacked social institutions such as ethnic

churches to assist them in the resettlement process. Later on, community organizations began to reflect more closely the immigrants' predominantly proletarian and peasant background, as well as their largely black and mulatto racial composition.

As New York's Dominican population swelled in the late 1960s and early 1970s, new social and political groups emerged. Many radical and liberal leaders were exiled in the United States to avoid political persecution in the Dominican Republic. The number of Dominican voluntary associations in New York multiplied; by the early 1980s, at least 125 of them were operating in the city, particularly in Washington Heights, where the bulk of the immigrants eventually settled. Self-help associations with various recreational, political, and cultural objectives proliferated. Formal organizations often revolved around the immigrants' place of origin, such as a province, town, or neighborhood in the Dominican Republic. For example, the Club de Tamborileños and the Asociación de Banilejos, both in New York, represented two Dominican hometowns. Informal networks of kin, friends, and neighbors helped to organize the community. Political ideology, party affiliation, and class interests reinforced ethnic ties.

Two of the three major political parties in the Dominican Republic were established abroad. In 1939, Juan Bosch founded the Partido Revolucionario Dominicano (PRD), the Dominican Revolutionary Party, in Havana, Cuba, which became the main group opposing Trujillo's dictatorship. In 1963, Joaquín Balaguer formed the Partido Reformista Social Cristiano (PRSC), the Social Christian Reformist Party, while exiled in New York City.

In 1973, Bosch resigned from the PRD and created the Partido de la Liberación Dominicana (PLD), the Dominican Liberation Party. During the 1970s, the two leading opposition parties, the PRD and the PLD, developed large followings in New York; San Juan, Puerto Rico; and other centers of the diaspora.

In the 1980s, Dominican Americans created various umbrella organizations to deal with their most pressing social problems in New York, which included education, housing, and health care. The largest of these organizations is Alianza Dominicana (Dominican Alliance), a comprehensive service and community-development agency founded in 1987, focusing on children, youth, and families. During this period, activists also mobilized the community to vote in local elections. This mobilization initiated a process of political empowerment that culminated in the election of several Dominicans to Manhattan school boards. In 1991, Washington Heights voters sent the first Dominican representative to the New York City Council, former schoolteacher Guillermo Linares. In 1996, Adriano Espaillat won the New York State Assembly seat from the 72nd district, which includes Washington Heights. Two important voluntary associations were created in the 1990s: the Dominican American National Roundtable (DANR) and Dominicans 2000. Founded in Washington, D.C., in 1997, DANR seeks to promote the educational, economic, cultural, and political interests of Dominican Americans through community empowerment, economic development, and planning. It includes representatives from most states with large Dominican populations, including New York, New Jersey, Rhode Island, Massachusetts, Pennsylvania, and Florida, as well as from Puerto Rico. Founded in New York in 1999, Dominicans 2000 is a community-based organization with a strong following among college and high school students, especially those enrolled at the City University of New York. Like DANR, it focuses on the educational advancement and political empowerment of the Dominican American community.

Settlement Patterns

The most outstanding feature of contemporary Dominican migration is its magnitude. In 1997, the U.S. Census Bureau found that nearly one out of ten persons of Dominican origin was living in the United States. Of these, 24 percent were born in the United States, a figure that speaks of a growing second generation. Furthermore, substantial Dominican communities have emerged in Puerto Rico, Venezuela, Spain, Curaçao, and the U.S. Virgin Islands since the 1980s. Unfortunately, many of the new destinations follow the path of the international trade in female sexual workers. In any case, the Dominican population has become increasingly diversified in its residential locations.

Secondly, the Dominican diaspora has expanded dramatically since the 1960s. Few Dominicans moved abroad before that date. In 1950, only 4,200 persons of Dominican birth were counted in the U.S. census. The U.S. Immigration and Naturalization Service (INS)—now called U.S. Citizenship and Immigration Services (CIS)—did not collect separate data for them before 1930 because the volume of Dominican immigrants was so low. But emigration from the Dominican Republic to the continental United States jumped tenfold between the 1950s and the 1960s (see Table 1). Thousands of Dominicans also moved to Puerto Rico after the mid-1960s. The outflow of people from the Dominican Republic continued to rise in the 1970s and 1980s, reaching unprecedented levels in the 1990s.

Compared to well-established U.S. Latina and Latino groups such as Mexicans and Puerto Ricans, large-scale immigration of Dominicans is relatively recent. More than 98 percent of the 845,387 Dominicans legally admitted to the continental United States between 1931 and 2000 arrived after 1961. Nearly half of those who moved to Puerto Rico did so in the 1990s (see Table 1). These statistics suggest that Dominican emigration is a massive and sustained movement of people that will continue unabated in the near future. In 2000, more than 55 percent of all the Dominican immigrants lived in the state of New York, with secondary concentrations in New Jersey, Florida, Puerto Rico, and Massachusetts (see Table 2). Small but vibrant Dominican communities have also mushroomed in Rhode Island, Pennsylvania, and Connecticut.

In the year 2000, most Dominican immigrants were living in New York City, San Juan, Puerto Rico; Miami, Florida; Bergen-Passaic, New Jersey; and Jersey City, New Jersey (see Table 3). Boston, Nassau-Suffolk, New York; Lawrence, Massachusetts; Providence, Rhode Island; and Middlesex-Somerset-Hunterdon, New Jersey, also have

TABLE 1. *Dominican Immigration to the Continental United States and Puerto Rico, 1931–2000*

YEARS	CONTINENTAL UNITED STATES	PUERTO RICO
1931–1940	1,150	n/a
1941–1950	5,627	n/a
1951–1960	9,897	n/a
1961–1970	93,292	12,278 (a)
1971–1980	148,135	19,781
1981–1990	252,035	28,811
1991–2000	335,251	54,025
Total	845,387	114,895

(a) The CIS does not provide separate figures for Dominican immigrants in Puerto Rico prior to 1966.

SOURCES: for the continental United States, U.S. Citizenship and Immigration Services, *Yearbook of Immigration Statistics, 2000*; for Puerto Rico, Duany, 2004.

TABLE 2. *Geographic Distribution of the Dominican Population in the Continental United States and Puerto Rico, by State or Territory, 2000*

STATE OR TERRITORY	NUMBER OF DOMINICAN RESIDENTS	PERCENT OF ALL DOMINICAN RESIDENTS IN THE U.S. AND P.R.
New York	455,061	55.4
New Jersey	102,630	12.5
Florida	70,968	8.6
Puerto Rico	56,146	6.8
Massachusetts	49,913	6.1
Rhode Island	17,894	2.2
Pennsylvania	12,186	1.5
Connecticut	9,546	1.2
Maryland	5,596	0.7
California	5,047	0.6
All other states	36,104	4.4
Total	821,091	100.0

SOURCE: U.S. Census Bureau, *Census 2000.*

substantial Dominican populations. The number of Dominican residents in some of these cities—especially New York and San Juan—now rivals the size of populations in many places in the Dominican Republic. As one informant told anthropologist Ninna Nyberg Sørensen, "New York is just another Dominican capital."

Social Origins

Scholars have debated the socioeconomic background of migrants from the Dominican Republic, especially their regional and class composition. In the early 1970s, several authors portrayed the migrants primarily as rural, poor, and illiterate. These pioneering studies documented the exodus of peasants from the Dominican countryside to the cities, especially to the capital Santo Domingo, and later to New York. Most of this research focused on rural communities in the Cibao region, such as Sabana Iglesia, Licey al Medio, Los Pinos, Juan Pablo, and La Amapola (the latter three are pseudonyms). In 1987, a survey of Dominicans in Puerto Rico found that nearly a third had been born in the Cibao region. The main reason for the massive out-migration from this region was the creation of a large pool of surplus workers who could not be absorbed by a declining agricultural economy.

In the late 1970s and early 1980s, a second wave of research depicted Dominican immigrants as predominantly urban, middle class, and educated. In 1974, a large-scale survey found that the vast majority of Dominican immigrants to the United States and Puerto Rico originated in urban areas. Other studies confirmed that most Dominicans had lived in their country's largest cities, especially Santo Domingo, Santiago, La Romana, San Pedro de Ma-

corís, and San Francisco de Macorís, prior to moving abroad. Furthermore, data from various sources revealed that the majority of the migrants belonged to relatively affluent social strata in the Dominican Republic, as measured by their occupational status and educational attainment. Before migrating, Dominicans tended to be skilled blue-collar or white-collar workers. The high costs of moving abroad—even illegally—prevented the poorest of the poor from leaving their country. The migrants' primary motivations were rising levels of unemployment and underemployment, as well as the desire for higher incomes and consumption levels. As many Dominicans put it, they move abroad *buscando mejor vida*—looking for a better life.

In the 1990s, Dominican emigration—both documented and undocumented—included a broad cross section of the sending society. Dominican migrants can no longer be represented exclusively as either middle or lower class, urban or rural, educated or illiterate. Recent CIS data suggest a bimodal distribution in the occupational backgrounds of Dominicans legally admitted to the United States (see Table 4). On the one hand, one out of four migrants held relatively skilled and well-paying jobs in the Dominican Republic, for example as professionals, technicians, managers, and administrators. Others worked in middle-level positions as sales and administrative support personnel. On the other hand, more than half were employed in low-skilled and low-paying occupations, particularly as operators, fabricators, laborers, and service workers. The small proportion of agricultural workers indicates that most were not rural dwellers.

Thus, contemporary migration from the Dominican Republic draws primarily on the urban working classes, not

TABLE 3. *Top Ten Metropolitan Areas of Dominican Concentration in the Continental United States and Puerto Rico, 2000*

METROPOLITAN AREA	NUMBER OF DOMINICAN RESIDENTS	PERCENT OF ALL DOMINICAN RESIDENTS IN THE U.S. AND P.R.
New York, N.Y.	424,847	51.7
San Juan, P.R.	45,560	5.5
Miami, Fla.	36,454	4.4
Bergen-Passaic, N.J.	36,360	4.4
Jersey City, N.J.	27,709	3.4
Boston, Mass.	25,057	3.1
Nassau-Suffolk, N.Y.	21,071	2.6
Lawrence, Mass.	19,055	2.3
Providence, R.I.	17,965	2.2
Middlesex-Somerset-Hunterdon, N.J.	15,467	1.9
All other areas	151,546	18.5
Total	821,091	100.0

SOURCE: U.S. Census Bureau, *Census 2000.*

TABLE 4. *Dominican Immigrants Admitted to the United States, by Occupation, 1996–2000*

OCCUPATION	NUMBER OF IMMIGRANTS	PERCENT OF ALL IMMIGRANTS
Professional and technical	5,132	15.1
Executive, administrative, and managerial	1,571	4.6
Sales	1,827	5.4
Administrative support	2,730	8.0
Precision production, craft, and repair	3,971	11.7
Operators, fabricators, and laborers	12,316	36.2
Service	4,464	13.1
Farming, forestry, and fishing	2,051	6.0
Total	34,062	100.0

NOTES: The figures do not include persons without occupations or with unreported occupations. The percentages in column 3 do not add up to 100 because of rounding.

SOURCE: U.S. Citizenship and Immigration Services. *Yearbook of Immigration Statistics, 1996–2000.*

the middle class or the peasantry. The basic causes for the sustained movement of Dominicans are the extensive labor market dislocations produced by a government development strategy that promotes tourism and export industrialization, but that creates insufficient jobs to replace those lost in agriculture and other sectors of the economy. Although the 1990s were a decade of rapid economic growth in the Dominican Republic, most people experienced a decline in their standards of living and were particularly distressed by the near-collapse in the provision of public services such as electricity, running water, housing, health care, and education.

Economic Incorporation

Sociologists Alejandro Portes and Luis E. Guarnizo have argued that Dominicans have created an incipient enclave economy in Washington Heights, characterized by a thriving network of small businesses catering to the immigrants and to the sending country. In the early 1990s, Dominicans owned nearly 20,000 businesses in New York City, mostly bodegas, supermarkets, garment sweatshops, restaurants, travel agencies, taxicab companies, remittance firms, and beauty parlors. Anthropologist Sarah Mahler counted an average of twelve Dominican businesses per block between 157th and 191st Streets in Upper Manhattan during the 1980s. The block I studied in 1993 had seven Dominican-owned businesses, including two bodegas, two beauty parlors, a restaurant, and a bakery. However, most Dominicans in New York City are poorly paid, unskilled workers, not business owners. En-

trepreneurs constitute only a small fraction of the Dominican labor force in Washington Heights, and most Dominicans do not work for themselves or their compatriots. As Ramona Hernández and Francisco Rivera-Batiz have shown, New York Dominicans have a relatively low rate of self-employment compared to other racial and ethnic groups, such as non-Hispanic whites and Cubans.

Table 5 presents the current occupational profile of Dominicans in the United States. The vast majority are service workers, operators, fabricators, and laborers. Conversely, few Dominican Americans are managers and professionals. The proportions of technical, sales, and administrative support workers, as well as the proportions in precision production, craft, and repair occupations, are much lower among Dominican immigrants than in the total U.S. population. Many Dominicans also experience a loss of occupational status upon moving abroad. For instance, 19.7 percent of recent immigrants had held jobs as managers and professionals in the Dominican Republic, while only 11.6 percent of all Dominicans in the United States held such jobs. Thus, Dominicans are predominantly found in the lower rungs of the American labor force, as blue-collar and service workers.

Table 6 shows how Dominicans cluster in three sectors of the U.S. labor market: retail trade, professional services, and manufacturing. Compared to the total U.S. population, Dominican immigrants are less likely to work in agriculture, construction, finance, insurance, real estate, or public administration, or in certain professional services such as education and health care. Since the mid-1970s, New York's economic restructuring has displaced many Dominicans from light manufacturing, especially the garment industry, to the low-wage and low-skilled service sector, and particularly to personal services jobs. Recent census data suggest that U.S. Dominicans are not massively moving up the occupational ladder, becoming

TABLE 5. *Occupational Distribution of the Dominican Labor Force in the Continental United States, 1996–1999 (in percentages)*

OCCUPATION	DOMINICANS	TOTAL U.S.
Managerial and professional	11.6	28.5
Technical, sales, and administrative support	25.7	29.4
Precision production, craft, and repair	4.7	10.8
Operators, fabricators, and laborers	30.2	14.5
Service	27.8	14.2
Farm, forestry, and fishing	—	2.6
Total	100.0	100.0

SOURCE: Levitt, 2001.

TABLE 6. *Industrial Distribution of the Dominican Labor Force in the Continental United States, 1997–2000 (in percentages)*

INDUSTRY	DOMINICANS	TOTAL U.S.
Agriculture, mining, and forestry	2.0	2.9
Construction	4.3	6.7
Manufacturing	17.5	15.5
Transportation and communications	8.5	5.8
Wholesale trade	4.5	3.8
Retail trade	23.3	17.3
Finance, insurance, and real estate	5.7	6.4
Business and repair services	7.0	6.9
Personal services	5.3	3.5
Professional services	20.0	26.9
Public administration	1.9	4.3
Total	100.0	100.0

SOURCE: Castro and Boswell.

entrepreneurs, or creating a diversified ethnic economy like Cubans have in Miami. Rather, most are barely surviving on the margins of a postindustrial economy.

The socioeconomic status of Dominicans in the United States, especially in New York City, is precarious. In 1997, Dominicans had the highest poverty rate (45.7 percent) of all the major ethnic and racial groups in New York City, including non-Hispanic whites, blacks, Puerto Ricans, and other Latinas and Latinos. The unemployment rates for Dominican men (18.9 percent) and women (18.6 percent) were also the highest of all groups. Moreover, Dominicans had the lowest average earnings of all workers. The scarcity of Dominicans in well-paid white-collar occupations such as in the professions and management is largely due to their low educational status and limited English-language proficiency. Only 4 percent of Dominicans twenty-five and older had completed college, compared to nearly 27 percent of all New Yorkers. Finally, Dominicans had the highest proportion (40.7 percent in 1990) of female-headed households in the city, which tend to be associated with poverty, welfare dependency, and other social problems.

Political Empowerment

Like other transnational migrants, Dominicans abroad become incorporated into the political structures of their host society as well as the sending society. In 1996, Leonel Fernández, the son of a Dominican immigrant to New York City, became president of his country of origin. That year, journalistic sources estimated that a third of the campaign funds in the Dominican Republic were raised overseas. The large volume of remittances (an estimated 1.5 billion U.S. dollars in 1999) confirms the migrants'

strong economic impact back home. The diaspora also plays an increasing role in Dominican domestic politics, as witnessed by widespread support for dual citizenship and voting abroad. To a lesser extent, diasporic communities have sought to influence U.S. foreign policy toward the Dominican Republic.

Dominican immigrants have a relatively low naturalization rate in the United States. In 1997, less than a third of all Dominican immigrants in the United States were U.S. citizens. Moreover, a large proportion of Dominicans entered the United States illegally or overstayed their nonimmigrant visas. In 1996, the CIS estimated that 56,000 undocumented Dominicans were living in the continental United States and another 34,000 in Puerto Rico. Thus, the vast majority of the immigrants are disenfranchised by their legal status.

Dominicans in the United States have not achieved political representation proportionate to their numbers. The U.S. House of Representatives does not yet have a Dominican member, although the New York State Assembly and City Council have had Espaillat and Linares, respectively. Several Dominicans have been elected to municipal office, including Marcus Devers (Lawrence, Massachusetts), Miguel Martínez (New York), Claribel Martínez-Marmolejos (San Juan, Puerto Rico), Diana Reyna (New York), Ramón Rosado (Atlantic City, New Jersey), Kennet Santana (Battle Creek City, Michigan), and Julia Silverio (Lawrence, Massachusetts).

Since the 1960s, leading politicians in the Dominican Republic have favored migration to the United States as a safety valve for rising unemployment and overpopulation. Furthermore, President Joaquín Balaguer used emigration to export political dissidents and excess workers during the first twelve years of his administration (1966–1978). In contrast, Dominican government officials have attempted to restrict Haitian immigration to the Dominican Republic, as well as return migration from the United States. Thus, immigration has officially been labeled as a problem, while emigration has traditionally appeared as a short-term solution for demographic and economic pressures, although it is problematic from a cultural and linguistic perspective. Popular terms referring to return migrants include *Dominican-York* (a native of New York City, as opposed to the Dominican Republic); *Joe* (an anonymous Americanized youth); and *cadenú* (literally, someone who wears gold necklaces, but figuratively linked to drug trafficking). All of these epithets imply Americanization, bad taste, and low status.

For years, the migrants considered themselves *dominicanos ausentes* (literally, absent Dominicans) In 1993, during the course of fieldwork in Washington Heights, this author found that most Dominican residents—including second-generation youth—disliked the popular term "Dominican American." Similarly, the pejorative Dominican-York is seldom used within New York's Dominican community, except by some committed activists. Dominicans have begun to claim a pan-ethnic category such as Hispanic or Latina and Latino, but they rarely describe themselves solely as American.

The Question of Race

A pressing issue for the Dominican American community is the reconfiguration of racial identities as a consequence of migration. Since 1980, the U.S. Census Bureau has asked U.S. residents to classify their race separately from their Hispanic origin. In 1990, 29.3 percent of Dominicans in the United States answered that they were white, while 30 percent considered themselves black. Only 1 percent of the Dominicans classified themselves as Native American. The most striking response was the high proportion choosing the "other" category—39.8 percent of the total. These figures parallel a broader trend among U.S. Hispanics—42.2 percent in 2000—who prefer the ambiguous racial term "other." Scholars have noted Dominicans' strong reluctance to call themselves black, both at home and in the diaspora. In the United States, most Dominicans consider themselves to be neither black nor white, but other, such as Hispanic, Spanish, Latina and Latino, or simply Dominican. Dominican migrants continue to persist on public recognition of racially mixed persons (mulattos, mestizos).

Cultural Adaptation

Racial prejudice and discrimination are two of the major reasons some groups of contemporary immigrants, such as Dominicans, do not assimilate quickly into U.S. culture but retain many cultural traditions from their nations of origin. Dominicans stay connected to the homeland through practices involving their space, such as renaming streets and schools, establishing businesses with the same names as those in the home country, redecorating inner and outer spaces, establishing hometown associations, and organizing ethnic parades and folk festivals. Immigrants have renamed several schools after distinguished Dominican figures like Salomé Ureña, Juan Pablo Duarte, and Gregorio Luperón in the Washington Heights neighborhood. The Corona section of Queens is commonly known as "Sabana Church" because of the large number of immigrants from Sabana Iglesia. In Santurce, Puerto Rico, Dominicans have established chains of popular cafeterias such as El Mangú (named for a Dominican staple made with boiled green plantain) and El Padrino (The Godfather). In Madrid, Spain, the Plaza de Aravaca is often associated with Lucrecia Pérez, a Dominican domestic worker murdered there in 1992.

Transnational connections are especially visible in the Dominican community of Washington Heights, the main focus of this section.

In Washington Heights, Dominican residents have a tendency to remain segregated from non-Hispanic whites, blacks, and other Latinas and Latinos such as Puerto Ricans and Colombians. Even when sharing the same neighborhoods with other racial and ethnic groups—such as African Americans or Ecuadorians—Dominicans frequently remain socially encapsulated. In one Washington Heights block I studied intensively, 79 percent of the residents were Dominican. Although residential segregation has many pernicious effects, it makes possible the consolidation of compact barrios, helps in the transformation of the urban landscape along transnational lines, and delivers some degree of political representation by concentration in certain electoral districts.

In 2000, Washington Heights and Inwood housed the largest concentration of Dominicans outside of the Dominican Republic—about one-fourth of New York City's Dominicans. Bodegas, *botánicas* (stores selling religious paraphernalia), restaurants, bakeries, travel agencies, gypsy (non-medallion) cabs, remittance agencies, and retail stores, along with dozens of voluntary associations, contribute to an unmistakable atmosphere of "Quisqueya Heights," which many Dominican residents now call their neighborhood. (Quisqueya is the indigenous name of the Caribbean island of Hispaniola, shared by the Dominican Republic and Haiti.) A community festival held during the 1990s was named "Quisqueya on the Hudson." It is here that Dominican transnational identity has taken shape most decisively; scholars tend to focus on this urban area as a microcosm of the immigrants' experience.

I spent part of the summer of 1993 studying the Dominican community of Washington Heights. In a typical block, street vendors sold oranges, corn, flowers, music cassettes, and the tropical ice cones Dominicans call *frío-fríos*. On hot summer days, small carts selling frío-fríos appeared on major street corners. Children opened fire hydrants and played with water on the sidewalks. The men usually spoke Spanish, listened to merengue, complimented young women passing by, played dominoes, drank *Presidente* beer, played the lottery, talked about Dominican politics, and read Dominican newspapers such as *El nacional*, *El siglo*, and *Listín diario*. Women took their children out in strollers, shopped at the bodegas, or talked with their neighbors in front of their buildings. Teenagers walked in groups to the local public school, bathed in the area's swimming pools, or listened to rap music on huge cassette players. Some people in the street appeared to be Mexican or Central American because of their accents, indigenous features, and small stature;

DANNY BAUTISTA. The Arizona Diamondbacks player celebrates a win with the flag of his native Dominican Republic. (Matthew Stockman/ALLSPORT/Getty Images)

however, most of the area's residents were Dominican immigrants.

Most residents took the subway to work in downtown Manhattan; others took the bus to New Jersey factories across the Hudson River. Many businesses, including Banco Dominicano, specialized in sending remittances to the Dominican Republic; taxi cabs, large dark-colored American cars, from Dominican-owned Riverside Radio Dispatcher, roamed the streets looking for potential customers. Ten Dominican newspapers, flown daily from the island, were available at a newsstand at the corner of 181st Street and Saint Nicholas Avenue.

Typical food from the Dominican Republic was available at many cafeterias and restaurants, while grocery stores imported tropical fruits and vegetables from the Caribbean; a discount beauty parlor sold a wide variety of Dominican brand names, such as Lafier and Capilo; and private telephone service to the Dominican Republic was offered by a large number of small businesses. Many store owners displaying their national origin by blasting merengue and salsa, sometimes *bachata* and *bolero*, Latin music on the sidewalk. Some businesses were local subsidiaries of Dominican Republic enterprises, such as Nitín Bakery; others sold Dominican drinks such as Cola Quisqueya, Refrescos Nacionales, and Cerveza Presidente.

The strong presence of immigrants from the Cibao region was reflected in commercial signs, such as Acogedor Cibao Supermarket, Cibao Vision Center, Cibao Meat Products, and Hielo Cibao. A Dominican immigrant who longed to have his own "little Cibao" in Washington Heights planted corn and black beans on Broadway Avenue and 153rd Street. During my fieldwork, a young man walked on the sidewalk with two roosters, a common sight in the Dominican countryside. Dozens of hometown associations carried Cibao place names, such as Moca, Esperanza, and Mao; some Dominicans even referred to Washington Heights as "El Cibao."

Maintaining their cultural traditions at home was important to immigrants; some tenants placed Spanish-language stickers on their apartment doors, especially with religious messages like "Jesus Christ is our only hope," "Christ will change your life," and "Let us build peace with Christ." Religious prints with images such as the Sacred Heart of Jesus and the Last Supper were often hung inside their homes on the walls; some families had calendars with a painting of the Virgin Mary, obtained in a local bodega. Some displayed the faceless ceramic dolls typical of the Dominican Republic, as well as plates painted in bright colors with folk themes from their country, usually a rural landscape, a peasant scene, the Cathedral of Santo Domingo, or a tropical beach. Such objects, even a Dominican flag or coat-of-arms in a visible place in the living room, re-created the iconography of the Dominican Republic in Washington Heights.

Many Dominican homes and businesses had small shrines (usually surrounded by flowers, lighted candles, food, and glasses filled with fresh water, wine, rum, and other alcoholic beverages) with images of Catholic saints and the Virgin Mary in a corner of the hall or a private room. The altars presented a wide range of religious images: Saint Claire, Saint Anthony of Padua, Saint Barbara, the Holy Child of Atocha, the Sacred Heart, the Sacred Family, and the Virgin of Fatima, as well as the most popular figures of the Virgin of Altagracia and Saint Lazarus. Like other Hispanic Catholics, many Dominicans believe that the saints will protect them from misfortune and help them to advance economically. A woman with a medallion of the Virgin of Altagracia around her neck told this author, "When you're away from your country, you need protection. And your country needs it too." Thus, the traditional Dominican devotion to the saints and the Virgin has been transplanted to Quisqueya Heights.

Contributions to the United States

Despite their relatively short time in the United States, Dominicans have made important contributions to American culture. Their most visible success has been in baseball, the national sport of the Dominican Republic. Record-setting hitter Sammy Sosa is only the most famous of a long roster of Dominican major leaguers, including Juan Marichal, Pedro Guerrero, Alex Rodríguez, and Pedro Martínez. With the exception of Cuba and Puerto Rico, no other country has exported as many professional baseball players to the United States as the Dominican Republic. San Pedro de Macorís, for example, is the hometown of several prominent sluggers. Today, nearly one out of four professional baseball players in the United States is Dominican.

The best-known musical tradition of the Dominican Republic is the merengue, which has replaced salsa in popularity among Latinas and Latinos in New York and in Puerto Rico itself. Dominicans have recorded and performed merengues in New York City since the 1920s. Alberto Beltrán, who sang with the legendary Cuban group La Sonora Matancera, popularized merengues such as "El negrito del batey" and "Compadre Pedro Juan" in the late 1950s. Accordionist Luis Kalaff and singer Primitivo Santos also moved to the city, helping to transplant merengue to the United States. Johnny Pacheco, a Dominican arranger and composer, was a driving force behind the explosion of Latin music in the 1960s, especially through the Fania recording label. In 1973, Dominican singer and bandleader Milly Quezada founded the group Milly, Jocelyn y los Vecinos in New York, and later developed a successful solo career. Today, New York City is one of the major centers of the international merengue music industry, rivaling Santo Domingo.

Restaurants and cafeterias specializing in Dominican food have contributed to New York's rich ethnic cuisines. In many cases, Dominican entrepreneurs took over old Cuban restaurants, such as Caridad and El Mambí, and refurbished their menus. It is now fairly easy to find the traditional mangú in any of several dozen eateries in Manhattan, the Bronx, and Queens. Other Dominican dishes include *sancocho*, a soupy stew made with various kinds of root vegetables, meats, and spices; *carne guisada*, or beef stew; *empanada de yuca*, or cassava turnover; and *habichuelas con dulce*, made with sweet beans, coconut milk, regular milk, sugar, and butter. A popular drink is *morir soñando* (die dreaming), which combines orange juice, milk, sugar, and ice. Favorite desserts include *pastelillos de guayaba* (guava pastries), *yaniqueques* (fried flour cakes), *dulce de coco* (coconut sweets), and *pan dulce relleno* (sweet stuffed bread).

Most Dominicans are raised as Roman Catholics. In New York, Boston, and other centers of the Dominican diaspora, immigrants often assert their Catholic faith even more strongly than in their home country. However, worship often takes the form of folk practices such as lighting candles, asking for blessings, and keeping a home altar for the saints, rather than institutionalized practices such as attending mass on Sundays. Several urban parishes have been renewed with thousands of Catholics (including some priests and nuns) from the Dominican Republic. Many of these churches now offer masses and other religious services in Spanish. The Virgin of Altagracia, the patron of the Dominican Republic, is a popular devotion among Dominicans in the United States and Puerto Rico. One Washington Heights church has been renamed Our Lady of Altagracia, and a procession in honor of the Virgin is held at Saint Patrick's Cathedral every year on January 21.

A small but distinguished group of Dominican intellectuals has lived in the United States since the beginning of the twentieth century. Among them, the respected literary critic Pedro Henríquez Ureña taught at the University of Minnesota (1916–1921) and at Harvard University (1940–1941). His sister Camila Henríquez Ureña was a professor at Vassar and Middlebury colleges for many years until 1960. Since then, other Dominican intellectuals have spent long periods of time in New York, including Viriato Sención, author of the controversial novel *Los que falsificaron la firma de Dios* (1992), translated as *They Forged the Signature of God* (1995); and the late Ilka Tanya Payán, a leading theater and television actress.

Dominican Americans have recently begun to penetrate the higher spheres of American culture. Some have become bilingual teachers and principals in New York's public school system. In 1992, Silvio Torres-Saillant, Ramona Hernández, and other scholars created the Dominican Studies Institute at the City University of New York. Several Dominican writers have established their reputations in the United States, most prominently Julia Alvarez, author of the critically acclaimed novels *How the García Girls Lost Their Accents* (1991) and *In the Time of the Butterflies* (1994). A new generation of Dominican American writers and artists has gained wider recognition, including Junot Díaz, the celebrated author of the short story collection *Drown* (1996), and Josefina Báez, a versatile artist, performer, and poet. Unfortunately, the general public is usually unaware of Dominican American cultural accomplishments, which remain on "the margins of the periphery," to use Torres-Saillant's trenchant phrase.

Future Challenges

At the beginning of the twenty-first century, the Dominican diaspora faces multiple challenges. First, the number of Dominicans living abroad, as well as the variety of their places of residence, will most likely continue to increase, including in various parts of the United States, Puerto Rico, and other countries of the Caribbean and Europe. Second, the immigrants and their descendants will suffer growing prejudice and discrimination against foreigners, especially those who are dark-skinned. Third, Dominican communities must organize themselves in ever more effective ways to articulate their collective needs and interests. Last, Dominicans abroad will have to renegotiate their political incorporation in the Dominican Republic as well as in the United States and other host countries.

To respond to such challenges, the Dominican diaspora has four decades of accumulated experience in the United States and Puerto Rico. In New York, the immigrants have created dozens of voluntary associations and community agencies to promote their social and economic well-being and political empowerment. In San Juan, Puerto Rico, Dominicans have begun to participate actively in municipal and state affairs. Elsewhere, they have elected a few public officials. Everywhere, community leaders have become aware of the strategic importance of overcoming internal divisions caused by class, color, ideology, region, and legal status, in order to face their shared adversity. However, socioeconomic and political differences continue to be major barriers to formal organization. Furthermore, coalitions with other ethnic and racial minorities—such as Puerto Ricans, African Americans, and Haitians—are still weak and sporadic. The future of the Dominican community in the United States depends in large measure on its capacity to overcome fragmentation and isolation from other groups.

The Dominican diaspora is currently revisiting its links with the homeland. An important step in this process has been the extension of dual citizenship to those living outside the Dominican Republic. However, the practical repercussions of this legal change remain unclear. Will Dominican citizens have the same privileges and obligations in the diaspora as on the island? How exactly will immigrants exercise the right to vote and be represented in the Dominican Republic? Will transnational efforts to organize Dominicans in the United States, Puerto Rico, and other countries be fruitful? What role will the social institutions of the Dominican Republic play in the immigrants' daily lives? How will the traditional discourse of Dominican identity be reconfigured once the gap between the nation of origin and the diaspora is reduced? The answers to such questions are urgent for Dominicans both at home and abroad.

In any case, the sustained exodus has already transformed the Dominican Republic—demographically, economically, culturally, and even juridically. The portion of the Dominican population living permanently or temporarily abroad, which sends millions of dollars back home and is increasingly adopting dual Dominican–U.S. citizenship, will continue to grow in the next few decades. It is therefore imperative to expand the political, cultural, and linguistic practices of the Dominican Republic to recognize the diaspora as an integral part of the nation. That expansion will require, among other measures, reexamining the popular stigma against the Dominican-York in Dominican society, as well as against the undocumented immigrant in Puerto Rican and American societies. More concretely, that expansion will require thinking through and guaranteeing citizen rights in more than one nation-state. Immigrant-receiving countries will have to combat xenophobia and racism through more concerted efforts by the forces of civil society, including non-governmental organizations and grassroots groups. Although the public agenda is long and difficult, the collective survival of the Dominican diaspora is at stake, as is the very fabric of multiethnic societies like the United States.

See also **Art, Dominican; Dominican Day Parade; Dominican Home Country Project; Dominican Studies Institute; Dominican Writers in the United States; Latino Identities and Ethnicities; Merengue; Playwrights, Caribbean; Poetry;** *and* **Washington Heights.**

BIBLIOGRAPHY

Austerlitz, Paul. *Merengue: Dominican Music and Dominican Identity*. Philadelphia: Temple University Press, 1997.

Castro, Max J., and Thomas D. Boswell. *The Dominican Diaspora Revisited: Dominicans and Dominican Americans in a New Century*. Occasional Paper No. 53. Miami: North-South Center, University of Miami, 2002.

Duany, Jorge. "Between the Nation and the Diaspora: Migration to and from Puerto Rico." In *Migration and Immigration: A Global View*, edited by Maura I. Toro-Morn and Marixsa Alicea. Westport, Conn.: Greenwood Press, 2004.

Duany, Jorge. *Quisqueya on the Hudson: The Transnational Identity of Dominicans in Washington Heights*. New York: CUNY Dominican Studies Institute, 1994.

Duany, Jorge. "Reconstructing Racial Identity: Ethnicity, Color, and Class among Dominicans in the United States and Puerto Rico." *Latin American Perspectives* 25, no. 3 (1998): 147–172.

Duany, Jorge, ed. *Los Dominicanos en Puerto Rico: Migración en la semi-periferia*. Río Piedras, P.R.: Ediciones Huracán, 1990.

Duany, Jorge, Luisa Hernández Angueira, and César A. Rey. *El Barrio Gandul: Economía subterránea y migración indocumentada en Puerto Rico*. Caracas, Venezuela: Editorial Nueva Sociedad, 1995.

Georges, Eugenia. *New Immigrants and the Political Process: Dominicans in New York*. Occasional Paper No. 45. New York: Center for Latin American and Caribbean Studies, New York University, 1984.

Graham, Pamela M. "Political Incorporation and Re-incorporation: Simultaneity in the Dominican Migrant Experience." In *Migration, Transnationalization, and Race in a Changing New York*, edited by Héctor R. Cordero-Guzmán, Robert C. Smith, and Ramón Grosfoguel, 87–108. Philadelphia: Temple University Press, 2001.

Grasmuck, Sherri, and Patricia R. Pessar. *Between Two Islands: Dominican International Migration*. Berkeley: University of California Press, 1991.

Guarnizo, Luis E. *"Los Dominicanyorks*: The Making of a Binational Society." *Annals of the American Academy of Political and Social Sciences* 533 (1994): 70–86.

Hendricks, Glenn L. *The Dominican Diaspora: From the Dominican Republic to New York City—Villagers in Transition*. New York: Teachers College Press, Columbia University, 1974.

Hernández, Ramona. *The Mobility of Workers under Advanced Capitalism: Dominican Migration to the United States*. New York: Columbia University Press, 2002.

Hernández, Ramona, and Francisco Rivera-Batiz. *Dominican New Yorkers: A Socioeconomic Profile, 1997*. New York: CUNY Dominican Studies Institute, 1997.

Itzigsohn, José, and Carlos Dore-Cabral. "The Manifold Character of Panethnicity: Latino Identities and Practices among Dominicans in New York City." In *Mambo Montage: The Latinization of New York*, edited by Agustín Laó-Montes and Arlene Dávila, 319–336. New York: Columbia University Press, 2001.

Levitt, Peggy. *The Transnational Villagers*. Berkeley: University of California Press, 2001.

Mahler, Sarah J. "La dinámica de la legalización en Nueva York: Un enfoque hacia los Dominicanos." In *Dominicanos ausentes: Cifras, políticas, condiciones sociales*, by Eugenia Georges, Eric M. Larson, Sara J. Mahler, et al., 139–182. Santo Domingo, D.R.: Fundación Friedrich Ebert: Fondo para el Avance de las Ciencias Sociales, 1989.

Pessar, Patricia R. *A Visa for a Dream: Dominicans in the United States*. Boston: Allyn and Bacon, 1995.

Portes, Alejandro, and Luis E. Guarnizo. *Capitalistas del trópico: La inmigración en los Estados Unidos y el desarrollo de la pequeña empresa en la República Dominicana*. Santo Domingo, D.R.: Facultad Latinoamericana de Ciencias Sociales, Programa República Dominicana, The Johns Hopkins University, 1991.

Ricourt, Milagros. *Power from the Margins: The Incorporation of Dominicans in New York City*. New York: Routledge, 2002.

Rodríguez de León, Francisco. *El furioso merengue del norte: Una historia de la comunidad Dominicana en los Estados Unidos*. New York: Editorial Sitel, 1998.

Sagás, Ernesto, and Sintia Molina, eds. *Global Perspectives on the Dominican Diaspora: The Transnational Dynamics of a Caribbean Migration*. Gainesville: University Press of Florida, 2004.

Sørensen, Ninna Nyberg. "Telling Migrants Apart: The Experience of Migrancy among Dominican Locals and Transnationals." Unpublished manuscript, Institute of Anthropology, University of Copenhagen, Denmark, 1994.

Torres-Saillant, Silvio. *El retorno de las yolas: Ensayos sobre diáspora, democracia y Dominicanidad*. Santo Domingo, D.R.: Librería La Trinitaria y Editorial Manatí, 1999.

Torres-Saillant, Silvio. *Diasporic Disquisitions: Dominicanists, Transnationalism, and the Community*. Dominican Studies Working Papers Series 1. New York: CUNY Dominican Studies Institute, 2000.

Torres-Saillant, Silvio, and Ramona Hernández. *The Dominican Americans*. Westport, Conn.: Greenwood Press, 1998.

Ugalde, Antonio, Frank D. Bean, and Gilbert Cárdenas. "International Migration from the Dominican Republic: Findings from a National Survey." *International Migration Review* 13, no. 2 (1979): 235–254.

U.S. Census Bureau, American FactFinder. *Census 2000*. Web site. www.census.gov/main/www/cen2000.html

U.S. Citizenship and Immigration Services. *Yearbook of Immigration Statistics, 1996–2000*. Web site. uscis.gov/graphics/shared/aboutus/statistics/Immigs.htm

JORGE DUANY

DOMINICAN STUDIES INSTITUTE. The Dominican Studies Institute opened at the City College campus of the City University of New York (CUNY) in August 1992 as a pilot project at the behest of local Dominican students, community leaders, and academics. The Institute was initially funded by a $78,000 development grant from W. Ann Reynolds, then chancellor of CUNY, and a $40,000 seed grant from the Aaron Diamond Foundation. Since then CUNY, the Rockefeller Foundation, the Ford Foundation, the Aaron Diamond Foundation, and private donations have funded the Institute. In 1994 it became part of CUNY.

At the time of the Institute's founding, Dominicans were the largest immigrant group in New York City, and the second largest Latino group. Census data from 1990 placed the Dominican diaspora in New York at roughly 350,000. The Institute claims there were closer to 800,000 Dominicans in New York when undocumented and uncounted immigrants are included. As it entered its third decade in the United States in the 1990s, the Dominican diaspora in New York City was growing exponentially and becoming increasingly organized politically.

At the same time, twin processes of maturation and marginalization were occurring. On the one hand, Dominicans were one of the most impoverished immigrant communities in New York, experiencing disproportionate rates of unemployment, high occupational segregation, high dropout rates, and high rates of juvenile imprisonment. On the other hand, they had established clear entrepreneurial niches in the local livery cab, small grocery store (bodega), and beauty services industries; they gained increasing visibility and power in the transnational political scene; and they sent increasing numbers of students on to higher education. In the 1990s, there were approximately ten thousand Dominican students in the CUNY system alone. Despite this, there were only two Dominicans on CUNY's permanent faculty. There were also few if any library holdings on Dominicans, and retention and graduation rates for Dominican students were relatively low. The institute's founding mandate, therefore, was both to document and to facilitate the process of community development.

The institute's founding director, Dr. Silvio Torres-Saillant, emigrated from the Dominican Republic. During his eight-year tenure as director, the institute sponsored over fifty national and international academic conferences, developed the first university-based Dominican studies library, published a series of research monographs, and received a three-year Rockefeller Foundation grant that enabled it to host visiting scholars from around the world. It also mounted several exhibits, established itself as a clearinghouse for information about the Dominican diaspora, and provided formal and informal mentoring to Dominican-diaspora students, activists, artists, and leaders of all stripes.

Among the conferences hosted by the Institute was "Dominican Writers in the Context of the Americas: A Dialogue on Literature and Cultural Identity," held in 1994 at the Americas Society. In 1995 the international conference, "The Two Nations of Quisqueya: Haitian-Dominican Relations at the Turn of the Century," exemplified the diaspora's desire to challenge traditional Dominican anti-Haitianism, fostering dialogue and collaboration instead. In June 2001 the Institute hosted "Up from the Margins: Diversity as a Challenge to the Democratic Nation," a major, two-part transnational conference funded by the Rockefeller Foundation and held in New York City and Santo Domingo. One of the many outcomes of the conference was the first public declaration, by Dominican vice president Milagros Ortiz Bosch, that Haitian and Dominican-Haitian children had the right of access to public education in the Dominican Republic regardless of their citizenship status. That declaration was followed by policy initiatives liberalizing access, the first of their kind.

The institute's monograph series began in 1994. Since then it has published demographic profiles of the community, a directory of Dominicanists, a Dominican studies resource guide, and several other historiographic, sociological, and literary monographs. In 1995 the institute issued the English-language translation of renowned Dominican historian Frank Moya Pons's *The Dominican Republic: A National History*.

In 1995 the institute was awarded a three-year Rockefeller Foundation Humanities Fellowships program to support visiting researchers working on Dominican history. A project entitled "Representation Versus Experience: Missing Chapters in Dominican History and Culture" supported research on subjects traditionally overlooked by Dominican historiography: the African diaspora, women, the poor, and dissenters in Dominican history and society. The institute hosted ten scholars from throughout the world between 1996 and 1999. Several of those fellows subsequently have published scholarly articles, research monographs, and books based on the work they did while at the Institute.

Throughout the institute's existence, Sarah Aponte has been its chief librarian and, from 1992 to 2001, its administrative coordinator. Under her direction, the library has become a central repository for archival, bibliographic, print media, and audiovisual materials related to the Dominican diaspora. Aponte published the first Dominican migration bibliography, *Dominican Migration to the United States, 1970–1997: An Annotated Bibliography*. In the fall of 2002, the library moved from the institute's administrative offices to City College's Cohen Library. It is the first and only university-based resource center dedicated to Dominican studies.

The institute has also been active in disseminating accurate information about the often-stigmatized Dominican diaspora in the United States to the media and to elected officials in both the Dominican Republic and the United States. In 1998, for example, the Institute issued a lengthy press release rebutting the *New York Times*' portrayal of Dominicans as primarily drug dealers. Similarly, the Institute has consistently rebutted negative portrayals of the diaspora by the Dominican media through the publication of newspaper and magazine articles in the Dominican Republic, and through presentations by the Institute's directors and affiliated researchers at conferences in the Dominican Republic. Finally, it was also instrumental in the development of the Dominican American National Roundtable, a national advocacy group located in Washington, D.C.

In 1998 the Institute was inducted into the Inter-University Program for Latino Research (IUPLR), thus establishing itself as a nationally recognized academic entity. The IUPLR is a national consortium of university-based Latina and Latino research centers headquartered at the University of Notre Dame.

In the spring of 2001, Dr. Ramona Hernández, also a Dominican immigrant, assumed directorship of the institute. She is the author of several scholarly works and a respected community advocate. Dr. Hernández was also the first Dominican appointed to the New York City Board of Education.

See also **Dominican American National Roundtable; Dominican Home Country Project; Dominican Writers in the United States;** *and* **Dominicans.**

BIBLIOGRAPHY

Aponte, Sarah. *Dominican Migration to the United States, 1970–1997: An Annotated Bibliography*. New York: CUNY Dominican Studies Institute, 1999.

Aponte, Sarah. "El Estudio de la Diáspora." *Estudios Sociales*. Santo Domingo, Dominican Republic. Forthcoming.

Itzigsohn, José, Carlos Dore Cabral, Esther Hernández Medina, et al. "Mapping Dominican Transnationalism: Narrow and Broad Transnational Practices." *Ethnic and Racial Studies* 22 (1999): 316–339.

Torres-Saillant, Silvio, and Ramona Hernández. *The Dominican Americans*. Westport, Conn.: Greenwood Press, 2000.

GINETTA E. B. CANDELARIO

DOMINICAN WRITERS IN THE UNITED STATES. Dominican literature in the United States can be traced as far back as the first half of the twentieth century, as politicians, scholars, and writers established themselves in this country, mainly for political reasons. These writers include Pedro, Max, and Camila Henríquez Ureña, who were the children of the poet laureate Salomé Ureña and Francisco Henríquez y Carvajal, the man who was president of the Dominican Republic at the start of the U.S. occupation of the country from 1916 to 1924. Pedro Henríquez Ureña first came to New York in 1901 at the age of sixteen with his brother Max and took courses at Columbia University. He left in 1904 and stayed in Mexico for almost a decade until he returned, first to Washington, D.C., and later to New York, to work as a journalist for various newspapers. In 1916, he began teaching at the University of Minnesota in Minneapolis, where he also obtained an M.A. degree and soon thereafter a PhD. After his graduation, Henríquez Ureña lived in Cuba, Mexico, Spain, and Argentina. He also stayed in the United States from 1940 to 1941, where, as a visiting professor at Harvard University, he delivered the prestigious Charles Eliot Norton Lectures, the texts of which were published in 1945 by Harvard University Press under the title *Literary Currents in Spanish America*. Henríquez Ureña died in Argentina in 1946.

Camila Henríquez Ureña received an MA from the University of Minnesota in 1918. Subsequently, she taught Spanish literature at Vassar College, in Poughkeepsie, New York, from 1942 to 1959. She focused her scholarly work on pedagogy and on feminist and Hispanic topics. After almost two decades of academic work, she moved to Cuba, where she joined the literacy campaign that the new revolutionary government had launched. There are several editions and compilations of Camila's work in Spanish, published by Cuban and Dominican organizations.

There were a number of other important writers in the first half of the twentieth century. José M. Bernard published a volume of verse entitled *Renuevos* (1907). Fabio Fiallo Cabral published a volume of short fiction entitled *Cuentos frágiles* (1908). Manuel Florentino Cestero published the book of poems *El canto del cisne* (1915) and a prose fiction work entitled *El amor en Nueva York* (1920). Jesusa Alfau Galván published a series of short articles and essays in the weekly *Las Novedades*. Gustavo Bergés Bordas published a collection of essays entitled *Cien días en Nueva York* (1925). Angel Rafael Lamarche wrote the short fiction collection *Los cuentos que Nueva York no sabe* (1949), published in Mexico. Virginia de Peña wrote the novels *Toeya*, *Atardecer en las montañas*, *Sobra de pasión*, *La hora del destino*, *Amores de Júpiter y Selene*, *Magia de primavera*, and *El fulgor de las estrellas*. Andrés Francisco Requena, after writing a few poems praising the Trujillo regime, wrote the novel *Cementerio sin cruces* (1951), which cost him his life because of its criticism of the dictatorship. These works were written in Spanish.

Contemporary literary works in Spanish have been promoted through the efforts of Silvio Torres Saillant, founding director of the Dominican Studies Institute at the City University of New York and subsequently director of the Latino–Latin American Studies Program at Syracuse University. Daisy Cocco-de Filippis, who in 2002 became provost at Hostos Community College, for years has hosted monthly meetings of women writers known as "La Tertulia." These gatherings have served not only as workshops to discuss works in progress but also as networking and support systems for the writers. These *tertulias* have produced anthologies such as *Tertuliando: dominicanas y amiga(o)s = Hanging Out: Dominican Women and Friends: Bilingual Text(o)s bilingües* (1997), a collection of the poetry and fiction of writers such as Yrene Santos, Zaida Corniel, Marianela Medrano, Miriam Ventura, Virginia Moore, Ynoemia del Villar, and other members of "La Tertulia." Another similar anthology is *Poemas del exilio y otras inquietudes = Poems of Exile and Other Concerns: A Bilingual Selection of the Poetry Written by Dominicans in the United States* (1988), which Cocco-de Filippis coedited with Emma Jane Robinett.

In addition to appearing in anthologies, some of these writers have published books of their own. Yrene Santos, an award-winning poet, has published the collections of poems *Desnudez del silencio* (1988), *Reencuentro* (1997) and *El incansable juego* (2002). Marianela Medrano, a poet and poetry therapist residing in Connecticut, has published *Oficio de vivir* (1986), *Los alegres ojos de la tristeza* (1987), *Regando esencias/The Scent of Waiting* (1998), and *Curada de espantos* (2002). The poet Julio Alvarado has published a collection of poems entitled *Fiesta Rota* (2003).

Along with the Dominican writers who publish in Spanish and those who write in English, there are also those who write in both languages. One of them is Alan Cambeira, a writer whose works are mainly dedicated to the home country. He is the author of *Quiénes son los dominicanos* (2002) and *Quisqueya la bella* (1997), two collections of essays on Dominican identity and culture, and *Azúcar: The Story of Sugar* (2003), a novel about the exploitation of sugarcane plantation workers in the Dominican Republic.

The works of Dominican writers who publish in English include, in chronological order, the fiction, poetry, and essays of Rhina Espaillat, Julia Alvarez, Junot Díaz, Loida Maritza Pérez, Josefina Báez, Angie Cruz, Nelly Rosario, and Annecy Báez. Recurring themes of their works are the feeling of loss and separation from the home country as well as the difficulties of cultural adaptation (Julia Alvarez); life in inner-city poverty, fragmentation of the family, and masculine sexual identity (Junot

Díaz); self-hatred and conflictive racial and sexual identities (Loida Maritza Pérez); the subversion of traditional notions of ethnicity (Josefina Báez); ambivalent feelings of anger and reconciliation with the home culture (Angie Cruz); and the subversion of traditional notions of gender and of the home culture (Nelly Rosario).

Rhina Espaillat and Julia Alvarez

Born in 1932 in Santo Domingo, Rhina Espaillat came with her family to the United States in 1939. At sixteen, she was already a published poet. Her poetry has been included in numerous literary magazines and anthologies and has received prestigious awards, including the T. S. Eliot Prize, the Richard Wilbur Award, the Sparrow Sonnet Prize, and three yearly prizes from the Poetry Society of America.

Julia Alvarez was born in New York in 1950. She spent her early childhood in the Dominican Republic until 1960, when her family moved back to New York to escape the Trujillo regime. She is the author of four novels, three collections of poetry, one collection of essays, one children's book, three young adult novels, and one cookbook, in addition to numerous poems, articles, and essays published in countless journals, magazines, and other publications. She is also the recipient of prestigious awards, fellowships, and other forms of recognition for her literary work. Her most celebrated works include the novels *How the García Girls Lost their Accents* (1991), *In the Time of the Butterflies* (1994), *¡Yo!* (1997), and *In the Name of Salomé* (2000). Her poem collections include *Homecoming* (1996), *The Other Side/El Otro Lado* (1996), and *The Woman I Kept to Myself* (2004).

Junot Díaz

Born in 1968 in the Dominican Republic, Junot Díaz moved with his parents to the United States in 1975. He holds a bachelor's degree from Rutgers University and an MFA in creative writing from Cornell University. He is the author of the best-selling short-story collection *Drown* (1996), which has been translated into twelve languages. He has also edited one anthology, *The Beacon Best of 2001: Great Writing by Women and Men of All Races and Colors.* His fiction has appeared in *Story*, *The New Yorker*, *The Paris Review*, *Time Out*, *Glimmer Train*, *African Voices*, four annual volumes of *Best American Short Stories* between 1996 and 2000, and the "Future of American Fiction" issue of *The New Yorker* in 1999. He has received a Pushcart Prize XXII, a Guggenheim Fellowship in 1999, a Lila Wallace–Reader's Digest Writers' Award, and the 2002 Pen/Malamud Award. Díaz taught in the MFA program at Syracuse University from 1997 to 2002, and then became an associate professor in the Writing and Humanistic Studies program at the Massachusetts Institute of Technology in Boston.

JUNOT DÍAZ.

Drown is a collection of stories about a boy growing up both in the impoverished Dominican barrios and in the inner cities of industrial New Jersey. The stories "Israel," "Aguantando," and "No Face" are set in the Dominican Republic, where little Yunior, his brother Rafa, and their mother Virta struggle with poverty and separation from her husband, who had migrated to the United States. The other stories are set in the United States and portray different stages of Yunior's coming of age. "Drown" and "Edison, New Jersey" describe the claustrophobic atmosphere of an industrial neighborhood, where life seems doomed and hopeless. Díaz's works reflect his Latino, African American, and global literary experiences. Although critics have perceived different influences in his writing, Díaz's success resides in the fact that he has crafted a new voice in the American literary landscape. Within the context of Dominican and other Latina and Latino writers, his work represents a generational shift in terms of his approach to the immigrant experience and his use of the language.

Loida Maritza Pérez

Loida Maritza Pérez was born in the Dominican Republic in 1963 and came to the United States with her family when she was three. Holding a BA from Cornell University, she is a recipient of the Pauline and Henry Louis Gates Fellowship for Djerassi Resident Artists Program (1996), the Ragdale Foundation's U.S.–Africa Writer's Project Award (1994), and the New York Foundation for the Arts Award (1992). She is the author of the novel *Geographies of Home* (1999), which narrates the life of a troubled Dominican family living in Brooklyn and deals with issues of poverty, domestic abuse, insanity, self-hatred, superstition, religious fanaticism, and conflictive racial and sexual identities. It is also the story of reconciliation with the self and with the home culture, in which religion is depicted as a place of tension between the contradictory feelings of repulsion and attraction towards the home culture. As Aurelia, the mother, comes to terms with her spiritual legacy, she uses it as a tool to address her family's needs. Her struggle is similar to that of her daughters, who are also confronting their own demons, and to that of Papito, the father, who is torn between his responsibility to his family and his religious devotion as an Adventist. While all these struggles are taking place, the home culture is represented in opposition to the civilized and rational universe that is glimpsed through Iliana's brief time in college.

Josefina Báez

Borin in 1960, Josefina Báez left her native town of La Romana to live in New York at the age of twelve, returning repeatedly to the Dominican Republic and spending extended periods of time in Dominican schools. A performer, writer, and educator, Báez has participated extensively in many international theatre festivals and workshops in Asia (particularly India), Latin America, Europe, and the Caribbean. She has devoted herself to a spiritual life under the guidance of Swami Guru Devanand Saraswati Ji Maharash. Her writing has been published in *Forward Motion Magazine, Brujula/Compass, Ventana Abierta, Tertuliando/Hanging Out, Vetas, Caribbean Connections: Moving North, Ojo Paralelo, Aquí es Manhattan, allá La Romana,* and *The Beacon Best of 2001: Great Writing by Women and Men of All Races and Colors.* She has taught in the Creative Arts Laboratory at Columbia University's Teachers College.

Báez is the author of the bilingual text for performance *Dominicanish* (2000), a non-traditional portrayal of the situation of a young immigrant woman in New York City who is learning English and, through her new language, new ways to relate to the world. In this process, traditional categories of identity, such as gender, race, ethnicity, and nationality, end up being subverted as the character/narrator opens up to alternative possibilities.

For Báez, her "hyphenated" condition enriches her in ways that could not have happened had she not migrated to New York. Furthermore, her creative work is the site for exploring possibilities in language, musical taste, sensual pleasures, and spiritual awakenings that are brought forth through exposure to multiple cultural stimuli. From this point of view, Dominicanness can no longer be reduced to stereotypical images and must include the contours of the "here" and "now" of the community in New York City.

Angie Cruz

Angie Cruz was born and raised in the Washington Heights section of New York City. She holds a bachelor's degree from Binghamton University and a Master of Fine Arts degree from New York University. Her fiction and activist work have earned her the New York Foundation of the Arts Fellowship, the Barbara Deming Memorial Fund Award, and The Bronx Writers' Center Van Lier Literary Fellowship. Cruz lives in New York City where she co-founded WILL: Women in Literature and Letters, a collective devoted to social change through artistic expression.

ANGIE CRUZ. (Lightstream)

Cruz's debut novel *Soledad* (2001) is the story of a Dominican adolescent, Soledad, who has escaped from what she describes as the loud, stifling, and waste-filled Dominican neighborhood of Washington Heights to live and attend school in the hip, downtown neighborhoods of New York City. When she is forced to return to the bedside of her mother Olivia, who has fallen into a deep, endless sleep, Soledad is confronted back in the old neighborhood with the conflictive culture and relatives that she had rejected. The memories of Soledad's haunted past intertwine with those of her mother, forcing the two of them to confront each other with an earnest attempt at rebuilding bridges. In this sense, although it is considered "the novel of Washington Heights" (Torres-Saillant 2003, p. 120), *Soledad* is also the story of cycles and reconciliation—a gradual process that begins with rejection and ends with the spiritual rebirth of its characters.

Nelly Rosario

Nelly Rosario was born in the Dominican Republic. Her parents moved to New York when she was three months old. She earned a bachelor's degree in engineering from MIT and an MFA in fiction from Columbia University. She has received numerous awards, including a 1999 Barbara Deming Memorial Fund Fellowship, The Bronx Writers' Center Van Lier Literary Fellowship for 1999–2000, two National Arts Club Writing Fellowships, the 1997 Hurston/Wright Award in Fiction, and the 1988 National Teachers in English Writing Award. Her work has appeared in *The Village Voice* and in the anthology of essays *Becoming American* (2000). Her novel, *Song of the Water Saints*, won the PEN Open Book Award "Beyond Margin" in 2002 and has been translated into Spanish by Emece Planeta under the title *El canto del agua* (2003). The *Village Voice Literary Supplement* chose her as one of seven "Writers on the Verge" for 2001.

Song of the Water Saints (2002) is a novel set mainly in the Dominican Republic, beginning in 1916, during the U.S. occupation of the country, and ending in 1999 in New York City. It is the story of four generations of unruly, headstrong women who struggle to make their dreams come true. The incessant wanderlust of the first woman, Graciela, leads her throughout the country in search of "a better life." Her daughter, Mercedes, more levelheaded than her impulsive mother, becomes a businesswoman. Despite her modest success, the economic situation of the Dominican Republic of the 1980s forces her and her family to move to New York and start anew as she looks after her granddaughter Leyla, who seems to have inherited Graciela's restlessness.

In this novel, the home culture is represented through the details of the everyday life of the working and rural classes. It avoids the pitfall of depicting the home culture

as either an exotic and unfamiliar place or an idealized Lost Eden. Its innovative treatment of both female and male characters suggests a questioning of the traditional notions of gender in the Dominican Republic. Her female characters are neither the passive victims of male abuse nor pure images of "perfection." Although they live in a patriarchal society, they pursue their dreams independently of the men with whom they are involved.

Annecy Báez

Annecy Báez was born in the Dominican Republic in 1958. She came to the United States with her family when she was three. As a teenager, she spent three years in Santo Domingo, where she attended secondary school. After graduation, she returned to New York and studied at Pace University, where she majored in psychology. She received her master's degree from Hunter School of Social Work in 1984 and her doctorate from New York University Ehrenkranz School of Social Work in 1995. She is the recipient of numerous grants and awards for her professional work as a clinical social worker.

Báez is the author of several poems and short stories dealing with teenagers' coming of age in the Bronx and in the Dominican Republic. In particular, she focuses on adolescent girls' conflicts with their mothers, their desire to explore beyond the confines of their protective family life, and their vulnerability in the face of life. She has developed her craft through participation in several workshops, including the Frederick Douglass Writing Center, New York University's continuing education creative writing courses, and the monthly "Tertulia" held by Daisy Cocco-de Filippis. Báez has published her poetry and fiction in the literary journals *Callaloo* and *Brújula*. She has also published a collection of short stories. Fully engaged by her social consciousness, her literary works are permeated with the stories and insights brought about through her professional experience and her understanding of two different cultures.

See also Alvarez, Julia; Díaz, Junot; Dominicans; Espaillat, Rhina; *and* Literature.

BIBLIOGRAPHY

PRIMARY SOURCES

Báez, Josefina. *Dominicanish: A Performance Text.* New York: I Ombe, 2000.

Cruz, Angie. *Soledad.* New York: Simon and Schuster, 2001.

Díaz, Junot. *Drown.* New York: Riverhead Books, 1996.

Pérez, Loida Maritza. *Geographies of Home.* New York: Penguin, 1999.

Rosario, Nelly. *Song of the Water Saints.* New York: Pantheon Books, 2002.

SECONDARY SOURCES

Cocco-de Filippis, Daisy. *La literatura dominicana al final del siglo: Diálogo entre la tierra natal y la diáspora.* Working Papers Series. New York: CUNY Dominican Studies Institute, 1999.

Cocco-de Filippis, Daisy, ed. *Tertuliando: dominicanas y amiga(o)s = Hanging out: Dominican women and friends: bilingual text(o)s bilingües, 1994–1996.* New York: Alcance, 1997.

Cocco-de Filippis, Daisy, and Emma Jane Robinett, eds. and trans. *Poemas del exilio y de otras inquietudes = Poems of Exile and Other Concerns: A Bilingual Selection of the Poetry Written by Dominicans in the United States.* New York: Alcance, 1988.

Cocco de Filippis, Daisy, and Franklyn Gutiérrez, eds. *Literatura dominicana en los Estados Unidos: Presencia temprana 1900–1950.* Santo Domingo: Editora Búho, 2001.

Maríñez, Sophie. "Dominicanish: La translocalización de los símbolos." Ventana: Listín Diario. Santo Domingo, June 17, 2001: 10.

Maríñez, Sophie. "El equilibrio de los sexos." Review of *Song of the Water Saints* by Nelly Rosario. Ventana: Listín Diario. Santo Domingo, March 2002: 3.

Torres-Saillant, Silvio. "Before the Diaspora: Early Dominican Literature in the United States." In *Recovering the U.S. Hispanic Literary Heritage*, edited by Maria Herrera-Sobek and Virginia Sanchez Korrol, 250–267. Houston: Arte Publico Press, 2000.

Torres-Saillant, Silvio. "La literatura dominicana en los Estados Unidos y la periferia del margen." *Punto y Coma* 3 (1991): 139–149. Reprinted in *Cuadernos de Poética* 7 (1993): 7–26.

Torres-Saillant, Silvio. "Writing Has to Be Generous: An Interview with Angie Cruz." *Calabash: A Journal of Caribbean Arts and Letters* 2, no. 2 (Summer/Fall 2003), New York University, pp. 108–127. library.nyu.edu/calabash/about.html

Torres-Saillant, Silvio, and Ramona Hernandez. *The Dominican Americans*. Westport, Conn.: Greenwood Press, 1998.

SOPHIE MARÍÑEZ

DOMINO PARK. *See* **Parque de Dominos.**

DOWNES V. BIDWELL. *Downes v. Bidwell*, 182 U.S. 244 (1901), decided by the U.S. Supreme Court on May 27, 1901, is regarded as the most important of the group of decisions known as the Insular Cases. Those decisions dealt with the issue of the constitutional status of the territories acquired by the United States at the end of the nineteenth century, including Hawaii, Puerto Rico, and the Philippines.

The specific issue in Downes was whether certain merchandise imported from Puerto Rico after the U.S. Congress had passed the Foraker Act (1900), which provided for a temporary civil government for the island, was exempt from the collection of duties in the port of New York. The Foraker Act authorized the imposition of duties upon goods imported into the U.S. mainland from Puerto Rico. The plaintiff had argued that Puerto Rico had become a part of the United States, after its acquisition from Spain. Therefore, the provision of the Foraker Act imposing duties upon its products violated the uniformity clause of the U.S. Constitution, which declares that "all duties, imposts, and excises shall be uniform throughout the United States."

The case involved broader questions as well. For example, did the U.S. Constitution apply of its own force in the newly acquired territories? What was the extent of the power Congress could exercise over them? The Court's decision, thus, addressed important issues of constitutional law and helped to begin constructing the framework within which the relationship between the United States and the peoples of the territories would eventually develop.

The Court was divided 5 to 4 in its final judgment. There was no single majority opinion. Justice Henry Billings Brown delivered the conclusion and judgment of the Court. Justice Edward Douglas White rendered a concurring opinion, joined by Justices George Shiras Jr. and Joseph McKenna, and Justice Horace Gray wrote separately concurring in the judgement. Chief Justice Melville Weston Fuller dissented, joined by Justices David Josiah Brewer, Rufus Wheeler Peckam, and John Marshall Harlan. The latter also filed a separate dissenting opinion.

The Court concluded that the uniformity clause of the U.S. Constitution did not extend to Puerto Rico. The island, Justice Brown wrote, belonged to but was not a part of the United States. Therefore, the phrase "throughout the United States" did not include Puerto Rico.

As a territory of the United States, Puerto Rico was subject to the plenary power of Congress. According to a majority of the Court, the plenary powers of Congress over the territories were grounded on the nation's inherent power to acquire territory, on the power to declare war, on the treaty making power of the federal government, and on the provisions of the territorial clause of the U.S. Constitution, contained in Article IV, section 3, which provides that "The Congress shall have Power to dispose of and make all needful Rules and Regulations respecting the Territory or other Property belonging to the United States."

The power of Congress, however, was not absolute, for according to the Court it was limited by the protection due to certain personal rights enjoyed by the inhabitants of the territories. Those personal rights were imbedded in the Constitution and were inherent in the system of government prevalent in the United States.

Justice White's concurring opinion was important, because its reasoning eventually became the position adopted by the Court in cases regarding territorial issues. He argued that it was evident that the Constitution applied to the territories. The question was which specific provisions applied. The answer, he posited, depended on the relationship of the particular territory to the United States. Justice White then proceeded to establish a distinction, up to that moment nonexistent in U.S. constitutional law, between what he called "incorporated" and "unincorporated" territories. Unincorporated territories belonged to, but were not a part of, the United States.

Justice White stated that the decision to incorporate a territory to the United States was a political decision to be made by the people of the United States, represented in Congress. It was not the immediate consequence of the mere acquisition of territory. Puerto Rico, he concluded, had been acquired by the United States, but Congress had not decided to incorporate it as part of the nation yet. "The result of what has been said," he added, "is that whilst in an international sense Porto Rico [sic] was not a foreign country, since it was subject to the sovereignty of and was owned by the United States, it was foreign to the United States in a domestic sense, because the island had not been incorporated into the United States, but was merely appurtenant thereto as a possession." In conclusion, the uniformity clause did not apply to Puerto Rico. The unincorporation doctrine elaborated by Justice White was finally adopted by the majority of the Court in *Dorr v. United States* in 1904.

Downes is also important because it contained the first of a series of vigorous dissents on the territorial question issued by Justice Harlan. He argued that Puerto Rico had become part of the United States at least since the ratification, in 1899, of the Treaty of Paris, by virtue of which Spain had ceded the island to the United States. Justice Harlan believed that the U.S. Constitution applied to all the peoples and all the territories over which the United States exercised its jurisdiction. He decried the doctrine adopted by the majority of the Court as a validation of a colonial system not authorized by the Constitution. Justice Harlan continued expressing his dissenting views on this question until his death in 1911.

The doctrine regarding territorial matters developed by the majority of the Court in the Insular Cases, starting with *Downes v. Bidwell*, is still cited as good law in federal court cases and official legislative and executive documents of the U.S. government. Some have argued that it is an anachronistic doctrine that perpetuates the relationship of political subordination that still defines the condition of the territories belonging to the United States and that it should be abolished. Federal courts, however, seem unwilling to take such a bold step and have on many occasions suggested that any substantial change in the relationship of the federal government to the territories is a matter reserved for Congress. In this sense, they have reaffirmed the basic rationale underlying the decision in *Downes*, including the highly influential concurring opinion penned by Justice White.

See also Foraker Act; Insular Cases; *and* Puerto Rico, Colonialism in.

BIBLIOGRAPHY

Rivera Ramos, Efrén. *The Legal Construction of Identity: The Judicial and Social Legacy of American Colonialism in Puerto Rico.* Washington, D.C.: American Psychological Association, 2001.

Torruella, Juan R. *The Supreme Court and Puerto Rico: The Doctrine of Separate and Unequal.* Río Piedras, Puerto Rico: Editorial Universitaria, 1985.

EFRÉN RIVERA RAMOS

D-Q UNIVERSITY–DAVIS. The D-Q University, whose initials stand for the Great Peacemaker (D), of the Iroquois Confederacy, and Quetzalcoatl, the Aztec spirit embodiment, was established in 1971 outside Davis, California, on land once home to the Wintun Peoples (Poowin and Patwin). Site of a former U.S. Army communications relay station, the 643 acres that make up the main campus were awarded to D-Q University in title under provision of the federal surplus property laws. In 1978 the university fell completely under American Indian control, a first. The university enrolled mostly indigenous and Chicano and Chicana students. In 2001 it came under the governance of a board of trustees.

D-Q University represents a site of common struggle for self-determination and control over resources and funding. Established during a period of intense debate about Indian autonomy and following the indigenous takeover of Alcatraz Island in 1969, D-Q began as a tribal college that included Chicanos and Chicanas as tribal people. In the 1990s it lost its accreditation and then regained it. Accreditation was often a topic of discussion. By the late 1970s D-Q University had achieved distinction as one of the most "audited" institutions of higher learning via harassing visits by federal auditors predicated on the belief that no real teaching or true learning was taking place. The volunteer efforts of many educators, some of them indigenous tribal leaders, disenchanted academics, and other friends and allies, secured the position of the university. Sometimes instructors were forced to leave campus and take their classrooms literally to the community, including the fields surrounding the university, where some students worked as day laborers, or the Sacramento city jail, where students were sometimes either wrongly held or incarcerated. These unusual classroom settings characterized the uniqueness of the D-Q experience, drawing as they did from the life experiences of an underserved student population. In the early twenty-first century, exchange and foreign students continued to make up some of the student body, and part-time as well as permanent faculty and staff continued to contribute to this unusual and interesting experiment in American higher education.

D-Q's academic survival and financial survival have been intertwined, as has been the case for most tribally controlled colleges and universities in the United States. Casino tribes and funding have thus far donated only a few thousand dollars of the estimated $20 million it would take to operate a full-fledged university of this size in its location. D-Q's land base, however, is secure as it has been deeded its site. The university functions as a community college and in 1994 was designated a land-grant institution. Its mission is to educate indigenous people and Chicanos and Chicanas in an environment sensitive to the perspectives and interests of people who are marginalized or ostracized by mainstream educational systems. American Indian languages are taught regularly, and the university hosts conferences of Indian nations; youth and elder gatherings; statewide meetings of MEChA (Movimiento Estudiantil Chicano de Aztlán), a Chicano student organization; powwows; concerts; and other ethnic and cultural activities. Seminars, academic conferences, and workshops are also part of the work D-Q contributes to the surrounding community. Its enrollment includes about six hundred main campus students and an additional nine hundred spread across four satellite campuses. Over one-half of the students are indigenous, and another 40 percent are Chicano and Chicana.

D-Q continues the ongoing dialogues between Chicanos and Chicanas and indigenous (or "enrolled," that is, officially listed as Indian by the U.S. government) people, given that Chicano and other Latino groups also claim indigenous heritage. Authenticating Indianness is not something the university has encouraged. Explaining differences and understanding uses of the Spanish language and of Catholicism and the impact of western European traditions are part of the curriculum at D-Q. For a period of time Dennis Banks, a co-leader of the American Indian Movement (AIM), and others visited or lived at the campus, thereby allowing younger indigenous students and scholars access to the political organizing AIM had undertaken in the 1970s.

From its atmosphere of cultural tolerance and historical sensitivity to teaching students basic skills that will allow them to transfer into four-year institutions, D-Q occupies a significant and symbolic role in northern California and, as some of its supporters suggest, throughout the land euphemistically labeled "Indian Country." Perhaps it could be argued that all of the continental United States was in fact Indian Country, but D-Q has attended to other needs. D-Q's Sequoyah Library Special Collections and Archives contains several important Native American women's papers, historical documents related to the establishment of D-Q, and first edition books dating to the institution's founding. As an alternative to mainstream educational practices and in fulfilling a valuable need among indigenous and Chicano and Chicana students, D-Q appears to have weathered the worst of times and survived through decades of discontent and renewal.

See also Higher Education.

BIBLIOGRAPHY

D Q University Website. www.dqu.cc.ca.us

Selden, Ron. " 'Persevere at All Costs': AIHEC Program Prepares New Generation of Leaders." *Tribal College* 16, no. 2 (Winter 2004):18–19.

Szasz, Margaret Connell. *Education and the American Indian: The Road to Self-Determination Since 1928*. Albuquerque: University of New Mexico Press, 1999.

Tribal College Journal Website. www.tribalcollegejournal.org

DEENA J. GONZÁLEZ

DREAM ACT. The DREAM (Development, Relief, and Education for Alien Minors) Act is a bill introduced in the U.S. Congress in 2001, and in revised form in 2003, to address the difficulties of immigration status and higher education access faced by undocumented youth. According to the Urban Institute's Jeffery S. Passel, it would benefit up to 65,000 students yearly who graduate from U.S. high schools and have lived in the country for over five years. This bill reflects political, legal, and educational struggles led by Latinas and Latinos against the criminalization of undocumented youth, the majority of whom were born in Latin America.

Undocumented migration to the United States rose dramatically during the 1980s and 1990s. Contributing factors include economic globalization and free trade agreements, civil wars, and growing U.S. demand for low-paid laborers. With the passage of the 1986 Immigration Reform and Control Act, millions of undocumented immigrants were legalized, and United States–Mexico border enforcement was intensified. Circular migration between the United States and Latin American countries of origin has declined, and more families with undocumented members are settling in the United States.

The increase in undocumented minors affects public schools. The federal government is responsible for immigration laws, but public education policy is developed largely at the state and municipal levels. Immigration restrictionists have worked to exclude the undocumented from state educational institutions. California's Proposition 187 (1994) banned undocumented immigrants from all public schools. Although it was voided in the courts, financial barriers were erected for the undocumented who sought higher education. In California, which is home to approximately 40 percent of all undocumented students in the United States, court decisions during the 1990s established that the undocumented were no longer considered "state residents" for determining public college tuition. Next, federal officials wrote this inequity into the Illegal Immigration Reform and Immigrant Responsibility Act of 1996 (IIRAIRA). Section 505 required any state that charges in-state tuition to undocumented immigrants to offer the same tuition rate to out-of-state residents. States that continued to classify their undocumented students as residents were hurt financially because they could no longer collect out-of-state tuition from any U.S. citizens.

Organizing for affordable college access for undocumented students began at the state level in the 1980s. The Leticia A. Network, named after an undocumented student in a California court case, included Latina and Latino educators, activists, parents, and students who fought against the state's restrictions. In 1991, Latino Legislative Caucus Chair Richard Polanco led the fight in the California legislature to restore affordable college access to

DREAM Act. College and high school students from El Salvador, Venezuela, and Bolivia rally at the U.S. Capitol in April 2004, urging Congress to pass the act. (Alex Wong/Getty Images)

dressing this issue had passed in seven states and were introduced or pending in eighteen states from New York to Hawaii. Courageous undocumented Latina and Latino youth played key roles in passing these bills by humanizing the plight of the undocumented. They emerged as political actors who educated their communities, spoke to their legislators, and testified at legislative hearings.

By 2000, elected officials across the United States were hearing about talented immigrant students in their districts who were unable to attend college. These students were vulnerable to abuse and deportation because they lacked lawful immigration status. In 2001, bills were introduced in Congress to eliminate federal barriers that prevented undocumented youth from attending college and to grant them legalization. The Student Adjustment Act was coauthored by Congress members Chris Cannon (R-UT), Howard Berman (D-CA), and a Latina, Lucille Roybal-Allard (D-CA). Its companion bill, the DREAM Act, introduced by Senators Orrin Hatch (R-UT) and Richard Durbin (D-IL), established upstanding undocumented youth as symbols of the American dream.

These efforts aimed to help undocumented youth of "good moral character" by deleting IIRAIRA Section 505. Students who have lived in the United States for at least five years and graduate from U.S. high schools or the equivalent could apply for a six-year conditional resident status. This status would become permanent after they completed two years of school or public service, such as college or military duty. The bills gained more than forty-five cosponsors in the Senate and 145 in the House of Representatives, and were endorsed by more than five hundred associations nationwide. Latina and Latino organizations that have led this struggle include the Mexican American Legal Defense and Education Fund and the National Council of La Raza. Undocumented youth and their peers, working as members of groups including the Coalition for Humane Immigrant Rights of Los Angeles, Latinos Unidos Siempre (Oregon), and Global Kids, Inc. (New York), have worked toward the passage of the DREAM Act.

The DREAM Act represents a remarkable bipartisan effort in the difficult climate of immigration reform after 9/11. Interracial coalitions have been formed through the conviction that children who are raised and educated in the United States should have the opportunity to become productive citizens. Latinas and Latinos have assumed leadership in the global pursuit of the human rights of undocumented youth, including the right to higher education based on merit as set forth in the 1948 Universal Declaration of Human Rights. Undocumented youth who fight for higher education demonstrate that they are not a social problem. They have much to contribute through their dedication to their families and communities, and their consciousness that transcends national boundaries.

undocumented students. Staff member Marco Firebaugh, a former activist with the Movimiento Estudiantil Chicano de Aztlán who came to the United States from Mexico at age four, worked on the bill. It was vetoed by Governor Pete Wilson. With the increase and dispersion of undocumented youth throughout the country during the 1990s, more teachers, elected officials, and neighbors knew valedictorians and student leaders who were prevented from contributing their full potential to their communities. When Firebaugh was elected to represent Southeast Los Angeles in the state assembly in 1998, he introduced a bill to waive out-of-state tuition for the state's undocumented high-school graduates. The first legislation of this kind, authored by Representative Rick Noriega, was signed into Texas law in 2001. California soon followed. According to the National Immigration Law Center, as of 2004, bills ad-

See also Ballot Propositions 187, 209, and 227; Higher Education; Immigration; Immigration Reform and Control Act of 186; and Movimento Estudiantil Chicauo de Aztlán.

BIBLIOGRAPHY

Alfred, Janice. "Denial of the American Dream: The Plight of Undocumented High School Students within the U.S. Educational System." *New York Law School Journal of Human Rights* 19 (2003): 615–650.

Galassi, Jennifer. "Dare to Dream? A Review of the Development, Relief, and Education for Alien Minors (DREAM) Act." *Chicano-Latino Law Review* 24 (2003): 79–94.

Passel, Jeffrey S. *Further Demographic Information Relating to the DREAM Act*. Washington, D.C.: Urban Institute, 2003.

Romero, Victor C. "Postsecondary School Education Benefits for Undocumented Immigrants: Promises and Pitfalls." *North Carolina Journal of International Law and Commercial Regulation* 27 (2002): 393–418.

Seif, Hinda. " 'Wise Up!' Undocumented Latino Youth, Mexican-American Legislators, and the Struggle for Higher Education Access." *Latino Studies* 2 (2004): 210–230.

HINDA SEIF

D'RIVERA, PAQUITO (b. 1948), musician. Paquito D'Rivera was born in Havana, Cuba. His father was Tito D'Rivera, the first Cuban to perform classical music on the saxophone. Tito predicted that his young son would one day develop his own style out of the classical technique and the musical traditions of Cuba.

As a teenager, Paquito D'Rivera formed and performed with various musical ensembles. He was one of the founding members of the Orquesta Cubana de Musica Moderna, which he conducted for two years. He was also a founding member and codirector of the innovative musical group Irakere, which developed an explosive mixture of jazz, rock, classical, and traditional Cuban music. The group toured extensively throughout America and Europe, winning one Grammy and garnering several nominations.

D'Rivera's instinctive rebelliousness, ferocious sense of humor, and intolerance of bureaucratic interference in the artistic process led him to leave Cuba for the United States in 1980. The same rebelliousness marks his musical style—a sharp-edged, boundary-pushing fusion of classical, Latino, and jazz. He has performed with many of the foremost musicians of the second half of the twentieth century, both classical and jazz. His own compositions reflect classical and Afro-Cuban influences, presented with cutting humor and technical perfection. D'Rivera names three jazz saxophonists as particular influences on his work: Paul Desmond, Lee Konitz, and Jackie McLean.

Before and after his tenure with Dizzy Gillespie's United Nations Orchestra, D'Rivera performed with a number of the most important musicians both in the jazz

PAQUITO DE RIVERA. At the 18th and Vine Festival in Kansas City, Kansas. (Michael Wildmann/Jazz Visions Photos)

and classical arenas. He has toured constantly with his Chamber Jazz Ensemble, the Paquito D'Rivera Big Bang, and the Paquito D'Rivera Quintet. He has also performed widely as a clarinet soloist in classical contexts or in association with some of the greatest concert-hall names. His collaboration with cellist Yo-Yo Ma is recognized worldwide.

As a composer, D'Rivera has gained well-deserved praise for his production in both popular and classical music. Among others, he has written *NW York Suite* (1989), the wind quintet *Aires Tropicales* (1994), the suite *Rivers* (1998), the *Panamericana Suite* (2000), *La Jicotea* (2002) for string quartet, and *Gran Danzon* (2002) for flute and orchestra.

D'Rivera has won six Grammys, including awards for his albums *Portraits of Cuba* (1996), *Tropicana Nights* (1999), and *Live at the Blue Note* (2001). In 2002, he won again as a guest artist on the recording of the Bebo Valdes Trio. He was also the first artist to win Latin Grammys in both classical and Latin jazz categories, for Stravinsky's

Historia del Soldado (Histoire du Soldat) and *Brazilian Dreams* in 2003.

In 2003 D'Rivera was awarded an honorary doctorate by the Berklee School of Music, which added to the numerous other awards he has received, including a Lifetime Achievement Award for his contribution to Latin music, along with Dizzy Gillespie and Gato Barbieri. The Jazz Journalists Association awarded D'Rivera the Clarinet of the Year 2004 award, an honor he has been nominated for on several occasions. D'Rivera's fiftieth anniversary as an artist was celebrated with several musical events in different countries. The highlights were at New York's Carnegie Hall, where he was surrounded by a constellation of jazz, Cuban, and classical music stars, and at Chicago's Millennium Park with the Grant Park Festival Orchestra.

D'Rivera has written an autobiography, *Mi vida saxual* (My Sax Life), and a novel, *Oh La Habana*. His journalism, expressing his opposition to Fidel Castro as well as to extremist attitudes among Cuban Americans, won an award for Outstanding Editorial Column in Spanish from the National Association of Hispanic Publications in 2001.

See also **Cuban Americans; Latin Grammys;** *and* **Music, Popular.**

BIBLIOGRAPHY

D'Rivera, Paquito. *Mi vida saxual.* Prologue by Guillermo Cabrera Infante and Fernando Trueba. Barcelona, Spain: Seix Barral, 2000.
D'Rivera, Paquito. *¡Oh, La Habana!* Spain: M&T Editores, 2004.
Paquito D'Rivera. www.paquitodrivera.com

ELBIO RODRÍGUEZ BARILARI

DROPOUTS AND RETENTION. Since 1970, the proportion of Latino and Latina high-school dropouts has remained significantly higher than that of any other racial or ethnic group in the United States. "In 1999, the dropout rate for White, non-Latino was 7.3 percent, compared to 12.6 percent for Black, non-Latinos and 28.6 percent for Latinos" (Rumberger and Rodriguez, p. 114). These numbers could increase in the future because of the projected increase in the Latino and Latina population. According to the 1997 census data, the number of white youth between the ages of eighteen and twenty-four is expected to decline by 4 percent, while the number of Latino and Latina youth is project to increase by 78 percent. This information, while crucial to gaining insight into the state of Latino and Latina education, cannot be fully understood outside of the social, political, economic, cultural, and historical context that produced it. In other words, the difficult relationship that Latinos and Latinas have had with the public education system must be taken into consideration; the statistical data cannot be read as the sole signifier of the "success" or "failure" of Latino and Latina students in school.

Among the many factors that contribute to the high Latino and Latina dropout rate are the history of segregation in public education, the imbalanced allocation of school funding, the inability of schools to deal effectively with language and cultural differences, grade retention, and the lack of a consistent definition of "dropout." The history of segregation is important because it reflects the problem of unequal distribution of resources, and locates the root of this problem in racial conflicts dating back to the turn of the twentieth century. Latino and Latina students have not only been attending schools with fewer resources, but certain institutional practices and mechanisms developed to exclude Latino and Latina students from white schools. Some of these mechanisms include standardized testing, segregation based on language proficiency, teaching practices that focused on the acculturation of students of color into an imagined homogeneous national community, and grade retention.

The development of standardized testing dates back to the late nineteenth and early twentieth centuries in the United States. It is plagued by a firm belief in "hereditarianism—the theory that individual and group differences in behavior (e.g., intelligence) can primarily be accounted for on the basis of genetics" (Valencia, Villarreal, and Salinas, p. 256). Its functions, according to Richard Valencia, Bruno Villarreal, and Moises Salinas, include: (1) the management of instruction—the sorting, monitoring, and grading of student achievement; (2) public accountability; and (3) the legitimization of the schooling process, or the sanctioning of a highly stratified public education system. These functions of standardized testing have important implications for the quality of education that Latinos and Latinas receive. The use of standardized testing to institutionalize a tracking system that segregates "successful" students from "unsuccessful" students allows educators and public school systems to ignore the disproportionate "failure" of Latino and Latina students in school. According to major reports and studies,

> two of the most significant academic achievement indicators, particularly in the schoolings of Chicano students, are (a) test performance in the content areas (especially reading) and (b) secondary school holding power (i.e., the "school systems' effectiveness in its ability to hold its students until they have completed the full course of study" [U.S. Commission on Civil Rights, 1971b, p. 8]).
>
> (Valencia, p. 5)

However, if—as some critics argue—standardized testing is culturally biased, then the mechanisms used to determine the careers of Latino and Latina students in public education must be reevaluated.

Moreover, the definition of a "dropout" must be clarified. According to some researchers, a dropout is a "person who is not currently enrolled in school and does not have a high school diploma or equivalent certificate" (Rumberger and Rodriguez, p. 16). The most commonly used terms to identify these students, according to Russell Rumberger and Gloria Rodriguez, include: (1) status dropout rate—the proportion of persons in an age group who have not completed high school and are not enrolled in school, regardless of when they dropped out; (2) event (or annual) dropout rate—the proportion of persons in an age group who drop out in a single year without completing high school; and (3) cohort (or longitudinal) dropout rate—the proportion of persons in a single age group or grade level who drop out over a specified period of time. A major obstacle in collecting accurate data is the inability of the states and local school districts to define "dropout" clearly and consistently. Despite the inadequate means of measuring enrollment, the current statistics reveal a frightening percentage of Latino and Latina students dropping out of school.

Latino and Latina students have shown little progress in high-school completion rates since 1970. In 2000, a report from the National Center for Educational Statistics revealed that 91.8 percent of white students, 83.7 percent of African American students, and 94.6 percent of Asian American students completed high school, while only 64.1 percent of all Latino and Latina students were reported to have completed secondary schooling (Table 1).

It is important to note, however, that there are significant differences among Latino and Latina subgroups. Table 2 breaks down the total percentage of Latino and Latina dropouts into three categories: foreign-born, first-generation U.S.–born, and second-generation (or later) U.S.–born.

The data reveal that "foreign born Latinos are more likely to be dropouts: 44.2% of Hispanic young adolescents born outside the United States were more likely to be dropouts" while U.S.–born Latinos and Latinas were more likely to complete secondary school (Espinoza-Herold, p. 28). Whether these figures are a result of the public education system's failure to address the social, cultural, and educational needs of Latinos and Latinas is debatable. What is unquestionable is that they reveal a disproportionate number of Latino and Latina students disengaging from their education.

See also **Education** *and* **Schools, Public.**

TABLE 1. *High-School Completion Rates and Number and Distribution of Completers Ages 18–24 Not Currently Enrolled in High School or Below by Background Characteristics: October 2000*

CHARACTERISTIC	COMPLETION RATE	POPULATION (THOUSANDS)	NUMBER OF COMPLETERS (THOUSANDS)	PERCENT OF ALL COMPLETERS
Total	86.5	25,138	21,743	100.0
SEX				
Male	84.9	12,460	10,580	48.7
Female	88.1	12,678	11,164	51.3
RACE/ETHNICITY				
White, non-Hispanic	91.8	16,502	15,145	69.7
Black, non-Hispanic	83.7	3,582	2,999	13.8
Hispanic	64.1	3,797	2,433	11.2
Asian/Pacific Islander	94.6	1,074	1,016	4.7
AGES				
18–19	84.0	6,718	5,645	26.0
20–21	86.4	7,363	6,359	29.2
22–24	88.1	11,057	9,739	44.8
REGION				
Northeast	89.1	4,265	3,799	17.5
Midwest	88.9	5,861	5,209	24.0
South	84.4	8,895	7,506	34.5
West	85.5	6,117	5,230	24.1

Because of rounding, subtotals may not add up to totals. Because of small sample sizes, American Indians and Alaska Natives are included in the totals but are not shown separately.
SOURCE: U.S. Department of Commerce, U.S. Census Bureau, Current Population Survey, October 2000. Cited in Espinoza-Herold, p. 25.

TABLE 2. *Status Dropout Rates and Number and Distribution of Dropouts of 16- through 24-Year-Olds, by Background Characteristics: October 2000*

CHARACTERISTIC	STATUS DROPOUT RATE (PERCENT)	NUMBER OF STATUS DROPOUTS (THOUSANDS)	POPULATION (THOUSANDS)	PERCENT OF ALL DROPOUTS	PERCENT OF POPULATION
Total	10.9	3,776	34,568	100.0	100.0
SEX					
Male	12.0	2,082	17,402	55.1	50.3
Female	9.9	1,694	17,166	44.9	49.7
RACE/ETHNICITY					
White, non-Hispanic	6.9	1,564	22,574	41.4	65.3
Black, non-Hispanic	13.1	663	5,058	17.6	14.6
Hispanic	27.8	1,456	5,237	38.6	15.1
Asian/Pacific Islander	3.8	54	1,417	1.4	4.1
AGE					
16	3.9	153	3,887	4.1	11.2
17	7.6	307	4,023	8.1	11.6
18	11.6	468	4,019	12.4	11.6
19	13.5	544	4,026	14.4	11.6
20–24	12.4	2,304	18,613	61.0	53.8
RECENCY OF IMMIGRATION					
BORN OUTSIDE THE 50 STATES AND THE DISTRICT OF COLUMBIA					
Hispanic	44.2	1,007	2,282	26.7	6.6
Non-Hispanic	7.4	140	1,907	3.7	5.5
FIRST GENERATION					
Hispanic	14.6	244	1,669	6.5	4.8
Non-Hispanic	4.6	84	1,837	2.2	5.3
SECOND GENERATION OR MORE					
Hispanic	15.9	205	1,286	5.4	3.7
Non-Hispanic	8.2	2,096	25,586	55.5	74.0
REGION					
Northeast	8.5	504	5,945	13.3	17.2
Midwest	9.2	741	8,058	19.6	23.3
South	12.9	1,597	12,337	42.3	35.7
West	11.3	933	8,228	24.7	23.8

Because of rounding, subtotals may not add up to totals. Because of small sample sizes, American Indians and Alaska Natives are included in the totals but are not shown separately. Individuals defined as "first generation" were born in the fifty states or the District of Columbia, and one or both of their parents were born outside the fifty states or the District of Columbia. Individuals defined as "second generation" were born in the fifty states or the District of Columbia, as were both of their parents.
SOURCE: U.S. Department of Commerce, U.S. Census Bureau, Current Population Survey, October 2000. Cited in Espinoza-Herold, p. 27.

BIBLIOGRAPHY

Espinoza-Herold, Mariella. *Issues in Latino Education: Race, School Culture, and the Politics of Academic Success.* Boston: Allyn and Bacon, 2003.

Rumberger, Russell, and Gloria Rodriguez. "Chicano Dropouts: An Update of Research and Policy Issues." In *Chicano School Failure and Success: Past, Present, and Future,* edited by Richard R. Valencia, 114–146. New York: Routledge/Falmer, 2002.

Valencia, Richard R., ed. *Chicano School Failure and Success: Past, Present, and Future.* New York: Routledge/Falmer, 2002.

Valencia, Richard, Bruno Villarreal, and Moises Salinas. "Educational Testing and Chicano Students: Issues, Consequences, and Prospects for Reform." In *Chicano School Failure and Success:*

Past, Present, and Future, edited by Richard R. Valencia, 253–309. New York: Routledge/Falmer, 2002.

MARISSA RAMIREZ

DRUG ABUSE. Latinos and Latinas have become the largest ethnic group in the United States. In July 2003, they numbered nearly 40 million (13.7 percent of the U.S. population). This Latino and Latina population has the youngest median age of any ethnic group reported in the U.S. census (median age 26.7 years, compared to 32 for

African Americans and 37 for whites). Almost 30 percent (29.2 percent) of Latinos and Latinas are age fourteen or younger, in comparison to 25.5 percent and 19.8 percent for African Americans and whites, respectively. If current immigration trends and birthrates continue, the size of the Latino and Latina population will continue to grow dramatically. Latinos and Latinas are a heterogeneous group, consisting of many races and nationalities. These demographic factors are critical to an understanding of trends in drug use and addiction among Latinos and Latinas in the United States. Moreover, there are several reasons that render any understanding of Latino and Latina drug use and addiction inconclusive. In addition to its rapid expansion, the Latino and Latina population in the United States is increasingly diverse, and future trajectories of immigration are unknown. These factors have important consequences for the prevalence of drug use and addiction.

The countries from which most of the Latinos and Latinas in the United States originate, Mexico and other Central American, South American, and Caribbean nations, have lower rates of illicit drug use than does the United States. Moreover, the United States has the highest rates of illicit drug use of any nation in the developed world. Therefore, the picture of Latino and Latina drug abuse and addiction in the United States is one of a heterogeneous group immigrating into a society in which drug use is a major social and health problem and in which the urban settings and neighborhoods to which Latino and Latina families relocate upon immigration tend to be the environments with the highest rates of drug use.

The high prevalence of drug use in the United States was sustained over the last thirty years of the twentieth century, with periods of increases and declines, despite concerted efforts by the U.S. government through the so-called War on Drugs. This War on Drugs has been conducted through several administrations, both Republican and Democratic, and if measured by the prevalence of drug use and misuse in the United States, it has been a dismal failure. According to the 2003 National Survey on Drug Use and Health, an estimated 19.5 million Americans, or 8.2 percent of the population aged twelve or older, are illicit drug users. Marijuana is the most widely used illicit drug. For example, in 2002 there were an estimated 2.6 million new marijuana users. This means that each day an average of seven thousand Americans try marijuana for the first time, and the majority of these new users (69 percent) are under age eighteen. Moreover, in 2003 an estimated 21.6 million Americans were classified as having substance dependence or abuse, which represents 9.1 percent of the total population aged twelve or older. Of these, 3.1 million were classified with dependence on or abuse of both alcohol and illicit drugs, 3.8 million were dependent on or abused illicit drugs but not alcohol, and 14.8 million were dependent on or abused alcohol but not illicit drugs.

Although these numbers are staggering, they are not the highest experienced in the United States during the late twentieth century. Instead, as reported by the annual Monitoring the Future Surveys conducted among high school students, the peak years for the use of illicit drugs among twelfth-grade students in the United States were between 1979 and 1981, with a prevalence of 65.6 percent for any illicit drug in 1981, 60 percent for marijuana in 1979 and 1980, and 93.2 percent for alcohol in 1979. From the early 1980s through the early 1990s there were small declines in drug use among the youth population; however, these rates began to increase again around 1997. All these changes took place in the midst of the War on Drugs, and it is apparent that experimentation with alcohol and other drugs is commonplace among the majority of the young people in the United States. This pattern of drug use is likely to have reverberations on adult consequences of drug use for decades to come in terms of demands on both treatment infrastructures and related health costs. The trends reported by the Monitoring the Future Study among high school students mirrors the adult trends reported by the National Survey on Drug Use and Health (formerly, the National Household Survey).

Given these high rates of drug use and experimentation among U.S. youth, drug abuse has become a major public health problem that reduces the productivity and quality of life of the American population. Drug users have inferior physical and mental health, and they are more likely to have problems with educational attainment and employment, an unstable family life, and heightened probability of criminal justice system involvement. Latinos and Latinas who live in the United States share this vulnerability. As an illustration of the magnitude of the problem, in the calendar year 1998 there were 542,544 emergency room episodes in the United States in which the primary reason for medical attention was drug ingestion. Among Latinos and Latinas between 1991 and 1998, emergency room admissions for drug use problems increased by 80 percent.

Drug abuse and addiction among the Latino and Latina population in the United States must be examined within the contextual background of trends in drug use and abuse in the United States. Additionally, examination of drug use and misuse among Latinos and Latinas is complicated by subgroup differences, regional differences, age differences, and the impact acculturation and exposure to U.S. society has on Latino and Latina immigrants, particularly younger ones. Therefore, the context of exit and entrance into the United States is relevant to understanding issues pertaining to drug use among Latinos and Latinas in the United States.

In terms of the context of entrance into the United States, national data illustrate that the Latino and Latina population mirrors the national trends illustrated above; that is, Latino and Latina youth and adults demonstrate similar years of peaks, reductions, and increases in drug use as those found among the general population. For example, the peak year for marijuana use among Latino and Latina twelfth-grade students were 1979 and 1980, as was the case for white non-Hispanics and blacks, and the lowest years were in the early 1990s for all the groups.

Although national data from surveys such as the Monitoring the Future Study, the National Survey on Drug Use and Health, and epidemiological studies throughout the United States can provide basic information about the extent of drug use and misuse among Latinos and Latinas, assessing the prevalence of drug use and addiction in the U.S. Latino and Latina population is complicated by three major factors. First, drug use patterns among immigrant Latinos and Latinas and those born in the United States are dramatically different. This is in part due to the fact that, despite marginal increases in some nations, such as Mexico, rates of substance use in countries of origin for Latinos and Latinas immigrating to the United States remain low, especially in comparison to the United States. None of the major ongoing national studies makes this important nativity distinction. All such information comes from smaller studies throughout the United States, which consistently demonstrate that the prevalence of drug use, abuse, and dependence is lower among immigrant Latinos and Latinas than their U.S.–born Latino and Latina counterparts.

Second, the Latino and Latina population in the United States is heterogeneous in terms of national origin as well as geographic location. Some groups, such as Puerto Ricans, tend to be in large metropolitan areas in the Northeast, whereas Mexicans, the largest Latino and Latina subgroup by far, are largely in the West but increasingly are moving to areas in the South, Midwest, and East. This heterogeneity makes evaluation of "overall" Latino and Latina drug abuse and addiction difficult if not impossible. Third, patterns of drug use among U.S.-born and immigrant Latinos and Latinas differ based on developmental age at the time of arrival in the United States, and these differing patterns persist after prolonged periods of residence in the United States. Immigrant and U.S.-born Latinos and Latinas have different preexisting social experiences and cultural knowledge, and this in turn produces different personal preferences and normative assumptions about drug use. Prevention and treatment efforts usually fail to consider these factors, and government policies such as the War on Drugs have especially failed to take these issues into account, with deleterious consequences for Latino and Latina communities and families.

Epidemiology of Drug Use among Latinos and Latinas in the United States

According to most epidemiologic studies, lifetime drug use rates for Latinos and Latinas fall between rates reported by white and black American adolescents and are lower than both groups for adults. For example, in the Monitoring the Future Study, the combined 2002 and 2003 data for high school seniors show that for lifetime marijuana use whites have higher rates than do Latinos and Latinas, who are followed by blacks (48.8 percent, 44.2 percent, and 40 percent, respectively). This pattern is repeated for annual marijuana use (37.9 percent, 31.1 percent, and 26.3 percent, respectively) as well as for almost all substances. For alcohol use, for example, the prevalence of having five or more drinks daily is 32.4 percent for whites, 25.9 percent for Latinos and Latinas, and 10.8 percent for blacks. Among adults the pattern changes slightly, with Latinos and Latinas reporting prevalence rates that are lower than those of whites and blacks. For example, results from the 2003 National Survey on Drug Use and Health indicate that lifetime use of any illicit drugs among persons aged eighteen to twenty-five years old was 65.1 percent for whites, 54.6 percent for blacks, and 52.2 percent for Latinos and Latinas, and a similar pattern was reported for past year and past month use. Among persons aged twenty-six years or older, the difference between Latinos and Latinas and both whites and blacks is larger. Therefore, for Latino and Latina adults the data seem to indicate lower rates of substance use than for whites and blacks, although the group designated as Asian on the National Survey on Drug Use and Health reported lower prevalence rates than Latinos and Latinas. As for the younger population, Latinos and Latinas tend to fall between the higher prevalence rates of whites and the lower rates of blacks and are closer to the higher group, whites.

There are two critical factors that are not addressed by any of the national data examining drug use patterns: nativity and national origin. First, these data sets make no distinctions with respect to nativity, combining immigrant, born outside the United States, and second generation, those born in the United States, Latinos and Latinas. Second, all Latino and Latina subgroups are combined as "Hispanic" without distinction of national origin. To the extent that immigrant and U.S.-born Latinos and Latinas have different rates of drug use, as is the case, and to the extent that there are some national-origin subgroup differences, interpretation of national data is problematic at best.

Studies examining U.S.-born and immigrant Latinos and Latinas have demonstrated that the latter exhibit much lower rates of substance use and abuse, and this has been found with adolescent and adult populations. This lower use among immigrant Latinos and Latinas has also been found in studies examining prison populations in California, with unauthorized (illegal) Latino and Latina immigrant arrestees less likely than members of all other groups to have been drug users.

Despite the fact that minority groups such as Latinos and Latinas in the United States show lower prevalence rates of drug use and abuse, epidemiological studies indicate that alcohol and other drug use (AOD), morbidity, and mortality vary by ethnicity or culture in seemingly paradoxical ways. As illustrated above, African Americans and Latinos and Latinas have lower overall rates of substance use than non-Hispanic whites; however, these same groups demonstrate higher rates of AOD-related morbidity and mortality than non-Hispanic whites. Moreover, minorities, including Latinos and Latinas, are overrepresented in AOD treatment facilities.

This paradox may result from ethnic variations in the processes by which substance use can lead to substance problems. For example, the accelerated progression from use to problem use seen among these minority populations could result from socioeconomic polarization, criminal justice problems, or the lack of appropriate treatment options. Moreover, Latino and Latina populations (despite overrepresentation in the treatment system) have been shown to chronically underutilize available substance abuse intervention services, which also may contribute to accelerated development of alcohol and other drug use problems.

Acculturation and Latino and Latina Drug Use

Consideration of Latino and Latina drug use patterns in the United States must separate adult and adolescent patterns for two major reasons. Adult patterns tend to be reflective of the patterns in the countries of origin, whereas for adolescents drug use takes a developmental process that is reflective of the influences of American society and peers as immigrant Latino and Latina youth assimilate or acculturate to greater or lesser degrees to American society. The fact is that adult Latino and Latina immigrants have lower rates of drug use that are more representative of the rates in their countries of origin. This is an important consideration given the younger median age of Latinos and Latinas in comparison to the U.S. population. Therefore, predicting future drug-related problems as well as prevention and treatment needs for Latinos and Latinas must be considered within the perspective of increased patterns of use based on the expectation that Latino and Latina youth will be assimilating to a society with greater normative drug use than is found in their countries of origin.

The epidemiological data presented above indicates that drug use among Latino and Latina adolescents is affected by their socialization experiences and the experiences of their families in their new environments. This socializa-

tion process has been described as acculturation. A core supposition is that acculturation simultaneously evolves in several critical areas, including the context of exit from one's nation of origin and entrance into the United States. These experiences can threaten the viability of families and relationships among family members. Acculturation is a discontinuous and idiosyncratic process, rather than a monolithic one, and has been described in the literature as segmented assimilation. This conceptualization assumes that the process of acculturation and assimilation is influenced by "localized" environments. For example, acculturation of a Latino or Latina youth from a family of recent Mexican immigrants in South Florida would be different than it would be in Kansas City, Missouri, due to the different sociocultural characteristics of these locations. To the extent that immigrants initially relocate to urban areas with higher rates of drug use, immigrant Latino and Latina youth are often exposed to drug use.

Regardless of the local environment where the process of acculturation develops, the family plays many important roles in the acculturation process and ultimately in the effect of U.S. drug use patterns on Latino and Latina youth. Acculturation-related stressors can ultimately cause drug use, or the family and its "traditional" values and behaviors can create buffers against adolescent drug use and misuse. Multiple research studies have illustrated the potential of the acculturation process to produce stress and conflicts in the family as adolescents become more acculturated into the values and behaviors of American society, and parents in turn become more authoritarian as they attempt to stop what they see as a downward progression into inappropriately liberal attitudes and behaviors. Moreover, the acculturation levels of both adolescents and their parents can contribute to greater rates of substance use, and the protectiveness or buffering of the family is greater for immigrant children than it is for those in the second generation. Studies have consistently demonstrated that the length of time lived in the United States has deleterious consequences for the drug use patterns of Latino and Latina children and adolescents, and the younger the child is at the time of immigration, the more likely he or she will resemble the drug use patterns of his or her American peers by late adolescence. Illicit drug use tends to increase with age among young persons, regardless of ethnic background, peaking among those eighteen to twenty years old and declining steadily after that point with increasing age. The Latino and Latina population includes a disproportionate number of younger people; thus, one can expect greater rates of drug use and addiction in this population.

The War on Drugs and Latino and Latina Drug Use

There are several negative consequences of the War on Drugs vis-à-vis the Latino and Latina population. As presented above, drug use and abuse varies across ethnic, minority, and immigrant populations; however, many of the punitive drug laws enacted through the War on Drugs are based on beliefs that certain communities of color commonly abuse drugs. This has created a situation among populations with relatively lower levels of drug use (for example, immigrant Latinos and Latinas) in which the likelihood of punitive consequences and engagement in the criminal justice system are more likely than treatment. The engagement in the criminal justice system then has further negative consequences through felony disenfranchisement laws that affect future employment possibilities and even the right to vote or to become U.S. citizens. Furthermore, justifications for a more restrictive immigration policy have often relied on associating socially unacceptable behaviors, such as welfare participation and illicit drug use, with illegal entry into the United States. Nevertheless, consistent with studies showing lower levels of drug use among immigrant Latinos and Latinas, studies of unauthorized (illegal) Latino and Latina immigrant arrestees in California indicate that this group is less likely than members of all other groups to have taken any drug (38.5 percent) or to have used multiple illicit drugs (18.7 percent). These data are within the context that, by comparison, 65.3 percent of all California arrestees used some illicit drug, and 32.7 percent engaged in poly-drug use.

The negative impact of high rates of incarceration on poorer communities, particularly black and Latino and Latina communities, is severe, resulting in social and economic insults that burden not only the individual offender but his or her family and community as well. The cumulative effect of mass incarceration on young men of color is to rob young people of their futures, children of their parents, and communities of economic capital. According to estimates by the U.S. Department of Justice, the lifetime probability of being incarcerated in a state or federal prison is four times higher for Latinos and Latinas than for white males and six times higher for black males than for white males. For example, in 2000 Latinos and Latinas constituted 12.5 percent of the U.S. population but 43.4 percent of all federal drug offenders. The major drug abuse and addiction issue with the Latino and Latina population is not high prevalence of drug use but the progression from use to abuse and addiction and the lack of attention to treatment, which is not addressed by the War on Drugs.

Final Thoughts

Latinos and Latinas are the largest and youngest ethnic minority group in the United States. This is a population that is diverse and increasingly dispersed throughout the United States. These patterns will continue as the three largest groups, Mexicans, Puerto Ricans, and Cubans,

continue to be supplanted by other Central and South American groups. Immigration and birthrates predict large increases in the Latino and Latina population, which is expected to triple in the first half of the twenty-first century to more than 96 million and 25 percent of the U.S. population.

Drug use and addiction patterns among the Latino and Latina population in the United States can be summarized thusly: (a) generally, Latinos and Latinas exhibit lower prevalence rates than does the general U.S. population, particularly lower than white non-Hispanics; (b) nativity is an important factor in understanding drug use and addiction patterns among Latinos and Latinas, with those born outside the United States exhibiting lower prevalence rates; (c) younger Latinos and Latinas tend to more closely resemble the higher prevalence rates found among white non-Hispanics; and (d) time lived in the United States and acculturation to U.S. society have deleterious effects on Latino and Latina drug use patterns, particularly for those who immigrated at younger ages. The relative youth of the Latino and Latina population in the United States (37 percent under the age of twenty years), disproportionately low incomes (23 percent below the poverty line), and relatively low levels of education (more than 42 percent of those eighteen years or older have not graduated from high school) are all factors portending increases in drug abuse and addiction.

Latinos and Latinas tend to underutilize drug abuse treatment services, even when these are available. Parental responses to Latino and Latina youth drug use tend to be punitive rather than treatment oriented. Given the context of drug use and abuse in Latino communities and the low availability and utilization of services, the most promising approaches to prevention are those that involve the larger community. This is especially important given the diversity of drug abuse problems based on nativity, acculturation, and geographic location. For example, the SAFE 2000 Community Partnership in El Paso, Texas, a city of about 590,000 people near the Mexican border, organized neighborhood task forces that emphasized community mobilization and training (including youth training) and the support of prevention activities. SAFE 2000 organized neighborhood task forces and their communities to take control of the substance abuse problems in their neighborhood. The structure of the SAFE 2000 partnership was developed to include three levels of representation and participation: city leaders, neighborhood members, and youth. These efforts provided education and parent-to-parent training programs, which can be critically important in Latino communities, and there is evidence that programs such as this can have positive impacts on drug abuse problems in these communities.

See also Alocholism; Assimilation and Acculturation; *and* Youth Culture.

BIBLIOGRAPHY

Bureau of Justice Statistics. *Lifetime Likelihood of Going to State or Federal Prison*. Special Report, NCJ-1600902. Washington, D.C.: U.S. Department of Justice, Office of Justice Programs, 1997.

Marcelli, Enrico A. "An Estimate of the Level and Determinants of Illicit Drug Use among Unauthorized Latino Immigrant Arrestees in California." *Journal of Drug Issues* 31, no. 2 (2001): 487–516.

U.S. Census Bureau. Table 1: Annual Estimates of the Population for the United States and for Puerto Rico, April 1, 2000, to July 1, 2004. www.census.gov/popest/states/tables/NST-EST2004-01.pdf

Staff of the Monitoring the Future Project, Institute for Social Research, University of Michigan. *Monitoring the Future National Survey Results on Drug Use, 1975–2003*. Vol. 1: *Secondary School Students*. National Institutes of Health Publication no. 04-5507. Bethesda, Md.: National Institute on Drug Abuse, 2003.

Substance Abuse and Mental Health Services Administration. *Mid-Year 1997 Preliminary Emergency Department Data from the Drug Abuse Warning Network*. Department of Health and Human Services Publication no. SMA 98–3228. Rockville, Md.: Department of Health and Human Services, Office of Applied Studies, 1998.

Substance Abuse and Mental Health Services Administration. *Results from the 2003 National Survey on Drug Use and Health: National Findings*. Office of Applied Studies, National Survey on Drug Use and Health Series H–25, Department of Health and Human Services Publication no. SMA 04–3964. Rockville, Md.: Department of Health and Human Services, Office of Applied Studies, 2004.

ANDRES G. GIL

DRUGS. Narcotics, stimulants, inebriants, and mind-altering substances have been used historically by peoples around the world to satisfy a variety of needs, including religious activities, public ceremonies, illnesses, pleasures, habits, and addictions. In the United States, drug use has long been present across the ethnic spectrum, including the white European American population. Yet there has been a tendency in this country to associate drug trafficking and consumption and their attendant negative connotations with Third World minorities, such as Asians, African Americans, and Hispanics. In the United States, "War on Drugs," Hispanics have been stigmatized as a group heavily involved in the drug culture. This view stems from highly publicized drug dealing and use among Hispanic youth gangs in U.S. cities and the involvement of Mexico and Colombia as supplier nations to the enormous U.S. drug market.

The racialization of narcotics is an old story in the United States, beginning with the first attempts at drug prohibition in the late nineteenth century, when states and municipalities passed laws and ordinances to limit commerce in cocaine, marijuana, and opium. Race and ethnicity played a central role in such legislation as Americans attributed the use of these substances to "depraved" minorities, especially the Chinese. Prohibitionists alarmed the public with allegations that perverse Asians lured white women to their opium dens and turned them into prostitutes. One example of an early ordinance is the San Francisco opium law of 1875, passed during a period of intense anti-Asian sentiment in California. In 1909, a state law in California outlawed the importation of smoking opium. African Americans came under scrutiny in the 1910s as newspapers published stories claiming that "cocaine-crazed Negroes" posed a great threat to society because they attacked white women.

During the 1920s and 1930s, marijuana use emerged as a social issue when prohibitionists labeled users, especially African Americans and poor Mexican immigrants, "decadent" people who corrupted the youth and engaged in criminal activity. In 1937, Congress passed the Marijuana Tax Act with the intent of stifling the distribution and consumption of marijuana. In the following decades, the United States government passed many other laws that dictated harsh, mandatory penalties for narcotics violations while giving greater powers to the police and prosecutors. During the turbulent 1960s, a period of youth rebellion, the Richard Nixon administration declared the War on Drugs. This "war" has been expanding ever since, with a number of highly disturbing consequences for Latinos and Latinas and other minorities.

Hollywood movies, television, and the print media have perpetrated the image of Hispanic youths as deviant drug users and traffickers, helping to lay the groundwork for stereotypes and discriminatory policies against the group. The public at large perceives that drug consumption is higher among Hispanics than white European Americans, yet survey data have shown that the use of marijuana is about the same for both groups and that the ingestion of inhalants, hallucinogens, and LSD is actually higher among European Americans. Only cocaine use is higher among Hispanics, but the level of consumption of this substance has dropped significantly among all groups.

Distorted perceptions of drug use and dealing have led to constant government surveillance and frequent police "operations" in poor *barrios* (neighborhoods), resulting in an escalation of violence and the placement of many innocent people in harm's way. During the 1990s, the situation worsened as the drug cartels of Mexico penetrated many Mexican American communities throughout the country, setting up sham businesses to hide their operations and hiring many local residents, especially gang members, to help in the distribution and sale of drugs. In the U.S. border region, violence and crime reached savage proportions. The November 4, 1997 *Washington Post* reported "mafia-style assassinations in San Diego, gangland shootouts on the streets of Phoenix, and grisly revenge kidnappings the length of the 2,000-mile border." According to this newspaper, the difference between the

U.S. borderlands and the U.S. interior is that violence and crime related to the drug trade is much more intense and vicious on the border. This view is shared widely by experts in the United States and Mexico.

The War on Drugs has led to an explosion in the population behind bars. Between 1970 and 2002, the number of prison and jail inmates in the United States skyrocketed from less than 200,000 to over 2 million. The Sentencing Project, a nonprofit organization concerned with reforming the criminal justice system, reports that from 1981 to 2001 the percentage of drug offenders in federal prisons increased from 25 percent to almost 60 percent. By 2001, approximately 6.6 million Americans were incarcerated or on probation or parole, an increase of more than 258 percent since 1980.

The alarming rise in the prison and jail population has been accompanied by equally disturbing disproportionate conviction and incarceration rates for African Americans and Hispanics. In 2001, blacks (39 percent) and Latinos and Latinas (29 percent) made up more than two-thirds of all federal prisoners although the two groups together composed less than a quarter of the United States population. European American males have a 4 percent chance of serving time at some point during their lives, while Latinos have a 16 percent chance and African American males a 29 percent chance. Critics of the War on Drugs have documented how the process used to send drug offenders to jail is riddled with racism and injustice. The problem begins with racial and ethnic profiling among law enforcement officials involved in making drug arrests and ends with harsh and discriminatory laws that mandate prison time for convicted drug offenders, many of whom of course are members of minority groups.

The call for reform of the drug policy in the United States has grown louder in the late twentieth century and the early twenty-first century. Judges, law enforcement officials, scholars, and many other knowledgeable observers have pointed out the ineffectiveness of the War on Drugs as well as its discriminatory nature. Some states have implemented minor changes, but the zero-tolerance approach remains the law of the land. Thus, for the foreseeable future the drug problem will remain one of the major social challenges confronting Hispanics in the United States.

See also Criminal Justice System.

BIBLIOGRAPHY

Bourgois, Philippe I. *In Search of Respect: Selling Crack in El Barrio*. Cambridge, U.K.: Cambridge University Press, 2002.

Glick, Ronald, and Joan Moore, eds. *Drugs in Hispanic Communities*. New Brunswick, N.J.: Rutgers University Press, 1990.

Kopstein, Andrea N. *Drug Use among Racial/Ethnic Minorities*. Rockville, Md.: National Institutes of Health, 1998.

Moore, Molly. "Tijuana Cartel Escalates Violence Along Border." *Washington Post*, November 4, 1997.

Sentencing Project. www.sentencingproject.org.

Suro, Roberto. "Dealers Exploiting Fellow Mexican Americans; Neighborhood Traffickers Damaging Lives—and Image—of Latinos." *Washington Post*, November 6, 1997.

OSCAR J. MARTÍNEZ

DUAL NATIONALITY. One of the most interesting characteristics of international migration in the early years of the twenty-first century is the proliferation of diasporas with dual nationality or citizenship—that is, groups of people who are nationals or citizens of two countries simultaneously. Few migrant groups have been as actively involved in this trend as Latinas and Latinos in the United States.

Most Latina and Latino expatriates became able to hold dual nationality during the 1990s: Mexicans (1996), Colombians (1991), Chileans (2003), Ecuadorians (1995), Dominicans (1998), and Costa Ricans (1995). The number of Latin American countries recognizing or debating some form of dual nationality more than doubled between 1996 and 2000. They include Mexico, the Dominican Republic, El Salvador, Guatemala, Nicaragua, Peru, Chile, Colombia, Uruguay, Argentina, Costa Rica, Ecuador, Bolivia, Panama, Honduras, and Paraguay. In the early 2000s, fourteen Latin American countries permitted their diasporas to retain their nationality or citizenship after acquiring another one. Worldwide, more than ninety countries had such laws. The United States tolerated dual citizenship, but neither formally recognized nor prohibited it. American critics of dual-citizenship laws and practices allege that it conflicts with migrants' allegiance as Americans; however, studies show that Latinas and Latinos with dual nationality are loyal U.S. citizens.

Some governments, like Mexico's, legally distinguish between dual nationality and dual citizenship. Whereas dual nationality encompasses social, economic, and civil rights, obligations, and privileges, dual citizenship enables expatriates to participate formally in their homelands' political processes by voting or, in some countries, by holding office. Nonetheless, both dual nationality and dual citizenship confer privileges and rights traditionally reserved for people living in the homeland, like government protection, access to public higher education, and voting. Furthermore, such laws also endow migrants with symbolic rights and responsibilities.

For Latinas and Latinos, the main expression of dual citizenship is the ability to participate in Latin American elections. By 2003, however, only Argentineans, Colombians, Hondurans, and Peruvians were able to cast absentee ballots in their homelands' elections. Mexicans, Chileans, and Dominicans were still unable to do so, despite constitutional reforms in their birth countries.

Various factors contributed to the enactment of these laws and the growing practice of dual nationality beginning in the 1990s. First, economic globalization led to an exponential increase in Latin American migration to the United States, while Latina and Latino political and economic clout continued to grow in both the United States and Latin America. The magnitude of the annual remittances contributed by their diasporas became a crucial factor that neither small nor large Latin American states could ignore. For Mexico, the nearly $14 billion in remittances sent by more than 10 million migrants represented the largest source of revenue after oil exports in 2003. Moreover, the growing political relevance of Latinas and Latinos, including their potential as allies in the pursuit of policy objectives concerning the United States, forced Latin American governments to court their diasporas and increased the influence of Latinas and Latinos in their homelands. Furthermore, democratization processes in Latin American countries such as Chile and Argentina put pressure on governments to reincorporate their emigrants into the political life of the country, while also empowering Latinas and Latinos to lobby for their reincorporation. Thus, governments were increasingly willing to adopt dual nationality laws to reinforce ties between diasporas and homelands.

A model of this trend is Mexico, which in 1996 enacted a law allowing Mexicans to retain, or reclaim, Mexican nationality when becoming citizens of another country. This law neither grants nor proscribes political rights, but constitutional reforms approved earlier in 1996 removed obstacles preventing Mexican expatriates from casting absentee votes in Mexico's elections. Yet, by 2004, expatriates were still lobbying for the approval of the legislation required to exercise the absentee vote.

Second, diaspora transnational lobbying and mobilizations played a key role in the enactment and implementation of dual nationality and citizenship laws. The Chilean Civic Center in the United States, for example, was instrumental in the recognition of dual nationality in Chile. Likewise, Dominicans in the northeast vigorously lobbied in the Dominican Republic for their political rights and managed to get the Congress there to recognize their right to vote from abroad. Furthermore, the activism of representatives of hundreds of U.S.-Mexican migrant hometown associations and coalitions like the Coalition for the Political Rights of Mexicans Abroad (CDPME)—formed by business leaders, professionals, academics, and activists—has been crucial in keeping the issue of political rights on the agenda of Mexico's federal executive and legislative branches, and in the opening of spaces for participation in state and local politics. In some cases, however, diasporas are so politically and economically influential in their home countries that they do not even need to mobilize to gain the right to participate in their homelands' elections, as in the case of U.S. Hondurans. Interestingly, by facilitating more transnational participation, dual nationality laws magnify diasporas' ability to influence homeland politics.

Third, the practice of dual nationality was facilitated by revolutionary advances in communications technology and transportation during the 1990s. Business deals, remittances, contributions to electoral campaigns, and fundraising for hometown projects were facilitated by electronic money transfers. Keeping in touch with the socioeconomic, religious, and political affairs of hometowns was easier, and direct participation more frequent, thanks to cheaper air travel and phone rates, online news, e-mail, cable television, and cellular phones. Hence, Latinas and Latinos and Latin American politicians could lobby each other as often as they wanted and wherever they wanted—for example, in Chicago, Bogotá, or their hometowns. Organization and mobilization capabilities for transnational political action were similarly enhanced by migrants' use of electronic networks and Web pages. In short, increasing international migration, democratization processes, and the growing clout and activism of Latinas and Latinos, as well as communications and transportation innovations, created new incentives, opportunities, channels, and pressures for the recognition and practice of dual nationality.

See also Citizenship *and* Migradólares and Remittances.

BIBLIOGRAPHY

Fitzgerald, David. *Negotiating Extra-Territorial Citizenship: Mexican Migration and the Transnational Politics of Community*. Center for Comparative Immigration Studies (CCIS) Monograph 2. La Jolla: University of California, San Diego, 2000.

Gilbertson, Greta, and Audrey Singer. "Naturalization under Changing Conditions of Membership: Dominican Immigrants in New York City." In *Immigration Research for a New Century: Multidisciplinary Perspectives*, edited by Nancy Foner, Ruben G. Rumbaut, and Steven J. Gold. New York: Russell Sage Foundation, 2000.

Jones-Correa, Michael. *Between Two Nations: The Political Predicament of Latinos in New York City*. Ithaca, N.Y.: Cornell University Press, 1998.

Martínez-Saldaña, Jesús, and Raúl Ross Pineda. "Suffrage for Mexicans Residing Abroad." In *Cross-Border Dialogues: U.S.–Mexican Social Movement Networking*, edited by David Brooks and Jonathan Fox. La Jolla: Center for U.S.–Mexican Studies and University of California, San Diego, 2002.

PATRICIA HAMM

DURAZO, MARÍA ELENA. *See* Latina Labor and Community Organizers